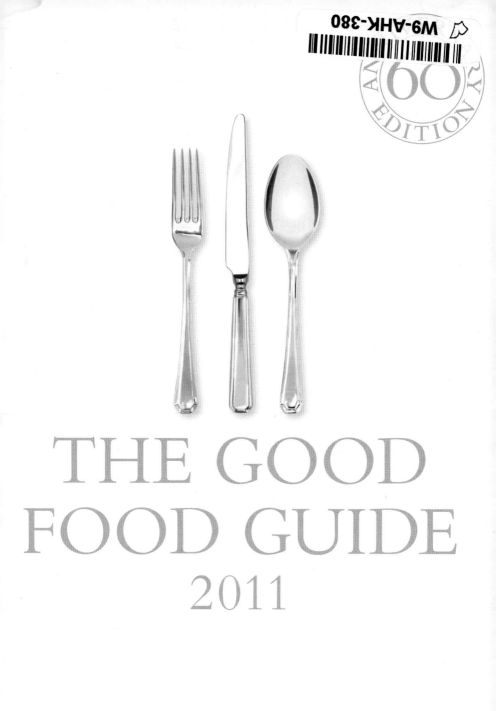

60 ANNIVERSARY EDITION

THE GOOD
FOOD GUIDE
2011

Distributed by Littlehampton Book Services Ltd
Faraday Close, Durrington, Worthing, West Sussex BN13 3RB

Copyright © Which? Ltd 2010

Base mapping by Cosmographics Ltd
Data management and export by AMA DataSet Limited, Preston
Printed and bound by Charterhouse, Hatfield

A catalogue record for this book is available from the British Library

ISBN: 978 1 84490 195 1

Consultant Editor: Elizabeth Carter
Managing Editor: Lisa Grey

The Good Food Guide makes every effort to be as accurate and up to date as possible.
All *Good Food Guide* inspections are anonymous but every Main Entry has been contacted
separately for details.

As we are an annual Guide, we have strict guidelines for fact-checking information
ahead of going to press, so some restaurants were dropped if they failed to provide the
information we required. Readers should still check details at the time of booking,
particularly if they have any special requirements.

Please send updates to: editors@thegoodfoodguide.co.uk or 2 Marylebone Road,
London NW1 4DF.

To submit feedback on any restaurant, please visit www.thegoodfoodguide.co.uk/feedback

FSC
Mixed Sources
Product group from well-managed
forests and other controlled sources

Cert no. SGS-COC-003131
www.fsc.org
© 1996 Forest Stewardship Council

"You can corrupt one man. You can't bribe an army."

Raymond Postgate, founder of
The Good Food Guide, 1951

Please turn to the page number
listed to find restaurant reviews
for the corresponding region.

7

Contents

Introduction

This edition of *The Good Food Guide* calls for a toast – for we celebrate 60 years of publication in 2011.

It's quite an achievement when you consider *The Good Food Guide*'s origins. The Guide emerged in the aftermath of the Second World War, in a country almost bankrupt, and still suffering the privations of rationing. For those who were able to eat out, the restaurant scene was in a dismal state, with many caterers taking full advantage of the customary British refusal to complain about awful food. A typical restaurant meal ran like this: soup from a tin; soggy steak; synthetic cream and tinned Empire fruit; tinned coffee.

We should raise our glasses too, therefore, to the memory of Raymond Postgate, the left-wing historian, wine connoisseur and crime writer, who founded the Guide and thereby helped rescue eating out in post-war Britain.

In the beginning…

In 1949, when Raymond Postgate started his 'campaign against cruelty to food', luncheon meat, false cream, margarine (or marge) that 'tasted as it did in 1919', and whalemeat rissoles were high on his hit list.

His campaign inspired an army of like-minded people to report on places where the food was decent – The Good Food Club was born, which, in turn, led to the publication of *The Good Food Guide* in 1951.

Postgate's aims were simple, among them to 'raise the standard of cooking in Britain' and 'to do ourselves all a bit of good by making our holidays, travels and evenings-out in due course more enjoyable'.

Although much has changed since then, when inclusion in *The Good Food Guide* meant 'any place where food could be eaten without nausea, where the helpings were not derisively tiny, and the staff not directly rude', the bare bones of Postgate's original Guide remain: the Guide is still based on the huge volume of feedback we receive from readers throughout the year, inspections are carried out anonymously and, importantly, the Guide is still independent.

Continuing to shape the modern British dining scene…

The Good Food Guide may be a veteran of the restaurant scene, but it has never stopped pushing the boundaries of dining out in the UK. From railing against convenience foods and the restaurants that served them in the 1970s, to coining the phrase 'modern British cooking' in the 1980s, the Guide and its readers have spotted culinary trends. It noted the emergence of Raymond Blanc in 1978, recognised Gordon Ramsay's star qualities in 1995, and, in 1997, hailed Heston Blumenthal as newcomer of the year.

Properly cooked food made from fresh ingredients has always been the Guide's main objective. From the very beginning it has worked to encourage restaurants to be part of their local food economy and establish a reputation for local and regional produce.

Has it succeeded? Chefs like Jimmy Graham of Ostlers Close in Cupar, and David Pitchford of Read's in Faversham have consistently been recognised in the Guide for supporting local food producers; they have appeared in the Guide for 28 and 25 years respectively. The food at Nigel Haworth's Northcote in Lancashire is famed for its strong northern accent, and Raymond Blanc is renowned for his organic kitchen garden at Le Manoir aux Quat'Saisons.

Building on this, in a move that takes seasonal/local to another level, this year we've seen a fierce new regionalism emerging, with some chefs sourcing all their fresh produce from within a strictly drawn-up area around their restaurants.

At L'Enclume, Simon Rogan has leased an organic farm and the produce he grows dictates his menu, while all the food he offers comes from within the boundaries of the county. He has, for example, eschewed olive oil in favour of Cumbrian-produced rapeseed oil. The same ambition can be seen in Stephen Harris of the Sportsman, who describes his commitment to the food produced in east Kent as pre-industrial cooking. Cornwall has always pretty much defined Nathan Outlaw's menu too, but he found the move to the St Enodoc Hotel presented the opportunity to explore modern fish cookery in greater depth. There, 80 per cent of the menu is now Cornish-landed fish – with oysters, mussels, clams, crabs, lobsters and foraged seashore vegetables and herbs also all coming from within five minutes of the restaurant.

But, in many ways, these are the exceptions. While quality of produce is far better than it used to be, we still have to do a lot more: the Guide continues to get complaints from restaurant-goers about jet-fresh asparagus, green beans and strawberries being served in winter, even in places that claim to use seasonal/local produce.

The future...

Six decades of publication have given the Guide a unique insight into eating out in Britain. More recently, it championed the pub's potential as a way for young chefs to make their name in the 1990s and, in 2010, we highlighted the trend for all-day dining shown by the emergence of good-quality eateries in the middle and lower price bands. As the many new entries in this 2011 edition show, this is a trend that continues to grow across the country.

This year we've seen a fierce new regionalism emerging, with some chefs sourcing all their fresh produce from within a strictly drawn-up area around their restaurants.

As a restaurant trend, open-to-view kitchens has been something of a slow burner, but the breaking down of the barrier between kitchen and dining room now seems to be growing apace. Some two decades ago, Clarke's, the River Café and a handful of Japanese restaurants were pioneers. The likes of Moro followed suit in the 1990s and, in the last ten years, such kitchens have become trademarks in places like Goodfellows in Wells and the Chef's Table in Tetbury. A flurry of new restaurants have now opened, all with their kitchens prominently positioned – and readers tell us they love the vibrancy, the relaxed conditions and the theatre of it all.

In contrast, each edition of the Guide throws up a selection of readers' restaurant complaints. Looking back over past editions of the Guide, it seems

poor service is a perennial and continuing problem. While good service can lift an indifferent meal, poor service can drag a good one down; it is a source of frustration to our readers and inspectors when restaurateurs do not place more importance on staff training and supervision. In restaurants where the bill can be more than £100 a head, it is particularly unacceptable. There is no point in the kitchen sending out exquisite dishes if the front-of-house staff can't make the experience memorable – the customer will always feel short changed.

And, most importantly … a thank you to our readers

Over the past 60 years, we as a nation have gone from being completely apathetic about food to having a total fascination with chefs, recipes, personalities and lifestyles. This may not have been exactly what Raymond Postgate had in mind, but UK produce, chefs and restaurants are now internationally renowned – and that is something of which he would have been very proud.

We have made it to 60 only with your help. We value all the reports we receive, so please keep them coming in because the restaurants listed in this book are, in our view, the best places in which to eat out this year – and that is on your say so. Without your efforts the Guide would not be what it is. We owe a very big thank you to everyone who fills in our online reader feedback form (www.thegoodfoodguide.co.uk/feedback), many of whom from the last year are acknowledged at the back of the Guide.

And, in this very special anniversary year, we have lots of exciting plans afoot, including a gorgeous recipe book. Do check out the website www.thegoodfoodguide.co.uk for up-to-date information on what we're up to – and keep in touch.

Good eating,

Elizabeth Carter, Consultant Editor

How to use the Guide

Each year *The Good Food Guide* is completely rewritten and compiled from scratch.
Our research list is based on the huge volume of feedback we receive from readers (the list of many of our contributors at the back of the book is testimony to this). This feedback, together with anonymous inspections, ensures that every entry is assessed afresh. To everyone who has used our feedback system (www.thegoodfoodguide.co.uk/feedback) over the last year, many thanks, and please keep the reports coming in.

Symbols

Restaurants that may be given Main Entry or Also Recommended status are contacted ahead of publication and asked to provide key information about their opening hours and facilities. They are also invited to participate in the £5 voucher scheme. The symbols on these entries are based on this feedback from restaurants, and are intended for quick, at-a-glance identification. The wine bottle symbol is an accolade assigned by the Guide's team, based on their judgement of the wine list available.

 Accommodation is available.

£30 It is possible to have three courses (excluding wine) at the restaurant for less than £30.

V There are more than three vegetarian main courses on the menu.

£5 OFF The restaurant is participating in our £5 voucher scheme. (Please see the vouchers at the end of the book for terms and conditions.)

The restaurant has a wine list that our inspector and wine expert have deemed to be exceptional.

£XX The price indicated on each review represents the average price of a three-course dinner, excluding wine.

Scoring

We believe that the restaurants included in this Guide are the very best in the UK; this means that a score of 1 is a significant achievement.

We reject many restaurants during the compilation of the Guide. Obviously, there are always subjective aspects to rating systems, but our inspectors are equipped with extensive scoring guidelines, so that restaurant bench-marking around the UK is accurate. We also take into account the reader feedback that we receive for each restaurant, so that any given review is based on several meals.

1/10   Capable cooking, with simple food combinations and clear flavours, but some inconsistencies.

2/10   Decent cooking, displaying good basic technical skills and interesting combinations and flavours. Occasional inconsistencies.

3/10   Good cooking, showing sound technical skills and using quality ingredients.

4/10   Dedicated, focused approach to cooking; good classical skills and high-quality ingredients.

5/10   Exact cooking techniques and a degree of ambition; showing balance and depth of flavour in dishes, while using quality ingredients.

6/10   Exemplary cooking skills, innovative ideas, impeccable ingredients and an element of excitement.

7/10   High level of ambition and individuality, attention to the smallest detail, accurate and vibrant dishes.

8/10   A kitchen cooking close to or at the top of its game – highly individual, showing faultless technique and impressive artistry in dishes that are perfectly balanced for flavour, combination and texture. There is little room for disappointment here.

9/10   This mark is for cooking that has reached a pinnacle of achievement, making it a hugely memorable experience for the diner.

10/10   It is extremely rare that a restaurant can achieve perfect dishes on a consistent basis.

You will notice that not all restaurants are scored: Also Recommended reviews are not scored but are worth a visit. Readers Recommend reviews are supplied by readers. These entries are the local, up-and-coming places to watch and represent the voice of our thousands of loyal followers.

Readers' Awards

The Good Food Guide has always recognised excellence and good service at restaurants throughout the UK. *The Good Food Guide* Restaurant of the Year award is run annually between March and May, and presents readers with the opportunity to nominate their favourite local establishment. For this year's award, members of the public were invited to nominate establishments for ten different regions, with the criteria that restaurants should be independently owned and offer regional or local produce. Nominations were submitted via our online feedback form (www.thegoodfoodguide.co.uk/feedback), and by postal vote. We received thousands of nominations and *The Good Food Guide* team picked the overall winner from the list of regional winners. All the regional winners were presented with a framed award by Jason Atherton.

The Readers' Restaurant of the Year (2011 edition)
THE SWAN, SOUTHROP

1. WALES – Slice, Swansea

2. EAST ENGLAND – Wiveton Bell, Norfolk

3. LONDON – The French Table, Surbiton

4. MIDLANDS – Saffron, Birmingham

5. NORTHERN IRELAND – Ginger Bistro, Belfast

6. NORTH EAST – Artisan, Hessle

7. NORTH WEST – Northcote, Langho

8   SCOTLAND – La Garrigue, Edinburgh

9. SOUTH EAST – Vanilla Pod, Marlow

10. SOUTH WEST – The Swan, Southrop

Editors' Awards

To mark the 60th anniversary of *The Good Food Guide*, this year's edition includes a special **Lifetime Achievement Award**. Presented in recognition of an unerring commitment to consistency, quality and seasonal produce, this award reflects the outstanding contribution that the chef has made to the UK dining experience.

Lifetime Achievement Award
Raymond Blanc, Le Manoir aux Quat'Saisons

It's been 32 years since the overnight success of Les Quat'Saisons and 27 years since Raymond Blanc opened Le Manoir aux Quat'Saisons, three decades that have earned him a reputation as a culinary giant. From moving away from the accepted French template to championing British produce and developing one of the most exemplary organic kitchen gardens in the country, few chefs can show such dedication and consistency or such an uncanny ability to read the mood of the times.

This year, *The Good Food Guide* team have allocated the following awards:

Best new entry 2011
Artichoke, Buckinghamshire

Best pub newcomer
Simon Bonwick, The Three Tuns, Oxfordshire

Wine list of the year
The Queensberry Hotel, Olive Tree Restaurant, Somerset

Best chef
Sat Bains, Restaurant Sat Bains, Nottinghamshire

Best up-and-coming chef
Mary-Ellen McTague, Aumbry, Greater Manchester

Best pub chef
Jason King, The Wellington Arms, Hampshire

Best fish restaurant
Restaurant Nathan Outlaw, Cornwall

Best value for money
delifonseca, Merseyside

Best use of local produce
Ode, Devon

Best family restaurant
Cwtch, West Wales

Longest-serving restaurants

The Good Food Guide was founded in 1951. Here is a list of restaurants that have appeared consistently since their first entry into the Guide.

The Connaught, London, 58 years
Gravetye Manor, East Grinstead, 54 years
Porth Tocyn Hotel, Abersoch, 54 years
Sharrow Bay, Ullswater, 50 years
Le Gavroche, London, 41 years
Summer Isles Hotel, Achiltibuie, 41 years
The Capital, London, 40 years
Ubiquitous Chip, Glasgow, 39 years
The Druidstone, Broad Haven, 38 years
Plumber Manor, Sturminster Newton, 38 years
The Waterside Inn, Bray, 38 years
White Moss House, Grasmere, 38 years
Isle of Eriska, Eriska, 37 years
Airds Hotel, Port Appin, 35 years
Farlam Hall, Brampton, 34 years
Corse Lawn House, Corse Lawn, 33 years
Hambleton Hall, Hambleton, 32 years
The Pier Hotel, Harbourside Restaurant, Harwich, 32 years
Grafton Manor, Bromsgrove, 31 years
Magpie Café, Whitby, 31 years
RSJ, London, 30 years
The Seafood Restaurant, Padstow, 30 years
Sir Charles Napier, Chinnor, 30 years

The Dower House, The Royal Crescent, Bath, 30 years
Kalpna, Edinburgh, 29 years
Le Caprice, London, 29 years
Little Barwick House, Barwick, 29 years
Moss Nook, Manchester, 29 years
Ostlers Close, Cupar, 28 years
The Cellar, Anstruther, 27 years
Le Manoir aux Quat'Saisons, Great Milton, 26 years
Clarke's, London, 26 years
Roade House, Roade, 26 years
Read's, Faversham, 25 years
The Three Chimneys, Isle of Skye, 25 years
Wallett's Court, St Margaret's-at-Cliffe, 25 years
Northcote, Langho, 24 years
ramsons, Ramsbottom, 24 years
Le Champignon Sauvage, Cheltenham, 22 years
Kensington Place, London, 22 years
Quince & Medlar, Cockermouth, 22 years
Silver Darling, Aberdeen, 22 years

Top 60 restaurants 2011

The Good Food Guide's Top 50 listing is now firmly established; a placing within it is greatly coveted by all chefs and restaurateurs serious about their business. To mark the Guide's 60th anniversary, we have extended it to a top 60 for this year.

1. The Fat Duck, Bray, Berkshire (10)
2. Gordon Ramsay, Royal Hospital Road, London (9)
3. Le Manoir aux Quat'Saisons, Great Milton, Oxfordshire (8)
4. L'Enclume, Cartmel, Cumbria (8)
5. Restaurant Nathan Outlaw, Rock, Cornwall (8)
6. Restaurant Sat Bains, Nottingham, Nottinghamshire (8)
7. Marcus Wareing at the Berkeley, London (8)
8. Le Champignon Sauvage, Cheltenham, Gloucestershire (8)
9. Pied-à-Terre, London (8)
10. The Square, London (8)
11. Hibiscus, London (8)
12. Alain Ducasse at the Dorchester, London (8)
13. Adam Simmonds at Danesfield House, Marlow, Buckinghamshire (8)
14. Whatley Manor, Easton Grey, Wiltshire (8)
15. Le Gavroche, London (8)
16. Tom Aikens, London (8)
17. Restaurant Martin Wishart, Edinburgh, Scotland (8)
18. The Waterside Inn, Bray, Berkshire (7)
19. Bohemia, St Helier, Jersey (7)
20. Fraiche, Oxton, Merseyside (7)
21. L'Atelier de Joël Robuchon, London (7)
22. Murano, London (7)
23. Anthony's Restaurant, Leeds, Yorkshire (7)
24. Fischer's Baslow Hall, Baslow, Derbyshire (7)
25. Gidleigh Park, Chagford, Devon (7)
26. Robert Thompson at the Hambrough, Ventnor, Isle of Wight (7)
27. Midsummer House, Cambridge, Cambridgeshire (7)
28. Tyddyn Llan, Llandrillo, Wales (7)
29. The Ledbury, London (7)
30. The Crown at Whitebrook, Whitebrook, Wales (7)

31. The Pass, Lower Beeding, West Sussex (7)

32. Mr Underhill's, Ludlow, Shropshire (7)

33. Michael Wignall at the Latymer, Bagshot, Surrey (7)

34. Hambleton Hall, Hambleton, Leicestershire & Rutland (7)

35. Andrew Fairlie at Gleneagles, Auchterarder, Scotland (7)

36. Simon Radley at the Chester Grosvenor, Chester, Cheshire (7)

37. The Creel, St Margaret's Hope, Scotland (7)

38. Harry's Place, Great Gonerby, Lincolnshire (7)

39. The Old Vicarage, Ridgeway, Derbyshire (7)

40. The Greenhouse, London (6)

41. The Kitchin, Edinburgh, Scotland (6)

42. Purnell's, Birmingham, West Midlands (6)

43. Artichoke, Amersham, Buckinghamshire (6)

44. The Sportsman, Whitstable, Kent (6)

45. Club Gascon, London (6)

46. ramsons, Ramsbottom, Greater Manchester (6)

47. The Yorke Arms, Ramsgill, Yorkshire (6)

48. La Bécasse, Ludlow, Shropshire (6)

49. The Hand & Flowers, Marlow, Buckinghamshire (6)

50. Galvin at Windows, London (6)

51. Chez Bruce, London (6)

52. Northcote, Langho, Lancashire (6)

53. Read's, Faversham, Kent (6)

54. The Cellar, Anstruther, Scotland (6)

55. Arbutus, London (6)

56. Zafferano, London (6)

57. The Peat Inn, Peat Inn, Scotland (6)

58. The Capital, London (6)

59. Seven Park Place, London (6)

60. Alimentum, Cambridge, Cambridgeshire (6)

London Explained

London is split into six regions: Central, North, East, South, West and Greater. Restaurants within each region are listed alphabetically. Each Main Entry and Also Recommended entry has a map reference.

The lists below are a guide to the areas covered in each region.

London — Central
Belgravia, Bloomsbury, Chinatown, Covent Garden, Fitzrovia, Green Park, Holborn, Hyde Park, Knightsbridge, Lancaster Gate, Marble Arch, Marylebone, Mayfair, Oxford Circus, Piccadilly, Soho, St James's Park, Trafalgar Square, Westminster

London — North
Belsize Park, Camden, Crouch End, Dalston, Euston, Golders Green, Hampstead, Highbury, Highgate, Islington, King's Cross, Primrose Hill, Stoke Newington, Swiss Cottage, Willesden

London — East
Barbican, Bethnal Green, Blackfriars, Canary Wharf, City, Clerkenwell, Hackney, Limehouse, Shoreditch, Spitalfields, Tower Hill, Wapping, Whitechapel

London — South
Balham, Battersea, Bermondsey, Blackheath, Clapham, East Dulwich, Elephant and Castle, Forest Hill, Greenwich, Putney, South Bank, Southwark, Tooting, Wimbledon

London — West
Chelsea, Chiswick, Earl's Court, Fulham, Hammersmith, Kensal Rise, Kensington, Knightsbridge, Maida Vale, Notting Hill, Paddington, Shepherd's Bush, South Kensington, Westbourne Park

London — Greater
Barnes, Croydon, Harrow-on-the-Hill, Kew, Richmond, Southall, Tottenham Hale, Twickenham, Wood Green

LONDON

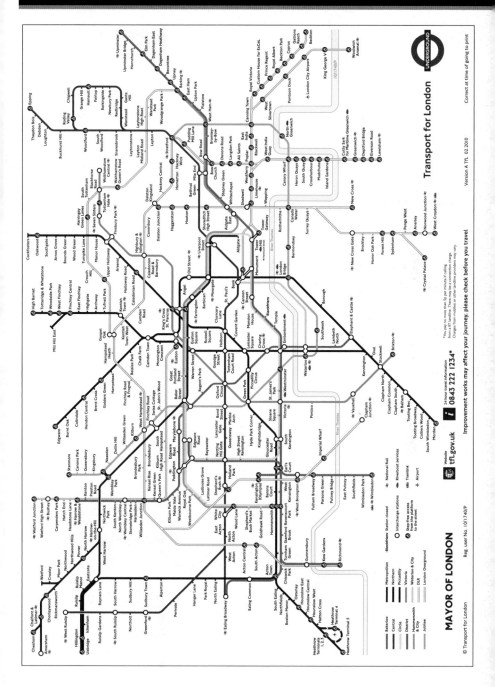

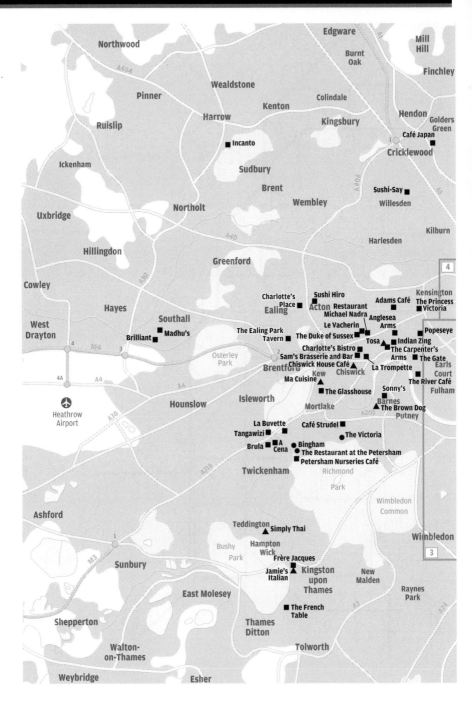

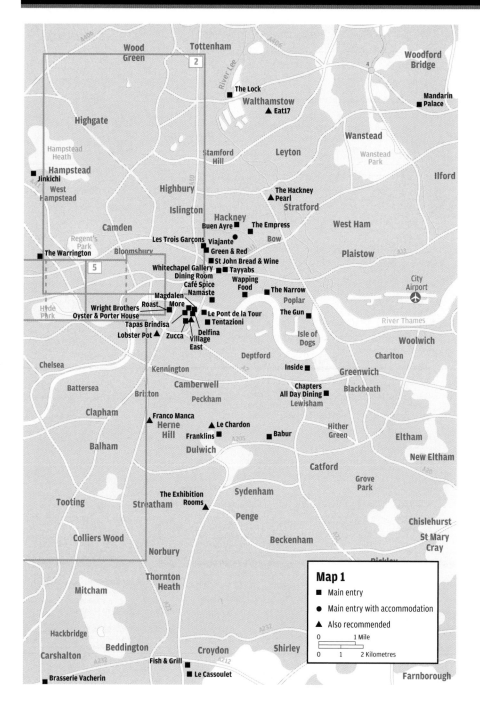

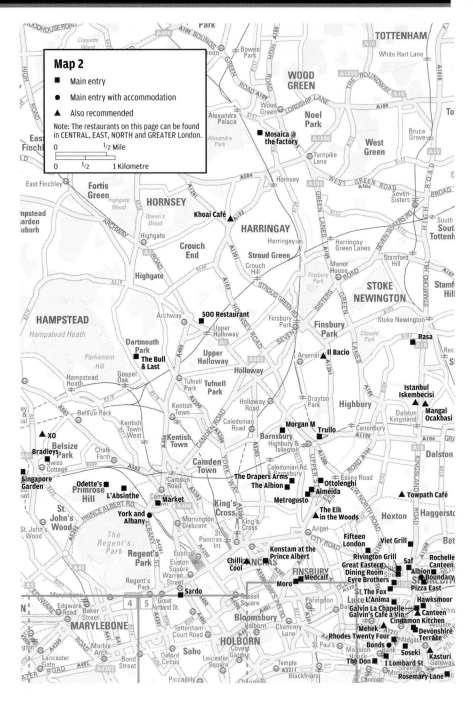

Map 2

- ■ Main entry
- ● Main entry with accommodation
- ▲ Also recommended

Note: The restaurants on this page can be found in CENTRAL, EAST, NORTH and GREATER London.

0   1/2 Mile

0   1/2   1 Kilometre

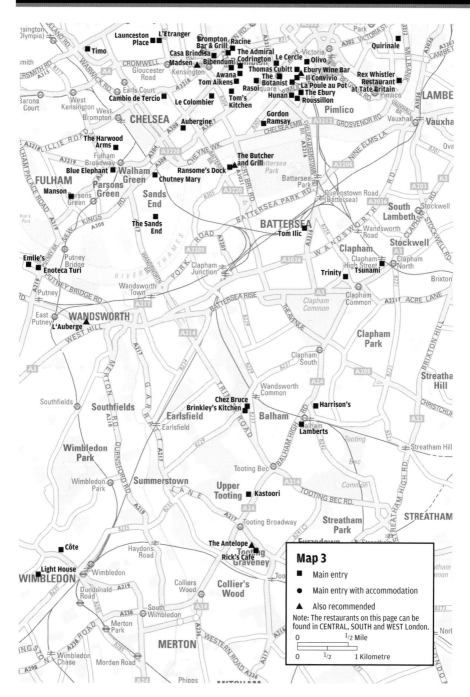

Map 3

- ■ Main entry
- ● Main entry with accommodation
- ▲ Also recommended

Note: The restaurants on this page can be found in CENTRAL, SOUTH and WEST London.

0   1/2 Mile

0   1/2   1 Kilometre

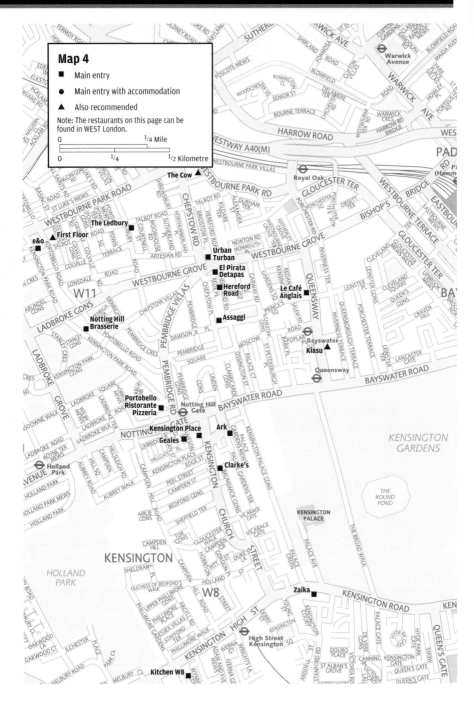

Map 4

- ■ Main entry
- ● Main entry with accommodation
- ▲ Also recommended

Note: The restaurants on this page can be found in WEST London.

0 — ¼ Mile
0 — ¼ — ½ Kilometre

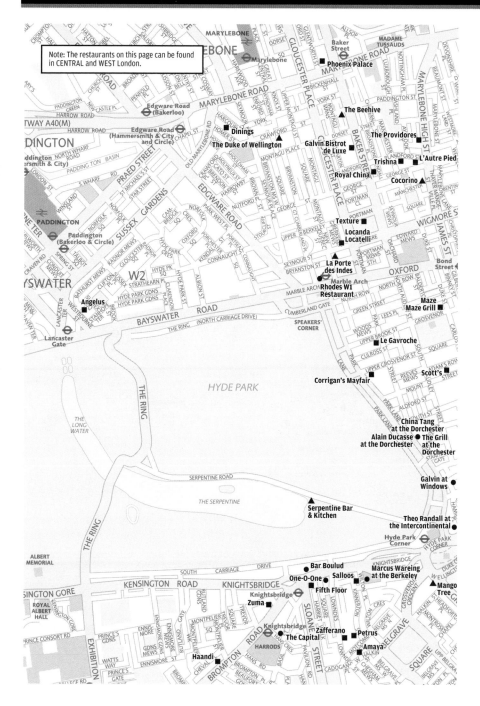

Note: The restaurants on this page can be found in CENTRAL and WEST London.

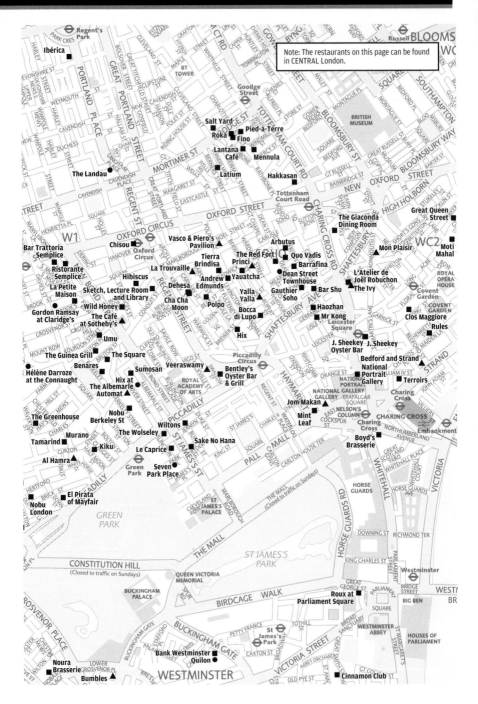

Note: The restaurants on this page can be found in CENTRAL London.

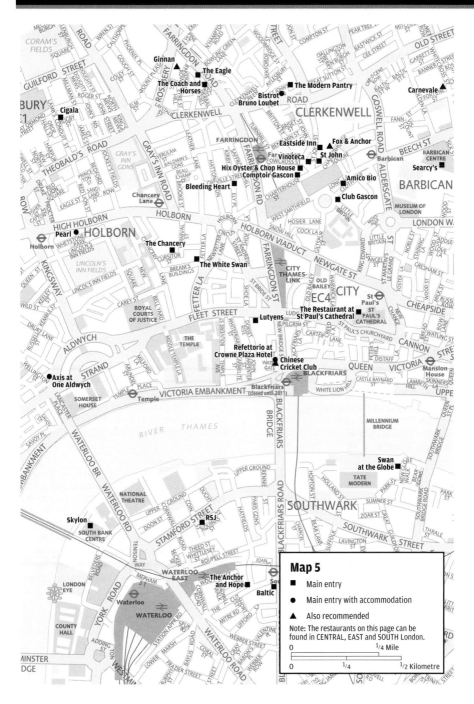

Map 5

■ Main entry

● Main entry with accommodation

▲ Also recommended

Note: The restaurants on this page can be found in CENTRAL, EAST and SOUTH London.

| 0 | | ¼ Mile |
| 0 | ¼ | ½ Kilometre |

ALSO RECOMMENDED

▲ Al Hamra

31-33 Shepherd Market, Green Park, W1J 7PT
Tel no: (020) 7493 1954
www.alhamrarestaurant.co.uk
⊖ Green Park, Hyde Park Corner, map 5
Lebanese £5 OFF

This busy Lebanese restaurant in Mayfair's Shepherd Market has been a local institution for over 25 years. It's reliably packed with punters who come back repeatedly for dishes such as bastorma (thin-sliced, dry-cured beef), pastries filled with lamb, onion and pine nuts (£7.50) and charcoal-grilled whole baby chicken with garlic sauce (£16.50); also don't miss the baba ganoush. Fish dishes are less well received. To finish, sticky baklava (£4.50) always hits the spot. House French is £15, but check out the Lebanese bottles. Open all week.

Alain Ducasse at the Dorchester

Definitive gastronomic destination
The Dorchester Hotel, 53 Park Lane, Hyde Park, W1K 1QA
Tel no: (020) 7629 8866
www.alainducasse-dorchester.com
⊖ Hyde Park Corner, map 4
Modern French | £75
Cooking score: 8

🍽 V

Alain Ducasse's reputation and achievements precede his restaurants. Here is an über-chef and global empire-builder who has not only trained a whole dynasty of talented young cohorts, but has also perpetuated the great discipline of haute cuisine. His interpretations of the classic French style are supremely subtle, making his dining room at the Dorchester a definitive destination of its kind – and the most obvious heir to the great London hotel kitchens (the last of which disappeared when Michel Bourdin retired from The Connaught in 2001). But while all the headlines and column inches go to the boundary-pushing young guns, 'high cooking' has also moved on and reinvented itself for inquisitive twenty-first century palates. Anyone in search of good food will not be disappointed here. Head chef Jocelyn Herland has absorbed every meticulous, methodical detail of the Ducasse credo – and it shows. A bowl of soft-boiled egg, crayfish and asparagus served with a superb sauce Nantua is truly heavenly, the flavours growing with every spoonful. Likewise, a dish of Limousin veal – two thick slices of delicate, pink-roasted loin, some slow-cooked meaty nuggets and an array of beautifully distinct vegetables in a delicate blanquette with an intense veal jus, poured at the table. The Achilles heel of the Ducasse style is accumulated richness, so bear this in mind when ordering. Perhaps that is why lighter dishes stand out in reports: perfectly braised halibut with Swiss chard and aubergine condiment, for example, with acidity provided by a citrus sauce that owes more to a Japanese ponzu than a classic agrumes. Surprisingly, desserts also aim for on-trend lightness – best of all are the soufflés, whether a lime-flavoured summer version with a white cheese and Szechuan pepper sorbet, or a winter creation of hazelnut with a pear granita. The expected parade of little extras gives notice that impeccable technique and spot-on flavours carry on right through to the very end. Service is drilled to perfection. Handsomely resourced imbibers will find a magnificent choice on the wine list, with real depth throughout France and elsewhere – although mere mortals may have to content themselves with the house selections at £25.
Chef/s: Jocelyn Herland. **Open:** Tue to Fri L 12 to 2, Tue to Sat D 6.30 to 10. **Closed:** Sun, Mon, 26 to 30 Dec, last 3 weeks Aug. **Meals:** Set L £39.50 (2 courses) to £45. Set D £55 (2 courses) to £75. Tasting menu £115 (8 courses). **Service:** 12.5%. **Details:** Cards accepted. 82 seats. Air-con. No mobile phones. Wheelchair access. Music. Children allowed.

Amaya

Sleek, slinky Indian
15 Halkin Arcade, Motcomb Street, Knightsbridge,
SW1X 8JT
Tel no: (020) 7823 1166
www.realindianfood.com
⊖ **Knightsbridge, map 4**
Indian | £40
Cooking score: 3

V

Amaya struts its stuff in a prime slice of
Belgravia real estate, flaunting its slinky assets
to a moneyed crowd: natural light streams in
from a glazed atrium, vibrant murals catch the
eye and a heady, aromatic scent wafts through
the air. Diners disport themselves in a vast
triangular dining area, which offers tantalising
views of the stunning theatre kitchen. 'Tiny
portions' designed for grazing and sharing are
the order of the day, with much depending on
the tandoor, sigri grill and tawa skillet. The
result is a racy repertoire that moves from
textbook tikkas and biryanis to Punjabi
chicken wing 'lollipops', venison seekh
kebabs, and char-grilled grouper in a pandan
leaf with a fiery peanut marinade. Stir-fried
tofu and Indian sweet white potato figure
among the inventive side dishes, and desserts
look westwards for, say, rhubarb semifreddo.
Wines start at £23.50.
Chef/s: Karunesh Khanna. **Open:** all week L 12.30 to
2.15 (2.45 Sun), D 6.30 to 11.30 (10.30 Sun). **Closed:**
25 Dec. **Meals:** alc (main courses £12 to £31). Set L
£19.50. Tasting menu £38.50. Gourmet menu £65.
Service: 12.5% (optional). **Details:** Cards accepted.
100 seats. Air-con. Separate bar. No music.
Wheelchair access. Children allowed.

Please send us your feedback

To register your opinion about any
restaurant listed in the Guide, or a new
restaurant that you wish to bring to our
attention, please visit the web address at
the bottom of the page. Your feedback
informs the content of the book and will be
used to compile next year's reviews.

Andrew Edmunds

On-song Soho treasure
46 Lexington Street, Soho, W1F OLW
Tel no: (020) 7437 5708
⊖ **Oxford Street, Piccadilly Circus, map 5**
Modern European | £25
Cooking score: 2

🍶 £30

Dedicated followers of fashion may come and
go, but Andrew Edmunds just keeps on
rolling, peddling its Dickensian, candlelit
charms to legions of devotees. The clubby
Soho interior smacks of a 70s wine bar
(especially if you're in the shadowy basement),
there's wood-chip on the walls and everyone
sits elbow-to-elbow, but who cares when the
kitchen is on song and the wines are hitting
the spot. The daily menu promises generosity
and value in the shape of goose rillettes with
red onion compote, plates of gnocchi with
Gorgonzola, walnuts and courgettes, pork
belly with celeriac mash, and – to finish – St
Clements and almond cake. Wine-loving
owner Andrew Edmunds has put together a
cracking list, bursting with quirky
discoveries, boutique bottles and bargains
galore. Prices start at £15 (£3 a glass).
Chef/s: Rebecca St John-Cooper. **Open:** all week L
12.30 to 3 (1 to 3.15 Sat and Sun), D 6 to 10.30
(10.15 Sun). **Closed:** 23 Dec to 2 Jan, Easter.
Meals: alc (main courses £10 to £19).
Service: 12.5% (optional). **Details:** Cards accepted.
58 seats. 4 seats outside. Air-con. No music. No
mobile phones. Children allowed.

Angelus

Bells-and-whistles flavours of France
4 Bathurst Street, Lancaster Gate, W2 2SD
Tel no: (020) 7402 0083
www.angelusrestaurant.co.uk
⊖ **Lancaster Gate, map 4**
Modern French | £45
Cooking score: 4

V

Angelus is a diverting mix of Gallic
informality and Victorian splendour. It
occupies a listed former pub, where the

original panelling and stained glass have been carefully preserved. A menu of adeptly cooked classic French brasserie dishes delivers plenty of big, punchy flavour. Butternut squash velouté with a goats' cheese and sage beignet is a great way to start, followed by the prix-fixe perhaps by roast breast of guinea fowl with creamed Savoy cabbage and tortellini. The bells-and-whistles carte brings on foie gras crème brûlée with caramelised almonds, with home-smoked cod, piquillo peppers and brandade to follow. Glazed lemon tart with basil ice cream makes a refreshing closer. The wine list is strongest in France, among the aristocracy of Burgundy and Bordeaux (vintages of the Saint-Emilion château go right back to the acclaimed 1959), but there are forays further afield too, including a productive one into Australia. Prices are high though, starting at £23.

Chef/s: Martin Nisbet. **Open:** all week 10am to 11pm (10pm Sun). **Closed:** 24 Dec to 3 Jan. **Meals:** alc (main courses £18 to £28). Set L £36. Set D £38. **Service:** 12.5% (optional). **Details:** Cards accepted. 40 seats. 12 seats outside. Air-con. Separate bar. Wheelchair access. Music. Children allowed.

Arbutus

Base ingredients turned to culinary gold
63-64 Frith Street, Soho, W1D 3JW
Tel no: (020) 7734 4545
www.arbutusrestaurant.co.uk
⊖ Tottenham Court Road, map 5
Modern European | £35
Cooking score: 6

Fine dining without tablecloths is the order of the day at Anthony Demetre and Will Smith's 'most appealing' bistro. Its Soho location ensures a lively atmosphere and nobody is here for privacy, whether they're seated at the bar (a great spot for eating alone) or along the neat row of closely ranked tables. Alan Christie has assumed day-to-day cooking activities, but Demetre's trademark approach, which turns base ingredients into culinary gold, persists. Meals are preceded by generous quantities of the crusty house bread and, perhaps, the day's aperitif, before diners face the choice between

the light – a moist, appealingly textured squid and mackerel 'burger' with sea purslane – and the not so light. Offal and cheap cuts are a strong feature of the menu, and one reader happily admitted defeat after tackling the signature main course of trotters on toast with a parcel of tripe. Marseilles-style bouillabaisse, with the components served separately, is an excuse for the kitchen to bring out its little copper pans, which also serve as a carriage for an excellent gratin dauphinois. Staff are 'brisk, efficient and personable' and thoughtful too, despite the rough and tumble of a Soho service; they are also knowledgeable about a user-friendly wine list which is available in its entirety by the carafe (from £5) as well as the bottle (£14.50).

Chef/s: Anthony Demetre and Alan Christie. **Open:** all week L 12 to 2.30 (3 Sun), D 5 to 11 (11.30 Fri and Sat, 10.30 Sun). **Closed:** 25 and 26 Dec, 1 Jan. **Meals:** alc (main courses £15 to £20). Set L £16.95. Pre-theatre set D £18.95. Sun L £16.95. **Service:** 12.5% (optional). **Details:** Cards accepted. 75 seats. Air-con. Separate bar. No music. Wheelchair access. Children allowed.

L'Atelier de Joël Robuchon

Sheer sense-jangling artistry
13-15 West Street, Covent Garden, WC2H 9NE
Tel no: (020) 7010 8600
www.joel-robuchon.com
⊖ Leicester Square, map 5
Modern French | £40
Cooking score: 7

V

The main action at Joël Robuchon's three-tiered Covent Garden pleasuredome takes place in the street-level Atelier – a fashionable space done out like a sushi bar with signature red and black colours, moody lighting and with the best seats as stools clustered around a counter. Chefs work hard in the open kitchen, and staff seem to have dispensed with the embarrassing conceptual spiel that used to greet diners as they perused the menu. On offer is a stunning line-up of jewel-like, highly original tasting plates, including Robuchon's signature dish – a beef and foie gras burger with lightly caramelised bell peppers. But that's just the beginning. This cornucopia of earthly delights might also include a dazzling layered construction of white crabmeat, guacamole and blood orange jelly tinged with coriander vinaigrette, tiny toasts topped with minced pig's trotter, crispy langoustine fritters with basil pistou, and luxury-laden caramelised scallop with kumquat emulsion and caviar. The terse descriptions give little away, but the results are as acutely calibrated as a Rolex watch. If the grazing format doesn't appeal, you can always take the conventional route in the monochrome first-floor dining room (La Table), where a carte and prestige tasting menus promise fillet sole with salsify, vanilla and cauliflower purée or free-range quail stuffed with foie gras and accompanied by Robuchon's emblematic truffle mash. Desserts such as a chocolate boule surprise with praline biscuit and Earl Grey ice cream also hit the heights for sheer sense-jangling artistry. The price for such remarkable food can take your breath away, although there is some relief in the fixed-price lunch and pre-theatre deals. Like Robuchon himself, the wine list is a globetrotter, with prestigious names across the range. Bottle prices start at £22, and around 20 are available by the glass (from £5). **Chef/s:** Olivier Limousin. **Open:** all week L 12 to 3, D 5.30 to 11. **Closed:** 25 and 26 Dec, 1 Jan. **Meals:** alc (main courses £16 to £39). Set L and pre-theatre D £22 (2 courses) to £27. Tasting menu £125. **Service:** 12.5% (optional). **Details:** Cards accepted. 43 seats. Air-con. Separate bar. Wheelchair access. Music. Children allowed. Car parking.

ALSO RECOMMENDED

▲ Automat

33 Dover Street, Mayfair, W1S 4NF
Tel no: (020) 7499 3033
www.automat-london.com
⊖ Green Park, map 5
North American

With booths, a buzzy atmosphere and pleasant staff, this characteristic American diner excels at brunch. Classics – say steak and eggs with home fries (£14), macaroni cheese, and waffles with blueberries and cream (£8) – rub shoulders with smoked brisket rolls and chicken paillard. Elsewhere, simple choices are best: crab cakes with guacamole (£11), New York strip steak and BBQ ribs. The split-level section overlooking the kitchen makes a brighter, livelier alternative to the traditional diner. House wine is £22. Open all week.

L'Autre Pied

Punchy food from a top young gun
5-7 Blandford Street, Marylebone, W1U 3DB
Tel no: (020) 7486 9696
www.lautrepied.co.uk
⊖ Bond Street, map 4
Modern European | £40
Cooking score: 6
£5 OFF

Having Fitzrovia thoroughbred Pied-à-Terre (see entry) as a big brother hasn't intimidated L'Autre Pied one jot. In fact this confident sibling continues to thrive on accessibility, fair value and high-class, seriously considered cooking. Inside, it forgoes edgy fashion statements in favour of elbow-to-elbow bare wooden tables, silk wallpaper and some chinoiserie gloss in the form of backlit painted panels and screens. Sharp but unbuttoned service matches the easy-going vibe, and one reporter even waxed lyrical about eating Sunday lunch out on the pavement. The mood may be dressed-down and it can often feel 'manic' at peak times, but there's no downsizing when it comes to the sophisticated food on the plate. Marcus Eaves is one of London's top young guns and his cooking packs a big seasonal punch, with strong, direct flavours and intelligently worked ideas. In spring, the kitchen celebrates wild garlic, Wye Valley asparagus, wood sorrel and young lamb, but also conjures subtly nuanced partnerships ranging from poached sea trout with cauliflower cream, sea purslane, Kaffir lime and lemongrass cream to slow-cooked veal cheek and crispy tongue with new season's peas, capers and mint. Picture-pretty desserts also ring true – poached Yorkshire

rhubarb might cosy up to baked Alaska and cardamom ice cream or nestle in with vanilla pannacotta and cinnamon foam. The well-chosen, cosmopolitan wine list leans towards Europe, with a fine selection from £23.
Chef/s: Marcus Eaves. **Open:** all week L 12 to 2.45 (3.30 Sun), D 6 to 10.45 (6.30 to 9.30 Sun). **Closed:** 1 week Christmas. **Meals:** alc (main courses £16 to £30). Set L and prer-theatre D £17.95 (2 courses) to £20.95. Sun L £26.50. Tasting menu £55 (7 courses). **Service:** 12.5% (optional). **Details:** Cards accepted. 53 seats. 12 seats outside. Air-con. Music. Children allowed.

Axis at One Aldwych
Thrilling interiors and straight-talking food
1 Aldwych, Covent Garden, WC2B 4RH
Tel no: (020) 7300 0300
www.onealdwych.com/axis
⊖ Covent Garden, map 5
Modern British | £30
Cooking score: 3

🛏

In a spectacularly conceived, subterranean space beneath the swish One Aldwych hotel, Axis puts on quite a show with its arty design features, Thai silk panels and slender tree trunks gilded with satin nickel. The interiors may be dressed to thrill, but the kitchen keeps its head, avoiding frills and furbelows in favour of a straight-talking menu of British staples and European classics. Come here if your palate warms to ham hock fritters with pease pudding, whole roast plaice with grilled potatoes and clam vinaigrette, or helpings of beef bourguignon with mash. Lunching ladies might opt for something lighter (perhaps a salad of endive, Cornish Blue and walnuts), although desserts heap on the cals with treacle sponge or cheesecake ice cream with toffee jelly. The concise wine list starts at £18.
Chef/s: Tony Fleming. **Open:** Mon to Fri L 12 to 2.30, Mon to Sat D 5.30 to 10.30 (5 to 10.30 Sat). **Closed:** Sun, bank hols, Christmas and New Year. **Meals:** alc (main courses £17 to £28). Set L and D £16.75 (2 courses) to £19.75. **Service:** 12.5% (optional). **Details:** Cards accepted. 92 seats. Air-con. Separate bar. Wheelchair access. Music. Children allowed.

Bank Westminster
Easy-eating brasserie food
45 Buckingham Gate, Westminster, SW1E 6BS
Tel no: (020) 7630 6644
www.bankrestaurants.com
⊖ St James's Park, map 5
Modern European | £40
Cooking score: 2

🛏 V

'Smart, stylish' Bank sits at the rear of the Crowne Plaza hotel and offers a big, boldly designed, light-washed space overlooking a very attractive courtyard. The easy-eating brasserie menu stays mainly with popular choices – Caesar salad with char-grilled chicken, for example, or chilli squid with Thai noodle salad – and breaks little new ground. But the cooking is dependable, ranging from salmon fishcakes with lemon and dill butter, via crispy dick with sesame and honey dressing to beef bourguignon with mash. Desserts are equally reassuring, perhaps chocolate brownies or baked New York cheesecake. The wine list opens at £15.50. There is a branch in Birmingham (see entry).
Chef/s: David Ferguson. **Open:** Mon to Fri 12 to 10.30, Sat D 5.30 to 10.30. **Closed:** Sun, 25 to 27 Dec, bank hols. **Meals:** alc (main courses £12 to £24). Set L and D £37.40 to £47.50. **Service:** 12.5% (optional). **Details:** Cards accepted. 120 seats. 20 seats outside. Air-con. Separate bar. No music. Wheelchair access. Music. Children allowed.

NEW ENTRY
Bar Boulud
French brasserie, New York style
Mandarin Oriental Hyde Park, 66 Knightsbridge, Knightsbridge, SW1X 7LA
Tel no: (020) 7201 3899
www.barboulud.com
⊖ Knightsbridge, map 4
French | £35
Cooking score: 4

🛏 V

This Knightsbridge spin-off from New York's superstar chef Daniel Boulud has proved a big hit. With its reasonable prices, simple food,

well-timed service and informal atmosphere, everything about Bar Boulud feels right: from the banquettes in the stylish bar to the tables clustered in front of the open-plan kitchen. The menu is so stuffed full of good things that you're planning a return visit before you've even ordered. From a dream line-up of brasserie dishes come Dorset crab salad with spring vegetables and five-herb citrus dressing, platters of shellfish, a charcuterie board with a standout coarse country pâté grand-père, a selection of meaty sausages, excellent pork belly and coq au vin. Not to be missed are the various burgers – 'the best in town', according to several readers. Desserts set out to delight, especially the lightest of Grand Marnier soufflés. The extensive but expensive wine list (from £21.50) is redeemed by a good selection by the glass.
Chef/s: Dean Yasharian. **Open:** all week L 12 to 3, D 5.30 to 11 (10 Sun). **Meals:** alc (main courses £12 to £23). Set L and D (5.30 to 7) £20 (3 courses). **Service:** 12.5% (optional). **Details:** Cards accepted. 169 seats. Air-con. Separate bar. Wheelchair access. Music. Children allowed.

NEW ENTRY

Bar Shu

Accomplished Sichuan cooking
28 Frith Street, Soho, W1D 5LF
Tel no: (020) 7287 6688
www.bar-shu.co.uk
⊖ Leicester Square, Tottenham Court Road, map 5
Chinese | £35
Cooking score: 4

V

Bar Shu is back after a closure due to a fire – and its return will be greeted with glee by lovers of Szechuan cooking. Far from being idle during the layoff, it has spawned Baozi Inn (25 Newport Court, WC2) and Ba Shan (24 Romilly Street, W1). At Bar Shu, you find yourself squeezed into small dining rooms with sturdy wood carvings and furniture, spread over three floors. The menu showcases some scary dishes featuring pig's blood and intestines. Flavours are full-on; sliced whelks

arrived with hot green Szechuan pepper and were rounded off by a pyrotechnical kick of wasabi. The kitchen can also deliver more delicate touches; sliced pork with softened silk gourd and lily bulbs was spot-on. Sweet-and-sour crispy sea bass was a visual treat, and 'bears paw' beancurd was an adroit mix of oil and chili. High pricing is a rub. Desserts and wines (from £18.90) are mere bit-part players.
Chef/s: Mr Xiao Zhong Zhang. **Open:** all week 12 to 11 (11.30 Fri and Sat). **Closed:** 24 and 25 Dec. **Meals:** alc (main courses £9 to £40). **Service:** 12.5%. **Details:** Cards accepted. 100 seats. Air-con. No mobile phones. Wheelchair access. Music. Children allowed.

Bar Trattoria Semplice

Straightforward Italian home cooking
22-23 Woodstock Street, Mayfair, W1C 2AP
Tel no: (020) 7491 8638
www.bartrattoriasemplice.com
⊖ Bond Street, map 5
Italian | £25
Cooking score: 3

V £30

Semplice ('simple') is the watchword and guiding principle at the casual sibling of Ristorante Semplice (see entry), tucked away just off Oxford Street. It feels like an upmarket café, and is dedicated to the freshest and most straightforward kind of Italian home cooking. Wooden boards of antipasti and cheeses are generally enjoyable, as are some of the regional Italian main dishes, like veal cooked in red wine with mashed potato or char-grilled tuna steak with tomato and rocket salad. Some people feel portions are controlled a little too agonisingly, and the appearance of a dessert trolley is something to be got over for others – although the chocolate torta and cheesecake are both good examples. Wines from £14.50.
Chef/s: Marco Torri and Marco Squillace. **Open:** Sun to Fri L 12 to 3 (12.45 to 3.45 Sun), D 6 to 11 (11.30 Fri, 6.15 to 9.30 Sun). Sat 12.30 to 11.30. **Closed:** 25 and 26 Dec, bank hols. **Meals:** alc (main courses £10 to £19). Set L £16.75 (2 courses). **Service:** 12.5%. **Details:** Cards accepted. 70 seats. 30 seats outside. Separate bar. Children allowed.

Barrafina

Spot-on tapas
54 Frith Street, Soho, W1D 4SL
Tel no: (020) 7813 8016
www.barrafina.co.uk
⊖ **Tottenham Court Road, map 5**
Spanish | £28
Cooking score: 4

V £30

The queues just won't die down at Sam and Eddie Hart's spot-on take on the classic tapas bar. It's authentically, some say irritatingly, reservation-free, with just two dozen vertiginous stools the length of the bar to accommodate its punters. Getting there as service begins is your best bet – or face hour-long waits. Any later and a chilled sherry and a few croquetas and pan con tomate 'para picar' will have to allay hunger pangs temporarily. The day's seafood specials are always worth ordering. Garlicky razor clams, dinky deep-fried chipirones and clams (each one individually checked for freshness by a keen-nosed chef) have all impressed. Trendier dishes such as mojama, pomegranate and chicory salad and some pricey, thickly battered zucchini flowers can't quite compete. You might miss the cold draught Cruzcampo, but an all-Iberian list of wines (from £15) and sherries, with everything by the glass, compensates.
Chef/s: Nieves Barragan. **Open:** all week L 12 to 3 (1 to 3.30 Sun), D 5 to 11 (5.30 to 10 Sun). **Closed:** 24 to 26 Dec, bank hols. **Meals:** alc (main courses £7 to £13). **Service:** 12.5% (optional). **Details:** Cards accepted. 23 seats. 10 seats outside. Air-con. No music. Children allowed.

READERS RECOMMEND

Barrica

Spanish
62 Goodge Street, Fitzrovia, W1T 4NE
Tel no: (020) 7436 9448
www.barrica.co.uk
'Great tapas selection, authentic Spanish atmosphere'

ALSO RECOMMENDED

▲ Bedford & Strand

1a Bedford Street, Covent Garden, WC2E 9HH
Tel no: (020) 7836 3033
www.bedford-strand.com
⊖ **Covent Garden, map 5**
Anglo-French

This jolly, good-natured Parisian-style wine bar does sterling service, mixing a passion for wine with a short menu of relaxed bistro food. The kitchen pumps out classic British dishes like potted crab (£7.50) and a well-reported chicken pie (£11.50). There's also the odd nod towards France – say Bayonne ham with rémoulade, côte de boeuf with béarnaise (£19.50), and apple and almond tart (£5.50) to finish. An eminently gluggable wine list opens with a Montepulciano d'Abruzzo at £19.50. Closed Sun.

▲ The Beehive

126 Crawford Street, Marylebone, W1U 6BF
Tel no: (020) 7486 8037
www.thebeehive-pub.co.uk
⊖ **Baker Street, map 4**
Gastropub

One of Marylebone's oldest pubs, the wood-floored Beehive is now part of the Claudio Pulze stable, but still plies its trade as a neighbourhood watering hole with a profitable new sideline in all-day food. Starters of deep-fried squid or mushroom risotto (£6) might give way to 'things of substance' such as Galloway steak sandwiches or plates of roast duck breast with herbed polenta, curly kale and carrot purée (£13.50). Simple desserts (£6.50) and cheese round things off. Meantime beers on tap; wines from £16.50. Open all week.

Benares

Innovative new-wave Indian
12a Berkeley Square, Mayfair, W1J 6BS
Tel no: (020) 7629 8886
www.benaresrestaurant.com
⊖ Green Park, map 5
Indian | £50
Cooking score: 4

V

The Rolls Royce showroom next door signals that the entry level at Atul Kochhar's new-breed Indian restaurant will be high. Inside, you feel cosseted in a swish room cloaked in dark wood and brown leather. The Indian cooking has a distinctive Western accent, so spicy soft-shell crab is paired with apple mille-feuille and lemongrass-cumin mayonnaise. At inspection, quail marinated in tomato chutney then cooked in the tandoor oven was stirred into life by subtle spicing, and though overcooking let down a pan-fried black bream (paired with crispy okra and tapioca mash), a racy mustard and tomato sauce lifted the dish. End with a delightful vanilla pudding infused with Jamaican dark rum, and passion-fruit sorbet. Service is silky smooth, but for all the trappings, the cooking seldom gets you shouting from the rooftops. Wines, from £18.50 are well researched, and a good match for the food; the list includes a quintet from the subcontinent.

Chef/s: Atul Kochhar. **Open:** all week L 12 to 2.30 (3 Sat and Sun), D 5.30 to 11 (6 to 10.30 Sun). **Closed:** 25 Dec. **Meals:** alc (main courses £20 to £45). Set L and D £24.95 (2 courses) to £29.95. Grazing Menu £69 (4 courses). **Service:** 12.5% (optional). **Details:** Cards accepted. 130 seats. Air-con. Separate bar. Wheelchair access. Music.

Bentley's Oyster Bar & Grill

Re-energised seafood institution
11-15 Swallow Street, Piccadilly, W1B 4DG
Tel no: (020) 7734 4756
www.bentleysoysterbarandgrill.co.uk
⊖ Piccadilly Circus, map 5
Seafood | £42
Cooking score: 4

The street-level Oyster Bar is an animated, marble-hued rendezvous for those who like their bivalves, crustacea and fish pie with a glass of something fizzy, while the main action takes place in the clubby upstairs Grill – a study in blues and whites, with William Morris flourishes, piscine paintings and nods to the building's Arts and Crafts heritage. Shrewdly sourced ingredients are at the heart of things, and the kitchen shows its worth with top-class grilled Dover sole and a textbook rendition of scallops with black pudding. Otherwise, expect anything from stuffed squid with chorizo and feta to Cornish fritto misto or lobster linguine. Meat eaters can content themselves with a mixed grill or eight-hour shoulder of lamb, while steamed apple sponge makes a comforting, sweet-toothed finale. 'Patchy' service has been reported this year. Delectable sherries and 'wines of the sea' lead off the expansive global list, which is stuffed with irresistible beauties. Bottle prices start at £19.50, and there's a commendable choice of 20 by the carafe and glass.

Chef/s: Brendan Fyldes. **Open:** Grill: Mon to Fri L 12 to 3, Mon to Sat D 6 to 11. Oyster Bar: all week 12 to 12 (10 Sun). **Closed:** 25 Dec. **Meals:** alc (main courses £17 to £29). **Service:** 12.5% (optional). **Details:** Cards accepted. 98 seats. 12 seats outside. Air-con. Separate bar. Wheelchair access. Music. Children allowed.

Bocca di Lupo

Buzzing, trendy trattoria
12 Archer Street, Piccadilly, W1D 7BB
Tel no: (020) 7734 2223
www.boccadilupo.com
⊖ **Piccadilly Circus, map 5**
Italian | £35
Cooking score: 4

V

Remember the name Jacob Kenedy. The ex-Moro chef packs them in nightly at this trendy Soho trattoria. The draw is 'fascinating regional dishes prepared fearlessly' (as one reporter put it), which might mean Tuscan lardo di Colonnata (cured pork fat) with grated walnuts, Roman fried lamb's brain with cauliflower or a Sicilian espresso granita. The majority of dishes are available in two sizes. The strong flavours and 'fantastic value' are very seductive, although some have found the presentation and finish wanting. Seats are at the bar or in the 'close but not cramped' dining room. Several readers have remarked on the noise – this is certainly not the place for an intimate tête-à-tête. Attentive service and a thrillingly Italophile wine list (with plenty of carafe and glass options) add to the buzz. Bottles start at £17.50.
Chef/s: Jacob Kenedy. **Open:** Mon to Sat L 12.30 to 3, D 5.30 to 11. **Closed:** Sun, 25 and 26 Dec. **Meals:** alc (main courses £9 to £25). **Service:** 12.5% (optional). **Details:** Cards accepted. 60 seats. Air-con. Wheelchair access. Music. Children allowed.

Symbols

🛏 Accommodation is available

£30 Three courses for less than £30

V More than three vegetarian main courses

£5 OFF £5-off voucher scheme

🍾 Notable wine list

NEW ENTRY

Boyd's Brasserie

Swanky bar/brasserie
8 Northumberland Avenue, Covent Garden, WC2N 5BY
Tel no: (020) 7808 3344
www.boydsbrasserie.co.uk
⊖ **Charing Cross, map 5**
British | £32
Cooking score: 3

V

The grand Victoria Hotel ceased operating decades ago, but its brown-beige marble foyer has been given a new lease of life with the creation of this swanky bar/brasserie. The deliberately populist British menu manages to undersell itself at almost every turn (steaks, burgers, prawn cocktail, omelettes), but the cooking is way above expectation: chunky fish soup with rouille, chicken and foie gras terrine or duck breast with duck leg hash are prepared and presented with real panache. Fish and chips delivers goujons of red snapper with a tomato and fennel ketchup, and if you can't make up your mind there's a selection of tapas-sized portions at bargain prices. With a large glass of house wine at £7, it represents great value for central London.
Chef/s: David Collison and Richard Hawthorne. **Open:** all week 12.30 to 10. **Closed:** 25 and 26 Dec. **Meals:** alc (main courses from £13 to £28). Set L and D £15.50 (2 courses) to £18.50. **Service:** 12.5% (optional). **Details:** Cards accepted. 70 seats. Air-con. Separate bar. Wheelchair access. Music. Children allowed.

ALSO RECOMMENDED

▲ Bumbles

16 Buckingham Palace Road, Belgravia, SW1W 0QP
Tel no: (020) 7828 2903
www.bumbles1950.com
⊖ **Victoria, map 5**
Modern British £5 OFF

Food was rationed when Bumbles opened near Victoria station, and British classics still feature – a testament to its spirit. The modern dining room is cosy, and the ambitious kitchen serves crowd-pleasers such as runny egg ravioli with pea foam, and pig's trotter stuffed with sweetbreads paired with crispy cuttlefish, as well as banana flambé and peanut praline. Fair pricing (3 courses from £10) and charming service make train delays less miserable. House wine £11.95. Closed Sat L and Sun.

▲ The Café at Sotheby's
34–35 New Bond Street, Mayfair, W1A 2AA
Tel no: (020) 7293 5077
www.sothebys.com
◑ Bond Street, Oxford Circus, map 5
Modern European £5 OFF

With tables spilling out into the foyer, this appendage of Sotheby's is a darling of the art crowd and Bond Street shoppers. Lobster club sandwiches (£18.50) are *de rigueur* here, but the lunch menu might also promise asparagus with baked feta and poppy seed dressing (£7.50) or confit duck with Parmesan polenta. Cool off with rosewater and Greek yoghurt pannacotta (£5.50) before hitting the galleries. Wines have been selected by Sotheby's own MW Serena Sutcliffe; prices from £19 (£5.25 a glass). Breakfast and afternoon tea, too. Open Mon to Fri.

READERS RECOMMEND
El Camino Mexicano
Mexican
25-27 Brewer Street, Soho, W1F 0RR
Tel no: (020) 7734 7711
www.elcamino.co.uk
'A lot of fun and great-value food in the heart of Soho'

Readers recommend

A 'readers recommend' review is a genuine quote from a report sent in by one of our readers. We intend to follow up these suggestions throughout the year to come.

Le Caprice
Classy modern brasserie fare
Arlington House, Arlington Street, Mayfair, SW1A 1RJ
Tel no: (020) 7629 2239
www.le-caprice.co.uk
◑ Green Park, map 5
Modern European | £45
Cooking score: 4

V

Le Caprice celebrates its thirtieth birthday in 2011, and it looks set to run and run – indeed a branch opened at The Pierre in New York in 2009. The fashion crowd may have moved on to sister restaurant Scott's (see entry), but reservations still remain hard to come by. Part of the secret lies in the cooking, which may not always be the very best, but generally achieves a satisfying consistency. Eggs Benedict, dressed crab with celeriac rémoulade, and calf's liver with crispy bacon and sage and onion mash, are typical of the classy modern brasserie fare it does so well, and the best seasonal ingredients also turn up in specials like John Dory with Sicilian artichokes, broad beans and mint, or Alphonso mango and pineapple with lemon sorbet. The wine list is sharply chosen, with good producers, highish prices and a reasonable selection by the glass. Bottles from £18.75.
Chef/s: Lee Bull. Open: all week L 12 to 3 (4 Fri and Sat), D 5.30 to 12 (12 to 11 Sun). Closed: 25 and 26 Dec, 1 Jan. Meals: alc (main courses £16 to £29). Pre/post-theatre set D £15.75 (2 courses) to £19.75. Service: 12.5% (optional). Details: Cards accepted. 70 seats. Air-con. Separate bar. No mobile phones. Music. Children allowed.

READERS RECOMMEND
Centre Point Sushi Café
Japanese
20-21 St Giles High Street, Soho, WC2H 8LN
Tel no: (020) 7240 6147
www.cpfs.co.uk
'Unassuming but charming, intimate, and truly excellent'

Cha Cha Moon

Super-stylish noodle bar
15-21 Ganton Street, Soho, W1F 9BN
Tel no: (020) 7297 9800
www.chachamoon.com
⊖ Oxford Circus, map 5
Pan-Asian | £18
Cooking score: 1

V £30

Sleek design meets canteen-style grazing at Alan Yau's take on a big-city noodle bar. Moody lighting, bamboo and rose-tinted glass set the tone, and the white-hot kitchen blasts out Hong Kong street food and pan-Asian plates to crowds crammed around communal tables. Come early to beat the queues waiting for the likes of Taiwan beef noodle soup, Fukian-style udon, chicken satay salad and yellow lamb curry. Zany cocktails are the stars of the drinks list, but you can also sup green tea, Tsingtao beer or wine (from £4.90 a glass).
Chef/s: Kim Choong Lee. **Open:** all week 12 to 11 (11.30 Fri and Sat, 10.30 Sun). **Closed:** 25 Dec. **Meals:** alc (main courses £6 to £9). **Service:** not inc. **Details:** Cards accepted. 144 seats. 70 seats outside. Air-con. No music. Wheelchair access. Children allowed.

The Chancery

Chic bolt hole in lawyerland
9 Cursitor Street, Holborn, EC4A 1LL
Tel no: (020) 7831 4000
www.thechancery.co.uk
⊖ Chancery Lane, map 5
Modern European | £34
Cooking score: 4

£5 OFF **V**

Legal eagles swoop on this popular local for some serious business-lunching (although new Saturday openings hold the promise of a more diverse clientele), and the deal-broking creates a buzz about the small, modern room with its wood floors and white walls. Chef Daniel Urzua Guerrero has recently arrived from sister restaurant The Clerkenwell (now closed) and there's certainly no shortage of skill coming out of the kitchen. A chilled terrine of smoked haddock, leek and potato paired with soft-boiled quails'eggs on hollandaise sauce displayed precise cooking, whilst a trio of pork – fillet, shredded hock spring roll and braised shin – showed inventiveness with cuts that had been selected from Smithfield that morning. There's a sense of fun about the desserts, which include a caramelised banana bavarois, and the wine list is a healthy mix of French and New World names. House selections start at £16.
Chef/s: Daniel Urzua Guerrero. **Open:** Mon to Fri L 12 to 2.30, Mon to Sat D 6 to 10.30. **Closed:** Sun, 24 Dec to 3 Jan. **Meals:** Set L and D £27.50 (2 courses) to £34. **Service:** 12.5% (optional). **Details:** Cards accepted. 55 seats. 10 seats outside. Air-con. Separate bar. Wheelchair access. Music. Children allowed.

China Tang at the Dorchester

Cantonese classics in a lavish setting
The Dorchester Hotel, 53 Park Lane, Hyde Park, W1K 1QA
Tel no: (020) 7629 9988
www.thedorchester.com
⊖ Hyde Park Corner, map 4
Chinese | £75
Cooking score: 3

🛏 **V**

Entrepreneur and style guru Sir David Tang is the brains – and the name – behind this slinky, expensively glamorous dining room in the bowels of the Dorchester Hotel. The menu covers familiar territory, with a selection of mainly Cantonese classics ranging from chicken in lemon sauce to lobster with ginger and spring onions, plus an array of dim sum (served in the evening as well as lunch). The kitchen is capable, and dishes such as carefully cooked Szechuan prawns and gai lan greens steamed with garlic have impressed. There is nothing here to scare the horses, and flavours can seem rather muted – although this may be a sop to the perceived tastes of the hotel clientele. Prices on the hefty wine list (from £25) take no prisoners, so stick to jasmine tea or beer unless someone else is paying.

Chef/s: Mr Yip Lam Law. **Open:** all week L 11.30 to 3.30 (11 to 4 Sat and Sun), D 5.30 to 11.30. **Closed:** 25 Dec. **Meals:** alc (main courses from £10 to £150). Set L £15 (2 courses). **Service:** 12.5% (optional). **Details:** Cards accepted. 180 seats. Air-con. Separate bar. Wheelchair access. Music. Children allowed.

Chisou

Style and substance in perfect harmony
4 Princes Street, Mayfair, W1B 2LE
Tel no: (020) 7629 3931
www.chisou.co.uk
⊖ **Oxford Circus, map 5**
Japanese | £40
Cooking score: 4

V

Proximity to Vogue House ensures a steady stream of fashionistas to keep Chisou busy – but don't be put off. This is a case of style and substance in perfect harmony. The menu is all-encompassing, with respectable selections of sushi, tempura, grills, rice and noodles. Set lunches aren't among the West End's cheapest Japanese offerings, but they are among the best. A nigiri selection has been described as 'impeccable': the rice treated as respectfully as the fish. Spinach and yuzu salad and chawan mushi are perennial favourites, while monkfish liver with ponzu and deep-fried tuna tataki show the chef's creative bent. The emphasis is on pure, clear flavours; luxurious 'western' embellishments are used with caution. Chisou quietly holds its own against more famous names, even if the modest blond wood décor doesn't. The saké offering is superb, and a sommelier is on hand to assist aficionados and novices alike. French wines from £14.90.
Chef/s: Kodi Aung. **Open:** Mon to Sat L 12 to 2.30 (3 Sat), D 6 to 10.15. **Closed:** Sun, bank hols, 2 weeks Aug, 2 weeks Christmas. **Meals:** alc (main courses £10 to £25). Set L £14. **Service:** 13% (optional). **Details:** Cards accepted. 70 seats. 6 seats outside. Air-con. Music. Children allowed.

Cigala

Unbuttoned Spanish hangout
54 Lamb's Conduit Street, Bloomsbury, WC1N 3LW
Tel no: (020) 7405 1717
www.cigala.co.uk
⊖ **Holborn, Russell Square, map 5**
Spanish | £28
Cooking score: 1
£30

Spanish cooking based on good raw materials has proved a winning formula here for ten years. The room hasn't changed either; the large windows give views of the bustle on the street and simple, white-clad tables add to the sense of light and space. You can graze your way through an extensive menu of classic tapas ranging from char-grilled chorizo and Jamón de Teruel to clams with white wine, garlic and parsley or pastel de bacalao (salt cod and potato fritters) with aïoli; otherwise opt for something more substantial, say grilled veal chop or a parillada of mixed seafood. The fascinating all-Spanish wine list opens at £16.50.
Chef/s: Jake Hodges. **Open:** all week 12 to 10.45 (12.30 to 10.45 Sat, 12.30 to 9.30 Sun). **Closed:** 24 to 26 Dec, Good Fri to Easter Mon. **Meals:** alc (main courses £12 to £19). Set L £16 (2 courses) to £18. **Service:** 12.5% (optional). **Details:** Cards accepted. 60 seats. 16 seats outside. Air-con. Separate bar. No music. Children allowed.

Cinnamon Club

Crowd-thrilling new-wave Indian
30-32 Great Smith Street, Westminster, SW1P 3BU
Tel no: (020) 7222 2555
www.cinnamonclub.com
⊖ **Westminster, map 5**
Indian | £45
Cooking score: 3

V

A business bolt hole *par excellence* and a favourite haunt of MPs and bureaucrats, the venerable enclaves of the Old Westminster Library – antique bookcases, mahogany panels and all – might seem like an odd setting for new-wave Indian cuisine. Since

2001, however, chef Vivek Singh has been thrilling the crowds with his subtle, multi-layered food and clever fusion of spicy Asian flavours with European ingredients and sharp culinary technique. Some dishes are 'blow-your-mouth-off hot', but the results can also be exquisitely satisfying. The fish 'tasting plate' of tandoori halibut, Norwegian king crab and wild African prawn is a stunner, but the kitchen also challenges the taste buds with 'hunter's-style' rabbit tikka, seared black bream with aubergine relish and vermicelli, and sides of masala chicken livers with cauliflower purée. The wine list suits the cuisine and prices are par for the location; bottles start at £21.

Chef/s: Vivek Singh. **Open:** Mon to Sat L 12 to 2.45, D 6 to 10.45. **Closed:** Sun, bank hols. **Meals:** alc (main courses £12 to £29). Set L and early D £19 (2 courses) to £22. **Service:** 12.5% (optional). **Details:** Cards accepted. 130 seats. Air-con. Separate bar. No music. No mobile phones. Children allowed.

Clos Maggiore
Happy eatery with good set deals
33 King Street, Covent Garden, WC2E 8JD
Tel no: (020) 7379 9696
www.closmaggiore.com
⊖ **Covent Garden, map 5**
French | £35
Cooking score: 2

V

'Beautiful setting – we were in the conservatory but dressed for winter with lighted trees and a big fire in the stove', enthused one couple of this Covent Garden stalwart. Clos Maggiore's modern French cooking lives up to the image: it is very passable, not expensive if you explore the various set deals, and is served with a willingness in a happy atmosphere. Raw materials are well sourced, and dishes are uncomplicated – say salad of English smoked eel and new potatoes, sea bass with a chorizo boulangère and Iberico chorizo sauce, or slow-cooked Charolais beef cheek. House wine is £18.50.

Chef/s: Marcellin Marc. **Open:** all week L 12 to 2.15, D 5 to 11 (10 Sun). **Closed:** 25 and 26 Dec. **Meals:** alc (main courses £17 to £20). Set L and D £19.50. **Service:** 12.5% (optional). **Details:** Cards accepted. 70 seats. Air-con. Music. Children allowed.

ALSO RECOMMENDED
▲ Cocorino
18 Thayer Street, Marylebone, W1U 3JY
Tel no: (020) 7935 0810
www.cocorino.co.uk
⊖ **Bond Street, map 4**
Italian

All-day opening and a flexible menu contribute to the appeal of this tiny, basic café owned by Francesco Mazzei (see L'Anima) and Linda Yau. It's split in two. The savoury side serves breakfasts of French toast and scrambled eggs, top-quality salads such as beetroot, pear and Gorgonzola (£4.50) or mortadella and Provolone cheese focaccia alongside aubergine Parmigiana and gnocchi all puttanese (£5.50), all to eat in or take away. The gelato side dispenses exquisite Italian ice creams, sorbets and frappés. Unlicensed. Open all week.

Corrigan's Mayfair
A joyous celebration of stellar ingredients
28 Upper Grosvenor Street, Mayfair, W1K 7EH
Tel no: (020) 7499 9943
www.corrigansmayfair.com
⊖ **Marble Arch, map 4**
Modern British | £55
Cooking score: 6

£5 OFF 🍷 **V**

Corrigan's is a restaurant of contrasts. The man behind it is Irish chef Richard Corrigan, a big name with a big personality, yet the décor of his Mayfair flagship is rather sedate – not at all what you might expect from such an ebullient character. But there is a 'lovely bar for pre-dinner Champagne', and the menus are a joyous celebration of stellar seasonal ingredients – from oysters and wild sea trout to Elwy Valley lamb and Cheltenham beetroot. Expect a cavalcade of creative and luxurious treats including tea-roasted veal sweetbreads and morels, hake with monk's beard and oyster linguine, and a gold-flecked 'millionaire's shortbread' just begging to be eaten. Game season is a good time to come for grouse pie or partridge with romesco sauce. Not everything on the plate is quite as exuberant as it sounds, although puddings get a universal round of applause. 'Ingratiating' staff can be distant – except when they're championing the wine list, which is a paean to 'natural' wines from small European producers working sustainably and biodynamically. Prices start high (£25) and soon shoot up. A £2 cover is levied on all bills (even the bargain lunch). Irritating, but the nibbles you get are superb.

Chef/s: Richard Corrigan and Chris McGowan. **Open:** Sun to Fri L 12 to 3 (4 Sun), all week D 6 to 11 (9.30 Sun). **Closed:** 25 and 26 Dec, 1 Jan. **Meals:** alc (main courses £22 to £36). Set L Mon to Fri £27 (3 courses). Sun L £27. **Service:** 12.5% (optional). **Details:** Cards accepted. 80 seats. Air-con. Separate bar. Wheelchair access. Music. Children allowed.

NEW ENTRY
Dean Street Townhouse
Boisterous British brasserie
69-71 Dean Street, Soho, W1D 3SE
Tel no: (020) 7434 1775
www.deanstreettownhouse.com
⊖ Leicester Square, Tottenham Court Road, map 5
British | £35
Cooking score: 4

⊏ V

It's fun, busy, everyone has a good time and the food is good – no whizzes or foams but seasonal British ingredients that taste the way they came on this earth. Dean Street Townhouse opened to a burst of enthusiasm in late 2009, and its profusion of art and close-set, white-clothed tables reminded one visitor of Langan's Brasserie in its 1980s heyday. It's got pizazz. It's also got superb twice-baked smoked haddock soufflé, delicious Blythburgh pork T-bone served with champ

and buttered carrots and excellent Creedy Carver duck breast with caramelised quince. A few dishes are bland, but they are rarely unacceptable. The only problem is that everyone wants to eat here at the same time – but the dining room is open all day with breakfast and afternoon tea extending choice. The wine list covers a good range of styles with prices from £15.25.

Chef/s: Stephen Tonkin. **Open:** all week 7am to 11.30pm (midnight Fri and Sat, 8am Sat and Sun). **Meals:** alc (main courses £11 to £27). **Service:** 12.5% (optional). **Details:** Cards accepted. 110 seats. 25 seats outside. Air-con. Separate bar. No mobile phones. Music. Children allowed.

Dehesa
Creative tapas and must-have charcuterie
25 Ganton Street, Oxford Circus, W1F 9BP
Tel no: (020) 7494 4170
www.dehesa.co.uk
⊖ Oxford Circus, map 5
Spanish/Italian | £25
Cooking score: 3

£5 OFF V £30

Whole hams in the window remind one of Dehesa's namesake – the woodland area where Spain's tastiest pigs roam (charcuterie should always be part of your plans). As for the rest, take your pick of gently priced tapas that are true to the spirit of the Italian and Spanish cuisines that inspire this contemporary tapas bar. Stuffed zucchini flowers are a signature dish here and at sister bar Salt Yard (see entry), while scallops with cauliflower purée, jamón and sherry caramel, and rice pudding with quince demonstrate Dehesa's creative but unshowy style. Bar stool seating and the odd cramped table don't encourage lingering. However the Italo-Spanish wine list (from £15) – big on indigenous grapes and by-the-glass options – certainly does.

Chef/s: Brent Loam. **Open:** all week 12 to 11 (5 Sun). **Closed:** 10 days Christmas and New Year. **Meals:** alc (tapas £3 to £7). **Service:** 12.5% (optional). **Details:** Cards accepted. 40 seats. 16 seats outside. Air-con. Music. Children allowed.

Dinings
Dinky but thrilling Japanese
22 Harcourt Street, Marylebone, W1H 4HH
Tel no: (020) 7723 0666
www.dinings.co.uk
⊖ Marylebone, map 4
Japanese | £55
Cooking score: 3

V

Dinings proves that bigger is not necessarily better: the tiny restaurant is crammed into a Marylebone town house, with a dinky sushi bar at street-level and a handful of tables in the basement. Overlook the seriously spartan décor and concentrate instead on the tapas-sized sharing plates that deliver a clever cocktail of Japanese flavours. The kitchen rarely puts a foot wrong with the likes of yellowtail tataki with truffle miso, the buttery citrus notes of sautéed scallops with yuzu garlic sauce or deliciously extravagant sushi rolls packed with seared Wagyu beef, foie gras and sweet soy sauce. Set menus help to keep lunchtime bills low, otherwise such skilled cooking does come at a price. Wines from £16.50 a bottle are well-matched to the food.
Chef/s: Masaki Sugisaki. **Open:** Mon to Fri L 12 to 2.30, all week D 6 to 10.30 (10 Sun). **Closed:** 25 to 27 Dec. **Meals:** Set L £12.50 (2 courses) to £17.50. Set D £40 (2 courses) to £58. **Service:** 10% (optional). **Details:** Cards accepted. 28 seats. Music. Children allowed.

ALSO RECOMMENDED
▲ The Duke of Wellington
94a Crawford Street, Marylebone, W1H 2HQ
Tel no: (020) 7723 2790
www.thedukew1.co.uk
⊖ Marylebone, Baker Street, map 4
Gastropub

It may look like an everyday boozer from the outside, but bookable wood tables in the bar and an upstairs dining room bear all the hallmarks of a modern-day gastropub. The menu changes daily, delivering robust and uncomplicated ideas that in spring could open with dressed crab on toast (£7.50), go on to

grilled calf's liver with swede purée, Savoy cabbage and Alsace bacon (£15) and finish with apple charlotte (£5.50). Good lunch and Saturday brunch deals. House wine is £15. Open all week.

Fifth Floor
Foodie heaven
Harvey Nichols, 109-125 Knightsbridge, Knightsbridge, SW1X 7RJ
Tel no: (020) 7235 5250
www.harveynichols.com
⊖ Knightsbridge, map 4
Modern British | £33
Cooking score: 3

V

Swan up to this Knightsbridge emporium's fifth floor, with its funky café, slinky leather-clad bar and über-minimalist, gleaming white dining room, and you are in foodie heaven. Chef Jonas Karlsson knows his clients and ratchets up the trendy components, tempting the assembled crowd with the likes of seared Rougie foie gras, pineapple salsa and pain d'épices croûtons, roast Icelandic cod with Puy lentils, glazed pork cheeks and palourde clams, or poached baby chicken with black rice pilaf. For sweet delectation, expect anything from 64 per cent Manjari chocolate fondant to spiced poached pumpkin with cinnamon ice cream. Alternatively, daily 'market menus' pull in provisions from the store's Foodmarket for the likes of creamed Jerusalem artichoke risotto, aged Parmesan and mizuna. The monumental wine list opens with irresistible own-label house selections (from £21.50), but moves rapidly into big-money territory: think Super Tuscans, blue-blooded Bordeaux and rare Aussie treasures.
Chef/s: Jonas Karlsson. **Open:** all week L 12 to 3 (4 Fri to Sun), Mon to Sat D 6 to 11. **Closed:** 25 and 26 Dec, Easter Sun. **Meals:** Set L and D £19.50 to £40. Sun L £19.50 (2 courses) to £24.50. **Service:** 12.5%. **Details:** Cards accepted. 125 seats. Air-con. Separate bar. No mobile phones. Wheelchair access. Music. Children allowed. Car parking.

Fino

Straight-up star tapas
33 Charlotte Street (entrance in Rathbone Street),
Fitzrovia, W1T 1RR
Tel no: (020) 7813 8010
www.finorestaurant.com
⊖ **Goodge Street, map 5**
Spanish | £25
Cooking score: 3
£30

The décor at Sam and Eddy Hart's spacious
basement restaurant has the kind of subtle,
understated chic that allows the quality of the
food to claim star status. This place has a strong
following. The menu is a straight-up list of
Spanish tapas, the quality of ingredients is
high, flavours are carefully balanced, and
service keeps the pace moving while retaining
a friendly attitude. There's a seasonal feel to
crisp-fried anchovies, grilled mackerel with
baby potatoes and jamón or grilled asparagus
with Payoyo cheese shavings, while hand-
sliced jamón de Jabugo, mushroom croquetas,
grilled quail, lamb cutlets with arroz blanco,
and chipirones (baby squid) are highly
regarded menu staples. A page of sherries by
the glass opens the all-Spanish wine list, with
bottles from £19.
Chef/s: Nieves Barragan. **Open:** Mon to Fri L 12 to 3,
Mon to Sat D 6 to 10.30. **Closed:** Sun, 25 and 26
Dec, bank hols. **Meals:** alc (tapas £6 to £22). Set L
£14.95 (2 courses) to £17.95. **Service:** 12.5%
(optional). **Details:** Cards accepted. 85 seats. Air-
con. Separate bar. Wheelchair access. Music.
Children allowed.

Please send us your feedback

To register your opinion about any
restaurant listed in the Guide, or a new
restaurant that you wish to bring to our
attention, please visit the web address at
the bottom of the page. Your feedback
informs the content of the book and will be
used to compile next year's reviews.

Galvin at Windows

Food that's as good as the views
Hilton Hotel, 22 Park Lane, Mayfair, W1K 1BE
Tel no: (020) 7208 4021
www.galvinatwindows.com
⊖ **Hyde Park Corner, Green Park, map 4**
French | £65
Cooking score: 6

The Galvin brothers' Mayfair branch has had a
good press this year, as it continues to wow
diners with its contemporary take on classical
French cooking. 'Elegant' seems a fair
description for this spacious, gracious golden
room on the twenty-eighth floor of the Park
Lane Hilton; 'impressive' neatly sums up the
plate-glass view over central London. Chef
André Garrett's determination is impressive,
too, and so is his consistency. His food
achieves a distinct blend of creativity and
fashion, backed up by a proper grounding in
the old ways. The long list of recommended
dishes gives an idea of the kitchen's mightily
impressive capabilities: pumpkin tortellini
with chestnut purée; duck and date
consommé with beetroot and foie gras; spiced
pigeon with swede and carrot écrasée (served
with foie gras boudin, an excellent macaroni
gratin and roasting jus); a searingly zingy
Kaffir lime granita with coconut foam. The
bread is always excellent, too. Fixed-price
lunches (with lots of complimentary
supplements) have been appreciated for
economy and performance, and the front-of-
house panache can hardly be faulted. The wine
list is very French and very strong on big-
hitting regions; drinkers are also well served
with an admirable by-the-glass selection and a
good choice of half-bottles. House wine
is £16.
Chef/s: André Garrett. **Open:** Sun to Fri L 12 to 2.30
(3 Sun), Mon to Sat D 6 to 10.30 (11 Thur to Sat).
Closed: bank hol Mon. **Meals:** Set L £22 (2 courses)
to £27. Set D £65. **Service:** 12.5% (optional).
Details: Cards accepted. 109 seats. Air-con.
Separate bar. No music. No mobile phones.
Wheelchair access. Children allowed. Car parking.

Galvin Bistrot de Luxe

Jollity and unwavering quality
66 Baker Street, Marylebone, W1U 7DJ
Tel no: (020) 7935 4007
www.galvinrestaurants.com
⊖ Baker Street, map 4
French | £30
Cooking score: 5

The Galvin brothers' Baker Street eatery revolutionised bistro dining in the capital when it opened in 2005, and it has gone from strength to dynamic strength. It's fair to say the place is buzzing – the reporter who took in a scene of 'heaving jollity reminiscent of a Toulouse-Lautrec painting' had it about right. The conviviality extends to Chris Galvin's assured French cooking – a typical route in might be crab lasagne with beurre nantais, confit duck leg with black pudding and salade lyonnaise, and rum baba with crème Chantilly to finish. It's a menu built around established standards, which bring people back because they know the quality won't waver from one visit to the next. Fish soup with rouille, steak tartare, escargots in garlic butter are all present and correct, but a swerve off the beaten track at main course might discover something like pavé of halibut with crushed potatoes and crab in soy and ginger vinaigrette. And to stumble upon oeuf à la neige served with a rose-shaped praline in twenty-first century London is somehow hugely reassuring. Drinking is mostly French. An extensive list of wines by the glass starts at £4.50, or you might opt for a pot lyonnais containing a third of a bottle.
Chef/s: Chris and Jeff Galvin. **Open:** all week L 12 to 2.30 (3.30 Sun), D 6 to 10.30 (11 Thur to Sat, 9.30 Sun). **Closed:** 25 and 26 Dec, 1 Jan. **Meals:** alc (main courses £12 to £19). Set L £15.50. Set D £17.50. **Service:** 12.5% (optional). **Details:** Cards accepted. 106 seats. 12 seats outside. Air-con. Separate bar. No music. Wheelchair access. Children allowed.

NEW ENTRY
Gauthier Soho

New home for a top chef
21 Romilly Street, Soho, W1D 5AF
Tel no: (020) 7494 3111
www.gauthiersoho.co.uk
⊖ Leicester Square, map 5
French | £27
Cooking score: 4

£5 OFF **V**

The latest venture from Alexis Gauthier, who used to cook at Roussillon in Chelsea (see entry), and still retains a business interest there, is in the charming old London town house where Richard Corrigan reigned for many years. Gauthier's style appears a little pared-down here, with simpler dishes – especially at lunch – on a menu that represents good value. A seared lobe of duck foie gras without a supplement is a fair enough proposition anyway, even if it is rather drowned out by its garnish of cold gingered diced mango. Halibut might be muscularly marinated in soy sauce before being lightly cooked, in an effect eerily similar to Chinese steamed fish, along with some spring veg and a sparse of reduction of fish stock. In the evenings things get a little more involved, with the likes of slow-roasted leg of Welsh lamb, served with turnips, almonds and sultanas, on offer. Complex dessert constructions at an early inspection included a chocolate Breton biscuit sandwich filled with strawberries, coconut velouté and sweet wine jelly. The wine list is predominantly French, with shorter shrift shown to Italy and the New World. Prices open at £18 a bottle (£5 a glass).
Chef/s: Alexis Gauthier and Gerard Virolle. **Open:** Mon to Fri L 12 to 2.30, Mon to Sat D 5.30 to 10.30. **Closed:** Sun, 25 and 26 Dec, bank hols. **Meals:** Set L £18 (2 courses) to £25. Set D £27 (3 courses) to £45. Tasting menu £70. **Service:** 12.5% (optional). **Details:** Cards accepted. 40 seats. Air-con. Music. Children allowed.

Le Gavroche

Gems from the haute cuisine jewel box
43 Upper Brook Street, Mayfair, W1K 7QR
Tel no: (020) 7408 0881
www.le-gavroche.co.uk
⊖ **Marble Arch, map 4**
French | £70
Cooking score: 8

🍷

The Gavroche is like a peerless old stage actor, probably titled, venerable, a little greyed perhaps, but still able to exude effortless class as the occasion demands. As London culinary fashion has hurtled on around it, the repertoire here, notwithstanding the fact that Michel Roux Jr, and now Rachel Humphrey, have sensitively updated it in recent years, has only come into sharper focus. There are people left in London who know what a *coeur d'artichaut Lucullus* is supposed to taste like, and are jubilant that you can still get your hands on one; and there are others for whom these gastronomic brilliants from the heritage jewellery box might exercise their fascination anew. Here's one reporter at work on the lunch menu: 'watercress soup with a poached egg was lovely and fresh-tasting, but paled in comparison with a quenelle of pike – so impressive to get that fish to taste this good'. Results no less spectacular are achieved with a main course of lamb offal (sweetbreads, tongue and kidney) in a rich, sweet jus, as also with a leg of rabbit with mushrooms in mustard sauce. Then there's the theatre of all the little service tables being wheeled around, wine being decanted with molecular precision, the sheer pin-sharp professionalism of it all. Can there be a 'but'? There can, and when there is, it tends to surface around dishes that fall surprisingly some way short of excellence. An unremarkable starter of mussels in a rather muddy curry cream sauce, in which the sea-freshness of the shellfish gets lost; sea bream on ratatouille that feels bogged down rather than lifted by its cooking. Then the cheeses arrive, and you're suddenly back in the upper echelons. Outside the confines of the set lunch, prices are frankly astronomical.

Come prepared, and the £26.80 required for a dessert of passion-fruit soufflé and white chocolate ice cream might just seem a mere trifle. Not so the wine list, where the entry prices are £22 for white, £30 for red, but then look at what you're being offered – a tremendous collection of vinous treasures with the emphasis on France. There are grand international hotels with less to offer.
Chef/s: Rachel Humphrey. **Open:** Mon to Fri L 12 to 2, Mon to Sat D 6.30 to 11. **Closed:** Sun, 23 Dec to 3 Jan, bank hols. **Meals:** alc (main courses £27 to £47). Set L £48.60 (including wine). Tasting menu £96 (£152 with wine). **Service:** 12.5% (optional). **Details:** Cards accepted. 65 seats. Air-con. Separate bar. No music. No mobile phones. Children allowed.

The Giaconda Dining Room

Imaginative food at fair prices
9 Denmark Street, Soho, WC2 H8LS
Tel no: (020) 7240 3334
www.giacondadining.com
⊖ **Tottenham Court Road, map 5**
Modern European | £28
Cooking score: 3

£30

When he opened in an unlikely part of London (Tin Pan Alley, London's famous music street), Paul Merrony was a man with a mission – elevating that humblest of eateries, the café, into a place where imaginative food could be bought at a reasonable price. Two years on, he describes his menu as 'Frenchish' but the cooking embraces far more than crisped pig's trotters with potatoes and egg mayonnaise and duck confit with lyonnaise potatoes. There's also linguine with crabmeat and nduja (a soft, spicy Calabrese salami) and braised tripe with chorizo, butter beans and paprika. Desserts such as Eton mess, cheerful service and wines (from £17) round off the experience.
Chef/s: Paul Merrony. **Open:** Mon to Fri L 12 to 2.15, D 6 to 9.15. **Closed:** Sat, Sun, bank hols. **Meals:** alc (main courses £11 to £18). **Service:** not inc. **Details:** Cards accepted. 32 seats. Air-con. No music. Children allowed.

Gordon Ramsay at Claridge's

Vintage opulence and modern food
Brook Street, Mayfair, W1K 4HR
Tel no: (020) 7499 0099
www.gordonramsay.com
⊖ Bond Street, map 5
Modern European | £70
Cooking score: 5

🍷 🍴 V

Claridge's has always been good at impressing, so enter via the hotel entrance rather than the restaurant's own, and pause to admire the Art Deco foyer and stately old-world opulence of a grand hotel. The sepulchrally lit dining room has less of the old-school tone, with its muted hues of peach and the odd tricksy number including big skirted lampshades hanging from the ceiling, but it's the sort of place in which there seems to be a waiter for every item – even the water. Steve Allen's menu promises a little more than it delivers – he is still some way off challenging the elite in this country. There's the clumsy over-gilding of some of the lilies and the occasional dish that seems like an intruder from an inferior restaurant – none of the components of a dish of steamed bass with scallop, cucumber and apple in an oscietre cream sauce were really strong enough in taste to be teamed with a horseradish mash. But many dishes are well reported, among them beef carpaccio with confit foie gras and a beetroot and horseradish ice cream, native lobster and salmon ravioli with lemongrass and coconut bisque, and beef Wellington (for two). From a strong base in France, the wine list turns up interesting bottles from all corners of the world. Prices are generally high, though they start at £22.50 for a Bordeaux Blanc.
Chef/s: Steve Allen. **Open:** all week L 12 to 2.45 (3 Sat and Sun), D 5.45 to 11 (6 to 10.30 Sun). **Meals:** Set L £30. Set D £70. Menu Prestige £80 (6 courses). **Service:** 12.5% (optional). **Details:** Cards accepted. 70 seats. Air-con. No music. Wheelchair access. Children allowed.

Great Queen Street

Buzzing vibes and no-frills food
32 Great Queen Street, Covent Garden, WC2B 5AA
Tel no: (020) 7242 0622
⊖ Covent Garden, map 5
British | £35
Cooking score: 2

The large dining room ('more pub than gastro' thought one reporter) buzzes with vitality. Bare boards and close-packed tables keep it simple and relaxed, and the no-frills modern British food pioneered by older sibling the Anchor & Hope (see entry) generally goes down well. 'This is traditional British food at its best', thought one visitor; 'Arbroath smokie and stewed mutton were both terrific', noted another, though a 'nice slice' of wild boar terrine suffered from being 'straight out of the fridge'. The cooking can be further undermined by variable service. A short, modern wine list offers some ten by the glass or carafe. House French is £12.50.
Chef/s: Tom Norrington-Davies and Sam Hutchins. **Open:** all week L 12 to 2.30 (3 Sun), Mon to Sat D 6 to 10.30. **Closed:** Christmas, bank hols. **Meals:** alc (main courses £11 to £25). **Service:** not inc. **Details:** Cards accepted. 60 seats. 8 seats outside. Separate bar. No music. Wheelchair access. Children allowed.

READERS RECOMMEND

Green's Restaurant & Oyster Bar

British
36 Duke Street, Mayfair, SW1Y 6DF
Tel no: (020) 7930 4566
www.greens.org.uk
'Simple, fresh ingredients cooked with care make this a winner for both fish and game. Decor comfortingly clubby if slightly dated.'

The Greenhouse

Romance and urban chic in Mayfair
27a Hay's Mews, Green Park, W1J 5NX
Tel no: (020) 7499 3331
www.greenhouserestaurant.co.uk
⊖ Green Park, map 5
Modern European | £70
Cooking score: 6
V

The Greenhouse has long been a reference address for a certain type and tone of central London dining out. A brisk culinary avant-gardism has been the name of the game through several changes of chef, and the location, down a secluded mews and through a shadowy garden, is about as romantic as Mayfair has to offer. The room has a sylvan air with its wall of twigs and green seating, but Antonin Bonnet's menus scream urban chic, and it all comes together to make a powerfully impressive experience. The lengthy carte will give the adventurous lots to think about. A Scottish langoustine is gently cooked in seaweed butter and accompanied by artichoke, bergamot and samphire, or there could be sautéed duck liver, counterpointed in early spring by rhubarb fondant and Chioggia beetroot. The set menu is pricey but, with the exception of the truffle starter, there are no supplements – not even for lobster in Amontillado sauce, or fillet of Aubrac veal in its own jus, with sweetcorn purée and black-sugar popcorn. An Anglo-French cheese selection is heftily supplemented, but then you may not be able to tear yourself away from desserts such as Amalfi lemon tart with basil sorbet, lime jelly and meringue. A commendable effort has been made to democratise what is essentially a rich person's wine list, with a broad array available by the glass. Bottles start comfortably north of £20 and aim for the stars.
Chef/s: Antonin Bonnet. **Open:** Mon to Fri L 12 to 2.30, Mon to Sat D 6.45 to 11. **Closed:** Sun, bank hols, 24 Dec to early Jan. **Meals:** Set L £25 (2 courses) to £29.70. Set D £70. Tasting menu £80. **Service:** 12.5% (optional). **Details:** Cards accepted. 70 seats. Air-con. Separate bar. No music. No mobile phones. Wheelchair access. Children allowed.

The Grill at the Dorchester

Confident food and baronial splendour
The Dorchester Hotel, 53 Park Lane, Hyde Park, W1K 1QA
Tel no: (020) 7629 8888
www.thedorchester.com
⊖ Hyde Park Corner, map 4
Modern British | £64
Cooking score: 4
V

The Grill Room's deliriously OTT décor is a somewhat garish reminder of the days when it was synonymous with smoked salmon and roast beef. But if you can withstand the Scottish baronial overkill of tartan-covered chairs, tartan panels and murals depicting Highland clansmen, there is some confident and satisfying British food to be had. The shiny trolleys still trundle round with their gargantuan slabs of animal protein, but chef Brian Hughson has imbued the cooking with some lighter shades and modern nuances of late. Sea bream might be served with garlic and shallot confit, clam vinaigrette and poached Scottish langoustines, while roast rump of Rhug Estate lamb could appear with cracked wheat, crushed minted peas and asparagus. Elsewhere, grilled Dover sole stands its ground, and strawberry soup with clotted cream mousse and basil sorbet is a bright take on an English summer classic. Wine prices are pretty scary, but this is the Dorchester – so be prepared to spend at least £40 on something serious.
Chef/s: Brian Hughson. **Open:** all week L 12 to 2.30 (12.30 to 3 Sat, 3.30 Sun), D 6.30 to 10.30 (11 Sat, 7 to 10.30 Sun). **Meals:** alc (main courses £19 to £47). Set L £21.50 (2 courses) to £25.50. Set D £25.50 (2 courses) to £29.50. Sun L £35. Tasting menu £60 (5 courses) to £80. **Service:** 12.5% (optional). **Details:** Cards accepted. 75 seats. Air-con. Separate bar. Wheelchair access. Music. Children allowed.

The Guinea Grill
Mighty helpings of old-school grub
30 Bruton Place, Mayfair, W1J 6NL
Tel no: (020) 7409 1728
www.theguinea.co.uk
⊖ Bond Street, map 5
British | £41
Cooking score: 2

Award-winning steak and kidney pies are sold by the truckload at this bastion of British Bulldog conservatism in the heart of W1. A doorman greets diners who pack the low-ceilinged dining rooms for mighty helpings of old-school grub – grills, Scotch steaks and a few more upbeat platefuls including rustic tomato tart with smoked bacon crisps or braised pork belly with caramelised apple and black pudding. For afters, lemon tart continues the wholesome traditional theme. The bar at the front heaves with Mayfair suits looking for sarnies to go with their pints of Young's, and there's also a decent spread of global wines from £19.50 (£5.95 a glass).
Chef/s: Mark Newbury. **Open:** Mon to Fri L 12.30 to 3, Mon to Sat D 6 to 10.30. **Closed:** Sun, bank hols, 25 to 28 Dec, 1 Jan, Easter. **Meals:** alc (main courses £15 to £33). Set L £25 (2 courses) to £35. Set D £42.50. Bar menu available. **Service:** 12.5% (optional). **Details:** Cards accepted. 47 seats. Air-con. Separate bar. No music.

Hakkasan
Cool Chinese with fascinating menus
8 Hanway Place, Fitzrovia, W1T 1HD
Tel no: (020) 7927 7000
www.hakkasan.com
⊖ Tottenham Court Road, map 5
Chinese | £50
Cooking score: 5

🍷 V

You approach down a narrow alley, then pass through a huge glass door and descend to the dimly lit hustle and bustle of this cool venue in the hub of London. The menu is long and fascinating, with Tong Chee Hwee applying the Alan Yau formula of bold experimental dishes supplemented by Chinese favourites and Western desserts. He takes all this in his stride, delivering all manner of refined and exquisite dishes from Jasmine tea-smoked chicken to Hong Kong-style baked lotus leaf Chilean sea bass with red dates, shiitake and enoki mushrooms and preserved vegetables, and tofu in various guises. Some love the ambience and elegance of the place, and praise the dim sum platter of scallop shu mai, har gau, Chinese chive dumpling and shimeji dumpling. Others lament the noisy, crowded atmosphere, the slightly inattentive staff and cooking 'that is competent rather than top'. Prices generally reflect the West End context, with wines contributing energetically to the cost – along with the 13% service charge. As well as a grand spread of Western wines, there are sakés with tasting-note pointers to consider too, and shochu and a range of appealing cocktails. Wines by the glass start at £6.40, with bottles from £29.
Chef/s: Tong Chee Hwee. **Open:** all week L 12 to 3.15 (4.15 Sat and Sun), D 6 to 11 (11.45 Thur to Sat). **Closed:** 25 and 26 Dec. **Meals:** alc (main courses £14 to £59). Set L £40. Set D £55 and £108. **Service:** 13% (optional). **Details:** Cards accepted. 220 seats. Air-con. Separate bar. Wheelchair access. Music.

Haozhan
Chinatown thriller
8 Gerrard Street, Soho, W1D 5PJ
Tel no: (020) 7434 3838
www.haozhan.co.uk
⊖ Leicester Square, map 5
Chinese | £25
Cooking score: 3

V £30

It's been all change on Gerrard Street in recent years as Chinatown restaurateurs race to be the first to update their offering. Haozhan, 'very smart and modern' with its jade and black interior, is a leader of the pack. While regionality holds sway elsewhere, this place plumps for modernity, and a fusion of dishes from China, Malaysia and Japan. 'Chef's recommendations' and attentive waiters encourage you to try something new. With coffee ribs, cheese lobster and Wagyu beef on the menu, there's certainly plenty to pique the interest. Playing it safer (and cheaper) are Sanpei chicken claypot, signature braised tofu, and the chilli quail and soft-shell crab appetisers. 'It's worth repeat visits', says one reporter. Specials and low prices (from £13.50) make the wine list tempting. **Chef/s:** Min Wei Lai. **Open:** all week 12 to 11.30 (midnight Fri and Sat, 11 Sun). **Closed:** 24 and 25 Dec. **Meals:** alc (main courses from £9 to £39). Set L £8 (2 courses) to £10. Set D £15.50 (2 courses) to £30. **Service:** 12.5% (optional). **Details:** Cards accepted. 80 seats. Air-con. No mobile phones. Wheelchair access. Music. Children allowed.

Hélène Darroze at the Connaught
Avant-garde, complex, thrilling
16 Carlos Place, Mayfair, W1K 2AL
Tel no: (020) 3147 7200
www.the-connaught.co.uk
⊖ **Bond Street, Green Park, map 5**
French | £75
Cooking score: 6

It's a fair bet that many of the Connaught's Edwardian customers might have been stopped in their tracks by what's going on today. The bold fabric patterns, the pair of Damien Hirst swirl paintings made from butterfly wings, the New World wines, and the fact that one woman chef has been succeeded by another in recent years. Is nothing sacred? Thankfully not, as this most institutional of all central London's grand-hotel institutions is on a creative swing as never before. Parisienne Hélène Darroze arrived here in 2008, and brought an ultra-refined French avant-garde tone to proceedings, in cooking that has both baffled and thrilled reporters. Menus are styled with a French headline and English subtitles for dishes such as pigeon and foie gras terrine with nori seaweed and dashi stock jelly, served with crispy pak choi, cucumber, green apple and beech mushrooms. Main courses ratchet the complexity still higher, bringing on many less

familiar ingredients, as in roasted Scottish scallops with an assemblage of quinoa, piquillo peppers and palm hearts, under a foaming layer of Asian-spiced lemon beurre blanc. Desserts hardly rest on their laurels either, with Champagne rhubarb compote and meringue served with Sarawak pepper ice cream and almond crumble. The Signature Menu offers an eight-course *tour d'horizon*. Wines? Yes, they've got some – hundreds, in fact. Start at £35, and the sky's the limit. **Chef/s:** Hélène Darroze. **Open:** Tue to Sat L 12 to 2.30 (11 to 3 Sat), D 6.30 to 10.30. **Closed:** Sun, Mon, 1 week Jan. **Meals:** Set L £35. Set D £75. Tasting menu £85. Sat brunch £32. **Service:** 12.5% (optional). **Details:** Cards accepted. 62 seats. Air-con. Separate bar. No music. No mobile phones. Wheelchair access. Children allowed. Car parking.

Hibiscus
Extraordinary cooking from a free spirit
29 Maddox Street, Mayfair, W1S 2PA
Tel no: (020) 7629 2999
www.hibiscusrestaurant.co.uk
⊖ **Oxford Circus, map 5**
Modern French | £70
Cooking score: 8

This carefully designed Mayfair dining room reminded one reader of prestigious Sergi Arola Gastro in Madrid – a surprisingly warm but featureless space with the odd flash of chi-chi glamour, where food is the primary source of pleasure. Claude Bosi's free-spirited culinary intelligence is in full flow here, creating extraordinary food that stuns the senses with a barrage of blistering seasonal flavours, left-field components and inspired re-runs of the bourgeois French classics. As a chef he lives on the edge, proffering luscious comfort as well as delivering full-frontal taste assaults and 'thought-provoking juxtapositions'. Your senses will be soothed by ravioli of hen's egg yolk and smoked potato with caramelised Cevennes onion and shavings of Bianchetto truffle, but you're likely to be seriously unnerved by the clash of raw bouquet shrimps with crunchy deep-fried shrimp heads, lychees, Galician sea urchins and another ravioli construction (this time involving kohlrabi and pig's trotter). Pork is from beasts reared by former Guide editor Jim Ainsworth, and it's treated in wondrous ways. A dramatic two-parter sees slow-cooked belly with white bean and pineapple purée (a rarefied take on the old pub standby gammon with pineapple) alongside rich eel in teriyaki sauce and pickled pineapple, before a signature warm sausage roll with black truffle dressing. Bosi also tackles fish with risk-taking brio – roast line-caught sea bass with confit fennel, a strident blood orange gel, Parmesan, truffle and fennel salad is a riot of fascinating, but disconcerting, textures and contrasts. He has also opened doors into the curious world of 'savoury' desserts – a fine tart of new season's parsnips with pear sauce, vanilla and smoked caramel ripple ice cream, for example. Excellent-value set lunches have also wowed, with standouts including a warm royale of Parmesan and candied walnuts with salsify velouté ('wonderful flavours', exclaimed the recipient). Service is well-informed and 'totally professional', and the sommelier's pin-sharp recommendations are always worth heeding when it comes to the formidable 40-page wine list. Posh Gallic treasures and country tipples rub shoulders with gems from Spain and Australia, and there's an admirable line-up of halves. Prices start at £19.75 (£6.50 a glass).

Chef/s: Claude Bosi. **Open:** Tue to Sat L 12 to 2.30, D 6.30 to 10 (6 Sat). **Closed:** Sun, Mon, Christmas, bank hols. **Meals:** Set L £24.50 (2 courses) to £29.50. Set D £70. Tasting menu £75 to £90 (7 courses). **Service:** 12.5% (optional). **Details:** Cards accepted. 48 seats. Air-con. No music. No mobile phones. Wheelchair access. Children allowed.

NEW ENTRY

Hix

Full-on flavours
66-70 Brewer Street, Soho, W1F 9UP
Tel no: (020) 7292 3518
www.restaurantsetcltd.co.uk
⊖ Piccadilly Circus, map 5
British | £35
Cooking score: 4

V

Mark Hix's gutsy take on real British cooking is distinguished by honesty, simplicity and full-on flavours. The menu changes daily, which means dishes can lack some of the exactness that comes with practice, but this is amply compensated for by the vibrance of cooking with the best produce. There are some very good things to eat here: Hix's own-smoked salmon, devilled lamb's kidneys, sublime deep-fried monkfish cheeks with caper mayo, rich and filling flat-iron steak with baked bone marrow. Foraged foods pop up regularly, with alexanders accompanying a whole flounder with cockles, or there could be a dessert of sea buckthorn berry posset. Praise, too, for good British cheeses, a superb Yorkshire rhubarb and Champagne jelly with ripple ice cream, and excellent bread. Pushing open the solid wood restaurant door can be intimidating, but inside it's welcoming and lively, and service is friendly without being overbearing. The well-constructed wine list offers plenty of choice. Prices open at £18.

Chef/s: Kevin Gratton. **Open:** all week 12 to 11 (10.30 Sun). **Closed:** 25 and 26 Dec, 1 Jan. **Meals:** alc (main courses £15 to £35). **Service:** 12.5% (optional). **Details:** Cards accepted. 70 seats. Air-con. Separate bar. Wheelchair access. Children allowed.

Mark Hix Hix

What is your earliest culinary memory?
Eating prawns straight out of the water when I used to catch them as a kid.

What food trends are you spotting at the moment?
Back to basics, simple food with no frills.

What would be your perfect birthday meal?
Lobster and chips.

How do you relax when out of the kitchen?
Fishing from my boat in Lyme Regis.

What do you wish you had known when you started out as a chef?
I wish I knew how much fun it would be.

What do you think is exciting about the British food scene?
It still has a long way to go but it's great that British producers are coming up with the goods.

Is there anything in the restaurant industry you would like to change?
Better colleges and basic training.

Hix at the Albemarle
Invigorated old-school charmer
Brown's Hotel, 30 Albemarle Street, Mayfair, W1S 4BP
Tel no: (020) 7518 4004
www.restaurantsetcltd.co.uk
⊖ Green Park, map 5
British | £50
Cooking score: 4

⊨ V

Brown's distinguished, old-school dining room received a shot in the arm and some judicious cosmetic treatment when British food champion Mark Hix moved in to take charge of the food. Two years down the line his ongoing exploration of our native larder continues to spring surprises – dressed crab with bittercress, Romney Marsh beets with Ragstone goats' cheese and wild herbs, and sea buckthorn posset, for instance. And then there are the food heroes themselves. Somerset applemaster Julian Temperley is just one who has been making his presence felt: a slug of his cider brandy goes into the Cornish shellfish soup, pork cheeks are braised in Burrow Hill scrumpy with split peas and Cumbrian black pudding, and his eau de vie cherries partner a dessert of Trinity burnt cream. Old hands will be pleased to hear that the time-honoured lunch trolley is still wheeled around: Tuesday might bring honey-glazed leg of Jimmy Butler's ham, for example. The well-spread, Eurocentric wine list starts at £26 (£7.50 a glass).
Chef/s: Lee Streeton and Mark Hix. **Open:** all week L 12 to 3 (12.30 to 4 Sun), D 5.30 to 11 (7 to 10.30 Sun). **Meals:** alc (main courses £15 to £40). Set L and D £25 (2 courses) to £30. **Service:** not inc. **Details:** Cards accepted. 80 seats. Air-con. Separate bar. No music. Wheelchair access. Children allowed.

Ibérica

Impeccable Spanish all-rounder
195 Great Portland Street, Fitzrovia, W1W 5PS
Tel no: (020) 7636 8650
www.ibericalondon.com
⊖ Regent's Park, Great Portland Street, map 5
Spanish | £32
Cooking score: 3

£5 OFF **V**

The Spanish credentials of this friendly bar/
deli/restaurant can't be faulted. Nacho
Manzano – a heavyweight chef in Asturias –
consults on the menu, nipping over regularly
for quality control. The light, spacious
ground-floor tapas bar is particularly strong
on cured hams and cheeses, but doesn't shy
away from the creative touches one might find
in the new Spain. Chorizo 'lollipops' with
pear allioli, fino-marinated rabbit and
sublime black rice with cuttlefish were
inspection highlights. Upstairs, the fine-
dining restaurant introduces the tastes and
textures of 'nueva cocina' in dishes such as
pigeon with quinoa and foie gras, as well as
Manzano's version of Asturian classics like
fabada. As you'd expect, all wines (and
sherries), from £15.50, are Spanish.
Chef/s: Santiago Guerrero. **Open:** all week 11.30am
to 11.30pm (6 Sun). **Closed:** 24 to 26 Dec, bank hols.
Meals: alc (main courses £5 to £38). **Service:** 12.5%
(optional). **Details:** Cards accepted. 130 seats. Air-
con. Separate bar. Wheelchair access. Music.
Children allowed.

ALSO RECOMMENDED

▲ The Ivy

1-5 West Street, Covent Garden, WC2H 9NQ
Tel no: (020) 7836 4751
www.the-ivy.co.uk
⊖ Leicester Square, map 5
British

Back in the Blair years, the Ivy really was the
hottest ticket in town, but it looks as if this
ageing Covent Garden diva is starting to lose
her puff as the A-listers move on to
playgrounds new. There is still a mood-lifting
charge about the place, with its clubby

luxuriance and jaunty waiters, but the food
now generates more catcalls than applause –
good pork belly with mash and cabbage, but
sub-standard prawn and avocado cocktail
(£12), kedgeree and salmon fishcakes with
sorrel sauce (£15.50). Lemon meringue pie
(£6.50) makes a decent finale. Wines from
£18.75. Open all week.

J. Sheekey Oyster Bar

Good-looking Sheekey offspring
33-34 St Martin's Court, Covent Garden,
WC2N 4AL
Tel no: (020) 7240 2565
www.j-sheekey.co.uk
⊖ Leicester Square, map 5
Seafood | £25
Cooking score: 4

V £30

Launched in 2008 to coincide with Sheekey's
tenth anniversary as part of Caprice Holdings,
this good-looking offspring sits right next
door to its auspicious parent and plays from
the same script. Perfectly placed to lure in the
theatre crowd, it has been designed around a
horseshoe-shaped dining bar, with a choice of
stools or tables and Alison Jackson's
photographs of thespian luminaries on the
wood-panelled walls. Sustainably sourced fish
is the backbone of a menu that cherrypicks
easy and affordable options from the full J.
Sheekey repertoire: uncluttered plates of
oysters and crustacea are star turns, fish pie
always has plenty of takers and the choice
might also stretch to scallops with wild garlic
and chilli, smoked haddock rarebit or shrimp
burgers with tomato relish. To finish, go for
British cheese, a savoury, or something sweet
such as spotted dick or pear and quince tart.
Everything on the drinker-friendly wine list
is available by the glass, carafe or bottle (from
£16.75).
Chef/s: Richard Kirkwood. **Open:** all week midday
to midnight (11pm Sun). **Closed:** 25 to 27 Dec, 1 Jan.
Meals: alc (main courses £10 to £29). Set L £25.50
(Sat and Sun only). **Service:** 12.5% (optional).
Details: Cards accepted. 33 seats. Air-con. Separate
bar. Wheelchair access. Music. Children allowed.

J. Sheekey

A seafood institution
28-32 St Martin's Court, Covent Garden,
WC2N 4AL
Tel no: (020) 7240 2565
www.j-sheekey.co.uk
⊖ Leicester Square, map 5
Seafood | £45
Cooking score: 4

V

Joseph Sheekey started selling shellfish in an alley off Charing Cross Road way back in 1896, and since then his brainchild has grown into a seafood institution beloved of theatregoers and the suited-and-booted brigade – there's even a liveried doorman on hand to usher the faithful into the very masculine, dark-panelled dining room. Plates of bivalves, fish pie and grilled Dover sole win over the old guard, but the kitchen also deals a fistful of contemporary aces in the shape of razor clams with broad beans and chorizo, pan-fried monkfish with caramelised chicory and citrus dressing, or a salad of baby lobster and Charlotte potatoes with pea shoots. If fish is out of the question, try ribeye steak or rump of lamb with caramelised beets and roast potatoes. For afters, Scandinavian iced berries with hot white chocolate rounds things off gently; otherwise cherry Bakewell tart might fill the gap. Fish-friendly big names dominate the global wine list (prices from £19.75).
Chef/s: Richard Kirkwood and Martin Dickinson. **Open:** all week L 12 to 3 (3.30 Sun), D 5.30 to 12 (6 to 11 Sun). **Closed:** 25 to 27 Dec, 1 Jan. **Meals:** alc (main courses £14 to £40). Set L (Sat and Sun only) £25.50. **Service:** 12.5% (optional). **Details:** Cards accepted. 107 seats. Air-con. Separate bar. No music. No mobile phones. Wheelchair access. Children allowed.

Average price

The average price listed in main-entry reviews denotes the price of a three-course meal, without wine.

ALSO RECOMMENDED

▲ Jom Makan

5-7 Pall Mall East, Trafalgar Square, SW1Y 5BA
Tel no: (020) 7925 2402
www.jommakan.co.uk
⊖ Charing Cross, Piccadilly Circus, map 5
Malaysian £5 OFF

The big, informal café-style eatery next door to the National Gallery's Sainsbury wing brings Malaysian cooking slap-bang into the centre of London. Newcomers might start with the well-known chicken satay skewers (£4), before exploring the likes of char-grilled salmon in spicy coconut sauce (£8.20) or nasi goreng kampung, a stir-fried rice dish with beef, fried anchovies and vegetables. The authentic finisher is sago gula melaka, tapioca topped with palm syrup and coconut cream (£3.50). Wines from £12.50. Open all week. A second branch is at the Westfield Centre, Shepherd's Bush.

Kiku

Dependable Japanese achiever
17 Half Moon Street, Mayfair, W1J 7BE
Tel no: (020) 7499 4208
www.kikurestaurant.co.uk
⊖ Green Park, map 5
Japanese | £40
Cooking score: 4

V

A branch of the Mikuniya Inn in Japan, Kiku arrived on the Mayfair scene in 1978 and has long been regarded as a reliable and sophisticated champion of traditional Japanese cuisine. Behind the classical exterior you'll find a modern, minimalist interior decked out in pale shades of bamboo and cream. Sushi fans can settle in at one of the capital's largest sushi bars, where nigiri, maki rolls and the like are produced in profusion. In the dining room, choose from structured kaiseki banquets or the carte, where dishes are organised by cooking techniques: grilled (maybe black cod in saké and miso paste); casseroled (perhaps taro and aubergine) and fried (from vegetable tempura to deep-fried

lemon sole). Other choices include classic soups, salads – sliced jellyfish, for instance – and hotpots such as shabu shabu (thinly sliced beef and assorted vegetables in stock, with a dipping sauce). There's a good choice of beers and sakés; alternatively, wines start at £14.50.
Chef/s: Hirofumi Shiraishi and Yoichi Hattori. **Open:** Mon to Sat L 12 to 2.30, all week D 6 to 10.15 (5.30 to 9.45 Sun). **Closed:** 25 and 26 Dec, 1 Jan. **Meals:** alc (main courses £15 to £65). Set L £15 (2 courses) to £20. Set D £20 (2 courses) to £30. **Service:** 12.5%. **Details:** Cards accepted. 100 seats. Air-con. Separate bar. Wheelchair access. Music. Children allowed.

The Landau
A grand hotel touting contemporary food
Langham Hotel, Portland Place, Oxford Circus, W1B 1JA
Tel no: (020) 7965 0165
www.thelandau.com
⊖ Oxford Circus, map 5
Modern European | £50
Cooking score: 6

🍴 V

Always one of the most enviably sited of grand central London hotels, the Langham sits on a bend in the upper reaches of Regent Street, opposite the BBC building. If it has often felt a little overlooked on the capital's dining scene, an £80m restoration, designed to emphasise the hotel's provenance in the mid-Victorian era, looks like money well spent. The Landau dining room has been fashioned from the old ballroom, with some light wood panelling, spindly modern chandeliers, and a vaulted wine corridor where you can dally and deliberate. Best of all, the culinary operation has been transformed. Ideas from the modern European repertoire are brought off with aplomb. Fish is sensitively handled, the treatments maximising its exemplary freshness, witness wild sea trout served with summer bean fricassee and cherry tomato butter. Meats include the prized Castle Mey Angus beef from the Prince of Wales' estate, perhaps served with a wild mushroom ragoût and sherry vinegar jus. Prior to that, you might have eaten something as classical as fine chicken liver and foie gras parfait with pear chutney and brioche, while desserts beguile with the likes of lavender pannacotta and strawberries. The wines that emerge from that cool store are served by a helpful and courteous sommelier. Prices are high, though. Bottles start at £29.
Chef/s: Graham Chatham. **Open:** Mon to Fri L 12.30 to 2.30, Mon to Sat D 5.30 to 10.30. **Closed:** bank hols. **Meals:** alc (main courses £21 to £38). Set L and D £21.50 (2 courses) to £28.50. **Service:** 12.5% (optional). **Details:** Cards accepted. 100 seats. Air-con. Separate bar. Wheelchair access. Music. Children allowed.

Lantana Café
Sunny brunch star
13 Charlotte Place, Fitzrovia, W1T 1SN
Tel no: (020) 7637 3347
www.lantanacafe.co.uk
⊖ Goodge Street, Tottenham Court Road, map 5
Café | £15
Cooking score: 1

£5 OFF V £30

The sun doesn't always shine on Charlotte Place, but it sure feels like it does at Aussie-style café Lantana. The tiny, modest spot dominates London's brunch scene and there are queues out of the door for Saturday's all-day offering: try the French toast with pears and pistachio mascarpone. Lunch might bring corn fritters with crispy bacon, avocado, rocket, tomato salsa and lime aïoli or a steak sandwich with beetroot, caramelised onion, crumbled Stilton and rocket. Impeccable Monmouth Coffee flat whites, and wine from £14.50.
Chef/s: Ben McRae. **Open:** all week 8 to 6 (9pm Thur and Fri, 9 to 5 Sat and Sun). **Closed:** 24 Dec to 1 Jan, bank hols. **Meals:** alc (main courses £4 to £13). **Service:** not inc. **Details:** Cards accepted. 25 seats. 10 seats outside. Air-con. Music. Children allowed.

Latium

Smart Italian
21 Berners Street, Fitzrovia, W1T 3LP
Tel no: (020) 7323 9123
www.latiumrestaurant.com
⊖ **Goodge Street, Tottenham Court Road, Oxford Circus, map 5**
Italian | £34
Cooking score: 2
£5 OFF **V**

Named after the region around Rome, Maurizio Morelli's restaurant is more of a pan-Italian outfit. It's a smart-looking place with Venetian blinds at the window, crisp linen on the tables and a predominant cappuccino tone in the décor. You might dine on Campania mozzarella with grilled zucchini and dried tomato, fillet of gurnard with wilted spinach in fennel broth, and roast guinea fowl with stewed borlotti beans, peppers and garlic leaves. Desserts aim for artistry with the likes of lime parfait wrapped in pineapple in a sauce of balsamic vinegar and mint. The Italian wine list starts at £16.
Chef/s: Maurizio Morelli. **Open:** Mon to Fri L 12 to 3, Mon to Sat D 6.30 to 10.30 (11 Sat). **Closed:** Sun, 25 and 26 Dec, 1 Jan, bank hols. **Meals:** Set L £15.50 (2 courses) to 20.50. Set D £28.50 (2 courses) to £33.50. **Service:** 12.5% (optional). **Details:** Cards accepted. 63 seats. Air-con. Wheelchair access. Music. Children allowed.

Locanda Locatelli

Celeb chef's elegant flagship
8 Seymour Street, Marble Arch, W1H 7JZ
Tel no: (020) 7935 9088
www.locandalocatelli.com
⊖ **Marble Arch, map 4**
Italian | £45
Cooking score: 4

🍷 **V**

Beloved of celebrities and Italophiles, Locanda Locatelli has settled into a very nice groove. It's notoriously hard to get a table but, especially at lunchtime, not impossible. Giorgio Locatelli's food has a clean, fresh feel to it. He buys well and puts produce, not his own ego,

to the fore. Bresaola with glorious olive oil, impeccably cooked lobster risotto and even tortellini in brodo are very, very elegant, even if fireworks are few. Salads, pasta and perfect bread easily outclass the mains such as duck breast with spelt or cod and lentils. Though expensive, Locanda Locatelli offers attentive service, 'a calm, very relaxing atmosphere' and a healthy attitude to families that other restaurants would do well to take note of. The wine list, all Italian and big on big reds, starts at £22 but really gets going near the £100 mark.
Chef/s: Giorgio Locatelli. **Open:** all week L 12 to 3 (3.30 Sat and Sun), D 6.45 to 11 (11.30 Fri and Sat, 10.15 Sun). **Closed:** bank hols, 25 to 26 Dec. **Meals:** alc (main courses £15 to £30). **Service:** 12.5% (optional). **Details:** Cards accepted. 82 seats. Air-con. No music. No mobile phones. Wheelchair access. Children allowed.

ALSO RECOMMENDED

▲ Mango Tree

46 Grosvenor Place, Belgravia, SW1X 7EQ
Tel no: (020) 7823 1888
www.mangotree.org.uk
⊖ **Victoria, Hyde Park Corner, map 4**
Thai £5 OFF

Ten years old but by no means over the hill, Mango Tree continues to pull in a raft of well-dressed diners (plus the odd celebrity) to its grand and glamorous dining room. Sweet-natured staff deliver starters such as green papaya salad with spicy lime sauce (£6.95), before main courses of barbecued duck curry (£13.95) and stir-fried scallops with basil and ginger sauce. Drink wine (from £19) or cocktails with an Asian kick. Pricey? Yes, but always a fun evening out. Open all week.

Readers recommend

A 'readers recommend' review is a genuine quote from a report sent in by one of our readers. We intend to follow up these suggestions throughout the year to come.

Marcus Wareing at the Berkeley

Among London's finest
The Berkeley, Wilton Place, Belgravia, SW1X 7RL
Tel no: (020) 7235 1200
www.marcus-wareing.com
⊖ Hyde Park Corner, Knightsbridge, map 4
Modern European | £75
Cooking score: 8

♠ ⊨ V

The restaurant that was once Pétrus is now proudly named after its culinary overlord, who has been making serious waves here over the past decade. To get there, bear right as you enter the main lobby of the Berkeley. At lunchtime, windows let in light, though there isn't any view to speak of, but the unique atmosphere of the evening, when the moody lighting simmers over wine-coloured upholstery and dark wood, is when the place comes into its own. You might want to go easy before you get here. Be advised that a full panoply of canapés, amuses, pre-desserts, post-desserts and bread will find its way to your table, as well as the stuff you've actually ordered. The whole drill is almost coaxing you to give in and go for the Menu Prestige (or equally inventive vegetarian Menu Gourmand), and indeed there are few better in London. Appetisers at a spring visit included fabulous taramasalata, marmalade-glazed foie gras en croûte and a tiny crab tart. Dishes from the main menu are inspired by novelty: witness an orientalised first course of creamy veal sweetbreads with ginger and garlic gastrique, pak choi and chopped cashews. Milk-fed Welsh lamb appears as several cuts in a main course, including some tiny chops, teamed with a miniscule ball of oozy burrata, the creaminess offset with some bitter herbs and nettles. Desserts are all about textural contrasts, seen in the likes of Granny Smith apple crème, served with spiced brioche crisps, popcorn and dots of salted caramel. The service keeps things at a formal level, well-versed in the niceties, but not quite extending to the relaxation of real conversation when needed. It would be hard to conceive of a more

comprehensive job being done in the wine department. Burgundy is analysed into its appellations, and there are Austrian Grüner Veltliners and Georgian Saperavi for the daring. It all starts at £25.
Chef/s: Marcus Wareing. **Open:** Mon to Fri L 12 to 2.30, Mon to Sat D 6 to 11. **Closed:** Sun, 1 Jan. **Meals:** Set L £38. Set D £75. Tasting menu £95 (7 courses). **Service:** 12.5%. **Details:** Cards accepted. 70 seats. Air-con. No music. No mobile phones. Wheelchair access. Children allowed.

Maze

Thrilling foodie destination
10-13 Grosvenor Square, Mayfair, W1K 6JP
Tel no: (020) 7107 0000
www.gordonramsay.com
⊖ Bond Street, map 4
Modern European | £40
New Chef

♠ V

It's been a turbulent year for Maze: Jason Atherton's decision to quit in April 2010 set alarm bells ringing, and then his lieutenant James Durrant announced he was moving on just as the Guide was going to press. No information was available regarding his successor, but it's likely that the kitchen will continue to conjure up an array of thrilling 'bijou' tasting dishes full of modish accents, eclectic components and dazzling flavours. Two hits from the recent past give some idea of the style: an über-fresh creation involving pearly white Salcombe crab, a ball of brown crab-and-toast sorbet, a tangle of sea herbs, tiny flowers and radishes on paper-thin discs of pickled mooli, and 'utterly wonderful', sticky Irish 'ox tongue 'n' cheek' with sweet raisin and caper dressing, pencil-thin carrots and a pot of potent horseradish pomme purée. The kitchen may be in flux, but this is still a sleek Mayfair showpiece, striking a pose somewhere between a top-end foodie destination and a big-money playground. Meanwhile, drinkers can look forward to top-drawer quaffing from a list that shimmers with class; expect Champagnes in luxurious abundance, wondrous Trimbach Rieslings, an encyclopaedic run through Bordeaux and Burgundy – even saké, if that's your bag. Prices rise skywards from £22 (£5 a glass). Note: Jason Atherton's new standalone restaurant is due to open on Pollen Street, Mayfair in late 2010.

Open: all week L 12 to 2.30, D 6 to 10.30. **Meals:** alc (main courses £9 to £14). Set L £28.50 (4 courses) to £42.50 (6 courses). Set D £65 (7 courses). **Service:** 12.5% (optional). **Details:** Cards accepted. 100 seats. Air-con. Separate bar. Wheelchair access. Music. Children allowed.

Maze Grill
A temple to red meat
10-13 Grosvenor Square, Mayfair, W1K 6JP
Tel no: (020) 7495 2211
www.gordonramsay.com
⊖ Bond Street, map 4
North American | £39
Cooking score: 4

V

Here is Gordon Ramsay Holdings' tribute to the American steakhouse, a modern temple to red meat. Sharing premises with Maze itself (see entry), it's fair to say it doesn't look much like an American steakhouse, with its contemporary beige colour scheme and posh glassware, but at least there are no tablecloths. After a little non-bovine appetite-whetter such as 'pigs on toast' or chorizo with confit tomato, it's time to square up to the big stuff, perhaps best enjoyed at the Butcher's Block, a communal oak table with ringside views of the kitchen. Choose your cut, breed, feed and level of maturity from a line-up that includes grass-fed Hereford, Aberdeen Angus, Casterbridge, Creekstone USDA and ninth-grade Wagyu for the big spenders. The steaks are cooked over coal and finished at a white-hot 650°C for perfect sealing; all the requisite trimmings are at hand, and a whole roasted garlic bulb on the side is a neat touch. If you've room after the beef, order a devilishly rich chocolate brownie with pistachio ice cream or an English strawberry sundae. An extensive list of the great and good from European and New World vineyards starts at £6.50.

Chef/s: Matt Bishop. **Open:** all week L 12 to 3 (3.30 Sun), D 5.45 to 11. **Meals:** alc (main courses £15 to £30). Set L £18 (2 courses) to £21. **Service:** 12.5% (optional). **Details:** Cards accepted. 90 seats. Air-con. Separate bar. Wheelchair access. Music. Children allowed.

NEW ENTRY
Mennula
Strong value-for-money Italian
10 Charlotte Street, Fitzrovia, W1T 2LT
Tel no: (020) 7636 2833
www.mennula.com
⊖ Goodge Street, map 5
Italian | £30
Cooking score: 4

£5 OFF **V**

The purple and white paint might be barely dry on this stylish, modern Sicilian newcomer, but Channel 4 were filming when we inspected, as part of Gordon Ramsay's *The F Word*, so this may thrust Mennula firmly into the spotlight. Santino Busciglio is Sicilian-born and Lancashire-raised, so hotpot-style cooking delivers braised lamb with vivid yellow maccheroni pasta, mint and rich jus. Equally fine is a chunky shellfish soup topped with mascarpone and almonds or a silky smoked venison carpaccio with pecorino, the smoothness cut with lemon. Traditional desserts such as cassata, cannoli or figs and peaches with zabaglione are must-tries. With abundant freebies including hot arancini, the eponymous salted almonds (mennula) and olives, not to mention a slate groaning with breads, it's strong value for money. The front-of-house team are razor sharp. A regional Italian wine list kicks off at £16 a bottle.

Chef/s: Santino Busciglio. **Open:** Sun to Fri L 12 to 3, all week D 6 to 11 (9.30 Sun). **Meals:** alc (main courses £12 to £25). Set L and D £17.50 to £19.50. **Service:** 12.5% (optional). **Details:** Cards accepted. 40 seats. 10 seats outside. Air-con. Music. Children allowed.

Mint Leaf

Cool subterranean Indian
Suffolk Place, Haymarket, SW1Y 4HX
Tel no: (020) 7930 9020
www.mintleafrestaurant.com
⊖ Piccadilly Circus, Charing Cross, map 5
Indian | £35
Cooking score: 2

£5 OFF **V**

Deep below Haymarket is one of London's most glamorous Indian restaurants. The cool cocktail bar is an attraction in itself, but most come for the contemporary Indian cooking. The moody (i.e. dark) interior sets the scene for dramatically presented food. Under a new chef, the format still offers seafood and grills in tasting portions alongside curry house standards, but portions have shrunk as bills have grown, so Mint Leaf has got to regain trust. Lamb and spinach curry, Hyderabadi biryani or a more creative dish of aubergine, cumin and goats' cheese are a step in the right direction. The global wine list starts at £19.
Chef/s: Vishal Rane. **Open:** Mon to Fri L 12 to 3, all week D 5.30 to 11 (6 to 10.30 Sun). **Closed:** 25 and 26 Dec, 1 and 2 Jan. **Meals:** alc (main courses £14 to £25). Set L £13.95 (2 courses) to £16.95. Set D £15 (2 courses) to £20. **Service:** 12.5% (optional).
Details: Cards accepted. 140 seats. Air-con. Separate bar. Wheelchair access. Music. Children allowed.

ALSO RECOMMENDED

▲ Mon Plaisir

21 Monmouth Street, Covent Garden, WC2H 9DD
Tel no: (020) 7836 7243
www.monplaisir.co.uk
⊖ Covent Garden, map 5
French

Opened in 1944, Mon Plaisir continues to be 'as French as it gets'. Tables in all four individual dining rooms are inches apart and filled with French memorabilia picked up from flea markets. The menu is designed to make you think you are on the other side of the Channel. Gratinée à l'oignon (£6.75) is the real thing, as are coq au vin, onglet de boeuf

with sauce bourguignonne (£16.95) and crème brûlée. Good-value lunch and theatre deals. House French is £16. Closed Sun.

Mooli's

Indian
50 Frith Street, Soho, W1D 4SQ
Tel no: (020) 7494 9075
www.moolis.com
'Great concept, good fun – love the Goan pork with pomegranate salsa'

Moti Mahal

Snazzy new-wave Indian
45 Great Queen Street, Covent Garden, WC2B 5AA
Tel no: (020) 7240 9329
www.motimahal-uk.com
⊖ Covent Garden, map 5
Indian | £40
Cooking score: 3

V

India's iconic Grand Trunk Road comes to Covent Garden in the shape of this snazzy venue, spread over two floors with a glassed-in kitchen for chef-watching downstairs. Service runs effortlessly, and the menu chugs its way through the northerly regions of the subcontinent, creatively re-inventing old flavours and giving due prominence to the tandoor. Dishes arrive in waves, with a 'cut your own' salad accompanying the first salvo and fresh-tasting breads later on. Recent highlights have included minty chapli kebabs moulded into flat patties, slow-cooked lamb nihari in a sealed pot, and kararee ghyein (crispy fried lotus stems tossed with peanuts and coriander). To finish don't miss the eye-opening assortment of halva, served warm with shards of solid 'condensed milk' shaved from a block – 'like truffle over pasta'. Global wines start at £27 (£6 a glass).
Chef/s: Anirudh Arora. **Open:** Mon to Fri L 12 to 3, Mon to Sat D 5.30 to 11. **Closed:** Sun, 25 and 26 Dec. **Meals:** alc (main courses £11 to £27). Set L £18. Set D £23. **Service:** 12.5% (optional). **Details:** Cards accepted. 90 seats. 10 seats outside. Air-con. Wheelchair access. Music. Children allowed.

Mr Kong
A king in Chinatown
21 Lisle Street, Soho, WC2H 7BA
Tel no: (020) 7437 7341
www.mrkongrestaurant.com
⊖ Leicester Square, map 5
Chinese | £15
Cooking score: 3

V £30

Like many of its neighbours, this Lisle Street old-timer deals in broadly based Cantonese cooking, although the encyclopaedic menu also branches out for Peking duck and stir-fried Szechuan-style prawns. Seafood is among the high points, from baked crabs and lobsters to steamed sea bass and Dover sole, but barbecued pork (char sui) and spare ribs are worth investigating too. If you want something more adventurous, go for the chef's specials: braised turbot with bitter melon and bean curd sticks in black bean sauce, say, or baked pork chop with onions and chilli bean sauce. There's also a specials list of vegetarian curiosities including vegetarian sweet-and-sour pork. House wine is £9.50.

Chef/s: K Kong and Y W Lo. **Open:** all week 12 to 2.45am (1.45am Sun). **Closed:** 24 and 25 Dec. **Meals:** alc (main courses £7 to £27). Set L and D £9.80 (2 courses) to £23.50 (4 courses). **Service:** 10%. **Details:** Cards accepted. 115 seats. Air-con. No music. No mobile phones. Children allowed.

Murano
Angela wows the crowds again
20 Queen Street, Mayfair, W1J 5PP
Tel no: (020) 7592 1222
www.gordonramsay.com
⊖ Green Park, map 5
Italian | £60
Cooking score: 7

V

Angela Hartnett MBE – the UK's most publicised female chef and Gordon Ramsay sidekick – has re-established her restaurant profile at this slick Mayfair destination and is wowing the crowds once again. Given that

Murano is named after the super-chic Venetian glassware, you might expect a certain suave exclusivity in the dining room – and that's exactly what it offers: arty frescoed panels, elaborate sculpted chandeliers and, of course, Murano hand-blown light fittings add extra gloss to the handsomely dignified surroundings. Angela Hartnett's affection for Mediterranean flavours and her nose for brilliant seasonal ingredients yield some fabulous results and startling marriages: caramelised veal sweetbreads are teamed with pickled quince, dandelion salad, honey and mustard dressing, while Scottish scallops appear alongside apple and cucumber salsa, pata negra ham, pumpkin purée and candied walnuts. Pasta is always a strong suit (perhaps braised rabbit pappardelle with confit lemons, black olive, mint and rocket), but other ideas show more imagination – hence the presence of anchovy tempura and grapefruit vinaigrette with a dish of braised halibut, capers and crosnes or roast Ibérico pork shoulder with pearl barley and salsify. Meals open with terrific breads, charcuterie nibbles and arancini balls, while a dozen miniature sorbets provide the prelude to exciting desserts such as chestnut moelleux with nashi pears and dry sherry ice cream. Excellent-value set lunches have also delivered first-class cooking in the form of deep-fried lamb's tongues with pearl barley ragù and salsa verde, duck egg on a salad of duck confit with wet polenta, and zingy orange tart. Faultless, on-the-ball service receives glowing praise, as does the auspicious Italian-accented wine list (despite some steep mark-ups). Prices start at £23.50 (£8 a glass).

Chef/s: Angela Hartnett. **Open:** Mon to Sat L 12 to 2.30, D 6.30 to 10.30. **Closed:** Sun, 1 week Christmas. **Meals:** Set L £30. Set D £60. Tasting menu £75 (8 courses). **Service:** 12.5% (optional). **Details:** Cards accepted. 45 seats. Air-con. Separate bar. No music. No mobile phones. Wheelchair access. Children allowed.

National Portrait Gallery, Portrait Restaurant

A feast for the eyes
St Martins Place, Trafalgar Square, WC2H 0HE
Tel no: (020) 7312 2490
www.searcys.co.uk
⊖ Leicester Square, Charing Cross, map 5
Modern British | £40
Cooking score: 2
£5 OFF **V**

There's no denying it is the glorious views over Trafalgar Square that give the Portrait Restaurant the wow factor. But spare a thought for the tireless kitchen team that has to please tourists, art lovers, suits and courting couples alike. Eccentric seasonal menus marrying old and new, homely and exotic, are the answer. Look out for the likes of beetroot tarte Tatin with Rosary goats' cheese, venison carpaccio, and blood orange Eton mess. Smart service and a user-friendly, predominantly Old World wine list (with plenty at the lower end, from £16.90) complete the package. Enjoy the views for less over breakfast or tea.
Chef/s: Katarina Todosijevic. **Open:** all week L 10 to 5, Thur and Fri D 5.30 to 10. **Closed:** 24 to 26 Dec. **Meals:** alc (main courses £14 to £21). Set L £20 (2 courses) to £25. Pre-theatre set D £14.50 (2 courses) to £18.50. Sun L £27. **Service:** 12.5% (optional). **Details:** Cards accepted. 90 seats. Air-con. Separate bar. No music. Wheelchair access. Children allowed.

Nobu Berkeley St

Uber-cool fashionistas' hangout
15 Berkeley Street, Mayfair, W1J 8DY
Tel no: (020) 7290 9222
www.noburestaurants.com
⊖ Green Park, map 5
Japanese | £70
Cooking score: 5
🍶 **V**

The glitz-strewn Berkeley Street outpost of Nobu's global empire seems to have overtaken its Park Lane sibling (see below) as the Japanese destination of choice for London's paparazzi-hungry fashionistas and wannabe hangers-on.

You'll probably need a rock drummer's earplugs to survive the braying throngs and booming soundtrack in the sexy ground-floor bar – although the famed saké-based Martini cocktails make amends. The food is a trademark mix of traditional Japanese cuisine overlaid with modish gestures and a fair smattering of South American-style tacos, ceviches and 'anti cuchos' (grilled skewers). Devotees of the Nobu brand won't be disappointed by the rock shrimp tempura, yellowtail sashimi with jalapeño and the relentlessly bastardised black cod in miso – or the exquisite, high-art sushi, salads and Euro-crossovers (octopus carpaccio with bottarga, say). This branch also has a wood oven, which can deliver all manner of eclectic specialities – think Iberian pork with spicy ponzu, duck breast with wasabi salsa, even paellas involving brown rice and miso – as well as specially designed tables for hibachi ('fire bowl') grills. Desserts are showtime spectaculars including OTT chocolate bento boxes and exotic fruity extravaganzas such as coconut pannacotta with lemongrass and milk sorbet, candied kumquats and vanilla-marinated pineapple. Exclusively imported sakés are an ever-enticing lure, although the swanky global wine list has treasures aplenty – especially in its bonus-busting 'reserve' section. Prices (from £32 a bottle, £7 a glass) are tailored to the moneyed international set.
Chef/s: Mark Edwards. **Open:** Mon to Fri L 12 to 2.15, all week D 6 to 11 (12 Thur to Sat, 9.15 Sun). **Closed:** bank hols. **Meals:** alc (main courses £5 to £32). Set L £26. Set D £21.75 to £32.75. **Service:** 15% (optional). **Details:** Cards accepted. 200 seats. Air-con. Separate bar. Music. Children allowed.

Nobu London

Thrilling Japanese fusion
Metropolitan Hotel, 19 Old Park Lane, Mayfair,
W1K 1LB
Tel no: (020) 7447 4747
www.noburestaurants.com
⊖ Hyde Park Corner, map 5
Japanese | £60
Cooking score: 5

🍶 V

When Nobu hit Mayfair in 1997, it heralded a new era of A-list dining in the capital. That crowd may have moved on to the Berkeley St branch, but there's no doubting that Nobu's take on Japanese cuisine still has the power to thrill – even if many of its iconic dishes have already entered gastro-folklore. If you're new to the sensory pleasures of scallop and smelt egg hand rolls, yellowtail sashimi with jalapeño dressing or silky black cod in miso, be prepared to be amazed by the sheer delicacy and clear-flavoured brilliance of these classics. However, it's worth crossing over into the daring world of the 'special dishes'; here are wondrous constructions of sea urchin tempura, crispy pork belly with spicy miso and ginger salsa, luxury-laden Wagyu and foie gras gyoza dumplings and the much-vaunted 'anti cuchos' skewers, which add some Latin fire to proceedings. The kitchen also has a sexy sting its tail with zany desserts such as 'green tea-ramisu' or the enigmatically titled 'banana split 3000' (a showboating collision of poached banana, hot chocolate foam, saffron crumble and torrone ice cream). The top-end global wine list offers a grand spread of grape varieties, although prices (from £24) are in keeping with the five-star setting; also check out the exclusively imported sakés. One final warning: the time limit on tables is enforced with samurai-like sternness.
Chef/s: Mark Edwards. **Open:** all week L 12 to 2.15 (12.30 to 2.30 Sat and Sun), D 6 to 10.15 (11 Fri and Sat, 9.15 Sun). **Closed:** 25 and 26 Dec. **Meals:** alc (main courses £6 to £33). Set L £55 to £65 (5 courses). Set D £75 to £95 (6 courses). **Service:** 15%

(optional). **Details:** Cards accepted. 150 seats. Air-con. Separate bar. No music. Wheelchair access. Children allowed.

Noura Brasserie

Spicy Lebanese favourite
16 Hobart Place, Belgravia, SW1W 0HH
Tel no: (020) 7235 9444
www.noura.co.uk
⊖ Victoria, map 5
Lebanese | £32
Cooking score: 3

£5 OFF V

The original branch of the Noura group is a bright, spacious venue that divides into formal restaurant and casual bar areas at lunchtime. In the evenings, all tables are smartly laid up, and the place is generally a hive of activity. Fixed-price menus are a popular way of experimenting with the Lebanese specialities, and hot and cold mezze get the nod. Among main courses, the lamb dishes, such as char-grilled cutlets, skewers and meatballs, are the stars, and the spices and seasonings are as vivid as you expect. Seafood dishes include grilled king prawns marinated in coriander, tomato, parsley and garlic. Finish with baklava, or one of the exotic homemade ice creams – milk and orange blossom, perhaps, or rosewater and lemon. Western European wines supplement the Lebanese offerings. House wine is £24.
Chef/s: Badih El Asmar. **Open:** all week 11.30am to 11.30pm. **Meals:** alc (main courses £12 to £23). Set L £18 (2 courses) to £24. Set D £22 (2 courses) to £30. **Service:** not inc. **Details:** Cards accepted. 130 seats. 30 seats outside. Air-con. No mobile phones. Wheelchair access. Music. Children allowed.

One-O-One

Top-end seafood cookery
Sheraton Park Tower, 101 Knightsbridge,
Knightsbridge, SW1X 7RN
Tel no: (020) 7290 7101
www.oneoonerestaurant.com
⊖ Knightsbridge, map 4
Seafood | £55
Cooking score: 6

🍽 V

Residing on the ground floor of the Sheraton
Park Tower hotel, One-O-One provides a
comfortable, tranquil backdrop to Breton chef
Pascal Proyart's stunningly rendered
contemporary fish cuisine. High-quality
ingredients are handled with originality,
combinations are well considered and the
results look stunning – especially the
signature 'petits plats'. To start, hand-dived
scallops paired with quivering slow-cooked
'onsen' quails' eggs, Charlotte potato
mousseline and crispy pork belly is a perfect
marriage of land and sea. Proyart can also
unleash some surprising flavour hits: wild sea
bass cooked in basil oil produced fish 'almost
floral flesh', beautifully offset by a superb
barigoule sauce and Parmesan compote.
Norwegian red king crabs from the Barents
Sea are his forte (perhaps paired with a
gazpacho jelly and Jabugo ham or potted and
served with artichokes, octopus, cockles and a
samphire gremolata dressing). There's also a
nod to the carnivorous tendency with the likes
of roast spring lamb with asparagus, wild
garlic gnocchi, olive and rosemary jus. To
finish, poached rhubarb in Grenadine with a
sublime ginger ice cream and mint foam has
been 'dangerously delicious', and the run of
desserts might also include a 'meli melo' of
summer red berries with chilled Champagne
sabayon. Service is alert as well as friendly, and
the carefully chosen wine list includes some
tempting fish-friendly bottles from £25.
Chef/s: Pascal Proyart. **Open:** all week L 12 to 2.30
(12.30 Sat and Sun), D 6.30 to 10. **Closed:** 25 and 26
Dec, 1 Jan. **Meals:** alc (main courses £26 to £37). Set

L £19. Set D £42. **Service:** not inc. **Details:** Cards
accepted. 50 seats. Air-con. Separate bar.
Wheelchair access. Music. Children allowed.

Pearl

Eye-popping dishes and affordable decadence
252 High Holborn, Holborn, WC1V 7EN
Tel no: (020) 7829 7000
www.pearl-restaurant.com
⊖ Holborn, map 5
Modern French | £58
Cooking score: 5

£5 OFF 🍽

'Decadence at an affordable price', is one take
on Pearl – a beautiful big-city dining room
occupying what was the old Pearl Assurance
banking hall. Inside, it's a glittering world of
Ionic columns and swathes of walnut
panelling, with hand-strung trails of pearly
beads dangling seductively from lofty
ceilings. The mood is sophisticated yet seldom
stuffy, service is attentive but never fawningly
intrusive, and Jun Tanaka's contemporary
French cuisine overlays razor-sharp technique
with visual spectacle. He creates what one
reader called 'sculptural masterpieces' – eye-
popping, arty dishes from an egalitarian
culinary palette that embraces ox tongue,
bone marrow and rabbit legs, as well as foie
gras and Périgord truffles. A fastidiously
fashioned, intense starter involving
caramelised langoustine with pig's cheek
tortellini, pineapple and black radish could set
the scene for an equally ambitious pairing of
perfectly timed halibut with chorizo, seared
squid, red pepper confit and chickpea fritters.
Pre-starters and extras are 'total heaven', while
desserts scale the heights with a stunningly
good version of tiramisu or an evocative
assemblage of caramelised apples with salted
caramel mousse, thyme ice cream and honey
jelly imbued with the scents of the garden. The
tasting menu with matching wines is deemed
'a real treat', and the clued-up sommelier
provides astute guidance when it comes to the
extensive, uppercrust list. Prices start at £26.

Chef/s: Jun Tanaka. **Open:** Mon to Fri L 12 to 2.30, Mon to Sat D 6 to 10. **Closed:** Sun, bank hols, 24 Dec to 5 Jan, 2 weeks Aug. **Meals:** Set L £26 (2 courses) to £29. Set D £49 (2 courses) to £58. Tasting menu £70. **Service:** 12.5% (optional). **Details:** Cards accepted. 80 seats. Air-con. Separate bar. Wheelchair access. Music. Children allowed.

La Petite Maison

Sharing's the name of the game
54 Brook Mews, Mayfair, W1K 4EG
Tel no: (020) 7495 4774
www.lpmlondon.co.uk
⊖ Bond Street, map 5
French | £60
Cooking score: 3

V

Offshoot of a long-standing restaurant in Nice, La Petite Maison delivers its own determined brand of Niçoise cooking via a hit-parade of 'light, colourful, uncomplicated dishes' designed for sharing. However, the smaller plates work best unshared – a salad of French beans and foie gras, perhaps, or a classic pissaladière (onion tart with anchovies). Even larger offerings like superb homemade pasta with squid, prawns and chorizo or a grilled veal chop 'might lead to a squabble'. Reporters have enjoyed the 'breezy, classy informality', and don't seem to mind the tightly packed tables and high decibel levels. Otherwise, the interior comprises burgundy leather seating, polished floorboards and an open kitchen delivering brasserie-style to the wedge-shaped room. French wines (plus some eye-catching Italians) start at £18.50.
Chef/s: Raphael Duntoye. **Open:** all week L 12 to 3 (12.30 to 3.30 Sat and Sun), D 6 to 11 (10.30 Sun). **Closed:** 25 and 26 Dec. **Meals:** alc (main courses £14 to £70). **Service:** 12.5% (optional). **Details:** Cards accepted. 85 seats. 16 seats outside. Air-con. Separate bar. No music. Wheelchair access. Children allowed.

NEW ENTRY
Pétrus

A brave revival
1 Kinnerton Street, Knightsbridge, SW1X 8EA
Tel no: (020) 7592 1609
www.gordonramsay.com
⊖ Knightsbridge, map 4
Modern French | £55
Cooking score: 5

🍾 **V**

There was a time when cooking of this calibre would have been showered with gongs, but such is the pace of the restaurant scene that Gordon Ramsay's brave revival of Pétrus, round the corner from its former incarnation in the Berkeley Hotel, falls short of the mark. Sure, the design is sleek and comfortable – neutral colours offset by claret tones, glass-fronted wine racks – and there's no doubting that this is a serious restaurant, run by a team of clued-up professionals. But it lacks the stamp of a hands-on chef/patron, the menu barely changes – apart from a few seasonal tweaks – and there is something rather impersonal (almost 'safe') about the execution. Crispy veal sweetbread with choucroute, carrots and a sherry vinegar sauce, a superb fillet of halibut with braised fennel and a slightly too-sweet citrus coriander sauce, and an orange meringue pie with clove ice cream were all perfectly fine, but lacked that extra edge you might expect for the money. The set lunch, however, is 'excellent value'. Fans of the original venue will recognise the wine list, which opens with a page of good stuff by the glass (from £5.50) and has France as its main focus, including a raft of biddable Pétrus vintages going back to 1924. It also accommodates the wider vinous world with largesse. Bottles from £25.
Chef/s: Sean Burbidge. **Open:** Mon to Sat L 12 to 2.30, D 6.30 to 10.30. **Closed:** Sun. **Meals:** Set L £25. Set D £55. Tasting menu £65. **Service:** not inc. **Details:** Cards accepted. 40 seats. Air-con. Separate bar. No music. No mobile phones. Wheelchair access. Children allowed.

Pho

Vietnamese
3 Great Titchfield Street, Fitzrovia, W1W 8AX
Tel no: (020) 7436 0111
'Superb-value Vietnamese food – fresh, healthy and packed with flavour'

Phoenix Palace

Winsome dim sum
3-5 Glentworth Street, Marylebone, NW1 5PG
Tel no: (020) 7486 3515
www.phoenixpalace.co.uk
⊖ Baker Street, map 4
Chinese | £25
Cooking score: 2
£5 OFF **V** £30

Although Phoenix Palace can seat almost 250 diners, weekend queues are a regular sight. Why? Because the elegantly furnished restaurant serves some of London's finest dim sum – delightful little morsels filled with anything from tender scallops to crunchy pork and peanuts. The wide-ranging carte is just as accomplished, offering popular Cantonese dishes as well as more intriguing chef's specials such as delicate steamed razor clams with garlic, or springbok with lotus roots and lily bulb in spicy XO sauce. Service is 'exceptionally efficient'. Drink jasmine tea, Tsing Tao beer or house wines from £15 a bottle (£4 a glass).
Chef/s: Marco Li. **Open:** all week 12 to 11.30 (11 to 10.30 Sun). **Closed:** 25 Dec. **Meals:** alc (main courses £9 to £88). Set L £15 (2 courses) to £20. Set D £25 (2 courses) to £30. **Service:** 12.5% (optional). **Details:** Cards accepted. 250 seats. Air-con. Separate bar. No mobile phones. Wheelchair access. Music. Children allowed.

Average price

The average price listed in main-entry reviews denotes the price of a three-course meal, without wine.

Pied-à-Terre

Serious dining for serious people
34 Charlotte Street, Fitzrovia, W1T 2NH
Tel no: (020) 7636 1178
www.pied-a-terre.co.uk
⊖ Goodge Street, map 5
Modern French | £72
Cooking score: 8
£5 OFF

A bijou Fitzrovia aristocrat, shoehorned into a low-key Victorian town house on media-saturated Charlotte Street, Pied-à-Terre trades on intimacy and purrs like a pedigree Persian cat. It may not be the most animated dining room in town, but co-owner David Moore's assured presence out front and his band of exceptionally drilled staff go about their business with real confidence, character and true professionalism. Shane Osborn is currently among the top players in London's premiership, and his brilliant cooking goes down a storm with the impeccably groomed 'sophisticats' who clearly enjoy being part of the show. This is serious dining for serious people. Canapés and amuse-bouches have a legendary reputation, and all the ancillary details – from terrific breads to the daintiest of petits fours – are just about as good as it gets. After the overtures, Osborn's culinary intelligence, razor-sharp imagination and peerless technique take flight as the kitchen wheels out a procession of miraculous dishes full of complexity and fascination: consider a starter of native Colchester oysters with pickled black radish, samphire, nori jelly, pennywort and toasted Ryvita – pure brilliance, clarity and cohesion. Or a richer, luxury-laden construction of pan-fried foie gras with fig and port purée, a salad of pomegranate, dried fig and toasted almonds. There's also a fascination with cute herbal embellishments – baby sorrel and semi-dried grapes added to carpaccio of scallops, sea purslane matched with pan-fried halibut, parsnip purée and fried ham hock, even lady's smock leaves and beetroot emulsion in a dish of Cornish mackerel (this from the preposterously good-value set lunch). Above all, Osborn's insistence on the very best produce (whatever its origin) runs through his endeavours like an ever-present leitmotif: Orkney lamb, Icelandic cod, Grelot onions, Anjou pigeon and fabulous cheeses are just some of the wares that find their way onto the plate. Like everything else that arrives from this starry kitchen, desserts are an absolute joy to behold and savour: ginger and chocolate mousse with chocolate feuillantine and a salad of orange and chestnuts, for example. The wine list comes in two volumes and it plays to the knowledgeable crowd with a fabulous choice of vintages and exemplary growers. Those partaking of the tasting menu also have the unlikely thrill of the sommelier's 'découverte' – each tipple tasted blind and then informatively revealed. Otherwise drink by the glass from £6.50 or bottle from £21. **Chef/s:** Shane Osborn. **Open:** Mon to Fri L 12 to 2.30, Mon to Sat D 6 to 11. **Closed:** Sun, last week Dec, first week Jan. **Meals:** Set L £23.50 (2 courses) to £29. Set D £57.50 (2 courses) to £71.50. Tasting menu £87 (10 courses). **Service:** 12.5% (optional). **Details:** Cards accepted. 40 seats. Air-con. Separate bar. Music. Children allowed.

El Pirata of Mayfair
Traditional tapas at rock-bottom prices
5-6 Down Street, Mayfair, W1J 7AQ
Tel no: (020) 7491 3810
www.elpirata.co.uk
⊖ Hyde Park Corner, map 5
Spanish | £20
Cooking score: 1
V £30

El Pirata deserves a rousing cheer and some celebratory olés for dishing up traditional tapas at rock-bottom prices in the moneyed enclaves of Mayfair. The congenial 'family atmosphere' (with the occasional celeb thrown in) wins everyone over, and it's perfect if you fancy grazing through some grilled wild asparagus, octopus with olive oil and paprika, or marinated chicken skewers with chorizo. If you're ravenous and are out to impress, there are also two sorts of paella for sharing. Spain reigns on the wine list, with prices from £15.95. **Chef/s:** Rosendo Gimbana. **Open:** Mon to Fri 12 to 11.30, Sat D 6 to 11.30. **Closed:** Sun, Easter and bank hols. **Meals:** alc (main courses £13 to £18). Set L £9.95 (2 courses). Set L and D tapas £14.95 to £19.50. **Service:** 10% (optional). **Details:** Cards accepted. 110 seats. 16 seats outside. Air-con. Separate bar. Wheelchair access. Music. Children allowed.

NEW ENTRY
Polpo
Italy's take on tapas
41 Beak Street, Soho, W1F 9SB
Tel no: (020) 7734 4479
www.polpo.co.uk
⊖ Piccadilly Circus, Oxford Circus, map 5
Italian tapas | £18
Cooking score: 3
V £30

Polpo rocks! There's an edgy feel to the rustic mix of wooden floors, chapel chairs, exposed brickwork, hanging light bulbs and menus doubling as table mats. And if you can squeeze in, either at the bar or on one of the mismatched tables, you're in for a treat. This is not your average tapas. Knowledgeable and unpretentious staff guide you through the menu of Venetian-inspired cicheti and small plates: salt cod on grilled polenta accompanied by, perhaps, broad bean, ricotta and mint bruchetta, could be followed by pork belly, radicchio and hazelnuts, or mackerel tartare with horseradish and carta di musica (flatbread). Service is perfectly timed and, if you've got a sweet tooth, round things off with chocolate and orange salami. House wines from £10 for a half-litre. **Chef/s:** Tom Oldroyd. **Open:** all week L 12 to 3 (4 Sat and Sun), Mon to Sat D 5.30 to 11. **Closed:** 25 Dec to 1 Jan. **Meals:** alc (main courses £5 to £7). **Service:** 12.5% (optional). **Details:** Cards accepted. 60 seats. Air-con. Separate bar. Wheelchair access. Music. Children allowed.

ALSO RECOMMENDED

▲ La Porte des Indes

32 Bryanston Street, Marble Arch, W1H 7EG
Tel no: (020) 7224 0055
www.laportedesindes.com
⊖ Marble Arch, map 4
Indian

There are echoes of Bollywood at this grandiose Indian with its cascading waterfalls, giant palms and bright colours. Conventional dishes like crab Malabar (£8.50) and chicken tandoori (£12) share the billing on the long menu with 'Les Indes Françaises', including poulet rouge (grilled chicken marinated in yogurt and red spices and served with a creamy sauce) and cassoulet de fruits de mer (£14). Finish with Alphonso mango and ginger kulfi (£6.90). Cocktails in the Jungle Bar; wines from £21. Open all week.

▲ Princi

135 Wardour Street, Soho, W1F 0UT
Tel no: (020) 7478 8888
www.princi.co.uk
⊖ Tottenham Court Road, map 5
Italian

Restaurateur Alan Yau and Italian baker Rocco Princi have joined forces and Soho loves the results. There's usually a wait for a table and sometimes even to get a look at the tempting displays of cannoli, pizza and focaccia. Throw in great coffee, friendly-if-frazzled Italian staff and a designer interior and you have a Soho Italian café for the twenty-first century. For a substantial lunch, try the Piemontese salt beef salad (£4) or aubergine parmigiana (£6). House wine from £17. Open all week.

The Providores

Exhilarating fusion trailblazer
109 Marylebone High Street, Marylebone, W1U 4RX
Tel no: (020) 7935 6175
www.theprovidores.co.uk
⊖ Baker Street, Bond Street, map 4
Fusion | £45
Cooking score: 4

♦ V

Foodie snobs may turn up their noses at the mere mention of fusion, but few would argue that Kiwi chef Peter Gordon can still cook this stuff better than just about anyone else in London. Since 2001, he has been throwing down the gauntlet in Marylebone, peppering his creations with obscure ingredients and highly charged assemblages. How about tataki of yellowfin tuna with kina pannacotta, wasabi tobiko, nori purée, lotus crisps and dashi jellies in the upstairs Providores restaurant, followed by Vietnamese mint sorbets, hokey-pokey ice cream and espresso-poached quince? These combos might read like cauldron-bubbling hocus-pocus, but the results are invariably exhilarating and full of surprises. Innovative Sunday roast dinners are a new wow. On the ground floor is the no-holds-barred Tapa Room (first come, first served) – a jam-packed grazing den where crowds get their global kicks from the likes of crispy crab, coconut and tapioca fritters with tea-smoked salmon and tamarind aïoli. Breakfast is a good call, too. The wine list is an incomparable tour of New Zealand's vineyards, with a supporting cast of terrific 'other world' bottles. Prices start at £17, and a beefed-up selection is now available by the glass or carafe.
Chef/s: Peter Gordon. **Open:** all week L 12 to 2.45, D 6 to 10. **Closed:** 25 Dec to 4 Jan, Easter Mon. **Meals:** alc (main courses £18 to £26). Sun D £29. **Service:** 12.5% (optional). **Details:** Cards accepted. 38 seats. Air-con. Separate bar. Wheelchair access. Music. Children allowed.

Quilon

Smart South Indian flavours
41 Buckingham Gate, Westminster, SW1E 6AF
Tel no: (020) 7821 1899
www.quilon.co.uk
⊖ St James's Park, Victoria, map 5
Indian | £40
Cooking score: 4
£5 OFF ⊨ V

In the subdued, corporate surrounds of the Crowne Plaza Hotel, Quilon can feel a touch sanitised – although there's no denying that the smartly attired, upscale dining rooms have a certain allure, especially for politicians and the business crowd. Beyond the decorative bling, the kitchen delivers a refined version of South Indian cuisine, plundering Kerala and the Malabar Coast for most of its inspiration. Indigenous ingredients and high-end western technique come together for a cavalcade of smartly groomed dishes with fascinating, pinpoint flavours. Seafood is naturally a strong suit, whether you fancy stir-fried oysters crusted with lentils and spices, batons of squid and shrimps cooked 'Alleppey style' or lobster with Kashundi mustard and cream sauce. Away from the sea there are other possibilities, including slow-cooked lamb with ground pistachios and chillies, vinegar-laced Goan chicken or roast duck spiked with kokum and cumin. Vegetarians also do well here: try soya beans and sprouted mung beans with spinach. The spice-friendly wine list starts at £20 – also note the choice of sakés.
Chef/s: Sriram Aylur. **Open:** Sun to Fri L 12 to 2.30 (12.30 to 3.30 Sun), all week D 6 to 11 (10.30 Sun). **Closed:** 25 Dec. **Meals:** alc (main courses £15 to £28). Set L £22. Set D £37. Sun L £22. **Service:** 10% (optional). **Details:** Cards accepted. 82 seats. Air-con. Separate bar. No mobile phones. Wheelchair access. Music. Children allowed.

Quirinale

Statesmanlike Italian
1 Great Peter Street, Westminster, SW1P 3LL
Tel no: (020) 7222 7080
www.quirinale.co.uk
⊖ Westminster, map 3
Italian | £36
Cooking score: 3

How apt that Quirinale – named after Italy's presidential palace – should stand within shouting distance of our own Houses of Parliament. No wonder it's a handy choice for power lunches and string-pulling over plates of pasta. The bright basement dining room strikes a statesmanlike pose with pastel colours and capacious leather banquettes, while Stefano Savio's kitchen gets the thumbs-up for its assured food. Top-end ingredients make their mark in dishes such as warm cauliflower timbale with egg and black truffle, or spaghetti with clams and bottarga, while mains stay with the old order – think pork saltimbocca, veal milanese or red mullet with cicerchie beans and cherry tomatoes. By contrast, desserts target the younger vote with Campari sorbets and liquorice tiramisu. Apart from an occasional cross-border foray, the wine list is true to its Italian roots; prices start at £18.
Chef/s: Stefano Savio. **Open:** Mon to Fri L 12 to 2.30, Mon to Sat D 6 to 10.30. **Closed:** Sun, 24 Dec to first Mon in Jan, Aug. **Meals:** alc (main courses £17 to £28). Set L and early D £19 (2 courses) to £23. **Service:** 12.5% (optional). **Details:** Cards accepted. 50 seats. Air-con. Music. Children allowed.

Average price

The average price listed in main-entry reviews denotes the price of a three-course meal, without wine.

Quo Vadis

Old-school Soho classic
26-29 Dean Street, Soho, W1D 3LL
Tel no: (020) 7437 9585
www.quovadissoho.co.uk
⊖ Tottenham Court Road, map 5
Modern British | £35
Cooking score: 2

£5 OFF 🍷

A Soho classic now in the hands of the Hart brothers (Barrafina, Fino, see entries). This, their first non–Hispanic venue, is wonderfully old–school. Stained glass windows, modern art and the buzz recall the Ivy and its ilk. So does the menu comprising classic grills and Mediterranean flavours. Among the former, Dover sole, oysters or rib of beef usually impress. Octopus and chorizo salad and tonka bean crème brûlée with pear show a trendier touch. Inconsistency is, sadly, still a problem that bedevils both service and food. The wine list's top picks from France and Spain open at £19.50.
Chef/s: Jean Philippe Patruno. **Open:** all week L 12 to 2.30 (12.30 Sun), D 5.30 to 10.30 (9.30 Sun). **Closed:** bank hols. **Meals:** alc (main courses £12 to £33). Set L and D £17.50 (2 courses) to £19.50. Sun L £39.50. **Service:** 12.5% (optional). **Details:** Cards accepted. 90 seats. 12 seats outside. Air-con. No music. Children allowed.

The Red Fort

Indian new-wave veteran
77 Dean Street, Soho, W1D 3SH
Tel no: (020) 7437 2115
www.redfort.co.uk
⊖ Tottenham Court Road, Leicester Square, map 5
Indian | £45
Cooking score: 2

V

Forced to close in 2009 due to a fire on Dean Street, the new-look Red Fort, dressed in warm shades of red and brown, is sleeker than before. However, the kitchen has stayed true to its roots, sending out rich, luxury dishes inspired by the Mughal tradition. You can eat royally here from a menu that references British ingredients including 'brawny' Herdwick lamb, salmon and venison. Dishes are subtly spiced, and chilled yoghurt flavoured with raspberry coulis makes a suitably creamy finale. Pricing is upmarket, but attentive staff soften the landing. Spice-friendly wines open at £25.
Chef/s: M. A. Rahman. **Open:** Mon to Fri L 12 to 3, all week D 5.30 to 11.30 (10.30 Sun). **Closed:** 25 Dec. **Meals:** alc (main courses £15 to £34). Set L £12 (2 courses) to £25. Set D £16 (2 courses) to £40. **Service:** 13% (optional). **Details:** Cards accepted. 80 seats. Air-con. Separate bar. No mobile phones. Wheelchair access. Music. Children allowed.

Rex Whistler Restaurant at Tate Britain

Drink to a national treasure
Millbank, Westminster, SW1P 4RG
Tel no: (020) 7887 8825
www.tate.org.uk
⊖ Pimlico, map 3
Modern British | £27
Cooking score: 2

🍷 £30

The basement restaurant at Tate Britain is a delightful lunchtime venue, worth incorporating into a day at an exhibition. Cornish fish and seafood are a strong feature, and there is a gently inventive note to dishes such as roasted wood pigeon with celeriac and Cox's apple rémoulade in red wine reduction, or Welsh lamb three ways with caramelised sweetbreads and carrots. A well-kept cheese selection and desserts such as chocolate tart with orange mascarpone round things off in style. The gazelle, leopard and snake bagged by the hunters in Rex Whistler's mural won't be on the menu. A wine list to suit a grand hotel has always been one of the glories of the place, with glasses and half-bottles supplementing a collection that is strong in the French classics. Good advice is on hand from the sommelier. Prices open at £4.35 a glass.
Chef/s: Richard Oxley. **Open:** all week L only 11.30 to 3. **Closed:** 25 and 26 Dec. **Meals:** alc (main courses £14 to £22). Set L £15.95 (2 courses) to

£19.95. **Service:** 12.5% (optional). **Details:** Cards accepted. 80 seats. 20 seats outside. Air-con. No music. No mobile phones. Wheelchair access. Children allowed.

Rhodes W1 Restaurant
Glitz, glamour and highfalutin food
Great Cumberland Place, Marble Arch, W1H 7DL
Tel no: (020) 7616 5930
www.rhodesw1.com
⊖ **Marble Arch, map 4**
Anglo-French | £50
Cooking score: 5

£5
OFF

First-timers be warned: don't venture into the Cumberland Hotel foyer or you may end up in Rhodes W1 Brasserie by mistake. Instead, look for the separate entrance leading to the fine-dining restaurant. This glitzy, cocooned room has glamour splashed all over it – thanks to Kelly Hoppen's decadent design (think sumptuous velvet fabrics, antique French chairs and glittering Spina chandeliers). Those chairs may have Gary's recipes printed on them, but anyone expecting cheery re-runs of heroic British dishes will be disappointed. Rhodes W1 looks to France for highfalutin inspiration – although its larder is packed with good things from Blighty. A finely pitched starter of sea trout fillet with crispy frogs' legs, pickled shallots, parsley risotto and garlic emulsion typifies the kitchen's enlightened, Anglo-French thinking. Elsewhere, precision-tuning is applied to meaty offerings including roast loin of veal (perhaps served with a Gallic ragoût of Chantenay carrots, snails and crosnes) or saddle of Balmoral venison with chestnuts and seasonal comrades-in-arms. Desserts run to a trendy take on traditional Scottish cranachan involving flapjack, iced whisky, honeycomb and raspberries, or pit dark chocolate délice against warm ginger parkin. The wine list oozes quality – especially in the French regions – but it's bedevilled by stiff mark-ups; prices start at £24.

Chef/s: Paul Welburn. **Open:** Tue to Fri L 12 to 2.15, Tue to Sat D 7 to 10.15. **Closed:** Sun, Mon, first 2 weeks Aug, last 2 weeks Dec. **Meals:** Set L £19.95 (2 courses) to £23.95. Set D £39.90 (2 courses) to £49.90. **Service:** 12.5% (optional). **Details:** Cards accepted. 45 seats. Air-con. Separate bar. Wheelchair access. Music. Children allowed.

Ristorante Semplice
Suave metropolitan Italian
9-10 Blenheim Street, Mayfair, W1S 1LJ
Tel no: (020) 7495 1509
www.ristorantesemplice.com
⊖ **Bond Street, Green Park, map 5**
Italian | £33
Cooking score: 5

♦ **V**

'What a find, a stone's throw from John Lewis!' exclaimed one reader after dining at this suave metropolitan Italian. Compared to some of its high-profile rivals in the capital, Semplice feels refreshingly civilised – although there's no holding back when it comes to the gold-frescoed interiors or slinky leather furnishings. Competitively priced set menus lure in the Bond Street shoppers and ladies who lunch on 'elegant' plates of linguine with mussels and samphire, generous saltimbocca and artisan Italian cheeses, but the kitchen also knows how to impress visitors who arrive after the stores close. Regional notes and imported ingredients point up the seasonal cooking, from Milanese-style monkfish with winter panzanella salad and poached quails' eggs to roast baby lamb with braised fennel, candied tomatoes and Rosso Pignoletto polenta. Elsewhere, pure-bred Fassone beef from Piedmont might be stuffed into ravioli with spinach sauce and aged ricotta or even fashioned into svizzere (Italian 'hamburgers'). To finish, crème brûlée spiked with Amaretto Disaronno is a good call. The all-Italian wine list was being updated as we went to press, but expect a fabulous range of bottles from vineyards great and small. Prices start at £19. Bar Trattoria Semplice is just around the corner (see entry).

Chef/s: Marco Torri. **Open:** Mon to Fri L 12 to 2.30, Mon to Sat D 7 to 10.30 (11 Sat). **Closed:** Sun, bank hols, 25 and 26 Dec. **Meals:** alc (main courses £19 to £29). Set L £22 (2 courses) to £29.50. **Service:** 12.5% (optional). **Details:** Cards accepted. 55 seats. 8 seats outside. Air-con. Wheelchair access. Music. Children allowed.

Roka

Chic sushi and robata fireworks
37 Charlotte Street, Fitzrovia, W1T 1RR
Tel no: (020) 7580 6464
www.rokarestaurant.com
⊖ **Goodge Street, map 5**
Japanese | £60
Cooking score: 4

V

A hit with the media crowd, trendy Roka is the London flagship of a global brand specialising in robatayaki cuisine. Take a ringside seat at the robata grill to watch the chefs at work. Char-grilling aside, it was actually the fresh glistening sushi and sashimi that wowed at inspection, with tuna tartare and extravagant beef gunkan proving the chef's palate is as sharp as his knives. Lamb cutlets with Korean spices were a whisker off overcooked, but the sweet meat couldn't be faulted. Creamy rice hot pot with king crab (a Roka original) is well worth trying. Prices soon mount up, so keep spending in check with the tasting menu. Service is 'exemplary', and staff are able to advise on the range of sakés, shochus and wines (from £24). Downstairs is a bar dedicated to trendy Japanese spirit shochu. Meanwhile, across town, a second branch serves the diners of Canary Wharf; tel: (020) 7636 5228.
Chef/s: Hamish Brown. **Open:** all week L 12 to 3.30 (12.30 to 4 Sat and Sun), D 5.30 to 11.30 (10.30 Sat and Sun). **Closed:** 25 Dec and 1 Jan. **Meals:** alc (main courses £13 to £68). **Service:** 13.5% (optional). **Details:** Cards accepted. 75 seats. 20 seats outside. Air-con. Separate bar. Wheelchair access. Music. Children allowed.

NEW ENTRY

Roux at Parliament Square

Hitting some impressive highs
Parliament Square, Westminster, SW1P 3AD
Tel no: (020) 7334 3737
www.rouxatparliamentsquare.co.uk
⊖ **Westminster, St James's Park, map 5**
Modern European | £55
Cooking score: 5

That old pedigree champion Le Gavroche has emerged from its Mayfair basement, been on an outing to the Houses of Parliament and pupped. The result is a squeaky-smart restaurant over two floors in the Royal Institute of Chartered Surveyors building. The bar still smelt of new paint at an early inspection and the design throughout is white and light. Staff are formal but warmly solicitous. You can even take your jacket off here, guys. Dan Cox has married the classical French technique of his mentor Michel Roux Jr with some ideas out of the classic modern British stable, and early results hit some impressive highs. Butter-poached langoustines are perfectly counterpointed with wafer-thin slices of Jabugo ham, offset with vivid purées of pea and baked onion. Main courses might deliver meltingly tender rack of Lune Valley spring lamb with baby artichokes and sun-dried tomatoes, while the equally gentle loin of veal comes with superb buttery roasted sweetbread and a mini-pan of smoky pomme mousseline. Dessert can be as classic as zingy lemon tart with yoghurt sorbet and a few raspberries, or as extravagant as jasmine tea custard with caramelised brioche and apricot compote. To explore the broadly based international wine list you'll need to be on more than the minimum wage, although there are some special Albert Roux selections from £20.
Chef/s: Dan Cox. **Open:** Mon to Fri L 12 to 2.30, Mon to Sat D 6 to 10.30. **Closed:** Sun, 25 and 26 Dec, bank hols. **Meals:** Set L £29.50. Set D £55. Tasting menu £65 (7 courses). **Service:** 12.5% (optional). **Details:** Cards accepted. 56 seats. Air-con. Separate bar. Wheelchair access. Music. Children allowed.

Royal China

Iconic dim sum
24–26 Baker Street, Marylebone, W1U 3BZ
Tel no: (020) 7487 4688
www.royalchinagroup.co.uk
⊖ Baker Street, map 4
Chinese | £30
Cooking score: 3

V

The Baker Street branch of this four-strong chain is an iconic stop on London's dim sum circuit – served daily from noon to 5pm (a long stretch sometimes resulting in jaded waiting staff). At inspection, one waiter seemed sapped of energy, choosing setting tables over interaction and topping up tea. The dim sum didn't disappoint, however. Prawn and chive dumplings were precisely pleated and delicately flavoured, a wholesome rice pot was generously packed with pork and salted fish and paper-thin, translucent cheung fun were as good as ever. Only egg custard tarts seemed tired. The spacious black and gilt interior raises Royal China well above rowdy Chinatown canteen level, without jettisoning the buzzy tea house atmosphere. House wine is £18. Branches in Queensway, Docklands and Fulham.
Chef/s: Mr Man and Master Hou. **Open:** all week 12 to 11 (11.30pm Fri and Sat, 11 to 10 Sun). **Closed:** 23 to 25 Dec. **Meals:** alc (main courses £6 to £90). Set L and D £30. **Service:** 13% (optional). **Details:** Cards accepted. 100 seats. Air-con. Separate bar. Wheelchair access. Music. Children allowed.

Rules

Britannia rules in Covent Garden
35 Maiden Lane, Covent Garden, WC2E 7LB
Tel no: (020) 7836 5314
www.rules.co.uk
⊖ Covent Garden, Leicester Square, Charing Cross, map 5
British | £36
Cooking score: 3

Now into its third century, the capital's longest running restaurant exudes the kind of plush velvety comfort that sends tourists into raptures – especially when it comes to politesse and platefuls of heartwarming true-Brit food. The kitchen occasionally casts its net beyond these shores for free-range chicken curry, venison osso bucco or chocolate soufflé, but its heart and soul are unfailingly loyal to the mother country. This is a world where dressed crab and game soup with quince jelly serve as patriotic preludes to thick-crusted steak and kidney pie, jugged hare or rack of Sussex lamb with spinach – not forgetting slabs of rare Belted Galloway beef and Rules' 'famous grouse'. For afters, memory lane beckons as orders are placed for golden treacle sponge or apple and blackberry crumble. Wines (including some corkers from the Rhône) start at £22; jugs of London tap water are free.
Chef/s: Richard Sawyer. **Open:** all week 12 to 11.45 (10.45 Sun). **Closed:** 4 days Christmas. **Meals:** alc (main courses £18 to £28). **Service:** 12.5% (optional). **Details:** Cards accepted. 89 seats. Air-con. Separate bar. No music. No mobile phones. Wheelchair access. Children allowed.

Sake No Hana

Cool and sexy Japanese
23 St James's Street, Mayfair, SW1A 1HA
Tel no: (020) 7925 8988
www.sakenohana.com
⊖ Green Park, map 5
Japanese | £30
Cooking score: 5

V

Alan Yau's Japanese restaurant, which resides on the first floor of the modernist Economist building, has just been through a re-vamp. The sushi bar has been relocated to the dining room, the sunken seating replaced by olive green banquettes and chairs with black leather, and the interior, designed by Kengo Kuma and based around cedar and tatami, now looks even more cool and sexy. There is a broader appeal to the menu, too, but with ample creativity to please the aficionado. At inspection a starter of crunchy razor clams served with a wasabi and soya dressing was a rousing success. Craftsmanship is applied

unstintingly, and dishes are beautifully presented – a trio of quail's breast lined up on top of a bed of leeks and spring onion looked spectacular. Plump and fatty otoro sushi sets the bar high, and a mixed vegetable tempura was pleasingly seasonal. Desserts are inventive, as in matsukaze (dried fruit) cake served with roasted tea ice cream. Staff are cheerful and well trained. Wines start from £25 and include an impressive selection of sakés, but note the high premiums.
Chef/s: Daisuke Hayashi. **Open:** Mon to Sat L 12 to 3, all week D 6 to 11 (11.30 Fri and Sat, 10.30 Sun). **Closed:** 25 Dec. **Meals:** alc (main courses from £9 to £80). Set D £55. **Service:** 13% (optional). **Details:** Cards accepted. 100 seats. Air-con. Separate bar. Wheelchair access. Music.

Salloos

Bastion of Pakistani cooking
62-64 Kinnerton Street, Knightsbridge, SW1X 8ER
Tel no: (020) 7235 4444
⊖ Knightsbridge, map 4
Pakistani | £50
Cooking score: 3

Owner Muhammed Salahuddin ('Saloo' to his friends) and chef Abdul Aziz have been in residence at this well-heeled Belgravia mews house since 1976, and their discreet first-floor restaurant remains a bastion of refined Pakistani cooking in the capital. The conservative menu seldom changes, but consistency and quality are never in doubt, with much depending on the output of the tandoor. Marinated lamb chops are the kitchen's most famous speciality, but the charcoal-fired oven also takes care of chicken tikka, shish kebabs and superb keema naans. Other notable dishes range from chicken jalfrezi and bhuna gosht to gurda masala (stir-fried kidneys in hot spices) and the emblematic haleem akbari (shredded lamb cooked for a day with whole wheatgerm and lentils). Vegetable sides are well worth a look, and there's cooling pistachio kulfi to finish. House wine is £19.50.

Chef/s: Abdul Aziz. **Open:** Mon to Sat L 12 to 2.30, D 7 to 11.15. **Closed:** Sun, 25 and 26 Dec. **Meals:** alc (main courses £16 to £20). **Service:** 12.5% (optional). **Details:** Cards accepted. 55 seats. Air-con. Separate bar. No music. No mobile phones.

Salt Yard

Off-the-wall tapas favourite
54 Goodge Street, Fitzrovia, W1T 4NA
Tel no: (020) 7637 0657
www.saltyard.co.uk
⊖ Goodge Street, map 5
Spanish/Italian | £25
Cooking score: 2
£5 OFF V £30

'It doesn't get much better than honey-drizzled courgette flowers stuffed with Monte Enebro cheese', insists a fan of this ebullient Spanish/Italian tapas hybrid. Graze at the elbow-to-elbow, street-level bar on hand-carved jamón Ibérico de Bellota, or venture downstairs if you want to explore the full menu. Unorthodox is the word for a choice that runs from confit Gloucester Old Spot pork belly with rosemary-scented cannellini beans to smoked wild mushrooms with olive oil-whipped potatoes, egg yolk and chorizo oil, via roasted scallops with cauliflower purée, hazelnuts and wild garlic leaf. For a left-field, sweet-toothed finale, consider turron parfait with poached dates and caramelised date ice cream. The Spanish/Italian wine list is a connoisseur's jewel box stuffed with great sherries and gems from reputable names and new-wave producers. Prices start at £15 (£3.75 a glass).
Chef/s: Ben Tish. **Open:** Mon to Fri L 12 to 3, Mon to Sat D 6 to 11 (5 Sat). **Closed:** Sun, 10 days Christmas, bank hols. **Meals:** alc (tapas £4 to £9). **Service:** 12.5% (optional). **Details:** Cards accepted. 75 seats. 6 seats outside. Air-con. Music. Children allowed.

Sardo

Sardinian star
45 Grafton Way, Fitzrovia, W1T 5DQ
Tel no: (020) 7387 2521
www.sardo-restaurant.com
⊖ Warren Street, map 2
Sardinian | £28
Cooking score: 4

£5 OFF ▲ V £30

One of the first restaurants in the capital to give Londoners a true taste of authentic Sardinian food and drink, Sardo has been preaching the native gospel since 1998. The cooking points up its peasant-style rusticity with touches of refinement, and all the details are in place – from the basket of pane carasau (brittle Sardinian flatbread) which opens proceedings to the sebadas (puff pastries filled with cheese and doused with honey) that round things off. In between there could be malloredus pasta with spicy salsiccia sarda (Sardinian sausage), grilled swordfish with rocket and tomatoes or grilled steak topped with Ovinfort (Sardinian blue cheese). Some have found the place rather 'mean-spirited', others have found the food 'very disappointing', but no such criticism can be levelled at the fascinating wine list. Little-known treasures from the island's growers are given full exposure, along with a healthy showing of classy bottles from the Italian mainland and France. Prices start at £14.50. The owners are planning to open a Sardinian deli/takeaway next door. From the same stable is Sardo Canale, 42 Gloucester Avenue, Primrose Hill, NW1; tel: (020) 7722 2800.
Chef/s: Roberto Sardu. **Open:** Mon to Fri L 12 to 3, Mon to Sat D 6 to 11. **Closed:** Sun, 24 to 27 Dec. **Meals:** alc (main courses £10 to £19). **Service:** 12.5% (optional). **Details:** Cards accepted. 60 seats. 10 seats outside. Air-con. No mobile phones. Music. Children allowed.

Also recommended

Also recommended entries are not scored but we think they are worth a visit.

Scott's

Star-spangled seafood
20 Mount Street, Mayfair, W1K 2HE
Tel no: (020) 7495 7309
www.scotts-restaurant.com
⊖ Green Park, map 4
Seafood | £46
Cooking score: 4

V

A glitzy Mayfair institution back in the 60s, Scott's re-emerged as a big player following a much publicised revamp a few years back. It plays to the crowds, and the setting works its magic for the A-listers and minor celebs who have taken the place to their hearts – and wallets. Star-spangled seafood is the culinary attraction, but the menu promises top-drawer renditions of the classics (Manx kipper pâté, lobster thermidor, poached sea trout with hollandaise) plus a sprinkling of foreign intruders in the shape of squid a la plancha, stone bass ceviche or cod fillet with Padrón peppers and chorizo. Meat eaters can also find satisfaction from pigeon on toast with raspberry dressing or roast veal with Brittany artichokes and borlotti beans. To conclude, go savoury (Welsh rarebit) or sweet (lemon curd cheesecake). French whites dominate the wine list, with prices from £24.
Chef/s: David McCarthy. **Open:** all week 12 to 10.30 (10pm Sun). **Closed:** 25 and 26 Dec, 1 Jan. **Meals:** alc (main courses £18 to £40). **Service:** 12.5% (optional). **Details:** Cards accepted. 120 seats. 10 seats outside. Air-con. Separate bar. No music. No mobile phones. Wheelchair access. Children allowed.

ALSO RECOMMENDED

▲ Serpentine Bar & Kitchen

Serpentine Road, Hyde Park, W2 2UH
Tel no: (020) 7706 8114
www.serpentinebarandkitchen.com
⊖ Hyde Park Corner, map 4
Modern British

The views take centre stage at this striking Hyde Park café with floor-to-ceiling windows overlooking the Serpentine's shimmering water and leafy borders. Food (ordered at the bar) is less of a marvel, but is fairly priced and generously portioned: think chorizo, new potato and soft-boiled egg salad (£7.50) or stone-baked pizzas topped with seafood (£9). The terrace is an idyllic alfresco dining spot – perfect for drinking wine (£14.50 a bottle) – however the no-bookings policy can lead to lengthy queues in clement weather. Open all week.

NEW ENTRY
Seven Park Place
High-end cooking with immense care
St James's Hotel and Club, 7-8 Park Place, Mayfair, SW1A 1LS
Tel no: (020) 7316 1600
www.stjamesclubandhotel.co.uk
⊖ Green Park, map 5
Modern French | £45
Cooking score: 6

£5 OFF 🍷 🛏️

Staff aplenty meet, greet and usher you through to a beautiful, intimate space behind the bar and brasserie. But the luxurious fittings of the dining room play second fiddle to William Drabble's cooking, and there's no doubt that everyone has come for the food. The menu is a set-price affair of five choices per course (less at lunch) or a gourmet table d'hôte of six courses, plus pre-starter and pre-dessert, all using high-end ingredients, and all cooked with immense care. A carpaccio of scallops is given zip and zing with a sharp but delicate lemon vinaigrette, while fresh morels are stuffed with a strong chicken mousse and served with crisped, boned chicken wings for texture and flavour. Roasted sea bass is invigorated with a rich red wine and tarragon jus, a memorable salty tang coming from an oyster beignet. Desserts are clever and innovative – a creamed rice pudding with dried, cooked and raw mango, enlivened with lime was a complete winner at inspection. This is not a restaurant to be taken lightly – William Drabble is a chef who deserves his hard-won reputation. The wine list, like the

clientele, is truly global. Prices start at £6.80 for a glass of house wine, but after that the sky's the limit.
Chef/s: William Drabble. **Open:** Tue to Sat L 12 to 2, D 7 to 10. **Closed:** Sun, Mon. **Meals:** Set L £24.50 (2 courses) to £29.50. Set D £39 (2 courses) to £45. **Service:** 12.5% (optional). **Details:** Cards accepted. 29 seats. Air-con. Separate bar. Wheelchair access. Music. Children allowed.

Sketch, Lecture Room and Library
Explosively designed pleasure palace
9 Conduit Street, Mayfair, W1S 2XG
Tel no: (020) 7659 4500
www.sketch.uk.com
⊖ Oxford Circus, map 5
Modern European | £59
Cooking score: 6

V

Sketch has the most explosive design of any restaurant in London, and it's a good part of the experience. Dining rooms and bars pop up all over the various levels, and it goes without saying that the Swarovski crystal bathrooms are not to be missed. The Lecture Room is decorated in an eye-popping, candy-coloured collision of orange, purple and crimson, with cream leather walls and ornate plaster mouldings. The aim is that 'every time you visit, something will have changed', a philosophy that extends to Jean-Denis Le Bras' extravagant interpretations of the Pierre Gagnaire template. Each course is comprised of a spectacular assemblage of small dishes: Sea Garden No 4 is an essay in fish that takes in Dover sole in Champagne, crab and malt whisky jelly, cuttlefish carpaccio, braised red mullet, clams and much more besides. At main course the lamb offering includes Indian-spiced roast leg, a shoulder dumpling, grilled rack and saddle, sheep's cheese and spinach velouté, and so forth. Individual items don't always deliver the hit-rate the outlay seems to warrant, and the fragmentary nature of it all can feel irksome to the sceptical, but there is a tremendous level of creative energy

here. And a tremendous bill, of course, which the ultra-fine list of wines, opening at £21, will do little to alleviate.
Chef/s: Jean-Denis Le Bras and Pierre Gagnaire. **Open:** Tue to Fri L 12 to 4, Mon to Sat D 6.30 to 12. **Closed:** Sun, 25 to 30 Dec, 2 weeks Aug, bank hols. **Meals:** alc (main courses £28 to £55). Set L £30 (2 courses) to £35. Tasting menu from £70 (7 courses). **Service:** 12.5% (optional). **Details:** Cards accepted. 50 seats. Air-con. Separate bar. No mobile phones. Wheelchair access. Music. Children allowed.

The Square
Pure, harmonious top-end cuisine
6-10 Bruton Street, Mayfair, W1J 6PU
Tel no: (020) 7495 7100
www.squarerestaurant.com
⊖ Green Park, map 5
Modern French | £75
Cooking score: 8
🍷

Philip Howard's status as one of the most gifted chefs in the land is all the more impressive because he has achieved a stellar reputation without parading himself in front of the TV cameras. He is a man of the kitchen who has dedicated himself to this sedate Mayfair dining room from the very beginning; every ounce of accumulated skill and devotion to the craft of cooking is channelled into dishes that are immaculately conceived, fastidiously worked through and hugely enjoyable. Showboating and fantastical molecular trickery have no place here; instead, diners can sit back and marvel at pure, harmonious top-end cuisine: 'it reminds you what eating out is supposed to be all about', observed one reader. Adorable amuse-bouches lead the charge, and some dishes are like old friends – the renowned lasagne of Dorset crab with a cappuccino of shellfish and Champagne foam is an enduring favourite. However, new menus always bring a tingle of anticipation: you can almost feel the spring sap rising as you consider a velouté of new season's garlic with a sauté of Somerset snails, frog's legs and morels. Overlaying bright, bouncy flavours with extreme richness is a favourite

device that also crops up in Howard's trademark salads – an assemblage of spring vegetables, Charolais beef, pea shoots and herbs, for instance, comes with goats' curd crostini and an unannounced cheese beignet for good measure. Elsewhere, the kitchen delivers blockbusting flavours with a vengeance, from a superbly balanced dish of slow-cooked pig's cheeks with sweet-and-sour belly and trotter pointed up with blood orange, chicory and star anise to a dark-hued autumnal plate of roast breast and croustillant of grouse with crushed root vegetables and elderberries. Desserts are handled with supreme dexterity, even if the results are a tad too busy at times – witness a flamboyant exploration of rhubarb involving tiny cubes of jelly with dollops of sorbet and fool, plus sablé and beignets. The cheeseboard is a slate of epic proportions, likewise the mighty 70-page wine list. France is explored in awesome detail, but an insistence on quality typifies the entire range, from little-known Champagnes to glorious stickies. Prices start at £21. Service remains studiously professional to a fault, although it has taken on a more chatty, lighter tone of late – which is all to the good.
Chef/s: Philip Howard. **Open:** Mon to Fri L 12 to 2.30, all week D 6.30 to 10 (10.30 Sat, 9.30 Sun). **Closed:** 25 Dec, 1 Jan, bank hols. **Meals:** Set L £30 (2 courses) to £35. Set D £75. Tasting menu £100. **Service:** 12.5% (optional). **Details:** Cards accepted. 75 seats. Air-con. No music. Wheelchair access. Children allowed.

Sumosan
Classy modern Japanese
26b Albemarle Street, Mayfair, W1S 4HY
Tel no: (020) 7495 5999
www.sumosan.com
⊖ Green Park, map 5
Japanese | £50
Cooking score: 4
V

A sophisticated family-run Japanese restaurant in the heart of Mayfair, Sumosan is suave in shades of soft purple with light oak flooring and macassar ebony tables – an apt setting for such a classy modern take on Japanese food. The swanky J bar below offers cocktails to kick off the evening, while Sumosan's menu lists sushi and sashimi, noodles and soups, and an engaging selection of modern/fusion dishes. For the undecided there are sushi and sashimi sets and tasting menus for tables of two or more. Teppanyaki grilled dishes include beef sirloin with sweet-potato purée and duck breast with buckwheat risotto. Lighter options take in mixed vegetable tempura, and a sashimi salad with Sumosan's special dressing. Naturally fish dominates, with choices ranging from familiar sushi to spicy somen noodles with lobster and baby asparagus, sea urchin risotto, or toro (fatty tuna) stuffed with foie gras. A decent selection of international wines starts at £27, but sakés and cocktails are a beguiling alternative.

Chef/s: Bubker Belkhit. **Open:** Mon to Fri L 12 to 2.45, all week D 6 to 11.30 (10.30 Sun). **Closed:** 25 and 26 Dec, Easter, bank hols. **Meals:** alc (main courses £8 to £55). Set menus from £22.50. **Service:** 15% (optional). **Details:** Cards accepted. 130 seats. Air-con. Separate bar. Wheelchair access. Music. Children allowed.

Tamarind

On sizzling form
20 Queen Street, Mayfair, W1J 5PR
Tel no: (020) 7629 3561
www.tamarindrestaurant.com
⊖ **Green Park, map 5**
Indian | £45
Cooking score: 5

£5 OFF V

A minor re-vamp to the wooden floor and bar has added further lustre to this already luxurious subterranean setting accented with subtle tones of browns and dusky gold. The room overflows with spirited conversation, helped along by the intuitive and responsive service. At inspection the kitchen was on sizzling form – serving up a trio of mushrooms (portobello, shiitake and oyster) that perfectly captured the smokiness of the tandoor oven, its flavours lingering beautifully on the palate. Main courses

excelled, especially sweet and plump tiger prawns cooked with tomatoes and peppers in a curry delicately spiced with toasted coriander. Vegetables are cooked with real care – witness a combo of broccoli, cauliflower, asparagus, red peppers and baby corn punctuated with cumin and crushed peppercorns. Dishes from the tandoor also shine, and kebabs are eminently likeable; tandoori-grilled quail marinated with ginger is a tried-and-tested combination, and staples such as basmati rice and nans are faultless. Desserts also adopt a reassuring stance, as in gulab jamun or tandoori pineapple spiced with chaat masala. Prices may be on the high side, but there is no denying the quality. The extensive wine list, which starts high from £26.50, is equally well-crafted and expensive.

Chef/s: Alfred Prasad. **Open:** Sun to Fri L 12 to 2.30 (3 Sun), all week D 5.30 to 11 (6 to 10.30 Sun). **Closed:** 25 and 26 Dec, 1 Jan. **Meals:** alc (main courses £15 to £28). Set L £16.50 (2 courses) to £18.95. Set D £52. Sun L £28. Tasting menu £78. **Service:** 12.5% (optional). **Details:** Cards accepted. 90 seats. Air-con. No mobile phones. Music.

Terroirs

Buzzy wine bar with French classics
5 William IV Street, Covent Garden, WC2N 4DW
Tel no: (020) 7036 0660
www.terroirswinebar.com
⊖ **Charing Cross, map 5**
French | £30
Cooking score: 3

V

'Incredible charcuterie, concise menu with something for everyone, all derived from French classics but including well-sourced British ingredients', is a knowledgeable verdict on this premier-league wine bar close to Charing Cross station. A little cellar-restaurant has been added since last year's Guide, all brick walls and wooden tables with a similar menu to the bright, buzzy wine bar. Cod with petits pois à la française pleased one regular reporter, as did buffalo mozzarella with lemon and mint, and a well-made crème caramel. Roast Landaise chicken with garlic

and watercress, and tarte Tatin 'still sizzling in a cast iron frying pan' have also been well received. The likeable modern wine list explores France and Italy, with insightful selections arranged by region and held together by bantering commentary. House wines start at £15.25.
Chef/s: Ed Wilson. **Open:** Mon to Sat 12 to 11. **Closed:** Sun, 24 to 28 Dec, 31 Dec to 3 Jan. **Meals:** alc (main courses £12 to £18). **Service:** 12.5% (optional). **Details:** Cards accepted. 75 seats. Air-con. Separate bar. Music. Children allowed.

Texture
Big-statement dining with Nordic nuances
34 Portman Street, Marble Arch, W1H 7BY
Tel no: (020) 7224 0028
www.texture-restaurant.co.uk
⊖ Marble Arch, map 4
Modern European | £60
Cooking score: 4

🍴 V

Agnar Sverrisson and Xavier Rousset are making a big statement at Texture – a confident destination with a fizzy Champagne bar out front and a sleek, white, ornately plastered dining room beyond. The menu references ingredients from Sverrisson's Nordic homeland. Expect complex culinary detailing in dishes such as poached halibut with Jerusalem artichoke 'textures'; elsewhere, a robust plateful of fallow deer with chocolate, cranberries, Brussels sprouts and red cabbage was winter fuel from heaven for one reader. There are cheeky touches, too: bacon popcorn literally pops up in a dish of char-grilled quail, while candied beetroot keeps company with a Valrhona chocolate ball. The set lunch is 'extraordinarily good value', but doesn't always showcase the kitchen's talents to good effect. However, there's no dumbing down where wine is concerned: Xavier Rousset's auspicious list breathes class, with French pedigree dripping from its opening pages and a healthy respect for the world's winemaking elite. Prices start at £16.50. The duo have also launched 28°–50° at 140 Fetter Lane, EC4 1BT, tel: (020) 7242 8877.

Chef/s: Agnar Sverrisson. **Open:** Tue to Sat L 12 to 2.30, D 6.30 to 10. **Closed:** Sun, Mon, 2 weeks Aug, 2 weeks Dec. **Meals:** alc (main courses £22 to £29). Set L £18.50 (2 courses) to £22. Set D £35 (2 courses) to £46. Tasting menu £59 (7 courses). **Service:** 12.5% (optional). **Details:** Cards accepted. 52 seats. Air-con. Music. Car parking.

Theo Randall at the InterContinental
Gutsy, alluring Italian flavours
InterContinental London Hotel, 1 Hamilton Place, Mayfair, W1J 7QY
Tel no: (020) 7318 8747
www.theorandall.com
⊖ Hyde Park Corner, map 4
Italian | £35
Cooking score: 6

£5 OFF 🍷 V

Having spent years playing a very impressive third fiddle at the River Café (see entry), Theo Randall has established a formidable reputation at his own gaff in the five-star setting of Park Lane's InterContinental Hotel. Sourcing top-drawer ingredients is in his blood, and a big budget means he can pick the very best for his gutsy, alluring dishes. There are bold gestures aplenty here, but also delicacy – especially in the starters. Plates of beef carpaccio with shaved violet artichokes, thinly sliced chicory shoots tinged with red wine vinegar or an exquisite combination of smoked eel with beetroots, dandelion and fresh horseradish all display an enviably clean, clear-sighted approach. Moving on, handmade pasta is a strength and the kitchen dishes up everything from herby green ravioli to spaghetti with Dorset blue lobster, San Marzano tomatoes and chilli. However, succulent wood-roasted specialities are the seasonal stars, whether it's Limousin veal chops, juicy monkfish with treviso tardivo or top-drawer guinea fowl stuffed with coppa di Parma, mascarpone and thyme, accompanied by braised Swiss chard and Castelluccio lentils. Randall's zucchini fritti are to die for, according to one devotee ('and I don't even like zucchini'), while desserts might offer a

choice of Amalfi lemon tart or sexy vanilla ice cream with chilled espresso. Prices are on the high side, although portions are ample and set lunches continue to offer fine value. Italy is a strong suit on the serious international wine list, with house selections from £20.
Chef/s: Theo Randall. **Open:** Mon to Fri L 12 to 3, Mon to Sat D 5.45 to 11. **Closed:** Sun, 25 to 28 Dec, bank hols. **Meals:** alc (main courses £20 to £35). Set L and D £23 (2 courses) to £27. **Service:** not inc. **Details:** Cards accepted. 124 seats. Air-con. Separate bar. Wheelchair access. Music. Children allowed. Car parking.

Tierra Brindisa
Premium Spanish provisions
46 Broadwick Street, Soho, W1F 7AF
Tel no: (020) 7534 1690
www.brindisatapaskitchens.com
⊖ Oxford Circus, map 5
Spanish | £20
Cooking score: 3

V £30

There's no mistaking the family likeness at this Soho offshoot of trailblazing Tapas Brindisa (see entry). Like its big daddy, Tierra is essentially about premium Spanish provisions, served up in a cramped dining room with a buzzy bar and an open kitchen. Brindisa trademarks including top-drawer Ibérico charcuterie, Padrón peppers, prawns in garlic, and Catalan spinach with pine nuts and raisins share the billing with some less familiar platefuls – perhaps scallops a la plancha with celeriac and crispy Serrano ham or braised beef cheeks with sweet potato mash. Country toast with tomatoes is a good lead-off, and you can close with obscure regional cheeses or Spanish flan with rhubarb compote. Drinkers can pick from a fine choice of sherries, esoteric digestifs and keenly chosen native wines from £15 (£3.75 a glass).
Chef/s: Sheldon Garcia. **Open:** Mon to Sat 12 to 10.30. **Closed:** Sun, 25 Dec. **Meals:** alc (tapas £5 to £13). Set L and D £25 (2 courses). **Service:** 12.5% (optional). **Details:** Cards accepted. 50 seats. 4 seats outside. Air-con. Separate bar. Wheelchair access. Music. Children allowed.

Trishna
Indian seafood star
15-17 Blandford Street, Marylebone, W1U 3DG
Tel no: (020) 7935 5624
www.trishnalondon.com
⊖ Marylebone, Bond Street, map 4
Indian/Seafood | £30
Cooking score: 3

V

The London sibling of a legendary seafood restaurant in Mumbai, classy Trishna courts the Marylebone vote with its sleekly pared-back good looks and adventurous piscine menu. Vegetable pakoras, sigri grills and tandooris set the ball rolling, along with light options such as wild mushroom salad with roasted garlic. After that, plump for Isle of Shuna mussels with coconut milk and turmeric, guinea fowl with fennel seeds and masoor lentils, or the signature Dorset brown crab with a garlicky, butter-rich sauce spiked with black pepper. To conclude, mango rice pudding with sweet chilli and pistachio rounds things off invitingly. The tasting menu is excellent value, and it comes with the option of fascinating beer recommendations for each dish. Wine flights are also on offer, and the full list kicks off at £17.10.
Chef/s: Karam Sethi. **Open:** Mon to Sat 12 to 2.45, D 6 to 10.45. **Closed:** Sun, 25 to 28 Dec, 1 to 3 Jan. **Meals:** alc (main courses £10 to £18). Set L £13.50 to £16.50. Set D £25 (2 courses) to £35. **Service:** 12.5% (optional). **Details:** Cards accepted. 60 seats. 10 seats outside. Air-con. Wheelchair access. Music. Children allowed.

ALSO RECOMMENDED
▲ La Trouvaille
12a Newburgh Street, Soho, W1F 7RR
Tel no: (020) 7287 8488
www.latrouvaille.co.uk
⊖ Oxford Circus, map 5
French £5 OFF

True to its name, this re-invented bistro/wine bar is a 'find' if you're a fan of slightly left-field French regional cooking. Head for the dining room for the likes of goats' cheese charlotte with pine needle emulsion followed by tomato-stuffed rack of lamb with gnocchi, preserved olives and coffee sauce; after that, perhaps tarte Tatin with a quenelle of milk jam and sea salt. Two-course lunches are £17.50, three-course dinners £35. Southern French organic/biodynamic wines start at £17.50. Open Mon to Sat L, Tue to Sat D.

Umu
Gilt-edged Kyoto cuisine
14-16 Bruton Place, Mayfair, W1J 6LX
Tel no: (020) 7499 8881
www.umurestaurant.com
⊖ Green Park, Bond Street, map 5
Japanese | £60
Cooking score: 5
🍷 V

Umu offers a luxurious version of traditional set-menu dining, and distantly recalls old Kyoto in its wood-toned, elegantly simple interior. Chefs in pillbox hats micro-slice the raw proteins in full view, while saké is served in glazed ceramic flasks and Japanese music plays in an atmosphere of studied calm. Traditional sushi and bento lunches are on offer, but the core of the operation is the repertoire of fixed-price banquets, which cover the full fascinating range of Japanese cuisine, from slivers of high-grade tuna in mukozuke dishes to exquisite mouthfuls such as grilled sea bream with Japanese turnip, shredded ginger and yuzu. The meltingly tender Wagyu beef appears with supporting flavours of blackberry and foie gras, while Japanese amberjack is among the less familiar fish options. In the season, you might finish with cherry blossom ice cream, or else push the boat out for chestnut Mont Blanc with mandarin and mango sorbet. An extravagantly broad selection of sakés should encourage experimentation. Grape wines include a white blend from the Shizen range, made from indigenous Japanese grape varieties by French consultant Denis Dubourdieu at £29. Prices are generally as sky-high as we've come to expect in this context.

Chef/s: Ichiro Kubota. **Open:** Mon to Fri L 12 to 2.30, Mon to Sat D 6 to 11. **Closed:** Sun, 24 Dec to early Jan, bank hols. **Meals:** alc (main courses £13 to £57). Set L from £25. Kaiseki tasting menu from £65. **Service:** 12.5% (optional). **Details:** Cards accepted. 67 seats. Air-con. No mobile phones. Wheelchair access. Music. Children allowed.

ALSO RECOMMENDED
▲ **Vasco & Piero's Pavilion**
15 Poland Street, Soho, W1F 8QE
Tel no: (020) 7437 8774
www.vascosfood.com
⊖ Oxford Circus, map 5
Italian

Soho remains Little Italy, even if it contains an ever-dwindling number of Italian restaurants. Vasco and Piero's bucks the trend by still going strong after four decades and by avoiding the 'red sauce' orthodoxy. On a daily changing, nominally Umbrian menu, dishes such as porchetta with rocket and pecorino (£9.50) or cod with farro and pesto (£18.50) are homely and accessible, but rarely hit the heights one expects of the price. Décor is unremarkable but pleasant, and chirpy staff enliven proceedings. Wines from £17.50. Pre-theatre menus, £19.50. Closed Sat L and Sun.

▲ **Veeraswamy**
Victory House, 99-101 Regent Street, Piccadilly, W1B 4RS
Tel no: (020) 7734 1401
www.veeraswamy.com
⊖ Piccadilly Circus, map 5
Indian

Britain's most venerable Indian restaurant is well into its ninth decade, although it now hits diners with a lavish contemporary look – think black granite flecked with gold leaf, silver jali screens and dramatic multi-coloured lighting. The cooking has also acquired a contemporary edge, but the kitchen can still deliver sound versions of classics such as lamb biryani (£23) or Lucknow-style chicken korma (£18). Starters might include flash–

grilled oyster kebabs, while desserts take in exotic sorbets, kulfi and 'black' galub jamun (£6.75). Wines from £23. Open all week.

The White Swan

Star in a gastropub galaxy
108 Fetter Lane, Holborn, EC4A 1ES
Tel no: (020) 7242 9696
www.thewhiteswanlondon.com
⊖ Chancery Lane, map 5
Modern British | £29
Cooking score: 3

£30
OFF

The White Swan was one of the first of a growing chain of London pubs to be opened by Tom and Ed Martin. It's a lively, narrow place on three levels. Crowds pack into the bar where decibel levels can be high, but you can climb the mirror-panelled staircase to the top-floor dining room for a more relaxed environment. The short menu reads simply and enticingly, and delivers the flavours it promises with creditable panache. Monkfish cheeks with garlic, tomato fondue and persillade is one way to start, followed by rump of Herdwick lamb, white polenta, curly kale and prune tapenade, with buttermilk pannacotta, poached rhubarb and shortbread to finish. The globetrotting wine list offers enjoyable quaffing at reasonable prices. House vino is £15.

Chef/s: Jon Coates. **Open:** Mon to Fri L 12 to 3, D 6 to 10. **Closed:** Sat, Sun, 25 and 26 Dec, bank hols. **Meals:** alc (main courses £10 to £18). Set L £25 (2 courses) to £29. Set D £22.25 (2 courses) to £29.35. **Service:** 12.5% (optional). **Details:** Cards accepted. 52 seats. Air-con. Separate bar. Music. Children allowed.

Wild Honey

'The best bargain lunches in London'
12 St George Street, Mayfair, W1S 2FB
Tel no: (020) 7758 9160
www.wildhoneyrestaurant.co.uk
⊖ Bond Street, Oxford Circus, map 5
Modern European | £35
Cooking score: 6

£5
OFF

The words 'bargain' and 'Mayfair' rarely find their way into the same sentence. Wild Honey, then, is a rare thing: a top-drawer W1 restaurant where you can snap up a deal. With set lunch menus under £20, it's no wonder that one reader exclaimed 'this must be the best bargain in London!' The carte changes weekly, delving into the British seasonal larder to produce creative bistro cooking with French leanings and particular attention paid to presentation. Heritage beets and ewes' milk ricotta salad is a light and fresh beginning, while smoked eel, chicken wings and sweetcorn 'really work'. Anthony Demetre's trademarks of 'wonderful balance and flavour combinations' are evinced by rose veal with polenta and endive, and hare with rhubarb and chestnut spätzle. But not all reports have been positive this year, and the 'gloomy' wood-panelled room adorned with contrasting modern art also comes in for some flak for its cramped tables. Service, described as 'pushy' has also let the side down. As at sister restaurant Arbutus (see entry) the concise list ('with lots under £30') is available in its entirety by the 250ml carafe.

Chef/s: Colin Kelly. **Open:** all week L 12 to 2.30 (3 Sun), D 6 to 11 (11.30 Fri and Sat, 10.30 Sun). **Closed:** 25 and 26 Dec, 1 Jan. **Meals:** alc (main courses £15 to £22). Set L £18.95. Sun L £25.50. **Service:** 12.5% (optional). **Details:** Cards accepted. 65 seats. Air-con. No music. Children allowed.

Wiltons

Blue-blooded British aristocrat
55 Jermyn Street, Mayfair, SW1Y 6LX
Tel no: (020) 7629 9955
www.wiltons.co.uk
⊖ Green Park, map 5
British | £70
Cooking score: 4

V

Old money feels very at home here. Though the kitchen prides itself on fabulous seafood and the best of English game, there is a nursery feel to the menu – daily lunchtime roasts are carved at the table, classic fish are poached, grilled or fried as requested, and meatier offerings are covered by steak, mixed grill and pies. The tasting menu offers a greater gastronomic challenge, but though the likes of ratatouille and confit of quail may be relished by the very competent kitchen, they seem somewhat out of keeping with the ethos of the restaurant. Most diners prefer to stick closer to home with lobster thermidor and omelette Arnold Bennett, with some crumble or cheese to finish. The wine list is stuffed with pedigree clarets and Burgundies and prices are eye-watering; even house offerings start at £8 a glass.
Chef/s: Andrew Turner. **Open:** Mon to Fri L 12 to 2.30, D 6 to 10.30. **Closed:** Sat, Sun, 24 Dec to 3 Jan, bank hols. **Meals:** alc (main courses £20 to £60). Set L £45. Tasting D £80 (8 courses). **Service:** 12.5% (optional). **Details:** Cards accepted. 100 seats. Air-con. No music. No mobile phones. Wheelchair access. Children allowed.

Please send us your feedback

To register your opinion about any restaurant listed in the Guide, or a new restaurant that you wish to bring to our attention, please visit the web address at the bottom of the page. Your feedback informs the content of the book and will be used to compile next year's reviews.

The Wolseley

High-impact all-day dining haven
160 Piccadilly, Mayfair, W1J 9EB
Tel no: (020) 7499 6996
www.thewolseley.com
⊖ Green Park, map 5
Modern European | £45
Cooking score: 2

V

'Jeremy King and Christopher Corbin have the magic touch' enthuses a regular, who adds that this high-impact building is the 'yardstick for all other restaurants I visit'. But popping into this car showroom-turned-grand café for a quick hamburger or sundae is almost unheard of; seven years on it's still hard to get a table, even for breakfast. International brasserie classics – steak frites, wiener schnitzel, or choucroute à l'alsacienne – are the Wolseley's stock-in-trade, alongside caviar, crustacea and an excellent banana split. Wines come from famous-name producers, starting at £19 and with plenty by the glass.
Chef/s: Julian O'Neill. **Open:** all week L 12 to 3 (3.30 Sat and Sun), D 5.30 to 12 (11 Sun). **Closed:** 25 Dec, August bank hol. **Meals:** alc (main courses £6 to £29). **Service:** 12.5% (optional). **Details:** Cards accepted. 150 seats. Air-con. Separate bar. No music. Wheelchair access. Children allowed.

ALSO RECOMMENDED

▲ Yalla Yalla

1 Green's Court, Piccadilly, W1F 0HA
Tel no: (020) 7287 7663
www.yalla-yalla.co.uk
⊖ Piccadilly Circus, map 5
Lebanese

Squeezing into this diminutive 'Beirut street food' café in an insalubrious Soho alleyway, it's tempting to order your chicken shawarma from the mouthwatering display to go, rather than suffer on one of the comically tiny stools. Once settled in, however, its charm takes over – 'there's real passion at work here'. From a reasonably priced choice of mezze, grills and wraps, chicken livers with pomegranate molasses (£3.50) and perfect ungreasy fritto misto (£5.50) show real care. A dozen Lebanese wines from £14.50. Open all week.

Yauatcha

Trendy tea parlour pulls the crowds
15-17 Broadwick Street, Soho, W1F 0DL
Tel no: (020) 7494 8888
www.yauatcha.com
⊖ Tottenham Court Road, map 5
Chinese | £35
Cooking score: 2

V

Alan Yau's trendy tea parlour is a stylish venue spread over two floors: a moodily lit basement restaurant, which comes into its own in the evening, and the white and neon ground-floor café serving a lengthy, largely Chinese tea list, beautiful cakes and an extensive selection of dim sum. Here reworked Chinatown staples – prawn dumplings, various cheung fun, lotus wrap, char sui bun – and larger plates including steamed wild prawn with homemade chilli sauce or braised veal momo-style (preserved beancurd, Chinese wine, star anise, cinnamon) appeal to a largely western crowd who, seven years on, still pack the place out.
Chef/s: Lee Che Liang. **Open:** all week 12 to 11.15 (11.30 Thur to Sat, 10.30 Sun). **Closed:** 24 and 25 Dec. **Meals:** alc (£9 to £34). Set L and D £40 to £60 (3 courses). **Service:** 12.5% (optional).
Details: Cards accepted. 194 seats. Air-con. Wheelchair access. Music. Children allowed.

Zafferano

Top Italian player
15 Lowndes Street, Belgravia, SW1X 9EY
Tel no: (020) 7235 5800
www.londonfinedininggroup.com
⊖ Knightsbridge, Hyde Park Corner, map 4
Italian | £45
Cooking score: 6

Zafferano has never been one for self-congratulation or big gestures, despite its reputation as one of the top Italian players in the capital. It retains a serious, understated

outlook – neatly clipped shrubs outside; exposed brick walls, sleek banquettes and stone floors in the effortlessly chic dining room. The main business in this very fine eatery has always been the food on the plate, and Andy Needham's cooking remains true to itself, following the calendar unerringly and treating ingredients with proper respect. Superbly fashioned pasta remains one of the kitchen's great strengths and a showcase for some unfussy artistry: consider linguine with lobster, veal shin ravioli with saffron or twisted strozzapreti with tomato, Tropea onions and rocket. There are lovely fresh salads, too (try the warm octopus version with celery and purple potatoes), plus a seasonally tuned roster of mains that might run from marvellous seafood (roast line-caught sea bass with Vernaccia wine and green olives) to emphatically flavoured meat and game (roast Gressingham duck with honey and mustard fruits). Desserts embrace everything from tantalisingly luscious tiramisu to buffalo ricotta cannoli with orange, chocolate and pistachio. The wine list is an Italian blockbuster from £22.
Chef/s: Andy Needham. **Open:** all week L 12 to 2.30 (3 Sat and Sun), D 7 to 11 (10.30 Sun). **Closed:** 1 week Christmas, 3 days New Year. **Meals:** alc (main courses £13 to 29). **Service:** 13.5%. **Details:** Cards accepted. 80 seats. Air-con. Separate bar. No mobile phones. Wheelchair access. Music.

L'Absinthe

Blissful bistro
40 Chalcot Road, Primrose Hill, NW1 8LS
Tel no: (020) 7483 4848
www.labsinthe.co.uk
⊖ Chalk Farm, map 2
French | £22
Cooking score: 3
£30

Jean-Christophe Slowik's neighbourhood bistro has spread a blanket of joy across Primrose Hill, and residents have been packing the place since it opened in 2007. Here are locally smoked salmon with sour cream, chicken liver parfait with port jelly and toast, backed up by mains such as duck confit with sauté potatoes. One reporter wondered about the serving temperatures – both the poached egg with leeks vinaigrette and the follow-up boeuf bourguignon with rice pilaff could have been hotter – but otherwise technique is sound. Finish with tarte Tatin and clotted Jersey cream, or with the house special, absinthe-laced crème brûlée. Wines are also sold retail, and the restaurant price is a standard £10 extra, which means that the further towards the summit you head, the better the value.
Chef/s: Christophe Fabre. **Open:** Tue to Sun L 12 to 2.30 (4 Sat and Sun), D 6 to 10.30 (9.30 Sun). **Closed:** Mon, Aug, 1 week Christmas. **Meals:** alc (main courses £10 to £16). Set L Tue to Sat £9.50 (2 courses) to £12.50. Sun L £14.95 (2 courses) to £18.50. **Service:** 12.5% (optional). **Details:** Cards accepted. 60 seats. 14 seats outside. Air-con. Wheelchair access. Music. Children allowed.

The Albion

Stylish pub with well-crafted food
10 Thornhill Road, Islington, N1 1HW
Tel no: (020) 7607 7450
www.the-albion.co.uk
⊖ Angel, Highbury and Islington, map 2
Gastropub | £27
Cooking score: 3
£5 OFF £30

This pretty, wisteria-covered Georgian building is hard to miss. It still operates as a pub, but it's a quietly stylish one attracting a mainly young, local crowd. Food, however, is placed firmly top of the agenda. Co-owner Richard Turner is now overseeing the kitchen and the cooking continues to gain approval from readers: simple things like Dorset crab on toast or pork belly ribs with fennel slaw preceding well-crafted main courses of lamb shank shepherd's pie or smoked haddock fishcake with spinach and poached egg. Check out the charcoal grill for a brace of quail, a cheeseburger or bacon chop. Staff are friendly and the wine list opens at £14.
Chef/s: Richard Turner. **Open:** all week L 12 to 3 (4 Sat and Sun), D 6 to 10 (9 Sun). **Meals:** alc (main courses £10 to £25). **Service:** 10% (optional). **Details:** Cards accepted. 102 seats. 110 seats outside. Wheelchair access. Music. Children allowed.

Almeida

Sleek Islington performer
30 Almeida Street, Islington, N1 1AD
Tel no: (020) 7354 4777
www.danddlondon.com
⊖ Angel, Highbury & Islington, map 2
Modern French | £33
Cooking score: 4
♪ V

'I saw Adrian Lester!' gasped a metropolitan sophisticate and fan of the *Hustle* actor, before regaining her cool in the D&D group's brasserie opposite Islington's namesake theatre. The spacious, breezy ambience of the place suits the mood of the food, as well as the district, with a repertoire of tried-and-true stalwarts enhanced with some neat creative flourishes. Dithering over the amply stocked charcuterie trolley is a good way to kick things off, and the meatier mains also score highly, whether for slow-braised suckling pig with caramelised apple, or deeply flavoured Barbary duck breast with endive Tatin and blood-orange sauce. Spring diners might enjoy a serving of poached wild halibut with broad beans and crushed peas in sorrel velouté. Champagne soup with seasonal strawberries is a refreshing finale, but there is also a gorgeously gooey take on crème brûlée. A set of sommelier's suggestions from £19.50 lead off a supremely well-constructed list that offers good drinking in Italy, Iberia and the southern hemisphere, as well as the classic French regions. Wines by the glass from £4.50. **Chef/s:** Alan Jones. **Open:** Tue to Sun L 12 to 2.30 (3.30 Sun), Mon to Sat D 5.30 to 10.30. **Closed:** 26 to 28 Dec, 1 Jan. **Meals:** Set L and theatre menu £15.95 (2 courses) to £18.95. Set D £27.50 (2 courses) to £32.50. Sun L £22.50 (2 courses) to £26.50. **Service:** not inc. **Details:** Cards accepted. 88 seats. 10 seats outside. Air-con. Separate bar. No music. Wheelchair access. Children allowed.

ALSO RECOMMENDED
▲ Il Bacio
178-184 Blackstock Road, Highbury, N5 1HA
Tel no: (020) 7226 3339
www.ilbaciohighbury.co.uk
⊖ Arsenal, map 2
Italian

The name means 'the kiss', and the warm embrace offered at this corner-site, family-run restaurant in Highbury is that of Sardinian cuisine. A cool interior with tiled floor and café-style tables is the setting for dishes such as carta musica crispbread served with Sardinian sausage, mushrooms and pecorino (£6.95), malloreddus pasta with swordfish, aubergine, tomato, garlic and chilli (£8.95), or a native fish stew, combining monkfish, swordfish, prawns, clams and mussels (£15.50). There's a full pizza menu too. House wines are £11.50. Open all week D, also Sat and Sun L.

Bradleys
Appealing Gallic eatery
25 Winchester Road, Swiss Cottage, NW3 3NR
Tel no: (020) 7722 3457
www.bradleysnw3.co.uk
⊖ Swiss Cottage, map 2
French | £35
Cooking score: 3
£5 OFF 🍾 🍴

Close by the Hampstead Theatre in Swiss Cottage, Simon Bradley's restaurant is not far off clocking up 20 years of service to the district. With its pretty courtyard garden, wood floors and light, airy ambience, it's an appealing place, good for pre-theatre dinners and value lunches too. The cooking is French in orientation, producing baby artichoke barigoule with goats' cheese fritter to start, and mains such as gurnard à la bourride with braised fennel or Gressingham duck with orange-glazed chicory and star anise. Side-orders include creamy dauphinoise, and desserts pull out the stops for the likes of pear Belle Hélène, or rhubarb soufflé with ginger ice cream. A thoroughly commendable wine list has always been one of the glories of the place, with stylistic classifications for the French-led selections. Prices start at £15.50. **Chef/s:** Simon Bradley. **Open:** Sun to Fri L 12 to 3 (10 to 5 Sun), Mon to Sat D 6 to 10.30 (11 Sat). **Closed:** 25 Dec to 3 Jan. **Meals:** alc (main courses £15 to £20). Set L £12.95 (2 courses) to £16.95. Set D £23.50. Sun L £22. **Service:** 12.5% (optional). **Details:** Cards accepted. 60 seats. Air-con. No music. No mobile phones. Children allowed.

The Bull & Last
Gorgeous gastrogrub and stonking ales
168 Highgate Road, Hampstead, NW5 1QS
Tel no: (020) 7267 3641
www.thebullandlast.co.uk
⊖ Tufnell Park, Kentish Town, map 2
Modern British | £30
Cooking score: 3

Kentish Town has a raft of good gastropubs but the forerunner is the Bull & Last, leading the way since it opened in 2008. It combines a

comfortably laid-back demeanour with mismatched pubby good looks and a kitchen that demonstrates a real flair for crafting a menu of seasonal, unfussy and full-flavoured dishes. Witness the unadulterated simplicity of warm Arbroath smokies with beetroot salad, followed by deep, meaty brisket pie or beer-battered haddock with outrageously good chips. Puds (rhubarb clafoutis with stem ginger ice cream) are top-notch and Sunday roasts are a homely treat. Even the bar snacks (Scotch eggs, crispy trotter won tons) alone are worth a visit. As with everything else, plenty of thought has been put into the stonking selection of ales and the wine list (bottles from £15).
Chef/s: Oliver Pudney. **Open:** all week L 12 to 3 (3.30 Sat, 12.30 to 3.45 Sun), D 6.30 to 10 (9 Sun). **Closed:** 25 to 26 Dec. **Meals:** alc (main courses £12 to £23). **Service:** not inc. **Details:** Cards accepted. 130 seats. 30 seats outside. Air-con. Separate bar. Music. Children allowed.

Café Japan
Fantastically fresh fish
626 Finchley Road, Golders Green, NW11 7RR
Tel no: (020) 8455 6854
www.cafejapan.co.uk
⊖ Golders Green, map 1
Japanese | £14
Cooking score: 3
£30

Sushi lovers flock to this pint-sized, no-frills café where the fish is as fresh as it comes in north-west London. The look is undeniably stark, but affable staff and a constant stream of punters ensure there is always a warm, cheerful air. The marbled beauty of fatty tuna (toro) is best sampled served over rice as nigiri, as are plump slices of salmon and sticky-sweet nuggets of grilled eel. Simple salads are elevated with zesty ginger dressing, jam-packed sushi rolls arrive filled with crispy deep-fried yellowtail, and hot dishes include the silky-salty sweetness of black cod in miso. Such top-quality fish is exceptionally good

value, with bento boxes further helping to keep prices down. Wines start at £12 a bottle; teetotallers can stick to green tea.
Chef/s: Hideki Sato. **Open:** Wed to Sun L 12 to 2, D 6 to 10 (9.30 Sun). **Closed:** Mon, Tue, 25 and 26 Dec. **Meals:** alc (main courses £7 to £20). Set L £7.50 (2 courses) to £12.50. Set D £12 (2 courses) to £17. **Service:** not inc. **Details:** Cards accepted. 36 seats. Air-con. Music. Children allowed.

ALSO RECOMMENDED
▲ Chilli Cool
15 Leigh Street, King's Cross, WC1H 9EW
Tel no: (020) 7383 3135
www.chillicool.com
⊖ Russell Square, King's Cross, map 2
Chinese £5 OFF

This modest Chinese restaurant continues to steam along, pleasing a mixed crowd of students and locals with its generous portions and fair prices. It's a far cry from Chinatown, not least in a menu which emphasises Szechuan cuisine. The kitchen aims for rapid turnover, sending out interesting chef's specials like fried beef with dry chilli and chilli powder (£8.80), generous hotpots along the lines of braised pot-steamed meat with mixed seafood (£19.80) and rice and noodle dishes. House wine is £9.90. Open all week.

READERS RECOMMEND
The Compass
Gastropub
58 Penton Street, London, N1 9PZ
Tel no: (020) 7837 3891
www.thecompassn1.co.uk
'The balance between good food, service and atmosphere is perfect and it deserves to be a huge success.'

The Drapers Arms
Re-energised Islington boozer
44 Barnsbury Street, Islington, N1 1ER
Tel no: (020) 7619 0348
www.thedrapersarms.com
⊖ Highbury & Islington, Angel, map 2
Gastropub | £24
Cooking score: 2

£5 OFF £30

Spacious and uncluttered, with a sheltered garden for fine weather, this re-energised Islington pub is proud of its roots as a watering hole, but is now primarily noted for its food. Daily changing menus deal in nicely judged, no-frills modern British dishes along the lines of smoked mackerel with celeriac and mustard or jellied ham and pig's head terrine. There's also a comforting familiarity about roast Middle White pork and cauliflower cheese or baked whole crab with chopped egg, parsley and breadcrumbs. Pear and blackcurrant jelly with custard is a good way to finish. House wine is £14.
Chef/s: Karl Goward. **Open:** all week L 12 to 3 (3.30 Sat and Sun), D 6 to 10 (9.30 Sun). **Meals:** alc (main courses £10 to £16). **Service:** 12.5% (optional). **Details:** Cards accepted. 130 seats. 45 seats outside. Separate bar. Music. Children allowed.

ALSO RECOMMENDED
▲ The Elk in the Woods
39 Camden Passage, Islington, N1 8EA
Tel no: (020) 7226 3535
www.the-elk-in-the-woods.co.uk
⊖ Angel, map 2
European

A 'lovely place down a cobbled street in Islington', this chic little restaurant is all stripped wood and antique mirrors. Food runs from breakfast to evening meals such as skewered quails wrapped in pancetta with sage and rosemary stuffing (£16.50) or fish pie. Diners rave about the frickadeller, served with roast bacon, gherkin, apple sauce and mormors potato salad with Gammel Dansk (£12.50). Puddings include homemade ice cream (£5). Wines from £16.

500 Restaurant
Genuine neighbourhood Italian
782 Holloway Road, Archway, N19 3JH
Tel no: (020) 7272 3406
www.500restaurant.co.uk
⊖ Archway, map 2
Italian | £25
Cooking score: 2

£30

The welcome is friendly and service attentive at this genuine neighbourhood Italian. The décor is agreeably understated: wooden floors, blue-grey walls and a lack of napery help crank up the volume and lend an informal air to proceedings. In the kitchen co-owner Mario Magli cooks with an earthy straightforwardness. Simple dishes such as risotto with smoked eel and parsley or oven-baked rabbit served with pistachios, black olives and sun-dried tomatoes are capably done, and a delicate mint-flavoured pannacotta with strawberry sauce is an appealing dessert. The all-Italian wine list includes some interesting bottles and prices are fair. House recommendations from £12.50.
Chef/s: Mario Magli. **Open:** Tue to Sat L 12 to 3, Tue to Sun D 5.30 to 10. **Closed:** Mon, 2 weeks Christmas. **Meals:** alc (main courses £9 to £15). **Service:** not inc. **Details:** Cards accepted. 30 seats. Wheelchair access. Music. Children allowed.

ALSO RECOMMENDED
▲ Istanbul Iskembecisi
9 Stoke Newington Road, Stoke Newington, N16 8BH
Tel no: (020) 7254 7291
www.istanbuliskembecisi.co.uk
⊖ Dalston Kingsland, map 2
Turkish

This smartly decorated Turkish restaurant is a stalwart of the local community, a welcoming place where nobody minds if your party booking stretches on into the night. Precisely seasoned, carefully prepared regional specialities come at ridiculously gentle prices, from lamb with hummus as a starter (£4), to mains such as iskender kebab, combining shish, kofte and lamb, served with grilled tomatoes and yoghurt, or grilled sea bass with salad and chips (£11). Set menus start at £11.50. Wines from £10. Open all week.

Jinkichi
Tokyo-style eatery
73 Heath Street, Hampstead, NW3 6UG
Tel no: (020) 7794 6158
www.jinkichi.com
⊖ Hampstead, map 1
Japanese | £25
Cooking score: 1

V £30

This cramped, no-frills restaurant provides little in the way of creature comforts. It has the ambience of a simple Tokyo eatery and the menu is easily navigated. Small dishes include good steamed fishcake with wasabi or more unusual items such as rocket, cheese and bonito flakes with ponzu dressing, while alongside sashimi and sushi choices there are the usual teriyaki, tonkatsu and tempura dishes. Prices are reasonable. A short list of sakés and shochu complements the brief wine list which starts at £23.
Chef/s: Atsushi Matsumoto. **Open:** Sat and Sun L 12.30 to 2, Tue to Sun D 6 to 11 (10 Sun). **Closed:** Mon, bank hols, Tue after bank hols. **Meals:** alc (main courses £8 to £16). **Service:** 10%. **Details:** Cards accepted. 40 seats. Air-con. No mobile phones. Children allowed.

READERS RECOMMEND
Juniper Dining
Modern British
100 Highbury Park, Islington, N5 2XE
Tel no: (020) 7288 8716
www.juniperdining.co.uk
'Modern, tastefully appointed and spacious restaurant. Staff very friendly and helpful. Superb food.'

ALSO RECOMMENDED
▲ Khoai Café
6 Topsfield Parade, Crouch End, N8 8PR
Tel no: (020) 8341 2120
⊖ Finsbury Park, map 2
Vietnamese

Cost-conscious Crouch Enders still show allegiance to their local Vietnamese, where steaming bowls of fragrant pho noodle soup cost little more than a fiver. Other punchy plates from the diverse menu include beef in betel leaves (£5.75) and char-grilled tiger prawns with green mango salad (£9.95). The zingy, chilli flavours are best suited to Vietnamese beer, though wine starts from £11.25 a bottle. Expect worn-in but comfortable surroundings. Open all week. A sister restaurant is at 362 Ballards Lane, Finchley, N12 0EE, tel no: (020) 8445 2039.

Konstam at the Prince Albert
Keeping it local
2 Acton Street, King's Cross, WC1X 9NA
Tel no: (020) 7833 5040
www.konstam.co.uk
⊖ King's Cross, map 2
Modern British | £30
Cooking score: 3

£5 OFF

Oliver Rowe's big idea was to set up a London neighbourhood restaurant and source most of his ingredients from within the M25. Diners have warmed to the fruits of his crusading labours – even though the interior of this one-time King's Cross boozer has been bizarrely tricked out with blue/green paintwork and swags of glittery metallic-chain artistry draped all around. As for the food, expect a daily menu that keeps it local, but adds a north European spin – perhaps Waltham Abbey chicken with wild garlic and walnut spätzle, pierogi dumplings stuffed with leeks and Spenwood cheese, or char-grilled Amersham pigeon accompanied by roast Crown Prince squash and braised chicory. Doughnuts with plum jam provide a lusty finish, and service comes with lashings of passion. Eurocentric wines (from £19) have further to travel than the food.

Chef/s: Oliver Rowe. **Open:** Mon to Fri and Sun L 12 to 2.30 (10.30 to 4 Sun), Mon to Sat D 6.30 to 10 (10.30 Fri and Sat). **Closed:** 24 Dec to 4 Jan. **Meals:** alc (main courses £12 to £20). Set L £15.75 (2 courses) to £18.75. **Service:** not inc. **Details:** Cards accepted. 44 seats. Air-con. No music. Wheelchair access. Children allowed.

ALSO RECOMMENDED

▲ Mangal Ocakbasi

10 Arcola Street, off Stoke Newington Road, Stoke Newington, E8 2DJ
Tel no: (020) 7275 8981
www.mangal1.com
⊖ Dalston, map 2
Turkish £5 OFF

Stoke Newington has no shortage of Turkish barbecues or 'ocakbasi', yet everyone descends on this one. Why? The answer becomes apparent on sampling the mixed mezze: the bright, fresh tomato salad, smokey aubergines and hummus positively sing with flavour. The generously proportioned kebabs (from £8), particularly the 'special mixed' with quail, speak of quality meat. This is an establishment that prides itself on doing just a few things, but doing them well. It's also cheap, BYO and pretty hectic. Open all week.

Market

Show-stealing British grub
43 Parkway, Camden, NW1 7PN
Tel no: (020) 7267 9700
www.marketrestaurant.co.uk
⊖ Camden Town, map 2
Modern British | £25
Cooking score: 2
£30
▼

A restaurant in colourful Camden Town should have heaps of character, and Market certainly does. Rustic furniture, warm woods and cheery staff all encourage a sense of bonhomie, but it is the resolutely British cooking that steals the show. Dan Spence may

no longer be involved, but a delicate plate of lemon sole with clams indicates a continued ability to handle subtle flavours, although most dishes on the concise menu have a bit more pluck: pig's cheeks with morcilla, faggots with mushy peas and tangy rhubarb cheesecake are representative of the gutsy style. Vegetarians won't be spoiled for choice, and wine fans will enjoy the succinct list (from £15.50 a bottle).

Chef/s: Charlie Bell and Davide del Gatto. **Open:** all week L 12 to 2.30 (1 to 3.30 Sun), Mon to Sat D 6 to 10.30. **Closed:** 24 Dec to 2 Jan, bank hols. **Meals:** alc (main courses £11 to £17). Set L £10 (2 courses). **Service:** 12.5% (optional). **Details:** Cards accepted. 50 seats. 4 seats outside. Air-con. Music. Children allowed.

Metrogusto

Eye-catching, tastebud-teasing Italian food
13 Theberton Street, Islington, N1 0QY
Tel no: (020) 7226 9400
www.metrogusto.co.uk
⊖ Angel, map 2
Italian | £28
Cooking score: 3
V £30
▼

After an absence of six months in 2009, Antonio Di Salvo has returned as executive chef of this lively Islington hot spot, a stylish place with tiled floors, undressed tables, a mix of black and white walls and a mass of pictures, including some striking modern art. 'Strikingly modern' might also describe the approach to Italian food, with dishes that catch the eye and intrigue the tastebuds in equal measure. A salad of tiger prawns comes with apple, celery and fennel, while pasta dishes include chocolate ravioli filled with caramelised braised veal. Mains keep to a more classical orientation, serving grilled bream with salsa verde, or dressing calf's liver with traditional Venetian agrodolce. Finish with ricotta cheesecake and caramelised orange. The Italian wine list opens at £18.50.

Chef/s: Antonio Di Salvo. **Open:** Sat and Sun L 11 to 3 (4 Sun), Tue to Sat D 6 to 10.30 (11 Fri, 10 Sat). **Closed:** Mon, 25 and 26 Dec, Easter, bank hols.

Meals: alc (£13 to £20). Set L and D £14.50 (2 courses) to £18.50. **Service:** 12.5% (optional). **Details:** Cards accepted. 60 seats. 8 seats outside. Air-con. Wheelchair access. Music. Children allowed.

Morgan M
Fastidious French food in Islington
489 Liverpool Road, Islington, N7 8NS
Tel no: (020) 7609 3560
www.morganm.com
⊖ Highbury & Islington, map 2
Modern French | £41
Cooking score: 6

A converted pub at the wrong end of Liverpool Road is hardly the site of choice for a top-end French restaurant, but the pithily monikered Morgan M (aka Meunier) has been quietly prospering here since 2003. Inside, all is bijou, affluent, bright and dressed-up, with frosted glass, burgundy tones and oak panelling – a suitably discreet, very Gallic backdrop for highly fastidious cooking that makes its mark through painstaking detail and classical technique. Ravioli of snails in Chablis with poached garlic and red wine jus is an inimitable signature dish, along with a trio of young Pyrenean lamb (the leg roasted, the shoulder confit, the cutlet grilled) accompanied by Jerusalem artichoke soubise and rosemary jus. Readers have also endorsed Morgan's take on rabbit stew ('beautifully sauced'), Challons duck (cooked pink) with a ragoût of Israeli couscous, salsify, liver ravioli and sauce grand veneur, and a dessert entitled 'all about chocolate' (a bonanza of tuile, ice cream, fondant and mousse, set off with a whisky-laced choc drink). There are also artfully constructed, seasonal tasting menus, including a veggie version featuring the likes of wild mushroom 'tourte' with poêlée of spinach and thyme beurre blanc. The patriotic French wine list allows room for a few tasty interlopers from Italy and Spain; prices start at £20.50 (£6.50 a glass).
Chef/s: Morgan Meunier and Sylvain Soulard. **Open:** Wed to Fri and Sun L 12.30 to 1.30, Tue to Sat D 7 to 8.30. **Closed:** Mon, 1 week Christmas. **Meals:** Set L £22.50 (2 courses) to £27.50. Set D £41. Sun L £41.

Tasting menu £45 to £50. **Service:** 12.5% (optional). **Details:** Cards accepted. 50 seats. Air-con. No mobile phones. Wheelchair access. Music. Children allowed.

Odette's
Confidence, sparkle... and dreamy desserts
130 Regents Park Road, Primrose Hill, NW1 8XL
Tel no: (020) 7586 8569
www.odettesprimrosehill.com
⊖ Chalk Farm, map 2
Modern British | £35
Cooking score: 5

Odette's has been a feature of the Primrose Hill landscape since the 1970s. It has long been a beacon of quality, and under Bryn Williams the modern British cooking is full of confidence and sparkle. Readers remain bemused by the eye-popping decor, with a throbbing yellow theme running through the wall tiles, seating and lights, but try to focus on what's on the plate. Fish is always good. Mackerel is much favoured, perhaps cured, roasted and elegantly presented alongside avocado, black olive and apple, or there might be a main course of sea bream, served with a tarte fine of aubergine, sweetcorn and basil. Meat dishes are not afraid to go for substance, as when loin of Elwy Valley mutton appears with a little shepherd's pie, salsify and puréed herbs. Desserts are even more of a treat than usual. A classic and generous rendition of tarte Tatin is enhanced with Calvados cream and apple jelly, or there could be ultra-trendy banana crumble with a peanut butter sandwich and salted caramel. Start with the sommelier's choice of wines by the glass (from £5), before exploring the intelligently constructed list. It may not be the most extensive, but there are great names aplenty.
Chef/s: Bryn Williams. **Open:** Tue to Sun L 12 to 2.30 (3 Sun), D 6 to 10.30. **Closed:** Mon, 1 week Christmas. **Meals:** alc (main courses £17 to £22). Set L and D £14 (2 courses) to £18. Sun L £20 (2 courses) to £25. **Service:** 12.5% (optional). **Details:** Cards accepted. 60 seats. 10 seats outside. Air-con. Separate bar. Music. Children allowed.

Ottolenghi

Hip deli-diner
287 Upper Street, Islington, N1 2TZ
Tel no: (020) 7288 1454
www.ottolenghi.co.uk
⊖ Angel, Highbury & Islington, map 2
Mediterranean | £30
Cooking score: 2

V

Guardian readers will be familiar with Yotam Ottolenghi's sunny, sexy 'new vegetarian' cooking and its Mediterranean and Middle Eastern influences. Meat is on the menu too, but there's no doubting the Islington deli-diner is the place to get your five-a-day. Feast your eyes on the meringue and cake mountains in the window, then jostle with the crowds to eye up the day's salads and mezze. Char-grilled salmon and salsa, lamb and pistachio kebab, and a salad of mixed beets are representative dishes. Food is served to go or at communal tables in the chic white space. Wines from £19.50. Branches in Belgravia, Notting Hill and Kensington.
Chef/s: Sami Tamimi. **Open:** all week L 11 to 3, Mon to Sat D 6 to 10 (10.30 Thur to Sat). **Closed:** 25 and 26 Dec, 1 Jan. **Meals:** alc (main courses £9 to £11). **Service:** not inc. **Details:** Cards accepted. 48 seats. 6 seats outside. Air-con. Wheelchair access. Music. Children allowed.

READERS RECOMMEND

El Parador

Spanish
245 Eversholt Street, Camden, NW1 1BA
Tel no: (020) 7387 2789
www.elparadorlondon.com
'Better tapas than I've ever had in Spain'

> **Readers recommend**
>
> A 'readers recommend' review is a genuine quote from a report sent in by one of our readers. We intend to follow up these suggestions throughout the year to come.

Rasa

Keralan veggie standard-bearer
55 Stoke Newington Church Street, Stoke Newington, N16 0AR
Tel no: (020) 7249 0344
www.rasarestaurants.com
⊖ Finsbury Park, map 2
Indian Vegetarian | £16
Cooking score: 2

V 💰£30

Since launching in Stoke Newington in 1994, the Rasa brand has spread as far as Newcastle and Brighton; some of its eateries are vegetarian, others specialise in seafood, but all are defined by the distinctive regional flavours of Kerala. Rasa N16 is the first-born and still the most impressive of the bunch, with its trademark pink livery, charming vibes and bright veggie food at knockdown prices. Cracking homemade chutneys and crispy nibbles start the show, before steamed idli cakes, dosas and curries ranging from stir-fried cabbage thoran to moru kachiyathu (mangoes, green bananas and green chillies cooked in a spicy yoghurt broth). House wine is £13.95. For details of other outlets visit www.rasarestaurants.com.
Chef/s: Rajan Karattil. **Open:** Sat and Sun L 12 to 3, all week D 6 to 10.30 (11 Fri to Sun). **Closed:** 25 to 27 Dec. **Meals:** alc (main courses £4 to £6). Set L and D £16. **Service:** 12.5% (optional). **Details:** Cards accepted. 48 seats. Air-con. Music. Children allowed.

Singapore Garden

Asian spice in suburbia
83 Fairfax Road, Swiss Cottage, NW6 4DY
Tel no: (020) 7328 5314
www.singaporegarden.co.uk
⊖ Swiss Cottage, map 2
Chinese | £30
Cooking score: 2

V

Although the menu is mainly taken up with mainstream Chinese dishes, there are some wonderful Malaysian and Singaporean flavours to be found at this upmarket Swiss

Cottage local. Plump fishcakes are fragrant with Kaffir lime leaves and Malay curries combine subtle spicing and tender meat, but the real show-stopper is the Singaporean national dish of fresh crab fried with chilli sauce, the crustacean's dainty white meat pepped up by hot, tangy gravy. The smart dining room looks good dressed in glossy Chinoiserie, though there are occasional discontented murmurs about the high prices – house wines start from a steep £17 a bottle. **Chef/s:** Kok Sum Toh. **Open:** all week L 12 to 3 (5 Sun), D 6 to 11 (11.30 Fri and Sat). **Closed:** 4 days at Christmas. **Meals:** alc (main courses £7 to £30). Set L £20 (3 courses). Set D £38 (4 courses). **Service:** 12.5% (optional). **Details:** Cards accepted. 85 seats. 12 seats outside. Air-con. Music. Children allowed.

Sushi-Say
Hospitable, personally run Japanese
33b Walm Lane, Willesden, NW2 5SH
Tel no: (020) 8459 7512
⊖ Willesden Green, map 1
Japanese | £20
Cooking score: 4
V £30

It says a great deal about Katsuharu and Yuko Shimizu's persistence and their natural talent for authentic Japanese food that they have been thriving in the backwaters of Willesden Green for more than 15 years. Their secret is to serve spanking fresh ingredients in clean-cut surroundings with a generous side order of sincere personal hospitality. An excellent choice of top-grade nigiri sushi and seaweed rolls promises everything from thickly sliced fatty tuna, turbot and horse mackerel to turbot, giant clams and sea urchin. Alternatively, investigate the wide-ranging carte, which offers gyoza dumplings, spinach with sesame sauce, and the curious delights of chawan mushi (savoury egg custard), as well as expertly rendered tempura, teriyaki and bowls of soba or udon noodles. Lunch plates and set dinners offer an affordable way into the repertoire. Teas, beer and saké are on-the-money, and Sushi-Say also has it own

homemade digestif (a palate-cleansing mix of vodka with pressed apple juice). House wine is £16. **Chef/s:** Katsuharu Shimizu. **Open:** Sat and Sun L 12 to 3.30, Tue to Sun D 6.30 to 10 (10.30 Sat, 6 to 9.30 Sun). **Closed:** Mon, 25 and 26 Dec, 1 Jan, bank hols, 1 week Easter, 2 weeks Aug. **Meals:** alc (main courses £9 to £25). Set L £11.90 to £18.50. Set D £22 (6 courses) to £37. **Service:** not inc. **Details:** Cards accepted. 40 seats. Air-con. No music. Wheelchair access. Children allowed.

NEW ENTRY
Trullo
Simple Italian with shining ingredients
300-302 St Paul's Road, Islington, N1 2LH
Tel no: (020) 7226 2733
www.trullorestaurant.com
⊖ Highbury and Islington, map 2
Italian | £24
Cooking score: 3
£30

A promising start for some Fifteen and River Café alumni, who have now flown the coop to launch their own simple Italian restaurant in a modest N1 spot. At inspection the daily menu featured seasonal ingredients like girolles and Amalfi lemons shining through in perfect pasta dishes, and San Marzano tomatoes in bright pappa pomodoro, while sea bass carpaccio and roast wood pigeon with potato and rocket displayed some capable cooking. The only hiccup was a tasty but solitary bruschetta of lardo, anchovy and cipolotti onions, mean for the money but happily not representative. A carafe of wine is £7.50 (bottles start at £15). **Chef/s:** Tim Siadatan. **Open:** Sat and Sun L 12.30 to 3, Tue to Sat D 7 to 11. **Closed:** Mon, 23 Dec to 3 Jan, last two weeks Aug. **Meals:** alc (main courses £8 to £17). **Service:** not inc. **Details:** Cards accepted. 38 seats. Music. Children allowed.

Visit us online

To find out more about
The Good Food Guide, please visit
www.thegoodfoodguide.co.uk

ALSO RECOMMENDED

▲ XO

29 Belsize Lane, Belsize Park, NW3 5AS
Tel no: (020) 7433 0888
www.rickerrestaurants.com
⊖ Belsize Park, map 2
Pan-Asian

XO aims to bring the West End closer to home for the residents of well-heeled Belsize Park. Part of the Ricker restaurant group, it's a sleek, clean-lined venue offering pan-Asian food. Japanese, Chinese and Thai references are all present and mostly correct, in dishes such as chicken and water chestnut dumplings (£6), prawn green curry and crispy duck in black vinegar (£19.50). Go west again at dessert stage for sticky toffee pudding with vanilla ice cream (£5.50). Varietally arranged wines start at £15.50. Open all week.

York & Albany

Slinky setting for Angela's Italian love affair
127-129 Parkway, Camden, NW1 7PS
Tel no: (020) 7388 3344
www.gordonramsay.com/yorkandalbany
⊖ Camden Town, map 2
Modern European | £35
Cooking score: 5

🍷 🍽 V

Having cracked the chi-chi Mayfair market with Murano (see entry), the Gordon Ramsay/Angela Hartnett roadshow rolled into Camden to open this 'complete lifestyle experience' in a majestic John Nash building. The York & Albany's heart is its cool, sedate dining room, slinkily done out in contemporary style. It's the perfect backdrop for Angela Hartnett's take on modern cuisine and her love affair with Italian flavours. Her star-spangled efforts depend on first-rate ingredients, which are given a spin before re-emerging as finely honed contemporary dishes with a truly individual stamp. To begin, breast of quail might be hazelnut-crusted and served atop a chorizo and pak choi risotto, while roasted pollack fillet appears in company with confit fennel, leek hearts, warm anchovy and

lemon vinaigrette. Italian-accented combos are balanced by big-hearted platefuls from the European mainstream – perhaps braised calf's cheek with parsnip purée and onion compote or Casterbridge côte de boeuf with sweet potato and thyme fondant, caramelised shallots and creamed mustard spätzle. For afters, saffron pannacotta sits alongside treacle sponge. The whole Y&A package also embraces an all-day bar, event spaces, bedrooms and Nonna's deli, which now has extra seating for punters wanting to partake of its pizzas. The Ramsay stable is noted for its wine lists and this is no exception – a terrific range of varietals from around the globe, with a great selection by the glass or carafe at prices that won't frighten the horses. Bottles start at £17.

Chef/s: Angela Hartnett. **Open:** Mon to Sat L 12 to 3, D 6 to 11, Sun 12 to 9. **Meals:** alc (main courses £17 to £22). Set L and early D £20. Sun L £25. **Service:** 12.5% (optional). **Details:** Cards accepted. 120 seats. 36 seats outside. Air-con. Separate bar. Wheelchair access. Music. Children allowed.

Albion

Stylish all-day caff
2-4 Boundary Street, Shoreditch, E2 7DD
Tel no: (020) 7613 7900
www.albioncaff.co.uk
⊖ Old Street, Liverpool Street, map 2
British | £20
Cooking score: 2

🍴 V £30

It's a lovely thought, all those tourists staying at Sir Terence Conran's Boundary Hotel and tucking into British grub such as 'breakfast baps', kippers and crumbles at the hotel's 'caff', Albion. Goodness only knows what they make of the knitted tea cosies. Locals have also fallen for the white-tiled all-day café and its friendly pricing, free Wi-Fi and on-site bakery. The cooking's homely – chicken pie, fish and chips, treacle tart – but high quality. The bad news is: you can't book. For something smarter, try the basement Boundary restaurant (separate entry). Wines from £16.25.
Chef/s: Ian Wood. **Open:** all week 8am to midnight. **Meals:** alc (main courses £6 to £12). **Service:** 12.5% (optional). **Details:** Cards accepted. 66 seats. 25 seats outside. Wheelchair access. Music. Children allowed.

NEW ENTRY
Amico Bio

Daring Italian vegetarian in the City
44 Cloth Fair, Barbican, EC1A 7JQ
Tel no: (020) 7600 7778
www.amicobio.co.uk
⊖ Barbican, map 5
Italian Vegetarian | £18
Cooking score: 1

V £30

'Vegetarian' and 'organic' aren't words one associates with City dining, but ex-Locatelli chef Pasquale Amico's family-friendly Italian shows healthy, vegetable cookery isn't just for hippies. This is not Italian food minus the meat: Amico dares to serve tofu, vegan cheeses, even seitan (mock duck). Technically, superb wholegrain rice risotto and overly-sweet seitan 'scaloppina milanese' are spot-on. Dishes are correctly priced too (unlike most restaurants' single 'veggie option'), but the meat-free secondi won't convince steak-lovers. Wines (from £12.50) are organic too.
Chef/s: Pasquale Amico. **Open:** Mon to Fri 12 to 10.30, Sat 5 to 10.30. **Closed:** Sun, bank hols.
Meals: alc (main courses £7 to £8). **Service:** not inc. **Details:** Cards accepted. 40 seats. Air-con. Separate bar. Wheelchair access. Music. Children allowed.

L'Anima

Confident, glossy Italian
1 Snowden Street, City, EC2A 2DQ
Tel no: (020) 7422 7000
www.lanima.co.uk
⊖ Liverpool Street, map 2
Italian | £47
Cooking score: 5

£5 OFF V

'A wonderful example of regional Italian cooking at its best', is how one reader summed up Francesco Mazzei's gorgeously sleek, high-gloss City restaurant (the name translates as 'soul'). Inside it is seriously handsome in a minimalist kind of way, with swathes of glass, white leather and stone picked out by shafts of light – just the ticket for Mazzei's confident take on the cuisine of his homeland. A signature dish of beef tagliata is a reinvention involving unctuous bone marrow, ovinsardo (sheep's cheese) and Magliocco wine sauce that shows off his feel for fine ingredients and bold, deep flavours. There is also plenty of breathtaking richness and clarity when it comes to stellar homemade pasta – perhaps herby lobster pappardelle or stracci with veal and pistachio ragù. Starters aim for true authenticity in the shape of char-grilled clams and mussels with n'duja (a spicy Calabrese salami) or octopus with cannellini beans and ricotta 'mustia'. Desserts play tricks on the classics – witness liquorice zabaglione or pannacotta with pomegranate and grappa. Also, don't miss the artisan cheeses, each served with a different relish (Taleggio with fig mustard, for example). Wines are kept in a

vast, glass-walled 'cave', and the list travels the length and breadth of Italy, picking up starry names along the way. Prices start at £18.
Chef/s: Francesco Mazzei and Luca Terraneo. **Open:** Mon to Fri L 11.45 to 3, Mon to Sat D 5.30 to 10.30 (11 Sat). **Closed:** Sun. **Meals:** alc (main courses £12 to £35). Set L £24.50 (2 courses) to £28.50.
Service: 12.5% (optional). **Details:** Cards accepted. 82 seats. Air-con. Separate bar. Wheelchair access. Music. Children allowed.

READERS RECOMMEND
Battery
Modern European
34 Westferry Circus, Canary Wharf, E14 8RR
Tel no: (020) 8305 3089
www.battery.uk.com
'Amazing views — perfect for special occasions'

NEW ENTRY
Bistro Bruno Loubet
Bruno's back in town
The Zetter, 86-88 Clerkenwell Road, Clerkenwell, EC1M 5RJ
Tel no: (020) 7324 4455
www.bistrotbrunoloubet.com
⊖ Farringdon, Barbican, map 5
Modern European | £30
Cooking score: 4

The restaurant at the Zetter Hotel is a bright, inviting space. Huge windows sweep the room and the involvement of Bruno Loubet means the food is on a sharp upward trajectory. All the rage in the 90s, Loubet has spent the past eight years down under, but his menu revisits classic French and European dishes. The hallmark of his cooking is high flavour – he's vastly skilled at coaxing every ounce of it out of cheap, unshowy cuts of meat and fish, turning something ordinary into something sublime. Recent successes have included beef daube provençale with mousseline potatoes, confit lamb shoulder with white beans, preserved lemon purée and a slick of green harissa, and perfectly timed pollack with squid, squid ink sauce and celeriac purée. Mackerel and piccalilli tart with green

gazpacho dressing is a good way to start, rice pudding pannacotta with marmalade makes a perfect finish, and readers applaud the prices. The wine list opens at £15.50.
Chef/s: Bruno Loubet. **Open:** all week L 12 to 2.30 (3 Sat and Sun), D 6 to 10.30 (10 Sun). **Closed:** 25 and 26 Dec. **Meals:** alc (main courses £12 to £18). **Service:** not inc. **Details:** Cards accepted. 75 seats. 25 seats outside. Air-con. Separate bar. Wheelchair access. Music. Children allowed.

Bleeding Heart
Romance and fine French dining
Bleeding Heart Yard, Greville Street, Clerkenwell, EC1N 8SJ
Tel no: (020) 7242 8238
www.bleedingheart.co.uk
⊖ Farringdon, map 5
Modern French | £30
Cooking score: 2
£5 OFF 🍾

Lady Elizabeth Hatton was the toast of seventeenth-century London society before being murdered (so the story goes) by her jilted lover in the cobbled courtyard that fronts this French restaurant, bistro and tavern. These days, romantic assignations generally pass without incident in the seductive, dreamily lit dining room, which is also a favourite for lunchtime business deals. The kitchen's modern interpretations yield attractive possibilities: smoked wild rabbit appears with red-wine pears, vanilla and beetroot vinaigrette, while roast hake fillet might be partnered by Jerusalem artichoke purée and a fricassee of salsify and ceps. After that, perhaps white rum pannacotta with a mint chocolate 'cigar'. The wine list caters for those who know their French vintages, but it also shines brilliantly in the New World (the proprietors own Trinity Hill Vineyard in Hawkes Bay). Prices from £16.95.
Chef/s: Peter Reffell. **Open:** Mon to Fri L 12 to 2.30, D 6 to 10.30. **Closed:** Sat, Sun, 23 Dec to 4 Jan. **Meals:** alc (main courses £13 to £25). **Service:** 12.5% (optional). **Details:** Cards accepted. 120 seats. 26 seats outside. Air-con. No music. No mobile phones. Children allowed.

Bonds
Banking on quality
Threadneedle Hotel, 5 Threadneedle Street, City,
EC2R 8AY
Tel no: (020) 7657 8090
www.theetoncollection.com
⊖ Bank, map 2
Modern French | £40
Cooking score: 6

£5 OFF 🍷 🍽

The monetary moniker emphasises the fact that Bonds is right in the fibrillating heart of London's recession-ravaged Square Mile: more precisely it occupies the bare bones of a grand old banking hall that now trades as a swanky boutique hotel. The dining room cleverly dovetails Victorian solidity with up-to-the-moment metropolitan chic – light streams in through a stained glass dome while diners sit amid imperious columns and gilded mirrors. Barry Tonks avoids artery-hardening culinary overkill in favour of a clean-cut, sensitive approach that fully exploits the contemporary French style, but weaves in a few details from the Mediterranean in the shape of pasta, risottos and gnocchi. Top-drawer ingredients provide the backbone for immaculately pretty, clean-as-a-whistle dishes ranging from Peterhead cod poached at 48°C with caramelised endive, orange and curly kale with its own beignet to slow-cooked Denham Estate venison with chestnut purée, vanilla-poached quinces and crosnes. Of course, there are rich, indulgent notes too – diver-caught scallops with smoked black pudding and parsley cream, foie gras 'a la plancha' with Medjool date purée, and an impeccable warm chocolate moelleux with almond milk sorbet (well worth the 15-minute wait). It's also worth investing in the heavyweight wine list, a deeply serious slate that pleases the City suits with high-end Champagnes, Bordeaux and Burgundies, but also scours the world's major growing areas. Those without bonuses to burn can seek solace in the house selections (from £16.50, £5.95 a glass).

Chef/s: Barry Tonks. **Open:** Mon to Fri L 12 to 2.30, D 6 to 10. **Closed:** Sat, Sun, bank hols. **Meals:** alc (main courses £13 to £20). Set L £15.50. Set D £17.50. **Service:** 12.5% (optional). **Details:** Cards accepted. 80 seats. Air-con. Separate bar. Wheelchair access. Music. Children allowed.

Boundary
Glamorous tribute to French brasserie cuisine
2-4 Boundary Street, Shoreditch, E2 7DD
Tel no: (020) 7729 1051
www.theboundary.co.uk
⊖ Old Street, Liverpool Street, map 2
French | £35
Cooking score: 4

🍽

Sir Terence Conran's Boundary (the high-end restaurant within his first hotel) bears all the hallmarks of a fashionable East London eatery. Cavernous basement – check. Bare brick – check. Converted warehouse – check. But where the design guru's stylish homage to French brasserie cuisine differs from the competition is in its sense of theatre. A glass-walled open kitchen, velvet chairs, Chagall-esque murals and shiny trolleys (for charcuterie, daily roasts and cheese) lend serious glamour. Both trendy locals and City types fit in just fine. The menu is admirably seasonal, with oysters, game and wild mushrooms appearing the very day you first crave them – in dishes from the pages of Elizabeth David. Bourgeois French classics – escargots, rognons de veau and crème caramel – play a starring role. The European wine list, from £18, has 80 wines under £35.

Chef/s: Ian Wood. **Open:** Tue to Fri and Sun L 12 to 3 (4 Sun), Mon to Sat D 6.30 to 10.30. **Meals:** alc (main courses £12 to £28). Set L £19.50. Set D £23.50. Sun L £23.50. **Service:** 12.5% (optional). **Details:** Cards accepted. 126 seats. Air-con. Separate bar. No mobile phones. Wheelchair access. Music. Children allowed.

Buen Ayre

Friendly grill with top-quality steaks
50 Broadway Market, Hackney, E8 4QJ
Tel no: (020) 7275 9900
www.buenayre.co.uk
⊖ Bethnal Green, map 1
Argentinian | £28
Cooking score: 1
£30

Grass-fed steaks from the pampas are this
friendly local's forte – diners cross town for
them. Food isn't served lickety-split – there's
just one man and one char-grill cooking all
those steaks, after all – but the staff are too nice
to get cross with. The deluxe 'parillada', a meat
feast of black pudding, ribeye and sausage atop
a tabletop brazier is the classic choice, with a
bottle of Malbec (from £13.10). Dessert is
usually a variation on a dulce de leche theme –
should you have room.
Chef/s: John Rattagan. **Open:** Thur to Sun L 12 to
3.30, all week D 6 to 10.30. **Closed:** 25 and 26 Dec, 1
Jan. **Meals:** alc (main courses £8 to £23).
Service: 12% (optional). **Details:** Cards accepted.
40 seats. 20 seats outside. Air-con. Wheelchair
access. Music. Children allowed.

Café Spice Namasté

Exotic high-profile Indian
16 Prescot Street, Tower Hill, E1 8AZ
Tel no: (020) 7488 9242
www.cafespice.co.uk
⊖ Tower Hill, map 1
Indian | £30
Cooking score: 2
£5 OFF **V**

'After 15 years, this restaurant just gets better
with age', commented a reporter of Cyrus
Todiwala's much-loved Tower Hill Indian.
Look for the orange banners outside, and be
prepared to have your taste buds awakened
with some traditional and modern
subcontinental recipes. A beetroot and
coconut samosa is a different way to start, and
you could follow on with tandoori pomfret in
Rajasthani masala, ostrich bhuna with chunks
of dried potato and pulao rice, or a memorable

rendition of the Anglo-Indian classic,
Country Captain. Finish with crème brûlée
aromatised with saffron, cardamom and
ginger. A cocktail list supplements the wines,
which start at £16.50.
Chef/s: Cyrus Todiwala. **Open:** Mon to Fri L 12 to 3,
Mon to Sat D 6.15 to 10.30 (6.30 Sat). **Closed:** Sun,
bank hols, 25 Dec to 1 Jan. **Meals:** alc (main courses
£14 to £18). Set L and D £22 (2 courses) to £30.
Service: 12.5% (optional). **Details:** Cards accepted.
140 seats. 40 seats outside. Air-con. Wheelchair
access. Music. Children allowed.

ALSO RECOMMENDED

▲ Canteen

2 Crispin Place, Spitalfields, E1 6DW
Tel no: (0845) 6861 122
www.canteen.co.uk
⊖ Liverpool Street, map 2
British

Now a four-strong chain, Canteen feeds the
capital's appetite for British classics such as
devilled kidneys, Marmite on toast and
Victoria sponge. The Spitalfields branch where
the nostalgic all-day concept made its debut
remains popular, though standards have
reportedly wobbled. Mainstays like potted
duck (£5.50), roast chicken (£9.50), macaroni
cheese and rice pudding (£5.25) won't
necessarily beat a decent home cook's
endeavours, but keen prices and a joyous list of
ales nevertheless make it a useful address.
Wines, from £12.50, include a few patriotic
English numbers. Open all week.

▲ Carnevale

135 Whitecross Street, Barbican, EC1 8JL
Tel no: (020) 7250 3452
www.carnevalerestaurant.co.uk
⊖ Barbican, map 5
Vegetarian £5 OFF

Cool Carnevale has been peddling
Mediterranean-style veggie food by the
Barbican for more than 15 years, and is still up
for the gig. The deli/takeaway does a roaring
trade during the day, while those wanting to
eat in can expect sunny flavours in abundance.

Quinoa, wild mushroom, spinach and chilli cakes (£6.25) could open the show, ahead of goats' cheese and butternut squash ravioli or stuffed red peppers with tomato and basil compote (£12.50). For afters, consider raspberry crème brûlée (£5.25). House wine is £14.50. Closed Sat L and Sun.

▲ Chinese Cricket Club

Crowne Plaza, 19 New Bridge Street, Blackfriars, EC4V 6DB
Tel no: (020) 7438 8051
www.chinesecricketclub.com
⊖ Blackfriars, map 5
Chinese £5 OFF

Despite its unusual name (in honour of the national Chinese team) and location (inside a Crowne Plaza hotel), the cooking here is far from shabby. Dim sum may be pricey, but black cod dumpling (£8.90), and dishes like king prawn with chilli and salt (£18) or spicy pak choi with cloud ear mushrooms won't leave you stumped. To end, try chocolate fondant paired with Szechuan pepper cream (£6.50). However, you may need to take the atmosphere with you. House wine £17. Closed Sun.

Cinnamon Kitchen

Original Indian creations
9 Devonshire Square, City, EC2M 4YL
Tel no: (020) 7626 5000
www.cinnamon-kitchen.com
⊖ Liverpool Street, map 2
Indian | £35
Cooking score: 4

V

The City-based offshoot of the Cinnamon Club (see entry) brings its trademark modern take on traditional Indian dishes to the Square Mile. The fusion of old and new in some quite original creations has considerable appeal and dishes come fully plated in the European style. Expect first-class ingredients and big flavours in dishes such as grilled mutton escalopes in a Rajasthani hunter-style dish or quail with red spices and Puy lentil salad, followed by French black-leg chicken with fresh fenugreek or

spiced and roasted red deer with stir-fried mushrooms. Elsewhere, roast rack of lamb might appear with saffron sauce and pilau rice. Among side dishes look out for curried marrow with mustard as well as the homemade chutneys. House wine is £18.
Chef/s: Abdul Yaseen. **Open:** Mon to Fri L 12 to 2.45, Mon to Sat D 6 to 12. **Closed:** Sun, bank hols.
Meals: alc (main courses £8 to £21). Set L and D £17.50 (2 courses) to £19. **Service:** 12.5% (optional). **Details:** Cards accepted. 110 seats. 40 seats outside. Air-con. Separate bar. No mobile phones. Wheelchair access. Music. Children allowed.

Club Gascon

Passion, innovation... and foie gras
57 West Smithfield, City, EC1A 9DS
Tel no: (020) 7796 0600
www.clubgascon.com
⊖ Barbican, Farringdon, St Paul's, map 5
Modern French | £60
Cooking score: 6
£5 OFF 🍴 V

Pascal Aussignac's passionate quest for the idiomatic flavours of southwest France is played out in a one-time Lyons tea house – now a jewel-like room with faux marble walls and blazingly colourful floral displays. He abandoned the concept of conventional courses long before 'grazing' became fashionable; instead, his thrill-inducing menus are built around clusters of sexy little platefuls arranged under headings such as 'la route du sel' and 'les pâturages'. At the heart of things is foie gras, and this rich, sensuous delicacy appears in six versions – perhaps served with sherry, aromatic kumquat and hazelnut 'crispies' or presented as carpaccio with liquorice, pears and lemon caviar. Aussignac's roots may be in Gascony, but he's also prepared to make cross-border sorties in search of radical ideas and obscure ingredients – vine shoot embers, cedar jelly, violet tea and more. This is the kind of place where you might eat a taster of seared yellowfin tuna with hibiscus jus and crisp rémoulade, move on to a sampling of Pertuis asparagus with honey meringue and Rivesaltes pearls, and continue with an assemblage of grilled veal sweetbread, bergamot and wild mushroom cannelloni. To conclude, who could resist the left-field prospect of a white 'chocobar' with frosted aloe vera, strawberries and Penja pepper? The restaurant is run with brisk efficiency – despite the odd gripe about 'posturing waiters' and 'stewed coffee' – and the all-French wine list is a minor miracle of regional diversity. Wondrous bottles from Jurançon, Madiran and Irouléguy stand out, but the classic varietals also shine and there's a fine selection of 'vins aux verres' from £6 a glass.

Chef/s: Pascal Aussignac. **Open:** Mon to Fri L 12 to 2, Mon to Sat D 7 to 10 (10.30 Fri and Sat). **Closed:** Sun, bank hols, 2 weeks Christmas and New Year. **Meals:** alc (main courses £13 to £20). Set L £20 (2 courses) to £28. Set D £28. Tasting menu £55. **Service:** 12.5% (optional). **Details:** Cards accepted. 40 seats. Air-con. Separate bar. Music. Children allowed.

The Coach and Horses
Dining pub with the right credentials
26-28 Ray Street, Clerkenwell, EC1R 3DJ
Tel no: (020) 7278 8990
www.thecoachandhorses.com
⊖ Farringdon, map 5
Gastropub | £25
Cooking score: 3
£5 OFF £30

'A local place to go with someone you want to have a good chat with over some lovely food', notes a reporter about this relaxed, wood-panelled dining pub, which comes with all the right credentials: real ales, a decent wine list with good choice by the glass, and a daily changing, ingredients-led menu. The charcuterie board with pickles and bread is a promising way to start, followed, perhaps, by rock turbot (aka catfish) with mussels, leeks and carrots mouclade or 'deliciously tender' pork belly with Puy lentils and sauerkraut. Readers have appreciated the good value of it all and have also praised the friendly service. House wine is £11.95.

Chef/s: Henry Herbert. **Open:** Sun to Fri L 12 to 3, Mon to Sat D 6 to 10. **Closed:** 24 Dec to 1 Jan, Easter weekend, bank hols. **Meals:** alc (main courses £11 to £16). Sun L £13 (2 courses) to £16. **Service:** 12.5% (optional). **Details:** Cards accepted. 70 seats. 40 seats outside. Separate bar. Music. Children allowed.

Comptoir Gascon
Perky bistro with a Gallic heart
61-63 Charterhouse Street, Clerkenwell, EC1M 6HJ
Tel no: (020) 7608 0851
www.comptoirgascon.com
⊖ Farringdon, Barbican, map 5
French | £30
Cooking score: 4
V

If you've enjoyed the food of south west France on holiday, Smithfield's Comptoir Gascon could be the place to rediscover it. More 'dressed down' than its stellar sibling, Club Gascon (see entry), there are no fine-dining trappings to detract from the robust regional food. The perky space with its chalkboards, deli shelves and pretty velvet seats is redolent of a small-town bistro, and the menu is quirkily divided up into 'mer', 'végétal', 'terre' and 'the best of duck'. Go for the latter if you are after a taste of the Gascon real stuff – foie gras, rillettes and confit are textbook. Alternatively, ring the changes with grilled lamb with aligot (a regional dish of potatoes and cheese), and round off with something simple like fruit crumble. Comptoir is recommended for dates and is also a handy daytime drop-in for breakfasts and teas. The wine list is proudly Gascon too, with house selections from £16.50.

Chef/s: Laurent Sanchis. **Open:** Tue to Sat L 12 to 2.30 (11 to 3 Sat), D 7 to 10 (11 Thur and Fri). **Closed:** Sun, Mon, 2 weeks Christmas and New Year, Easter weekend. **Meals:** alc (main courses £8 to £15). **Service:** 12.5% (optional). **Details:** Cards accepted. 35 seats. 6 seats outside. Air-con. Wheelchair access. Music. Children allowed. Car parking.

Devonshire Terrace

Cool City dining
9 Devonshire Square, Liverpool Street, EC2M 4WY
Tel no: (020) 7256 3233
www.devonshireterrace.co.uk
⊖ Liverpool Street, map 2
Modern European | £25
Cooking score: 1

V £30

A collage of smartly appointed, flexible spaces, this cool restaurant/bar sits snugly in the Devonshire Square development close to Liverpool Street. Eat alfresco on the one of the terraces or stake your claim in the spacious central dining room. The menu is short and sweet, offering world tapas (think crab spring rolls or rabbit rillettes) ahead of pumpkin and feta salad or meat and fish with pick-your-own sauces (perhaps confit duck with Madeira jus or cod fillet with mixed pepper salsa). Strawberry cheesecake could close the show. Drinks range from big-spender fizz to global wines (from £15).
Chef/s: Justin Abbott Charles. **Open:** Mon to Fri B 7 to 11, L 12 to 3, D 6 to 11. **Closed:** Sat, Sun, 25 and 26 Dec, bank hols. **Meals:** alc (main courses £10 to £19). **Service:** 12.5% (optional). **Details:** Cards accepted. 78 seats. 90 seats outside. Air-con. Separate bar. Wheelchair access. Music. Children allowed.

The Don

Blue-chip wines and vibrant food
The Courtyard, 20 St Swithin's Lane, City, EC4N 8AD
Tel no: (020) 7626 2606
www.thedonrestaurant.co.uk
⊖ Bank, map 2
Modern British | £35
Cooking score: 2

Once the headquarters of the Sandeman fortified wine company, the Don is now a City destination for vibrant contemporary food, a fittingly splendid wine list and artwork by John Hoyland RA. Choose between restaurant or bistro dining, the former ranging from scallops in the shell with lime and vanilla beurre blanc, through roast suckling pig on rosemary mash with a black pudding and apple tart, to dark chocolate and mint marquise with coffee bean sauce. A satisfied autumn customer wrote in praise of the pot-roast pheasant with roast beetroot, apricots and bread sauce. In the Bistro, simpler fare along the lines of grilled lamb burger with caramelised red onion and chips is offered. There simply isn't world enough and time to do the wine list justice. It represents a comprehensive global tour, with due diligence paid to France, but with roll calls of classic fortified wines adding depth, together with bottles from the owners' New Zealand winery Trinity Hill, and even a Chardonnay/Riesling/Muscat blend from China. Prices start at £16.95. The Don is sister to the Bleeding Heart (see entry).
Chef/s: Matthew Burns. **Open:** Mon to Fri L 12 to 3, D 6 to 10. **Closed:** Sat, Sun, 23 Dec to 2 Jan. **Meals:** alc (main courses £14 to £28). **Service:** 12.5% (optional). **Details:** Cards accepted. 130 seats. Air-con. Separate bar. No music. No mobile phones.

The Eagle

Still flying high
159 Farringdon Road, Clerkenwell, EC1R 3AL
Tel no: (020) 7837 1353
⊖ Farringdon, map 5
Gastropub | £20
Cooking score: 2

V £30

'It was good to return to the Eagle after some time, and it does not disappoint. Four of us had main courses only, belly of lamb, pork and beans, risotto and grilled sardines. All were very good indeed, fresh and tasty. We voted the pork and beans a real hit, with wonderful succulent flavours – a superb dish'. This was the conclusion of someone happy to find this genre-defining gastropub (which celebrates 20 years in 2011) still flying high, the quirky, bare-boarded room pretty much as it's always been with blackboard menus and service that's 'fine and efficient'. House wine is £13.

Chef/s: Ed Mottershaw. **Open:** all week L 12.30 to 3 (3.30 Sat and Sun), Mon to Sat D 6.30 to 10.30. **Closed:** 1 week Christmas, bank hols (except Good Fri D). **Meals:** alc (main courses £8 to £15). **Service:** not inc. **Details:** Cards accepted. 60 seats. 24 seats outside. Music. Children allowed.

Eastside Inn

Inventive take on French bistro classics
40 St John Street, Clerkenwell, EC1M 4AY
Tel no: (020) 7490 9240
www.esilondon.com
⊖ Farringdon, map 5
French | £30
Cooking score: 3

£5 OFF

Originally a two-handed operation, Björn van der Horst's restaurant had an air of occasion, but with prices to match it was no surprise the adjoining bistro drew the customers and its menu is now served in both rooms. The original bistro is still the preferred spot, a relaxed, noisy affair with a central, open-to-view kitchen pumping out an inventive take on classic French bistro food. It's delivered in an unfussy style that perfectly echoes the surroundings of plain walls, bare boards and unclothed tables. Not all is textbook French, for instance a starter of tender baby squid set off by a light ragoût of cocoa beans and rocket, but duck rillettes or a main course of braised rabbit with tagliatelle and mustard sauce will reorientate you, as will desserts such as apple tart. Wines start at £19.50 a bottle (£5.50 a glass).
Chef/s: Björn van der Horst. **Open:** Mon to Fri L 12 to 3, D 7 to 11. **Closed:** Sat, Sun, 24 Dec to 3 Jan, bank hols. **Meals:** alc (main courses £13 to £18). Set L £15 (2 courses). **Service:** 12.5% (optional). **Details:** Cards accepted. 28 seats. Air-con. Separate bar. No mobile phones. Wheelchair access. Music. Children allowed.

Also recommended

Also recommended entries are not scored but we think they are worth a visit.

The Empress

Useful all-day venue
130 Lauriston Road, Hackney, E9 7LH
Tel no: (020) 8533 5123
www.theempressofindia.com
⊖ Mile End, Bethnal Green, map 1
Modern British | £25
Cooking score: 3

£30

Located near the gates to Victoria Park, the Empress is a useful local bistro combining Gallic good looks (red banquettes, chandeliers and bentwood chairs) with proudly British good cooking. By day, it plays café to locals with a user-friendly menu of casual 'brunchy' dishes (for example omelettes and cheeseburgers) and afternoon teas, combined with dishes more representative of the kitchen's loftier aims (smoked haddock 'brandade' cake with sorrel and curry cauliflower foam being a case in point). As day turns to night, café turns bar/restaurant and the punters pop in for draught beers or cocktails before a smart dinner of, say, gazpacho, guinea fowl with celeriac dauphinoise, and classic trifle. Prices befit a local spot with well-chosen global wines from £15.
Chef/s: Ajo Plunkett. **Open:** Mon to Sat L 12 to 3 (9 to 4 Sat), D 6 to 10. Sun 9 to 9. **Closed:** 25 Dec. **Meals:** alc (main courses £12 to £17). **Service:** 12.5% (optional). **Details:** Cards accepted. 60 seats. 20 seats outside. Separate bar. Wheelchair access. Music. Children allowed.

Eyre Brothers

Exploring the flavours of Iberia
68-70 Leonard Street, Shoreditch, EC2A 4QX
Tel no: (020) 7613 5346
www.eyrebrothers.co.uk
⊖ Old Street, map 2
Modern European | £30
Cooking score: 2

The warehouse conversion in which David and Robert Eyre's City eatery is housed is very twenty-first century. Soft lights, lots of textural surfaces and colourful urban artworks make a good backdrop for the food, which explores the flavours, seasonings and textures of Spain and Portugal. Hare soup with jamón and red wine is a fortifying way to start, or there could be pulpo (octopus), served Gallega-style with boiled potatoes, pimentón, garlic and olive oil. Mains bring on feijoada de bacalhau (salt cod and pinto bean stew) with cockles and clams, as well as grilled Longhorn beef with piquillo peppers, served with potatoes roasted in goose fat. The Iberian wines that make up the list represent a wonderful introduction to some of Europe's most exciting styles. Prices start at £16.

Chef/s: David Eyre and João Cleto. **Open:** Mon to Fri L 12 to 3, Mon to Sat D 6.30 to 10.30. **Closed:** Sun, Christmas to New Year. **Meals:** alc (main courses £12 to £27). **Service:** 12.5% (optional). **Details:** Cards accepted. 70 seats. Air-con. Separate bar. Wheelchair access. Music. Children allowed.

Fifteen London
Jamie's trendy trattoria
15 Westland Place, Shoreditch, N1 7LP
Tel no: (020) 3375 1515
www.fifteen.net
⊖ Old Street, map 2
Italian | £37
Cooking score: 3

'Good, rustic Italian grub' is what to expect at Fifteen's ground-floor trattoria (pricier, finer dining is available downstairs), where the young chefs are trained as part of the charitable Jamie Oliver Foundation. The menu focuses on 'wonderful, fresh and seasonal ingredients', their unadulterated flavours allowed to sing through in 'simply marvellous' dishes such as beetroot-cured salmon with shaved fennel, green beans and smoked eel crème fraîche or ravioli of speck, Jersey Royals and broad beans in sage butter broth. White chocolate crème brûlée proves a fine finale to evening meals, while breakfast (perhaps Arbroath smokies with lemon butter) is served from 7.30am. Friendly and professional staff complement the buzzy, welcoming feel of the place. House wine is £19.

Chef/s: Andrew Parkinson. **Open:** all week L 12 to 3 (3.30 Sun), D 6 to 9.30. **Closed:** 25 and 26 Dec, 1 Jan. **Meals:** alc (main courses £16 to £23). **Service:** 12.5% (optional). **Details:** Cards accepted. 65 seats. Air-con. Separate bar. Wheelchair access. Music. Children allowed.

ALSO RECOMMENDED
▲ Fox & Anchor
115 Charterhouse Street, Smithfield, EC1M 6AA
Tel no: (020) 7250 1300
www.foxandanchor.com
⊖ Barbican, Farringdon, map 5
Gastropub

This impressive, recently renovated late Victorian pub has been serving Smithfield Market traders for years, and is as good for a pint and a gossip as it is for robust food that reflects its comfortable down-to-earth informality. Breakfast is available from 8am; at other times there could be Maldon oysters, Scotch eggs and pork pies, or excellent fried skate knobs with ketchup tartare (£5.95), a roast of the day with duck-fat roast potatoes (£14.95) and jam sponge and custard. Wines from £14.50. Accommodation. Open all week.

The Fox
Terrific cooking in an East End boozer
28 Paul Street, City, EC2A 4LB
Tel no: (020) 7729 5708
www.thefoxpublichouse.com
⊖ Old Street, Liverpool Street, map 2
Gastropub | £29
Cooking score: 3
£30

There is a welcome lived-in feel to the dining room above this lively East End boozer. The dark-wood interior is simple, the short menu straightforward, although it deviates from standard British fare into the Med. It's hard to imagine what the old-time Cockney geezers would have made of a deep-fried courgette flower served with a piquant raw tomato sauce, but it goes down well with the young media types who now fill the place. In addition, rabbit, with its meat falling off the bone, arrives in a stew with peppers, bacon and a buttery saffron mash. Hazelnut charlotte with praline and vanilla sauce is a delightful end. Service is energetic and friendly. Wines from £14.

Chef/s: Amanda Pritchett. **Open:** Sun to Fri L 12 to 3 (4 Sun), Mon to Sat D 6 to 10. **Closed:** bank hols. **Meals:** alc (main courses £10 to £17). **Service:** 12.5% (optional). **Details:** Cards accepted. 35 seats. 21 seats outside. Separate bar. Music. Children allowed.

NEW ENTRY

Galvin La Chapelle

Stunning dining room with captivating food
35 Spital Square, Spitalfields, E1 6DY
Tel no: (020) 7299 0400
www.galvinrestaurants.com
⊖ Liverpool Street, map 2
French | £45
Cooking score: 6

The Galvin brothers would be hard-pushed to find a more stunning interior to launch their latest restaurant. Splendidly converted from a former girls' school, it is seen as one of the most attractive dining rooms in London. The vaulted ceiling and dramatic stone arches give the room gravitas, and natural light streams down from the tall windows. The menu offers a range of modern French dishes from the Galvin stable. Flavours and timings are notably good: silky sheets of Dorset crab lasagne are served with an earthy velouté of mousseron. Some dishes can be rich, although sound materials and technical ability provide the impetus. An assiette of veal, for example, arrived with its cheek braised, brain deep-fried, belly slow-cooked and sweetbread pan-fried, finished off with a carrot and cumin purée and diable sauce. Desserts are just as captivating; mille-feuille of raspberry ticked all the boxes. Service generally manages the correct mix of attention and knowledge. The wine list is expensive, with France taking the lion's share. Prices start from £18 and travel all the way to £19,500 for a 1961 Hermitage La Chapelle.

Chef/s: Chris and Jeff Galvin. **Open:** all week L 12 to 2.30, D 6 to 10 (10.30 Thurs to Sat, 9.30 Sun). **Closed:** 25 and 26 Dec, 1 Jan. **Meals:** alc (main courses from £14 to £26). Set L £19.50 (2 courses) to £25.50. **Service:** 12.5% (optional). **Details:** Cards accepted. 110 seats. Air-con. Separate bar. No music. Wheelchair access. Children allowed.

NEW ENTRY

Galvin's Café à Vin

Affordable Galvin offshoot
35 Spital Square, Spitalfields, E1 6DY
Tel no: (020) 7299 0404
www.galvinrestaurants.com
⊖ Liverpool Street, map 2
Modern European | £26
Cooking score: 4

£30

The Galvin brothers have pitched their third camp in Spital Square with a two-handed operation that also takes in the chic La Chapelle (see entry). What is on offer in the more modest, tightly packed Café à Vin is very much in tune with the London times: simple, affordable, flexible. One reporter started with wild garlic soup with pieces of chorizo and razor clams and loved every mouthful. Indeed, raw materials are almost eerily fine, with the eloquent flavour of char-grilled quail singing out next to a bundle of leaves, bean shoots, lardons and broad beans. From the wood-fired oven, a pizza of pipérade, chorizo, salted ricotta and basil is the real thing, served on the thinnest crust and bursting with flavour, while fish might be smoked haddock with wilted leeks, ratte potatoes and poached egg. Meals end strongly with the likes of île flottante with rhubarb and almonds. Wines from £18.

Chef/s: Chris and Jeff Galvin. **Open:** all week B 8 to 11.30 (9 to 11.30 Sat and Sun), L 12 to 3, D 6 to 10.30 (9.30 Sun). **Closed:** 25 and 26 Dec. **Meals:** alc (main courses £7 to £15). Set L and D £14.95 (2 courses). **Service:** 12.5% (optional). **Details:** Cards accepted. 38 seats. 32 seats outside. Air-con. Separate bar. Wheelchair access. Music. Children allowed.

ALSO RECOMMENDED
▲ Ginnan
1 Rosebery Court, Rosebery Avenue, Clerkenwell, EC1R 5HP
Tel no: (020) 7278 0008
www.ginnan.co.uk
⊖ Angel, Farringdon, map 5
Japanese

A low-lit room with sectioned-off tables has been the Clerkenwell setting for this efficient Japanese restaurant and takeaway since 1991. Outside catering is also offered. As well as the expected sushi and sashimi variations, there is a carte of traditional dishes such as grilled aubergine spread with sweet miso paste (£5.50), salmon teriyaki, and grilled pork loin with ginger and soy (£9.50). Bento lunches are also popular, while set dinners come at £25 or £33. Open Mon to Fri L, all week D.

Great Eastern Dining Room
Impeccably hip all-rounder
54-56 Great Eastern Street, Shoreditch, EC2A 3QR
Tel no: (020) 7613 4545
www.rickerrestaurants.com
⊖ Old Street, map 2
Pan-Asian | £35
Cooking score: 3
£5 OFF **V**

The bold black-and-red dining room in this converted fabric warehouse sets off a menu that plunders China, Thailand, Malaysia and Japan in a pan-Asian style that is Will Ricker's trademark. Evenings get a noisy start at the bar, a high-decibel playground for a young, affluent crowd. It's the kind of menu that encourages sharing, whether dim sum of chilli salt squid or wasabi prawns, salads of warm chicken and coconut, soft-shell crab and jalapeño tempura, or curries and roasts like rack of ribs with black pepper sauce. Desserts are mostly orientalised versions of western ideas, and there's a fittingly stylish wine list with lots of southern-hemisphere bottles. House wines are £16.

Chef/s: Andy Hearnden. **Open:** Mon to Fri L 12 to 4, Mon to Sat D 6 to 12 (1am Sat). **Closed:** Sun, bank hols. **Meals:** alc (main courses £12 to £24). Set L £15 (2 courses) to £17. Set D £19 (2 courses) to £23. **Service:** 12.5% (optional). **Details:** Cards accepted. 70 seats. Air-con. Separate bar. No mobile phones. Music. Children allowed. Car parking.

Green & Red
Part-party, part-restaurant
51 Bethnal Green Road, Bethnal Green, E1 6LA
Tel no: (020) 7749 9670
www.greenred.co.uk
⊖ Liverpool Street, map 1
Mexican | £25
Cooking score: 2
£30

With its basement bar and street-level Mexican diner, Green & Red is part-party, part-restaurant. Scorning naff Tex-Mex and the ubiquitous burrito, its USP is Jaliscan home cooking (Jalisco being the home of tequila; tequila being Green & Red's *raison d'être*). Of the 'small dishes', superfood salad with jicama (a turnip-like root) and chayote (squash), and octopus ceviche were good at inspection, but palate fatigue set in with underpowered braised lamb shank and pork belly. Menu fatigue is another problem – even for the occasional visitor. At least the 200-strong tequila list, a true labour of love, has the power to revive. House wine from £15.50.
Chef/s: Erick Medina Guisa. **Open:** all week D 5.30 to 11 (1am Fri and Sat, 10.30 Sun). **Closed:** bank hols, 1 week Christmas. **Meals:** alc (main courses £11 to £15). Set D £18.50 (2 courses) to £25. **Service:** 12.5% (optional). **Details:** Cards accepted. 70 seats. Air-con. Separate bar. Wheelchair access. Music. Children allowed.

Visit us online
To find out more about *The Good Food Guide*, please visit www.thegoodfoodguide.co.uk

The Gun
Popular Docklands gastropub
27 Coldharbour, Canary Wharf, E14 9NS
Tel no: (020) 7515 5222
www.thegundocklands.com
⊖ Canary Wharf, map 1
Gastropub | £30
Cooking score: 3

Part of Tom and Ed Martin's ever-expanding gastro-empire, this rejuvenated eighteenth-century dockers' pub benefits from a fabulous Thames-side location (and spectacular views of the O2 arena from both bar and covered terrace). The kitchen pumps out modern seasonal British dishes with the odd nod towards France: mackerel with confit shallot tart, beetroot and horseradish cream shares the stage with black Périgord truffle macaroni cheese, and roast saddle of rabbit with black pudding, braised leg and shoulder and 'Scotch broth'. Desserts range from chocolate and clementine tart to apple Bakewell tart. From May to September, the terrace becomes A Grelha, a Portuguese restaurant serving food cooked on a barbecue. House wine is £15.
Chef/s: Mark Fines. **Open:** all week L 12 to 3 (4 Sat and Sun), D 6 to 10. **Closed:** 25 Dec. **Meals:** alc (main courses £15 to £19). **Service:** 12.5% (optional). **Details:** Cards accepted. 80 seats. 100 seats outside. Separate bar. Wheelchair access. Music. Children allowed.

ALSO RECOMMENDED
▲ The Hackney Pearl
11 Prince Edward Road, Hackney, E9 5LX
Tel no: (020) 8510 3605
www.thehackneypearl.com
⊖ Hackney Wick, map 1
Modern British

In unlovely Hackney Wick, an area now popular with artists, the Hackney Pearl fits right in with its vintage Formica tables and school chairs. The cool café/bar's food is surprisingly ambitious, with cuttlefish and polenta (£11), veal skirt steak and chips (£12), and loquat tart (£4.50) all appearing. The short menu is supplemented by panini, scrambled egg brunches and cakes. Even better is a great-value (if limited) wine list from £14.10. Closed Mon.

Hawksmoor
'The best meat in London'
157 Commercial Street, City, E1 6BJ
Tel no: (020) 7247 7392
www.thehawksmoor.co.uk
⊖ Liverpool Street, Aldgate East, map 2
British | £38
Cooking score: 3

'I've been going here for a couple of years, and think it's the best meat available in London, whether in a steak restaurant or not.' That's one uncompromising verdict on this British steakhouse. It certainly ticks all the boxes: the beef is dry-aged for at least 35 days, you can choose from a range of cuts and weights, and standards are very high indeed. If beef isn't your bag, perhaps chicken, bacon chops or even lobster might fit the bill. Start with Tamworth belly ribs, London-cure smoked salmon or 'great grilled squid', and finish with strawberry trifle or London stout float. 'Really friendly staff' do their stuff, and the international wine list features plenty of sturdy reds; prices from £22.
Chef/s: Richard Turner. **Open:** all week L 12 to 3 (11 to 4 Sat and Sun), Mon to Sat D 6 to 10.30. **Closed:** Christmas, bank hols. **Meals:** alc (main courses £10 to £120). **Service:** 12.5% (optional). **Details:** Cards accepted. 106 seats. Air-con. Separate bar. Wheelchair access. Music. Children allowed.

Hix Oyster & Chop House
Plain Brit virtues
35-37 Greenhill Rents, Cowcross Street, Clerkenwell, EC1M 6BN
Tel no: (020) 7017 1930
www.restaurantsetcltd.co.uk
⊖ Farringdon, map 5
British | £35
Cooking score: 4

Mark Hix's bare-boarded, Brit-style bistro achieves a stylish informality that embraces the service as much as the food, a formula that attracts a full house. Much is made of the careful sourcing, with reassuring pointers such as Wye Valley asparagus, South Devon Ruby Red beef, Blythburgh pork and native oysters. The kitchen makes a virtue out of plain food, but takes dishes way beyond the meat-and-two-veg approach. Salted ox cheek is served with green split-pea and dandelion salad, asparagus is teamed with ham hock and wild herb salad, while flavour is everything in grilled Eyemouth brill teamed with sea purslane, a Somerset Barnsley chop with grilled kidney and rosemary, and hanger steak with baked bone marrow. Welsh rarebit is a savoury alternative to Jersey creamed rice with Yorkshire rhubarb. Wines, beers and ciders come from all over and show discrimination; a few wines are available by the glass, and bottles start at £17.50.

Chef/s: Tom Hill. **Open:** Mon to Fri L 12 to 3, Mon to Sat D 5.30 to 11. Sun 12 to 9. **Closed:** 25 and 26 Dec, 1 Jan. **Meals:** alc (main courses £13 to £36). Pre-theatre D £15.95 (2 courses) to £19.95.
Service: 12.5% (optional). **Details:** Cards accepted. 65 seats. 10 seats outside. Air-con. No music. No mobile phones. Children allowed.

ALSO RECOMMENDED

▲ Kasturi

57 Aldgate High Street, Whitechapel, EC3N 1AL
Tel no: (020) 7480 7402
www.kasturi-restaurant.co.uk
⊖ Aldgate, map 2
Indian

Wedged in among Aldgate's fibrillating financial institutions, flashily appointed Kasturi offers pain relief in the form of skilfully rendered Indian regional food for those who don't fancy braving touristy Brick Lane. Pitch-perfect tandooris and koh-e-avadh (an elegant take on rogan josh made with lamb shanks) line up alongside a trio of traditional biryanis (from £8.95), popular curry house stalwarts such as chicken dhansak and a few unusual specialities including a starter of crab masala (£4.95). Good-value thalis too (from £15.95). House wine is £15.95. Closed Sun.

Pascal Aussignac Club Gascon

Could you give us a very simple recipe?
Take a tulip from your garden. Wash it. Stuff it with some risotto or cooked tapioca and steam everything for three minutes. You will be amazed.

What would be your perfect birthday meal?
French fries from my mum and grilled duck hearts.

How do you relax when out of the kitchen?
Gardening and socialising.

What do you think is exciting about the British food scene?
The variety of food made by great specialists.

What is your favourite restaurant and why?
Busaba Eathai because I love their squid and the buzz of the place. Very good value as well.

Where do you see cooking/food/restaurants in 60 years' time?
Hope people will still enjoy eating as we eat even if the general quality of food has lost a lot of taste already.

The Larder

Modern British
91-93 St John Street, Clerkenwell, EC1M 4NU
Tel no: (020) 7608 1558
www.thelarderrestaurant.com
'A really special place that everyone should try
if they get the chance'

NEW ENTRY

Lutyens

A Conran classic
85 Fleet Street, City, EC4Y 1AE
Tel no: (020) 7583 8385
www.lutyens-restaurant.com
⊖ Chancery Lane, St. Pauls, Temple, map 5
French | £40
Cooking score: 4

Named after the building's architect Sir
Edwin Lutyens, this second venture from Sir
Terence Conran and Peter Prescott (see
Boundary) is a large, busy operation. There's a
sense of space and airiness in the restaurant
proper and despite cheek-by-jowl tables it
doesn't feel packed. The appeal of the menu
(much of it written in gastronomic Franglais)
is not hard to spot. It delivers good renditions
of dishes that soothe rather than challenge in a
well-considered mix of fish and shellfish (a
Conran speciality) with upmarket brasserie
ideas. The straightforwardness of the cooking
is another confidence-booster – the repertoire
runs from lobster mousse via jambon persillé
to Dover sole. The kitchen also presses the
comfort button for classics as diverse as
escalope of veal Holstein and calf's liver with
cèpes bordelaise. Puddings such as an intense
blackcurrant jelly served with madeleines and
crème Chantilly confirm a commitment to
simple, well-executed basics. Service from
plentiful staff is efficient. The substantial wine
list opens at £16.
Chef/s: David Burke. **Open:** Mon to Fri L 12 to 3, D 6
to 10. **Closed:** Sat, Sun, 25 to 29 Dec, bank hols.
Meals: alc (main courses £12 to £37). Set L and D
£16.50. **Service:** 12.5% (optional). **Details:** Cards
accepted. 115 seats. Air-con. Separate bar. No
music. Wheelchair access. Children allowed.

Medcalf

No gimmicks, just Brit food
40 Exmouth Market, Clerkenwell, EC1R 4QE
Tel no: (020) 7833 3533
www.medcalfbar.co.uk
⊖ Farringdon, map 2
Modern British | £25
Cooking score: 1

£30

An Exmouth Market stalwart, Medcalf trades
on its bubbly location, stark functionality and
honest grub. The best advice is to drop in at
lunchtime if you want to sample first-class
renditions of dishes with a strong British
flavour. There's nothing flashy about the
presentation and no gimmicks either – just
beetroot and grilled goats'cheese salad, braised
veal shin with pearl barley and curly kale, and
steamed chocolate pud with custard to finish.
Service gets mixed reports. House
wine £15.25.
Chef/s: Andrew Fila. **Open:** all week L 12 to 3 (4 Sat
and Sun), Mon to Sat D 6 to 10 (5.30 Thur, 5.30 to
10.30 Fri and Sat). **Closed:** 24 Dec to 3 Jan, Easter
Sun and Mon. **Meals:** alc (main courses £10 to £22).
Service: 12.5% (optional). **Details:** Cards accepted.
80 seats. 40 seats outside. Air-con. Wheelchair
access. Music.

ALSO RECOMMENDED

▲ Mehek

45 London Wall, City, EC2M 5TE
Tel no: (020) 7588 5043
www.mehek.co.uk
⊖ Moorgate, Liverpool Street, map 2
Indian £5 OFF

'The best Indian meal we have had in ages' is a
typical response to the food on offer at this
smart, spacious, professionally run venue on
the London Wall. Bengali tiger-fish tikka
cooked in the tandoor (£6.20) is an
interesting curtain-raiser, while chef's special
main dishes include guinea fowl bilash and
tandoori squab garnished with peppers and
tomatoes (£13.50), the marinades and spices
being notable for their deep, precise flavours.
Wines from £14.50. Open Mon to Fri.

The Modern Pantry

Kaleidoscopic fusion flavours
47-48 St John's Square, Clerkenwell, EC1V 4JJ
Tel no: (020) 7553 9210
www.themodernpantry.co.uk
⊖ Farringdon, map 5
Fusion | £34
Cooking score: 3

£5
OFF

Anna Hansen shot to fame as one of the co-founders of The Providores (see entry), but she's now running her own fusion gaff in trendy Clerkenwell. The premises – once a Georgian town house and steel foundry – is split into a fashion-conscious, all-day café/deli with communal tables and two more formal dining rooms upstairs (limited opening hours). Expect a kaleidoscope of world ingredients and flavour clashes – say grilled quail with mole sauce, plantain fritter and tomatillo salsa, Vietnamese-style braised pig's cheeks or pan-fried gilthead bream with umeboshi potato gratin, confit leeks and grilled nori, followed by a 'bombe' of habanero meringue, passion-fruit ice cream and pistachio cake. Anglo-Antipodean breakfasts and weekend brunch are an irresistible lure for the locals, and the compact global wine list is a model of good taste, with ungreedy mark-ups and plenty by the glass or carafe. Bottles start at £14.
Chef/s: Anna Hansen. **Open:** Café all week 8am to 11pm (10pm Mon, from 9 Sat, 10 to 10 Sun), Restaurant Tue to Fri and Sun L 12 to 3 (4 Sun), Tue to Sat D 6 to 10.30. **Closed:** 24 to 28 Dec, bank hols. **Meals:** alc (main courses £14 to £20). Set L £17.50 (2 courses) to £21.50. Sun L £17.50 (2 courses) to £22.50. **Service:** 12.5% (optional). **Details:** Cards accepted. 60 seats. 24 seats outside. Air-con. Separate bar. Wheelchair access. Music. Children allowed.

Moro

Sheer palate-tingling excitement
34-36 Exmouth Market, Clerkenwell, EC1R 4QE
Tel no: (020) 7833 8336
www.moro.co.uk
⊖ Farringdon, map 2
Spanish/North African | £50
Cooking score: 4

One man bemoaned the fact that the hard surfaces make Moro one of the capital's shoutier restaurants ('I wish I'd brought my megaphone'), so maybe it isn't the best location for an intimate tryst, but what the acoustics lack in subtlety, the cooking more than makes up for in sheer palate-tingling excitement. Moro specialises in Moorish Spanish cooking, and the tapas or mezze (as you will) taken at a long zinc bar may well induce you to bag a table and go the whole hog. That 'hog' might be the wood-roasted pork with 'amazingly crisp crackling, and very tender, perfectly cooked meat' enjoyed by one reporter, while charcoal-grilling is the preferred treatment for lamb, served with chickpeas and cauliflower fried in harissa. To start, there could be a dish of fideos – mussels, clams and prawns with allioli – while sweet things include a heaven-scented rosewater and cardamom ice cream. Wines from the Iberian peninsula open at £14. A new tapas bar, Morito, was due to open next door as we went to press.
Chef/s: Samuel and Samantha Clark. **Open:** Mon to Sat L 12.30 to 2.30, D 7 to 10.30. **Closed:** Sun, 23 Dec to 2 Jan, Easter, bank hols. **Meals:** alc (main courses £16 to £20). **Service:** 12.5% (optional). **Details:** Cards accepted. 106 seats. 18 seats outside. Air-con. Separate bar. No music. Wheelchair access. Children allowed.

The Narrow
Dapper riverside gastropub
44 Narrow Street, Limehouse, E14 8DP
Tel no: (020) 7592 7950
www.gordonramsay.com
⊖ Limehouse, map 1
Gastropub | £25
Cooking score: 2
£30

This was Gordon Ramsay's first venture into the world of gastropubs and it's easy to imagine he arrived with a tick-list: riverside views – tick; interesting history – tick; dapper décor – tick; trendily nostalgic British food – tick. From the à la carte menu you could try chicken and ham hock terrine with beetroot chutney, followed by braised ox cheek pie or braised neck of Cornish lamb with pearl barley and smoked bacon risotto and gremolata. Bar meals fill in the gaps with favourites such as devilled whitebait, sardines on toast or ham, egg and chips. Treacle pudding with bay leaf custard is a typical dessert. Wine starts at £18 a bottle.
Chef/s: John Collin. **Open:** all week L 11.30 to 3 (12 to 4 Sat and Sun), D 6 to 11 (5.30 to 11 Sat, 5.30 to 10.30 Sun). **Meals:** alc (main courses £12 to £17). Set L and early D £18 (2 courses) to £22.
Service: 12.5% (optional). **Details:** Cards accepted. 70 seats. 40 seats outside. Air-con. Separate bar. Wheelchair access. Music. Children allowed. Car parking.

1 Lombard Street
Cultured City high-roller
1 Lombard Street, City, EC3V 9AA
Tel no: (020) 7929 6611
www.1lombardstreet.com
⊖ Bank, map 2
Modern European | £65
Cooking score: 6
🍾

This remodelled, neo-classical banking hall holds a special place in the social mores of the City, and it's quite a set-up. Amid the spectacular, cathedral-like Georgian interior with its dazzling Pietro Agostini domed ceiling is a full-throttle bar/brasserie that feeds and waters the traders with Asian-tinted French food washed down with gulps of Cristal. By contrast the fine-dining restaurant is the soul of discretion – a calm, civilised and rather exclusive inner sanctum dominated by the baroque excesses of Titian's *Rape of Europa*. Herbert Berger's food fits the setting like a velvet glove, although his luxurious, technically astute and high-gloss haute cuisine is also open to the exotic thrills of wasabi, Thai papaya pickle and Szechuan peppercorns. White radish, ginger and lime vinaigrette add their special zing to spiced carpaccio of tuna, while a dish of squab pigeon takes a different turn with chorizo and chickpea casserole, roasted salsify and Rioja reduction. Of course, there is much from the pure-bred French repertoire, perhaps a fricassee of native lobster and langoustines scented with tarragon, chervil and shellfish beurre blanc, or veal fillet with caramelised foie gras, a ragoût of sweetbreads, sorrel and Champagne sauce. Desserts also flit between different worlds, offering William pear with nougat mousseline and warm Cassis sabayon alongside a feuillantine of caramelised Granny Smith apple with Guinness ice cream and glazed hazelnuts. Friendly mark-ups are a feature of the superb wine list, which puts France first but offers a great global spread – notably from the USA, Italy and Spain. Halves and by-the-glass selections abound, with bottle prices starting around £20.
Chef/s: Herbert Berger. **Open:** Mon to Fri L 12 to 2.30, D 6 to 10. **Closed:** Sat, Sun, 25 and 26 Dec, 1 Jan, bank hols. **Meals:** alc (main courses £24 to £29). Set L £28 (2 courses) to £34. Set D £25.
Service: 12.5% (optional). **Details:** Cards accepted. 60 seats. Air-con. Separate bar. No music. Wheelchair access. Children allowed.

Average price

The average price listed in main-entry reviews denotes the price of a three-course meal, without wine.

NEW ENTRY
Pizza East
Totally serious about pizza
56 Shoreditch High Street, Shoreditch, E1 6JJ
Tel no: (020) 7729 1888
www.pizzaeast.com
⊖ Liverpool Street, Old Street, map 2
Italian | £22
Cooking score: 2

V £30

Modelled on a trendy Californian pizzeria, the Soho House Group's huge industrial-chic eatery feels 'absolutely right for now'. It's as fashion-conscious as its fans, but is totally serious about pizza. 'Roughly Italian-American', it's not all about the authenticity of the margherita (although that's excellent). Instead, elastic, smoky dough is topped with the likes of veal meatballs, lemon and sage. Olives, Italian salumi (preserved meats) and cheese are impressive, and a better bet than the under-sized, over-seasoned chicken livers and woefully inauthentic bagna cauda served at inspection. Save room for puds – the doughnuts and chocolate sauce are terrific. Perky, family-friendly service gets a thumbs-up too.
Chef/s: Jon Pollard. **Open:** all week midday to midnight (10am Sat and Sun, 1am Thur, 2am Fri and Sat). **Closed:** 25 and 26 Dec. **Meals:** alc (main courses £6 to £25). **Service:** 12.5% (optional). **Details:** Cards accepted. 200 seats. Air-con. Separate bar. Wheelchair access. Music. Children allowed.

Refettorio at the Crowne Plaza Hotel
Authentic Italian with carefully sourced food
19 New Bridge Street, City, EC4V 6DB
Tel no: (020) 7438 8052
www.refettorio.com
⊖ Blackfriars, map 5
Italian | £35
Cooking score: 2

V

This refectory-style dining room within the Crowne Plaze hotel – 'one of the few authentic Italian restaurants in London', suggests one aficionado – has built up a loyal following of fans who keep returning for the simple, modern Italian food. The dining room is split into two areas, and the staff can set a steady pace at busy times. The simplicity, along with careful sourcing, can be seen in the selection of Italian charcuterie and cheeses, in smoked mozzarella with roasted beetroots and rocket salad, in a pasta dish of pappardelle with chicken livers, sage and brandy, and in main courses like sea bream with salted new potatoes and fennel salad. The all-Italian wine list opens in Puglia at £16.
Chef/s: Alessandro Bay. **Open:** Mon to Fri L 12 to 2.30, Mon to Sat D 6 to 10.30 (10 Fri and Sat). **Closed:** Sun. **Meals:** alc (main courses £17 to £24). Set D £23. **Service:** 12.5% (optional). **Details:** Cards accepted. 110 seats. Air-con. Separate bar. Wheelchair access. Music. Children allowed.

NEW ENTRY

The Restaurant at St Paul's Cathedral

Chic eatery in a crypt
St Paul's Cathedral, St Paul's, EC4M 8AD
Tel no: (020) 7248 2469
www.restaurantatstpauls.co.uk
⊖ St Paul's, map 5
Modern British | £26
Cooking score: 2
£5 OFF V £30

The crypt beneath St Paul's Cathedral is an atmospheric lunch spot. Frequented by a City crowd, it nevertheless feels special enough for an 'occasion' meal – the painted stone walls, bone-handled knives and Danish furniture being the very definition of understated chic. Chef Candice Webber's menus fuse some very English ingredients with Italian and French culinary traditions. The result is very effective in perfectly fried potato gnocchi with peas, broad beans and buffalo mozzarella or Cornish grey mullet with mussels and spiced bisque. The honey ice and gingerbread 'sandwich' is considered a must-try. The wine list is half French, with house at £16.25.
Chef/s: Candice Webber. **Open:** all week L 12 to 3. **Closed:** 25 Dec, Good Fri. **Meals:** Set L £20 (2 courses) to £26. **Service:** 10% (optional). **Details:** Cards accepted. 48 seats. Air-con. No music. Wheelchair access. Children allowed.

Rhodes Twenty Four

Skyline vistas and gussied-up Brit food
Tower 42, 25 Old Broad Street, City, EC2N 1HQ
Tel no: (020) 7877 7703
www.rhodes24.co.uk
⊖ Liverpool Street, map 2
British | £55
Cooking score: 4

Once you have negotiated the security checks, take the lift to the 24th floor, where jaw-dropping panoramic vistas await (bag a window seat for grandstand views over the city's skyline). With Gary Rhodes' name above the door, you might expect re-inventions of the British gastronomic vernacular with a

splash of haute cuisine on the side – and you wouldn't be wrong. This is the world of gussied-up mutton suet pudding, oxtail cottage pie and beef fillet with crispy bone marrow and sloe gin cabbage, although the likes of pan-fried halibut with slow-cooked veal and citrus risotto prove that the kitchen isn't stuck in the nostalgia groove. Shrewdly sourced regional ingredients are the building blocks, but it requires real confidence and gusto to transform them into dishes that justify their rather dizzying price tags, and recent reports suggest that this is not always the case. Big names from France dominate the diverse wine list, with prices (from £21) pitched at deep pockets.
Chef/s: Adam Gray. **Open:** Mon to Fri L 12 to 2.30, D 6 to 10. **Closed:** Sat, Sun, bank hols, 24 Dec to 3 Jan. **Meals:** alc (main courses £17 to £30). **Service:** 12.5% (optional). **Details:** Cards accepted. 75 seats. Air-con. Separate bar. No mobile phones. Wheelchair access. Music. Children allowed. Car parking.

Rivington Grill

High-provenance Brit grub
28-30 Rivington Street, Shoreditch, EC2A 3DZ
Tel no: (020) 7729 7053
www.rivingtongrill.co.uk
⊖ Old Street, map 2
British | £28
Cooking score: 2
V £30

In arty Shoreditch, where restaurants jockey for the most extravagant concept award, Rivington Grill feels refreshingly, well, normal. It's a British bistro of sorts, serving quaint fare of high provenance from breakfast to dinner both at the bar and in the dining room. The 'on toast' section is fun: cod chitterlings with caper mayonnaise or haggis and HP sauce swing the foodie vote. Mains range from decent fish and chips to more ambitious Dover sole with pennywort and fennel. Pudding continues in a retro-Brit vein with 'burnt cream' or apple crumble. Snippy service lets the side down. House wine is £16.25. There's a sibling in Greenwich.

Chef/s: Simon Wadham. Open: all week L 12 to 3 (11 to 4 Sat and Sun), D 6 to 11 (10 Sun). Closed: 25 and 26 Dec, 1 Jan. Meals: alc (main courses £13 to £27). Sun L £19.75. Service: 12.5% (optional). Details: Cards accepted. 80 seats. Air-con. Separate bar. Music. Children allowed.

NEW ENTRY
Rochelle Canteen
No-frills East End hideaway
Rochelle School, Arnold Circus, E2 7ES
Tel no: (020) 7729 5677
www.arnoldandhenderson.com
⊖ Liverpool Street, map 2
Modern British | £18
Cooking score: 2
£30

As the 'canteen' in the title suggests, this East End hideaway is a basic operation with communal tables, restricted opening hours and no alcohol licence. That doesn't stop it filling up. The terse menu betrays the influence of St John (see entry – co-owner Margot Henderson is married to St John's Fergus), but steers an international course taking in lamb harrira, bream with puntarelle and anchovy, onglet steak and chips, and trifle. Staffing is minimal, it's noisy and dishes run out frustratingly early sometimes, but such downsides are counterbalanced by good looks and charm. The courtyard is heaven in the summer. BYO with corkage £5.
Chef/s: Margot Henderson. Open: Mon to Fri B 9.30 to 11, L 12 to 3. Closed: Sat, Sun, bank hols. Meals: alc (main courses £9 to £19). Service: not inc. Details: Cards accepted. 42 seats. 42 seats outside. No music. Wheelchair access. Children allowed.

READERS RECOMMEND
Rosa's Spitalfields
Thai
12 Hanbury Street, Spitalfields, E1 6QR
Tel no: (020) 7247 1093
www.rosaslondon.com
'Wonderful food and great service all for a very reasonable price'

Rosemary Lane
The secret's out
61 Royal Mint Street, Tower Hill, E1 8LG
Tel no: (020) 7481 2602
www.rosemarylane.btinternet.co.uk
⊖ Tower Hill, map 2
Modern European | £30
Cooking score: 3

'I used to come here for secret meetings', confides a diner. 'The secret's out now.' Indeed, in an area poorly served for business-quality lunching, tiny, wood-panelled Rosemary Lane enjoys 'hidden gem' status. Cristina Anghelescu's France-meets-California cooking is clean and vibrant; the ingredients healthy, colourful and cooked *à la minute*. The cucumber salad with tuna tataki at inspection had clearly been cut just seconds before. Lemon sole with sauce vierge and gloriously smokey confit aubergine was perfectly timed. 'Dinner party cooking' is the worst you could say. It's a shame the menu changes just quarterly, but the tasting menu (Saturdays only) shows more of what Anghelescu can do. A likeable wine list, strong on France and California, is kindly priced, with recession-era expense accounts in mind. House wine £15.
Chef/s: Cristina Anghelescu. Open: Mon to Fri L 12 to 2.30, Mon to Sat D 5.30 to 10 (6 Sat). Closed: Sun. Meals: alc (main courses £11 to £20). Set L and D £15 (2 courses) to £18. Service: 12.5% (optional). Details: Cards accepted. 30 seats. Air-con. Music. Children allowed.

Saf
Raw talent
152 Curtain Road, Shoreditch, EC2A 3AT
Tel no: (020) 7613 0007
www.safrestaurant.co.uk
⊖ Old Street, map 2
Vegetarian | £27
Cooking score: 4
£5 OFF V £30

Utterly mystifying to those who love roast meat but the ultimate in menu-roaming freedom for those who don't, Saf specialises in

raw vegan food. Few items are heated beyond 48°C and where there might be a problematic ingredient (rice, cheese, bread) there is always an ingenious solution. If you don't live 'raw', it can take a while to process the realities of, say, a lasagne made with raw bolognese, sage pesto and macadamia ricotta. It will be clever, complex and fresh, but it won't be hot. Equally, the success of Saf's take on sushi – vegetable maki with shiitake, cucumber and avocado – depends very much on the diner's fondness for 'rice' made from tiny chips of raw parsnip. The pill is sugared with an abundance of fresh flavours, low-lit industrial style and a still-hip Shoreditch location. Wine, also available to carry out, includes biodynamic and organic bottles from £19. A 'botanical' cocktail list is annotated with humour and supplemented with non-alcoholic 'elixirs'.
Chef/s: Matt Downes. **Open:** all week L 12 to 3 (4 Sun), D 6 to 11 (10.30 Sun). **Closed:** 25 and 26 Dec, 1 Jan. **Meals:** alc (main courses £12 to £14). Sun L £12.95. **Service:** 12.5% (optional). **Details:** Cards accepted. 83 seats. 26 seats outside. Air-con. Wheelchair access. Music. Children allowed.

St John

Inspiring nose-to-tail champ
26 St John Street, Clerkenwell, EC1M 4AY
Tel no: (020) 7251 0848
www.stjohnrestaurant.com
⊖ Farringdon, map 5
British | £36
Cooking score: 6

A mere glance at the day's menu inspires the true foodie to reverie. Seasonal, nostalgic and creative, the unmistakeable St John idiom has changed the way we eat. Founder Fergus Henderson's nose-to-tail philosophy means an emphasis on offal. Whether ox tongue and chicory or pig's tail with watercress, 'there's much to discover'. Vegetarians and pescetarians don't have much choice, but such is the quality of brill with tartare sauce or lentils and goats' curd, they won't feel short-changed. Rare seasonal finds like woodcock, pennywort and kid beg to be ordered. 'Dishes are simple in composition but supremely well-

cooked', reports one fan. Come pudding, it's hard not to recommend the highly digestive lemon sorbet with vodka, but Bakewell tart or Eccles cake and Lancashire cheese usually win. Service is charming – when it wants to be. The fascinating French wine list (from £19.60) suits the robust fare well. The St John 'empire' expands this year with the opening of the St John Hotel off Leicester Square.
Chef/s: Chris Gillard. **Open:** Sun to Fri L 12 to 3 (1 to 3 Sun), Mon to Sat D 6 to 11. **Closed:** bank hols. **Meals:** alc (main courses £14 to £24). **Service:** 12.5% (optional). **Details:** Cards accepted. 110 seats. No mobile phones. Children allowed.

St John Bread & Wine

Supporting the English cause
94-96 Commercial Street, Spitalfields, E1 6LZ
Tel no: (020) 7251 0848
www.stjohnbreadandwine.com
⊖ Liverpool Street, map 1
British | £28
Cooking score: 3
£30

St John's Spitalfields sibling benefits from a more varied crowd and menu than at the Smithfield mothership, so you won't find butch blokes baying for blood and bone marrow here. Instead, you'll find a daily changing blackboard menu comprising small and large plates with breakfast, salads, seafood and English seasonal curiosities (alexanders and cobnuts) as central as the nose-to-tail stuff. If your dining partner agrees, the pies, roasts and steamed puddings for two are recommended. The food looks as plain as the descriptions sound ('salad', 'swede cake', 'chocolate ice cream') but the delivery is consistent and good. Intriguing French country and table wines (from £19.60) suit the mood and are available to take away, along with excellent home-baked bread and cakes.
Chef/s: James Lowe. **Open:** all week L 12 to 4, D 6 to 10.30 (9 Sun). **Closed:** 25 Dec to 1 Jan, bank hols. **Meals:** alc (main courses £10 to £46). **Service:** not inc. **Details:** Cards accepted. 56 seats. Air-con. Separate bar. No music. No mobile phones. Wheelchair access. Children allowed.

Searcy's

Flexible food for culture vultures
Level 2, Barbican Centre, Silk Street, Barbican,
EC2Y 8DS
Tel no: (020) 7588 3008
www.barbican.org.uk
⊖ Barbican, Moorgate, map 5
Modern British | £29
Cooking score: 3

£5 £30
OFF

The narrow, L-shaped dining room overlooking St Giles' Cripplegate church from Level 2 of the Barbican is just what is needed to complement the Centre's cultural offerings. Flexibility is there in the form of breakfasts from 10am, and bar snacks along the lines of venison and ale pie or slow-roast pork belly sandwich, while the restaurant offers a greatest hits list of modern British cooking. Scallops with dry-cured bacon, cauliflower and pea shoots, brawn with parsely, braised ox cheeks with celeriac mash, and venison with braised red cabbage, parsnip purée and blackcurrant sauce are typical of the consistent output – and good quality is to the fore. The wine list is arranged by style and offers a good mix, with prices from £18.
Chef/s: Darren Archer. **Open:** Mon to Fri L 12 to 2.30, Mon to Sat D 5 to 10.30. **Closed:** Sun, 24 to 26 Dec. **Meals:** Set L £17.50 (2 courses) to £20. Set D £24.50 (2 courses) to £28.50. **Service:** not inc. **Details:** Cards accepted. 70 seats. Air-con. Separate bar. No mobile phones. Wheelchair access. Music. Children allowed. Car parking.

Soseki

City stunner with sustainable fish
20 Bury Street, City, EC3A 5AX
Tel no: (020) 7621 9211
www.soseki.co.uk
⊖ Liverpool Street, Bank, map 2
Japanese | £45
Cooking score: 3

From the makers of the Moshi Moshi sushi chain, this City dazzler evokes the distant spirit of a Taishō-period teahouse – complete with gorgeous screens, exotic fabrics and stunning 1920s Kyoto antiques. The food is based on 'kaiseki-kappo' (literally 'cutting and cooking'); chefs and diners face each other across a counter and ingredients-led banquets are constructed according to strict traditional principles. The owners are keen on promoting sustainably sourced fish and ethical ingredients, which also show up strongly on the innovative sushi menus and the contemporary carte. An appetiser of Cornish spider crab with daikon gyoza and yuzu honey dressing might appear beside a salad of rare Wagyu beef, wood sorrel, pickled celeriac, samphire and tosazu jelly, with mains involving steaming, simmering, grilling and braising (perhaps suckling pig with black miso broth, ginko nut and mustard greens). Sakés, shochu and wines start at £21.
Chef/s: Paul Greening and Shu Inagaki. **Open:** Mon to Fri L 12 to 2.30, D 6 to 10. **Closed:** Sat, Sun, bank hols, Christmas to New Year. **Meals:** alc (main courses £10 to £45). Set L and D £25. Kaiseki menu £45 to £60. **Service:** 12.5% (optional). **Details:** Cards accepted. 60 seats. Air-con. Separate bar. Wheelchair access. Music.

NEW ENTRY

Tayyabs

A Punjabi meat-lover's paradise
83-89 Fieldgate Street, Whitechapel, E1 1JU
Tel no: (020) 7247 9543
www.tayyabs.co.uk
⊖ Whitechapel, Aldgate East, map 1
Pakistani | £14
Cooking score: 2

V £30

One of London's most enduringly popular restaurants, this 35-year-old veteran is the capital's foremost purveyor of Pakistani-style grilled meat. There are plenty of other pretenders in the area, but none can convincingly replicate Tayyabs' signature lamb chops. The naan breads, seekh and shami kebabs, mutton tikka and dry meat curry are also exemplary. Service can be a bit brusque at peak times, when the army of waiters struggles to keep pace with rampant demand and the narrow aisles between tables are jam-packed with queues of hungry hopefuls. Prices are remarkably fair, and though no alcohol is served, you're welcome to BYO and no corkage is charged.

Chef/s: Wasim and Saleem Tayyab. **Open:** all week midday to midnight. **Meals:** alc (main courses £5 to £13). **Service:** not inc. **Details:** Cards accepted. 250 seats. Air-con. Wheelchair access. Music. Children allowed.

ALSO RECOMMENDED
▲ Towpath Café
42 De Beauvoir Crescent, Dalston, N1 5SB
Tel no: (020) 7254 7606
⊖ Old Street, map 2
Café

Food writer Lori de Mori and photographer Jason Lowe's quirky canalside café is best saved for a sunny day, as there's little space under cover. The part-British, part-Italian menu changes daily but is as basic as the set-up – usually a soup, salad, bruschetta and a grilled cheese sandwich. Tomato and farro salad (£4.50), chard bruschetta, (£3), broad bean and mint salad, and blood orange posset (£3.50) is simple stuff, but a lesson in joyful, seasonal cooking. Service is kindly but disorganised. House wine from £14.95. Open Tue to Sun, breakfast and lunch only.

Les Trois Garçons
High-camp glamour and decent cooking
1 Club Row, Shoreditch, E1 6JX
Tel no: (020) 7613 1924
www.lestroisgarcons.com
⊖ Liverpool Street, map 1
Modern French | £46
Cooking score: 3
£5
OFF

It may occupy an unremarkable corner in the City, but you can't miss this flamboyant former pub. Inside it's a hotchpotch of high-camp glamour and Gothic shadows where a modern French-inspired menu offers some decent cooking. Starters include home-cured foie gras in Sauternes 'au torchon' with pear and raisin chutney, or lemon-and-lime dressed

fresh crab with aubergine and white miso caviar, lotus root crisps and a marinated mooli and radish salad. Mains see roasted pork belly, honey-cured and ginger-braised shoulder and smoked ham croquettes served in a ginger broth, or there could be a straightforward slow-braised rib of beef with pomme purée, spinach and confit onion. Desserts bring on vanilla crème brûlée with honey truffle cake and blood orange sorbet. Mainly French wines start at £22.

Chef/s: Michael Chan. **Open:** Mon to Sat D only 7 to 12. **Closed:** Sun, Christmas, New Year, bank hols, 2 weeks Aug. **Meals:** Set D £27 to £45.50. Tasting menu £62. **Service:** 12.5% (optional). **Details:** Cards accepted. 80 seats. Air-con. Wheelchair access. Music. Children allowed.

NEW ENTRY
Viajante
A brilliantly eccentric restaurant
Cambridge Heath Road, Bethnal Green, E2 9NF
Tel no: (020) 7871 0461
www.viajante.co.uk
⊖ Bethnal Green, map 1
Modern European | £60
Cooking score: 5
🛏 V

The kitchen grabs the gritty urban view, diners view the kitchen; it's probably the best arrangement, given the not entirely salubrious area. Nuno Mendes bowled almost everybody over with his innovative, provocative cooking at Bacchus. Now he's moved into the ground floor of Bethnal Green's Victorian town hall (transformed into a boutique hotel), and in an economically spare setting is offering cooking that essays a further degree of experimentation. There's the edgy concept of no written menu on arrival, just a check on likes, dislikes and a choice of three (at lunch), six, nine or twelve courses. It's creative, confident stuff full of twists, turns and surprising technique, with a strong sense of freshness, flavour and balance. Standouts from a six-course lunch were: squid tartare with squid ink granita, pickled radishes and samphire and dill oil; a spring garden salad

with ribbons of leeks, carrots, peas, broad beans, couscous and a pea velouté; lemon sole with shavings of raw asparagus and a confit egg yolk which melted into a pool of coconut tapioca; the highly flavoured brown butter served with bread; a mini crema Catalana as a petit four. Sharper service and better English (if each dish is to be recited at table) would help. The modern wine list opens at £20.
Chef/s: Nuno Mendes. **Open:** all week L 12 to 2.30, D 7 to 9.30. **Closed:** 25 and 26 Dec, 1 Jan. **Meals:** Set L £25 (3 courses) or £45 (6 courses). Set D £60 (6 courses), £75 (9 courses) or £85 (12 courses). **Service:** not inc. **Details:** Cards accepted. 36 seats. Air-con. Separate bar. No mobile phones. Wheelchair access. Music.

Viet Grill

Stunning vibes and street food
58 Kingsland Road, Shoreditch, E2 8DP
Tel no: (020) 7739 6686
www.vietnamesekitchen.co.uk
⊖ Old Street, map 2
Vietnamese | £16
Cooking score: 2

£5 OFF **V** £30

Just a few years after its last snazzy refurb, Viet Grill on Kingsland Road's 'Pho Mile' has been revamped again, this time with a French colonial look. With its bold foliage murals it looks stunning, and easily overshadows its cheaper, canteen-style neighbours. The menu is an enticing balance of contemporary Vietnamese specials and street food, the former taking in lobster and crab 'Saigon ceviche' or lemongrass mackerel in banana leaves. Paired with spice-friendly wines (in smart glasses) from the Malcom Gluck-selected list (from £14.50) it makes a destination or date place. One quibble – when the joint's jumping, it gets very, very noisy.
Chef/s: Vinh Bu. **Open:** Mon to Sat L 12 to 3, D 5.30 to 11 (11.30 Fri and Sat). Sun 12 to 10.30. **Closed:** 23 Dec to 4 Jan. **Meals:** alc (main courses £6 to £9). Set L and D £9.50 (2 courses) to £20. **Service:** 12.5% (optional). **Details:** Cards accepted. 150 seats. Air-con. Separate bar. Music. Children allowed. Car parking.

Vinoteca

Brilliant wine and vibrant flavours
7 St John Street, Farringdon, EC1M 4AA
Tel no: (020) 7253 8786
www.vinoteca.co.uk
⊖ Farringdon, Barbican, map 5
Modern European | £25
Cooking score: 3

🍷 £30

'Be prepared to wait and muck in', advises a fan of Vinoteca – a vibrant venue that is regularly rammed with enthusiasts seeking an interesting tipple to drink or take home. This place is proud of its wares – not surprising given that the wine list runs to some 250 bins with quality across the board. The owners stay on top of emerging trends and offer an exemplary choice by the glass; alternatively choose a bottle (from £12.95) to go with something smart from the menu. The food has ambition, with punchy flavours gracing a short repertoire packed with interest. Wood pigeon with pea and pancetta fricassee or grilled squid with chilli oil and preserved lemons could catch the eye, before poached brill with Manila clams, fregola and chorizo. Desserts could include strawberry and rhubarb crumble with crème fraîche.
Chef/s: John Murray. **Open:** Mon to Sat L 12 to 2.45, D 5.45 to 10 (6 Sat). **Closed:** Sun, Christmas and some bank hols. **Meals:** alc (main courses £9 to £16). **Service:** 12.5% (optional). **Details:** Cards accepted. 40 seats. 6 seats outside. Music. Children allowed.

Symbols

🛏 Accommodation is available

£30 Three courses for less than £30

V More than three vegetarian main courses

£5 OFF £5-off voucher scheme

🍷 Notable wine list

Wapping Food

Industrial-chic food arena
Wapping Hydraulic Power Station, Wapping,
E1W 3SG
Tel no: (020) 7680 2080
www.thewappingproject.com
⊖ Wapping/Shadwell, map 1
Modern European | £35
Cooking score: 3

£5
OFF

The cavernous, converted power station that houses Wapping Food demands big personality from its incumbents and that's exactly what it gets. The kitchen team specialises in vervy assemblies of mainly Mediterranean ingredients such as a starter of mackerel, new potato, mustard fruits and radicchio, then roast plaice with chermoula mussels and chickpeas, with liquorice ice cream to finish. There are occasional misfires – one huge, claggy pumpkin 'gnocchi' [sic] by way of veggie main course – but simple presentation and fair prices usually excuse them. Staff aren't shy and retiring either, confidently taking guests through the less familiar reaches of an exciting wine list that is, proudly, all Australian. Prices start at £16.50.
Chef/s: Camron Emirali. **Open:** all week L 12 to 3 (1 to 3.30 Sat, 1 to 4 Sun), Mon to Sat D 6.30 to 11 (7 Sat). **Closed:** 23 Dec to 3 Jan, bank hols. **Meals:** alc (main courses £14 to £20). Set L and D £35.50 (3 courses) to £49.50. **Service:** 12.5% (optional). **Details:** Cards accepted. 150 seats. 50 seats outside. Separate bar. Wheelchair access. Music. Children allowed. Car parking.

Whitechapel Gallery Dining Room

A great display of light, seasonal cooking
77-82 Whitechapel High Street, Whitechapel,
E1 7QX
Tel no: (020) 7522 7896
www.whitechapelgallery.org
⊖ Aldgate East, map 1
Modern British | £30
Cooking score: 3

£5
OFF

'Delicious, courteous, adventurous', is how one reporter summed up the restaurant in this landmark art gallery – the by-product of a whopping £13.5m expansion programme. It's a small, light, street-facing room with lots of pale wood, mirrors and tightly packed tables and a kitchen that champions seasonal British produce. Simple modern dishes like char-grilled rump of Romney Marsh lamb with wild garlic potato terrine, roasted red pepper and saffron dressing or roast suprême of free-range chicken accompanied by summer vegetables, tomato and tarragon toast and a nettle-scented consommé are typical of the light, uncluttered approach. Flavours are well-balanced, as can be seen in desserts such as Victoria plums teamed with macerated blackberries, plum wine jelly, mint and honeydew melon soup. The sharply focused wine list starts at £12.50.
Chef/s: Michael Paul. **Open:** Tue to Sun L 12 to 2.30, Wed to Sat D 6 to 11. **Closed:** Mon, 24 Dec to 2 Jan. **Meals:** alc (main courses £15 to £18). Set L £18 (2 courses) to £23. **Service:** 12.5% (optional). **Details:** Cards accepted. 50 seats. Air-con. Wheelchair access. Music. Children allowed.

READERS RECOMMEND

The Abbeville

Gastropub
67-69 Abbeville Road, Clapham, SW4 9JW
Tel no: (020) 8675 2201
www.theabbeville.co.uk
'Exceptionally tasty, hearty, home-cooked food and great real ale'

The Anchor & Hope

Eye-poppingly fine ingredients
36 The Cut, South Bank, SE1 8LP
Tel no: (020) 7928 9898
⊖ Waterloo, Southwark, map 5
Gastropub | £29
Cooking score: 3

£30

This reliably excellent gastropub alongside the Young Vic is usually filled to capacity with a noisy scrum of diners, drawn by its ability to source eye-poppingly fine ingredients, determinedly rustic but skilful cooking, generous portions and enthusiastic, knowledgeable service. Recent highlights have included tender strips of griddled ox heart with zingy celeriac rémoulade, a gargantuan lasagne for two containing epically rich beef ragù, silky béchamel and succulent chunks of liver, and woodcock roasted to pink perfection, the head cleaved neatly in half, with a little spoon to pick out the brains. At inspection, churros con chocolate were worthy of Madrid. Some old favourites on the wine list have gone up by a fiver or so, but the gluggable house bottles are still excellent value at £12.50. You can't book, so get there early or expect to wait in the bar.
Chef/s: Jonathon Jones. **Open:** Tue to Sat L 12 to 2.30, Sun L at 2 (1 sitting), Mon to Sat D 6 to 10.30. **Closed:** Christmas, New Year, bank hols. **Meals:** alc (main courses £9 to £24). Sun L £30. **Service:** not inc. **Details:** Cards accepted. 50 seats. 24 seats outside. Air-con. Separate bar. Wheelchair access. Music. Children allowed.

ALSO RECOMMENDED

▲ The Antelope

76 Mitcham Road, Tooting, SW17 9NG
Tel no: (020) 8672 3888
www.antic-ltd.com/antelope
⊖ Tooting Broadway, map 3
British £5 OFF

Church chairs, stuffed foxes and other oddments lend this huge pub an air of granny chic. There's a brand new garden and a hidden games room where you'll sometimes find live comedy, film screenings or quiz nights. Expect classic London gastropub fare such as grilled sardines with white bean, bread and pepper salad (£5.50) followed by braised Gloucester Old Spot pig's cheeks with polenta (£12). Bar food might include Catalan chicken with baked potato chips and aïoli (£7). Wines start at £13.50. Open all week.

▲ L'Auberge

22 Upper Richmond Road, Putney, SW15 2RX
Tel no: (020) 8874 3593
www.ardillys.com
⊖ East Putney, map 3
French

The black-and-white frontage in leafy Putney hides a dyed-in-the-wool local French restaurant, where residents gather to be reminded just how satisfying real Gallic food can be. Wine takes a star role in the cooking. Snails baked with mushrooms in Monbazillac and cream (£8.75) might be followed by duck breast sauced with Banyuls and figs, accompanied by crushed potatoes and black olives (£15.75), while desserts such as chestnut cream and whisky gâteau (£6.75) send you away happy. House wines are £15.25. Open Tue to Sat D only.

Babur

Ethnic art meets culinary innovation
119 Brockley Rise, Forest Hill, SE23 1JP
Tel no: (020) 8291 2400
www.babur.info
map 1
Indian | £26
Cooking score: 2
£5 OFF £30

Vivid 'kalamkari' dyed fabrics, hand-woven 'kantha' table runners and antique print blocks give an ethnic arty edge to this innovative contemporary Indian on Brockley Rise. Tikkas and biryanis are overshadowed by a raft of trendy crossover ideas ranging from tamarind-glazed quail breast, 'dum-cooked' rabbit in a pot with star anise and ginger broth, and black cod in spiced mustard sauce with mustard mash. Vegetables might include crispy fried potatoes with dried mango powder, while desserts such as carrot halva in yoghurt soup end meals with an adventurous flourish. Sunday lunch is a leisurely family buffet, cocktails are worth sipping, and the wine list starts at £16.50.
Chef/s: Jiwan Lal. **Open:** all week L 12 to 2.30 (4 Sun), D 6 to 11.30. **Closed:** 26 Dec. **Meals:** alc (main courses £10 to £15). Sun L buffet £10.95.
Service: not inc. **Details:** Cards accepted. 72 seats. Air-con. No mobile phones. Wheelchair access. Music. Children allowed.

Baltic

Buzzy Eastern European eatery
74 Blackfriars Road, Southwark, SE1 8HA
Tel no: (020) 7928 1111
www.balticrestaurant.co.uk
⊖ Southwark, map 5
Eastern European | £25
Cooking score: 2
£5 OFF £30

This vast room gussied up with abstract artwork has a buzz about it. The menu is based on Eastern Europe – confit of goose leg with beetroot and sour cherry, for example – but it can stray beyond these borders, say with a dish of delicious seared scallops paired with a purée

of chickpeas and butternut squash finished off with chilli. The repertoire is modern, yet rooted in tradition. Nalesniki crêpe filled with yoghurt, honey and fruit makes a creamy finish. When busy, the service is easily put off its stride. Polish vodka heads the drink list, with wines from £14.50.
Chef/s: Piotr Repinski. **Open:** Mon to Sat L 12 to 3, D 5.30 to 11. Sun 12 to 10.30. **Closed:** 24 to 27 Dec. **Meals:** alc (main courses £8 to £18). Set L and D £14.50 (2 courses) to £17.50. **Service:** 12.5% (optional). **Details:** Cards accepted. 100 seats. Air-con. Separate bar. Wheelchair access. Music. Children allowed.

Brinkley's Kitchen

Affordable crowd-pleaser
35 Bellevue Road, Wandsworth, SW17 7EF
Tel no: (020) 8672 5888
www.brinkleys.com
⊖ Balham, map 3
Modern European | £28
Cooking score: 1
£30

Part of John Brinkley's admirable empire, 'B's Kit' does the business on Bellevue Road with its neighbourhood vibes and easily priced victuals. The open kitchen sends out a zesty assortment of dishes with influences from all over – don't be surprised to see steamed chicken dim sum and teriyaki beef challenging Euro contenders such as calf's liver with pancetta or grilled monkfish and scallop spiedini. Burgers are a star turn and puds might include hot toffee cake. Brinkley's refreshing wine policy means that all bottles come with astonishingly low mark-ups (prices from £11).
Chef/s: Paolo Zanca. **Open:** all week L 12 to 4 (11 to 4 Sat and Sun), Mon to Sat D 6 to 11. **Closed:** 24 to 28 Dec. **Meals:** alc (main courses £8 to £23). Set L £12 (2 courses). Set D £15 (2 courses).
Service: 12.5% (optional). **Details:** Cards accepted. 60 seats. 20 seats outside. Air-con. Separate bar. Wheelchair access. Music. Children allowed.

London's Italian bargains

Good ingredients cost. That's why, outside of neighbourhood red sauce joints, eating Italian is a pricey business. Stellar produce is key, from the oil in your focaccia to the truffles on your taglierini.

However, there are ways of trying London's best Italian restaurants without spending your last euro.

At **Murano** in soigné Mayfair, Angela Hartnett does an excellent value set lunch at £30 for three courses. By lavishing her ingredients, both workaday and gourmet, with the attention they deserve, she delivers dishes that are more than the sum of their parts – just watch the wine list!

River Café alumnus **Theo Randall at the InterContinental** does a £27 three-course lunch that's also available pre- and post-theatre, and that never skimps on terrific ingredients.

At the casual end, trendy **Pizza East** is more than a pizzeria. Its salumi and cheese boards are excellent while its cheapest pizza, the margherita, is arguably its best. Meanwhile, at **Princi** in Soho, just a fiver or so will buy you a pasta, salad or antipasti dish at any time of day.

In the mid-range, Holloway Road's **500 Restaurant** and newcomer **Zucca** in Bermondsey have won plaudits for honest, affordable cooking that you can return to time and again.

ALSO RECOMMENDED
▲ The Butcher and Grill
39-41 Parkgate Road, Battersea, SW11 4NP
Tel no: (020) 7924 3999
www.thebutcherandgrill.com
map 3
Modern European

Ethically reared meat is the main draw at this bar-restaurant and bespoke butcher's shop. A family-friendly establishment with a no-frills approach to cooking, this a perfect place for steak flashed on the grill and served simply with chips, maybe with green peppercorn sauce (£12.75 for ribeye; £2.75 for chips). Other butcher's counter choices are sausages and lamb cutlets (£17.50), while alternatives include tagliatelle with feta, cherry tomatoes, broad beans and olives (£10.50) and crab risotto. Wines start at £14.50. Closed Sun. Also at 33 High Street, Wimbledon SW19 5BY, tel no: (020) 8944 8269.

Chapters All Day Dining
User-friendly brasserie
43-45 Montpelier Vale, Blackheath, SE3 OTJ
Tel no: (020) 8333 2666
www.chaptersrestaurants.com
map 1
Modern British | £25
Cooking score: 3
£30

Its name sums up what it does. The room is awash with natural light and accented with exposed brickwork, and there is a casual neighbourhood vibe; good-natured staff make a difference. The broad menu holds few surprises – the speciality is prime steaks cooked in a Josper charcoal oven. At a test meal, a trio of lightly baked scallops paired with chorizo and a sweet chilli dressing was right on the money. Equally competent was pan-fried sea bream with a spicy couscous and rose harissa, while blood orange and vanilla cream trifle with an espuma of blood orange was a cut above what you would expect from similar establishments. The wine list, which starts at £15.50, is easily navigable.

Chef/s: Trevor Tobin. **Open:** Mon to Sat 8am to 11pm, Sun 9am to 10pm. **Closed:** first week Jan. **Meals:** alc (main courses £9 to £24). **Service:** 12.5% (optional). **Details:** Cards accepted. 100 seats. 20 seats outside. Air-con. Separate bar. Wheelchair access. Music. Children allowed.

ALSO RECOMMENDED

▲ Le Chardon

65 Lordship Lane, East Dulwich, SE22 8EP
Tel no: (020) 8299 1921
www.lechardon.co.uk
map 1
French £5
OFF

Amid a wealth of Victorian tiling (it was a grocer's shop back in the old days) is an oasis of unreconstructed Frenchness, sure to be a hit with a sizeable chunk of the London restaurant-going constituency. They return eagerly for duck foie gras with brioche, prune and red onion chutney (£10.45), salmon with mussel and saffron sauce (£12.95) and crêpes suzette properly flamed with Grand Marnier (£5.95). Wines, not all French, start at £13.95. Open all week, from breakfast onwards.

Chez Bruce

Big-hitting neighbourhood star
2 Bellevue Road, Wandsworth, SW17 7EG
Tel no: (020) 8672 0114
www.chezbruce.co.uk
⊖ **Balham, map 3**
Modern British | £43
Cooking score: 6
🍾

'Some of the best food in London' is the reason why throngs of supporters continue to pack into Bruce Poole's personable local restaurant. This is a neighbourhood eatery of the best sort with a very special atmosphere; some say it's cramped, but a planned refurbishment should provide more elbow-room. The cooking pleases, excites and soothes in equal measure and the kitchen's strength is in its balance of straightforwardness, clever ideas and exact, rounded flavours. An avidly reported meal proves the point: after a foie gras and onion

tart, the happy recipients got their fill of duck breast on a bed of potato, beets, parsnips, shallots and French beans, as well as Cornish bream with a Spanish bean casserole and razor clams. To finish, an exemplary crème brûlée was simply perfect. Food such as this works magnificently because every component and ingredient is on-song. On other occasions, the kitchen has also hit the heights with a robust risotto bianco with snails, gésiers (gizzards), duck hearts and red wine, and rump of veal with chanterelles, calf's tongue, spätzle and thyme. Bruce Poole's sommelier blows diners away with a staggeringly good wine list that mixes top-flight names with representatives from lesser-known regions. A goodly clutch of house selections starts at £17.95.
Chef/s: Bruce Poole and Matt Christmas. **Open:** all week L 12 to 2.30 (3 Sat and Sun), D 6.30 to 10 (10.30 Fri and Sat, 7 to 9.30 Sun). **Closed:** 24 to 26 Dec, 1 Jan. **Meals:** Set L Mon to Fri £19.50 (2 courses) to £25.50. Set L Sat and Sun £32.50. Set D £31.50 (2 courses) to £42.50. **Service:** 12.5% (optional). **Details:** Cards accepted. 75 seats. Air-con. No music. No mobile phones. Wheelchair access.

Côte

Go-getting Gallic brasserie
8 High Street, Wimbledon Village, Wimbledon, SW19 5DX
Tel no: (020) 8947 7100
www.cote-restaurants.co.uk
⊖ **Wimbledon, map 3**
French | £25
Cooking score: 2
£30

The original branch of a go-getting Gallic brasserie chain that is spreading like wildfire across the capital and beyond, Côte brings a touch of Parisian *ooh-la-la* to the streets of Wimbledon. Robust French flavours, cheery continental vibes and brilliant value for money are the main inducements, with lunch and evening menus offering a glut of bourgeois classics from pissaladière or warm Roquefort and endive salad to steak haché, roast duck breast with griottine cherry sauce

and much-loved desserts including apple tarte fine or dark chocolate mousse. Breakfasts and weekend brunch are equally enticing for the locals, and the all-French wine list starts at £13.95. Visit www.cote-restaurants.co.uk for details of other branches.
Chef/s: Lucasz Horynski. **Open:** all week 8am to 11pm (9am to 11pm Sat, 9am to 10.30pm Sun). **Closed:** 25 Dec. **Meals:** alc (main courses £9 to £18). Set L and D £9.95 (two courses) to £11.90. **Service:** 12.5% (optional). **Details:** Cards accepted. 90 seats. 8 seats outside. Air-con. Wheelchair access. Music. Children allowed.

Delfina

Fashionable flavours and shining ingredients
50 Bermondsey Street, Southwark, SE1 3UD
Tel no: (020) 7357 0244
www.thedelfina.co.uk
⊖ London Bridge, map 1
Fusion | £25
New Chef
£5 £30
OFF

A short walk from London Bridge Station brings you to this former chocolate factory and its smart white-walled dining space, which houses regularly changing art exhibitions. As we went to press we learned that the restaurant was in the process of appointing yet another new chef. It's likely that the simple approach, focusing on assemblages in which the top-quality ingredients are allowed to shine will continue. Previously, the short menu offered main courses ranging from beef and pork belly burger with apple and tomato relish to cod with mussel, Kaffir lime and coconut sauce, crushed Jersey Royals and samphire, with sharing slates of charcuterie, fish or vegetables making a light lunch or a simple start. Opening times may be limited, but Delfina is tailor-made for contemporary private parties.
Open: Sun to Fri 8am to 5pm (11.30 to 5 Sun), Fri D 7 to 10. **Closed:** Sat, 25 to 31 Dec, bank hols. **Meals:** alc (main courses £10 to £15). **Service:** 12.5% (optional). **Details:** Cards accepted. 80 seats. 12 seats outside. Wheelchair access. Music. Children allowed.

Emile's

An enduring favourite
96-98 Felsham Road, Putney, SW15 1DQ
Tel no: (020) 8789 3323
www.emilesrestaurant.co.uk
⊖ Putney Bridge, map 3
Anglo-French | £27
Cooking score: 1
£5 £30
OFF

Well away from the dreary parade of chain eateries found on Putney High Street, reporters thoroughly enjoy the 'genuine personal approach' at Emil Fahmy's well-established restaurant. The menu is a monthly changing mix of French and British classics – think seared foie gras and the ever-popular individual beef Wellington. For one reporter, a meal that opened with an 'exquisite crispy piece of pork belly', went on to lamb rump with minted hazelnut crust, and finished with lavender pannacotta, was 'a bargain' for the quality of the food. House wine is £13.75.
Chef/s: Andrew Sherlock. **Open:** Mon to Sat D only 7.30 to 11. **Closed:** Sun, banks hols, 24 to 30 Dec, 2 Jan, Easter Sat. **Meals:** Set D £23.50 (2 courses) to £26.50. **Service:** not inc. **Details:** Cards accepted. 100 seats. No mobile phones. Music. Children allowed.

Enoteca Turi

Popular Italian with devoted local fans
28 Putney High Street, Putney, SW15 1SQ
Tel no: (020) 8785 4449
www.enotecaturi.com
⊖ Putney Bridge, map 3
Italian | £35
Cooking score: 3
🍷 V

Restaurateur Giuseppe Turi celebrates 21 years in Putney in 2011, and his popular Italian still puts the emphasis firmly on traditional country cooking. No wonder he has a devoted local following. Neatly dressed tables, a feeling of comfort and space, and on-the-ball waiting staff set the tone for such dishes as warm salad of veal kidneys with baby spinach, lemon and rosemary dressing, delicate gnocchi with Apulian plum tomato, stracciatella and basil or a main course of Abruzzi-style slow-cooked lamb with courgettes, asparagus, spring onion and a brodettato (egg and lemon) sauce. Elsewhere there could be a selection of cured meats, wonderful seafood linguine, and 'excellent wine suggestions at reasonable prices' to go with each course. The impressive range of Italian wines comes with detailed tasting notes, giving an exhaustive picture of what is happening in Italian viticulture nowadays. Bottles from £16.

Chef/s: Massimo Tagliaferri. **Open:** Mon to Sat L 12 to 2.30, D 7 to 10.30 (11 Fri and Sat). **Closed:** Sun, 25 and 26 Dec, 1 Jan. **Meals:** alc (main courses £13 to £25). Set L £15.50 (2 courses) to £18.50. Set D £25.50 (2 courses) to £29.50. **Service:** 12.5% (optional). **Details:** Cards accepted. 85 seats. Air-con. No mobile phones. Wheelchair access. Music. Children allowed.

ALSO RECOMMENDED

▲ Franco Manca

4 Market Row, Brixton, SW9 8LD
Tel no: (020) 7738 3021
www.francomanca.co.uk
⊖ Brixton, map 1
Italian £5 OFF

This Brixton Market pizzeria proves that pizza, done well, is a thing of wonder. Toppings are restricted to just six choices, for example organic tomato, mozzarella and basil (£5.30) or home-cured Gloucester Old Spot (£6.10). But it's the chewy sourdough crust, characterised by a perfectly bubbled and lightly charred 'cornicione' (edge) that Franco Manca really wows. Only its intransigence on certain matters (no white coffees, no reservations, no desserts and just two wines, £9.20) may irk. Closed Sun. The Chiswick branch opens evenings – 144 Chiswick High Road, W14; tel: (020) 8747 4822.

Franklins

British food with a beating heart
157 Lordship Lane, East Dulwich, SE22 8HX
Tel no: (020) 8299 9598
www.franklinsrestaurant.com
map 1
British | £29
Cooking score: 2
£5 OFF £30

A farm shop across the road has beefed up the patriotic British offering at this exemplary Dulwich destination. With a rumbustious wine bar out front and a bare-bones dining room beyond, it's a thumpingly good neighbourhood destination offering food without airs or graces. The kitchen turns tricks with down-home ingredients from the native larder – serving ox tongue with pease pudding, cod with mash and parsley sauce and pork belly with red cabbage. To finish, vanilla blancmange has been 'sensationally good'; alternatively pick a classic Brit savoury (perhaps Scotch woodcock). The short, sharp wine list starts at £14. Note that Franklins' sister restaurant in Kennington has closed.

Chef/s: Ralf Wittig. **Open:** all week 12 to 10.30 (10am to 10.30pm Sat). **Closed:** 25 and 26 Dec, 1 Jan. **Meals:** alc (main courses £14 to £21). Set L £13.50 (2 courses) to £16.50. **Service:** not inc. **Details:** Cards accepted. 65 seats. 12 seats outside. Separate bar. No music. Wheelchair access. Children allowed.

Harrison's

A happy local eatery
15-19 Bedford Hill, Balham, SW12 9EX
Tel no: (020) 8675 6900
www.harrisonsbalham.co.uk
⊖ Balham, map 3
Modern British | £26
Cooking score: 1
V £30

Since opening in July 2007, this bustling eatery, an offshoot of Sam's Brasserie in Chiswick (see entry), has become a much loved and frequented Balham favourite. The kitchen is firmly in touch with today's trends and well-reported dishes have included seared salmon burger with wasabi mayo and venison escalopes with braised red cabbage. Set lunches, early-bird dinners, weekend brunch and Sunday night jazz add to the appeal. House wine is £14.50.

Chef/s: Nick Stones. **Open:** all week L 12 to 4 (9 to 4 Sat and Sun), D 6 to 10.30 (6.30 to 10.30 Sat, 6.30 to 10 Sun). **Closed:** 24 to 29 Dec. **Meals:** alc (main courses £11 to £20). Set L £12.50 (2 courses) to £15.50. Set D £14 (2 courses) to £17. Sun L £20.50. **Service:** 12.5% (optional). **Details:** Cards accepted. 90 seats. 10 seats outside. Air-con. Separate bar. Wheelchair access. Music. Children allowed.

Inside

Stylish bistro
19 Greenwich South Street, Greenwich, SE10 8NW
Tel no: (020) 8265 5060
www.insiderestaurant.co.uk
map 1
Modern European | £28
Cooking score: 1
£30

A stripped wood floor, small modern artworks and a general air of understated chic distinguish Guy Awford's stylish Greenwich restaurant. Tagliatelle with prawns, followed by wild halibut with roast aubergine and garlic greens in a tomato coulis sent one pair of seafood-lovers away happy, or there might be seared beef fillet in bourguignon jus with a potato and onion galette. Finish with rum baba, or pecan tart with whipped cream. House wines are Languedoc blends at £14.50.

Chef/s: Guy Awford and Brian Sargeant. **Open:** Tue to Sun L 12 to 2.30 (3 Sun), Tue to Sat D 6.30 to 11. **Closed:** Mon, 24 Dec to 2 Jan. **Meals:** alc (main courses £13 to £19). Set L £11.95 (2 courses) to £15.95. Set D £16.95 (2 courses) to £20.95. Sun L £17.95 (2 courses) to £21.95. **Service:** not inc. **Details:** Cards accepted. 36 seats. Air-con. No mobile phones. Wheelchair access. Music. Children allowed.

Kastoori

Tooting's Gujarati treasure
188 Upper Tooting Road, Tooting, SW17 7EJ
Tel no: (020) 8767 7027
www.kastoorirestaurant.com
⊖ Tooting Broadway, Tooting Bec, map 3
Indian Vegetarian | £21
Cooking score: 3
V £30

Manoj and Dinesh Thanki's Gujarati-style restaurant is considered one of the most consistent addresses for vegetarian food in London. Décor is plain but vivid – bright colours and Hindu sculptures add a touch of exoticism – while the kitchen takes its cue from the owners' native Katia Wahd (a temperate region famed for its tomatoes). The good-value menu moves from mainstay appetisers such as puris and samosas to intriguing vegetable curries (try the special tomato curry or mutter panir) and speciality dishes inspired by the Thanki family's time in Uganda – perhaps matoki (a green banana curry) or kasodi (sweetcorn in coconut milk with a ground peanut sauce). Finish in traditional style with kheer, an aromatic rice pudding. House wine is £11.95.

Chef/s: Manoj Thanki. **Open:** Wed to Sun L 12.30 to 2.30, all week D 6 to 10.30. **Closed:** 25 and 26 Dec. **Meals:** alc (main courses £6 to £7). **Service:** not inc. **Details:** Cards accepted. 82 seats. Air-con. Separate bar. No mobile phones. Music. Children allowed. Car parking.

Lamberts

Gutsy local restaurant
2 Station Parade, Balham, SW12 9AZ
Tel no: (020) 8675 2233
www.lambertsrestaurant.com
⊖ Balham, map 3
British | £30
New Chef
£5 OFF

It's inevitable that chefs move around, and we learned of Ryan Lowery's appointment too late to respond with an inspection. Hopefully this gutsy local restaurant will continue to offer a brand of straightforward cooking based on good seasonal produce – with dishes along the lines of baby beetroot salad with horseradish crisp and punchy main courses of nut-crusted pollack fillet with red wine shallots, turnip mash and roasted swede or slow-roasted Saddleback pork belly with green lentils, salsify and trotter fritters. There's been praise for the Herdwick mutton, too. House wine is £16. Reports please.

Chef/s: Ryan Lowery. **Open:** Sat and Sun L 12 to 3 (5 Sun), Tue to Sat D 7 to 10.30. **Closed:** Mon, 25 and 26 Dec, 1 Jan. **Meals:** alc (main courses £16 to £18). Set L and D £17 (2 courses) to £24. Sun L £24. **Service:** 12.5% (optional). **Details:** Cards accepted. 53 seats. Air-con. Wheelchair access. Music. Children allowed.

Light House
Good-value global food
75-77 Ridgway, Wimbledon, SW19 4ST
Tel no: (020) 8944 6338
www.lighthousewimbledon.com
⊖ Wimbledon, map 3
Modern European | £30
Cooking score: 3

£5 OFF

The leafy suburban surroundings provide most of this restaurant's faithful customers, who for over a decade have loved its 'excellent value, interesting menu and helpful staff'. A sleek, understated interior sets the tone for a modern repertoire crammed with international flavours. Starters typically range from grilled tuna with papaya, green beans, chilli, tamarind and coriander to a red wine-braised pork and apple faggot with potato purée. After that, maybe a simple grilled ribeye with chips, red wine and rosemary gravy or fresh spaghetti with red pepper and tomato pesto and goats' cheese. Desserts have a similar scope, from pear clafoutis to tonka bean pannacotta. The set lunch offers excellent value. House wines are priced from £14.50.

Chef/s: Chris Casey. **Open:** all week L 12 to 2.45 (3 Sun), Mon to Sat D 6 to 10.30 (10.45 Fri and Sat). **Closed:** 24 to 27 Dec. **Meals:** alc (main courses £12 to £23). Set L £11.50 (2 courses) to £14.50. Early set

D £14.50 (2 courses) to £18.50. Sun L £18.50 (2 courses). **Service:** 12.5% (optional). **Details:** Cards accepted. 75 seats. 14 seats outside. Air-con. Wheelchair access. Music. Children allowed.

ALSO RECOMMENDED

▲ Lobster Pot
3 Kennington Lane, Elephant and Castle, SE11 4RG
Tel no: (020) 7582 5556
www.lobsterpotrestaurant.co.uk
⊖ Kennington, map 1
Seafood £5 OFF

Celebrating 20 years in 2011, this very French, very nautical and very idiosyncratic restaurant continues to delight with its maritime sound effects, an interior resembling a trawler cabin and house specialities of bouillabaisse (£20.50) and plateaux de fruits de mer. Elsewhere there are oysters gratinated with a Champagne sauce (£11.50), fillet of grouper with Cajun spices and white butter sauce and French duck stew with sweet-and-sour sauce and flageolet beans. Try tarte Tatin (£8.50) for dessert. House French £17.50. Closed Sun and Mon.

Magdalen
Earthy flavours and astute cooking
152 Tooley Street, Southwark, SE1 2TU
Tel no: (020) 7403 1342
www.magdalenrestaurant.co.uk
⊖ London Bridge, map 1
Modern British | £30
Cooking score: 3

James Faulks' double-decker of a restaurant is a highly useful south London bolt hole with plenty of buzz and uncluttered vibes – especially in the handsome upstairs room. The kitchen does a good line in unusual things on toast – perhaps roast quail with snails and garlic or veal kidneys with spinach and onion purée. It's also happy to celebrate the humbler things of life – ham and parsley terrine, baked rabbit with shallots and mustard, or lamb's tongues with white beans, stewed tomatoes and rosemary are some possibilities from the ingredients-led daily menu. Earthy flavours and astute cooking are the keys, and there's no fussing around when it comes to desserts either: steamed marmalade pudding with custard is par for the course. The wine list has some 'interesting' bottles at fair prices, from £19 (£4.75 a glass).

Chef/s: James Faulks. **Open:** Mon to Fri L 12 to 2.30, Mon to Sat D 6.30 to 10. **Closed:** Sun, bank hols, 2 weeks Aug, 10 days Christmas. **Meals:** alc (main courses £14 to £24). Set L £15.50 (2 courses) to £18.50. **Service:** 12.5% (optional). **Details:** Cards accepted. 90 seats. 6 seats outside. Air-con. Wheelchair access. Music. Children allowed.

READERS RECOMMEND

Maltings Café

Mediterranean
169 Tower Bridge Road, Bermondsey, SE1 3NA
Tel no: (020) 7378 7961
www.maltingscafe.co.uk
'This simple and unpretentious café offers a daily changing blackboard menu – try the orange polenta cake'

NEW ENTRY

More

Versatile café with big ideas
104 Tooley Street, Southwark, SE1 2TH
Tel no: (020) 7403 0635
www.moretooleystreet.com
⊖ **London Bridge, map 1**
Modern European | £28
Cooking score: 2
£30

You have to hand it to Theodore Kyriakou and Paloma Campbell – they don't stop. The founders of Livebait and the Real Greek have, for their third act, opened this simple, funky café close to London Bridge Station and across the road from More London and the Hilton Hotel. It's a versatile space, serving breakfast onwards, with an open bar/kitchen and dressed-down service going hand in hand with simple, well-prepared Mediterranean dishes. Grilled squid, chorizo, rocket and avocado salad with a romesco dressing and baked aubergine 'imam bayaldi' with herbed

goats' cheese are typical choices. The package also includes a good-value set lunch and Sunday brunch. House wine is £15.50.

Chef/s: Theodore Kyriakou. **Open:** Mon to Fri 7.30am to 11pm, Sat 12 to 11. **Closed:** Sun, bank hols. **Meals:** alc (main courses £13 to £17). Set L and D (to 7pm) £12.50 (2 courses). **Service:** 12.5% (optional). **Details:** Cards accepted. 32 seats. Air-con. Separate bar. Wheelchair access. Music. Children allowed.

READERS RECOMMEND

Numero Uno

Italian
32 Tooting Bec Road, Tooting, SW17 8BD
Tel no: (020) 8767 9395
'Delicious, generously proportioned classics – just leave room for the puds!'

Platform

Modern British
56-58 Tooley Street, Southwark, SE1 2SZ
Tel no: (020) 7403 6388
www.platformse1.co.uk
'An amazing restaurant. It is very original – food direct from the farm!'

Le Pont de la Tour

French favourite by the river
36d Shad Thames, Bermondsey, SE1 2YE
Tel no: (020) 7403 8403
www.lepontdelatour.com
⊖ **Tower Hill, London Bridge, map 1**
Modern French | £43
Cooking score: 3
£5 OFF ♦ V

Picture-postcard views of the Thames and Tower Bridge (the restaurant's namesake) are a huge bonus at this South Bank fixture – just pray that the weather's kind and you can bag a seat on the terrace. Inside, the choice is between the special-occasion, yellow-walled dining room and the high-decibel bar/grill. Either way, the accent is predominantly French, simplicity is the key and fish is a major player. Plump for the restaurant and you can look forward to starters of West Mersea oysters or seared scallops with cauliflower alongside an assiette of Vendée quail with boudin noir. After that, poached halibut with braised Swiss chard and Champagne caviar sauce might sit next to a 'cushion' of Yorkshire venison with braised red cabbage. Desserts promise flambés, brûlées and chocolate marquise souped up with liquorice cream. France leads on the mighty wine list, although the auspicious selection has been infiltrated by some cracking German reds, Slovenian obscurities and rare gems from the Antipodes. Prices start at £22.

Chef/s: Lee Bennett. **Open:** all week L 12 to 3 (4 Sat and Sun), D 6 to 11 (10 Sun). **Meals:** Set L £26.50 (2 courses) to £31.50. Set D £42.50. Sun L £27.50. **Service:** not inc. **Details:** Cards accepted. 110 seats. 70 seats outside. Separate bar. No mobile phones. Wheelchair access. Music. Children allowed.

Ransome's Dock
Dreamy dining by the Thames
35-37 Parkgate Road, Battersea, SW11 4NP
Tel no: (020) 7223 1611
www.ransomesdock.co.uk
map 3
Modern British | £33
Cooking score: 3
£5 OFF

Dreamy meals out on the riverside terrace are one of the enduring pleasures at Martin and Vanessa Lam's Battersea stalwart – although food and wine never play second fiddle to the views. The Lams have always championed regional produce, and their meticulous sourcing yields Lincolnshire smoked eel, Elwy lamb, free-range Creedy Carver duck and much more. Char-grilled quail comes with a salad of dandelion, dates and oranges, venison and chestnut pie is served with buttered Brussels sprout tops, and desserts might run to poached quince with gingerbread and clotted cream. But any patriotism is tempered by a broad-minded approach that accommodates polenta as well as bubble and squeak, while giving the nod to Elizabeth David's generous bourgeois style – her spinach and ricotta gnocchi is a perennial

favourite. Martin Lam's brilliant wine list is a model of quality over showiness, with a procession of stellar names from France, Italy and California in particular, plus a wondrous choice of halves. A page of house selections starts at £14.50 (£5.25 a glass).

Chef/s: Martin and Vanessa Lam. **Open:** all week L 12 to 5 (3.30 Sun), Mon to Sat D 5 to 11. **Closed:** Christmas, Aug bank hol. **Meals:** alc (main courses £12 to £23). Set L £15.50 (2 courses). Sun L £22.50. **Service:** 12.5% (optional). **Details:** Cards accepted. 55 seats. 24 seats outside. Separate bar. Wheelchair access. Music. Children allowed.

Rick's Café
Friendly Tooting treat
122 Mitcham Road, Tooting, SW17 9NH
Tel no: (020) 8767 5219
⊖ Tooting Broadway, map 3
Modern European | £26
Cooking score: 1
£5 OFF £30

'Such a friendly and welcoming little place, no pretensions at all, just what you want for a local restaurant', sums up one regular, catching the tone of this Tooting favourite. Other pluses are the 'wonderfully fresh and tasty' cooking and 'excellent value'. Reporters have enjoyed salt cod and mackerel croquettes, twice-baked goats' cheese soufflé with rhubarb compote, gnocchi with 'little Spanish sausages in a delicate tomato sauce', and sea bass with spinach, soy sauce and ginger. Finish with Baileys chocolate mousse. House Spanish is £12.50.

Chef/s: Ricardo Gibbs. **Open:** Tue to Fri L 12 to 3 (10 to 3 Sat and 10 to 4 Sun), Tue to Sat D 6 to 11. **Closed:** Sun, Mon, 25 and 26 Dec, 1 Jan. **Meals:** alc (main courses £7 to £13). **Service:** 12.5% (optional). **Details:** Cards accepted. 35 seats. No mobile phones. Wheelchair access. Music. Children allowed.

Also recommended

Also recommended entries are not scored but we think they are worth a visit.

Roast

Barnstorming foodie patriot
Floral Hall, Stoney Street, Southwark, SE1 1TL
Tel no: (0845) 034 7300
www.roast-restaurant.com
⊖ London Bridge, map 1
British | £38
Cooking score: 3
£5 OFF

New Brit foodie patriotism is alive and kicking at Roast – a barnstorming eatery in Borough Market's Floral Hall, overlooking the gastronomic mêlée below. Self-styled 'head cook' Lawrence Keogh plunders the stalls, but also plucks the best from artisan producers across the land – check the back of the menu to find out who's behind the grub on your plate. The seasonal haul might bring wild garlic and spinach soup, hot Scotch egg with pea shoots, peppered red deer fillet with quince jelly, or pollack with smoked mackerel fritters and watercress sauce – not forgetting mighty roasts. Neal's Yard Dairy does the cheese lobby proud, and for pud there might be Yorkshire rhubarb crumble. Breakfast is a top deal for the market crowd, and the drinks list champions all things British. Wines start at £23, with plenty of affordable stuff by the glass.
Chef/s: Lawrence Keogh. **Open:** all week L 12 to 2.45 (3.45 Thur to Sat, 11.30 to 6 Sun), Mon to Sat D 5.30 to 10.30 (6 to 10.30 Sat). **Closed:** 25 and 26 Dec, 31 Dec and 1 Jan. **Meals:** alc (main courses £14 to £30). Set L and D £26 (3 courses).
Service: 12.5%. **Details:** Cards accepted. 125 seats. Air-con. Separate bar. Wheelchair access. Music. Children allowed.

RSJ

Well-supported South Bank veteran
33 Coin Street, Southwark, SE1 9NR
Tel no: (020) 7928 4554
www.rsj.uk.com
⊖ Waterloo, Southwark, map 5
Modern British | £30
Cooking score: 3
£5 OFF 🍷 V

The dear old RSJ, stalwart of many a Guide gone by (see the longest-serving list at the front) continues to draw support from readers. 'We usually come before going to the National Theatre. They always ensure that we are served in plenty of time to go on to the performance', is one typical comment; 'it is good value for money', is another. The cooking is driven by well-sourced produce, intelligent simplicity and assured execution in dishes such as fresh crab linguine with ginger, garlic and chilli or roast rump of lamb with spring vegetables, minted Jersey Royals and lamb jus. Desserts such as rhubarb and lemon posset and ginger shortbread are equally well-made. The Loire is explored in great depth by the superbly organised wine list, supplemented by bottles from the rest of France, with just a handful from elsewhere. Prices start at £16.95.
Chef/s: Ian Stabler and Alex Lovett. **Open:** Mon to Fri L 12 to 3, Mon to Sat D 5.30 to 11. **Closed:** Sun, 24 to 27 Dec, Good Fri. **Meals:** alc (main courses £15 to £19). Set L and D £16.95 (2 courses) to £18.95.
Service: 12.5% (optional). **Details:** Cards accepted. 90 seats. 12 seats outside. Air-con. No music. Children allowed.

Skylon

The setting's the star

Southbank Centre, Belvedere Road, South Bank, SE1 8XX

Tel no: (020) 7654 7800

www.skylonrestaurant.co.uk

⊖ Waterloo, map 5

Modern European | £45

Cooking score: 2

This vast space on level 3 of the Royal Festival Hall is a symphony of harmonious tones (olives, greys, browns, a dash of carmine) with floor-to-ceiling windows giving a sweeping view of the Thames (obscured partially in summer by trees). It houses a bar, a casual but pricey brasserie/grill – lobster risotto, burgers, onglet steak and confit duck leg – and a more formal restaurant, distinguished by its white-clothed tables. Here a spring lunch took in crispy soft-shelled crab with heritage tomatoes, shaved fennel and aïoli, and confit organic salmon with spring vegetables à la grecque, guacamole and shellfish mousseline. House wine is £21.

Chef/s: Helena Puolakka. **Open:** Restaurant all week L 12 to 2.30 (4 Sun), Mon to Sat D 5.30 to 10.30. Grill all week 12 to 11 (10.30pm Sun). **Closed:** 25 Dec. **Meals:** alc (main courses £12 to £30). Grill Set L £15 (2 courses) to £18. Grill theatre menu £22.50 (2 courses) to £19. Restaurant Set L £23.50 (2 courses) to £27.50. Restaurant Set D £40 (2 courses) to £45. Sun L £28.50 (2 courses) to £31.50. **Service:** 12.5% (optional). **Details:** Cards accepted. 94 seats. Air-con. Separate bar. Wheelchair access. Music. Children allowed.

NEW ENTRY

Swan at the Globe

English classics with a contemporary edge

21 New Globe Walk, Bankside, SE1 9DT

Tel no: (020) 7928 9444

www.swanattheglobe.co.uk

⊖ Blackfriars, London Bridge, Mansion House, map 5

Modern British | £30

Cooking score: 4

Slightly too posh to be classed as a gastropub and rather too good for a pre-theatre dine-and-dash, this first-floor brasserie in Shakespeare's Globe gives English classics a contemporary edge. Fashionably simple and mostly seasonal, a Northumbrian pan haggerty may appear on the menu alongside baked trout or roast pork chop with fennel and apple salad. A superlative côte de boeuf, chosen from a handful of French favourites, impressed at inspection, served on a wooden board with grilled mushrooms lacquered with meat jus, watercress and a silky bowl of pommes mousseline. The stunning vista across the river to St Paul's is a major bonus, though you're unlikely to get a window seat unless you demand one when booking. On the downside, poor acoustics make the room noisy when full, and slightly intrusive music can irritate when it isn't. There is an excellent wine list starting at £16.

Chef/s: Kieren Steinborn. **Open:** all week L 12 to 2.30 (11 Sat, 11 to 5 Sun), Mon to Sat D 6 to 10. **Closed:** 1 Jan. **Meals:** alc (main courses £12 to £19). Sun L £17.95 (2 courses) to £19.95. **Service:** 12.5% (optional). **Details:** Cards accepted. 90 seats. Separate bar. Wheelchair access. Music. Children allowed.

Tapas Brindisa

Palate-teasing taste of Spain
18-20 Southwark Street, Southwark, SE1 1TJ
Tel no: (020) 7357 8880
www.brindisatapaskitchens.com
⊖ Borough, London Bridge, map 1
Tapas | £20
Cooking score: 3
V £30

The mother ship of a bristling Spanish foodie armada, cheery Tapas Brindisa goes about its business just steps away from Borough Market's edible cornucopia. Set in a defunct potato warehouse with mirrored walls, jam-packed tables and concrete floors, it dishes up authentic tapas fashioned from top-drawer imported provisions. Come here for acorn-fed Ibérico charcuterie, cured fish, artisan cheeses and rustic breads, plus an array of hot and cold dishes ranging from cups of green pea soup with Manchego to roast butternut squash with rosemary via pan-fried sea bass with beetroot and orange salad or crispy pork belly with quince sauce. Desserts don't stray far from crema catalana and turrón mousse, but there's plenty to lift the spirits among the Spanish sherries and regional wines (from £15.75). Siblings Casa Brindisa and Tierra Brindisa are out of the same mould (see entries).
Chef/s: Esperanza Anonuevo. **Open:** Mon to Sat L 12 to 3 (4 Fri and Sat), D 5.30 to 11. Sun 12 to 10. **Closed:** 25 and 26 Dec, 1 Jan. **Meals:** alc (tapas from £5 to £13). **Service:** 12.5% (optional). **Details:** Cards accepted. 45 seats. 25 seats outside. Separate bar. Wheelchair access. Music. Children allowed.

Please send us your feedback

To register your opinion about any restaurant listed in the Guide, or a new restaurant that you wish to bring to our attention, please visit the web address at the bottom of the page. Your feedback informs the content of the book and will be used to compile next year's reviews.

Tentazioni

Artful Italian food and conviviality
Lloyds Wharf, 2 Mill Street, Bermondsey, SE1 2BD
Tel no: (020) 7237 1100
www.tentazioni.co.uk
⊖ Bermondsey, London Bridge, map 1
Italian | £42
Cooking score: 3
£5 OFF **V**

The shimmering red colour scheme at Riccardo Giacomini's Italian restaurant near Tower Bridge is by no means the least striking aspect of the place. An evening might well be accompanied mellifluously by an opera singer, and there are jazz and special wine-themed occasions. It makes for a thoroughly convivial operation, and the artful modern Italian cooking on offer enhances that impression. Fish and meat partnerships are favoured. An open lasagne of black pasta is topped with king scallops, veal sweetbreads and artichokes for a thought-provoking starter, while mains might include a pairing of beef fillet and lobster tail with spinach and lemony hollandaise. Fine Italian cheeses and ice creams conclude things satisfyingly, and there is an enterprising listing of mostly Italian wines, from £13.
Chef/s: Riccardo Giacomini. **Open:** Mon to Fri L 12 to 3, Mon to Sat D 6.30 to 10.45. **Closed:** Sun, 25 to 28 Dec, bank hols. **Meals:** alc (main courses £13 to £23). Set L £11.95 (2 courses) to £15. **Service:** 12.5% (optional). **Details:** Cards accepted. 50 seats. Wheelchair access. Music. Children allowed.

Tom Ilic

Big on gutsy meat cookery
123 Queenstown Road, Battersea, SW8 3RH
Tel no: (020) 7622 0555
www.tomilic.com
map 3
European | £25
Cooking score: 2
£5 OFF £30

Tom Ilic has previous form at this Battersea site, having cooked up a storm here when it was the Stepping Stone. His eponymous restaurant got off to a good start, but recent reports have been mixed. There's no doubting Ilic's flair, particularly when it comes to all things porcine – the signature starter of braised pig's cheeks and chorizo and a gutsy main course of seared scallops with pork belly both do his talent justice – but imprecise cooking and scrappy presentation mar other dishes. Service can also be listless. When on form, however, it's a dream local restaurant. Wines from £14.75.

Chef/s: Tom Ilic. **Open:** Wed to Sun L 12 to 2.30 (3.30 Sun), Tue to Sat D 6 to 10.30. **Closed:** Mon. **Meals:** alc (main courses £13 to £17). Set L £14.50 (2 courses) to £16.95. Set D and Sun L £16.95 (2 courses) to £21.50. **Service:** 12.5% (optional). **Details:** Cards accepted. 62 seats. Air-con. Separate bar. Wheelchair access. Music. Children allowed.

Trinity
Neighbourhood high-achiever
4 The Polygon, Clapham, SW4 0JG
Tel no: (020) 7622 1199
www.trinityrestaurant.co.uk
⊖ Clapham Common, map 3
Modern European | £35
Cooking score: 4
£5
OFF

In the heart of Clapham's old town, opposite the library and close to the Common, Trinity is a high-achieving neighbourhood restaurant. Chic and stylish, it opens up at the front for summer lunches, and is a place that means business, as is evident from Adam Byatt's imaginative modern European menus. A reporter who began with crackled pig's trotter on toasted sourdough with fried quails' eggs and gribiche applauded its intensity and winning combinations. Mackerel might appear two ways, cold tartare and hot grilled, with beetroot and horseradish, before a main course selection that mobilises today's slow, gentle cooking temperatures to great effect – either in rabbit loin with figs, pistachios, chanterelles and tarragon gnocchi, or blade of beef braised in Guinness. 'Rich and superb' was the verdict on the irresistible Valrhona chocolate 'hot-pot' dessert served with fig and

honey ice cream, and there are Neal's Yard Dairy cheeses for the savoury of tooth. Good drinking starts at £19 a bottle.

Chef/s: Adam Byatt and Jo Sharratt. **Open:** Tue to Sun L 12.30 to 2.30 (4 Sun), Mon to Sat D 6.30 to 11. **Closed:** 24 to 28 Dec. **Meals:** alc (main courses £16 to £28). Set L £15 (2 courses) to £20. Set D (Mon to Thur, by prior booking only) £20. Sun L £25. Tasting menu £38. **Service:** 12.5% (optional). **Details:** Cards accepted. 65 seats. Air-con. No music. Wheelchair access. Children allowed.

Tsunami
Fusion-tinged Japanese food
5-7 Voltaire Road, Clapham, SW4 6DQ
Tel no: (020) 7978 1610
www.tsunamirestaurant.co.uk
⊖ Clapham North, map 3
Japanese | £26
Cooking score: 2
V £30

A sleek oriental fixture down by Clapham's railway sidings, Tsunami celebrates its tenth birthday in 2011. Since opening, the kitchen has honed its style, flattering its affluent audience with fashionable Japanese food and flashes of fusion in the shape of 'semi-grilled' oysters with pan-fried foie gras, truffle mayo and black caviar, wasabi lamb, or roasted pork belly with Chinese water spinach and piri-piri hoisin. Fans of sushi, sashimi, tempura and claypot sizzlers are well served, and there's black cod in miso for those who can't make it to Nobu (see entry). Snazzy cocktails and sakés bolster an eclectic choice of wines from £16. There's a branch at 93 Charlotte Street, W1T 4PY, tel: (020) 7637 0050.

Chef/s: Ken Sam. **Open:** Sat and Sun L 12.30 to 4, all week D 6 to 10.30 (11 Fri, 5.30 to 11 Sat, 6 to 9.30 Sun). **Closed:** 25 to 27 Dec. **Meals:** alc (main courses £8 to £18). Set L £10.50. **Service:** 12.5% (optional). **Details:** Cards accepted. 80 seats. 28 seats outside. Air-con. Separate bar. Wheelchair access. Music. Children allowed.

ALSO RECOMMENDED
▲ Village East

171-173 Bermondsey Street, Southwark, SE1 3UW
Tel no: (020) 7357 6082
www.villageeast.co.uk
⊖ London Bridge, map 1
Modern European

A big, bustling warehouse conversion not far
from London Bridge, Village East offers a
versatile style of modern brasserie cooking,
complete with an open-plan kitchen and
cocktail bars. Reverse the wording of the
name, and you'll appreciate the New York
styling of the place. The range encompasses
soft-shell crabs with watermelon and wasabi
(£11.40), roast pheasant breast with smoked
bacon, creamed kale and celeriac (£15.40),
and chocolate tart with mixed berry compote
(£5). Wines from £3.80 a glass. Open all
week.

Wright Brothers Oyster & Porter House

Aficionado's guide to oysters
11 Stoney Street, Southwark, SE1 9AD
Tel no: (020) 7403 9554
www.wrightbros.eu.com
⊖ London Bridge, map 1
Seafood | £25
Cooking score: 2
£30

Head down the alleyways across from
Borough Market to find this good-natured
bar and eating house; 'it's like a scene out of
Dickens', thought one visitor. Inside there's
exposed brickwork, and you eat perched at a
wooden counter or at communal tables –
perfect for slurping some of the finest oysters
around. If you want a change from bivalves,
the kitchen can also turn out a very competent
fish soup with rouille, a Med-influenced dish
of razor clams with chorizo and chickpeas that
hit all the right notes for one visitor, and a
decent beef and Guinness pie. Wines start from
£18.50. The Wright Brothers have also taken
their mollusc concept to Cornwall with the

opening of the Ferryboat Inn, Helford
Passage, near Falmouth, tel: (01326) 250625 –
reports please.
Chef/s: Phillip Coulter. **Open:** all week L 12 to 3 (4
Sat and Sun), D 6 to 10.30 (9 Sun). **Closed:** 25 and
26 Dec, bank hols. **Meals:** alc (main courses from
£10 to £22). **Service:** not inc. **Details:** Cards
accepted. 35 seats. No music. Wheelchair access.
Children allowed.

NEW ENTRY
Zucca
Vibrant Italian bursting with flavours
184 Bermondsey Street, Bermondsey, SE1 3TQ
Tel no: (020) 7378 6809
www.zuccalondon.com
⊖ London Bridge, Borough, map 1
Italian | £22
Cooking score: 3
£30

If vibrant Italian cooking bursting with fresh
flavours, close-set tables, plenty of noise and
an open-plan kitchen sounds familiar, it's
because the team behind this modern Italian
restaurant are ex-River Café (see entry). Zucca
fritti – battered and deep-fried pumpkin,
crisp and golden on the outside, soft and
fragrant within – is an unmissable antipasti
treat, as is a plate of grilled octopus, tender
from long cooking, and enhanced by its final
moments on the charcoal grill. Pastas such as
rigatoni with courgettes and pecorino have
less of a wow factor, but mains of slow-cooked
rabbit with pancetta, or grilled monkfish with
caponata raise the bar once more. Portions are
huge, rendering dessert (pannacotta, et al)
redundant, but prices are small enough to
make customers want to return again and
again. A glass of house wine is £4.50.
Chef/s: Sam Harris. **Open:** Tue to Sun L 12.30 to 3,
Tue to Sat D 6.30 to 10. **Closed:** Mon. **Meals:** alc
(main courses £7 to £15). **Service:** not inc.
Details: Cards accepted. 60 seats. Air-con. No
music. Wheelchair access. Children allowed.

Adams Café

Handy local drop-in
77 Askew Road, Shepherd's Bush, W12 9AH
Tel no: (020) 8743 0572
www.adamscafe.co.uk
⊖ Ravenscourt Park, Stamford Brook, map 1
North African | £17
Cooking score: 1
£5 OFF £30

Abdel and Frances Boukraa have run Adam's Café for 21 years. It's a café by day and reasonably priced Tunisian restaurant by night. Their customers are a loyal bunch, drawn back time and again by a menu that runs the gamut of North African cuisine with plenty of couscous and tagines. Otherwise, there are grills of, say, merguez sausages or marinated swordfish. Start with brik au thon (filo pastry with tuna, egg and herb filling); desserts are not a strong suit. House wine is £11.50.
Chef/s: Sofiene Chahed. **Open:** Mon to Sat D only 7 to 11. **Closed:** Sun, bank hols. **Meals:** Set D £14.50 (2 courses) to £16.95. **Service:** 12.5% (optional). **Details:** Cards accepted. 60 seats. Children allowed.

The Admiral Codrington

Jam-packed Chelsea bolt hole
17 Mossop Street, Chelsea, SW3 2LY
Tel no: (020) 7581 0005
www.theadmiralcodrington.com
⊖ South Kensington, map 3
Modern British | £27
Cooking score: 3
£5 OFF **V** £30

In the 10 years the Admiral Codrington has appeared in the Guide not much has changed. You still need to elbow your way through the crush of drinkers to get to the narrow dining area, and the single-sheet menu hasn't altered much over the years either. The cooking is cosmopolitan, taking in three 'well-prepared and nicely presented' scallops (served with celeriac, roasted chestnuts and crispy pancetta) or foie gras and chicken liver parfait as starters, and an 'extremely good and excellent-value' coq au vin or slow-roasted lamb shoulder for

mains. Side orders of hand-cut chips are praised, service is 'very keen and friendly' and the compact, intelligently put together wine list offers a dozen by the glass; bottles start at £15.
Chef/s: Fred Smith. **Open:** all week L 12 to 2.30 (3.30 Sat, 4 Sun), D 6.30 to 11 (7 to 10.30 Sun). **Closed:** 25 and 26 Dec. **Meals:** alc (main courses £11 to £20). **Service:** 12.5% (optional). **Details:** Cards accepted. 50 seats. 25 seats outside. Air-con. Separate bar. Wheelchair access. Music. Children allowed.

Anglesea Arms

Lively gastrogrub
35 Wingate Road, Shepherd's Bush, W6 0UR
Tel no: (020) 8749 1291
⊖ Ravenscourt Park, map 1
Gastropub | £33
Cooking score: 2

The Anglesea Arms deftly combines the qualities of a traditional pub with a bright, exposed dining area that fuses British cooking with European influences. There was a huge cheer when it dropped its no-booking policy. The compact menu is a lively affair: starters range from pig's head terrine to pigeon breast with grilled Jerusalem artichokes, Kentish leaves and pear. Main courses see the likes of skate wing with cima di rape (a slightly bitter Italian green leaf) and anchovy dressing or braised quails with polenta and gremolata. Apple and blackberry crumble with custard hits the spot for dessert. House wine is £15.50.
Chef/s: Matt Cranston. **Open:** all week L 12.30 to 2.45 (3 Sat, 3.30 Sun), D 7 to 10.30 (6 to 9 Sun). **Closed:** 24 to 27 Dec. **Meals:** alc (main courses £11 to £18). **Service:** 12.5% (optional). **Details:** Cards accepted. 85 seats. 22 seats outside. Air-con. Separate bar. No music. Wheelchair access. Music. Children allowed.

Average price

The average price listed in main-entry reviews denotes the price of a three-course meal, without wine.

Ark

Likeable local Italian
122 Palace Gardens Terrace, Notting Hill, W8 4RT
Tel no: (020) 7229 4024
www.ark-restaurant.com
⊖ **Notting Hill Gate, map 4**
Italian | £32
Cooking score: 2
£5 OFF

Ablaze with flowers when the summery
terrace is in full bloom, this likeable Italian
also strikes a sunny pose with its Roman
blinds, skylights and painted panelling. The
kitchen makes its own breads and pasta
(chestnut tagliatelle with wild mushrooms
and pecorino is a good shout in winter), and
there are strong seasonal notes throughout the
menu. Fillet of sea bass might be served with
Jerusalem artichoke purée, crispy leeks and
tomato salsa, confit of duck comes with
roasted chicory and orange sauce, and there's a
special feast for truffle aficionados during the
autumn. The all-Italian wine list scours the
home country for top names. Prices start
at £15.
Chef/s: Daniele Cefero. **Open:** Tue to Sat L 12 to 3,
Mon to Sat D 6.30 to 11. **Closed:** Sun, bank hols.
Meals: alc (main courses £7 to £35). Set L £12.50 (2
courses) to £15.50. **Service:** 12.5% (optional).
Details: Cards accepted. 65 seats. 10 seats outside.
Air-con. Separate bar. Wheelchair access. Music.
Children allowed.

Assaggi

Superior Italian home cooking
The Chepstow, 39 Chepstow Place, Notting Hill,
W2 4TS
Tel no: (020) 7792 5501
⊖ **Notting Hill Gate, map 4**
Italian | £60
Cooking score: 4
V

The location has its own charm – you climb
the stairs to a room above a pub in a quiet
residential area. No standing on ceremony
here, just a gentle buzz of people enjoying
superior Italian home cooking in bright,

friendly surroundings. Ingredients are the key
when food is this simple, and Nino Sassu
doesn't let anybody down on that front.
Antipasti range from stuffed squid, burrata
with grilled aubergine or pecorino with San
Daniele ham and rocket, while main dishes are
straightforward – say, grilled sea bass, fritto
misto and calf's liver. A keen sense of season
and an indulgent touch with classic Italian
desserts (the tiramisu is legendary) add
sparkle. The wine list – apart from
Champagne and port – is an all-Italian love
affair, with useful, concise descriptions to help
you through the less familiar names. Prices
start at £21.95 the bottle (£5 the glass).
Chef/s: Nino Sassu. **Open:** Mon to Sat L 12.30 to
2.30 (1 to 2.30 Sat), D 7.30 to 11. **Closed:** Sun, 2
weeks from 24 Dec, bank hols. **Meals:** alc (main
courses £19 to £27). **Service:** not inc. **Details:** Cards
accepted. 40 seats. Air-con. No music. Children
allowed.

Aubergine

Well-heeled French grandee
11 Park Walk, Chelsea, SW10 0AJ
Tel no: (020) 7352 3449
www.auberginerestaurant.co.uk
⊖ **South Kensington, map 3**
Modern French | £68
Cooking score: 4

This long-running French restaurant lost
some of its vim in the past couple of years, and
Christophe Renou was recruited in late 2009
to inject new life back into the place. The
dining room is awash with warm ochre, and
you are well looked after by an enthusiastic
team. The cooking is modern French, so sea
bass is paired with confit of pork belly and
chlorophyll. Aubergine caviar and vegetable
confit made an ornate start, and cheeses are
well worth the detour at the end, but
imprecise seasoning let down a frisée salad
with lardons, poached egg and grainy mustard
dressing, as well as sirloin steak with béarnaise.
There is undoubted skill in the kitchen, but it
needs to be more consistent. Predominantly
French wines, which start from £25, suffer
from steep premiums. Aubergine's out-of-

town sibling at the Compleat Angler Hotel in Marlow has failed to live up to its early promise, judging by feedback.
Chef/s: Christophe Renou. **Open:** Tue to Sat L 12 to 2.30, D 7 to 10.45. **Closed:** Sun, Mon, 23 Dec to 5 Jan, bank hols, Easter Sat. **Meals:** Set L £18.50 (2 courses) to £25. Set D £25 (2 courses) to £34. **Service:** 12.5% (optional). **Details:** Cards accepted. 50 seats. Air-con. Separate bar. Music. Children allowed.

Awana
Suave Malaysian high-flyer
85 Sloane Avenue, Chelsea, SW3 3DX
Tel no: (020) 7584 8880
www.awana.co.uk
⊖ South Kensington, map 3
Malaysian | £48
Cooking score: 1

V

Inspired by traditional Malaysian teak houses – with some suave, Sloane-friendly intervention – Awana is a swanky-looking amalgam of lush silk panels and delicate glass screens, with burgundy leather seating and hardwood surfaces. The menu pitches native favourites such as beef rendang, nasi lemak and laksa alongside more esoteric specialities – perhaps rojak buah (sour fruit salad with tamarind sauce) or kambing betis (cumin-spiced lamb shank with pumpkin, sweet potato and lemongrass). There's also a satay bar for casual bites. A short but flashy wine list starts at £19.
Chef/s: Mark Read and Lee Chin Soon. **Open:** all week L 12 to 3, D 6 to 11 (11.30 Thur to Sat, 10.30 Sun). **Closed:** 25 and 26 Dec, 1 Jan. **Meals:** alc (main courses £11 to £25). Set L £12.50 (2 courses) to £15. Set D £35 (3 courses) to £45 (5 courses). **Service:** 12.5% (optional). **Details:** Cards accepted. 100 seats. Air-con. Separate bar. Music. Children allowed. Car parking.

Bibendum
Icon with a magical mood
Michelin House, 81 Fulham Road, South Kensington, SW3 6RD
Tel no: (020) 7581 5817
www.bibendum.co.uk
⊖ South Kensington, map 3
French | £48
Cooking score: 4

🍾 V

The old Michelin building plies its trade via a ground-floor Oyster Bar with Edwardian racing scenes in the tiled walls, and a gorgeous first-floor dining room, where light streams through the massive windows, some stained in cobalt-blue. Matthew Harris maintains a refined version of rustic French cooking, with the odd drift into other European modes. You might start with soused herrings in beetroot and horseradish wrapped around new potato and red onion salad, before making a southerly beeline for beef soaked in a deep rich sauce of mushrooms and garlic, or sautéed rabbit with balls of stuffing. Finish with lemon tart, or chocolate fondant with griottine cherries. The wine list is formidable in both range and price. France is the trump suit, but Spanish, Italian and Australian showings are all great. The bidding opens at £19.95.
Chef/s: Matthew Harris. **Open:** all week L 12 to 2.30 (12.30 to 3 Sat and Sun), D 7 to 11 (10.30 Sun). **Closed:** 25 and 26 Dec, 1 Jan. **Meals:** alc (main courses £17 to £30). Set L and D £26 (2 courses) to £29.50. Sun L £29.50. **Service:** 12.5% (optional). **Details:** Cards accepted. 90 seats. Air-con. Separate bar. No music. No mobile phones. Children allowed.

Readers recommend

A 'readers recommend' review is a genuine quote from a report sent in by one of our readers. We intend to follow up these suggestions throughout the year to come.

Blue Elephant

Extravagant Thai fantasies
3-6 Fulham Broadway, Fulham, SW6 1AA
Tel no: (020) 7385 6595
www.blueelephant.com
⊖ Fulham Broadway, map 3
Thai | £35
Cooking score: 1

V

Guaranteed to transport you momentarily to the land of a thousand temples, London's most glamorous and extravagantly decorated Thai restaurant weaves its magic with cascading waterfalls, a veritable jungle of luxuriant greenery, carp ponds and a gilt-edged bar. The kitchen's tour of the culinary repertoire is equally exotic, promising stir-fried 'running crocodile' with palm hearts, sea bass grilled in a bamboo case, and poached lobster 'swimming in a sea of vegetables and perfumed mushrooms' – as well as regulation soups, curries and noodles. Wines start at £20. **Chef/s:** Surapol Sriaim. **Open:** all week L 12 to 2.30 (2.15 Sun), D 7 to 11.30 (6.30 Fri, 6 Sat, 6.30 to 10.30 Sun). **Closed:** 25 and 26 Dec, 1 Jan. **Meals:** alc (main courses £11 to £28). Set L £12 (2 courses) to £15. Set D £35 to £39. Sun L £30. **Service:** 12.5% (optional). **Details:** Cards accepted. 300 seats. Air-con. Separate bar. No mobile phones. Wheelchair access. Music. Children allowed.

The Botanist

Buzzy, trendy brasserie
7 Sloane Square, Chelsea, SW1W 8EE
Tel no: (020) 7730 0077
www.thebotanistonsloanesquare.com
⊖ Sloane Square, map 3
Modern European | £30
New Chef

Inspired by famous botanist Sir Hans Sloane (who gave the surrounding square its name) this big, boisterous, buzzy boozer from brothers Ed and Tom Martin is appropriately kitted out with displays of pressed flowers, pinned insects and framed pages from Victorian horticultural journals. David Bone took over just as the Guide was going to press, but expect a similar range of brasserie-style dishes along the lines of red mullet and blood orange escabèche with pickled anchovy, grilled 35-day aged Angus ribeye steak with chips and béarnaise, and desserts such as churros with spiced caramel parfait and a toffee crab apple. This action-packed space is also open for breakfast and gets rammed for post-work drinks; cocktails are a hot ticket and global wines start at £14.50.
Chef/s: David Bone. **Open:** all week L 12 to 4, D 6 to 10.30. **Closed:** 25 and 26 Dec. **Meals:** alc (main courses £11 to £22). Set D £19 (2 courses) to £24. **Service:** 12.5% (optional). **Details:** Cards accepted. 84 seats. 8 seats outside. Air-con. Separate bar. Wheelchair access. Music. Children allowed.

Brompton Bar & Grill

Up-to-the-minute, earthy British food
243 Brompton Road, South Kensington, SW3 2EP
Tel no: (020) 7589 8005
www.bromptonbarandgrill.com
⊖ South Kensington, map 3
Modern British | £28
Cooking score: 2

V £30

The zinc-topped bar and uniform line of tables-for-two against a banquette make this the very image of a modern London brasserie. Opposite the Brompton Oratory, it's a great bolthole for up-to-the-minute British cooking that's earthy and easy to understand. Start with a dozen oysters, or lentil and smoked bacon soup, before going on to the house fish stew, grilled halibut with gremolata, or roasted calf's sweetbreads and kidneys with mustard onions. Finish with rhubarb fool and ginger shortbread, or crème caramel. Wines open with a Spanish white and a French red blend at a mere £10.
Chef/s: Gary Durrant. **Open:** all week L 12 to 3 (3.30 Sat and Sun), D 6 to 10.30 (10 Sun). **Closed:** 24 to 27 Dec. **Meals:** alc (main courses £13 to £22). Set L and D (until 7.30) £15 (2 courses) to £17.50. **Service:** 12.5% (optional). **Details:** Cards accepted. 60 seats. Air-con. Separate bar. Wheelchair access. Music. Children allowed.

Bryn Williams Odette's

What is your earliest culinary memory?
Making bread at the local bakery. I visited the local bakery at the age of nine and loved it.

What is the best dish on your menu?
Pan-fried turbot, braised oxtail and cockles.

How do you relax when out of the kitchen?
I like diving, it's relaxing, deep sea diving, keeping fit...

What do you wish you had known when you started out as a chef?
How hard you have to work all the time, one cannot have an 'off' day, always on your feet.

What is your favourite restaurant and why?
Roka at the moment, it has great atmosphere and the food is great.

What do you think is exciting about the British food scene?
What London offers is versatile, one can have great food from different cuisines.

READERS RECOMMEND

The Butcher's Hook

Gastropub
477 Fulham Road, Fulham, SW6 1HL
Tel no: (020) 7385 4654
www.thebutchershook.co.uk
'This looks a pretty standard old-type pub... but the flair in the cooking is outstanding'

Le Café Anglais

Unbuttoned, no-nonsense enjoyment
8 Porchester Gardens, Notting Hill, W2 4DB
Tel no: (020) 7221 1415
www.lecafeanglais.co.uk
⊖ Bayswater, map 4
Anglo-French | £40
Cooking score: 5

Rowley Leigh launched the Café in 2007 amid a blaze of expectation, having fed Kensington and Notting Hill for 20 years. This operation feels quite as zeitgeisty as Kensington Place did when it opened, and there is the same atmosphere of unbuttoned, no-nonsense enjoyment here as at Whiteley's. The huge menu deals in brasserie favourites from both sides of the Channel, with some more new fangled ideas scattered about for good measure. Pike boudin with fines herbs has the whiff of Elizabeth David about it, but there may also be chicken with a sage and onion pudding, or else get seriously meaty with partridge choucroute served with frankfurters, ventrèche and morteau sausage. Finish with a bouquet of ices, or with grilled pineapple, coconut sorbet and chilli syrup. It's all cooked and presented with great panache, and is a powerful lure for the area. Wines are a classy Franco-Italian bunch, chosen with food friendliness in mind. Prices start at £17.50.
Chef/s: Rowley Leigh and Colin Westal. **Open:** all week L 12 to 3.30, D 6.30 to 11 (11.30 Fri and Sat, 10.15 Sun). **Closed:** 25 and 26 Dec, 1 Jan. **Meals:** alc (main courses £9 to £30). Set L (Mon to Fri) £16.50 (2 courses) to £19.50. Set D £35. Sun L £24.50. **Service:** 12.5% (optional). **Details:** Cards accepted. 160 seats. Air-con. Separate bar. No music. Wheelchair access. Children allowed. Car parking.

Cambio de Tercio

Inventive Spanish on top form
163 Old Brompton Road, Earl's Court, SW5 0LJ
Tel no: (020) 7244 8970
www.cambiodetercio.co.uk
⊖ Gloucester Road, map 3
Spanish | £38
Cooking score: 5

There is much to enjoy in this informal restaurant, its discreet matador theme accented by black slate and leather against a backdrop of vividly coloured walls. Service too, is welcoming 'in a family sort of way'. The menu kicks off with tapas before moving onto main courses and desserts. At inspection the kitchen was on top form with a fearlessly inventive streak that goes beyond standard Spanish fare. To start, a lollipop of Manchego cheese, followed by Spanish potato and chorizo omelette 'El Bulli 1998' – deconstructed layers of caramelised onion and egg yolk, topped off by potato foam with a drizzle of chorizo oil, which was no mere out-take of the restaurant that pioneered experimental cooking. The kitchen is equally deft with the classics; a casserole of monkfish with griddled razor clams, broad beans, asparagus tips and parsley jus perfectly captured the flavours and textures of Basque cuisine. Desserts are equally fun – a witty gin and tonic on a plate coupled a Bombay Sapphire gelée with tonic water sorbet and lime foam. The wine list goes from £18 right up to £750 for a Pingus 1988 and engineers a grand tour of Spain with some noteworthy and rare labels. From the same stable are the tapas bar Tendido Cero opposite at 174 Old Brompton Road, tel: (020) 7370 3685 and Tendido Cuatro at 108-110 New Kings Road, SW6 4LY, tel:(020) 7371 5147.
Chef/s: Alberto Criado. **Open:** all week L 12 to 2.30, D 6.30 to 11.30 (11 Sun). **Closed:** 20 Dec to 5 Jan, 15 to 30 Aug. **Meals:** alc (main courses £18 to £23). **Service:** 12.5% (optional). **Details:** Cards accepted. 45 seats. 12 seats outside. Air-con. Wheelchair access. Music. Children allowed.

The Capital

Classical French food that won't shock
22 Basil Street, Knightsbridge, SW3 1AT
Tel no: (020) 7591 1202
www.capitalhotel.co.uk
⊖ Knightsbridge, map 4
French | £55
Cooking score: 6

The small dining room at the Capital has gone through a fair few decorative transformations over the years, and has currently settled on a neutral background, with light panelling, small monochrome pictures and chandeliers that are too big for the space. The aim seems to be not to shock – and that might well be the axiom of new chef Jérôme Ponchelle, who arrived to take over from Eric Chavot in November 2009. Under Ponchelle, the food has veered back towards a more classical French style, with avant-garde flourishes largely banished amid an almost archaic culinary approach. Roast fillet of lamb grande-mère emphasises the point, with its herb-crusted collops of bright pink meat, blandly creamy dauphinoise, mushrooms, bacon and croûtons. Guinea fowl breast is cooked gently in butter, and served with a portion of gooey macaroni cheese. The odd nod to more contemporary London modes is evident in a fine starter of seared scallops on braised lentils with a rich curry sauce, while a dessert of muscovado meringue with tropical fruits and a powerful mango and turmeric sorbet struck clear, ringing notes. A small selection of pedigree French cheeses is mostly well-kept. Service is sweetly charming, but doesn't get quite everything right. The wine list is bristling with excellent growers, and many mature vintages (Marcel Deiss Gewürztraminer 2006 served by the glass, hooray!). Prices open at £25.
Chef/s: Jérôme Ponchelle. **Open:** all week L 12 to 2.30, D 6.45 to 11 (10.30 Sun). **Meals:** alc (main courses £22 to £35). Set L £27.50 (2 courses) to £33. Tasting menu £70. **Service:** 12.5% (optional). **Details:** Cards accepted. 34 seats. Air-con. Separate bar. No music. Children allowed. Car parking.

The Carpenter's Arms
Pub full of bright, fresh flavours
89-91 Black Lion Lane, Hammersmith, W6 9BG
Tel no: (020) 8741 8386
www.carpentersarmsw6.co.uk
⊖ Stamford Brook, Ravenscourt Park, map 1
Gastropub | £27
Cooking score: 2

£30

This small corner pub has been given a
modern makeover, with light walls, good
pictures and mirrors, and it also boasts a walled
garden at the back for summer eating. The
fabled 'Modern European Cookbook' is
ransacked to bring an array of bright, fresh
flavours to Hammersmith. A platter of
Spanish charcuterie with olives and almonds is
a tasty, tapas-y way to begin, and there might
be seared tuna in romesco, roast pollack with
shrimps and wild garlic, or Tamworth pork
loin with portobello mushrooms to follow. A
dozen wines by the glass (from £4.25) head up
a short list that finds room for a German
Riesling and a pink Prosecco.
Chef/s: Steven Carbery. **Open:** all week L 12 to 2.30
(12.30 to 3.30 Sat, 12.30 to 5 Sun), D 6.30 to 10 (7
Sat, 7 to 9 Sun). **Meals:** alc (main courses from £10
to £17). Set L £12.50 (2 courses) to £15.50.
Service: 12.5% (optional). **Details:** Cards accepted.
48 seats. 46 seats outside. Separate bar. Music.
Children allowed.

Casa Brindisa
Homage to Iberian tapas
7-9 Exhibition Road, South Kensington, SW7 2HE
Tel no: (020) 7590 0008
www.casabrindisa.com
⊖ South Kensington, map 3
Spanish | £25
Cooking score: 3

V £30

Following in the footsteps of Tapas Brindisa
and Soho sibling Tierra Brindisa (see entries),
this homage to Iberian food picks up the
theme but adds a basement deli and ground-
floor 'jamónería' to the buzzy, atmospheric
mix. Top-drawer artisan provisions form the
backbone of the menu, and the fired-up open
kitchen dispenses old Brindisa favourites plus
some less familiar treats. Charcuterie, obscure
cheeses and country breads are bolstered by
patatas with allioli, chickpea and spinach stew,
and beetroot-marinated salmon with
pistachio vinaigrette. For something more
filling, try Iberian pork tenderloin with
Oloroso sherry and roasted apple, or rare fillet
steak with caramelised onion and Torta de
Barros cheese on toast. To finish, confit quince
with Manchego ice cream turns a classic
partnership on its head. Wash it all down with
cracking sherries and Spanish regional wines
(from £15.75).
Chef/s: Leonardo Rivera. **Open:** all week 12 to 11 (10
Sat and Sun). **Meals:** alc (tapas £5 to £22).
Service: 12.5% (optional). **Details:** Cards accepted.
62 seats. 8 seats outside. Air-con. Separate bar.
Wheelchair access. Music. Children allowed.

Le Cercle
Elegance and exquisite small dishes
1 Wilbraham Place, Belgravia, SW1X 9AE
Tel no: (020) 7901 9999
www.lecercle.co.uk
⊖ Sloane Square, map 3
Modern French | £40
Cooking score: 5

£5 OFF 🍷 V

Just off Sloane Street, this offshoot of Club
Gascon (see entry) makes the most of its
basement setting – marble floors, high
ceilings, neutral colours and careful lighting
create a feeling of elegance and space. Florent
Fabulas has been promoted to head chef, a
seamless move that has done nothing to
disturb the rhythm of the kitchen or the pick-
and-mix style of the menu. Seasonality is
characteristic of the output, which is largely
rooted in the culinary traditions of southwest
France and delivered in a procession of
exquisite and inventive small dishes. There are
no conventional starters, and the idea is to
graze your way through the menu, choosing
from four groups. 'Végétal' may supply a white
asparagus velouté with pea ice cream, from
'marin' comes skate wing with sweet peppers

and fennel broth, while 'fermier' delivers braised ox cheek, Jerusalem artichoke gratin and liquorice jus, and 'plaisir' a squab pigeon with spicy caramel and pistachio pastilla. Prices are reasonable and the set lunch and dinner options offer good value. The all-French wine list lays out a quality selection from all regions and also encompasses some serious bottles from mature vintages. Prices from £20.

Chef/s: Florent Fabulas. **Open:** Tue to Sat L 12 to 3, D 6 to 11. **Closed:** Sun, Mon, 23 Dec to 1 Jan. **Meals:** alc (main courses £8 to £18). Set L £15. Set D £17.50. **Service:** 12.5% (optional). **Details:** Cards accepted. 80 seats. Air-con. Separate bar. Wheelchair access. Music. Children allowed.

NEW ENTRY
Charlotte's Bistro
Slick neighbourhood bistro
6 Turnham Green Terrace, Chiswick, W4 1QP
Tel no: (020) 8742 3590
www.charlottes.co.uk
⊖ Turnham Green, map 1
Modern British | £28
Cooking score: 2
£30

Slicker than most bistros, this newcomer (related to Charlotte's Place, Ealing – see entry) boasts a split-level dining room topped off by a glass roof and backed up by accommodating service. The menu may be predictable but it's appealing, and prices fair. Wild mushroom risotto has been praised, or there could be smoked haddock and sweetcorn chowder to start. For mains, beef onglet comes with hand-cut chips, caramelised onion and garlic aïoli, or there's bouillabaisse with rouille. Lime and lemongrass tart paired with crème fraîche sorbet is a good way to finish. Wines, arranged by style, start from £16.

Chef/s: Cameron Hill. **Open:** all week L 12 to 3, D 5.30 to 9.45. **Meals:** alc (main courses £12 to £16). Set L £12 (2 courses) to £15. Early D (5.30 to 7) £25. Sun L £16.50 (2 courses) to £19.50. **Service:** 12.5% (optional). **Details:** Cards accepted. 60 seats. Air-con. Separate bar. Music. Children allowed.

NEW ENTRY
Charlotte's Place
Good ideas and impressive cooking
16 St Matthew's Road, Ealing, W5 3JT
Tel no: (020) 8567 7541
www.charlottes.co.uk
⊖ Ealing Broadway, Ealing Common, map 1
Modern European | £29
Cooking score: 3
V £30

Charlotte's Place is a cheery eatery laid out over two floors and lifted right out of its neighbourhood restaurant niche by cooking that tends to impress. It may not be particularly polished or refined – but the manner in which raw materials are combined demonstrates skill. Even when dishes are as simple as game terrine with red onion marmalade, and cod fillet with shallot purée, boulangère potatoes and pea shoots, they have a straightforwardness about them that is appealing. These good ideas are backed up by honest-tasting desserts such as apple and rhubarb crumble, and white chocolate cheesecake with blood-orange sorbet. House wine is £16.

Chef/s: Greg Martin. **Open:** all week L 12 to 3, D 6 to 9.45. **Closed:** 26 Dec to 3 Jan. **Meals:** alc (main courses £12 to £17). Set L £12 (2 courses) to £15. Early D (6 to 7) £25 (3 courses). Sun L £16.50 (2 courses) to £19.50. **Service:** 12.5% (optional). **Details:** Cards accepted. 54 seats. 10 seats outside. Air-con. Music. Children allowed.

ALSO RECOMMENDED
▲ Chiswick House Café
Chiswick House, Burlington Lane, Chiswick, W4 2QN
Tel no: (020) 8995 6356
www.chgt.org.uk
⊖ Chiswick Park, map 1
Café

This lovely modern café in the beautiful grounds of Chiswick House delivers exactly what it promises. The menu is locally sourced, seasonal and packed with honest, freshly cooked dishes you want to eat; prices are fair and service is polite. At lunchtime there's a full array of sandwiches, salads, soups and the like, as well as fish pie and seasonal stews. To drink, expect a tempting array of non-alcoholic tipples as well as local beer and wine (from £4.75 a glass). Open all week for breakfast, lunch and tea.

Chutney Mary

Glamorous contemporary Indian
535 King's Road, Fulham, SW10 0SZ
Tel no: (020) 7351 3113
www.realindianfood.com
⊖ Fulham Broadway, map 3
Indian | £33
Cooking score: 3

V

Visitors are instantly seduced by the ethnic exoticism, sensuous sparkle and many-coloured opulence of this Chelsea Indian, but its food has also taken on a new vivacity and contemporary edge of late. Chef Siddharth Krishna is firing on all cylinders and creating dishes that are shot through with invigorating flavours and unexpected contrasts: crispy rock shrimps are served with lime and chilli chutney, crushed yam and lentil kebabs are stuffed with yoghurt and red onion, and Keralan-style roast duck comes with black pepper sauce and sweet potato crumble. More conventional ideas also feature in the guise of tandoori prawns with a shrimp paste marinade, genuine lamb shank vindaloo, and a version of chicken tikka masala tweaked with caramelised tomato sauce. The wine list has been intelligently tailored to the food, with prices from £21.
Chef/s: Siddharth Krishna. **Open:** Sat and Sun L 12.30 to 3, all week D 6.30 to 11.30 (10.30 Sun). **Meals:** alc (main courses £15 to £24). Set L and D (Sun to Thur only) £22. **Service:** 12.5% (optional). **Details:** Cards accepted. 110 seats. Air-con. No music. Wheelchair access. Children allowed.

Clarke's

Honesty, simplicity and full-on flavours
124 Kensington Church Street, Notting Hill, W8 4BH
Tel no: (020) 7221 9225
www.sallyclarke.com
⊖ Notting Hill Gate, High Street Kensington, map 4
Modern British | £40
Cooking score: 4

🍾 **V**

Split between ground floor and airy basement at the Notting Hill end of Church Street, Sally Clarke's restaurant celebrates 26 years in the Guide this year and for all that time her cooking has been distinguished by honesty, simplicity and full-on flavours. Her menu, broadly modern British with Italian leanings, is market-orientated – the tone is firmly set by a plate of buffalo mozzarella with blood orange, pomegranate, puntarelle (chicory), toasted walnuts and balsamic dressing. After that, the kitchen might produce a baked fillet of Cornish black bream with a sauce of tumeric and coriander, spiced Umbrian lentils and steamed winter greens, as well as a beautifully roasted Aylesbury duck breast with apple and sage sauce. Desserts maintain the balance with a sophisticated dark chocolate soufflé cake with candied ginger cream and brazil nut brittle, and a trio of British cheeses in perfect condition. There's something to please all palates on the well-chosen wine list, from mature clarets to pickings from Sally's beloved California. Prices start at £17.
Chef/s: Sally Clarke. **Open:** all week L 12.30 to 2 (12 Sat), Mon to Sat D 6 to 10. **Closed:** 8 days Christmas and New Year, bank hols. **Meals:** alc (main courses £17 to £19). Set D £39.50. Sun L £32. **Service:** 12.5% (optional). **Details:** Cards accepted. 80 seats. Air-con. No music. No mobile phones. Wheelchair access. Children allowed.

Sally Clarke Clarke's

What is your earliest culinary memory?
Lettuce and sugar sandwiches made by my mother after school.

What would be your perfect birthday meal?
January is not easy - and so soon after Christmas - so usually a restrained affair. But my favourite is crab salad, roasted chicken, and blood oranges for dessert.

What do you think is exciting about the British food scene?
That more and more people are wanting to know where their food comes from, and more and more are growing their own.

How do you relax when out of the kitchen?
I relax when I am in the kitchen... But sleep, go to the opera and eat in other people's restaurants.

What is your favourite restaurant and why?
Chez Panisse, Berkeley, California, because it is the best in the world and always has been (for 35-plus years).

Le Colombier
French through and through
145 Dovehouse Street, Chelsea, SW3 6LB
Tel no: (020) 7351 1155
www.lecolombier-sw3.co.uk
⊖ South Kensington, map 3
French | £35
Cooking score: 2

Didier Garnier's dyed-in-the-wool Chelsea bistro is a bastion of unreservedly bourgeois French cooking, and its bustling atmosphere and appealing repertoire draws a loyal following. It helps that it looks the part – its wide covered terrace leads into a dining room of polished floorboards and close-set, white-clothed tables. Salads such as crab or warm goats' cheese, and feuilleté d'escargots vie for attention alongside mains such as cannon of lamb provençale and veal chop with thyme and garlic. Equally familiar desserts include tarte au citron. House French is £17.50.
Chef/s: Philippe Tamet. **Open:** all week L 12 to 3 (3.30 Sun), D 6.30 to 10.30 (10 Sun). **Meals:** alc (main courses £17 to £29). Set L £19 (2 courses) to £25.70. Sun L £23. **Service:** 12.5% (optional). **Details:** Cards accepted. 42 seats. 30 seats outside. No music. Wheelchair access. Children allowed.

ALSO RECOMMENDED
▲ The Cow
89 Westbourne Park Road, Westbourne Park, W2 5QH
Tel no: (020) 7221 0021
www.thecowlondon.co.uk
⊖ Royal Oak, map 4
Gastropub

Part of Tom Conran's mini foodie empire, this boozer-turned-gastropub has been restyled with plenty of urban pizazz. Its strapline is 'domestic and foreign cooking; oysters and Guinness', and you can't get much fairer than that. If fruits de mer aren't your thing (a platter for two costs £36 while oysters start at £9.50 for six), you could plump for imaginative pasta dishes or a patriotic main course of smoked eel with mash, bacon and horseradish (£17) Wines from £21. Open all week.

The Duke of Sussex
Local with Brit classics and tapas
75 South Parade, Chiswick, W4 5LF
Tel no: (020) 8742 8801
⊖ Chiswick Park, map 1
Gastropub | £25
Cooking score: 2

'Packed on a bitterly cold night' testifies to the popularity of this lively gastropub on the Chiswick/Acton borders. Crowds drink and mingle in the bar (and the garden in summer), while diners populate the high-ceilinged, chandelier-hung dining room. The attraction is upbeat British classics mixed with Spanish tapas: razor clams with chorizo and chilli, pinchos morunos (skewers of marinated pork), Old Spot pork belly with escalivada and salsa picante or chicken pie for two, with churros and chocolate or sticky toffee pudding for dessert. Reports on service are mixed. The short wine list offers a bunch of eminently drinkable bottles from £14.25.
Chef/s: Chris Payne. **Open:** Tue to Sun 12 to 10.30 (9.30 Sun). Mon D only 6 to 10.30. **Closed:** 25 Dec. **Meals:** alc (main courses £10 to £16). **Service:** not inc. **Details:** Cards accepted. 65 seats. 130 seats outside. Separate bar. Wheelchair access. Music. Children allowed.

e&o
Sleek style-dining
14 Blenheim Crescent, Notting Hill, W11 1NN
Tel no: (020) 7229 5454
www.rickerrestaurants.com
⊖ Ladbroke Grove, map 4
Pan-Asian | £40
Cooking score: 3

V

Part of the trendsetting Will Ricker stable, e&o is a place of sharp-edged design, sexily lit, predominantly black, with a be-seen cocktail bar at the front and a sleek monochrome dining area for those who penetrate intrepidly into the interior. Expect trademark Ricker pan-Asian grazing, on a menu that proceeds from Chinese-style dim sum through sashimi and sushi to Malaysian curries, all capably rendered by Simon Treadway. Steamed toothfish in black bean, beef tahoon with yuzu koshu, and soft-shell crab with asparagus and candied peanuts are among the less familiar offerings, though desserts will largely reorient you to western modes with banoffee pie or brandy snaps filled with pistachio cream. The varietally ordered wine list starts at £16.
Chef/s: Simon Treadway. **Open:** Mon to Fri L 12 to 3, D 6 to 11. Sat 12 to 11. Sun 12.30 to 10.30. **Closed:** 24 to 27 Dec, 29 and 30 Aug, Aug bank hol. **Meals:** alc (main courses £11 to £25). Set L £19. **Service:** 12.5% (optional). **Details:** Cards accepted. 84 seats. 16 seats outside. Air-con. Separate bar. Music. Children allowed.

NEW ENTRY
The Ealing Park Tavern
Charmer with complete-steal meals
222 South Ealing Road, Ealing, W5 4RL
Tel no: (020) 8758 1879
www.ealingparktavern.com
⊖ South Ealing, Northfields, map 1
Modern British | £25
Cooking score: 3

The ramshackle charm of this building, with its period features and wood-panelled dining room, makes it appear more Oxbridge refectory than west London boozer. An open kitchen reveals a young team working harmoniously, and it all translates well on the plate. At inspection, a soft-shell crab with salt and chilli squid and crab mayonnaise was well-balanced against tangy pickled vegetables, while stuffed guinea fowl with potato galette had a luxurious richness coaxed out by anchovy and oil. Imaginative desserts included a cassava doughnut with coconut ice cream, as well as salt-caramel and chocolate marquise with raspberry sorbet. Prices seem a complete steal. House wine £13.95.
Chef/s: Jane Collins. **Open:** all week L 12 to 3 (4 Sun), D 6 to 10 (9.30 Sun). **Closed:** 25 Dec, 1 Jan. **Meals:** alc (main courses £10 to £18). **Service:** 12.5%. **Details:** Cards accepted. 120 seats. 60 seats outside. Separate bar. Children allowed.

ALSO RECOMMENDED

▲ Ebury Wine Bar

139 Ebury Street, Belgravia, SW1W 9QU
Tel no: (020) 7730 5447
www.eburywinebar.co.uk
⊖ Victoria, map 3
Modern European £5 OFF

The décor is pure gentleman's club, with dark green colour scheme and trompe l'oeil paintings, but this wine bar/restaurant was considered a ground-breaker when it opened in 1957 and it continues to move with the times. Expect all-day bar food in the front wine bar – the likes of seared scallops with beetroot and horseradish purée (£9.50) and grilled calf's liver with polenta croquette, stuffed onions and sage jus (£16.95) in the restaurant. The impressive wine list offers monthly promotions and more than 30 by the glass. House wine £14.50. Open daily.

The Ebury

Bright, buzzy brasserie with city food
11 Pimlico Road, Chelsea, SW1W 8NA
Tel no: (020) 7730 6784
www.theebury.co.uk
⊖ Sloane Square, Victoria, map 3
Modern European | £30
Cooking score: 2

V

On a wedge-shaped site at an intersection, and handy for the Royal Court and Victoria Palace theatres, the Ebury is a bright, buzzy brasserie with big windows and an informal vibe. Christophe Clerget has his finger on the pulse of modern London eating, offering wooden boards of nibbles to share (mezze, seafood, charcuterie or cheeses), as well as generous portions of brasserie staples such as meltingly tender lamb shank, steamed mussels with smoked bacon, and salmon fishcakes with spinach and hollandaise. Finish off with lemon tart and raspberry sorbet. A short, French-led wine list opens at £16 a bottle. **Chef/s:** Christophe Clerget. **Open:** all week L 12 to 3.30 (11 to 4 Sat and Sun), D 6 to 10.30 (10 Sun). Bar menu available. **Closed:** 25 Dec. **Meals:** alc (main courses £11 to £20). Set L and early D £16.50 (2 courses) to £19.50. **Service:** 12.5% (optional). **Details:** Cards accepted. 60 seats. Air-con. Separate bar. Music. Children allowed.

L'Etranger

A chef who loves luxury
36 Gloucester Road, South Kensington, SW7 4QT
Tel no: (020) 7584 1118
www.etranger.co.uk
⊖ Gloucester Road, South Kensington, map 3
Modern French | £55
Cooking score: 4

£5 OFF 🍶 V

Fusion is an 'F' word one rarely hears these days, but could South Kensington's subtly opulent L'Etranger be the place to rehabilitate it? The jury's still out. For some, the 'French meets Japanese' cuisine is 'a bit of everything or nothing'; for others, it's the best of both worlds. Chef Jerome Tauvron can't say no to luxury: foie gras, Wagyu beef and truffles crop up repeatedly, but a set lunch proves he can also work to a budget. Inspection steered a middle course and was largely impressed by cleanly fried shrimp tempura, fail-safe miso black cod, and tender lamb shoulder. L'Etranger's all-out luxury and flash presentation have dated, but fine technique and produce save it – with the exception of a gimmicky 'Death by Chocolate'. More compelling is the 'never knowingly undersold' wine list (from £20) making Montrachet Grand Crus a snip – of sorts. **Chef/s:** Kingshuk Dey and Jerome Tauvron. **Open:** all week L 12 to 3, D 6 to 11 (10 Sun). **Meals:** alc (main courses £17 to £55). Set L £16.50. Sat and Sun L £18.50 (2 courses) to £22.50. **Service:** 12.5% (optional). **Details:** Cards accepted. 64 seats. Air-con. No music. Music. Children allowed.

Average price

The average price listed in main-entry reviews denotes the price of a three-course meal, without wine.

ALSO RECOMMENDED

▲ First Floor

186 Portobello Road, Notting Hill, W11 1LA
Tel no: (020) 7243 0072
www.firstfloorportobello.co.uk
⊖ Notting Hill Gate, map 4
Modern European

With its chandelier, flouncy curtains and eye-popping décor, the First Floor is some way off what you may be expecting a converted old boozer to look like. A lengthy menu of modern European dishes suits the Notting Hill scene to a T. Seared scallops on salsify and vanilla purée with fennel beurre blanc (£8.50), marinated lamb gigot with garlic roast potatoes and minted yoghurt (£15.95) and chocolate fondant with strawberry compote (£6.50) are what to expect. Wines from £14.50. Closed Sun D.

The Gate

Vibrant veggie favourite
51 Queen Caroline Street, Hammersmith, W6 9QL
Tel no: (020) 8748 6932
www.thegate.tv
⊖ Hammersmith, map 1
Vegetarian | £25
Cooking score: 2
£5 OFF V £30

This long-standing Hammersmith vegetarian restaurant – once the studio of the artist Sir Frank Brangwyn – uses a wide variety of techniques and influences to create dishes such as Indo-Iraqi potato cake, haloumi kibi, rotolo of butternut squash, goats' cheese and basil, or winter vegetable and chickpea tagine with pomegranate and quinoa salad. It's the kind of food to please meat-eaters and veggies alike, all the way to a chocolate and hazelnut version of Eton mess. Organic Italian house wines are £16.50 (£4.50 a glass).
Chef/s: Mariusz Wegrodzki. **Open:** Mon to Fri L 12 to 2.30, Mon to Sat D 6 to 10.30 (11 Sat). **Closed:** Sun, 24 Dec to 1 Jan, bank hols. **Meals:** alc (main courses £11 to £16). **Service:** 12.5% (optional). **Details:** Cards accepted. 59 seats. 36 seats outside. Air-con. Music. Children allowed.

Geales

Much more than a chippy
2 Farmer Street, Notting Hill, W8 7SN
Tel no: (020) 7727 7528
www.geales.com
⊖ Notting Hill Gate, map 4
Seafood | £25
Cooking score: 1
£30

The black-and-white check tablecloths and paper napkins give a nostalgic nod to Geales' past as a proper chippy, but the current 'poshed-up' version has much more to offer. There's a great selection of shellfish – a lovely soft-shell crab tempura, moules marinière, even lobster thermidor for those that want it – but the focus is still on the classic fish and chips, the fish either grilled or cooked in the lightest of batter, the chips crisp, hot and moreish. Steaks and salads are available for non-fish eaters, as is red wine (from £3.95 a glass), but they're sideshows to the main attraction.
Chef/s: Garry Hollihead. **Open:** Tue to Sun L 12 to 2.30 (5 Sat and Sun), all week D 6 to 10.30 (5 to 10.30 Sat, 5 to 10 Sun). **Closed:** 25 and 26 Dec, 31 Dec. **Meals:** alc (main courses £11 to £27). Set L £9.95 (2 courses) to £15. Set D £15 (2 courses) to £20. **Service:** 12.5% (optional). **Details:** Cards accepted. 80 seats. 20 seats outside. Air-con. No music. Wheelchair access. Children allowed. Car parking.

Gordon Ramsay

A world-class restaurant experience
68-69 Royal Hospital Road, Chelsea, SW3 4HP
Tel no: (020) 7352 4441
www.gordonramsay.com
⊖ Sloane Square, map 3
Modern French | £90
Cooking score: 9
🍷 V

Gordon Ramsay's reputation may have taken a severe battering of late, but there's little doubt his illustrious Chelsea flagship is still the nearest thing to a world-class restaurant experience currently on offer in the capital. He may not sweat over the stoves these days, but Hospital Road remains close to his heart and those who have been delegated to run the show on his behalf go about their duties with consummate skill and gilt-edged metropolitan style. Much is down to the magisterial presence and gleeful, hand-rubbing bonhomie of irrepressible Jean-Claude Breton (indubitably 'the best maître d' in the UK'), a genial overlord who orchestrates his staff brilliantly and applies litres of French polish to ensure that every customer feels 'like a millionaire'. Meanwhile, head chef Clare Smyth interprets the Ramsay style with supreme confidence and knows how to sing with her master's voice – matching peerless technique and attention to detail with breathtaking freshness and picture-perfect presentation. Look no further than an astonishing dish of sautéed foie gras with roasted veal sweetbreads tinged with Cabernet Sauvignon vinegar and mollified with a spoonful of foamed almond velouté. Perfect. The kitchen can still deliver masterly renditions of the tried-and-trusted compositions that have become Ramsay signatures over the years, and these benchmarks of modern haute cuisine should be treasured – even though the kitchen has to withstand jibes about its lack of boundary-pushing edge. That said, a tour of GR's greatest hits might yield some truly memorable results: poached ravioli of lobster, langoustine and salmon in a velouté enhanced with the most delicate tinges of lemongrass and chervil, or a true classic involving the finest Cornish lamb with confit shoulder and a meticulous assemblage of Provençal vegetables, baby spinach and thyme jus. Delve deeper into the repertoire and you will also uncover some unexpected gems with more modish inflections – perhaps a remarkable, clear-flavoured combo of meaty roast monkfish with chorizo couscous, baby squid, artichokes and spiced tomato jus or a gorgeous dessert of Granny Smith apple parfait with blackberry foam, honeycomb and cider sorbet. Incidentals point up the sheer class of the place – whether it's a frog's leg lollipop on a coffee spoon of crushed potato or a heavenly take on

piña colada sucked through a glass straw. As for wine, a crack team of sommeliers is on hand to guide diners through the intricate byways of the awe-inspiring list. Rarities and fabulous French vintages abound, but take counsel if you are after something with a more earthly price tag. Around £23 is the bottom line, with glasses from £5.50.

Chef/s: Clare Smyth. **Open:** Mon to Fri L 12 to 2.30, D 6.30 to 11. **Closed:** Sat, Sun, 1 week Christmas. **Meals:** Set L £45. Set D £90. Tasting menu £120 (7 courses). **Service:** 12.5%. **Details:** Cards accepted. 45 seats. Air-con. Separate bar. No music. No mobile phones. Wheelchair access. Children allowed.

Haandi

Top-end Indian food near Harrods
136 Brompton Road, Knightsbridge, SW3 1HY
Tel no: (020) 7823 7373
www.haandi-restaurants.com
⊖ Knightsbridge, map 4
Indian | £25
Cooking score: 4

£5 OFF **V** £30

Drop in from the Brompton Road or use the entrance on Cheval Place to reach this London outpost of a Nairobi-based Indian restaurant group. Given that Haandi's near neighbour is Harrods, you can expect swish trappings and a platinum-card vibe in the vividly decorated dining room – with the added visual distraction of a theatrical kitchen in full flow. The menu leans towards top-end Punjabi cuisine, with the tandoor given plenty of use and most other dishes prepared and served in 'haandis' (wide-bellied, narrow-necked pots). If you want to venture beyond the ginger-spiked adraki lamb chops, rogan josh and murgh makhani, the menu also trips its way through Bombay street snacks, Goan fish masala, and South Indian Chennai chicken with coconut, curry leaves and mustard seeds. To conclude, freshen up with pistachio kulfi or slices of sumptuous Alphonso mango in season. House Italian is £14.95. A second London branch is at 301-303 Hale Lane, Edgware; tel (020) 8905 4433.

Chef/s: Ratan Singh. **Open:** all week L 12 to 3, D 5.30 to 11. **Closed:** 25 Dec. **Meals:** alc (main courses £7 to £14). Set L £12.95. **Service:** 12.5% (optional). **Details:** Cards accepted. 65 seats. Air-con. Music. Children allowed.

The Harwood Arms

Remarkable British victuals
Walham Grove, Fulham, SW6 1QP
Tel no: (020) 7386 1847
www.harwoodarms.com
⊖ Fulham Broadway, map 3
Gastropub | £30
Cooking score: 5

The Harwood Arms – the result of a premier-league partnership between Aussie star Brett Graham from the Ledbury (see entry) and Berkshire pub entrepreneur Mike Robinson – is now in full flow, serving pints of ale and stupendous Scotch eggs for the drinkers, and feeding everyone else with some remarkable British victuals. And with ex-Ledbury chef Stephen Williams revved-up in the kitchen, it's still raising the bar for gastropub food in the capital. Pulling neat strokes is one of the Harwood's trademarks – serving little prawn toasts with bowls of butternut squash and thyme soup, deploying pheasant for a novel Kiev, and filling 'technically strong', sugar-coated doughnuts with bittersweet marmalade. Poor pastrywork can sometimes let the side down, but reporters have found plenty of top-drawer stuff to applaud – including prettily presented poached salmon with 'broken eggs', braised shoulder of English mutton with creamed broccoli and celeriac purée, and an exquisitely simple dessert of Earl Grey ice cream with homemade Garibaldi biscuits. This place is the real deal – especially when you factor in courteous service, top-notch coffee and a wine list that offers serious drinking at very keen prices from £15.50.
Chef/s: Stephen Williams. **Open:** all week L 12 to 3 (4 Sun), D 6.30 to 9.30 (7 to 9 Sun). **Closed:** 25 to 28 Dec. **Meals:** alc (main courses £15 to £17). **Service:** 12.5% (optional). **Details:** Cards accepted. 60 seats. Separate bar. Music. Children allowed.

Hereford Road

Bullish British cooking
3 Hereford Road, Notting Hill, W2 4AB
Tel no: (020) 7727 1144
www.herefordroad.org
⊖ Bayswater, map 4
British | £24
Cooking score: 4
£5 OFF £30

Look for the black awning above what used to be a Notting Hill butcher's shop and you'll find Tom Pemberton's characterful neighbourhood restaurant, which he opened in 2007. The food is old British, with one or two notes of daring cosmopolitanism in the shapes of pigeon, pork and foie gras terrine, or veal breast with fennel and aïoli. Otherwise, expect heartily sustaining creations such as ox cheek and onion pie for two, and a range of offal starters, from devilled lamb's kidneys to ox heart with horseradish. It all felt 'wonderfully unpretentious' to one January diner, not to mention exemplary value, which may well be something to do with the tendency of the cheaper cuts of meat to deliver more flavour. There is fish too, perhaps lemon sole, served with salsify and black butter, and sturdy old English puddings such as sticky date or apple crumble. The wines are a sound international jumble, with prices from £18, or £3.50 for a small glass.
Chef/s: Tom Pemberton. **Open:** all week L 12 to 3 (4 Sun), D 6 to 10.30 (10 Sun). **Closed:** 25 and 26 Dec. **Meals:** alc (main courses £10 to £14). Set L £13 (2 courses) to £15.50. **Service:** not inc. **Details:** Cards accepted. 66 seats. 8 seats outside. Air-con. Wheelchair access. Music. Children allowed.

Please send us your feedback

To register your opinion about any restaurant listed in the Guide, or a new restaurant that you wish to bring to our attention, please visit the web address at the bottom of the page. Your feedback informs the content of the book and will be used to compile next year's reviews.

Hunan

Regional Chinese flavours
51 Pimlico Road, Chelsea, SW1W 8NE
Tel no: (020) 7730 5712
www.hunanlondon.com
⊖ Sloane Square, map 3
Chinese | £40
Cooking score: 3

V

Inside this neutral coloured room, adventurous diners can enjoy a no-choice menu, which takes in a dozen dishes from various regions in China. Flavours can be big: pepper igniting a hot-and-sour soup, salt bringing to life a diced chicken in a lettuce wrap, and a chicken won ton spiced up by red chilli. Braised pork belly with preserved vegetables is rich, whereas steamed scallop with cucumber and water chestnut showed the kitchen also has a sensitive side. Contrasting textures appear in the form of a jellyfish roll, as well as slow-cooked pork tongue in soy sauce. Best of all are crunchy tempura-like French beans. Service is attentive and informed. The carefully chosen wine list starts at £15.
Chef/s: Michael Peng. **Open:** Mon to Sat L 12.30 to 2.30, D 6.30 to 11. **Closed:** Sun, Christmas, 2 weeks July, bank hols. **Meals:** Set L and D from £38.80. **Service:** 12.5% (optional). **Details:** Cards accepted. 48 seats. Air-con. Music. Children allowed.

Il Convivio

Sleek and slick modern Italian
143 Ebury Street, Chelsea, SW1W 9QN
Tel no: (020) 7730 4099
www.etruscarestaurants.com
⊖ Victoria, Sloane Square, map 3
Italian | £35
Cooking score: 2

This beautifully converted Georgian town house in the heart of Belgravia is home to a sleek and slick Italian restaurant whose bilingual menu strides boldly through the Italian culinary canon while throwing in some smart modern ideas. The literary canon is referenced too; Dante coined the term 'convivio', meaning a meeting of minds over food and drink, and lines from his poetry adorn the red walls. On the plate, expect the likes of beef carpaccio with celery and basil-infused virgin olive oil followed by pan-fried fillet of wild sea bass with Mediterranean vegetables and rocket pesto. Desserts include pineapple carpaccio with exotic fruits and vanilla syrup. Wines from £13.50
Chef/s: Lukas Pfaff. **Open:** Mon to Sat L 12 to 3, D 6.30 to 10.30. **Closed:** Sun, bank hols, 25 Dec to 3 Jan. **Meals:** alc (main courses £13 to £28). Set L £17.50. Tasting menu £49.50. **Service:** 12.5% (optional). **Details:** Cards accepted. 65 seats. Air-con. Separate bar. Music. Children allowed.

Indian Zing

Cool venue, exciting food
236 King Street, Hammersmith, W6 0RF
Tel no: (020) 8748 5959
www.indianzing.co.uk
⊖ Ravenscourt Park, map 1
Indian | £22
Cooking score: 4

£5 OFF **V** £30

Designed in accordance with the harmonious mystical principles of Vastu Shastra, Manoj Vasaikar's purple-fronted Hammersmith venue is a cool customer indeed. This is a 'top spot' and its creative take on regional cuisine is exciting, refreshingly light and 'never old-fashioned'; Zing is also one of the few Indians in the capital to respect free-range and organic produce. Recommendations are thick on the ground, from appetite-sharpening shot glasses of raw mango, mint and cucumber frappé to a cheeky take on English fruit crumble for afters. In between, banana flower patties with a zesty green coriander sauce and 'utterly dreamy' warm prawn and aubergine kharphatla are hits, likewise 'gymkhana' lamb chops and velvety wild boar vindaloo with 'standout' lemon and ginger rice. Sides are also in a league of their own – fabulous aubergine raita and a dish of bottle gourd with pumpkin and lentils, for example. Wines from £15.
Chef/s: Manoj Vasaikar. **Open:** all week L 12 to 3 (1 to 4 Sun) D 6 to 11 (5 to 10 Sun). **Meals:** alc (main courses £9 to £18) Set L £12 (2 courses) to £15.

Service: 12.5% (optional). **Details:** Cards accepted. 61 seats. 22 seats outside. Air-con. No mobile phones. Wheelchair access. Music. Children allowed.

Kensington Place
Still delivering the goods
201-209 Kensington Church Street, Notting Hill, W8 7LX
Tel no: (020) 7727 3184
www.kensingtonplace-restaurant.co.uk
⊖ Notting Hill Gate, Kensington High Street, map 4
Modern European | £25
Cooking score: 4
🍷 £30

A west London landmark since 1987, Kensington Place continues to deliver the goods in its slick, professional style. The large room with its floor-to-ceiling windows is a booming but bright space, and new chef Daniel Phippard brings on board a sackload of culinary influences from across the Channel – for example in a starter of Loch Duart salmon ballottine with oyster vinaigrette and pickled vanilla cucumber. The menu is quite short and the kitchen generally steers a course towards tried and tested flavours – serving pot-roasted chicken with leek étouffée, mash and black trompettes, for example. However, it isn't afraid to stick its head above the parapet: stone bass has been enlivened with oxtail, while pineapple carpaccio might appear as a dessert in company with coconut sorbet, Thai basil and Szechuan pepper. The wine list is exciting, affordable and full of serious-minded global possibilities. A dozen by-the-glass selections get things rolling, with bottles from £17.50.
Chef/s: Daniel Phippard. **Open:** all week L 12 to 3 (3.30 Sat and Sun), D 6.30 to 10.30 (11 Fri and Sat, 10 Sun). **Closed:** 1 Jan. **Meals:** Set L £16.50 (2 courses) to £19.50. Set D £21.50 (2 courses) to £25. Sun L £16.50. **Service:** not inc. **Details:** Cards accepted. 96 seats. Air-con. Wheelchair access. Music. Children allowed.

ALSO RECOMMENDED
▲ Kiasu
48 Queensway, Bayswater, W2 3RY
Tel no: (020) 7727 8810
www.kiasu.co.uk
⊖ Bayswater, map 4
Pan-Asian

The word kiasu in the Chinese Hokkien dialect means 'afraid to be second best' and this restaurant has won a loyal following with its quest for perfection. The food is predominantly Singaporean and Malaysian – to be precise, it hails from the Straits of Malacca and neighbouring countries. Try Vietnamese spring rolls (£4.50) followed by nasi lemak – a traditional Straits dish comprising coconut rice, crispy anchovies, chicken curry, prawn sambal, achar pickle and egg (£8). Finish with a traditional dessert such as pulut hitam, a black rice pudding (£2.80). Wines start at £11.50. Open all week.

NEW ENTRY
Kitchen W8
Sophisticated brasserie
11 Abingdon Road, Kensington, W8 6AH
Tel no: (020) 7937 0120
www.kitchenw8.com
⊖ High Street Kensington, map 4
Modern European | £32
Cooking score: 5

Philip Howard of The Square (see entry) was brought in to sex up this restaurant which had failed to ignite the neighbourhood – and given the brisk business at the time of inspection his efforts seem to have worked. The dining room is smart yet informal and has a large collection of artwork. On the menu, dishes such as roast monkfish tail with Jerusalem artichokes and Swiss chard help ensure the culinary compass is pointing in the right direction. Craftsmanship is evident from the off, with a feather-light salt cod beignet, and superbly made pasta is a feature – ravioli of smoked ham hock sitting atop some pickled cabbage and finished off with pea foam, for example. The kitchen's versatility allows you to taste each element in complex dishes, witness a silken fillet of Cornish haddock with smoked gnocchi, petite pieces of chorizo, razor clams and celery. Cheese is worth a punt, but save room for dessert – a passion-fruit tart with fresh mango and lime-infused cream is pure deliciousness. Service, too, bubbles with enthusiasm. The nifty wine list starts at £14.95, with a Reserves collection offered without any premiums.

Chef/s: Mark Kempson. **Open:** all week L 12 to 2.30 (12.30 to 3 Sun), D 6 to 10.30 (6.30 to 10 Sun). **Closed:** bank hols. **Meals:** alc (main courses £17 to £22). Set L £17.50 (2 courses) to £19.50. Set D £21.50 (2 courses) to £24.50. Sun L £25. **Service:** 12.5% (optional). **Details:** Cards accepted. 80 seats. Air-con. Wheelchair access. Children allowed.

Launceston Place

Traditional and innovative food
1a Launceston Place, South Kensington, W8 5RL
Tel no: (020) 7937 6912
www.launcestonplace-restaurant.co.uk
⊖ Gloucester Road, map 3
Modern British | £46
Cooking score: 4

This neighbourhood restaurant located in a quiet backwater of ever-so-smart Kensington consists of a series of interconnecting rooms unflashily decorated in neutral caramels, creams and dark grey. Drawing on the best of the European repertoire – anything from cep risotto and crispy suckling pig to innovative hot-smoked halibut with wild fennel – Tristan Welch offers fixed-price lunch and dinner options (with supplements) plus a six-course tasting menu. The results can be uneven, but few would argue with well-timed scallops roasted with aromatic herbs and 'amazing' salt marsh lamb served with crackling, sea beets and salt-baked potatoes. At dessert stage, rice pudding is given a twist, emerging as a soufflé with a trendy raspberry ripple ice cream. Service can be 'extremely polite and helpful' but also 'too slow for a business lunch'. While the food is good value, drinks, including water and coffee can 'really bump up the bill'. Wines from £19.50.

Chef/s: Tristan Welch. **Open:** Tue to Sun L 12 to 2.30 (3 Sun), all week D 6 to 10.30 (6.30 Sun). **Meals:** Set L £20. Set D £46. Sun L £26. Tasting menu £60. **Service:** 12.5% (optional). **Details:** Cards accepted. 65 seats. Air-con. Separate bar. No music. No mobile phones. Wheelchair access. Children allowed.

The Ledbury

Astonishing food from an Aussie star
127 Ledbury Road, Notting Hill, W11 2AQ
Tel no: (020) 7792 9090
www.theledbury.com
⊖ Notting Hill Gate, Westbourne Park, map 4
Modern European | £65
Cooking score: 7

🍾 V

The Ledbury's über-cool, soigné dining room radiates affluence and old-school Notting Hill breeding, but it also manages to meld moneyed sophistication with the personable attributes of a proper neighbourhood eatery. Aussie frontman Brett Graham responds to the surrounds by dressing his astonishing food with a designer's brio, allowing luxurious finery to shine and re-inventing some of the old rustic ways for today's inquisitive palates. His talent for injecting outrageous thrills into earthy practices might see celeriac baked in ash with wood sorrel, shoulder of Pyrénean milk-fed lamb cooked for 24 hours, or loin of Sika deer baked in Douglas Fir with beetroot, bone marrow and malt. Even an intricately worked dish of Hereford snails in a mousseline of herbs is hard-wired to the soil with pickled carrots, cep marmalade and roasted oxtail juices. Like most auteur chefs, Graham flaunts his hottest signature dishes (flame-grilled mackerel with cucumber, Celtic mustard and shiso, say) and also has a magic box of favourite ingredients: liquorice, for example, is not only paired famously with scallops, but also adds its dark tones to poached breast and confit pigeon with Cevennes onions and foie gras. When it comes to ringing the changes, the daring possibilities seem endless: a pressing of suckling pig could arrive with spätzle, morels and a reduction of dried

chicory or with spring onions, mangosteen and molasses – depending on personal whims or the demands of the season. The set lunch has proved a real diamond for outstanding value and unabashed quality of late (no crunch-busting pauperism here). One reader came away with drool-inducing memories of a warm salad of Middle White pork with apple and spring truffles followed by crusted monkfish cooked in bonito butter with cauliflower and seaweed; after that, a sublime coconut pannacotta stuffed with tiny cubes of gariguette strawberries sealed the deal. Service seems to have perked up after last year's wobbles, with 'caring attention' and unobtrusive manners now the order of the day. A page of brilliant wines by the glass (from £7.50) fronts the weighty list, which has plenty of half-bottles and treasures in abundance – from patrician white Burgundies to beefy Californian reds. Bottles start at £24.
Chef/s: Brett Graham. **Open:** Tue to Sun L 12 to 2.30, all week D 6.30 to 10.30 (7 to 10 Sun). **Closed:** 24 to 27 Dec, 1 Jan, Aug bank hol. **Meals:** Set L £22.50 (2 courses) to £27.50. Set D £55 (2 courses) to £65. Tasting menu £75 (8 courses). Sun L £40. **Service:** 12.5% optional. **Details:** Cards accepted. 65 seats. 25 seats outside. Air-con. No music. Wheelchair access. Children allowed.

ALSO RECOMMENDED
▲ Madsen
20 Old Brompton Road, South Kensington, SW7 3DL
Tel no: (020) 7225 2772
www.madsenrestaurant.com
⊖ South Kensington, map 3
Scandinavian £5 OFF

The clean-lined glass frontage of this relaxed Scandinavian brasserie stands out from the touristy eateries around South Kensington tube. It's strong on eco ethics and design; an interior of blond woods is set against white walls and classic Poul Henningsen lighting. The food follows suit, offering a modern take on traditional Scandinavian themes. The evening carte delivers classic sweet-cured herring with dill-marinated potatoes and

mustard cream (£6.96), and fillet of plaice teamed with beurre noisette and a tomato, onion and parsley salad (£16.75). Lunch is even simpler, 'entirely smørrebrød', though with smaller versions of the traditional open sandwich, called 'smushi'. European wines from £17.25. Open all week.

READERS RECOMMEND
The Mall Tavern
Gastropub
71-73 Palace Gardens Terrace, Notting Hill, W8 4RU
Tel no: (020) 7229 3374
www.themalltavern.com
'Brilliant Victorian curiosity shop decor, delicious traditional British food'

NEW ENTRY
Manson
Metropolitan vibes, elegant food
676 Fulham Road, London, SW6 5SA
Tel no: (020) 7384 9559
www.mansonrestaurant.co.uk
⊖ Parsons Green, map 3
Modern European | £27
Cooking score: 4
£30

The team behind top-drawer gastropub the Sands End (see entry) has created a more sophisticated, grown-up experience with their exciting new venture. Manson's slick, light, metropolitan interior comes complete with booths and a noticeably laid-back atmosphere. There are no white cloths on the tables and the simplistic tone of the menu belies the big-city elegance of the food dished up by talented ex-Ramsay chef Gemma Tuley. Ceviche-style trout tartare with roe and tomato consommé and an English tomato salad with lavender and honey dressing are perfect warm-weather starters, whilst a tripartite dish of Sussex rabbit – rolled saddle, pressed meat and offal faggot – served with macaroni cheese is exemplary, although rice pudding with a jammy rhubarb compote and granita has been less well-schooled. House wine is £13.50.

Chef/s: Gemma Tuley. **Open:** Mon to Fri L 12 to 3 (10 to 4 Sat), D 6 to 10.30. Sun 12 to 9.30. **Closed:** 25 and 26 Dec. **Meals:** alc (main courses £12 to £25). Set L £12.50 (2 courses) to £16. **Service:** 12.5% (optional). **Details:** Cards accepted. 62 seats. 8 seats outside. Air-con. Separate bar. Music. Children allowed.

Notting Hill Brasserie
Highly valued local destination
92 Kensington Park Road, Notting Hill, W11 2PN
Tel no: (020) 7229 4481
www.nottinghillbrasserie.com
⊖ Notting Hill Gate, map 4
Modern European | £45
Cooking score: 4

Equally useful for big-occasion bashes and cool romantic assignations to the accompaniment of live jazz, the capacious Notting Hill Brasserie is a highly valued destination in swish W11. It occupies the plush, dramatically lit ground floor of three knocked-together terraced houses, with lofty corniced ceilings, well-spaced tables and eye-catching floral displays – just the ticket if you have money to spend. The food is certainly not the cheapest in the neighbourhood, but it's well worth the outlay for confidently rendered dishes such as pan-fried sea bass with pumpkin purée, wild mushroom risotto and red wine sauce, or slow-cooked beef fillet with triple-cooked chips and béarnaise. Round off with something classic such as chocolate fondant or tarte Tatin with Calvados sauce. Good-value lunches bring some financial relief, and Sunday is a family get-together: parents looking to relax can even entrust their little darlings to the nanny in charge of the kiddies' play area. The international wine list kicks off with house selections from £18.
Chef/s: Karl Burdock. **Open:** Tue to Sun L 12 to 3 (4 Sun), all week D 7 to 11 (10.30 Sun). **Closed:** 26 and 27 Dec, 1 and 2 Jan. **Meals:** alc (main courses £19 to £30). Set L £16.50 (2 courses) to £23. Sun L £29.50 (2 courses) to £36.50. **Service:** 12.5%.
Details: Cards accepted. 110 seats. Air-con. Separate bar. Music. Children allowed.

Olivo
Showcase for Sardinian specialities
21 Eccleston Street, Belgravia, SW1W 9LX
Tel no: (020) 7730 2505
www.olivorestaurants.com
⊖ Victoria, map 3
Sardinian | £31
Cooking score: 1

Dark blue and sandy hues set a cheery tone in the original branch of Mauro Sanna's olive-themed mini-chain, where the food combines unshowy rustic Italian cooking with some specialities from Sardinia. Marinated tuna carpaccio is a good way to start, before a signature dish of malloredus pasta with an Italian sausage ragù. Mains might feature the likes of roast rabbit wrapped in Parma with polenta, and you could finish with poached pears garnished with mascarpone and crumbled amaretti. Sardinian house wines (from £18.50) top the short Italian-led list.
Chef/s: Sandro Medda. **Open:** Mon to Fri L 12 to 2.30, all week D 6 to 10.30 (6.30 to 10.30 Sun). **Closed:** bank hols. **Meals:** alc (main courses £15 to £19). Set L £21.25 (2 courses) to £25. **Service:** not inc. **Details:** Cards accepted. 40 seats. Air-con. No music. Children allowed.

El Pirata Detapas
Neighbourhood tapas bar
115 Westbourne Grove, Notting Hill, W2 4UP
Tel no: (020) 7727 5000
www.elpiratadetapas.co.uk
⊖ Notting Hill Gate, Bayswater, map 4
Spanish | £20
Cooking score: 3
£5 OFF **V** £30

This neighbourhood tapas bar's chef has done time at El Bulli, and it shows. Endive salad with Valdéon cheese – so far, so conventional – has a trendy foam dressing, while octopus carpaccio is dotted with spheres of clementine 'caviar' and paprika. Omar Allibhoy's mastery of technique is even better when applied to tapas classics: an individual tortilla, cooked to order, was perfectly runny inside, while ham croquetas were as crisp without as they were creamy within. Reports, however, suggest such heights aren't always hit. Its straitlaced, 15-year-old Mayfair sibling (El Pirata, see entry) could teach it a thing or two. The all-Iberian wine list, from £13.50 (£3.50 a glass) shows a special affection for Tempranillo and 'native varieties'. Tasting menus showcase the greatest hits.

Chef/s: Omar Allibhoy. **Open:** all week L 12 to 3, D 6 to 11 (12 to 11 Sun). **Closed:** 25 to 28 Dec, last weekend Aug. **Meals:** alc (tapas £3 to £12). Set L £9. Set D £25. **Service:** 10% (optional). **Details:** Cards accepted. 88 seats. Air-con. Separate bar. Wheelchair access. Music. Children allowed.

Popeseye

Steak and chips – but what steak!
108 Blythe Road, Kensington, W14 0HD
Tel no: (020) 7610 4578
www.popeseye.com
⊖ Olympia, map 1
Steaks | £20
Cooking score: 1
£5 OFF £30

Since 1995 Ian Hutchinson has been serving the denizens of W14 honest-to-goodness steak and chips and nothing more. But it's some steak – prime grass-fed Aberdeen Angus from the Highlands, hung for a minimum of two weeks to ensure maximum flavour and tenderness, with cuts ranging from 6 oz to 30 oz of popeseye (rump), sirloin or fillet. With no starters and a perfunctory choice of puddings and cheese, it is all served in a simply decorated dining room with the grill open to view in the corner. Wines focus on fine clarets, with basic house red at £12.50. There's another branch at 277 Upper Richmond Road, Putney SW15; tel: (020) 8788 7733.

Chef/s: Ian Hutchinson. **Open:** Mon to Sat D only 6 to 10. **Closed:** Sun, bank hols. **Meals:** alc (steaks £10 to £45). **Service:** 12.5% (optional). **Details:** Cash only. 34 seats. Air-con. Wheelchair access. Music. Children allowed.

NEW ENTRY

Portobello Ristorante Pizzeria

Eat-me pizza for sharing
7 Ladbroke Road, Notting Hill, W11 3PA
Tel no: (020) 7221 1373
www.portobellolondon.co.uk
⊖ Notting Hill Gate, map 4
Italian | £30
Cooking score: 1
V

You need to be in a sociable mood to enjoy the noisy, cramped rooms, and to share the 'pizzametro', a pizza by the metre with various toppings that shouts 'eat me'. The kitchen does a good job, too, when it comes to earthy scilatelli pasta with king prawns and porcini, or charcoal-grilled sea bream. Service can lose the plot when busy. The front terrace is fabulous for sunny days, and lemon sorbet makes a pleasant end. Wines start from £14.50.

Chef/s: Franco Ferro. **Open:** all week L 12 to 3.30 (4 Sat and Sun), D 6 to 11 (10.30 Sun). **Meals:** alc (main courses £9 to £20). Set L £12.50. **Service:** 12.5% (optional). **Details:** Cards accepted. 60 seats. 30 seats outside. Air-con. Music. Children allowed.

La Poule au Pot

Irrepressible Gallic charmer
231 Ebury Street, Belgravia, SW1W 8UT
Tel no: (020) 7730 7763
⊖ Sloane Square, map 3
French | £50
Cooking score: 2
V

For more than 40 years, this irrepressible grand-mère among London's bistros has worked its magic, thanks to a seductive blend of clutter and close-packed tables, lace-draped windows and magnums of house wine. It's universally prized as a dream ticket for Francophiles and as a hearts-and-flowers rendezvous *par excellence* for processions of doting couples. Bonhomie rules, French is the lingua franca and there's no disguising what's on the menu. The kitchen doesn't care a jot about fashion, relying instead on the flavours of old – la soupe à l'oignon, les escargots, bouillabaisse and, naturally, la poule au pot in all its bourgeois glory. To finish, it has to be crème brûlée or tarte Tatin. Wines – French, of course – start at £16.75.

Chef/s: Francesco Villa and Chris Golebiowski. **Open:** all week L 12.30 to 3 (4 Sat and Sun), D 6.45 to 11.15 (10 Sun). **Closed:** 25 and 26 Dec, 1 Jan. **Meals:** alc (main courses £16 to £25). Set L £18.75 (2 courses) to £22.75. **Service:** 12.5% (optional). **Details:** Cards accepted. 65 seats. 36 seats outside. Air-con. No music. No mobile phones. Wheelchair access. Children allowed.

The Princess Victoria

Smart pub with big-hearted food
217 Uxbridge Road, Shepherd's Bush, W12 9DT
Tel no: (020) 8749 5886
www.princessvictoria.co.uk
⊖ **Goldhawk Road, Shepherd's Bush, map 1**
Gastropub | £27
Cooking score: 3

£30

Since opening in June 2008, this Victorian watering hole has become an assured, congenial establishment, much favoured by a young, affluent crowd. The bar, where you can eat oysters, potted crab and homemade pork and herb sausages, buzzes with noise and chatter, while the stately dining room impresses with its centrepiece oak table and high ceilings. The kitchen puts its faith in big-hearted dishes, which could mean braised ox faggots and onion gravy with bubble and squeak. Starters might include beef shin and vegetable soup with pearl barley and bone marrow dumplings, while desserts are equally robust offerings like sticky toffee pudding. Well-chosen wines from £14.50.

Chef/s: James McLean. **Open:** all week L 12 to 3 (4.30 Sun), D 6.30 to 10.30 (9.30 Sun). **Closed:** 25 to 28 Dec. **Meals:** alc (main courses £9 to £18). Set L £12.50 (2 courses) to £15. **Service:** not inc. **Details:** Cards accepted. 170 seats. 40 seats outside. Air-con. Separate bar. Music. Children allowed. Car parking.

Racine

Bastion of cuisine bourgeoise
239 Brompton Road, Knightsbridge, SW3 2EP
Tel no: (020) 7584 4477
www.racine-restaurant.com
⊖ **Knightsbridge, South Kensington, map 3**
French | £40
Cooking score: 4

£5 OFF

Racine is one of a vanishing breed among London restaurants – it is dedicated wholesale to serving the traditional French dishes of cuisine bourgeoise. Henry Harris emerged from the kitchens at Harvey Nichols in 2002 to run his own operation, a kind of neighbourhood restaurant – if indeed the Brompton Road quite counts as a neighbourhood. Visitors to the Kensington museums, at any rate, will give thanks for Bayonne ham with celeriac rémoulade, calf's brains with black butter and capers, and fortifying main courses such as grilled veal chop with pickled walnuts in Roquefort butter. The front-of-house approach is as businesslike and efficient as you would expect in any Parisian restaurant *du quartier*, and the daily changing prix-fixe menu is a bargain. Desserts such as poached rhubarb with rosewater and crème fraîche sorbet end things on a light note. Wine prices open at £18.

Chef/s: Henry Harris. **Open:** all week L 12 to 3 (3.30 Sun), D 6 to 10.30 (10 Sun). **Closed:** 25 Dec. **Meals:** alc (main courses £15 to £26). Set L and early D £15 (2 courses) to £17.50. **Service:** 14.5% (optional). **Details:** Cards accepted. 60 seats. 4 seats outside. Air-con. No music. Children allowed.

Please send us your feedback

To register your opinion about any restaurant listed in the Guide, or a new restaurant that you wish to bring to our attention, please visit the web address at the bottom of the page. Your feedback informs the content of the book and will be used to compile next year's reviews.

Rasoi

A spicy treat for the taste buds
10 Lincoln Street, Chelsea, SW3 2TS
Tel no: (020) 7225 1881
www.rasoi-uk.com
⊖ Sloane Square, map 3
Indian | £58
Cooking score: 5

£5 OFF 🍾 V

Rasoi is unmistakably Indian – the trendy retro flock wallpaper and ethnic artefacts even hint at old-school curry house – but the point about Vineet Bhatia is that he has been redefining the culinary genre in London since his early days. The results may not be to everyone's taste, but they certainly challenge the vindaloo and lager clichés. Look for the discreet entrance in a street just off the King's Road and ring the bell to get in. Once inside, expect the unexpected: this is a place where round plates are the exception not the rule, where meals come with amuse-bouches and pre-desserts, and top-drawer service helps to create a top-drawer vibe. Results were uneven at inspection, but there was no arguing with the refreshing lemon and mint drink served with steamed idli cakes, the home-smoked tandoori salmon (part of a seafood medley) that has been Bhatia's signature dish for many years, or a truffled potato khichdi offered with subtly spiced duck tikka. Elsewhere there are good lunch deals – note the excellent-value platter with lamb seekh kebab, the aforementioned salmon, chicken tikka and duck confit samosa, naan and black dhal – and a seven-course tasting menu with optional wine pairings. Westernised desserts are not a strong suit. The upmarket wine list offers plenty to match the spicy food, with a good selection by the glass, some serious reds and prices from £25.

Chef/s: Vineet Bhatia. **Open:** Mon to Fri L 12 to 2.30, Mon to Sat D 6 to 11. **Closed:** Sun, 25 and 26 Dec, 1 Jan. **Meals:** alc (main courses £28 to £38). Set L £21 (2 courses) to £26. Set D £48 (2 courses) to £58. Tasting menu £83 (7 courses). **Service:** 12.5% (optional). **Details:** Cards accepted. 50 seats. Air-con. No music. No mobile phones. Children allowed.

Restaurant Michael Nadra

New-look Chiswick favourite
6-8 Elliott Road, Chiswick, W4 1PE
Tel no: (020) 8742 0766
www.restaurant-michaelnadra.co.uk
⊖ Turnham Green, map 1
Modern European | £32
Cooking score: 4

Michael Nadra's restaurant has changed its name from Fish Hook and has moved away from its pescatarian theme. The dining room is smart, with black leather banquettes making up for the tight table spacing. It's a place to enjoy rather than worship food. The cooking is contemporary, with cross-cultural influences popping up, as in an 'ultra-fresh' seared yellowfin tuna paired with a tempura of soft-shell crab. Closer to home but equally deft, a juicy grilled Devon pork chop arrived with olive oil mash enlivened by a thyme jus. Fish is an obvious strength, producing a 'lovely piece' of sea bass with saffron crab ravioli in a basil-infused bisque. The upbeat style continues with a textbook apple tarte Tatin with cinnamon and Calvados ice cream. The wine list starts from £15, reaches out to every corner of the globe, and has plenty of choices under £30.

Chef/s: Michael Nadra. **Open:** all week L 12 to 2.30 (3.30 Sat and Sun), D 6 to 10 (10.30 Fri and Sat). **Closed:** 25 and 26 Dec. **Meals:** alc (main courses £17 to £22). Set L £13.50 (2 courses) to £16. Set D £16.50 (2 courses) to £19. **Service:** 12.5% (optional). **Details:** Cards accepted. 52 seats. Air-con. Wheelchair access. Music. Children allowed.

Symbols	
🛏	Accommodation is available
£30	Three courses for less than £30
V	More than three vegetarian main courses
£5 OFF	£5-off voucher scheme
🍾	Notable wine list

The River Café
Relentlessly consistent Italian icon
Thames Wharf, Rainville Road, Hammersmith, W6 9HA
Tel no: (020) 7386 4200
www.rivercafe.co.uk
⊖ **Hammersmith, map 1**
Italian | £65
Cooking score: 6

The sad death of Rose Gray in 2010 was a reminder of just how influential the restaurant that she co-founded with friend Ruth Rogers in 1987 has been over the years. Their shared philosophy has survived untarnished and the River Café experience remains relentlessly consistent, as the cavernous Hammersmith dining hall regularly heaves with foodie punters. Famously, eating here doesn't come cheap – although perks such as half-portions, the house fizzy water and the option of choosing either antipasti (a fritto misto of borage, polenta and radicchio, perhaps) or primi (risotto alla vongole) can ease the financial pain. The main pleasure of the place is not the river (you won't have a sniff of it, unless a sunny day coincides with space on the terrace), but the fact that everything on the plate is good. This is one of the capital's most fashion-forward Italian menus – defined by emblematic seasonal flavours – and just about everything begs to be eaten. Fresh herbs, leaves and vegetables lighten main courses such as veal shin slow-roasted with thyme and spring garlic in Soave Classico (accompanied by Swiss chard, broad beans and gremolata), while fish dishes are sparkling fresh – perhaps char-grilled monkfish and scallops on a rosemary stick with zucchini fritti, rocket, anchovy and rosemary sauce. To finish, the notorious Chocolate Nemesis and silky ice creams round things off with spoonfuls of lush luxury. Wines start at £17.50 (£4.50 a glass), and the list makes thorough reading for Italophiles on any budget.
Chef/s: Ruth Rogers. **Open:** all week L 12.30 to 3, Mon to Sat D 7 to 11. **Closed:** 23 Dec to 3 Jan, bank hols. **Meals:** alc (main courses £28 to £36).

Service: 12.5% (optional). **Details:** Cards accepted. 116 seats. 80 seats outside. Separate bar. No music. Wheelchair access. Children allowed. Car parking.

Roussillon
Polished Gallic jewel
16 St Barnabas Street, Chelsea, SW1W 8PE
Tel no: (020) 7730 5550
www.roussillon.co.uk
⊖ **Sloane Square, map 3**
Modern French | £60
Cooking score: 6
£5 OFF 🍷 **V**

Noted for its measured civility, calm confidence and sophistication, this fixture of the Chelsea scene continues to show its class with highly assured modern French cuisine. Following Alexis Gauthier's move to Gauthier Soho (see entry), new chef Daniel Gill has stepped up to the mark with surprising ease, and delicate pre-starter offerings set the tone for a menu full of high-end ingredients. Early reports suggest he can match his predecessor's prowess with food that is precision-tuned and full of delicate colours, textures and contrasts. A dish of sautéed langoustines and expertly poached lobster is set off with startling beetroot embellishments (raw, cooked and puréed), while griddled foie gras is complemented by the punchy sweetness of mango and Pedro Ximénez sherry. To finish, Louis XV – a classic chocolate mousse and praline concoction – is as good a version as you'll find in London. So far, so impressive. However, the kitchen has something exceptional up its sleeve – a high-end vegetarian menu that challenges the ingrained French loathing for meatless frivolities. Expect to revel in seasonal truffles, morels, asparagus and herbs, all cooked with due care and attention. Wines from southern France (including the Roussillon region, of course) loom large on the eye-opening, palate-challenging 400-bin list, which roams the world in search of quality. Rare tipples abound and there is a comprehensive choice by the glass (from £6.50).

Chef/s: Daniel Gill. **Open:** Mon to Fri L 12 to 2.30, Mon to Sat D 6.30 to 10. **Closed:** Sun, 25 Dec to 5 Jan. **Meals:** Set L £35 (includes half-bottle of wine). Set D £48 (2 courses) to £60. Tasting menu £65 (vegetarian), £78 (non-vegetarian). **Service:** 12.5% (optional). **Details:** Cards accepted. 70 seats. Air-con. No music. No mobile phones. Children allowed.

Sam's Brasserie & Bar
All-singing, all-dancing venue
11 Barley Mow Passage, Chiswick, W4 4PH
Tel no: (020) 8987 0555
www.samsbrasserie.co.uk
⊖ Chiswick Park, Turnham Green, map 1
Modern European | £26
Cooking score: 3
V £30

Sam Harrison's big brasserie carved out of a former Sanderson wallpaper factory has a lively café atmosphere. Roast bone marrow on toast with parsley and shallot salad, and braised pork cheek with sweet potato purée, honey roast parsnips and cider jus are typical of the now familiar modern British brasserie dishes on offer. Ingredients are good and results have pleased across the board. A 'comforting' dish of poached smoked haddock with champ mash, poached egg and hollandaise sauce has topped the list of recent recommendations, with milk chocolate torte and banana ice cream getting the thumbs up for dessert. Set lunches are good value. The wine list offers a well-chosen global selection with bottles from £14.50.
Chef/s: Ian Leckie. **Open:** all week L 12 to 3 (4 Sat and Sun), D 6.30 to 10.30. **Closed:** 24 Dec to 28 Dec. **Meals:** alc (main courses £11 to £19). Set L £12.50 (2 courses) to £15.50. Set D £14.50 (2 courses) to £17.50. Sun L £21. **Service:** 12.5% (optional). **Details:** Cards accepted. 100 seats. Air-con. Separate bar. Wheelchair access. Music. Children allowed.

Also recommended
Also recommended entries are not scored but we think they are worth a visit.

The Sands End
Achingly simple comfort food
135-137 Stephendale Road, Fulham, SW6 2PR
Tel no: (020) 7731 7823
www.thesandsend.co.uk
⊖ Fulham Broadway, map 3
British | £25
Cooking score: 2
V £30

This may be the residential heart of Fulham, but step inside this unassuming pub and it could be the Cotswolds. Mismatched tables and chairs, bare floorboards, blackboard menus – there's no doubt the Sands End is enjoying the benefits of a twenty-first century revamp. Ideas are unfussy, and much of the food is achingly simple comfort food at its best: Welsh rarebit, Scotch eggs and crackling in the bar, roast venison and 28-day ribeye steak with triple-cooked wedges and béarnaise sauce in the dining room. There's also the 'best and most agreeable service I've come across in a long time' and a good-value wine list from £14.70.
Chef/s: Tim Kesset. **Open:** Mon to Fri L 12 to 3, D 6 to 10.30. Sat and Sun 12 to 10. **Closed:** 25 and 26 Dec. **Meals:** alc (main courses £13 to £20). Set L £12.50 (2 courses) to £16.50. Sun L £16.95. **Service:** 12.5% (optional). **Details:** Cards accepted. 60 seats. 16 seats outside. Air-con. Separate bar. Wheelchair access. Music. Children allowed.

NEW ENTRY
Sushi Hiro
Impeccable sushi
1 Station Parade, Ealing Common, W5 3LD
Tel no: (020) 8896 3175
⊖ Ealing Common, map 1
Japanese | £18
Cooking score: 3
£30

Small and spartan, Sushi Hiro makes its own rules. One couple were turned away at 1pm because the restaurant was shutting early, without warning. However, the effort of a return visit was more than justified by sushi and sashimi of impeccable quality. There's often just one chef on, and he'll take as long as need be. Express service is not the Sushi Hiro way. Don't let these warnings put you off: this is some of the capital's best-quality and best-value Japanese food. From a menu limited to sushi and sashimi, an inspector was wowed by an attractively chequered, pressed mackerel sushi, by tofu pockets filled with perfect rice, and the chef's sashimi choice (including sweet prawns and glistening sardines). Credit cards aren't accepted, so come prepared.

Chef/s: Mr Funakoshi. **Open:** Tue to Sun L 11 to 3, D 4.30 to 9.30. **Closed:** Mon. **Meals:** alc (sushi from £3). Set L and D £10 to £18. **Service:** not inc. **Details:** Cash only. 20 seats. Air-con. Separate bar. Music. Children allowed.

The Thomas Cubitt

Dapper Belgravia gastropub
44 Elizabeth Street, Belgravia, SW1W 9PA
Tel no: (020) 7730 6060
www.thethomascubitt.co.uk
⊖ Victoria, map 3
Gastropub | £34
Cooking score: 3

Named in honour of Thomas Cubitt, the Victorian master builder who gave Belgravia Square its good looks, this lavishly re-fashioned town house now operates as a dapper gastropub on two levels. The oak-floored bar and street terrace get rammed with well-heeled drinkers and snackers ('be prepared to fight the chaotic crowds', warns a reader), but things are more civilised in the handsome upstairs dining rooms. There's a well-considered modern flavour to the cooking, which might yield pressed duck and pistachio terrine with raspberry jelly ahead of pan-fried stone bass with oyster pot pie, baby fennel and lemon preserve, or peppered wild venison fillet with black cabbage and creamed morels. Sea salt caramel and chocolate tart with peanut parfait makes a typically trendy finale. The extended, knowledgeably chosen wine list starts at £16 (£4 a glass).

Chef/s: Phillip Wilson. **Open:** Sun to Fri L 12 to 3 (4 Sun), Mon to Sat D 6 to 10. **Closed:** 25 Dec to 1 Jan. **Meals:** alc (main courses £15 to £27). Set D £17.50 (2

courses) to £25. Sun L £18.50. **Service:** 12.5% (optional). **Details:** Cards accepted. 50 seats. Air-con. Separate bar. Music. Children allowed.

Timo

Dignified, affable Italian
343 Kensington High Street, Kensington, W8 6NW
Tel no: (020) 7603 3888
www.timorestaurant.net
⊖ High Street Kensington, map 3
Italian | £32
Cooking score: 2

£5 OFF **V**

An affably run Italian in the heart of Kensington, Timo receives plaudits from readers for its 'dignified welcome, calm atmosphere and good service, not to mention a lunch menu that's astonishingly good value'. A brown-toned interior with hanging light-pods and smart table settings is the scene for offerings such as pumpkin and squash risotto, plaice in Vermentino wine with prawns and baby artichokes, and veal escalopes in lemon sauce. Among the desserts are crème caramel with amaretti and chocolate, and tiramisu. A fine, expansive wine list divides Italy painstakingly into its regions, with prices starting at £17, and plenty by the glass.

Chef/s: Franco Gatto. **Open:** Mon to Sat L 12 to 2.30, D 7 to 11. **Closed:** Sun, 24 to 26 Dec, bank hols. **Meals:** alc (main courses £7 to £24). Set L £13.90 (2 courses) to £16. **Service:** not inc. **Details:** Cards accepted. 48 seats. 2 seats outside. Air-con. Separate bar. Music. Children allowed.

Tom Aikens

Dazzling flavours from a white-hot talent
43 Elystan Street, Chelsea, SW3 3NT
Tel no: (020) 7584 2003
www.tomaikens.co.uk
⊖ South Kensington, map 3
Modern French | £65
Cooking score: 8

V

Having survived a financial scare during the downturn, Tom Aikens is still afloat and it's business as usual at his discreet Chelsea flagship – a light-filled, monochromatic room where understated design gestures allow the food to hold centre stage. Canapés set the bar high – a tiny square of cod pannacotta dipped in tomato dust and served on a spoon, a Parmesan beignet, and a cauliflower and beetroot confection in a shot glass with a straw. After that, diners now have a choice of inspired, high-end creations and self-styled Tom's Classics – simpler ideas pulled from the Euro mainstream (think langoustine risotto, baked sea bass with heritage tomatoes and warm rice pudding with poached pear). There are suggestions of hesitant bet-hedging in this arrangement, and the results aren't always on target – judging by one reader's chewy rack of lamb with Parmesan mash. Aikens has certainly cooled down since those early maverick days when he played like Jackson Pollock and threw everything at the plate, but he remains a white-hot talent and his food can still blow your socks off: consider an outrageously good starter of roast hand-dived scallops arranged with spiced mango purée and tiny morsels of confit duck in different forms. The search for exquisitely amalgamated, 'dazzle-in-the-mouth' flavours is a recurring theme that can also yield John Dory with cauliflower purée, mint oil and pickled grapes, loin of lamb marinated in ewe's cheese with dried green olive or a fabulous combination of marinated pigeon poached in cinnamon and coffee with pigeon confit. To finish, the kitchen might conjure up a seriously deconstructed île flottante involving baked and poached meringue with salted popcorn and caramel ice cream. Service is very proper, but can become intrusive and overbearing – you may be pressured into ordering superfluous side dishes, for example. New sommelier Sebastien Morice worked at Tom Aikens alongside legendary Gearoid Devaney, although the list has lost some of its depth and authority since he took over the reins, with prices (from £25) heading ever upward; also be prepared to spend at least £10 if you order by the glass.

Chef/s: Tom Aikens. **Open:** Mon to Fri L 12 to 2.30, Mon to Sat D 6.45 to 10.45. **Closed:** Sun, bank hols, last 2 weeks Aug, 24 Dec to 5 Jan. **Meals:** alc (main

courses £25 to £40). Set L £23 (2 courses) to £29. Tasting menu £80. **Service:** 12.5% (optional). **Details:** Cards accepted. 54 seats. Air-con. Separate bar. Wheelchair access. Music. Children allowed.

Tom's Kitchen
Brasserie food for strapping appetites
27 Cale Street, Chelsea, SW3 3QP
Tel no: (020) 7349 0202
www.tomskitchen.co.uk
⊖ **Sloane Square, South Kensington, map 3**
Modern British | £40
Cooking score: 4

V

It's situated just around the corner from his exclusive fine-dining flagship (see entry above), but Tom Aikens' streetwise Kitchen is a gastronomic world away – this deafening whitewashed space feeds noisy crowds with trencherman brasserie food. Following the departure of chefs Rob Aikens and Julien Maisonneuve, the top job has passed to Richard Robinson – a safe pair of hands who knows the repertoire inside out. Steak tartare and moules marinière line up alongside coronation crab salad with toasted almonds, although big boys with strapping appetites might go straight for shepherd's pie, venison casserole with cranberries or Loch Duart salmon with choucroute, roasted carrots and sherry vinegar sauce. Locals kick-start their working day with breakfast, and dressed-down crowds pile in for weekend brunch and Sunday roasts. The wine list promises good drinking from £19.50 (£5 a glass). Never one to let the grass grow, Tom Aikens has opened a branch of Tom's Kitchen (with a canopied summertime terrace) in the stately surrounds of Somerset House, WC2R 1LA, tel: (020) 7845 4646 – reports please.

Chef/s: Richard Robinson. **Open:** all week L 12 to 3 (10 to 4 Sat and Sun), D 6 to 11. **Meals:** alc (main courses £11 to £22). **Service:** not inc. **Details:** Cards accepted. 74 seats. Air-con. Separate bar. Wheelchair access. Music. Children allowed.

ALSO RECOMMENDED

▲ Tosa

332 King Street, Hammersmith, W6 0RR
Tel no: (020) 8748 0002
www.tosauk.com
⊖ **Ravenscourt Park, Stamford Brook, map 1**
Japanese

The interior may be modest, and service subdued, but locals come here for the tasty morsels of yakitori skewers like pork loin with shiso leaf (£2.30) or chicken and onion grilled over charcoal. Agedashi tofu features expertly deep-fried beancurd served with a dashi sauce. Yellow tail nigiri and prawn and mixed vegetable tempura (£9) don't let the side down either. Finish with chestnut ice cream, and wash it down with saké or Sapporo beer. House wine £13.50. Open all week.

La Trompette

Hitting new heights
5-7 Devonshire Road, Chiswick, W4 2EU
Tel no: (020) 8747 1836
www.latrompette.co.uk
⊖ **Turnham Green, map 1**
Modern European | £40
Cooking score: 6
🍸

La Trompette fits snugly among the boutiques of Devonshire Road, its discreet blue frontage announcing one of the outstanding *restaurants du quartier* of village London. Its four-square look, with simply set tables on a bare wood floor, belies the fireworks that are going on here. 'Service is consistently efficient and friendly', says a reporter, 'but with that extra attention – appropriate, not overwhelming – you expect in a great restaurant.' James Bennington's cooking mixes and matches diverse European techniques to produce dishes of formidable impact. A starter of ham hock terrine with a perfect poached egg balanced on a potato cake, topped with hollandaise, is a promise of great things to come. Main courses pull out all the stops: a daube of pork with beetroot and Hispi cabbage in mustard sauce achieves wonderful balance but, just occasionally, too many disparate flavours can seem to unsettle a dish, as when a roast breast of fine poulet noir arrives with chorizo risotto, courgette fritters and a liberal application of strongly zesty gremolata. Fruit compositions at dessert stage, however, are aptly judged, as in a prune crème brûlée with Granny Smith sorbet. A wondrous wine list could be a model for others, were it not so triumphantly comprehensive. France is accorded its full dignity, but there is a strong showing of quality German wines, interesting finds from central and eastern Europe, and a majestic New World array (glasses from £3.50).
Chef/s: James Bennington. **Open:** all week L 12 to 2.30 (12.30 to 3 Sun), D 6.30 to 10.30 (7 to 10 Sun). **Closed:** 25 and 26 Dec, 1 Jan. **Meals:** Set L £19.50 (2 courses) to £23.50. Set D £34.50 (2 courses) to £39.50. Sun L £29.50. **Service:** 12.5% (optional). **Details:** Cards accepted. 72 seats. 16 seats outside. Air-con. Wheelchair access. Children allowed.

Urban Turban

Mumbai street food, tapas-style
98 Westbourne Grove, Westbourne Park, W2 5RU
Tel no: (020) 7243 4200
www.urbanturban.uk.com
⊖ **Royal Oak, Bayswater, Queensway, map 4**
Indian | £20
Cooking score: 2
£5 OFF **V** £30

Vineet Bhatia's second London restaurant (see also Rasoi), Urban Turban aims to introduce western diners to the food typically peddled by India's informal street eateries. The rich hues and textures of the décor reflect the liveliness of the cooking, which comes in tapas-style portions and sharing platters. Alongside familiar options such as samosas, chicken tikka and lamb seekh kebab, there might be tandoori prawns with a chilli and coriander risotto, Mumbai fried fish with coriander and lime juice, and 'pizaan' – naan bread served pizza-style with a choice of toppings. To finish, maybe cardamom pannacotta with fresh berries and rose coulis. Wines from £20.

Chef/s: Vineet Bhatia. **Open:** Sat and Sun L 12.30 to 3.30 (1 to 3.30 Sun), all week D 5 to 11 (10 Sun). **Closed:** 25 and 26 Dec, 1 Jan. **Meals:** alc (main courses £7 to £14). **Service:** not inc. **Details:** Cards accepted. 140 seats. Air-con. Separate bar. Wheelchair access. Music. Children allowed.

Le Vacherin
Classic French cooking
76-77 South Parade, Chiswick, W4 5LF
Tel no: (020) 8742 2121
www.levacherin.co.uk
⊖ Chiswick Park, map 1
French | £35
Cooking score: 4

It's the combination of classic French bistro-style food and atmosphere that draws one enthusiastic reader back to Malcolm John's neighbourhood restaurant overlooking Acton Green. A recent design revamp has softened some of the old 'car-showroom acoustics' and it all feels gentler and cosier, although this hasn't lessened the impact of the food. This is the place to come for the French cooking of old, from onion soup based on concentrated stock to feather-light île flottante. In between, you might find it hard to choose from richly satisfying main courses such as duck confit with salsify gratin or sea bass with mussels in a saffron and garlic broth. The cheese that gives the restaurant its name is a favourite, baked in a serving for two with Bayonne ham and all the trimmings. Fixed-price menus represent great value for the quality of food. The wine list is entirely French and, as well as covering the headline regions, it forages into lesser-known byways such as the southwest, Corsica and Savoie.
Chef/s: Malcolm John. **Open:** Tue to Sun L 12 to 3 (4 Sun), all week D 6 to 10 (11 Fri and Sat). **Closed:** 25 and 26 Dec, 1 Jan, bank hols. **Meals:** alc (main courses £12 to £21). Set L £15 (2 courses) to £17. Set D £22.50. Sun L £19.50. **Service:** 12.5% (optional). **Details:** Cards accepted. 72 seats. Air-con. Separate bar. No mobile phones. Wheelchair access. Music. Children allowed.

The Warrington
Branded Ramsay gastropub
93 Warrington Crescent, Maida Vale, W9 1EH
Tel no: (020) 7592 7960
www.gordonramsay.com
⊖ Maida Vale, Warwick Avenue, map 1
Gastropub | £33
Cooking score: 2
£5 OFF

An impressive Victorian boozer, complete with grand Art Nouveau features and stained glass windows provides the backdrop for this Gordon Ramsay gastropub, where the food bangs an Anglo-European drum. Dishes might include a neat seared trout with celeriac rémoulade and gremolata, dense braised ox-cheek pie with verdant crushed peas, and sticky toffee pudding for dessert. While the Ramsay name guarantees consistency (plus a few extra quid on the bill), the menu smacks of branded uniformity rather than individuality or passion. Readers, however, enjoy it as a dependable local option – especially as the wine list offers an exhaustive global tour, with prices from £14.25. Ramsay's first gastropub, the Narrow, is still trading (see entry), but the Devonshire in Chiswick has closed.
Chef/s: Simon Levy. **Open:** Thur to Sun L 12 to 2.30 (3 Sun), all week D 6 to 10 (10.30 Fri and Sat, 9 Sun). **Meals:** alc (main courses £14 to £20). Set L and D £18 (2 courses) to £22. **Service:** 12.5% (optional). **Details:** Cards accepted. 70 seats. Air-con. Music. Children allowed.

Zaika
Flavours to kick-start the taste buds
1 Kensington High Street, Kensington, W8 5NP
Tel no: (020) 7795 6533
www.zaika-restaurant.co.uk
⊖ High Street Kensington, map 4
Indian | £30
Cooking score: 3
£5 OFF

The former bank building facing Hyde Park makes a dramatically ornamented setting for the contemporary Indian cooking on offer at Zaika. Oak panelling and ornate masonry at the window surrounds add the right feeling of opulence, and the cooking, under chef and new TV star Sanjay Dwivedi, is full of fresh, invigorating flavours. Spice-crusted seared tuna and crushed ratte potatoes with coriander and fennel seeds are a kick-start to the taste buds, and mains pile on the style with breast of Goosnargh duck accompanied by garlic and chilli mash, crisp-fried okra, cloves and black cardamom. More traditional offerings include lamb rogan josh, while desserts take in a thought-provoking assemblage of chocolate samosa, coconut cheesecake and a ginger biscuit. Wines start from £21.

Chef/s: Sanjay Dwivedi. **Open:** Tue to Sun L 12 to 2.45, all week D 6 to 10.45 (9.45 Sun). **Closed:** 25 and 26 Dec. **Meals:** alc (main courses £17 to £25). Set L £20 (2 courses) to £25. Tasting menu £42. **Service:** 12.5% (optional). **Details:** Cards accepted. 80 seats. Air-con. Separate bar. Music. Children allowed.

kumquat relish. Otherwise, there are sizzling-fresh dishes from the robata grill, such as pork skewers in yuzu mustard miso, specialities such as the show-stopping roasted lobster with green chilli and garlic hojiso (Japanese mint) butter, as well as tempura and raw fish items. Finish with jasmine tea crème brûlée with strawberry ice cream, or green tea and azuki bean doughnuts with kinako (toasted soybean) ice cream. Saké aficionados are extravagantly served by the drinks list, as are lovers of fine international wines with plenty of cash to splash. Prices open at £22 for a Languedoc blend.

Chef/s: Ross Shonhan. **Open:** all week L 12 to 2.15 (12.30 to 3.15 Sat and Sun), D 6 to 10.45 (10.15 Sun). **Closed:** 25 Dec, 1 Jan. **Meals:** alc (main courses £14 to £75). Tasting menu £96. **Service:** 15% (optional). **Details:** Cards accepted. 147 seats. Air-con. Separate bar. Wheelchair access. Music. Children allowed.

Zuma

Supremely stylish jet setter
5 Raphael Street, Knightsbridge, SW7 1DL
Tel no: (020) 7584 1010
www.zumarestaurant.com
⊖ Knightsbridge, map 4
Japanese | £60
Cooking score: 5

V

The feeling of entering a supremely stylish grotto is hard to resist on arriving at Zuma, the London branch of an international group that includes outposts in Hong Kong, Istanbul, Dubai and Miami. A low-lit, contemplative atmosphere is created with pinewood screens and natural rock, and the spaces include a generously stocked saké bar, sushi counter and the main dining room, where the kitchen is open to view in the Japanese manner. Menus are divided along traditional lines, with new dishes grouped helpfully together. Recent additions have included a tataki of the sought-after Wagyu sirloin, served with black truffle ponzu sauce, grilled octopus with spicy black bean dressing, and gloriously fruity duck breast with umeboshi plum, mango and

A Cena

Smart neighbourhood Italian
418 Richmond Road, Twickenham, TW1 2EB
Tel no: (020) 8288 0108
www.acena.co.uk
⊖ Richmond, map 1
Italian | £35
Cooking score: 2
£5 OFF

Wedged in among a row of chi-chi boutiques at the foot of Richmond Bridge, A Cena looks every inch the affluent suburban Italian. The interior is understated and the kitchen runs with the seasons, changing its menus each day and pleasing Twickenham's smart set with the likes of smoked haddock carpaccio with baby San Marzano tomatoes, or roast rump of Welsh lamb with braised onions, mint and roast aubergine purée. Pasta is a decent shout – perhaps tagliatelle with brown shrimps, rocket and chilli – while desserts might usher in caramel pannacotta or coffee granita with hazelnut whipped cream. Well-researched Italian regional wines start at £16.
Chef/s: Nicola Parsons. **Open:** Tue to Sun L 12 to 2.30, Mon to Sat D 7 to 10.30. **Closed:** Christmas. **Meals:** alc (main courses £13 to £21). Sun L £25. **Service:** not inc. **Details:** Cards accepted. 65 seats. Air-con. Separate bar. Wheelchair access. Music. Children allowed.

Bingham

Adventurous food by the river
61-63 Petersham Road, Richmond, TW10 6UT
Tel no: (020) 8940 0902
www.thebingham.co.uk
⊖ Richmond, map 1
Modern British | £39
Cooking score: 5
£5 OFF ♦ ⊨

The Bingham is a boutique hotel with class to spare. Gentle pastels in the dining room are easy on the spirits, and the riverside view through large picture windows is a tonic. Shay Cooper is an adventurous chef, with the self-confidence to put some daring culinary ideas into practice, and the technical skill to bring

them off. You might start with a smoked eel risotto, its richness offset with the cutting edge of tomatoes in vinaigrette and jelly, or with a chunk of brill fillet and a scallop, their sweetness pointed up with a handful of poached grapes, and substance provided by ricotta gnocchi and a light bread sauce. Mains maintain the pace, with less obvious meat cuts adding interest (try glazed veal cheek with crisp tongue, red wine salsify, truffle mash and gribiche sauce), while monkfish comes bedecked with razor clams, squid and fennel marmalade in a seafood bisque. Valrhona chocolate mousse with vanilla rice pudding and pink grapefruit sorbet has all the right elements of taste and texture to end a meal with a flourish. A great selection of wines by the glass (from £6) opens a list that is strong in the classics of France and Italy, but has expansive global reach too. Georgia's Saperavi is an interesting, savoury red for the curious (albeit at £44).
Chef/s: Shay Cooper. **Open:** all week L 12 to 2.30 (12.30 to 4 Sun), Mon to Sat D 7 to 10. **Closed:** first week Jan. **Meals:** Set L £19.50 (2 courses) to £23. Set D £32 (2 courses) to £39. Sun L £36. Tasting menu £55. **Service:** 12.5% (optional). **Details:** Cards accepted. 36 seats. 12 seats outside. Air-con. Separate bar. Wheelchair access. Music. Children allowed. Car parking.

Brasserie Vacherin

NEW ENTRY
Slice of France in commuter-land
12 High Street, Sutton, SM1 1HN
Tel no: (020) 8722 0180
www.brasserievacherin.co.uk
map 1
French | £22
Cooking score: 2
£30

Malcolm John (the man behind Croydon's Le Cassoulet and Fish & Grill, and Chiswick's Le Vacherin – see entries) brings his winning formula to Sutton – and appears to have got it spot-on. It's a real brasserie, open from breakfast (at 8am) onwards, and looks like everyone's idea of one – red banquettes, polished floorboards, French prints – with a menu of Gallic favourites. Expect escargot de Bourgogne or moules marinière, mains like pot-roast Label Rouge poussin with artichoke, tomato, lemon and couscous, or perhaps chateaubriand with roast bone marrow for two to share. Wines are equally patriotic, with bottles from £15.50.

Chef/s: Matthew Stone. **Open:** all week L 12 to 5, D 6 to 11 (10.30 Sun). **Closed:** 25 Dec. **Meals:** alc (main courses £11 to £19). Set L and D £14 (2 courses) to £16.95. Sun L £14.95. **Service:** 12.5% (optional). **Details:** Cards accepted. 75 seats. 40 seats outside. Air-con. Wheelchair access. Music. Children allowed.

Brilliant
Shining Punjabi star
72-76 Western Road, Southall, UB2 5DZ
Tel no: (020) 8574 1928
www.brilliantrestaurant.com
⊖ Hounslow West, map 1
Indian | £25
Cooking score: 3
£5 OFF V £30

The Anands take an intergenerational approach to the family business. First, there's an ingrained respect for the traditions on which Brilliant was founded 36 years ago, but then there's also a marked ambition to move it forward – witness the jazzy décor and lighter, healthier cooking. Fans of Brilliant's Punjabi cuisine 'with a Kenyan slant' can still get their cumin chicken and masala lamb (as assured as ever at inspection) and stunning specials such as 'superb' Amritsar fish, and they can also cut back on calories, thanks to low-cal versions of methi chicken or tandoori salmon. But please, forget your diet for dessert: exemplary gulab jamun and rasmalai dispel the myth that Indian restaurant puds are best avoided. House wine (£11), Indian beers and lassis complete the offering.

Chef/s: Jasvinderjit Singh and Gulu Anand. **Open:** Tue to Fri L 12 to 2.30, Tue to Sun D 6 to 11.30. **Closed:** Mon, 25 Dec. **Meals:** alc (main courses £5 to £14). **Service:** 10%. **Details:** Cards accepted. 225 seats. Air-con. Separate bar. Wheelchair access. Music. Children allowed. Car parking.

ALSO RECOMMENDED

▲ The Brown Dog
28 Cross Street, Barnes, SW13 0AP
Tel no: (020) 8392 2200
www.thebrowndog.co.uk
map 1
Gastropub

Hidden away down the narrow streets of well-heeled Little Chelsea, this hound-friendly pub is a local favourite. With Polaroids of cute canine faces, copper lights and a red lacquered ceiling, there's plenty of character. Food is simple and honest, say English asparagus wrapped in Parma ham and served with a free-range poached egg (£8.25), or rump of lamb, harissa-roasted vegetables and lemon mint couscous (£16.50). Steamed date pudding with honeycomb ice cream (£5) makes a great finish. Wines from £15.75. Open all week.

Brula
Perfect local with recession-busting prices
43 Crown Road, St Margarets, Twickenham, TW1 3EJ
Tel no: (020) 8892 0602
www.brula.co.uk
⊖ Richmond, map 1
French | £29
Cooking score: 3
£30

'A perfect local', sums up many readers' affection for Brula – in fact some are even happy to endure lengthy train rides for a taste of its friendly hospitality, recession-defying prices and dependable bourgeois cooking. In a setting of sturdy pews and stained glass windows, the faithful get their fill of 'inventive, professionally delivered' dishes from the French archives – fricassee of Burgundian snails and poached duck egg 'en meurette' (in a red wine sauce), slow-cooked belly pork with Agen prune sarladaise, and wild sea bass with brandade, almond and sage beurre noisette. Desserts stay on track for the likes of clafoutis with griottine cherries or chocolate bavarois with orange crème anglaise, and the French regional wine list opens with vins de pays at £14.75. Brula is also much in demand for birthdays and other celebratory bashes, when staff pull out all the stops.

Chef/s: Jamie Russel. **Open:** all week L 12 to 3, Mon to Sat D 6 to 10.30. **Closed:** 26 to 30 Dec. **Meals:** alc (main courses £10 to £18). Set L £11.50 (2 courses) to £14. Sun L £20. **Service:** 12.5% (optional). **Details:** Cards accepted. 45 seats. 8 seats outside. No music. Wheelchair access. Children allowed.

La Buvette

Good-value Gallic comfort food
6 Church Walk, Richmond, TW9 1SN
Tel no: (020) 8940 6264
www.labuvette.co.uk
⊖ Richmond, map 1
French | £17
Cooking score: 3
£5 OFF £30

Formerly the refectory of the next-door St Mary Magdalene church, La Buvette is a smart, bright room with crisply dressed tables and a walled courtyard for summer dining. It deals in classic French dishes with occasional external influences, such as a starter of Moroccan-style crab pastilla with harissa. Otherwise, expect suitably rich fish soup with rouille, croûtons and Gruyère, juicy onglet steak and chips with a well-dressed shallot salad, and properly served French cheeses. Desserts might include prune and almond tart with brandy cream. It's essentially good-value Gallic comfort food served in a comfort setting, which goes a long way to explain the popularity of the place. A single-page listing of French wines takes us from Languedoc house blends at £14 to the 2004 vintage of Clos Fourtet, a fine Saint-Emilion at £68.25, with lots served by the glass.

Chef/s: Buck Carter. **Open:** all week L 12 to 3, D 6 to 10. **Closed:** 25 and 26 Dec, Good Fri, Easter Sun. **Meals:** alc (main courses £11 to £19). Set L £13.25 (2 courses) to £15. Set D £17.75 (2 courses) to £19.75. Sun L £17.75. **Service:** 12.5% (optional). **Details:** Cards accepted. 46 seats. 34 seats outside. No music. No mobile phones. Wheelchair access. Children allowed.

Café Strudel

Elegant Viennese cuisine in East Sheen
429 Upper Richmond Road West, East Sheen, SW14 7PJ
Tel no: (020) 8487 9800
www.cafestrudel.co.uk
⊖ Richmond, map 1
Austrian | £35
Cooking score: 2
£5 OFF

Step into a little enclave of old Vienna at this Austrian restaurant in East Sheen, where ornately framed mirrors, café-style chairs and a dark wood bar recreate a certain *fin de siècle* atmosphere. Elegantly presented dishes are bulked with the fortifying carbohydrate of Mitteleuropa, with frittaten pancake strips in the chicken soup, spätzle in the gulasch and with the schnitzeln. It's all brought off with a light touch though, even for the apfel im schlafrock ('apple in a nightgown'), a baked apple stuffed with dried apricots and prunes, served with cinnamon ice cream. Wines from Austria and Hungary dominate the list, from £9.99.

Chef/s: Yacine Bengazahl. **Open:** Tue to Sun L 12 to 3, Tue to Sat D 6 to 9.30. **Closed:** Mon, 25 Dec. **Meals:** alc (main courses £14 to £18). **Service:** 12.5%. **Details:** Cards accepted. 36 seats. 10 seats outside. Wheelchair access. Music. Children allowed.

READERS RECOMMEND

The Cambria

Gastropub
40 Kemerton Road, Camberwell, SE5 9AR
Tel no: (020) 7737 3676
'Glamorous interior, down-to-earth staff and delicious food from jerk chicken with all the trimmings to great-value burger and chips, plus enormous Sunday roasts.'

Le Cassoulet

Like being in Paris
18 Selsdon Road, Croydon, CR2 6PA
Tel no: (020) 8633 1818
www.lecassoulet.co.uk
map 1
French | £17
Cooking score: 3
£30

'Just like being in Paris: elegant service, knowledgeable staff and great tastes of quality ingredients well prepared,' exclaimed a reporter – and the comments are all the more remarkable because the setting is south Croydon. The décor is 'stylish and comfortable' and the fixed-price menus split allegiance between classic and modern French cooking. Everyone mentions the scallops with black pudding ravoli, and the sea bream, brown crab and pear tortellini, but slow-cooked veal cheeks with risotto milanese and the duck and pork cassoulet also get the thumbs-up. Praise too for good-value lunches delivering the likes of roasted wild garlic and ham hock soup, guinea fowl, and pot au chocolat, the homemade bread and the tarte Tatin for two. House French is £15.50. Part of Malcolm John's growing south London empire.
Chef/s: Philip Amponsa. **Open:** all week L 12 to 3 (3.30 Sun), D 6 to 10.30 (11 Fri and Sat, 10 Sun). **Meals:** Set L £16.50. Set D £27.50. Sun L £19.50. **Service:** 12.5% (optional). **Details:** Cards accepted. 55 seats. Air-con. Separate bar. Wheelchair access. Music. Children allowed. Car parking.

READERS RECOMMEND

The Depot

Modern British
Tideway Yard, Mortlake High Street, Barnes, SW14 8SN
Tel no: (020) 8878 9462
www.depotbrasserie.co.uk
'There can hardly be a nicer setting on a summer's evening with the Thames flowing by. The food has been consistently good.'

ALSO RECOMMENDED

▲ Eat17

28-30 Orford Road, Walthamstow, E17 9NJ
Tel no: (020) 8521 5279
www.eat17.co.uk
⊖ Walthamstow Central, map 1
British £5 OFF

There aren't too many salubrious eating options in Walthamstow, so it's vital that the ones there are will please everybody. Eat17 succeeds with an all-day menu that starts with crumpets or fry-ups (£6.50) and finishes on cocktails, wine (from £13) and fair bistro cooking – pork chop with creamed cabbage (£11) and lemon tart (£4.50). In between come burgers and 'tidbits' such as mini macaroni cheese or fishcakes. Trendy interiors endear it to local professionals and mums. Open all week.

▲ The Exhibition Rooms

69-71 Westow Hill, Crystal Palace, SE19 1TX
Tel no: (020) 8761 1175
www.theexhibitionrooms.com
map 1
Modern European

The venue is a belated homage to the Great Exhibition site that graced Crystal Palace in the Victorian era, hinted at in the design themes of mirrored arches, stone planters and old-fashioned furniture. A range of modern brasserie dishes is offered, from crab and prawn cakes with Thai salad and ponzu dressing (£7.50) to new season's lamb with ratte potatoes and mint jus (£17) and desserts such as pear tart and cinnamon anglaise (£5.50). Sunday lunch is a treat. Wines from £15. Open all week.

Fish & Grill
It's all in the name
48-50 South End, Croydon, CR0 1DP
Tel no: (020) 8774 4060
www.fishandgrill.co.uk
map 1
Modern British | £23
Cooking score: 3

V

Following the success of Le Cassoulet and Le Vacherin (see entries), empire builder Malcolm John decided to cement his reputation in Croydon with this casual, unpretentious eatery: 'what a wonderful surprise', exclaimed one local gleefully. As you might guess from the name, the emphasis is on fish and grills: monkfish tail and line-caught sea bass have pleased piscophiles, while meat fans have rated the carefully sourced Aberdeen Angus steaks, veal chops and hand-diced burgers. Well-reported starters have included a gratin of scallops and spinach, shellfish bisque, and Montgomery Cheddar and leek tart, with bread-and-butter pudding, lemon meringue pie and sherry trifle getting the vote when it comes to desserts. The no-nonsense wine list kicks off with house selections from £15.50.
Chef/s: Jason Nott. **Open:** all week 12 to 11. **Closed:** 25 Dec. **Meals:** alc (main courses £12 to £32). Set L £11.95 (2 courses) to £14.95. Sun L £15.95. **Service:** 12.5% (optional). **Details:** Cards accepted. 70 seats. 6 seats outside. Air-con. Separate bar. Wheelchair access. Music. Children allowed.

> ★ READERS' RESTAURANT OF THE YEAR ★
> LONDON

The French Table
Ever-popular neighbourhood veteran
85 Maple Road, Surbiton, KT6 4AW
Tel no: (020) 8399 2365
www.thefrenchtable.co.uk
map 1
French | £32
Cooking score: 4

Ten years on, the Guignard's 'neighbourhood gem' of a French restaurant continues to please – for warmth, informality and spontaneity.

The surroundings are clean-cut, modern and well-dressed and the food is 'creative and accomplished'. It makes an excellent lunch spot with its 'something-of-a-steal' pricing and dishes such as terrine of ham hock and pheasant with piccalilli, or suckling pig with parsnip purée, red onion chutney and thyme jus. At dinner the directness of much of the cooking is welcome, from a duo of foie gras – a brûlée and a more traditional pâté – with lovely soft brioche, via excellent rack of lamb teamed with pumpkin and chestnuts ('the sides of deep-fried broccoli with chickpeas and caramelised carrots were lovely') to warm praline cake with pistachio ice cream. Homemade breads raise expectation from the off, and the globetrotting wine list offers reasonable mark-ups and bottles from £14.95.
Chef/s: Eric Guignard. **Open:** Tue to Sun L 12 to 2.30, Tue to Sat D 7 to 10.30. **Closed:** Mon, 26 to 28 Dec, 2 weeks end Aug. **Meals:** alc (main courses £12 to £19). Set L £16.50 (2 courses) to £19.50. Set L Sat and Sun £24.50. **Service:** 12.5% (optional). **Details:** Cards accepted. 50 seats. Air-con. No mobile phones. Music. Children allowed.

Frère Jacques
Upbeat waterfront brasserie
10-12 Riverside Walk, Kingston-upon-Thames, KT1 1QN
Tel no: (020) 8546 1332
www.frerejacques.co.uk
map 1
French | £23
Cooking score: 2

£5 £30

Frère Jacques' riverside setting is a great boon, and visitors enjoy sitting under the permanent awning as the world drifts by; alternatively retreat indoors if the elements intrude. Either way, the kitchen dishes up a well-tried mix of bourgeois French provincial food with a few international add-ons. Snails in garlic butter, charcuterie with celeriac rémoulade and whole salt-baked sea bream compete with more upbeat offerings including slow-roast rump of spring lamb with Jerusalem artichoke, beetroot and garlic confit or grilled

sea bass fillet with sun-blush tomatoes and chilli butter. Glazed lemon tart and rhubarb crumble are typical desserts. Vins de pays start at £9.95 a carafe.
Chef/s: Gerhard Peleschka. **Open:** all week 12 to 11. **Closed:** 26 Dec, 1 Jan. **Meals:** alc (main courses £10 to £20). Set L and early D £9.90 (2 courses). **Service:** 12.5% (optional). **Details:** Cards accepted. 60 seats. 140 seats outside. Air-con. Wheelchair access. Music. Children allowed. Car parking.

The Glasshouse
Pleasing the eye and the palate
14 Station Parade, Kew, TW9 3PZ
Tel no: (020) 8940 6777
www.glasshouserestaurant.co.uk
⊖ Kew Gardens, map 1
Modern European | £40
Cooking score: 5
🍶

The big glass frontage creates a pleasantly airy ambience, and Bruce Poole's influence as owner (see entry, Chez Bruce, London) ensures the menus have an appealing contemporary edge. New chef Daniel Mertl is another deft practitioner of the modern European style in the tradition of his predecessors. His dishes are full of deep flavour and, presented with sculptural flair, they please the eye as well as the palate. Proceedings might open with a ham and Gruyère torte with braised endive and warm truffle vinaigrette, before moving on to roast saddle of lamb with kidneys, pomme cocotte and garlic purée. The aura of sunnier climes that runs through dishes such as fillet of black bream with pepper compote, grilled courgettes and gremolata is cheering, and dank British winter days will be further brightened by steamed syrup sponge or Black Forest trifle. The wine list zips smartly about the globe, with good selections by the glass and half-bottle; even Germany gets a fair shake of the quality stick. Regional French selections from such byways as Madiran, Cabardès and Bellet are worth exploring. Prices open at £18.

Chef/s: Daniel Mertl. **Open:** all week L 12 to 2.30 (3 Sun), D 6.30 to 10.30 (7 Sun). **Closed:** 24 to 26 Dec, 1 Jan. **Meals:** Set weekday L £18.50 (2 courses) to £23.50. Set D £34 (2 courses) to £39.50. Sat L £20 (2 courses) to £25. Sun L £29.50. **Service:** 12.5% (optional). **Details:** Cards accepted. 65 seats. Air-con. No music. No mobile phones. Children allowed.

Incanto
Italian favourite on the up
41 High Street, Harrow-on-the-Hill, HA1 3HT
Tel no: (020) 8426 6767
www.incanto.co.uk
⊖ Harrow-on-the-Hill, map 1
Italian | £28
Cooking score: 3
£5 OFF V £30

'Very few local restaurants care about their food like these chaps', enthused a reporter on this popular neighbourhood Italian with a 'beautifully designed interior'. Tradition meets modernity on a menu that offers a great antipasti selection of Italian cured meats, 'simple but very well executed' ravioli with egg and black truffle (the yolk beautifully soft within), a 'fabulous' assiette of winter pasta – aubergine and sun-dried tomato, butternut squash and buffalo ricotta, mushrooms and hazelnut – and slow-cooked braised belly of Old Spot pork with Derbyshire black pudding and spicy nduja (Calabrian sausage) sauce. New chef Marcus Chant has certainly raised the game, and service is excellent. The predominantly Italian wine list opens at £15.50.
Chef/s: Marcus Chant. **Open:** Tue to Sun L 12 to 2.30 (12.30 to 4 Sun), Tue to Sat D 6.30 to 10.30. **Closed:** Mon, bank hols. **Meals:** alc (main courses £14 to £19). Set L £15.95 (2 courses) to £19.95. Set D £18.95 (2 courses) to £22.50. Sun L £13.95. **Service:** 12.5% (optional). **Details:** Cards accepted. 68 seats. Air-con. Wheelchair access. Music. Children allowed.

ALSO RECOMMENDED
▲ Jamie's Italian

19-23 High Street, Kingston-upon-Thames, KT1 1LL
Tel no: (020) 8912 0110
www.jamiesitalian.com
map 1
Italian

Be prepared to queue for a table at peak times outside this outpost of Jamie O's Italian chain. Accessible and keenly priced, this is a logical extension of what he's been promoting in all those TV programmes and cookbooks over the years. Expect fresh ingredients, clear flavours and a few cheery gimmicks (mains cooked under a hot brick, for instance). Typical choices are spaghetti bolognese, asparagus risotto (£6.65 or £10.25) and lamb 'lollipops' cooked under the aforementioned brick, with a minted sauce (£13.95). Wines from £14.95. Open all week.

The Lock
Enticing eatery by the canal
Heron House, Hale Wharf, Ferry Lane, Tottenham Hale, N17 9NF
Tel no: (020) 8885 2829
www.thelockrestaurant.com
⊖ Tottenham Hale, map 1
Modern British | £20
Cooking score: 5
£5 OFF £30

'In the reaches of Tottenham next to the canal', might be one way to describe the location of this restaurant; 'a chaotic area that is being transformed prior to the 2012 Olympics', might be another. But wherever, this smart, modern eatery is worth a trip for very sound cooking. The dining room is spacious and attractive with comfortable leather chairs, while the cooking has the hallmarks of proper technique and a pleasing directness even in the cheapest menu option. There is a vein of English cookery in lunch dishes of poached smoked haddock with baked egg or good butcher's sausages and mash. Running parallel to it is an expressive contemporary streak, that yields dishes such as well-timed sea bass with crushed Jerusalem artichokes and ratte potatoes, sautéed baby vegetables and confit of banana shallots, or Old Spot pork cutlet with dauphinoise potatoes, wilted spinach and lyonnaise onions with French wholegrain mustard sauce. When everything works the approach can be remarkably expressive – bread is first-class, for example, and desserts have been praised. A modern wine list offers a fair selection at pocket-friendly prices. Bottles are from £14.50.
Chef/s: Adebola Adeshina. **Open:** Tue to Fri and Sun L 12 to 2 (5 Sun), Tue to Sat D 6 to 10. **Closed:** Mon, 1 week Dec. **Meals:** alc (main courses £10 to £25). Set L £12.50 (2 courses) to £15.50. Set D £17.50 (2 courses) to £26. Sun L £10. **Service:** 10%.
Details: Cards accepted. 56 seats. 25 seats outside. Separate bar. Wheelchair access. Music. Children allowed. Car parking.

ALSO RECOMMENDED
▲ Ma Cuisine

9 Station Approach, Kew, TW9 3QB
Tel no: (020) 8332 1923
www.macuisinebistrot.co.uk
⊖ Kew Gardens, map 1
French £5 OFF

Gingham-clothed tables, Gallic posters and rustic chairs set the scene in this patriotically French 'bistrot', which is part of John McClements' South London empire. The kitchen dishes up everything from duck rillettes to bowls of bouillabaisse and also makes room for the likes of braised chicory and Roquefort gratin (£5), beefy pot au feu and baked sea bass with fennel and Pernod (£18). For afters, perhaps tarte Tatin (£4.95). Wines from £13. Open all week. A second outlet is at 6 Whitton Road, Twickenham, tel: (020) 8607 9849.

Madhu's

Chic, high-class Indian
39 South Road, Southall, UB1 1SW
Tel no: (020) 8574 1897
www.madhus.co.uk
map 1
Indian | £20
Cooking score: 3

V £30

Sibling to Brilliant on Western Road (see entry), Madhu's is run by the Anand family with genuine confidence and style. Following a high-gloss makeover, the interior now oozes contemporary chic – although the kitchen has resolutely resisted any temptation to emulate its flashy new-wave cousins in the capital. What it offers is pitch-perfect food that scales heights few other local curry houses can dream of. Dishes are generous to a fault, expertly spiced and zingingly fresh, whether you plump for one of the Southall staples (tandoori lamb chops, butter chicken, masala fish) or something from the family's East African back catalogue – perhaps nyamah choma (a Masai warrior's dish of char-grilled marinated ribs). Veggies also do well, with unusual specialities such as karela gourd with potatoes and pomegranate. Beer and lassi suit the chilli-spiked food, although wines start at a very affordable £9.
Chef/s: Rakesh Verma. **Open:** Mon and Wed to Fri L 12.30 to 3, Wed to Mon D 6 to 11.30. **Closed:** Tue. **Meals:** alc (main courses £5 to £11). Set L and D £18 (2 courses) to £20. **Service:** not inc. **Details:** Cards accepted. 105 seats. Air-con. Wheelchair access. Music. Children allowed.

NEW ENTRY
Mandarin Palace

Knocking spots off Chinatown
559-561 Cranbrook Road, Ilford, IG2 6JZ
Tel no: (020) 8550 7661
⊖ Gants Hill, map 1
Chinese | £25
Cooking score: 2

£5 OFF **V** £30

A night out off Gant's Hill roundabout would surely be nobody's first choice, but this three-decades-old Cantonese restaurant has made it so. Ornately decorated with fans and screens, its traditional looks are reflected in cooking that is at its most impressive in barbecued meats and luxurious seafood. The well-known names on the French-leaning wine list (from £15) are a good match. Dim sum also knocks Chinatown's offerings into a cocked hat: on the tick-list are steamed fish balls, pork congee and duck's chins with chilli. The friendly hostess welcomes guests, old and new, with equal bonhomie.
Chef/s: K.W. Chong. **Open:** all week L 12 to 4 (6.30 Sun), D 6.30 to 11.30 (midnight Fri and Sat). **Closed:** 25 Dec. **Meals:** alc (main courses £7 to £16). Set L £8. Set D £22.50. **Service:** 10%. **Details:** Cards accepted. 120 seats. Air-con. Separate bar. No mobile phones. Wheelchair access. Music. Children allowed. Car parking.

Mosaica @ the factory

Funky flavour-fest
Chocolate Factory, Clarendon Road, Wood Green, N22 6XJ
Tel no: (020) 8889 2400
www.mosaicarestaurants.com
⊖ Wood Green, map 2
Modern European | £30
Cooking score: 3

£5 OFF

Housed in a New York-style shabby-chic loft space adorned with festoons of lights and a jumble of furniture, Mosaica has its finger on the pulse of contemporary London dining. A daily changing menu revolves around modern European ideas, with simple starter pairings such as portobello mushroom and Gorgonzola, or sardines and gremolata backed up by main courses that aim for taste and substance, such as Gloucester Old Spot pork belly with red cabbage and mustard mash. It all adds up to an infectiously vibrant venue in a part of north London where exciting eating is a little thin on the ground. Round things off in retro style with profiteroles and warm chocolate sauce, or raspberry and almond tart with Cornish ice cream. A concise wine list starts at £13.50.

Chef/s: Steven Goode. **Open:** Tue to Fri and Sun L 12 to 2.30 (1 to 4 Sun), Tue to Sat D 6.30 to 9.30 (7 to 10 Sat). **Closed:** Mon. **Meals:** alc (main courses £13 to £18). **Service:** 10% (optional). **Details:** Cards accepted. 80 seats. 40 seats outside. Air-con. Wheelchair access. Music. Children allowed. Car parking.

Petersham Nurseries Café
Arcadian eatery with sunny food
Church Lane, off Petersham Road, Richmond, TW10 7AG
Tel no: (020) 8605 3627
www.petershamnurseries.com
⊖ Richmond, map 1
Modern British | £45
Cooking score: 4

Picture the scene: a ramshackle greenhouse with sand and dirt on the floor, a mishmash of battered tables that look as if they've been used for potting-up plants, some oriental sculptures, exotic orchids in full boom and waitresses padding about in wellies. Welcome to the Petersham Nurseries Café – a remarkable lunch-only eatery linked to a high-profile garden centre in Richmond's self-styled Arcadia. It makes a quirky, but entirely appropriate, setting for Skye Gyngell's poised and innovative cooking, which is defined by seasonal pickings and refreshingly unexpected, sunny flavours. Despite limited hours and far-from-cheap prices, it's become the darling of the local green set, who pack in for plates of crab with kohlrabi, fennel and verjus dressing, baked chicory with mâche and roasted pumpkin, or slow-cooked chicken

with olives and thyme. Slabs of pork belly with farro grains and salsa verde have also gone down well, and there might be 'proper' almond tart to finish. Wines start at £16.

Chef/s: Skye Gyngell. **Open:** Wed to Sun L only 12 to 2.30. **Closed:** Mon, Tue, 24 Dec to 3 Jan. **Meals:** alc (main courses £19 to £25) Set L Wed to Fri £27 (2 courses) to £29.50. **Service:** 12.5% (optional). **Details:** Cards accepted. 90 seats. No music. Wheelchair access. Children allowed. Car parking.

The Restaurant at the Petersham
River views and stately dining
Nightingale Lane, Richmond, TW10 6UZ
Tel no: (020) 8940 7471
www.petershamhotel.co.uk
⊖ Richmond, map 1
Modern British | £39
Cooking score: 4

Fabulous vistas of the Thames and Petersham Meadow are the trump cards at this dependable Gothic-style hotel, which also boasts England's largest Portland stone staircase. You can enjoy the panoramic riverside prospect from the stately comfort of the olde-worlde dining room, while sampling Alex Bentley's food. He is happy to send out plates of smoked salmon, grilled veal cutlets and Dover sole meunière for Richmond's old guard, as well as upping the tempo for those who prefer something with a bit more zing – perhaps seared scallop and smoked eel with fennel and orange salad or 'seven-spice' duck breast with endive tarte Tatin, beetroot purée and date sauce. To finish, it's worth the wait for raspberry and pear soufflé tart. Lunchtime callers have also eaten well – although some reckon you're paying 'quite a bit' for the view. The international wine list starts at £19.50.

Chef/s: Alex Bentley. **Open:** all week L 12 to 2.15 (12.30 to 3.30 Sun), D 7 to 9.45 (8.45 Sun). **Closed:** 25 and 26 Dec, 1 Jan. **Meals:** alc (main courses £15 to £26). Set L £18.50 (2 courses) to £25.50. Sun L £32. **Service:** 10% (optional). **Details:** Cards accepted. 70 seats. Air-con. Separate bar. No music. Wheelchair access. Children allowed. Car parking.

Kitchen tables

The chance to get up close and (almost) personal with the kitchen staff in smart restaurants is a trend that looks likely to stay. When Gordon Ramsay opened his chef's table at **Claridge's** in 2001, the notion was an extension of the private room, with the chef cooking you a bespoke menu in front of your very eyes.

Recent years have seen the concept elaborated. You aren't necessarily being offered a different menu to the main dining room now, but the thrill of observing the brigade at work is like seeing food TV brought to three-dimensional life.

East London's **Viajante** sees the kitchen dominating, with tables positioned so that diners get to see Nuno Mendes and his team preparing a tasting menu full of culinary fireworks. At the South Lodge Hotel near Horsham, where Matt Gillan is head chef, an entire small restaurant, **The Pass**, has been built alongside the kitchen, complete with live TV feed.

The new movement is as much about allowing diners to share the whole experience as it is about allowing the kitchen to show off. At **21212** in Edinburgh, one end of the dining-room is a floor-to-ceiling glass panel, behind which Paul Kitching can be seen calmly instructing his staff. The effect is a little like being able to see backstage at a theatre.

ALSO RECOMMENDED

▲ Simply Thai
196 Kingston Road, Teddington, TW11 9JD
Tel no: (020) 8943 9747
www.simplythai-restaurant.co.uk
map 1
Thai £5 OFF

For years locals have kept Patria Weerapan's compact restaurant a closely guarded secret, but exposure on Gordon Ramsay's *F Word* has meant it is now harder than ever to book a table. Variable service is compensated by 'the best Thai food in town'. Start, perhaps, with a fragrant Scottish scallop salad with lime, lemongrass, fresh apples and a coconut cream dressing (£6.95), go on to pork belly braised in aromatic spices with pickled bamboo shoots (£12.95) and finish with Thai sticky rice pudding with fresh mango (£5.50). House wine is £13.95. Open Tue to Sun D only.

Sonny's
Upmarket local eatery with lively cooking
94 Church Road, Barnes, SW13 0DQ
Tel no: (020) 8748 0393
www.sonnys.co.uk
map 1
Modern European | £30
Cooking score: 3
£5 OFF

Opened in 1986 when the idea of upmarket but affordable neighbourhood restaurants was still a novelty in London, Sonny's has maintained a consistent standard over the years. The dining room is cream with good pictures and smartly dressed tables, and the restaurant offers a lively modern European style of cooking, with a separate bar menu of simpler dishes. Grilled sardines with tomato and olive bruschetta, or spiced crab spring rolls with Indian-spiced coleslaw provide the necessary starting kick, before confit pork belly with cider-braised cheek, spring greens and glazed prunes. Desserts to spoil yourself with include vanilla cheesecake, chocolate tart with raspberries and crème fraîche, or rhubarb and custard brûlée. House French is £13.50.

Chef/s: Owen Kenworthy. **Open:** all week L 12 to 3 (4 Sun), Mon to Sat D 7 to 10.30 (11 Fri and Sat). **Closed:** 25 to 28 Dec, bank hols. **Meals:** alc (main courses £11 to £23). Set L £13.50 (2 courses) to £15.50. Set D £15.50 (2 courses) to £18.50. Sun L £21.50 (2 courses) to £24.50. **Service:** 12.5% (optional). **Details:** Cards accepted. 100 seats. Air-con. Separate bar. Wheelchair access. Music. Children allowed.

Tangawizi
Colourful, classy Indian cooking
406 Richmond Road, Richmond, TW1 2EB
Tel no: (020) 8891 3737
www.tangawizi.co.uk
⊖ Richmond, map 1
Indian | £25
Cooking score: 2

V £30

Hard by Richmond Bridge on the fringes of East Twickenham, Tangawizi strikes a colourful pose with its lilac frontage and multi-hued interiors – all saffron, purple and gold tones. The cooking aims a notch or two higher than your average suburban curry house, and the kitchen shows ambition by adding a mango dressing to grilled marinated paneer, cooking lamb with mustard seeds, curry leaves and coconut milk, and dishing up grilled fillet of sea bream with spiced potatoes. Otherwise, expect classy renditions of the usual suspects including vegetable samosas, chicken jalfrezi and prawn masala. House wine is £11.95. Plans are afoot to expand and take over the premises next door.
Chef/s: Surat Singh Rana. **Open:** all week D only 6 to 11 (10.30 Sun). **Closed:** 25 and 26 Dec, 1 Jan. **Meals:** alc (main courses £7 to £13). **Service:** not inc. **Details:** Cards accepted. 50 seats. Air-con. Wheelchair access. Music. Children allowed.

The Victoria
TV chef's popular all-rounder
10 West Temple, East Sheen, SW14 7RT
Tel no: (020) 8876 4238
www.thevictoria.net
⊖ Richmond, map 1
Modern British | £26
Cooking score: 3

£5 OFF £30

Regulars are clearly delighted to have TV chef Paul Merrett's upmarket gastropub-with-rooms close to home, and most are drawn here by the food: 'their steaks are outstanding, I love the crispy duck and black pudding salad starter, their oysters come with a totally yummy watermelon shot and their thrice-cooked chips are stonking', drools one reader. Elsewhere, Merrett's Scotch eggs are a winner, and the all-round package also runs to 'blinding' weekend breakfasts, great Sunday roasts, good-value lunches, 'bargain-price' early-bird dinners and summertime barbecues. Puds are a good call too – perhaps white chocolate pannacotta with gooseberry fool and ginger madeleines. Locals appreciate the bar for morning coffee and pastries, and the kid-friendly ambience extends to an outdoor play area. Wines start at £16, and there's a handy selection by the glass (from £3.95).
Chef/s: Paul Merrett. **Open:** Mon to Sat L 12 to 2.30 (8.30am to 3pm Sat), D 6 to 10 (10.30 Sat). Sun 12 to 8. **Meals:** alc (main courses £13 to £15). Set L and early D £12.50 (2 courses). Sun L £22. **Service:** 12.5% (optional). **Details:** Cards accepted. 88 seats. 36 seats outside. Air-con. Separate bar. Music. Children allowed. Car parking.

ENGLAND

Bedfordshire, Berkshire,
Buckinghamshire, Cambridgeshire,
Cheshire, Cornwall, Cumbria, Derbyshire,
Devon, Dorset, Durham, Essex,
Gloucestershire & Bristol,
Greater Manchester,
Hampshire (inc. Isle of Wight),
Herefordshire, Hertfordshire, Kent,
Lancashire, Leicestershire and Rutland,
Lincolnshire, Merseyside, Norfolk,
Northamptonshire, Northumberland,
Nottinghamshire, Oxfordshire, Shropshire,
Somerset, Staffordshire, Suffolk, Surrey,
Sussex – East, Sussex – West,
Tyne & Wear, Warwickshire,
West Midlands, Wiltshire, Worcestershire,
Yorkshire

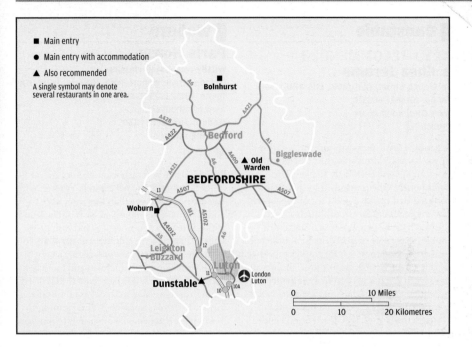

- ■ Main entry
- ● Main entry with accommodation
- ▲ Also recommended

A single symbol may denote
several restaurants in one area.

Bolnhurst

Bedford

Biggleswade

▲ Old Warden

BEDFORDSHIRE

Woburn

Leighton Buzzard

Luton

Dunstable ▲

London Luton

0		10 Miles
0	10	20 Kilometres

■ Bolnhurst

The Plough

Fiercely seasonal food with a big heart
Kimbolton Road, Bolnhurst, MK44 2EX
Tel no: (01234) 376274
www.bolnhurst.com
Modern British | £30
Cooking score: 5

Martin and Jayne Lee are not only consummate innkeepers but also savvy restaurateurs who have managed to create a fully functioning top-end eatery in a country pub without resorting to prissy amuse-bouches or needless frippery. The kitchen is pitched behind the bar and Martin's brigade delivers fiercely seasonal dishes with a big heart and bold flavours. It's food with real immediacy and impact – whatever the season. In winter, there might be something as simple as roast chicken broth with herb dumplings or a fine boozy dish of Denham Estate venison with beetroot purée and celeriac; come April you might find a delicately wobbly Robiola goats' cheese terrine or a natural-born summation of springtime in the shape of pink new season's lamb loin, green Norfolk asparagus, lightly roasted Jersey Royals and creamy sweetbreads finished with a sweet buttery sauce redolent of wild garlic. To conclude, the soufflés are 'a dream', or you might be tickled by a slab of lemon parfait gift-wrapped in a tuile with sweetly astringent red cherry compote. The whole show is run with clear-sighted efficiency by a young team who also know their way around the cracking wine list. Choice is global, prices (from £13.50) are exemplary and a dozen come by the glass.
Chef/s: Martin Lee. **Open:** Tue to Sun L 12 to 2, Tue to Sat D 6.30 to 9.30. **Closed:** Mon, 26 Dec to 9 Jan. **Meals:** alc (main courses £12 to £25). Set L £14 (2 courses) to £18. **Service:** not inc. **Details:** Cards accepted. 80 seats. 30 seats outside. No music. Wheelchair access. Children allowed. Car parking.

Send your reviews to: www.thegoodfoodguide.co.uk

Dunstable

ALSO RECOMMENDED
▲ Chez Jerome

26 Church Street, Dunstable, LU5 4RU
Tel no: (01582) 603310
www.chezjerome.co.uk
French £5 OFF

A genuine local 'pick-me-up', this sociable bistro comes complete with stuccoed walls, brick arches and cosy little alcoves. The neighbourly vibe is matched by generous cooking that makes a good fist of top-notch raw materials ('gigantic, sublimely sweet' scallops have been a standout). Starters of moules marinière or goats' cheese soufflé with sun-dried tomatoes (£6.15) could be followed by calf's liver with pomme purée, onions and 'boozy' Bordeaux jus (£14.95) or grilled sea bass fillet with basil dressing. Desserts such as crème brûlée (£4.25) are an afterthought. House wine is £12.50. Closed Sun D and Mon.

Old Warden

ALSO RECOMMENDED
▲ Hare & Hounds

High Street, Old Warden, SG18 9HQ
Tel no: (01767) 627225
www.hareandhoundsoldwarden.co.uk
Gastropub

The houses in Old Warden were once home to workers on the Shuttleworth Estate, and the Hurts' singular-looking country inn is based in one of them. A bar menu of superior traditional pub food supplements the more adventurous dining options, which might take in crab spring rolls with a soy, lime and chilli dip (£7), braised Scotch lamb shank with roasted red pepper and garlic polenta (£15), or Norfolk pigeon with dauphinoise and braised red cabbage. Wines from £12.50. Closed Sun D and Mon.

Woburn

Paris House

Wittily reinvented classics
London Street, Woburn Park, Woburn, MK17 9QP
Tel no: (01525) 290692
www.parishouse.co.uk
Modern European | £59
Cooking score: 5

V

Paris House was transported, timber by timber, from the French capital to grace Woburn Estate more than a century ago. Today it sits resplendent, an oasis of black and white amid grazing muntjacs and lush green acres. Following the untimely death of Peter Chandler, the restaurant was taken over by Alan Murchison (of L'Ortolan and La Bécasse fame – see entries). He has given the civilised dining room a classy makeover and installed former L'Ortolan sous-chef Phil Fanning to head up the kitchen. His mission is to reinvent 'these you have loved' classics for the twenty-first century: one stunning parody involves superbly moist smoky ham terrine, a soft-boiled quail's egg, pineapple three ways (including chewy jellied 'sweets') and 'crisps' fashioned from purple potatoes. Gammon, egg and chips, anyone? Witty strokes abound, whether it's a 'cheese and pickle sandwich' involving gingerbread and blue cheese mousse, 'Thierry's chocolate orange' or a deconstructed banoffi pie with condensed milk ice cream. The 'tasting menu' format can be rather baffling, although impeccably drilled French staff provide guidance from the outset. The serious wine list starts from £18.
Chef/s: Phil Fanning. **Open:** Wed to Sun L 12 to 2, Tue to Sat D 7 to 9. **Closed:** Mon, 25 Dec to 8 Jan. **Meals:** alc (main courses £19 to £29). Set L £24 (2 courses) to £32 (6 courses). Set D £49 (2 courses) to £89 (10 courses). **Service:** 10% (optional). **Details:** Cards accepted. 30 seats. Separate bar. Wheelchair access. Music. Children allowed. Car parking.

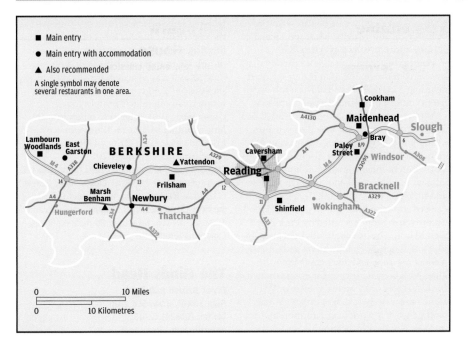

Key:
- ■ Main entry
- ● Main entry with accommodation
- ▲ Also recommended

A single symbol may denote several restaurants in one area.

0   10 Miles
0   10 Kilometres

▌Bray

The Fat Duck

The stuff of genius
1 High Street, Bray, SL6 2AQ
Tel no: (01628) 580333
www.thefatduck.co.uk
Modern British | £150
Cooking score: 10

🍷 V

The bespectacled wizard of Bray is everywhere these days, sprinkling fairy dust on TV, fronting supermarket campaigns and re-vitalising roadside eateries. In the vox pop charts he is up there with Gordon Ramsay, and even has his own F-word – fun. Heston Blumenthal has also imbued the UK's most astonishing restaurant with the jovial vibe of a true people's palace: the punters who congregate in this hospitable oak-beamed dining room come to be entertained and enchanted, but above all to experience unadulterated foodie pleasure. This is cooking as fantastical public showmanship, not solemn

ritual – you may not 'get' every dish, but you'll never forget the edgy thrills of Blumenthal's gastronomic fairground. Every sense is challenged in this wondrous phantasmagorical world, and you'll need them all as a barrage of scents, colours, sounds and flavours bombard you in precisely orchestrated waves: eyes wide open, taste-buds tuned, olfactory organs at the ready, let the show begin. As ever, the 'novel ice-breaker' is a billowing, nitrogen-fuelled display known as the 'lime grove': nitro-poached lime and vodka mousse sprinkled with powdered green tea and finished with a puff of citrus spray. Once primed, your palate is now ready for the sublime simplicity of a tiny blob of Pommery mustard ice cream balancing on a deep-purple puddle of red cabbage gazpacho. Anyone who has watched *Heston's Feasts* will be familiar with Blumenthal's foibles – his obsession with scientific methodology and gastro-anthropology, his academic forays into the dusty annals of *ars culinaria*, his love of children's bedtime stories – and the ever-evolving tasting menu now features several of the show's greatest hits, often date-stamped for historical authenticity. Most spectacular of all is the 'mock turtle soup' (circa 1850), a brilliantly conceived, outrageous parody that slips in references to the Mad Hatter's tea party including a make-believe gold-leaf fob watch that becomes a miso-like flavour bomb as it melts in a teacup of hot water. Blumenthal also knows how to probe our nostalgia synapses, hitting just the right nerves and making it count: the 'sound of the sea', for example, evokes potent memories of childhood seaside holidays – edible 'sand' shot through with umami, nuggets of cured fish, foraged seaweed and samphire – all to the famed iPod soundtrack, now re-recorded by Pink Floyd's Nick Mason. The onslaught of visual puns, in-jokes and sleights of hand amazes and unsettles in equal measure, and few people leave the Duck with their sensory apparatus unscathed. But it isn't all kooky surreal theatre or Willy Wonka dreamscapes; a razor-sharp culinary intelligence is at work here, summoning up a procession of 'world-beating' dishes for the bedazzled throngs. Consider a minuscule square of roast foie gras with a slick of rhubarb purée, braised kombu seaweed and thin slivers of crab biscuit, or three small pieces of Anjou pigeon with a smooth purée of black pudding and a challenging confit of umbles (edible innards). This is the stuff of genius. Of course, such heady, 'eat me' potions can only be taken in small doses, and the effects can be evanescent – although new levels of lingering richness have been noted of late. Sometimes a tiny detail makes all the difference – perhaps the most exquisitely tender snails in *that* savoury porridge, or a few drops of Manni olive oil added to a dish of creamy salmon poached to blackness in liquorice gel and served with artichokes, vanilla mayonnaise and golden trout roe. It goes without saying that most of this cannot be replicated anywhere else, although the petits fours manqué ought to be hugely marketable – especially the 'whisk(e)y wine gums' set on a map of Scotland (with a USA insert for Jack Daniel's), and the bag of 'sweet shop' goodies including apple pie caramel with an edible wrapper and even a chocolate playing card.

Inspired wine matches (from £90) are part of the experience, and the list is staggering in its breadth, with glorious vintages and mouthwatering possibilities including sherries and saké. Prices may sting, but shelling out £40 for a bottle of something serious really shouldn't trouble your conscience – just remember where you are. Note: Dinner by Heston Blumenthal at London's Mandarin Oriental Hotel is due to launch around December 2010.

Chef/s: Heston Blumenthal. **Open:** Tue to Sun L 12 to 2, Tue to Sat D 7 to 9.30. **Closed:** Mon, 2 weeks Christmas. **Meals:** Tasting menu L and D £150. **Service:** 12.5% (optional). **Details:** Cards accepted. 40 seats. Air-con. No music. No mobile phones. Children allowed.

The Hinds Head
Great British pub food
High Street, Bray, SL6 2AB
Tel no: (01628) 626151
www.hindsheadbray.com
British | £25
New Chef
£30

While the Fat Duck continues to deliver the most revolutionary food in the land, Heston Blumenthal's innkeeping aspirations are alive and well at this centuries-old hostelry along the road. Sturdy oak panelling, beams and blazing fires point up its heritage as a boozer, although most people are here to eat – either in the bar or the light-filled dining room. Chef Clive Dixon left as the Guide was going to press and no information was available regarding his successor. However, it is likely that self-styled 'seasonal British tavern cuisine' will remain the kitchen's stock-in-trade – think warming soups, pies, hotpots and comforting nursery desserts. No changes are expected to the wine list, with prices from £17.50. Heston recently acquired another pub on Bray's High Sreet, the Crown, tel: (01628) 621936. Reports please.

Open: all week L 12 to 2.30 (4 Sun), Mon to Sat D 6.30 to 9.30. **Closed:** 25 and 26 Dec. **Meals:** alc (main courses £14 to £30). **Service:** 12.5%

(optional). **Details:** Cards accepted. 140 seats. Air-con. Separate bar. No music. Children allowed. Car parking.

The Waterside Inn
The old grand things done perfectly
Ferry Road, Bray, SL6 2AT
Tel no: (01628) 620691
www.waterside-inn.co.uk
French | £120
Cooking score: 7

☰ V

The combination of French haute cuisine in an English pastoral setting remains undimmed in its appeal. Even if the culinary neighbours in Bray are a bit more flash these days than they were, it was the Waterside that put the place on the map in the early 1970s. Alain Roux presides over a kitchen that is unashamedly about doing the old grand things to the utmost of everyone's abilities, and service matches that to a nicety. The tone may have become increasingly anachronistic over the years, calling to mind a well-to-do fancy-dress party rather than the machinations of a high-end restaurant – although this merely adds to the gentrified sense of fun. While your waiter garnishes your glass of water with a lime slice, great labours are taking place backstage. They could well be pot-cooking medallions of lobster in white port, to be served with gingery vegetable julienne (go large for £86 as a main course). Soufflés are the most billowingly light and regally risen examples of the genre to be found anywhere, founded on langoustines perhaps, their flavour deepened by an accompanying truffled langoustine cassolette. Dishes for two at main may be a whole braised turbot or saddle of milk-fed lamb, and the preparations are virtually always as classical as can be. Fillets of rabbit on celeriac fondant with glazed chestnuts in Armagnac sauce seems, in the context, daringly radical. What you are paying for – apart from faultless commitment to quality ingredients – is the sheer unblinking attention to detail that everything receives, through to the grande assiette dessert

selections and the fabulous petits fours. Wines are an encyclopedic array, although mere mortals will probably require a loan extension. Whites start at £21, reds from £27.
Chef/s: Alain Roux. **Open:** Wed to Sun L 12 to 2 (2.30 Sun), D 7 to 10, also Tue D 1 Jun to 31 Aug. **Closed:** Mon, 26 Dec for four or five weeks, bank hols. **Meals:** alc (main courses £49 to £70). Set L £41.50 (2 courses) to £56.50. Sun L £72. Menu exceptionnel £112.50 (5 courses). **Service:** 12.5%. **Details:** Cards accepted. 70 seats. Air-con. Separate bar. No music. No mobile phones. Car parking.

▮ Caversham

NEW ENTRY
Mya Lacarte
Popular neighbourhood restaurant
5 Prospect Street, Caversham, RG4 8JB
Tel no: (01189) 463400
www.myalacarte.co.uk
British | £38
Cooking score: 2

£5
OFF

The café-like exterior and underwhelming décor of this popular local restaurant belie its skilfully rendered food and friendly service. French chef Remy Joly taps into the UK's regional network and creates menus that are tuned in to the prevailing zeitgeist. His main courses in particular show good technical skill: at inspection, a Watlington pork platter (belly, cheek and kidney) and Scottish scallops with Hampshire oxtail both impressed with their deep, rich flavours, contrasting textures and clean presentation. Capably executed starters and desserts also point up the backpacking all-British theme, from Yattendon rabbit loin or baked goats' cheese with Basingstoke watercress, Goring Heath leaves and North Yorkshire rhubarb dressing to gooseberry crumble with Shropshire double cream. Wines from £13.95.
Chef/s: Remy Joly. **Open:** all week L 12 to 3 (4 Sun), Mon to Sat D 5 to 10.30. **Closed:** 25 and 26 Dec, 1 Jan. **Meals:** alc (main courses £5 to £21). Set L and D (Set D Mon to Wed only) £13.50 (2 courses) to £16.95. **Service:** not inc. **Details:** Cards accepted. 34 seats. Music. Children allowed.

▌Chieveley

The Crab at Chieveley

Skilful seafood in a surprising setting
Wantage Road, Chieveley, RG20 8UE
Tel no: (01635) 247550
www.crabatchieveley.com
Seafood | £38
Cooking score: 3

 £5 OFF ⊨ V

An isolated hilltop in rural Berkshire is the unlikely setting for this seafood restaurant, which gets its fish daily from the Devon markets. The interconnecting dining rooms share a rather hackneyed décor – low-beamed ceilings strung with fishing nets and shells. Lobster and crab feature heavily alongside French classics on an extensive seafood menu expanded by Goosnargh duck, aged beef fillet and lamb. But reports run hot and cold, ranging from 'poorly cooked soufflé, terrible Dover sole' to 'a delicately rich scallop boudin with chive beurre blanc, and a creamy cauliflower risotto topped with a precisely timed sea bass fillet and salsa verde – the highlight of lunch.' Service is knowledgeable and efficient. The affordable wine list has carafes from £13.95.
Chef/s: Jamie Hodson. **Open:** all week L 12 to 2.30, D 6 to 10 (9 Sun). **Meals:** alc (main courses £19 to £45). Set menu £15.95 (2 courses) to £19.95. Sun L £23. Tasting Menu £60 (8 courses). **Service:** 10% (optional). **Details:** Cards accepted. 90 seats. 40 seats outside. Separate bar. Wheelchair access. Music. Children allowed. Car parking.

Symbols

⊨ Accommodation is available

£30 Three courses for less than £30

V More than three vegetarian main courses

£5 OFF £5-off voucher scheme

🍾 Notable wine list

▌Cookham

Maliks

Hot spot for spices and stars
High Street, Cookham, SL6 9SF
Tel no: (01628) 520085
www.maliks.co.uk
Indian | £40
Cooking score: 2

V

Malik Ahmed is used to welcoming stars of the entertainment and sporting worlds at this creeper-covered restaurant near the Thames, where antiques, flowers and lots of dark wood set a tone a world away from most urban Indian eateries. Nor do the menus plough the usual furrows. Instead, expect a char-grilled marinated duck breast to start, or king prawns in sweet-sour tamarind sauce, followed perhaps by lamb halim with lentils, ginger and garlic, or fried marinated red mullet with mushrooms and peppers. Clear, vivid spicing and accurate cooking impress, as do desserts such as frini (creamed rice pudding) with coconut ice cream. House French is £15, or drink lassi.
Chef/s: Malik Ahmed and Shapon Miah. **Open:** all week L 12 to 2.30 (3 Sun), D 6 to 11 (10.30 Sun). **Closed:** 25 and 26 Dec. **Meals:** alc (main courses £8 to £16). Set L £12 (2 courses). Set D £21 (2 courses) to £30. Sun L £10. **Service:** 10% (optional). **Details:** Cards accepted. 70 seats. No mobile phones. Wheelchair access. Music. Children allowed. Car parking.

▌East Garston

Queen's Arms Hotel

Stylish old inn with simple food
Newbury Road, East Garston, RG17 7ET
Tel no: (01488) 648757
www.queensarmshotel.co.uk
British | £26
Cooking score: 2
⊨ £30

The interior of this whitewashed old inn has been revamped with style: it's all very open and done out in soothing colours with board floors, period furnishings, old prints on the walls, subtle lighting and polished wood tables. Simple dishes but no pub clichés describes the cooking, with the likes of sea trout with crushed Jersey Royals, creamed pea, bacon and wilted lettuce reflecting both sound buying and seasonal ingredients. Start with pork and sage pâté with caramelised apple, crackling and star anise jus and finish with vanilla pannacotta and raspberry compote. Wines from £15.25.

Chef/s: Kevin Chandler, Gary Burns and Chris Hancock. **Open:** all week L 12 to 2.30 (4 Sun), D 6.30 to 9.30 (9 Sun). **Closed:** 25 Dec. **Meals:** alc (main courses £11 to £18). **Service:** not inc. **Details:** Cards accepted. 45 seats. 20 seats outside. Separate bar. No music. Wheelchair access. Children allowed. Car parking.

∎ Frilsham
The Pot Kiln

Gutsy country gem
Frilsham, RG18 0XX
Tel no: (01635) 201366
www.potkiln.co.uk
Gastropub | £26
Cooking score: 1
£30

This gem of a rural pub was built in 1700 and Mike and Katie Robinson are proud to claim they are the third-ever owners. It's a fantastic resource for the local community, with a welcoming feel, real ales taken seriously and a kitchen noted for its gutsy country cooking. Game is a passion, with hare ragù on tagliatelle with aged Parmesan and Wiltshire truffle served alongside fresh Cornish fish and pub classics including local beef and roe deer burger. House wine is £12.95.

Chef/s: Mike Robinson. **Open:** Wed to Mon L 12 to 2 (2.45 Sun), Wed to Sat and Mon D 7 to 9. **Closed:** Tue. **Meals:** alc (main courses £13 to £17). Set L £14.50 (2 courses) to £19.50. **Service:** 10% (optional). **Details:** Cards accepted. 45 seats. 100 seats outside. Separate bar. No music. No mobile phones. Children allowed. Car parking.

∎ Lambourn Woodlands

NEW ENTRY
The Hare Restaurant

Confident cooking and flavoursome food
Ermin Street, Lambourn Woodlands, RG17 7SD
Tel no: (01488) 71386
www.theharerestaurant.co.uk
Modern British | £34
Cooking score: 2
£5 OFF **V**

Traditional and contemporary influences rub shoulders in the décor and menus of this refurbished former village inn set in the Berkshire Downs. Paul Reed's confident, technically sound cooking, based on prime, seasonal and regional ingredients, shows in flavoursome, well executed mains of calf's liver with bubble and squeak and roast rump of spring lamb with tabbouleh and baba ganoush. Exemplary desserts include rhubarb and custard crème brûlée and apple and pear crumble. The set lunch menu changes weekly, whilst the lounge menu includes excellent classic poached egg dishes – Benedict, florentine and royale (with smoked salmon). Diners can mix and match menus. House wines start at £17 (£4.50 a glass).

Chef/s: Paul Reed. **Open:** Tue to Sun L 12 to 2 (2.30 Sun), Tue to Sat D 7 to 9 (9.30 Fri and Sat). **Closed:** Mon, bank hols, 2 weeks Jan/Feb, 2 weeks July/Aug. **Meals:** alc (main courses from £15 to £22). Set L £20 (2 courses) to £26. Set D £20 (2 courses) to £32. Sun L £26. **Service:** not inc. **Details:** Cards accepted. 75 seats. 30 seats outside. Separate bar. Wheelchair access. Music. Children allowed. Car parking.

Please send us your feedback

To register your opinion about any restaurant listed in the Guide, or a new restaurant that you wish to bring to our attention, please visit the web address at the bottom of the page. Your feedback informs the content of the book and will be used to compile next year's reviews.

Maidenhead

NEW ENTRY

Boulters Restaurant & Bar

Ambitous restaurant on an island
Boulters Lock Island, Maidenhead, SL6 8PE
Tel no: (01628) 621291
www.boultersrestaurant.co.uk
Modern British | £35
Cooking score: 2
£5 OFF

Set on an island commanding idyllic views of the Thames, Boulter's restaurant is light, airy and tastefully decorated, with well-spaced tables and luxuriously upholstered chairs. Daniel Woodhouse's cooking successfully combines classical French techniques with bold innovations, such as brandade soup with slow-poached egg and beef cheek ravioli with snails. Perfectly timed sea bream fillet and breast of black-leg chicken show sensitive handling of fish and meat dishes. Although pastry needs a lighter touch, other desserts such as sticky toffee soufflé with Earl Grey ice cream are well executed. Wines start £15.75.
Chef/s: Daniel Woodhouse. **Open:** Wed to Sun L 12 to 3, Wed to Sat D 7 to 10. **Meals:** alc (main courses £13 to £20). Set L £14.95 (2 courses) to £19.95. Sun L £29.95. Tasting menu £65. **Service:** 12.5% (optional). **Details:** Cards accepted. 150 seats. 75 seats outside. Air-con. Separate bar. Wheelchair access. Music. Children allowed. Car parking.

Marsh Benham

ALSO RECOMMENDED

▲ The Red House

Marsh Benham, RG20 8LY
Tel no: (01635) 582017
www.theredhousepub.com
Gastropub

Laurent Lebeau, former executive chef for Group Chez Gérard, has downsized to this beautifully situated, off-the-beaten-track thatched pub (although it's not far from the M4). He offers a modern brasserie menu of sound British classics, which spans everything from split-pea and smoked ham soup (£4.95),

steak and kidney pudding (£12.75), and haddock in beer batter with hand-cut chips and peas, to good steaks and roast Label Anglais chicken with roast potatoes, braised leeks and gravy. Wines from £13.50. Open all week. Reports please.

Newbury

The Vineyard at Stockcross

A class act
Newbury, RG20 8JU
Tel no: (01635) 589400
www.the-vineyard.co.uk
Modern European | £70
Cooking score: 6
£5 OFF ☖ ⇌ V

Despite is oenophilic name, the Vineyard is actually a plush, modern hotel off a B-road on the outskirts of Newbury, with an interior of muted but deep British comfort. Following the departure of supremo John Campbell, the kitchen is now in the hands of Daniel Galmiche. He has sidestepped the restless culinary ambition of his predecessor and introduced a style that is a mix of the familiar and the gently inventive. Most reporters endorse the three-course lunch, which has included braised belly of free-range pork with 'delicate' black pudding tortellini, apple and celery, and a superb coffee and clementine soufflé (marbled with bitter chocolate) with clementine sorbet. They also appreciate the flexibility of the fixed-price repertoire – including different choices at lunch and dinner – and the fact that the carte is bolstered by tasting options. Prices rise in the evening, when the menu might also feature carpaccio of milk-fed veal with basil, veal sweetbread and grapefruit dressing, and steamed fillet of John Dory with honey and chilli glaze, fennel and broad beans. The split-level dining room is a class act, too, its grapevine balustrade echoing the establishment's name and giving a nod to the Vineyard's spectacular 2,300-bin wine list. Expect a star-spangled collection from California (including representatives from owner Sir Peter Michael's winery) with some 50 bottles under £25.

Chef/s: Daniel Galmiche. **Open:** all week L 12 to 2, D 7 to 10. **Meals:** Set L £20 (2 courses) to £30. Set D £60 (2 courses) to £70. Sun L £37. L tasting menu £46. D tasting menu £97. **Service:** not inc. **Details:** Cards accepted. 90 seats. Air-con. Separate bar. Wheelchair access. Music. Children allowed. Car parking.

▌Paley Street
The Royal Oak
Upper-tier pub food
Paley Street, SL6 3JN
Tel no: (01628) 620541
www.theroyaloakpaleystreet.com
Gastropub | £45
Cooking score: 5

£5 OFF 🍷

The oak-beamed, whitewashed pub in a village near Maidenhead presses all the right buttons for devotees of the genre. Comfortable armchairs and an open log fire cheer the soul, and hand-pumped cask ales are an essential part of the picture. Nick Parkinson, Sir Michael's son, oversees the operation with eagle-eyed attention to detail, and numerous ringing endorsements continue to bolster the reputation of Dominic Chapman's seasonally based English cooking. Almost everybody loves to start with one of the now-famous Scotch eggs, a £3 nibble whose succulence and savour banish all thought of monstrosities in supermarket packets. After that, it's on to pickled Cornish herrings with beetroot, horseradish and watercress, or a bowl of thick, restorative Jerusalem artichoke soup, before mains such as cutlet and liver of Welsh salt marsh lamb, served with braised lettuce and champ. Heritage ways with meat have also seen hare and trotter pie crop up, while puddings are an honour roll of bread-and-butter, rhubarb trifle and lemon posset, with fine English cheeses the alternative. Just when you think the experience is complete, you turn to the wine list, and fresh hosannas ring out. From the excellent choice by the glass (from £2.90 for 125ml), to the run of first-growth clarets in four figures, it's an unexpected classic.

Chef/s: Dominic Chapman. **Open:** all week L 12 to 2.30 (3.30 Sun), Mon to Sat D 6.30 to 9.30 (10 Fri and Sat). **Closed:** 26 Dec, 1 Jan. **Meals:** alc (main courses £13 to £24). Set L £17.50 (2 courses) to £21. **Service:** 12.5% (optional). **Details:** Cards accepted. 50 seats. 30 seats outside. Air-con. Separate bar. Wheelchair access. Music. Children allowed. Car parking.

▌Reading
London Street Brasserie
Generous, comforting food
2-4 London Street, Reading, RG1 4SE
Tel no: (01189) 505036
www.londonstbrasserie.co.uk
Modern European | £29
Cooking score: 3

£30

'Consistently good local restaurant with strong client base and excellent service', is one regular's fond verdict on this fixture of the Reading scene. Paul Clerehugh is not about to rock an exceedingly steady ship, and his food remains true to the spirit of generosity, wholesome flavour and comfort. His menus are a mixed bag of contemporary European ideas: fish soup or partridge and ham hock terrine could be followed by a well-reported sea bass with garlic king shrimp skewer, Mediterranean vegetables and salsa verde or rabbit saddle baked in pancetta and served with a potato cake and light cider cream. Desserts might feature an excellent hot chocolate fondant with vanilla ice cream. Lunch menus are very good value. Wines from a wide-ranging list start at £18.

Chef/s: Paul Clerehugh. **Open:** all week 12 to 10.30 (11 Fri and Sat, 10 Sun and Mon). **Closed:** 25 Dec. **Meals:** alc (main courses £12 to £22). Set L and D £14.95 (2 courses) to £18.90. **Service:** not inc. **Details:** Cards accepted. 80 seats. 24 seats outside. Separate bar. Wheelchair access. Music. Children allowed.

▌Shinfield

L'Ortolan

Sheer prosperity and top-end food
Church Lane, Shinfield, RG2 9BY
Tel no: (01189) 888500
www.lortolan.com
Modern French | £47
Cooking score: 6

It stands proud at the end of a sweeping gravel drive with mature gardens resplendent all around. Once inside, guests can soak up the sheer prosperity of it all, from the clubby lounge and boldly decorated bar to the summery conservatory and smartly attired, sober dining room overseen by supremely professional staff. The kitchen delivers top-end, cultured French food in the modern idiom, with a full complement of extras – perhaps a cup of intense foaming parsnip velouté with curry oil, an intermezzo of calamansi fruit jelly with coconut foam, and jellied petits fours with coffee. In between, expect a procession of 'consistently outstanding' dishes. High points from recent meals have included an exceedingly smart Jerusalem artichoke salad with crispy Parmesan risotto and pickled mushrooms, and a beautifully cohesive dish of crispy pork belly offset by spiced pumpkin purée, caramelised kohlrabi and sage gnocchi – not forgetting a dessert of spiced pear with a tantalising trio of candied pistachio, rosemary jelly and quince sorbet. The cheeseboard has been deemed 'sensational', and the French-centred wine list offers an aristocratic spread starting at £20; note the increasing numbers of organic bottles. Chef/patron Alan Murchison is in empire-building mood, with La Bécasse, Ludlow and the re-launched Paris House, Woburn (see entries) already on board.
Chef/s: Alan Murchison. **Open:** Tue to Sat L 12 to 2, D 7 to 9. **Closed:** Sun, Mon, 25 Dec to 7 Jan.
Meals: Set L £24 (2 courses) to £29. Set D £56 (2 courses) to £65. Gourmand menu £69.
Service: 12.5% (optional). **Details:** Cards accepted. 62 seats. Separate bar. Wheelchair access. Music. Children allowed. Car parking.

▌Yattendon

ALSO RECOMMENDED
▲ The Royal Oak

The Square, Yattendon, RG18 0UF
Tel no: (01635) 201325
www.royaloakyattendon.co.uk
Modern British

New owners have made a promising early impression at this wisteria-clad, sixteenth-century inn facing the village square. Oliver Cromwell dined here on the eve of the Battle of Newbury and the classic beamed and rug-strewn tiled bar and the adjoining lounge and dining rooms have been spruced up without losing their ancient charm and character. These days, the food is bang up-to-date – lobster risotto with prosciutto (£9) perhaps followed by char-grilled ribeye steak with chips and béarnaise (£17.50). To finish, try vanilla and peach parfait with peach jelly (£6). Wines from £13. Open all week.

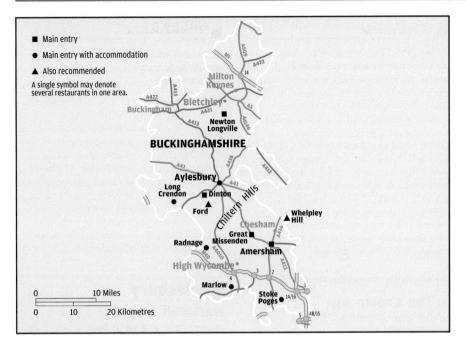

- ■ Main entry
- ● Main entry with accommodation
- ▲ Also recommended

A single symbol may denote
several restaurants in one area.

BUCKINGHAMSHIRE

| 0 | 10 Miles |
| 0 | 10 | 20 Kilometres |

▌Amersham

NEW ENTRY

Artichoke
What a comeback!
9 Market Square, Amersham, HP7 ODF
Tel no: (01494) 726611
www.artichokerestaurant.co.uk
Modern British | £40
Cooking score: 6

Fire damage in 2008 meant months of closure,
but Laurie and Jacqueline Gear's beloved
Artichoke is back – and better than ever.
During the extended time out, the narrow
beamed room has been given a newly-minted
feel with cool glass panels, pictures and bare
walnut tables. It's a tight fit, but the whole set-
up gels – an affable blend of serious intent and
neighbourly good humour. Laurie Gear has
also been absorbing new ideas – especially
from superstar René Redzepi at Noma in

Copenhagen – and the result is a transparent
culinary style that can accommodate anything
from smoked quails' eggs to gorse flowers. It's a
busy, highly worked approach, although the
intricacy never gets out of hand and every
detail makes sense; flavours have room to
breathe and cohesive natural empathy is the
key. The theme of beetroot and goats' cheese is
explored in an eye-popping starter involving
'deliriously sexy' beetroot sorbet, whole baby
beets resembling Lilliputian maroon pears, a
micro-thin disc of the raw root, mounds of
wispy whipped cheese dusted with beetroot
powder and a tangle of lemon thyme.
Elsewhere the sheer rightness of the food
shows in pitch-perfect poached brill on pokey
sea spinach beside a slab of wobbly white
onion mousse (cleverly 'seasoned' with crispy
crumbled Serrano ham), all surrounded by a
golden drizzle of 'chutney-pungent' pear
vinegar dressing. Other dishes are an
apotheosis of the season – an end-of-year
blockbuster of Chiltern venison ('so tender')
with glazed pears, pontack (elderberry
ketchup), Savoy cabbage and pumpkin

gnocchi, or warm walnut tart with cranberry sorbet, say. Set lunch brings some humbler offerings to the table, but no dumbing down – witness a textbook blanquette of English rose veal with a hillock of butter-smooth mash and fresh-as-a-daisy carrots. The wine list is pure class, a knowledgeable collection from forward-looking producers around the globe. Prices start at £19 (£5.50 a glass).

Chef/s: Laurie Gear. **Open:** Tue to Sat L 12 to 1.30, D 6.30 to 11 (6.15 Fri and Sat). **Closed:** Sun, Mon, 1 week Christmas, 1 week end Apr, 2 weeks Aug, bank hols. **Meals:** alc (main courses £17 to £23). Set L £18.50 (2 courses) to £22.50. Set D £32 (2 courses) to £39.50. Tasting menu £56 (7 courses). **Service:** 12.5% (optional). **Details:** Cards accepted. 24 seats. 4 seats outside. Air-con. No mobile phones. Music. Children allowed.

ALSO RECOMMENDED

▲ The Crown Inn

16 High Street, Amersham, HP7 0DH
Tel no: (01494) 721541
www.thecrownamersham.com
British

An affluent inn-with-rooms for our times, the Crown makes its brick-fronted presence felt on Old Amersham's main drag. Recent reports are mixed, but the kitchen still does the right thing by rustling up rough-hewn dishes from seasonal British ingredients. Typical offerings might include chicken liver and beetroot salad (£5.80), grilled hake with purple sprouting broccoli (£17.50) and new season's lamb and tomato stew. To finish, elderflower sorbet bobbing in a glass of ginger beer (£5.90) is a novel idea. 'Slap Bang' lunches are stonkingly good value, and wines start at £15. Closed Sun D.

▲ Gilbey's

1 Market Square, Amersham, HP7 0DF
Tel no: (01494) 727242
www.gilbeygroup.com
Modern British

A faithful servant of Old Amersham for many years, Gilbey's is still the model of a dependable neighbourhood bistro. The setting – a converted grammar school with a lovely courtyard garden – is a big plus, and the kitchen plays with a straight bat. The lively menu might take in pork and pink peppercorn terrine (£7.75), confit duck with red onion tarte Tatin (£16.95) and lemon tart with cranberry and orange sorbet (£6.85). The Gilbey family are also wine importers, so expect plenty of good stuff from £13.95. Open all week.

■ Aylesbury

Hartwell House

Opulent hotel with smart food
Oxford Road, Aylesbury, HP17 8NR
Tel no: (01296) 747444
www.hartwell-house.com
Modern European | £37
Cooking score: 4

£5 OFF ⊨ V

Reposing in 90 acres of beautifully tended grounds, Hartwell was a bolthole for the French monarchy during the Napoleonic period. It is now an opulent hotel, and the primrose-coloured dining-room is smartness itself, from the staff to the food. Daniel Richardson uses ingredients from the hotel's gardens and orchards, as well as the surrounding counties. The fixed-price menus are especially popular. Expect a certain level of country-house richness, for instance wood pigeon on cassoulet with parsley purée and game jus, perhaps followed by John Dory with buttered leeks, girolles and rösti in white wine sauce. To finish, consider mandarin and cranberry cheesecake with mandarin sorbet and a ginger biscuit. The wine list is stuffed

with classic drinking. A page of 'vineyard values' offers financial relief, and the Spanish house wines, at £19.95, are impressive.
Chef/s: Daniel Richardson. **Open:** all week L 12.30 to 1.45, D 7.30 to 9.45. **Meals:** alc (main courses £22 to £29). Set L £22.95 (2 courses) to £29.95. Set D £37 (3 courses). Sun L £32.95. **Service:** 12.5%.
Details: Cards accepted. 60 seats. Separate bar. No music. No mobile phones. Wheelchair access. Children allowed. Car parking.

■ Dinton

La Chouette
Quirky Belgian auberge
Westlington Green, Dinton, HP17 8UW
Tel no: (01296) 747422
www.lachouette.co.uk
Belgian | £29
Cooking score: 2
🍷 £30

For more than 20 years, tireless chef/patron Frédéric Desmette has presided over this one-off, 'rare-breed' restaurant – an idiosyncratic Belgian 'auberge' deep in rural Buckinghamshire. It's a strangely alluring, time-warp bubble with quirks aplenty – even if some visitors find the owner's straight-talking, opinionated demeanour rather unsettling. Aside from cooking, Desmette spends his hours painting and photographing wildlife: pictures of his beloved owls (*chouettes*) fill the endearingly old-fashioned dining room, where customers can enjoy Belgian and French bourgeois food from the world of *Larousse Gastronomique*. Flemish-style asparagus and turbot with a sauce of Duvel beer rub shoulders with fresh-tasting skate salad, duck breast with morels and veal kidney with mustard, before crêpes, fruity sorbets and chocolate confections close proceedings. The wine list is a French wonder, with glories from Alsace to Madiran, a huge choice of superb Burgundies and much more to distract. Vins de pays are £15.
Chef/s: Frédéric Desmette. **Open:** Mon to Fri L 12 to 2, Mon to Sat D 7 to 9. **Closed:** Sun. **Meals:** alc (main courses £15 to £18). Set L £16 (3 courses). Set D £33 (4 courses) to £42. **Service:** 12.5% (optional).

Details: Cards accepted. 35 seats. Separate bar. No mobile phones. Music. Children allowed. Car parking.

■ Ford

ALSO RECOMMENDED
▲ The Dinton Hermit
Water Lane, Ford, HP17 8XH
Tel no: (01296) 747473
www.dintonhermit.co.uk
Gastropub £5 OFF

'It feels like driving into a showpiece farmyard', complete with pristine barns (now used for accommodation), but this extended country boozer in the windy wilds of the Aylesbury Vale earns its living from good hospitality, locally brewed ales and generous, satisfying food. Garlicky wild mushrooms on toast with a poached egg and shaved Parmesan (£5.75) makes a wholesome starter; mains might feature slow-braised lamb shank with colcannon (£14) or some fresh fish, before nursery puds such as treacle sponge (£5.50) round things off. Wines from £16 (£3.75 a glass). Open all week.

■ Great Missenden

La Petite Auberge
Paragon of French virtues
107 High Street, Great Missenden, HP16 0BB
Tel no: (01494) 865370
www.lapetiteauberge.co.uk
French | £36
Cooking score: 3
£5 OFF

A *chère amie* to the people of Great Missenden, the Martels' ever-reliable paragon of French virtues has been conversing amicably in Gallic tones for more than two decades. Madame is on first-name terms with most of her customers in the 'petite' warm-toned dining room, and chef/patron Hubert feeds the chatty assembled company with an ingrained repertoire of skilfully wrought, satisfying dishes. The food is deeply unfashionable, but no one cares when there are generous, carefully arranged plates of juicy duck breast with blackcurrant sauce, fillet of turbot with anchovies and capers or veal sweetbreads with green Chartreuse on offer. Precisely timed scallops on julienne of carrot and leeks tinged with a light soy dressing is about as racy as it comes, while desserts revert to type with – say – nougatine glacé or apple chaud-froid and cinnamon ice cream. The concise, all-French wine list starts at £16.50.

Chef/s: Hubert Martel. **Open:** Mon to Sat D only 7 to 10. **Closed:** Sun (except Mothering Sun L), 2 weeks Christmas, 3 weeks Easter, bank hols. **Meals:** alc (main courses £17 to £20). **Service:** not inc. **Details:** Cards accepted. 30 seats. No music. No mobile phones. Wheelchair access. Children allowed.

Little Marlow

READERS RECOMMEND

The Queens Head

Gastropub
Pound Lane, Little Marlow, SL7 3SR
Tel no: (01628) 482927
www.marlowslittlesecret.co.uk
'Cosy pub with exceptional service and almost all food sourced locally'

Long Crendon

Angel Restaurant

Engaging inn with generous platefuls
47 Bicester Road, Long Crendon, HP18 9EE
Tel no: (01844) 208268
www.angelrestaurant.co.uk
Modern British | £32
Cooking score: 2

A veteran provider of hospitality on the Buckinghamshire/Oxfordshire border, the Angel started life as a local inn – although it now flourishes as an engaging country restaurant-with-rooms. Inside it sports several distinctive dining areas, which regularly get packed to the gunnels. A specials board above the bar spells out the day's fish (sea bass, monkfish et al), but there is also plenty for

those with a taste for generous platefuls of red meat. Start with crispy duck salad, proceed to rump of lamb on curly kale with ratatouille and save room for, say, Calvados-spiked rice pudding. The fascinating wine list casts its net wide for classy names and lesser-known grape varieties, with lots available by the glass and 50cl pichet. Bottles prices start at £15.50.

Chef/s: Trevor Bosch. **Open:** all week L 12 to 2.30, Mon to Sat D 7 to 9.30. **Meals:** alc (main courses £14 to £29). Set L and D £14.95 (2 courses) to £21.95. Sun L £18.50. **Service:** not inc. **Details:** Cards accepted. 70 seats. 25 seats outside. Air-con. Separate bar. Wheelchair access. Music. Children allowed. Car parking.

Marlow

Adam Simmonds at Danesfield House

Magnificent food with new impetus
Henley Road, Marlow, SL7 2EY
Tel no: (01628) 891010
www.danesfieldhouse.co.uk
Modern European | £55
Cooking score: 8

Completely rebuilt at the end of the nineteenth century, this sparklingly white Italianate mansion stands in 65 acres with views to the river Thames. The interior will look familiar to frequenters of country house hotels, with plenty of polished wood, tapestries and huge fireplaces, although a more contemporary feel has been brought to bear on the Oak Room – now named after its chef. Adam Simmonds has perfected a culinary style full of understated personal flourishes and painstaking attention to detail, offering the seasonal best alongside impeccably sourced meat and fish. All these ingredients are translated into dishes with real poise. Everything on the plate is there for a purpose – there is no over-complication – and the results are strikingly vivid. Indeed, his cooking has such exactitude that he creates flavours where others would lose them – in a confit foie gras with yellow peaches, hazelnut purée and

Condrieu jelly; in a slow-cooked fillet of wild salmon with pea purée, wild strawberries and green almonds; in poached fillet of turbot with tiny cubes of vibrant lemon verbena pannacotta, asparagus purée, girolles and crunchy peanuts. These are alpha dishes, but the sheer vitality of the ingredients shines through at every turn: 'I am still thinking about the starter of langoustine with cucumber which we both ordered; just a remarkable and clever combination of delicate ingredients', mused one reporter who also sampled magnificent main courses of veal sweetbread and anchovy tortellini, and slow-cooked loin of lamb with tomato-spiced couscous. The verdict: 'just outstanding'. As for dessert, try not to miss the milk chocolate, banana and rum mille-feuille with banana parfait or the extraordinary concentration of chilled coconut and mango in a rice pudding with mango parfait, coconut jelly and olive caramel. Masterful wine service is on hand to guide diners through the impressive, varietally arranged wine list, even if it is just matching a series of glasses (from £7 to £17) to your meal. There are no budget options, with prices starting at £25 for an Australian Chardonnay and a French Merlot.

Chef/s: Adam Simmonds. **Open:** Fri and Sat L 12 to 2, Tue to Sat D 7 to 9.30. **Closed:** Sun, Mon, 2 weeks Christmas, 2 weeks Aug. **Meals:** Set L and D £55 (3 courses). Tasting menu £68.50. **Service:** 12.5% (optional). **Details:** Cards accepted. 26 seats. Separate bar. No music. No mobile phones. Wheelchair access. Car parking.

The Hand & Flowers
A beacon of quality
126 West Street, Marlow, SL7 2BP
Tel no: (01628) 482277
www.thehandandflowers.co.uk
Modern British | £35
Cooking score: 6

Tom and Beth Kerridge opened this roadside inn (with rooms a little way along the road) in 2005 and have achieved remarkable results in a comparatively short time. Unsuspecting

visitors who know nothing of its reputation come away in a state of breathless excitement, while those in the know rate it as one of Buckinghamshire's beacons of quality. It all looks so unassuming, and yet the calibre of the materials lifts the place to another level. Tom Kerridge's skill has something to do with it too, of course, witnessed in dishes such as a memorable slow-cooked shoulder and rump of lamb with smoked aubergine. Meals might begin enterprisingly with Cornish mackerel tartare with avruga caviar, radish and black pepper toast, or with something as apparently straightforward as an omelette, but all lushed up with smoked haddock and Parmesan. It's the accuracy of cooking and the sheer impact on the palate that impress readers, as when sea bass fillet is partnered with belly pork, cockles, pickled apple and honey gravy. The lavender pannacotta with whisky jelly and honeycomb continues to be mentioned in dispatches. A good spread of house wines comes by the glass (from £3.95), carafe or bottle (£15.50).

Chef/s: Tom Kerridge. **Open:** all week L 12 to 2.30 (3.30 Sun), Mon to Sat D 6.30 to 9. **Closed:** 24 to 26 Dec. **Meals:** alc (main courses £16 to £25). Set L £10 (2 courses) to £13.50. **Service:** not inc.
Details: Cards accepted. 50 seats. 25 seats outside. Music. Children allowed. Car parking.

★ READERS' RESTAURANT OF THE YEAR ★
SOUTH EAST

Vanilla Pod
House of hidden delights
31 West Street, Marlow, SL7 2LS
Tel no: (01628) 898101
www.thevanillapod.co.uk
Modern European | £40
Cooking score: 5

£5 OFF **V**

Once T.S. Eliot's out-of-town domicile, this unremarkable two-storey dwelling is now home to one of Marlow's most consistent and likeable gastronomic performers. Step through the black door into a discreet, narrow dining room with heavy-clothed round tables and French doors opening out onto a pretty back garden – a suitably warm-hearted backdrop for Michael Macdonald's highly assured, technically astute and seasonally sympathetic cooking. Buttered Brussels sprouts partner poached quail, and roast fillet of cod is robustly shored up with lentils and pickled shallots, while date purée and wild mushrooms are natural end-of-year companions for roasted duck breast. To follow, a dessert of apple financier with hot buttered cinnamon rum also radiates winter warmth. Value for money is exceptional at this level, particularly the weekly changing set lunch menu, which might work its way through celeriac risotto with truffle and potato foam, roast pork fillet wrapped in fennel seeds, and caramel pears with spiced bread and tonka bean pannacotta – all leaving change from a £20 note. Courteous staff go about their business politely, and front of house has been strengthened by the arrival of Mickael Metmayer from London high flyer Pied-à-Terre (see entry). The French-leaning wine list succeeds in offering affordable quality across the board, with prices commendably reined back. Selections start at £19.50 (£4.50 a glass). **Chef/s:** Michael Macdonald. **Open:** Tue to Sat L 12 to 2, D 7 to 10. **Closed:** Sun, Mon, 24 Dec to 6 Jan. **Meals:** Set L £15.50 (2 courses) to £19.50. Set D £35 (2 courses) to £40. Gourmand menu £50 (8 courses). **Service:** not inc. **Details:** Cards accepted. 36 seats. 10 seats outside. Air-con. Separate bar. No music. Children allowed.

▊ Newton Longville
The Crooked Billet
Cheery pub with stupendous wines
2 Westbrook End, Newton Longville, MK17 0DF
Tel no: (01908) 373936
www.thebillet.co.uk
Modern British | £28
Cooking score: 2
£5 OFF ▎ £30

Newton Longville's allotment holders provide a bumper crop for this thatched hostelry, which has evolved into a cheery landmark dedicated to artisan produce: the Gilchrists buy wisely, smoke bacon and hams,

make preserves and bake impressively. They also know how to procure from abroad – witness a gorgeous starter of Serrano ham with shaved two-year Gouda, celeriac rémoulade and truffled honey, although more intricately worked dishes can be let down by the details: sea bream with sweet clams, beetroot purée and lemon beurre blanc has been marred by 'leaden, unseasoned' olive oil mash. Spicy homemade gingerbread with caramelised apples is a moreish dessert, and the cheese trolley is unrivalled in these parts. The Billet is also recommended as a lunchtime pit-stop for, say, chimney-smoked duck sausages and mash with a pint of ale. Pride of place, however, goes to the stupendous 200-bin wine list – a treasure for curious imbibers, with almost everything available by the glass and friendly prices from £13.75. **Chef/s:** Emma Gilchrist. **Open:** Tue to Sun L 12 to 2 (4 Sun), Mon to Sat D 7 to 9.30 (10 Fri and Sat). **Meals:** alc (main courses £14 to £28). Set L £16.75 (2 courses) to £21. Set D £18.75 (2 courses) to £23. Sun L £24.75. Tasting menu £65. **Service:** not inc. **Details:** Cards accepted. 60 seats. 50 seats outside. Separate bar. No music. Wheelchair access. Children allowed. Car parking.

▊ Radnage
The Three Horseshoes
Intriguing seasonal dishes
Horseshoe Road, Bennett End, Radnage, HP14 4EB
Tel no: (01494) 483273
www.thethreehorseshoes.net
Modern British | £40
Cooking score: 3
£5 OFF 🛏

'Lovely spot, super views, casual vibes, comfy scrubbed-up rustic interior, serious precise food'. So writes one reporter, happy to support Simon Crawshaw's neat, uncluttered inn hidden in the depths of the Chilterns. Freshness and timing really make the most of excellent raw materials, and seasonal menus offer an intriguing array of dishes: seared scallop and braised pork belly with mulled wine reduction and cauliflower purée, for example, or a main course of Barbary duck breast with sautéed foie gras, black pudding and deep-fried celeriac and potato purée. There's an 'excellent Sunday roast' too. Treats to finish include caramelised bananas with a waffle or peanut butter ice cream with hot chocolate sauce. The modest wine list covers a lot of territory with some 14 by the glass and bottles from £15. **Chef/s:** Simon Crawshaw and James Norie. **Open:** Tue to Sun L 12 to 2.30 (3 Sun), Mon to Sat D 7 to 9.30. **Meals:** alc (main courses £14 to £19). Set L Tue to Sat £13.50 (2 courses) to £17.50. Set D £14 (2 courses) to £19. Sun L £25. **Service:** 10% (optional). **Details:** Cards accepted. 65 seats. 120 seats outside. Separate bar. No mobile phones. Wheelchair access. Music. Children allowed. Car parking.

■ Stoke Poges

NEW ENTRY
Stoke Place, The Garden Room
Precise food in a chi-chi getaway
Stoke Green, Stoke Poges, SL2 4HT
Tel no: (01753) 534790
www.stokeplace.co.uk
Modern British | £32
Cooking score: 4

Thankfully, John Betjeman's 'friendly bombs' didn't fall on this lavish William and Mary mansion set in landscaped parkland north of Slough. Following a trendy revamp, Stoke Place is now a chi-chi boutique getaway and it sports a refreshingly airy restaurant with views. The winsome Garden Room lives up to its name with lacquered cream-and-green tables, bare floors and leafy, botanically themed wallpaper – perfect for precise modern food with seasonal accents. Accuracy and sharp technique show in dishes such as delicate plum tomato consommé, earthy confit rabbit and wild mushroom terrine with pickled grapes and raisin purée, or seared beef fillet with spring vegetables, pearl barley and pine nut emulsion. For dessert, chocolate

ganache with silky cherry sorbet has provided gentle satisfaction. The excellent-value set lunch also proves its worth with, say, seared salmon (daringly cooked *'à point'*) partnered by zingy, citrus-scented couscous, braised baby fennel and vierge dressing. Fifty global wines start at £16.50. **Chef/s:** Craig Van der Meer. **Open:** all week L 12 to 3, Mon to Sat 7 to 10. **Meals:** alc (main courses £16 to £19). Set L £15 to £19.50. Sun L £19.50. Tasting menu £50. **Service:** 12.5% (optional). **Details:** Cards accepted. 48 seats. 30 seats outside. Air-con. Separate bar. Wheelchair access. Music. Children allowed. Car parking.

■ Whelpley Hill

ALSO RECOMMENDED
▲ The White Hart
High Street, Whelpley Hill, HP5 3RL
Tel no: (01442) 833367
Modern European £5 OFF

Dedicated Guide followers might recall Ali Al-Sersy from Mims in Barnet (and, briefly, Fulham Road). Now he's back, this time bringing his brand of dramatic modern cuisine to a bucolic Chilterns boozer: expect crab balls impaled on lolly sticks, desserts crowned with candy floss and a liberal helping of towers and daubs. Typical dishes might include seared scallops with beetroot and horseradish foam (£6.50), slow-braised leg and saddle of rabbit with root vegetable confit and lemon essence (£14) and a 'brilliantly deconstructed' apple cheesecake (£5). House wine is £13.50. Closed Mon. More reports please.

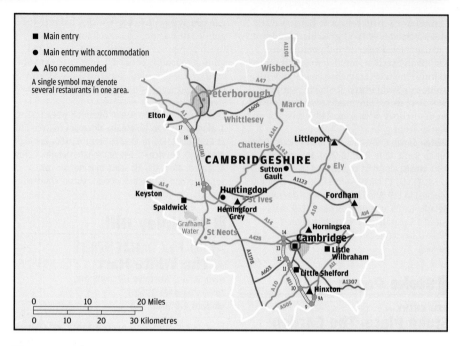

▌Cambridge

Alimentum

High-impact dishes

152-154 Hills Road, Cambridge, CB2 8PB

Tel no: (01223) 413000

www.restaurantalimentum.co.uk

Modern European | £35

Cooking score: 6

£5 OFF ♨

A cosmopolitan dining room/bar with a shot of funk, Alimentum is tricked out in slinky black and red, with smoked glass, blissful air conditioning and a soundtrack of groovy beats. Since taking over as co-owner, chef Mark Poynton has upped his game, sending out high-impact dishes bursting with bullish ambition, strong counterpoints and big visual statements. Most eye-popping of all is a starter that arrives in a Kilner jar filled with smoke. Once opened, it reveals a layer of pond-green cucumber jelly topped with a sublime fillet of almost raw-almost cooked, ethereally smoky trout ('an absolute revelation'), a ball of creamy horseradish, sweet briny shrimps, slivers of pungent radish and a sinuous pea tendril. Other dishes appear as high drama on designer plates and slates. This is cooking that makes its point with bold brushstrokes, not gentle watercolour dabs: stone bass fillet coated in shiny black nigella seeds with twirls of marinated carrot, blobs of vibrant green coriander mousse and braised red lentils, for example, or a trio of veal fillet, belly and kidney with courgettes, basil and capers. Desserts are also roller-coaster rides for the senses – perhaps banana parfait accompanying a four-part homage to lime (including tiny squares of clear-as-glass jelly and contorted, gossamer-thin caramel). Polite staff do their best to keep the customers satisfied, but a touch more confidence and swing would work wonders in energising the mood. Breads and cheeses are top drawer, and the lively modern wine list is noted for its 'eco' recommendations, enticing global range and ungreedy mark-ups. Around 15 tasty house selections open the account from £16.50 (£4.50 a glass).

Chef/s: Mark Poynton. **Open:** all week L 12 to 2.30 (4 Sun), Mon to Sat D 6 to 10. **Closed:** 23 Dec to 2 Jan, bank hols. **Meals:** alc (main courses £18 to £21). Set L £13.50 (2 courses) to £16.50. Set D £15.50 (2 courses) to £18.50. Tasting menu £55. **Service:** 12.5% (optional). **Details:** Cards accepted. 64 seats. Air-con. Separate bar. Wheelchair access. Music. Children allowed.

Cotto
Civilised city eatery
183 East Road, Cambridge, CB1 1BG
Tel no: (01223) 302010
www.cottocambridge.co.uk
European | £35
Cooking score: 3
V

A civilised refuge from the studenty mayhem of East Road, Cotto occupies a tall brick town house that works brilliantly as an all-purpose eatery. At lunchtime its bakery/café feeds town and gown, but three evenings a week the gorgeous, light-filled upstairs room becomes a good-natured, gregarious restaurant – exactly what is required in a university city. Hans Schweitzer's satisfying food inhabits the unfashionable world of mousselines and beurre blancs – although he drops in the occasional sweetbread tempura to liven things up. His breads are 'mind-boggling' and he cooks with generosity, delivering new season's asparagus in buttery pastry, pearly-white turbot with rich Champagne sauce, sautéed veal kidneys dijonnaise and textbook apple tarte fine with salted caramel ice cream encased in a geodesic dome of spun sugar. Service is the embodiment of *festina lente*, an irresistible combination of energy, charm, panache and good grace. Wines start at £17.50. **Chef/s:** Hans Schweitzer. **Open:** Tue to Sat L 9 to 3, Thur to Sat D 7 to 9. **Closed:** Sun, Mon, 25 and 26 Dec, first week Jan, Aug. **Meals:** alc (main courses £8 to £17). Set L £12 (2 courses) to £18. Set D £35. **Service:** not inc. **Details:** Cards accepted. 60 seats. 15 seats outside. Wheelchair access. Music. Children allowed. Car parking.

Midsummer House
Dazzling food with tricks and treats
Midsummer Common, Cambridge, CB4 1HA
Tel no: (01223) 369299
www.midsummerhouse.co.uk
Modern European | £65
Cooking score: 7

'A unique out-of-London restaurant with great finishing touches', is one reader's view of Midsummer House; 'just brilliant', is another straight-talking plaudit. On a more prosaic level, Daniel Clifford's enchanting Victorian villa by the river Cam is quite simply a 'breath of fresh air', secreted in a tranquil world of its own, with a warm conservatory dining room overlooking a quaint walled garden. Every element rings true in this fully rounded dining experience, from the prompt, flawless service to the tiniest details of the dazzlingly good food. Clifford knows how to summon up the seasons and create dishes that are complex, but naturally in tune – each component relevant and in its rightful place. The overall effect can be breathtaking: 'my confit sea bass with soya bean cassoulet and caramelised squid was true heaven on a stylish fork!' drooled one reporter. Challenging partnerships appear with startling regularity – roast pineapple adds a sharp, fruity edge to a combo of cod brandade and pork belly, while peanuts and pistachios find their way into an elaborate dish of turbot with scallop, cos lettuce, asparagus and vanilla. Of course, it isn't all cutting-edge tricks and treats; there's also room for pungent thrills of the more traditional kind in the shape of, say, slow-cooked daube of beef with port and beetroot purée or veal kidney rendered in its own fat with snails and parsley. As for desserts, prepare for some fantastical, many-layered delights: a kaleidoscopic conceit of figs and dates, mulled wine and gingerbread ice cream with cinnamon and caramelised walnuts is as warmly perfumed and nostalgic as a Christmas pomander. If something more modish is required, try pear tarte Tatin with vanilla, garlic and bay leaf. The lengthy wine list matches the food for serious intent, but it's bedevilled by pain-inducing mark-ups;

expect to pay at least £40 for a decent New World bottle, or three figures for something with vintage French pedigree.

Chef/s: Daniel Clifford. **Open:** Wed to Sat L 12 to 1.45, Tue to Sat D 7 to 9.30. **Closed:** Sun, Mon, 1 week Christmas, 1 week Apr, 2 weeks Aug. **Meals:** Set L £29.50 (2 courses) to £35. Set D £47.50 (2 courses) to £65. Tasting menu £85. **Service:** 12.5% (optional). **Details:** Cards accepted. 44 seats. Separate bar. No music. Wheelchair access. Children allowed.

ALSO RECOMMENDED
▲ The Cambridge Chop House

1 King's Parade, Cambridge, CB2 1SJ
Tel no: (01223) 359506
www.chophouses.co.uk
British

A meat cleaver logo, bare boards and butcher's blocks in the window – there's no doubting the gutsy intentions of this easy-going eatery directly opposite King's College. Assorted sausages with mash are the front-runners, but the true-Brit menu also features goats' cheese, pear and honey tart (£6), suet puds, roasts and beef cheek braised in beer (£15). To finish, it has to be Cambridge burnt cream (£5). Wines from £14, and local cask beers too. Open all week. The St John's Chop House is nearby at 21-24 Northampton Street, tel: (01223) 353110.

▌Elton

ALSO RECOMMENDED
▲ The Crown Inn

8 Duck Street, Elton, PE8 6RQ
Tel no: (01832) 280232
www.thecrowninn.org
Gastropub

With its thatched roof, oak beams and log fire the Crown looks every inch the village pub. Its easy-going approach is just the ticket too, whether you fancy a pint and a snack or a full-blown meal. The lively menu picks up ideas from all over, taking in starters of filo tart filled with ham hock, leeks and mushrooms (£6) and mains of steak and kidney pie or sea bass and salmon with paella and seafood bisque (£16.50). House wine £15.95. Closed Sun D, Mon L.

▌Fordham

ALSO RECOMMENDED
▲ The White Pheasant

21 Market Street, Fordham, CB7 5LQ
Tel no: (01638) 720414
www.whitepheasant.com
Gastropub

This seventeenth-century inn has few airs and graces, but its food is far removed from your average pub fare. A typical meal might be pork terrine with pineapple jam, ham consommé, pork scratchings and cider sorbet (£8.95) followed by rosemary-roast rump of lamb with pickled and sautéed Jerusalem artichokes, crushed peas and mint, red wine and five-spice (£18.95). To finish, maybe chocolate délice with raspberry sorbet. Wines start at £13.95. Closed Mon.

▌Hemingford Grey

ALSO RECOMMENDED
▲ The Cock

47 High Street, Hemingford Grey, PE28 9BJ
Tel no: (01480) 463609
www.cambscuisine.com
Modern British

Part traditional village pub, part country restaurant, this prettily located hostelry is worth knowing about, not least because it is just north of the frenetic A14. Add to this blackboard menus offering homemade sausages with a choice of mash and sauces, fresh fish, plus a choice of more cosmopolitan dishes, say chicken breast with chorizo croquettes and mushroom sauce (£14), and it makes for an attractive package. Set lunch (not Sun) is £11/15 for two/three courses. House wine is £14. Open all week.

Hinxton

ALSO RECOMMENDED
▲ The Red Lion Inn

32 High Street, Hinxton, CB10 1QY
Tel no: (01799) 530601
www.redlionhinxton.co.uk
Gastropub £5 OFF

This neat-looking inn just minutes from the M11/A11 is a proper all-rounder. Drinkers congregate in the beamed and boarded bar, while the food in the rustic dining room aims beyond pub grub – maybe ham hock and petit pois terrine with homemade piccalilli (£6), then tranche of turbot with fine bean cassoulet and ham velouté (£18). Also expect comfort food like steak and Woodforde's Wherry ale pie. House wine is £12.75. Accommodation. Open all week.

Horningsea

ALSO RECOMMENDED
▲ The Crown & Punchbowl

High Street, Horningsea, CB25 9JG
Tel no: (01223) 860643
www.thecrownandpunchbowl.co.uk
Modern British

A Georgian country inn 10 minutes' drive from Cambridge, the Crown & Punchbowl has all the classic accoutrements, from the stolid wood furniture to the crackling log fire. Matching a three-way choice of sausage, sauce and flavoured mash (£11.95) is a fun way to go at lunch, while the printed evening menu might offer crab and crayfish tian (£7.95), venison steak with celeriac and potato gratin in juniper and redcurrant sauce (£16.95), and pear and almond tart with cinnamon ice cream (£6.75). Wines from £14.95. Closed Sun D.

Huntingdon

The Old Bridge Hotel

Menus with a taste of the Med
1 High Street, Huntingdon, PE29 3TQ
Tel no: (01480) 424300
www.huntsbridge.com
Modern British | £30
Cooking score: 3
🍷 🚗

Overlooking the river Ouse, the Old Bridge is a tastefully extended, ivy-clad eighteenth-century building. At its heart is the Terrace, an easy-on-the-eye conservatory restaurant with white-clothed tables and a breezy, modern feel. The kitchen brings touches of the Mediterranean to menus that offer fine fresh seafood, perhaps in a salad of Dorset crab with fennel, red pepper and pomegranate dressing. Shrewd buying of main-course meats brings saddle of Denham Castle lamb with a mini lamb suet pudding, and slow-roast pork belly with sesame, spring greens, spiced parsnip purée and pork dim sum. A passion for wine shows in winning selections from all regions, with plenty to suit most palates and pockets, including some mature bottles. The changing house line-up of a dozen or so by the glass or bottle (from £14.95) offers good value.
Chef/s: Simon Cadge. Open: all week L 12 to 2.15 (2.30 Sun), D 6 to 10. Meals: alc (main courses £13 to £25). Set L £15 (2 courses) to £19.50. Service: not inc. Details: Cards accepted. 80 seats. 25 seats outside. Air-con. Separate bar. No music. No mobile phones. Wheelchair access. Children allowed. Car parking.

Keyston

The Pheasant

Foodie thatched pub
Village Loop Road, Keyston, PE28 0RE
Tel no: (01832) 710241
www.thepheasant-keyston.co.uk
Modern British | £28
Cooking score: 2

It may have a thatched roof, beams and an open fire, but this is no unchanging olde-worlde pub. A nicely judged mix of unpretentious modern British and Mediterranean ideas informs the menus, say boudin noir with caramelised apple, or brill with pappardelle, cuttlefish, gremolata and brown shrimps. Reports this year have differed quite markedly, suggesting some inconsistencies in standards (perhaps due to pressure, since the Pheasant was runner-up in Gordon Ramsay's *F Word* search for the best independent local restaurant), but at its best the cooking is simple and effective. Wines are arranged by style, making it easy to find one's way around the high-class modern offerings. A dozen classy, affordable house selections come by the bottle (from £15.50).
Chef/s: Jay Scrimshaw and Liam Goodwill. **Open:** all week L 12 to 2.30, Mon to Sat D 6.30 to 9.30. **Meals:** alc (main courses £15 to £21). Set L and D £14.50 (2 courses) to £19.50. Sun L £15.50 (2 courses) to £19.50. **Service:** not inc. **Details:** Cards accepted. 80 seats. 61 seats outside. Separate bar. Music. Children allowed. Car parking.

Little Shelford

Sycamore House

Endearing home from home
1 Church Street, Little Shelford, CB22 5HG
Tel no: (01223) 843396
Modern British | £27
Cooking score: 2

Michael and Susan Sharpe had the idea of running a modest restaurant from their own home long before it became the stuff of reality

TV shows. They live upstairs and have converted the ground floor of this 300-year-old property into an endearing country dining room. Four nights a week, they serve dinner – a four-course affair that generally begins with soup or a savoury tart (crab and tomato, say). A salad provides the mid-course break before mains such as grilled sea trout with salsa verde or crispy duck with spring onions and soy. A good choice of desserts – iced raspberry terrine, warm chocolate pudding – closes the show. House wine is £14.50.
Chef/s: Michael Sharpe. **Open:** Wed to Sat D only 7.30 to 9. **Closed:** Sun, Mon, Tue, Christmas to New Year. **Meals:** Set D £26.50 (3 courses). **Service:** not inc. **Details:** Cards accepted. 24 seats. No music. No mobile phones. Children allowed. Car parking.

Little Wilbraham

The Hole in the Wall

Quintessential country pub
2 High Street, Little Wilbraham, CB21 5JY
Tel no: (01223) 812282
www.the-holeinthewall.com
Modern European | £23
No Score

Every tourist's idea of the quintessential English country pub, with logs piled high in the inglenook and dried hops draped around its ancient beams, the Hole in the Wall plays to a dedicated local following with fine real ales, a good slate of wines (from £14) and accomplished modern cooking. The kitchen had to pare back its efforts for a few months in early 2010 while chef Chris Leeton was out of action, but we are pleased to announce that he returned to the stoves just as the Guide was going to press, and we anticipate a return to top form before too long. Progress reports please.
Chef/s: Chris Leeton. **Open:** Tue to Sun L 12 to 2, Tue to Sat D 7 to 9. **Closed:** Mon, 2 weeks Jan, 2 weeks Oct. **Meals:** alc (main courses £11 to £17). **Service:** not inc. **Details:** Cards accepted. 60 seats. 20 seats outside. No music. Wheelchair access. Children allowed. Car parking.

Littleport

ALSO RECOMMENDED
▲ The Fen House
2 Lynn Road, Littleport, CB6 1QG
Tel no: (01353) 860645
Anglo-French

David Warne's highly individual Fenland restaurant is a whitewashed Georgian inn with an open fire and an array of personal mementoes and pictures, which makes it feel very much like dining with friends. A hardworking kitchen produces four-course menus of modern Anglo-French cooking (£38.25). The bill of fare might be spiced belly pork with cucumber and mint yoghurt, then poached turbot with grapes, sauced with red wine and port, with cheeses intervening before buttermilk and vanilla cream with apricot compote. Wines from £15.50. Open Fri and Sat D only.

Spaldwick

NEW ENTRY
The George of Spaldwick
Cracking modern pub food
5-7 High Street, Spaldwick, PE28 0TD
Tel no: (01480) 890293
www.georgeofspaldwick.co.uk
Modern British | £24
Cooking score: 2
£30

Tired and hungry travellers should take note of this rambling, cream-washed fifteenth-century pub and pull off for some cracking modern pub food. It's served in the high-raftered converted barn or traditional bar, where wonky walls, thick beams and huge fireplaces blend effortlessly with leather sofas, chunky tables and contemporary artwork. Darrell Haylett's monthly menus work with the seasons and trawl Europe for inspiration, offering Polebrook asparagus with roast garlic mayonnaise, braised hake with rhubarb and onion compote, chump of lamb with pea shoots and balsamic dressing, or classic haddock and chips with pea purée. Desserts include carrot and walnut cake with mascarpone ice cream. House wine from £12.95.
Chef/s: Darrell Haylett. Open: all week L 12 to 2.30, D 6 to 9.30. Closed: 1 Jan. Meals: alc (main courses £11 to £22). Sun L £14. Service: not inc. Details: Cards accepted. 105 seats. 52 seats outside. Air-con. Separate bar. Wheelchair access. Music. Children allowed. Car parking.

Sutton Gault

The Anchor Inn
Remote Fenland treasure
Bury Lane, Sutton Gault, CB6 2BD
Tel no: (01353) 778537
www.anchor-inn-restaurant.co.uk
Modern British | £25
Cooking score: 2
£5 OFF ⊑ V £30

Don't be fooled by the Fenland desolation or the chilly winds blowing across the Hundred Foot Drain, all is snug and infectiously hospitable inside this engaging country inn-with-rooms. Casks of real ale, head-cracking beams and scrubbed pine tables are all in place, and if you're lucky the sunlight will stream in as you feast on food with its roots in the region. Generous plates of local asparagus with crispy air-dried ham or Bottisham smoked duck with roasted figs, followed by hake fillet with spinach crème fraîche, minty crushed Jersey Royals and a salad of wickedly pungent wild garlic are the kinds of dishes to expect. To finish, perhaps summery Pimm's jelly with a ball of yoghurt ice cream. House wine is £14.30.
Chef/s: Adam Pickup and Will Mumford. Open: all week L 12 to 2 (Sun 2.30), D 7 to 9, (6.30 to 9.30 Sat, 6.30 to 8.30 Sun). Meals: alc (main courses £10 to £22). Set L £11.95 (2 courses) to £15.95. Service: not inc. Details: Cards accepted. 65 seats. 20 seats outside. No music. No mobile phones. Wheelchair access. Children allowed. Car parking.

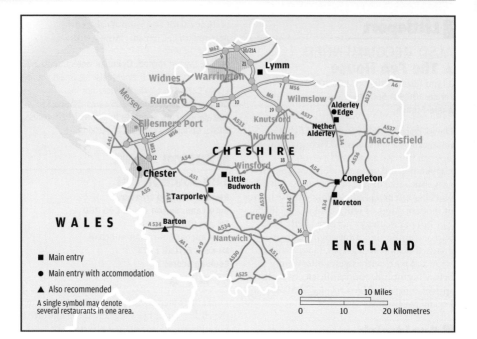

Main entry
Main entry with accommodation
Also recommended
A single symbol may denote several restaurants in one area.

Alderley Edge

NEW ENTRY
Alderley Edge Hotel
A local institution
Macclesfield Road, Alderley Edge, SK9 7BJ
Tel no: (01625) 583033
www.alderleyedgehotel.com
Modern British | £44
Cooking score: 3

🛏 V

The dining room at the Alderley Edge Hotel has become something of a local institution and continues to please a loyal band of followers from South Manchester and beyond: fans reckon the food is 'exceptional' and applaud the staff for raising their game to match the kitchen's efforts. There's a choice of menus ranging from value-for-money lunches, vegetarian and lounge menus to the pricier carte and six-course tasting extravaganzas – the latter delivering contemporary dishes such as roasted scallop with confit salmon, Granny Smith apple, caviar and toasted bacon powder followed by fillet of mature beef cooked sous-vide for 48 hours with braised ox cheek and truffle potato espuma. To conclude, pear and tonka bean custard with limoncello ice cream and caramelised pastry might suffice. House wines start at £17.50.

Chef/s: Christopher Holland. **Open:** all week L 12 to 2 (4 Sun), Mon to Sat D 7 to 10. **Closed:** 1 Jan.
Meals: alc (main courses £22 to £24). Set L £17.95 (2 courses) to £21.95. Set D £29.95 (3 courses). Tasting menu £54.50 (6 courses). **Service:** not inc.
Details: Cards accepted. 56 seats. 24 seats outside. Air-con. Separate bar. Wheelchair access. Music. Children allowed. Car parking.

Average price

The average price listed in main-entry reviews denotes the price of a three-course meal, without wine.

Barton

ALSO RECOMMENDED
▲ The Cock O' Barton
Barton Road, Barton, SY14 7HU
Tel no: (01829) 782277
www.thecockobarton.co.uk
Modern European

A venerable drinkers' den dating back to medieval times, the legendary Cock has moved with the times and now trades as a fashion-conscious restaurant and bar. The new kitchen team rejects local British flavours in favour of Eurocentric dishes along the lines of gin- and juniper-cured salmon tartare with quail's egg (£7.95), rump of lamb with niçoise potatoes and Kalamata olives (£16.95), and apple mille-feuille with cinnamon cream (£5.50). A crowd-pleasing daytime menu also promises salads, sharing platters and the like. Wines from £13.75. Closed Mon.

Chester

1539 Restaurant & Bar
A good bet for local produce
Watergate Square, Chester, CH1 2LY
Tel no: (01244) 304611
www.restaurant1539.co.uk
Modern British | £30
Cooking score: 1

£5
OFF

Overlooking the green expanse of the Roodee, 1539 must cater for sedate business lunches as well as the barely contained madness of racedays. Not surprisingly, it steers a middle course, turning produce from the best local sources into dishes with a populist bent, notably roast monkfish with curry spices and well-handled calf's liver with a rich onion sauce. Service is cool but well-meaning, and if all the tables with a racecourse view are taken, there's always the open kitchen for entertainment. Wine is from £2.75 a glass, though you'd have to drink a lot of it to imagine that the overbearing soundtrack is appropriate.

Chef/s: Glenn Morrill. Open: Mon to Fri L 12 to 2.30 (3.30 Fri), D 6 to 10. Sat 12 to 10, Sun 12 to 7. Closed: 25 and 26 Dec, 1 Jan. Meals: alc (main courses £12 to £25). Set L and D £27.50. Sun L £12.50. Service: not inc. Details: Cards accepted. 160 seats. 40 seats outside. Air-con. Separate bar. Wheelchair access. Music. Children allowed. Car parking.

Simon Radley at the Chester Grosvenor
This is serious cooking
Eastgate, Chester, CH1 1LT
Tel no: (01244) 324024
www.chestergrosvenor.com
Modern European | £69
Cooking score: 7

🍷 🍽 V

Chester's grandest restaurant has a spirit which must be entered into. Luxury comes as standard in a dining room that glows green and gold, and even the walls are padded. The cheese trolley trundles past marble pillars; raised voices are a rarity. But it is not old-fashioned in every aspect. Simon Radley's food applies modern technique to staidly luxurious ingredients such as fillet of Aberdeenshire beef. Radley likes a joke – a dish called 'cheek to cheek' combines those of monkfish and pig – but this is serious cooking. To start, scallops are served with bittersweet caramelised chicory and Bellota ham in two different guises, a pallid foam (beer, perhaps?) the only unnecessary indulgence. Rabbit comes as a cool, soft-set daube with a whipped pâté of the liver and a glistening Agen prune; the proximity of the bread trolley is handy. Main courses are intensely flavoured, with rich stickiness a feature of both the beef dish (poached fillet with chicken mousse-stuffed brisket, snails and sauce poivrade) and pollack, cooked until pearly, sprinkled with mushroom dust and served with samphire and an outrageously oozy mushroom raviolo. Desserts have improved since our last inspection, with each taking a theme – rhubarb or coffee, for example – and investigating it thoroughly.

'Rhubarb and custard' involves a pannacotta rich with vanilla seeds alongside jelly and a fun-to-smash sugar tube of rhubarb purée. 'Arabica' is a more grown-up bombe of coffee-scented mascarpone with latte ice cream and crystal-clear Amaretto jelly. Some reporters baulk at the prices, but there's no arguing with the sheer class or sophistication of the food. The wine list, from £25, is very French, very large and very impressive, with careful notes from sommelier Garry Clark to aid navigation. Lots of Burgundy, Champagne from smaller houses and the occasional focus on particular grapes make it a very worthwhile read.

Chef/s: Simon Radley. **Open:** Tue to Sat D only 6.30 to 9.15 (6 Sat). **Closed:** Sun, Mon, 25 and 26 Dec, 1 to 11 Jan. **Meals:** Set D £69, Tasting menu £80. **Service:** 12.5% (optional). **Details:** Cards accepted. 46 seats. 40 seats outside. Air-con. Separate bar. No music. No mobile phones. Wheelchair access. Car parking.

▌Congleton

L'Endroit
A lovely French find
70-72 Lawton Street, Congleton, CW12 1RS
Tel no: (01260) 299548
www.lendroit.co.uk
French | £25
Cooking score: 3
£5 OFF £30

Readers report that they are almost as likely to see chef/proprietor Eli Leconte collecting mushrooms in local woods as passing through L'Endroit's cheerful, cosy dining room. Between foraging and keeping his own bees, he cooks a reassuringly French bistro menu, though the light black pudding served to start is in the style of his native Belgium. Game features strongly, and an end-of-season lunch packed with woodcock mousse, mallard and game consommé is a popular tradition. For something less visceral on the side, cauliflower cheese is an unexpected hit. 'Really good' house wine starts at £12.25, and there's a small terrace outside on which to drink it.

Chef/s: Eli Leconte. **Open:** Tue to Fri L 12 to 2, Tue to Sat D 6 to 9.30 (10 Fri and Sat). **Closed:** Sun, Mon, last week Feb, first week Mar, 1 week Jun, 1 week Sept. **Meals:** alc (main courses £12 to £17). Set L £11.95 (2 courses). **Service:** not inc. **Details:** Cards accepted. 36 seats. 12 seats outside. Wheelchair access. Music. Children allowed. Car parking.

▌Little Budworth

Cabbage Hall
Glam dining pub with French fancies
Forest Road, Little Budworth, CW6 9ES
Tel no: (01829) 760292
www.cabbagehallrestaurant.com
Modern British | £30
Cooking score: 2
£5 OFF V

It's a roadside restaurant, but not as we know it. A refurbishment has freshened Robert Kisby's glamorous dining pub, where a rather large variety of menus, peppered with French, allow customers to stick with pub food or go for something showier. Elaborate signature dishes include a rich lobster risotto smelling of roasted shells, but Kisby is also keen on providing mixed plates and assemblies, some with a homespun air. On inspection, a 'retro pub platter', which amounts to dinner for two, was a little sad in places but delivered fun in the form of a mini chicken Kiev and little 'cottage pies' stuffed into potato skins. The wine list starts at an accessible £15.95, though there's a brief 'chef's cellar' selection for those with deeper pockets.

Chef/s: Robert Kisby. **Open:** all week 12 to 10 (8 Sun). **Closed:** 5 to 15 Jan. **Meals:** alc (main courses £15 to £23). Set L and D £14.95. **Service:** not inc. **Details:** Cards accepted. 70 seats. 40 seats outside. Separate bar. No mobile phones. Wheelchair access. Music. Children allowed. Car parking.

Raymond Postgate's legacy

Raymond William Postgate's best memorial is the book he began 60 years ago in the front room of his house in Finchley. His editorship of *The Good Food Guide* was a long one: he minded the nation's stomach for 20 years. Yet it started as a sideline, for he was also a classical scholar, economist, social historian, journalist and a crime writer – his most famous novel being *Verdict of Twelve*, published in 1940.

At the end of the eighteenth century the reputation of British food was high, considered better than in France, yet by 1950 it had sunk to being among the worst in the world. Postgate determined to reverse the situation. Mock cream, synthetic custard, margarine masquerading as butter – the bad victuals and bad habits encouraged by years of rationing fuelled Postgate's 'campaign against cruelty to food'. It resulted in the Good Food Club, and the subsequent recommendations of decent places to eat from people all over the country became the 'first mapping of an unexplored country' – the 1951 *Good Food Guide*.

He was convinced a more enlightened general public could bring the force of public opinion to bear on British catering and have the desired effect. He was right. Raymond Postgate's legacy is the growing reputation of British food and restaurants – nowadays, one even hears the odd niggle that eating in France is not what it was.

▌Lymm
The Church Green
Restaurant food in a country pub
Higher Lane, Lymm, WA13 0AP
Tel no: (01925) 752068
www.thechurchgreen.co.uk
Modern British | £45
New Chef

Aiden Byrne's pub has settled into a rhythm in the past year, providing pints for drinkers, pub food for lunchers and something a bit fancier in its dark, contemporary dining room. In the bar, there's not a word to be said against a puffy, burnished steak pie and chips, delivered with cheer, but readers note that restaurant portions can be 'inadequate' and main dishes 'pricey'. At inspection it was hard to disagree, though the upside was a well-made cep risotto with a smoky sherry jelly and a beautifully presented, if scanty, plate of Goosnargh duck with red cabbage purée and dried red fruit. But changes occurred as the Guide went to press with the opening of second venture Aiden Byrne at Hillbark Hotel and Roger Calhau now cooking at the pub. Wines from £16.40. Reports please.
Chef/s: Roger Calhau. **Open:** all week L 12 to 3, D 6 to 9.30. **Closed:** 25 Dec. **Meals:** alc (main courses £10 to £28). Set L and D £28.50. Sun L £15. Tasting menu £68 (7 courses). **Service:** not inc.
Details: Cards accepted. 80 seats. 120 seats outside. Air-con. Separate bar. Wheelchair access. Music. Children allowed. Car parking.

▌Moreton
Pecks
A thoroughly affable experience
Newcastle Road, Moreton, CW12 4SB
Tel no: (01260) 275161
www.pecksrest.co.uk
Modern British | £35
Cooking score: 3

£5 OFF **V**

A long-established village restaurant not far from local landmark Mow Cop Castle, Pecks takes an idiosyncratic approach. Dinner is

served at 7.30 for 8, and the drill is a five-course menu, with choice at each stage, of dishes that are paraded before you in theatrical display. April diners might have progressed from smoked haddock, leek and potato soup, through wild boar and mushroom pâté with cheese shortbreads and ginger compote, to shin of Hereford beef with spring onion mash in red wine jus, before being offered a dessert selection and then cheeses. It's a thoroughly affable experience, with friendly service and an international list of reasonably priced wines (from £14.50) to match. By the time we go to press, a block-paved patio area for outdoor dining should have come into commission.
Chef/s: Les Wassall. **Open:** Tue to Sun L 12 to 2 (3 Sun), Tue to Sat D 7.30 for 8 (1 sitting). **Closed:** Mon, 25 to 30 Dec. **Meals:** alc (main courses £9 to £23). Set L £14.95 (2 courses) to £17.95. Set D Tue and Wed £36.50 (5 courses), Thur and Fri £39.95 (7 courses), Sat £44.95 (7 courses). Sun L £18.25. **Service:** not inc. **Details:** Cards accepted. 110 seats. Air-con. Separate bar. Wheelchair access. Music. Children allowed. Car parking.

▌Nether Alderley
The Wizard
Charming pub with deft British dishes
Macclesfield Road, Nether Alderley, SK10 4UB
Tel no: (01625) 584000
www.ainscoughs.co.uk
Modern British | £25
Cooking score: 2
£30

With internal twists and turns to rival Hogwarts, the fabric of the Wizard remains true to its sixteenth century origins. The pub's clientele, however, is a thoroughly modern mix of walkers, who come for the nearby sandstone ridge, and nouveau riche attracted to the wagtastic village below. They both enjoy the considerable charm of low beams, log fires and a menu which, though guilty of ill-advised Mediterranean dabblings, copes deftly with British dishes. From the blackboard, a salad of hot-smoked trout with horseradish dressing has the right amount of

zing; follow, perhaps, with a slow-cooked lamb shank with parsnip mash and sticky red wine jus. Wine is from £12.50 a bottle.
Chef/s: Paul Beattie. **Open:** Mon to Fri L 12 to 2, D 6.30 to 9.30. Sat 12 to 10, Sun 12 to 8. **Meals:** alc (main courses £9 to £25). **Service:** not inc. **Details:** Cards accepted. 90 seats. 40 seats outside. Music. Children allowed. Car parking.

▌Tarporley
Fox & Barrel
Friendly pub with enterprising food
Foxbank, Cotebrook, Tarporley, CW6 9DZ
Tel no: (01829) 760529
www.foxandbarrel.co.uk
Gastropub | £24
Cooking score: 2
£5 OFF V £30

This highly attractive Cheshire pub makes a good impression right from the start, and a friendly welcome is guaranteed. Traditional touches prevail, like beams and a real fire, and it successfully combines enterprising food alongside its role as a local. There's little doubt that the kitchen can deliver unfussy dishes with skill and dexterity: you might start with a dish of scallops, cauliflower purée and caper dressing, before tackling a belly-warming steamed suet pud packed with venison, beef and shallots or sea bream with braised lentils, winter vegetables and a red wine butter sauce. After that, banoffi mille-feuille makes a satisfying finish. The contemporary wine list offers decent value from £13 a bottle.
Chef/s: Richard Cotterill. **Open:** all week 12 to 9.30 (9 Sun). **Closed:** 25 Dec. **Meals:** alc (main courses £8 to £17). **Service:** not inc. **Details:** Cards accepted. 100 seats. 110 seats outside. Separate bar. No music. Children allowed. Car parking.

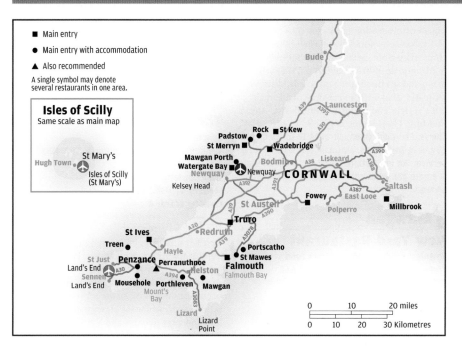

- ■ Main entry
- ● Main entry with accommodation
- ▲ Also recommended

A single symbol may denote several restaurants in one area.

Isles of Scilly
Same scale as main map

■ Falmouth

NEW ENTRY

Rick Stein's Fish & Chips

Upmarket chippy... with a Champagne bar
Events Square, Discovery Quay, Falmouth,
TR11 3AX
Tel no: (01841) 532700
www.rickstein.com
Seafood | £20
Cooking score: 1
£30

Rick Stein's first foray outside of Padstow, this bustling seafood café is slap bang on the waterfront in Falmouth's Events Square and opposite the National Maritime Museum. Upstairs, the Champagne and oyster bar offers crab, lobster and langoustines, but downstairs is a more traditional fish and chip restaurant with white tiles, slate floor and closely packed oak benches. Cornish suppliers are used as much as possible and local fish including hake, John Dory and sea bass are either roasted over charcoal, grilled or fried in beef dripping and

can be accompanied by homemade chips, curry sauce, mushy peas and tartare sauce. House recommendations from £15.
Chef/s: Fergus Coyle. **Open:** all week L 12 to 2.30, D 5 to 9. **Closed:** 25 and 26 Dec. **Meals:** alc (main courses £9 to £16). **Service:** not inc. **Details:** Cards accepted. 80 seats. 40 seats outside. Air-con. Separate bar. No music. Wheelchair access. Children allowed.

■ Fowey

Sam's

Lively great-value brasserie
20 Fore Street, Fowey, PL23 1AQ
Tel no: (01726) 832273
www.samsfowey.co.uk
North American | £24
Cooking score: 1
V £30

There are no airs and graces at this lively brasserie in the heart of Fowey. The décor is no-frills, with bare wood tables and a 'quite pubby menu'. But there's an endless flow of

eager customers drawn by generous portions and value-for-money burgers and fish and chips. Also note specials such as moules marinière, deep-fried calamari with garlic mayo and sea bass with a 'quite refreshing' aromatic salad with a herb dressing. Finish with apricot and Cointreau bread-and-butter pudding. House wine is £12.95.
Chef/s: Phil Kidd. **Open:** all week 12 to 10. **Closed:** 25 and 26 Dec. **Meals:** alc (main courses £8 to £20). **Service:** not inc. **Details:** Cards accepted. 65 seats. Separate bar. Wheelchair access. Music. Children allowed.

Mawgan

New Yard Restaurant
Townies' dream, with first-rate food
Trelowarren Estate, Mawgan, TR12 6AF
Tel no: (01326) 221595
www.trelowarren.com
Modern British | £24
Cooking score: 3
£5 OFF £30

Trelowarren estate is the kind of rural picture townies dream about. The restaurant in the old stable yard reinforces the image with its blazing winter fire, alfresco summer tables and strongly rooted policy of sourcing the majority of its ingredients from within a 15-mile radius. Olly Jackson has stamped his mark on the kitchen, with reporters praising 'first-rate' soups (say pumpkin with crème fraîche) and the 'careful cooking' of pan-fried pigeon breast with orange salad and pomegranate molasses, mackerel with beetroot, new potatoes and horseradish, superb local venison, excellent duck confit and good Sunday roasts. Homemade bread, warm chocolate mousse and strawberry pavlova all get the thumbs-up. Service is attentive. Wines from £15.
Chef/s: Olly Jackson. **Open:** all week L 12 to 2 (2.30 Sun), Mon to Sat D 7 to 9. **Closed:** Mon from end Sept to Whitsun. **Meals:** alc (main courses £13 to £18). Set L £15.95 (2 courses) to £19.50. Set D £23.50. Sun L £17.95. **Service:** not inc.

Details: Cards accepted. 50 seats. 20 seats outside. Wheelchair access. Music. Children allowed. Car parking.

Mawgan Porth

NEW ENTRY
The Scarlet Hotel
Spectacular clifftop hotel
Tredragon Road, Mawgan Porth, TR8 4DQ
Tel no: (01637) 861800
www.scarlethotel.co.uk
Modern British | £35
Cooking score: 4
£5 OFF

Ben Tunnicliffe last appeared in the Guide in 2008 at the Abbey Restaurant, Penzance, but he is now established under the ecologically sound roof of this new hotel. The building has been designed to make the most of natural light – spectacular sea views from its clifftop location are a given – and Scarlet's ethos also includes a commendable commitment to local suppliers. A spring inspection dinner opened with lobster risotto with broad beans and went on to lamb (slightly tough fillet, tasty belly and good sweetbreads) with asparagus, peas and fondant potato and a 'rather overpowering' onion purée, but things ended on a high note with 'big, chunky, really gooey' chocolate fondant accompanied by a salted lemon délice and yoghurt sorbet. Homemade bread is excellent, service could be sharpened up, and the up-to-date wine list is arranged by style, with bottles from £18.50.
Chef/s: Ben Tunnicliffe. **Open:** all week L 12 to 2, D 7 to 9.30. **Closed:** 5 weeks Jan/Feb. **Meals:** alc (main courses £15 to £28). Set L 16.50 (2 courses) to £19.50. **Service:** not inc. **Details:** Cards accepted. 80 seats. 30 seats outside. Separate bar. No mobile phones. Wheelchair access. Music. Car parking.

Nathan Outlaw Restaurant Nathan Outlaw

Could you give us a very simple recipe?

A simple salad: shredded white cabbage, brown shrimps, dill, gherkins, lemon juice and a few chopped shallots. Mix together and season. A lovely refreshing salad with no cooking required.

Is there anything in the restaurant industry that you would like to change?

I would like to see more young people coming into the front of house as a career.

What would be your perfect birthday meal?

Whole char-grilled mackerel fresh from the sea with seasonal salad leaves and Cornish Earlies, eaten on the beach with family and friends.

What is your favourite restaurant and why?

Hix Oyster & Chop House is my favourite. I always come out inspired by the menu. It's always different when I have been, and super-seasonal which I love!

▮ Millbrook

The View

Outstanding clifftop package
Treninnow Cliff Road, Millbrook, PL10 1JY
Tel no: (01752) 822345
www.theview-restaurant.co.uk
Modern British | £28
Cooking score: 2
£5 OFF £30

'Would that there were more places like it', enthused one reporter of this clifftop restaurant with its gorgeous coastal views. The décor may be basic, but the overall package is outstanding. Very fresh seafood, mostly from Looe Harbour, makes up the bulk of the menu and is treated with respect and without flamboyance – delicate crab, lime and Parmesan risotto to start, followed, perhaps, by turbot with tiger prawns and ginger. Equal care is taken handling meat: 'very tender and delicious' best end of lamb, for instance. Strawberry jelly and almond biscuits add interest to vanilla mousse. House wine is £13.95.
Chef/s: Matt Corner. **Open:** Wed to Sun L 12 to 2, D 7 to 9. **Closed:** Mon, Tue, Feb. **Meals:** alc (main courses £12 to £19). **Service:** not inc. **Details:** Cards accepted. 45 seats. 30 seats outside. No mobile phones. Music. Children allowed. Car parking.

▮ Mousehole

2 Fore Street

Family-run local treasure
2 Fore Street, Mousehole, TR19 6PF
Tel no: (01736) 731164
www.2forestreet.co.uk
Modern British | £27
Cooking score: 2
£30

'The sort of local family-run restaurant we should treasure', is one reader's verdict on Joe Wardell's refreshingly unpretentious eatery close to Mousehole's harbour front. Neutral colours and distressed wooden tables set the tone for clear-flavoured, no-nonsense dishes with a bias towards Cornish seafood – think

Newlyn scallops in the shell with toasted walnut and thyme butter or roast cod with bouillabaisse. Crab and chilli linguine wins friends at lunchtime, Cornish ribeye and chips gets the evening vote, and chocolate tart with caramelised pear is an ever-popular pud. Joe is a gregarious host, and he is supported by exceptionally kind staff who are great with kids. Wines start at £13.95 (£3.85 a glass).

Chef/s: Joe Wardell. **Open:** all week L 12 to 3, D 6 to 9.30. **Closed:** 3 Jan to 6 Feb. **Meals:** alc (main courses £12 to £16). **Service:** not inc. **Details:** Cards accepted. 36 seats. 22 seats outside. Music. Children allowed.

Padstow

Custard

Popular diner with fashionable food
1st Floor, 1a The Strand, Padstow, PL28 8AJ
Tel no: (01841) 532565
www.custarddiner.com
Modern British | £28
Cooking score: 2
£5 £30
OFF

This first-floor eating house is an understandably popular venue that pulls in the crowds with high-quality food. Take your pick from a fashionable modern medley, perhaps grilled sardines with olive tapenade, devilled tomatoes and watercress or Cornish pollack wrapped in Parma ham and served with a purée of chorizo, white beans, capers and aïoli. Meat dishes include glazed pork belly and rump steak with chips and béarnaise. Though results can occasionally prove inconsistent, service is enthusiastic and the no-nonsense wine list is reasonably priced, with Sicilian house opening the account at £14.95. Breakfast too.

Chef/s: Daniel Gedge. **Open:** Tue to Sun L 12 to 2.30, D 6 to 9.30. **Closed:** Mon, Sun D Sept to Mar, Jan, Easter, 1 week Sept. **Meals:** alc (main courses £10 to £20). **Service:** not inc. **Details:** Cards accepted. 65 seats. Air-con. Music. Children allowed.

Paul Ainsworth at No. 6

Accomplished cooking and top-value lunches
6 Middle Street, Padstow, PL28 8AP
Tel no: (01841) 532093
www.number6inpadstow.co.uk
Modern British | £28
Cooking score: 6
£5 £30
OFF

Paul Ainsworth has been cooking at this pint-sized restaurant-with-rooms for six years, the last two as chef/patron, and has maintained a tenacious local following for his highly crafted, regionally based cooking. The menu is written in understated modern fashion, but what turns up on the plate is always considerably more expressive. Devilled local lamb's kidneys with wild mushrooms on brioche might vie for your attention with a dynamic duo of Dave Thomasson scallops and Charles MacLeod black pudding among starters. Main courses stretch out expansively in the direction of cod with Porthilly mussels, chickpeas and chorizo, or ox cheek and tongue in beef soup with carrot and swede. The overall impression is of carefully judged balance, supporting an array of eloquent flavours. If you manage to swerve desserts such as blackberry Bakewell with butterscotch sauce and vanilla ice cream, the serving of fine British cheeses with raisin and treacle bread and truffle honey will surely prove irresistible. The fixed-price lunch is exemplary value. An excellent wine list opens with 11 by the glass, starting with Chilean Sauvignon and Merlot at £4, with the bulk of the list very fairly priced and full of interesting growers.

Chef/s: Paul Ainsworth. **Open:** Tue to Sat L 12 to 2, D 6 to 10. **Closed:** Sun (except L in summer), Mon, 24 to 26 Dec, Jan. **Meals:** alc (main courses £13 to £18). Set L £10 (2 courses) to £13.50. Sun L £18. **Service:** not inc. **Details:** Cards accepted. 42 seats. Music. Children allowed.

Rick Stein's Café

Feel-good crowd-pleaser
10 Middle Street, Padstow, PL28 8AP
Tel no: (01841) 532700
www.rickstein.com
Seafood | £23
Cooking score: 1

An informal outpost of the TV chef's empire, Rick Stein's Café sees diners tightly packed between whitewashed walls, where lively artwork and shiny service set the tone for a feel-good operation. As you might expect, seafood dominates a menu of crowd-pleasing dishes – at inspection a generous portion of mussels in chilli, tomato and parsley was followed by goujons of plaice served with a salsa verde mayonnaise. A short wine list opens at £4 a glass. If you book in advance, be sure to avoid the hefty cancellation fees.
Chef/s: David Sharland and Ross Geach. **Open:** all week L 12 to 3, D 6.30 to 9. **Closed:** 25 and 26 Dec, 1 May. **Meals:** alc (main courses £11 to £17). Set L and D £22.20. **Service:** not inc. **Details:** Cards accepted. 36 seats. 14 seats outside. Music. Children allowed.

St Petroc's Bistro

Rick Stein's cut-price chummy eatery
New Street, Padstow, PL28 8EL
Tel no: (01841) 532700
www.rickstein.com
European | £30
Cooking score: 2

A senior member of Rick Stein's Cornish dynasty, this chummy bistro-with-rooms was set up as a cut-price alternative to the Seafood Restaurant (see entry) and has established a life of its own over the years. The mood is as bright and breezy as a Padstow summer's day, colourful paintings line the walls, and the courtyard gets rammed when the sun is out. Local fish waxes strongly on the menu – perhaps fried squid in olive oil with smoked pimentón and garlic mayo or bourride of gurnard with salt cod and prawns. The no-nonsense line-up also runs to whole baked

Camembert, ribeye with béarnaise sauce and desserts including pear and almond tart. Wines start at £17.95.
Chef/s: Paul Harwood and David Sharland. **Open:** all week L 12 to 2, D 6.30 to 9.30. **Closed:** 25 and 26 Dec, 1 May. **Meals:** alc (main courses £13 to £21). Set L (winter only) £17.50. **Service:** not inc. **Details:** Cards accepted. 56 seats. 36 seats outside. Separate bar. Music. Children allowed.

The Seafood Restaurant

Stein's old-stager
Riverside, Padstow, PL28 8BY
Tel no: (01841) 532700
www.rickstein.com
Seafood | £54
Cooking score: 3

The Seafood Restaurant was the first of Rick Stein's extensive interests and it's still a must-do on many people's Padstow itineraries. Built around an altar-like seafood bar in the centre, where chefs assemble the groaning platters of fruits de mer, served classically with mayonnaise and shallot vinegar, it's a spacious, loquacious venue on the waterfront. Adventures into more ambitious dishes often meet with sulks, and the prices still feel hard to justify when so many of the menu items are landed so locally – thus a bouillabaisse of sea bass, gurnard, monkfish, langoustine and mussels, served with rouille and Parmesan seems like better value at £28.50 than the £34.50 asked for a piece of baked turbot with hollandaise. White wines start at £18.50, reds at £19.95.
Chef/s: Stephane Delourme and David Sharland. **Open:** all week L 12 to 2, D 7 to 10. **Closed:** 25 and 26 Dec, 1 May. **Meals:** alc (main courses £17 to £45). Winter Set L £28.50. Tasting menu £65.50 (6 courses). **Service:** not inc. **Details:** Cards accepted. 90 seats. 22 seats outside. Air-con. Separate bar. No music. Wheelchair access.

Penzance

The Bay

A breath of fresh sea air
Hotel Penzance, Britons Hill, Penzance, TR18 3AE
Tel no: (01736) 366890
www.bay-penzance.co.uk
Modern British | £29
Cooking score: 3
£5 OFF ⬚ V £30

Most readers seem to enjoy themselves at this light, modern dining room housed in an Edwardian hotel – 'we cannot fault any part of the restaurant' notes one, while another declares 'my family and I had a really great time'. Rooftop views to Penzance Harbour and Mount's Bay are a plus, and menus lean towards seafood and bistro favourites such as mussels in a shallot, garlic and cider cream sauce, or wood pigeon with pea purée, black pudding and rosemary and juniper oil. Roast fillet of skate wing with aubergine, garlic and herb purée is a typical main course, or there could be loin of wild rabbit with orange caramelised fennel, figs and Cornish hog pudding. House wine is £15.75.
Chef/s: Ben Reeve. **Open:** Sun to Fri L 12 to 2, all week D 6 to 9. **Closed:** first 2 weeks Jan. **Meals:** Set L £12.50 (2 courses) to £17. Set D £24 (2 courses) to £29.95. Sun L £15.50. **Service:** not inc.
Details: Cards accepted. 40 seats. 10 seats outside. Air-con. Separate bar. No mobile phones. Wheelchair access. Music. Children allowed. Car parking.

Harris's

Cheery eatery with fiercely loyal fans
46 New Street, Penzance, TR18 2LZ
Tel no: (01736) 364408
www.harrissrestaurant.co.uk
Modern European | £29
Cooking score: 2
£5 OFF £30

The building that houses Roger and Anne Harris's side–street restaurant has been in the catering business continuously since 1860; the couple have been running it for around a quarter of that time, having set up in 1972. What their fiercely loyal regulars appreciate is reliable, unpretentious food and an unfailingly cheery atmosphere in which to eat it. Seafood dishes are always a strong suit – 'crab florentine was spectacular, grilled Dover sole with chive butter was timed to perfection, and the sea bass was as fresh as tomorrow'. Meat eaters might still enjoy a grilled fillet steak with béarnaise. If it ain't broke...Wines start at £14.95.
Chef/s: Roger Harris. **Open:** Tue to Sat L 12 to 2, Mon to Sat D 7 to 9.30. **Closed:** Sun, Mon during Oct to May, 25 and 26 Dec, 1 Jan, 3 weeks winter.
Meals: alc (main courses £12 to £30). **Service:** 10%.
Details: Cards accepted. 40 seats. Separate bar. No mobile phones. Music. Children allowed.

Perranuthnoe

ALSO RECOMMENDED
▲ Victoria Inn
Perranuthnoe, TR20 9NP
Tel no: (01736) 710309
www.victoriainn-penzance.co.uk
Gastropub

The Victoria lays claim to being the oldest pub in Cornwall. Dating from the twelfth century, and painted a fetching shade of pink, it's in an unspoilt coastal village about five miles east of Penzance, and is a welcoming place with bare wood tables and cheering, locally based cooking. Curry-spiced crab and potato salad with mango and lime chutney (£7.50), Cornish ribeye steak with chips, onion rings and aïoli (£16.95) and lemon crème brûlée with poached plums in mulled wine syrup (£5.25) are on the bill of fare. Wines from £14.50. Closed Sun D.

Average price

The average price listed in main-entry reviews denotes the price of a three-course meal, without wine.

Porthleven

Kota

Fusion pizazz and friendly staff
Harbour Head, Porthleven, TR13 9JA
Tel no: (01326) 562407
www.kotarestaurant.co.uk
Fusion | £27
Cooking score: 2
£5 OFF 🍴 £30

Cornwall barely gets more picture-postcard than this. The sunny yellow building that houses Kota is a converted 300-year-old cornmill and sits right on Porthleven's harbour. Chef/co-owner Jude Kereama has been here five years now and combines local materials with ideas from his native New Zealand, and plenty more besides. Scallops could appear with belly pork, soy ginger and cider apple purée, wild sea bass with Thai spiced bouillabaisse and prawn won tons. Otherwise, a duo of duck in noodles has been 'mightily impressive', there's good sticky toffee pudding for dessert and staff 'are very friendly and efficient'. House wine is £12.95.
Chef/s: Jude Kereama. **Open:** Fri and Sat L 12 to 2, Mon to Sat D 5.30 to 9. **Closed:** Sun (exc bank hols and Mother's Day), 1 Jan to 8 Feb. **Meals:** alc (main courses £12 to £19). Set L and D £14 (2 courses) to £19.50. **Service:** not inc. **Details:** Cards accepted. 34 seats. Separate bar. Wheelchair access. Music. Children allowed.

Portscatho

Driftwood

Breathtaking sea views and seasonal food
Rosevine, Portscatho, TR2 5EW
Tel no: (01872) 580644
www.driftwoodhotel.co.uk
Modern European | £42
Cooking score: 5

🍴

A plum coastal location, breathtaking sea views and a private beach are big selling points at Paul and Fiona Robinson's personally run boutique hotel high above Rosevine. Huge expanses of plate glass make the most of the panoramic vistas in the simply appointed, wood-floored restaurant, while seaside yellow and blue colours point up the sunny theme. Fresh-from-the-boats seafood gets a good airing on Chris Eden's finely judged seasonal dinner menus – perhaps hand-dived Falmouth scallops with squid, cauliflower, sherry and pine nuts, or brill with pumpkin and ginger purée, chanterelles and crab. Those with other preferences might fancy a flag-waving salad of Cheltenham and golden beetroot, with heritage carrots, quince and walnuts or the homespun flavours of crisp Gloucester Old Spot pork belly with chestnuts, Brussels sprouts and marjoram. Lobsters and chateaubriand for two can be arranged with 24 hours' notice. Meals end with a variety of 'inventive yet delicious' desserts – a mini sherry and raisin soufflé worked for one visitor, otherwise caramelised banana with gingerbread and salted peanut ice cream sounds like fun. It would also be a shame to miss the array of West Country cheeses served with homemade digestive biscuits, membrillo jelly, figs and hazelnuts. The carefully chosen 60-bin wine list jumps between Europe and the New World, with prices from £16.
Chef/s: Chris Eden. **Open:** all week D only 7 to 9.30. **Closed:** 6 Dec to 3 Feb. **Meals:** Set D £42. **Service:** not inc. **Details:** Cards accepted. 34 seats. Separate bar. No mobile phones. Music. Children allowed. Car parking.

Rock

Nathan Outlaw Seafood & Grill

Pin-sharp Cornish seafood
St Enodoc Hotel, Rock Road, Rock, PL27 6LA
Tel no: (01208) 863394
www.nathan-outlaw.com
Seafood | £28
Cooking score: 4
£5 OFF 🍴 £30

This relaxed eatery is the casual alternative to Nathan Outlaw's new self-named restaurant in the St Enodoc Hotel. It makes the most of dramatic views over the Camel estuary and the rugged Cornish countryside, and seafood is the culinary star. Head chef Peter Biggs takes full advantage of the local haul, from hand-dived scallops to skate and wreckfish. Outlaw's home-smoked salmon is a signature starter, or you might plump for crab 'on toast' with pumpkin-seed dressing. After that, there might be pollack fillet (with cucumber, saffron and Porthilly mussels) or black bream (with Pink Fir potatoes and oyster cream). Irreproachable sourcing, refreshingly dressed-down ideas and pin-sharp execution also define proceedings when it comes to meat and seasonal game – perhaps a warm salad of wood pigeon with pickled shallots and celeriac, or local venison with parsnips and spring greens. Desserts such as lemon posset with rhubarb compote also stay with the unshowy programme. Everything on the carefully chosen 40-bin wine list is available by the glass, with bottle prices from £18.

Chef/s: Peter Biggs. **Open:** all week L 12 to 2, D 6 to 9.30. **Closed:** mid Dec to early Feb. **Meals:** alc (main courses £12 to £18). Set L and D £15 (2 courses) to £18. **Service:** not inc. **Details:** Cards accepted. 60 seats. 20 seats outside. Separate bar. No mobile phones. Music. Children allowed. Car parking.

★ **BEST FISH RESTAURANT** ★

Restaurant Nathan Outlaw

Awe-inspiring food from a top talent
St Enodoc Hotel, Rock Road, Rock, PL27 6LA
Tel no: (01208) 863394
www.nathan-outlaw.com
Modern British/Seafood | £55
Cooking score: 8

£5 OFF ♦ ⊏ V

Having staked a claim in Rock with Nathan Outlaw Seafood & Grill (see entry), the West Country's top-ranking chef has gone the whole hog and moved his prestigious restaurant from its old base in Fowey. Set in the grand surrounds of the St Enodoc Hotel, the new standalone dining room feels more serene and less demanding on the senses than its forebear (think muted tones, grey pinstripe chairs and splashes of orange and yellow),

although it has the requisite estuary views and a terrace for alfresco carousing. Meals begin with an amuse-bouche – perhaps a mouthful of soused mackerel with tomato jam – before the kitchen casts off and gives a truly awe-inspiring display of premier-league fish cookery. Eating here is 'an education in seafood', observed one reader who worked her way through a raft of incredible, impeccably executed dishes. Natural intensity and clear flavours are the hallmarks, and nothing overpowers, cloys or distracts from the real business on the plate: it might be a dish of lemon sole with caper and potato dumplings and an ever-so-subtle parsley sauce (a world away from the glue of yesteryear), or perhaps unimpeachable red mullet, squid, mushroom and tomato all piled on top of ravioli-like squid ink pasta. The choice of fish could also run to equally sharp compositions involving sea bass with crab sauce and sea vegetables or John Dory with brown shrimps, cucumber and oyster sauce. The menus are now laid out in tasting format, which means that meatiness intensifies as you proceed towards, say, an unbelievably delicate combo of lamb cooked three ways with asparagus, sweetbreads and tiny cubes of mint jelly dotted around the plate. Before dessert, you can slip in a cheese course – an all-British affair listed in order of strength. Finally, two puddings arrive – 'little gifts on the plate' in the shape of a 'sandcastle' of vanilla cheesecake with strawberries and mint followed by a knockout bitter chocolate mousse with pistachios and cherries. Service is totally relaxed, genuine and knowledgeable – especially if you need guidance regarding the wine list. This is a slate worthy of the food, with a peerless choice from around the globe, whether you are after a 'creamy white' or a 'chewy red'. Prices start at £24 (£7.50 a glass).

Chef/s: Nathan Outlaw and Gordon Gray. **Open:** Fri and Sat L 12.30 to 2, Tue to Sat D 7 to 9. **Closed:** Sun, Mon, 6 weeks from mid Dec to early Feb. **Meals:** Set L £27.50 (2 courses) to £32.50. Set D £45 (2 courses) to £55. Tasting menu £75. **Service:** 10% (optional). **Details:** Cards accepted. 26 seats. Separate bar. No mobile phones. Music. Car parking.

St Ives

Alba

Mediterranean zing by the harbour
Old Lifeboat House, Wharf Road, St Ives, TR26 1LF
Tel no: (01736) 797222
www.thealbarestaurant.com
Modern European | £24
Cooking score: 3

£5 OFF £30

Bracing views are one of the perennial talking points at this tasteful conversion of the St Ives lifeboat house, with tables on the upper level commanding the best vistas across the harbour. There's also plenty of stimulating eye candy in the form of contemporary canvases by local artists. Meanwhile, most attention downstairs is on the open kitchen, where chefs conjure up lively dishes with some noticeable Mediterranean zing. Fish is always a good call (perhaps fillet of grey mullet with leek and saffron risotto, linguine with crab and chilli, or a cassoulet of gurnard with chorizo and haricots blancs), while those with other preferences might be taken by pan-fried pigeon breast with choucroute or beef and ale stew with horseradish dumplings. For afters, warm almond tart with poached pear should suffice. House wines start at £12.95 (£3.50 a glass).
Chef/s: Grant Nethercott. **Open:** all week L 12 to 2, D 5.30 to 9.30. **Closed:** 25 and 26 Dec. **Meals:** alc (main courses £11 to £19). Set L and D £13.50 (2 courses) to £16.50. **Service:** not inc. **Details:** Cards accepted. 65 seats. Air-con. Wheelchair access. Music. Children allowed.

Blas Burgerworks

Eco-friendly boho burger joint
The Warren, St Ives, TR26 2EA
Tel no: (01736) 797272
www.blasburgerworks.co.uk
Burgers | £15
Cooking score: 1

V £30

An infectiously laid-back ambience – 'backstreet boho chic' is how co-owner Marie Dixon describes it – imbues this committed eco-friendly operation, where the communal tables are made of reclaimed wood, the burgers from naturally reared free-range beef or chicken and the char-grilled fish is from non-pressurised marine stocks. Get stuck into a bacon and cheese (Cornish Blue or Davidstow Cheddar) burger, a vegan tofuburger with tahini, or whatever fish has come in that day. Finish with Willy Waller's ice creams, made in St Ives, or a chocolate brownie made with Green & Black's. A handful of wines, from £13.50.
Chef/s: Sally Cuckson, Marie Dixon and Sarah Newark. **Open:** Tue to Sun D only 6 to 10 (all week D 5 to 10 during school hols). **Closed:** Nov to mid Dec, mid Jan to mid Feb, first week May. **Meals:** alc (main courses £8 to £10). **Service:** not inc. **Details:** Cards accepted. 30 seats. Wheelchair access. Music. Children allowed.

Porthminster Beach Café

Funky beach hangout
Porthminster Beach, St Ives, TR26 2EB
Tel no: (01736) 795352
www.porthminstercafe.co.uk
Seafood | £35
Cooking score: 4

V

This striking Art Deco building beneath the slopes of Porthminster Point is the kind of funky beach hangout that would fire up owner Mick Smith's ozone-addicted Aussie mates. It's much more than just a seaside café – fabulous views are a given, but the kitchen also rises to the occasion by offering a world tour of upbeat dishes with a fusion undercurrent and bold, freewheeling flavours. Cornish seafood is the star: Indonesian-style monkfish curry amazed one reader, but the choice extends to spiced black bream fillets with crab noodle salad or baked hake with salt cod croquettes, smoked tomato and langoustine velouté. Meat dishes also stake their claim (perhaps West Country venison with crispy Parma ham and celeriac purée), and desserts are in keeping – especially the 'black berry' tasting plate and showstopping caramelised banana with cinnamon meringues, pistachio ice cream, banana pudding and cinder toffee. A cherry-picked, worldwide wine list starts at £12.95. The same team also runs the seasonal Porthgwidden Beach Café.

Chef/s: Isaac Anderson and Tom Pryce. **Open:** all week L 11 to 5, D 6 to 10. **Meals:** alc (main courses £13 to £20). **Service:** not inc. **Details:** Cards accepted. 80 seats. 80 seats outside. Separate bar. No mobile phones. Wheelchair access. Music. Children allowed.

St Andrew's Street Bistro
Relaxed, tucked-away bistro
16 St Andrew's Street, St Ives, TR26 1AH
Tel no: (01736) 797074
Modern European | £20
Cooking score: 2

V £30

Tucked away down a narrow street behind the harbour, this agreeable evenings-only restaurant occupies a former pilchard works. The double-height space is lined with modern art (for sale) and the menu is now fixed price, offering excellent value across the board. Pork, cumin and cinnamon meatballs with a rich tomato sauce is a good way to start, while the main course line-up runs from oven-roasted salmon with mash to venison burger with French fries and salad. Service is at a pace that's suited to such a relaxed setting. House wine is £10, or you can BYO.

Chef/s: Matt Knight. **Open:** all week D only 6 to 11. **Closed:** Nov. **Meals:** Set D £15 (2 courses). **Service:** not inc. **Details:** Cards accepted. 70 seats. Wheelchair access. Children allowed.

ALSO RECOMMENDED
▲ Alfresco
The Wharf, St Ives, TR26 1LF
Tel no: (01736) 793737
www.stivesharbour.com
Modern British £5 OFF

Outdoor seats are obviously a big draw when it's sunny, but even on a rain-soaked day, nothing can dim Alfresco's 'winning combination' of harbour views, bustling vibes and carefully crafted food. Local flavours shine through in 'wonderfully presented' dishes such as scallops on celeriac rémoulade with pancetta crackling and raisin purée (£6.95), John Dory with crab cakes and sweetcorn velouté, or fillet of beef with wild mushrooms, Cornish blue cheese gratin and port jus (£18.95). Caramelised banana with peanut butter ice cream (£5.95) is a typically lively dessert. House wine is £12.95. Open all week.

St Kew
St Kew Inn
Pubby vibes and unfussy, flavourful food
St Kew, PL30 3HB
Tel no: (01208) 841259
www.stkewinn.co.uk
Gastropub | £25
Cooking score: 3

£30

Guide veteran Paul Ripley always fancied owning a pub, and he got his chance when this grand old fifteenth-century Cornish hostelry came on the market in 2008. He has preserved the inn's tasteful pubby virtues, its cosy vibes, flagstone floors and real ales, but has added his own brand of unpretentious, populist grub to the mix. The kitchen delivers what one reader called 'full flavours and unfussy food' – perfectly cooked pheasant pie and chicken pot au feu, as well as beer-battered cod cheeks and plates of crisp pork belly, Boston baked beans and black pudding – not forgetting a few things 'on toast', bowls of fish pie to share, and puds such as crème caramel with Agen prunes. House recommendations from £13.

Chef/s: Paul Ripley. **Open:** all week L 12 to 2, Mon to Sat D 6.30 to 9. **Closed:** 25 Dec. **Meals:** alc (main courses £10 to £19). Sun L £15 (2 courses) to £19.50. **Service:** not inc. **Details:** Cards accepted. 70 seats. 80 seats outside. Separate bar. No music. No mobile phones. Children allowed. Car parking.

▋ St Mawes
Hotel Tresanton
Pure pleasure
27 Lower Castle Road, St Mawes, TR2 5DR
Tel no: (01326) 270055
www.tresanton.com
Modern European | £38
Cooking score: 4

'We did not realise that such places existed in England', reports a visitor, adding 'the food here is really top drawer'. The location is stunning, with amazing sea views from the summer dining terrace, and owner Olga Polizzi has injected a chic Mediterranean feel. Add to this the contentment of lunch and dinner, and the result is pure pleasure. A May lunch produced a generous wedge of foie gras and chicken liver parfait with apple chutney and a lovely dish of monkfish, samphire, green beans, quails' eggs and salsa verde. Elsewhere local lobster, simply grilled, has been pronounced superb and local lamb praised – perhaps best end with spinach and potato croquette, tomato and borlotti beans with basil. Desserts shine too, especially a well-reported vanilla pannacotta. House wine is £20.
Chef/s: Paul Wadham. **Open:** all week L 12.30 to 2.30, D 7 to 9.30. **Closed:** 2 weeks Jan. **Meals:** alc (main courses £17 to £22). Set L £26.50 (2 courses) to £35. Set D £42. Sun L £35. **Service:** not inc. **Details:** Cards accepted. 40 seats. 40 seats outside. Separate bar. No music. Wheelchair access. Car parking.

▋ St Merryn
Rosel & Co
Easy-going eatery with simple, tasty food
The Dog House, St Merryn, PL28 8NF
Tel no: (01841) 521289
www.roselandco.co.uk
Modern British | £30
Cooking score: 4

Zane Rosel's brand of straightforward cooking based on good seasonal produce is proving a winning formula at this rustic, wooden dining room, which shares a building with the Dog House Bar. It's all very casual: an easy mix of close-packed tables, local art on the walls, and a partial view of the kitchen. The menu is short and to the point with simplicity evident in a dish of asparagus with well-made egg yolk ravioli and miso butter sauce and 'good, tasty flavours' coming through in a main course of pork fillet and belly served with apple sauce, mustard and spring greens. A few details, such as 'nicely cooked' monkfish overpowered by too much wild garlic, and chorizo dominating a dish of cod with mussels, peas and lettuce, have let the side down. For dessert, baked apple with vanilla parfait and almond crumble is an outright winner. The wine list offers plenty of affordable drinking from £15.
Chef/s: Zane Rosel. **Open:** Tue to Sat D only 7 to 9. **Closed:** Sun, Mon, Dec to Feb. **Meals:** Set D £25 (2 courses) to £30. **Service:** not inc. **Details:** Cards accepted. 30 seats. Separate bar. No mobile phones. Music. Children allowed.

Readers recommend

A 'readers recommend' review is a genuine quote from a report sent in by one of our readers. We intend to follow up these suggestions throughout the year to come.

Treen
The Gurnard's Head
Going from strength to strength
Treen, TR26 3DE
Tel no: (01736) 796928
www.gurnardshead.co.uk
Modern British | £27
Cooking score: 3

£5 OFF 🍴 £30

It's five years since the Inkin brothers' bold refurbishment of this large coastal pub on the winding road to St Ives, but the Gurnard's Head continues to go from strength to strength. Former sous chef Bruce Rennie now heads the kitchen and keeps things pubby with lunchtime offerings of beef and ale stew or ham, egg and chips, but you can expect a few modern twists and turns in the evening. Possibilities are confit duck with apple and walnut to start, followed by cod with crushed potatoes, mussels, leeks, lemon and cucumber vinaigrette or pork loin with mashed potatoes, broccoli, sage, cider and mustard. To finish there may be bread-and-butter pudding and ginger ice cream or good British artisan cheeses. An excellent global wine list offers some 16 by the glass, and bottles from £15.50.
Chef/s: Bruce Rennie. **Open:** all week L 12.30 to 2 (2.30 Sun), D 6 to 9.30. **Closed:** 24 and 25 Dec, first week Jan. **Meals:** alc (main courses £13 to £17). Sun L £18 (2 courses) to £23. **Service:** not inc.
Details: Cards accepted. 60 seats. 35 seats outside. Separate bar. No mobile phones. Music. Children allowed. Car parking.

Truro
Tabb's
Beguiling Cornish stalwart
85 Kenwyn Street, Truro, TR1 3BZ
Tel no: (01872) 262110
www.tabbs.co.uk
Modern British | £30
Cooking score: 4

£5 OFF

Nigel Tabb continues to win over tourists and the denizens of Truro with his beguiling restaurant in a converted pub, and all-comers feel at ease amid the soothing lilac shades and fresh flowers as they sample the fruits of his labours. Spanking fresh, locally landed fish has been given an emphatic thumbs-up – notably seared fillet of red mullet on warm potato salad with garlic soup and basil oil, and a main of grilled red gurnard with crisp polenta, shredded leeks, cockles and a delicate chive sauce. The 'outstanding' quality of baked cannon of lamb and roast Terras Farm duck breast has delighted meat eaters, and everyone adores the vegetables (moreish boulangère potatoes and inspired courgette tempura in particular). Cornish cheeses are kept in their prime, while desserts and petits fours owe much to Nigel's training as a chocolatier. The commendable 40-bin wine list opens with house selections from £14.95; a pokey Portuguese Irreverente also hit the spot for one reporter.
Chef/s: Nigel Tabb. **Open:** Tue to Sat D only 6.45 to 9.30. **Closed:** Sun, Mon, 1 week Jan, 1 week Oct. **Meals:** alc (main courses £15 to £21). **Service:** not inc. **Details:** Cards accepted. 30 seats. Separate bar. No mobile phones. Music. Children allowed.

Wadebridge

The Orchard
Bright, value-for-money eatery
Polmorla Road, Wadebridge, PL27 7ND
Tel no: (01208) 812696
www.theorchardrestaurant.co.uk
Modern British | £28
Cooking score: 1
£5 OFF **V** £30

'The food is wonderful, very fresh and local. It is imaginatively cooked, the menu changes frequently so there's always something new', enthuse regulars to this slick, bright and unfussy restaurant that offers value-for-money café food by day and a full-blown modern restaurant at night. Daytime offerings range from sandwiches to good burgers with homemade chips and crayfish linguine. Evening menus offer the likes of crab ravioli with saffron and butter sauce, confit duck leg with wholegrain mustard mash, and apple tarte Tatin. House wine from £16.
Chef/s: Lee Brine. **Open:** Mon to Sat L 11.30 to 2.30, Wed to Sat D 6.30 to 9.30. **Closed:** Sun, 5 to 30 Jan.
Meals: alc (main courses £14 to £19). Set L £13 (2 courses) to £18. Set D £21 (2 courses) to £26.
Service: not inc. **Details:** Cards accepted. 40 seats. No mobile phones. Music. Children allowed.

READERS RECOMMEND

Bridge Bistro
Modern British
4 Molesworth Street, Wadebridge, PL27 7DA
Tel no: (01208) 815342
'**Chef is Phil Wakeling (ex No 6 in Padstow) and every course had the wow factor**'

Watergate Bay

Fifteen Cornwall
Pukka Cornish destination
On the beach, Watergate Bay, TR8 4AA
Tel no: (01637) 861000
www.fifteencornwall.co.uk
Italian | £26
Cooking score: 4
£30

On the beach overlooking one of Cornwall's funkiest surfing destinations, this is the hip West Country outpost of Jamie Oliver's Fifteen Foundation (a training programme for disadvantaged youngsters) and Fifteen London (see entry). Jaw-dropping sandscapes, sunsets and crashing Atlantic waves add to the thrill of it all, and the food passes muster on all counts. Seasonal Cornish ingredients and Italian provisions are the impeccable building blocks, bread is baked each day and the results are straight and true. Breakfast is worth considering, while lunches offer vigorous rustic dishes such as pappardelle with Tregothnan Estate vension ragù and Selvapiana olive oil, or brill with aubergine caponata, sprouting broccoli and wild garlic aïoli. To finish, classic Amalfi lemon tart with Rodda's clotted cream has been heartily endorsed. Dinner offers slightly more upbeat dishes in a five-course tasting format (think pot-roasted balsamic Primrose Herd pork with a borlotti bean, cavolo nero and artichoke stew). The global wine list is a canny selection of elite, unusual bottles from £19.50 (£5 a glass).
Chef/s: Andy Appleton. **Open:** all week L 12 to 2.30, D 6.15 to 9.15. **Meals:** alc (main courses £12 to £23). Set L £26. Set D £55 (5 courses). **Service:** not inc.
Details: Cards accepted. 100 seats. Air-con. Wheelchair access. Music. Children allowed. Car parking.

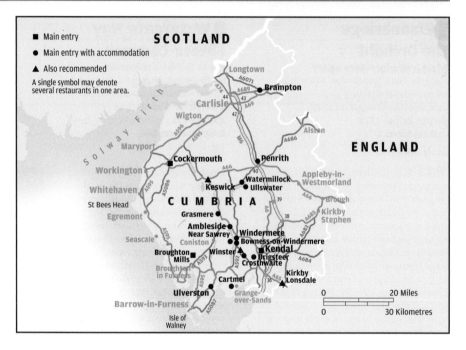

◼ Ambleside

The Drunken Duck Inn

Handsome all-rounder
Barngates, Ambleside, LA22 0NG
Tel no: (015394) 36347
www.drunkenduckinn.co.uk
Modern British | £32
Cooking score: 2

⌾ ⊨ V

If you're hankering after country pub virtues, the Drunken Duck has them in spades: stunning Lakeland views, fishing rights, an on-site brewery, wood fires and grub with a regional accent – plus annals of history under its belt. Walkers, tourists and ale buffs are wowed by the place, piling in for pints of the real stuff and wholesome lunchtime victuals (think cob sandwiches, wild mushrooms on toast and beef in ale). Come evening and there's confit rabbit terrine and duck parfait with fig chutney and seared venison loin with Puy lentils, sweet potato purée and pied bleu mushrooms. To conclude, perhaps rhubarb and duck-egg custard tart. Wine is also taken seriously here, and the impressive, well annotated list kicks off with around 20 house selections from £19.50 (£4.95 a glass).

Chef/s: Luke Shaw. **Open:** all week L 12 to 3, D 6.30 to 9 (6 Fri and Sat). **Closed:** 25 Dec. **Meals:** alc (main courses £13 to £25). **Service:** not inc. **Details:** Cards accepted. 52 seats. 20 seats outside. Separate bar. No music. Wheelchair access. Children allowed. Car parking.

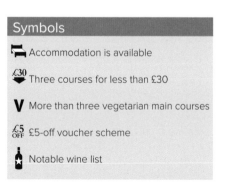

Symbols

⊨ Accommodation is available

£30 Three courses for less than £30

V More than three vegetarian main courses

£5 OFF £5-off voucher scheme

⚑ Notable wine list

Bowness-on-Windermere

Linthwaite House

Precise, full-blooded food
Crook Road, Bowness-on-Windermere, LA23 3JA
Tel no: (015394) 88600
www.linthwaite.com
Modern British | £50
Cooking score: 5

£5 OFF 🍷 🛏 V

Spectacular views across Lake Windermere come with the territory at Linthwaite House – a one-time Edwardian gentleman's residence set in 15 acres of enchanting woodland with its own tarn. Local boy Richard Kearsley knows his way around the region when it comes to sourcing top-drawer ingredients, and his dependable network provides the kitchen with everything from hand-churned butter to rare-breed lamb from the fells. You can eat casually from the Terrace menu, but the main business takes place in two opulent dining rooms that parade their cultured demeanour with mirrors, prints and antiques. The cooking is a sure match for its surroundings, offering precise but full-blooded dishes with one eye on the latest trends. A pairing of pan-roasted scallops with sticky chicken wing, parsnip salsa and cumin foam is right up there, likewise a voguish combo of line-caught sea bass fillet with braised beef shin and Puy lentils. There is also room for well-tried partnerships in the shape of Holker Estate venison with some of its favourite companions – red onion tart, damson purée, port and chocolate jus. Desserts tend to be fun-loving bonanzas – warm carrot cake paired with candied orange, carrot jellies and candied walnuts, for example. The wine list explores classic grape varieties in depth, pulling in prestigious growers and satisfying the traditionalists with an awesome showing of big, beefy reds. Prices start at £21.
Chef/s: Richard Kearsley. **Open:** all week L 12.30 to 2, D 7 to 9. **Meals:** Set L £14.95 (2 courses) to £19.95. Set D £36 (2 courses) to £49 (4 courses). Sun L £24.95. **Service:** not inc. **Details:** Cards accepted.

60 seats. 40 seats outside. Separate bar. No mobile phones. Wheelchair access. Music. Children allowed. Car parking.

Brampton

Farlam Hall

Consistency and attention to detail
Brampton, CA8 2NG
Tel no: (016977) 46234
www.farlamhall.co.uk
Modern British | £43
Cooking score: 3

🛏

Regulars writing in to praise the well-oiled machine that is Farlam Hall are unanimous in their enthusiasm for the consistency and attention to detail that always distinguish a visit here. It's a large Victorian house set in expansive gardens incorporating an ornamental lake, and that consistency may owe something to the fact that the Quinion family has been running it since the mid-1970s. The fixed-price dinner menu changes every evening, and always offers a choice of three starters and mains, with a sorbet in between. Start, perhaps, with pheasant and pistachio terrine with toasted fruit loaf and plum chutney, and follow it up with grilled fillets of lemon sole, garnished with coconut and banana, in a white wine and dill cream sauce. English cheeses precede dessert. Wines by the glass start at £5.25.
Chef/s: Barry Quinion. **Open:** all week D only 8 to 8.30. **Closed:** 25 to 30 Dec, 4 to 13 Jan. **Meals:** Set D £43 (4 courses). **Service:** not inc. **Details:** Cards accepted. 40 seats. No music. No mobile phones. Wheelchair access. Car parking.

Brigsteer

NEW ENTRY

The Wheatsheaf

Whitewashed inn with up-to-date food
Brigsteer, LA8 8AN
Tel no: (015395) 68254
www.thewheatsheafbrigsteer.co.uk
Gastropub | £23
Cooking score: 2

£5 OFF 🍴 V £30

The Lyth and Winster Valleys abound with traditionally whitewashed Lake District inns whose exteriors belie their transformation into modern foodie pubs. Light oak floors, matching tables and leather sofas give the Wheatsheaf its attractive contemporary feel. A seasonally changing blackboard menu is equally up to scratch in ambition and execution while avoiding most of the clichés of Cumbrian pub standards. Choose from the likes of a zinging tomato soup with homemade bread roll, local lamb with roast garlic mash, or sea bass fillet with buttered samphire. Lemon meringue pie or white chocolate cheesecake finish things in satisfying style. House wine from £13.95.
Chef/s: Lee Rowbotham. **Open:** all week L 12 to 2 (2.30 Sun), D 5.45 to 9 (6 Sat and Sun). **Meals:** alc (main courses £10 to £19). Set L and D £12 (2 courses) to £15. **Service:** not inc. **Details:** Cards accepted. 56 seats. 20 seats outside. Separate bar. No mobile phones. Wheelchair access. Car parking.

Broughton Mills

NEW ENTRY

Blacksmiths Arms

A tucked-away treasure
Broughton Mills, LA20 6AX
Tel no: (01229) 716824
www.theblacksmithsarms.com
Gastropub | £20
Cooking score: 2

£5 OFF

Tucked away down a country lane three miles up the Lickle Valley from Broughton-in-Furness, the Blacksmiths is a treasure from the

moment you duck your head through its crooked doorway, wander its oak-lined passages and squeeze into the tiny, one-table bar. The best of three dining rooms has an ancient, smoke-blackened range and the menu features dependable dishes such as terrine of ham hock and black pudding, a melting pot of Flookburgh potted shrimps, herb-crusted lamb with a balsamic and red wine sauce, or a golden-topped steak pie. Wash it down with a pint of Hawkshead Bitter or Mothbag from Barngates Brewery. House wine from £11.95.
Chef/s: Paul McKnight. **Open:** Tue to Sun L 12 to 2, D 6 to 9. **Meals:** alc (main courses £10 to £17). **Service:** not inc. **Details:** Cards accepted. 40 seats. 24 seats outside. Separate bar. No music. Wheelchair access. Children allowed. Car parking.

Carlisle

READERS RECOMMEND

David's Restaurant

British
62 Warwick Road, Carlisle, CA1 1DR
Tel no: (01228) 523578
'Steaks simply sublime, beautiful terrines and homemade desserts'

Cartmel

L'Enclume

Nature meets the avant-garde
Cavendish Street, Cartmel, LA11 6PZ
Tel no: (015395) 36362
www.lenclume.co.uk
Modern European | £60
Cooking score: 8

£5 OFF 🍷 🍴

Simon Rogan's northern star is waxing ever more strongly out in the Cumbrian backwoods as his food blazes into the gastronomic stratosphere. In the past L'Enclume has been likened to the Fat Duck (see entry), but comparisons are invidious and unhelpful; while Blumenthal turns to scientific methodology and analysis, Rogan now looks out of his window for inspiration. 'Our identity through our surroundings' is his mantra, and the Lake District really is his larder – in fact he is aiming to cultivate or rear just about everything from his latest project, Howbarrow Farm across the valley. Few chefs have such a passionate dedication to nature or their home turf, although Rogan calls on the latest equipment to tease astonishing contrasts from a host of archaic ingredients that could easily have fallen from the pages of Dorothy Hartley's *Food in England*: pickled apples, sweet cicely, lady's smock, St George's mushrooms, fat hen (chenopodium) and other wayside gleanings are given new life in this converted Lakeland smithy. Two menus are offered (8 or 13 courses) and the procession reads like a truncated litany from the outer limits of British gastronomy as sense-tingling combinations follow each other in dazzling profusion; here are heady fragrances, incredible textures and flavours you never dared imagine – all conceived with intelligence and natural empathy. The sheer breadth of this thrilling food can be gauged immediately from two opening salvos: the perennial 'grown-up yolk from the golden egg' (a whimsy involving delicate chicken velouté encased in glittery golden carrageen gel, with hot mustard mayo masquerading as the 'white') and a construction of young peas, pea purée, chocolate mint and wild sorrel, layered together and generating a 'wonderful riff'. Elsewhere Rogan creates limpid vegetable and herb broths entirely from natural juices, smokes eel in a glass dome over lovage and juniper, and conjures extraordinary effects from two varieties of carrot with a little ham fat and nasturtium flowers. At the heart of the menu is seasonality – monkfish cheeks with bay cockles and broad bean leaf leading quite naturally into another springtime barnstormer of new season's lamb (from nearby Holker Hall) with curds and whey and a little puffed pearl barley for texture. Towards the end comes the famous 'experamenthol frappé' (pear meringue with eucalyptus ice cream and powdered coffee) – a stroke of linguistic genius as well the perfect curtain-raiser for sea buckthorn with basil chocolate and tiny, crunchy, fizzy 'rocks'. The unfussy mood in the rough-walled, stone-floored dining room is sustained by engaging and genuinely committed staff; no one feels intimidated here, although the auspicious wine list is on hand to steady any first-time nerves. A heavyweight French contingent leads the charge, but also note the excellent choice of half-bottles and stickies. House selections start at £21 (£4 a glass).

Chef/s: Simon Rogan. **Open:** Wed to Sun L 12 to 1.30, all week D 6.45 to 9. **Meals:** Set L £25 (3 courses). Set menu £60 (8 courses) to £80 (13 courses). **Service:** not inc. **Details:** Cards accepted. 50 seats. Air-con. No music. No mobile phones. Wheelchair access. Car parking.

Rogan and Company

Heart-warming brasserie
The Square, Cartmel, LA11 6QD
Tel no: (015395) 35917
www.roganandcompany.co.uk
Modern European | £25
Cooking score: 4

£5 OFF £30 ↓

The sibling establishment to L'Enclume (see entry above), Rogan and Co is just round the corner. Here Simon Rogan offers a more informal brasserie-style menu in a heart-warmingly traditional bar with low beams and an upstairs dining room. The straightforward British cooking produces some engaging results. Meat main courses were particularly praised by reporters who ate haunch of venison on roasted roots and fell-bred beef sirloin with béarnaise sauce. To start, there may be something as sustaining as a bowl of roast pumpkin soup with a dollop of nutmeg crème fraîche, or pickled herrings with potato salad, and you might finish in fine style with bread-and-butter pudding and vanilla ice cream, or a good British cheese plate with onion marmalade and quince jelly. The wine list opens at £13.40.

Chef/s: Adam Wesley. **Open:** Tue to Sun L 12 to 2.30, D 6.30 to 9. **Closed:** Mon. **Meals:** alc (main courses £10 to £19). **Service:** not inc. **Details:** Cards accepted. 80 seats. Air-con. Separate bar. Wheelchair access. Music. Children allowed.

COCKERMOUTH

▊ Cockermouth
Quince & Medlar
Veteran Lakeland veggie
13 Castlegate, Cockermouth, CA13 9EU
Tel no: (01900) 823579
www.quinceandmedlar.co.uk
Vegetarian | £27
Cooking score: 4

V £30

Colin and Louisa Le Voi's neighbourly
vegetarian restaurant has been quietly
flourishing in Cockermouth for 22 years, and
the Victorian setting still retains a certain
elegance and intimacy, backed up by all-round
integrity and that personal touch. The food is a
world away from the sexy global pyrotechnics
of some trendy veggie haunts, but it scores
with pleasing homely rusticity; there's
nothing to scare the horses when it comes to
wild mushroom pâté with home-baked oat
biscuits or rocket and ricotta cheese in a crisp
pastry case, partnered by spiced plum and
kumquat chutney. Mains tend to have less
textural vibrancy ('baby food' comes to mind),
but the likes of red onion wrapped in
aubergine slices or parsnip and cheese roulade
are capably executed. To finish, try the warm
raspberry flapjack with crème anglaise. The
wine list comes with an organic/vegetarian/
vegan tag; prices start at £12.90.
Chef/s: Colin Le Voi. Open: Tue to Sat D only 7 to
9.30 (6.30 Sat). Closed: Sun, Mon, 24 to 26 Dec.
Meals: alc (main courses £14). Service: not inc.
Details: Cards accepted. 26 seats. No mobile
phones. Music.

READERS RECOMMEND
The Pheasant
Gastropub
Bassenthwaite Lake, Cockermouth, CA13 9AY
Tel no: (017687) 76234
www.the-pheasant.co.uk
'Set three or four course dinners change daily
and the service is attentive'

▊ Crosthwaite
The Punch Bowl
Stylish country pub with spot-on food
Lyth Valley, Crosthwaite, LA8 8HR
Tel no: (015395) 68237
www.the-punchbowl.co.uk
British | £25
Cooking score: 3

£5 OFF ▊ V £30

From the outside this may seem a traditional
Lyth Valley inn with a 'great location next to
the church', but once through the door you'll
find a smart interior of slate or polished oak
floors, oatmeal walls and a welcome lack of
clutter. The kitchen shows sound talent, and
the results have pleased: Manx scallops on the
half-shell, grilled with bacon, parsley and
breadcrumbs, and a salad of crab, smoked
salmon and a carpaccio of langoustine proved
'fresh and light', while a generous portion of
venison haunch with black rice and a wine
sauce with a hint of chocolate was 'spot-on'.
Others have praised the beef bourguignon for
two. However, lapses in service have marred
enjoyment. House wine is £16.95.
Chef/s: Chris Meredith and Peter Howarth. Open:
all week L 12 to 6, D 6 to 9.30. Meals: alc (main
courses £14 to £19). Service: not inc. Details: Cards
accepted. 95 seats. 60 seats outside. Wheelchair
access. Music. Children allowed. Car parking.

▊ Grasmere
The Jumble Room
Global flavours and good vibes
Langdale Road, Grasmere, LA22 9SU
Tel no: (015394) 35188
www.thejumbleroom.co.uk
Global | £30
Cooking score: 2

£5 OFF ▊

Andy and Christine Hill have certainly
imbued their laid-back restaurant-with-
rooms with bags of 'feel-good' personality:
fun-filled, arty decoration adds to the good
vibrations (check out the LP-covered loos) and
Andy is reckoned to be the 'best front-of-

house manager in Cumbria'. In the kitchen, things are equally upbeat, with big-hearted global flavours stuffed into a lively menu that might backpack from Herdwick lamb loin with a jamboree of aromatic Lebanese inflections to South African dithoise chicken with roasted pumpkin, sticky beets and chilli jam, by way of smoked haddock soufflé and locally reared steak with Madeira sauce. The owners' organic allegiances extend to the worldwide wine list, which opens at £11.95. **Chef/s:** Christine Hill and David Clay. **Open:** Sat and Sun L 12 to 3, Wed to Mon D 5 to 11. **Closed:** Tue, 20 to 26 Dec. **Meals:** alc (main courses £13 to £24). **Service:** not inc. **Details:** Cards accepted. 48 seats. 8 seats outside. No mobile phones. Wheelchair access. Music. Children allowed.

White Moss House
Seasonal food and seductive wines
Rydal Water, Grasmere, LA22 9SE
Tel no: (015394) 35295
www.whitemoss.com
British | £40
Cooking score: 5

The stone house – once owned by William Wordsworth – has been in Peter and Sue Dixon's capable hands for 31 years. Peter's enthusiasm for locally sourced, organic and free-range food is as strong as ever, while his assured, quality-conscious style exudes and inspires confidence. The format never changes – a five-course dinner served at a single sitting, with dishes assiduously following the seasons. In March this could mean leek and lovage soup to start, then West Coast sea bass poached with Champagne in the Aga with sorrel and saffron sauce, followed by Goosnargh chicken breast cooked in natural yoghurt, old white Burgundy and thyme and served with an abundance of vegetables. Sticky toffee pudding with pecan toffee sauce or apple crumble ice cream could be offered ahead of a plate of British cheeses. Immense effort and care have gone into the excellent wine list. French regional classics take star

billing, but there is much to seduce elsewhere. A page of personally selected wines starts at £13.95.
Chef/s: Peter Dixon. **Open:** Thur to Sat D only 8pm (1 sitting). **Closed:** Sun to Wed, Dec, Jan. **Meals:** Set D £39.50 (5 courses). **Service:** not inc. **Details:** Cards accepted. 18 seats. Separate bar. No music. Children allowed. Car parking.

Kendal
Bridge Street Restaurant
Calm reassurance and appealing food
1 Bridge Street, Kendal, LA9 7DD
Tel no: (01539) 738855
www.one-bridgestreet.co.uk
Modern British | £25
Cooking score: 3

Highly polished wooden tables, oatmeal-coloured walls and a welcome lack of clutter create a mood of calm reassurance in this listed Georgian building overlooking the river Kent. Julian Ankers is an accomplished cook with a raft of appealing ideas up his sleeve: crab and lentil tartlet is topped with a soft poached egg and served with lime butter, saddle of venison comes with a caramelised pear tarte Tatin, spinach and ruby port sauce, and poached halibut is dressed up with baby vine tomatoes and 'poddled pea stew'. Everything is underpinned by first-class raw materials, mostly from the region. To finish there are old-school desserts ranging from apple and rhubarb crumble to homemade ice creams, and the choice of artisan cheeses includes some enterprising local names. The diverse wine list promises good-value drinking from £13.50.
Chef/s: Julian Ankers. **Open:** Wed to Sat L 12 to 1.30, 6 to 9. **Closed:** Sun to Tue, 25 and 26 Dec, 1 and 2 Jan. **Meals:** alc (main courses £12 to £23). Set L and D (5.30 to 6.30) £12 (2 courses) to £17. **Service:** not inc. **Details:** Cards accepted. 36 seats. 8 seats outside. Air-con. Separate bar. No mobile phones. Wheelchair access. Music. Children allowed.

Keswick

ALSO RECOMMENDED
▲ Swinside Lodge

Grange Road, Newlands, Keswick, CA12 5UE
Tel no: (017687) 72948
www.swinsidelodge-hotel.co.uk
Modern British £5 OFF

The pretty Georgian residence set in tranquil gardens is now a warm and welcoming hotel. Dinner in the candlelit dining room is a classical four-course affair (£40), with plenty of local flavours apparent in the likes of roast fillet of Cumbrian lamb served with goats' cheese and sun-dried tomato potato, stuffed courgettes, butternut squash and braised shallots. Terrines, Asian-style fiscakes and soufflés are offered as nibbles, there's always a soup course, and dark chocolate truffle cake with Kirsch cherries is a recommended dessert. House wine is £17.50. Open all week D only.

Kirkby Lonsdale

ALSO RECOMMENDED
▲ The Sun Inn

6 Market Street, Kirkby Lonsdale, LA6 2AU
Tel no: (015242) 71965
www.sun-inn.info
Gastropub

Owners Lucy and Mark Fuller have done a grand job transforming this historic, white-painted Cumbrian boozer into a thriving gastro-inn with boutique bedrooms. Visitors can eat in the old-fashioned bar or the brasserie-style dining room from a lively menu that roams its way through the likes of Lancashire haggis with smoked cheese and mustard sauce (£5.95), rare-breed sirloin steak, and sea bass with spinach and shellfish potato pie (£16.95). Round off with, say, vanilla pannacotta, Calvados jelly and apple sorbet (£4.25). Wines from £12.95. Closed Mon L.

Near Sawrey

Ees Wyke

Beatrix Potter bolthole
Near Sawrey, LA22 0JZ
Tel no: (015394) 36393
www.eeswyke.co.uk
Anglo-French | £33
Cooking score: 2

The Lees' Georgian country house, with commanding views to Esthwaite Water, basks in all the majesty the Lakes have to offer and it makes a favourable impression on visitors. The five-course dinner begins in the lounge at 7.30. Richard Lee's approach is to perk up interest using excellent-quality raw materials, although the repertoire plays a fairly safe modern European tune. Simplicity is the key: wild mushrooms with a creamy chervil sauce perhaps, then tiger prawns in garlic, sherry and olive oil and chilli, followed by veal slow-cooked with bacon, onion and mushroom. Sticky toffee sponge and regional cheeses could complete the picture. House wine is £19.50.
Chef/s: Richard Lee. **Open:** all week D only 7.30 (1 sitting). **Meals:** Set D £33 (5 courses). **Service:** not inc. **Details:** Cards accepted. 16 seats. Separate bar. No music. No mobile phones. Car parking.

Penrith

George and Dragon

Estate pub with a landmark restaurant
Clifton, Penrith, CA10 2ER
Tel no: (01768) 865381
www.georgeanddragonclifton.co.uk
Gastropub | £23
Cooking score: 2
£5 OFF £30

The low-roofed, whitewashed pub sits at the heart of the owner's estate, which supplies many fresh ingredients for the kitchen. It is both a village hostelry and a landmark restaurant and has a loyal local following which warmly appreciates the kitchen's achievements. A richly savoury, twice-baked soufflé starter is a technically impressive feat, or there may be fried mackerel in a tomato stew with crisp-cooked onions. Blackboard specials flesh out the main menu, which offers a superior burger of shorthorn beef, or perhaps hake in mussel and saffron broth with mash, before favourite desserts like sticky toffee pudding and fudge sauce, or apple and cinnamon crumble. A fine, stylistically sorted wine list kicks off with house Italian at £13. **Chef/s:** Paul McKinnon. **Open:** all week L 12 to 2.30 (3 Sun), D 6 to 9.30 (9 Sun). **Closed:** 26 Dec. **Meals:** alc (main courses £9 to £19). Sun L £10.95. **Service:** not inc. **Details:** Cards accepted. 90 seats. 40 seats outside. Separate bar. Wheelchair access. Music. Children allowed. Car parking.

▌Ullswater

Sharrow Bay

Prestige and traditional expectations
Ullswater, CA10 2LZ
Tel no: (01768) 486301
www.sharrowbay.co.uk
Modern British | £70
Cooking score: 5

🍸 🗮 V

The lakeside location is a dream, and everything looks much the same inside this archetypal 'country house hotel': gilded screens, cherubic candlesticks and Staffordshire pottery provide the trappings, although time hasn't stood still since the golden era of Francis Coulson and Brian Sack. That said, traditional expectations remain high – especially when it comes to shelling out for the meandering six-course dinner. While standards are spot-on in dishes such as tender venison fillet with juniper and rosemary sauce, tastes do not always come through as they should and there are also some eyebrow-raising repetitions: risottos, in particular, appear with relentless regularity. But diners can generally forgive any aberrations when there's ample comfort from the likes of spinach and Stilton soufflé with roasted onion or tournedos of Aberdeen Angus beef with a little steak and kidney pud and deep Burgundy sauce. Francis Coulson's

'icky sticky toffee sponge' remains a classic throwback to Sharrow Bay's peerless heyday, but not the clunking coconut Alaska – just rescued by the chilli hit of a pineapple salsa. Blue-blooded pedigree runs through the heavyweight wine list, with its deep French centre and global spread. Prices start at £17.50. **Chef/s:** Colin Akrigg. **Open:** all week L 1 to 3, D 7.30 for 8 (1 sitting). **Meals:** Set L £25. Set D £70 (6 courses). Sun L £43. **Service:** not inc. **Details:** Cards accepted. 50 seats. Air-con. No music. No mobile phones. Wheelchair access. Car parking.

▌Ulverston

The Bay Horse

Romantic charmer with breathtaking views
Canal Foot, Ulverston, LA12 9EL
Tel no: (01229) 583972
www.thebayhorsehotel.co.uk
Modern British | £30
Cooking score: 3

🗮 V

Once a stopover for stagecoaches crossing the sands and mudflats of Morecambe Bay at low tide, this pedigree retreat by the water's edge still has the power to entrance visitors with its glorious estuary views and romantic sunsets. 'Dinner at eight' is the drill in the Conservatory restaurant, and the kitchen shows its mettle with skilfully wrought dishes ranging from smoked duck breast and mango salad with passion-fruit vinaigrette to medallions of venison on spiced beetroot with port and Madeira sauce, or rack of salt marsh lamb with a Dijon mustard and herb crust. Sandwiches and 'light bites' are also served in the bar at lunchtime. Engaging staff have the knack of making visitors 'feel spoiled', and the wine list is also source of delight – especially for fans of South African winemaking. Prices start at £16.50. **Chef/s:** Robert Lyons and Chris Hogan. **Open:** all week L 12 to 4 (3 Mon), D 7.30 for 8 (1 sitting). **Meals:** alc (main courses £14 to £26). Set D £24 (2 courses) to £30. **Service:** not inc. **Details:** Cards accepted. 80 seats. 16 seats outside. Separate bar. No mobile phones. Wheelchair access. Music. Car parking.

▌Watermillock

Rampsbeck Country House Hotel

Seductively situated lakeside mansion
Watermillock, CA11 0LP
Tel no: (017684) 86442
www.rampsbeck.co.uk
Anglo-French | £47
Cooking score: 3

£5 OFF ☖ ☷ ☶

'It was all rather grand', noted a reporter of this imposing mansion seductively situated on Ullswater's western shore, 'a big country house that feels out of time now'. In the 'near ballroom' of a dining room the menu turns up anything from flavoursome carrot soup and tarragon foam to an impressive risotto of John Dory and shrimp. Uneven results have varied from poorly timed roast teal and an over-reduced shellfish reduction to a reporter's fabulously fresh slab of turbot accompanied by three tempura oysters finely cooked on a bed of spinach and crushed broad beans that bore comparison with the best. Reports are unanimous in their praise of very fine amuse-bouches, the outstanding petits fours, and the 'highly attentive but never stuffy' service. The auspicious wine list starts at £15.95 a bottle.
Chef/s: Andrew McGeorge. **Open:** all week L 12 to 1.15, D 7 to 8.30 (9 Fri and Sat). **Closed:** 3 to 28 Jan. **Meals:** Set L £24 (2 courses) to £29.95. Set D £47 (3 courses) to £52.50. Sun L £24 (2 courses) to £29.95. **Service:** not inc. **Details:** Cards accepted. 40 seats. Separate bar. No mobile phones. Wheelchair access. Music. Children allowed. Car parking.

▌Windermere

Gilpin

Beguiling retreat with brilliant food
Crook Road, Windermere, LA23 3NE
Tel no: (015394) 88818
www.gilpinlodge.co.uk
Modern British | £53
Cooking score: 6

£5 OFF ☖ ☷ V

Following some subtle re-branding, Gilpin Lodge has become Gilpin Hotel and Lake House – or Gilpin, if you prefer. Otherwise, it's business as usual at this early Edwardian retreat on a tranquil wooded hilltop overlooking Windermere. Long-serving custodians the Cunliffe family have learned the art of balancing professionalism with personable charm and intimacy – something not lost on their faithful following. In truth, fans of Gilpin love everything about the place, from drinks in the chic Champagne bar to meals in one of the four candlelit dining rooms. Lunch brings an easy choice of please-yourself dishes from roast beef fillet with béarnaise to beer-battered haddock, but dinner allows chef Russell Plowman to flex his muscles and show his talent for brilliantly executed modern cuisine. Signature specialities might include organic sea trout with fennel, carrot and orange purée enhanced with star anise nage or a tribute to local sourcing in the form of roast loin and shank of Gatelands Farm rose veal with butternut squash purée and gnocchi. If something 'classic' is required, the kitchen can also conjure up brill on the bone with chive sauce mousseline or coq au vin prepared with Goosnargh chicken. Meals are interspersed with dainty extras and conceits, while desserts promise anything from passion-fruit soufflé with dark chocolate sorbet to apple pie with cider sorbet and cinnamon foam. The prestigious wine list is built on interest, appeal and value, rather than a roll call of ancient vintages. Choice is global, half-bottles show up well and there is plenty of fine drinking for around £25.

Chef/s: Russell Plowman. **Open:** all week L 12 to 2, D 6.30 to 9.15. **Meals:** alc L (main courses £12 to £21). Set L £27 (3 courses). Set D £52.50 (5 courses). Sun L £30. **Service:** not inc. **Details:** Cards accepted. 60 seats. 25 seats outside. Separate bar. No music. No mobile phones. Wheelchair access. Car parking.

Holbeck Ghyll

Spectacular views and fantastic wine
Holbeck Lane, Windermere, LA23 1LU
Tel no: (015394) 32375
www.holbeckghyll.com
Modern British | £60
Cooking score: 5

£5 OFF ♦ 🍷 V

There is often an element of uncertainty about country house hotels of this magnificence when they change hands. Will the original intentions be abandoned in order to maximise profit? Will the talented chef be allowed to show his potential? Holbeck Ghyll's strengths are its setting – spectacular views over Windermere and Langlands Fell – and the fantastic wine list. However, while David McLaughlin has remained at the stove, recent reports indicate that the food is now prepared with varying degrees of attention to detail. Of course there are good dishes – a tian of crab with avocado and pink grapefruit from the lunch menu, well-timed scallops, served with celeriac and balsamic vinegar – but fierce cooking has marred a good piece of sea bass (although the accompanying braised fennel and artichokes in a vermouth sauce was excellent) and best end of Cumbrian lamb was overdone (despite being promised pink), the dish 'bland and the meat lacking any real flavour'. The cheese trolley remains superb, but it would help if the person manning it knew something about the stuff itself. France remains the main focus of the fabulous wine list, with some fine vintages from notable producers, but quality is evident throughout. Prices from £27.55.
Chef/s: David McLaughlin. **Open:** all week 12.30 to 2, 7 to 9.30. **Closed:** 2 to 21 Jan. **Meals:** Set L £60. Set D £32. Gourmet menu £78 (7 courses).

Service: not inc. **Details:** Cards accepted. 50 seats. 35 seats outside. Separate bar. No music. No mobile phones. Wheelchair access. Car parking.

Jerichos at the Waverley

Cooking that aims to please
College Road, Windermere, LA23 1BX
Tel no: (015394) 42522
www.jerichos.co.uk
Modern British | £32
Cooking score: 5

♦ 🛏

'This was a first-rate dining experience' sums up the way most visitors feel about this centrally located restaurant-with-rooms, which appears to go from strength to strength – perhaps because the kitchen is more interested in cooking to please customers than to entertain itself. Chris and Jo Blaydes are experienced restaurateurs and over the years Chris has gradually refined his version of modern British cooking. Confit of guinea fowl with an 'impressively light' rösti potato, creamed Savoy cabbage and bacon with a reduced red wine glaze has shone, likewise the quality of the mature, prime Scotch beef that is served with grilled tomatoes, mushrooms, reduced Cabernet wine sauce and 'straw fries' of an 'equally high standard'. Local produce shows up in slow-roasted, de-boned knuckle of Lune Valley lamb served with smoked butter mashed potato, roasted roots, glazed greens and port wine sauce. Puddings might include orange, honey and prune parfait with homemade sorbet and sweet glazed orange segments. Wines are arranged in groups according to what food they go with (from smoked fish to lamb and duck) in an entertainingly wide-ranging collection with prices from £15.
Chef/s: Chris Blaydes and Tim Dalzell. **Open:** Fri to Wed D only 7 to 8.30. **Closed:** Thur, 24 to 26 Dec, 1 Jan, last 2 weeks Nov, first week Dec. **Meals:** alc (main courses £16 to £24). **Service:** not inc. **Details:** Cards accepted. 28 seats. Music. Car parking.

The Samling
Comforting tradition and modern style
Ambleside Road, Windermere, LA23 1LR
Tel no: (01539) 431922
www.thesamlinghotel.co.uk
Modern British | £55
Cooking score: 4

£5 OFF 🛏

Set high above Lake Windermere, this elegant Victorian villa exudes comforting tradition and stylish modernism in equal measure – something that also applies to the food on the plate. Dishes are spelt out in terse menuspeak, with main ingredients getting top billing – brill, Hawkshead venison, Herdwick mutton – and the kitchen reveals its star-chasing intentions with an eight-course 'Gourmand' extravaganza. Top marks for silky potato and smoked haddock soup with soft-boiled quail's egg and a starter of scallops with slivers of sticky chicken wing, fresh-tasting parsley root and sweet raisin purée, but alpha-minus for pork belly and cod cheek terrine where meat trumped fish and the stiletto of crackling failed to stab home. To follow, slices of Goosnargh duck were outstandingly tender, but the accompanying confit leg pudding was depressingly lukewarm, while the pick of desserts was a sharp lemon tart with pine nut parfait. The Samling experience is overtly expensive and classy, although service can veer from 'suave to homely'. Wines start at £25.
Chef/s: Nigel Mendham. **Open:** all week L 12 to 1.30, D 7 to 9.30. **Meals:** Set L £19.50 (2 courses) to £25. Set D £55 (3 courses). Sun L £38 (3 courses). Gourmand menu £67. **Service:** not inc. **Details:** Cards accepted. 22 seats. 12 seats outside. Separate bar. No mobile phones. Music. Children allowed. Car parking.

■ Winster

ALSO RECOMMENDED
▲ The Brown Horse Inn
Winster, LA23 3NR
Tel no: (015394) 43443
www.thebrownhorseinn.co.uk
Gastropub £5 OFF

An on-site microbrewery is the latest addition to this enterprising inn-with-rooms overlooking the Lyth Valley. The pub also has a flourishing garden and smallholding, which provides valuable ingredients for the kitchen. Eat in the beamed bar or the dining room from a menu that features honest dishes such as ham hock terrine with celeriac rémoulade and pickled eggs (£6.25), dry-aged steaks with twice-cooked chips, and roast curried cod with Puy lentils (£14.95). Real ales rule, but there are also gluggable wines from £13.95. Open all week.

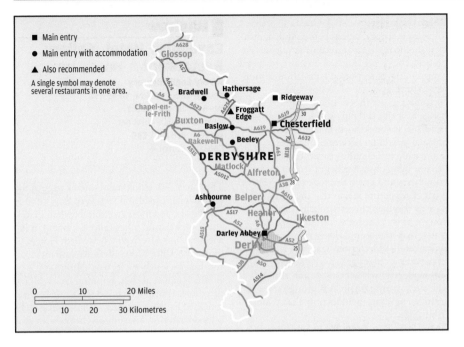

■ Ashbourne

Callow Hall
Imposing Peak District pile
Mappleton Road, Ashbourne, DE6 2AA
Tel no: (01335) 300900
www.callowhall.co.uk
Modern British | £42
Cooking score: 3

A fine Victorian pile resting in 34 acres of garden, fields and woodland, Callow Hall is what most people would expect a country house hotel to be. It is now owned by Von Essen Hotels, but Anthony Spencer (son of the former owners) continues to head the kitchen. Not all reports have been positive this year, but at its best his cooking exudes and inspires quiet confidence. Chicken liver terrine with fig and orange chutney could start a lunch, followed by grilled fillet of salmon with thyme-scented, slow-roast courgettes and peppers, puréed potatoes and white wine fumé, with sticky toffee chocolate pudding to finish. House wine is £18.95. As we went to press, Von Essen was planning a 'full refurbishment' of the hotel.

Chef/s: Anthony Spencer. **Open:** all week L 12 to 2, D 7.15 to 9. **Meals:** alc (main courses £17 to £22). Set L £16.95 (2 courses) to £19.95. Set D £29.95 (2 courses) to £42. Sun L £28.95. **Service:** not inc. **Details:** Cards accepted. 70 seats. 20 seats outside. Separate bar. No mobile phones. Wheelchair access. Music. Children allowed. Car parking.

The Dining Room
An intimate dining odyssey
33 St John Street, Ashbourne, DE6 1GP
Tel no: (01335) 300666
www.thediningroomashbourne.co.uk
Modern European | £37
Cooking score: 4

A creaking wooden gate makes for a humble entrance to the Dining Room, a tiny restaurant housed in an endearingly wonky seventeenth-century building. Inside, low-beamed ceilings and crisp linen set the scene for an intimate dining odyssey; with only six tables, booking is essential. Guests all arrive for a single sitting, before being guided, dish by dish, through the ambitious set menus. At his best, chef Peter Dale can orchestrate a brave chorus of flavours: potted Ross-shire salmon served with a pipette of compressed cucumber, goats' cheese and pink grapefruit perhaps, or smoked pig's cheek with foie gras snow and sea buckthorn-berry purée. Expect unusual interludes between courses – homemade still elderflower lemonade served in a test tube, or a refresher of frozen Essex gooseberry and green tea, for example. This spirit of adventure means that the odd misfire is easily forgiven; sweetcorn and popcorn doughnut was one noble mistake on a 16-course inspection meal. Desserts are every bit as intricate – elderflower-macerated strawberries, cherry cake and blueberry lemonade jelly with chocolate and almond soil was a worthy finale. A thorough wine list, arranged by style, includes house selections from £18.

Chef/s: Peter Dale. **Open:** Tue to Sat D only 7 (1 sitting). **Closed:** Sun, Mon, 1 week over Shrove Tue, 1 week Sept, last 2 weeks Dec. **Meals:** Set weekday D £37 (7 courses). Sat D £45 (16 courses). **Service:** not inc. **Details:** Cards accepted. 16 seats. No mobile phones. Wheelchair access. Music.

Bakewell

READERS RECOMMEND
Piedaniel's
French
Bath Street, Bakewell, DE45 1BX
Tel no: (01629) 812687
www.piedaniels-restaurant.com
'Good food – so much so we returned two days later for another delicious meal'

Baslow
Cavendish Hotel, Gallery Restaurant
A very English eatery
Church Lane, Baslow, DE45 1SP
Tel no: (01246) 582311
www.cavendish-hotel.net
Modern British | £39
Cooking score: 4

The Cavendish Hotel stands on the edge of the Chatsworth Estate and feels very English: it is small scale, and more comfortable than grand, although its ducal inheritance is evident in the ancestral portraits from Chatsworth House lining the walls. The Gallery Restaurant continues serenely on its way, despite yet another change of chef, winning fans with its agreeable atmosphere, good food, and service provided by 'pleasant staff'. The cooking style is broad-ranging, maybe cod cheeks with veal risotto and pea purée alongside oxtail soup with horseradish and Bakewell beer dumplings to begin. Among main courses there might be smoked haddock tortellini served with grilled black pudding, celeriac purée and a poached duck egg or six-hour braised saddle of lamb with a mini shepherd's pie. Puddings are popular, be they chocolate délice or iced Bakewell cream slice. More informal meals in the Garden Room have also been praised. House wine is £15.70.

Chef/s: Wayne Rogers. **Open:** all week L 12 to 2.30, D 6.30 to 10. **Meals:** Set L and D £30.25 (2 courses) to £39.45. **Service:** 5%. **Details:** Cards accepted. 50 seats. Separate bar. No mobile phones. Music. Children allowed. Car parking.

Fischer's Baslow Hall
Stunning food in a starry retreat
Calver Road, Baslow, DE45 1RR
Tel no: (01246) 583259
www.fischers-baslowhall.co.uk
Modern European | £72
Cooking score: 7

🍷 🛏

Don't be taken in by the tall chimneys, mullioned windows and gabled wings, Baslow Hall was actually erected in 1907 for a local vicar with an appetite for all things archaic. Since 1988 it has been in the hands of Max and Susan Fischer, whose painstaking approach to hospitality has transformed the place into a starry retreat without the turgid, stiff-collared formality that often blights country hotels. Much depends on the food, and the kitchen is capable of great things – although high prices are becoming a bugbear with readers. The 'menu du jour' has delivered some cracking stuff including a heavenly Yorkshire blue cheese pannacotta with hazelnut tuile and spiced pear sorbet, as well as classic roast pheasant breast wrapped in Parma ham with sauerkraut and Madeira sauce. However, it pays to throw financial caution to the wind and go for the high-end 'gourmet menu', which is a dazzling showcase for Rupert Rowley's true talents. Fashionable meat/fish pairings are something of a calling card – witness pan-fried scallops with braised oxtail, parsnip purée and black pudding or crispy pork cheek with langoustine, carrot and star anise. Like everything else, mains take their cue from judicious seasonal sourcing and top-drawer raw materials, but there is a free-thinking imagination at work here: loin of wild venison might be sharpened up with blackberry vinegar and sloe gin, while mango and coriander are used to enhance poached fillet of turbot and a fricassee of lobster and squid. The Anglo-European cheeseboard gets full marks, closely followed by 'extremely competent' desserts such as cheeky Mississippi mud pie with mandarin sorbet and pistachio 'soil'. Service is generally in tune with the Fischers' diligence, although there have been gripes about 'obsequious', clumsy staff. The worldwide wine list is as classy as they come, although you will need a fat wallet to enjoy its deepest French treasures; look to the New World for the best value. House recommendations start at £21 (£5 a glass).
Chef/s: Rupert Rowley. **Open:** Tue to Sun L 12 to 1.30, Mon to Sat D 7 to 8.30. **Closed:** 25 and 26 Dec. **Meals:** Set L £28 (2 courses) to £33. Set D £42 (2 courses) to £48. Gourmet D £72. Sun L £38. Tasting menu £68. **Service:** not inc. **Details:** Cards accepted. 40 seats. Separate bar. No music. No mobile phones. Car parking.

Rowley's
Lively brasserie with comfort food
Church Lane, Baslow, DE45 1RY
Tel no: (01246) 583880
www.rowleysrestaurant.co.uk
Modern British | £30
Cooking score: 1

£5 OFF

Purple walls and flamboyant canvases might seem a bit incongruous in a former pub on the fringes of the Peak District; however Rowley's has made a name for itself as a lively destination for diners returning from a stroll in the Chatsworth Estate. Reports have been mixed of late, and an inspection highlighted inconsistencies on the menu. A starter of ham hock, quails' eggs and capers was let down by an uninspired main of slow-cooked chicken leg with wilted baby gem and spring vegetables. Pork chop with mashed potato and rich wholegrain mustard sauce proved a more satisfying example of the comfort food on offer here. A respectable wine list opens with house selections from £16.
Chef/s: Rupert Rowley. **Open:** all week L 12 to 2 (2.30 Sat, 3 Sun), Mon to Sat D 5.30 to 9 (6 to 10 Fri and Sat). **Closed:** 1 Jan. **Meals:** alc (main courses £13 to £19). Set L £19.50 (2 courses) to £23.50. **Service:** not inc. **Details:** Cards accepted. 60 seats. 12 seats outside. Separate bar. Wheelchair access. Music. Car parking.

▌Beeley

The Devonshire Arms

Well-to-do country inn
Devonshire Square, Beeley, DE4 2NR
Tel no: (01629) 733259
www.devonshirebeeley.co.uk
Gastropub | £25
Cooking score: 3

🛏 V £30

This renovated country inn on the edge of the Chatsworth Estate makes the most of its 250-year-old building. There's a bar with all the appeal of a traditional village pub, or you can move into the contemporary brasserie where plate glass, bright colours and modern furniture reflect the Duchess of Devonshire's hand in the décor. There's an all-day menu and lunchtime sandwiches, as well as a carte that delivers good flavours from well-sourced ingredients. Cauliflower and curd cheese mousse with ham hock roulade may be among starters, while well-presented main courses include slow-cooked chicken leg with Punjabi spinach curry and spicy basmati rice or a pubby ham, egg and chips. While the food is given the thumbs-up, reports indicate that service continues to let the side down. House wine is £14.95.
Chef/s: Alan Hill and Daniel Farrand. **Open:** all week L 12 to 3, D 6 to 9.30. **Meals:** alc (main courses £10 to £22). Sun L £13.95. **Service:** not inc. **Details:** Cards accepted. 77 seats. 60 seats outside. Separate bar. Music. Children allowed. Car parking.

▌Bradwell

NEW ENTRY

The Samuel Fox Inn

A favourite come rain or shine
Stretfield Road, Bradwell, S33 9JT
Tel no: (01433) 621562
www.samuelfox.co.uk
Gastropub | £25
Cooking score: 1

£5 OFF 🛏 £30

Named after a local lad who made his fortune in umbrella sales, the Samuel Fox stays true to its origins as a village pub. Regulars chat at the bar, while a dining area wraps around in a horseshoe shape – the luckier tables can claim the Bradwell Edge escarpment as a backdrop. A dish of lamb with Henderson's Relish hash (a local speciality, for the uninitiated) wowed one visitor, with other hearty mains including cottage pie or pan-fried salmon on crushed new potatoes. A good stock of desserts provide a fitting conclusion. House wines start at £15 a bottle.
Chef/s: Charles Curran. **Open:** all week L 12 to 2, D 6 to 9 (9.30 Fri and Sat, 9 Sun). **Meals:** alc (main courses £9 to £16). Set L £12 (2 courses) to £15. **Service:** not inc. **Details:** Cards accepted. 45 seats. 20 seats outside. Wheelchair access. Music. Children allowed. Car parking.

▌Buxton

READERS RECOMMEND

Nat's Kitchen

Modern British
9-11 Market Street, Buxton, SK17 6JY
Tel no: (01298) 214642
www.natskitchen.co.uk
'Always good and service never lets me down'

Chesterfield

NEW ENTRY

Non Solo Vino

Enterprising wine shop and eatery
417 Chatsworth Road, Brampton, Chesterfield,
S40 3AD
Tel no: (01246) 276760
www.nonsolovino.co.uk
Italian | £27
Cooking score: 3

£5 £30
OFF

Peter Gately and Andrea Sgaravatto's Italian wine shop-cum-restaurant is a real find, and an enterprising addition to the local scene. The menu changes often enough to keep regulars amused, and there have been good reports of scallops with cauliflower purée, apple fondant and wholegrain mustard ice cream, pitch-perfect Carnaroli risottos packed with crab and parsley or wild mushrooms, and a rich chocolate fondant with Carnation milk ice cream. Roast rack of lamb comes with its shoulder braised and herb-crusted, while sea trout is served with pickled fennel, potato and fennel boulangère and sorrel foam. Service is reckoned to be 'top notch', and the whole of Italy is covered by the wine list, which features some reputable producers. Bottles start at £10.50, and 16 come by the glass – thanks to a high-tech Enomatic preservation system.
Chef/s: Matt Bennison. **Open:** Tue to Sat L 12 to 2.30, D 7 to 11. **Closed:** Mon, Sun, 25 and 26 Dec, Easter Sun. **Meals:** alc (main courses from £10 to £20). **Service:** not inc. **Details:** Cards accepted. 36 seats. Air-con. Separate bar. Wheelchair access. Music. Children allowed. Car parking.

ALSO RECOMMENDED

▲ The Old Post

43 Holywell Street, Chesterfield, S41 7SH
Tel no: (01246) 279479
www.theoldpostrestaurant.co.uk
Modern British £5
OFF

This fifteenth-century building, a former post office, continues to do sterling service as an intimate restaurant run by a friendly and efficient husband-and-wife team. The cooking has a modern slant, and reporters are eager to sing the praises of fixed-price lunches (£13.25 for two courses) and dinners (£23.50 for two courses). Terrine of feathered game, a darne of salmon with a tapenade crust and sauce vierge, and pannacotta with rhubarb have all been applauded. House wine is £14.95. Open Wed to Fri and Sun L, Tue to Sat D. No credit cards.

Darley Abbey

Darleys

Finely crafted food in an unlikely setting
Darley Abbey Mills, Haslams Lane, Darley Abbey,
DE22 1DZ
Tel no: (01332) 364987
www.darleys.com
Modern British | £35
Cooking score: 4

Housed in a brick-built former cotton mill right on the edge of the river Derwent, Darley's is one of Derbyshire's more idiosyncratic dining experiences: 'beautiful setting; excellent cooking; very interesting menu', ran one reader's notes, but another reports poor service and lack-lustre food. When on form Jonathan Hobson's kitchen can conjure up interesting combinations in dishes such as a home-cured venison with chocolate jelly and pickled red cabbage, or duck confit and pumpkin terrine with orange and anise foam. Things get toned down a little when the likes of wild sea bass with sautéed cabbage and bacon take centre stage, while desserts might include semolina pancakes with a cassis-poached pear and blackcurrant tea ice cream. It all comes with a decent, brasserie-style wine list opening at £14.50 (£3.75 a glass).
Chef/s: Jonathan Hobson and Mark Hadfield. **Open:** all week L 12 to 2 (2.30 Sun), Mon to Sat D 7 to 9.30. **Closed:** bank hols, 2 weeks after 25 Dec. **Meals:** alc (main courses £18 to £22). Set L £15.95 (2 courses) to £17.95. Sun L £20. **Service:** not inc. **Details:** Cards accepted. 65 seats. Air-con. Separate bar. Music. Children allowed. Car parking.

Derby

READERS RECOMMEND

Zest

Modern British
16d George Street, Derby, DE1 1EH
Tel no: (01332) 381101
www.restaurantzest.co.uk
'Refreshingly original, well executed modern British fare and very good value for money'

Froggatt Edge

ALSO RECOMMENDED
▲ The Chequers Inn

Froggatt Edge, S32 3ZJ
Tel no: (01433) 630231
www.chequers-froggatt.com
Gastropub

Year in, year out, this sixteenth-century Peak District inn remains a popular choice for walkers and tourists drawn by the warm, friendly atmosphere, the unpretentious cooking and splendid views. Goats' cheese with polenta chips, poached egg and hollandaise (£6) might precede lamb shank with braised winter vegetables (£15) or smoked haddock and parsley fishcake. Finish with Bakewell pudding and custard (£5.50). House wine is £14.25. Accommodation. Open all week.

Hathersage

The George Hotel

Rugged romance and confident cooking
Main Road, Hathersage, S32 1BB
Tel no: (01433) 650436
www.george-hotel.net
Modern British | £36
Cooking score: 4

£5 OFF 🍴

Former patron Charlotte Brontë found inspiration for her novel *Jane Eyre* while staying at the George Hotel, and to this day it's a place in keeping with the rugged romance of the Peak District. Stone floors, oak-beamed ceilings and roaring fires provide welcome respite for wanderers from the windswept heaths and valleys outside. Meanwhile, Helen Heywood's confident kitchen attracts its own followers from Sheffield and beyond – an inspection starter of smoked duck breast, hazelnut salad and toasted apple brioche was a worthy prelude to a main of pan-fried salmon, served with aubergine and olive-stuffed courgette. Elsewhere, slow-roast five-spiced belly pork with jasmine sticky rice and steamed pak choi represents the occasional deviation from a modern British menu. Traditional desserts hit the right note – warm treacle tart with clotted ice cream, or perhaps coconut rice pudding with glazed pineapple skewers. A comprehensive wine list starts at £14 a bottle.
Chef/s: Helen Heywood. **Open:** all week L 12 to 2.30, D 6.30 to 10 (7 to 10 Sat and Sun). **Meals:** Set L and D £28.65 (2 courses) to £35.75. Sun L £19.95. **Service:** not inc. **Details:** Cards accepted. 50 seats. Separate bar. No mobile phones. Music. Children allowed. Car parking.

Ridgeway

The Old Vicarage

Stellar food and a slice of Arcadia
Ridgeway Moor, Ridgeway, S12 3XW
Tel no: (0114) 2475814
www.theoldvicarage.co.uk
Modern British | £60
Cooking score: 7

£5 OFF 🍷

A beguiling slice of Arcadia just eight miles from Sheffield's sprawling conurbation, this enchanting converted vicarage is squirrelled away amid wild-flower meadows and hidden copses, with lovely walks and gardens laid out by a Victorian horticulturist. Tessa Bramley is an inspired presence in the kitchen, a real expert who understands the garden and wild expanses, sources meticulously from the region and moves confidently through the tangled world of modern cuisine. Her food is complex and seasonal, with an instinctive feel for what is right and natural on the plate: consider a risotto of chestnuts and cob nuts with thyme-roasted beetroot and roast garlic 'spumanti' or a celebration of Yorkshire rhubarb involving a ginger-scented parfait, crisps, a sorbet and star anise syrup. Other stellar examples of her fully focused craft might include saddle of hare on exotically spiced red cabbage with mulled pear purée and a gin-and-tonic jelly or roast fillet of locally reared Charolais beef with caramelised shallots, glazed chicken wing and potato purée spiked with goose liver. She also allows exotic embellishments to make an impact, without surrendering to 'fusion' – tinges of lemongrass relish are applied to pan-fried langoustines, mango granita sets off a risotto of Whitby crab, and caramelised pecans partner ravioli of goats' cheese and dates. As meals draw to a close, English themes return in the guise of old-fashioned puddings with custard, fruit tarts stuffed with Cox's Orange Pippins, slabs of Yorkshire parkin and seasonal ice creams tinged with sweet woodruff from the garden – all contrived into elaborate confections. Finally, unpasteurised cheeses from the cream of British makers take to the stage. Tessa remains the quintessential country host and her staff win everyone over with their enthusiasm and warmth. Wines are sourced through the restaurant's own importing business, and the intelligently chosen list culminates in a roll call of fabulous rare vintages. Big-name European estates and boutique New World growers share the spoils, but for best value go to the page headed '20 basic everyday gluggers for under £20'.

Chef/s: Tessa Bramley and Nathan Smith. **Open:** Tue to Fri L 12.30 to 2, Tue to Sat D 6.30 to 9.30 (6 Sat). **Closed:** Sun, Mon, 26 Dec to 5 Jan. **Meals:** Set L £30 (2 courses) to £40. Set D £60 (4 courses). Tasting menu £65. **Service:** not inc. **Details:** Cards accepted. 40 seats. 16 seats outside. Separate bar. No music. No mobile phones. Wheelchair access. Children allowed. Car parking.

Grow-your-own chefs

An increasing number of chefs are swapping whites for green; the benefit of part-timing as a son of the soil (or employing a gardener) is that you get to cook with the freshest fruit and vegetables.

There are kitchen gardens and kitchen gardens: at **Le Manoir aux Quat'Saisons**, Raymond Blanc's little plot produces 90 types of vegetable and more than 70 herb varieties. You can taste it on every plate.

At **Northcote,** head gardener Andrew Mellin has overseen the gardens' conversion to the organic system. Garden salad is exactly that, while seasonal herbs and leaves go into a light 'foragers'' soup. There are chickens, too.

Winteringham Fields is set in the agricultural heartland of the east, so it's fitting that chef-patron Colin McGurran can select potatoes, roots, pumpkins and tomatoes from the vegetable patch and fruit from the trees in the traditional country garden.

Meanwhile, the gardens at **Mallory Court** are as much for strolling as for harvesting, but the Warwickshire weather is kind to the crops of soft fruit used by chef Simon Haigh in delicate, balanced dishes.

If you can't grow out, grow up. Space is limited in Fitzrovia, so Shane Osborn and the team at **Pied-à-Terre** have created a garden on the roof to supply herbs, edible flowers and veggies to the kitchen.

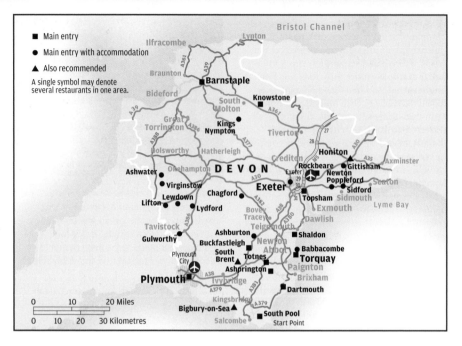

Ashburton

Agaric

Unaffected natural flavours

30 North Street, Ashburton, TQ13 7QD
Tel no: (01364) 654478
www.agaricrestaurant.co.uk
Modern British | £35
Cooking score: 4

Nick and Sophie Coiley's unprepossessing restaurant is a hotbed of industrious foodie enterprise, where diners sit surrounded by shelves of home-produced comestibles – an apt backdrop for food that sings with unaffected natural flavours and immediacy. Local produce is at the heart of things, from a warm salad of pigeon breast with beetroot and raspberry vinegar to twice-baked Jerusalem artichoke and Devon Blue cheese soufflé. Roasted duck breast with steamed and crispy leg is one of Nick's standout mains (perhaps served with a sauce of rhubarb or plums), although he is equally confident tackling an elaborately worked dish of lamb shoulder poached in red wine, stuffed with tapenade then fried in a rosemary crust with cornichon and caper sauce as embellishment. Fish also receives thoughtful treatment – matching steamed turbot with grilled fennel and orange hollandaise feels entirely right – while desserts such as warm pancakes with rhubarb and almond purée are true to the season. The zesty, 30-bin wine list is filled with intriguing bottles at fair prices; house selections start at £17.95.

Chef/s: Nick Coiley. **Open:** Wed to Fri L 12 to 2, Wed to Sat D 7 to 9.30. **Closed:** Mon, Tue, Sun, 2 weeks Aug, 3 weeks Christmas. **Meals:** alc (main courses £15 to £19). Set L £14.95 (2 courses). **Service:** not inc. **Details:** Cards accepted. 28 seats. 15 seats outside. Separate bar. No music. No mobile phones. Wheelchair access. Children allowed.

Ashprington

NEW ENTRY
The Vineyard Café
Quirky alfresco eatery
Sharpham Estate, Ashprington, TQ9 7UT
Tel no: (01803) 732178
www.thevineyardcafe.co.uk
Modern British | £20
Cooking score: 1
£5 OFF **V** £30

Sharpham Estate is a famous foodie enclave noted for its vineyard and cheeses, and it also sports a quirky café with unrivalled views over to the river Dart. You can eat outside or under cover in the marquee, and every climatic change is catered for: parasols in summer, rugs for your knees on chilly days. Rosie Weston cooks in a mobile trailer and her food is fresh, seasonal and locally inclined. Highlights include green pea, mint and Sharpham Rustic cheese fritters, pork belly on bean and chorizo cassoulet, dressed Dartmouth lobster and 'any of her puddings'. Wines from the vineyard start at £9.25 (£3.50 a glass).
Chef/s: Rosie Weston. **Open:** all week L 12 to 2.30 (2.45). **Closed:** Oct to Easter. **Meals:** alc (main courses £9 to £16). Set L £15 (2 courses). **Service:** not inc. **Details:** Cards accepted. 60 seats outside. Wheelchair access. Children allowed. Car parking.

Ashwater
Blagdon Manor
Hospitable hidden gem
Ashwater, EX21 5DF
Tel no: (01409) 211224
www.blagdon.com
Modern British | £38
Cooking score: 2

Hidden away in glorious countryside a few miles north of Launceston, this seventeenth-century Devon longhouse could be a model of its kind. Run as a modest hotel and restaurant, the well-managed operation offers just the sort of hospitality that travellers appreciate.

Nothing is posh or grand, indeed the scale is personable, almost homely. Steve Morey's fixed-price menus are built on an abundance of regional ingredients. Pigeon breast appears with cabbage, sesame seeds, lentils and rosemary, monkfish with olives, sun-blushed tomatoes and saffron creamed potatoes, and meals are rounded off with the likes of hot caramel soufflé with brazil nut brittle ice cream and florentine biscuits. House wine is £14.
Chef/s: Steve Morey. **Open:** Fri to Sun L 12 to 1.30, Wed to Sun D 7 to 9. **Closed:** Mon, Tue, Jan. **Meals:** Set L £17 (2 courses) to £20. Set D £33 (2 courses) to £38. Sun L £25. **Service:** not inc. **Details:** Cards accepted. 28 seats. Separate bar. No music. No mobile phones. Wheelchair access. Car parking.

Babbacombe

NEW ENTRY
The Cary Arms
Chic seaside pub with hearty food
Beach Road, Babbacombe, TQ1 3LX
Tel no: (01803) 327110
www.caryarms.co.uk
Gastropub | £28
Cooking score: 2

Engage low gear and disappear down the unnervingly steep cliff road to reach Peter and Lana de Savary's chic seaside pub-with-rooms, which stands above the beach and a world away from touristy Torquay. Refurbished in 2009, it successfully blends traditional pub trappings (rustic bar, real ales, log fires) with swish boutique bedrooms and a cracking chalkboard menu chock-full of hearty dishes that champion local suppliers. In the kitchen, Ben Kingdon delivers hake with chorizo and wild garlic pesto, roast duck with bacon and shallot sauce, steak and Otter Ale pie, and rhubarb and ginger crumble. Glorious terraces and plashing waves make it perfect for summer alfresco dining; otherwise, just take in the stunning views across Babbacombe Bay. Wines from £14.50.

Chef/s: Ben Kingdon. **Open:** all week L 12 to 3, D 6.30 to 9. **Meals:** alc (main courses £10 to £19). **Service:** not inc. **Details:** Cards accepted. 48 seats. 100 seats outside. Music. Children allowed. Car parking.

Barnstaple

James Duckett at the Old Custom House

A godsend for the neighbourhood
9 The Strand, Barnstaple, EX31 1EU
Tel no: (01271) 370123
www.jamesduckett.co.uk
Modern European | £30
Cooking score: 2

£5
OFF

The oldest building on Barnstaple's Strand was indeed once the custom house – before doing duty as a tobacconist and tearoom – but nowadays it's home to James Duckett's passionately run, 'spot-on' neighbourhood restaurant. Local produce is close to his heart, and he wows the punters with everything from creamed Hallwood Farm Jerusalem artichokes with artichoke crisps to daube of West Country beef with wild mushrooms and parsnip purée. Elsewhere, Creedy chicken leg is stuffed with black pudding and served on pearl barley risotto, while a bonanza of local shellfish goes into a saffron-tinged ragoût. To finish, the pyramid of lime parfait with caramelised figs is a showstopper. Keenly priced wines start at £14.50.
Chef/s: James Duckett. **Open:** Tue to Sat L 12 to 2.30, D 7 to 10. **Closed:** Sun, Mon, 26 Dec, first 2 weeks Jan. **Meals:** alc Fri and Sat D (main courses £14 to £24). Set L £12 (2 courses) to £15. Midweek set D £21 to £26. Tasting menu £65. **Service:** not inc. **Details:** Cards accepted. 52 seats. 16 seats outside. No mobile phones. Wheelchair access. Music. Children allowed.

Visit us online

To find out more about
The Good Food Guide, please visit
www.thegoodfoodguide.co.uk

Bigbury-on-Sea

ALSO RECOMMENDED
▲ The Oyster Shack

Milburn Orchard Farm, Stakes Hill, Bigbury-on-Sea, TQ7 4BE
Tel no: (01548) 810876
www.oystershack.co.uk
Seafood

A little way off the A379 is this quirky, hugely popular seafood restaurant, where crabs and lobsters from Salcombe, and oysters with various dressings (or none at all), are the main draw. 'Our crabs are not dressed', advises the menu. 'We simply crack them and you do the rest' – the rest involving mayonnaise, bread, and onion and cucumber chutney. Favourite dishes are sold by imperial measurements, such as moules marinière by the pound (£9.50, or £11.45 with skinny chips), and prawns Marie Rose by the pint (£6). Wines from £14.95. The Shack is also open for breakfasts, from 9am. Closed Sun D.

Buckfastleigh

Riverford Field Kitchen

Organic farm where cooking shines
Wash Barn, Buckfastleigh, TQ11 0JU
Tel no: (01803) 762074
www.riverford.co.uk
British | £23
Cooking score: 4

£30

If you want to see where your food is coming from, take a tour of the organic farm before dropping into the 'field kitchen' to sample the fruits of Riverford's agricultural endeavours. Hungry punters sit at communal tables, and sharing is the order of the day as large bowls are passed around. The blackboard menu is mostly veggie, although one meat dish is generally on show: grilled chermoula leg of lamb on chickpeas, tomatoes, peppers and parsnip purée passed with flying colours at inspection. Chef Jane Baxter has a red-hot CV and it shows in the sheer quality and vigour of her food: 'I've never tasted vegetables as good', exclaimed one reader – perhaps referring to roast saffron potatoes with almonds and thyme or braised carrots with beetroot, lentils, mint and feta. Queue up for puds, which might include rhubarb and maple syrup pavlova. The organic wine list starts at £14.95. **Chef/s:** Jane Baxter. **Open:** all week L 1pm (1 sitting), Tue to Sat D 7.30 (1 sitting). **Closed:** 23 Dec to 15 Jan. **Meals:** Set L £17.50 (2 courses). Set D £22.50 (3 courses). **Service:** not inc. **Details:** Cards accepted. 64 seats. No music. Wheelchair access. Children allowed. Car parking.

▮ Chagford
Gidleigh Park
Assured cooking in a blissful setting
Chagford, TQ13 8HH
Tel no: (01647) 432367
www.gidleigh.com
Modern European | £45
Cooking score: 7
£5 OFF 🍷 🍴 V

The Gidleigh package is quite something, for first-timers and old hands alike. The hotel is approached via a tortuous, scarily narrow roadway that winds through woodland and across streams, until a broad-fronted black-and-white house rises magisterially on the hillside before you. Built in the Edwardian era, it's all wood-panelled Elizabethan pastiche inside, with a pair of interconnecting dining rooms. The views over the descending land from a little terrace are almost as appetising as Michael Caines' food, from superb canapés onwards. It should be acknowledged that it all comes at quite a cost – especially if you are ordering from the carte. What you get is cooking of immaculate polish, demonstrating formidable attention to detail throughout. A vivid green risotto is infused with essence of nettles, diced snails and tiny mushrooms, and further garnished with plump crayfish and battered frogs' legs, a triumphant first-course performance. That might be followed by a complex construction involving a boudin of John Dory set about with whole chunks of the fish and some langoustines, balanced on a piece of thick-cut

belly pork, with wisps of gingered apple purée, segments of pink grapefruit, and dabs of a chicken stock and vanilla jus. It could so easily be a car-crash, and yet the balance and technically near-flawless execution (could the pork belly have been a mite crisper?) are hugely impressive. Nor do desserts aim to cosset you simply with creamy blandness. A banana parfait comes sandwiched between squares of dark frozen chocolate, adorned with an exhilaratingly sour lime sorbet. Eating from the cheaper lunch menu delivers good stuff too, perhaps a tripartite dish of roast duckling breast, confit leg and a duck stew with fennel and bacon, but portions are noticeably lighter. An army of service staff is fully on the ball, and the wine list is inevitably stuffed with VIP producers at top-dollar prices. Glass prices open at £8.50 for the excellent Sancerre of Henri Bourgeois. **Chef/s:** Michael Caines and Ian Webber. **Open:** all week L 12 to 2.30, D 6.30 to 9.30. **Meals:** Set L £35 (2 courses) to £45. Set D £95 (3 courses). Sun L £35. Tasting menu £115 (7 courses). **Service:** not inc. **Details:** Cards accepted. 52 seats. Separate bar. No music. No mobile phones. Wheelchair access. Car parking.

▮ Dartmouth
The Seahorse
Lively eatery with wonderful fish
5 South Embankment, Dartmouth, TQ6 9BH
Tel no: (01803) 835147
www.seahorserestaurant.co.uk
Seafood | £45
Cooking score: 4
£5 OFF 🍷

The main attraction of any waterside restaurant called the Seahorse is likely to be fish, and on that score Mitch Tonks' lively eatery overlooking Dartmouth quayside comes up trumps. The menu does not shy away from adventure and may turn up roasted mackerel with North African spices, or local cuttlefish braised in Chianti with borlotti beans, but skate roasted with black butter suggests more traditional treatments are in evidence too. A starter of Bismarck pickled herrings impressed one visitor – 'much more solid than traditional soused herrings' – as did a well-timed sea bream cooked 'al cartoccio' (in paper) with chilli, roasted garlic, rosemary and olive oil. Cornish lamb chops or a single rib of South Devon beef should please meat eaters. For dessert, sticky toffee pudding has been praised yet again. The wine list is packed with good bottles and stretches to some prestigious offerings, from £18.

Chef/s: Mitch Tonks and Mat Prowse. **Open:** Wed to Sat L 12 to 3, Tue to Sat D 6 to 10. **Closed:** Sun, Mon. **Meals:** alc (main courses £15 to £25). Set L £15 (2 courses) to £20. **Service:** not inc. **Details:** Cards accepted. 40 seats. 4 seats outside. Air-con. Wheelchair access. Music. Children allowed.

▌Exeter
Michael Caines at ABode Exeter
Grown-up chic and full-flavoured food
Royal Clarence Hotel, Cathedral Yard, Exeter, EX1 1HD
Tel no: (01392) 223638
www.michaelcaines.com
Modern European | £46
Cooking score: 5

🍷 V

Grown-up chic is what you get the moment you walk through the doors of the Royal Clarence Hotel. The smart bar sets the tone, while the restaurant has a cool, contemporary look with polished boards and bold canvasses inspired by Exeter Cathedral, which you can see through the windows. Fixed-price menus offer an appealing repertoire of full-flavoured dishes that often include some unusual but accomplished combinations: perhaps a starter of salmon confit with Puy lentils, herb purée, horseradish and Parmesan sauce and, for main course, a prettily presented sea bream with Thai purée, stir-fried shiitake mushrooms, mangetout and lemongrass foam. Elsewhere, Tom Williams-Hawkes makes good use of well-sourced produce from the region's abundant larder, perhaps serving Brixham-landed John Dory with crushed olive potato,

baby leeks, roasted langoustine and shellfish bisque, or loin of local lamb with fondant potato, onion and thyme purée and tapenade sauce. Desserts are indulgent and beautifully crafted, for instance white chocolate and vodka with plum jus, pepper tuile and yoghurt sorbet. House wine is £22.50.

Chef/s: Tom Williams-Hawkes. **Open:** Mon to Sat L 12 to 2.30, D 6 to 10. **Closed:** Sun. **Meals:** alc (main courses £20 to £25). Set L £14.50 (2 courses) to £19.50. Set D £14.95 (2 courses) to £19.95. **Service:** 12% (optional). **Details:** Cards accepted. 60 seats. Air-con. Separate bar. No mobile phones. Wheelchair access. Music. Children allowed.

▌Gittisham
Combe House
Splendour and food with pizzazz
Gittisham, EX14 3AD
Tel no: (01404) 540400
www.combehousedevon.com
Modern British | £48
Cooking score: 5

🍷 🍴 V

From the moment you begin the mile-long meander up the drive, Combe House begins to exert its impossibly romantic charms. Arab horses canter in the grounds, pheasants break cover and then the eye-popping, Grade I-listed manor comes into view. It's a sight to behold in all its Elizabethan splendour, although the whole place is run with a mix of personable good humour and common courtesy – no furtive tiptoeing or doffing-of-caps pomposity here. Outside, there's serious horticultural enterprise at work in the restored Victorian kitchen garden, and chef Hadleigh Barrett takes full advantage of the harvest. Sourcing is important here, and a list of regional suppliers is posted on the menu, which promises confident displays of culinary invention in the shape of, say, scallops with parsnip and vanilla purée and spiced raisins. Mains also show what the kitchen can do with first-class ingredients garnered from Devon's larder and beyond: slow-roast loin of venison is paired with balsamic Puy lentils and caramelised apple, while sea bass keeps

company with crushed ratte potatoes, smoked eel and tarragon, a drizzle of lemon oil and a few olives. There is also plenty of measured pizazz when it comes to desserts such as carpaccio of pineapple with pineapple parfait, coconut and Malibu sorbet. The underground cellars are put to profitable vinous use, and the prestigious list (from £18) avoids snobbery in favour of superb drinking at fair prices.
Chef/s: Hadleigh Barrett. **Open:** all week L 12 to 2, D 7 to 9.30. **Closed:** first 2 weeks Jan. **Meals:** Set L £27 (2 courses) to £32. Set D £48. Sun L £35. **Service:** not inc. **Details:** Cards accepted. 75 seats. Separate bar. No mobile phones. Wheelchair access. Music. Children allowed. Car parking.

Gulworthy
The Horn of Plenty
Ravishing views and high-flying food
Gulworthy, PL19 8JD
Tel no: (01822) 832528
www.thehornofplenty.co.uk
Modern European | £47
New Chef
£5 OFF 🍴

Pause at the creeper-clad front entrance of this Georgian manor house to admire the fine views along the wooded Tamar Valley. Inside, it is decorated in traditional county-house style and there are 'wonderful views from the dining room and terrace'. Reporters have emerged full of praise for accurately cooked pot-roast wood pigeon with mushroom tortellinis and garlic and truffle sauce, and fillet of cod with a saffron and white wine velouté. Raw materials are from the top drawer. As we went to press we learned that Peter Gorton had sold the Horn of Plenty, but he will remain as a consultant for the next 18 months. Stuart Downe is staying on as head chef and the emphasis is likely to remain on West Country produce cooked in a refined modern way. Reports please.
Chef/s: Stuart Downe. **Open:** all week L 12 to 2, D 7 to 9. **Meals:** Set L £26.50. Set D £47. **Service:** not inc. **Details:** Cards accepted. 60 seats. 18 seats outside. Air-con. No mobile phones. Music. Children allowed. Car parking.

Honiton
ALSO RECOMMENDED
▲ **The Holt**
178 High Street, Honiton, EX14 1LA
Tel no: (01404) 47707
www.theholt-honiton.com
Modern British

At the western end of this charming market town's high street, not far from the river Gissage, the Holt is a bustling pub/restaurant offering some engaging modern British dishes. Expect the likes of poached salmon with apple purée and spiced lentils (£5.50), followed by glazed pork cheek with 'nose to tail' terrine, smoked mash and sherry vinegar sauce (£14.50), with passion-fruit shortcake and Greek yoghurt sorbet (£5.50) to finish. Wines from £13. Closed Sun and Mon.

Kings Nympton
NEW ENTRY
The Grove Inn
'Tremendous pub' oozing character
Kings Nympton, EX37 9ST
Tel no: (01769) 580406
www.thegroveinn.co.uk
Gastropub | £22
Cooking score: 2
£5 OFF 🍴 V £30

This seventeenth-century pub bang in the middle of a picturesque village oozes character. Being off the beaten track it has to please a variety of customers, and succeeds with its all-day breakfast, surf and turf, and steaks and sandwiches – but other dishes on the blackboard menus show a serious intent. Start, perhaps, with an unusual laverbread soup bursting with flavour, followed by fruity and spicy Moroccan-style lamb served in an authentic tagine dish. To finish, a fresh lemon burnt cream was 'mouth-wateringly creamy – though the brûlée topping was unrelentingly hard'. Wines in this 'tremendous pub' start at £14.50.

Chef/s: Deborah Smallbone. **Open:** Tues to Sun L 12 to 2 (2.30 Sun), Tues to Sat D 7 to 9. **Closed:** 25 Dec. **Meals:** alc (main courses £10 to £17). Sun L £9 to £16 (3 courses). **Service:** not inc. **Details:** Cards accepted. 28 seats. 24 seats outside. Separate bar. No music. No mobile phones. Wheelchair access. Children allowed.

■ Knowstone
The Masons Arms
Dreamy thatched pub with impeccable food
Knowstone, EX36 4RY
Tel no: (01398) 341231
www.masonsarmsdevon.co.uk
Modern British | £38
Cooking score: 6

Mark Dodson cut his culinary teeth in the world of mousselines and veloutés, before upping sticks and moving to this dreamy thatched pub on the fringes of Exmoor – although he wasn't about to give it all up for ploughman's and pies. He opted for a straight-talking approach but kept a handle on his culinary skills, teasing clear natural flavours from shrewdly sourced ingredients and allowing impeccable craftsmanship to do the rest. The result is a pared-back seasonal menu that might open with foie gras and wood pigeon breast tinged with blueberry jus or a re-invented kedgeree involving Parmesan risotto, flaked smoked haddock and poached egg. There's also no attempt to scare the horses when it comes to big-hearted, easy-to-manage main courses such as fillet of sea bass with lentils and roasted garlic or roulade of pork belly with braised red cabbage and apple compote. Pretty desserts are pitched a few notches up from banoffi pie, but no one should baulk at the prospect of iced Amaretto parfait with vanilla-poached plums or a trio of chocolate confections. If a light lunch is required, the kitchen can also oblige by offering home-cured gravlax, wild duck with orange sauce and chocolate brownie for a modest outlay. The succinct wine list promises sound drinking from France and the New World; house recommendations start at £13.60 (£4.75 a glass).

Chef/s: Mark Dodson. **Open:** Tue to Sun L 12 to 2, Tue to Sat D 7 to 9. **Closed:** Mon, first 2 weeks Jan. **Meals:** alc (main courses £17 to £23). Sun L £33.50. **Service:** not inc. **Details:** Cards accepted. 30 seats. 16 seats outside. Separate bar. No music. No mobile phones. Children allowed. Car parking.

■ Lewdown
Lewtrenchard Manor
Vibrant seasonal cooking
Lewdown, EX20 4PN
Tel no: (01566) 783222
www.lewtrenchard.co.uk
Modern British | £51
Cooking score: 6

£5 OFF ♦ ⊨

For many years gabled Lewtrenchard Manor was home to the Gould family – a colourful breed who included a gambler and explorer among their ranks, as well as Victorian reverend-cum-writer Sabine Baring-Gould (author of *Onward, Christian Soldiers*). Despite the remote location, chef/patron Jason Hornbuckle manages to garner an impressive array of West Country produce, in addition to pickings from the manor's restored walled kitchen garden. Seasonal awareness and vibrant contemporary strokes colour just about every finely-honed dish, be it a pressing of slow-cooked chicken leg with truffle marshmallow and crisp ham, or a dessert of fig and butter puff pastry with a mulled wine parfait sphere, crème fraîche and spiced biscotti. In between, caramelised pollack comes with curry-scented cauliflower, palourde clams and almond emulsion, while honey-roast duck breast appears in a more exotic guise with its own sausage, salsify, sesame-scented pak choi and a sauce of honey and lavender. If you want something more personalised, the Purple Carrot private room offers a bespoke experience, with split-screen TVs and viewing areas providing live action from the kitchen. The well-rounded global wine list explores France in depth, but gives space to lively names and mature vintages from elsewhere. A dozen house selections start at £19 (£4.50 a glass).

Chef/s: Jason Hornbuckle and Carl Maxfield. **Open:** all week L 12 to 2, D 7 to 9. **Meals:** Set L £15 (2 courses) to £19. Set D £35 (2 courses) to £55. Sun L £22.50. Tasting menu £75. Light menu available. **Service:** not inc. **Details:** Cards accepted. 65 seats. Separate bar. No mobile phones. Wheelchair access. Music. Children allowed. Car parking.

ALSO RECOMMENDED
▲ The Harris Arms
Portgate, Lewdown, EX20 4PZ
Tel no: (01566) 783331
www.theharrisarms.co.uk
Gastropub £5 OFF

Andy and Rowena Whiteman's homely pub makes the perfect pit-stop with fantastic rolling Devon views from the decked terrace and a menu that champions West Country produce. Hearty dishes take in classics like ham, egg and chips (£9.95) alongside more imaginative offerings, perhaps pigeon with beetroot risotto and red wine sauce (£6.50), and roast loin and braised shoulder of wild venison with Madeira sauce. House wine £15. Closed Sun D and Mon.

▌Lifton
The Arundell Arms
Civilised sporting retreat
Fore Street, Lifton, PL16 0AA
Tel no: (01566) 784666
www.arundellarms.com
Modern British | £35
Cooking score: 4
£5 OFF 🍷 🛏 V

This is undoubtedly one of England's major sporting hotels. It has a quintessentially gentrified English feel, and has changed little over the years. Anne Voss-Bark has now yielded the management to her son, Adam Fox-Edwards, but her quiet influence can still be felt. Steven Pidgeon remains at the helm in the kitchen, and he bases his classical cooking on sound local produce. Start maybe with grilled fillet of sea bream with lentils, spinach and tempered scallop (fish comes from Looe

and St Ives). For main course there might be roasted best end of English lamb, or pan-fried cutlet of turbot. Finish with a comforting pudding such as rhubarb parfait with marinated oranges. The wine list has a core of French classics with a good selection from other Old World and New World vineyards. There are plenty of half-bottles, and plenty by the glass. House wines start at £16.
Chef/s: Steven Pidgeon. **Open:** all week L 12 to 2.30, D 7 to 10. **Meals:** alc (main courses £17 to £30). Set L £18 (2 courses) to £22.50. Set D £34.95. Sun L £18 (2 courses) to £24. **Service:** not inc. **Details:** Cards accepted. 100 seats. 40 seats outside. Separate bar. No mobile phones. Wheelchair access. Music. Children allowed. Car parking.

▌Lydford
The Dartmoor Inn
Charmer with local leanings
Moorside, Lydford, EX20 4AY
Tel no: (01822) 820221
www.dartmoorinn.com
Modern British | £28
Cooking score: 3
£5 OFF 🛏 £30

The Burgess family's cracking rural inn comes with a full quota of nooks and crannies, and even has its own boutique. It also supports Devon produce in a big way, with a list of suppliers displayed on the specials board. The kitchen serves a mix of upmarket pub grub and ambitious restaurant-style food ranging from mushroom and thyme risotto cakes or scallop and courgette flower fritters to rump of lamb with Indian spices and saffron sauce. Confit duck leg with red cabbage in a red wine sauce and rhubarb sorbet with a shortbread biscuit have been well received, although some reports suggest inconsistencies in the kitchen. Bottles on the short wine list start at £14.50.
Chef/s: Andrew Honey and Philip Burgess. **Open:** Tue to Sun L 12 to 2.30 (3 Sat and Sun), Mon to Sat D 6 to 10. **Meals:** alc (main courses £10 to £27). Set L and D £16.50 (2 courses) to £21.50. Sun L £26.50.

Service: not inc. **Details:** Cards accepted. 70 seats. 18 seats outside. Separate bar. No music. No mobile phones. Children allowed. Car parking.

∎ Newton Poppleford

Moores'

Personally run local eatery
6 Greenbank, High Street, Newton Poppleford, EX10 0EB
Tel no: (01395) 568100
www.mooresrestaurant.co.uk
Modern British | £32
Cooking score: 1

£5 OFF 🍴

A converted village shop up on the 'green bank' overlooking the High Street, Jonathan and Kate Moore's personally run local eatery is a model of tasteful domesticity, and the food rings true. Sound local ingredients are the building blocks for regularly changing menus that might yield pork and rabbit rillettes with cranberry compote followed by roast monkfish with chunky ratatouille, or Devon fillet steak partnered by beetroot and herb dauphinoise and wild mushroom jus. Summer pudding makes a good finish. House wine is £12.95.
Chef/s: Jonathan Moore. **Open:** Tue to Sun L 12 to 1.30 (1 Sat), Tue to Sat D 7 to 9.30 (10 Sat). **Closed:** Mon, first 2 weeks Jan, bank hols. **Meals:** Set L £14.95 (2 courses) to £19.90. Midweek set D £17.50 (2 courses). Weekend set D £22.50 (2 courses) to £27.50. Sun L £14.95. **Service:** not inc.
Details: Cards accepted. 32 seats. 12 seats outside. No mobile phones. Wheelchair access. Music. Children allowed.

∎ Plymouth

Tanners

Stunning building, bang-up-to-date food
Prysten House, Finewell Street, Plymouth, PL1 2AE
Tel no: (01752) 252001
www.tannersrestaurant.com
Modern British | £39
Cooking score: 3

V

Chris and James Tanner certainly picked a prime location in Plymouth to ply their trade. Their stunning restaurant is housed in Prysten House, the oldest surviving domestic building in the city. It dates from 1490 and stands close to the Barbican. In a setting of tapestry-covered stone walls, worn flagstones, ancient beams and vaults the brothers deliver modern British dishes from a menu that's bang up to date and bristling with local meats, line-caught fish and seasonal vegetables. Plump, juicy scallops served with roasted chorizo, peppers and confit lemon, lamb chump with asparagus, peas, broad beans and mint, and a refreshing iced Tamar Valley strawberry parfait are typical of the style. A Verre de Vin system allows for a wide choice of wines by the glass, starting at £3.75; elsewhere, bottles on the carefully annotated list begin at £13.95.
Chef/s: Chris and James Tanner. **Open:** Tue to Sat L 12 to 2.30, D 7 to 9.30. **Closed:** Sun, Mon, 24 to 31 Dec, first 2 weeks Jan. **Meals:** alc (main courses £10 to £23). Set L £17.50 (2 courses) to £22.50. Set D £30 (2 courses) to £39. **Service:** not inc.
Details: Cards accepted. 60 seats. Separate bar. No mobile phones. Wheelchair access. Music. Children allowed.

ALSO RECOMMENDED
▲ Lemon Tree Café & Bistro
2 Haye Road South, Plymouth, PL9 8HJ
Tel no: (01752) 481117
www.lemontreecafe.co.uk
Modern European £5 OFF

'A little gem in one of Plymouth's suburbs', is how one reader describes this very promising bistro. Lunch brings warm pigeon salad with toasted pumpkin, sunflower and sesame seeds (£6.95) or penne pasta with crispy bacon in a creamy mushroom, tomato and chilli sauce; otherwise the must-book, three-course dinner (£24.95) might begin with smoked pork accompanied by apple and beetroot relish. Sea bass fillet with lemon, garlic and thyme is a possible main course, before rhubarb, ginger and almond crumble. House wine £12.95. Closed Sun and Mon.

READERS RECOMMEND
Shallyns
Modern British
5 Old Town Street, Plymouth, PL1 1DA
Tel no: (01752) 221115
www.shallyns.com
'Best restaurant in Plymouth – welcoming staff, great quality food and value for money'

▮ Rockbeare
The Jack in the Green
Devon food champion
London Road, Rockbeare, EX5 2EE
Tel no: (01404) 822240
www.jackinthegreen.uk.com
Modern British | £30
Cooking score: 3
£5 OFF **V**

Paul Parnell is the long-time custodian of this beguilingly unassuming roadside pub. Inside expect to find a traditional bar with local real ales, a series of more contemporary dining areas and a menu from a dependable kitchen team that reveals plenty of conscientious effort in the sourcing of seasonal Devon produce.

The cooking bristles with up-to-the-minute ideas as well as classical variations, with dishes as diverse as home-smoked duck breast with a fig tart and port jus or slow-braised pork belly with hot-pickled pineapple, lamb and vegetable hotpot or fish and chips. Everyone praises the desserts, whether chocolate mousse and mandarin sorbet or banana parfait with pecan cake, white chocolate and lime caramel. Staff are 'always very welcoming'. House wine is £15.50.
Chef/s: Mat Mason and Scott Paton. **Open:** all week L 12 to 2, D 6 to 9 (9.30 Thur to Sat). **Closed:** 25 Dec to 5 Jan. **Meals:** alc (main courses £10 to £24). Set L and D £19.50 (2 courses) to £25. Sun L £24.50.
Service: not inc. **Details:** Cards accepted. 130 seats. 80 seats outside. Air-con. Separate bar. Wheelchair access. Music. Children allowed. Car parking.

▮ Shaldon
★ BEST USE OF LOCAL PRODUCE ★
Ode
An organic gem
21 Fore Street, Shaldon, TQ14 0DE
Tel no: (01626) 873977
www.odetruefood.co.uk
Modern British | £32
Cooking score: 5
£5 OFF

True food values and a passion for sourcing the finest seasonal Devon produce are at the heart of Tim and Clare Bouget's tiny restaurant, which occupies the ground floor of their three-storey Georgian town house. Using ethically reared meats, line-caught fish and local organic fruit and vegetables, and inspired by his global travels, Tim injects vivid flavours and some bold combinations into his innovative modern British cooking. Dinner may kick off with an intensely flavoured black olive tapenade appetiser, served with homemade flatbread. Seared squid with shaved fennel, radish salad and a zingy Asian dressing or delicately steamed fillet of sole with ginger, turmeric, lime and coconut milk may follow. Equally impressive main courses range from beautifully cooked rump of Manx

Loaghtan lamb with potato gratin, celeriac purée and thyme jus, to squeaky-fresh sea bass with spider crab, basil quinoa, warm tomato and lemon olive oil, while rhubarb crumble tart with poached meringue or a plate of artisan farmhouse cheeses make a fitting finale. Ode is certified by the Soil Association, and the 100% organic wine list starts at £18.50.

Chef/s: Tim Bouget. **Open:** Thur and Fri L 12 to 1.30, Wed to Sat D 7 to 9.30. **Closed:** Sun to Tue, 2 weeks Oct, bank hols. **Meals:** alc (main courses £17 to £22). Set L £17.50 (2 courses) to £21.50. **Service:** not inc. **Details:** Cards accepted. 24 seats. No mobile phones. Wheelchair access. Music. Children allowed. Car parking.

▌ Sidford

NEW ENTRY
The Salty Monk
Homemade food to be proud of
Church Street, Sidford, EX10 9QP
Tel no: (01395) 513174
www.saltymonk.co.uk
Modern British | £40
Cooking score: 4
£5 OFF 🛏

Situated opposite St Peter's Church, this cream building with faux-Gothic windows was originally a salt house used by the Benedictine monks who traded the stuff at Exeter Cathedral. The tables in the sophisticated dining room overlooking a landscaped garden are impeccably laid, and both Annette and Andy Witheridge take pride in their food and service. Both were trained as chefs, but Andy is in charge of the kitchen. He attracts a loyal following for good-value lunch and dinner menus and for his eight-course tasting extravaganza on Friday and Saturday nights. A typical lunch might start with a salad of marinated seared scallops with homemade tomato and chilli pasta ribbons, go on to roast breast of duck on a spicy cassoulet, and finish with apple and fig tarte Tatin with walnut and orange pastry. Everything – from the bread to the ice creams and petits fours – is homemade. House wines are £14.75.

Chef/s: Andy Witheridge. **Open:** Thurs to Sun L 12 to 2.30, all week D 6 to 9. **Closed:** 2 weeks Nov, Jan. **Meals:** Set L £25 (2 courses) to £29.50. Set D £36.50 (2 courses) to £39.50. Tasting menu £49 (8 courses). **Service:** not inc. **Details:** Cards accepted. 32 seats. 16 seats outside. Separate bar. Wheelchair access. Music. Children allowed. Car parking.

▌ South Brent

ALSO RECOMMENDED
▲ The Turtley Corn Mill
Avonwick, South Brent, TQ10 9ES
Tel no: (01364) 646100
www.avonwick.net
Gastropub £5 OFF

Today's incarnation of this comfortably appointed mill house by the banks of the river Glazebrook is an affable inn with a kitchen that mixes old favourites with more modern ideas. Tried-and-tested dishes include homemade Scotch eggs with plum chutney (£5.95) and chicken, mushroom and leek pie, but the menu might also flag up the likes of wild sea bass with fennel risotto or char-grilled Thai beef salad (£12.95). For afters, perhaps blueberry cheesecake or seasonal fruit crumble (£5.95). House wine is £13.95. Open all week. Accommodation.

▌ South Pool

NEW ENTRY
The Millbrook Inn
Buzzy pub peddling Devon produce
South Pool, TQ7 2RW
Tel no: (01548) 531581
www.millbrookinnsouthpool.co.uk
Modern British | £28
Cooking score: 2

Drive down steep-sided lanes to reach this 400-year-old pub (or, if the tide is right, arrive by boat from Salcombe, mooring in the pretty creek that juts into the village). There's a rustic bar with a buzzy vibe and monthly changing menus celebrating local produce, from Start Bay crab and Teign mussels to British White Beef reared at nearby Diptford. Pig's trotter

patties ahead of seafood casserole or whole cock crab with aïoli, are typical choices, with strawberry pithivier and clotted-cream ice cream as a fine finale. Sunday roasts (and jazz) have been endorsed. Wines from £14.
Chef/s: Jean-Philippe Bidart. **Open:** all week L 12 to 2, D 7 to 9. **Meals:** alc (main courses £11 to £24). Set L £15 (2 courses) to £20. **Service:** 10% (optional). **Details:** Cards accepted. 38 seats. 48 seats outside. No music. Children allowed.

∎ Topsham
La Petite Maison
Happy vibes and accomplished food
35 Fore Street, Topsham, EX3 0HR
Tel no: (01392) 873660
www.lapetitemaison.co.uk
Modern European | £36
Cooking score: 4

£5
OFF

Everyone mentions the wonderfully warm welcome, engagingly friendly service and happy vibes that pervade this centuries-old building a stone's throw from the river Exe in fashionable Topsham. True to the name, there's something of the French auberge about this 'petite maison', and it displays its heritage with white stucco, a bow window and other homely touches. The tone may be Gallic, but native West Country ingredients including Lyme Bay crab, free-range Creedy Carver duck and outdoor-reared Somerset pork define proceedings on Douglas Pestell's seasonal menu. Typically accomplished dishes might run to seared pigeon breast with parsnip purée, red wine jus and an accompanying croûton topped with warm foie gras, or a satisfying combination of sea bass fillet and monkfish with chive potato cake and chive beurre blanc. To finish, warm almond and apricot tart with Amaretto mascarpone cream went down a treat with one reader. French names loom large on the even-handed wine list, which opens with house selections from £16.95 (£4.25 a glass).

Chef/s: Douglas Pestell and Sarah Bright. **Open:** Tue to Sat L 12.30 to 2, D 7 to 10. **Closed:** Sun, Mon, 26 Dec. **Meals:** Set L and D £29.95 (2 courses) to £35.95. **Service:** not inc. **Details:** Cards accepted. 26 seats. No mobile phones. Music. Children allowed.

∎ Torquay
The Elephant
Sleek, imaginative cooking
3-4 Beacon Terrace, Torquay, TQ1 2BH
Tel no: (01803) 200044
www.elephantrestaurant.co.uk
Modern British | £45
Cooking score: 5

£5
OFF

Downstairs for fixed-price menus delivering modern British brasserie dishes, upstairs for dinner in 'The Room' and views across Torbay harbour. The Elephant wears its style where you can see it. But Simon Hulstone is a technician who manages to do the set-piece modern dishes with more *élan* than others. What awaits you upstairs is sleek, imaginative cooking along the lines of John Dory with parsnip purée and a spring onion and sultana verjus butter, or Torbay scallops with lemon and cabbage risotto. Dishes are rooted reliably in the region, a main course rump of new season's lamb with summer vegetables and thyme gnocchi, for example, followed by locally grown raspberries in a mille-feuille with vanilla ice cream. Service is declared 'friendly' and the interior modish, with a smart cocktail bar adjoining the restaurant. This year, however, the ground-floor brasserie has drawn criticism for 'minute portions' and one visitor noted that 'everything was extra, even bread with soup', on the fixed-price menu. House wine is £15.50.
Chef/s: Simon Hulstone. **Open:** Brasserie Tue to Sat L 12 to 2, D 6.30 to 9. Restaurant Tue to Sat D only 6.30 to 9. **Closed:** Sun, Mon, first 2 weeks Jan. **Meals:** Brasserie Set L £16.50 (2 courses) to £29.50. Set D £27 (2 courses) to £32.50. Restaurant Set D £45 (3 courses). Tasting menu £55. **Service:** 10% (optional). **Details:** Cards accepted. 74 seats. Separate bar. Wheelchair access. Music. Children allowed.

Totnes

Effings

Delightful deli/café
50 Fore Street, Totnes, TQ9 5RP
Tel no: (01803) 863435
www.effings.co.uk
Modern European | £21
Cooking score: 2

£30

Not to be missed when browsing Totnes's eclectic range of shops is this little deli-cum-café, situated just below the East Gate arch on the main street. There are just five tables tucked away behind laden shelves and a deli-counter chock-full of charcuterie and cheeses, so you may need to time your arrival for noon to bag a table for lunch. This is superior food: a plate of delicious homemade terrines and pâtés served with dressed leaves and crispy bread, perhaps, or look to the daily chalkboard for spinach, mozzarella and Parmesan tart, kedgeree or roast poussin. Booking is essential for the themed set dinners. House wine is £13.75. **Chef/s:** Karl Rasmussen. **Open:** Mon to Sat 9 to 5 (L 12 to 2.15). **Closed:** Sun, 25 and 26 Dec, 1 Jan, bank hols. **Meals:** alc (main courses £8 to £14). **Service:** not inc. **Details:** Cash only. 12 seats. No music. No mobile phones. Wheelchair access. Children allowed.

NEW ENTRY

The Kingsbridge Inn

Sophisticated modern food amid the history
9 Leechwell Street, Totnes, TQ9 5SY
Tel no: (01803) 863324
www.thekingsbridgeinn.com
Modern British | £27
Cooking score: 2

V £30

Step inside this seventeenth-century inn at the top of trendy Totnes to find painted stone walls, beams and a flagstone floor all brought up to date to create a sophisticated place to eat. Simon Greene cooks a short menu of modern dishes based on locally sourced raw materials.

Dinner might start with char-grilled Brixham scallop with cauliflower and vanilla purée, go on to roast lamb rump, confit shoulder with tomato and aubergine ragoût or pan-fried pollack with olive potatoes, chorizo and almond butter, and finish with bay leaf pannacotta with Pedro Ximénez baby pears. House wines are £12.95.
Chef/s: Simon Greene. **Open:** all week L 12 to 2.30, D 6.30 to 9. **Meals:** alc (main courses £12 to 19). Sun L £10. **Service:** not inc. **Details:** Cards accepted. 40 seats. 20 seats outside. Separate bar. Music. Children allowed.

Virginstow

Percy's Country Hotel

Food doesn't get more local than this
Coombeshead Estate, Virginstow, EX21 5EA
Tel no: (01409) 211236
www.percys.co.uk
British | £40
Cooking score: 4

'It's a smart and sophisticated place to dine and stay', noted a visitor to Tina and Tony Bricknell-Webb's country hotel. It's also a thriving concern, a 130-acre organic farm which is virtually 'a living pantry' – raw materials rarely get as local as this. Tina cooks, and dinner is a limited-choice affair – main items on the menu are simply recited to guests on arrival – with Tony an amiable front-of-house host. The quality of the enterprising food is undeniably good, from the homemade breads and the amuse of pumpkin and mixed grain broth, via a squid, scallop and sweet-cure bacon salad with mustard and honey, to a main course of pink lamb, and finale of lemon tart with homemade cardamom ice cream. Waits between courses proved 'excruciating' for one reporter – although he concluded that 'this is in many ways an exceptional place'. Wines begin at £20.
Chef/s: Tina Bricknell-Webb. **Open:** all week D only 7 to 9. **Meals:** Set D £40. **Service:** not inc.
Details: Cards accepted. 24 seats. Separate bar. No music. No mobile phones. Wheelchair access. Car parking.

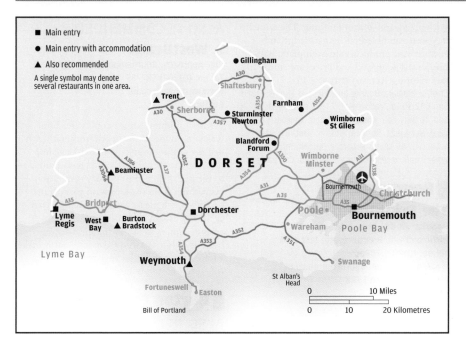

- ■ Main entry
- ● Main entry with accommodation
- ▲ Also recommended

A single symbol may denote several restaurants in one area.

DORSET

■ Beaminster

▲ The Wild Garlic
4 The Square, Beaminster, DT8 3AS
Tel no: (01308) 861446
www.thewildgarlic.co.uk
British £5 OFF

Mat Follas was the 2009 winner of the BBC's *MasterChef* series, and opened on this pretty little square in the town centre not long after being garlanded. Chunky wood tables, fish pictures and a green colour scheme are the backdrop for an unbuttoned approach and an atmosphere of cool relaxation. Seasoning can be erratic, but ingredients are good. The chalkboard menu offers the likes of squid and English chorizo salad (£8), Barnsley chops with pesto and crushed new potatoes (£15), and passion-fruit and rosewater pannacotta (£6). Wine from £14. Open Mon to Sat L, Wed to Sat D.

■ Blandford Forum

Castleman Hotel
Food that deserves attention
Chettle, Blandford Forum, DT11 8DB
Tel no: (01258) 830096
www.castlemanhotel.co.uk
Modern British | £25
Cooking score: 2
🍷 🛏 £30

This lovely old building is a former dower house, much enlarged and remodelled in Victorian times. Its elegant proportions and period features have survived conversion to a hotel and restaurant, providing plenty to catch the eye. The food, too, certainly deserves its share of attention. The kitchen garden provides much of the produce, as do the surrounding estates – witness local pheasant served as a starter, or as a main course braised with chorizo, red wine, Puy lentils and tomato. Other choices include chicken liver parfait with marrow and red pepper chutney, and sea bass with dill and lemon butter. Finish

with bread-and-butter pudding. The wine list has been assembled with knowledge and enthusiasm; producers are exemplary, half-bottles show up well and prices are eminently fair. House selections start at £13.
Chef/s: Barbara Bourke and Richard Morris. **Open:** Sun L 12.30 to 2, all week D 7 to 9.30. **Closed:** 25, 26 and 31 Dec, Feb. **Meals:** alc (main courses £10 to £20). Set L £21. **Service:** not inc. **Details:** Cards accepted. 45 seats. Separate bar. No music. Wheelchair access. Children allowed. Car parking.

Bournemouth

The Print Room
Popular all-day brasserie
Richmond Hill, Bournemouth, BH2 6HH
Tel no: (01202) 789669
www.theprintroom-bournemouth.co.uk
Modern European | £22
Cooking score: 2

A buzzy atmosphere, friendly service, all-day opening and good-value, flexible menus make this airy contemporary brasserie and bar an understandably popular spot. The repertoire is wide-ranging, taking in starters of wild mushrooms on toasted brioche with duck egg and red onion jam, and main courses of crab linguine, lobster thermidor and roast peppered duck breast with orange marmalade, fondant potato and Swiss chard. Eggs Benedict is a fixture on both the breakfast and afternoon menu, while desserts are variations on old favourites such as pear and praline crumble. Nine house wines (from £3.25 a glass, £16.50 a bottle) head the extensive list.
Chef/s: Michael Lecouteur. **Open:** all week 8am to 10pm. **Meals:** alc (main courses £8 to £28). Set L £12.50 (2 courses) to £15.50. Sun L £11.95. **Service:** 10% (optional). **Details:** Cards accepted. 145 seats. Separate bar. Wheelchair access. Music. Children allowed.

ALSO RECOMMENDED
▲ WestBeach
Pier Approach, Bournemouth, BH2 5AA
Tel no: (01202) 587785
www.west-beach.co.uk
Seafood

'Thank goodness some people care about returning trade on the beach front, rather than just the passing tourist', enthused a visitor returning to this glass-fronted restaurant close to the pier. Fish is the culinary inspiration – everything from scallops with garlic butter (£10) via fish pie to whole roasted sea bass (£18.50). Steaks and a Sunday roast are among choices to satisfy the meat-eating brigade, while Barford Farm ice creams make a refreshing alternative to griottine cherry roly-poly. House wine £15.50. Open daily.

Burton Bradstock

ALSO RECOMMENDED
▲ Hive Beach Café
Beach Road, Burton Bradstock, DT6 4RF
Tel no: (01308) 897070
www.hivebeachcafe.co.uk
Seafood

Perched on the headland between a scruffy car park and a beach of fine-ground shingle, the Hive Beach is a proper seafood café, open for breakfasts and lunches, plus Friday and Saturday evenings in the spring and summer. Order your food at the counter, and wait for one of the waiting staff to shout your number. Big Martini glasses of crab and crayfish cocktail (£5.95) start you off, while mains run from mackerel fillets in caper cream sauce (£10.95) to grilled half-lobsters with garlic chive butter (£19.95) served with brilliant chunky chips. Wines from £13.50. Open all week.

▌Dorchester

Sienna

Beguiling little restaurant with big aspirations
36 High West Street, Dorchester, DT1 1UP
Tel no: (01305) 250022
www.siennarestaurant.co.uk
Modern British | £39
Cooking score: 4

It's easy to walk past the Browns' unassuming restaurant at the end of Dorchester's High Street. However, the intimate 15-cover dining room – done out with wooden tables, candles and bright artwork – is the setting for some serious culinary aspirations. Russell Brown's format is a brief fixed-price menu with generally five choices at each stage (three at lunch), and the repertoire celebrates local Dorset producers and the seasons. On arrival, guests are served jugs of iced water ('still a rarity in British restaurants'), and an amuse-bouche, say prosciutto and wild garlic pesto pizza and a quail's egg with fresh English asparagus salad. At inspection, a starter of char-grilled rump of Jurassic Coast rose veal with white beans, Arbequina olive oil and pickled carrot was followed by fillet of turbot with seared scallops, braised lettuce, bacon and shallots. West Country cheeses can be ordered as a supplement; also look for the Selvática chocolate tasting plate, which includes an oozing bitter chocolate tart and a 'fun' milk chocolate shake to be slurped through a straw. Service from Eléna Brown is 'superb'. An affordable wine lists kicks off at £16.15.
Chef/s: Russell Brown. **Open:** Tue to Sat L 12 to 2, D 7 to 9. **Closed:** Sun, Mon, 2 weeks spring and autumn. **Meals:** Set L £21.50 (2 courses) to £24.50. Set D £32.50 (2 courses) to £39. Tasting menu £48.50 (6 courses). **Service:** not inc. **Details:** Cards accepted. 15 seats. Air-con. No mobile phones. Music.

▌Farnham

The Museum Inn

Modern cooking with top-drawer ingredients
Farnham, DT11 8DE
Tel no: (01725) 516261
www.museuminn.co.uk
Modern British | £33
Cooking score: 3

🛏

This handsome seventeenth-century inn is noted for modern British cooking using top-drawer regional produce. Ambitious dishes feature some unusual combinations and, while intense foams and purées are generally successful, they may come as a surprise in this remote rural location. A hog's head starter with chorizo, caper purée, apple and crispy pig's ear could be followed by an inspired roast 'tikka' cod loin with coconut purée, spiced yellow peas and shallot bhaji, while a tropical fruits dessert arrives in the form of coconut parfait, mango jelly, pineapple spring roll and chocolate ice cream. However, 'a huge portion' of pork belly with a mound of mash and braised red cabbage was considered 'not a June lunchtime dish'. Bar meals feature beef burgers or fish and chips with mushy peas and tartare sauce. House wines from £17.50.
Chef/s: Owen Sullivan. **Open:** all week L 12 to 2.30 (3 Sun), D 7 to 9 (9.30 Fri and Sat). **Closed:** 25 Dec. **Meals:** alc (main courses £15 to £22). Bar menu available. **Service:** not inc. **Details:** Cards accepted. 90 seats. 36 seats outside. Separate bar. Wheelchair access. Children allowed. Car parking.

Gillingham

Stock Hill House

Austrian flavours in a Dorset domicile
Stock Hill, Gillingham, SP8 5NR
Tel no: (01747) 823626
www.stockhillhouse.co.uk
Modern European | £40
Cooking score: 5

🛏 V

It's 25 years since Peter and Nita Hauser took over as custodians of this tranquil Victorian domicile, and visitors still marvel at their sheer professionalism in the hospitality stakes. Set in lovely landscaped grounds, Stock Hill House looks and feels comfortingly homely but at the same time immaculate in the classic style of chintz, antiques, salmon-pink walls and William Morris wallpaper. Peter has stayed close to his Austrian roots, patriotically flagging up dishes from his native land alongside European classics, and his revealing, supremely crafted food proves that familiar things still have the power to surprise. 'You spend a lifetime hating the idea of rollmops and then discover Hauser's pickled dill herring on poached fennel with red onion cream', wrote one convert; others have spoken highly of home-cured ox-tongue dressed in olive oil (a real favourite), calf's liver pâté with crab apple jelly, copybook goulash, plates of sweetbreads in various forms and lemon sole stuffed with smoked salmon on couscous 'risi e bisi'. Sumptuous desserts range from a 'truly amazing' trio of crèmes brûlées to classic chocolate parisienne and iced candied fruit with rum passata. 'Lazy lunches' are highly praised, service is superbly drilled, and there are some unusual mid-European wines on the international list. House selections start at £22.
Chef/s: Peter Hauser. Open: Tue to Sun L 12.30 to 2, all week D 7.30 to 9. Meals: Set L £17.50 (2 courses) to £21. Set D £40 (3 courses). Sun L £29.
Service: not inc. Details: Cards accepted. 24 seats. 12 seats outside. No music. No mobile phones. Children allowed. Car parking.

Lyme Regis

Hix Oyster & Fish House

Simplicity is the watchword
Cobb Road, Lyme Regis, DT7 3JP
Tel no: (01297) 446910
www.restaurantsetcltd.co.uk
Seafood | £30
Cooking score: 4

Perched high up overlooking Lyme Bay, this coastal outpost of Mark Hix's stable of restaurants provides fabulous all-round views of the Cobb and Jurassic coastline from every table. Although access can be a challenge – 'no adjacent parking, off a steep hill, down steep steps' – there's 'lovely food, good service' as a reward. Alongside the simple styling there's a modern British menu that screams its seasonal and local credentials via the day's oysters and daily catch. The kitchen deals in simple presentations that capture the essence of the main ingredient: herb-baked Manx queenie scallops with wild garlic butter or herring roes with capers. To follow, grilled lobster is served with chips and buttered ramsons (wild garlic), and whole lemon sole comes with béarnaise sauce. Puddings carry on the theme of simplicity with the likes of Yorkshire parkin with butterscotch sauce and vanilla ice cream. House wine is £16.
Chef/s: Seldon Curry. Open: all week L 12 to 2.30 (3 Fri to Sun), D 6.30 to 10 (6 Fri to Sun). Closed: Mon (Sept to Jun), 25 and 26 Dec, first 3 weeks Jan.
Meals: alc (main courses £13 to £40). Set weekday L £17 (2 courses) to £21. Service: 12.5% (optional).
Details: Cards accepted. 45 seats. 8 seats outside. Air-con. No music. No mobile phones. Wheelchair access. Children allowed.

NEW ENTRY
The Mill Tea & Dining Room
Lovely eatery with skilled food
Mill Lane, Lyme Regis, DT7 3PU
Tel no: (01297) 445757
www.teaanddiningroom.com
British | £30
Cooking score: 2
£5
OFF

Relaxed and informal, this restored mill beside the River Lym makes a lovely little eatery. There are just seven tables in the tiny dining room, with the courtyard and riverside garden extending space in fair weather. Seasonal ingredients are simply prepared, whether a crab sandwich or a stunning smoked salmon and fennel tart for lunch, or a light Dorset apple cake to accompany afternoon tea. At dinner (booking essential), Anthony McNamara's kitchen skills are showcased in dishes such as braised beef shin and oyster pie, roast hake with clams and capers, and hot chocolate pudding with pink grapefruit. Open for breakfast too. Wines from £12.50.
Chef/s: Anthony McNamara. **Open:** Tue to Sun L 12 to 4.30 (5 Sun), Tue to Sat D 6.30 to 10. **Closed:** Mon (except bank hols), 3 to 28 Jan. **Meals:** alc (main courses £13 to £18). Set L £15 (2 courses) to £18. **Service:** not inc. **Details:** Cards accepted. 24 seats. 32 seats outside. Separate bar. Wheelchair access. Music. Children allowed. Car parking.

▮ Sturminster Newton
Plumber Manor
A treasured English retreat
Sturminster Newton, DT10 2AF
Tel no: (01258) 472507
www.plumbermanor.com
Anglo-French | £30
Cooking score: 2
🛏

A Jacobean manor set in its own garden and surrounded by countryside, Plumber Manor is a treasured place. It has been in the Prideaux-Brune family since the seventeenth century

and exudes Englishness in everything from the family portraits on the walls to the cooking, which eschews all culinary fads and fashions. Chicken liver pâté with onion marmalade followed by a pairing of pigeon and partridge breasts on a black pudding bubble and squeak are typical of the style. Pudding might be a medley of lemon and ginger crunch, chocolate torte, mini meringues and fresh berries. Wines start at £16.50.
Chef/s: Brian Prideaux-Brune. **Open:** Sun L 12 to 2, all week D 7.30 to 9. **Closed:** 26 Jan to 4 Mar. **Meals:** Set D £26 (2 courses) to £30. Sun L £23. **Service:** not inc. **Details:** Cards accepted. 65 seats. No music. Wheelchair access. Children allowed. Car parking.

▮ Trent
ALSO RECOMMENDED
▲ The Rose and Crown
Trent, DT9 4SL
Tel no: (01935) 850776
www.roseandcrowntrent.co.uk
Gastropub

This unpretentious, part-thatched pub in an archetypal Dorset village has a history going back to medieval times and portrays its age with beams, flagstones and large fireplaces. The kitchen deals in full-blooded modern dishes – local wood pigeon breast with crispy bacon and port syrup (£6.25), then slow-roasted belly pork with colcannon mash and a grain mustard cream sauce or calf's liver and bacon with balsamic sauté potatoes (£14.50). To finish, consider baked marshmallow and vanilla cheesecake with honeycomb ice cream (£5.75). House wine is £12.95. Closed Mon.

Average price

The average price listed in main-entry reviews denotes the price of a three-course meal, without wine.

West Bay
Riverside Restaurant
Ever-popular seafood veteran
West Bay, DT6 4EZ
Tel no: (01308) 422011
www.thefishrestaurant-westbay.co.uk
Seafood | £30
Cooking score: 3

Arthur Watson and family have been in the seafood business for nigh on 50 years, and continue to feed hordes of tourists, families and fish fans with excellent maritime victuals fresh from the Dorset boats. Cross the walkway over the water to reach this 'plain-looking but brilliant' place if you have an appetite for hefty helpings of seafood as refreshingly unadorned as the surroundings. Keep it simple with a plate of grilled turbot or lemon sole with new potatoes; otherwise explore one of the more exotic specials – perhaps monkfish curry or baked cod with chorizo and chickpeas. For afters, banana split or pear tarte Tatin with homemade rum and raisin ice cream should go down a treat. House wine is £12.95. Ring to check opening times in winter.
Chef/s: George Marsh. **Open:** Tue to Sun L 12 to 2.15, Tue to Sat D 6.30 to 9 (9.30 Fri and Sat). **Closed:** Mon, 28 Nov to 12 Feb. **Meals:** alc (main courses £11 to £24). Set L £17.50 (2 courses) to £22.50. **Service:** not inc. **Details:** Cards accepted. 80 seats. 20 seats outside. Separate bar. No music. No mobile phones. Wheelchair access. Children allowed.

Weymouth
ALSO RECOMMENDED
▲ Crab House Café
Ferryman's Way, Portland Road, Weymouth, DT4 9YU
Tel no: (01305) 788867
www.crabhousecafe.co.uk
Seafood

'Not a place to dress up, much more flip-flops than stilettos', advises a visitor to this zany wooden beach shack overlooking Chesil

Beach. Very fresh fish is the main focus – including oysters from their farm in the Fleet lagoon and whole crabs, which come complete with a hammer (£18.95). Delicious home-smoked eel mousse (£5.95), whole brill baked with Portland prawn butter (£18.25) and very good desserts are other attractions on the twice-daily changing menus. Wine from £13.90. Closed Sun D, Mon and Tue.

Wimborne St Giles
NEW ENTRY
The Bull Inn
Gutsy Brit cooking
Coach Road, Wimborne St Giles, BH21 5NF
Tel no: (01725) 517300
www.bullinnwsg.com
Modern British | £23
Cooking score: 2
🛏 £30

In a sleepy village deep in the Cranborne Chase, ex-Museum Inn head chef Matt Davey has teamed up with Mark Thornton – with the intention of putting the recently spruced-up Bull firmly on Dorset's culinary map. The village local now sports an open-to-view kitchen in the smart, open-plan bar/dining area. Here Matt makes good use of local produce and his gutsy modern British dishes are big on flavour. Start with tomato, borlotti bean, cabbage and chorizo soup, then follow with fish stew, saffron potatoes, grilled leeks and aïoli or venison pie with red onion and game jus, and finish with honey and lavender pannacotta with raspberry compote. New bedrooms, too. Wine from £16.50 (£4.20 a glass).
Chef/s: Matt Davey. **Open:** all week L 12 to 2.30 (3.30 Sun), D 6 to 9.30 (7 to 9.30 Sun). **Meals:** alc (main courses £8 to £19). **Service:** 10% (optional). **Details:** Cards accepted. 64 seats. 46 seats outside. No music. Wheelchair access. Children allowed. Car parking.

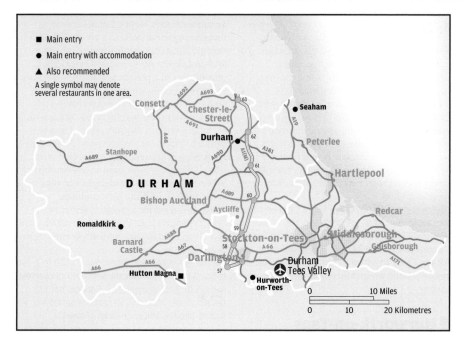

Legend:
■ Main entry
● Main entry with accommodation
▲ Also recommended
A single symbol may denote several restaurants in one area.

■ Durham

Bistro 21

Pleasant, friendly bistro
Aykley Heads House, Aykley Heads, Durham,
DH1 5TS
Tel no: (0191) 3844354
www.bistrotwentyone.co.uk
Modern British | £33
Cooking score: 2

V

This well-established bistro was the second restaurant added to Terry Laybourne's portfolio in 1996. It offers a friendly and professional welcome, and generally the kitchen suceeds in its efforts to deliver confident, unpretentious food. However, although the cooking is 'consistently good', one regular complains that 'it lacks imagination and varies little from one visit to the next'. Fried duck egg with truffle oil and radish makes a comforting starter, followed by sirloin steak, chicken ballottine or haddock and triple-cooked chips, with chocolate pots

and churros to finish. The bistro has a pleasant ambience and a lovely outdoor courtyard. A bottle of Georges Duboeuf house wine is £11.60.
Chef/s: Robbie Bell. **Open:** Mon to Sat L 12 to 2.30, D 6 to 10. **Closed:** Sun, 25 and 26 Dec, 1 Jan, Easter Mon. **Meals:** alc (main courses £15 to £26). Set L and D £15.50 (2 courses) to £18. **Service:** 10%.
Details: Cards accepted. 70 seats. 20 seats outside. Separate bar. Wheelchair access. Music. Children allowed. Car parking.

Gourmet Spot

Adventurous restaurant with big ideas
The Avenue, Durham, DH1 4DX
Tel no: (0191) 3846655
www.gourmet-spot.co.uk
Modern European | £36
Cooking score: 2

£5 OFF 🛏

'Amazing service from entering the restaurant to leaving; on arrival a warm greeting, and staff had brilliant knowledge of menu', exclaimed a reporter in florid mood. Despite yet another change of chef, this remains a restaurant with big ideas and the cooking steers the course it set at the beginning: adventurous menus heavily influenced by fashionable techniques. Presentation is 'beautiful', whether red mullet served with carrot, ginger and coconut velouté, spiced lentils and saffron foam, a main course duck breast with butter-roast potato, Jerusalem artichoke purée, roast salsify and lavender jus or mango cheesecake with ginger crumble, lime jelly and roast pineapple sorbet. House wine is £16.50.

Chef/s: Stephen Hardy. **Open:** Tue to Sat D only 5 to 10. **Closed:** Sun, Mon, 25 to 28 Dec, 1 to 12 Jan. **Meals:** alc (main courses £15 to £25). Set D £27 (2 courses) to £35. **Service:** 10% (optional). **Details:** Cards accepted. 24 seats. Separate bar. No mobile phones. Wheelchair access. Music. Car parking.

▌Hurworth-on-Tees

NEW ENTRY
Kenny Atkinson at The Orangery
Something special for Darlington
Rockliffe Hall, Hurworth-on-Tees, DL2 2DU
Tel no: (01325) 729999
www.rockliffehall.com
Modern British | £45
Cooking score: 5

≠ V

An impressive new hotel demands an impressive chef, and Kenny Atkinson is it. His new home (he lives in the grounds) is Rockliffe Hall, just outside Darlington, and his presence is a huge boost. The old orangery has become the kind of dining room you'd expect in this reassuringly expensive resort, but the bland luxury of shot silk and golf-course views is tempered by a trio of extraordinary soft-focus still lifes of cheese and fruit. They may have an air of the 1970s, but Atkinson's food is determinedly of-the-moment in terms of both fashions and seasons. A late-spring inspection was very green, from

an unfortunately sloppy but otherwise likeable pea pannacotta to a vivid wild garlic velouté. To start, pork belly with pineapple and cauliflower purée boasted crackling reminiscent of a polished tabletop and bonus cubes of fabulous smoked eel, while a main course of turbot with a lobster risotto and foamy pink bisque just survived enthusiastic seasoning with its flavours intact. Dessert might be Atkinson's as-seen-on-TV take on strawberry jelly, a Martini glass filled with jelly, light elderflower mousse and crumbs of expertly made shortbread; light but very sweet indeed. Like the surroundings, Atkinson's food feels special without being out of reach, though the wine list (which starts at £19, £5 a glass) has definite potential for expansion.

Chef/s: Kenny Atkinson. **Open:** Sun L 12.30 to 2, Tue to Sat D 6.45 to 9.30. **Meals:** Set D £45 (3 courses). Sun L £30. Tasting menu £65. **Service:** not inc. **Details:** Cards accepted. 50 seats. Separate bar. No mobile phones. Music. Children allowed.

▌Hutton Magna

The Oak Tree Inn
Warm welcome and food with flair
Hutton Magna, DL11 7HH
Tel no: (01833) 627371
Modern British | £32
Cooking score: 2

The Rosses' whitewashed country pub is snuggled in a row of terraced cottages, and is run with all the warmth and welcome you would hope to find in such an establishment. Alastair Ross once worked at the Savoy in London, and brings a sharp seasonal sense and plenty of flair to his modern British repertoire. Start with a salt cod fishcake seasoned with garlic and saffron, before moving on to roast breast of guinea-fowl with confit leg, olive oil mash and rosemary-scented vegetables. Baked vanilla cheesecake with poached plums and pistachio ice cream makes a fitting finale. Good selections of teas, bottled beers and malt whiskies supplement the value-conscious wine list, which starts at £12.50.

Chef/s: Alastair Ross. **Open:** Tue to Sun D only 6 to 9 (5 to 8 Sun). **Closed:** Mon, 25 and 27 Dec, 31 Dec, 1 and 2 Jan. **Meals:** alc (main courses £18 to £20). **Service:** not inc. **Details:** Cards accepted. 20 seats. No mobile phones. Music. Car parking.

Romaldkirk
The Rose & Crown
Olde-worlde village charmer
Romaldkirk, DL12 9EB
Tel no: (01833) 650213
www.rose-and-crown.co.uk
Modern British | £33
Cooking score: 3

£5
OFF

Set in the picture-postcard surroundings of the village green with its ancient oaks, this creeper-clad inn exudes charm of the olde-worlde variety. Christopher and Alison Davy have been running the place for nigh on 22 years, with Christopher still taking care of matters in the kitchen. While lunch in the bar brings straightforward dishes like Welsh rarebit with grilled back bacon and salad or steak, kidney and mushroom pie, dinner in the elegant dining room ('it looked superb') is a sedate four-course affair. The quality of raw materials is consistently high in such dishes as baked crab soufflé with light parsley cream, and wood pigeon with creamed parsnip tartlet, juniper sauce and grilled pancetta. Good regional cheeses and desserts such as hot chocolate brownie have impressed. House wine is £16.95.
Chef/s: Christopher Davy and Andrew Lee. **Open:** Sun L 12 to 1.45, all week D 7.30 to 9.15. **Closed:** 24 to 26 Dec. **Meals:** Set D £32.50 (4 courses). Sun L £17.75. Bar menu available. **Service:** not inc. **Details:** Cards accepted. 24 seats. 24 seats outside. Separate bar. No music. No mobile phones. Wheelchair access. Children allowed. Car parking.

Seaham
Seaham Hall, The White Room
Lord Byron's Walk, Seaham, SR7 7AG
Tel no: (0191) 5161400
www.seaham-hall.com
Modern European | £50
Cooking score: 5

It's a tough call running a grand hotel on the remote Durham coast – small signs like garden weeds and tired chair upholstery suggest the strain. But in the White Room, dinner glides smoothly with various menus adequately showcasing Max Wilson's skills. At inspection, a pre-starter of cucumber pannacotta was an impressive launch pad for a meal that was mostly highs. Scallops were neatly paired with sweet carrot purée and crisp carrot curls. Even better, a perfectly timed cut of lemon sole with razor clam, clam butter and miniature leaves presented a beautiful mix of fresh, grassy summer flavours. Sea bass and lobster atop asparagus and shaved fennel with lobster consommé poured from a teapot was equally accomplished. Local Spennymoor lamb – a mix of loin and braised shoulder – was lifted by a wild garlic and pearl barley risotto and expertly cooked kidney. At dessert, a rich slab of flourless chocolate cake, teamed with caramel ice cream, narrowly trumped the honey mousse and almond ice cream. Engaged service, an elegant room and an exhaustive wine list with plenty of half bottles and some 20 by the glass, add to an experience that is sophisticated without showing off.
Chef/s: Max Wilson. **Open:** Sun L 12 to 2, all week D 7 to 10. **Meals:** Set D £50 (3 courses) to £80 (7 courses). Sun L £30. **Service:** not inc. **Details:** Cards accepted. 45 seats. Air-con. Separate bar. No mobile phones. Wheelchair access. Music. Children allowed. Car parking.

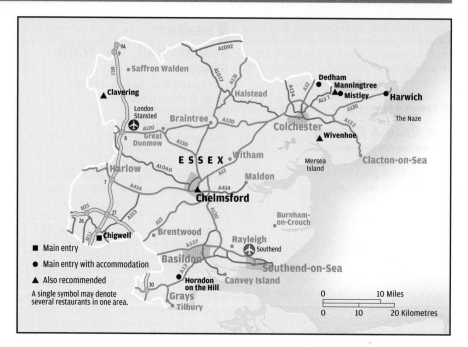

- ■ Main entry
- ● Main entry with accommodation
- ▲ Also recommended

A single symbol may denote several restaurants in one area.

0		10 Miles
0	10	20 Kilometres

■ Chelmsford

ALSO RECOMMENDED
▲ Barda

30-32 Broomfield Road, Chelmsford, CM1 1SW
Tel no: (01245) 357799
www.barda-restaurant.com
Modern European £5 OFF

Funky Barda has plenty of street cred in Chelmsford's West End, with its sleek, clean lines, decked patio and eclectic Med/Asian food. Light lunches set the scene for more ambitious dinner offerings ranging from seared beef salad with mooli, coriander and lotus root (£7) to slow-braised pork cheeks or cod fillet on samphire with enoki mushrooms and wild herb butter (£18). Finish in upbeat mood with desserts such as lemon and Tequila mousse with lemongrass granita (£6). Wines from £14. Closed Sat L, Sun D and Mon.

■ Chigwell

The Bluebell

Catering for all appetites
117 High Road, Chigwell, IG7 6QQ
Tel no: (020) 8500 6282
www.thebluebellrestaurant.co.uk
Modern European | £30
Cooking score: 1

Despite several recent changes of chef, Greg Molen's restaurant (located in a converted 400-year-old building) maintains its popularity among a certain clientele. Menus cater for all appetites, from typically complex dishes like hot Scotch egg served on a celeriac and apple rémoulade with honey-roast pork belly, smoked venison and watercress salad, or wild sea bass fillet on lemon spätzle with a pesto and Parma ham minestrone to more classic chicken liver and foie gras pâté, or loin of pork with creamed potatoes and grain mustard jus. Fresh blueberry and frangipane tart with lemon curd ice cream is one way to finish. House wine £15.50. More reports please.

Chef/s: Gavin Maguire. **Open:** Tue to Fri and Sun L 12 to 3.45 (6.30 Sun), Tue to Sat D 6.45 to 1am. **Closed:** Mon. **Meals:** alc (main courses £18 to £26). Set L £15.95 (2 courses) to £19.95. Set D and Sun L £24.95. **Service:** not inc. **Details:** Cards accepted. 95 seats. Air-con. No mobile phones. Music. Children allowed.

Clavering

ALSO RECOMMENDED
▲ The Cricketers

Clavering, CB11 4QT
Tel no: (01799) 550442
www.thecricketers.co.uk
Gastropub £5 OFF

The Olivers (parents of Jamie) run a tight ship at their smart country inn-with-rooms, with Jamie's own local certified organic garden supplying the vegetables, herbs and salads. It's a thoroughly homely, pubby place, with fixed-price menus (£23.95 for two courses, £29.95 for three) the principal business. Expect the likes of steamed mussels in white wine, shallots and lemon, followed by slow-braised shank of Suffolk lamb with creamy champ, and iced amaretti and almond tortoni with raspberry sauce to finish. House wines are £14.25. Open all week.

Dedham
The Sun Inn

Ancient inn with Med flavours
High Street, Dedham, CO7 6DF
Tel no: (01206) 323351
www.thesuninndedham.com
Mediterranean | £23
Cooking score: 3
£5 OFF 🛏 V £30

As you drive through the pretty Constable-country village, you can't miss this sunny yellow fifteenth-century inn. There's a congenial bar, a large timbered and beamed dining room and a spacious patio, but menus

are rather more cutting edge than you might expect to find in a country pub. Local and regional suppliers play a role, their produce worked into a modern version of classic Med cuisine with a strong Italian accent. Among successes have been red mullet with curly kale, chickpeas and mint, and grilled Tuscan-style sausages with spinach and soft polenta. Desserts have ranged from apple, lemon and almond tart to rhubarb and ice cream. Excellent drinking is to be had by the glass and carafe on a list with an interesting Mediterranean emphasis; bottles from £13.50.

Chef/s: Ugo Simonelli. **Open:** all week L 12 to 2.30 (3 Sat and Sun), D 6.30 to 9.30 (10 Fri and Sat, 9 Sun). **Closed:** 25 and 26 Dec. **Meals:** alc (main courses £9 to £18). Set L and D £10.50 (2 courses) to £13.50. **Service:** not inc. **Details:** Cards accepted. 60 seats. 60 seats outside. Music. Children allowed. Car parking.

Harwich
The Pier at Harwich, Harbourside Restaurant

Classic seafood and fine estuary views
The Quay, Harwich, CO12 3HH
Tel no: (01255) 241212
www.milsomhotels.com
Seafood | £28
Cooking score: 2
£5 OFF 🛏 £30

There's a traditional look to the menu at this long-standing first-floor seafooder with fine views over the Stour and Orwell estuaries. The classic approach brings lobster bisque with cream and brandy or an impeccably timed local Dover sole. There are some foreign forays, too, including Thai-flavoured salmon cake served with home-smoked salmon, tomato and coriander salsa and tzatziki, and a couple of meat options for those who must – perhaps a straightforward Dedham Vale sirloin steak served with fat chips. Tables are sensibly spaced, there are crisp white cloths and service from 'friendly young staff' is on the ball. House wine is £16.

Chef/s: Chris Oakley. **Open:** all week L 12 to 2, D 6 to 9.30. **Meals:** alc (main courses £15 to £35). Set L £19.50 (2 courses) to £25. Sun L £27. **Service:** 10%. **Details:** Cards accepted. 70 seats. 40 seats outside. Air-con. Separate bar. No mobile phones. Music. Children allowed. Car parking.

▌Horndon on the Hill

The Bell Inn
Medieval pub with up-to-date food
High Road, Horndon on the Hill, SS17 8LD
Tel no: (01375) 642463
www.bell-inn.co.uk
Modern European | £29
Cooking score: 2

🛏 £30

Disappointments are rare at this popular Essex inn-cum-hotel, parts of which date back to the fifteenth century. Run by the same family for over 50 years, it's still at the heart of village life: the hot cross buns hanging in the saloon bar are tokens of a local tradition dating back 90 years. But there's nothing antiquated about the food served in the restaurant. Assertive European flavours are the hallmarks of dishes ranging from monkfish poached in citrus oil with orange reduction and confit Parmentier potatoes to pan-fried duck breast on spinach with poached pear. Start with a warm terrine of Essex wood pigeon, and round off with layered cherry and Baileys crème brûlée. British pub grub and real ales do duty in the bar. Wines start at £12.95.
Chef/s: Stuart Fay. **Open:** all week L 12 to 1.45 (2.15 Sun), D 6.30 to 9.45 (7 Sun). **Closed:** 25 and 26 Dec, bank hol Mon. **Meals:** alc (main courses £9 to £22). Bar menu available. **Service:** not inc. **Details:** Cards accepted. 80 seats. 36 seats outside. Separate bar. No music. Wheelchair access. Children allowed. Car parking.

▌Manningtree

ALSO RECOMMENDED
▲ Lucca Enoteca
39-41 High Street, Manningtree, CO11 1AH
Tel no: (01206) 390044
www.luccafoods.co.uk
Italian

It's a rare thing, a high street pizzeria that's not a chain. This spin-off from the Mistley Thorn (see entry) is a popular local resource – a warm and friendly place dealing in wood-fired pizzas with toppings that range from the classic margherita or quattro stagioni (£6.25-£8.25) to the creative salsiccia – homemade fennel sausages with tomatoes, red onion and fior di latte mozzarella (£7.95). The menu offers a few pasta dishes and salads too, plus wood-fired roasts on Saturdays and Sundays. Italian wines from £13.95. Open all week.

▌Mistley

The Mistley Thorn
Upbeat eatery with piscine pickings
High Street, Mistley, CO11 1HE
Tel no: (01206) 392821
www.mistleythorn.com
Modern European | £25
Cooking score: 2

🛏 £30

With terracotta tiles on the floor and interesting artwork to distract the eye, this Georgian inn has shaken off its boozy shackles and re-invented itself as an 'upscale bistro-style restaurant'. Fish fans do well here, and the specials list spotlights prime piscine pickings from the Mersea boats; expect anything from grilled squid with shaved fennel and sprouting broccoli salad to roast cod on chickpeas with romesco sauce. Meanwhile, the regular menu satisfies all-comers with the likes of roast free-range duck breast with wilted cavolo nero and salsa verde or spinach and ricotta crespelle. Fig and frangipane tart is a typically Eurocentric dessert, and global wines start at £14.95.

Chef/s: Sherri Singleton. **Open:** all week L 12 to 2.30 (3.30 Sat, 5 Sun), D 6.30 to 9.30 (6 Fri to Sun). **Meals:** alc (main courses £8 to £17). Set L £12.95 (2 courses) to £15.95. Set D Sun and Mon £25 (3 courses for 2 people). Sun L £15.95. **Service:** not inc. **Details:** Cards accepted. 70 seats. 12 seats outside. Separate bar. Wheelchair access. Music. Children allowed. Car parking.

West Mersea

READERS RECOMMEND
The Company Shed
Seafood
129 Coast Road, West Mersea, CO5 8PA
Tel no: (01206) 382700
'The freshly caught seafood is excellent value and well worth the wait – you can also bring your own bread and wine'

Wivenhoe

ALSO RECOMMENDED
▲ The Bake House
5 High Street, Wivenhoe, CO7 9BJ
Tel no: (01206) 824569
www.thebakehouserestaurant.co.uk
Modern European

Having managed this converted bakery for two years, Simon Hirst and Sue Harris decided to buy the place, and are maintaining its reputation for friendly hospitality and locally sourced food. Native ingredients appear in the shape of, say, deep-fried Colchester oysters with lemon couscous (£6.50), sirloin of beef with red wine sauce, and rump of lamb with spiced aubergines (£16.95). Fishcakes are bestsellers, and lemon posset (£5) makes a refreshing finale. Wines from £14.95. Open Wed to Sat D and Sun L. Note: Simon Hirst and Sue Harris have also re-launched the legendary Warehouse Brasserie in Colchester – reports please.

Fine dining on a shoestring

'Special offers' and 'fine dining' are unlikely bedfellows but there are some good deals around if you know where to look. The seasonal lunch at Lancashire's **Northcote** is always a fair deal at £25 for three courses with coffee, but check their website www.northcote.com, where there may be a £5-off voucher, and it's an even better deal.

You *can* have it all with 'all in' lunch deals. The best of the bunch is arguably at **Le Gavroche**. Just £48 gets you three courses of classic French cuisine, half a bottle of wine, mineral water and coffee. A similar set lunch offer at **Galvin at Windows** for £42 also includes a sweeping view across London.

Outside London, **The Kitchin** in Edinburgh impresses with a set lunch at £24.50 for three courses that might include squid with wild garlic gnocchi, and St George's mushrooms and pork and foie gras terrine. Whereas at **Anthony's Restaurant** in Leeds, one can sample Anthony Flinn's dazzling dishes, including sardines with pomelo salad or braised pig's cheeks with squid ink risotto and squid crackers at £24 for three courses.

Tom Kerridge at **The Hand and Flowers** in Marlow is most generous of all. His set lunch might not include all the bells and whistles, but £10 for two courses can't be bad.

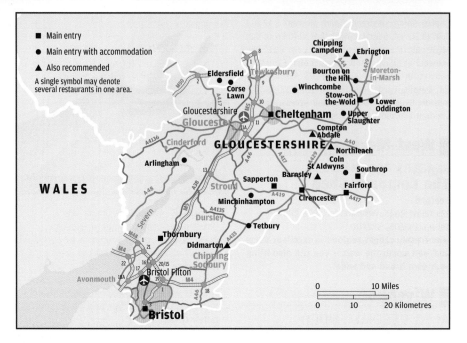

Legend:
- ■ Main entry
- ● Main entry with accommodation
- ▲ Also recommended

A single symbol may denote several restaurants in one area.

Arlingham

The Old Passage

Confident seafood cookery
Passage Road, Arlingham, GL2 7JR
Tel no: (01452) 740547
www.theoldpassage.com
Seafood | £30
Cooking score: 3

£5 OFF

Sitting on an ox-bow bend in the river Severn, the Old Passage is so named because it was here that you could cross the ford to the Forest of Dean and the wilds of Wales. The views are altogether sumptuous, and you won't lack for diversion in Mark Redwood's confident seafood cookery either. An overnight guest enjoyed a regal start to the day in the form of a smoked haddock soufflé. Otherwise, the menus offer the likes of chilli-spiked potted shrimps, sea bream with cockles, clams, parsnip and vanilla purée and a shellfish sauce, or classics such as lobster thermidor. To finish, the lemon meringue pie comes enterprisingly with fennel ice cream. Gloucestershire's Three Choirs wines take their places among a usefully varied list. Prices start at £17.50.
Chef/s: Mark Redwood. Open: Tue to Sun L 12 to 2 (2.30 Sun), Tue to Sat D 6.30 to 9. Closed: Mon, 25 and 26 Dec. Meals: alc (main courses £17 to £24). Set L £15 (2 courses) to £20. Service: not inc. Details: Cards accepted. 50 seats. 20 seats outside. Air-con. Wheelchair access. Music. Children allowed. Car parking.

Barnsley

ALSO RECOMMENDED
▲ The Village Pub

Barnsley, GL7 5EF
Tel no: (01285) 740421
www.thevillagepub.co.uk
Modern British

Now under the same ownership as Calcot Manor in Tetbury (see entry), this village pub has had new life breathed into it after a sympathetic refurbishment. The Cotswold stone, open fires and flagstones remain, but sumptuous fabrics and a stylish new bar add a contemporary edge. Enjoy 'Scotch' quails' eggs (£3) with a pint or feast on modern pub food created from British produce: mussels with cider, parsley and cream (£5.50) could be followed by slow-roast belly of pork with root vegetable gratin (£14). House wine £15.75. Open all week.

■ Bourton on the Hill

Horse & Groom
Proper inn with proper food and drink
Bourton on the Hill, GL56 9AQ
Tel no: (01386) 700413
www.horseandgroom.info
Modern British | £26
Cooking score: 2
🛏 £30

Brothers Tom and Will Greenstock are no strangers to innkeeping and have put their talents to good use at this Cotswold stone pub perched on a hill. Having saved the lovely Georgian building from dereliction, they are cementing its reputation as a proper inn serving proper food and drink. Local sourcing is close to their heart, and the seasonal menu makes its point with dishes such as roast rack of Old Farm lamb with home-grown mustard greens, chilli jam and horseradish. There's also plenty of industrious home curing on show: salt cod fritters receive a dollop of rouille, and salted Dexter beef comes with parsley dumplings. As for desserts, consider apple, rhubarb and flapjack crumble. House wine is £12.95.
Chef/s: Will Greenstock. **Open:** all week L 12 to 2 (2.30 Sun), Mon to Sat D 7 to 9 (9.30 Fri and Sat). **Closed:** 25 Dec, 1 week Jan. **Meals:** alc (main courses £10 to £21). **Service:** not inc. **Details:** Cards accepted. 70 seats. 50 seats outside. Separate bar. No music. Children allowed. Car parking.

Visit us online

To find out more about
The Good Food Guide, please visit
www.thegoodfoodguide.co.uk

■ Bristol

The Albion
Bold, no-nonsense cooking
Boyces Avenue, Clifton, Bristol, BS8 4AA
Tel no: (0117) 9733522
www.thealbionclifton.co.uk
Gastropub | £30
Cooking score: 3

Set back from the street on the edge of one of Clifton's grandest squares, this listed seventeeth-century inn occupies a corner of Bristol often described as the city's answer to Notting Hill. Walk through the cobbled courtyard (a great sheltered alfresco dining area) to the handsome pub with its wooden floors, log fire and trendy colour scheme. Grab a stool at the bar for a pint of local ale and snacks such as foie gras on toast, or take a seat in the dining area for chef Clarke Oldfield's bold, no-nonsense modern British cooking – smoked Cornish trout with scrambled eggs, say, then beef and mushroom pie with mash, followed by chocolate fondant with fig and rum ice cream. Wines from £15.50, including ten by the glass (from £3.80).
Chef/s: Clarke Oldfield. **Open:** Tue to Sun L 12 to 3 (4 Sun), Tue to Sat D 7 to 10. **Closed:** 25 and 26 Dec, 1 Jan. **Meals:** alc (main courses £16 to £24). Set L £18 (2 courses) to £24. Set D £24 (2 courses) to £30. Sun L £28. **Service:** 10% (optional). **Details:** Cards accepted. 100 seats. 40 seats outside. Wheelchair access. Music. Children allowed.

Bell's Diner
Inventive cooking at full throttle
1-3 York Road, Montpelier, Bristol, BS6 5QB
Tel no: (0117) 9240357
www.bellsdiner.com
Modern European | £35
Cooking score: 4
£5 OFF

A one-time grocer's shop in Bristol's Montpelier district is the setting for Christopher Wicks' highly idiosyncratic restaurant – a telling mix of reclaimed features, auction room curios and striking modern food. Fans have praised his daring culinary approach, which marries experimental conceits such as tea fluid gel with sound breadmaking, classic technique and consommés. A modish starter of two-hour poached duck egg with Ibérico ham and pea sorbet blew one reporter away, and the invention continues with palate-challenging combos such as wood pigeon with almonds, foie gras, oloroso sherry and Muscatel grapes or beef with pickled vegetables, watercress and black truffle. Wicks also has an inspired way with vegetables (cooking salsify with a splash of grenadine, for example), and his creative momentum remains at full throttle for desserts such as compressed pineapple with white chocolate snow, coriander sorbet and coconut gel. The attentive sommelier's knowledge of the 'exploratory' wine list also does the restaurant credit. Prices start at £15.50.

Chef/s: Christopher Wicks and Alex Collins. **Open:** Tue to Fri L 12 to 2.30, Mon to Sat D 6.30 to 12.30. **Closed:** Sun, 24 to 31 Dec, bank hols. **Meals:** alc (main courses £15 to £20). Tasting menu £45. **Service:** 10% (optional). **Details:** Cards accepted. 60 seats. No mobile phones. Music. Children allowed.

Bordeaux Quay
Versatile harbourside landmark
V-Shed, Canons Way, Bristol, BS1 5UH
Tel no: (0117) 9431200
www.bordeaux-quay.co.uk
Modern European | £30
Cooking score: 2

There have been a number of changes at this landmark building on Bristol's harbourside. A new management team has arrived from Murrays of Clevedon (see entry, Somerset) and there has been a noticeable improvement in the service. Downstairs, the brasserie is the place for more informal dining (from weekend breakfast pancakes to moules-frites, excellent fish stew and curried lamb), but there is a more pronounced Italian slant to the cooking upstairs. Here seasonal produce steers the menu – tagliatelle with morels, thyme and Parmesan, then rump of lamb with wild garlic

dauphinoise and Hispi cabbage, and Yorkshire rhubarb and yoghurt pannacotta to finish. House wine from £17.

Chef/s: Liz Payne. **Open:** Tue to Fri and Sun L 12 to 3 (4 Sun), Tue to Sat D 6.30 to 10. **Closed:** Christmas. **Meals:** alc (main courses £14 to £23). Set L £21.50 (2 courses) to £25. Set D £25.50 (2 courses) to £28.50. Sun L £14.50. **Service:** 10% (optional). **Details:** Cards accepted. 200 seats. Separate bar. Wheelchair access. Music. Children allowed.

Café Maitreya
Vibrant veggie favourite
89 St Mark's Road, Easton, Bristol, BS5 6HY
Tel no: (0117) 9510100
www.cafemaitreya.co.uk
Vegetarian | £23
Cooking score: 4

£5 OFF **V** £30

Maitreya means 'universal love' in Sanskrit and the innovative, vibrant cooking at this neighbourhood restaurant has certainly won the affections of the veggie fraternity. It occupies a corner spot in a bustling street that also houses a huge Asian supermarket, and its purple walls are hung with striking local artwork. The small open kitchen delivers interesting and well-defined flavours from predominantly organic and wild ingredients. A creamy, full-flavoured smoked ricotta terrine studded with capers and raisins (to be spread on toasted brioche) makes for a very satisfying starter, with a slightly tart poached quince purée cutting through the richness. An individual bake of finely diced trompette mushrooms, Puy lentils and chopped hazelnuts, layered with spinach and butternut squash purée is a stampede of textures and flavours, while rosehip, Champagne and pineapple trifle provides a light, refreshing finale. House wine from £12.50.

Chef/s: Mark Evans. **Open:** Wed to Sat L 12 to 3, D 6.30 to 9.45 (6 Sat). **Closed:** Mon, Tue, Sun, 24 Dec to 1 Jan, last 2 weeks Aug. **Meals:** alc (main courses £10 to £13). Set L £9.95 (2 courses) to £12.95. Set D £19.95 (2 courses) to £22.95. **Service:** not inc. **Details:** Cards accepted. 55 seats. Separate bar. Wheelchair access. Music. Children allowed.

Casamia

Slibing chefs full of surprises
38 High Street, Westbury on Trym, Bristol,
BS9 3DZ
Tel no: (0117) 9592884
www.casamiarestaurant.co.uk
Italian | £28
Cooking score: 5
£5 OFF £30 ✔

Only the large storage vessels of liquid nitrogen next to the pots of herbs in the pretty courtyard garden hint at what's to come at this unassuming neighbourhood restaurant. With its terracotta tiles and fresco-style paintings, Casamia still has reminders of its traditional Italian trattoria past – but for the past four years, brothers Peter and Jonray Sanchez-Iglesias have well and truly put this place on the culinary map, thanks to their innovative cooking style and ultra-modern techniques. Their epigrammatic tasting menus give little away and the creative dishes are full of surprises. A starter of hot and earthy beetroot risotto arrives with a scoop of iced yoghurt and is topped with razor-thin slices of pickled fennel and finely chopped pistachios to create a dish of genuine textural complexity. A confit leg and breast of roast quail is cooked sous-vide before being placed on a small 'nest' of crisp, dried angel-hair pasta with celery leaves and a drizzle of quail jus. For dessert, succulent English strawberries are flavoured with tarragon and meadowsweet and presented in a billowing cloud of ice-cold liquid nitrogen with a 'summer's day aroma'. The predominantly Italian wine list is modern in tone, with a good range by the glass from £4. **Chef/s:** Jonray and Peter Sanchez-Iglesias. **Open:** Fri and Sat L 12.15 to 2, Tue to Sat D 7 to 9. **Closed:** Sun, Mon, 25 and 26 Dec, bank hols. **Meals:** L tasting menu £35 (6 courses). D tasting menu £40 (8 courses) to £65. **Service:** not inc. **Details:** Cards accepted. 40 seats. Separate bar. No mobile phones. Wheelchair access. Music. Children allowed.

Culinaria

Bristol's culinary royals
1 Chandos Road, Redland, Bristol, BS6 6PG
Tel no: (0117) 9737999
www.culinariabristol.co.uk
Modern British | £32
Cooking score: 4
🍾

Stephen and Judy Markwick are restaurant royalty in Bristol and – more than three decades down the line – they are not about to relinquish their kingdom. Over the years they have gained legions of followers by taking a genuinely unaffected approach to things, rather than wallowing in some 'imposed, expensive faux-luxury'. Fans reckon that 'few chefs source and cook fish as well as Stephen Markwick', although the results can be deceptively simple: a dish of grilled scallops in their shells doused with garlic butter, fillet of pollack with crab sauce, even fishcakes with tomato and pomegranate salsa. The bright, user-friendly repertoire also embraces plates of mezze, Provençal fish soup, and Mendip venison with spiced beetroot, gherkins and sour cream, with desserts promising the likes of prune and Armagnac tart or warm rice pudding with rhubarb – it's as if the ghosts of Elizabeth David and Jane Grigson are hovering somewhere near the stove. Service is 'outstanding', likewise the wine list – a succinct worldwide slate with pin-point choices in every region and a helpful showing of half-bottles. Prices start at £15.50. (£3.25 a glass). **Chef/s:** Stephen Markwick. **Open:** Thur to Sat L 12 to 2, D 6.30 to 9.30. **Closed:** Sun to Wed, 2 weeks Christmas, 1 week spring, 2 weeks summer, 1 week autumn. **Meals:** alc (main courses £13 to £18). Set L £15.50 (2 courses) to £20. **Service:** not inc. **Details:** Cards accepted. 30 seats. No music. Wheelchair access. Children allowed.

NEW ENTRY
Flinty Red
Fine-tuned food and wine
34 Cotham Hill, Bristol, BS6 6LA
Tel no: (0117) 9238755
www.flintyred.co.uk
European | £25
Cooking score: 3

V £30

Described by one reader as being 'a far cry
from provincial English city restaurants',
Flinty Red has a distinctly European feel
about it. Run in conjunction with an
independent wine shop, the emphasis is on
shared plates and small dishes, with lots of
interesting tipples to sample. The menu is
broadly Italian and French and you can eat at
tables or at the marble bar. Ingredients are
impeccably sourced and the menu encourages
experimentation and sharing. Bold flavour
combinations can be expected in rabbit and
walnut ravioli with wild garlic and Parmesan,
followed by grilled quail, Muscat raisins and
watercress. Round things off with rhubarb
and blood orange with buttermilk pudding.
The interesting modern wine list changes
frequently and starts at £12 (£3 a glass).
Chef/s: Matthew Williamson. **Open:** Tue to Sat L 12
to 3, Mon to Sat D 6.30 to 10. **Closed:** Sun, 25 to 28
Dec, first week Jan, bank hols. **Meals:** alc (main
courses from £10 to £16). **Service:** not inc.
Details: Cards accepted. 36 seats. Separate bar.
Music. Children allowed.

Greens' Dining Room
Delightful, good-value local eatery
25 Zetland Road, Bristol, BS6 7AH
Tel no: (0117) 9246437
www.greensdiningroom.com
Modern British | £28
Cooking score: 3

£30

The green awning and big shopfront
windows announce one of Bristol's best-loved
neighbourhood restaurants. It's 'always a
delight', according to one regular who notes
that 'the front-of-house staff are charming and

well-informed, and the food punches well
above its weight in terms of value and class.'
The Green team produces dishes in the
modern European vein, with the emphasis on
seasonality. A satisfying winter meal
proceeded from potato pancakes with sour
cream and caviar, through lemon sole with
beurre blanc, capers and double-cooked chips,
to alight on Seville orange curd tart at the end.
The rump of beef with rosemary, served with
dauphinoise, is well reported too, while the set
supper menu looks particularly good value. A
single-page wine slate is appealing in every
way. Prices are kept on a leash, and there is an
imaginative selection of international
growers, with Spanish house selections
at £13.95.
Chef/s: Andrew and Simon Green. **Open:** Tue to Sat
L 12.30 to 3, Tue to Sat D 6.30 to 10.30. **Closed:** Sun,
Mon, 23 Dec to 5 Jan, last 2 weeks Aug. **Meals:** alc
(main courses £9 to £15). Set L £10 (2 courses). Set
D £21.50 (2 courses) to £27.50. **Service:** not inc.
Details: Cards accepted. 38 seats. 14 seats outside.
No mobile phones. Music. Children allowed.

Lido
Punchy flavours poolside
Oakfield Place, Clifton, Bristol, BS8 2BJ
Tel no: (0117) 9339533
www.lidobristol.com
Eclectic | £29
Cooking score: 3

£5 £30
OFF

Tucked down a quiet residential street in the
heart of leafy Clifton, this Victorian lido
reopened in 2008 as an open-air swimming
pool, spa and bustling restaurant. Window
seats overlooking the heated infinity pool are
hotly prized and this striking location sets the
scene for ex-Moro chef Freddy Bird's robust
seasonal Italian and North African-inspired
cooking. There is much use of the kitchen's
wood-fired oven, including a starter of wood-
roast scallops served in their shell with a green
pool of sweet herb and garlic butter. A main
course of quails roasted the same way with
peppers, aubergine salad and seasoned
yoghurt delivers big flavours, as do the delicate

and freshly churned ice creams including Pedro Ximénez and raisin or salted-butter caramel. Wines from £14.
Chef/s: Freddy Bird. **Open:** all week L 12 to 3, Mon to Sat D 6 to 10. **Closed:** 25 and 26 Dec. **Meals:** alc (main courses £14 to £21). Set L and D £29.50. **Service:** not inc. **Details:** Cards accepted. 108 seats. 40 seats outside. Separate bar. Music. Children allowed.

riverstation

Tip-top ingredients cooked with respect
The Grove, Bristol, BS1 4RB
Tel no: (0117) 9144434
www.riverstation.co.uk
Modern European | £28
Cooking score: 3
£5 OFF   £30

Restaurants on Bristol's harbourside come and go, but riverstation has remained constant for more than a decade. Occupying a former 1950s river-police station, the place is modern and minimalist with lots of floor-to-ceiling glass, wood and steel. Downstairs there's a lively café/bar, but upstairs is the bright and airy restaurant with a partially open kitchen. Only the very best seasonal produce will do here and tip-top ingredients are handled with respect in the Mediterranean and French dishes that change daily. Start with smoked mozzarella and cauliflower frittata with rocket before moving on to a perfectly balanced smoked haddock 'choucroute' with morteau sausage and Gewürztraminer sauce. Finish with lemon syllabub with blood oranges. A regularly changing and intelligently written wine list starts at £14.95.
Chef/s: Peter Taylor. **Open:** Sun to Fri L 12 to 2.30 (3 Sun), Mon to Sat D 6 to 10.30 (11 Fri and Sat). **Closed:** 24 to 26 Dec. **Meals:** alc (main courses £13 to £20). Set L £12 (2 courses) to £14.50. Set D £14.75 (2 courses) to £18.50. Sun L £16 (2 courses) to £19.50. **Service:** not inc. **Details:** Cards accepted. 120 seats. 30 seats outside. Air-con. Separate bar. No music. Wheelchair access. Children allowed.

NEW ENTRY
Rockfish Grill

Stylish seafood and meat too
128-130 Whiteladies Road, Bristol, BS8 2RS
Tel no: (0117) 9737384
www.rockfishgrill.co.uk
Seafood | £30
Cooking score: 4
£5 OFF

Owner Mitch Tonks used to cook at this address when it was part of his FishWorks chain but this restaurant and fishmongers is very different to its former incarnation. With its linen curtains, sandy driftwood floors and tables and sea-green leather button-back banquettes, it's a stylish yet informal place with walls dotted with photos of Tonks and fishermen in his beloved Brixham. This is the sort of place where you can just pop in for a plate of oysters and a glass of wine or dive into the daily changing menu. It's not just fish and seafood here, and the meat dishes are certainly worthy of attention, with most cooked over the charcoal fire. Scallops roasted in the shell with white port and garlic might be followed by turbot roasted on the bone with hollandaise sauce. Leave room for seasonal desserts such as Yorkshire rhubarb trifle. Wines from £17.
Chef/s: Jake Platt and Mitch Tonks. **Open:** Tue to Sat L 12 to 2.30, D 6 to 10. **Closed:** Sun, 25 and 26 Dec, bank hols. **Meals:** alc (main courses £12 to £28). Set L and early D £15 (2 courses) to £20. **Service:** not inc. **Details:** Cards accepted. 42 seats. Air-con. Wheelchair access. Music. Children allowed.

ALSO RECOMMENDED
▲ Zazu's Kitchen

45 Jamaica Street, Bristol, BS2 8JP
Tel no: (0117) 9232233
www.zazuskitchen.com
European

A haven in Bristol's bohemian quarter, this laid-back all-day café delivers quality food in a setting of scrubbed pine tables, book-lined shelves and sofas. The tiny open kitchen moves up a gear at night, when it turns into a candlelit bistro serving locally sourced modern European food. The well-priced set menu (£19 for three courses) offers the likes of pea and mint soup and harissa-spiced rump of lamb with sweet potato purée and broad beans. House wine starts at £8 a carafe. Open all week, Fri and Sat D.

Cheltenham

Le Champignon Sauvage
Thrilling tastes from a high-achiever
24-26 Suffolk Road, Cheltenham, GL50 2AQ
Tel no: (01242) 573449
www.lechampignonsauvage.co.uk
Modern French | £55
Cooking score: 8

Sitting tight to the pavement on Suffolk Road, the Champignon is hard to miss, but twenty-three years of continuous high achievement is altogether impossible to ignore. What must have seemed a daring venture in the speculative late 80s has blossomed into one of the UK's destination restaurants. There is nothing unduly ostentatious about the operation that David and Helen Everitt-Matthias run. To be sure, this is a smart place with quality appointments, including some striking abstract artworks. It's colourful where others are determinedly monochrome, with well-spaced tables in place of the serried ranks favoured elsewhere. But what the Champignon has always been about, first and foremost, is excellent cuisine. David's style has developed over the years, acquiring greater complexity, some would say a greater degree of metropolitan shine, but the same enjoyment of thrilling tastes and textures from unusual ingredients informs the menus today as it has always done. Readers remember the outstanding 3D precision of it all, even when the object of attention is a modern classic such as scallops with cauliflower purée, served with smoked freshwater eel and apple. The prized Dexter beef is offered in two guises – corned and tartare – as a starter, with wasabi cream and pickled shimeji, spinning glorious

variations on something so everyday (corned beef and horseradish, anyone?) that we can only admire the daring. Dishes can look as bold as the aforementioned artworks – carpaccio of pig's head with puréed pear, pavé of cod on squid-ink risotto – yet still avoid undue pretension. And the incorporation of other culinary traditions adds depth, rather than striving desperately for novelty, witness the wood pigeon with its pastilla, chermoula and accompanying carrot tagine. Bitter and savoury notes ring through the dessert options, to great effect in the opinion of a reporter who took the chocolate and olive tart with fennel ice cream. The only thing that could now go wrong is a wine list that looks dull and unaffordable. Perish the thought. Starting at an almost silly £12, here is a collection of cannily chosen, thought-provoking bottles, halves and glasses that offer fruitful, purposeful drinking throughout.
Chef/s: David Everitt-Matthias. Open: Tue to Sat L 12.30 to 1.15, D 7.30 to 8.30. Closed: Sun, Mon, 10 days Christmas, 3 weeks Jun. Meals: Set L £25 (2 courses) to £30. Set D Tue to Fri £25 (2 courses) to £30. Sat D £45 (2 courses) to £55. Service: not inc. Details: Cards accepted. 38 seats. Air-con. Separate bar. No mobile phones. Music. Children allowed.

Lumière
Serious Cheltenham contender
Clarence Parade, Cheltenham, GL50 3PA
Tel no: (01242) 222200
www.lumiere.cc
Modern British | £42
Cooking score: 4
£5 OFF V

Since taking over this understated Cheltenham favourite in 2009, Jon Howe and Helen Aubrey have re-established Lumière as a serious gastronomic contender in the town. The place trades on intimacy, with purple colours, floral displays and modern art in the contemporary dining room. By contrast, Jon's food's all about on-trend culinary complexity and confident gestures. A plate of Jimmy Butler's pork (poached loin, faggot, confit belly) with mash, pumpkin purée and white pudding crumble bedazzled one enthusiastic recipient, while others have singled out a cheeky corned beef terrine with *pain d'épices* and mustard cream, and Balmoral venison with sweet peppered swede, cavolo nero, dark chocolate and raspberry sauce ('a work of art'). Cleverly deconstructed apple and blackberry crumble with sorbet, jelly, parfait and a wonderful little doughnut makes a 'triumphant' finale, and Valrhona chocolate fondant served on a slate with toasted pistachios and 'space dust' has also elicited 'wows'. The wine list is a serious tome with prices from £20.

Chef/s: Jon Howe. **Open:** Wed to Sat L 12 to 2, Tue to Sat D 7 to 9. **Closed:** Sun, Mon, 2 weeks Jan. **Meals:** Set L £19 (2 courses) to £22. Set D £36 (2 courses) to £42. Tasting menu £42 to £55. **Service:** not inc. **Details:** Cards accepted. 32 seats. Air-con. No mobile phones. Music.

The Royal Well Tavern

Tucked-away bistro with seasonal food
5 Royal Well Place, Cheltenham, GL50 3DN
Tel no: (01242) 221212
www.theroyalwelltavern.com
Modern British | £27
Cooking score: 4
£5 OFF **V** £30

A short stroll from the Promenade, this tucked-away bistro may look like a gastropub with its burgundy leather banquettes and polished wooden floors, but it is more akin to a bustling Paris brasserie. The Elizabeth David books on the bar hint at what's to come and the straight-talking menu is fiercely seasonal, with well-sourced ingredients treated in simple fashion. New chef Andrew Martin eschews fancy tricks in favour of full-blooded dishes along the lines of courgette fritters with mint yoghurt, bouillabaisse, steak-frites or saddle of rabbit with sweetcorn, leeks and carrots. Elsewhere, a starter of sautéed lamb's kidneys on a bed of creamed onions and thyme could be followed by poached wild sea trout with peas, braised baby gem, lemon oil and crayfish. To finish, vanilla-speckled poached rhubarb arrives with a zingy rhubarb sorbet,

or you might go for walnut and salted caramel tart. The wine list is an exclusively French collection that kicks off at £16 (£4 a glass).
Chef/s: Andrew Martin. **Open:** all week L 12 to 3 (10 to 3.30 Sun), Mon to Sat D 5 to 10 (10.30 Fri and Sat). **Closed:** 25 and 26 Dec. **Meals:** alc (main courses £9 to £60). Set L and D £10 (2 courses) to £12.50. **Service:** 10% (optional). **Details:** Cards accepted. 46 seats. Air-con. Separate bar. Wheelchair access. Music. Children allowed.

ALSO RECOMMENDED
▲ Brosh
8 Suffolk Parade, Cheltenham, GL50 2AB
Tel no: (01242) 227277
www.broshrestaurant.co.uk
Eastern Mediterranean

Raviv Hadad's stylishly appointed restaurant offers the cuisine of the eastern Mediterranean and North Africa, so Cheltenham now knows its brik from its bazargan. Ftut, a Yemeni beef soup (£6.95), is a fine restorative in winter, while mains might take in partridge with preserved lemons, saffron and green olives, or venison with tzimmes (honeyed carrots) and Marsala sauce (£18.95). Desserts are fragrant with rosewater and spices. Wines from £12.95. Open Wed to Sat D.

■ Chipping Campden
ALSO RECOMMENDED
▲ Eight Bells Inn
Church Street, Chipping Campden, GL55 6JG
Tel no: (01386) 840371
www.eightbellsinn.co.uk
Modern British

Built in 1380 to house stonemasons working on the nearby church, this inn is steeped in antiquity, but the menu has a modern edge. A diverse list of fuss-free dishes takes in anything from oriental-style duck and noodle stir-fry with hoi sin sauce (£6.95) to classic surf and turf or prime fillet of pork stuffed with apricot and chestnut and served with lyonnaise potatoes (£16). Wines start at £14.50. Accommodation. Open all week.

Cirencester

Made by Bob

Good-natured café/deli
The Corn Hall, Unit 6, 26 Market Place,
Cirencester, GL7 2NY
Tel no: (01285) 641818
www.foodmadebybob.com
Mediterranean | £25
Cooking score: 3

£5 OFF **V** £30

A godsend for Cirencester, this jolly, good-natured café/deli does sterling service to the community, providing relaxed modern brasserie dishes and daily breakfasts – and it's 'fantastic to watch it cooked in front of you'. Simplicity is evident in a well-reported pancetta and sage risotto or wild mushroom, spinach and ricotta tart, but all this indicates that attention is focused where it should be: raw materials are of good quality, and tastes and textures properly considered. Bob Parkinson's heart is seemingly in the Mediterranean world of linguine with garlic sausage, tomatoes, pecorino and basil or breast of chicken with deep-fried polenta, field mushrooms and salsa verde. Desserts include a sublime apple and rhubarb granita, as well as praline and orange parfait. The short, thoughtfully assembled wine list starts at £14.25.
Chef/s: Bob Parkinson and Ben Round. **Open:** Mon to Sat 7.30am to 10pm (10.30 Sat), L 12 to 3.
Closed: Sun. **Meals:** alc (main courses £10 to £18). **Service:** not inc. **Details:** Cards accepted. 45 seats. Wheelchair access. Music. Children allowed.

Coln St Aldwyns

The New Inn

Honest pub food
Main Street, Coln St Aldwyns, GL7 5AN
Tel no: (01285) 750651
www.new-inn.co.uk
British | £30
Cooking score: 2

£5 OFF 🛏

In one of Gloucestershire's prettiest villages, this creeper-covered, sixteenth-century inn really looks the part. Amid beams and flagstones you can sample real ales and a workmanlike version of honest pub food – simple stuff for lunch (deli boards of cold meats, fish and chips), a touch more elaboration in the evening. Much of the repertoire has a cosmopolitan feel, say lime-scented crab and char-grilled pepper tian, although more robust game dishes also win votes. Reporters have found it 'costly by local standards', but the food satisfies and service runs well. House wine £14.50.
Chef/s: Oliver Addis. **Open:** all week L 12.30 to 2.30 (3 Sun), D 7 to 9 (9.30 Fri and Sat, 6.30 to 8 Sun). **Meals:** alc (main courses £10 to £19). Sun L £15. **Service:** not inc. **Details:** Cards accepted. 50 seats. 80 seats outside. Separate bar. No mobile phones. Wheelchair access. Music. Children allowed. Car parking.

Compton Abdale

ALSO RECOMMENDED
▲ The Puesdown Inn

Compton Abdale, GL54 4DN
Tel no: (01451) 860262
www.puesdown.cotswoldinns.com
Modern British £5 OFF

A cottage façade and backdrop of stunning countryside add to the appeal of this rejuvenated one-time local boozer set back from the A40. Although still a pub, especially when the sun shines and the garden comes into its own, this is also a forward-looking restaurant with a liking for seasonal produce. Look for tian of crab and avocado (£8), slow-cooked belly of Gloucester Old Spot (£15) and tarte Tatin (£6.25). Lighter lunch dishes and pizzas also available. Wine from £12.75. Accommodation. Closed D on Sun and Mon.

Corse Lawn
Corse Lawn House Hotel
Classic cuisine at a gracious retreat
Corse Lawn, GL19 4LZ
Tel no: (01452) 780771
www.corselawn.com
Anglo-French | £33
Cooking score: 3
£5 OFF ⓘ ⏗ V

When the Hines took over this listed Queen Anne residence in 1978, they set about fostering a sense of gracious Englishness that has suffused the place ever since. Meanwhile, the cooking has moved on – although the food served diligently in the sedate dining room still ploughs an Anglo-French furrow, with conscientious sourcing at its heart (a policy that now embraces sustainable fish). Here is a country retreat that's happy to offer sound renditions of caramelised onion tart, slow-cooked pork belly with cider, and abundant local game alongside more upbeat ideas (grilled fillet of gurnard with couscous and saffron sauce, say). A cavalcade of puddings ends proceedings in classic style – raspberry pavlova, honey and walnut tart, and so on. Simpler menus are also available in the bistro. The wine list delves deep into the aristrocratic French regions, and the result is an assured, price-conscious selection oozing class; elsewhere, look for prestigious numbers from Italy and Australia. Prices start at £17.20 (£4.60 a glass), with more than 50 half-bottles on show.
Chef/s: Andrew Poole and Martin Kinahan. **Open:** all week L 12 to 2, D 7 to 9.30. **Closed:** 24 to 26 Dec. **Meals:** alc (main courses £13 to £23). Set L £22.50 (2 courses) to £25.50. Set D £32.50. Sun L 25.50. Set bistro L and D £15 (2 courses) to £20. **Service:** not inc. **Details:** Cards accepted. 70 seats. 40 seats outside. Separate bar. No music. No mobile phones. Wheelchair access. Children allowed. Car parking.

Didmarton
ALSO RECOMMENDED
▲ The Kings Arms
The Street, Didmarton, GL9 1DT
Tel no: (01454) 238245
www.kingsarmsdidmarton.co.uk
Gastropub

A seventeenth-century coaching inn with a foot firmly in the gastropub camp, the Kings Arms is 'well-decorated and atmospheric' inside, with simple décor and heritage colours. Dishes range from sturdy pub favourites such as ham, egg and chips (£8.95) or sausages and mash to imaginative options such as ratatouille-stuffed baby squid on lemon and garlic mashed potato (£13.95) or pigeon and blackberry pie. Finish with banoffi pie (£5.85). Wines start at £14.75. Open all week.

Ebrington
ALSO RECOMMENDED
▲ The Ebrington Arms
Ebrington, GL55 6NH
Tel no: (01386) 593223
www.theebringtonarms.co.uk
Modern British £5 OFF

A sixteenth-century inn built from Cotswold stone, this village pub is cosy, 'a little cramped' even, but big on atmosphere with crackling fires in winter and the option of a beer garden for fine days. Expect straightforward dishes with 'impressive flavour combinations' from a 'clearly talented' chef. Ham hock and parsley terrine with piccalilli and olive toasts (£6) followed by pan-fried fillets of grey mullet with truffled new potatoes, wilted spinach and salsa verde (£13) are typical of the style. Puds might include raspberry and praline pannacotta (£5). Wines start at £16. Accommodation. Open all week.

Also recommended
Also recommended entries are not scored but we think they are worth a visit.

Eldersfield
The Butchers Arms

Local sourcing with a vengeance
Lime Street, Eldersfield, GL19 4NX
Tel no: (01452) 840381
www.thebutchersarms.net
Modern British | £35
Cooking score: 4

Squirreled away on the border between
Gloucestershire and Worcestershire, the
Winter family's two-room pub has valiantly
rejected olde-worlde tweeness and defied
'gastro' improvement. This is the real thing,
four centuries old, with real ales drawn from
the cask in the pint-sized bar and a minuscule
dining room where tables are at a premium. It
may be genuinely archaic, but diners 'step into
the twenty-first century' when it comes to the
food on the plate. James Winter sources local
produce with a vengeance, be it Philip
Houldey's lamb, wild salmon netted from the
Severn or rare-breed Middle White pork from
Huntsham Farm. The result is a commendably
short, seasonal menu bursting with sharply
executed ideas: breast of grouse is served with
black pudding and beetroot relish, roast and
confit mallard comes with bashed neeps and
quinces. Cornish fish also gets a good outing
(brill with lobster ravioli and buttered chard)
and puds such as damson ice cream are true to
the cause. Around 40 wines kick off at £15.50.
Chef/s: James Winter. **Open:** Wed to Sun L 12 to 1,
Tue to Sat D 7 to 8.45. **Closed:** Mon, first week Jan,
last week Aug. **Meals:** alc (main courses £16 to £21).
Service: not inc. **Details:** Cards accepted. 24 seats.
No music. No mobile phones. Wheelchair access.
Car parking.

Fairford
Allium

Stylish, first-rate cooking
1 London Street, Fairford, GL7 4AH
Tel no: (01285) 712200
www.allium.uk.net
Modern British | £43
Cooking score: 6

'We would always choose it for our Last
Supper', admitted one couple who regularly
make the pilgrimage to Erica and James
Graham's much-loved restaurant by Fairford's
market square. Allium is held in high
affection, and its gussied-up seventeenth-
century frontage looks instantly appealing –
although a thoroughly modern tone prevails
inside. There's a vivid sense of seasonality
about the food here, and James is keen to flaunt
his allegiances. He serves local rabbit with
wild garlic, embellishes Phillip Kinch's rose
veal with marrowbone and morels, and even
finds room for the freshwater zander in a dish
with Claydon Lake crayfish. This is food
where clarity and freshness go hand in hand,
witness perfectly timed cod loin with pea
purée, white asparagus and chive flowers or
turbot with clams and sea vegetables.
Elsewhere, earthier influences come into play
– chicken and wild mushroom terrine is
pointed up with red onion marmalade, and
suckling pig gets an aromatic kick from star
anise and fennel. On-trend themes re-surface
in desserts such as blood orange délice with
beetroot sorbet, a sweet take on sushi or the
zany Snickers 2010. Local cheeses and home-
baked breads are up to the mark, and the
Francophile wine list is a well-judged
collection with prices from £16 (£3.85 a
glass).
Chef/s: James Graham. **Open:** Wed to Sun L 12 to 2,
Tue to Sat D 7 to 9. **Closed:** Mon, 25 to 28 Dec.
Meals: Set L £22.50 (2 courses) to £25. Set D £36.50
(2 courses) to £42.50. Sun L £25. Tasting menu £65.
Service: not inc. **Details:** Cards accepted. 34 seats.
Separate bar. No mobile phones. Music. Children
allowed.

David Everitt-Matthias Le Champignon Sauvage

What do you wish you had known when you started out as a chef?
The importance of attention to detail.

What is your earliest culinary memory?
Going wild food gathering with my Auntie Pat when I was six years old.

Where do you see cooking/food/restaurants in 60 years' time?
Chefs will have more knowledge of their products. The restaurant scene will be more relaxed, less formal service, less pomposity. Equipment will have a big effect on the techniques of cooking.

If you were having a dinner party for six people, who would you invite?
Yamamoto Tsunetomo (seventeenth-century samurai), Roy Lichtenstein, Stieg Larsson, Audrey Hepburn, Chet Baker, Humphrey Bogart.

What would be your perfect birthday meal?
Calves' sweetbreads, scallops, roasted chicken, treacle pudding.

What is the best dish on your menu?
Fillet of sewin, baby beetroot, wood sorrel and lovage velouté.

▌Lower Oddington

The Fox Inn
Sturdily agreeable pub food
Lower Oddington, GL56 OUR
Tel no: (01451) 870555
www.foxinn.net
Gastropub | £23
Cooking score: 1
🍴 V £30

Creeper-clad and built from Cotswold stone, this is a quintessential British pub tweaked for the twenty-first century. Rug-strewn floors and a judicious amount of rustic knick-knackery keeps the interior somewhere between gastropub and village inn. Expect sturdily agreeable pub food: a square of puff pastry topped with sweet, grilled peppers and goats' cheese made a satisfying starter at inspection, followed by a steak and kidney pie with a rich, dark sauce and plenty of freshly cooked vegetables. House wine is £13.75.
Chef/s: Ray Pearce. **Open:** all week L 12 to 2.30 (3.30 Sun), D 6.30 to 10 (7 to 9.30 Sun). **Closed:** 25 Dec. **Meals:** alc (main courses £11 to £17). **Service:** not inc. **Details:** Cards accepted. 80 seats. 80 seats outside. Separate bar. No music. Wheelchair access. Children allowed. Car parking.

▌Minchinhampton

The Ragged Cot
Country charmer with robust cooking
Cirencester Road, Minchinhampton, GL6 8PE
Tel no: (01453) 884643
www.theraggedcot.co.uk
Gastropub | £25
Cooking score: 2
£5 OFF 🍴 £30

Spruced up and brimming with bucolic charm, this centuries-old coaching inn is pitched beside 600 acres of National Trust land, and there's a distinct *Country Living* vibe about the cottage-style bar with its snug alcoves, wood-burning stoves and pints of Ringwood Best on draught. You can eat here, or at rustic oak tables in the unpretentious dining room. Emma Berriman makes

admirable use of home-grown and allotment vegetables – as well as local meat and game – for a short, no-nonsense menu with robust Brit overtones. Smoked haddock Scotch egg with tomato and thyme compote might give way to roast duck with crushed peas, wilted spinach and Madeira jus, while puds could run to apple crumble with rhubarb ice cream. House wine is £14 (£3.80 a glass).
Chef/s: Emma Berriman. **Open:** all week L 12 to 3 (4 Sun), Mon to Sat D 6 to 9 (10 Fri and Sat). **Meals:** alc (main courses £11 to £15). **Service:** not inc. **Details:** Cards accepted. 80 seats. 100 seats outside. Separate bar. Wheelchair access. Music. Children allowed. Car parking.

Northleach

ALSO RECOMMENDED
▲ The Wheatsheaf Inn
West End, Northleach, GL54 3EZ
Tel no: (01451) 860244
www.cotswoldswheatsheaf.com
Modern British £5 OFF

New life and vigour has been breathed into this seventeenth-century Cotswold stone coaching inn. Set in the heart of Northleach, it's an atmospheric gem offering a classy mix of flagstone floors, open fires and inviting food, say devilled kidneys on toast (£5) or red mullet with fennel and cucumber salad, followed by roast pork loin with braised lentils (£16). To finish, perhaps goats' curd and cherries (£5). Wines from £16. Open all week. Accommodation. Reports please.

Sapperton
The Bell at Sapperton
Well-supported local
Sapperton, GL7 6LE
Tel no: (01285) 760298
www.foodatthebell.co.uk
Gastropub | £30
New Chef

Paul Davidson and Patricia LeJeune have built up a loyal following since taking over this attractive, stone-built pub/restaurant 11 years

ago, and their kitchen puts a lot of effort into sourcing decent materials, from locally foraged wild garlic and mushrooms to Dorset crabs, Hereford beef and Neal's Yard Dairy cheeses. Staff are on the ball, although there have been complaints of late about 'rushed service' due to the pressures of a second sitting. The enterprising wine list offers plenty of choice from £16 (£3.75 a glass). Note: chef Ivan Reid left as the Guide was going to press, and his replacement, Christopher Lee, was yet to take up his post. Reports please.
Chef/s: Christopher Lee. **Open:** all week L 12 to 2.15, D 7 to 9.30 (6.30 to 9 Sun). **Closed:** 25 Dec. **Meals:** alc (main courses £12 to £21). **Service:** not inc. **Details:** Cards accepted. 65 seats. 40 seats outside. No music. No mobile phones. Wheelchair access. Car parking.

Southrop

★ READERS' RESTAURANT OF THE YEAR ★
NATIONAL WINNER

The Swan at Southrop
What a country restaurant should be
Southrop, GL7 3NU
Tel no: (01367) 850205
www.theswanatsouthrop.co.uk
Modern British | £27
Cooking score: 4

V £30

'Every now and again, you find a place that embodies the spirit of what a country restaurant should be about. The dream is to find a combination of excellence across food, service, ambience and high-quality local produce. The Swan at Southrop has this. There is nowhere that my family and I would rather dine in the world.' Even those readers who stop short of eulogy are variously impressed, seduced or simply gratified by the Snows' custody of this seventeenth-century, creeper-clad Cotswold pub, where 'the fires are always lit, the seats are comfortable, the space between the tables is good, and you can park outside'. Combining informality with sound but simple cooking is a style that Sebastian Snow has successfully developed. The menu runs from good old fish and chips and the 'great' Swan burger, to 'phenomenal' tempura prawns, ox cheek bourguignon, confit of goose leg, and duck cassoulet, with raspberry bread-and-butter pudding a favourite dessert. House wine is £14.

Chef/s: Sebastian Snow. **Open:** all week L 12 to 3, Mon to Sat D 6 to 10. **Closed:** 25 Dec. **Meals:** alc (main courses £12 to £18). Set L and D £13 (2 courses) to £16. **Service:** not inc. **Details:** Cards accepted. 65 seats. 25 seats outside. Separate bar. No music. Children allowed.

▮ Stow-on-the-Wold

The Old Butcher's
Gutsy, straight-talking food
7 Park Street, Stow-on-the-Wold, GL54 1AQ
Tel no: (01451) 831700
www.theoldbutchers.com
Modern British | £25
Cooking score: 3
£30

If Stow-on-the-Wold evokes antiques and *Country Life* magazine, The Old Butcher's may surprise. Its walls may be Cotswold stone, but at its heart is a slick modern restaurant with a metropolitan edge. Bistro furniture and smooth, knowledgeable service set the tone for gutsy, straight-talking cooking that trumpets the quality of its ingredients. Superb homemade breads struck a winning note at inspection; hot on their heels, piquillo peppers stuffed with salt cod typified the simple, hearty style. A main course of venison and cabbage Gascogne was perfectly executed – dark, intense, wintry food followed by cosy Venetian rice pudding with plump white raisins, vanilla and tart blood orange. A sensible list of wines starts at £14.

Chef/s: Peter Robinson. **Open:** all week L 12 to 2.30, Mon to Sat D 6 to 9.30 (10 Sat). **Closed:** 1 week Oct, 1 week May. **Meals:** alc (main courses £12 to £18). Set L £12 (2 courses) to £14. **Service:** not inc. **Details:** Cards accepted. 45 seats. 12 seats outside. Air-con. Separate bar. Wheelchair access. Music. Children allowed.

▮ Tetbury

Calcot Manor, The Conservatory
Full country house package
Tetbury, GL8 8YJ
Tel no: (01666) 890391
www.calcotmanor.co.uk
Modern British | £35
Cooking score: 2
🛏

In a former life this centuries-old building was a farmhouse, but nowadays it's a contemporary country house hotel, complete with spa and conference facilities. The Conservatory restaurant (there's also an informal pub, the Gumstool Inn) has fairly bland, neutral décor and the set-up seems to have lost some of its edge: offhand service and a lack of care have been cited, although the kitchen still puts its faith in seasonal supplies. Whole grilled Dover sole with hollandaise and roast venison with winter root vegetable stew are typical centrepieces. Start with dressed Dorset crab with lemon and dill mayonnaise and finish with caramelised lemon tart. The wine list opens with a good choice by the glass (including 100ml tasting measures from £3.55); bottles from £23.25.

Chef/s: Michael Croft. **Open:** all week L 12 to 2, D 7 to 9.30 (9 Sun). **Meals:** alc (main courses £17 to £24). Set L £19.50 (2 courses) to £23.50. **Service:** not inc. **Details:** Cards accepted. 80 seats. 15 seats outside. Air-con. Separate bar. No mobile phones. Wheelchair access. Music. Car parking.

The Chef's Table
Deli/bistro with a French accent
49 Long Street, Tetbury, GL8 8AA
Tel no: (01666) 504466
www.thechefstable.co.uk
French | £35
Cooking score: 4

Simple pine tables and an open-plan kitchen in the upstairs dining room emphasise the laid-back tone at this deli-cum-bistro in the centre of Tetbury, and Michael Bedford has nailed his colours firmly to the rustic French mast. Plates of charcuterie or moules marinière (with mussels from the Fowey estuary) might be the preludes to hearty main dishes such as duck cassoulet with smoked bacon and Toulouse sausage, or the day's fresh fish served with creamy mash and garlic butter. In the light of such a simple approach, it is all the more impressive when reporters describe the end product as 'quite superb', and, as always, it's the quality of the ingredients themselves that defines the food. Finish with textbook crème brûlée and pistachio ice cream, or choose from a fabulous menu of European cheeses. House wines are £17.15, or £19.50 for a litre carafe.

Chef/s: Michael Bedford. **Open:** Mon to Sat L 12 to 2.30, Wed to Sat D 7 to 9.30. **Closed:** Sun, 25 and 26 Dec, 1 Jan. **Meals:** alc (main courses £16 to £20). **Service:** not inc. **Details:** Cards accepted. 55 seats. Music. Children allowed.

▌Thornbury

Ronnies

Low-key gem
11 St Mary Street, Thornbury, BS35 2AB
Tel no: (01454) 411137
www.ronnies-restaurant.co.uk
Modern European | £30
Cooking score: 4

£5
OFF

Ron Faulkner's well-appointed restaurant hidden away in a shopping precinct has a low-key ambience, but its reputation is founded on quality cooking. The short carte and even shorter set menus are peppered with ideas that attempt to please all palates – a policy that seems to work well judging by the endorsements for scallops wrapped in Italian bacon with garlic purée and sage butter, roasted belly pork with Clonakilty black pudding and beetroot chutney, and wild mushroom risotto with black chanterelles, Champagne and truffle oil. Elsewhere there could be brill with saffron and mussel chowder or beef Wellington. For dessert, apple and blackberry crumble has been

praised. A good-value international wine list (from £15) is forthrightly set out by style, with a few special bottles added for treats.

Chef/s: George Kostka. **Open:** Tue to Sun L 12 to 2.30, Tue to Sat D 6.30 to 9.30 (10.30 Fri and Sat). **Closed:** Mon, 25 and 26 Dec, 1 Jan. **Meals:** alc (main courses £14 to £20). Set L £9.75 (2 courses) to £12.75. Set D £16 (2 courses) to £19. Sun L £16.75 (2 courses) to £19.75. **Service:** not inc. **Details:** Cards accepted. 62 seats. Wheelchair access. Music. Children allowed.

▌Upper Slaughter

Lords of the Manor

Dishes full of fascination
Upper Slaughter, GL54 2JD
Tel no: (01451) 820243
www.lordsofthemanor.com
Modern British | £55
Cooking score: 6

🍷 🍴

Despite its name, Upper Slaughter is one of a handful of 'thankful villages', small communities that somehow sustained no loss of life in either of the World Wars. At its centre is this handsome Cotswold house of honey-coloured stone, built as a rectory in the seventeenth century and surrounded by eight acres of walled gardens, parkland and a lake. A low-ceilinged, neutral dining room forms the backdrop for Matt Weedon's polished contemporary cooking, which is informed by an assiduously listed roll call of local suppliers. Choice on the fixed-price menus is wide, and the dishes are full of fascination: start perhaps with wood pigeon mi-cuit, with a pastilla of the leg meat, pigeon tartare, beetroot sorbet, pickled mushrooms and fig purée. Mains proceed with the likes of roasted pollack teamed with braised chicken wings, clams and creamed leeks in a chicken and thyme jus, or Longhorn beef, the rib accompanied by snails, artichokes and hedgehog mushrooms in cep velouté. Beguile the senses with desserts such as dark chocolate and truffle oil custard presented with chocolate croquant and truffle honey ice cream. A majestic wine list travels the known world, but look to the Sommelier's Value Selection near the back for price relief – the bidding opens at £19.50.

Chef/s: Matt Weedon. **Open:** Sun L 12 to 2, all week D 7 to 9.30. **Meals:** Sun L £35. Set D £55. Tasting menu £65 (7 courses) to £95 (10 courses). **Service:** 10% (optional). **Details:** Cards accepted. 60 seats. Separate bar. No music. No mobile phones. Wheelchair access. Car parking.

■ Winchcombe

5 North Street
Pint-sized eatery with stellar food
5 North Street, Winchcombe, GL54 5LH
Tel no: (01242) 604566
www.5northstreet.com
Modern European | £36
Cooking score: 6

V

Kate and Marcus Ashenford's 'supremely welcoming' little restaurant is a pint-sized eatery squeezed into a centuries-old, slightly crooked building on Winchcombe's main drag. It's run as a low-key family affair, with an easy-going attitude to ordering: diners are offered a choice of fixed-price menus, mixing and matching is encouraged and meals are priced accordingly. Marvellous home-baked mini loaves and a couple of amuse-bouches open proceedings – perhaps a cup of soup and dinky Welsh rarebit with rhubarb compote. After that, you might be treated to a starter of hand-dived scallop and sautéed foie gras with creamed cauliflower, sweet braised onion and beetroot syrup, followed by breast and leg of quail with cep dumplings, celeriac fondant, pickled grapes and grenadine reduction. To conclude, perhaps a many-faceted assemblage involving caramel cheesecake, pineapple, peanut brittle, blood orange and rosemary sorbet and white balsamic – a riot of contrasts and textures. Sadly, 'very amateurish' staff are sometimes at odds with Kate Ashenford's personable approach to proceedings out front, and, while Marcus is capable of great things in the kitchen, there has been the odd gripe about overblown, unbalanced flavours. The modest, eclectic wine list is regularly updated with

inviting bin ends; prices start at £20. Note that the restaurant doesn't attract or expect huge numbers, especially at lunchtime – so book ahead to make sure they're open.
Chef/s: Marcus Ashenford. **Open:** Wed to Sun L 12.30 to 1.30, Tue to Sat D 7 to 9. **Closed:** Mon, 2 weeks Jan, 1 week Aug. **Meals:** alc (main courses £15 to £22). Set L £22 (2 courses) to £26. Set D £36 (3 courses) to £46. Sun L £31. **Service:** not inc. **Details:** Cards accepted. 26 seats. Wheelchair access. Music. Children allowed.

Wesley House
Lively, confident British cooking
High Street, Winchcombe, GL54 5LJ
Tel no: (01242) 602366
www.wesleyhouse.co.uk
Modern British | £33
Cooking score: 3

£5 OFF 🛏 **V**

The proprietor of this fifteenth-century half-timbered gem has been running it as a small hotel for nigh on two decades with seemingly consummate ease. Of the two dining rooms, the bar/grill enjoys the minimum formality that comes with a please-all menu and value-for-money pricing, while the restaurant is grander in style, but not in approach. Here the cooking is confident modern British, with the kitchen taking a lively approach to whatever comes its way. This could include a starter of fricassee of forest mushrooms and spinach with free-range poached egg or main courses such as venison with gratin potato, potted Savoy cabbage and red wine sauce. Warm Bakewell sponge with Amaretto ice cream rounds things off. The wine list comes with lots of options by the glass; bottles from £16.50.
Chef/s: Martin Dunn. **Open:** all week L 12 to 2, Mon to Sat D 6.30 to 9.30 (10 Fri and Sat). **Meals:** alc (main courses £14 to £25). Set L £12.50 (2 courses) to £25.50. Set D £19.50 (2 courses) to £24.50. **Service:** not inc. **Details:** Cards accepted. 80 seats. Air-con. Separate bar. No mobile phones. Wheelchair access. Music. Children allowed.

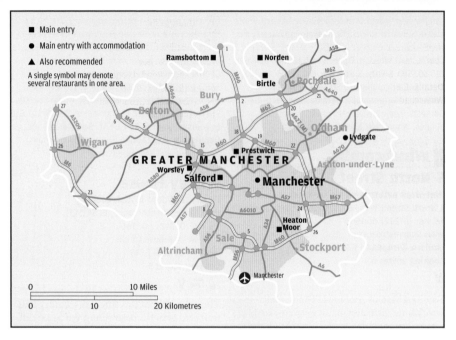

- ■ Main entry
- ● Main entry with accommodation
- ▲ Also recommended

A single symbol may denote several restaurants in one area.

▌Altrincham

READERS RECOMMEND

Dilli

Indian

60 Stamford New Road, Altrincham, WA14 1EE

Tel no: (0161) 9297484

www.dilli.co.uk

'The menu is a world away from your high street curry house, and the kitchen has a skill and lightness of touch with the spicing'

Symbols

🛏 Accommodation is available

£30 Three courses for less than £30

V More than three vegetarian main courses

£5 OFF £5-off voucher scheme

🍾 Notable wine list

▌Birtle

The Waggon at Birtle

Ex-pub scores with local ingredients

131 Bury and Rochdale Old Road, Birtle, BL9 6UE

Tel no: (01706) 622955

www.thewaggonatbirtle.co.uk

Modern British | £25

Cooking score: 2

£5 OFF £30

This former pub 'in the middle of nowhere on the main road between Bury and Rochdale' has been knocked through to create a restaurant that scores because it is prepared to invest in decent local ingredients. Tempura of Chadwick's Bury black pudding with apple, bacon, Lancashire cheese salad and mustard vinaigrette made a good start to one meal, and plaice, with a caper, lemon and herb butter sauce was an 'absolutely lovely piece of fish, perfectly cooked'. Steaks have been well endorsed, too, though elsewhere there have been complaints of muted flavours and poor vegetables. House wine is £13.50.

Chef/s: David Watson. **Open:** Wed to Sat D 6 to 9.30 (10 Sat), Sun 12.30 to 7.30. **Closed:** Mon, Tue, 26 Dec for 2 weeks, 2 weeks end Jul/Aug. **Meals:** alc (main courses £10 to £20). Set D £13.50 (2 courses) to £15.50. Sun L £10.50. **Service:** not inc. **Details:** Cards accepted. 50 seats. Separate bar. Wheelchair access. Music. Children allowed. Car parking.

▌Heaton Moor

NEW ENTRY

Damson

A great little local place
113 Heaton Moor Road, Heaton Moor, SK4 4HY
Tel no: (0161) 4324666
www.damsonrestaurant.co.uk
Modern European | £28
Cooking score: 2

🍾 £30

Done out in plummy purple, Damson is a peach of a local. It embodies the idea of the 'great little place round the corner', say readers, but seals city-centre smart (a legacy of co-owner Steve Pilling's long service in Manchester hospitality) and serves adventurous dishes such as a starter of foie gras with pineapple fluid gel. But more attention to the basics is needed; at inspection, a vegetable and chervil soup looked summery but suffered a surfeit of onion, while asparagus and pea pappardelle didn't show the pasta to advantage. Main courses such as grilled sea bass with orzo, tomatoes and chilli are more solid. House wines from £13.95.
Chef/s: Sally Shawarby and Simon Stanley. **Open:** all week L 12 to 2.45, D 5.30 to 9.30 (10 Fri and Sat). **Closed:** 25 and 26 Dec, 1 Jan. **Meals:** alc (main courses £10 to £19). Set L and D £12 (2 courses) to £15. Sun L £14.95. **Service:** not inc. **Details:** Cards accepted. 52 seats. 16 seats outside. Air-con. Wheelchair access. Music. Children allowed.

▌Lydgate

The White Hart

Worth the journey
51 Stockport Road, Lydgate, OL4 4JJ
Tel no: (01457) 872566
www.thewhitehart.co.uk
Modern British | £27
Cooking score: 4

£5 OFF 🍽 V £30

It's fair to say the White Hart is a little off the beaten track. One pair of lunchers, having been grievously misled by their SatNav, phoned in and received reliable directions from a human being in the old-fashioned way. The journey is worth it for the engaging country-pub ambience of ancient beams, the award-winning gardens, and for Paul Cookson's lively modern British food, offered in the bar and restaurant areas. Expect to start with something like tandoori sea bass accompanied by roast garlic and shallot raita and tomato and onion-seed chutney, before moving on to honey-roast Goosnargh duck and mango, served with chilli and coriander couscous, or roast lamb rump with goats' cheese and spinach ravioli, aubergine purée and balsamic onions. Finish with spiced plum tart and cinnamon ice cream. An enterprising wine list suits the culinary ambition, with Australian house blends at £14.90.
Chef/s: Paul Cookson. **Open:** Mon to Sat L 12 to 2.30, D 6 to 9.30. Sun 1 to 7.30. **Closed:** 26 Dec, 1 Jan. **Meals:** alc (main courses £13 to £24). Set L £13.50. Sun L £19.95. **Service:** not inc. **Details:** Cards accepted. 44 seats. 60 seats outside. Separate bar. No music. Children allowed. Car parking.

▊ Manchester

Chaophraya
High-quality Thai food
19 Chapel Walks, Manchester, M2 1HN
Tel no: (0161) 8328342
www.chaophraya.co.uk
Thai | £25
Cooking score: 2

V £30

Named after the great river, Chaophraya remains Manchester's best choice for Thai, served either downstairs in the bar or with napery in the restaurant. The setting is stylish and (for the most part) calm, the menu extensive. Sizzling dishes may be run-of-the-mill, but seafood and sauces are a particular strength, and vibrant salads worth exploration. Choo chi gong khao klong – king prawns still sweet after a dip in the deep fryer and served with a rich curry sauce and red rice – works well; peer past the display of Thai ingredients into the open kitchen and see it being made. House wine from £14.95.
Chef/s: Thanyanan 'Pum' Phuaknapo. **Open:** all week 12 to 11 (11.30 Fri and Sat). **Closed:** 25 Dec. **Meals:** alc (main courses £9 to £30). Set D £20 to £50. **Service:** 10% (optional). **Details:** Cards accepted. 120 seats. Air-con. Separate bar. Music. Children allowed.

The French at the Midland Hotel
Decades of ritual and splendour
16 Peter Street, Manchester, M60 2DS
Tel no: (0161) 2363333
www.qhotels.co.uk
Anglo-French | £57
Cooking score: 2

🛏

The service ritual is as lavish as the décor in Manchester's most gloriously old-fashioned dining room. At the heart of the hotel where Rolls met Royce, its Belle Époque splendour has lured high-profile diners for decades. At tables cluttered with covetable silver, regulars and see-and-be-seeners pick their way through a menu that offers joy and disappointment in equal measure. To start, tortellini of veal shank with crisp air-dried ham are light and intensely savoury, but halibut with braised leeks and baby onions is let down by barely cooked alliums. The setting, service and laden bread trolley almost (but not quite) justify the ambitious pricing, which extends to a wine list that starts at £23.
Chef/s: Paul Beckley and Gary Jenkins. **Open:** Tue to Sat D only 7 to 10.30. **Closed:** Sun, Mon, 1 week Aug, 1 week Sept, 26 Dec to 6 Jan. **Meals:** alc (main courses £23 to £75). Set D £29 (2 courses) to £35. **Service:** not inc. **Details:** Cards accepted. 46 seats. Air-con. Separate bar. No mobile phones. Wheelchair access. Music. Children allowed.

Gabriel's Kitchen
Great for grown-ups and kids
265 Upper Brook Street, Manchester, M13 OHR
Tel no: (0161) 2760911
www.themoderncaterer.co.uk
Modern British | £15
Cooking score: 2

V £30

Gabriel's Kitchen, run by genial Liverpudlian chef Peter Booth, makes fine use of a narrow slip of space near Manchester's universities. A tiny open kitchen fills the canteen-style café (now open some evenings) with the promise of hot lunch dishes such as truffled pappardelle with flat mushrooms and parsley or sausage and mash with onion gravy; you'll also get chunky sandwiches and wraps containing, for example, good Lancashire cheese. Booth's commitment to feeding kids healthily (the place is named after his son) is borne out by a children's menu featuring carrot sticks, bean purée and fruit as well as a chocolate and walnut brownie. As at Booth's Gallery Café (see entry), the appeal is simple, carefully sourced food. House wine £11.
Chef/s: Peter Booth. **Open:** all week 9am to 5pm (9am to 9pm Fri and Sat, 10am to 5pm Sun). **Closed:** 25 and 26 Dec. **Meals:** alc (main courses £9 to £10). **Service:** not inc. **Details:** Cash only. 38 seats. 12 seats outside. No mobile phones. Wheelchair access. Music. Children allowed.

The Gallery Café

An unusually good café
Whitworth Art Gallery, Oxford Road, Manchester,
M15 6ER
Tel no: (0161) 2757497
www.themoderncaterer.co.uk
Modern British | £15
Cooking score: 2
£5 OFF **V** £30

Visitors to the Whitworth are just as likely to be here for its unusually good café as its quirky art collections. Chef Peter Booth (also of the nearby Gabriel's Kitchen, see entry) took over this small operation in 2005, and brought with him an enthusiasm for fresh food and intelligent sourcing. The room is small, square and simple, with blackboards showing what's in season, as well as listing affordable lunch possibilities from ham hock terrine and sausage casserole to vegan-friendly sandwiches on good bread. Everything, including some choice dry goods and cakes with an air of superior school fête about them, is available to take away.
Chef/s: Matthew Brame and Peter Booth. **Open:** Mon to Sat L 11.30 to 3.30, Sun 12 to 2.30. **Closed:** 25 Dec. **Meals:** alc (main courses £8 to £9). **Service:** not inc. **Details:** Cash only. 40 seats. 24 seats outside. No music. No mobile phones. Wheelchair access. Children allowed. Car parking.

Greens

Manchester's default veggie option
43 Lapwing Lane, West Didsbury, Manchester,
M20 2NT
Tel no: (0161) 4344259
www.greensdidsbury.co.uk
Vegetarian | £23
Cooking score: 2
V £30

This contemporary suburban restaurant keeps on keeping on, no surprise since it has little real competition in its field – namely, global vegetarian food with, at best, a polished edge. The frequent presence of celebrity co-owner Simon Rimmer adds piquancy to an experience that includes old favourites like the

house take on duck pancakes, done with deep-fried oyster mushrooms and plum sauce (recently pronounced 'disappointing' by some readers) or Cheshire cheese sausages or a 'nibble' of vegetarian black pudding – not the travesty it sounds – with a sharp mustardy dip. Pleasantly fashionable environs, featuring floral-print wallpaper, lots of wood and confident but well-mannered staff, enhance the experience. Wines by the glass start at £3.75.
Chef/s: Simon Rimmer, Bob Short, Barry Heath. **Open:** Tue to Sun L 12 to 2 (3 Sat, 12.30 to 3.30 Sun), all week D 5.30 to 10.30. **Closed:** 25 and 26 Dec, bank hols. **Meals:** alc (main courses £11 to £12). Set D £15.95 (3 courses). Sun L £15.95. **Service:** not inc. **Details:** Cards accepted. 84 seats. 10 seats outside. Air-con. Separate bar. Music. Children allowed.

The Lime Tree

Much-loved local favourite
8 Lapwing Lane, West Didsbury, Manchester,
M20 2WS
Tel no: (0161) 4451217
www.thelimetreerestaurant.co.uk
Modern British | £25
Cooking score: 3
£30

Much-loved for its sunny aspect and abundance of greenery, the Lime Tree's popularity began before West Didsbury became all the rage. As a mid-range independent that does most things right, it has endured. To start, oysters Rockefeller or a crab salad with Bloody Mary vinaigrette showcase the kitchen's abilities with fish. Main courses, such as roast suckling pig with bubble and squeak and a port jus, often make use of produce from the restaurant's own smallholding near Macclesfield. It's not all trad British, though; spanking-fresh hake is done Spanish-style with chorizo and patatas bravas, and the Cajun spices come out for a lunchtime take on Caesar salad. There's nothing groundbreaking here, but things do move on: readers suggest an improvement in service this year. The smart contemporary wine list confidently balances ambition and value, with France and Italy showing up strongly. Prices are fair, with house recommendations kicking off at £15.50 (£3.75 a glass); also look for the great value monthly 'picks'. **Chef/s:** Jason Parker and Jason Dickinson. **Open:** Tue to Fri and Sun L 12 to 2.30, all week D 5.30 to 9 (10 Thur to Sat). **Closed:** 25 and 26 Dec, 1 Jan. **Meals:** alc (main courses £11 to £17). Set L and D £13.95 (2 courses) to £15.95. Sun L £17.95. **Service:** not inc. **Details:** Cards accepted. 75 seats. 15 seats outside. Wheelchair access. Music. Children allowed.

Michael Caines at ABode Manchester

Smooth city-centre dining
107 Piccadilly, Manchester, M1 2DB
Tel no: (0161) 2005678
www.michaelcaines.com
Modern European | £40
Cooking score: 4

🛏 V

The basement of a former Victorian cotton merchant's warehouse a few minutes from Piccadilly station provides the atmospheric space for Michael Caines' fine-dining venture within the Manchester branch of the ABode hotel group. Long-time collaborator Ian Matfin interprets the Caines style admirably, offering ample choice from grazing, tasting and à la carte menus. The deftness that creates a colourful starter of intensely flavoured razor clams and squid with fresh herbs and chorizo jam sometimes slips – as in a poorly seasoned dish of roast cod cheeks with bland carrot and cumin purée and tarragon foam. But meltingly tender saddle of venison, partnered by creamed Savoy cabbage, potato galette and a bitter chocolate sauce has been perfectly balanced. Reporters have criticised the 'Lilliputian portions on the grazing menu', and though not especially ungenerous for the price, the line between small portions and parsimony might be too fine for some. House wine is £21.95.

Chef/s: Ian Matfin. **Open:** Mon to Sat L 12 to 2.30, D 6 to 10. **Closed:** Sun, 25 to 30 Dec. **Meals:** alc (main courses £19 to £23). Set L £12. Set D £14.95 (2 courses) to £19.95. **Service:** 12% (optional). **Details:** Cards accepted. 74 seats. Air-con. Separate bar. No mobile phones. Wheelchair access. Music. Children allowed.

The Modern

Creative cooking and cool cocktails
Urbis, Cathedral Gardens, Manchester, M4 3BG
Tel no: (0161) 6058282
www.themodernmcr.co.uk
Modern British | £27
Cooking score: 3
£30

A lift whisks you up to this shimmering glass and steel venue spread over the upper floors of Manchester's iconic Urbis complex (the cityscape comes as standard). The Modern is a fiercely fashionable destination, with radical cocktails and modish mixes on offer in the bar, and a blend of subdued jazz and reinvented British food in the streamlined restaurant. Regional accents speak loudly on the menu, which has delivered unctuous veal tongue with onion purée and radish salad, a hunk of Cheshire ribeye with shallots, red wine reduction and fat beef-dripping chips, and nostalgia-inducing sherry trifle with poached rhubarb. Potted Loch Fyne mackerel and grilled Menai Straits sea bass with parsley root purée and sorrel butter should please the fish fans, while Sunday lunch brings whole roast chickens to the table for carving and sharing. Funky wines start at £15.30.

Chef/s: Paul Faulkner. **Open:** all week L 12 to 3, Mon to Sat D 5 to 10. Bar menu available. **Closed:** 25 and 26 Dec. **Meals:** alc (main courses £10 to £23). Set L and early D £12 (2 courses) to £15. Sun L £25 (2 courses). **Service:** not inc. **Details:** Cards accepted. 56 seats. Air-con. Separate bar. Wheelchair access. Music. Children allowed.

Moss Nook

Sliver-service charmer
2 Trenchard Drive, Ringway Road, Moss Nook,
Manchester, M22 5NA
Tel no: (0161) 4374778
www.mossnookrestaurant.co.uk
European | £45
Cooking score: 3
£5 OFF

The modern world passes by overhead – Manchester airport's flight paths seem perilously close – but the Moss Nook, sitting squat by a busy road, feels untouched. Its first consecutive entry in the Guide was in 1982, and the spirit (and perhaps some of the fabric) of the place remains the same. Heavy drapes, cut glass and ornate woodwork cocoon diners revisiting the Nook's textbook cheese soufflé with red pepper sauce or herb-crusted local lamb with chicken and tarragon mousse. It's all competently produced and served with exemplary friendliness and ease; readers comment on the lack of airs and graces which makes new customers feel part of the club (a tip for first-timers: the entrance is through the little garden at the back). Plenty of old-fashioned but nonetheless welcome extras, along with the outmoded but luxurious décor, justify high-ish prices which extend to an 'excellent' wine list. Bottles start at £19.50.
Chef/s: Kevin Lofthouse. **Open:** Tue to Sat L 12 to 1.30, D 7 to 9.30. **Closed:** Sun, Mon, 2 to 10 Jan. **Meals:** alc (main courses £17 to £30). Set L £15 (2 courses) to £21. Set D £33 (2 courses) to £40. Tasting menu £38.50 (7 courses). **Service:** not inc. **Details:** Cards accepted. 65 seats. 20 seats outside. Air-con. No music. No mobile phones. Car parking.

Second Floor

Stylish city food and rooftop views
Harvey Nichols, 21 New Cathedral Street,
Manchester, M1 1AD
Tel no: (0161) 8288898
www.harveynichols.com
Modern European | £35
Cooking score: 4

Second Floor, with its beguiling views of rooftops and the Wheel of Manchester, is a stylish designer-led dining room tucked behind a lively bar/brasserie. A black-and-white colour scheme and a huge expanse of window set the trendy tone, while well-spaced, impeccably dressed tables and attentive, formal service give notice of the level of ambition in the kitchen. Stuart Thomson has settled in well. His modern European-biased menus are based on superior ingredients and there is plenty that appeals. Manx scallops with saffron risotto and pickled trompettes, for example, was a vibrant and colourful starter at inspection, while the star main course comprised a perfectly timed wild sea bass served with crab, black olive, potatoes and sauce vierge. Others have enjoyed slow-cooked beef, saddle of rabbit wrapped in Parma ham and served with some good choucroute and a smear of fig purée, and roasted peanut parfait with rice crispy crunch and Guanaja chocolate. The thrilling global wine list is trendy enough for any Mancunian fashionista, but also gives full rein to top-end Champagnes and classics from the French regions. Harvey Nics' own-label house selections are £18, and it's worth looking out for the discounted 'wine shop' selections.
Chef/s: Stuart Thomson. **Open:** all week L 12 to 3 (4 Sun), Tue to Sat D 6 to 10. **Closed:** 25 Dec, 1 Jan. **Meals:** alc (main courses £16 to £23). Set L £25. **Service:** 10% (optional). **Details:** Cards accepted. 35 seats. Air-con. Separate bar. No mobile phones. Wheelchair access. Music. Children allowed.

ALSO RECOMMENDED

▲ Red Chilli

70 Portland Street, Manchester, M1 4GU
Tel no: (0161) 2362888
www.redchillirestaurant.co.uk
Chinese

With six branches in the north, trend-conscious Red Chilli is spreading its fiery message to an increasing number of fans. Blisteringly hot, anatomically challenging Szechuan dishes form the bedrock of the menu, from 'husband and wife lung' (£4) and baked intestines with green chilli (£7.50) to poached salty duck and dan-dan noodles in soup. Support comes from authentic Cantonese and Beijing staples such as stir-fried eel with coriander (£10), and the spring onion bread is unmissable. Wines from £14. Open all week. A second Manchester outlet is at 403–419 Oxford Road, M13 9WL, tel: (0161) 2731288.

▲ Vermilion

Lord North Street, Manchester, M40 8AD
Tel no: (0161) 2020055
www.vermilioncinnabar.com
Pan-Asian

Industrial east Manchester is not the most obvious place to locate what is arguably the city's most opulent restaurant. Part cocktail bar, part restaurant, the black lacquered floor, vast copper-varnished timbered ceiling, pearl curtains and dramatic lighting give an ethereal film-set quality, which Chadchai Jamjang's Asian-influenced food tiptoes through. Expect dishes like Thai fishcakes (£6.90), Karai fish (£11.50) or tandoori mixed grill and seafood platters (from £16.95) as well as good vegetarian choices and westernised desserts. House wine £19. Closed Sat L.

▮ Norden

Nutters

Good local food at reasonable prices
Edenfield Road, Norden, OL12 7TT
Tel no: (01706) 650167
www.nuttersrestaurant.co.uk
Modern British | £34
Cooking score: 3

V

Today's incarnation of the nineteenth-century Wolstenholme Hall overlooking Ashworth Moor is as an affable restaurant and bar. 'This is not cutting edge gastronomy but minor celeb chef Andrew Nutter cooks good food at very reasonable prices', noted one regular. While the cooking style focuses on the modern, it also concentrates on using carefully sourced, top-notch ingredients from the abundant local larder. Goosnargh duck confit with Lancashire potato pancakes and crispy croûtons is one way to start, then perhaps herb-crusted fillet of Tabley Brook beef, 'well hung, very flavoursome and cooked rare', with some slow-roasted blade and a vine tomato and basil confit served alongside. A hit for one reporter was whimberry cheesecake, but there are also simple crowd-pleasers such as sticky toffee pudding. House wine is £14.50.
Chef/s: Andrew Nutter. **Open:** Tue to Sun L 12 to 2 (4 Sun), D 6.30 to 9.30. **Closed:** Mon, 1 to 2 days after Christmas and New Year. **Meals:** alc (main courses £15 to £21). Set L £13.95 (2 courses) to £16.95. Gourmet D £38 (6 courses). Sun L £22.50. **Service:** not inc. **Details:** Cards accepted. 154 seats. Air-con. Separate bar. No mobile phones. Wheelchair access. Music. Children allowed. Car parking.

Prestwich

★ BEST UP-AND-COMING CHEF ★
MARY-ELLEN McTAGUE

NEW ENTRY

Aumbry

Gem with good cooking at its heart
2 Church Lane, Prestwich, M25 1AJ
Tel no: (0161) 7985841
www.aumbryrestaurant.co.uk
British | £26
Cooking score: 4

£5 OFF £30

Saké

Naming a restaurant after an ecclesiastical store cupboard might seem kooky, but readers reckon this aumbry is 'a little gem'. Co-owner and chef Mary-Ellen McTague has form locally (at ramsons) and nationally (at the Fat Duck), but she is treading with care: this is a small, tentative first project done on a modest budget, but with good cooking at its heart. The open kitchen at the back of a cottagey dining room sends out measured quantities of excellent bread, interesting starters such as mini black pudding-clad Scotch eggs ('a triumph' with mushroom relish) and main courses garnished with silky vegetable purées: roast mallard comes with the pumpkin version and a parcel of braised leg, for example. Portions have been boosted since the early days and the brief menu should grow as Aumbry flourishes – likewise the rather limited wine list, which currently includes house selections from £13.50. There are also plans to provide more facilities upstairs.
Chef/s: Mary-Ellen McTague and Laurence Tottingham. **Open:** Wed to Sun L 12 to 3 (4 Sun), Wed to Sat D 7 to 9.30. **Closed:** Mon, Tue, first 2 weeks Jan. **Meals:** alc (main courses £12 to £19). Sun L £18.50 (2 courses) to £22.50. Tasting menu £45. **Service:** not inc. **Details:** Cards accepted. 26 seats. Separate bar. Wheelchair access. Music. Children allowed.

The Japanese rice wine, saké, is winning new converts among Western drinkers. Not only is it the obvious accompaniment to sushi, tempura and grilled meats, its relative lack of acidity compared to grape wine makes it an altogether gentler proposition to drink on its own.

Quality saké is made from polished *shinpaku-mai* rice, a high-starch variety, fermented in spring water with the addition of a rice-mould, *koji*. It comes in a variety of styles, from dry to sweet, and there are even sparkling ones now, too.

The taste is a little like fino sherry, but with fruitier overtones (sometimes compared to banana), and the alcoholic strength, typically around 15%, is also in the light sherry range.

Saké is traditionally taken slightly warm from a *choko*, or earthenware cup, but the best grades are drunk at room temperature, so as to preserve all their aromatic nuances. The style known as *ginjo-shu*, made from less vigorously polished rice than the premium grades, is usually served chilled, like white wine.

Japanese table etiquette requires guests to pour saké for each other. The polite way of receiving it is to hold the cup up to the *tokkuro*, or jug, as it is poured for you.

You may not need to go to a Japanese eatery to try saké. Some Western restaurants now have saké listings.

Ramsbottom

ramsons

Civilised Italian sophistication
18 Market Place, Ramsbottom, BL0 9HT
Tel no: (01706) 825070
www.ramsons-restaurant.com
Italian | £50
Cooking score: 6

£5 OFF 🍷 V

With one foot in Ramsbottom and one in Italy, Chris Johnson's lovely little restaurant offers an extremely civilised way to eat Italian food. Neither Johnson nor chef Abdulla Naseem brooks compromise when it comes to suppliers or execution. The former are either the finest nearby producers (who send, for example, hand-reared rose veal or St Asaph lamb) or Italian purveyors of, say, carnaroli rice or San Marzano tomatoes – destined for soup 'like you've never tasted'. This is not a kitchen that embarks on complication for the sake of it: flourishes, such as a sliver of duck ham with the much-loved appetiser of duck liver parfait with brioche toast and quince compote, must earn their place. Dinner might continue with saffron tajarin (slender Piedmontese pasta with wild rabbit ragù and basil infusion), pausing for a separate course of vegetables or salad, then on to halibut with lemon mash, pea purée and a cream sauce spiked with Prosecco – fish cookery is Naseem's particular strength. Italian or British cheeses, each carefully matched with an accompanying chutney, jam or jelly, are as alluring as the fondant made with the best from Tuscan chocolate house Amedei. As a sop to the traditionalists, Chris Johnson recently introduced a new 'ramsons classics' menu promising the likes of prawn tortellini with seafood bisque, flashed fillet of Cheshire beef with dauphinoise potatoes and red wine sauce, and 'la pannacotta' with Fragolina grape purée. Out on the floor, experience shows, particularly in Chris's 'priceless' ability to match dishes with something from an extraordinary and lovingly compiled wine list, which includes a rainbow of Italian fizz as well as some very serious bottles. House vino is £20.
Chef/s: Abdulla Naseem. **Open:** Wed to Sun L 12 to 2.30 (1 to 3.30 Sun), Tue to Sat D 7 to 9.30. **Closed:** Mon. **Meals:** Set L £24 (2 courses) to £30. Set D £30 (2 courses) to £40. Sun L £30. **Service:** not inc. **Details:** Cards accepted. 34 seats. Air-con. No mobile phones. Music. Children allowed.

Sanmini's

Homespun South Indian flavours
Carrbank Lodge, Ramsbottom Lane, Ramsbottom, BL0 9DJ
Tel no: (01706) 821831
www.sanminis.com
Indian | £26
Cooking score: 3

V £30

Run by a husband-and-wife medic team – with their grown-up kids on hand to serve – Sanmini's is a true family affair. This amenable eatery occupies a good-looking Victorian gatehouse, and the food has all-round appeal for carnivores and veggies alike. The owners have distilled their love of homespun South Indian cooking into a modest menu of distinctive, subtly spiced dishes: starters of crispy cashew and spinach pakoras or fish vadai (tuna and lentil cakes) could give way to equally vivid mains from Chennai potato masala to Chettinad chicken. Also check out Mini's 'tiffin specialities' – vibrant street snacks including dosas, uthappam and steamed idli with sambar. Lunch for a tenner is a bargain. The only downsides seem to be an unchanging menu and the difficulty of getting a table. House wine is £13.95.
Chef/s: Sundara Moorthy, Mr Balraj, Mr Sathyanand. **Open:** Tue to Sun L 12 to 2 (2.30 Sat and Sun), D 6.30 to 9.30 (10.30 Fri to Sun). **Closed:** Mon. **Meals:** alc (main courses £8 to £13). Set L Tue to Fri £10. Thalis £20. **Service:** not inc. **Details:** Cards accepted. 30 seats. Separate bar. Wheelchair access. Music. Children allowed.

ALSO RECOMMENDED

▲ Hideaway

16-18 Market Place, Ramsbottom, BL0 9HT
Tel no: (01706) 822005
www.ramsons-restaurant.com
Italian £5 OFF

A self-styled 'enoteca con cucina' secreted in the basement below ramsons (see entry), Hideaway offers a candlelit backdrop for Louise Varley's four-course, single-sitting suppers (£20). There's no choice, but a typical meal might take in antipasto misto, cauliflower soup with Gorgonzola and a rustic centrepiece such as slow-roast shoulder of St Asaph lamb with rosemary chips and Savoy cabbage. After that, perhaps Trentino pear tart or artisan Italian cheeses. The dining area adjoins ramsons' glorious wine cellars, and browsing is encouraged. Half-litre jugs of house vino are £10. Open Tue to Sat D.

■ Salford

NEW ENTRY

The Mark Addy

Hearty British food by the river
Stanley Street, Salford, M3 5EJ
Tel no: (0161) 8324080
www.markaddy.co.uk
British | £30
Cooking score: 2
£5 OFF

Robert Owen Brown is Manchester's premier wandering chef, but his latest perambulations have come to a halt across the border in Salford. His hearty British style (signature snack: chips with buttery tarragon sauce) fits well into the Mark Addy's dark and slightly shabby vaulted interior overlooking the murky Irwell, though outside on the sunny terrace, the heart may yearn for something lighter. Start with dab fishcakes, potted beef or a row of salty-sweet but hefty blue cheese bhajias, followed by a Barnsley chop with beetroot and quince, or a saffron-infused dish of crisp-skinned sea bass with lemon, tomatoes and fennel. Wines start at £12, leaving change for a Manchester tart. **Chef/s:** Robert Owen Brown. **Open:** Mon to Sat L 12 to 3, D 5 to 9.30 (10 Fri and Sat). Sun 12 to 6. **Meals:** alc (main courses £9 to £18). **Service:** not inc. **Details:** Cards accepted. 80 seats. 60 seats outside. No music. Children allowed. Car parking.

■ Worsley

Grenache

Warmth and generous cooking
15 Bridgewater Road, Walkden, Worsley, M28 3JE
Tel no: (0161) 7998181
www.grenacherestaurant.co.uk
Modern British | £30
New Chef
£5 OFF

Bucking the current trend on Britain's high streets, owner Hussein Abbas turned a defunct estate agent's into a warm-hearted contemporary restaurant and bar specialising in self-styled 'decadent dining'. Inside, Grenache exudes safe, suburban chic – a suitably relaxed backdrop for cooking with plenty of generosity and bold modern flavours. Stephen Hildebrandt arrived just as the Guide went to press, too late for us to receive any feedback. He was previously at Stock Restaurant in Manchester. Reports please. House wines – Grenache, of course – start at £11.75 (£3.15 a glass). **Chef/s:** Stephen Hildebrandt. **Open:** Sun L 2 to 6, Wed to Sat D 5.30 to 9 (9.30 Fri and Sat). **Closed:** Mon, Tue, 25 and 26 Dec, 1 Jan. **Meals:** alc (main courses £11 to £22). Set D and Sun L £13.95 (2 courses) to £16.95. **Service:** not inc. **Details:** Cards accepted. 34 seats. Air-con. Separate bar. Wheelchair access. Music. Children allowed.

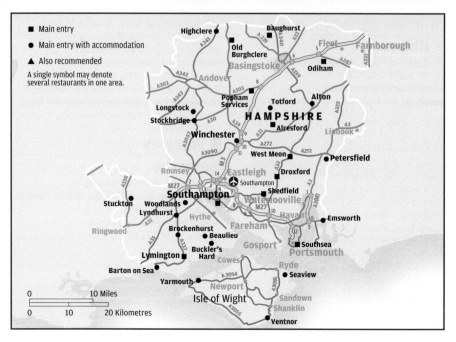

- ■ Main entry
- ● Main entry with accommodation
- ▲ Also recommended

A single symbol may denote several restaurants in one area.

Highclere
Baughurst
Old Burghclere
Fleet
Farnborough
Basingstoke
Odiham
Andover
Popham Services
Alton
Totford
Longstock
HAMPSHIRE
Stockbridge
Alresford
Liphook
Winchester
West Meon
Petersfield
Romsey
Eastleigh
Droxford
Southampton
Shedfield
Stuckton
Woodlands
Waterlooville
Lyndhurst
Hythe
Havant
Emsworth
Ringwood
Fareham
Brockenhurst
Beaulieu
Gosport
Southsea
Lymington
Buckler's Hard
Portsmouth
Barton on Sea
Cowes
Ryde
Yarmouth
Seaview
Newport
Isle of Wight
Sandown
Shanklin
Ventnor

0 ___ 10 Miles
0 ___ 10 ___ 20 Kilometres

■ Alresford

Caracoli
Buzzy, versatile café
15 Broad Street, Alresford, SO24 9AR
Tel no: (01962) 738730
www.caracoli.co.uk
Modern British | £17
Cooking score: 1
£30

'There should be more of these places', noted a fan of this versatile café, 'especially as it offers an alternative to bland high street brands'. Caracoli comes with a buzzy atmosphere and friendly staff 'who take time to talk about products'. Lunches include local smoked trout, spinach and crème fraîche tart or fish pie stuffed with salmon, crayfish and scallops. For dessert try a cake – perhaps apple and cinnamon or orange and passion fruit (£2.15) – or fruit tart (£3.15). Sunday brunch offers eggs Benedict or smoked haddock kedgeree, while for dinner on Fridays there could be slow-roasted pork belly. Wines from £13.50.

Chef/s: Alex Thomelin. **Open:** all week 8.30am to 5pm (10 to 5 Sun). Fri D 6 to 9. **Closed:** 25 Dec. **Meals:** alc (main courses £5 to £8). **Service:** not inc. **Details:** Cards accepted. 37 seats. 30 seats outside. Air-con. Wheelchair access. Music. Children allowed.

■ Alton

The Anchor Inn
Big helpings of posh comfort food
Lower Froyle, Alton, GU34 4NA
Tel no: (01420) 23261
www.anchorinnatlowerfroyle.co.uk
Modern British | £26
Cooking score: 2
£30

This scrubbed-up inn draws a well-heeled clientele with a credo of high-quality ingredients cooked simply and served generously. An unashamedly nostalgic menu name-checks local suppliers and kicks off with the likes of devilled whitebait or mushrooms on toast. The theme of posh, patriotic comfort food is reflected in main courses of beer-battered haddock with chunky chips, roast partridge with bread sauce, and a well-made pie of beef braised in Stairway ale from excellent local brewery Triple fff, whose beers can also be supped at the bar. Spotted dick and jam roly-poly loom large among the puddings. The nicely composed wine list starts at £14.50. Sister establishment to the Peat Spade Inn, Longstock and Queen's Arms Hotel, Garston (see entries).

Chef/s: Kevin Chandler. **Open:** all week L 12 to 2 (4 Sun), Mon to Sat D 6.30 to 9.30. **Meals:** alc (main courses £11 to £19). **Service:** not inc. **Details:** Cards accepted. 74 seats. Separate bar. No music. Wheelchair access. Children allowed. Car parking.

▌Barton on Sea

Pebble Beach

Glorious clifftop eatery where fish stars
Marine Drive, Barton on Sea, BH25 7DZ
Tel no: (01425) 627777
www.pebblebeach-uk.com
French | £30
Cooking score: 3

🍽 V

Given its glorious clifftop location looking out towards the Needles, it's no surprise that fish plays a starring role at this bright and breezy eatery-with-rooms. Holidaymakers pack the terrace when the sun's out, but the place appeals whatever the weather. Scallops, langoustine, crab and lobsters every which way are the top shouts, but there is much more besides. Breton-style fish soup is a robust version, skate wing comes with crisp onion rings, black butter and capers, and there is sea bass 'en papillote' for those who like a bit of drama on the plate. Meat eaters and veggies also do well with the likes of duck braised in red wine with blackcurrants, veal cutlet with morels and roasted shallots or carrot, Emmental and chervil gateau on a bed of pea risotto. Lemon parfait filled with hot raspberries and topped with crunchy meringue makes a fine finish. Service is 'first class and very friendly'. Well-chosen wines start at £15 (£3.95 a glass).

Chef/s: Pierre Chevillard. **Open:** all week L 11 to 2.30 (12 to 3 Sun), D 6 to 11 (6.30 to 10.30 Sun). **Closed:** 1 Jan. **Meals:** alc (main courses £13 to £34). **Service:** not inc. **Details:** Cards accepted. 90 seats. 36 seats outside. Air-con. Separate bar. No mobile phones. Wheelchair access. Music. Children allowed. Car parking.

▌Baughurst

★ BEST PUB CHEF ★ JASON KING ★

The Wellington Arms

Likeable country dining pub
Baughurst Road, Baughurst, RG26 5LP
Tel no: (0118) 9820110
www.thewellingtonarms.com
Modern British | £25
Cooking score: 3

£30

With its low ceilings and beams, tiled floor, unclothed tables and chalkboard menu, the Wellington is exactly what you might expect to find in a genuine village hostelry. Jason King and Simon Page run a tight ship, keeping beehives, maintaining a herb garden and fostering an army of hens, as well as sourcing some of the best regional produce in the area. They make admirable use of the harvest, knocking out dishes that are carefully crafted, unpretentious and full of flavour. Reports have praised a host of things, from flawlessly timed scallops on minted crushed peas to properly rendered roast pork with crackling, new potatoes and apple sauce. For afters, treat yourself to a wedge of flourless dark chocolate cake with espresso ice cream. Wines start at £18 (£5.50 a glass).

Chef/s: Jason King. **Open:** all week L 12 to 2 (4 Sun), Mon to Sat D 7 to 9.30 (6 Fri). **Meals:** alc (main courses £11 to £18). Set L £15 (2 courses) to £18. **Service:** 10% (optional). **Details:** Cards accepted. 23 seats. 20 seats outside. No mobile phones. Music. Children allowed. Car parking.

Beaulieu

Montagu Arms Hotel, Terrace Restaurant

Intriguing food worth a detour
Palace Lane, Beaulieu, SO42 7ZL
Tel no: (01590) 612324
www.montaguarmshotel.co.uk
Modern British | £50
Cooking score: 6

£5 OFF 🍷 🍽

With its lush gardens and front-facing views over Beaulieu's lake, this highly regarded and very famous Georgian hotel is worth a detour in its own right, but Matthew Tomkinson's cooking is proving quite a draw too. The setting may be classic country house, but contemporary menus conjure up some intriguing, sharply honed ideas, from slow-cooked oxtail and celeriac lasagne to a four-part pork showpiece involving braised cheek, stuffed cabbage, confit belly and roast fillet. Raw materials are spot-on, timing is impressive and dishes are marked by clarity of flavour, no matter how busy they look: for example, a well reported escalope of sea bass with smoked bacon, sweet shallots, red chicory, sprouting broccoli and Jerusalem artichokes. Recommended desserts include a perfect banana soufflé accompanied by banana ice cream, butterscotch sauce and honeycomb – although readers have been quick to point out that all this comes at a price. The wine list avoids the usual country house style, swapping long runs of pedigree Bordeaux and Burgundy for a more eclectic approach that mixes Old and New World names with thoughtfulness and enthusiasm. House selections start at £19.50, and a dozen are offered by the glass (from £5.10).
Chef/s: Matthew Tomkinson. Open: Wed to Sun L 12 to 2.30, Tue to Sun D 7 to 9.30. Meals: alc (main courses £18 to £35). Set L £17.50 (2 courses) to £22.50. Sun L £27.50. Tasting menu £70.
Service: not inc. Details: Cards accepted. 50 seats. 25 seats outside. Separate bar. No mobile phones. Wheelchair access. Music. Car parking.

Brockenhurst

Simply at Whitley Ridge

Keeping it simple
Beaulieu Road, Brockenhurst, SO42 7QL
Tel no: (01590) 622354
www.whitleyridge.co.uk
Modern British | £25
Cooking score: 4

🍽 V £30

Following the high-profile launch of Lime Wood in Lyndhurst (see entry), this mellow Georgian country house has taken on a new role as the reincarnation of Simply Poussin on Brookley Road. The setting is lovely to behold, with manicured lawns and giant New Forest oaks, although the interior shuns traditional swags-and-tails for clean-lined modernity. Unadorned brasserie food is the name of the game, with handpicked garden produce supplementing local supplies. Menus are flexible, the cooking shows a light modern touch and dishes 'burst with flavour': the 'larder and garden' might provide a salad of Sopley Farm asparagus, poached egg and croûtons, 'the Solent' could offer hake fillet with brown shrimps, Dorset cockles and broad beans, while 'the forest' brings venison with St George's mushrooms, Chantenay carrots and port dressing. For a simple finish try local rhubarb jelly with Brockenhurst honey and clotted-cream ice cream. The wine list is equally accessible, with plenty by the glass. Bottles start at £15.
Chef/s: James Golding. Open: all week L 12 to 3, D 6.30 to 10. Meals: alc (main courses £8 to £20). Set L £12.50 (2 courses) to £17.50. Set D £20 (2 courses) to £25. Sun L £27.50. Tasting menu £65.
Service: 12.5% (optional). Details: Cards accepted. 60 seats. 60 seats outside. Separate bar. No mobile phones. Wheelchair access. Music. Children allowed. Car parking.

Buckler's Hard
The Master Builder's
Versatile venture in a pretty village
Buckler's Hard, SO42 7XB
Tel no: (01590) 616253
www.themasterbuilders.co.uk
Modern British | £30
Cooking score: 2

Business has been brisk since Hillbrooke Hotels spruced up the former house of master shipbuilder Henry Adams in May 2009. Set in a pretty village, with lawns running down to the Beaulieu river, it draws a varied clientele of tourists and boating types for bowls of mussels, Lymington crab mayonnaise sandwiches, and fish and chips in the bar – not forgetting summer barbecue treats. Cooking moves up a gear at dinner in the restaurant next door – a plate of rock oysters, perhaps, then New Forest venison with chocolate jus, or skate wing with cauliflower purée, and warm pear and almond cake with cinnamon ice cream to finish. Wines from £14.50.
Chef/s: Neil Dowson. **Open:** all week L 12 to 2, D 7 to 9. **Meals:** alc (main courses £10 to £19). Sun L £19.50. **Service:** not inc. **Details:** Cards accepted. 80 seats. 30 seats outside. Separate bar. Music. Children allowed. Car parking.

Droxford
The Bakers Arms
Distinctly superior pub food
High Street, Droxford, SO32 3PA
Tel no: (01489) 877533
www.thebakersarmsdroxford.com
Gastropub | £23
Cooking score: 3
£30

The white-fronted country inn stands next to the old village bakehouse, a mere hundred yards from the river Meon. It's a delightful setting for some distinctly superior pub fare from a pair of much-travelled chefs. Traditional fish soup with garlic croûtons and rouille is one way to start, and main dishes run

a broadly based course from gurnard with crushed potatoes, brown shrimps and preserved lemon to local venison steak with polenta and damson sauce. Those in the market for top-notch sausages and mash with onion gravy will not be sent away empty – especially if they conclude with treacle tart or apple crumble and custard. The short wine list opens with a good selection by the glass, from £3.30 for Chilean Merlot rosé.
Chef/s: Adam Cordery and Richard Harrison. **Open:** Tue to Sun L 12 to 2 (3 Sun), Tue to Sat D 7 to 9. **Closed:** Mon. **Meals:** alc (main courses £11 to £17). Set L and D £13. Sun L £13.95. **Service:** not inc. **Details:** Cards accepted. 35 seats. 16 seats outside. No music. Children allowed. Car parking.

Emsworth
Fat Olives
Admirable little restaurant
30 South Street, Emsworth, PO10 7EH
Tel no: (01243) 377914
www.fatolives.co.uk
Modern British | £32
Cooking score: 3

'Cheerful', 'relaxed' and 'informal' are words that crop up frequently when reporters talk about this admirable little restaurant in a fisherman's cottage by Emsworth quayside. Julia Murphy's warmth out front is the perfect foil for her husband's seasonal food, which takes many of its cues from the Med. 'Fat' olives naturally start the show and fish gets plenty of votes (scallops with lardons and pea purée, for example). Meat dishes such as venison loin with dauphinoise and butternut squash are also heartily endorsed, likewise desserts: 'my wife would go just to eat the rhubarb beignets and custard'. The short, global wine list opens at £13.75.
Chef/s: Lawrence Murphy. **Open:** Tue to Sat L 12 to 1.45, D 7 to 9.15. **Closed:** Sun, Mon, 2 weeks Christmas, 2 weeks Jun. **Meals:** alc (main courses £15 to £23). Set L £16.75 (2 courses) to £18.75. **Service:** not inc. **Details:** Cards accepted. 24 seats. 10 seats outside. Wheelchair access. Music. Children allowed.

36 On The Quay

A dream ticket for visitors
47 South Street, Emsworth, PO10 7EG
Tel no: (01243) 375592
www.36onthequay.co.uk
Modern French | £49
Cooking score: 6

A large seventeenth-century cottage overlooking the bay in this Hampshire fishing village, 36 is a continuing testament to Ramon and Karen Farthing's high ideals. It runs like clockwork, with proficient and knowledgeable front-of-house staff who are fully clued-up about the menus, and exudes the kind of intimate atmosphere that people love. 'I visit every time I have an excuse to', confesses one reporter, who notes that a lot of work goes into the relatively small range of each menu. One happily reported dinner went from a cornucopian assemblage of roasted pigeon breast on braised onion and pine-nut compote, with steamed beetroot, black pudding and warm plum chutney, to a main course of three cuts of pork – loin, belly and cheek – accompanied by shallot Tatin and bubble and squeak. Fish is adventurously treated too, witness gently steamed lemon sole paupiettes sent out with crab, mushroom and leek lasagne, and a pea cream sauce. Dessert variations might include an apple study that takes in Bramley brûlée, Granny Smith sorbet and Cox's tart, dressed in cinnamon yoghurt. The wine list is full of interest too, arranged stylistically with an eye to food pairings, and replete with top-drawer producers. Prices start at £17.95.
Chef/s: Ramon Farthing. **Open:** Tue to Sat L 12 to 1.45, D 7 to 9.30 (6.45 Sat). **Closed:** Sun, Mon, first 2 weeks Jan, 1 week May, 1 week Oct. **Meals:** Set L £21.95 (2 courses) to £26.95. Set D £39.95 (2 courses) to £48.95. **Service:** not inc. **Details:** Cards accepted. 50 seats. Separate bar. No music. No mobile phones. Wheelchair access. Children allowed. Car parking.

Highclere

Marco Pierre White's Yew Tree Inn

Smart country inn
Hollington Cross, Andover Road, Highclere, RG20 9SE
Tel no: (01635) 253360
www.theyewtree.net
British | £40
New Chef

It may look like just another old white-painted country inn on the fast-running A343, but the Marco Pierre White signage on the front announces that the Yew Tree is a restaurant by any other name. True, it sells real ale but the bar is a modern marble-topped affair, and, while the dark beams and fireplaces are classic inn, white linen and black leather banquette seating reinforce the dining focus. Those familiar with Marco Pierre White's style will also be familiar with the menu's brasserie format of Morecambe Bay potted shrimps, Wheeler's of St James's fish pie or ribeye with béarnaise sauce. We heard of a change of chef too late to respond with an inspection, but the kitchen has always interpreted the Marco Pierre White mode reasonably well and we feel that this will not change. Service is friendly and attentive, and the globetrotting wine list (with France to the fore) opens at £15.95.
Chef/s: Matthew Cuthbert. **Open:** all week L 12 to 2.30 (3 Sun), D 6 to 9.30 (9 Sun). **Meals:** alc (main courses £15 to £23). Set L £15.50 (2 courses) to £18.50. Sun L £19.95. Sun D £15.50 (3 courses). **Service:** not inc. **Details:** Cards accepted. 80 seats. 35 seats outside. Separate bar. No music. Children allowed. Car parking.

▌Isle of Wight

The George Hotel

Elegant brasserie with a fish focus
Quay Street, Yarmouth, Isle of Wight, PO41 0PE
Tel no: (01983) 760331
www.thegeorge.co.uk
Modern European | £30
New Chef

🛏

Dire Straits bassist John Illsley is co-owner of this elegant boutique hotel; his paintings adorn the walls of the lovely dining room overlooking the Solent, and the band's music often provides the soundtrack to proceedings. New chef Liam Finnegan earned his stripes at Bath Priory and Gidleigh Park (see entries), and it will be interesting to see what impact he has on the food here – given that culinary ambitions have been scaled back in recent years from serious haute cuisine to modern brasserie food with strong European influences. With Yarmouth harbour just a stone's throw away, it's likely that fish will continue to play a starring role on the menu. House wine is £16.45 (£4.50 a glass). Reports please.
Chef/s: Liam Finnegan. **Open:** all week L 12 to 3, D 7 to 10. **Meals:** alc (main courses £12 to £28). **Service:** not inc. **Details:** Cards accepted. 70 seats. 100 seats outside. Air-con. Separate bar. Wheelchair access. Music. Children allowed.

Robert Thompson at the Hambrough

Astonishing food from a true artist
Hambrough Road, Ventnor, Isle of Wight, PO38 1SQ
Tel no: (01983) 856333
www.thehambrough.com
Modern French | £55
Cooking score: 7

£5 OFF 🍷 🛏 V

There's nothing like a dreamy sea view to induce a feeling of relaxed contentment, and the Hambrough's position on a clifftop overlooking the Channel on the eastern side of the Isle of Wight maximises that happy state. This handsome Victorian house has been coaxed into the boutique hotel age with seven guest rooms, and the light, unfussy styling of the restaurant provides a head-clearing space in which to enjoy Robert Thompson's astonishing food. Thompson is one of those chefs who has managed to redefine what modern British cooking can aspire to; he pays his dues when it come to local and seasonal sourcing, but also knows how to conjure up new contrasts and lift prosaic raw materials into an entirely new dimension. The results are truly startling. Dishes exhibit an artist's eye for composition, both visually and on the palate, witness a starter of seared yellowfin tuna with veal tenderloin, served with green beans bound in a hazelnut mayonnaise with a further dressing of lemon vinaigrette. Following up might be a piece of roast organic venison from Windmill Wood, alongside an endive tarte Tatin, winter cabbage and roasted chestnuts or a dish of pan-fried fillet of plaice with linguine, palourde clams, sautéed wild mushrooms and almond velouté. Flavours throughout are deep and striking, with all manner of subtly woven textures competing for attention. The dramatic tasting menu is an obvious way to splash out and enjoy the whole repertoire, especially if it culminates in a show-stopping chocolate- and coffee-rich gâteau Opéra (with pre-desserts beforehand, of course). Staff are generously applauded for their all-round professionalism, and the weighty wine list provides plenty to chew over whether you are after an obscure terroir or a classic vintage. The range is global, with particularly strong contributions from the Italian regions and Bordeaux; there's also an exciting choice by the glass (from £6.50). Bottles start at £19 for a Spanish Macabeo. The Hambrough team also run the informal Pond Café in Bonchurch, tel: (01983) 855666 – reports please.
Chef/s: Robert Thompson. **Open:** Tue to Sat L 12 to 1.30, D 7 to 9.30. **Closed:** Sun, Mon, 1 to 17 Nov, 27 Dec to 27 Jan. **Meals:** Set L £22 (2 courses) to £26. Set D £48 (2 courses) to £55. **Service:** not inc. **Details:** Cards accepted. 45 seats. Air-con. No mobile phones. Music. Children allowed.

The Seaview Hotel

Lovely seaside hotel with island food
High Street, Seaview, Isle of Wight, PO34 5EX
Tel no: (01983) 612711
www.seaviewhotel.co.uk
Modern British | £27
Cooking score: 2

This lovely seaside hotel harbours a smart, modern dining room – pleasant and comfortable, but rather at odds with the charm and style of the rest of the building. The cooking is slightly retro – expect posh comfort food and no-nonsense fish platters (from Solent day boats), plus generous side dishes of excellently cooked vegetables (from the hotel's own farm). An April meal produced a rich crab ramekin, a salad of seared scallops and squid, an enormous pie filled with soft braised beef and a pungent medley of wild mushrooms, and a pair of perfectly cooked John Dorys. Desserts are not a strong point and service is variable. House wine £12.95. **Chef/s:** David Etchell Johnson. **Open:** all week L 12 to 2.30 (3 Sat and Sun), D 6.30 to 9.30 (9.45 Sat). **Closed:** 21 to 27 Dec. **Meals:** alc (main courses £13 to £17). Sun L £19.95. **Service:** not inc. **Details:** Cards accepted. 100 seats. 35 seats outside. Air-con. Separate bar. Wheelchair access. Music. Children allowed. Car parking.

Longstock

The Peat Spade Inn

Popular country inn with unusual flair
Village Street, Longstock, SO20 6DR
Tel no: (01264) 810612
www.peatspadeinn.co.uk
Modern British | £26
Cooking score: 2

You can see why this place is popular. A country inn with unusual flair, it can be thought of as a gentrified pub in two parts: where drinkers are welcome, and a smart dining room delivering a menu of contemporary brasserie-style dishes. Basic

materials are well sourced (many locally) and well handled, the kitchen coming up with chicken liver parfait with red onion marmalade ahead of lemon sole with brown shrimp and caper and parsley butter, or duck breast with sauté potatoes and purple sprouting broccoli. For dessert there might be chocolate brownie and honeycomb swirl ice cream. Wines from £15.25. From the same stable as the Anchor Inn, Alton, and Queen's Arms Hotel, Garston (see entries). **Chef/s:** Simon Tear. **Open:** all week L 12 to 2 (2.30 Sar, 3.30 Sun), D 7 to 9 (9.30 Fri and Sat). **Closed:** 25 Dec. **Meals:** alc (main courses £12 to £20). **Service:** not inc. **Details:** Cards accepted. 45 seats. 35 seats outside. Wheelchair access. Music. Children allowed. Car parking.

Lymington

Egan's

Well-loved family restaurant
24 Gosport Street, Lymington, SO41 9BE
Tel no: (01590) 676165
Modern British | £28
Cooking score: 2

'There should be more small family restaurants like this in the UK', notes a regular to John and Debbie Egan's relaxed neighbourhood restaurant.'It is a place where you can eat every week', adds a fan who is drawn by daily changing menus and the value for money they offer. Even on the carte the well-wrought cooking keeps things within sensible bounds and is built around carefully considered combinations such as lobster and shrimp sausage with leeks, mussels, and shellfish bisque or venison saddle with griottine cherry sauce. Chocolate torte is a fondly remembered dessert. The equally good-value wine list opens at £14.95. **Chef/s:** John Egan. **Open:** Tue to Sat L 12 to 2, D 6.30 to 10. **Closed:** Sun, Mon, 2 weeks from 25 Dec. **Meals:** alc (main courses £15 to £19). Set L £13.95 (2 courses) to £15.95. **Service:** not inc. **Details:** Cards accepted. 50 seats. 20 seats outside. Separate bar. No mobile phones. Wheelchair access. Music. Children allowed.

Lyndhurst

NEW ENTRY

Lime Wood, The Dining Room

Country house with fine-tuned cooking
Beaulieu Road, Lyndhurst, SO43 7FZ
Tel no: (023) 8028 7167
www.limewoodhotel.co.uk
Modern British | £48
Cooking score: 6

🍷 ☎ V

It has been a while coming, but this grand venture is finally open in the heart of the New Forest. Following a £30m redevelopment, what was Le Poussin at Parkhill has been brilliantly transformed into a boutique country house retreat for our times thanks to design guru David Collins. The interiors (including an inner courtyard with a retractable glass roof) are guaranteed to wow, but foodie ambition is centred on the ash-panelled Dining Room with its leather hues, carved chandeliers and stunning views over the Italianate-style garden. Luke Holder's fine-tuned, ingredients-led cooking is pointed up with organic produce and foraged wild stuff: here you will find everything from a garden salad with frogs' legs, snails, nettles and wild garlic to iced parfait of New Forest cobnuts and honey praline with lavender caramel. There's a commendable lightness of touch about his ambitiously conceived dishes, but also clear-minded good sense – witness halibut fillet served with samphire and a Poole Bay cockle and chorizo dressing, or delicate Warborne Farm organic milk lamb teamed with broad beans, peas and rainbow chard. Wallet-friendly prices at lunch and tasting options bolster the output. Staff are exemplary, while the globetrotting wine list offers plenty of interest by the glass. Bottles from £16.
Chef/s: Luke Holder. **Open:** all week L 12 to 2, D 7 to 9.30 (10 Fri and Sat). **Meals:** Set L £18 (2 courses) to £25. Set D £38 (2 courses) to £48. Sun L £35. **Service:** 12.5% (optional). **Details:** Cards accepted. 70 seats. 30 seats outside. Air-con. Separate bar. No music. Wheelchair access. Children allowed. Car parking.

Micheldever, Popham Services

Little Chef Popham

Chuffed to bits with Little Chef
West-bound on the A303, Micheldever, Popham Services, SO21 3SP
Tel no: (01256) 398490
www.littlechef.co.uk/heston.php
British | £15
Cooking score: 1
£30

Heston Blumenthal's heavily hyped makeover of Little Chef is a 'massive improvement' by all accounts. Done out in the brazen style of an all-American diner, it is now a welcome pit stop for travellers on the A303 – and others who fancy the detour. Star turns are the Olympic Breakfast and braised ox cheeks with mash and rich wine sauce; trifle with popping candy gets an honourable mention too. Wines from £2.75 a glass. The branch on the A64 between Tadcaster and York has also been praised, and there's a third outlet on the A14 at Kettering.
Chef/s: Jo Cleaver. **Open:** all week 7am to 10pm. **Meals:** alc (main courses £6 to £13). **Service:** not inc. **Details:** Cards accepted. 84 seats. Air-con. Wheelchair access. Music. Children allowed. Car parking.

Odiham

NEW ENTRY

St John

Lashings of luxury
83 High Street, Odiham, RG29 1LB
Tel no: (01256) 702697
www.stjohn-restaurant.co.uk
Modern European | £30
Cooking score: 4

V

No relation to the famous London restaurant of the same name, this is a chic, upmarket place on Odiham's Georgian high street. The dining room is expensively decorated: abstract art on smooth white walls, black leather-upholstered banquettes, heavy linen napery. The cooking is fairly elaborate, with several tasters between courses, and a strong focus on luxury ingredients – witness a generous portion of lobster with perfectly al dente orzo pasta in lobster coral sauce with green beans and lashings of brandy. Plaudits, too, for cod cheeks on cauliflower purée with capers and pancetta, and an interesting take on the Scotch egg: a quail's egg encased in black pudding and crisp batter, served on a smear of ketchup alongside an unctuous slab of pork belly. Desserts range from the traditional (Bakewell tart with clotted cream and lavender honey) to the unusual (chilled melon and gin soup with melon jellies). The wide-ranging wine list starts at £15 and offers ample temptation, but some mark-ups seem a bit steep.

Chef/s: Steven James. **Open:** Mon to Sat L 12 to 3, D 6 to 12. **Closed:** Sun, 1 Jan. **Meals:** alc (main courses £17 to £26). Set L and D £16.95 (2 courses) to £23.50. **Service:** 12.5% (not inc). **Details:** Cards accepted. 50 seats. 12 seats outside. Air-con. Wheelchair access. Music.

▌Old Burghclere

Dew Pond

Dreamy views and clear flavours
Old Burghclere, RG20 9LH
Tel no: (01635) 278408
www.dewpond.co.uk
Anglo-French | £32
Cooking score: 3

£5
OFF

Fashioned from a pair of sixteenth-century drovers' cottages, Keith and Julie Marshall's idyllic domain on the Berkshire/Hampshire border really does have its own dew pond – plus equally dewy-eyed views out towards Watership Down. Inside, the tone in the dining rooms has been lightened up of late, but Keith's food hasn't been sidetracked in the process. Acutely judged, measured cooking is his style, with clear flavours much in evidence and no trendy flimflam. He is happy to serve field mushrooms on olive toast as a starter, as well as tackling roast scallops with black pudding and butternut squash purée. After

that, the choice might include best end of Hampshire lamb with crispy shoulder confit or halibut fillet with fennel pollen, shrimp butter sauce and grilled courgettes. To finish, local cheeses vie with caramelised lemon tart and sticky toffee pudding. Wines start at £15.50.

Chef/s: Keith Marshall. **Open:** Tue to Sat D only 7 to 9.30. **Closed:** Sun, Mon, 2 weeks Christmas and New Year. **Meals:** Set D £32 (3 courses). **Service:** not inc. **Details:** Cards accepted. 45 seats. Separate bar. No music. Wheelchair access. Children allowed. Car parking.

▌Petersfield

JSW

Pure panache
20 Dragon Street, Petersfield, GU31 4JJ
Tel no: (01730) 262030
www.jswrestaurant.com
Modern British | £50
Cooking score: 6

▲ ⊨ V

JSW stands for Jake Saul Watkins, chef/proprietor of this highly personal restaurant-with-rooms in a converted seventeenth-century coaching inn. Understatement is the theme in the dining room, but the show comes with oodles of style and panache. What impresses about JSW's cooking is the unadorned contemporary approach and keen eye for seasonal ingredients (organic meat, fish from the Solent day boats and the best French poultry). There are no absurdly cluttered plates, no superfluous garnishes, just finely honed modern dishes bristling with flavour and clarity. A starter of scallops with lightly spiced mussels and razor clams might set the tone, before ox cheek (simmered for 18 hours and served with curly kale and mash) or perhaps a dish of honey-roasted duck, cooked two ways and sent out with an earthy duo of lentils and chicory. Meals end on a high note with exquisite desserts such as banana parfait with honeycomb and mini cinnamon doughnuts or a savarin with apple mille-feuille and caramelised apple purée. Drinker-friendly prices are a major bonus when it

comes to the awesome wine list. The mighty tome is also bolstered by one of the best collections of half-bottles you're likely to see. House recommendations start at £16.50 (£4.75 a glass).
Chef/s: Jake Watkins. **Open:** Tue to Sat L 12 to 1.30, D 7 to 9.30. **Closed:** Sun, Mon, 2 weeks Jan, 2 weeks Jun. **Meals:** Set L £19.50 (2 courses) to £25. Set D Tue to Thur £25 (2 courses) to £29.50, Fri and Sat £38.50 (2 courses) to £47. **Service:** not inc. **Details:** Cards accepted. 60 seats. 28 seats outside. No music. No mobile phones. Wheelchair access. Children allowed. Car parking.

ALSO RECOMMENDED
▲ The Harrow Inn
Steep, Petersfield, GU32 2DA
Tel no: (01730) 262685
www.harrow-inn.co.uk
Gastropub

Nostalgia is part of the charm at this unspoilt sixteenth-century inn, which has been with the same family since 1929. There are two simple bars – one Tudor with an inglenook, the other Victorian – plus a large cottage garden, and loos located across the road in the old stables. The Rayburn-cooked food fits the bill, whether split-pea and ham soup (£4.70), flans and quiches, ham-off-the-bone ploughman's (£9) or gooey treacle tart. House wine £12. No food Sun D.

■ Portsmouth
READERS RECOMMEND
Abarbistro
Modern British
58 White Hart Road, Portsmouth, PO1 2JA
Tel no: (023) 9281 1585
www.abarbistro.co.uk
'The fish and chips are the best in Portsmouth'

■ Shedfield
Vatika
Avant-garde Indian food in a vineyard
Wickham Vineyard, Botley Road, Shedfield, SO32 2HL
Tel no: (01329) 830405
www.vatikarestaurant.com
Indian | £40
Cooking score: 5
🍷 V

The highly individual Vatika is the brainchild of Atul Kochhar of Benares fame (see entry, London), and offers a similar style of Brit-inflected modern Indian food, from the more than capable hands of Jitin Joshi. There's also the bonus of picture-window views of the surrounding Wickham Vineyard. It's a winning formula, not least because the clarity and vivacity of the cooking makes such a powerful case. Dishes are built around interesting pairings – mackerel with orange, pork with artichoke, sea bass with peas – and then further developed with judicious use of Indian spices. The peas with that sea bass are mashed into a kind of dhal and seasoned with cumin, the dish sauced with a reduction of coconut, while tandoori chicken breast might come with peppers in tikka masala dressing and roasted onion sauce. Vegetarian options are inspired too – perhaps curried asparagus with barley and garlic risotto and Parmesan – and all dishes comes with a suggestion for an appropriate accompanying glass. Desserts might take in a combination of ginger beer granita with lime syrup and melon foam. An exhilaratingly widespread wine list gathers up some of the best growers in its various regions, not forgetting the aromatic varietals made on the doorstep, as well as a handful from India itself. Prices start at £17.
Chef/s: Jitin Joshi. **Open:** Fri to Sun L 12 to 2.30, Wed to Sat D 6 to 10. **Closed:** Mon, Tue, 25 Dec. **Meals:** alc (main courses £15 to £25). Set L £19.95 (2 courses) to £24.95. Set D £24.95. **Service:** 12.5% (optional). **Details:** Cards accepted. 40 seats. 20 seats outside. Air-con. No music. Wheelchair access. Children allowed. Car parking.

▌Southampton

NEW ENTRY
Namaste Kerala
Affordable South Indian food
4a Civic Centre Road, Southampton, SO14 7FL
Tel no: (023) 8022 4422
www.namaste-kerala.co.uk
Indian | £14
Cooking score: 1
£30

An upstairs oasis of reasonably priced South Indian fare in the culinary desert of central Southampton. The dining room is modest and functional, but the traditional vegetarian staples of Kerala are cooked with care and flair, from skilfully spiced sambars to perky pachadi. The handmade breads (vellappam, paratha) are also commendable. When perusing the menu, steer clear of familiar Punjabi-style meat curries (though these are perfectly decent) and home in on the authentic Keralan dishes, which are the kitchen's strongest suit. A smaller but equally good sister restaurant, Kairali, lurks in the suburban wasteland of Burgess Road, near the university. House wine £12.95.
Chef/s: Abdul Muneer. **Open:** all week L 12 to 2.30, D 6 to 11. **Closed:** 24 to 26 Dec. **Meals:** alc (main courses £6 to £12). Set L buffet £7.95. **Service:** not inc. **Details:** Cards accepted. 65 seats. Air-con. Separate bar. Music. Children allowed.

ALSO RECOMMENDED
▲ The White Star Tavern
28 Oxford Street, Southampton, SO14 3DJ
Tel no: (023) 8082 1990
www.whitestartavern.co.uk
Modern British £5 OFF

Drinkers and diners generate a lively buzz at this vibrant tavern-with-rooms on Southampton's restaurant row. Menus are based on sound ingredients and the repertoire is a promising mix of classic brasserie dishes jazzed up with a few voguish flourishes. Ham hock terrine with piccalilli (£6.50), and slow-roast pork belly with organic leek champ cake,

grain-mustard sabayon and cider gravy (£14.50) show the range. Dark chocolate and thyme fondant with parsnip ice cream (£5) is a typically eclectic dessert. House wine £14. Open all week.

▌Southsea
Montparnasse
Sound food with intense flavours
103 Palmerston Road, Southsea, PO5 3PS
Tel no: (023) 9281 6754
www.bistromontparnasse.co.uk
Modern European | £34
Cooking score: 4

Smart-yet-relaxed and enduringly popular, Montparnasse has moved on from the robust French bistro cooking which made its name, but the modern European cuisine is still Francophile to the core. Nikolas Facey has maintained the quality of the kitchen's output since Kevin Bingham left to launch Restaurant 27 a few blocks away (see entry). The menu features dishes such as white onion soup studded with miniature blue cheese doughnuts and topped with squiggles of cider syrup. A springtime main course of roast lamb fillet with tomato and mint chutney and a drizzle of rosemary jus exemplifies the 'intense flavours' of well-sourced ingredients. At inspection, a hot chocolate pudding with caramel ice cream and banana cake didn't disappoint, either. The wine list opens with some good-value, gluggable glasses from £2.95 and bottles from £15.25.
Chef/s: Nikolas Facey. **Open:** Tue to Sat L 12 to 1.30, D 7 to 9.30. **Closed:** Sun, Mon, 25 and 26 Dec, 1 Jan. **Meals:** Set L and D £28.50 (2 courses) to £33.50. **Service:** not inc. **Details:** Cards accepted. 30 seats. Music. Children allowed.

Average price

The average price listed in main-entry reviews denotes the price of a three-course meal, without wine.

NEW ENTRY
Restaurant 27
Chef's impressive solo venture
27a South Parade, Southsea, PO5 2JF
Tel no: (023) 9287 6272
www.restaurant27.com
Modern French | £35
Cooking score: 5

After a decade's service behind the stoves at the popular Montparnasse (see entry), Kevin Bingham has ratcheted his ambitions up a notch in this solo venture. The sparsely furnished dining room is comfortable, though of barn-like proportions, which does seem to induce hushed whispers in timid diners. Bingham, who dubs his style 'global French', has undoubtedly drawn inspiration from *McGee on Food and Cooking* – witness sundry gels, foams, jellies and illogical-sounding pairings of ingredients – but the dishes sampled at inspection were well-conceived and built on good old Gallic technique, with a commendable focus on textural contrasts. A starter of blowtorched goats' cheese was sweetened with vibrant pumpkin jam, strewn with crunchy, salty green olive crumble, enriched with a dusting of ground macadamia nuts and enlivened with a sprinkle of pea shoots. A signature dish of '30-hour' pork belly hit the target, the rich, fatty meat aptly cut by a sour rhubarb gel, spiked with fragrant, kaffir lime-infused pork jus and underpinned by an earthy parsnip purée. Puddings have impressed too, especially a stridently flavoured strawberry jelly given darker undertones by a subtle and intriguing black olive caramel ice cream and topped with creamy lime mousse and spiky-sharp lime sugar crystals. An interesting wine list starts at £15, with some interesting options under £30.
Chef/s: Kevin Bingham. **Open:** Sun L 12 to 2.30, Wed to Sat D 7 to 9.30. **Closed:** Mon, Tue, 25 and 26 Dec. **Meals:** Set D £35. Sun L £25. **Service:** not inc. **Details:** Cards accepted. 30 seats. Separate bar. Music. Children allowed.

▌Stockbridge
The Greyhound Inn
Good looks and foodie aspirations
31 High Street, Stockbridge, SO20 6EY
Tel no: (01264) 810833
www.thegreyhound.info
Modern British | £30
Cooking score: 4

🍷 🛏

Everybody has a good word to say about the Greyhound; indeed, some reckon 'there's no place like it'. With a little garden overlooking the clear waters of the river Test, a full contingent of low beams, timbers and a roaring fire in the bar, plus bags of atmosphere throughout, this gentrified fifteenth-century inn certainly puts on a convincing show. Its unpretentious approach is matched by some appealingly soothing food, and the menu offers a familiar run through the modern brasserie catalogue: seared scallops with linguine or fishcake with poached egg and chive beurre blanc are regularly endorsed starters, while main courses embrace good steaks, cannon of Welsh lamb or sea bass with brown shrimp risotto, tomato and broad bean velouté. To finish, the house ice creams are highly rated, or you could put your money on plum tarte Tatin with cinnamon ice cream. Real ale buffs are well served, but the Greyhound really scores with its astutely chosen wine list. France gets top billing, but good drinking abounds and prices are very easy on the wallet. House selections start at £15.
Chef/s: Norelle Oberin. **Open:** all week L 12 to 2 (2.30 Fri to Sun), Mon to Sat D 7 to 9 (9.30 Fri and Sat). **Closed:** 24 to 26 Dec, 1 Jan. **Meals:** alc (main courses £12 to £21). Bar menu available.
Service: not inc. **Details:** Cards accepted. 50 seats. Separate bar. No music. Children allowed. Car parking.

Stuckton

The Three Lions

Superlative ingredients treated with respect
Stuckton, SP6 2HF
Tel no: (01425) 652489
www.thethreelionsrestaurant.co.uk
Anglo-French | £35
Cooking score: 5

£5 OFF 🍷 ⊨ V

Mike Womersley was once at the cutting edge of London cuisine, cooking alongside the likes of Gordon Ramsay and Marco Pierre White. But in the mid-90s he decamped to establish this 'English auberge' in a farmhouse on the New Forest's western fringe. Fast-forward 15 years and the cooking style might now be uncharitably described as retro – it hasn't changed a jot. A few readers have reported disappointing dinners, but a test meal found much to praise. A starter of sautéed kidneys, liver and faggot came in lip-smackingly rich gravy. To follow, a perfectly pink duck breast fanned out over rich blueberry jus with a warm afterglow of cinnamon also impressed, as did a magnificent Angus fillet steak and a palate-popping lime parfait. It isn't cheap, but the ingredients are invariably of superlative quality and treated with the respect they deserve. The food is matched by an enlightened wine list that favours elite independent growers from across the globe. There's an impressive choice – especially in the £20 to £30 bracket – and ample scope for big spenders. The downside is the dated décor: salmon-pink woodchip walls clash with tomato-coloured, Provençal-print curtains and yellow pine furniture, while the 1980s pop music reminds us that retro can be decidedly uncool.
Chef/s: Mike Womersley. **Open:** Tue to Sun L 12 to 2, Tue to Sat D 7 to 9. **Closed:** Mon, last 2 weeks Feb. **Meals:** alc (main courses £18 to £25). Set L £19.75. Set D £24.75. **Service:** not inc. **Details:** Cards accepted. 60 seats. 10 seats outside. Separate bar. No mobile phones. Wheelchair access. Music. Children allowed. Car parking.

Totford

NEW ENTRY

The Woolpack Inn

Spruced-up country boozer
Totford, SO24 9TJ
Tel no: (0845) 2938066
www.thewoolpackinn.co.uk
Modern British | £23
Cooking score: 2

£5 OFF ⊨ V £30

Standing beside an old drovers' road in the Candover Valley, the spruced-up Woolpack is enjoying a new lease of life – thanks to chef/landlord Brian Ahearn (ex-Thomas Cubitt in London – see entry). Old stagers such as ham, fried duck egg and chips keep the punters happy in the rustic, scrubbed-wood bar, but it's worth settling into the plush dining area if you fancy something more ambitious. Seasonal game and fish specials bolster a menu that might take in beetroot and goats' cheese soufflé with orange salad, smoked pork belly with spring greens, rhubarb and cider jus, and chocolate fondant with mocha sauce. Sunday roasts and summer barbecues complete the package. Wines from £14.
Chef/s: Brian Ahearn. **Open:** all week L 12 to 3 (4 Sat, 4.30 Sun), D 6.30 to 10 (8 Sun). **Meals:** alc (main courses £9 to £17). Set L £11 (2 courses) to £14.50. **Service:** 10% (optional). **Details:** Cards accepted. 100 seats. 50 seats outside. Wheelchair access. Music. Children allowed. Car parking.

West Meon

The Thomas Lord

A remarkable country pub
High Street, West Meon, GU32 1LN
Tel no: (01730) 829244
www.thethomaslord.co.uk
Gastropub | £26
Cooking score: 3

£30

'A genuine local, refreshingly free of affectation, resolutely faithful to its pub roots and a place of true food integrity', comments a reporter of this remarkable country pub. Here

local means local. Seasonal ingredients, including herbs and vegetables from the pub's potager, eggs from their hens and quails, are matched by produce from small-scale producers and farms in the area. Sensibly compact, concisely scripted menus change each session to offer the likes of warm bacon-rolled pig's head with apple purée then, perhaps, venison fillet teamed with roasted beetroot, quince and onion gravy. There's a popular range of local brewery ales on tap, while the wine list carries a pair from Hampshire vineyards; prices from £14.50.
Chef/s: Gareth Longhurst. **Open:** Tue to Sun L 12 to 2 (3 Sat and Sun), D 7 to 9 (9.30 Fri and Sat). **Closed:** Mon. **Meals:** alc (main courses £11 to £18). **Service:** not inc. **Details:** Cards accepted. 62 seats. 50 seats outside. Separate bar. No music. Wheelchair access. Children allowed. Car parking.

▋ Winchester

The Black Rat
Quality not frippery
88 Chesil Street, Winchester, SO23 0HX
Tel no: (01962) 844465
www.theblackrat.co.uk
Modern British | £32
Cooking score: 3

At first glance you might be forgiven for thinking this was a run-of-the-mill city boozer, with its rather unkempt look and busy roadside location. In reality, this early eighteenth-century building is a charming restaurant with cheerful, idiosyncratic décor creating a contemporary feel. Simple table settings indicate that the focus is on the quality of what you eat rather than unnecessary frippery. Menus could open with a good bouillabaisse and finish with a Welsh rarebit made with local ale. Along the way, expect braised duck hearts with confit potatoes and sorrel, roast partridge with Jerusalem artichoke, kale and sloe gin, as well as desserts such as home-baked madeleines with butterscotch sauce. The wide-roaming wine list is realistically priced with house tipples at £16.50.

Chef/s: Chris Bailey. **Open:** Sat and Sun L 12 to 2, all week D 7 to 9.30. **Closed:** 23 Dec to 8 Jan, 2 weeks Easter, 2 weeks end Oct/Nov. **Meals:** alc (main courses £17 to £22), Set L £19.50 (2 courses) to £23.50. **Service:** not inc. **Details:** Cards accepted. 60 seats. 18 seats outside. Separate bar. Music.

The Chesil Rectory
A highly attractive prospect
1 Chesil Street, Winchester, SO23 0HU
Tel no: (01962) 851555
www.chesilrectory.co.uk
Modern British | £27
Cooking score: 4
£30

One of Winchester's oldest buildings, with a 'wonderful fifteenth-century interior', is a highly attractive prospect. 'Completely un-Disneyfied' thought one reporter, who approved of the good-sized tables 'with a civilised distance between them' and the 'outstanding welcome'. The repertoire has a regional feel, the aim being to combine first-rate, well-sourced raw materials with uncomplicated modern cooking to produce a 'Great British Dining' menu with broad appeal. From the complex to the straightforward, many dishes 'have been superb': ham hock salad with perfectly poached egg and mustard dressing, a flavour-packed tomato and cheese tart, slow-cooked belly of local pork with parsnip potato purée, beetroot and crackling, and a 'brilliantly executed 'cottage pie from the set-price lunch. Desserts maintain the standard with a 'sublime' lemon mousse with shortbread biscuits and a 'first-rate' chocolate fondant with milk sorbet. An enterprising and fairly priced wine list from around the world opens at £19.95.
Chef/s: Damian Brown. **Open:** all week L 12 to 2.30 (3 Sun), Mon to Sat D 6 to 9.30 (10 Fri and Sat). **Closed:** 1 week Christmas, 1 week Aug. **Meals:** alc (main courses £12 to £18). Set L and early D £14.95 (2 courses) to £19.95. **Service:** not inc. **Details:** Cards accepted. 75 seats. Separate bar. Music. Children allowed.

Hotel du Vin & Bistro

Simple classics with please-all appeal
14 Southgate Street, Winchester, SO23 9EF
Tel no: (01962) 841414
www.hotelduvin.com
European | £30
Cooking score: 3

🍷 🛏 V

Found in a delightful, sympathetically restored Georgian town house, the dining room has trademark polished tables, bare floorboards and lots of vinous paraphernalia – if the setting is recognisable Hotel du Vin, so too is the style of food. Its broad European sweep goes from pâté de campagne to beer-battered pollack with pea purée and tartare sauce, from scallops with cauliflower risotto to confit pork belly with porcini sauce and spring greens. Simple classics have a please-all appeal, for example moules marinière and 'Botham' burger with pommes frites and homemade ketchup, but the kitchen also turns out bream 'en papillote' with wild rice pilau. Finish with hazelnut parfait and white chocolate ice cream. The wine list is packed full of good ideas from around the world, from affordable basics to classic French appellations. House wine is £15.95.
Chef/s: Adam Fargin. **Open:** all week L 12 to 1.45 (2.30 Sat and Sun), D 7 to 9.45 (10.45 Sat and Sun). **Meals:** alc (main courses £14 to £21). Set L and D £10 (2 courses). Sun L £25. **Service:** 10% (optional). **Details:** Cards accepted. 65 seats. 40 seats outside. Separate bar. No music. Wheelchair access. Children allowed. Car parking.

▌Woodlands

NEW ENTRY

Hotel TerraVina

A wine-lover's delight
174 Woodlands Road, Woodlands, SO40 7GL
Tel no: (023) 8029 3784
www.hotelterravina.co.uk
Modern European | £35
Cooking score: 4

🍷 🛏

Owned by Gerard Basset, Master of Wine and co-founder of the Hotel du Vin chain, there are no prizes for guessing this chic, edge-of-the New Forest boutique hotel is an oenophile's delight. The modern dining room comes with a glass-fronted cellar, simply dressed tables and a central high-backed banquette offering views over the open kitchen or veranda and garden. The room's inspiration may be a laid-back Californian wine lodge, but the cuisine is modern European, as in pan-fried wild sea bass teamed with provençale vegetables, violet artichokes, confit potato, pesto dressing and poached oyster, or a more classic ribeye of beef with chateaubriand sauce and hand-cut chips. Crafted from the best local and organic produce, the cooking is accomplished but occasionally 'tries too hard to impress'. Wine advice is spot-on, and 'not at all snooty', the list itself a corker with a bias towards smaller producers. Bottles from £15.50.
Chef/s: Alan Haughie. **Open:** all week L 12 to 2, D 7 to 9.30. **Meals:** alc (main courses £16 to £22). Set L £19.50 (2 courses) to £26. **Service:** not inc. **Details:** Cards accepted. 56 seats. 26 seats outside. Air-con. Separate bar. No music. Wheelchair access. Children allowed. Car parking.

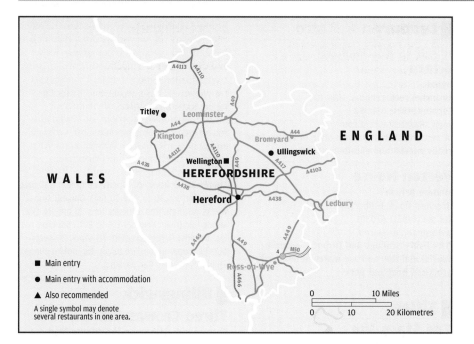

- ■ Main entry
- ● Main entry with accommodation
- ▲ Also recommended

A single symbol may denote several restaurants in one area.

0		10 Miles
0	10	20 Kilometres

▉ Hereford

Castle House

Swish food in a swanky setting
Castle Street, Hereford, HR1 2NW
Tel no: (01432) 356321
www.castlehse.co.uk
Modern British | £30
Cooking score: 5

♟ ⇌

A handsome Regency town dwelling close to Hereford's ancient and modern tourist attractions, the Castle House is now a seriously swish getaway with a swanky dining room overlooking the remains of the old castle moat. Chef Claire Nicholls has found her niche here, fashioning clever contemporary dishes from locally sourced ingredients and allowing the creative juices to flow. She pairs braised boneless chicken wings with seared scallops, spring vegetables and toasted hazelnuts, matches rack of lamb with Puy lentils, home-dried tomatoes and tapenade, and gives sea bream an Asian shake-up with Bombay potatoes, pak choi, peanuts and ginger emulsion. Her Herefordshire beef is also reckoned to be particularly fine – the fillet might be served with local asparagus, carrot fondant, wild mushrooms and new potatoes, while ribeye steaks get home-cut chips and all the trimmings. To finish, try the kitchen's take on rhubarb and custard (if it's in season) or go for something more zany such as confit of lemon and green olive parfait with mascarpone and pecan ice and a basil wafer. It's all 'tremendous value for money' – a virtue that also applies to the informative, knowledgeably assembled wine list: expect a broad palette, taking in big-name Bordeaux and Burgundies as well as exciting tipples from Italy, Australia and South Africa. House selections kick off at £15 (£3.75 a glass).
Chef/s: Claire Nicholls. **Open:** all week L 12 to 2 (12.30 Sun), D 7 to 10 (9 Sun). **Meals:** alc (main courses £12 to £24). Sun L £24. Tasting menu £49 (7 courses). **Service:** not inc. **Details:** Cards accepted. 28 seats. 24 seats outside. Air-con. Separate bar. No mobile phones. Wheelchair access. Music. Children allowed. Car parking.

Ledbury

Sitara
Indian
19 High Street, Ledbury, HR8 1DS
Tel no: (01531) 630088
www.sitararestaurant.com
'A restaurant with its own style of Indian food, really special and excellent value'

Verzon House
Modern British
Hereford Road, Ledbury, HR8 2PZ
Tel no: (01531) 670381
www.verzonhouse.com
'The fish – scallops and turbot – deserve special mention and are matched by locally produced beef and pork'

Titley

The Stagg Inn
Herefordshire pub star
Titley, HR5 3RL
Tel no: (01544) 230221
www.thestagg.co.uk
Modern British | £29
Cooking score: 5

Steve and Nicola Reynolds are now into their second decade as custodians of this Herefordshire inn, and continue to base their enterprise on industrious home production and keen sourcing: Steve bakes his own bread, cures chorizo and makes black pudding – perhaps served with a poached duck egg from his mum's brood of Khaki Campbells. Her Middle White pigs also live in the village (hunks of their belly meat might appear on the plate with apple and brawn salad), and Steve's larder is bulked out with vegetables from smallholdings and locally bagged game. But this isn't simply homespun rusticity and honest endeavour for its own sake: the cooking has sharpness and flair when it's required – as in a rump of Byton lamb with slow-cooked shoulder and fennel purée.

Seafood takes a back seat, while desserts offer chocolate meringue with satsuma cream, or blackcurrant compote, blood orange sorbet and citrus syrup. A stupendous wood-boarded trolley loaded with 20 regional cheeses gets rave reviews, although the same cannot be said of the sometimes 'sullen, ill-mannered' service. Thankfully there are no complaints regarding the exemplary wine list. Growers and grape varieties have been chosen with unfailing intelligence, and prices (from £13.50) are ungreedy to a fault.
Chef/s: Steve Reynolds. Open: Tue to Sun L 12 to 2, Tue to Sat D 6.30 to 9 (9.30 Sat). Closed: Mon, 2 weeks Jan/Feb, first 2 weeks Nov, 25 and 26 Dec. Meals: alc (main courses £15 to £19). Service: not inc. Details: Cards accepted. 70 seats. 20 seats outside. Separate bar. No music. No mobile phones. Children allowed. Car parking.

Ullingswick

Three Crowns Inn
Cottage pub with up-to-the-minute food
Ullingswick, HR1 3JQ
Tel no: (01432) 820279
www.threecrownsinn.com
Modern British | £26
Cooking score: 4

Follow tiny, twisting lanes through the Herefordshire countryside to find this half-timbered, centuries-old cottage pub. Hop-garlanded beams, high-backed settles and locally brewed ales create a suitably bucolic mood in the bar, although some have found the place 'downtrodden' rather than appealingly rustic. However, there's nothing archaic about Brent Castle's food; he taps into the local network for supplies and lets his imagination rip when it comes to bright culinary ideas – despite the odd gripe about 'badly overcooked' dishes. He also rings the changes and follows the calendar, although some items such as a soufflé of Little Hereford cheese are seldom rubbed off the blackboard. Around Christmas you might find roast woodcock with a risotto of its liver followed by winter fruit compote with rice pudding ice cream, while lemon sole with nettles, garlic and red peppers has pleased summer visitors. House wine is £14.50. The owners did not send us a current menu or wine list, so some details may have changed.

Chef/s: Brent Castle. **Open:** Tue to Sun L 12 to 3, D 7 to 10. **Closed:** Mon, 25 and 26 Dec. **Meals:** alc (main courses £15). Set L (not Sun) £12.95 (2 courses) to £14.95. **Service:** not inc. **Details:** Cards accepted. 75 seats. 30 seats outside. No music. Wheelchair access. Children allowed. Car parking.

▌Wellington

The Wellington

Good value, heart-on-sleeve cooking
Wellington, HR4 8AT
Tel no: (01432) 830367
www.wellingtonpub.co.uk
Gastropub | £27
Cooking score: 2

Reporters continue to applaud Ross Williams' rustic pub, singling out for praise the 'excellent value for money' and 'charming service'. Don't expect refined cuisine here: direct, earthy, heart-on-sleeve dishes are the order of the day, and it's all fuelled by a dedication to well-sourced local and seasonal produce. Rabbit ravioli with grain mustard and cream sauce won over one reporter. Fillet of sea bass is served with wild mushroom and Puy lentil salad, while calf's liver comes with crispy pancetta, buttered mash and sage butter. Cheeses are from Herefordshire and desserts are uncomplicated offerings such as pannacotta with poached fig. Wines start at £13.

Chef/s: Ross Williams. **Open:** Tue to Sun L 12 to 2 (12.30 Sun), Mon to Sat D 7 to 9. **Closed:** 25 and 26 Dec. **Meals:** alc (main courses £12 to £18). Sun L £17.50. **Service:** not inc. **Details:** Cards accepted. 70 seats. 20 seats outside. Separate bar. Music. Children allowed. Car parking.

Great trolleys

For the most part, trolleys belong in supermarkets, but there is a particularly old-fashioned thrill in having bread, dessert, cheese or petits fours wheeled over to your table. Here follow some of our favourites.

A mind-boggling array of house-baked breads is offered by a man with a white glove and a sharp knife at Manchester's **The French at the Midland Hotel.** Down the M56 in Chester, **Simon Radley at the Chester Grosvenor** is also home to an impressive selection of breads – which even includes banana bread.

The offbeat presentation of Simon Rogan's dishes at **L'Enclume** (test tubes, spinal tap needles and specially made serving pieces are all employed) makes the familiarity of a straightforward cheese trolley all the more comforting. Large helpings of a mainly French selection are encouraged, as they are at **Le Gavroche**.

Marcus Wareing at the Berkeley gives chocolates similarly smart treatment; diners pluck them from the sculptural glass bowls of the bonbon trolley.

To round things off, **Alain Ducasse at the Dorchester** offers the saintly option – a trolley loaded with herbs ready for a purifying hot-water infusion – as well as mignardises galore.

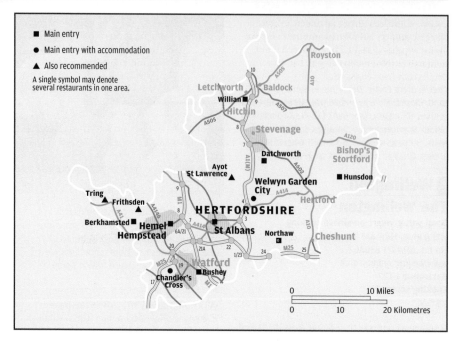

- ■ Main entry
- ● Main entry with accommodation
- ▲ Also recommended

A single symbol may denote several restaurants in one area.

■ Ayot St Lawrence

ALSO RECOMMENDED
▲ The Brocket Arms

Ayot St Lawrence, AL6 9BT
Tel no: (01438) 820250
www.brocketarms.com
Gastropub

A favourite haunt of walkers and literary pilgrims visiting George Bernard Shaw's house (National Trust), this emblematic, centuries-old hostelry is a real ale stronghold and atmospherically gregarious re-fuelling point. Chef Andrew Knight (ex-Auberge du Lac, see entry) has forsaken haute cuisine for humble cuts, with a menu that pitches shepherd's pie, battered pollack and Guinness-braised ox cheek against seared scallops with cauliflower purée or pea and broad bean risotto. Play safe with the straight-talking pub-style dishes, and finish with fragrant rose petal brûlée. Two courses £16.95; wines from £13.30. Closed Sun D.

■ Berkhamsted

The Gatsby

Deco decadence and pretty food
Rex Cinema, 97 High Street, Berkhamsted, HP4 2DG
Tel no: (01442) 870403
www.thegatsby.net
Modern European | £33
Cooking score: 2

£5 OFF **V**

Housed within a fabulously restored Art Deco cinema, the Gatsby is a full-on destination in its own right. The booming bar is for cocktail kicks; ascend some steps to reach the plush dining room, tricked out with sculpted ceilings and original mirrored pillars. The kitchen deals in neatly plated arrangements – as you might expect from a chef with Le Gavroche and L'Escargot on his CV. Little gratins of scallops and caramelised leeks sit in their shells on a bed of salt, and a creamy fricassee of seafood is intricately embellished with turned vegetables – although

Lincolnshire pork fillet and confit belly with black pudding mash strikes an earthier chord. To finish, chocolate fondant oozes impressively. Wines start at £15.25.
Chef/s: Matthew Salt. **Open:** all week L 12 to 2.30, D 5.30 to 10.30 (9.30 Sun). **Closed:** 25 and 26 Dec. **Meals:** alc (main courses £14 to £25). Set L £13.95 (2 courses) to £18.90. Sun L £14.95. **Service:** not inc. **Details:** Cards accepted. 65 seats. 50 seats outside. Air-con. Separate bar. No mobile phones. Wheelchair access. Music. Children allowed. Car parking.

ALSO RECOMMENDED
▲ Eat Fish
163-165 High Street, Berkhamsted, HP4 3HB
Tel no: (01442) 879988
www.eatfish.co.uk
Seafood £5 OFF

Occupying a prime site on Berkhamsted High Street, this local favourite dishes up decent helpings of spanking fresh fish in jolly surroundings. Tapas bowls and lobster platters are just the job for sharing, and the menu also goes walkabout for lively assemblages including chilli and coriander crab cakes (£6) or stone bass with braised fennel and chorizo (£16). Meat eaters get their fill from ribeye and chips, while sweet-toothed punters drool over sticky toffee pudding (£5). House wine is £14. Open all week. There's also a sibling in Bedford.

▌Bushey
St James
Local asset with great staff
30 High Street, Bushey, WD23 3HL
Tel no: (020) 8950 2480
www.stjamesrestaurant.co.uk
Modern British | £35
Cooking score: 1

A laudable local asset since 1997, St James creates a pleasing vibe with its halo motifs and uncomplicated food. The kitchen sends out a mixed bag of accessible dishes ranging from scallops with pear and ginger purée to Arctic roll with raspberry jelly, plus substantial mains such as grilled halibut on smoked haddock and potato chowder or venison loin with parsnip crumble and braised red cabbage. Professional staff are praised to the skies, and the food is bolstered by some quaffable French and Italian wines from £15.50.
Chef/s: Calvin Hill. **Open:** Mon to Sat L 12 to 3, D 6.30 to 10. **Closed:** Sun, 25 and 26 Dec, bank hols. **Meals:** alc (main courses £16 to £22). Set L £14.95 (2 courses). Set D £16.95 (2 courses). Sun L £24.50. **Service:** 12.5% (optional). **Details:** Cards accepted. 90 seats. 20 seats outside. Air-con. Separate bar. No mobile phones. Wheelchair access. Music. Children allowed. Car parking.

▌Chandler's Cross

NEW ENTRY
The Clarendon
Animated vibes, deeply satisfying food
Redhall Lane, Chandler's Cross, WD3 4LU
Tel no: (01923) 270009
www.theclarendon.co.uk
Modern European | £28
Cooking score: 5
£5 OFF £30

A load of cash has obviously been lavished on this pristine-looking restaurant and bar, with its fresh-faced brick frontage, sculpted topiary and funky outdoor space. Inside, the Clarendon is stuffed with kooky novelties – pop art, a bust of the Queen Mum on the bar, black chandeliers the size of oil drums in the brick-walled, bare-tabled dining room. It's unashamedly populist, but the set-up also allows room for the finer things: linen napkins, excellent bread, good strong coffee. Chef Anthony Boyd has been lured away from the Glasshouse in Kew (see entry, Greater London) to head up the open-to-view kitchen, and fans will recognise some of the dishes on his keenly priced menu: the warm duck salad with deep-fried truffled egg, burnished crispy mackerel with sweet mustard, and an unctuous 'tasting of pork' with pungent choucroute, prunes and sage leaves, for example. He has lost none of his zest for deeply satisfying, big-city food without bells and whistles, although some dishes are a touch simpler than before. Silky foie gras and chicken liver parfait topped with braised green lentils (another Boyd classic) is pure pleasure, likewise a hunk of pearly cod with buttery mash, sprouting broccoli and shrimps. Desserts play with a straight bat – perhaps citrusy lemon posset, topped with a matrix of blood orange segments and a golf-ball marmalade doughnut. The wine list strikes a lively note, with prices from £14.50.

Chef/s: Anthony Boyd. **Open:** all week L 12 to 3 (5 Sun), D 6 to 10 (9 Sun). **Closed:** 25 Dec. **Meals:** alc (main courses £10 to £18). **Service:** 10% (optional). **Details:** Cards accepted. 99 seats. 80 seats outside. Air-con. Separate bar. Wheelchair access. Music. Children allowed. Car parking.

The Grove, Colette's
Head-turning surrounds and eye-catching food
Chandler's Cross, WD3 4TG
Tel no: (01923) 807807
www.thegrove.co.uk
Modern European | £62
Cooking score: 5

Once the bolthole of choice for an aristocratic weekend out of town, the Grove has re-invented itself as a premier-league hospitality destination; instead of lords and ladies, you are more likely to encounter the England football team ensconced within its illustrious porticoed enclaves. Colette's is the hotel's gastronomic flagship and very grand it is too – an ever-so-trendy, head-turning space with a moody bar, vast canvases and larger-than-life sculptures. The kitchen is also out to impress, with no shortage of foams, dusts and eye-candy applied to its elaborately constructed dishes. Native seasonal ingredients get a good airing on the dauntingly priced dinner menu, although they often find themselves in unfamiliar company: Aylesbury duck breast appears with turnips, pistachios and caramelised satsuma, while organic Lincolnshire pork cutlet is matched with Scottish langoustines, butternut squash, sage and golden raisins; elsewhere, coconut-

poached brill might come to the table with korma couscous, spinach pastilla and steamed mussels. Also look out for seasonal treats including free-range Creedy Carver duck 'tea' and plates of truffles with violet artichokes, duck egg, salsify and cep purée. To conclude, have fun with the kitchen's wacky 'toffee crisp' or try the set Earl Grey cream with milk froth, green cardamom and orange granita. The wine list is a suitably bullish slate, promising serious drinking at serious prices (from £26).

Chef/s: Russell Bateman. **Open:** Tue to Sat D 7 to 9.30 (and Sun D on bank hols). **Closed:** Sun and Mon. **Meals:** Set D £62. Tasting menu £77 (6 courses). **Service:** not inc. **Details:** Cards accepted. 40 seats. Air-con. Separate bar. Wheelchair access. Music. Car parking.

▌Datchworth
The Tilbury
Serious eatery with patriotic inclinations
Brookbridge Lane, Datchworth, SG3 6TB
Tel no: (01438) 815550
www.thetilbury.co.uk
Modern British | £29
Cooking score: 4
£30

Paul Bloxham has set himself up as a champion of regional produce, and puts his money where his mouth is at this classily refurbished village hostelry. Once a local boozer, it now also trades as a serious eatery with strong patriotic inclinations – and a smokehouse to boot. 'Pub classics' are outshone by an upbeat menu that touts anything from local beef tataki with coriander shoots and ponzu dressing to guinea fowl 'in a jar' with sauerkraut. The Tilbury's 'plate of Old Spot pig' is a porcine bonanza, while fish fans might fancy roast rock bass with cockles, mussels, tomato and garlic confit. Readers have also endorsed old favourites such as Corneybury Farm onglet steak with chips, and few can resist the glazed lemon tart with Seville orange marmalade ice cream. Sunday roasts go down a treat, likewise the global wines (from £13.95). Paul has also re-launched the Blue Anchor in St Albans (see entry).

Chef/s: Paul Bloxham and Ben Crick. **Open:** all week L 12 to 3 (5 Sun), Mon to Sat D 6 to 11. **Meals:** alc (main courses £10 to £23). Set L £13.95 (2 courses) to £16.95. Set D £18.95 (2 courses) to £23.50. Sun L £19.95. **Service:** not inc. **Details:** Cards accepted. 70 seats. 40 seats outside. Separate bar. No mobile phones. Wheelchair access. Music. Children allowed. Car parking.

▌Frithsden

ALSO RECOMMENDED
▲ The Alford Arms
Frithsden, HP1 3DD
Tel no: (01442) 864480
www.alfordarmsfrithsden.co.uk
Gastropub

The blueprint for a group that now includes five Home Counties gastropubs, the Alford Arms defined the house style – a combination of country locations, folksy interiors and enterprising food. Deep in National Trust woodland, it serves seasonal 'small plates' and big dishes ranging from herb-crusted local rabbit croquettes with spiced cauliflower dip (£6.75) to pan-fried sea bream with beetroot purée, pickled cucumber and chervil dressing (£14.50). Desserts might include rhubarb and ginger crumble (£5.25). House wine £13.50. Open all week.

▌Hemel Hempstead

NEW ENTRY
Restaurant 65
Proper, honest food
65 High Street, Old Town, Hemel Hempstead, HP1 3AF
Tel no: (01442) 239010
www.restaurant65.com
Modern European | £28
Cooking score: 1
£5 OFF £30

A diamond in Hemel's foodie wasteland, this thoroughly likeable, pint-sized dining room is everything a decent local restaurant should be. Congeniality rules and Grant Young does a grand job in his tiny kitchen, taking time and care over his 'proper, honest food'. A 'drop-dead delicious' starter of stonkingly fresh chicken livers on black pudding with mustard and chive sauce could be followed by a hunk of roasted salmon on a cake of wilted spinach and saffron-crushed potatoes. Warm apple and almond tart with a slick of green apple purée makes a fine finish. House French is £13.

Chef/s: Grant Young. **Open:** Tue to Fri and Sun L 12 to 2 (12.30 to 2.30 Sun), Tue to Sat D 7 to 9. **Closed:** first week Jan, 1 week Jul. **Meals:** alc (main courses £14 to £17). Set L £14.95 (2 courses) to £19.95. **Service:** 12.5% (optional). **Details:** Cards accepted. 28 seats. Music. Children allowed. Car parking.

ALSO RECOMMENDED
▲ Cochin Cuisine
61 High Street, Old Town, Hemel Hempstead, HP1 3AF
Tel no: (01442) 233777
www.thecochincuisine.com
Indian £5 OFF

A world away from the town's 'one pot' curry houses, Cochin brings a taste of Kerala's coastal cuisine to Hemel Hempstead. The setting is a light room done out in pastel shades of sky-blue, and the kitchen goes for seafood in a big way: try nadan meen char (£8.90), a 'toddy shop' special of kingfish with tamarind. Gentle but acute spicing also shows in silky medhu vadai 'doughnuts' (£3) and nadan kohzi (£5.75) – a home-style chicken curry bursting with natural flavours. Wines from £9.95; also lassi and beer. Open all week.

Symbols

🛏 Accommodation is available

£30 Three courses for less than £30

V More than three vegetarian main courses

£5 OFF £5-off voucher scheme

🍷 Notable wine list

Hunsdon

Fox & Hounds

Relaxed village local with first-class ingredients
2 High Street, Hunsdon, SG12 8NH
Tel no: (01279) 843999
www.foxandhounds-hunsdon.co.uk
Gastropub | £25
Cooking score: 2

V £30

It still has the air of a village local, albeit with a menu taking in sweet-and-sour mackerel and penne with braised wild rabbit ragù, but combined with an unpretentious, contemporary look, it all adds up to a distinctive yet relaxed hostelry. James Rix's modern menus, showcasing first-class raw materials, reveal realistic ambition and the resulting clear focus is much appreciated, especially in the evening when a winter dinner could bring char-grilled harissa-marinated squid with preserved lemon and rocket, whole roast partridge with braised lentils, and pannacotta with Yorkshire rhubarb. A short, to-the-point wine list opens at £13.50.
Chef/s: James Rix. **Open:** Tue to Sun L 12 to 2.30 (3 Sat, 3.30 Sun), Tue to Sat D 6.30 to 10. **Closed:** Mon. **Meals:** alc (main courses £9 to £19). Set L £12.50 (2 courses). Set D £13.50 (2 courses). Sun L £21.50 (2 courses) to £25.50. **Service:** 10% (optional). **Details:** Cards accepted. 80 seats. 60 seats outside. Separate bar. Music. Children allowed. Car parking.

Northaw

NEW ENTRY
The Sun at Northaw

Jolly regional champion
1 Judges Hill, Northaw, EN6 4NL
Tel no: (01707) 655507
www.thesunatnorthaw.co.uk
Gastropub | £25
Cooking score: 3

£5 £30
OFF

Artisan provisions, 'field fare' and sustainable fish loom large at this jolly champion of produce from England's eastern counties, which has been tricked out in fashionably folksy style with boxes of veg, cookbooks and reclaimed tables. Oliver Smith arrived here armed with a natural-born appetite for seasonal food and a rallying cry of 'Ingredients! Ingredients! Ingredients!' A 'wondrous' starter of Jerusalem artichokes, pickled walnuts, soft goats' cheese and crisp red radishes in a tangle of thyme typifies his ingenious way of doing things; elsewhere venison comes with an incisive sauce of sea buckthorn berries, and whole flounder is scattered with sweet cockles and alexanders. Moreish nibbles include crispy sweetbreads with green sauce, free-range Label Anglais chicken (from Essex) is a revelation and heaps of fresh-as-a-daisy vegetables are a given. Handmade cheeses, hand-pulled ales and handpicked wines (from £14.50) complete a splendid package.
Chef/s: Oliver Smith. **Open:** Tue to Sun L 12 to 3 (4 Sat, 5 Sun), Tue to Sat D 6 to 10. **Closed:** Mon. **Meals:** alc (main courses £12 to £19). Sun L £22 (2 courses) to £28. **Service:** not inc. **Details:** Cards accepted. 90 seats. 60 seats outside. Separate bar. Wheelchair access. Music. Children allowed. Car parking.

St Albans

NEW ENTRY
The Blue Anchor

Pubby attributes and vigorous cooking
145 Fishpool Street, St Albans, AL3 4RY
Tel no: (01727) 855038
www.theblueanchorstalbans.co.uk
Gastropub | £22
Cooking score: 2

£5 **V** £30
OFF

Following the success of the Tilbury at Datchworth (see entry), Paul Bloxham is applying his Midas touch to this sturdy red-brick boozer in a genteel quarter of St Albans. The new place has pubby attributes aplenty, but vigorous cooking is now the major draw. Daily menus fuse regional ingredients with sunny Med flavours, promising anything from sprue (first pickings) asparagus with a Bantam egg or rare-breed bavette and chips to juicy free-range chicken and wild mushroom sausages with braised lentils and punchy romesco salsa. Also check out the specialist British charcuterie, and don't miss the jokey take on 'jelly and ice cream' if it's offered. Commendable wines from £10.

Chef/s: Paul Bloxham, Ben Crick and Mark Thurlow. **Open:** Tue to Fri L 12 to 2.30, D 5.30 to 10. Sat 11 to 11, Sun 11 to 6. **Closed:** 26 Dec, 1 Jan. **Meals:** alc (main courses £9 to £16). Set L and early D £12.95 (2 courses). **Service:** not inc. **Details:** Cards accepted. 60 seats. 60 seats outside. Air-con. Separate bar. No mobile phones. Wheelchair access. Music. Children allowed. Car parking.

Darcy's
Racy food in cool surrounds
2 Hatfield Road, St Albans, AL1 3RP
Tel no: (01727) 730777
www.darcysrestaurant.co.uk
Global | £35
Cooking score: 2

£5
OFF

The 'coolest' restaurant in St Albans occupies a weatherboarded one-time smithy just off the town's main drag. Inside, it's a suave combination of moody cocktail bar and dining rooms spread over two floors. Aussie chef Ruth Hurren is at home with sun-baked global flavours, serving sexy salads dramatically in black pottery bowls, partnering smoked kangaroo with 'native' pepper jus and steaming miso cod in banana leaves. She also dreams up some clear, bright Euro-accented ideas (seared mackerel with beetroot pesto) and gives local ingredients a fusion spin – Wobbly Bottom goats' cheese on a disc of sourdough and hazelnut dukkah with preserved quince, say. Amazing-value set menus feed the local ladies who lunch, and the wine list has some quaffable stuff from £13.50. **Chef/s:** Ruth Hurren. **Open:** all week L 12 to 2.30 (3.30 Sun), D 6 to 10 (9 Sun). **Closed:** 26 and 27 Dec, 1 and 2 Jan. **Meals:** alc (main courses £12 to £24). Set L and early D £11.90 (2 courses) to £14.90. Sun L £16.90 (2 courses) to £19.90. **Service:** 12.5% (optional). **Details:** Cards accepted. 90 seats. 20 seats outside. Air-con. Separate bar. Wheelchair access. Music. Children allowed.

Lussmanns
Chic brasserie dining
Waxhouse Gate, Off High Street, St Albans, AL3 4EW
Tel no: (01727) 851941
www.lussmanns.com
Modern British | £22
Cooking score: 1

V £30

One of Andrei Lussmann's group of chic Hertfordshire brasseries (also in Hertford and Bishop's Stortford). Like its relatives, the menu races through starters (grilled squid with fresh chilli and rocket), salads, pasta (rabbit and chestnut mushroom linguine), fish, steaks and burgers. There are also specials such as venison with mash and leek crisp, and a few puddings including warm chocolate and walnut brownie. Menus are keen to promote provenance and seasonality, and service 'is second to none'. Wines from £14.25. **Chef/s:** Nick McGowan. **Open:** all week 12 to 10 (10.30 Fri and Sat, 9.30 Sun). **Closed:** 25 and 26 Dec. **Meals:** alc (main courses £7 to £17). Set L and D £10.95 (2 courses) to £13.95. **Service:** not inc. **Details:** Cards accepted. 100 seats. 10 seats outside. Air-con. Wheelchair access. Music. Children allowed.

▌Tring

ALSO RECOMMENDED
▲ The Green House
50 High Street, Tring, HP23 5AG
Tel no: (01442) 823993
www.thegreenhousetring.co.uk
Vegetarian

This easy-going, green-fingered local veggie ticks all the right eco boxes, and its summery conservatory vibe is perfectly in tune with the fresh, invigorating food on offer. The kitchen shows care with the details, creating a raft of global flavours from parsnip sushi rolls stuffed with tiny sprouting seeds to barley risotto with Kabocha squash and baby spinach (£9.50). Start with flaky butternut squash and ricotta samosas (£5.25) and finish with a slice of special apple pie, 'made raw' and served with almond cream (£5.95). Organic wines from £14.95. Closed Mon.

▌Welwyn Garden City

Auberge du Lac

Star-studded dishes and awesome wines
Brocket Hall, Welwyn Garden City, AL8 7XG
Tel no: (01707) 368888
www.aubergedulac.co.uk
Modern French | £55
Cooking score: 6

£5 OFF ⌀ ▭ V

Half-hidden amid the manicured grounds of Brocket Hall – an aristocratic country retreat turned gold-standard hospitality venue/ conference centre/golf complex – Auberge du Lac is housed in a Hansel and Gretel hunting lodge right next to an ornamental lake. Phil Thompson sails confidently through the tricky waters of intricate modern cuisine, fashioning star-studded dishes that dovetail artisan British ingredients with contemporary French technique and influences from the Orient. He serves paupiettes of home-smoked salmon and spiced Cornish crab with yuzu cream and pickled cockles, but counterbalances any arcane tendencies with some back-to-the-roots blockbusters – slow-roast rump of Devon Vale beef with Madeira-braised snails, parsnip, blue cheese and Guinness reduction, for example. To finish, a clever fruit and cheese alliance of poached pear, white chocolate, Roquefort and olive oil is in tune with the zeitgeist, although Thompson is equally at home with rhubarb and custard soufflé. Brilliant-value lunches (including two glasses of superior wine) maintain the tempo with the likes of warm confit morteau sausage, spiced lentil and marinated carrot salad or grey mullet with crushed Jersey Royals, watercress and razor clam butter. The awe-inspiring, 700-bin list is a stately procession through the wine-making world, exploring France in depth before giving due consideration to Italy, Austria, Australia and beyond. Prices start at £22.

Chef/s: Phil Thompson. **Open:** Tue to Sat L 12 to 2.30, D 7 to 9.30. **Closed:** Sun, Mon, last week Dec, first week Jan. **Meals:** Set L £32.50. Set D £55. Tasting menu £65. **Service:** 10% (optional). **Details:** Cards accepted. 70 seats. 40 seats outside. Air-con. Separate bar. No mobile phones. Wheelchair access. Music. Children allowed. Car parking.

▌Willian

The Fox

Agreeable gastropub with star seafood
Willian, SG6 2AE
Tel no: (01462) 480233
www.foxatwillian.co.uk
Gastropub | £28
Cooking score: 2

£30 ⬛

Cliff and James Nye's contemporary-styled pub-restaurant by the village green is close to Letchworth and the A1 and draws folk from afar with its fish-inspired menus. There are close associations with the north Norfolk coast (the Nyes also own the White Horse at Brancaster Staithe – see entry), and the menu bristles with freshly delivered Cromer crab, Brancaster mussels and oysters, smoked salmon and haddock from Letzer's Smokery, alongside the likes of cod with spring onion and tiger prawn risotto. Elsewhere, there could be chicken liver and foie gras parfait, venison with blackberry jus, and blackberry Eton mess with almond caramel. Don't miss the Food Barn out back for local meats and deli goodies to take home. House wine is £14.50 a bottle (£2.50 a glass).

Chef/s: Chris Jones. **Open:** all week L 12 to 2 (2.45 Sun), Mon to Sat D 6.45 to 9 (6.30 to 9.15 Sat). **Meals:** alc (main courses £9 to £19). **Service:** 10% (optional). **Details:** Cards accepted. 65 seats. 16 seats outside. Separate bar. No mobile phones. Wheelchair access. Music. Children allowed. Car parking.

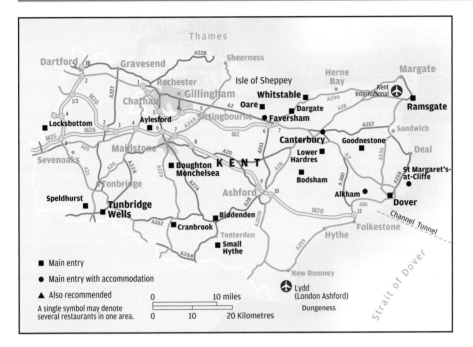

Alkham
The Marquis at Alkham
Food with flair and care
Alkham Valley Road, Alkham, CT15 7DF
Tel no: (01304) 873410
www.themarquisatalkham.co.uk
Modern British | £28
Cooking score: 4

£5 OFF £30

As the name suggests, the Marquis was once a pub, but internally all trace of its former use is gone. The decoration in this ambitious, fairly formal restaurant-with-rooms is all stripped woodwork and neutral colours. In the kitchen Charles Lakin cooks carefully sourced ingredients with flair – slices of crisp pig's trotter stuffed with ham hock and topped with fried quails' eggs, served with a pungent cauliflower piccalilli is a signature dish. The food looks the part too, whether it's seared loin of venison Wellington with cocotte potato, sauerkraut, red wine jus and mushroom foam, or a carrot cake enlivened by blood orange

sorbet, compote and cream cheese frosting. Interesting Kentish beers and ciders add spice to a wine list structured to appeal to all pockets. France is the main focus, with strong global support. House wine is £14.75.
Chef/s: Charles Lakin. **Open:** Tue to Sun L 12 to 2.30 (6 Sun), Mon to Sat D 6.30 to 9.30. **Meals:** Set L £15.50 (2 courses) to £19.50. Set D £18.95 (2 courses) to £24.95 or £31.50 (2 courses) to £39.50. Tasting menu £50 (6 courses). **Service:** not inc. **Details:** Cards accepted. 60 seats. 35 seats outside. Separate bar. Wheelchair access. Music. Children allowed. Car parking.

Aylesford
Hengist

'A fantastic all-round experience'
7-9 High Street, Aylesford, ME20 7AX
Tel no: (01622) 719273
www.hengistrestaurant.co.uk
Modern French | £30
Cooking score: 4

The décor is curiously mixed – ancient beams, timbered walls and exposed brick, offset by lots of contemporary touches – but in the kitchen the emphasis is placed firmly on an up-to-the-minute menu with plenty of touchstone ideas and good ingredients. It's a 'fantastic all-round experience'. Chef Daniel Hatton takes full account of Kentish produce and supplies from further afield in dishes such as oak-smoked cod brandade beignet with cauliflower three ways, thyme dressing and candied citrus fruits, and a taster of local farmed venison (braised shoulder, hotpot and roast loin) served with creamed cabbage, poached grapes and bitter chocolate jus. Desserts are elaborate creations such as iced passion-fruit parfait with glazed chestnut purée, and passion-fruit jelly and Kentish cobnuts, and the cheese selection is to be applauded – all are from the south-east of England. House wine is £14.50.
Chef/s: Daniel Hatton. Open: Tue to Sun L 12 to 2.30 (4 Sun), Tue to Sat D 6.30 to 10.30. Closed: Mon. Meals: Set L £12.95 (2 courses) to £14.95. Set D £19.95 (2 courses) to £25.50. Sun L £18.50. Service: 12% (optional). Details: Cards accepted. 70 seats. Air-con. Separate bar. No mobile phones. Wheelchair access. Music. Children allowed. Car parking.

Biddenden
The West House

Clever food without flimflam
28 High Street, Biddenden, TN27 8AH
Tel no: (01580) 291341
www.thewesthouserestaurant.co.uk
Modern European | £35
Cooking score: 5

Here is a restaurant that runs in its own way and at its own speed, with a casual demeanour that belies the sharpness of the food coming from the kitchen. Graham Garrett's cooking is technically assured, intelligent and instinctively true: mackerel fillet and Rye Bay scallop sit comfortably with rhubarb chutney potatoes, while parsley root purée and three-cornered garlic seem like happy companions for line-caught sea bass. Graham's grounding with Irish supremo Richard Corrigan may explain a liking for bold, earthy flavours – fried pig's head with roast belly, twice-cooked duck egg, anchovy and caper vinaigrette, for example. He is also brave enough to serve pickled wood pigeon in a salad with Jerusalem artichokes and hazelnuts, and provides sweetness for cured duck foie gras in the shape of caramel pineapple and wine jelly. The results are crisp, clear-flavoured and refreshingly free of flimflam. To finish, turn back time with 'all the fun of the fair' – a helter-skelter of toffee apple pannacotta, candyfloss and a popcorn shot; otherwise saffron-poached pear with bread pudding and turrón ice cream might suffice. The global wine list opens with 17 house selections from £4.50 a glass, £11 a carafe.
Chef/s: Graham Garrett. Open: Tue to Fri and Sun L 12 to 2, Tue to Sat D 7 to 9 (9.30 Fri and Sat). Closed: Mon, 2 weeks Christmas to New Year, 2 weeks summer. Meals: Set L £22 (2 courses) to £25. Set D £29.50 (2 courses) to £35. Sun L £29.50 (2 courses) to £35. Service: 12.5% (optional). Details: Cards accepted. 32 seats. No music. No mobile phones. Wheelchair access. Music. Children allowed. Car parking.

ALSO RECOMMENDED

▲ The Three Chimneys

Hareplain Road, Biddenden, TN27 8LW
Tel no: (01580) 291472
www.thethreechimneys.co.uk
Gastropub

A true country classic, this picture-perfect Kentish pub dates from the sixteenth century and has a rambling interior full of low beamed ceilings, wonky brick floors, old settles and evening candlelight. Expect 'consistently great, beautifully presented British food' and 'friendly, efficient' service. A typical meal might comprise salmon and smoked haddock fishcakes (£7.95) followed by pan-roasted duck breast with bubble and squeak mash and rich port jus (£15.95). Wines start at £15.50. Open all week.

▌Bodsham

Froggies at the Timber Batts

Traditional pub, classic French food
School Lane, Bodsham, TN25 5JQ
Tel no: (01233) 750237
www.thetimberbatts.co.uk
French | £35
Cooking score: 1

The beamed and timbered pub with its inglenook fireplace is a joy to behold, while rustic pine tables with candles enhance the dining area. French food is the name of the game, as indicated none too delicately by the name, with stuffed mussels, duck magret in sauce bigarade, and grilled ribeye steaks with béarnaise all bearing handsome witness. The lack of pretension appeals, all the way through to a finishing glass of cassis sorbet anointed with crème de cassis. House wines from a relative's vineyard in the Loire are £17.
Chef/s: Joël Gross. **Open:** all week L 12 to 2.15 (3 Sun), D 7 to 9.30 (9 Sun). **Closed:** 24 Dec to 3 Jan. **Meals:** alc (main courses £15 to £24). Set L £16 (2 courses) to £20. Sun L £20 (2 courses) to £25. **Service:** not inc. **Details:** Cards accepted. 50 seats. 50 seats outside. Separate bar. Music. Children allowed. Car parking.

▌Boughton Monchelsea

The Mulberry Tree

Heroic Kentish food champion
Hermitage Lane, Boughton Monchelsea,
ME17 4DA
Tel no: (01622) 749082
www.themulberrytreekent.co.uk
Modern British | £28
Cooking score: 4
£30

Secreted away in the Kent countryside, this self-styled 'contemporary restaurant and bar' has staked its claim as a local food champion – and it's also moving into serious home production. The kitchen garden is now in full swing, Middle White pigs root around in the grounds, and plans are afoot for an orchard and duck rearing. If there were any doubts about provenance, Alan Irwin's seasonal menus are strewn with named ingredients. Heronden Estate pigeon breasts appear with spiced peppers, Broadstairs lemon sole comes with tarragon, spinach and a gratin of Whitstable shellfish, while winter truffles add a luxurious earthiness to poached and roasted haunch of Tenterden rose veal. But this isn't simply a heroic effort to 'go local', the cooking is astute, unaffected and totally convincing. To finish, explore the Kentish cheeses, and satisfy any sweet cravings with, say, upside-down blackcurrant and hibiscus cheesecake. Almost everything on the 60-bin wine list is available by the glass; bottles start at £13.25.
Chef/s: Alan Irwin. **Open:** Tue to Sun L 12 to 2 (2.30 Sun), Tue to Sat D 6.30 to 9 (9.30 Fri and Sat). **Closed:** Mon. **Meals:** alc (main courses £15 to £21). Set L and D £12.95 (2 courses) to £15.95. Sun L £18.95. **Service:** not inc. **Details:** Cards accepted. 50 seats. 40 seats outside. Separate bar. Wheelchair access. Music. Children allowed. Car parking.

Canterbury

The Goods Shed
Good food from the market
Station Road West, Canterbury, CT2 8AN
Tel no: (01227) 459153
www.thegoodsshed.net
Modern British | £30
Cooking score: 2

The cavernous brick-built Victorian railway shed opened in 2002 as the only daily farmers' market in the country. As a venue for fresh local produce it is second to none, and the raised restaurant, which runs the length of the market, sources as much as possible from the various stalls. Scrubbed wooden tables and junk-shop chairs define its casual nature, and the daily changing blackboard menu could deliver good fishcakes with tartare sauce, then local cod with brown shrimps and summer herbs, or confit of duck leg with braised cabbage and apples. House wine is £13.50 (£4.80 a glass).

Chef/s: Rafael Lopez. **Open:** Tue to Sun L 12 to 2.30 (3 Sat and Sun), D 6 to 9.30. **Closed:** Mon, 25 to 27 Dec, 1 and 2 Jan. **Meals:** alc (main courses £11 to £20). **Service:** not inc. **Details:** Cards accepted. 60 seats. No music. No mobile phones. Wheelchair access. Children allowed. Car parking.

Michael Caines at ABode Canterbury
Dining in another dimension
High Street, Canterbury, CT1 2RX
Tel no: (01227) 826684
www.michaelcaines.com
Modern European | £30
Cooking score: 5

The ABode chain's Canterbury branch is to be found on the medieval high street. Its restaurant is a cream-coloured, bare-floorboarded room with well-spaced tables and a gentle buzz animating the air. Toby Lin, formerly sous-chef, took up the reins in 2009 and has taken the food into another dimension. What impresses across the ABode

group is the freedom of expression each head chef has within a finely wrought 'house' style. A first course of organic salmon cooked in slow motion to achieve a kind of warm sashimi texture is garnished with wasabi-spiked Greek yoghurt, salmon eggs, honey and soy, a dish of disparate elements that comes together beautifully on the palate. Gressingham duck appears in a trio line-up as a chunk of crackle-skinned breast, a sliver of seared foie gras and a perfectly made mini spring roll of confit leg. Desserts mobilise a lot of chocolate, but it is superb chocolate, perhaps in the form of a warm moelleux crammed with rum-soaked raisins and served with smoothly concentrated pistachio ice cream. The fixed-price lunch menu remains one of Kent's bargains – despite rather modest portions. Details such as breads and petits fours are all persuasively classy, and service is a model of discreet efficiency. The wine list is arranged helpfully by grape variety, with an excellent choice by the glass. House selections are £20.50.

Chef/s: Toby Lin and Jean-Marc Zanetti. **Open:** all week L 12 to 2.30 (12.30 Sun), Mon to Sat D 6 to 10. **Meals:** alc (main courses £19 to £24). Set L £12. Set D £20 (2 courses) to £25. Sun L £14.95. **Service:** 12% (optional). **Details:** Cards accepted. 70 seats. Air-con. Separate bar. No mobile phones. Wheelchair access. Music. Children allowed. Car parking.

Cranbrook

Apicius
Artistry and big-statement cooking
23 Stone Street, Cranbrook, TN17 3HF
Tel no: (01580) 714666
www.restaurant-apicius.co.uk
Modern European | £32
Cooking score: 6

Timothy Johnson and Faith Hawkins' tenure of this fifteenth-century weaver's cottage has been something of a slow-burner, and it took a while to convince the local crowd that their intentions were serious. Thankfully, Kent's foodies now recognise that something gastronomically significant is going on here. The restaurant takes its name from Roman

chef Apicius, whose *De Re Culinaria* ranks as the world's oldest surviving recipe book. But you won't find any liquamen or dormice on Tim Johnson's menus; instead he stages a contemporary one-man show, quietly winning over an appreciative audience with his bold approach and keen prices. The sheer culinary artistry can dazzle, although ideas are never outlandish for the sake of it. Smoked haddock brandade with saffron rice and a soft-boiled quail's egg sounds conventional, until you discover that the brandade is deep-fried for maximum textural effect; elsewhere, smoked venison might appear as the main player in a Yuletide salad with chestnuts, beetroot, cranberry jelly, melon and pickled mushrooms. Tim's dishes 'burst with love', according to one ardent admirer: perhaps he was talking about roast John Dory with crushed new potatoes, a niçoise garnish and a drizzle of thyme oil or rustic braised chuck of beef with a tuberous trinity of turnips, carrots and celeriac. When it comes to desserts, the kitchen takes a cheeky tilt at the classics, pitching chocolate fondant alongside a raspberry and orange drink, or presenting lime pannacotta with olive oil emulsion and lavender lemonade infusion. Faith Hawkins' affable presence out front is much appreciated, likewise the concise, carefully considered wine list. Prices start at £18 (£4.50 a glass).
Chef/s: Timothy Johnson. **Open:** Wed to Fri and Sun L 12 to 2, Wed to Sat D 7 to 9. **Closed:** Mon, Tue, 2 weeks Christmas and New Year, 2 weeks summer. **Meals:** Set L £22.50 (2 courses) to £26.50. Set D £27 (2 courses) to £32. Sun L £26.50. **Service:** 12.5% (optional). **Details:** Cards accepted. 26 seats. Air-con. No music. No mobile phones. Wheelchair access.

Readers recommend

A 'readers recommend' review is a genuine quote from a report sent in by one of our readers. We intend to follow up these suggestions throughout the year to come.

▌Dargate
The Dove Inn
Full-of-flavour food
Plum Pudding Lane, Dargate, ME13 9HB
Tel no: (01227) 751360
Gastropub | £25
Cooking score: 2
£5 OFF £30

The atmosphere might be typical English country pub – scrubbed wooden tables, bare floorboards and a real fire – but you can expect some sound modern British cooking here. Care goes into the sourcing of ingredients, and compact menus allow Phillip MacGregor leeway to produce some good food: accurately timed ribeye steak with horseradish, perhaps, or roasted saddle of Romney Marsh lamb with Savoy cabbage and pumpkin purée. Flavours shine through in a starter of foie gras terrine with goats' cheese and hazelnuts, and you can finish with a perfect vanilla crème brûlée. Good-value pub dishes such as smoked haddock macaroni with poached egg could appear on the lunchtime blackboard. House wine is £14.
Chef/s: Phillip MacGregor. **Open:** Tue to Sun L 12 to 2.30, Tue to Sat D 7 to 9. **Closed:** Mon, one week Feb. **Meals:** alc (main courses £12 to £19). **Service:** not inc. **Details:** Cards accepted. 22 seats. 20 seats outside. No mobile phones. Wheelchair access. Music. Children allowed. Car parking.

▌Dover
The Allotment
Mightily satisfying urban bistro
9 High Street, Dover, CT16 1DP
Tel no: (01304) 214467
www.theallotmentdover.com
Modern British | £24
Cooking score: 3
£5 OFF £30

David Flynn's urban bistro is certainly attempting to kick-start Dover's restaurant scene. Menus feature some well-wrought, internationally influenced dishes – spicy pork casserole with couscous and Andalusian lamb with dauphinois potatoes left one pair of diners feeling mightily satisfied. Local ingredients receive a fair outing, whether it is Dungeness mackerel with grain mustard dressing, or slow-roasted shoulder of Canterbury lamb. Puddings, in the shape of baked blueberry cheesecake or lemon posset, will prove hard to resist. Some have found the front-of-house approach a little distracting and others have detected the disconcerting 'ping' of the microwave, but plaudits continue to outweigh grievance. A spread of wines sold at the uniform price of £17 (£4 a glass) is a neat idea.

Chef/s: David Flynn. **Open:** Tue to Sat 8.30am to 11pm. **Closed:** Sun, Mon, 24 Dec to 11 Jan. **Meals:** alc (main courses £8 to £16). **Service:** not inc. **Details:** Cards accepted. 26 seats. 26 seats outside. Wheelchair access. Music. Children allowed.

▌Faversham

Read's

Fine-dining grandee
Macknade Manor, Canterbury Road, Faversham, ME13 8XE
Tel no: (01795) 535344
www.reads.com
Modern British | £52
Cooking score: 6

🍷 🍴 V

'The consistency of this restaurant is truly admirable', runs one glowing report of David and Rona Pitchford's long-serving gastronomic grandee. Since 1977, they have been doing great things in this lovely Georgian manor, which comes complete with guest rooms, five acres of well-nurtured grounds and a bountiful walled kitchen garden. Seasonal pickings make a telling contribution to David's larder, in tandem with sensitively sourced produce from home and abroad (smoked eel is imported because British stocks are endangered, salmon is organically reared, and lamb is from Kentish pastures). Dishes are tagged on the menu with quotes from Gandhi, Miss Piggy, *et al*, but there's nothing frivolous about the refined,

careful compositions flowing from the kitchen. Starters often show an affection for the Med, be it smoked haddock arancini balls or a plate of Langhirano Parma ham with caramelised figs. After that, a fulsome British tone emerges – say, slow-braised pork belly with a purée of Cox's apples and red onion marmalade, or locally reared Gressingham duck breast with orange purée, blackberries and almond potatoes. To conclude, Read's emblematic deep lemon tart with blackcurrant sorbet is a must if it's on; otherwise orange and rhubarb soufflé with ginger parkin and poached rhubarb is worth the 20-minute wait. The whole experience is enhanced by 'wonderfully attentive staff', who orchestrate meals at just the right pace. A sampler of 60 'best buys' provides affordable entry into the 'simply superb' wine list – a 300-bin blockbuster that puts France first, but shows real depth and knowledge across the range. Prices start at £18.

Chef/s: David Pitchford. **Open:** Tue to Sat L 12 to 2, D 7 to 9. **Closed:** Sun, Mon, 25 and 26 Dec, first week Jan, 2 weeks early Sept. **Meals:** Set L £24. Set D £52. Tasting menu £52. **Service:** not inc. **Details:** Cards accepted. 55 seats. 24 seats outside. Separate bar. No music. No mobile phones. Wheelchair access. Children allowed. Car parking.

▌Goodnestone

The Fitzwalter Arms

No-frills local with cut-above grub
The Street, Goodnestone, CT3 1PJ
Tel no: (01304) 840303
www.thefitzwalterarms.co.uk
Gastropub | £25
Cooking score: 3

£5 OFF £30 ⬇

David Hart is keeping things on track at this no-frills village pub in an 'end of the road location'. It remains very much a local, with people popping in just for a drink, although the blackboard menu gives notice that the food here is a cut above the norm for a boozer. Seasonal menus are sourced from a network of local suppliers. In winter you might find hare, roast partridge or a 'splendidly crisped' belly of pork with intense rhubarb purée; in spring, expect rack of salt marsh lamb with garden mint, topped and tailed by pickled herring with potato salad, and vanilla pannacotta with strawberries. Not all reporters have taken to the very basic décor, and not all experiences have been positive, but 'the place deserves encouragement.' House wine is £13.

Chef/s: David Hart. **Open:** Wed to Mon L 12 to 2 (2.30 Sun), Mon and Wed to Sat D 7 to 9. **Closed:** Tue, 25 Dec, 1 Jan. **Meals:** alc (main courses £12 to £20). Set L £15.50 (2 courses) to £17.50. **Service:** not inc. **Details:** Cards accepted. 28 seats. 24 seats outside. Separate bar. No mobile phones. Music. Children allowed.

▍Locksbottom
Chapter One
Seriously good food at local prices
Farnborough Common, Locksbottom, BR6 8NF
Tel no: (01689) 854848
www.chaptersrestaurants.com
Modern European | £32
Cooking score: 5

A gastronomic landmark in Kent's commuterland since 1996, this striking mock-Tudor building is still a favourite with local foodies, who relish its tempting cocktail of smart cosmopolitan surrounds and serious food at local prices. Much depends on Andrew McLeish's cooking, which is supremely accomplished and full of up-to-the-minute strokes but also sits easily on the palate. Reporters continue to eat very well here, heaping praise on a silky Jerusalem artichoke velouté with roast gnocchi and an ever-popular dish of poached and roasted quail with roast foie gras, braised red cabbage and raisin jus. Elsewhere, a rustic plateful of pot-roast organic pork belly with choucroute, caramelised onions, salsify and apple jus has also been given an enthusiastic nod. Blood orange trifle is a winning dessert, although those with adventurous tastes might be swayed by poached plum with a cannelloni of quark mousse and honey-tinged lavender ice cream. At lunchtime (Sundays excepted), you can eat even more affordably in the casual brasserie from a menu that touts seared tuna niçoise, goats' cheese risotto and warm chocolate brownie. France leads the way on the wine list, although serious varietals from elsewhere feature prominently. Prices start at £15.50 (£4.50 a glass).

Chef/s: Andrew McLeish. **Open:** all week L 12 to 2.30 (2.45 Sun), D 6.30 to 10 (11 Fri and Sat, 9 Sun). **Closed:** first few days Jan. **Meals:** Set L £18.50. Set D £32. Sun L £19.95. **Service:** 12.5% (optional). **Details:** Cards accepted. 120 seats. 16 seats outside. Air-con. Separate bar. Wheelchair access. Music. Children allowed. Car parking.

▍Lower Hardres
The Granville
A proper pub with interesting ideas
Street End, Lower Hardres, CT4 7AL
Tel no: (01227) 700402
www.thegranvillecanterbury.com
Gastropub | £28
Cooking score: 4
£30

A few miles out of Canterbury, the Granville is a proper roadside pub with a winter fire, a bar for drinkers and a blackboard menu of modestly ambitious cooking. It's the sister establishment to the Sportsman (see entry, Whitstable). Certain dishes have become fixtures over the years, but they're interesting ones, for instance the starter of smoked widgeon with mustard fruits. For main, a serving of whole bream seasoned with rosemary and garlic is well timed, and coq au vin is generous, correctly rustic and full of flavour. The homemade focaccia is not to be missed, but leave room for a pudding such as the flourless chocolate cake. A concise list of well-chosen wines describes an arc from Australian Chardonnay at £13.95 to premier cru Pommard at £41.95.

Chef/s: Jim Shave. **Open:** Tue to Sun L 12 to 2 (2.30 Sun), Tue to Sat D 7 to 9. **Closed:** Mon, 25 and 26 Dec, 1 Jan. **Meals:** alc (main courses £10 to £22). **Service:** not inc. **Details:** Cards accepted. 50 seats. 40 seats outside. Air-con. Separate bar. Wheelchair access. Music. Children allowed. Car parking.

Oare

The Three Mariners

Cheerful pub with enticing food
2 Church Road, Oare, ME13 0QA
Tel no: (01795) 533633
www.thethreemarinersoare.co.uk
Gastropub | £25
Cooking score: 3
£30

A welcoming bar and a big working fireplace greet customers to this cheerful pub that's unpretentious enough for walkers to call in. The kitchen knows how to put an enticing yet straightforward selection of dishes together, and the place seems to fill up most nights with an enthusiastic crowd. Simplicity is the key to the operation and good ingredients (mostly local) are evident in a plump fillet of cod accurately timed and served with parsley sauce on a bed of ratte potatoes and leeks, and in slices of tender, pink roast veal with a porcini sauce. Start with smooth Cullen skink with chunks of smoked haddock and a Welsh rarebit croûton and finish with gooey mango pavlova with lime ice cream. Weekday set lunches look good value. House wine is £12.50.
Chef/s: John O'Riordan. **Open:** Tue to Sun L 12 to 2.30 (3.30 Sun), Tue to Sat D 6.30 to 9. **Closed:** Mon. **Meals:** alc (main courses £12 to £15). Set L £11 to £15. **Service:** not inc. **Details:** Cards accepted. 50 seats. 30 seats outside. Separate bar. Music. Children allowed. Car parking.

Ramsgate

Age & Sons

Local bright spark
Charlotte Court, Ramsgate, CT11 8HE
Tel no: (01843) 851515
www.ageandsons.co.uk
Modern British | £24
Cooking score: 3
£30

This one-time wine warehouse was originally called Page & Sons, but the 'P' dropped off the sign and current incumbent Toby Leigh decided to run with the truncated name. Since then, Age & Sons has been making waves, with much attention focused on the vaulted top-floor restaurant. Here visitors can delve into a sharp seasonal menu that favours local ingredients. Fish fans could drift towards, say, herring roes with rhubarb, cucumber and capers, or brill with purple sprouting broccoli and brown shrimps. Meat-eaters might prefer pigeon breast salad followed by pig's 'face' with prune sauce, mash and Savoy cabbage. After that, rice pudding with milk jam and blackberries sounds suitably comforting. Light bites are served in the ground-floor café, and there's a funky basement bar for cocktails. Wines start at £14.50 (£4 a glass).
Chef/s: Toby Leigh. **Open:** Tue to Sun L 12 to 3, Tue to Sat D 6.30 to 9.30. **Closed:** Mon, 25 to 28 Dec. **Meals:** alc (main courses £10 to £17). Set L £12 (2 courses) to £15. Set D £19 (2 courses) to £25. Sun L £18. **Service:** not inc. **Details:** Cards accepted. 60 seats. 40 seats outside. Separate bar. Music. Children allowed.

ALSO RECOMMENDED

▲ Eddie Gilbert's

32 King Street, Ramsgate, CT11 8NT
Tel no: (01843) 852123
www.eddiegilberts.com
Seafood £5 OFF

The combination of ground-floor fishmonger and takeaway chippy with a pleasant, informal seafood restaurant upstairs is proving popular. Fish is very fresh and portions are generous, whether a plate of battered cod and chips (cooked in beef dripping), mussels with Kentish cider, shallots and cream (£4.95) or well-timed turbot with steamed samphire in a lightly curried mussel cream (£16.50). There are meat options for those who must, plus regional cheeses, potent bottled ales from Ramsgate brewer Gadds, and wines from £12. Closed Sun D and Mon.

St Margaret's-at-Cliffe

The Bay Restaurant

Informal eating and excellent ingredients

The White Cliffs Hotel, High Street, St Margaret's-at-Cliffe, CT15 6AT

Tel no: (01304) 852229

www.thewhitecliffs.com

Modern British | £25

Cooking score: 2

£5 OFF ⊨ £30

The smaller sibling of Wallett's Court (see entry) offers informal eating in the wood-floored dining room of this rejuvenated inn. Cooking follows unfussy brasserie lines. The kitchen's approach is to perk up interest using excellent-quality produce, much of it local. Reports have praised starters such as smoked haddock fish fingers with pea shoots, pear purée and mint vinaigrette, and mains like sea bream with a sea-salt crust, sea lettuce salsa verde and smoked garlic purée, as well as rump of new season's Romney Marsh lamb and excellent steaks reared in the nearby Alkham Valley. Meals end on a high note with rose blancmange and hot rhubarb compote. House wine is £14.95.

Chef/s: Gavin Oakley. **Open:** all week L 12 to 2, D 7 to 9. **Meals:** alc (main courses £9 to £20). Set D £25. Sun L £10. **Service:** not inc. **Details:** Cards accepted. 40 seats. 40 seats outside. Separate bar. Wheelchair access. Children allowed. Car parking.

Wallett's Court

Elegant surroundings and prime ingredients

Westcliffe, St Margaret's-at-Cliffe, CT15 6EW

Tel no: (01304) 852424

www.wallettscourt.com

Modern British | £40

Cooking score: 1

♦ ⊨

The Oakley family have run this seventeenth-century former farmhouse since 1976 and it exudes a graciously traditional elegance with its weathered timbers, Jacobean staircase and white-clothed tables in the dining room. A new chef is maintaining the tradition of sourcing prime British ingredients, offering mackerel fillet with a warm salad of Jersey Royals, chorizo and lemon jus for lunch, and Kentish chicken or pavé of Sussex Red sirloin at dinner. Early reports have been unhappy with timing and seasoning, but service remains good and the wine list (from £16.95) is a well-rounded global collection that brims with fine growers. More reports please.

Chef/s: Ryan Tasker. **Open:** all week L 12 to 2, D 7 to 9. **Closed:** 25 and 26 Dec. **Meals:** Set L £19.50 (2 courses) to £25. Set D £32 (2 courses) to £40. Sun L £25. **Service:** not inc. **Details:** Cards accepted. 80 seats. 20 seats outside. Separate bar. Wheelchair access. Music. Car parking.

Small Hythe

Richard Phillips at Chapel Down

Showcase for local food and local wine

Chapel Down Vineyard, Small Hythe, TN30 7NG

Tel no: (01580) 761616

www.richardphillipsatchapeldown.co.uk

Modern British | £35

Cooking score: 3

£5 OFF

Wealden vistas and views over Chapel Down Vineyard lure punters to Richard Phillips' 'wonderfully quirky', first-floor eatery – an up-to-the-minute showcase for Kentish winemaking and top-notch regional produce. The kitchen keeps it local, with plenty of votes for the slow-cooked belly of Landrace pork with creamed cabbage, apple and sage compote, although readers have also given the nod to crab and fennel risotto with diver-caught scallops. Elsewhere, rib of Ardington beef appears with woodland mushrooms and Barkham Blue cheese dauphinoise, while recent crowd-pleasing finales have included a 'fab' sharing dessert and perfectly constructed brioche bread-and-butter pud with milk chocolate and vanilla custard. Fans of Sunday brunch have also endorsed eggs florentine and juicy salt-crusted leg of Romney Marsh lamb. 'Delicious' Chapel Down wines head the good-value list; prices start at £15.30.

Chef/s: Richard Phillips and Jose Azevedo. **Open:** all week L 12 to 3 (4 Sun), Thur to Sat D 6.30 to 10.30. **Meals:** alc (main courses £14 to £20). Set L £12.95 (2 courses) to £14.95. Sun L £19.95. **Service:** not inc. **Details:** Cards accepted. 60 seats. 16 seats outside. Air-con. Separate bar. Music. Children allowed. Car parking.

█ Speldhurst
George & Dragon
A fine feel for flavour
Speldhurst, TN3 0NN
Tel no: (01892) 863125
www.speldhurst.com
Gastropub | £27
Cooking score: 4
£5 OFF £30

The front of this early thirteenth-century inn – 'the second oldest in the country' according to proprietor Julian Leefe Griffiths – creates a good, solid impression, while inside it really looks the part of the olde-worlde country pub. Ambition does not outrun culinary skills, which include a fine feel for flavour and excellent local meat (including succulent lamb and pheasant). Scallops are seared and served with butternut squash and sage risotto, and pigeon breasts appear as a starter with smoked bacon and Puy lentils. Mains appeal to hearty appetites with the likes of coq au vin with mash and winter greens or fillet of sea bream with shellfish butter, braised fennel and new potatoes. Seasoning and timing are accorded due consideration and most dishes seem to deliver what they promise. Toffee and apple tart with caramel ice cream is a good choice for pudding. A wide-ranging wine list starts at £14.
Chef/s: David Friend. **Open:** all week L 12 to 2.30 (3.30 Sun), Mon to Sat D 7 to 9.30 (6.30 Sat). **Closed:** 1 Jan. **Meals:** alc (main courses £11 to £19). **Service:** 12.5% (optional). **Details:** Cards accepted. 110 seats. 110 seats outside. Separate bar. Wheelchair access. Music. Children allowed. Car parking.

█ Tunbridge Wells
NEW ENTRY
The Black Pig
'Just what a dining pub should be'
18 Grove Hill Road, Tunbridge Wells, TN1 1RZ
Tel no: (01892) 523030
www.theblackpig.net
Gastropub | £25
Cooking score: 2
£5 OFF £30

'I think the Black Pig is just what a dining pub should be – lovely sunny dining room, homemade bread, interesting food and service by interested staff,' observed a reporter about this urban branch of the George & Dragon at Speldurst (see previous entry). The menu works the piggy theme with a board of ham hock and loin of pork with Lord of the Hundreds (a mild hard cheese), as well as Italian and Spanish charcuterie, but there's also 'very fresh' lemon sole with wild garlic butter, plus good steaks, seasonal game and Eton mess to finish. House wine is £13.50.
Chef/s: Graham Overall. **Open:** Mon to Thur L 12 to 2.45, D 7 to 10. Fri to Sun 12 to 10 (9 Sun). **Closed:** 25 Dec, 1 Jan. **Meals:** alc (main courses £10 to £17). **Service:** 10% (optional). **Details:** Cards accepted. 70 seats. 40 seats outside. Separate bar. Wheelchair access. Music. Children allowed. Car parking.

Thackeray's
Inventive, complex French food
85 London Road, Tunbridge Wells, TN1 1EA
Tel no: (01892) 511921
www.thackerays-restaurant.co.uk
Modern French | £50
Cooking score: 4
V

For a decade Richard Phillips and his team have been delivering inventive, modern French cooking in the handsome white-clapboard Georgian house that was once home to novelist William Makepeace Thackeray. The kitchen draws on quality produce from the region for a repertoire of deliberately

complex, busy dishes with lots happening on the plate. Although the results look stunning, flavours can sometimes get confused in the process – a starter of rabbit and ham ballottine, for example, is presented with pea and mint mousse, poached quails' eggs, celeriac rémoulade *and* piccalilli. Elsewhere, a perfectly timed but ungenerous piece of baked turbot comes with a wild mushroom crust, fricassee of mussels, and a basil and saffron velouté, while desserts pile on the components for the likes of lemon verbena délice with passion-fruit jelly, crème fraîche sorbet and exotic fruit salsa. Service is spot on, and the interiors are a pitch-perfect blend of ancient and modern. The global wine list oozes quality, with house selections from £14.95.
Chef/s: Christopher Bower. **Open:** Tue to Sun L 12 to 2.30, Tue to Sat D 6.30 to 10.30. **Closed:** Mon. **Meals:** alc (main courses £20 to £29). Set L £16.50 (2 courses) to £17.50. Set D £24.50 (2 courses) to £26.50. Sun L £28.50. **Service:** 12.5% (optional). **Details:** Cards accepted. 78 seats. 30 seats outside. Air-con. Separate bar. Wheelchair access. Music. Children allowed.

▋Whitstable

JoJo's
Tapas star gets bigger
2 Herne Bay Road, Whitstable, CT5 2LQ
Tel no: (01227) 274591
www.jojosrestaurant.co.uk
Tapas | £20
Cooking score: 3
V £30

Paul Watson and Nikki Billington have successfully moved from Tankerton Road to this former supermarket overlooking the North Sea and are settling back into the simple tapas formula that has made JoJo's such a big hit. The long, low, white building has given them the space to expand, with an all-day café for salads, sandwiches and cakes and a bar now part of the deal. The licence was not in place at inspection, but the popular BYO policy will remain (£2 corkage, £5 for Tesco-bought wines). Wood floors, beams and rustic tables create an unfussy look, the focal points being

JoJo's trademark open kitchen and the spectacular sea views. The menu continues to deal in old favourites such as calamari deep-fried in beer batter, mutton and feta koftas with spicy tomato sauce and tzatziki, patatas bravas, garlicky hummus, and exemplary Italian charcuterie, as well as fish specials – say Dover sole or plaice – grilled in lemon butter. Booking essential. Note cash only.
Chef/s: Nikki Billington and Adam Taylor. **Open:** Wed to Sun L 12.30 to 2.30 (3.30 Sun), Tue to Sat D 6.30 to 10. **Closed:** Mon. **Meals:** alc (tapas £3 to £9). **Service:** not inc. **Details:** Cash only. 60 seats. Separate bar. No mobile phones. Wheelchair access. Music. Children allowed.

The Sportsman
Extraordinary food in a no-frills pub
Faversham Road, Seasalter, Whitstable, CT5 4BP
Tel no: (01227) 273370
www.thesportsmanseasalter.co.uk
Modern British | £35
Cooking score: 6

Trekking out from Whitstable over the bleak, blustery marshes to a weather-beaten pub might seem like a labour of love, but the Sportsman is no ordinary boozer. Inside it's as cheery as can be, with warming fires, bare boards and real ales, although everyone comes to eat these days. Stephen and Phil Harris have created something remarkable here – a stellar destination that dispenses with fine-dining trappings (expect bare tables and paper napkins), but delivers extraordinary food by feeding off its locality and sustaining its efforts with self-reliant enterprise. 'Take us as we are' is the message, loud and clear. Stephen cures his own hams from local pigs, bakes bread, churns butter and even produces his own sea salt. Above all, he respects the seasons. In winter, a 'salmagundi' inspired by the flamboyant salads of Elizabethan times sees smoked egg yolk and beetroot among an array of appropriate vegetables, while fabulous widgeon is overlaid with earthy Puy lentils and the sweet-sharp lusciousness of quince sauce. And then there's the fish – perhaps baked hake fillet with crispy bacon, intense green parsley sauce and a briny oyster dressing, or brill topped with a nugget of smoked pork surrounded by a potent vin jaune sauce. To conclude, you might indulge in cream-cheese ice cream with meringue, pear purée and ginger cake crumbs. The wine list is full of keenly priced goodies, with prices from £13.95.

Chef/s: Stephen Harris and Dan Flavell. **Open:** Tue to Sun L 12 to 2 (2.30 Sun), Tue to Sat D 7 to 9. **Closed:** Mon, 25 and 26 Dec, 1 Jan. **Meals:** alc (main courses £15 to £22). Tasting menu £55. **Service:** not inc. **Details:** Cards accepted. 50 seats. No mobile phones. Wheelchair access. Music. Children allowed. Car parking.

Wheelers Oyster Bar
One-off seaside gem
8 High Street, Whitstable, CT5 1BQ
Tel no: (01227) 273311
Seafood | £30
Cooking score: 4

'This is a one-off and very enjoyable', enthused a visitor who left this unprepossessing gem with a big smile on her face. Delia Fitt's long-standing family restaurant does Whitstable proud. Whether you sit at one of four bar stools at the counter in the tiny Victorian oyster bar, or squeeze into the 16-seater parlour, you will appreciate Mark Stubbs's cheerful passion for fish. His dishes bear evidence of serious thought, with flair and originality running strongly through the short menu. Lots of influences are at work: five-spiced roast scallops are teamed with crispy oriental pork belly, caramelised onion purée and a honey and soy dressing, while a main-course monkfish is served spiced and roasted with crab crushed potatoes and an Indonesian seafood chowder. Service is genial, booking essential and the restaurant unlicensed, so BYO.

Chef/s: Mark Stubbs. **Open:** Thur to Tue 1 to 7.30 (7 Sun). **Closed:** Wed, 11 to 28 Jan. **Meals:** alc (main courses £18 to £22). **Service:** not inc. **Details:** Cards accepted. 16 seats. Air-con. No music. Wheelchair access. Children allowed.

Williams & Brown Tapas
A taste of Spain
48 Harbour Street, Whitstable, CT5 1AQ
Tel no: (01227) 273373
www.thetapas.co.uk
Spanish | £23
Cooking score: 2

£5 OFF V £30

This corner site on trendy Harbour Street is a simple place with close-packed tables and bar-stool seating at marble counters running the length of the windows – it really captures the feel of eating in a Spanish tapas bar. Christopher Williams aims to serve good, simple food using the best local ingredients, supplemented by quality Spanish suppliers. Char-grilled mackerel fillets à la plancha and Goods Shed pork belly with sage jus could appear alongside straightforward classics such as chorizo baked in red wine, albondigas (meatballs), patatas bravas and deep-fried squid. House wine is £14.50.

Chef/s: Christopher Williams, Andy Cozens and Antonio Julio. **Open:** all week L 12 to 2 (2.30 Sat and Sun), D 6 to 9 (9.45 Sat). **Closed:** Mon and Tue from Jan to end Mar. **Meals:** alc (main courses £6 to £14). **Service:** 10% (optional). **Details:** Cards accepted. 31 seats. 6 seats outside. Air-con. No mobile phones. Music. Children allowed.

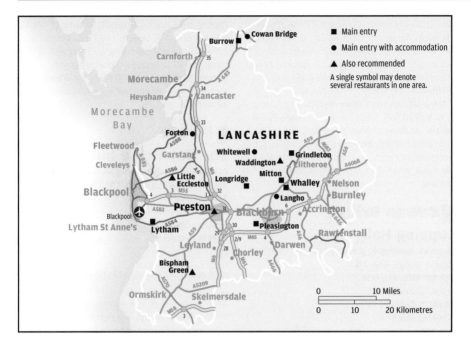

■ Bispham Green

ALSO RECOMMENDED
▲ The Eagle & Child

Malt Kiln Lane, Bispham Green, L40 3SG
Tel no: (01257) 462297
www.ainscoughs.co.uk
Gastropub £5
OFF

Once part of Lord Derby's estate, the
Georgian building by the village green also
boasts a farm shop, housed in the barn next
door. An enterprising vein of modern British
cooking brings on crispy lamb salad dressed in
lime and coriander (£6.50), seared salmon
cutlets in mango and chilli salsa with purple
sprouting broccoli (£14), and indulgent
desserts such as chocolate and caramel slice
topped with crushed pistachios (£4.50). Bar
menu available. House wines are £13. Open
all week.

■ Burrow

The Highwayman

Twenty-first century local
Burrow, LA6 2RJ
Tel no: (01524) 273338
www.highwaymaninn.co.uk
British | £22
Cooking score: 3
£30

Pitched out in the borderlands where
Lancashire meets Yorkshire and Cumbria, the
Highwayman still poses as a big-hearted
North Country local, although lavish
refurbishment has also given it a clean-cut
foodie persona. Photos of the region's 'food
heroes' line the walls and the menu reads like
an inventory of local enterprise: William
Hunter's deep-fried parsnip fritters, Port of
Lancaster smoked fish, Sillfield Farm dry-
cured bacon, Tomlinson's Yorkshire rhubarb.
In addition, the kitchen stands and delivers
plates of home-cured rare-breed meats with
homemade pickles, braised ox-cheek pudding

and jam roly-poly. It's the kind of stuff pub diehards dream of. By contrast, the 60-bin wine list is a cut above local boozer, with serious drinking from £13.95. Related to the Three Fishes, Mitton, and the Clog and Billycock, Pleasington (see entries).
Chef/s: Michael Ward. **Open:** Mon to Sat L 12 to 2, D 6 to 9 (5.30 Sat). Sun 12 to 8.30. **Closed:** 25 Dec. **Meals:** alc (main courses £9 to £21). Sun L £15 (2 courses) to £19.50. **Service:** not inc. **Details:** Cards accepted. 120 seats. 40 seats outside. Separate bar. No music. Wheelchair access. Children allowed. Car parking.

Cowan Bridge
Hipping Hall
Assured cooking in a lovely setting
Cowan Bridge, LA6 2JJ
Tel no: (01524) 271187
www.hippinghall.com
Modern British | £50
Cooking score: 4

This small yet distinguished seventeenth-century house appeals to those who want peace and are happy left to their own devices. The interiors are done out in loosely defined period style and the high-beamed Tudor dining hall is simply designed, with well-spaced tables. Of a summer's evening, drinks in the garden followed by dinner in the grand hall is a pleasing experience, but others have complained of finding that same room cold in winter when the fire was allowed to go out early in the evening. Brent Hulena is now heading the kitchen and his menus are short and strongly seasonal. Dishes typical of his style are scallops with roast cauliflower purée and caper emulsion, halibut with cockle chowder, saffron farfalle and broad beans or roast loin of Lakeland veal with a tortellini of the shin, served alongside butter beans, spring cabbage and celeriac purée. Apple and bee pollen financier with apple bavarois and rosemary sorbet makes a delicate finale. House wine is £22.

Chef/s: Brent Hulena. **Open:** Fri to Sun L 12 to 1.45, all week D 7 to 9. **Closed:** 3 to 7 Jan. **Meals:** Set L £29.50 (3 courses). Set D £49.50 (3 courses). Tasting menu £62.50 (8 courses). **Service:** not inc. **Details:** Cards accepted. 30 seats. Separate bar. No mobile phones. Wheelchair access. Music. Children allowed. Car parking.

Forton
The Bay Horse Inn
Competent kitchen using local ingredients
Bay Horse Lane, Forton, LA2 0HR
Tel no: (01524) 791204
www.bayhorseinn.com
Gastropub | £30
Cooking score: 3

'It is very convenient that the Bay Horse is only a mile off junction 33 of the M6', noted a business traveller who stayed overnight at this traditional-looking, Georgian coaching inn. He thoroughly enjoyed a seafood salad with tarragon dressing, moved on to a plate of 'very fresh' halibut served with dill-marinated cucumber, peas, broad beans, watercress and a red wine reduction, and rounded things off with an excellent lemon posset and shortbread. The menu also promises the likes of black pudding with soused onions and English mustard, 12-hour braised pork belly with cider sauce, and chocolate pot with peanut butter ice cream. There's no doubt this is a competent kitchen using good local and regional materials – aged Cumbrian beef, Goosnargh duck, Lancashire cheese – but one couple caught in last winter's heavy snow reported 'a lack of goodwill' in the hospitality department. House wine is £14.95.
Chef/s: Craig Wilkinson. **Open:** Tue to Sun L 12 to 2 (3 Sun). Tue to Sat D 6.30 to 9 (9.30 Sat). **Closed:** Mon. **Meals:** alc (main courses £12 to £23). Set L £16.95 (2 courses) to £20.95. **Service:** not inc. **Details:** Cards accepted. 60 seats. 60 seats outside. Separate bar. Wheelchair access. Music. Children allowed. Car parking.

▌Grindleton

NEW ENTRY
The Duke of York Inn
Food with imagination and skill
Brow Top, Grindleton, BB7 4QR
Tel no: (01200) 441266
www.dukeofyorkgrindleton.com
Modern British | £25
Cooking score: 3

£5 OFF £30

A re-vamped nineteenth-century pub in the beautiful Ribble Valley that still manages to maintain its olde-worlde charm (and serve good beer to its locals), while offering food that shows imagination and skill. Much is made of locally sourced produce such as golden beetroot risotto with red beetroot foam, or hotpotch of Paythorne Saddleback pork, a clever medley of all things porcine – glazed cheek, belly, mini pork pie, sausage and more besides. Fish features too, with dishes such as the starter of scallops with homemade black pudding and pea mousse that shone at inspection, or king prawn tagliolini with spring onion, chilli and samphire. Puddings are of the sticky toffee variety and there is cheese from the region. The wine list has plenty to offer, starting at £13.50.
Chef/s: Michael Heathcote. **Open:** Tue to Sun L 12 to 2, D 6 to 9 (5 to 8 Sun). **Closed:** Mon, 25 Dec. **Meals:** alc (main courses £12 to £25). Set L and D (6 to 7 Tue to Fri) £9 (2 courses) to £11.50. Set D £19.50 (2 courses) to £25. Sun L £14.50 (2 courses) to £17.50. **Service:** not inc. **Details:** Cards accepted. 70 seats. 30 seats outside. Separate bar. Wheelchair access. Children allowed. Car parking.

▌Langho

★ READERS' RESTAURANT OF THE YEAR ★
NORTH WEST

Northcote
Regional food with a vengeance
Northcote Road, Langho, BB6 8BE
Tel no: (01254) 240555
www.northcote.com
Modern British | £46
Cooking score: 6

🍷 ⇌ V

'Northcote serves superb food in pleasant, unstuffy surroundings and the service is always excellent', pronounced one reader. This adjudication is echoed in other reports. The kitchen is headed by Lisa Allen, under the guidance of Nigel Haworth, and the great strength here lies in the quality of the regional supplies, from meat and game right down to the herbs, fruit and vegetables grown in their own kitchen garden. A reporter praised the four-course set-lunch served on Easter Monday: English pea soup with white onion cream and ham sandwich; carpaccio of pigeon, pickled cranberries and smoked hazelnuts; new season's lamb wrapped in butter puff pastry with butterbeans, baked celeriac and pak choi; rhubarb cheesecake with vanilla crumble ice cream and coffee with mini Eccles cakes. Others have endorsed the langoustine ravioli, black pudding with buttered trout and mustard and nettle sauce, Whitby cod, Herdwick mutton, and the Lancashire hotpot (which must be pre-ordered).'Exquisite bread rolls are worth a visit alone'. A separate vegetarian menu brings veggie cooking to life. The wine list gets its teeth into most regions, while keeping the overall length under control. There are plenty of half-bottles, interesting choices by the glass, and prices are better value than you might expect. Bottles from £20.
Chef/s: Nigel Haworth and Lisa Allen. **Open:** all week L 12 to 1.30 (2 Sun), D 7 (6.30 Sat) to 9.30 (9 Sun). **Closed:** 25 Dec. **Meals:** alc (main courses £18 to £35). Set L £24.50. Set D £55 (5 courses). Sun L £40 (4 courses). Tasting menu £75 (8 courses).

Service: not inc. **Details:** Cards accepted. 60 seats. Separate bar. Wheelchair access. Music. Children allowed. Car parking.

Little Eccleston

ALSO RECOMMENDED
▲ The Cartford Inn
Cartford Lane, Little Eccleston, PR3 0YP
Tel no: (01995) 670166
www.thecartfordinn.co.uk
Gastropub £5 OFF

Beside the Wyre river in a quiet corner of the Fylde Peninsula stands this handsomely renovated seventeenth-century coaching inn. It succeeds admirably on all counts – as a bustling bar, a relaxed pubby brasserie, and a place to lay your head. A lengthy repertoire covers the likes of Morecambe Bay shrimps, wood platters of, say, Fleetwood seafood (£8.95) and more substantial steaks, homemade burgers and lamb hotpot with red cabbage (£9.50). House wine £13.95. Closed Mon L.

Longridge
Longridge Restaurant
Heathcote's with a twist
104-106 Higher Road, Longridge, PR3 3SY
Tel no: (01772) 784969
www.heathcotes.co.uk
Modern British | £38
Cooking score: 3
£5 OFF V

Once the jewel in Paul Heathcote's toque, Longridge is now ably run day-to-day by manager Kath Bell and her head-chef husband Chris. Cool, tranquil décor, the central booking system and a cabinet full of awards reflect Heathcote's continued ownership, but something has shifted. Now friendly as well as professional, the atmosphere in this stone-built cottage above Preston is gratifyingly comfortable. British dishes are slimmed down and moved on, so black pudding comes with a jellied 62°C duck egg and fresh apple purée, and the classic Heathcote's bread-and-butter

pudding, with a crunchy top and jammy apricots, is ever-present. Texture is sometimes an issue – cauliflower purée blurred soggily with a butter sauce for beautifully poached salmon, for example – but dishes have plenty of style. Wines from £3.85 a glass.
Chef/s: Chris Bell. **Open:** Wed to Sun L 12 to 2.30 (7.45 Sun), Wed to Sat D 6 to 10. **Closed:** Mon, Tue, 4 to 6 Jan. **Meals:** alc (main courses £17 to £28). Set L £14.50 (2 courses) to £19. Sun L £22.50. Tasting menu £55 (6 courses). **Service:** not inc. **Details:** Cards accepted. 60 seats. Separate bar. Music. Children allowed. Car parking.

Lytham

NEW ENTRY
Hastings Eating and Drinking House
Clever mix of informal and formal dining
26 Hastings Place, Lytham, FY8 5LZ
Tel no: (01253) 732400
www.hastingslytham.com
Modern British | £28
Cooking score: 3
£5 OFF V £30

You won't have to do battle to find good things to eat at Hastings. Light bites to tempt include 'delicately seasoned' potted Lytham shrimps with a toasted crumpet and – for those nostalgic about the seaside location – a jar of local cockles in vinegar and olive oil. The all-day brunch menu offers old favourites and there's plenty of Lancashire produce in evidence: fish and chips, locally sourced steaks and grills. Serious eaters can head to the 1066 dining room, where foie gras with spiced apple purée may feature alongside local chump of lamb with wild garlic and morels. Desserts are of the classic variety, with offerings of tarte Tatin and sticky toffee pudding. A well-balanced wine list kicks off £12.95.
Chef/s: Warrick Dodds. **Open:** Tue to Sun 11 to 10 (11pm Fri and Sat, 7.30pm Sun). **Closed:** Mon. **Meals:** alc (main courses £9 to £23). Set L £9.95. Set D £12.95. **Service:** not inc. **Details:** Cards accepted. 140 seats. 32 seats outside. Air-con. Separate bar. Wheelchair access. Music. Children allowed.

Mitton

The Three Fishes

A beacon of Lancashire quality
Mitton Road, Mitton, BB7 9PQ
Tel no: (01254) 826888
www.thethreefishes.com
British | £25
Cooking score: 3
V £30

A 400-year-old inn set in a rugged piece of Lancashire hinterland between the Hodder and the Ribble, the Three Fishes offers the full country-pub package, with terrace seating in summer, log fires in winter and a range of cask ales and guest beers. The décor looks distinctly more upscale than the standard pub, though, and the cooking has made it a beacon of quality with strong local support. The generous fish pie is justly celebrated by readers, and comes topped with Kirkham's Lancashire cheese, and there are fortifying cold-weather dishes such as oxtail braised in red wine with mash and winter veg. Start with Morecambe Bay shrimps or black pudding with caramelised onions, and don't miss the bread-and-butter pudding with proper custard. Chilean house wines are £13.95.
Chef/s: Simon Bower. **Open:** all week L 12 to 2, D 6 to 9 (5.30 to 9 Sat, 8.30 Sun). **Closed:** Dec. **Meals:** alc (main courses £9 to £20). Sun L £15 (2 courses) to £19.50. **Service:** not inc. **Details:** Cards accepted. 140 seats. 40 seats outside. Separate bar. Wheelchair access. Children allowed. Car parking.

Pleasington

The Clog and Billycock

Pressing all the dining pub buttons
Billinge End Road, Pleasington, BB2 6QB
Tel no: (01254) 201163
www.theclogandbillycock.com
British | £21
Cooking score: 3
£30

'Another of Nigel Haworth's Ribble Valley Inns, which presses all the dining pub buttons for me. As with the others, there's a heavy reliance on local ingredients, good pricing and friendly and eager young staff. What's not to like?' Thus run the notes of one winter visitor, who enjoyed a meal of warm, perfectly tender pheasant salad with orange and pomegranate dressing, slow-baked pig's trotter stuffed with black pudding and served with mash and good gravy, and 'three decent slices' of artisan Lancashire cheeses. The flexible menus also deliver generous elm-wood sharing plates, sandwiches, a good choice of steaks, pies and traditional English pancakes. Local real ales and a decent slate of carefully considered wines from £13.95 complete the picture.
Chef/s: Johnny Gilmore. **Open:** all week L 12 to 2 (8.30 Sun), D 6 to 9 (5.30 Sat). **Closed:** 25 Dec. **Meals:** alc (main courses £9 to £20). Sun L £15 (2 courses) to £19.50. **Service:** not inc. **Details:** Cards accepted. 130 seats. 50 seats outside. Separate bar. No music. Wheelchair access. Children allowed. Car parking.

Preston

ALSO RECOMMENDED
▲ Bangla Fusion

Liverpool Old Road, Much Hoole, Preston, PR4 5JQ
Tel no: (01772) 610800
www.banglafusion.co.uk
Indian £5 OFF

A cut above the local competition, this sumptuous Indian 'fusion' eatery outside Preston is still wowing the crowds with its combination of plush surrounds, jolly staff and a menu that challenges provincial curry house clichés. Tikkas and baltis (from £7.45) play second fiddle to a contingent of signature and creative specials including cremeguru steak marinated in fennel with almond sauce or rajshah scallops in a garlicky tomato sauce (£15.95). Sunday 'family' lunches run until 6pm. House wine is £12.25. Closed Mon to Fri L.

> **Also recommended**
> Also recommended entries are not scored but we think they are worth a visit.

Waddington

ALSO RECOMMENDED
▲ Waddington Arms

West View, Clitheroe Road, Waddington, BB7 3HP
Tel no: (01200) 423262
www.waddingtonarms.co.uk
Gastropub £5 OFF

Village pub, restaurant and hotel all rolled into one, the Waddington is a valuable local resource and an agreeable stopover for visitors to the Ribble Valley. Reliable hands in the kitchen conjure up robust, full-flavoured dishes like Earl Grey tea-smoked duck breast with fennel and radish salad (£5.50), Lancashire hotpot or steak ale and mushroom pie (£10.50), as well as desserts such as sticky toffee pudding with toffee sauce and banoffi ice cream (£4.25). Well-kept ales, too, and a short, global wine list with prices from £12.50. Open all week.

Whalley
Food by Breda Murphy

Appealingly simple cooking
Abbots Court, 41 Station Road, Whalley, BB7 9RH
Tel no: (01254) 823446
www.foodbybredamurphy.com
Modern British | £22
Cooking score: 2

V £30

Tucked in beside the railway arches in an attractive Ribble Valley village, Breda Murphy's restaurant and deli is a daytime venue, with fortnightly themed evenings on Fridays and Saturdays. The cooking is appealingly simple, using quality ingredients for dishes such as prosciutto-wrapped chicken and leek terrine with spiced pears, and fish pie made with haddock, salmon and prawns under a topping of champ potato and Lancashire cheese. Desserts such as baked chocolate cheesecake with orange caramel sauce will prove hard to resist, as may cheeses from the deli counter. A short list opens with wines by the glass from £2.75.

Chef/s: Gareth Bevan. **Open:** Tue to Sat L 10 to 6, Fri and Sat D 7 to 9.30 (themed nights, twice monthly). **Closed:** Sun, Mon, 25 Dec to 6 Jan. **Meals:** alc (main courses £7 to £14). Set D £42.50 (5 courses). **Service:** not inc. **Details:** Cards accepted. 50 seats. 20 seats outside. No mobile phones. Wheelchair access. Music. Children allowed. Car parking.

Whitewell
The Inn at Whitewell

A grand inn for all seasons
Whitewell, BB7 3AT
Tel no: (01200) 448222
www.innatwhitewell.com
Modern British | £28
Cooking score: 3

The fourteenth-century manor house was transformed during the 1700s into a coaching inn, and remains every inch the welcoming village hostelry, albeit a fairly grand one. Eat in the bar or restaurant. Either way, the modern British cooking of Jamie Cadman presents a satisfying prospect. A crab salad with pickled cucumber, seasoned with coriander seed and mint, offered a nice balance of sweetness and acidity for one reporter. Main courses of duck breast with black pudding mash, pancetta and redcurrant sauce, and seared tuna with a beansprout and mangetout salad in sesame, ginger and soy dressing impressed too, even though the tuna was a few shades further on than the requested rare. Finish with a trio of well-kept British and Irish cheeses. The wine list has some very flash bottles, but starts comfortably enough at £12.99.

Chef/s: Jamie Cadman. **Open:** all week L 12 to 2, D 7.30 to 9.30. **Meals:** alc (main courses £15 to £25). **Service:** not inc. **Details:** Cards accepted. 70 seats. 30 seats outside. Separate bar. No music. Wheelchair access. Children allowed. Car parking.

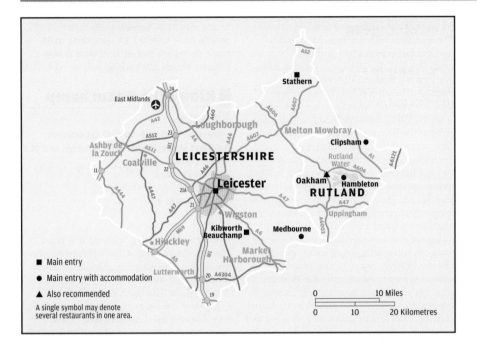

Clipsham

The Olive Branch

Crowd-puller with first-class food
Main Street, Clipsham, LE15 7SH
Tel no: (01780) 410355
www.theolivebranchpub.com
Gastropub | £30
Cooking score: 3

♦ ⊨ V

'Sitting outside in the shade on a warm summer day for our meal was delightful' volunteered one visitor to this pretty country pub not far from the A1. The cheerful, idiosyncratic décor is in good taste, and the place certainly pulls in the crowds. That's hardly surprising, given that the cooking is first class. The menu changes on a daily basis to reflect what is readily available and mixes pub standards such as fish, chips and minted peas with some more interesting options, perhaps braised shoulder of lamb with rosemary and cannellini bean cassoulet. Local cheeses and homemade ice creams and sorbets get the thumbs-up, too. An enterprising array of wines is grouped by style, with prices from £15.
Chef/s: Sean Hope. **Open:** all week L 12 to 2 (3 Sun), D 7 to 9.30 (9 Sun). **Meals:** alc (main courses £12 to £24). Set L £16.95 (2 courses) to £19.95. Set D £27.50. Sun L £25. **Service:** not inc. **Details:** Cards accepted. 48 seats. 24 seats outside. Separate bar. Wheelchair access. Music. Children allowed. Car parking.

Hambleton

Hambleton Hall

Crystal-clear seasonal flavours
Hambleton, LE15 8TH
Tel no: (01572) 756991
www.hambletonhall.com
Modern British | £70
Cooking score: 7

♦ ⊨ V

Standing proud like some *petit château* in middle England, Hambleton Hall towers over glorious terraces and topiary, wondrous flowerbeds and landscaped features. Owners Tim and Stefa Hart celebrated the hotel's thirtieth birthday in 2010, and their stewardship of this fabulous Victorian edifice overlooking Rutland Water has been a triumph. The place is held in the highest regard as one of England's archetypal country house retreats, where civilised comfort is the order of the day and staff are superlative in their personal attentions. Chef Aaron Patterson has been a key figure in the set-up since taking over the stoves way back in 1992, and his appetite for fine seasonal food is still as keen as ever. Hambleton's menus are some of the prettiest you're likely to see, beautifully illustrated with delicate watercolours (a collage of game-bird feathers, dark sloes and rusty oak leaves tells you that it's winter). These evocative seasonal images frame an array of perfectly tuned, calendar-friendly ideas full of promise: poached and roasted squab with cep purée and pumpkin-flavoured gnocchi; roast loin of fallow deer with gin and tonic jelly, passion fruit and chocolate flavoured sauce; line-caught sea bass with 'variations of parsley'. Hambleton's own kitchen garden provides the components for a seasonal salad dressed with truffle oil vinaigrette, while a farm near Oakham supplies veal (the fillet might be partnered by sweetbread raviolo and morels). Dazzling, crystal-clear flavours and a perfect sense of balance are the hallmarks, although artistry really comes to fore with desserts – hence the advice that they may take 'up to 25 minutes to prepare'. The result could be poached pear with gingerbread parfait and blackberries, or comfortingly exotic chocolate and olive truffle with salted caramel, pistachios and baked banana. 'Lunch for less' weekday menus live up to their billing, and the illustrious wine list has drooling possibilities on every page. Its allegiances are with 'the little guys', independent winemakers who are producing prodigiously good stuff across the globe. Popular 'wines of the moment' start at £18, positively encouraging exploration.

Chef/s: Aaron Patterson. **Open:** all week L 12 to 2, D 7 to 9.30. **Meals:** alc (main courses £32 to £40). Set L £20 (2 courses) to £25. Set D £37. Sun L £41.50.

Tasting menu £65. **Service:** 12.5% (optional). **Details:** Cards accepted. 64 seats. Separate bar. No music. No mobile phones. Wheelchair access. Children allowed. Car parking.

▮ Kibworth Beauchamp

Firenze
Florentine food with bags of satisfaction
9 Station Street, Kibworth Beauchamp, LE8 0LN
Tel no: (0116) 2796260
www.firenze.co.uk
Italian | £32
Cooking score: 3
£5 OFF 🍾

Kibworth Beauchamp is a long way from Florence, but Lino and Sarah Poli have been injecting Italian sunshine and native flavours into this Leicestershire backwater for more than a decade. The result is a 'real eating out experience', staged in a setting that positively encourages relaxed congeniality. Lino's domain is the kitchen, and he serves up classic food with bags of satisfaction on the plate and nothing to raise eyebrows. Menus are rotated with the seasons, so autumn might bring bruschetta with wild mushrooms and poached egg ahead of pastas including pumpkin gnocchi or garganelle with game ragù. Secondi are equally big-hearted offerings ranging from braised lamb shank with saffron risotto to roast leg of rabbit in cured ham with soft polenta and porcini. Artisan Italian cheeses are authentically pointed up with chestnut honey and mostarda di Cremona (mustard-spiced fruit preserve), and the well-bred wine list also scours the home country for peerless growers from Lombardy to Sicily. The 'Firenze selection' offers around 15 tipples from £15.75. The Polis also run Boboli, an all-day eatery in nearby Kibworth Harcourt.

Chef/s: Lino Poli and Stuart Batey. **Open:** Mon to Sat L 12 to 3, D 7 to 11. **Closed:** Sun, bank hols, 25 and 26 Dec, 1 Jan. **Meals:** alc (main courses £16 to £27). Set L £13.50 (2 dishes). Set D Mon to Thur £17.50 (2 courses) to £22.50. **Service:** not inc. **Details:** Cards accepted. 60 seats. No mobile phones. Wheelchair access. Music. Children allowed.

▋ Leicester

Entropy

Appealing all-day food
42 Hinckley Road, Leicester, LE3 0RB
Tel no: (0116) 2259650
www.entropylife.com
Modern British | £25
Cooking score: 4
£5 £30
OFF

Tom Cockerill pitched his camp in this Leicester suburb a decade ago and over time has reworked both the premises and his own cooking style. What he and his wife Cassandra are offering is very much in tune with modern times, at least for those who don't expect three lots of appetisers and a pre-dessert with their dinner. It's two shops knocked together, both of which have been simply decorated with lots of pale wood and an on-view kitchen. The food has broad appeal, not least because it is offered all day. Sensible, unfussy dishes include game broth with root vegetable and pearl barley or ox heart served with ratte potatoes, red chard and chilli oil, followed by Dexter steak and smoked oyster pie or roast free-range chicken. Equally well-handled desserts have included duck egg crème brûlée with peanut butter cookies. Good weekend breakfasts, too. The short, modern wine list starts at £13.95.
Chef/s: Tom Cockerill. **Open:** all week 10.30am to 10pm (9.30am to 10pm Sat, 9.30am to 7pm Sun). **Closed:** 25 and 26 Dec, 1 Jan. **Meals:** alc (main courses £9 to £24). **Service:** not inc. **Details:** Cards accepted. 62 seats. 32 seats outside. Air-con. Music. Children allowed.

ALSO RECOMMENDED

▲ Bobby's

154-156 Belgrave Road, Leicester, LE4 5AT
Tel no: (0116) 2660106
www.eatatbobbys.com
Indian Vegetarian

Named after an old Bollywood blockbuster, the Lakhani family's eatery has been plying its trade since 1976 and is queen of the hill on Belgrave Road. It has brushed up its looks over the years, but still serves some of the best Indian veggie food in the city. Farsan snacks (from £3.50) are the star turns; also try the Mysore dosas, paneer specials, the dhal panchratna made from five sorts of lentils, and Gujarati undhiyu with dumplings (£4.50). House wine is £8.95, but lassi is a better bet. Don't leave without some sweetmeats. Open all week.

READERS RECOMMEND

Maiyango

Modern European
13-21 St Nicholas Place, Leicester, LE1 4LD
Tel no: (0116) 2518898
www.maiyango.com
'Eclectic food and cocktails in a trendy hotel'

▋ Medbourne

Horse & Trumpet

A change of tack
12 Old Green, Medbourne, LE16 8DX
Tel no: (01858) 565000
www.horseandtrumpet.co.uk
Modern British | £27
Cooking score: 3
£30

The stately honey-stone façade and trim thatched roof still speak of solid reliability, but things are on the move inside this sedate country restaurant. Following a change of tack, the 'all-new' menu has moved away from intricate foams, gels and powders into the conventional world of chicken and shallot terrine, pappardelle with broad beans, and sea bass with samphire and chive butter sauce. Ingredients are sound and the cooking is professional, but dishes now lack any real thrills or invention: fresh-tasting crab and pea shoot omelette (a current hit) is fashioned like a Chinese egg roll, succulent confit duck is from a big bird, and there is textbook crème brûlée to finish. Meanwhile, a few bells and whistles from the old days add some zing to proceedings (don't miss the petits fours). Wines start at £17.95 (£3.70 a glass).

Chef/s: Gary Magnani. **Open:** Tue to Sun L 12 to 1.45
(2 Sun), Tue to Sat D 7 to 9. **Closed:** Mon, first week
Jan. **Meals:** alc (main courses £11 to £18). Tasting
menu £35 (6 courses). **Service:** not inc.
Details: Cards accepted. 40 seats. 15 seats outside.
No mobile phones. Wheelchair access. Music.
Children allowed.

Oakham

ALSO RECOMMENDED
▲ Lord Nelson's House Hotel, Nick's Restaurant

11 Market Place, Oakham, LE15 6DT
Tel no: (01572) 723199
www.nicksrestaurant.co.uk
Modern European £5 OFF

History looms large at this charm-laden local
favourite in a Grade II-listed building
opposite Oakham School. The foodie focus is
now on light lunches and affordable set
dinners (£15.95 for two courses), which offer
conventional bistro-style food ranging from
smoked salmon and ricotta roulade to roast
poussin on chorizo mash. By contrast, the
carte deals in elaborate, 'over-egged' dishes
such as stuffed lemon sole fillets with lobster
sausage, Jerusalem artichoke purée, fennel
confit, lobster and basil potato (£16.95). Wines
from £14.95. Open Wed to Sat L, Thur to Sat
D.

Symbols

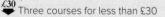

🛏 Accommodation is available

£30 Three courses for less than £30

V More than three vegetarian main courses

£5 OFF £5-off voucher scheme

🍾 Notable wine list

Stathern

Red Lion Inn
Revitalised village pub championing local food
2 Red Lion Street, Stathern, LE14 4HS
Tel no: (01949) 860868
www.theolivebranchpub.com
Gastropub | £25
Cooking score: 2
£30

The people behind the Olive Branch,
Clipsham (see entry) were responsible for
revitalising this seventeenth-century village
boozer – and they did a grand job without
loosing a gastropub wrecking ball on the
place. All is as it should be, with locally
brewed ales on tap, deliberately rustic interiors
and a menu that doubles as a suppliers' map of
the region. Belvoir pigeon breast comes with
pearl barley, a schnitzel of Old Dalby veal is
served with hash browns, or you could feast
on faggots with sage and onion rösti. The
kitchen also dishes up fish and chips with
gusto and pleases pud fans with, say, Rearsby
treacle tart. Wines start at £13.75.
Chef/s: Edward Leslie. **Open:** all week L 12 to 2 (3
Sun), Mon to Sat D 6 to 9 (7 to 9 Mon, 6 to 9.30 Fri,
7 to 9.30 Sat). **Meals:** alc (main courses £12 to £18).
Set L and D £13.50 (2 courses) to £16.50. Sun L
£18.50. **Service:** not inc. **Details:** Cards accepted.
60 seats. 60 seats outside. Separate bar.
Wheelchair access. Music. Children allowed. Car
parking.

Wing

READERS RECOMMEND
The Kings Arms
Modern British
Top Street, Wing, LE15 8SE
Tel no: (01572) 737634
www.thekingsarms-wing.co.uk
'Family-run pub flying the flag for local
produce'

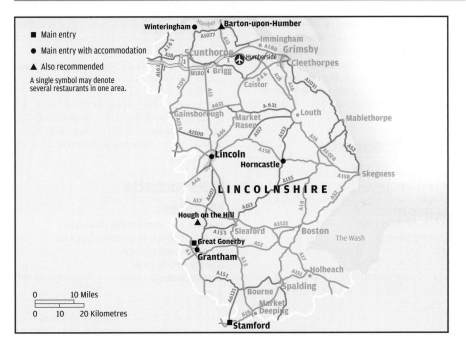

- ■ Main entry
- ● Main entry with accommodation
- ▲ Also recommended

A single symbol may denote
several restaurants in one area.

Winteringham ● ▲ Barton-upon-Humber
A1077
Humber
Immingham
A180 Grimsby
Scunthorpe
A18
Humberside ✈ Cleethorpes
A161 2 3 5
M180 4 Brigg
A15 Caistor
A46 A16
A1031
A631 Louth
Gainsborough Market Mablethorpe
Rasen
A1500 A46 A157 A153 A16
A158
●Lincoln A1028
Horncastle ● A52
A155 Skegness
L I N C O L N S H I R E A158
A17 A153 A16
Hough on the Hill ▲
A1121
A153 Sleaford Boston
Great Gonerby ■ A52 The Wash
Grantham ●
A151
A151 Holbeach
Bourne Spalding
Market
Deeping
■ Stamford

0 — 10 Miles
0 — 10 — 20 Kilometres

■ Barton-upon-Humber

ALSO RECOMMENDED
▲ Elio's

11 Market Place, Barton-upon-Humber, DN18 5DA
Tel no: (01652) 635147
www.elios-restaurant.co.uk
Italian

An Italian family affair for more than 25 years,
this easy-going trattoria-with-rooms owes
much to its caring owners. Main man Elio
Grossi dons his whites for old-school menus
that might run from Parma ham with melon
(£8.25) to cassata siciliana (£5.75). Pasta and
pizzas are good calls, and it's worth checking
the specials board if fish is your bag: char-
grilled tuna with Mediterranean vegetables
(£14.95) is typical. Weekday set menus are
good value, and the all-Italian wine list kicks
off with house selections from £12.25 a litre.
Open Mon to Sat D only.

■ Grantham

Chequers Inn
Honest country boozer
Main Street, Woolsthorpe by Belvoir, Grantham,
NG32 1LU
Tel no: (01476) 870701
www.chequersinn.net
Modern British | £26
Cooking score: 1
£5 OFF 🛏 £30

Real ales, real fires and a cricket pitch add
some English rustic cred to this country
boozer in the shadow of Belvoir Castle. The
bar deals in pub grub, but it's worth putting on
your glad rags for a cosy meal in the Chequers'
converted bakehouse. Classics such as Stathern
bangers and mash go hand in hand with the
likes of crispy lamb's sweetbreads with port
syrup or roast cod fillet with mussel and
saffron ragoût. Desserts might include orange
and cardamom rice pudding. House wine
is £14.

Chef/s: Mark Nesbit. **Open:** all week L 12 to 2.30 (4 Sun), D 6 to 9.30 (8.30 Sun). **Meals:** alc (main courses £9 to £19). Set L £11.50 (2 courses) to £15. Set D £13.50 (2 courses) to £16.50. Sun L £11.95 (2 courses). **Service:** not inc. **Details:** Cards accepted. 100 seats. 60 seats outside. Separate bar. No mobile phones. Wheelchair access. Music. Children allowed. Car parking.

Great Gonerby

Harry's Place

An absolute gem
17 High Street, Great Gonerby, NG31 8JS
Tel no: (01476) 561780
Modern French | £56
Cooking score: 7

£5
OFF

For 23 years, the formula of a two-person operation and short menu of impeccable judgement has not altered. Harry's Place has just three tables – and people love its lack of flourish and expense accounts. 'Having now visited this wonderful restaurant several times, we can only describe Harry's Place as an absolute gem' and 'you feel more like a guest at an intimate dinner party rather than a paying customer' are typical comments. The food is cooked by Harry and served by Caroline. The real point of all this is that the cooking is extremely good. One couple enjoyed – an understatement – a meal that included 'simply divine' salt marsh teal served with fresh blueberries and a Madeira jus, and 'the freshest' halibut with 'beautifully cooked' fresh vegetables and pancetta crisps. Other meals have produced chilled chicken livers in spiced sherry aspic with Cumberland sauce and candied lemon, then filleted loin of Jacob's lamb served with a fresh leek and onion sauce, tarragon hollandaise and a sauce of white olive, Madeira, rosemary, thyme and tarragon, followed by a dessert of cherry brandy jelly with yoghurt and black pepper. It is a well-loved repertoire. Reasonably enough, dishes that win fans are not lightly abandoned, but they do change and there is no way they could be called old-fashioned. In fact, most reckon that Harry Hallam's cooking is becoming

more expressive and bolder as the years roll by. The all-European wine list extends to one handwritten side of A4 opening with Riojas at £20 (white) and £26 (a Reserva red), but choice is sufficient to match what is on the menu that day.

Chef/s: Harry Hallam. **Open:** Tue to Sat L 12.30 to 2, D 7 to 8.30. **Closed:** Sun, Mon, 1 week from 25 Dec, bank hols. **Meals:** alc (main courses £35 to £39). **Service:** not inc. **Details:** Cards accepted. 10 seats. No music. Car parking.

Horncastle

Magpies

Warmth and gastronomic pleasures
71-75 East Street, Horncastle, LN9 6AA
Tel no: (01507) 527004
Modern British | £38
Cooking score: 5

Caroline and Andrew Gilbert's Horncastle hideaway is the personification of an English provincial restaurant full of warmth, honest intent and gastronomic pleasures. The mood is mellow and Andrew's respectful food is defined by clear flavours, pin-sharp accuracy and a feel for what is right on the plate. He also sets great store by local ingredients: corn-fed chicken from nearby Ashby Puerorum might be pot-roasted and served with bean cassoulet and herb dumplings, while a dish of smoked eel on toasted brioche with wild mushrooms and black truffle dressing owes a debt to Hall Farm in Great Carlton. The kitchen also makes telling use of Lincoln Red beef and game from the Wolds countryside – perhaps saddle of fallow deer on spiced parsnip purée with fig and mustard-seed tart and a sauce enriched with Cacao Barry. To conclude, one reader was staggered by a confection of mango, passion-fruit coulis and mango sorbet, although winter visitors might prefer a festive assiette comprising traditional sherry trifle, iced pudding bombe with Turkish delight sorbet and a chocolate and chestnut truffle roulade. The wine list is a connoisseur's treat and a godsend for those with humbler needs: top-flight vintages from the French regions share the limelight with seriously gluggable stuff from Italy, the Americas and elsewhere. Around 20 house recommendations start at £15.95. Note that Magpies now has letting rooms if you fancy lingering.

Chef/s: Andrew Gilbert. **Open:** Wed to Fri and Sun L 12 to 2, Wed to Sun D 7 to 9.30. **Closed:** Mon, Tue. **Meals:** alc L only (main courses £14.95). Set D £38 (3 courses). **Service:** not inc. **Details:** Cards accepted. 34 seats. 5 seats outside. Air-con. Separate bar. No mobile phones. Wheelchair access. Music. Children allowed.

▌Hough on the Hill

ALSO RECOMMENDED
▲ The Brownlow Arms
High Road, Hough on the Hill, NG32 2AZ
Tel no: (01400) 250234
www.thebrownlowarms.com
Gastropub

A traditional English country inn dating from the seventeenth century, where a log fire, beams, polished tables and a civilised atmosphere are major draws. Dinner is the main event and there's little doubt that the kitchen can deliver unfussy dishes with skill and dexterity: to start you might choose ox tongue with pickled walnut and celeriac rémoulade (£6.25), go on to medallions of venison with creamed chestnut mushrooms (£19.95), and finish with orange marmalade sponge (£6.50). House wine £14.95. Open Sun L, Tue to Sat D. Accommodation.

▌Lincoln

The Old Bakery
Charming restaurant with great ingredients
26-28 Burton Road, Lincoln, LN1 3LB
Tel no: (01522) 576057
www.theold-bakery.co.uk
Modern European | £35
Cooking score: 2

£5 OFF 🛏

This charming and characterful restaurant is situated close to Lincoln Cathedral. The kitchen is proud of its raw materials, which are

provided by a well-established network of suppliers. These might show up at dinner in a straightforward starter of beef tartare and carpaccio of venison with a slow-poached duck egg and smoked confit shallot tarte Tatin. The choice at main course might be between butter-poached free-range chicken with gratin potato mousse served with onion and sprouts coleslaw or slow-roasted lamb shank with char-grilled polenta, honey-glazed celeriac and carrots with lamb jus. Lunch is a simpler affair. Wines are varied and sensibly priced, starting with house French at £13.95.

Chef/s: Ivano de Serio. **Open:** Tue to Sun L 12 to 2, D 7 to 9. **Closed:** 26 Dec, 1 Jan. **Meals:** alc (main courses £15 to £21). Sun L £16.50. Tasting menu £43 (5 courses) to £60 (9 courses). **Service:** not inc. **Details:** Cards accepted. 75 seats. Air-con. Wheelchair access. Music. Children allowed.

ALSO RECOMMENDED
▲ Wig & Mitre
32 Steep Hill, Lincoln, LN2 1LU
Tel no: (01522) 535190
www.wigandmitre.com
Modern British £5 OFF

In the old part of town within sight of the castle, the Wig & Mitre is a paragon of flexible dining, open all day, every day, with assorted eating and drinking areas spread over two higgledy-piggledy floors. Drop by for breakfast, or order something light from the all-day menu. Otherwise, look to the seasonal carte for coarse country pâté (£5.95) and slow-cooked collar of pork with English mustard mash, caramelised apples and cider apple brandy sauce (£13.95). House wine is £13.45. Open all week.

Average price

The average price listed in main-entry reviews denotes the price of a three-course meal, without wine.

Scunthorpe

San Pietro

Italian
11 High Street East, Scunthorpe, DN15 6UH
Tel no: (01724) 277774
www.sanpietro.uk.com
'All in all, a wonderful experience – fantastic welcome and quality'

Stamford

Jim's Yard

Terrific neighbourhood eatery
3 Ironmonger Street, Stamford, PE9 1PL
Tel no: (01780) 756080
www.jimsyard.biz
Modern European | £25
Cooking score: 2

£5 OFF £30

Full of people and full of life, Jim's Yard is a terrific, 'irresistibly charming' neighbourhood eatery housed in a cluster of seventeenth-century stone cottages, with a bright, buzzy conservatory and French doors opening onto a plant-filled courtyard. A lot of care and thought has gone into the details (note the lovely French Laguiole cutlery), and satisfaction is guaranteed when it comes to honest, clear-flavoured dishes such as asparagus risotto, confit chicken with punchy chorizo cassoulet or salmon with saffron potatoes and niçoise vegetables. Skilful desserts on red glass plates add a final touch of drama to proceedings. Wines start at £13.95. A sibling, Jim's Bistro, is at 52 Broadway, Peterborough PE1 1SB, tel: (01733) 341122.
Chef/s: James Ramsay. **Open:** Tue to Sat L 12 to 2.30, D 6.30 to 9.30 (6 Fri and Sat). **Closed:** last week Dec, first week Jan, last week Jul, first week Aug. **Meals:** alc (main courses £9 to £17). Set L 13.50 (2 courses) to £16.50. **Service:** not inc. **Details:** Cards accepted. 65 seats. 20 seats outside. Air-con. Separate bar. Wheelchair access. Music. Children allowed.

Winteringham

Winteringham Fields

Unique charm and culinary finesse
Silver Street, Winteringham, DN15 9ND
Tel no: (01724) 733096
www.winteringhamfields.com
Modern European | £75
Cooking score: 5

£5 OFF 🍷 🖵 V

The beguiling restaurant-with-rooms that famously put Lincolnshire on the foodie map seems to have finally regained some of its stature and equilibrium. Germain and Annie Schwab were always going to be a hard act to follow, but supporters reckon that Winteringham can still deliver 'unique charm' and culinary finesse – witness a euphorically reported lunch that yielded an exquisite amuse-bouche of anchovy tuile with 'revelatory' tarragon ice cream on a sweetcorn base, wickedly luxurious seared scallops on scrambled egg with caviar and truffles ('possibly the best starter I have ever eaten'), and near-perfect belly pork with apple rémoulade and tempura squid. Those who come for dinner have even more high-calibre strokes to consider – perhaps Cornish halibut (cooked at 50°C) with truffle mousse, Puy lentils, langoustine crêpes and artichoke barigoule, or a dessert of dark chocolate coulant with parsnip ice cream and raspberries. The whole experience is crowned by service that has that magic blend of formality and friendliness. If you are staying over, take time to wallow in the wine list, which is packed with distinguished names from around the globe – whether you are after a top-end Mersault, a South African Sumaridge Merlot or a Tasmanian Pinot Grigio. Prices start at £24.
Chef/s: Colin McGurran. **Open:** Tue to Sat L 12 to 3, D 7 to 10. **Closed:** Sun, Mon, 2 weeks Dec/Jan, 3 weeks Aug. **Meals:** Set L £35 (2 courses) to £39.95. Set D £65 (2 courses) to £75. **Service:** not inc. **Details:** Cards accepted. 60 seats. Air-con. Separate bar. No music. No mobile phones. Wheelchair access. Children allowed. Car parking.

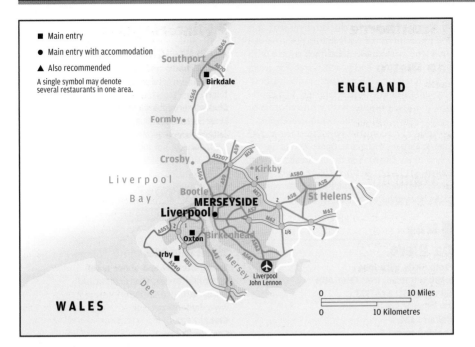

- ■ Main entry
- ● Main entry with accommodation
- ▲ Also recommended

A single symbol may denote several restaurants in one area.

■ Birkdale

Bistrot Vérité
Rustic food with big flavours
7 Liverpool Road, Birkdale, PR8 4AR
Tel no: (01704) 564199
French | £25
Cooking score: 3
£30

This small, lively bistro, a white-fronted venue with a few tables outside, is in photogenic Birkdale village and is dedicated to rustic French cooking. Daily changing menus (chalked on the board in the evenings) offer inspired choice, from pissaladière topped with red onion, tomatoes and Brie to a pairing of boudin noir and smoked morteau sausage with caramelised apple. The food delivers plenty of flavour without pretension, for instance roasted leg of corn-fed chicken in creamy mushroom and tarragon sauce, or chateaubriand for two with béarnaise, the sorts of dishes that once sustained many a village bistro the length and breadth of

France. Finish with caramelised banana and rum crêpes. A brief wine list starts at £14.95. Carafes are also available.
Chef/s: Marc Vérité. **Open:** Tue to Sat L 12 to 1.30, D 5.30 to 9.30. **Closed:** Sun, Mon, 25 and 26 Dec, 1 week Feb, 1 week Aug. **Meals:** alc (main courses £9 to £16). **Service:** not inc. **Details:** Cards accepted. 45 seats. 16 seats outside. Air-con. Music. Children allowed.

Michael's
Gently upbeat cooking
47 Liverpool Road, Birkdale, PR8 4AG
Tel no: (01704) 550886
www.michaelsbirkdale.co.uk
Modern European | £25
Cooking score: 2
£5 OFF £30

Michael Wichmann rules the roost in this two-roomed restaurant in Birkdale village. He has a strong local following for what is a neighbourhood bistro-style restaurant mixing old favourites with lively additions.

This may explain why chicken liver parfait, and pheasant breast with champ potatoes share the menu with smoked haddock risotto with minted pea sauce and poached free-range egg, or salmon with Thai red curry sauce, cashew rice and minted Chinese cabbage. The gentle, upbeat style continues with white chocolate crème brûlée with rhubarb and strawberry compote. The compact wine list starts at £13. **Chef/s:** Michael Wichmann. **Open:** Wed to Sat D only 6 to 10. **Closed:** Sun to Tue. **Meals:** alc (main courses £11 to £21). Set D £13.95 (2 courses) to £16.95. **Service:** not inc. **Details:** Cards accepted. 32 seats. Wheelchair access. Music. Children allowed.

■ Irby

Da Piero

From Sicily with love

5 Mill Hill Road, Irby, CH61 4UB
Tel no: (0151) 6487373
www.dapiero.co.uk
Italian | £30
Cooking score: 5

£5
OFF

'Sicily on a plate' was one reader's fond assessment of the food at Piero and Dawn Di Bella's remarkable little restaurant in the nether reaches of the Wirral. It's a place that generates real warmth and affection, not least because of its honesty and genuinely passionate approach to Italian cooking. Piero is a single-minded perfectionist when it comes to sourcing ingredients, and his hand-crafted culinary endeavours take their cue from his native Catania as he plunders family recipes for inspiration: his mother handed down the secrets of a disarmingly simple cotelette di carne, and his way with mussels is also rooted in the old traditions. The result is a world away from anglicised trattoria clichés, whether it's a textbook version of caponata served authentically lukewarm or a fabulously rich chocolate semifreddo. In between, pasta gets rave reviews – perhaps 'sublimely subtle' linguine with lemon sauce or Piero's signature penne with hand-minced wild venison ragù. Fans also adore the lightly fried scallops with salmoriglio dressing, gutsy homemade

Sicilian-style sausages with braised Umbrian lentils and wonderfully aromatic pesce al cartuccio (mixed seafood baked in paper). Dawn's affable presence out front fosters a genuine sense of family goodwill and open-hearted generosity. Wines from £15.75. **Chef/s:** Piero Di Bella. **Open:** Tue to Sat D only 6 to 11 (12 Sat). **Closed:** Sun, Mon, 25 and 26 Dec, 1 and 2 Jan, 2 weeks Aug. **Meals:** alc (main courses £14 to £22). **Service:** not inc. **Details:** Cards accepted. 22 seats. Music. Children allowed.

■ Liverpool

★ BEST VALUE FOR MONEY ★

NEW ENTRY

delifonseca

Small, friendly and above a deli

12 Stanley Street, Liverpool, L1 6AF
Tel no: (0151) 2550808
www.delifonseca.co.uk
Global | £21
Cooking score: 2

£5
OFF V £30

'Small and friendly' is how readers accurately describe the global bistro above Candice Fonseca's well-stocked deli. During daylight hours its capacious booths are a popular refuge from the nearby shopping streets, and beefed-up sandwiches – perhaps a falafel wrap or a muffuletta – provide much-needed fuel. In the evening attention turns to a blackboard packed with local goodies transformed into interesting international dishes. Vegetarians have plenty to choose from – although they miss a treat in the Cumbrian mutton mappas, a many-layered South Indian curry served with sag aloo and fragrant rice. To conclude, try the exceptional chocolate brownie. Wine is from £3.30 a glass, and for £6 cheery staff will pop the cork on bottles from downstairs, which are available at shelf price. A new delifonseca is planned for Brunswick Dock. **Chef/s:** Saul O'Reilly. **Open:** Mon to Sat 12 to 9 (9.30 Fri and Sat). **Closed:** Sun, 25 Dec to 1 Jan, bank hols. **Meals:** alc (main courses £7 to £14). **Service:** not inc. **Details:** Cards accepted. 48 seats. Air-con. Music. Children allowed.

The London Carriage Works

Satisfying menus, thick with local produce
Hope Street Hotel, 40 Hope Street, Liverpool,
L1 9DA
Tel no: (0151) 7052222
www.thelondoncarriageworks.co.uk
Modern British | £40
Cooking score: 3

🛏 V

A recent extension to the Hope Street Hotel,
to which Liverpool's best-known restaurant is
appended, hasn't altered the dining room but
may have rebooted its profile. There are now
more residents to come down to a menu thick
with local produce, served in ex-industrial,
gussied-up surrounds. Dishes balance smart
presentation with the need to satisfy, so a
terrine of organic pork with zingy green
peppercorns and an apricot compote might
come as a neat but hefty slab, and pheasant
breast is given presence with an array of
accompaniments including parsnip purée,
trompettes, kale, potatoes and quince jelly –
though a cheese plate was rather parsimonious.
Reports suggest that inconsistency remains a
feature, but a local team tries hard to please.
The easily navigated wine list (from £14.95)
takes account of a decent range of styles.
Chef/s: Paul Askew. **Open:** all week L 12 to 5, D 5 to
10. **Meals:** alc (main courses £12 to £29). Set L and
D £15 (2 courses) to £20. Sun L £25. **Service:** not
inc. **Details:** Cards accepted. 70 seats. Air-con.
Separate bar. Wheelchair access. Music. Children
allowed.

Panoramic

Foodie button-pusher with views
34th Floor, West Tower, Brook Street, Liverpool,
L3 9PJ
Tel no: (0151) 2365534
www.panoramicliverpool.com
Modern European | £48
Cooking score: 2

If you're turned on by 'dining in widescreen',
ascend to the rarefied reaches of Liverpool's
West Tower for a 360-degree window on the
world (well, five counties anyway). Currently

the UK's 'tallest restaurant', Panoramic delivers
what it promises, with the bonus of sleek
surrounds and a menu that pushes lots of
foodie buttons – albeit with lofty prices. Pithy
dish descriptions spell out the trendy details –
say 'scallops' (suckling pig tortellini, apple
pannacotta) ahead of 'beef fillet' (blade, pak
choi, violet potato, caper and raisin sauce).
After that, a confection of sweet potato
cheesecake with tonka bean ice cream and
lemon jelly might catch the eye. Global wines
start at £17.50.
Chef/s: Chris Marshall. **Open:** all week L 12 to 2.30,
D 6 to 10. **Closed:** bank hols (exc Good Friday).
Meals: alc (main courses £18 to £32). Set L £20.
Service: 10% (optional). **Details:** Cards accepted.
52 seats. Air-con. Separate bar. No mobile phones.
Wheelchair access. Music. Children allowed.

The Side Door

Welcoming, good-value little bistro
29a Hope Street, Liverpool, L1 9BQ
Tel no: (0151) 7077888
www.thesidedoor.co.uk
Modern European | £30
Cooking score: 2

£5 OFF

Between the two cathedrals, near the
universities and handy for theatre-goers, this
small bistro is a cheap and informal alternative
to the grander eateries on Hope Street. Spread
over the ground floor and basement, with
house clearance furniture, deep red and cream
walls, bare floorboards and cheerful service,
it's a welcoming place. Start perhaps with
monkfish with shellfish cream spaghetti (fish
fresh from Fleetwood), and follow with
tender pink lamb with butterbean purée,
char-grilled courgettes and salsa verde.
Cooking is simple and presentation unfussy.
Puddings such as blood orange and Amaretto
tart are highly praised. Wines start at £13.75.
Chef/s: Sean Millar. **Open:** Mon to Sat L 12 to 2.30
(2 Sat), D 6 to 10. **Closed:** Sun, 24 to 27 Dec, 1 Jan,
bank hols. **Meals:** alc (main courses £11 to £16). Set
D £17.95 (2 courses) to £19.95. **Service:** 10&
(optional). **Details:** Cards accepted. 55 seats. Air-
con. No mobile phones. Music. Children allowed.

60 Hope Street

Skilful cooking and 'bang-on' service
60 Hope Street, Liverpool, L1 9BZ
Tel no: (0151) 7076060
www.60hopestreet.com
Modern British | £36
Cooking score: 3

🍷 V

Housed in a slice of Georgian architecture not far from the Philharmonic Hall, this contemporary dining room has been stripped down with bare floorboards and painted walls; the booming acoustic isn't to everyone's taste, but the cooking shows skill in abundance – witness a favourably reported meal that took in three perfectly seared scallops with celeriac purée and saffron vinaigrette, followed by fillet of Cumbrian beef accompanied by a mini casserole of braised shin with herb dumplings and a single Carlingford oyster. Elsewhere, pan-fried wild duck breast might appear with a gyoza dumpling of confit leg, although the kitchen also shuns fashion by dishing up deep-fried hake with homemade black pudding and ketchup, sole véronique and such like. Desserts are not a strong point, but deep-fried jam sandwich served with a very rich Carnation milk ice cream has its fans. Service is 'bang-on' and the wine list turns up a host of interesting bottles from all corners of the world. Serious drinking opportunities abound, regardless of your palate or pocket; prices start at £15.95.

Chef/s: Damien Flynn. **Open:** Mon to Fri L 12 to 2.30, Mon to Sat D 5 to 10.30. **Closed:** Sun, bank hols. **Meals:** alc (main courses £13 to £30). Set L and D £19.95. **Service:** not inc. **Details:** Cards accepted. 150 seats. 12 seats outside. Air-con. Separate bar. Music. Children allowed.

Spire

Lively contemporary food
1 Church Road, Liverpool, L15 9EA
Tel no: (0151) 7345040
www.spirerestaurant.co.uk
Modern European | £26
Cooking score: 4

£5 OFF £30

Just a walk from Penny Lane in Liverpool's re-energised Wavertree district, Spire is making its mark on the city's restaurant scene thanks to stylish vibes and lively contemporary food. The interior is all exposed brickwork, polished floors and abstract art, with a wrought-iron staircase linking the two dining rooms. Matt Locke's cooking occasionally underwhelms, although the consensus is firmly in his favour – witness glowing reports of tempura squid with Moroccan noodles, 'posh' fish pie, and Goosnargh duck (perhaps served with garlic potatoes, maple-roasted parsnips, mustard and juniper sauce). His menus might also bring on board the likes of smoked haddock and lemon croquettes with sauce gribiche, roast chump of lamb with pease pudding, and char-grilled vegetable linguine with seared haloumi. To finish, lemon pannacotta with lime ice cream and excellent home-baked shortcake has been heartily endorsed. Set menus feature simple pickings from the carte, and the wine list offers a global spread at fair prices from £12.50.

Chef/s: Matt Locke. **Open:** Tue to Fri L 12 to 2.30, Mon to Sat D 6 to 9 (9.30 Fri and Sat). **Closed:** Sun, 1 to 15 Jan. **Meals:** alc (main courses £13 to £17). Set L £9.95 (2 courses) to £12.95. Set D £12.95 (2 courses) to £15.95. **Service:** not inc. **Details:** Cards accepted. 68 seats. Air-con. No mobile phones. Music. Children allowed.

Oxton

Fraiche

Mind-boggling food, sense-tingling thrills
11 Rose Mount, Oxton, CH43 5SG
Tel no: (0151) 6522914
www.restaurantfraiche.com
Modern French | £40
Cooking score: 7

Do the smart thing and book well ahead if you want to experience the sense-tingling thrills of Marc Wilkinson's extraordinary food. His pint-sized, 14-cover restaurant is secreted away in a conservation village a few miles from Birkenhead, but it has blasted into the national spotlight since opening a few years back. This is very much Wilkinson's home turf, and he has siphoned all his energy and passion into making Fraiche a special work-in-progress, suffusing the dining room with subdued tones, commissioning the weird and wonderful glass artwork and training up the staff. His latest addition is a shop selling produce from the kitchen as well as arty bits and bobs. The culinary format is three tasting menus of increasing complexity – Elements, Signature and Bespoke (an unpredictable cavalcade of surprises running to some 14 courses). Much of Marc's inspiration comes from the Spanish gastronomic avant-garde, but this is a deeply personal, experimental trip that knows no frontiers. His audacious, 'who dares wins' approach reaps huge rewards at every turn, whether it's a dish of seared scallops with pineapple, dehydrated smoked olive oil and 'coal' or an oft-reported success story involving lemon sole with mussels, radish and seaweed. Given that it's a one-man show in the kitchen, the results are truly mind-boggling. Dish descriptions are epigrammatic, which allows plenty of room for the imagination to run riot: what are we to make of 'smoked olive and mushroom textures' in a dish with the enigmatic moniker 'autumn'? To finish, excited punters have mentioned the delights of lemongrass ice cream, a dessert based around carrot cake and even a miraculously deconstructed Sachertorte – although cheeses 'with contrasting flavours' also have a special allure. This is cooking on the edge – risky, experimental stuff with arcane technical innovation behind the scenes and startling results on the plate. Fraiche is also blessed with some of the warmest, most enthusiastic staff you could wish for, with Marc's other half Gemma making a sizeable contribution to the relaxed vibe. The wine list packs in a huge amount of high-quality drinking from the world's vineyards, with agreeable prices to suit big spenders and everyday tipplers alike. House selections from £19 set the tone.
Chef/s: Marc Wilkinson. **Open:** Fri and Sat L 12 to 1.30, Wed to Sun D 7 to 9 (6 to 8 Sun). **Closed:** Mon, Tue, 25 Dec, first 2 weeks Jan. **Meals:** Set L £23.50 (3 courses). Set D £40 (3 courses). Bespoke menu £60. **Service:** not inc. **Details:** Cards accepted. 14 seats. 8 seats outside. Separate bar. No mobile phones. Wheelchair access. Music. Children allowed.

Wallasey

READERS RECOMMEND

Peninsula Dining Room

Modern British
3 Grosvenor Road, Wallasey, CH45 2LW
Tel no: (0151) 6398338
www.peninsula-dining-room.co.uk
'A great local restaurant – there is always something unusually delicious on offer'

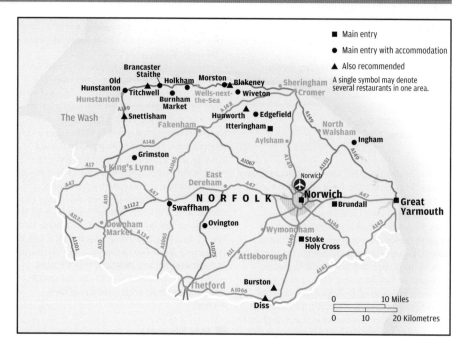

Blakeney

ALSO RECOMMENDED
▲ The Moorings
High Street, Blakeney, NR25 7NA
Tel no: (01263) 740054
www.blakeney-moorings.co.uk
Modern British

'Fresh local ingredients and simple, accurate cooking' bring droves of diners to this bistro-style café which sits a few yards up the hill from Blakeney's historic quay. Local produce fuels the menu, from game terrine with a caramelised apple, onion and caraway seed relish (£5.95) to roast rack of Norfolk lamb with a herb crust, wilted spinach and caramelised garlic jus (£18.50). Seafood also features strongly in dishes such as cod, cockle and shrimp chowder or roast monkfish with pancetta and pea purée (£17.50). Wines start at £14.50.

Brancaster Staithe
The White Horse
Popular pub with fabulous views
Brancaster Staithe, PE31 8BY
Tel no: (01485) 210262
www.whitehorsebrancaster.co.uk
Modern British | £25
New Chef

This popular north Norfolk coastal pub admirably combines the role of a traditional local with a real dining experience. Scrubbed pine furniture and a winter fire give it a rural feel. Beyond the public bar are the dining areas: a lounge bar/restaurant leading on to a large conservatory and terrace, where views over the salt marshes are nothing short of stunning. As we went to press, we learnt that chef Rene Llupar had left and his replacement not yet appointed. It is likely that the crowd-pleasing, fashionable menus driven by local raw materials and seasonal seafood will continue, offering simple classics such as

Brancaster mussels poached in white wine, cream and parsley or local venison pie. House wine is £13.95. Reports please.

Open: all week L 12 to 2, D 6.30 to 9. **Meals:** alc (main courses £8 to £19). **Service:** not inc. **Details:** Cards accepted. 100 seats. 130 seats outside. Separate bar. No music. No mobile phones. Wheelchair access. Children allowed. Car parking.

▌ Brundall
The Lavender House
Foodie haven in a thatched cottage
39 The Street, Brundall, NR13 5AA
Tel no: (01603) 712215
www.thelavenderhouse.co.uk
Modern British | £40
Cooking score: 3

🍷 V

This pretty thatched cottage has played host to restaurants since the 60s, but local champion Richard Hughes has raised its foodie profile since arriving in 2002. Dinner is a supremely relaxed 'evening of discovery' that opens with a little palate sharpener, before the kitchen shows its ambition with a 'tasting' of Shropham pork, celery root purée and capers or herb-crusted salt cod with butter-bean stew. After that, expect anything from crusted loin and pastilla of Edgefield venison with beetroot and juniper to fillet and shin of Barnard's beef with winter vegetables and beef tea (a favourite with readers). Smoked potato purée is a signature accompaniment, and Euro-inclined desserts might feature iced brown sugar parfait with Victoria plums. A private dining room named after Austrian winemaking legend Willi Opitz points up the restaurant's vinous inclinations. The high-class list naturally includes incomparable stickies from the man himself, along with top names from elsewhere. Prices start at £18.95.
Chef/s: Richard Knights. **Open:** Sun L 12 to 3, Tue to Sat D 6 to 11. **Closed:** Mon. **Meals:** Set D £39.95 (5 courses). Tasting menu £58. Sun L £25. **Service:** not inc. **Details:** Cards accepted. 50 seats. Separate bar. No music. Wheelchair access. Music. Children allowed. Car parking.

▌ Burnham Market
The Hoste Arms
Smart inn with good service
The Green, Burnham Market, PE31 8HD
Tel no: (01328) 738777
www.hostearms.co.uk
Modern British | £25
Cooking score: 2

🍷 ⊨ V £30

Adored by prosperous weekenders, this much-extended seventeenth-century inn is a tribute to founder Paul Whittome, who sadly died in July 2010. It encompasses various dining areas, including a refurbished 'Moroccan garden' restaurant – although the most favoured spot is the wood-panelled room by the bar, overlooking Burnham's elegant green. In addition to gastropub staples, the menu is peppered with oriental flourishes, from tempura oysters and fishcakes with wasabi mayo to pad thai stir-fries. Elsewhere, the kitchen has delivered sound renditions of succulent pork tenderloin on butternut squash purée with Parma ham, and passion-fruit custard tart with mojito granita. Service earns nothing but praise. The well-constructed wine list has an excellent global range, whether you are after an everyday quaffer or something iconic. Prices start at £15.50 (£3.80 a glass).
Chef/s: Aaron Smith. **Open:** all week L 12 to 2, D 6 to 9. **Meals:** alc (main courses £12 to £20). **Service:** not inc. **Details:** Cards accepted. 130 seats. 100 seats outside. Air-con. Separate bar. No music. Wheelchair access. Children allowed. Car parking.

▌ Burston
ALSO RECOMMENDED
▲ The Burston Crown
Mill Road, Burston, IP22 5TW
Tel no: (01379) 741257
www.burstoncrown.com
Gastropub

Dubbed 'the friendliest pub in Norfolk' by one first-timer, this cracking local is the hub of a village famous for a school strike in the 1920s.

Bypass the regular pubby menu and home in on the specials board for some generous, big-hearted cooking with 'honest intent'. Hits have included a salad of black pudding, bacon and fried quail's egg (£6.50), Moroccan chicken with sweet potatoes, and garlicky confit duck with bubble and squeak (£13.50). Puds (£5) are old favourites. Live music, real ales and unusual wines (from £13). Closed Sun D.

Diss

ALSO RECOMMENDED
▲ Weavers Wine Bar & Eating House
Market Hill, Diss, IP22 4JZ
Tel no: (01379) 642411
www.weavers-diss.com
Modern British

William Bavin has been presiding over this well-regarded local eating house since 1987, and has kept the lovely old Tudor beamed building in good shape. Sound seasonal ingredients find their way into unchallenging dishes along the lines of Norfolk mussels in garlic butter, poached pigeon breast with rhubarb compote, and baked salmon with Arbroath smokie mousseline. For afters, perhaps lemon and ginger cheesecake. Lunch is £15.95, dinner £21.95 (for 3 courses); Saturday dinner is a carte. Well-considered Adnams wine list from £12.95. Open Tue to Fri L, Mon to Sat D.

Symbols

🛏 Accommodation is available

£30 Three courses for less than £30

V More than three vegetarian main courses

£5 OFF £5-off voucher scheme

🍷 Notable wine list

Edgefield
The Pigs
Gutsy food in a proper pub
Norwich Road, Edgefield, NR24 2RL
Tel no: (01263) 587634
www.thepigs.org.uk
Gastropub | £22
Cooking score: 1
🛏 £30

Bar billiards, darts, local ales and gutsy food with a Norfolk drawl are the calling cards at this bucolic pub-with-rooms in a village south of Holt. The kitchen procures produce from the county's 'food heroes' for a quirky menu that offers tapas-style 'iffits' (potted rabbit, crispy pigs' ears, smoked prawns), hefty platefuls of Edgefield game suet pudding or mutton hotpot, and nostalgic sweets ranging from lardy cake to baked Norfolk Biffin apples. There are plenty of kiddie distractions for under-age 'piglets' to enjoy as their grown-up charges dip into the wine list (from £15.50).
Chef/s: Tim Abbott. **Open:** Mon to Sat L 11 to 2.30 (12 to 3 Sat), D 6 to 9. Sun 12 to 9. **Meals:** alc (main courses £10 to £18). **Service:** not inc. **Details:** Cards accepted. 80 seats. 60 seats outside. Separate bar. Wheelchair access. Music. Children allowed. Car parking.

Great Yarmouth
Seafood Restaurant
A seaside jewel
85 North Quay, Great Yarmouth, NR30 1JF
Tel no: (01493) 856009
www.theseafood.co.uk
Seafood | £35
Cooking score: 2
£5 OFF

'Great Yarmouth is not renowned for its eating places and this is a real jewel', noted one visitor to Christopher and Miriam Kikis' welcoming seafood restaurant, which is now in its thirty-second year. With its comfortable, safe and well-tried style, the kitchen goes in for starters such as pan-fried scallops with bacon or crab

claws with garlic butter, followed by mains ranging from grilled skate with black butter to scampi provençale with rice. What gets the show off to a cracking start is the high-quality materials and the kitchen's sheer consistency. Sensibly, the wine list is tilted towards whites, with bottles starting at £16.50.
Chef/s: Christopher Kikis. **Open:** Mon to Fri L 12 to 1.45, Mon to Sat D 6.30 to 10.30. **Closed:** Sun, 2 weeks Christmas, 2 weeks May, bank hols. **Meals:** alc (main courses £11 to £30). **Service:** not inc. **Details:** Cards accepted. 40 seats. Air-con. Separate bar. No mobile phones. Wheelchair access. Music. Car parking.

Grimston
Congham Hall, The Orangery
Modern country house cooking
Lynn Road, Grimston, PE32 1AH
Tel no: (01485) 600250
www.conghamhallhotel.co.uk
Modern British | £40
Cooking score: 3
🛏 V

A short drive from Sandringham, Congham Hall is an elegant Georgian manor house set in 40 acres of grounds, which include a wonderful working kitchen garden (some of the 700 varieties of herbs grown there are used to good effect in the kitchen). The Orangery restaurant, which overlooks lawns and parkland, is the backdrop for a modern country house style of cooking based on local seasonal produce, including game from the Sandringham Estate. At a test dinner, Cromer crab with lemon mayonnaise, pickled spring vegetables and garden herbs preceded pan-seared John Dory with white asparagus, pink grapefruit and Champagne sauce. Desserts are worth leaving room for, especially a deliciously creamy vanilla pannacotta with roasted plums and basil foam. The wine list opens with house recommendations from £20, and there's more good-value drinking for those wanting to delve deeper.
Chef/s: David Hammond. **Open:** all week L 12 to 2, D 7 to 9. **Meals:** alc (main courses £23 to £27). Set L £16.25 (2 courses) to £20.75. Set D £35. Sun L £23.

Gourmand Menu £65. **Service:** not inc. **Details:** Cards accepted. 50 seats. 24 seats outside. Separate bar. No music. No mobile phones. Wheelchair access. Children allowed. Car parking.

Holkham
The Victoria
Quirky colonial hotel
Park Road, Holkham, NR23 1RG
Tel no: (01328) 711008
www.victoriaatholkham.co.uk
Modern British | £31
Cooking score: 1
🛏

The Victoria is a handsomely proportioned, quirkily decorated hotel owned by Viscount Coke, heir to the Holkham Estate. Behind an intimate bar are two grander dining areas: one woody and baronial, with Rajasthani carvings; the second tiled and light, overlooking the garden and fields. Breezy, amenable staff ensure that a relaxed vibe prevails. Local game and seafood feature strongly in the expertly presented yet variable food, which ranges from lobster and crab bisque, via chicken breast with mash, to sublime lemon tart. Wines from £15.50.
Chef/s: Shayne Woods. **Open:** all week L 12 to 2.30, D 7 to 9 (9.30 Fri and Sat). **Meals:** alc (main courses £12 to £20). **Service:** not inc. **Details:** Cards accepted. 40 seats. 40 seats outside. Air-con. Separate bar. Music. Children allowed. Car parking.

Hunworth
ALSO RECOMMENDED
▲ The Hunny Bell
The Green, Hunworth, NR24 2AA
Tel no: (01263) 712300
www.thehunnybell.co.uk
Gastropub £5 OFF

Under the same ownership as the Wildebeest Arms, the Mad Moose and Mackintosh's Canteen (see entries), the Hunny Bell is a friendly place with a beamed main bar and winter wood burners, and neatly combines the roles of rustic pub and contemporary restaurant. Nicely turned-out English staples include Morston mussels or pressed ham hock and green peppercorn terrine with piccalilli (£5.95), followed by roast chump of spring lamb with local turnips, asparagus, broad beans and mint jus (£17.25), and raspberry Bakewell tart (£5.50). House wine is £13.95. Open all week.

Ingham

NEW ENTRY

The Ingham Swan

Proper boozer with broad-minded food
Sea Palling Road, Ingham, NR12 9AB
Tel no: (01692) 581099
www.theinghamswan.co.uk
Modern European | £29
Cooking score: 2

Daniel Smith made his name cooking at the Wildebeest Arms (see entry), but upped sticks to take over this tidy-looking village local on the outer limits of the Norfolk Broads. The thached Swan still feels like a proper boozer, with cheery vibes, five Woodforde's ales on tap and a full complement of ancient timbers, but the food tells a different story. There are echoes of the Wildebeest days on the menu, which takes a broad-minded, eclectic view of things: pork belly is jazzed up with ras-el-hanout and matched with crispy squid, grilled sea bass is partnered by local asparagus and tomato sauce vierge, and there's coconut pannacotta with strawberry sorbet and mango ravioli to finish. House wines start at £14.
Chef/s: Daniel Smith. **Open:** Tue to Sun L 12 to 2 (4 Sun), Mon to Sat D 7 to 9. **Closed:** 25 and 26 Dec. **Meals:** alc (main courses £9 to £25). Set D £15.95 (2 courses) to £19.95. **Service:** not inc. **Details:** Cards accepted. 50 seats. 30 seats outside. Music. Children allowed. Car parking.

Itteringham

The Walpole Arms

Well-run hostelry with sunny flavours
The Common, Itteringham, NR11 7AR
Tel no: (01263) 587258
www.thewalpolearms.co.uk
Gastropub | £27
Cooking score: 2

Out in the Norfolk backwoods, on the fringes of Holkham Estate, the Walpole Arms is a really well-run hostelry with attributes aplenty – not least a cookery school set up by Norfolk gastro-legend David Adlard. Ale buffs and quiz fans mingle in the rough-hewn beamed bar, sun-seekers head for the terrace and foodies throng in the rustic, brick-walled dining room. The daily menu is packed with sharp seasonal dishes built around local ingredients (from Morston mussels to Gunton Hall venison), although Med flavours give the food its real kick. Expect anything from red mullet escabèche or grilled lamb with chickpea and spinach salad to homemade Catalonian sausage with blackeye beans and spring cabbage. For afters, perhaps saffron-poached pear with orange-flower rice pudding. House wines start at £13.95 (£3.50 a glass).
Chef/s: Jamie Guy. **Open:** all week L 12 to 2 (2.30 Sun), Mon to Sat D 7 to 9. **Closed:** 25 Dec. **Meals:** alc (main courses £11 to £19). Sun L £17.95 (2 courses) to £21.95. **Service:** not inc. **Details:** Cards accepted. 85 seats. 60 seats outside. Separate bar. Wheelchair access. Music. Children allowed. Car parking.

■ Morston

Morston Hall

Class act by the coast
The Street, Morston, NR25 7AA
Tel no: (01263) 741041
www.morstonhall.com
Modern British | £55
Cooking score: 5

♦ 🍾 🛏

It may sound and look rather grand with its high walls, stately brick-and-flint façade and pretty gardens, but Morston Hall doesn't lord it – just the opposite, in fact. This is a very professional set-up with a caring heart, and its overall comfort factor should increase even further once a second lounge is up and running for drinks and socialising. Galton Blackiston's way of doing things is to map out a no-choice, four-course menu each evening, and deploy acute seasonal flavours and local ingredients to telling effect – although some visitors have found the results a tad 'safe'. A terrine of locally foraged mushrooms with parsley purée and pear chutney could set the tone, before grilled fillet of sea bream on brown shrimp risotto with tarragon beurre blanc. Rack of salt marsh lamb, venison and squab are also emphatically 'Norfolk' – the latter served in two guises with Puy lentils, carrot purée and Alsace bacon. To conclude, passion-fruit tart with vanilla ice cream and orange madeleine has been praised, although you might prefer to savour the artisan cheeses with homemade cheese biscuits, quince jelly and walnut bread. A page of top-drawer wines by the glass (from £4) offers an easy introduction to the joys of the fascinating list – a labour of love that has been helpfully laid out by grape variety (note the starry Trimbach Rieslings). Bottle prices start at £19.
Chef/s: Galton Blackiston, Richard Bainbridge and Samantha Wegg. **Open:** Sun L 12.30 for 1 (1 sitting), all week D 7.30 for 8 (1 sitting). **Closed:** 25 and 26 Dec, Jan. **Meals:** Set D £55 (4 courses). Sun L £33. **Service:** not inc. **Details:** Cards accepted. 50 seats. No music. No mobile phones. Wheelchair access. Children allowed. Car parking.

■ Norwich

1Up at the Mad Moose

Upscale pub/restaurant
2 Warwick Street, Norwich, NR2 3LD
Tel no: (01603) 627687
www.themadmoose.co.uk
Modern British | £28
New Chef

£30

It's all change in the kitchen of this upscale pub/restaurant hidden away in one of Norwich's residential enclaves. Eden Derrick has moved to sister venue the Wildebeest Arms (see entry) and his replacement is well-known Norfolk chef Nick Anderson. Dinner in the first-floor 1Up Restaurant is now a carte and the cooking has taken on a different complexion, with regional ingredients and seasonal flavours at the heart of things. Lowestoft herrings 'two ways' with parsley jelly and beetroot salad might give way to roast rack and spiced shoulder of local lamb with spring carrots, Norfolk asparagus and garlic jus. After that, perhaps 'textures of rhubarb and ginger'. Eclectic wines start at £13.95.
Chef/s: Nick Anderson. **Open:** Sun L 12 to 3, Mon to Sat D 7 to 10. **Closed:** 25 and 26 Dec. **Meals:** alc (main courses £14 to £18). Sun L £16.50 (2 courses) to £20. **Service:** not inc. **Details:** Cards accepted. 42 seats. Separate bar. Music. Children allowed.

NEW ENTRY

Roger Hickman's

A stylish addition to the Norwich scene
79 Upper St Giles Street, Norwich, NR2 1AB
Tel no: (01603) 633522
www.rogerhickmansrestaurant.com
Modern British | £35
Cooking score: 5

£5 OFF ♦ V

Following a spell feeding the holiday crowds at the Victoria, Holkham (see entry), Roger Hickman has returned to his old stamping ground. Eagle-eyed Guide readers may recognise the address as the site of one-time legend Adlards (where Hickman was head chef), and the intimate dining room still exudes discreet elegance and personable civility. Hickman's food is all about clean, sharply defined, seasonal flavours – just consider a beautifully arranged salad of perky asparagus with pea shoots, tiny fronds of fennel, soft-poached quails' eggs, pickled chanterelles and a few dabs of earthy cep purée, or an uncluttered dish of sweetly timed halibut fillet on a crisp rösti surrounded by a herb-strewn pea casserole. The kitchen is equally confident with muscular ideas, sending out combos of braised shin and roast fillet of beef with confit garlic and wilted spinach, for example, before closing the show with artful puds such as pineapple tarte Tatin with black pepper ice cream. Dinner also comes dressed up with cheeky appetisers and pre-desserts – watch out for the amazing 'egg yolk' (a trompe l'oeil flavour-bomb of golden-yellow passion-fruit purée encased in a film of agar). The wine list is exemplary; pricing, variety and growers are spot-on, whether you fancy Charles Melton's Rose of Virginia or a classy Trimbach Gewürztraminer. Thirteen house selections start at £16 (£4.50 a glass). **Chef/s:** Roger Hickman. **Open:** Tue to Sat L 12 to 2.30, D 7 to 10. **Closed:** Sun, Mon, bank hols, 1 to 9 Jan, 23 to 31 Aug. **Meals:** Set L £16 (2 courses) to £19. Set D £30 (2 courses) to £35. **Service:** not inc. **Details:** Cards accepted. 40 seats. Air-con. Music. Children allowed.

Tatlers
Lovely eatery with enthusiastic fans
21 Tombland, Norwich, NR3 1RF
Tel no: (01603) 766670
www.butlersrestaurants.co.uk
Modern British | £24
Cooking score: 3
£30

'Warm welcome; excellent service; fresh, local produce; skilful cooking,' is one enthusiastic verdict on this Georgian town house in a lovely setting near the gates of the cathedral. The cooking is never less than steady, with reports speaking favourably of 'sumptuous'

parsnip soup, and smoked haddock fishcake with a fresh langoustine and a light dill sauce, as well as mains of local pigeon breast with black pudding, lardons and a good salad, and a combo of new season's lamb – rump, fillet, tongue and sweetbreads – with sweet potato purée and purple sprouting broccoli. Classic vanilla crème brûlée is all it should be, or you could have 'the best chocolate brownies I have ever tasted'. The wine list is sensibly priced and probably has something for everyone. House recommendations from £15. **Chef/s:** Adam Jarvis. **Open:** Mon to Sat L 12 to 2, D 6 to 9 (10 Fri and Sat). **Closed:** Sun, 25 and 26 Dec. **Meals:** alc (main courses £10 to £22). Set L and D £12 (2 courses) to £16. **Service:** 10% (optional). **Details:** Cards accepted. 68 seats. Separate bar. No mobile phones. Music. Children allowed.

ALSO RECOMMENDED
▲ Mackintosh's Canteen
Unit 410, Chapelfield Plain, Norwich, NR2 1SZ
Tel no: (01603) 305280
www.mackintoshscanteen.co.uk
British

From the makers of Mad Moose and the Wildebeest Arms (see entries), this easy-going, all-day canteen occupies two floors in the one-time Mackintosh's confectionery factory. If you're after more than breakfast or an afternoon cuppa, the brasserie menu offers some lively, eclectic stuff including smoked chicken salad with chorizo (£6.95), macaroni cheese and sea bass fillet on saffron and Parmesan risotto (£13.95), followed by Norfolk cheeses and desserts such as coffee and Armagnac pannacotta (£5.75). House wines are £14.95 (£5 a glass). Open all week.

READERS RECOMMEND
Vine Thai Cuisine
Thai
7 Dove Street, Norwich, NR2 1DE
Tel no: (01603) 627362
www.vinethai.co.uk
'Zesty Thai flavours in Norwich's tiniest boozer'

Old Hunstanton

The Neptune
Seriously good food
85 Old Hunstanton Road, Old Hunstanton,
PE36 6HZ
Tel no: (01485) 532122
www.theneptune.co.uk
Modern British | £42
Cooking score: 5
£5 OFF 🛏

Swapping the Isle of Wight for the flat
expanses of the Norfolk coast seems to have
paid dividends for Kevin and Jacki
Mangeolles, who have transformed this
seventeenth-century inn into a cool
restaurant-with-rooms, noted for its mellow
vibes and seriously good food. Local
fishermen play their part by providing
maritime pickings, and customers reap the
benefit in the form of some startlingly vivid
ideas – say grilled mackerel and crab salad
fashionably dovetailed with slivers of
watermelon, or a 'magnificent', exceptionally
fresh piece of turbot accompanied by avocado
mousse, with a poached oyster topped with
baby leeks adding extra depth to the dish.
Norfolk's farmers also make a valuable
contribution – loin of Courtyard Farm pork
comes to the table in good company with wild
mushrooms, Savoy cabbage and creamed
potatoes, while a duo of pan-fried ribeye and
braised beef is dressed up with Binham Blue
cheese butter, shiitake mushrooms and
pumpkin seeds. To finish, reporters have
praised the sublime cinnamon bavarois on a
bed of apple sponge with poached figs and a
sorbet of walnut and yoghurt. Jacki
Mangeolles gives a winning 'professional
performance' out front, as well as tending to
the well-constructed wine list; expect a broad
global spread with a page of house selections
from £17.50 (£5 a glass).
Chef/s: Kevin Mangeolles. **Open:** Sun L 12 to 2, Tue
to Sun D 7 to 9. **Closed:** Mon, 2 weeks Nov, 3 weeks
Jan. **Meals:** Set L £20.50 (2 courses) to £25. Sun L
£25 (3 courses). **Service:** not inc. **Details:** Cards
accepted. 24 seats. Separate bar. No mobile
phones. Music. Car parking.

Ovington

The Café at Brovey Lair
Fusion fish ... and more
Carbrooke Road, Ovington, IP25 6SD
Tel no: (01953) 882706
www.broveylair.com
Pan-Asian/Seafood | £53
Cooking score: 6
£5 OFF 🛏 V

'Tina and Mike Pemberton are wonderfully
welcoming hosts, which is probably only to be
expected as the restaurant is situated in their
home', observed one reader. They also run
Brovey Lair in their own way, discussing likes
and dislikes over the phone and attending to
all the details. First-timers are surprised by the
whole set-up, but adore everything about the
place, from the elegantly combined kitchen
and dining room to the fantastic California-
style breakfasts for those staying over. Tina
cooks a no-choice set menu (hence the
negotiations when booking) and her skill at
the teppan grill is much admired; her
invigorating fusion style even evokes 'warm
memories of China nights with a hint of a
spice'. Exciting seafood cookery is her
penchant, although she is also as sharp as a
Global knife when it comes to vegetables.
Flavours hit you from the very start, whether
it's carpaccio of marinated tuna in sashimi
sauce with shredded daikon or 'exquisite' stir-
fried tiger prawns on green papaya salad. Next
comes a soup (perhaps beetroot), before
another piscine dazzler is brought to the table:
teppanyaki monkfish on squid ink noodles
with shiitake mushrooms and stir-fried
asparagus has been applauded. Desserts are
also frequently mentioned in dispatches –
bitter chocolate mocha truffle torte with
raspberries and organic ice cream, for
example. House wine is £17.50.
Chef/s: Tina Pemberton. **Open:** all week L by
appointment only, all week D 7.45 (1 sitting) by
appointment only. **Closed:** 25 Dec. **Meals:** Set L and
D £52.50 (4 courses). **Service:** 10%. **Details:** Cards
accepted. 20 seats. 20 seats outside. Air-con. No
mobile phones. Wheelchair access. Music. Car
parking.

Snettisham

ALSO RECOMMENDED
▲ The Rose & Crown

Old Church Road, Snettisham, PE31 7LX
Tel no: (01485) 541382
www.roseandcrownsnettisham.co.uk
Gastropub £5 OFF

Behind the summery, flower-decked façade of this atmospheric fourteenth-century inn a narrow, twisting corridor leads to a warren of oak-beamed rooms with red-tiled floors, inglenook fireplaces and ancient cushioned settles. Perfect for quaffing Norfolk-brewed ales and tucking into some cracking pub food, perhaps Holkham sausages and mash with onion gravy (£9.95), or something more adventurous like black bream with champ, curly kale and salsa verde (£12.25), or even courgette risotto with lemon, thyme and goats' cheese. Desserts may include white chocolate and coconut crème brûlée (£5). House wine £13.50. Accommodation. Open all week.

Stoke Holy Cross
The Wildebeest Arms

Consistent, imaginatively conceived food
82-86 Norwich Road, Stoke Holy Cross, NR14 8QJ
Tel no: (01508) 492497
www.thewildebeest.co.uk
Modern European | £29
Cooking score: 2

♠ V £30

Striking yellow tones and a fondness for Africana mark out this open-plan pub/restaurant to the south of Norwich. Chef Eden Derrick hotfooted it from the Mad Moose (see entry) to head up the kitchen, and he is shoring up the Wildebeest's culinary reputation following Dan Smith's departure. Consistency is the watchword and the food is imaginatively conceived, even if the results on the plate sometimes lack impact. Norfolk ingredients often court unlikely bedfellows (honey-glazed Scott's Field pork belly with crispy squid and saffron-pickled onions, for

example), and the eclectic theme continues with dishes such as longshore cod fillet with asparagus and orzo pasta, chorizo and pipérade. Desserts keep it seasonal with the likes of lavender crème brûlée, roast figs and honey ice cream. There is a passion about wine here too, and the interesting, global list (from £15.95) includes some beauties from the New World plus a fine spread of house selections.
Chef/s: Eden Derrick. Open: all week L 12 to 2 (12.30 to 2.30 Sun), D 7 to 9. Closed: 25 and 26 Dec. Meals: alc (main courses £13 to £19). Set L £14.95 (2 courses) to £18.50. Set D £19.95 (2 courses) to £21.50. Service: not inc. Details: Cards accepted. 90 seats. 35 seats outside. Separate bar. Wheelchair access. Music. Children allowed. Car parking.

Swaffham
Strattons

Flamboyant eco champ
4 Ash Close, Swaffham, PE37 7NH
Tel no: (01760) 723845
www.strattonshotel.com
Modern British | £40
Cooking score: 3

🛏 V

'A country house in a town' just about sums up the Scotts' Palladian-style villa, which is protected by a ring of lush garden from the centre of Swaffham. Reporters continue to applaud the eco-friendly stance, with recycling, food miles and local supplies all part of the remit, while the flamboyant interior and unusual sculptures impress first-time visitors. Simon Linacre-Marshall now heads the kitchen, offering plenty of interest on menus that could open with fishcakes with chilli aïoli, sweet cucumber pickle, fennel slaw and red pepper pâté, go on to venison loin with sour cherry sauce, fondant potatoes and roasted vegetables, and finish with lemon meringue tart or a taster of British cheeses. Organic wines feature on the well-annotated wine list. Prices start from £17.
Chef/s: Simon Linacre-Marshall. Open: all week L 12 to 2.30, D 6.30 to 9. Closed: 20 to 26 Dec. Meals: alc (main courses £16 to £26). Service: not

inc. **Details:** Cards accepted. 28 seats. 12 seats outside. Separate bar. No mobile phones. Music. Children allowed. Car parking.

Titchwell

ALSO RECOMMENDED
▲ Titchwell Manor

Titchwell, PE31 8BB
Tel no: (01485) 210221
www.titchwellmanor.com
Modern European

This large, roadside Victorian redbrick house has been artfully styled to the point where it oozes rustic sophistication. A series of atmospheric rooms sport clattering bare boards, open fires and leather sofas, while the garden conservatory offers a more formal dining option. Rustic sophistication is pretty much the tone of the cooking too. Typical choices include six Brancaster oysters (£6), fisherman's pie (£10), or (from the £40 seven-course Conservatory Restaurant menu) belly and tenderloin of pork with bulgur wheat and maple syrup. Wines start at £15.50. Accommodation. Open all week.

Wiveton

Wiveton Bell

Splendid inn that keeps it local
Blakeney Road, Wiveton, NR25 7TL
Tel no: (01263) 740101
www.wivetonbell.co.uk
Gastropub | £26
Cooking score: 2

Local ingredients get top billing at this splendidly rejuvenated Norfolk inn overlooking Wiveton's green and church. The cooking follows unfussy brasserie lines, with menus advertising the likes of Biston ham hock served with piccalilli or goats' cheese and red onion marmalade crostini ahead of breast of farm chicken with dauphinoise potatoes,

white wine, shallots, chestnuts and local wild mushrooms, or shoulder of lamb cooked in white wine and served with garlic mash. Fresh fish has been praised, a smoked Norfolk Dapple cheeseburger much enjoyed, and meals end on a high note with desserts such as sticky toffee pudding or lemon posset. A fairly priced wine selection starts in Chile at £13.95. **Chef/s:** Jamie Murch. **Open:** all week L 12 to 2.15 (2.45 Sun), D 6 to 9. **Closed:** 25 and 26 Dec. **Meals:** alc (main courses £12 to £18). **Service:** not inc. **Details:** Cards accepted. 60 seats. 50 seats outside. Separate bar. No music. No mobile phones. Children allowed. Car parking.

ALSO RECOMMENDED
▲ Wiveton Farm Café

Wiveton Hall, Wiveton, NR25 7TE
Tel no: (01263) 740515
www.wivetonhall.co.uk/cafe.htm
Café

Decked out like a 'folksy doll's house', this funky daytime café is part of an admirable local food enterprise built around Wiveton Hall. Chef Alison Yetman made her name at Guide favourite Yetman's, and has lost none of her zest for farm-to-table cooking. Blackboard lunch menus move from pork and game terrine with apple chutney (£7.50) to grilled sea bass, butter beans, aïoli and sprouting broccoli (£13.50). Puds include pannacotta with orange and rhubarb compote (£4.50). Tapas is served Friday and Saturday evenings; there are delightful afternoon teas, too. House wine £12.50. Open all week Apr to Oct.

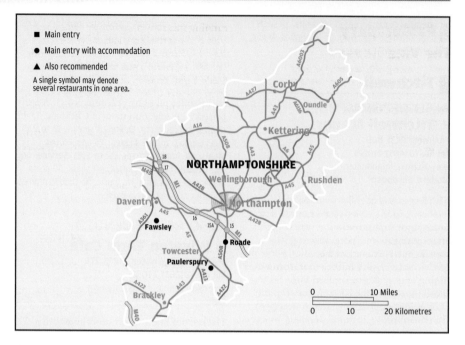

▋Fawsley

Equilibrium at Fawsley Hall

Inventive food with extraordinary flavours
Fawsley, NN11 3BA
Tel no: (01327) 892000
www.fawsleyhall.com
Modern British | £59
Cooking score: 6

£5
OFF

Fawsley Hall sits in a world of its own at the
end of a single-track road, but it is no
backwater. As a modern country house hotel it
has to work hard to keep the roof repaired and
achieves this via conferences, weddings and a
spa. It is best to be aware of this. One diner was
surprised to be shown to a 'small, dull side
room' instead of the magnificent Tudor
kitchen that houses Equilibrium, which had
been booked for a private function. However,
it says something about Nigel Godwin's
cooking that the food overcame the room.
There is real invention here, with innovative
concepts supported by sound techniques. The
tasting menu of seven small courses is a
speciality, but there's also a seasonal carte. At a
spring dinner the latter delivered a 'quite
extraordinary combination of flavours' in a
dish of sewin (sea trout) with rhubarb, spiced
lentils, duck liver and pistachio. That was
followed by a superb poached and roasted loin
of rabbit with a 'cannelloni' of the braised meat
wrapped in thin strips of carrot, while a
luscious banana pannacotta and pineapple
sorbet accompanied peanut parfait for a
perfect finish. The wine list is an engaging mix
of classic French and fresh international
flavours, with bottles from £24.50.
Chef/s: Nigel Godwin. **Open:** Tue to Sat D only 7 to
9.30. **Closed:** Sun, Mon, 24 to 26 Dec, 31 Dec.
Meals: Set D £59 (5 courses). Tasting menu £79 (7
courses). **Service:** 12.5% (optional). **Details:** Cards
accepted. 26 seats. Separate bar. No mobile
phones. Wheelchair access. Music. Car parking.

Paulerspury
The Vine House

Lively cooking with an army of fans
100 High Street, Paulerspury, NN12 7NA
Tel no: (01327) 811267
www.vinehousehotel.com
Modern British | £30
Cooking score: 3

£5 OFF

A 300-year-old limestone house in an unruffled Northants village, the Vine House has a loyal army of followers. The place is an especial delight in fine weather, when a table inside a kind of summerhouse in the garden comes into its own. Marcus Springett's cooking is lively modern British, with Mediterranean and east-Asian influences used to good effect. Home-smoked Loch Duart salmon dressed in toasted sesame seeds and wasabi is a typical way to start. One reporter found no fault with a meal that progressed from wild garlic and rocket gnocchi to saddle of lamb with crushed peas and salsa verde. The determination to make an impact is sustained through to desserts such as passion-fruit jelly with dark chocolate sauce. Wines start at £16.95.
Chef/s: Marcus Springett. **Open:** Tue to Sat L 12 to 1.30, Mon to Sat D 7 to 9. **Closed:** Sun. **Meals:** Set L and D £26.95 (2 courses) to £29.95. **Service:** 12.5%. **Details:** Cards accepted. 33 seats. No music. No mobile phones. Wheelchair access. Children allowed. Car parking.

Roade
Roade House

A quarter-century in the Guide...
16 High Street, Roade, NN7 2NW
Tel no: (01604) 863372
www.roadehousehotel.co.uk
Modern British | £34
Cooking score: 4

£5 OFF

Clocking up a quarter-century in the Guide is no mean feat, and we congratulate the Kewleys on achieving it. They have been running this converted former village pub – now a comfortable restaurant-with-rooms – since 1983 and although it isn't that far from the M1, a spirit of great tranquillity prevails. Sleek, light, modern design makes the place feel city-smart, and Chris's cooking seals the deal. Influences are drawn from far and wide, producing grilled spiced mackerel with hummus and preserved lemon relish to start, followed by seared cod with a salt cod fishcake in prawn and mussel chowder or roast breast of pheasant with a parcel of its leg meat, accompanied by leek purée and cranberries in red wine and port sauce. Dishes make consummate sense, with clean, clear flavours standing out all the way through to homely desserts such as ginger sponge and custard or apple and blueberry crumble tart. Wines are grouped by style, with prices from £15.50.
Chef/s: Chris Kewley. **Open:** Mon to Fri and Sun L 12 to 2, Mon to Sat D 7 to 9.30. **Closed:** bank hols, 26 to 31 Dec. **Meals:** Set L £20 (2 courses) to £23. Set D £26 (2 courses) to £31. Sun L £20. **Service:** not inc. **Details:** Cards accepted. 50 seats. Air-con. Separate bar. No music. Wheelchair access. Children allowed. Car parking.

Rushton

READERS RECOMMEND
Rushton Hall

Modern British
Rushton, NN14 1RR
Tel no: (01536) 713001
www.rushtonhall.com
'Grand country house with faultless food'

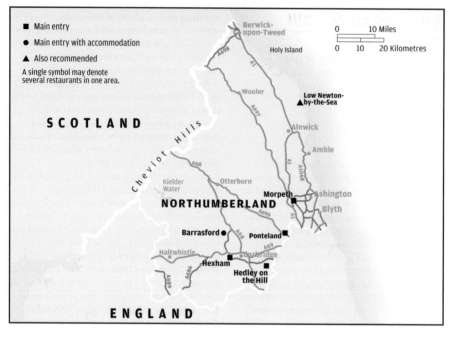

Barrasford

The Barrasford Arms

Local gastro grub cuts the mustard
Barrasford, NE48 4AA
Tel no: (01434) 681237
www.barrasfordarms.co.uk
Gastropub | £23
Cooking score: 2

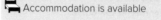

With the ruins of Haughton Castle and Hadrian's Wall just a hike away, the Barrasford Arms (circa 1870) isn't short on heritage. It also cuts the mustard as a gastropub with a sound reputation for unfussy food, thanks to Tony Binks' feel for locally sourced ingredients. A warm salad of Northumberland rabbit and black pudding is dressed up with apple and vanilla purée, North Shields halibut is given some Mediterranean warmth with sweet pepper and chorizo stew, and diehards can get stuck in to platefuls of suet-crusted steak, mushroom and ale pie. To finish, rice pudding with damson compote should set you up for some roaming. Corney & Barrow house wines are £13.50.

Chef/s: Tony Binks. **Open:** Tue to Sun L 12 to 2 (3 Sun), Mon to Sat D 6.30 to 9. **Closed:** 26 and 27 Dec, bank hols. **Meals:** alc (main courses £10 to £22). Set L £11.50 (2 courses) to £14.50. Sun L £13.50 (2 courses) to £16. **Service:** not inc. **Details:** Cards accepted. 65 seats. 40 seats outside. Separate bar. Wheelchair access. Music. Children allowed. Car parking.

Symbols

Accommodation is available

£30 Three courses for less than £30

V More than three vegetarian main courses

£5 OFF £5-off voucher scheme

Notable wine list

■ Hedley on the Hill
The Feathers Inn
Fashionably traditional food
Hedley on the Hill, NE43 7SW
Tel no: (01661) 843607
www.thefeathers.net
Gastropub | £30
Cooking score: 2

£5 OFF

This stone-built former drovers' inn has a beautiful hilltop village location and a welcoming family atmosphere. Locals fill the bar and local ingredients fill the daily changing menu. The cooking is fashionably traditional: you could kick off with potted North Sea brown shrimps with toast, watercress and lemon or homemade black pudding with a poached egg and devilled gravy, followed by braised roe deer with sprouting broccoli and dauphinoise potatoes, then rhubarb meringue pie for dessert. Service is 'friendly and efficient.' There's a great selection of beers and wines to wash it all down (from £11). **Chef/s:** Rhian Cradock. **Open:** Tue to Sun L 12 to 2 (2.30 Sun), Mon to Sat D 6 to 8.30 (8 Mon). **Closed:** 2 weeks Jan. **Meals:** alc (main courses £8 to £15). Sun L £12 to £17. **Service:** not inc. **Details:** Cards accepted. 40 seats. 24 seats outside. No music. Children allowed. Car parking.

■ Hexham
Bouchon Bistrot
Appealing bistro with no-frills French classics
4-6 Gilesgate, Hexham, NE46 3NJ
Tel no: (01434) 609943
www.bouchonbistrot.co.uk
French | £25
Cooking score: 4

£5 OFF £30

Just off the market square, in a rather stolid-looking stone building, Gregory Bureau's appealing French bistro offers unpretentious country cooking, the sort of place that would be populated with people eating *en famille* over the Channel. There are no-frills classic

offerings such as plates of charcuterie, king prawns in garlic butter, and roast chicken with green beans, bacon and tarragon cream sauce, but also some showier stuff too. Turbot with mussels in a lightly spiced jus, served with saffron pomme purée is one such, and there might also be lamb tagine with couscous and chickpeas for those ready to venture a little further afield. Finish with rum baba, tarte Tatin, or – spectacularly – with a clafoutis of griottine cherries served with pistachio ice cream and green Chartreuse. The mostly French wine list starts at £12.95 (£3.25 a glass). **Chef/s:** Nicolas Duhill. **Open:** Tue to Sat L 12 to 2, D 6 to 9.30. **Closed:** Sun, Mon, 10 days Feb. **Meals:** alc (main courses £12 to £19). Set L £9.95 (2 courses) to £12.95. Set D £12.95 (2 courses) to £14.95. **Service:** not inc. **Details:** Cards accepted. 150 seats. Air-con. Wheelchair access. Music. Children allowed. Car parking.

■ Low Newton-by-the-Sea
ALSO RECOMMENDED
▲ The Ship Inn
Newton Square, Low Newton-by-the-Sea, NE66 3EL
Tel no: (01665) 576262
www.shipinnnewton.co.uk
Gastropub

The whitewashed inn is set in a square of fishermen's cottages facing the sandy beach, and comes complete with its own micro-brewery next door. Its locally sourced menu is naturally big on seafood, including fresh dressed crab with herb salad (£8.50 as a starter), followed perhaps by sea bass in lemon butter with olive mash, chilli and fennel salsa, and roasted cherry tomatoes (£16.50). Finish with the 'serious' chocolate brownie, served with cream (£4.50). Wines from £14.25. Open all week, with seasonal variations (phone to check). Cash only.

█ Morpeth

Black Door Bar & Dining Rooms

Characterful restaurant with traditional food
59 Bridge Street, Morpeth, NE61 1PQ
Tel no: (01670) 516200
www.blackdoorbaranddiningrooms.co.uk
Modern British | £25
Cooking score: 2

V £30

This characterful restaurant comprises three floors of rustic furniture and eclectic décor, with plenty of room for lounging and drinking. A highlight of the menu is the 'to die for' chunky triple-cooked chips. 'Moist, flaky' haddock encased in a crisp batter impressed one reader, as did a hearty plateful of steak and kidney pudding. More ambitious offerings include sugar-cured salmon with fennel, honey and mustard, followed by crispy confit duck with smoked bacon and heritage potatoes. Desserts sing from the same traditional/classic songsheet with the likes of sticky toffee pudding or crème brûlée. An international wine list opens at £9.75
Chef/s: David Kennedy. **Open:** all week L 12 to 3 (5 Sun), Mon to Sat D 5 to 9.30. **Closed:** 25 to 26 Dec, 1 to 2 Jan. **Meals:** alc (main courses £7 to £11). **Service:** not inc. **Details:** Cards accepted. 90 seats. Air-con. Separate bar. Wheelchair access. Music. Children allowed.

█ Ovington

READERS RECOMMEND
Winships Restaurant
Modern European
Main Road, Ovington, NE42 6DH
Tel no: (01661) 835099
www.winships-ovington.co.uk
'Each course was beautifully presented and simply scrumptious'

█ Ponteland

Café Lowrey

An understated bistro with flair
33-35 The Broadway, Darras Hall, Ponteland, NE20 9PW
Tel no: (01661) 820357
www.cafelowrey.co.uk
Modern British | £25
Cooking score: 4

£30

Set in the well-to-do estate of Darras Hall, a couple of miles from Newcastle airport, Ian Lowrey's place is an understated, softly lit venue, with some diverting artworks on display. It's the very image of a modern bistro, and the cooking reflects that, with a host of simple but effective dishes. Chilli salt squid or crayfish cocktail are among the starters, with mains such as fishcakes and chips with parsley sauce, or duck confit with mustard mash, rosemary and thyme jus following on. As in all bistros, there is occasionally something a little grander – perhaps pheasant breast wrapped in Parma ham with braised Savoy cabbage – but desserts return to the tried-and-true with treacle tart or plum crumble and vanilla ice cream. It's all done with appreciable flair, and comes with a short wine list at wholly reasonable prices. Bottles start at £13.95.
Chef/s: Ian Lowrey. **Open:** Sat and Sun L 12 to 2, Tue to Sat D 5.30 to 10 (6 Sat). **Closed:** bank hols. **Meals:** alc (main courses £13 to £23). Set L and D £13.50 (2 courses) to £16.95. **Service:** not inc. **Details:** Cards accepted. 70 seats. Air-con. Wheelchair access. Music. Children allowed. Car parking.

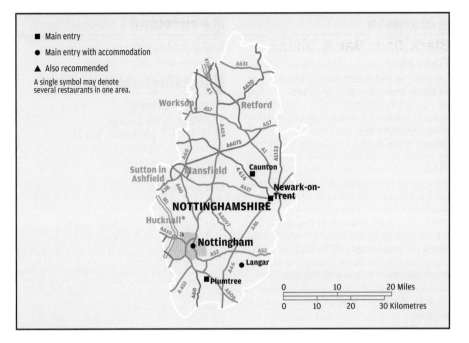

- ■ Main entry
- ● Main entry with accommodation
- ▲ Also recommended

A single symbol may denote several restaurants in one area.

■ Caunton

Caunton Beck

Pub that pulls out all the stops
Main Street, Caunton, NG23 6AB
Tel no: (01636) 636793
www.wigandmitre.com
Modern British | £27
Cooking score: 2

£5 OFF **V** £30

It still lives up to its title of freehouse, dispensing real ales and pub hospitality, but elsewhere this extended sixteenth-century cottage pulls out all the stops for customers in search of food. The day begins at 8am with breakfast and food is available all day. Unusual considering that, apart from the odd car, bountiful birdsong and a babbling beck, this is a peaceful, rural spot. The kitchen prides itself on good ingredients and the expertise shows in twice-baked smoked haddock and spring leek soufflé, and lemon and marjoram roast leg of chicken with sauté of courgettes and sun-blushed tomatoes. Wines from £13.45.

Chef/s: Valerie Hope and Andy Pickstock. **Open:** all week 8am to 10pm. **Meals:** alc (main courses £13 to £16). Set L and D £12.50 (2 courses) to £14.95. Sun D £22.50. **Service:** not inc. **Details:** Cards accepted. 84 seats. 32 seats outside. Separate bar. No music. Wheelchair access. Children allowed. Car parking.

■ Langar

Langar Hall

Peaceful idyll with professional food
Church Lane, Langar, NG13 9HG
Tel no: (01949) 860559
www.langarhall.com
Anglo-French | £35
Cooking score: 4

For more than 25 years, Imogen Skirving has imbued this distinctive early-Victorian mansion with her own personality – in fact Langar Hall still feels a bit like some rather grand family home from days gone by. After a leisurely drive past medieval ponds and croquet lawns, guests enter a world where marble pillars, crystal chandeliers and statues are the backdrop to a peaceful idyll that comes with some very creditable, professionally executed food. Langar lamb remains the star of the show (perhaps served as a trio accompanied by bubble and squeak, smoked garlic, carrot and swede mash), although char-grilled haunch of venison or steamed halibut fillet with vermouth sauce might also tempt. Begin rustically with braised pig's cheek and ox tongue with celeriac rémoulade, and finish in fancy style with passion-fruit soufflé and bitter chocolate sorbet. The well-spread wine list includes a clutch of Imogen's personal recommendations from £19.95.

Chef/s: Gary Booth. **Open:** all week L 12 to 2, D 7 to 9.30 (6.30 to 10 Fri and Sat, 6.30 to 8.30 Sun). **Meals:** alc (main courses £12 to £28). Set L £15 (2 courses) to £20. Set D £20 (2 courses) to £25. Sun L £27.50. **Service:** 10% (optional). **Details:** Cards accepted. 70 seats. 20 seats outside. Separate bar. No music. Wheelchair access. Children allowed. Car parking.

Newark-on-Trent

Café Bleu
Colourful bistro favourite
14 Castle Gate, Newark-on-Trent, NG24 1BG
Tel no: (01636) 610141
www.cafebleu.co.uk
Modern European | £29
Cooking score: 1
£5 OFF £30

Down by the riverside and close to the castle ruins, colourful Café Bleu has been Newark's favourite bistro for more than 15 years. Tables outside are at a premium, the happy atmosphere is helped along by live jazz and the food strikes a vibrant note. The kitchen casts its net wide, pulling in seared tuna loin with tabbouleh, as well as chicken ballottine with tarragon mousse or braised blade of beef with parsnip purée and foie gras cream. For dessert, tarte Tatin with five-spice ice cream might appeal. House wines are £12.95.

Chef/s: Mark Cheseldine. **Open:** all week L 12 to 2.30 (2 Sat, 3 Sun), Mon to Sat D 7 to 9.30 (6.30 to 10 Sat). **Closed:** 25 to 30 Dec, 2 to 5 Jan. **Meals:** alc

(main courses £9 to £19). **Service:** not inc. **Details:** Cards accepted. 80 seats. 50 seats outside. Wheelchair access. Music. Children allowed.

Nottingham

French Living
A patriotic foodie package
27 King Street, Nottingham, NG1 2AY
Tel no: (0115) 9585885
www.frenchliving.co.uk
French | £20
Cooking score: 1
£30

The traditional English take on a French city bistro is alive and well in this bustling red-brick eatery in the basement of a well-stocked deli/café. The main menu, supplemented by blackboard set deals, combines basic crowd-pleasers (gratinée à l'oignon, moules), with classic regional dishes (tartiflette, cassoulet toulousain). There's also onglet (steak) with shallot and veal sauce and wild boar casserole in a rich red wine sauce, with tartelette au chocolat or excellent unpasteurised Gallic cheeses to finish. House French is £10.50.

Chef/s: Jeremy Tourne. **Open:** Tue to Sat L 12 to 2 (2.30 Sat), D 6 to 10. **Closed:** Sun, Mon, 25 Dec to 1 Jan. **Meals:** alc (main courses £12 to £17). Set L £8.50 (2 courses) to £10.50. Pre-theatre set D £7.90 (1 course) to £12.50. Set D £21.50. **Service:** not inc. **Details:** Cards accepted. 40 seats. Air-con. Music. Children allowed.

Hart's
Edgy food that's full of life
Standard Court, Park Row, Nottingham, NG1 6GN
Tel no: (0115) 9110666
www.hartsnottingham.co.uk
Modern British | £35
Cooking score: 5
£5 OFF 🍷 🚃 V

'Elegant' seems a fair description of this spacious, gracious contemporary dining room which occupies the ground floor of the delightfully understated (and listed) former General Hospital. This is Tim Hart's

Nottingham venture (see also Hambleton Hall, Leicestershire and Rutland) and his determination is impressive. So too, 14 years on, is his consistency. Chefs may come and go, but the menu always has an edge that gives life to many dishes. It's particularly strong on local produce and seasonal ingredients – reports have praised a 'robust' partridge terrine, and described smoked eel with beetroot, liquorice and apple soaked in rose water as 'exemplary in terms of its balance and counterpoint of flavour'. Fish cookery includes fried hake with sauté potatoes, spinach, beurre noisette and toasted hazelnuts ('a simple dish but perfectly executed'), and success continues with roast duck breast, fondant potato, celeriac purée and red cabbage forestière, via the good-value set lunch – 'seared tuna was as good as it gets and was worth twice the price' – right through to Yorkshire rhubarb and custard with gingerbread ice cream. The knowledgeably assembled wine list is defined by value and diversity, with bottles from £17.50.
Chef/s: Tom Earle. **Open:** all week L 12 to 2, D 6 to 10 (9 Sun). **Closed:** 1 Jan. **Meals:** alc (main courses £16 to £23). Set L £13.95 (2 courses) to £16.95. Set D £25. Pre-theatre £18 (2 courses). Sun L £22. **Service:** 12% (optional). **Details:** Cards accepted. 80 seats. 15 seats outside. Separate bar. No music. No mobile phones. Wheelchair access. Children allowed.

NEW ENTRY
The Larder on Goosegate
Seasonal food that makes a big impact
1st Floor, 16-22 Goosegate, Hockley, Nottingham, NG1 1FE
Tel no: (0115) 9500111
www.thelarderongoosegate.co.uk
Modern British | £25
Cooking score: 2
£5 OFF £30

This listed Victorian building was once home to a small herbalist's shop, the first outlet in the Boots the Chemist empire. The kitchen makes the most of seasonal (and local) ingredients, and has really made an impact with a repertoire that kicks off with beetroot, spring onion and creamy goats' curd salad or asparagus with soft poached egg and smoked Poacher Cheddar – Ewan McFarlane was a vegetarian for 10 years and that shines through on his menus. Grilled sole with lemon zest mash, sea kale and brown shrimp butter could follow, or choose from a steak menu that features 100% grass-fed Aberdeen Angus aged on the bone for 28 days. Finish with caramel parfait. Wines from £12.
Chef/s: Ewan McFarlane. **Open:** Tue to Sun L 12 to 2.00 (2.30 Sun), Tue to Sat D 6 to 10. **Closed:** Mon, first week Jan. **Meals:** alc (main courses £10 to £19). Set L and D £12.95 (2 courses) to £14.95. **Service:** not inc. **Details:** Cards accepted. 60 seats. Air-con. Music. Children allowed.

Restaurant 1877
Interesting menu and excellent service
128 Derby Road, Canning Circus, Nottingham, NG1 5FB
Tel no: (0115) 9588008
www.restaurant1877.com
Modern British | £25
Cooking score: 2
£30

Looking smart and fashionable, this modern-day 'traditional English restaurant' gets marks for its excellent service and interesting menu. It sets its sights on an appealing mix of both established and contemporary ideas, with excellent regional produce featuring prominently but not exclusively. Chicken liver pâté or asparagus with poached egg and hollandaise lead on to main courses such as wild sea bass with saffron potatoes, vanilla leeks and lobster sauce or honey-glazed duck breast with pot-roast potato, wilted spinach and orange sauce. Bakewell tart makes a good finish. Wine from £16.
Chef/s: Tony Baxter. **Open:** Sat and Sun L 12 to 2, Mon to Sat D 5 to 10. **Closed:** 25 and 26 Dec, 1 Jan. **Meals:** alc (main courses £10 to £17). Set L and pre-theatre D £9.95. Sun L £9.95 (2 courses) to £16.95. **Service:** 10% (optional). **Details:** Cards accepted. 65 seats. Air-con. Wheelchair access. Music. Children allowed.

Restaurant Sat Bains

Breathlessly original food from a star chef
Lenton Lane, Nottingham, NG7 2SA
Tel no: (0115) 9866566
www.restaurantsatbains.com
Modern European | £69
Cooking score: 8

It sounds almost too surreal to be true: a boundary-pushing restaurant-with-rooms in a collection of converted barns near the Nottingham ring road, with electricity pylons and a flyover for company and an English-born Sikh turning out breathlessly original food. Mind you, Sat Bains is very much his own man, a chef who is always moving onward and upward. His daring culinary style continues to evolve beyond the shock of the new as he explores the telling possibilities of taste, texture and temperature: if that smacks of dry, arcane alchemy, fear not – this is thrilling stuff, guaranteed to make you think about food afresh. Three tasting menus of increasing complexity are now colour-coded to highlight the dominant tastes in each tersely described dish – allowing diners to plot a fascinating course from, say, a clever amuse of sweetcorn velouté floated with crunchy popcorn to a restrained sweet/sour finale involving al dente Yorkshire rhubarb with tarragon and basil granita – the gentlest of 'warm-downs' for the palate. Lifting standouts from the cohesive whole almost misses the point, but two star turns from recent meals prove why Sat Bains is heading towards the very top of the gastronomic tree. First, a perfectly balanced dish of organic salmon matched with oyster emulsion, parsley, radish and passion fruit, then a combination of magnificently tender Cumbrian lamb with lemon confit, goats' cheese and black olive that swept through the entire 'taste spectrum'. As this unique culinary odyssey proceeds, the savoury main event is followed by a 'crossover' – nothing to do with fusion, but an interface intended to recalibrate the taste-buds before sweetness takes over: it might be a dish of tiny figs with a blob of pine-nut ice cream and a sprinkling of English Parmesan. Desserts avoid the predictable sugar rush and calorie overload with some revelatory creations: taste the magic as bland rapeseed oil jelly is shocked into fizzy life on the tongue, thanks to a combination of rich chocolate ice cream, perfumed candied violets and rose petals. Service continues to improve, and it has taken on a more relaxed, engaging tone of late; all the details are in place – even if the corporate hotel Muzak grates. The carefully annotated wine list is a gem although there's precious little below £25, but glorious drinking awaits in the upper regions.
Chef/s: Sat Bains. **Open:** Tue to Sat D only 7 to 8.30. **Closed:** Sun, Mon, 1 week spring, 2 weeks summer, 2 weeks winter. **Meals:** Tasting menu £55 (5 courses, Tue to Thur only), £69 (7 courses), £85 (10 courses). **Service:** 12.5%. **Details:** Cards accepted. 42 seats. Air-con. Separate bar. Music. Car parking.

World Service

Complex dishes with first-class ingredients
Newdigate House, Castle Gate, Nottingham, NG1 6AF
Tel no: (0115) 8475587
www.worldservicerestaurant.com
Modern British | £40
Cooking score: 3
£5
OFF

Behind the high front wall in a street close to the castle is an architectural and decorative hotchpotch. A Japanese-style pebble garden and paved terrace give way to a modern extension to seventeenth-century Newdigate House, where a panelled bar, restrained colours and oriental artefacts create a look that coalesces into contemporary. Dishes can often be complex – perhaps organic salmon with cucumber, liquorice, tomato and gazpacho dressing, followed by duck breast with carrot and ginger purée, pak choi, confit potato, picked carrot and spiced port sauce – but materials are first-class and the kitchen competent. Puddings include warm cherry Bakewell with vanilla yoghurt and yoghurt sorbet. House wine is £16.

Chef/s: Garry Hewitt. **Open:** all week L 12 to 2 (2.30 Sun), 7 to 10 (6.30 Sat, 7 to 9 Sun). **Closed:** 25 and 26 Dec, first week Jan. **Meals:** alc (main courses £16 to £24). Set L £13 (2 courses) to £17.50. Set D Sun only £16.50 (2 courses) to £21. Sun L £18. **Service:** 10% (optional). **Details:** Cards accepted. 80 seats. 30 seats outside. Air-con. Separate bar. Music.

ALSO RECOMMENDED
▲ Delilah
15 Middle Pavement, Nottingham, NG1 7DX
Tel no: (0115) 9484461
www.delilahfinefoods.co.uk
Café

This amply stocked, independent deli in the centre of Nottingham has been plying its trade for six years, and its nine-stool food counter at the back of the shop draws a loyal following. The cooking might be described as Mediterranean with additions, offering breakfast of poached eggs with hollandaise sauce, crispy pancetta and thick rustic toast (£5.95) then rest-of-the-day selections of sandwiches, cheese and charcuterie platters and the likes of bruschetta with char-grilled chorizo, feta and red peppers (£5.95) or classic niçoise salad (£7.95). Wines from £12.95. Open all week.

▲ Iberico World Tapas
Shire Hall, High Pavement, Nottingham, NG1 1HN
Tel no: (0115) 9410410
www.ibericotapas.com
Spanish/Tapas £5 OFF

Out of the stable that owns World Service (see entry) this vaulted, elaborately tiled basement below the old courthouse is the sort of place where the congenial atmosphere and well-practised menu draw the crowds. Choice is divided between Iberian classics and world tapas – in other words tortilla (£4.50), chorizo or gambas à la plancha alongside Italian charcuterie, agedashi tofu or black cod with spicy miso (£8). Finish with sweet yuzu yogurt, rhubarb compote and ginger biscuit (£5). House wine is £15.50. Closed Sun and Mon.

▮ Plumtree
Perkins
Plenty to choo-choo choose from
Station House, Station Road, Plumtree, NG12 5NA
Tel no: (0115) 9373695
www.perkinsrestaurant.co.uk
Modern European | £28
Cooking score: 2
V £30

It's all change at this former Victorian railway station – a complete refurbishment has seen the addition of a private dining room and chef's table and there's a longer, flexible menu format. 'Perkins sleepers' are tapas-style selections to share – the classic of prawn salad, plaice goujons and lemon mayonnaise, their own smokehouse mushroom and Brie on garlic toast 'was beautifully presented and extremely tasty'. Navarin of lamb has been praised, but the new menu format has drawn some criticism, and inspection highlighted some bland and ill-conceived dishes. However, chocolate fondant is 'well worth the extra 10 minutes' wait' and good service goes a long way to make amends. House wine £14.50.
Chef/s: Sarah Newham. **Open:** all week L 12 to 2 (3.30 Sun), Mon to Sat D 6 to 10. **Meals:** alc (main courses £10 to £21). Set L £12 (2 courses) to £14.50. Set D £18.50 (2 courses) to £21.50. Sun L £14.95 (2 courses) to £18.50. **Service:** not inc. **Details:** Cards accepted. 76 seats. 20 seats outside. Air-con. Separate bar. Wheelchair access. Music. Children allowed. Car parking.

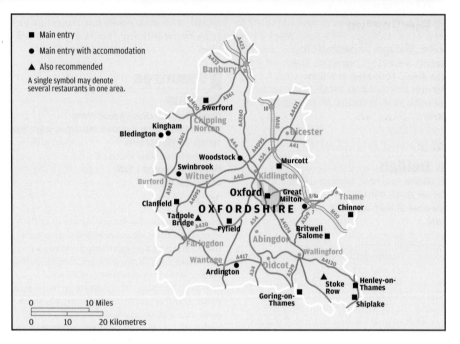

- ■ Main entry
- ● Main entry with accommodation
- ▲ Also recommended

A single symbol may denote several restaurants in one area.

0   10 Miles
0   10   20 Kilometres

■ Ardington

The Boar's Head

Pretty timber-framed all-rounder
Church Street, Ardington, OX12 8QA
Tel no: (01235) 833254
www.boarsheadardington.co.uk
Modern British | £30
Cooking score: 3

£5 OFF 🛏

Set in an unspoiled village on the Oxon/Berks border, the half-timbered Boar's Head manages to combine its dual roles as local hostelry and upscale eatery with agility. Bright primary colours set a cheering tone in the dining area, and Bruce Buchan's food strikes many alluring modern British chords. Confit of lightly spiced salmon with lentils, or a classic teaming of scallops, black pudding and foie gras might be the prelude to a carefully worked main course such as medallions of roe deer with fig Tatin and fondant potato. Readers are happy to note that the kitchen can adapt to individual requests, and meals end indulgently with, say, steamed date and walnut pudding with toffee sauce and vanilla ice cream. Wines from an extensive list start at £16.90.
Chef/s: Bruce Buchan. **Open:** all week L 12 to 2 (4 Sun), D 7 to 9.30 (8.30 Sun). **Closed:** 26 Dec, 1 Jan. **Meals:** alc (main courses £17 to £25). Set L £15 (2 courses) to £18.50. Sun L £23.50. Tasting menu £39.50. **Service:** not inc. **Details:** Cards accepted. 35 seats. 32 seats outside. Separate bar. Wheelchair access. Music. Children allowed. Car parking.

Symbols

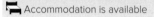

🛏 Accommodation is available

£30 Three courses for less than £30

V More than three vegetarian main courses

£5 OFF £5-off voucher scheme

🍾 Notable wine list

Bledington

The Kings Head Inn

Sensitive cooking in an idyllic spot
The Green, Bledington, OX7 6XQ
Tel no: (01608) 658365
www.thekingsheadinn.net
Modern British | £25
Cooking score: 2

🛏 £30

The setting is as attractive as ever: a honey-hued sixteenth-century former cider house overlooking Bledington's green. It's no backwoods watering hole, however, but a strongly rooted enterprise, a combination of pub and serious restaurant. Raw materials are consistently good (meat comes from the family farm at Fifield) and unflashy elements, such as chicken liver parfait or Baltic-cured sea trout with beetroot relish and sour cream, are allowed to shine. Straightforward main courses bring whole baked lemon sole with brown shrimp dressing or free-range chicken breast with chorizo and leek tartiflette, with caramelised rhubarb and custard with rhubarb schnapps to finish. House wine is £14.
Chef/s: Charlie Loader. **Open:** all week L 12 to 2 (2.30 Sat and Sun), D 7 to 9 (9.30 Fri and Sat). **Closed:** 25 and 26 Dec. **Meals:** alc (main courses £10 to £20). Sun L £13. **Service:** not inc. **Details:** Cards accepted. 76 seats. 44 seats outside. Separate bar. Wheelchair access. Music. Children allowed. Car parking.

Britwell Salome

The Goose

Smartly converted country pub
Britwell Salome, OX49 5LG
Tel no: (01491) 612304
www.thegoosebritwellsalome.com
Modern British | £33
Cooking score: 4

V

Following chef Ryan Simpson's move to Orwells in Shiplake (see entry), there has been something of a shake-up at this smartly converted country pub. You can now choose from 'light meals' (aka sublime bar food such as gooey-centred Scotch egg on spinach with celeriac purée and bacon foam), a keenly priced set menu, or the more adventurous carte – or indeed a mix from all three. A main course of precisely cooked turbot tranche resting on braised fennel with Jersey Royals, flavourful red wine jus and lemon beurre blanc shows the style, and a perfectly executed apricot soufflé proves that the kitchen has plenty of know-how in the technical department. Service is generally solicitous, if a mite confused at times. Behind its modest brick frontage, the Goose offers comfy sofas and small wooden tables in the bar, and more formality in the diminutive, low-beamed restaurant; otherwise, there is space out on the patio. Wine starts at £16.50, but watch out for bin-end deals.
Chef/s: John Footman. **Open:** Tue to Sun L 12 to 2.30 (3.30 Sat and Sun), Tue to Sat D 7 to 9.30. **Closed:** Mon, 3 to 18 Jan, 2 to 17 Aug. **Meals:** alc (main courses £11 to £25). Set L and D £14.95 (2 courses) to £17.95. Sun L £21.95 (2 courses) to £25.95. **Service:** not inc. **Details:** Cards accepted. 40 seats. 20 seats outside. Separate bar. Music. Children allowed. Car parking.

Chinnor

The Sir Charles Napier

One-off, irresistible charmer
Sprigg's Alley, Chinnor, OX39 4BX
Tel no: (01494) 483011
www.sircharlesnapier.co.uk
Modern British | £35
Cooking score: 4

🍾

Whether it's a dreamy repast under the pergolas or a snug-as-a-bug winter's evening amid the surreal sculptures and crazy curios, the Napier never seems to fail. That said, those who visit this heartfelt homage to hospitality expecting a 'quickie' are likely to be disappointed; time – and plenty of it – is of the essence, and ever-dutiful Julie Griffiths is not about to rush anyone. The kitchen continues on its merry seasonal way, serving up local lamb cutlets with crushed peas in

springtime, juicy Cornish lobsters with samphire during the summer and game by the bagful come winter – perhaps 'unbelievably moist' mallard with a deep, dark riot of beetroot, quince purée and elderberry jus. There are also bountiful harvests of foraged fungi (how about char-grilled giant puffball with salsa verde?) and signs of some increasingly assured fish cookery – a gentle fricassee of sweet freshwater crayfish with chanterelles and lovage, for example. Puds are invariably a treat (peanut butter parfait with blackcurrant sorbet is a current wow) and the big tray of ripe cheeses whiffs invitingly. The wine list shows an oenophile's passion, with France, California and the Antipodes shining particularly brightly. Tantalising house selections start at £15.95 (£4 a glass).
Chef/s: Sam Hughes. **Open:** Tue to Sun L 11.30 to 2.30 (3.30 Sun), Tue to Sat D 6 to 9.30. **Closed:** Mon, 4 days Christmas. **Meals:** alc (main courses £17 to £28). ·Set L Tue to Fri £14.50 (2 courses). Set D Tue to Thur £15.50 (2 courses). **Service:** 12.5% (optional). **Details:** Cards accepted. 70 seats. 60 seats outside. Air-con. Separate bar. No mobile phones. Music. Children allowed. Car parking.

▌Clanfield

Clanfield Tavern
Pub that ticks the right boxes
Bampton Road, Clanfield, OX18 2RG
Tel no: (01367) 810223
www.clanfieldtavern.com
Gastropub | £20
Cooking score: 2
£5 £30
OFF

This low-slung, seventeenth-century Cotswold village inn ticks all the right boxes, with its crackling winter fires, flagstoned floors and low oak beams. The interior might suggest Dr Johnson's local watering hole, but there's nothing portentously archaic about the food on offer these days. Seared smoked Shetland trout with capers and cress, braised pork belly with pickled pear, cabbage and cider gravy, and iced passion-fruit soufflé with poached apricots could well be the order of the

day. Dishes are annotated with suggested beer matches, but for wine buffs the list opens at £12.50.
Chef/s: Nick Seckington. **Open:** Tue to Sun L 12 to 3, Tue to Sat D 6 to 9 (9.30 Fri and Sat). **Closed:** Mon. **Meals:** alc (main courses £8 to £25). Set L £10 (2 courses). Set D £12.95 (2 courses). Sun L £14.95. **Service:** not inc. **Details:** Cards accepted. 90 seats. 40 seats outside. Separate bar. No mobile phones. Wheelchair access. Music. Children allowed. Car parking.

▌Fyfield

The White Hart
Assured cooking with a Mediterranean touch
Main Road, Fyfield, OX13 5LW
Tel no: (01865) 390585
www.whitehart-fyfield.com
Modern British | £27
Cooking score: 2
£5 £30
OFF

The fifteenth-century White Hart is an immaculately maintained pub with a kitchen that cares about the provenance of its supplies, so much so that the owners have developed a large kitchen garden. Mediterranean influences loom large on the daily changing menus, as in a neat starter of sautéed baby squid with couscous and gremolata. The quality also shows in homespun dishes such as slow-roasted belly of pork with celeriac purée, cider jus and the crispiest of crackling or braised lamb shoulder with dauphinoise potatoes, Savoy cabbage, beer and bacon. To finish, there are treats including apple and Calvados mousse with cinnamon shortbread. The wine list provides fair back-up at prices starting from £16.
Chef/s: Mark Chandler. **Open:** Tue to Sun L 12 to 2.30 (3.30 Sun), Tue to Sat D 6.45 to 9.30. **Closed:** Mon. **Meals:** alc (main courses £12 to £20). Set L £15 (2 courses) to £18. Sun L £17 (2 courses) to £20. **Service:** not inc. **Details:** Cards accepted. 45 seats. 50 seats outside. Separate bar. Music. Children allowed. Car parking.

Goring-on-Thames

Leatherne Bottel

Delightful waterside dining

The Bridleway, Goring-on-Thames, RG8 0HS

Tel no: (01491) 872667

www.leathernebottel.co.uk

Modern European | £45

Cooking score: 3

£5 OFF

There's a sense of true dedication about Julia Abbey's bucolic restaurant on the banks of the Thames (waterside tables in summer offer a spectacular view), and she's still drawing the crowds 14 years on. The feel is relaxed, and menus of a sensible length keep things simple but maintain interest, focusing on showing off good raw materials. A winter meal produced marinated beetroot with soft goats' cheese curd, salad shoots and good honeyed hazelnut dressing, and a successful partnership of roast fillet of wild sea bass with crab and herb risotto and sweet chilli jam. That meal finished with dark chocolate délice with raspberry pâté and gianduja (hazelnut chocolate) ice cream. The French-led wine list (with shorter selections from elsewhere) opens with house vin de pays at £20.

Chef/s: Julia Abbey. **Open:** all week L 12 to 2.15 (3 Sun), Mon to Sat D 7 to 9 (9.30 Sat). **Meals:** alc (main courses £16 to £25). Set L £14.50 (2 courses) to £18.50. Sun L £29.50. Tasting menu £65. **Service:** 10%. **Details:** Cards accepted. 40 seats. 60 seats outside. Separate bar. No music. No mobile phones. Wheelchair access. Children allowed. Car parking.

Please send us your feedback

To register your opinion about any restaurant listed in the Guide, or a new restaurant that you wish to bring to our attention, please visit the web address at the bottom of the page. Your feedback informs the content of the book and will be used to compile next year's reviews.

Raymond Blanc Le Manoir aux Quat'Saisons

What is your earliest culinary memory?

My childhood was probably a cliché of French rural life. It established the foundation and structure of my approach as much to cuisine as to people. At the age of seven, my father took me to the garden, made me take a handful of earth, look at it, smell it, taste it! And of course, I was very much involved in all the toiling in the garden, whilst my friends were playing football. Then the vegetables would be picked, topped and tailed and cooked by Maman Blanc and much of it bottled for the winter. This was a true cottage industry. From the age of seven, I was also a hunter-gatherer across the woods and fields of Franche-Comté. All was for the taking: mushrooms, chanterelles, wild asparagus, escargots, frogs. All that we picked would be handed to Maman Blanc for a simple creative act of cooking and the rest sold on the side of the road. This was the foundation of my philosophy and my cooking and also made me a rich man by the age of ten!

What would be your perfect birthday meal?

My sixtieth birthday last year, where four of my best friends, chefs: Gary Jones, Bruno Loubet, Michael Caines and Clive Fretwell cooked a special menu for me... I had to wait 60 years for it.

Great Milton

Le Manoir aux Quat'Saisons

'Close to heaven'
Church Road, Great Milton, OX44 7PD
Tel no: (01844) 278881
www.manoir.com
Modern French | £95
Cooking score: 8

🍷 🍴 V

Raymond Blanc's enchanting homage to the blue-blooded good life continues to cast a spell, more than three decades after Le Manoir opened its doors deep in the sleepy Oxfordshire countryside. The mellow stone manor house is an absolute dream, a vision of loveliness and pure escapism sustained by the prospect of unbridled cosseting and pleasure – if only for a few hours. 'Très calme' is one way of describing its uniquely enthralling atmosphere, and there are gently seductive distractions all around – whether you are taking a lazy stroll through the fragrant gardens, trying your hand at croquet or partaking of that most English pastime, afternoon tea. Everyone squirrels away their own special memories, but it is the food that garners most ecstatic comments: 'close to heaven' and 'Olympic gold for a voyage of discovery' are just two superlative verdicts from recent feedback. The kitchen reflects Raymond Blanc's all-embracing vision of 'sustainable harmony' and it can deliver world-class food. By definition the cooking adheres to the modern French credo, but it also courts influences from distant lands – witness braised Cornish brill with scallops, wild asparagus and wasabi, a terrine of langoustines with Japanese savoury custard or exquisite fruit-filled ravioli with Kaffir lime leaves and coconut jus. Clarity, lightness, balance and natural intensity are the culinary watchwords for food that doesn't demand finicky analysis. There are no sense-jarring collisions or scary 'nitro' shocks here. Instead, diners can relish the unashamed gratification of enlightened

food without attitude – perhaps beetroot terrine with horseradish and dill cream, a heaven-sent marriage of scallops with sea kale and cauliflower three ways, or a good-natured seasonal classic involving roast Laverstoke lamb loin with vegetables, sweet garlic purée and a spoonful of roasting juices. As you might expect, desserts make the prettiest impression – perhaps three little tempters fashioned from Valrhona chocolate Grand Cru or the finest croustade pastry with caramelised Braeburn apples, honey and ginger ice cream. Super-smooth, ever-attentive service contributes to 'one of the most enjoyable dining experiences you could imagine', and helpful sommeliers play their full part in proceedings. The fabulous wine list celebrates French regional diversity in loving detail, acknowledging the great and the good as well as 'terroir' innovation. Otherwise it shows off gems from across the globe, with a tilt towards the Manoir's increasingly green agenda. Prices rise skywards from £30.

Chef/s: Raymond Blanc and Gary Jones. Open: all week L 12 to 2.30, D 7 to 10. Meals: Set L £52.50. Set menus L and D £95 to £125. Service: not inc. Details: Cards accepted. 90 seats. Air-con. Separate bar. No music. No mobile phones. Wheelchair access. Children allowed. Car parking.

Henley-on-Thames

NEW ENTRY

The Three Tuns

Touchstone ideas and clear flavours
5 Market Place, Henley-on-Thames, RG9 2AA
Tel no: (01491) 411588
Modern British | £30
Cooking score: 5

The building is centuries old and its charm lies in its tiny size. Visitors enthuse about the unpretentious informality of what was, by all accounts, 'a bit of a beat-up old boozer'. Simon Bonwick was last seen cooking at the Black Boys Inn, Hurley, but is now to be spotted through a hatch working away in what he describes as 'the smallest kitchen I have ever worked in'. It's his first solo venture and reports praise the short, contemporary menu with plenty of touchstone ideas, good ingredients and clear flavours – think 'simply perfect' torchon of goose liver with intense peach chutney, and 'first-class' goats' curd given texture with pickled roots and macadamia nuts. Main courses might offer a brilliantly rendered piece of beef cheek 'of the deepest burgundy colour', served with pommes purée 'as good as Joël Robuchon's' or a clean-flavoured dish of hake with crushed potatoes 'tartare' and hake bouillon. Desserts can also be first-rate, judging by a refreshingly light lemon posset with lemon curd madeleines, and a 'rich and inviting' chocolate mousse 'Michel Cluizel'. House recommendations from £14.

Chef/s: Simon Bonwick. **Open:** Tue to Sat L 12 to 2, D 6 to 9. **Closed:** Mon, 1 week Christmas, 1 week Aug. **Meals:** alc (main courses £13 to £16). **Service:** not inc. **Details:** Cards accepted. 24 seats. 10 seats outside. Separate bar. No music. No mobile phones. Wheelchair access. Children allowed.

READERS RECOMMEND

Le Parisien

French
50 Bell Street, Henley-on-Thames, RG9 2BG
Tel no: (01491) 571115
www.brillant.co.uk
'Small local restaurant run by chef/patron Philippe Brillant – his cooking is excellent'

▌Kingham

The Kingham Plough

Upper-crust country pub
The Green, Kingham, OX7 6YD
Tel no: (01608) 658327
www.thekinghamplough.co.uk
Modern British | £28
Cooking score: 3
🛏 £30

Behind a honey-hued façade by Kingham's handsome green, this renovated Cotswold pub sports scrubbed beams, rattan flooring and a shabby-chic dining room with leather

chairs fashionably 'in tatters'. Moneyed locals sip wine, or occasionally ale, at the little bar. Chef Emily Lampson (née Watkins) has an unfussy approach, treating prime ingredients with consideration. In spring, fluffy scrambled duck egg on toast might be boosted by flavoursome St George's mushrooms. Main courses could be poached cod paired with 'scotched' salt-cod quail's egg, or expertly fried lamb's sweetbreads and breast lifted by luscious gravy (though glutinous mash and salty spring greens provided little counterbalance). Rhubarb baked Alaska on dry sponge has also disappointed. At inspection, staff were prompt and willing, but other reports cite 'unresponsive' service. House wine is £16.

Chef/s: Emily Lampson. **Open:** all week L 12 to 2 (2.30 Sun), Mon to Sat D 7 to 9. **Closed:** 25 Dec. **Meals:** alc (main courses £12 to £24). **Service:** not inc. **Details:** Cards accepted. 74 seats. 24 seats outside. Separate bar. No music. Wheelchair access. Children allowed. Car parking.

▌Murcott

The Nut Tree Inn

Food with deep seasonal goodness
Main Street, Murcott, OX5 2RE
Tel no: (01865) 331253
www.nuttreeinn.co.uk
Modern British | £35
Cooking score: 5
£5
OFF

Such has been the Nut Tree's success since Michael and Imogen North took over this prodigiously picturesque sixteenth-century thatched pub in 2006, that it has recently opened an extension and sheltered patio. So, as well as the low-ceilinged bar (replete with beams, real ales, leather armchairs and loquacious locals), and the equally snug dining room, there's now a sleek new space with quarry-tiled floor, white walls and reclaimed brick fireplace. Whatever the location, Michael North's food shines with seasonal goodness and remarkable depth of flavour. Salmon is smoked on the premises, and much of the beef and pork is home-reared. Perhaps start with grilled scallops, cauliflower 'couscous' and curry oil, followed by a rich, gorgeously fatty slab of crisp-topped belly pork (from pigs that forage in the large garden), accompanied by potato purée, apple gravy and a vernal assembly of pea shoots, asparagus, peas and broad beans. 'Scrummy' passion-fruit soufflé has been much-lauded, as has the 'friendly and attentive' service. Further options include a well-priced set lunch and bar snacks (wild mushrooms on toast, say). Wines (from £15.95) show up well, especially the 'perfectly chosen' selection to match the tasting menu.

Chef/s: Michael North. **Open:** Tue to Sun L 12 to 2.30 (3 Sun), Tue to Sat D 7 to 9. **Closed:** Mon. **Meals:** alc (main courses £16 to £25). Set L and D £15 (2 courses) to £18. **Service:** not inc. **Details:** Cards accepted. 60 seats. 60 seats outside. Music. Children allowed. Car parking.

Oxford
The Anchor Inn
A terrific gastropub package
2 Hayfield Road, Oxford, OX2 6TT
Tel no: (01865) 510282
www.theanchoroxford.com
Gastropub | £23
Cooking score: 2
£5 OFF   £30

Run by a 'brilliant team', the Anchor is squirrelled deep in leafy Hayfield, hard by the canal and well away from the hum of the city. It's evolved into a terrific gastropub under the stewardship of Jamie and Charlotte King, who have raised the local bar when it comes to food. Pigeon breast with pea risotto was 'spring on a plate' for one visitor, and the seasonally tuned menu also advertises game faggots with honey-roast parsnips, roast hake with vine tomatoes, olives and capers, and desserts such as pannacotta with poached rhubarb. Log fires, board games, quiz nights, real ales and quaffable wines (from £13.50) complete an admirable pub package.

Chef/s: Jamie Cottrell. **Open:** all week L 12 to 2.30 (3 Sun), D 6 to 9.30 (6.30 to 8.30 Sun). **Closed:** 25 and 26 Dec. **Meals:** alc (main courses £10 to £15).

Set L Mon to Fri £12.95 (2 courses). **Service:** not inc. **Details:** Cards accepted. 70 seats. 40 seats outside. Separate bar. Wheelchair access. Music. Children allowed. Car parking.

NEW ENTRY
Ashmolean Dining Room
Versatile rooftop restaurant
Beaumont Street, Oxford, OX1 2PH
Tel no: (01865) 553823
www.ashmoleandiningroom.com
Mediterranean | £25
Cooking score: 2
V   £30

Contrasting with its hoard of antiquities, Oxford's recently renovated Ashmolean Museum boasts a spanking new rooftop restaurant. The light-filled, glassy space comes complete with an open terrace and lawn, fine views and seating for solo diners, couples or large groups. Equally versatile is the Mediterranean-slanted menu, where sharing plates of freshly fried salt-cod croquettes could precede 'small dishes' of skilfully seared char-grilled squid with rocket salad, choice charcuterie and cheeses, or larger plates such as a resoundingly fresh chermoula-marinated bream with plentiful lentils and peppers. Exemplary tarte au citron makes a fitting finale. The refreshingly pertinent wine list starts at £14.50 a bottle.

Chef/s: Arun Manickan. **Open:** Tue to Sun L 12 to 3 (10 to 6 Sun), Tue to Sat D 6 to 10. **Closed:** Mon, 24 to 26 Dec. **Meals:** alc (main courses £10 to £45). Set L and D £18.50 (2 courses) to £23. **Service:** 10% (optional). **Details:** Cards accepted. 106 seats. 100 seats outside. Wheelchair access. Music. Children allowed.

Please send us your feedback

To register your opinion about any restaurant listed in the Guide, or a new restaurant that you wish to bring to our attention, please visit the web address at the bottom of the page. Your feedback informs the content of the book and will be used to compile next year's reviews.

Branca

Lively all-day Italian
111 Walton Street, Oxford, OX2 6AJ
Tel no: (01865) 556111
www.branca-restaurants.com
Italian | £23
Cooking score: 1
£5 OFF **V** £30

With its animated atmosphere, all-day opening and good lunch and supper deals, this populist Italian brasserie pleases everyone. The setting is a revamped Victorian building with lots of light and space. Order from a menu that promises a mixed bag of contemporary ideas: roasted Piedmontese peppers with buffalo mozzarella, and pork cutlet with Parmesan herb breadcrumbs and a tomato and chilli salsa might feature alongside risottos, pastas and pizzas. Desserts include profiteroles with chocolate semifreddo. A short Italian wine list opens at £14.55.
Chef/s: Michael McQuire. **Open:** all week 12 to 11. **Meals:** alc (main courses £9 to £17). Set L and D £10.65 (2 courses). Sun L £11.45. **Service:** not inc. **Details:** Cards accepted. 100 seats. Air-con. Separate bar. Wheelchair access. Music. Children allowed.

Cherwell Boathouse

A riverside stalwart
50 Bardwell Road, Oxford, OX2 6ST
Tel no: (01865) 552746
www.cherwellboathouse.co.uk
Modern British | £26
Cooking score: 1
£5 OFF £30

Readers continue to endorse this Oxford stalwart – taken by the river setting, the punts for hire, good cooking and affordable prices. Menus, whether fixed price or à la carte, do not give a lot of choice – perhaps three items per course – but most people find something to their liking, served in 'pleasingly modest but not ungenerous portions'. Confit potato and goats' cheese terrine might be followed by crisp sea bass fillet with aromatic vegetables and crayfish butter, and there could be poached tamarillos with pink pannacotta to finish. France anchors the exceptional wine list, but there's a balance between the classics and the modern – and fine value too. Some 16 are offered by the glass and bottles start at £12.75.
Chef/s: Carson Hill. **Open:** all week L 12 to 2 (2.30 Sat and Sun), D 6 to 9.30. **Closed:** 25 to 30 Dec. **Meals:** alc (main courses £10 to £19). Set L £19 (2 courses) to £23.50. Set D £20 (2 courses) to £25.50. Sun L £23.50. **Service:** not inc. **Details:** Cards accepted. 65 seats. 40 seats outside. Separate bar. No music. Wheelchair access. Children allowed. Car parking.

Gee's

A landmark to linger in
61 Banbury Road, Oxford, OX2 6PE
Tel no: (01865) 553540
www.gees-restaurant.co.uk
British | £32
Cooking score: 2
V

A notable Oxford landmark, Gee's is a conservatory restaurant out in the north of the city, not far from fashionable Summertown. It's the kind of place that's thoroughly agreeable to linger in on a bright sunny day, and readers appreciate the fact that they never feel rushed. The menu is divided into brasserie-style sections, comprising modern British dishes cooked with accuracy and care. Favoured specialities include quails' eggs in hollandaise on puff pastry, watercress soup, blade of Rofford Farm beef served with roast roots and mash, and the nostalgic apple and hazelnut crumble. A short list of reasonably priced wines opens at £14.95.
Chef/s: Ben Aslin. **Open:** all week L 12 to 2.30 (3.30 Sun), D 5.45 to 10 (10.30 Fri and Sat, 6 to 10 Sun). **Closed:** 25 Dec. **Meals:** alc (main courses £15 to £24). Set L £13.95 (2 courses) to £16.95. Set D £22 (2 courses) to £25. Sun L £21 (2 courses) to £24. **Service:** 12.5% (optional). **Details:** Cards accepted. 85 seats. 40 seats outside. Air-con. Separate bar. Wheelchair access. Music. Children allowed.

Jamie's Italian

Pared-down brasserie
24-26 George Street, Oxford, OX1 2AE
Tel no: (01865) 838383
www.jamiesitalian.com
Italian | £25
Cooking score: 1

V £30

The original of a steadily growing Italian brasserie chain sees Jamie O back in *Naked Chef* mode. Not only are recipes pared down to their bare essentials, there's also a 90s loft conversion feel to the two-tiered space. But there are reports that the brand may be spreading itself too thin, for poor maintenance and lacklustre cooking are recent complaints here. At its best, Italian breads and a 'plank' of cured meats or Italian cheese makes a great sharing starter, folowed by a fiery penne arrabiata or a rose veal Parmigiana, and lemon ricotta cheesecake to finish. House wine is £15.35. For other branches see website.
Chef/s: David Bargione. **Open:** all week 12 to 11 (10.30pm Sun). **Closed:** 25 and 26 Dec. **Meals:** alc (main courses £6 to £17). **Service:** 10% (optional). **Details:** Cards accepted. 220 seats. Air-con. Wheelchair access. Music. Children allowed.

ALSO RECOMMENDED

▲ Edamamé

15 Holywell Street, Oxford, OX1 3SA
Tel no: (01865) 246916
www.edamame.co.uk
Japanese

Close by the entrance to New College, Edamamé serves up affordable Japanese 'home cooking' to hordes of students, tourists and academics. Menus rotate through the week, with a full sushi selection on Thursday evenings. Otherwise, choose from the likes of shogayaki (strips of pork loin in soy and ginger), takoyaki (octopus wrapped in a pancake with a fruity sauce), or ever-popular teriyaki salmon. Expect to pay £4 to £9 per dish. Ice-cold Japanese beers, plum wine and saké (from £3.50) are the things to drink. Open Wed to Sun L, Thur to Sat D.

READERS RECOMMEND

The Fishes

Gastropub
North Hinksey, Oxford, OX2 0NA
Tel no: (01865) 249796
www.fishesoxford.co.uk
'One of the most welcoming and inclusive pubs'

The Old Parsonage

Modern British
1 Banbury Road, Oxford, OX2 6NN
Tel no: (01865) 310210
www.oldparsonage-hotel.co.uk
'Beautiful place and stunning food to match'

The Mole Inn

Gastropub
Toot Baldon, Oxford, OX44 9NG
Tel no: (01865) 340001
www.moleinntootbaldon.co.uk
'Would rate as one of the best pubs I have visited for a very long time'

■ Shiplake

NEW ENTRY
Orwells

Panache, promise and picture-perfect plates
Shiplake Row, Shiplake, RG9 4DP
Tel no: (01189) 403673
www.orwellsatshiplake.co.uk
Modern British | £50
Cooking score: 5

Ryan Simpson is a restless young talent. After attracting bountiful praise at the Goose in Britwell Salome, he moved on and decamped to this smart former pub set amid pristine Oxfordshire countryside. Venerable beams, oak flooring, bare brick, white walls and a seductive blues soundtrack define the bar area, where classy gastropub food incorporates the likes of crayfish cocktail followed by muntjac and hazelnut burger. However, Simpson's creativity is given full expression in 'the Room', a diminutive bright new conservatory overlooking a grassy garden (with open fields beyond). Here, assertive flavours are combined with panache, on picture-perfect plates where

the seasons and wild food are given due prominence. Succulent pork belly is matched with plump lobster morsels perched on sea beet, with a soy sauce reduction amplifying the Chinese influence – and the salinity. Still better, a dainty main course of immaculate plaice on pak choi forms a perfect marriage with salty-sour verjuice, joined by a happy congregation of sultanas, St George's mushrooms and artichokes – a low-carb masterpiece. To finish, chewy pink praline tart is lifted immeasurably by an astringent sorrel sorbet. Capable staff add to the allure of this promising new venture. House wine is £14.
Chef/s: Ryan Simpson. **Open:** all week L 11.30 to 3, D 6.30 to 9.30. The Room Tue to Sat D only 7 to 9.30. **Closed:** 1 week Christmas, first 2 weeks Jan, first 2 weeks Sept. **Meals:** alc (main courses £16 to £23). Set L £10 (2 courses) to £15.50. Sun L £19.95. **Service:** not inc. **Details:** Cards accepted. 45 seats. 30 seats outside. Separate bar. Wheelchair access. Music. Children allowed. Car parking.

Stoke Row

ALSO RECOMMENDED
▲ The Crooked Billet
Newlands Lane, Stoke Row, RG9 5PU
Tel no: (01491) 681048
www.thecrookedbillet.co.uk
Gastropub

A vintage star of film and TV, this lop-sided country cottage pub (circa 1672) is a magnet out in the sticks, treasured for its kooky charms and high-class boho atmosphere, music events and creative food. Local and faraway ingredients are given a lively spin on the handwritten menus. Crispy wild mushroom risotto cakes (£7) or oysters Benedict could give way to roast cod with tempura prawns and chilli soy broth (£17) or rack of lamb with 'bashed' roots. Desserts might include vanilla pannacotta with mango and orange soup (£5). Eclectic wines from £16.95. Open all week.

Swerford
The Masons Arms
Stylish roadside eatery
Banbury Road, Swerford, OX7 4AP
Tel no: (01608) 683212
www.masons-arms.com
Modern British | £25
Cooking score: 2
£5 OFF £30

Formerly a Masonic lodge, this Oxford stone roadside eatery has a stylish rustic interior and lovely views from its garden. Chef/proprietor Bill Leadbeater has a fondness for classic techniques and old-fashioned cuts of meat, but dishes have a modern edge. The menu is divided into 'pub grub' (chicken korma; ham, egg and chips), specials (maybe 28-day hung Exmoor ribeye steak with fries, rocket and beetroot relish) and a great-value set-price menu offering the likes of duck terrine with plum chutney followed by seared fillet of black bream with baby spinach and cream sauce. Wines start at £14.
Chef/s: Bill Leadbeater. **Open:** all week L 12 to 2 (3 Sun), Mon to Sat D 7 to 9 (8.30 Sun). **Closed:** 25 and 26 Dec. **Meals:** alc (main courses £8 to £19). Set L £15 (2 courses) to £18. Set D £20 (2 courses) to £26. Sun L £18. **Service:** not inc. **Details:** Cards accepted. 75 seats. 40 seats outside. Separate bar. Wheelchair access. Music. Children allowed. Car parking.

Swinbrook

NEW ENTRY
The Swan Inn
Idyllic stone pub
Swinbrook, OX18 4DY
Tel no: (01993) 823339
www.theswanswinbrook.co.uk
Modern British | £25
Cooking score: 2
🛏 £30

Following a decade developing the Kings Head at nearby Bledington (see entry), Archie and Nicola Orr-Ewing jumped at the chance to breathe new life into this idyllic stone pub in the Windrush Valley, owned by the Dowager Duchess of Devonshire. The Swan has rustic country charm aplenty and to many it's the perfect country pub – worn flagstones, thick beams, old settles, crackling log fires, bantams in the graden and a dreamy riverside location overlooking the village cricket pitch. Seasonal menus combine pub classics with more adventurous dishes brimming with local ingredients, including aged beef from Archie's family farm in Fifield. Wild rabbit terrine with pickled mushrooms, haunch of roe deer with cottage pie, braised red cabbage and tarragon jus, and chocolate nutty cookies with raspberry ripple ice cream show the style. Wines from £14.

Chef/s: Giles Lee. **Open:** all week L 12 to 2 (2.30 Sat and Sun), D 7 to 9 (9.30 Sat and Sun). **Closed:** 25 and 26 Dec. **Meals:** alc (main courses £10 to £18). **Service:** not inc. **Details:** Cards accepted. 65 seats. 40 seats outside. Wheelchair access. Music. Children allowed. Car parking.

▊ Tadpole Bridge

ALSO RECOMMENDED
▲ The Trout at Tadpole Bridge

Tadpole Bridge, SN7 8RF
Tel no: (01367) 870382
www.troutinn.co.uk
Gastropub £5 OFF

A seventeenth-century inn that's a summertime favourite – you can sit outside and enjoy rustic views of the river Thames and eat food that focuses on good quality produce. All tastes are indulged here, whether it's for crayfish with citrus mayonnaise (£7.95), steamed beef and ale pudding, ribeye steak with fat chips and green peppercorn sauce (£18.95) or half a dozen oysters, and breast of pigeon with pigeon livers and sweet potato chips. House wine is £14.50. Open all week. Accommodation.

▊ Woodstock

The Feathers
Old-school charm and fine food
Market Street, Woodstock, OX20 1SX
Tel no: (01993) 812291
www.feathers.co.uk
Modern British | £39
Cooking score: 4

🛏 V

Plum in the centre of this fetching market town, the Feathers has been cobbled together from four seventeenth-century houses. Its succession of diminutive dining rooms – all wood panelling, yellow wallpaper, standard lamps and background classical music – exude old-school charm. A year into his tenure, Marc Hardiman shows great technical skill and juxtaposes textures with verve. Choose from a supplement-strewn set dinner or the five-course tasting menu. In May, the latter delivered a pre-starter pea velouté that was a veritable distillate of spring. Creamy scallops matched with 'cauliflower textures' (deep-fried, 'couscous' and 'carpaccio'), and new-season's lamb (juicy loin, stewed breast in a breadcrumbed parcel, deep-fried sweetbread and kidney served quiveringly rare) were textural triumphs. Flavours can occasionally be restrained, though not the faultless finale: properly tart passion-fruit soufflé tempered with raspberry ripple ice cream. Service is polite, friendly, but sometimes achingly slow. The hotel's gin bar/bistro has also attracted praise. The long, approachable wine list starts at £17 a bottle.

Chef/s: Marc Hardiman. **Open:** Tue to Sun L 12 to 2.30 (3 Sun), Mon to Sat D 7 to 9.30. **Meals:** alc (main courses £11 to £24). Set L and D £35 (2 courses) to £39.95. Sun L £29. **Service:** 10% (optional). **Details:** Cards accepted. 46 seats. 60 seats outside. Separate bar. No mobile phones. Wheelchair access. Music. Children allowed.

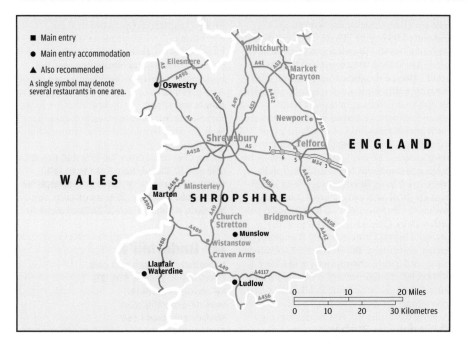

- ■ Main entry
- ● Main entry accommodation
- ▲ Also recommended

A single symbol may denote several restaurants in one area.

Whitchurch
Ellesmere
Market Drayton
● Oswestry
Newport
Shrewsbury
Telford
E N G L A N D
W A L E S
■ Marton
Minsterley
S H R O P S H I R E
Church Stretton
Bridgnorth
● Munslow
Wistanstow
Craven Arms
Llanfair Waterdine
● Ludlow

| 0 | 10 | 20 Miles |
| 0 | 10 | 20 | 30 Kilometres |

■ Llanfair Waterdine

The Waterdine

A serious restaurant in pub clothing
Llanfair Waterdine, LD7 1TU
Tel no: (01547) 528214
www.waterdine.com
Modern British | £33
Cooking score: 4

At the Adams's seventeenth-century longhouse, low-beamed ceilings, plain furniture and bare tables retain the atmosphere of a country pub, but there the resemblance just about comes to an end. The gloriously out-of-the-way location, right on the border of Wales and England, means that diners are not taken without a booking. In the kitchen there is little doubt that Ken Adams can deliver unfussy dishes with skill and dexterity. He is a regionalist par excellence; his short menu features homegrown or local produce (with fresh fish delivered from Cornwall). Clean, clear flavours speak for themselves in dishes

such as goats' cheese gnocchi with fresh tomato sauce and walnut salad, roast loin of organic mountain lamb with courgettes and Jabron potatoes, and mulberry cheesecake. Wine from £18.50.
Chef/s: Ken Adams. **Open:** Thur to Sun L 12 to 1.30, Tue to Sat D 7 to 8.30. **Closed:** Mon, 1 week spring, 1 week autumn. **Meals:** Set L £22.50 (3 courses). Set D £32.50 (3 courses). Sun L £22.50. **Service:** not inc. **Details:** Cards accepted. 20 seats. Separate bar. No music. No mobile phones. Car parking.

■ Ludlow

La Bécasse

A great culinary adventure
17 Corve Street, Ludlow, SY8 1DA
Tel no: (01584) 872325
www.labecasse.co.uk
Modern French | £45
Cooking score: 6

Restaurateur Alan Murchison did wonders for Ludlow's flagging foodie reputation in 2007, when he launched this top-end eatery in the

oak-panelled, stone-walled surrounds of a historic coaching inn. There has been a fine restaurant on this site for a good few years (it used to be Claude Bosi's original Hibiscus), and La Bécasse maintains the tradition with what chef Will Holland describes as a 'modern British interpretation of classic French cuisine'. In practice that means serving halibut with braised oxtail and artichoke in a cep velouté, or embellishing poached mallard with a mousse of Puy lentils, sweet-and-sour celeriac, a boudin of confit duck leg, and a sauce combining Seville orange with sherry vinegar. It all adds up to a great adventure, perhaps best appreciated via the 'menu du jour' taste-athon. One reporter who took the plunge admitted he was utterly dumbstruck as each astonishing course was placed in front of him, until a dish of venison with blackberry and beetroot purée, wimberry compote and bitter salted chocolate tuile finally out-dazzled everything for sheer flavour and colour. Among the brilliantly crafted desserts on that occasion was a caramel parfait with apple and blackberry compote and sweet sage granité of memorable intensity. An expanding list of fine wines opens at £19.
Chef/s: Will Holland. **Open:** Wed to Sun L 12 to 2, Tue to Sat D 7 to 9 (9.30 Sat). **Closed:** Mon, 2 weeks Christmas and New Year. **Meals:** alc (main courses £20 to £30). Set L £25 (2 courses) to £29. Set D £49 (2 courses) to £55. Tasting menu £60. Surprise menu £85. **Service:** 10% (optional). **Details:** Cards accepted. 35 seats. Separate bar. No mobile phones. Music. Children allowed. Car parking.

NEW ENTRY
Green Café
Friendly café with good local lunches
Mill on the Green, Ludlow, SY8 1EG
Tel no: (01584) 879872
Modern British | £16
Cooking score: 1
£30

Trendily Spartan décor and a relaxed atmosphere characterise this café in a converted mill beside the river Teme – the riverside terrace gives views onto Dinham

bridge. Lunch is the main event, with everything on the short menu seasonally or locally inspired, from pickled herrings with a potato salad and a refreshing beetroot and horseradish crème fraîche, via pheasant ravioli with green salad to a highly praised squid, red mullet and borlotti bean stew. At other times there's a varied, but not extensive, cake menu. Staff are friendly and attentive. House wine is £16.
Chef/s: Clive Davis. **Open:** Tue to Sun 10 to 5, D Sat only 6 to 10. **Closed:** Mon, 5 Jan to 10 Feb. **Meals:** alc (main courses £8 to £12). **Service:** not inc. **Details:** Cash only. 30 seats. 28 seats outside. No music. Wheelchair access. Children allowed.

Mr Underhill's
Beautifully run, with real care
Dinham Weir, Ludlow, SY8 1EH
Tel no: (01584) 874431
www.mr-underhills.co.uk
Modern European | £60
Cooking score: 7

Chris and Judy Bradley celebrate the thirtieth anniversary of Mr Underhill's in 2011. Barely a year has passed without Guide readers reporting warmly on the quality that sets it apart: the 'real care and attention lavished on each course and each table'. Given the personal nature of the hospitality at this restaurant-with-rooms, it's no surprise that each party receives a menu with their name on it. It's a guide to the eight courses that are taken, dietary requirements permitting, by each table in the restaurant, though not everybody needs the reference material. The Bradleys have generations of regulars who are as familiar with the calming views over the gardens and weir as with the signature duck liver custard with a contrasting glaze of, say, spices or lemongrass. On paper, dinner may sound like a slog. There are olive gougères to get through, not to mention a delicate cone containing a preparation of smoked salmon, a little vegetable-based soup, a pretty fish course such as organic Shetland salmon with spiced apple and smoked haddock cream and, perhaps, a fabulous slow-roasted fillet of Marches beef with a tiny braised beef pie, or roast rack and shoulder of spring lamb with garden sorrel. However, just as Bradley uses his judgement and experience to choose the best of local produce, he balances the menu so that energies are preserved for a Yorkshire rhubarb sponge with custard ice cream, and dessert proper, perhaps a melting 'hot fondant' fruit tart, or the excellent cheese plate. If there is the odd tiny niggle – at inspection some courses were a little cold – it is brushed lightly away by the pleasure of being in a beautifully run dining room. Judy Bradley is a constant reassuring presence, able to linger and chat or leave well alone. Her expertise is particularly apparent when it comes time to hand over the wine list, a labour of love which has a friendly lower end from £16.50 to balance some truly special bottles.

Chef/s: Chris Bradley. **Open:** Wed to Sun D only 7.30 (1 sitting). **Closed:** Mon, Tue, 25 and 26 Dec, 1 Jan, 1 week June, 1 week end Oct/early Nov. **Meals:** Set D £52.50 to £59.50 (8 courses). **Service:** not inc. **Details:** Cards accepted. 30 seats. 30 seats outside. Separate bar. No music. No mobile phones. Children allowed. Car parking.

Marton
Gartells at the Sun Inn
Pubby hospitality, real ales, honest food
Marton, SY21 8JP
Tel no: (01938) 561211
www.suninn.org.uk
Modern British | £25
Cooking score: 1

£5 £30
OFF

Almost on the Welsh border, this old stone inn is capably run by the Gartell family who have cemented its reputation for pubby hospitality, real ales and honest food. Basic grub is served in the bar, but the restaurant aims higher, with the likes of tea-smoked chicken on celery, apple and walnut salad, slow-roast pork belly with stir-fried vegetables and spicy coconut sauce, and gilthead bream with roast peppers

and courgettes. For afters, try iced lemon parfait or sticky toffee pud. Wines from hands-on independent growers start at £14.40.

Chef/s: Peter Gartell. **Open:** Wed to Sun L 12 to 2, Tue to Sat D 7 to 9.30. **Closed:** Mon (exc bank hols). **Meals:** alc (main courses £8 to £19). Sun L £13.95 (2 courses) to £16.95. Bar menu available. **Service:** not inc. **Details:** Cards accepted. 55 seats. 25 seats outside. Separate bar. Wheelchair access. Music. Children allowed. Car parking.

Munslow
The Crown Country Inn
Historic pub with posh comfort food
Corvedale Road, Munslow, SY7 9ET
Tel no: (01584) 841205
www.crowncountryinn.co.uk
Modern British | £25
Cooking score: 3

£5 V £30
OFF

Set in an Area of Outstanding Natural Beauty between Wenlock Edge and the Clee Hills, this Grade II-listed building was once a 'hundred house' where justice was meted out to local wrongdoers. Sympathetically restored and updated, it retains grand inglenooks, flagstone floors and carved beams that reputedly date from Tudor times. Food is served in the bar and the first-floor restaurant; either way, expect a balance of posh comfort food (grilled ribeye with roasted vine tomatoes, a griddled flat mushroom and straw potatoes) and classics with an international twist – maybe roast breast and confit leg of Gressingham duck with sweet potato and ginger purée and sherry, spring onion and green peppercorn jus. Finish with vanilla crème brûlée, fresh pineapple and a crisp homemade brandy snap. Wines start at £13.95.

Chef/s: Richard Arnold. **Open:** Tue to Sun L 12 to 2, Tue to Sat D 6.45 to 8.45. **Closed:** Mon, Christmas. **Meals:** alc (main courses £14 to £19). Set D £15 (2 courses) to £18. Sun L £18.95. **Service:** not inc. **Details:** Cards accepted. 50 seats. 20 seats outside. Separate bar. No mobile phones. Music. Children allowed. Car parking.

Oswestry

Sebastians

Haute cuisine with frills
45 Willow Street, Oswestry, SY11 1AQ
Tel no: (01691) 655444
www.sebastians-hotel.co.uk
French | £38
Cooking score: 3

This homely restaurant-with-rooms has been run by the Fishers for over 20 years. Housed in a sixteenth-century inn, it's cosy in winter with real log fires, while summer brings drinks on the courtyard terrace. Old-fashioned chairs and smart linen set a traditional tone in the dining room, where the monthly changing menu is stoically written in French, with English subtitles: think haute cuisine, with added frills in the form of appetisers and palate-cleansing sorbets. Sliced saddle of rabbit with herb risotto and tomato and wine jus is a typical starter, followed by fillet of beef on celeriac purée with slow-braised pork cheek and a red wine sauce. Pear clafoutis with beer ice cream brings things to a classic but quirky close. The French-led wine list opens at £16.95.
Chef/s: Richard Jones. **Open:** Tue to Sat D only 6.30 to 9.30. **Closed:** Sun, Mon, 1 week Christmas. **Meals:** Set D £19.95 to £37.50. **Service:** not inc. **Details:** Cards accepted. 40 seats. 20 seats outside. Separate bar. No mobile phones. Music. Children allowed. Car parking.

Symbols

Accommodation is available

£30 Three courses for less than £30

V More than three vegetarian main courses

£5 OFF £5-off voucher scheme

Notable wine list

Will Holland La Bécasse

What is the best dish on your menu?
Parmesan crusted scallops, spiced parsnip and spinach, lime emulsion, coconut velouté.

What would be your perfect birthday meal?
My dad's lasagne followed by Viennetta! It's what I always chose when I was allowed to choose my birthday dinner!

If you were having a dinner party for six people, who would you invite?
Marco Pierre White, Ferran Adrià, Ferran Adrià's translator, the ghost of Keith Floyd, Remy the rat from Ratatouille, Delia Smith.

What do you think is exciting about the British food scene?
The wealth of great produce our country offers and the genuine move from chefs to make the most of it.

What is your favourite restaurant and why?
The Ledbury. The best, most exciting food I've eaten in the UK in the last few years. The flame-grilled mackerel dish is out of this world.

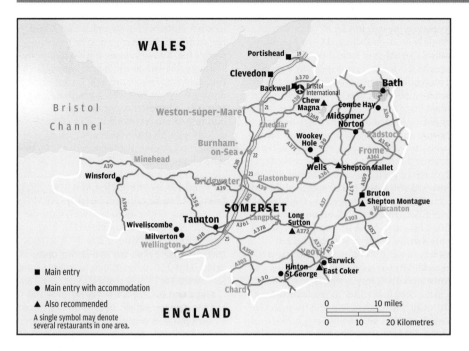

Backwell

NEW ENTRY
The New Inn
Smart pub with high standards
86 West Town Road, Backwell, BS48 3BE
Tel no: (01275) 462199
www.newinn-backwell.co.uk
Modern European | £28
Cooking score: 3

£30

The oldest pub in this village close to Bristol has been given the full gastropub makeover with heritage colours and exposed brick and stone. The bar area has comfortable leather chairs and sofas, local ales and snacks such as pork rillette with beetroot chutney, while the L-shaped restaurant touts pine tables, flickering church candles and confident cooking that majors in local produce. A starter of caramelised veal sweetbreads with chicory, carrot purée and golden raisins might be followed by wild sea bass with black pudding gnocchi, leeks, chives and Mornay sauce.

Standards remain high for desserts such as passion-fruit brûlée with chocolate and coconut mousse. Wines from £13.95.
Chef/s: Nathan Muir. **Open:** all week L 12 to 3 (4 Sun), D 6 to 9.30 (10 Fri and Sat, 9 Sun). **Closed:** 25 Dec. **Meals:** alc (main courses £12 to £19). Set L £15 (2 courses) to £19.50. Set D £20 (2 courses) to £27.50. Sun L £12.50. **Service:** not inc.
Details: Cards accepted. 40 seats. 60 seats outside. Separate bar. Music. Children allowed. Car parking.

Barwick
Little Barwick House
Polished restaurant-with-rooms
Rexes Hollow Lane, Barwick, BA22 9TD
Tel no: (01935) 423902
www.littlebarwickhouse.co.uk
Modern British | £40
Cooking score: 6

Tim and Emma Ford's polished restaurant-with-rooms is invitingly pitched on a secluded hillside with three acres of grounds

to distract the eye. Inside, all is just so: the brightly lit, high-ceilinged Georgian dining room is a picture of formality, although assured service quickly dispels any stiffness. Tim's cooking depends on assiduously sourced produce, allowing him to ring the changes and adapt his menus each day. The result is an array of dishes defined by unfaltering consistency, balance and spot-on seasoning; there are no foams, smears or daubs here – instead the kitchen follows classical dictates to the letter. A starter of perfectly timed Cornish scallops is enriched with chive butter sauce, while mains offer anything from supremely tender local beef fillet garnished with onion confit and lifted by a deep Madeira truffle reduction to pink-roasted roe deer with braised red cabbage and beetroot purée. To finish, an exquisite trio of raspberry sablé, mousse and sorbet reveals exemplary patisserie skills. Emma Ford looks after the acclaimed wine list, which spans the globe and has prices to suit all pockets. Glasses start at £5.25.
Chef/s: Tim Ford. **Open:** Wed to Sun L 12 to 2, Tue to Sat D 7 to 9.30. **Closed:** Mon, 3 weeks from 25 Dec. **Meals:** Set L £21.95 (2 courses) to £25.95. Set D £34.95 (2 courses) to £39.95. Sun L £27.95. **Service:** not inc. **Details:** Cards accepted. 56 seats. Air-con. Separate bar. No music. No mobile phones. Wheelchair access. Children allowed. Car parking.

▌Bath

The Bath Priory
Vivid food from an ambitious chef
Weston Road, Bath, BA1 2XT
Tel no: (01225) 331922
www.thebathpriory.co.uk
Modern European | £65
Cooking score: 4

🍷 ⛷ V

'It's easy to get bowled over by the setting', reports a visitor to this handsome manor house nestling in pretty gardens about a mile from Bath city centre. Executive chef Michael Caines (see entry, Gidleigh Park) has promoted Sam Moody, and reports this year indicate that the restaurant has taken on a new level of culinary ambition. Moody cooks vivid modern dishes with the emphasis on sound raw materials. Meats appear to be well-timed (as in a fine loin of venison with spiced pear compote, braised salsify and red wine jus), and fish, delivered from Cornwall, is treated innovatively: sea bass with parsnip and ginger purée and ginger sauce, for example. A lightness of touch is evident, as in a first course of scallops with shallot purée and bacon velouté, while chocolate orange confit mousse with orange sorbet and dark chocolate ice cream reveals 'a very talented pastry chef'. As for wine, masses of French stuff will intimidate the uninitiated, but there are enterprising explorations too, with Italy, the US and Australia particularly well represented. Prices from £27.
Chef/s: Michael Caines and Sam Moody. **Open:** all week L 12 to 2.30, D 6 to 9.30. (6.30 to 9.45 Fri and Sat). **Meals:** Set L £24 (2 courses) to £30. Set D £54 (2 courses) to £65. Sun L £39. Tasting menu £90 (7 courses). **Service:** not inc. **Details:** Cards accepted. 80 seats. 40 seats outside. Separate bar. No music. No mobile phones. Wheelchair access. Car parking.

Casanis
A plateful of Provence
4 Saville Row, Bath, BA1 2QP
Tel no: (01225) 780055
www.casanis.co.uk
French | £30
Cooking score: 1

Situated in a pretty pedestrian street in the heart of Bath, Casanis is every bit as charming as its surroundings. Pastel shades, chandeliers and crisp white tablecloths give a romantic, airy feel. Jill Couvreur runs front of house, while her husband Laurent cooks bistro classics with a Provençal slant: seafood bisque or salt cod brandade, with rabbit and mustard fricassee or a 'beautifully pink' rack of lamb with herb crust to follow. For dessert, a 'superb' lavender crème brûlée is a staple. The exclusively-French wine list starts at £15.25.
Chef/s: Laurent Couvreur. **Open:** Tue to Sat L 12 to 2, D 6 to 10. **Closed:** Sun, Mon, 25 to 29 Dec, first week Jun, 1 week Aug. **Meals:** alc (main courses £11 to £24). Set L £13.50 (2 courses) to £17. Set D £17 (2

courses) to £21. **Service:** not inc. **Details:** Cards accepted. 54 seats. 14 seats outside. Separate bar. Music. Children allowed.

Dukes Hotel, Cavendish Restaurant
Tasteful restaurant with ambitious food
Great Pulteney Street, Bath, BA2 4DN
Tel no: (01225) 787960
www.dukesbath.co.uk
Modern British | £35
Cooking score: 2

In the basement of a Palladian-style town house, this small, relaxed restaurant is tastefully decorated with period furniture and framed prints on the cream walls. In the kitchen, Fran Snell is committed to sourcing locally, with venison coming from the Mendips and beef from the Chew Valley. There is no lack of ambition in dishes such as breast of wood pigeon with a bonbon of the leg, beetroot and hazelnuts. Similarly, a breast of chicken might be served with a ravioli of the leg meat and accompanied by Wye Valley asparagus, morels and sweetcorn. A concise wine list starts at £17.
Chef/s: Fran Snell. **Open:** Fri to Sun L 12 to 2, all week D 6.30 to 10 (9 Mon, Sun). **Meals:** alc (main courses £14 to £24). Set L £12.95 (2 courses) to £15.95. Sun L £14.95 (2 courses) to £19.95. **Service:** not inc. **Details:** Cards accepted. 36 seats. 34 seats outside. Separate bar. No mobile phones. Music. Children allowed.

King William
Big on comfort food
36 Thomas Street, Bath, BA1 5NN
Tel no: (01225) 428096
www.kingwilliampub.com
Gastropub | £27
Cooking score: 2

Past reports suggested that Charlie Digney's casual and unpretentious city pub suffered from inconsistency, but the King William appears to be on 'very good form at the moment'. Meat is still the thing the kitchen does best – meltingly tender lamb shanks, pork belly, and juicy, well-flavoured steak with béarnaise sauce, the latter accompanied by superb triple-cooked chips. Despite the focus on meat, vegetarian choices are always interesting and original, say Jerusalem artichoke gratin, and vegetable accompaniments are well handled. Puddings impress less. House wine is £13.50.
Chef/s: Adie Ware. **Open:** all week L 12 to 3, D 6 to 10 (9.30 Sun to Tue). **Meals:** alc (main courses £12 to £20). Set L £15 (2 courses) to £20. **Service:** not inc. **Details:** Cards accepted. 60 seats. Separate bar. Music. Children allowed.

The Marlborough Tavern
Smart city gastropub
35 Marlborough Buildings, Bath, BA1 2LY
Tel no: (01225) 423731
www.marlborough-tavern.com
Gastropub | £25
Cooking score: 3

Once a run-down city watering hole, the Marlborough Tavern has been teleported into the gastropub age in a smart makeover that is in keeping with its location a few steps from the Royal Crescent. Although drinkers are still welcome, eager diners are drawn by the commitment to local, seasonal produce. Homemade beef burgers or beer-battered Cornish pollack with mushy peas, caper mayonnaise and hand-cut chips are served alongside whole lemon sole with brown shrimp and caper butter, and roast breast of Creedy Carver chicken on a smoked bacon and white bean cassoulet with wild mushrooms, seasonal greens and a soft herb and chicken dressing. For dessert, perhaps chocolate bread-and-butter pudding with vanilla ice cream. House wine £14.20.
Chef/s: Richard Knighting. **Open:** all week L 12.30 to 2.30 (4 Sat and Sun), D 6 to 9.30 (9 Sun). **Closed:** 25 Dec. **Meals:** alc (main courses £10 to £22). **Service:** not inc. **Details:** Cards accepted. 70 seats. 60 seats outside. Wheelchair access. Music.

Minibar

Classic tapas and contemporary twists
1 John Street, Bath, BA1 2JL
Tel no: (01225) 333323
www.bathminibar.com
Spanish | £20
Cooking score: 2

V £30

'Ideal for snack meals', writes a reporter who goes on to comment that Minibar is 'basically a tapas bar with outstanding cold meats and hot croquettes'. The most is made of the small upstairs space, with spotlights, bar stools at stainless steel counters, lots of mirrors and a picture window with views overlooking the city. The menu mixes tapas staples – pan con tomate, calamares fritos, tortilla – with more contemporary ideas, say chorizo egg soufflé, crispy garlic and soy chicken, or duck liver pâté served with Cognac-marinated raisins and truffle oil. All 12 bottles on the wine list are Spanish. Prices open at £16.50.
Chef/s: Alex Grant. **Open:** Mon to Sat L 12 to 3, D 6 to 10. **Closed:** Sun, 23 Dec to 4 Jan. **Meals:** alc (tapas from £6 to £8). **Service:** not inc.
Details: Cards accepted. 20 seats. Air-con. Music. Children allowed.

★ WINE LIST OF THE YEAR ★

The Queensberry Hotel, Olive Tree Restaurant

Serene comfort and knockout flavours
4-7 Russel Street, Bath, BA1 2QF
Tel no: (01225) 447928
www.thequeensberry.co.uk
Modern British | £38
Cooking score: 4

£5 OFF

'Not what you might expect' is the Queensberry's understated slogan. And in this serenely comfortable Georgian town house hotel, there are indeed a few modest surprises: notably, the innovative and assured twists on a deceptively traditional-looking menu. In the restaurant, the basement gloom is lifted with discreet lighting and a palette of cream and

blue. Chef Nick Brodie focuses on local ingredients such as rose veal, Cornish crab and West Country cheeses, then throws Eastern spicing into the mix without ever heading too far down the fusion route. This results in some knockout flavours, such as a beautiful Indian-inspired starter of gurnard with curried Puy lentils and tiny, crisp onion bhajis. A more classic confit of duck was tender, rich and deeply savoury. Desserts take the oriental theme a little further: a green tea pannacotta, for example, with just the right amount of wobble, served with caramelised Alphonso mango. The wine list is an object-lesson in its unstinting commitment to quality, combined with a genuine attempt to be inclusive. Nearly three dozen wines by the glass lead you in to a list that is structured imaginatively by wine style ('Nutty Whites' to 'Sweet-and-Sour Reds'), and is teeming with pedigree producers. Bottle prices start at £16, standard glasses at £4.50.
Chef/s: Nick Brodie. **Open:** Tue to Sun L 12 to 2 (12.30 to 2.30 Sun), all week D 7 to 10. **Meals:** alc (main courses £15 to £25). Set L £16 (2 courses) to £19.50. Sun L £19.50. **Service:** 10% (optional).
Details: Cards accepted. 60 seats. Air-con. Separate bar. Music. Children allowed.

The Royal Crescent Hotel, The Dower House

One of Bath's hidden glories
16 Royal Crescent, Bath, BA1 2LS
Tel no: (01225) 823333
www.royalcrescent.co.uk
Modern European | £60
Cooking score: 4

Tucked away behind the Royal Crescent Hotel in a leafy and secluded garden, the Dower House is one of Bath's hidden glories. The modern cooking may seem at odds with the grand style of the hotel, but it is well executed and there is a confidence in the kitchen. The sunny terrace makes for an excellent alfresco option, but the contemporary dining room is comfortable and staff are efficient and chatty. The kitchen's use of trendy foams appears to have been relegated to the sidelines in place of a more classic, produce-driven approach. A roasted squab pigeon with soused vegetables, Puy lentils, celeriac and raisin purée might be followed by pan-fried stone bass with sauté langoustine, confit frogs' legs and warm saffron jelly. Rhubarb and vanilla mousse with gingerbread ice cream adds a seasonal fruitiness to the dessert menu. The wine list is a brilliantly intelligent selection of fine bottles with a broad global spread and plenty to suit all pockets and palates; South America and the Antipodes offer the best choice for those on a tight budget. Prices start at £20 (£5.50 a glass).

Chef/s: Luke Richards. **Open:** all week L 12.30 to 1.45, D 7 to 10. **Meals:** Set L £15.50 (2 courses) to £18.50. Set D £50 (2 courses) to £60. Sun L £35. **Service:** not inc. **Details:** Cards accepted. 40 seats. 40 seats outside. Air-con. Separate bar. No mobile phones. Wheelchair access. Music. Children allowed. Car parking.

The White Hart Inn
Packed with things you want to eat
Widcombe Hill, Widcombe, Bath, BA2 6AA
Tel no: (01225) 338053
www.whitehartbath.co.uk
Gastropub | £28
Cooking score: 3
🛏 £30

Its close proximity to Bath's railway station and the city's rugby ground makes the White Hart a favoured watering hole for locals and visitors alike. The backpackers' hostel above also adds to its quirkiness, but none of this should distract from the consistent and well-priced food cooked by veteran Bath chef Rupert Pitt and his team. The separate dining area of this light and airy pub is smart and 'New England' in style, whilst the pretty walled garden has a Provençal feel. The assertive seasonal menu is short, but packed with things you want to eat: ham hock, potato and parsley croquettes with rémoulade might precede slow-braised lamb shank with roasted aubergines and Moroccan spiced chickpeas. House wines start at £13.90 (£3.50 a glass).

Chef/s: Rupert Pitt, Jason Horn, Rachel Milsom and Luke Gibson. **Open:** all week L 12 to 2, Mon to Sat D 6 to 10 (9 Mon and Tue). **Closed:** 25 and 26 Dec, bank hols. **Meals:** alc (main courses £11 to £15). **Service:** not inc. **Details:** Cards accepted. 50 seats. 50 seats outside. Wheelchair access. Music. Children allowed.

ALSO RECOMMENDED

▲ The Garrick's Head
7-8 St Johns Place, Bath, BA1 1ET
Tel no: (01225) 318368
www.garricksheadpub.com
Gastropub £5 OFF

Sister to the King William (see entry), this city pub is right by Bath's Theatre Royal. Deep colours and bare wood floors create an upmarket, gastropub vibe. Food is simple and to-the-point: meat tends to be put on the char-grill rather than slow-cooked. You could start with smoked haddock chowder (£7) then follow with a no-nonsense steak and chips (£18) or maybe lemon sole with crushed olive and herb potatoes, kale and hollandaise sauce. Finish with chocolate and hazelnut bread-and-butter pudding. Wines are priced from £13.50. Open all week.

▲ Yak Yeti Yak
12 Pierrepont Street, Bath, BA1 1LA
Tel no: (01225) 442299
www.yakyetiyak.co.uk
Nepalese

Wherever you sit in the basement of this eighteenth-century town house – on traditional floor cushions or conventional chairs – you will be served authentic Nepalese cooking. Look for pork or vegetable momos (steamed dumplings, from £4.95), bhutuwa lamb (with spices and tomato and spring onion, £7.80) and fascinating vegetable dishes including aloo tamar (potatoes with bamboo shoots and black-eyed peas). Finish with spiced chiyaa (tea) ice cream (£4.20). House wine is £13.90. Open all week.

Bruton
At the Chapel
A fascinating venture
High Street, Bruton, BA10 0AE
Tel no: (01749) 814070
www.atthechapel.co.uk
Modern British | £25
Cooking score: 2
£5 OFF **V** £30

There's much to enjoy at this 'beautifully converted' chapel. Now a bakery, bar, café and restaurant, it is light and airy with an open-plan kitchen and 'helpful, welcoming staff'. A new chef is at the helm, but the modern British brasserie cooking continues in the same vein with a menu that revels in seasonal materials and crowd-pleasers such as burgers and steaks, plus exemplary breads, pastries and pizzas from the wood-fired oven. Recent successes have included pâté with thick, warm toast 'straight from the bakery', and char-grilled leg of lamb with carrots and potato. House wine is £13. Accommodation is in the pipeline.
Chef/s: Steven Horrell. **Open:** Tue to Sun 9 to 3 (10 to 4 Sun), D 6 to 9.30. **Closed:** Mon, 25 and 26 Dec. **Meals:** alc (main courses £10 to £19). **Service:** not inc. **Details:** Cards accepted. 84 seats. Separate bar. No music. Wheelchair access. Children allowed.

Chew Magna

ALSO RECOMMENDED
▲ **The Pony & Trap**
Knowle Hill, Chew Magna, BS40 8TQ
Tel no: (01275) 332627
www.theponyandtrap.co.uk
Modern British £5 OFF

A short drive from Bristol, this white-fronted nineteenth-century inn flies the flag for local produce. Quarry-tiled floors and beams keep the feel in the bar traditional, but the dining room sports a more contemporary look, has stunning views of the valley below and delivers up-to-date European cooking. Pork, rabbit and pistachio terrine with green tomato chutney (£6) is one possible starter, followed

by roast rack of lamb with creamed Italian black cabbage and pesto (£15.50). House wine £11.95. Closed Mon.

Clevedon
Murrays
Top-notch goodies for foodies
87-93 Hill Road, Clevedon, BS21 7PN
Tel no: (01275) 341555
www.murraysofclevedon.co.uk
Italian | £26
Cooking score: 4
£5 OFF **V** £30

This 'light and airy' restaurant, and its first-class deli next door, draws savvy locals and visitors with its civilised, cheerful character and focus on top-drawer produce. A seasonally focused menu is based on local supplies (with a little help from Italy) and manages to push all the right buttons. The very reasonably priced menu at lunch (and some weekday evenings) offers a couple of daily specials as well as a selection of more mainstream Italian fare – 'very tender and nicely gamey' wood pigeon with potatoes and roast vegetables, and well-timed sea bass fillets with sautéed potatoes and spinach, followed by excellent figs with hazelnut ice cream or amaretti tart. Otherwise, the carte may produce Umbrian lentil and mushroom tart, followed by osso bucco (from free-range Devon rose veal) or roast wild Mendip hare wrapped in speck with a juniper and redcurrant sauce. Prices on the all-Italian wine list start at £14.50.
Chef/s: Reuben Murray. **Open:** Tue to Sat L 12 to 2, D 6 to 9.30. **Closed:** Sun, Mon, 25 and 26 Dec. **Meals:** alc (main courses £10 to £23). Set L and D £15 (2 courses) to £20. **Service:** not inc. **Details:** Cards accepted. 70 seats. Air-con. Separate bar. Wheelchair access. Music. Children allowed.

Combe Hay
The Wheatsheaf
Popular inn with sophisticated food
Combe Hay, BA2 7EG
Tel no: (01225) 833504
www.wheatsheafcombehay.com
Modern British | £35
Cooking score: 4

£5 OFF 🛏

'The location is beautiful, the décor stylish and the service is relaxed but professional', gives some hint that this attractive sixteenth-century inn is very popular. Commitment to local produce permeates the menu, and for one group of regulars things just get better and better, a March meal bringing 'yummy bread, a big selection of fresh fish dishes and divine desserts'. Typically, you might find potted organic salmon with spelt crostini and cornichon salad, rump of spring lamb with braised belly, sauce gribiche and garlic purée, and Alphonse mango rice pudding with mango sorbet. Most reporters are happy, but some mention small portions at steep prices, and service errors 'when the owner is not around'. The wine list presents a considered European line-up from £14.95.
Chef/s: Lee Evans. **Open:** Tue to Sun L 12 to 2.30 (3 Sun), Tue to Sat D 6.30 to 9 (10 Fri and Sat). **Closed:** Mon (except bank hols). **Meals:** alc (main courses £12 to £20). Set L £13.95. Sun L £18.95. **Service:** 10% (optional). **Details:** Cards accepted. 55 seats. 100 seats outside. Music. Children allowed. Car parking.

East Coker
ALSO RECOMMENDED
▲ Helyar Arms
Moor Lane, East Coker, BA22 9JR
Tel no: (01935) 862332
www.helyar-arms.co.uk
Gastropub £5 OFF

This traditional fifteenth-century village inn dispenses real ales and pub hospitality, but is equally focused for visitors in search of food. Sourcing as much as he can locally, Mathieu

Eke cooks in a relatively straightforward style, with no needless gilding of lilies. Chicken liver parfait comes with carrot and orange marmalade and homemade bread (£5.95) and the kitchen also dishes up slow-cooked belly pork, rack of lamb with dauphinoise potatoes (£16), ploughman's, good ham sandwiches and homemade ice creams. House wine is £13.75. Open all week. Accommodation.

Hinton St George
The Lord Poulett Arms
Atmospheric inn with delightful fare
High Street, Hinton St George, TA17 8SE
Tel no: (01460) 73149
www.lordpoulettarms.com
Gastropub | £24
Cooking score: 3

🛏 £30

There's no denying that Steve Hill and Michelle Paynton have scored a hit with this vigorously re-energised and instantly alluring hamstone inn. Part of the attraction is the fact that the Lord Poulett still functions as a local hostelry: there a real ales on tap in the flag-floored bar, a boules 'piste' in the garden and opportunities for seductive lounging among the florally garlanded outdoor expanses. The kitchen tips its hat to pub grub – think textbook versions of toad in the hole, fish and chips, and a first-class local steak with béarnaise and triple-cooked chips – but there are vivid contemporary ideas, too. Gilthead bream with celeriac purée, black olive and almond crumbs could lead on to cumin- and apple-glazed pork belly with roasted beetroot and polenta-crusted potatoes. After that, perhaps molten Valrhona chocolate tart – or elderflower 'snowcone' with macerated strawberries for a summertime finale. House wines from £13.
Chef/s: Gary Coughlan. **Open:** all week L 12 to 2.30, D 7 to 9.15. **Closed:** 25 and 26 Dec, 1 Jan. **Meals:** alc (main courses £10 to £24). Sun L £16 (2 courses) to £19. **Service:** not inc. **Details:** Cards accepted. 60 seats. 60 seats outside. Separate bar. No music. Wheelchair access. Children allowed. Car parking.

Long Sutton

ALSO RECOMMENDED
▲ The Devonshire Arms
Long Sutton, TA10 9LP
Tel no: (01458) 241271
www.thedevonshirearms.com
Gastropub

An outwardly rather grand former hunting lodge on a Somerset village green, the Devonshire is kitted out in appealing rustic style with bare wooden tables and a blackboard menu. The modern British cooking scores plenty of hits with the likes of Cornish mussels steamed over Long Sutton cider with chilli, garlic and thyme (£5.90), shoulder of hogget with minted new potatoes and green beans (£14.80), and ginger sticky toffee pudding with Grand Marnier caramel sauce and lime-leaf ice cream (£5.95). Wines from £14.50. Open all week. Accommodation.

Midsomer Norton
The Moody Goose at the Old Priory
Creative cooking with flair
Church Square, Midsomer Norton, BA3 2HX
Tel no: (01761) 416784
www.theoldpriory.co.uk
Modern European | £42
Cooking score: 4

🛏 V

Readers with long memories will recall that the Moody Goose used to be in Bath. That was until 2005, when the Shores happened upon the Old Priory and relocated. It's not hard to see why, as you survey Somerset's rolling acres from the partly twelfth-century house. Stephen's cooking, with its contemporary Anglo-French creative flair, survived the journey intact. A salad of smoked goose, cranberry compote and pain d'épices introduces us neatly to the titular bird, and then it's on to steamed brill with marinated fennel and green beans, or venison with golden beetroot and wilted spinach. There is an agreeable disinclination to gild the lily in the cooking, so dishes make sense – all the way through to hot chocolate fondant with raspberry sorbet or the plate of apple variations. Nine house selections, from £18.50 for a Chilean Carmenère rosé, head up a compact, fairly-priced list.
Chef/s: Stephen Shore. Open: Mon to Sat L 12 to 1.15, D 7 to 9.30. Closed: Sun, 25 Dec. Meals: alc (main courses £18 to £24). Set L £22.50 (2 courses) to £28.50. Set D £32.50. Service: not inc. Details: Cards accepted. 32 seats. Wheelchair access. Music. Children allowed. Car parking.

Milverton

NEW ENTRY
The Globe
Pleasing made-over coaching inn
Fore Street, Milverton, TA4 1JX
Tel no: (01823) 400534
www.theglobemilverton.co.uk
Modern British | £25
Cooking score: 2

£5 🛏 £30
OFF

This former coaching inn in a conservation village has had a contemporary makeover. Some feel its heart has been ripped out – although modern pine tables and high-backed leather chairs give it a pleasing atmosphere and a well-travelled couple reported 'as good a meal as we've had anywhere' here. At a test lunch, a starter of tempura tiger prawns with sweet chilli sauce pleased, as did a main course of shoulder of lamb with rosemary stuffing and redcurrant jelly sauce. Head chef Kaan Atasoy's classic crème brûlée was first-rate. The short wine list kicks off at £11.50.
Chef/s: Mark Tarry and Kaan Atasoy. Open: Tue to Sun L 12 to 2, Mon to Sat D 6.30 to 9 (7 Fri and Sat). Meals: alc (main courses £8 to £ 18). Sun L £8.50. Service: not inc. Details: Cards accepted. 54 seats. Separate bar. Wheelchair access. Music. Children allowed. Car parking.

Portishead
The Lockhouse
Estuary views and inspiring food
Lockside, Portishead, BS20 7AF
Tel no: (01275) 397272
www.thelockhouseportishead.co.uk
Modern European | £25
New Chef
£5 OFF £30

The glass-structured restaurant and terrace extension to the tiny lock keeper's cottage on the marina at Portishead makes the most of its location, with commanding estuary views. It's an atmospheric venue even on rainy days, and offers a range of bar snacks as well as restaurant dining. Fish soup with Gruyère or lime-dressed salmon ceviche are inspiring ways to start, with mains such as honey-glazed duck breast, baby onions and salsify to follow on. One aficionado reckons they do 'the best risotto in the southwest', perhaps a version with courgette fritters, lemon and mint. Rosewater pannacotta with rhubarb closes the deal, with wines from £15.50. New chef David McGuff was due to start as we went to press – reports please.
Chef/s: David McGuff. **Open:** Mon to Sat L 12 to 3, D 6 to 10. Sun 12 to 9. **Meals:** alc (main courses £9 to £24). Set L £14.95. **Service:** not inc. **Details:** Cards accepted. 60 seats. 32 seats outside. Air-con. Separate bar. Wheelchair access. Music. Children allowed. Car parking.

Shepton Mallet
ALSO RECOMMENDED
▲ Blostin's
29-33 Waterloo Road, Shepton Mallet, BA4 5HH
Tel no: (01749) 343648
www.blostins.co.uk
Anglo-French

Nick and Lynne Reed are continuing their affable double act in this cosy conversion of three cottages and a sweet shop, where visitors can expect a cordial welcome, all the courtesies of home and some generous Anglo-French food of the comforting kind. Fixed-price

dinners (£20.95 for three courses) might open with butternut squash soup, before pork fillet with Savoy cabbage and peppercorn sauce or trout with creamy leeks. To finish, perhaps treacle and walnut tart. House wine is £14. Open Tue to Sat D only.

Shepton Montague
ALSO RECOMMENDED
▲ The Montague Inn
Shepton Montague, BA9 8JW
Tel no: (01749) 813213
www.themontagueinn.co.uk
Gastropub £5 OFF

Local supplies are vigorously championed in this very rural pub, where friendly staff 'take a pride in serving'. Confit of duck seems to be a signature dish, served in a variety of ways – perhaps in winter with a cassoulet of cannellini beans, root vegetables and garlic sausage. Elsewhere there could be dill and beetroot-cured gravadlax (£6.95), slow-baked belly pork with potato and leek cake (£14.95) and dark chocolate mousse with Cointreau jelly and citrus curd (£5.50). House wine is £13.95. Closed Sun D.

Taunton
The Castle at Taunton
A bastion of British cooking
Castle Green, Taunton, TA1 1NF
Tel no: (01823) 272671
www.the-castle-hotel.com
Modern British | £40
Cooking score: 4

As the Guide celebrates its 60th anniversary, it is interesting to note that this bastion of British cooking is the only restaurant in this edition to have been listed in the 1951 original. The Chapman family has been the custodian of this magnificent castle (a former Norman fortress) in the centre of Taunton since 1950 – their chef Richard Guest has clocked up 12 years. He takes raw materials seriously (menus open with a list of local suppliers), presentation is a strong suit and, at their best, dishes are full of interest and flavour, among them breaded lamb's sweetbreads with sauce gribiche and an anchovy and olive salad, and honey-roast belly of ham with sweet and spiced vegetables and parsley sauce. Standards can seesaw a little, but among the successes have been an impressive trio of beef, an apple mille-feuille, and a selection of good-condition West Country cheeses. The wine list is a source of pride, honouring France thoroughly, with reliable selections from elsewhere. Prices from £18.

Chef/s: Richard Guest. **Open:** Tue to Sat L 12.30 to 2, D 7 to 9.30. **Closed:** Sun, Mon. **Meals:** alc (main courses £15 to £26). Set L and D £17.95 (2 courses) to £22.95. **Service:** 12.5% (optional). **Details:** Cards accepted. 70 seats. 30 seats outside. Separate bar. No mobile phones. Wheelchair access. Music. Children allowed. Car parking.

The Willow Tree

Top ingredients and big-impact dishes
3 Tower Lane, Taunton, TA1 4AR
Tel no: (01823) 352835
Modern British | £30
Cooking score: 6

Darren Sherlock and Rita Rambellas's waterside restaurant was once the Taunton moathouse. It's a seventeenth-century building with an inglenook and an outdoor terrace, suavely decorated, with good pictures and gentle lighting. The kitchen uses the best regional fare, from Quantock venison to Brixham fish, along with some of Britain's most outstanding dairy produce. Darren Sherlock's cooking style is unfussy modern British, with menus that read agreeably and relatively simple dishes that deliver major impact. To start, you might be offered a poached duck egg, garnished with ham lardons and sliced potato, each element playing its allotted part, while a favoured main course sees monkfish garnished with ribbons of courgette in an opulent sauce of mussels, saffron and caviar. The trend for serving lamb in two presentations is celebrated with a little moussaka alongside a portion of the roast loin,

with accompaniments of sautéed spinach and smoked aubergine purée. Spring is a good time to come, as Sherlock is a dab hand with rhubarb, best seen in the full four-part assiette of cheesecake, trifle, consommé and a flavoured goats' cheese ice cream. Wines on a carefully chosen list start at £16.95.
Chef/s: Darren Sherlock. **Open:** Tue to Sat D only 6.30 to 9. **Closed:** Mon, Sun, 26 to 31 Dec, Jan, Aug. **Meals:** Set D Tue and Wed £24.50, Thur to Sat £29.50. **Service:** not inc. **Details:** Cards accepted. 30 seats. 10 seats outside. Separate bar. No mobile phones. Music. Children allowed.

■ Wells

Goodfellows

A good fellow indeed
5 Sadler Street, Wells, BA5 2RR
Tel no: (01749) 673866
www.goodfellowswells.co.uk
Modern European | £37
Cooking score: 5
£5 OFF

'Wells is very lucky to have this place', reckoned a fan of Adam and Martine Fellows' flexible, two-pronged venue just a few steps from the cathedral – no wonder it's a local favourite that continues to please a loyal band of followers. Goodfellows itself is an upmarket seafood restaurant occupying a compact, split-level space, with an open-to-view kitchen and a more intimate area reached via a spiral staircase – the atmosphere is always congenial and the service friendly. Whether you choose from the six-course tasting menu, daily-changing set deal or short carte, the quality of the cooking rarely falters, delivering excellent seared tuna carpaccio with avocado purée, Brixham crab with sesame tuile and pomegranate dressing, and John Dory with saffron-braised fennel, coriander mash, olive and anchovy velouté. 'Superb puddings' such as chilled white chocolate and passion fruit soup with dark chocolate sponge and grenadine sorbet have also pleased the punters. The casual Sadler Street Café is run in tandem, serving coffee, cakes and good-value brasserie-style dishes

(say shoulder of lamb or grey mullet, plus a choice from the patisserie counter). The short, global wine list opens at £16.50.
Chef/s: Adam Fellows. **Open:** Tue to Sat L 12 to 2, Wed to Sat D 6.30 to 9.30. **Closed:** Sun, Mon, 25 to 27 Dec. **Meals:** alc (main courses £12 to £23). Set L £16.50 (2 courses) to £19.50. Set D £29 (2 courses) to £35. Tasting menu £55. **Service:** not inc.
Details: Cards accepted. 35 seats. Air-con. No mobile phones. Wheelchair access. Music. Children allowed.

The Old Spot
Welcoming neighbourhood favourite
12 Sadler Street, Wells, BA5 2SE
Tel no: (01749) 689099
www.theoldspot.co.uk
Modern European | £28
Cooking score: 4

£30

The Georgian building looks the part, and its back windows give views of the cathedral's magnificent west front. Reporters appreciate the bonhomie and efficiency, and the modern European cooking has made the restaurant many friends. Start perhaps with an effective pairing of Devon Blue and beetroot in hazelnut dressing, before going on to roast pollack with olive oil mash, fennel provençale and gremolata, or the ever-popular duck confit, served with lentils and braised leeks and sauced with Madeira. It's confident food that avoids any gilding of the lily. A copybook prune and almond tart is accompanied by irresistible cream from a local farm, while chocoholics might go for a warm mousse served with praline and crème fraîche. A canny, concise wine list keeps prices within bounds, and opens with a spread of five whites, five reds and a rosé by the glass from £3.50.
Chef/s: Ian Bates. **Open:** Wed to Sun L 12.30 to 2.30, Tue to Sat D 7 to 10.30. **Closed:** Mon, 1 week Christmas. **Meals:** Set L £12.50 (2 courses) to £15. Set D £23.50 (2 courses) to £27.50. Sun L £18.50 (2 courses) to £21.50. **Service:** not inc. **Details:** Cards accepted. 50 seats. No music. No mobile phones. Children allowed.

■ Weston-super-Mare

The Cove
British
Birnbeck Road, Weston-super-Mare, BS23 2BX
Tel no: (01934) 418217
www.the-cove.co.uk
'The quality of ingredients is high and the preparation of them excellent'

■ Winsford
The Royal Oak
Revitalised village local
Halse Lane, Winsford, TA24 7JE
Tel no: (01643) 851455
www.royaloakexmoor.co.uk
Gastropub | £20
Cooking score: 1

£30

Dating from the twelfth century, this thatched pub in the heart of the Exmoor National Park has really come to life since Ed and Kirsty Hoskins moved in and revitalised the place. Food is based around judicious sourcing of local ingredients, pleasing the diehards with the likes of steak and ale pie or ham, egg and chips, but also offering a plate of Exe Valley smoked salmon, comforting braised lamb suet pudding with parsley mash and rosemary gravy, and West Country cheeses. House wine is £13.50
Chef/s: Gregory Herbert. **Open:** all week L 12 to 2.30, D 6.30 to 9.30. **Meals:** alc (main courses £8 to £16). **Service:** 10% (optional). **Details:** Cards accepted. 66 seats. 20 seats outside. Separate bar. No mobile phones. Wheelchair access. Music. Children allowed. Car parking.

Average price

The average price listed in main-entry reviews denotes the price of a three-course meal, without wine.

Wiveliscombe

10 The Square

Inspiring dreams of Tuscany
10 The Square, Wiveliscombe, TA4 2JT
Tel no: (01984) 629128
www.gardneredwards.co.uk
Italian | £18
Cooking score: 4

Sally Edwards' cleverly renovated town house now functions as a boutique retreat, design showpiece and food store, with an unfussy lunchtime café attached. Her cooking takes its cue from home-grown produce and knowledgeably sourced Italian imports, offering a simple slate of peasant-style dishes ranging from roast butternut squash soup to zabaglione with baked rhubarb. In between, expect anything from warm Umbrian lentil salad with beetroot and goats' cheese to fishcakes with mustard cream. Antipasti and pastas are also good shouts. The café is housed in a converted barn with a delightful walled courtyard – perfect for some wistful dreams of Tuscany. A dozen wines start at £13.50 (£3.50 a glass).
Chef/s: Sally Edwards. **Open:** Tue to Sat L 10 to 3. **Closed:** Sun, Mon. **Meals:** alc (main courses £7 to £9). **Service:** not inc. **Details:** Cards accepted. 30 seats. 50 seats outside. Separate bar. Music. Children allowed. Car parking.

Wookey Hole

The Wookey Hole Inn

Quirky village pub
High Street, Wookey Hole, BA5 1BP
Tel no: (01749) 676677
www.wookeyholeinn.com
Gastropub | £30
Cooking score: 1

The Wookey Hole is something to see. Outwardly a traditional timbered country inn, inside it assaults the senses (in the nicest possible way) with a riot of colour, and there's even a sculpture garden. Glastonbury, you're reminded, can't be far away. Locally sourced produce, not to mention 'love and peace', are offered on menus that run from tempura tiger prawns with lime and coriander crème fraîche via rump of lamb with Savoy cabbage, pancetta and walnuts, to date and pecan pudding with toffee sauce and clotted cream. Wines start at £13.95.
Chef/s: Ivan Keable. **Open:** all week L 12 to 2.30 (3 Sun), Mon to Sat D 7 to 9.30. **Closed:** 25 and 26 Dec. **Meals:** alc (main courses £14 to £24). Sun L £19.50. **Service:** not inc. **Details:** Cards accepted. 60 seats. 100 seats outside. Music. Children allowed. Car parking.

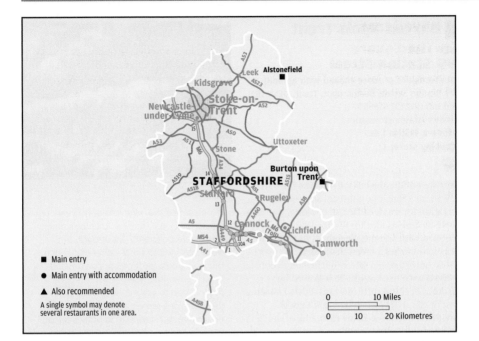

■ Alstonefield

The George

Idyllic village pub
Alstonefield, DE6 2FX
Tel no: (01335) 310205
www.thegeorgeatalstonefield.com
Gastropub | £25
Cooking score: 2

£30

Perched above Dovedale in the heart of the Peak District National Park, the George is an eighteenth-century former coaching inn that remains a true village hostelry. A reader lucky enough to live in a neighbouring village returns regularly for dishes such as scallops on borlotti bean and chestnut purée, and fillet steak with fondant potatoes, wild mushrooms and horseradish butter. Dishes don't shy away from piling up the layers, but always to good effect, as when sea bass comes with braised lettuce, a galette of potato, peas, fennel and a white wine and tarragon sauce. Reporters' favourite desserts include the matching lemon duo of posset and sorbet – 'light, stacked full of lemony flavour and very refreshing'. A compact wine list starts with house French at £12 a bottle.

Chef/s: Chris Rooney. **Open:** all week L 12 to 2.30, D 7 to 9 (6.30 to 8 Sun). **Closed:** 25 Dec. **Meals:** alc (main courses £8 to £20). **Service:** not inc. **Details:** Cards accepted. 44 seats. 60 seats outside. Separate bar. No music. No mobile phones. Wheelchair access. Children allowed. Car parking.

Symbols

🛏 Accommodation is available

£30 Three courses for less than £30

V More than three vegetarian main courses

£5 OFF £5-off voucher scheme

🍾 Notable wine list

Burton upon Trent

NEW ENTRY
99 Station Street
Staffordshire produce cooked with aplomb
99 Station Street, Burton upon Trent, DE14 1BT
Tel no: (01283) 516859
www.99stationstreet.com
Modern British | £25
Cooking score: 1

£30

Situated in the shadow of Burton's breweries, 99 Station Street might seem an unlikely location for modern British cooking, but it's a worthy ambassador for Staffordshire produce cooked with aplomb. Sprightly, unpretentious service matches a menu that doesn't overcomplicate – a starter of chicken liver pâté served with toast might be followed by sautéed beef in a mild mustard sauce. The wine list opens at £12 a bottle, but it's good manners to choose an ale from one of the venerable local brewers.
Chef/s: Daniel Pilkington. **Open:** Wed to Sun L 11.30 to 2.30 (12 to 2.30 Sun), Wed to Sat D 6 onwards. **Closed:** Mon, Tues, 25 Dec to 1 Jan, bank hols. **Meals:** alc (main courses £10 to £21). Set L £8.50 (2 courses) to £9.95. Sun L £16.95. **Service:** not inc. **Details:** Cards accepted. 36 seats. Air-con. Music. Children allowed.

Leek

READERS RECOMMEND
Qarma Tandoori
Indian
Cross Street, Leek, ST13 6BL
Tel no: (01538) 387788
www.the-qarma.com
'All in all a great experience at a fantastic price'

Wine lists then and now

In one sense, the wine lists of 60 years ago would look oddly familiar to today's diner. They were principally about claret and Burgundy, and lots of it, some of it dating back decades, most of it priced beyond reach. Even now, many restaurateurs still feel obliged to accord the red wines of these regions pre-eminence, as though no list that didn't ascend to bottles priced in three and four figures could be taken seriously.

The rest of France was there too, at least as far down as the southern Rhône (Châteauneuf-du-Pape), though there wasn't much from the deep south. There was Champagne, but virtually no other sparkling wines.

The plethora of German wines seen then (Hocks and Moselles, as they were known) have now all but disappeared from restaurant wine lists, even though what Germany has to offer these days is far superior to the wines of 60 years ago. There was perhaps some Chianti and Barolo from Italy, as well as the traditional fortified wines, sherry, port and Madeira. The world beyond Europe's boundaries was largely unexplored territory.

If diners in the 1950s could have seen wines from the United States, South America, Australia, New Zealand and South Africa on offer, they would have thought a brave new world was on its way. And so, indeed, it was.

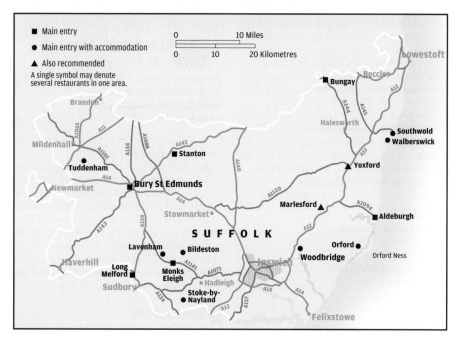

- ■ Main entry
- ● Main entry with accommodation
- ▲ Also recommended

A single symbol may denote
several restaurants in one area.

0   10 Miles

0   10   20 Kilometres

Lowestoft

Brandon

Mildenhall

Tuddenham

Newmarket

Bungay

Beccles

Halesworth

Southwold
Walberswick

Stanton

Yoxford

Bury St Edmunds

Stowmarket

Marlesford

Aldeburgh

SUFFOLK

Lavenham   Bildeston

Orford
Woodbridge

Orford Ness

Haverhill

Long
Melford

Monks
Eleigh

Hadleigh

Ipswich

Sudbury

Stoke-by-
Nayland

Felixstowe

■ Aldeburgh

The Lighthouse

Aldeburgh's top performer
77 High Street, Aldeburgh, IP15 5AU
Tel no: (01728) 453377
www.lighthouserestaurant.co.uk
Modern British | £25
Cooking score: 2

£5 OFF V £30

The pack leader on Aldeburgh's foodie main
drag has been feeding the throngs for more
than 15 years, and now combines bare-tabled
café bonhomie with a sunny, fully rounded
restaurant experience. Consistency is the
watchword, and the kitchen knows its niche
market – dishing up lively pan-European
dishes and spanking fresh seafood from the
Aldeburgh boats. Perfectly caramelised
scallops on grainy homemade hummus with
bacon is a neat trick, lamb rump might be
served with okra and cumin sauce, and cod
fillet could appear on shrimp risotto. Fish soup
is a fixture, and desserts could feature

refreshing lime tart. A tasty list from local
merchant Marcl Wines has oodles of good
drinking from £14.95
Chef/s: Guy Welsh. **Open:** all week L 12 to 2 (2.30
Sat and Sun), D 6 to 10. **Meals:** alc (main courses £9
to £18). **Service:** not inc. **Details:** Cards accepted.
100 seats. 15 seats outside. Air-con. No music. No
mobile phones. Wheelchair access. Children
allowed.

152 Restaurant

Unbuttoned neighbourhood eatery
152 High Street, Aldeburgh, IP15 5AX
Tel no: (01728) 454594
Modern European | £24
Cooking score: 1

£5 OFF £30

A popular pit-stop wedged in an alley
between the beach and the High Street, 152 has
the free-flowing, unbuttoned vibe of a
neighbourhood eatery in full swing. The
interior is light, rustic and uncluttered, and
the food generates enthusiastic feedback –

chunky sweet-cured rollmops with sun-blush tomato dressing, Dingley Dell ham hock terrine, sweet-tasting scallops with celeriac purée, and slow-cooked pork belly have all been given the thumbs-up. Service gets full marks for bubbly good humour, and the place is great for kids. Quaffable wines start at £14.50.

Chef/s: Chris Easters. **Open:** all week L 12 to 3, D 6 to 10. **Meals:** alc (main courses £10 to £18). **Service:** not inc. **Details:** Cards accepted. 52 seats. 30 seats outside. No music. No mobile phones. Wheelchair access. Children allowed.

Regatta

Breezy seaside brasserie
171 High Street, Aldeburgh, IP15 5AN
Tel no: (01728) 452011
www.regattaaldeburgh.com
Modern British | £25
Cooking score: 1

£30

In summer it can feel like France at Robert Mabey's nautically themed bastion of the Aldeburgh scene. A breezy brasserie vibe prevails and the food aims to please: home-smoked fish makes a big contribution (oaky 'Bradan Rost' salmon with mascarpone and chilli chutney has impressed), and the regular repertoire spans everything from pheasant and pistachio terrine to chickpea and butternut squash curry. Also check out the specials – perhaps crispy pork belly and squid salad, or a clever combo of meaty sea bass and oil-rich mackerel on couscous. Family-friendly desserts include sticky toffee pud, and wines start at £14.

Chef/s: Robert Mabey. **Open:** all week L 12 to 2, D 6 to 10. **Closed:** 24 to 26 Dec, 31 Dec, 1 Jan. **Meals:** alc (main courses £10 to £18). **Service:** not inc. **Details:** Cards accepted. 95 seats. Air-con. No music. Children allowed.

Also recommended

Also recommended entries are not scored but we think they are worth a visit.

▲ The Aldeburgh Market Café

170-172 High Street, Aldeburgh, IP15 5EY
Tel no: (01728) 452520
www.thealdeburghmarket.co.uk
Modern British £5 OFF

Peter Hill and Sara Fox of the Lighthouse (see entry) have added another string to their Aldeburgh bow with this terrific venture – a fishmongers, deli, greengrocers and livewire daytime café under one roof. The Market is a fiercely local foodie enterprise with an eclectic edge: have Buck's Fizz and kedgeree (£6.75) for breakfast, fill up with seafood laksa or fish pie (£8.75) at lunchtime, enjoy lemon and polenta cake (£2.95) for tea. Drinks range from organic tomato juice to Suffolk beers and wine (£3.25 a glass). Open all week.

▌ Bildeston

The Bildeston Crown

Slick mix of ancient and modern
High Street, Bildeston, IP7 7EB
Tel no: (01449) 740510
www.thebildestoncrown.com
Modern British | £35
Cooking score: 4

At first glance, the Crown might look like just one more timber-framed, fifteenth-century Suffolk hostelry – albeit a fine example of the genre. But inside it has been spiffingly revitalised with huge paintings, prints and mirrors adding some exclusivity and contemporary pizazz to its heavily beamed rooms. The main business is undoubtedly food, with back-to-the-roots themes ably expressed in unfussy 'Crown Classics' such as braised Red Poll beef faggot with artichoke mash or mutton hotpot with red cabbage. But this isn't provincial backwater cooking – other dishes trumpet a much more vigorous modern British style, with telling use of local and regional produce in starters such as cumin-roasted scallops with cauliflower

velouté, and mains of poached and roasted breast of pheasant served with its confit leg and sprouts. Lobster Caesar salad and 'very good game pies' have been heartily endorsed, and desserts from rhubarb crumble to goats' milk pannacotta with balsamic figs also earn their share of plaudits. House wines start at £18 (£4.75 a glass).
Chef/s: Chris Lee. **Open:** all week L 12 to 3, D 7 to 10. **Meals:** alc (main courses £14 to £24). Set L and D £22 (3 courses). Sun L £25. **Service:** not inc. **Details:** Cards accepted. 80 seats. 40 seats outside. Separate bar. No music. Wheelchair access. Children allowed. Car parking.

Bungay
Earsham Street Café
Local favourite for lunch and snacks
13 Earsham Street, Bungay, NR35 1AE
Tel no: (01986) 893103
Modern British | £25
Cooking score: 2
V £30

The Earsham Street Café remains, in the view of one reporter, what it has always been: an unassuming café, smart and stylish within, serving snacks and light dishes during the day alongside a fuller lunch menu. Local and regional materials play an increasing role in a cooking style that embraces salmon, ginger and chilli fishcakes, sticky pork belly with mango, spring onion and cherry tomato salad, and venison and pancetta bourguignon with celeriac purée. Desserts might include ginger syrup cheesecake with dark chocolate sauce. Service is friendly, and wines are priced from £14.
Chef/s: Stephen David. **Open:** Mon to Sat 9.30 to 4.30. **Closed:** Sun, 25 and 26 Dec, bank hols. **Meals:** alc (main courses £10 to £17.50). **Service:** not inc. **Details:** Cards accepted. 45 seats. 30 seats outside. Wheelchair access. Music. Children allowed.

Bury St Edmunds
Maison Bleue
A breath of Gallic fresh air
30-31 Churchgate Street, Bury St Edmunds, IP33 1RG
Tel no: (01284) 760623
www.maisonbleue.co.uk
Seafood | £29
Cooking score: 4
£30

There's no doubting readers' affection for Regis Crépy's long-serving French seafood restaurant, which remains a 'breath of fresh air' in the region – right down to the snazzy cosmopolitan décor, with its contemporary artworks and designer radiators affixed to the walls like exhibits from Tate Modern. No such trendy ostentation afflicts the cooking, which is firmly in the European tradition – with a few worldly embellishments on the side. Halibut might be paired with cauliflower, Dijon mustard tapenade and green olive sauce, while sea bass could arrive on the plate with cream of horseradish and pan-fried celery. Meat eaters are not forgotten (a dish of pigeon breast with Cabernet Sauvignon sauce, honey and cranberry-tinged red cabbage has been well received), and desserts such as apple and butterscotch tart have also impressed. Service comes with smiles and unmistakable French accents, set menus are excellent value, and the well-chosen, fish-friendly wine list has plenty of sound drinking from £13.20 (£3.10 a glass).
Chef/s: Pascal Canevet. **Open:** Tue to Sat L 12 to 2.30 (2 Sat), D 7 to 9.30. **Closed:** Sun, Mon, Jan, 2 weeks Jul/Aug. **Meals:** alc (main courses £14 to £27). Set L £16.95 (2 courses) to £18.95. Set D £28.95. **Service:** not inc. **Details:** Cards accepted. 65 seats. No mobile phones. Music. Children allowed.

NEW ENTRY
Pea Porridge
A perfect neighbourhood restaurant
28-29 Cannon Street, Bury St Edmunds, IP33 1JR
Tel no: (01284) 700200
www.peaporridge.co.uk
Modern British | £27
Cooking score: 3

£5 £30
OFF

This winsome eatery in a quiet residential street seems to be everyone's vision of a perfect neighbourhood restaurant. Formed from a cottage and a bakery (note the splendid old oven), it comprises three delightfully unpretentious dining rooms, all with wooden floors, exposed brick, old pine tables, and open fires in cold weather. Equally simple and unfussy is Justin Sharp's modern British cooking. He reveals a deft touch with quality ingredients and, with a nod towards Mediterranean shores, allows key flavours to shine through. Daily menus may bring crab cakes with baby tomatoes, a zingy chilli and red onion salsa and caramelised lime, followed by perfectly pink lamb rump with aubergine caponata, salsa verde, anchovy and mint, with blueberry and almond tart to finish. Wines from £13.95 a bottle.
Chef/s: Justin Sharp. **Open:** Tue to Sat L 12 to 2, D 6.30 to 10. **Closed:** Mon, Sun. **Meals:** alc (main courses £12 to £19). Set L £12 (2 courses) to £15. **Service:** not inc. **Details:** Cards accepted. 44 seats. 8 seats outside. Wheelchair access. Music. Children allowed.

Please send us your feedback

To register your opinion about any restaurant listed in the Guide, or a new restaurant that you wish to bring to our attention, please visit the web address at the bottom of the page. Your feedback informs the content of the book and will be used to compile next year's reviews.

▮ Lavenham
The Great House
Revitalised French favourite
Market Place, Lavenham, CO10 9QZ
Tel no: (01787) 247431
www.greathouse.co.uk
Modern French | £32
Cooking score: 4

Veteran supporters of the timber-framed Great House still remember it as a genuine 'French country restaurant' dishing up bourgeois food in surroundings that were as Gallic as a pack of Gauloises. A serious makeover in 2008 changed all that, although the owners have managed to preserve much of the venue's civilised charm amid the new-found, clean-lined modernity. The food has also taken a quantum leap forward, and readers have been quick to applaud the 'absolutely exquisite' dishes emanating from Regis Crépy's kitchen. Contemporary flavours now define the repertoire, from carpaccio of hand-dived scallops marinated in Cabernet Sauvignon to a praline and fromage blanc tartlet with verbena sorbet. In between, indigenous Suffolk ingredients also pop up regularly – perhaps grilled Woodbridge pigeon breasts on red cabbage stew with beetroot sauce – and local fish is sensitively handled (steamed fillet of turbot marinated in olive oil with black truffle and rosemary, say). Suffolk beers line up alongside a hefty, French-led wine list with house selections from £13.20.
Chef/s: Regis Crépy. **Open:** Wed to Sun L 12 to 2.30, Tue to Sat D 7 to 9 (9.30 Fri and Sat). **Closed:** Mon, Jan, 2 weeks summer. **Meals:** alc (main courses £15 to £24). Set L £16.95 (2 courses) to £19.95. Set D £31.95. Sun L £31.95. **Service:** not inc. **Details:** Cards accepted. 50 seats. 24 seats outside. No mobile phones. Wheelchair access. Music. Children allowed. Car parking.

Long Melford

Scutchers

Hall house with nicely balanced cooking
Westgate Street, Long Melford, CO10 9DP
Tel no: (01787) 310200
www.scutchers.com
Modern British | £26
Cooking score: 2
£5 OFF £30

The Barretts have been here since 1991 and in the past few years have injected a contemporary feel into their fifteenth-century hall house to match the tone of their food. Nick Barrett strikes a good balance between innovation and the need to satisfy some of his more conservative customers. Own hot-smoked salmon on scrambled egg with watercress purée is one way to start, followed by roast loin of lamb with caramelised onions, rösti potatoes and minty gravy, with chocolate sponge pudding and real vanilla custard to finish. Service is 'friendly and efficient', and the restaurant is cheerful yet elegant in a smart-casual way. House wine is £16.
Chef/s: Nicholas Barrett. **Open:** Tue to Sat L 12 to 2, D 7 to 9.30. **Closed:** Sun, Mon, 24 to 26 Dec. **Meals:** alc (main courses £18 to £24). Set L and D £20 (2 courses) to £26. **Service:** not inc. **Details:** Cards accepted. 65 seats. 40 seats outside. Air-con. No music. Wheelchair access. Children allowed. Car parking.

Marlesford

ALSO RECOMMENDED
▲ Farmcafé & Foodmarket

Main Road (A12), Marlesford, IP13 0AG
Tel no: (01728) 747717
www.farmcafe.co.uk
Modern British

For dedicated local sourcing and sheer, unbranded enterprise, Paul Thomas's remarkable roadside café/shop is a refuelling point *par excellence*. All-day breakfasts are the business – anything from Suffolk fry-ups to Orford kippers and devilled kidneys (£5.90)

– and lunch brings pasta, ham hock hash (£7.90), skate with capers, braised oxtail and the like, plus old-fashioned nursery puds (£4.90). Baguettes and sandwiches are also available to take out. Drinks range from zingy fresh fruit smoothies to Calvors Suffolk lager and wines (from £11.90). Open all week.

Monks Eleigh

The Swan Inn

Globetrotting gastropub food
The Street, Monks Eleigh, IP7 7AU
Tel no: (01449) 741391
www.monkseleigh.com
Gastropub | £22
Cooking score: 3
£30

Polished wood floors and subtle sage tones may suggest a trendy modern eatery, but the medieval Swan Inn is still a local watering hole, complete with a thatched roof and real ales on tap. Carol and Nigel Ramsbottom run the place as a double act – she greets everyone as if they were old friends, while he mans the stoves. British, Mediterranean and oriental influences bed happily together on the blackboard menu, and East Anglian fish is always a strong suit – perhaps dressed Cromer crab or whole roast sea bass with ginger and coriander butter. The kitchen also sends out emphatically flavoured dishes ranging from spicy Thai pork to braised lamb knuckle with Puy lentil sauce or Italian-style sweet and sour duck leg. Close the show with, say, hot caramelised fig tart. House wine is £13.50.
Chef/s: Nigel Ramsbottom. **Open:** Tue to Sun L 12 to 2, Tue to Sat D 7 to 9. **Closed:** Mon, 25 and 26 Dec, 2 weeks school summer hols. **Meals:** alc (main courses £9 to £20). Set L and D £13.75 (2 courses) to £17.75. **Service:** not inc. **Details:** Cards accepted. 40 seats. 24 seats outside. No music. Children allowed. Car parking.

> **Also recommended**
> Also recommended entries are not scored but we think they are worth a visit.

Orford

The Trinity, Crown and Castle

Laid-back, foodie hotel
Orford, IP12 2LJ
Tel no: (01394) 450205
www.crownandcastle.co.uk
Modern British | £30
Cooking score: 4

🍽 V

Dating from the sixteenth century – though you wouldn't know it from the Victorian façade – the Crown and Castle operates as a hotel with a very likeable restaurant noted for its appealing informality and laid-back atmosphere – not surprising given that Ruth Watson (Channel 4's *Country House Rescue*) and husband David are old hands at the hospitality game. It's the kind of place that revels in local produce, including game and fish, although it garners Carlingford Lough oysters and tuna from much further away – the latter might appear as 'nearly sashimi' alongside salmon and a hijiki (seaweed) and carrot salad. After that, rump of Suffolk lamb with broad bean sauce or Orford sea bass with niçoise salad and aïoli are good seasonal shouts, with rosewater and cardamom pannacotta or hot treacle tart to finish. The Trinity also dishes up self-styled 'pub lunches' (Mon to Sat) when the kitchen hits the value-for-money button with 'wild-ish' mushrooms on toast, short-crust pies and a 'jelly of the day'. An informative, modern wine list starts at £15.95.
Chef/s: Nick Thacker and Ruth Watson. **Open:** all week L 12.15 to 2.15, D 6.45 to 9.15. **Closed:** 4 to 6 Jan. **Meals:** alc (main courses £15 to £21). **Service:** not inc. **Details:** Cards accepted. 50 seats. Separate bar. No music. No mobile phones. Wheelchair access. Car parking.

Average price

The average price listed in main-entry reviews denotes the price of a three-course meal, without wine.

ALSO RECOMMENDED

▲ Butley Orford Oysterage

Market Hill, Orford, IP12 2LH
Tel no: (01394) 450277
www.butleyorfordoysterage.co.uk
Seafood

'Never fails us' noted a fan of this basic eatery, famed for its locally bred Butley Creek oysters and incomparable oak-smoked fish – try a selection of both for £10.50. Elsewhere there could be griddle squid (£7.90) or smoked eel on toast to start, while mains such as lemon sole with a prawn and vermouth sauce (£14) get the thumbs-up. Treacle tart with cream (£4.50) has also pleased reporters. Expect crowds and queues in summer. Fish-friendly wines from £14.75. Open all week in season, but limited winter hours.

Southwold

The Crown Hotel

London by the seaside
90 High Street, Southwold, IP18 6DP
Tel no: (01502) 722275
www.adnams.co.uk/hotels
Modern British | £30
Cooking score: 2

🍷 🍽

Flagship of brewer and wine fashionista Adnams, the Crown has been luring foodies from their metropolitan dwellings since the 80s and the crowds just keep on coming. The main action takes place in the Parlour, where the 'no bookings' policy means queues at the bar. It's worth the hassle, because the kitchen knows its way around the Suffolk food network and sends out some typically vibrant dishes: seared chicken livers and beans on toast, pea and mint tart with pea shoot salad, and polenta-crusted plaice with tapenade potato are just the ticket for trend-sensitive, cosmopolitan palates. Smoked salmon terrine and 'beautifully cooked' roast partridge have been applauded and there could be peach Melba Knickerbocker glory for a dizzy high-cal finale. The stellar wine list bristles with beauties and tasty numbers from around the globe. Get sampling with a few well-chosen glasses from the 'verre de vin' house selection; otherwise, bottles start at £14.50.

Chef/s: Robert Mace. **Open:** all week L 12 to 2 (2.30 Sat, 3 Sun), D 6.30 to 9 (6 to 9.30 Sat, 7 to 9 Sun). **Meals:** alc (main courses £13 to £17). **Service:** not inc. **Details:** Cards accepted. 96 seats. 32 seats outside. Separate bar. No music. No mobile phones. Wheelchair access. Children allowed. Car parking.

Sutherland House
High style, low food miles
56 High Street, Southwold, IP18 6DN
Tel no: (01502) 724544
www.sutherlandhouse.co.uk
Modern British | £22
Cooking score: 2

Bits of this highly visible Southwold landmark date back to 1455, although its skull-cracking beams and mighty fireplaces now play second fiddle to funky artwork and menus that are tuned in to the local network. Food miles matter here, and the menu is explicit when it comes to distances travelled: rabbit (one mile), Blythburgh pork (four miles), calf's liver (28 miles), scallops (Scotland). The results on the plate could range from roast pigeon breast with red onion and pickled cabbage to pan-fried Orford cod with rapeseed oil mash, sprouting broccoli and lobster foam. Desserts such as Suffolk pear Bakewell tart generally stay close to home. House wine is £15.95.

Chef/s: Dan Jones. **Open:** Tue to Sun L 12 to 3, D 7 to 9 (9.30 Fri and Sat). **Closed:** Mon, 25 Dec, 2 to 15 Jan. **Meals:** alc (main courses £9 to £22). Set L £10 (2 courses) to £13. Sun L £12.95. **Service:** not inc. **Details:** Cards accepted. 48 seats. 42 seats outside. No mobile phones. Wheelchair access. Music. Children allowed.

Visit us online
To find out more about *The Good Food Guide*, please visit www.thegoodfoodguide.co.uk

Stanton
The Leaping Hare
Vineyard restaurant with fine local produce
Wyken Vineyards, Stanton, IP31 2DW
Tel no: (01359) 250287
www.wykenvineyards.co.uk
Modern British | £26
Cooking score: 1

This striking 400-year-old timbered barn also houses an informal café and country store and is part of an estate that includes an Elizabethan manor with gardens and vineyard. Fine local produce contributes to short lunch and weekend dinner choices, perhaps a terrine of game from the estate, served with piccalilli and medlar jelly, then daube of beef with grain-mustard mash and red cabbage. The cooking can be undermined by variable service. Wines from £16.

Chef/s: Jon Ellis. **Open:** all week L 12 to 2.30, Fri and Sat D 7 to 9.30. **Closed:** 25 Dec to 5 Jan. **Meals:** alc (main courses £13 to £25). Set L £15.95 (2 courses) to £18.95. **Service:** not inc. **Details:** Cards accepted. 45 seats. 20 seats outside. Separate bar. No music. No mobile phones. Wheelchair access. Children allowed. Car parking.

Stoke-by-Nayland
The Crown
Affluent inn with seasonal food
Park Street, Stoke-by-Nayland, CO6 4SE
Tel no: (01206) 262001
www.crowninn.net
Modern British | £25
Cooking score: 2

Following its refit in 2003, the affluent Crown is now part country inn, part boutique hotel – although it has retained pubby virtues, real ales and a feel for good food. The kitchen depends on regional producers for seasonal menus that pitch standards such as smoked haddock fishcakes or faggots and mash alongside more upbeat ideas – say braised pig's cheeks with butter beans and chorizo or wild

rabbit with cavolo nero and Parmesan polenta. After that, apple, pear and hazelnut crumble is a good call. Wine-matching suggestions accompany each dish, and the list is noted for its painless mark-ups (prices start at £13.95); also take time to browse their wine shop.
Chef/s: Mark Blake. **Open:** Mon to Sat L 12 to 2.30, D 6 to 9.30 (10 Fri and Sat), Sun 12 to 9. **Closed:** 25 and 26 Dec. **Meals:** alc (main courses £11 to £20). **Service:** not inc. **Details:** Cards accepted. 130 seats. 100 seats outside. Separate bar. No music. Wheelchair access. Children allowed. Car parking.

Tuddenham

NEW ENTRY
Tuddenham Mill
Exciting food in a gorgeous setting
High Street, Tuddenham, IP28 6SQ
Tel no: (01638) 713552
www.tuddenhammill.co.uk
Modern British | £40
Cooking score: 4

£5 OFF 🍴

The setting is glorious – a beautifully restored eighteenth-century watermill standing in gorgeous countryside on the Suffolk/Cambridgeshire border. Inside, everything is pristine and modern, yet the place is small enough to have retained a personality behind the gloss. The first-floor dining room offers huge oak beams, the illuminated mill wheel, views across the millpond and Paul Foster's undoubtedly talented cooking. The young chef previously worked with Sat Bains in Nottingham (see entry) and he brings great technical skill, flair and precision to the Tuddenham Mill kitchen, creating visually exciting dishes that combine unusual ingredients and deliver thrilling textures and flavours. A memorable meal in early summer produced Cornish crab with cauliflower, coconut, coriander and lime, a dish of lemon sole with pork belly, asparagus, broad beans and pickled mushrooms, and fennel pannacotta with black olive and iced tea. House wine is £18.

Chef/s: Paul Foster. **Open:** all week L 12 to 2.15 (3 Sun), D 6.30 to 9.30. **Meals:** alc (main courses £18 to £24). Sun L £24. Tasting menu £70. **Service:** not inc. **Details:** Cards accepted. 50 seats. 30 seats outside. Separate bar. No mobile phones. Wheelchair access. Music. Children allowed. Car parking.

Walberswick
The Anchor
Dream team in a Suffolk getaway
The Street, Walberswick, IP18 6UA
Tel no: (01502) 722112
www.anchoratwalberswick.com
Modern British | £23
Cooking score: 2

£5 OFF 🍴 £30 🍷

Walberswick was doing 'Hampstead on Sea' long before the Sunday supplements, so it's no surprise that its getaway *du jour* is the spiffingly re-energised Anchor. Mark and Sophie Dorber are a dream team: he made his name as London's beer guru, she is a savvy cook who understands big-boned local flavours. Her succinct seasonal menu speaks of careful sourcing: sharing platters, West Mersea oysters, rabbit stew with Savoy cabbage and root mash; she also strays further afield for Brazilian-style pork feijoada, but brings it all back home with gingerbread and lemon curd. Gold-standard world beers are supported by wines from local heroes Adnams, with prices from £13.50 (£3.75 a glass).
Chef/s: Sophie Dorber. **Open:** all week L 12 to 3, D 6 to 9 (10 Fri and Sat). **Closed:** 25 Dec. **Meals:** alc (main courses £11 to £23). **Service:** not inc. **Details:** Cards accepted. 100 seats. 120 seats outside. Separate bar. No music. Wheelchair access. Children allowed. Car parking.

Woodbridge

NEW ENTRY

The Crown at Woodbridge

Quirky, charming bolthole with wow factor
Thoroughfare, Woodbridge, IP12 1AD
Tel no: (01394) 384242
www.thecrownatwoodbridge.co.uk
Modern European | £25
Cooking score: 3

⊟ V £30

With seventeenth-century period charm and quirky urban design (including a boat hull suspended over the granite-topped bar), the Crown has been wowing locals and Suffolk-coast visitors since it opened in July 2009. Stephen David's menu draws its inspiration from across Europe. It may look ambitious, but results on the plate are sound, revealing good technical skills, depth of flavour and a policy of using the best local produce available. Note a light dish of Butley Creek smoked eel, served with wilted spinach and scrambled egg on a toasted muffin, followed by Orford cod with chorizo, piquillo pepper and butter-bean cassoulet. Desserts include ginger pannacotta with roasted rhubarb and brandy snap. Wines from £14.50.
Chef/s: Stephen David and Luke Bailey. **Open:** all week L 12 to 2.15, D 6.15 to 9. **Meals:** alc (main courses £10 to £23). **Service:** not inc. **Details:** Cards accepted. 80 seats. 24 seats outside. Separate bar. No mobile phones. Wheelchair access. Music. Children allowed. Car parking.

The Riverside

Meals and movies by the river
Quayside, Woodbridge, IP12 1BH
Tel no: (01394) 382174
www.theriverside.co.uk
Modern British | £25
Cooking score: 1

£5 OFF £30

Well into its third decade, this ultra-reliable Woodbridge warhorse is as zesty as ever. Embedded in the cinema/arts complex by the river, it's never short of custom – thanks in part to special 'dinner and film' deals most nights. Sound ingredients, decent local sourcing and sharp presentation typify confident dishes such as seared scallops with smoked garlic dressing and onion jam, Ketley Farm ribeye and chips or boozy cider-braised pork with pear tarte Tatin. Desserts promise the likes of Baileys cheesecake with butterscotch 'caviar', and the respectable wine list starts at £14.
Chef/s: Chris Lynch. **Open:** all week L 12 to 2.15 (12.30 to 2.30 Sun), Mon to Sat D 6 to 9.30 (10.30 Fri and Sat). **Closed:** 25 and 26 Dec, 1 Jan. **Meals:** alc (main courses £8 to £22). Set D with film £30. **Service:** not inc. **Details:** Cards accepted. 55 seats. 30 seats outside. Air-con. Separate bar. Wheelchair access. Music. Children allowed. Car parking.

Yoxford

ALSO RECOMMENDED
▲ Main's Restaurant

High Street, Yoxford, IP17 3EU
Tel no: (01728) 668882
www.mainsrestaurant.co.uk
Modern European £5 OFF

Nancy Main and Jason Vincent have transformed Yoxford's drapery shop into a left-field neighbourhood eatery and bubbly local asset – check out the 'pauper's nights' and bread-making classes. Ingredients from near and far are deployed for appetising daily menus that might run from warm pigeon salad with shards of jamón crisp (£6.50) to asparagus and Parmesan brûlée or slow-roast beef ribs with wild garlic mash (£13). Gooseberry tart with elderflower ice cream (£5) makes a summery finale. Wines from £13.50. Open Tue to Sat D only.

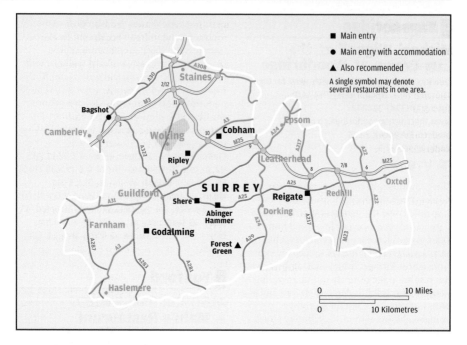

▌Abinger Hammer

Drakes on the Pond

High-class village restaurant
Dorking Road, Abinger Hammer, RH5 6SA
Tel no: (01306) 731174
www.drakesonthepond.com
Modern British | £44
Cooking score: 5

Drakes on the Pond is easily found on the A25 Dorking to Guildford road. You would be forgiven for thinking the surrounding gently rising countryside and the fishing lake would inspire a sleepy version of country house cooking, but John Morris's sights have always been trained higher than that. The focal point is the bright, low-ceilinged dining room with its well-spaced tables and 'lovely, welcoming' service. Ideas come thick and fast, as in first courses such as a tian of fresh white crab and creamed coconut teamed with a tempura of soft-shell crab and fresh mango salsa, or a classic combination of chicken liver parfait with Sauternes jelly, white truffle brioche and

date and apple chutney. Mains command attention for the quality of their raw materials: slow-cooked belly of pork with fondant potato, black pudding, crackling and pancetta cream, or for example, cannon of lamb served alongside potato and celeriac dauphinois, spinach, pea purée, roast vine tomatoes and red wine jus. To finish, a trio of chocolate – brownie, brûlée, Nutella ice cream – is impressively executed. House wine is £17.95.
Chef/s: John Morris. **Open:** Tue to Sat L 12 to 1.30, D 7 to 9.30. **Closed:** Sun, Mon, 25 and 26 Dec, bank hols. **Meals:** alc (main courses £24 to £30). Set L £21.50 (2 courses) to £24.95. **Service:** not inc. **Details:** Cards accepted. 32 seats. Air-con. No music. No mobile phones. Wheelchair access. Children allowed. Car parking.

Visit us online

To find out more about
The Good Food Guide, please visit
www.thegoodfoodguide.co.uk

▌Bagshot

Michael Wignall at the Latymer

Complex, elaborately worked food
Pennyhill Park Hotel, London Road, Bagshot,
GU19 5EU
Tel no: (01276) 471774
www.pennyhillpark.co.uk
Modern European | £58
Cooking score: 7

🍴 V

Pennyhill Park is one of those sprawling country retreats that attracts celebs and PR opportunities like a social magnet – whether it's starring in a James Bond movie, showing off F1 racer Lewis Hamilton or hosting the England rugby team. Château-style grounds designed by a French landscape gardener surround the greatly extended Victorian edifice – a silky-smooth operation that flaunts luxurious comfort on a grand scale, with a spa, country club and dining options including Michael Wignall's signature Latymer Restaurant. His clubby dining room is etched with antiquity (think oak beams, carved panelling and mullioned windows), but the food never takes a backward glance. The carte and tasting menus overlap, although there are some subtle variations – a starter of roast calf's sweetbread with Comté fondue, black-eyed peas, pumpkin purée and spiced velouté, for example, might be adorned with dinky Hereford snails for those taking the elaborate ten-course route. Wignall loves complexity and elaborately worked constructions on the plate: just imagine the sheer work involved in producing a six-part dish of Portland crab cannelloni with sugar-snap jelly, octopus pressé, samphire tempura, poached Scottish langoustine and smoked haddock brandade, or an equally intricate bonanza built around slow-cooked Lancashire suckling pig with crispy ears, seared foie gras, salsify, honey-glazed parsnip and roast Belgian endive, but also involving deep-fried consommé and lavender jus. To conclude, how about the 'continental breakfast'? This outrageous wake-up call is a world away from coffee and croissants in your hotel bedroom, a measured parody involving a parfait of cornflakes, yoghurt sorbet, a smear of pink grapefruit jelly, a squirt of pain au chocolat foam and more besides. Alternatively, a clever dessert exploring the gustatory possibilities of rhubarb and lemongrass with a dusting of basil powder might satisfy those seeking heightened sensory distraction. The cheeseboard is magnificent, or you can get your dairy fix from a playful mousse of Crottin de Périgord with microcosmic cheesy accompaniments – a film of cucumber, marinated celery and Granny Smith apple. A dozen wines by the glass (from £8.50) head the serious wine list; there is fine drinking to be had, but mark-ups are steep. Bottles start at £25.

Chef/s: Michael Wignall. **Open:** Tue to Fri L 12 to 2, Tue to Sat D 7 to 9.30. **Closed:** Sun, Mon, 1 to 15 Jan. **Meals:** Set L £25 (2 courses) to £32. Tasting menu L £58. Set D £58 (3 courses). Tasting menu D £78. **Service:** 12.5% (optional). **Details:** Cards accepted. 45 seats. 10 seats outside. Air-con. Separate bar. No music. No mobile phones. Wheelchair access. Car parking.

▌Cobham

NEW ENTRY

The Old Bear

Destination gastropub with fine credentials
High Street, Cobham, KT11 3DX
Tel no: (01932) 862116
www.theoldbearcobham.co.uk
Modern British | £30
Cooking score: 4

Although it dates from 1719, this is an up-tempo food-led pub with a modern, cosmopolitan vibe and genuine gastro credentials. Interiors come sympathetically remodelled, with fashionable touches such as leather seating alongside low beams, winter fires and oak floors, but the dining room retains a cosy, more traditional look. Nathan Green arrived here from Arbutus (see entry, London) and his modern British cooking is driven by high-quality local and seasonal

produce. He delivers bold flavours, with a sprinkling of dishes such as spiced pig's head with chickpea purée, coriander cress and crispy ears giving the nod to his Soho days. Sharing plates are also a feature (slow-cooked rib of Longhorn beef with triple-cut chips, for example) and fish could include line-caught sea bream, perhaps teamed with chorizo, red pepper pipérade and gnocchi. Rice pudding is a typically old-fashioned dessert. By-the-glass wines include eight from an Enomatic preservation unit; otherwise the well-selected global list opens at £17.50 a bottle. Related to the Albion in Islington (see entry, London).
Chef/s: Nathan Green. **Open:** all week L 12 to 3 (4 Sat), 6 to 10 (9 Sun). **Meals:** alc (main courses £11 to £19). Set L and D £15 (2 courses) to £18.
Service: 10% (optional). **Details:** Cards accepted. 120 seats. 80 seats outside. Separate bar. Music. Children allowed. Car parking.

▌Forest Green

ALSO RECOMMENDED
▲ The Parrot Inn
Forest Green, RH5 5RZ
Tel no: (01306) 621339
www.theparrot.co.uk
Gastropub

Overlooking the village green and with an interior that looks the rustic part with beams, flagstones and old tables in a network of knocked-through rooms, the Parrot conforms to everyone's idea of a classic country pub. The kitchen keeps customers satisfied with uncluttered modern dishes and shows a laudable commitment to top-class raw materials (the meat is sourced from owner Charles Gotto's farm nearby). Coarse pork terrine comes with fruit chutney (£5.95), and mutton shank with mash and kale (£14). There's also a well-stocked farm shop. Wine £14.95. Open all week.

▌Godalming
La Luna
Inventive Italian food and sensational wine
10-14 Wharf Street, Godalming, GU7 1NN
Tel no: (01483) 414155
www.lalunarestaurant.co.uk
Italian | £26
Cooking score: 4
£5 OFF ▐ V £30

La Luna celebrates ten years at Godalming in 2011. From the start it gained plaudits – and a devoted loyal following – for its modern setting and for serving Italian food to an appreciated formula: a concise menu that follows the native style (four courses with pasta or risotto coming second) and juxtaposes classics like gnocchi with Gorgonzola or minestrone with trendier offerings including poached duck egg with baby spinach, crispy root vegetables and horseradish dressing or mackerel with squid casserole and crushed parsley potato. Elsewhere there could be wild mushroom and butternut squash risotto or Sicilian casarecce (pasta) with fennel seed and pork sausage and sprouting broccoli, and mains of calf's liver with sautéed curly kale and parsnip purée. Efficient staff work the tables with consummate skill, uncorking bottles from a sensational all-Italian list that opens in Sicily at £13, goes on to a carefully selected choice under £30 and includes some real gems elsewhere.
Chef/s: Valentino Gentile. **Open:** Tue to Sat L 12 to 2, D 7 to 10. **Closed:** Sun, Mon. **Meals:** alc (main courses £10 to £19). Set L £11.95 to £14.50.
Service: not inc. **Details:** Cards accepted. 50 seats. Air-con. Music. Children allowed.

Average price

The average price listed in main-entry reviews denotes the price of a three-course meal, without wine.

Reigate

The Westerly
Buoyant bistro with something for everyone
2-4 London Road, Reigate, RH2 9AN
Tel no: (01737) 222733
www.thewesterly.co.uk
Modern British | £29
Cooking score: 4
£5 OFF | £30

This modern bistro just off Reigate's High Street is a tribute to the dedication and professionalism of Jon and Cynthia Coomb. The décor is simple, with wooden floors and plain tables making a low-key backdrop for some accomplished modern country cooking. The short carte is peppered with ideas that attempt to please all palates – a policy that seems to work well as crowds of regulars keep the mood buoyant. Rich, tasty morsels of mustard-crumbed pig's head on a well-made sauce gribiche made a strong opener at inspection. For main course a creamy bourride of bream, monkfish and red mullet with mussels and clams showed great assurance, and pudding turned up a perfectly textured treacle and almond tart. Wines are grouped by style, with a 13-strong selection by the glass, 375ml or 500ml pot Lyonnaise; the list reveals a commendable effort to source interesting bottles at ungrasping mark-ups (from £15). **Chef/s:** Jon Coomb. **Open:** Wed to Fri L 12.30 to 3, Tue to Sat D 7 to 10. **Closed:** Sun, Mon, 25 Dec for 10 days. **Meals:** alc (main courses £16 to £20). Set L £17.50 (two courses) to £19.50. **Service:** not inc. **Details:** Cards accepted. 45 seats. Air-con. No music. Children allowed.

ALSO RECOMMENDED
▲ Tony Tobin @ The Dining Room
59a High Street, Reigate, RH2 9AE
Tel no: (01737) 226650
www.tonytobinrestaurants.co.uk
Modern European £5 OFF

Tony Tobin's welcoming first-floor restaurant is still going strong, drawing loyal locals for its calm and soothing décor and attentive service, as well as for reasonably priced lunches (two courses, £12.50) and weekday evening set menus (three courses, £19.50). The cooking follows a contemporary European route typified by a set à la carte (two courses, £28.50) that might bring vodka-marinated salmon with chilli, lime and pink peppercorns, then roast pork fillet with black pudding, apple purée and mustard sauce. Wine from £16.95. Closed Sat L and Sun D.

Ripley

Drake's Restaurant
Cutting-edge, big-attitude food
The Clock House, High Street, Ripley, GU23 6AQ
Tel no: (01483) 224777
www.drakesrestaurant.co.uk
Modern British | £46
Cooking score: 6
£5 OFF

Steve Drake's restaurant occupies a clock-fronted Georgian house in a suitably timeless Surrey village. Good local artworks help create an air of relaxed refinement in the low-ceilinged dining room, where service is 'unobtrusively attentive' and there is a 'rarefied and hushed air' to proceedings. The food is cutting-edge, the fixed-price menus offering artfully composed pile-ups of ingredients that are big on attitude; Steve calls it 'artisan cooking'. A plump and immaculately timed roast scallop appears with a portion of braised pig's cheek and ceps, dressed with pear and saffron relish, while seared duck foie gras could be accompanied by peppered pineapple; the unctuous offal also turns up in a dish of wood pigeon with celeriac, salted cherries and olives. Main courses bring some cute, high-end pairings to the table – perhaps lamb with nettles, peas, chicory and grapefruit or a dish of brill with cauliflower, cucumber and turmeric. Readers are occasionally put off by the determinedly dinky dimensions of some dishes, but the technical wizardry is so great that we should perhaps trust the chef's judgement on that. A voyage of discovery at dessert stage might take in the beautifully juxtaposed flavours of beetroot parfait with mandarin sorbet, chocolate crumbs and a gel of star anise or saffron-poached pear with chocolate sandwich and perry gel. Prices on the opulent wine list start at £17.

Chef/s: Steve Drake. **Open:** Tue to Fri L 12 to 1.30, Tue to Sat D 7 to 9 (9.30 Fri and Sat). **Closed:** Sun, Mon, 2 weeks Jan, 2 weeks Aug, bank hols (exc Good Friday). **Meals:** Set L £21 (2 courses) to £26. Set D £38.50 (2 courses) to £46. Tasting menu £60. **Service:** not inc. **Details:** Cards accepted. 40 seats. Children allowed. Car parking.

Shere

Kinghams
An exceedingly steady ship
Gomshall Lane, Shere, GU5 9HE
Tel no: (01483) 202168
www.kinghams-restaurant.co.uk
Modern British | £33
Cooking score: 2

£5
OFF

'Pretty well unchangeable' is one returning visitor's verdict on this seventeenth-century cottage restaurant, an enduring stalwart of the Surrey dining scene. After 18 years, Paul Baker is not about to rock an exceedingly steady ship, and his food remains true to the spirit of wholesome flavour and comfort. Well-timed scallops and chorizo with a minted salad of courgettes, broad beans, pea shoots and smoked chilli crème fraîche, and mains of thick, pink slices of lamb wrapped in a thyme mousse and aubergines and served with a full-flavoured baby caper and shallot sauce suit the tone of the place, but results can be hit and miss. Service, however, is excellent. House wine is £15.95.

Chef/s: Paul Baker. **Open:** Tue to Sun L 12 to 2 (4 Sun), Tue to Sat D 7 to 11. **Closed:** Mon, 25 Dec to 6 Jan. **Meals:** alc (main courses £13 to £20). Set L and D £16.95 (2 courses) to £22.90. Sun L £23.95. **Service:** not inc. **Details:** Cards accepted. 48 seats. 16 seats outside. Wheelchair access. Music. Children allowed. Car parking.

ALSO RECOMMENDED
▲ The William Bray
Shere Lane, Shere, GU5 9HS
Tel no: (01483) 202044
www.thewilliambray.co.uk
Gastropub

Bright and relaxed, with a simple menu, this substantial Edwardian pub in the centre of Shere is a great local asset. Whether you are taking advantage of the outside tables or sitting in the bar or dining room, all is busy, convivial and unreservedly good-natured. A crowd-pleasing, fashionable menu offers pub classics such as shepherd's pie or a good burger (£9.95) alongside black bream with salsa verde (£13.50) and pannacotta with blackberry sorbet (£6.95). House wine £15.50. Open all week.

Woking

Sands at Bleak House
Modern British
Chertsey Road, Woking, GU21 5NL
Tel no: (01483) 756988
www.sandsatbleakhouse.co.uk
'The whole evening was a sheer delight... I cannot recommend this restaurant enough'

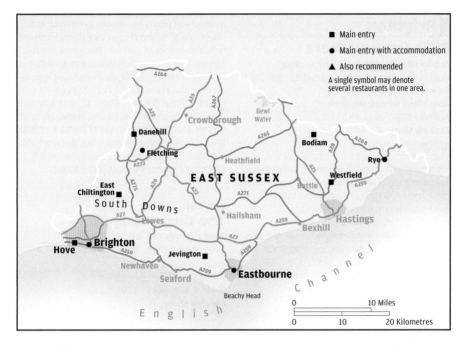

■ Bodiam

NEW ENTRY
The Curlew

Spruced-up ex-pub with interesting food
Junction Road, Bodiam, TN32 5UY
Tel no: (01580) 861394
www.thecurlewrestaurant.co.uk
Modern British | £29
Cooking score: 3

£30

This spruced-up, white-weatherboarded former pub stands at a lonely crossroads on the Kent/Sussex border close to Bodiam Castle. Inside, wooden floors, leather chairs and jazzy Paul Smith striped fabrics combine well with cool grey and blue-painted panelling and quirky wall coverings. It makes a suitably restrained setting in which to sample Neil McCue's imaginative modern British cooking. With Romney Marsh lamb, micro-herbs and salads from Appledore, and fish from south-coast day boats the seasonal menus reveal plenty of local interest, some unusual combinations and a feel for flavours and textures. Slow-cooked duck egg served with smoked haddock, bacon, shrimps and capers is a typical starter, followed perhaps by a beautifully timed lamb shoulder with lamb 'bacon', artichoke and mint dripping, or duck breast with rhubarb, beetroot and goats' cheese. For dessert, try a delicious combination of nutmeg milk pudding and treacle tart. Wines from £14.70.
Chef/s: Neil McCue. **Open:** Wed to Sun L 12 to 2, D 6 to 9.30 (9 Sun). **Closed:** Mon, Tue, 27 Dec to mid Jan, one week spring, one week autumn. **Meals:** alc (main courses £15 to £17). Set L £16 (2 courses) to £20. **Service:** not inc. **Details:** Cards accepted. 64 seats. 32 seats outside. No mobile phones. Music. Children allowed. Car parking.

Average price

The average price listed in main-entry reviews denotes the price of a three-course meal, without wine.

Brighton

Bill's Produce Store

Foodie market with good Brit cooking
The Depot, 100 North Road, Brighton, BN1 1YE
Tel no: (01273) 692894
www.billsproducestore.co.uk
British | £20
Cooking score: 2

V £30

This high-class food market and popular all-day eatery is based in a flamboyantly converted bus garage. The kitchen produces honest, generous British food using quality ingredients. Breakfast could bring smoked mackerel with spinach, tomatoes and poached egg; otherwise, expect the legendary fish finger sandwiches, good beef lasagne, mezze and salad plates. For supper, look out for mussels steamed in beer, fish pie or Cumberland sausage and mash, with workmanlike renditions of fruit pavlova and warm chocolate brownie for dessert. House wine £13.95. There is a branch in Lewes and more are planned.
Chef/s: Jane Hill. **Open:** all week 8 to 5 (9 to 5 Sun), D 5 to 10. **Closed:** 25 Dec. **Meals:** alc (main courses £8 to £14). **Service:** not inc. **Details:** Cards accepted. 96 seats. Air-con. No music. Wheelchair access. Music. Children allowed.

Due South

Easy-going seafront eatery
139 Kings Road Arches, Brighton, BN1 2FN
Tel no: (01273) 821218
www.duesouth.co.uk
Modern European | £25
Cooking score: 2

V £30

'We were fortunate to get a window table upstairs with a nice view of beach and sea', wrote one who was happy to find this seafront restaurant in a Victorian arch under the promenade. It's easy-going inside, the décor simple and unfussy. Fresh ingredients and good combinations feature on a modern menu that may offer, as a first course, warm lamb's tongue with confit potatoes, salted mackerel dressing and mint oil or a main of sea bass with fishcake, buttered spinach and warm tartare. Simple fish and chips have been praised, as have desserts such as rhubarb and cardamom pannacotta. House wine is £14.50.
Chef/s: Michael Bremner. **Open:** all week L 12 to 3, D 6 to 10. **Closed:** 25 and 26 Dec. **Meals:** alc (main courses £10 to £28). Set L £10 (2 courses) to £15. Sun L £25. **Service:** 10% (optional). **Details:** Cards accepted. 52 seats. 40 seats outside. Air-con. Wheelchair access. Music. Children allowed.

NEW ENTRY
The Ginger Dog

Food that fits the bill
12-13 College Place, Brighton, BN2 1HN
Tel no: (01273) 620990
www.gingermanrestaurants.com
Modern European | £30
Cooking score: 3

£5 OFF

If Brighton's eating-out scene still lags a little way behind what its locals would support, the indefatigable Ben McKellar has been the best thing to happen to it over the past 15 years. His talent lies in spotting a geographical gap in the market and filling it with another well-trained chef, another pleasantly laid-back venue, and food that fits the bill to a T. His latest venture was once a back-street pub with sports TV, but is now a back-street pub with great staff and a menu of compelling, uncomplicated food. Start with a serving of cold, lightly pickled wild sea trout with assertively mustardy beetroot rémoulade, and continue with a satisfying, flavourful main course such as roasted veal rump, served with an oozy garlic croquette, spring veg and a high-gloss Marsala sauce. Dessert could be passion-fruit custard tart with mascarpone ice cream. A slate of wines starts at £3.75 a glass.
Chef/s: Ben McKellar and Robin Koehorst. **Open:** all week L 12 to 2 (3 Fri, 12.30 to 3 Sat, 12.30 to 4 Sun), D 6 to 10. **Closed:** 25 Dec. **Meals:** alc (main courses £10 to £18). Set L and D £10. **Service:** 12.5% (optional). **Details:** Cards accepted. 30 seats. Separate bar. Music. Children allowed.

The Ginger Pig

Buzzy local asset with straightforward food
3 Hove Street, Brighton, BN3 2TR
Tel no: (01273) 736123
www.gingermanrestaurants.com
Modern British | £25
Cooking score: 4

£30
▼

Reports have branded the Ginger Pig a great neighbourhood asset, and the place certainly has a good buzz. There's an unpretentious, contemporary look to both bar and dining area, and seasonal raw materials are good – the menu is not so long on ingredients that it loses focus. Starters such as baby squid stuffed with chickpea, onion and confit lemon with black pudding and fennel salad is perfectly cooked, while venison and smoked bacon terrine with celeriac proves to be a simple rustic dish. Similarly, a main course of braised lamb suet pudding with cauliflower mash and stout gravy, and char-grilled Scotch ribeye with dripping chips, field mushrooms and garlic and parsley butter have been appreciated precisely for their straightforward virtues. Desserts include peanut butter and white chocolate parfait. Prices on the well-spread wine list start at £14.
Chef/s: Dave Metterill and Ben McKellar. **Open:** all week L 12 to 2 (3 Fri, 12.30 to 3 Sat, 12.30 to 4 Sun), D 6.30 to 10. **Closed:** 25 Dec. **Meals:** alc (main courses £9 to £20). Set L £10. **Service:** not inc. **Details:** Cards accepted. 60 seats. 35 seats outside. Separate bar. Wheelchair access. Music. Children allowed.

Gingerman

Impressive fashionable cooking
21A Norfolk Square, Brighton, BN1 2PD
Tel no: (01273) 326688
www.gingermanrestaurants.com
Modern European | £30
Cooking score: 3

This was the first of Ben McKellar's ever-growing group of restaurants and pubs and for many it's still the most intimately agreeable. It's a smallish, low-ceilinged room in the centre of town, with intelligently chatty service and some impressive cooking. A fashionably urban dish offers plaice goujons with a pea shooter, caper and nori hash, perhaps followed by fillet of local beef with celeriac gratin, broccoli purée, salsify crisps and red wine sauce, or a multi-layered vegetarian rösti dish. Desserts relax into slightly more classic bistro mould with Drambuie chocolate mousse and almond shortbread, or rhubarb gratin with pecan crumble ice cream. Ridgeview Sussex sparklers crop up among the fizzes on a quality list that starts at £14.
Chef/s: Simon Neville-Jones and Ben McKellar. **Open:** Tue to Sun L 12.30 to 1.30, D 7 to 9.15. **Closed:** Mon, 2 weeks Jan. **Meals:** Set L £15 (2 courses) to £18. Set D £26 (2 courses) to £30. **Service:** not inc. **Details:** Cards accepted. 32 seats. Air-con. Music. Children allowed.

The Restaurant at Drakes

Sheer culinary impact
43-44 Marine Parade, Brighton, BN2 1PE
Tel no: (01273) 696934
www.drakesofbrighton.com
Modern British | £37
Cooking score: 6

£5
OFF

Fine dining in Brighton was set on a new course when the basement restaurant at this seafront hotel opened in 2005. What the place lacks in sea views (you can have your fill of those in the ground-floor cocktail bar after all), it more than makes up for in sheer culinary impact. It's a white-tiled, light space with comfortable banquette seating, and appealing service that behaves as though we're all on the same side. Andrew MacKenzie is a talented, intuitive chef, and composes dishes with an obvious eye for balance. Seasonal game cookery is especially appreciated by reporters, but all meats are top-quality, including the 21-day aged Irish beef fillet, which comes fully accoutred with potato rösti, a faggot of the shin meat mixed with pork, roast carrots, spinach and a sauce enriched with bone marrow and truffle. Daring starters

have included tempura frogs' legs with puréed garlic and hazelnut salad, while robust fish treatments have taken in Loch Duart salmon with artichoke barigoule. Soufflés with a scoop of ice cream dropped in are a must – perhaps blackcurrant or rum and raisin – or there may be lemon meringue pie with mascarpone custard. Wines by the glass start at £5.50.
Chef/s: Andrew MacKenzie. **Open:** all week L 12.30 to 1.45, D 7 to 9.30. **Meals:** Set L and D £28 (2 courses) to £37. Sun L £25. Tasting menu £50 (5 courses). **Service:** 12.5% (optional). **Details:** Cards accepted. 44 seats. Air-con. Separate bar. No mobile phones. Music. Children allowed.

Terre à Terre
Funky veggie maverick
71 East Street, Brighton, BN1 1HQ
Tel no: (01273) 729051
www.terreaterre.co.uk
Vegetarian | £28
Cooking score: 3

V £30

In recent times, this rule-breaking veggie has reined in some of its maverick tendencies, but it still knows how to assault the taste buds and challenge preconceptions about flesh-free food – the trick is to plunder the world larder with free abandon. Smoked sakuri soba (a chilled Japanese collation involving noodles, umeboshi plums, smoked tofu, white miso, pomegranate 'beads', wasabi cashews) is a typically full-on starter, likewise a main called Sodden Socca (hot chickpea pancakes with piquant caponata, marmara tapenade, thyme, saffron and orange dressing). For a sweet hit, finish with Bum (a little sheep's cheesecake with sambuca-soaked raisins, rosemary lemon syrup, black grapes, fennel, orange zest and almond biscotti). Also look out for special themed evenings, such as 'Mumbai Mondays'. The mood is pure Brighton (offbeat, extrovert, funky, colourful), kids do well and the organically inclined wine list is totally in tune with the restaurant's philosophy. Prices start at £17.50 a bottle (£13.95 a carafe).

Chef/s: Dino Pavledis. **Open:** Tue to Sun L 12 to 4.30, D 5 to 10.30 (11 Sat, 10 Sun). **Closed:** Mon (exc bank hols), 25 and 26 Dec. **Meals:** alc (main courses £11 to £15). **Service:** 10% (optional). **Details:** Cards accepted. 100 seats. 15 seats outside. Air-con. Wheelchair access. Music. Children allowed.

ALSO RECOMMENDED
▲ La Marinade
77 St Georges Road, Brighton, BN2 1EF
Tel no: (01273) 600992
www.lamarinaderestaurant.co.uk
Modern European £5 OFF

The outer reaches of Kemptown village, probably all of about 15 minutes' walk from central Brighton, are home to a handful of quirky neighbourhood restaurants, none more so than Nick Lang's single-handed operation. On two bright yellow floors, a repertoire of tried-and-true dishes takes in the likes of seared local scallops with morcilla and balsamic dressing (£7.50), roast guinea fowl with seared foie gras, truffled mash and wild mushrooms in Marsala jus (£13.50), and a rather racy lemon and lime posset (£4.95). Wines from £3.95 a glass. Open Thur to Sat L, Tue to Sat D.

▲ TABLE
Jubilee Square, Brighton, BN1 1GE
Tel no: (01273) 900383
www.tablebrighton.com
Modern European

The restaurant at the Brighton branch of the boutique myhotel chain has its own entrance off a big square next to the recently built Jubilee Library. It's handy for shows at the Theatre Royal (there's a good-value pre-theatre deal of two courses and a glass of wine for £12.50), and the menus are all about the kind of informal brasserie eating that Brighton loves. Think deep-fried devilled whitebait with fennel, red onion and orange salad (£5), braised lamb shoulder with baby onions, peas and lettuce (£12.50), and Amalfi lemon tart with crème fraîche (£4.50). Wines from £12.50. Open all week L, Fri to Sun D.

Danehill
The Coach and Horses
Pub classics in a soul-soothing setting
School Lane, Danehill, RH17 7JF
Tel no: (01825) 740369
www.coachandhorses.danehill.biz
Gastropub | £25
Cooking score: 2

£30

A country pub serving the local communities of Danehill and Chelwood Gate since the mid-nineteenth century, the Coach and Horses boasts a sun terrace at the back and lovely gardens with views of the South Downs at the front. It makes a soul-soothing, bucolic setting for the modern British cooking on offer, which ranges from spicy Portland crab and saffron risotto with sweet chilli and Parmesan to pub staples such as steak and kidney pie, with local pheasant and prune terrine to begin, and apple and cranberry crumble with cinnamon crème fraîche for afters. An imaginative international list opens with South African house wines at £13.75.
Chef/s: Lee Cobb. **Open:** all week L 12 to 2 (2.30 Sat and Sun), D 7 to 9 (5 to 8 Sun). **Meals:** alc (main courses £11 to £19). Bar menu available. **Service:** not inc. **Details:** Cards accepted. 60 seats. 100 seats outside. Separate bar. Wheelchair access. Music. Children allowed. Car parking.

East Chiltington
The Jolly Sportsman
Pub with unfussy modern cooking
Chapel Lane, East Chiltington, BN7 3BA
Tel no: (01273) 890400
www.thejollysportsman.com
Gastropub | £28
Cooking score: 2

V £30

The weather-boarded exterior of this rural pub has been painted a 'Farrow and Ballish green', and inside there's a small traditional bar and a contemporary dining room leading onto a delightful garden. It provides a congenial backdrop for modern cooking that makes a conscientious use of local materials. At its best the kitchen can deliver unfussy dishes with skill and dexterity: to start you might choose chorizo and crayfish linguine or a well reported twice-baked cheese soufflé stuffed with baked courgettes, before full-bodied main courses such as char-grilled calf's liver with bacon, colcannon and sweet-and-sour onions or 'lovely venison'. House wine is £14.25.
Chef/s: Alistair Doyle. **Open:** all week L 12 to 2.30 (3 Sun), D 6.45 to 9.30 (10 Fri and Sat). **Closed:** 25 and 26 Dec. **Meals:** alc (main courses £10 to £20). Set L £12 (2 courses) to £15.75. Sun L £18.50. **Service:** not inc. **Details:** Cards accepted. 100 seats. 40 seats outside. Air-con. Separate bar. No music. Wheelchair access. Children allowed. Car parking.

Eastbourne
Mirabelle at the Grand Hotel
Starry seaside hotel with skilled food
Jevington Gardens, Eastbourne, BN21 4EQ
Tel no: (01323) 412345
www.themirabelle.co.uk
Modern European | £38
Cooking score: 5

£5 OFF   ☐ V

The pristine white edifice on the Eastbourne seafront looks like a stack of meringues, and is one of the grandest seaside hotels to be found anywhere. It's justly proud of its starry heritage, having hosted Claude Débussy while he was finishing his composition *La Mer*, fittingly. Are there still ghostly echoes of the BBC Palm Court Orchestra, which used to broadcast live from here every Sunday evening? The pastel-hued Mirabelle overlooks the promenade, and is an elegant setting for the highly skilled cooking of Gerald Röser. His modern British dishes spurn rackety combinations in favour of gentle cosseting, perhaps with smoked ham hock terrine and sauce gribiche, salmon and asparagus in chervil vinaigrette, or pinkly roasted rump of lamb with a thyme-scented jus. One reporter was full of praise for a dinner that featured a trio of fish served on fennel 'sauerkraut' with new potatoes and spinach, followed by plum and star anise ice cream with caramelised plum compote. Richer dessert tastes might be satiated by a chocolate version of crème brûlée with hazelnut biscotti. A second dining room, the Garden Restaurant, serves slightly more traditional fare. The monster wine list is a work of art, finding quality producers in Chile and Portugal as well as the expected crus classés. Prices open at £21.75.

Chef/s: Gerald Röser. **Open:** Tue to Sat L 12.30 to 2, D 7 to 10. **Closed:** Sun, Mon, first 2 weeks Jan. **Meals:** Set L £19.50 (2 courses) to £22. Set D £38 (3 courses). Tasting menu £56. **Service:** 10%. **Details:** Cards accepted. 50 seats. Air-con. Separate bar. No mobile phones. Wheelchair access. Music. Children allowed. Car parking.

■ Fletching
The Griffin Inn
A restorative inn for all seasons
Fletching, TN22 3SS
Tel no: (01825) 722890
www.thegriffininn.co.uk
Modern European | £30
Cooking score: 3
£5 OFF ♦ 🍴

A very English inn for all seasons, the sixteenth-century Griffin is blessed with restorative attributes aplenty. In summer, entrancing views from the splendid tiered garden over the Ouse Valley are 'a sight for sore eyes'; in winter there are log fires ablaze in the snugly beamed interior. The bar dispenses real ales and touts an upbeat blackboard menu, while the equally homely restaurant aims higher with ambitious seasonal dishes and a special liking for fish. You might be offered cumin-spiced scallops with crushed chickpeas and crispy seaweed ahead of brill with creamed celeriac, tapenade and vincotto, although the kitchen is equally at home with meatier possibilities (fillet of Fletching beef with foie gras butter, or rump of lamb with spinach risotto cake and lentil jus, say). To conclude, perhaps quince and pear frangipane tart. The Griffin's final ace is its terrific, knowledgeably assembled and 'fairly priced'

wine list. Eclectic choices abound, with house selections from £13.85 and around 20 by the glass.

Chef/s: Andrew Billings and Onik Minassian. **Open:** all week L 12 to 2.30 (3 Sat and Sun), Mon to Sat D 7 to 9.30. **Closed:** 25 Dec. **Meals:** alc (main courses £15 to £24). Sun L £30. **Service:** 10% (optional). **Details:** Cards accepted. 60 seats. 35 seats outside. Separate bar. No music. No mobile phones. Wheelchair access. Music. Children allowed. Car parking.

■ Hastings
READERS RECOMMEND
Maggie's Fish & Chips
Seafood
Rock-a-Nore Road, Hastings, TN34 3DW
Tel no: (01424) 430205
'Exceptionally fresh fish, tasting like it has just come straight off the boat'

■ Hove
The Foragers
Likeable local with keen prices
3 Stirling Place, Hove, BN3 3YU
Tel no: (01273) 733134
www.theforagerspub.co.uk
Gastropub | £26
Cooking score: 2
£5 OFF V £30

Easily spotted on a quiet Hove street, this corner pub has two dining rooms and a sheltered all-weather garden. Mismatched tables emphasise the rusticity in the light-filled front bar, where you can glimpse the chefs at work. Keenly priced menus foreshadow the cooking's direct style. There is no artifice, just decent cooking of the main ingredients (many locally sourced) evident in a starter of mustard-cured mackerel with apple and beetroot, and in honey-glazed pig's cheek with beer-braised carrots and pickled cabbage. Desserts bring Sussex pond pudding and custard tart. Service is solicitous and easy-going, and house wine is £12.80.

Chef/s: Jake Northcoate-Green. **Open:** all week L 12 to 3 (4 Sat and Sun), Mon to Sat D 6 to 10. **Closed:** 25 Dec. **Meals:** alc (main courses £11 to £19). Set L £12 (2 courses) to £15. **Service:** not inc. **Details:** Cards accepted. 90 seats. 90 seats outside. Separate bar. Wheelchair access. Music. Children allowed.

NEW ENTRY

Graze Restaurant
Beautiful tasting dishes
42 Western Road, Hove, BN3 1JD
Tel no: (01273) 823707
www.graze-restaurant.co.uk
Modern British | £30
Cooking score: 5

£5
OFF

Graze is a small, intimate, affable restaurant at the Hove end of Western Road, split between a narrow ground-floor room and a basement space with a rather glamorous private area. Kate Alleston runs a tight but infectiously good-humoured ship out front, and the place has become reliably busy. As you might guess from the restaurant's name, grazing is a major theme on the menu: a combo of seared tuna crusted in pepper and anise (timed to the second) with smoked anchovy tapenade, potato fondant and quails' eggs certainly provides ample food for thought as well as gustatory excitement. There are conventional main courses too, as well as seven-course tasting menus in vegetarian and omnivorous versions. Cooking skills are pretty impressive and dishes are beautifully presented – witness a steamed sea bream fillet on sin-dark cavolo nero purée, with chunks of Jerusalem artichoke and a razor-clam cooked '*au gratin*' on the half-shell. Elsewhere, juicy, flavourful organic venison appears as a hunk of gamey meat wrapped in pancetta with a pile of buttery mash and a rather delicate Madeira sauce. Wines are a small, intelligent selection, with some nice by-the-glass offerings. Bottles start at £13.95.
Chef/s: Gethin Jones. **Open:** Tue to Sun L 12 to 2 (4 Sun), Tue to Sat D 6.30 to 9.30. **Closed:** Mon, 25 and 26 Dec, 1 Jan. **Meals:** alc (main courses £14 to £18).

Set L £14 (2 courses) to £20. Set D £16 (2 courses) to £22. Sun L £13.50. Tasting menu £35 (7 courses). **Service:** 12.5% (optional). **Details:** Cards accepted. 50 seats. 4 seats outside. Separate bar. No mobile phones. Music. Children allowed.

The Real Eating Company
A foodie paradise
86-87 Western Road, Hove, BN3 1JB
Tel no: (01273) 221444
www.real-eating.co.uk
Modern British | £23
Cooking score: 2

V £30

Nothing could whet the appetite more than browsing through this foodie paradise. You might opt for breakfast, graze on charcuterie or choose something more substantial. The menu highlights the kitchen's cosmopolitan approach and commitment to good shopping and sourcing; daily specials, in particular, follow the market. A winter salad of pear, walnut and Colston Bassett Stilton makes a perfect start, ahead of Barnsley lamb chop with bubble and squeak and buttered winter greens, or a simple roast free-range chicken. Sticky toffee pudding with hot vanilla custard might head up desserts, and there are superb cheeses from Neal's Yard Dairy. House wine is £14.75. There is another branch at 18 Cliffe High Street, Lewes, BN7 2AJ; tel: (01273) 402650.
Chef/s: Lisa Walker. **Open:** all week 9 to 6 (4 Sun), Tue to Sat D 6.30 to 9.30. **Closed:** 25 Dec. **Meals:** alc (main courses £7 to £16). **Service:** 12.5% (optional). **Details:** Cards accepted. 40 seats. 14 seats outside. Air-con. Wheelchair access. Music. Children allowed.

READERS RECOMMEND

Coriander
Global
5 Hove Manor Parade, Hove, BN3 2DF
Tel no: (01273) 730850
www.corianderbrighton.co.uk
'Skilfully fusing flavours from ingredients that are mostly local and often organic'

Jevington

The Hungry Monk

Quality and value on the plate
Jevington, BN26 5QF
Tel no: (01323) 482178
www.hungrymonk.co.uk
Modern European | £36
Cooking score: 2
£5
OFF

For 43 years this popular cottage restaurant has been dispensing high-quality cooking with a resolute focus on value on the plate. Interiors are traditionally English, with ceilings as beamed as you would expect in the intimate dining room and cosy sitting rooms, but the kitchen is far from retro, using sound British ingredients to create modern European dishes. Starters such as seafood fritto misto and mains of crisp breast of duckling or rabbit roasted in prosciutto with leek and ricotta and mild mustard sauce are typical choices. This is the home of banoffi pie, but there's also lemon meringue posset. House wine from £17.50.
Chef/s: Gary Fisher. **Open:** Tue to Sun L 12 to 2, all week D 6.45 to 9.30. **Closed:** 24 to 26 Dec, bank hols. **Meals:** Set L £18.95 (2 courses) to £21.95. Set D £28.90 (2 courses) to £35.50. Sun L £29.95. **Service:** 12.5% (optional). **Details:** Cards accepted. 82 seats. Air-con. Separate bar. No music. Children allowed. Car parking.

Rye

The George in Rye

Well-to-do inn with good ingredients
98 High Street, Rye, TN31 7JT
Tel no: (01797) 222114
www.thegeorgeinrye.com
Modern European | £26
New Chef
🖃 V £30

The revitalised George on Rye's High Street belongs to the new breed of well-to-do inns, combining gentrified country décor with food based around judicious sourcing of ingredients. An atmospheric bar with a winter fire leads to a sheltered courtyard garden; here

good-value daytime offerings range from mussels and Rye Bay fish and chips to duck confit and Romney Marsh lamb burgers. Dinner in the small restaurant is pricier – perhaps ham hock terrine with piccalilli followed by spiced sea bass with Puy lentils. We were notified about the arrival of a new chef too late to respond with an inspection; reports please. House wine is £18.
Chef/s: Paul Gordon. **Open:** all week L 12 to 3 (3.30 Fri to Sun), D 6.30 to 9.30 (10.30 Fri to Sun). **Meals:** alc (main courses £14 to £17). Set L £12.50 (2 courses) to £14.95. **Service:** not inc. **Details:** Cards accepted. 40 seats. 20 seats outside. Separate bar. Music. Children allowed.

Landgate Bistro

Excellent local fish and game
5-6 Landgate, Rye, TN31 7LH
Tel no: (01797) 222829
www.landgatebistro.co.uk
Modern British | £26
Cooking score: 3
£30

A mood of bonhomie prevails at Martin Peacock and Nilla Westin's homely restaurant in a pair of interconnecting Georgian cottages. He cooks, while she takes care of business out front. Local produce is used to good effect on their short menus. Fish and game, in particular, are excellent, showing up in decent, robust versions of well-tried dishes: Rye Bay scallops wrapped in home-cured bacon and served with a sherry and shallot sauce, say, or a main course of breast and sage-stuffed leg of guinea fowl with spinach and mustard mash. Grilled whole Dover sole and Romney Marsh lamb (served with French beans and gratin potatoes) have also been endorsed, although regulars would like to see some new puddings. House wine is £13.90.
Chef/s: Martin Peacock. **Open:** Sat and Sun L 12 to 3, Wed to Sat D 7 to 9. **Closed:** Mon, Tue, Christmas and New Year. **Meals:** alc (main courses £11 to £18). Set L £12.30 (2 courses) to £15.30. Set D (Wed and Thur only) £15.30 (2 courses) to £18.30. **Service:** not inc. **Details:** Cards accepted. 32 seats. Separate bar. No mobile phones. Music. Children allowed.

Webbe's at the Fish Café

Easy-going seafood eatery
17 Tower Street, Rye, TN31 7AT
Tel no: (01797) 222226
www.webbesrestaurants.co.uk
Seafood | £25
Cooking score: 2

£30

The ground floor of this unusual four-storey brick building houses an easy-going eatery where on-the-ball service and an open kitchen convey the feel of a businesslike operation. As the name suggests, seafood dominates proceedings, with an extensive list of starters ranging from deep-fried sprats with lemon and parsley, via scallop, potato and watercress chowder to chicken liver parfait with red onion marmalade. Main courses might take in grilled fillets of lemon sole with wild garlic and spring vegetables, with sirloin of beef a token meat option. While there is no doubting the kitchen's skills, reports suggest under-par dishes can slip through the net. A more formal restaurant is upstairs, with limited evening opening. Wines from £13.95.
Chef/s: Matthew Drinkwater. **Open:** all week L 12 to 2 (3 Sat and Sun), D 6 to 9 (10.30 Fri to Sun). **Closed:** 24 to 26 Dec. **Meals:** alc (main courses £13 to £22). **Service:** not inc. **Details:** Cards accepted. 52 seats. Children allowed.

Westfield
The Wild Mushroom

Discreet country restaurant
Woodgate House, Westfield Lane, Westfield, TN35 4SB
Tel no: (01424) 751137
www.wildmushroom.co.uk
Modern British | £32
Cooking score: 2

£5 OFF

A converted Victorian farmhouse provides the setting for this likeable country restaurant, noted for its discreet sophistication, relaxed charm and capably executed food. Smoked quail and foie gras salad is a favourably

reported starter, although wild mushroom and butternut squash risotto might seem more apt – given the fungal moniker. Main courses accentuate the contemporary theme, as the kitchen matches wild sea bass with linguine, salsify, Jerusalem artichoke and basil velouté, or partners roast loin of venison with cassis sauce and caramelised pear. To finish, orange mousse with chocolate ganache, lemon curd and mint syrup is a typical choice. House wine is £15.95.
Chef/s: Chris Weddle. **Open:** Tue to Sun L 12 to 2 (3 Sun), Tue to Sat D 6 to 9 (10.30 Fri and Sat). **Closed:** Mon, 25 Dec for 2 weeks. **Meals:** alc (main courses £12 to £19). Set L £15.95 (2 courses) to £18.95. Sun L £22.50. Tasting menu £32. **Service:** not inc.
Details: Cards accepted. 40 seats. Separate bar. No mobile phones. Wheelchair access. Music. Children allowed. Car parking.

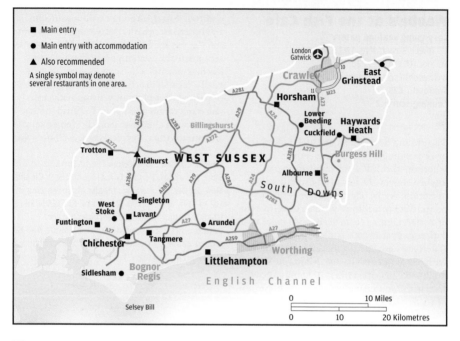

- ■ Main entry
- ● Main entry with accommodation
- ▲ Also recommended

A single symbol may denote
several restaurants in one area.

■ Albourne

The Ginger Fox

Convivial country pub star
Muddleswood Road, Albourne, BN6 9EA
Tel no: (01273) 857888
www.gingermanrestaurants.com
Modern British | £25
Cooking score: 4

£30

'A country inn with "city restaurant" standards', is how one reader summed up this West Sussex branch of Ben McKellar's little empire (see also Gingerman, the Ginger Dog and the Ginger Pig, Brighton). Originally called Shaves Thatch, the building now sports a tidy new roof (complete with an effigy of our vulpine friend stalking a pheasant) and an interior that has been tricked out for maximum country-loving conviviality – 'it really works', added another fan. The scenery is great, service is bright as a button, and the cooking derives from a natural-born instinct for local flavours, without fuss or contrivance.

Rye Bay scallops with Seville orange and fennel could be followed by haunch of venison with Puy lentils, Jerusalem artichokes and Banyuls vinegar. The kitchen isn't slavishly patriotic, though – hence the presence of sesame beef and spiced enoki mushroom salad, roast monkfish with harissa potatoes, and toffee banana cornetto with espresso ice cream. Real ales do duty at the bar, and quaffable wines start at £14 (£3.70 a glass).

Chef/s: David Keats and Ben McKellar. **Open:** all week L 12 to 2 (12.30 to 4 Sat and Sun), D 6 to 10 (6.30 Sat and Sun). **Closed:** 25 Dec. **Meals:** alc (main courses £9 to £20). Set L £10 (2 courses). **Service:** not inc. **Details:** Cards accepted. 55 seats. 90 seats outside. Separate bar. Wheelchair access. Music. Children allowed. Car parking.

Arundel

Arundel House

Spot-on restaurant-with-rooms
11 High Street, Arundel, BN18 9AD
Tel no: (01903) 882136
www.arundelhouseonline.com
Modern British | £32
Cooking score: 2

£5 OFF 🍷 🛏

This restaurant-with-rooms in picture-perfect Arundel is designed like a boutique hotel, and makes a day out at the nearby Castle all the more memorable. Carefully composed modern British dishes are attractively presented and big on flavour. Seared salmon on kohlrabi rémoulade with pesto gives a good kick-start to the palate, while mains such as roast loin of venison on sweet potato mash with a blackberry and whisky reduction showcase quality local meats. Popular desserts run to bitter chocolate fondant with orange ice cream, or brioche-and-butter pudding with clotted cream. It all comes with a wine list of exemplary pedigree that offers imaginative selections throughout, from French classics to southern-hemisphere varietals, at mark-ups that are nowhere near what you might be expecting. Prices from £14.95 (£4.50 a glass).
Chef/s: Luke Hackman. **Open:** Tue to Sat L 12 to 2, D 7 to 9. **Closed:** Sun, Mon, 24 to 31 Dec, bank hols. **Meals:** Set L £16 (2 courses) to £22. Set D £22 (2 courses) to £28. **Service:** 10% (optional). **Details:** Cards accepted. 32 seats. Music.

READERS RECOMMEND

The Town House

Modern British
65 High Street, Arundel, BN18 9AJ
Tel no: (01903) 883847
www.thetownhouse.co.uk
'We did not stop mmm-ing for the duration of the meal'

Chichester

Field & Fork

Superior café/restaurant in a cultural glory
Pallant House Gallery, 9 North Pallant, Chichester, PO19 1TJ
Tel no: (01243) 770827
www.fieldandfork.co.uk
Modern British | £24
Cooking score: 2

£5 OFF **V** £30

The Pallant Gallery is one of the cultural glories of Chichester, and in Field & Fork it has a rather superior café/restaurant. Outside catering supplements the on-site operation, and there's a sun-trap courtyard for alfresco meals. Straightforward modern European dishes include smoked eel fillets on fennel ceviche, grilled halibut with truffle mash and asparagus, and well-timed lamb noisettes with ratatouille and anchovies. A fig tart at inspection wasn't good, but lavender crème brûlée with almond and orange tuiles may be a better bet. A short wine list does the job, opening at £14.95.
Chef/s: Sam Mahoney. **Open:** Tue to Sun L 12 to 3 (11.30 Sun), Wed to Sat D 6 to 10.30. **Closed:** Mon, 25 and 26 Dec, 1 Jan. **Meals:** alc (main courses £10 to £15). Set D £19.95 (2 courses) to £26.95. Sun L £21.95. **Service:** not inc. **Details:** Cards accepted. 38 seats. 40 seats outside. Air-con. No mobile phones. Wheelchair access. Music. Children allowed.

Cuckfield

Ockenden Manor

Top-end cooking with panache
Ockenden Lane, Cuckfield, RH17 5LD
Tel no: (01444) 416111
www.hshotels.co.uk
Modern French | £51
Cooking score: 6

£5 OFF 🛏

Very much a country hotel on a human scale – regardless of its nine acres of pristine landscaped grounds – Ockenden Manor still manages to bristle with chimneys and exude an air of aristocratic gentility. Inside, the hotel is feeling the benefit of some tidy refurbishment, and chef Stephen Crane now goes about his business in a brand new kitchen. Whether his spruced-up surroundings will inspire even greater feats of culinary accomplishment remains to be seen; suffice to say that the cooking is top-end stuff delivered with a sure hand, confidence and panache. Restrained intricacy is one of his trademarks, be it an assiette of Longhorn beef with crunchy vegetables, a bone marrow bonbon and horseradish cream, or a vividly contrasted pairing of hot and cold Selsey crab with crispy sweet potato tempura and oriental salad. Local and seasonal flavours also come together in centrepieces such as saddle of Balcombe venison with buttered kale, Jerusalem artichokes and caramelised apple. Desserts aim for precision-tuned artistry in the shape of, say, cinnamon crème brûlée with quince compote and apple sorbet. The lengthy wine list is notable for an abundance of serious bottles at serious prices. France leads the way, but other countries are amply represented. Ten house selections at £22 (£5.75 a glass) offer the best value.

Chef/s: Stephen Crane. **Open:** all week L 12 to 2, D 6.30 to 9. **Meals:** Set L £15.50 (2 courses) to £21.75. Set D £51 (3 courses). Sun L £33.50. **Service:** not inc. **Details:** Cards accepted. 45 seats. 20 seats outside. Separate bar. No music. No mobile phones. Wheelchair access. Children allowed. Car parking.

▌East Grinstead

Gravetye Manor

The show goes on

Vowels Lane, East Grinstead, RH19 4LJ

Tel no: (01342) 810567

www.gravetyemanor.co.uk

Modern British | £53

Cooking score: 4

🍶 🚃

You might think that this vision of Elizabethan enchantment and Victorian horticultural innovation would go on forever, but Gravetye Manor almost succumbed in 2010 as the financial plague reaped its harvest. Thankfully, the prospect of losing such a

beloved friend was too much for one devoted customer – a hedge fund high-flier who stumped up the money and saved the day. Following the shake-up, the toque has been handed to long-serving culinary lieutenant Rupert Gleadow, who is keeping things right on track. Irish beef and Cornish seafood supplement local supplies, and the cooking has maintained its sense of ambition. A starter of home-smoked salmon with crab tian and beetroot purée could precede loin of organic pork with spiced braised belly, Bury black pudding and Madeira jus or pavé of halibut with celeriac gratin, pickled baby vegetables, coriander purée and Pineau des Charentes. For dessert, readers have singled out the bread-and-butter pudding with white chocolate ice cream. Gravetye's majestic wine list remains a joy to behold; good breeding and glorious drinking are its hallmarks, whether you are after a vintage Bordeaux or a sprightly New World yearling. Prices start at £25.

Chef/s: Rupert Gleadow. **Open:** all week L 12 to 2, D 6.30 to 9.30. **Meals:** Set L £20 (2 courses) to £25. Set D £37. **Service:** 12.5%. **Details:** Cards accepted. 45 seats. 25 seats outside. Separate bar. No music. No mobile phones. Wheelchair access. Car parking.

▌Funtington

Hallidays

Village restaurant with notable food

Watery Lane, Funtington, PO18 9LF

Tel no: (01243) 575331

www.hallidays.info

Modern British | £35

Cooking score: 2

£5 OFF

The Stephensons' village restaurant occupies a row of fourteenth-century thatched flint cottages at the lower reaches of the South Downs National Park, about four miles out of Chichester. Under low beamed ceilings, smartly dressed tables are adorned with fresh flowers, and Andrew's locally based cooking achieves some notable results. Start with home-cured gravadlax or a warm salad of pigeon, bacon and hazelnuts. Mains might offer a whole grilled lemon sole with brown shrimps, or honey-glazed duck breast with wild rice and mango salsa, while the crème brûlée comes with berry sorbet, shortbread and a glass of dessert wine. Wines from the main list start at £15.

Chef/s: Andrew Stephenson. **Open:** Wed to Fri and Sun L 12 to 1.30. Wed to Sat D 7 to 9.30. **Closed:** Mon, Tue, 1 week Mar, 2 weeks Aug. **Meals:** alc (main courses £16 to £19). Set L £13 (2 courses) to £18. Set D £20 (2 courses) to £25. Sun L £22. **Service:** not inc. **Details:** Cards accepted. 24 seats. 4 seats outside. Separate bar. Wheelchair access. Music. Children allowed. Car parking.

▌Haywards Heath

Jeremy's Restaurant at Borde Hill
Fine food from an old hand
Balcombe Road, Haywards Heath, RH16 1XP
Tel no: (01444) 441102
www.jeremysrestaurant.com
Modern European | £35
Cooking score: 4
£5
OFF

'As much delicious home-baked bread as you want' is just one of the things that pleases reporters about this agreeably relaxed restaurant at the entrance to Borde Hill Garden. Those with itchy green fingers can wander the verdant spaces, while armchair gardeners might prefer to gaze from the windows of the dining room or go alfresco if the weather allows. As an old hand at the restaurant game, Jeremy Ashpool moves with the times, although his style is one of gradual change rather than revolution, with dishes based on impressive ingredients from local rabbit via Bury black pudding to free-range pork (served with langoustine and a mango and spring onion salsa). Readers relish everything they are offered, from beautifully cooked confit cod with Puy lentils and shallots in red wine and venison with cauliflower cheese and Madeira jus to 'best in the world' sticky toffee pudding. Well-trained staff are unobtrusive but friendly, and the wine list offers decent drinking from £17.

Chef/s: Jeremy Ashpool and Richard Cook. **Open:** Tue to Sun L 12.30 to 2.30 (3 Sun), Tue to Sat D 7 to 9.30. **Closed:** Mon, first two weeks Jan. **Meals:** alc (main courses £15 to £24). Set L £17.50 (2 courses) to £22.50. Set D £20 (2 courses) to £25. Sun L £29. **Service:** not inc. **Details:** Cards accepted. 60 seats. 40 seats outside. Separate bar. No mobile phones. Wheelchair access. Children allowed. Car parking.

▌Horsham

Restaurant Tristan
Cracking quality and bright ideas
3 Stans Way, Horsham, RH12 1HU
Tel no: (01403) 255688
www.restauranttristan.co.uk
Modern European | £36
Cooking score: 5
£5
OFF

The first-floor restaurant in Horsham's old town is a mixture of ancient and modern, with small abstract paintings offset by the original sixteenth-century beams of a large open hall. It feels expansive and eccentric, and the amicable front-of-house staff add to the appeal. Tristan Mason opened here in 2008 and set a cracking pace straight off, one that he has maintained in modern European dishes that are full of colour, acute intelligence and great technical capabililty. Prices seem eminently reasonable for the quality, especially at lunch, as legions of readers attest. The subtle art of combination is celebrated in productions like red mullet with pata negra ham, or rabbit and tiger prawn with 'cocky-leeky' garnish, and the bright ideas continue in mains such as John Dory with truffle risotto, salsify and pickled shimeji mushrooms. Menu descriptions are voguishly terse, but enticing enough anyway. 'Daube of beef, bavette, oyster fritter, parsley root' sounds worth a punt. Parsley may crop up again at dessert in an ice cream with caramelised walnuts, to accompany banana tarte Tatin in lemon sauce. The short, serviceable wine list opens at £17 for a South African Sauvignon Blanc.

Chef/s: Tristan Mason. **Open:** Tue to Sat L 12 to 2.30, D 6.30 to 9.30. **Closed:** Sun, Mon, 25 Dec for 2 weeks, last week Jul, first week Aug. **Meals:** Set L

£12 (2 courses) to £16. Set D £28 (2 courses) to £36.
Tasting menu £50. **Service:** 12.5% (optional).
Details: Cards accepted. 38 seats. No mobile
phones. Wheelchair access. Music. Children
allowed.

Lavant
The Earl of March
Inspirational views and terrific food
Lavant, PO18 0BQ
Tel no: (01243) 533993
www.theearlofmarch.com
Modern British | £30
Cooking score: 4

As you gaze out towards Goodwood, over the
lovely prospect of the South Downs, it's easy
to see why William Blake was inspired to pen
Jerusalem here. A lot has changed since 1803,
but the views are still inspirational and the
Earl of March has a new-found reputation as a
hostelry with terrific food. Main man Giles
Thompson earned his stripes as executive chef
at The Ritz, before decamping to Sussex and
filling his larder with regional produce. The
result is an inviting checklist of finely honed,
seasonal dishes: grilled Sussex haloumi is
paired with Tangmere red pepper mousse,
steaks are from beasts reared in the Rother
Valley and Southdown lamb cutlets are fired
up with devil sauce. Fish is also handled with
exemplary flair, witness diver-caught scallops
with white bean purée, black pudding and
truffle oil. Desserts could usher in lemon and
goats' curd tart with pear caramel. Lunch bites
are served in the bar, and the well-spread wine
list starts at £16.50.
Chef/s: Giles Thompson and Mattie Thumshirn.
Open: all week L 12 to 2.30 (4 Sun), Mon to Sat D
5.30 to 9.30. **Meals:** alc (main courses £12 to £20).
Set L and early D £17.95 (2 courses) to £22.95.
Service: not inc. **Details:** Cards accepted. 60 seats.
40 seats outside. Separate bar. Wheelchair access.
Music. Children allowed. Car parking.

Littlehampton
East Beach Café
Imaginative, family-friendly menus
Sea Road, Littlehampton, BN17 5GB
Tel no: (01903) 731903
www.eastbeachcafe.co.uk
Modern British | £27
Cooking score: 3

£5 OFF   £30

The Thomas Heatherwick-designed structure
– built of rusted metal to resemble washed-up
driftwood – is unmissable, smack bang on the
seafront. With the windows thrown open, the
independent seaside café is lovely and airy
inside. No surprise it's popular with families
and 'a little noisy' at the weekend. Fast and
efficient service keep things ticking over and
guests, young and old, are treated with
respect. From an imaginative, all-purpose
menu, the fish and chips (crisp batter, proper
chips) pass muster, while salt-and-pepper
squid, moules marinière and crab linguine put
an international spin on things. The wine list
(from £13.95) is suitably seafood-friendly and
very quaffable. If you're passing by, it's worth
popping in just for a slice of superb homemade
cake.
Chef/s: David Whiteside. **Open:** all week L 12 to 3
(3.30 Sun), all week D (Jun to Aug) 6.30 to 8.30,
Thur to Sat D (Sept to Jun) 6.30 to 8.30. **Closed:** 16
to 25 Dec. **Meals:** alc (main courses £9 to £17).
Service: not inc. **Details:** Cards accepted. 60 seats.
Wheelchair access. Music. Children allowed. Car
parking.

Average price

The average price listed in main-entry
reviews denotes the price of a three-
course meal, without wine.

Lower Beeding

NEW ENTRY

The Pass

Food to take the breath away

South Lodge Hotel, Brighton Road, Lower
Beeding, RH13 6PS

Tel no: (01403) 891711

www.southlodgehotel.co.uk

Modern British | £60

Cooking score: 7

£5 OFF ⊨ V

The South Lodge began life as a private
residence in the Victorian era, when
enterprising polymath Frederick DuCane
Godman set about turning it into a home fit
for his ceramic collection. An upscale hotel
since 1985, it now boasts a pair of dining rooms
– the traditional panelled Camellia, and a
daring high-tech enterprise, the Pass. This
extends the idea of the chef's table into a whole
small restaurant, with high olive-green
banquettes to observe the kitchen action,
which is also relayed on screens for the wall-
facers. Followers of the copious cookery
programming on TV will love it, but if you're
wondering whether it all sounds a bit of a
gimmick, banish that thought. In Matt Gillan
(formerly of the Vineyard at Stockcross – see
entry), South Lodge has a spectacularly gifted
chef. The format is a series of fixed-price
menus of varying numbers of courses, with
dishes effectively interchangeable between
them as you wish. A small serving of white
onion risotto is flawless for texture, timing
and seasoning, barely needing its minimal
garnish of morels and toasted pine nuts. A
parfait of rabbit and duck livers is sandwiched
between wafer-thin slices of pain d'épices,
surrounded by compoted prunes and cubes of
apple jelly. The main course might be grey
mullet accompanied by seasonal veg, or a roll
of confit duck leg, with creamed cabbage and
bacon, chunks of cumin-spiced polenta and
baby turnips, but the quality of ingredients,
the precision seasoning and the lustrous
intensity of it all take the breath away. To
conclude, there could be trifle served in a
tumbler, composed of layers of mango,
pistachio sponge, vanilla cream, anise, and
pistachio ice cream. With three kinds of salt to
sprinkle on the fabulous homemade breads,
and truffled cream cheese for dipping mini-
grissini into, the incidentals are all of the same
order. Staff contribute to the whole polished
experience, and there are some good wines,
though there could be more by the glass, and
mark-ups are on the tough side. House wine
is £25.

Chef/s: Matt Gillan. **Open:** Wed to Sun L 12 to 2, D 7
to 9. **Closed:** Mon, Tue, first 2 weeks Jan. **Meals:** Set
L £28 (4 courses) to 38. Set D £60 (6 courses) to
£70. Sun L £35. **Service:** 10% (optional).
Details: Cards accepted. 22 seats. Air-con. Separate
bar. No music. Children allowed. Car parking.

Midhurst

ALSO RECOMMENDED

▲ The Duke of Cumberland Arms

Henley, Midhurst, GU27 3HQ

Tel no: (01428) 652280

Gastropub £5 OFF

Trout ponds and herb beds ornament the
landscaped gardens of this wisteria-clad,
fifteenth-century hostelry down a tiny
wooded lane. The Duke of Cumberland is a
low-beamed, folksy real ale pub with a
vengeance, but the food has modern
aspirations. It delivers scallops with herb
risotto or hot chorizo, new potato and olive
salad (£7.95) alongside slow-cooked brisket
with horseradish mash (£15.95) and haggis
with buttered swede. For afters, perhaps
chocolate fondant (£5.95). House wine is
£11.50. Closed Sun D and Mon D.

Please send us your feedback

To register your opinion about any
restaurant listed in the Guide, or a new
restaurant that you wish to bring to our
attention, please visit the web address at
the bottom of the page. Your feedback
informs the content of the book and will be
used to compile next year's reviews.

▌Sidlesham

The Crab & Lobster

British food of some distinction
Mill Lane, Sidlesham, PO20 7NB
Tel no: (01243) 641233
www.crab-lobster.co.uk
Modern British | £32
Cooking score: 3

🛏

This cream-painted former pub on the edge of
the Pagham Harbour nature reserve, is 350
years old, as may be seen from the low-
ceilinged, stone-flagged interior. Now a
stylish restaurant-with-rooms, the emphasis is
on carefully cooked modern British food of
some distinction. Seafood dishes are well-
received, whether a classic starter of whitebait
with lemon mayonnaise, or a main course of
hake with samphire and sun-dried tomatoes.
Meat mains such as slow-roasted Old Spot
pork belly with bubble and squeak in pear and
cider cream sauce also hit the spot. One reader
felt desserts let the side down a little, but there
are fine English cheeses with quince jelly to
compensate. A concise international wine
selection opens at £14.50.
Chef/s: Macolm Goble and Simon Haynes. **Open:** all
week L 12 to 2.30 (12.30 Fri and Sat), D 6 to 9.30 (10
Fri and Sat, 9 Sun). **Meals:** alc (main courses £15 to
£27). **Service:** not inc. **Details:** Cards accepted. 48
seats. 50 seats outside. No mobile phones.
Wheelchair access. Music. Children allowed. Car
parking.

Symbols

🛏 Accommodation is available

£30 Three courses for less than £30

V More than three vegetarian main courses

£5 £5-off voucher scheme
OFF

🍾 Notable wine list

▌Singleton

NEW ENTRY

The Partridge Inn

Lovely village pub with hearty grub
Singleton, PO18 0EY
Tel no: (01243) 811251
www.thepartridgeinn.co.uk
Gastropub | £24
Cooking score: 1

V £30

This lovely, friendly pub in a gorgeous village
by the foothills of the South Downs is quite a
contrast to its upmarket sibling, the Earl of
March in nearby Lavant (see entry). Here you
can expect hearty pub grub that majors in old-
time favourites: whitebait, game terrine or
melon with Parma ham to start, followed by
the likes of bangers and mash, macaroni cheese
and wholetail scampi with splendid hand-cut
chips. True British puds run from spotted dick
via treacle tart to Eton mess, and there are
well-kept local ales and a dozen wines by the
glass from £3.50.
Chef/s: Andrew Hotstone. **Open:** all week L 12 to 2
(3 Sat and Sun), D 6 to 9 (9.30 Fri and Sat).
Meals: alc (main courses £10 to £20). **Service:** not
inc. **Details:** Cards accepted. 75 seats. 100 seats
outside. Separate bar. Wheelchair access. Music.
Children allowed. Car parking.

▌Tangmere

Cassons

Good food near Goodwood
Arundel Road, Tangmere, PO18 0DU
Tel no: (01243) 773294
www.cassonsrestaurant.co.uk
Modern British | £35
Cooking score: 2

£5
OFF

This restaurant beside the A27 has low-
beamed ceilings and a king-sized inglenook.
It feels suitably 'cottagey' and is home to some
accomplished cooking. Vivian Casson keeps
tabs on fashionable preparations and
presentation, but doesn't lose sight of the
importance of good quality materials, from

mixed seafood in a bouillabaisse sauce with spinach and new potatoes to venison fillet with wild mushrooms served with green beans, red cabbage, celeriac velouté, fondant potato, port and juniper sauce. First courses include goats' cheese wrapped in ratatouille on a red pepper garnish, and desserts take in rhubarb tarte Tatin. House wine is £18.

Chef/s: Vivian Casson. **Open:** Wed to Sun L 12 to 2 (2.30 Sun), Tue to Sat D 7 to 10. **Closed:** Mon, 25 and 26 Dec, 1 Jan. **Meals:** Set L £17 (2 courses) to £21. Set D £27 (2 courses) to £35. Sun L £17.50. **Service:** not inc. **Details:** Cards accepted. 36 seats. 16 seats outside. Separate bar. No mobile phones. Wheelchair access. Music. Children allowed. Car parking.

▌Trotton

The Keepers Arms
Dyed-in-the-wool Sussex pub
Terwick Lane, Trotton, GU31 5ER
Tel no: (01730) 813724
www.keepersarms.co.uk
Gastropub | £27
Cooking score: 2
£5 OFF £30

A mid-seventeenth century village inn between Petersfield and Midhurst, the Keepers Arms is every inch the Sussex country pub. A brace of winter fires, a beamed and timbered bar and a light, contemporary dining room establish the mood. The cooking acknowledges current trends, as well as offering tried-and-true pub dishes, so whether you're in the mood for fish and chips or a herb-crusted fillet of bream with celeriac rösti and semi-dried tomatoes, you won't put the kitchen off its stroke. Finish, perhaps, with Bakewell tart and drink from a 50-strong wine list that starts at £15.

Chef/s: Charlotte Piper-Hodgson. **Open:** all week L 12 to 2 (2.30 Sun), D 6.30 to 9 (7 to 9 Sun). **Closed:** 25 and 26 Dec. **Meals:** alc (main courses £10 to £22). **Service:** not inc. **Details:** Cards accepted. 48 seats. 30 seats outside. Separate bar. No mobile phones. Wheelchair access. Music. Children allowed. Car parking.

▌West Stoke

West Stoke House
Cool and chic
Downs Road, West Stoke, PO18 9BN
Tel no: (01243) 575226
www.weststokehouse.co.uk
Modern British | £45
Cooking score: 6
▐ ▄

This popular restaurant-with-rooms is the old dower house of the Goodwood estate, and it stands in seven acres of well-kept gardens – perfect for a post-lunch stroll. Inside, it is cool and chic, a fitting backdrop for Darren Brown's cooking, which is unmistakably contemporary. Most dishes are complex: potted foie gras, for example, is finely complemented by smoked duck breast, confit duck leg, cherries, pear chutney and toasted hazelnut and prune bread. Equally well considered have been fish main courses such as fillet of halibut, which comes teamed with confit rabbit leg, tagliatelle, cep purée, kale and chive foam. Meats might include impressive roast fillet of beef partnered by braised snails, parsley and marrow bone risotto, garlic purée, Parmesan crisps and foam, while dessert brings apple mousse with poached apple, brandy-snap, green apple sorbet and cider jelly. Elsewhere, a well-reported winter lunch took in leek and chive velouté with black pudding ravioli and truffle foam, excellent pan-fried sea bream with aubergine caviar, spinach, and anchovy frite, and apricot frangipane tart with apricot compote and apricot sorbet. Service is 'impeccable'. Wines continue to hit the spot – long on quality, short on pretension – and it's good to see a decent selection by the glass at reasonable prices. House wine is £16.

Chef/s: Darren Brown. **Open:** Wed to Sun L 12.30 to 2, D 7 to 9. **Closed:** Mon, Tue, 24 to 26 Dec, 1 Jan. **Meals:** Set L £22.50 (2 courses) to £27.50. Set D £37.50 (2 courses) to £45. Sun L £32.50. **Service:** not inc. **Details:** Cards accepted. 30 seats. Separate bar. No mobile phones. Wheelchair access. Music. Children allowed. Car parking.

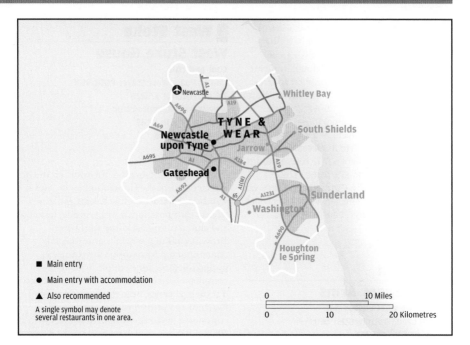

- ■ Main entry
- ● Main entry with accommodation
- ▲ Also recommended

A single symbol may denote
several restaurants in one area.

0   10 Miles

0   10   20 Kilometres

Gateshead

Eslington Villa

Loyally supported Victorian retreat
8 Station Road, Low Fell, Gateshead, NE9 6DR
Tel no: (0191) 4876017
www.eslingtonvilla.co.uk
Modern British | £24
Cooking score: 3
£5 OFF 🛏 V £30

Eslington is a late Victorian mansion in a
couple of acres of well-maintained gardens. It
has smart but informal dining areas in the
main house and the conservatory, and a loyal
band of regular customers. Andrew Moore
cooks a menu of modern brasserie-style
dishes, with starters built around the likes of
crab fritters with tomato and chilli jam, and
vodka-cured sea trout with beetroot
carpaccio. Fortifying main courses may
include roast venison loin with cep purée in
red wine sauce, or sea bream wrapped in
Parma ham with saffron risotto. Chocolate
mousse and brandied cherries is a fittingly
stylish way to finish. A well-presented
modern wine list opens with eight house
wines from £16.95 a bottle (£4.25 a glass).
Chef/s: Andrew Moore. **Open:** Sun to Fri L 12 to 2
(3.30 Sun), Mon to Sat D 7 to 10 (6.30 to 10 Sat).
Closed: bank hols. **Meals:** Set L £17.50 (2 courses)
to £19.50. Set D £20.50 (2 courses) to £24.50. Sun L
£19. **Service:** not inc. **Details:** Cards accepted. 80
seats. 20 seats outside. Separate bar. Wheelchair
access. Music. Children allowed. Car parking.

Newcastle upon Tyne

Blackfriars Restaurant

Britain's oldest eating house?
Friars Street, Newcastle upon Tyne, NE1 4XN
Tel no: (0191) 2615945
www.blackfriarsrestaurant.co.uk
British | £25
Cooking score: 3
£5 OFF £30

There are not many inner-city former
monasteries operating as restaurants in the
UK, so we must treasure one that is. The

dining room at Blackfriars was once the monks' refectory and, since it was built in 1239, it might just be Britain's oldest eating house. The menus offer a take on traditional British dishes, such as black pudding with crispy bacon, fried potato and a poached egg, loin of Scottish venison with braised red cabbage and port sauce, or rainbow trout with green beans and béarnaise. The odd foreign note creeps in with butternut squash risotto, or halibut and wilted pak choi, but by pudding stage you're back to sticky toffee or apple and rhubarb crumble. Dishes are annotated with broad-brush wine suggestions; bottles start at £15.
Chef/s: Troy Terrington. **Open:** all week L 12 to 2.30 (4 Sun), Mon to Sat D 6 to 10. **Closed:** bank hols. **Meals:** alc (main courses £9 to £21). Set L £12 (2 courses) to £15. Sun L £11. **Service:** 10% (optional). **Details:** Cards accepted. 72 seats. 50 seats outside. Air-con. Separate bar. Music. Children allowed.

Brasserie Black Door
Relaxed venue with prime food
Biscuit Factory, Stoddart Street, Newcastle upon Tyne, NE2 1AN
Tel no: (0191) 2605411
www.blackdoorgroup.co.uk
Modern British | £25
Cooking score: 3

V £30

'This is a really charming venue and a very relaxing and enjoyable place', was the verdict of a reporter who enjoyed a good-value express lunch at this spacious contemporary brasserie on the ground floor of a converted biscuit factory. There's nothing flashy about the presentation, and no gimmicks, just prime materials confidently cooked. That express lunch produced mackerel escabèche, breast of free-range chicken with potato purée, and banana and pecan bread pudding, but elsewhere the carte could offer deep-fried soft-shell crab with avocado and crab mayonnaise, chicken, mushroom and chorizo pie, and hazelnut nougatine with chocolate

cream, orange and pistachio. Sunday lunch is popular. The short wine list has a wide global reach. Prices from £14.50.
Chef/s: David Kennedy. **Open:** all week L 12 to 2 (3 Sun), Mon to Sat D 7 to 9.30 (10 Sun). **Closed:** 25 and 26 Dec, 1 Jan. **Meals:** alc (main courses £11 to £19). Set L £10 (2 courses) to £12.95. Set D £18.95. Sun L £8.95. **Service:** 10% (optional). **Details:** Cards accepted. 100 seats. Air-con. Separate bar. Wheelchair access. Music. Children allowed. Car parking.

Café 21
Serious eating and stylish drinking
Trinity Gardens, Quayside, Newcastle upon Tyne, NE1 2HH
Tel no: (0191) 2220755
www.cafetwentyone.co.uk
Modern British | £38
Cooking score: 3

V

The twenty-first anniversary of Café 21 was too good an opportunity to pass up – and that's what dominated the agenda in 2010 at Terry Laybourne's quayside brasserie. Both bar and dining area make upbeat venues for some serious eating and stylish drinking. The former might involve crab lasagne with chive butter sauce, followed by either turbot braised in Chardonnay or grilled breast of Goosnargh duckling with black olives in red wine. Finish with old-fashioned knickerbocker glory, or a more newfangled chocolate tart with macadamia brittle ice cream. The separate vegetarian menu is good to see – cheese and spinach soufflé received one reader's thumbs-up. A useful international wine collection opens at £15.80 (£4.10 a glass), for house Duboeuf.
Chef/s: Chris Dobson. **Open:** Mon to Sat L 12 to 2.30, D 5.30 to 10.30. Sun 12 to 8.30. **Closed:** 25 and 26 Dec, 1 Jan, Easter Mon. **Meals:** alc (main courses £15 to £29). Set L and D £16 (2 courses) to £19.50. Sun L £21.50. **Service:** 10% (optional). **Details:** Cards accepted. 100 seats. Separate bar. Wheelchair access. Music. Children allowed.

Fisherman's Lodge

A hidden surprise
Jesmond Dene, Jesmond, Newcastle upon Tyne,
NE7 7BQ
Tel no: (0191) 2813281
www.fishermanslodge.co.uk
Modern British | £35
Cooking score: 3

£5
OFF

'Arriving here is a bit like Alice falling down
the rabbit hole', remarked a visitor, surprised
to find a traditional-looking Victorian lodge
with a contemporary interior in such a rural
setting, yet only minutes from the centre of
Newcastle. New chef/co-proprietor Alan
O'Kane delivers a light, modern British style
with much use of seasonal produce. Slow-
cooked eggs, truffle toast, asparagus and
bacon, followed by monkfish with tomato
jam and confit fennel, then exotic fruit terrine,
were the components of a successful lunch in
June. Elsewhere, roasted rump of lamb with
shoulder and leg cottage pie has been well
reported, likewise sea trout confit with pea
mousse and crayfish tail salad. Service needs
better training: 'at these prices, things should
be a lot slicker!' House wine is £19.50.
Chef/s: Alan O'Kane. **Open:** all week L 12 to 2.30,
Mon to Sat D 6 to 9.30. **Closed:** 25 and 26 Dec, 1
Jan. **Meals:** alc (main courses £18 to £28). Set L and
D £16.50 (2 courses) to £18.50. Sun L £18.50.
Service: 10% (optional). **Details:** Cards accepted.
60 seats. 16 seats outside. Separate bar. Wheelchair
access. Music. Children allowed. Car parking.

Jesmond Dene House

Kitchen full of craft and care
Jesmond Dene Road, Newcastle upon Tyne,
NE2 2EY
Tel no: (0191) 2123000
www.jesmonddenehouse.co.uk
Modern European | £50
Cooking score: 5

🛏

A country house in a city is something of a
paradox, yet it is an accurate description of this
Arts and Crafts house in a leafy river park not
far from Newcastle city centre. It's now a
lavishly converted contemporary hotel (the
dining room was being given a fresh new look
as we went to press) and under the guidance of
Pierre Rigothier, craft and care continue to
hold sway in the kitchen. Lateral thinking
provides some intriguing combinations, such
as the marinated mango, espelette (chilli)
pepper and balsamic vinegar accompanying
grilled scallops or the watercress jelly, Avruga
caviar and gin and grapefruit granité served
with steamed oysters. Everyone, though,
wants an old favourite once in a while, as often
as not given a new twist: venison loin is
sweetly foiled by confit quince, chanterelles
and celeriac and coffee sauce, while fillet of
beef is fortified with bone marrow, girolles,
panisse (a chickpea flour cake) and sauce
Périgueux. Desserts might bring chocolate
sablé with chocolate crémeux and spiced
poached pear. Lunch is good value, a policy
that extends to the well-spread wine list, with
decent drinking form £16.
Chef/s: Pierre Rigothier. **Open:** all week L 12 to 2
(12.30 to 2.30 Sat, 12.30 to 3.15 Sun), D 7 to 9.30 (10
Sat). **Meals:** alc (main courses £14 to £40). Set L
£25. Set weekday D £26. Sun L £23. **Service:** 10%
(optional). **Details:** Cards accepted. 45 seats. 20
seats outside. Separate bar. No mobile phones.
Wheelchair access. Music. Children allowed. Car
parking.

▌South Shields

READERS RECOMMEND
Colmans

Fish and Chips
182-186 Ocean Road, South Shields, NE33 2JQ
Tel no: (0191) 4561202
www.colmansfishandchips.com
**'Their famous scampi was totally historic,
sweet langoustine tails in a light batter,
fantastic.'**

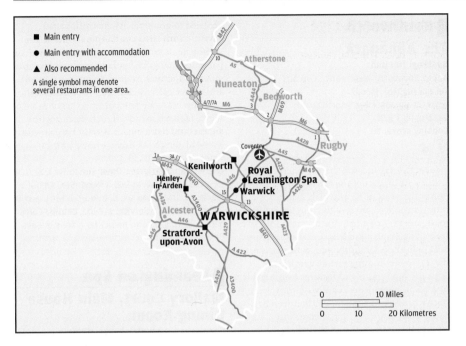

■ Henley-in-Arden

The Bluebell

Comfort classics and cooking with care
93 High Street, Henley-in-Arden, B95 5AT
Tel no: (01564) 793049
www.bluebellhenley.co.uk
Modern British | £25
Cooking score: 4

£30

'It appears to be the place to be seen in locally', noted a reader of the Taylors' 500-year-old former coaching inn on Henley's Tudor high street. Oodles of original features contribute to the cheering atmosphere, and it's run with great aplomb. Much of the kitchen produce comes from the owners' expanding allotment, and the pick of local suppliers provides the rest. On a cold night, one reporter was glad to be served with a hearty winter vegetable soup swirled with pesto, followed by braised lamb shank with dauphinoise, accompanied by devilled kidneys. Whisky-jellied oranges and blood orange sorbet made for an impeccably refreshing conclusion. Great care is taken over these dishes, and fish cookery is equally sharp (try sea bass fillet with a crab and ginger cream sauce). There's also a listing of pies and 'comfort classics', as befits the pub ethos. A short wine list offers a good geographical spread, with most things available by the glass (from £3.85).

Chef/s: Rob Round. **Open:** Tue to Sun L 12 to 2.30 (3.30 Sun), Tue to Sat D 6 to 9.30. **Closed:** Mon. **Meals:** alc (main courses £10 to £25). **Service:** not inc. **Details:** Cards accepted. 50 seats. 50 seats outside. Wheelchair access. Music. Children allowed. Car parking.

Please send us your feedback

To register your opinion about any restaurant listed in the Guide, or a new restaurant that you wish to bring to our attention, please visit the web address at the bottom of the page. Your feedback informs the content of the book and will be used to compile next year's reviews.

Kenilworth

The Almanack

Bustling, fun pub
Abbey End North, Kenilworth, CV8 1QJ
Tel no: (01926) 353637
www.thealmanack-kenilworth.co.uk
Gastropub | £28
Cooking score: 1

V £30

The retro sofas and armchairs from the 1960s and 70s are all part of the fun at this bustling pub at the heart of Kenilworth, where morning coffee comes with complimentary toast, and the colourful dining room looks into an open-plan kitchen. Extensive menus deal in the best local produce, with roasts of the day, including free-range gammon, ethically bred meats and fish from sustainable sources all in evidence. Cod with chorizo and butter beans, or 28-day aged Aberdeen beef rump with chips and blue cheese sauce, are among the options. Wines are from £13.75.
Chef/s: Kuba Fijak. **Open:** all week 8am to 10pm. **Meals:** alc (main courses £10 to £16). **Service:** not inc. **Details:** Cards accepted. 100 seats. 40 seats outside. Air-con. Separate bar. Wheelchair access. Music. Children allowed. Car parking.

Restaurant Bosquet

Ever-popular Gallic charmer
97a Warwick Road, Kenilworth, CV8 1HP
Tel no: (01926) 852463
French | £32
Cooking score: 4

Bernard and Jane Lignier have been charming everyone since 1981, and their cosily intimate converted house is 'all the better for being resolutely French', according to one reporter. They run things with great personal affection and irreproachable devotion to duty, adding a generous helping of bonhomie and never bowing to stiff-collared formality. Bernard's cooking takes its inspiration from the kitchens of his native south-west France: earthy richness and generosity are his watchwords, game and foie gras have their say, and his chips

are fried in goose fat. Menus follow the seasons, with wintery offerings including game pâté en croûte with walnut salad or roast partridge on truffled polenta with mandarin sauce giving way to spring lamb, basil confit and provençale vegetables, or boneless saddle of rabbit with crayfish tails in a sherry-laced sauce. Desserts are mostly standards such as lemon tart, and the patriotically French wine list heads south for some prime pickings. Prices start at £16.50.
Chef/s: Bernard Lignier. **Open:** Tue to Fri L 12 to 1.15, Tue to Sat D 7 to 9.15. **Closed:** Sun, Mon. **Meals:** alc (main courses £20 to £22). Set L and D Tue to Fri £31.50. **Service:** not inc. **Details:** Cards accepted. 26 seats. No music. No mobile phones. Children allowed.

Leamington Spa

Mallory Court, Main House Dining Room

Sophisticated country house dining
Harbury Lane, Leamington Spa, CV33 9QB
Tel no: (01926) 330214
www.mallory.co.uk
Modern British | £40
Cooking score: 5

V

Immaculately landscaped gardens and gracious terraces form the backdrop to this distinguished Lutyens-style mansion, which comes complete with trademark topiary, pitched roofs and mullioned windows. It's a pedigree package for fans of the country house experience – with the added incentive of some highly accomplished food. The dining room in the self-styled Main House is kitted out with the obligatory oak panelling, tapestry carpets and soft lights, although Simon Haigh's cooking aims for something more contemporary in tone. Luxury ingredients and fashionable cheffy flourishes are woven into a sophisticated 'country house' repertoire that also gives the nod to local and seasonal raw materials. At the top end expect the likes of foie gras bonbon with a salad of smoked duck and duck pastilla or fillet of beef with veal shin, morels and Madeira sauce; for something more humble, consider a pressing of ham hock with pickled red cabbage and prune purée, or braised ox cheek with red wine sauce. Fish receives eclectic treatment – perhaps sesame-crusted tuna with dressed crab and oriental dressing or John Dory with curried lentils – while desserts usher in the fruity delights of damson soufflé with apple strudel and apple sorbet. The wine list is a weighty tome that opens with bottles from nearby Welcombe Hills Vineyard; otherwise, expect broadly spread international selections from £18.50.

Chef/s: Simon Haigh. **Open:** Sun to Fri L 12 to 1.30, all week D 6.30 to 8.45 (9.30 Sat, 8.30 Sun). **Meals:** Set L £22.50 (2 courses) to £27.50. Set D £39.50. Sun L £35. **Service:** not inc. **Details:** Cards accepted. 50 seats. 25 seats outside. Separate bar. No mobile phones. Wheelchair access. Music. Children allowed. Car parking.

Stratford-upon-Avon

Malbec

Up-to-the-minute bistro cooking
6 Union Street, Stratford-upon-Avon, CV37 6QT
Tel no: (01789) 269106
www.malbecrestaurant.co.uk
Modern European | £28
Cooking score: 2

£5 OFF £30

Simon Malin's restaurant in a Stratford terrace has flagstoned floors, light wood panelling, bare tables and a vaulted cellar dining area which all create an unaffected, laid-back ambience. Up-to-the-minute Anglo-French bistro cooking is the order of the day, celebrating such modern classic dishes as roast Gressingham duck breast with parsnip purée and Madeira sauce, or Cornish black bream with olive crushed potatoes and creamed leeks. Glasses of Manzanilla sherry might set you up for something like sautéed chestnut mushrooms with a poached egg, and a meal might conclude with textbook crêpes suzette. The short wine list opens at £14.75.

Chef/s: Simon Malin. **Open:** Tue to Sat L 12 to 1.45, D 7 to 9 (9.30 Fri and Sat). **Closed:** Sun, Mon, 1 week Oct, bank hols and following Tue. **Meals:** alc (main courses £13 to £19). Set L £12 (2 courses) to £15. **Service:** not inc. **Details:** Cards accepted. 38 seats. Music. Children allowed.

Warwick

Rose & Crown

Crowd-pulling, down-to-earth pub
30 Market Place, Warwick, CV34 4SH
Tel no: (01926) 411117
www.roseandcrownwarwick.co.uk
Gastropub | £27
Cooking score: 1

V £30

While the food at this re-energised town-centre pub draws the crowds, the place retains its comfortable down-to-earth informality. Sensibly planned menus feature a sharp assortment of modern dishes supported by the kitchen's determination to buy seasonal and British where possible. There's something to eat at almost any time of the day, whether free-range back bacon muffins for breakfast, shared charcuterie or cheese deli boards, tempura squid, whole roast plaice with salsa verde or great 28-day dry-aged Aberdeenshire steaks. Wines from £13.75. More reports please.

Chef/s: Russell Clarke. **Open:** all week 8am to 10pm (9.30 Sun). **Meals:** alc (main courses £11 to £20). **Service:** not inc. **Details:** Cards accepted. 45 seats. 30 seats outside. Air-con. Separate bar. Wheelchair access. Music. Children allowed.

READERS RECOMMEND

Tailors

Modern British
22 Market Place, Warwick, CV34 4SL
Tel no: (01926) 410590
www.tailorsrestaurant.co.uk
'A small restaurant serving fantastic modern British cuisine. Novel and interesting interpretations of dishes packed full of flavour and excellently presented.'

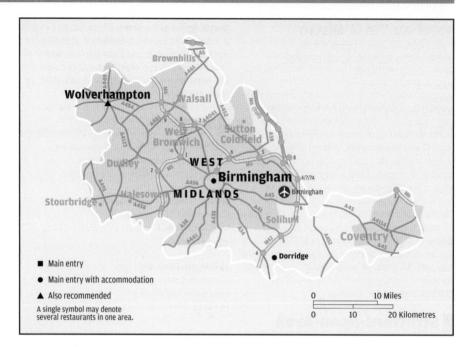

- ■ Main entry
- ● Main entry with accommodation
- ▲ Also recommended

A single symbol may denote several restaurants in one area.

0   10 Miles
0   10   20 Kilometres

▌Birmingham

Edmunds

Swish contemporary cooking
6 Central Square, Brindleyplace, Birmingham,
B1 2JB
Tel no: (0121) 6334944
www.edmundsbirmingham.com
Modern European | £40
Cooking score: 6

£5 OFF ▮ V

Brindleyplace is a canalside business and leisure development in the centre of Birmingham, the kind of smart, uptempo environment that needs at least one outstanding restaurant, and this is it. Andy Waters named the place in honour of his late father, and it's a stylish, classy venue, artfully lit, with lots of gentle wood tones and mirrors. Menus are fixed-price, with no supplements until cheese, and the cooking style is as swish and contemporary as the surroundings. Dishes are built up of many ingredients, but precise presentations and sharp flavours ensure that there is no confusion. A maritime starter combining a king prawn, smoked halibut and Cornish crab comes with pickled cucumber and a caviar dressing for emphasis, and if you're continuing on the same tack into main courses, you might find lemon sole adorned with a seared scallop, gem lettuce, walnuts and lemon butter. Beef from Scotland and lamb from Cornwall may crop up among meats, the latter served as breast and loin, with mint jelly, swede fondant and crushed peas. The alluring dessert options offer Valrhona chocolate délice or black cherry cheesecake. An inspiring, comprehensive list of quality wines suits the mood, with a good glass selection from £4.75, and a roll call of fine young clarets for the splashers-out.

Chef/s: Andy Waters. **Open:** Mon to Fri L 12 to 2, Mon to Sat D 7 to 10. **Closed:** Sun, 1 week in Jan/April/Aug/Oct. **Meals:** Set L £19 (2 courses) to £21.50. Set D £36 (2 courses) to £39.50. Tasting menu £55. **Service:** 10% (optional). **Details:** Cards accepted. 40 seats. Air-con. Wheelchair access. Music. Children allowed.

Hotel du Vin & Bistro
Branded bistro with opulent wines
25 Church Street, Birmingham, B3 2NR
Tel no: (0121) 2000600
www.hotelduvin.com
European | £35
Cooking score: 2

🍾 ⊏ V

You can always be sure of interesting architectural heritage at the various branches of the Hotel du Vin chain, and the Birmingham outlet is located in what was a Victorian eye hospital. The familiar menu structure offered throughout the group brings on a list of classics such as braised beef with dumplings and red cabbage, or seafood crêpes full of mussels, cockles and crab, alongside modern brasserie offerings such as Serrano ham and celeriac rémoulade in truffle oil, perhaps followed by fillet of red snapper with mushroom and fennel duxelle in tarragon beurre blanc. Wines from the famously extensive list are as opulent here as elsewhere in the chain, from £14.
Chef/s: Nick Turner. **Open:** all week L 12 to 2 (12. 30 to 2.30 Sat, 1 to 3 Sun). D 6 to 10 (10.30 Fri and Sat, 7 to 10 Sun). **Meals:** alc (main courses £11 to £20). Sun L £25. **Service:** 10% (optional). **Details:** Cards accepted. 96 seats. Separate bar. No mobile phones. Wheelchair access. Children allowed.

Jyoti's Vegetarian
Zingy treats and rock-bottom prices
1045 Stratford Road, Hall Green, Birmingham, B28 8AS
Tel no: (0121) 7785501
www.jyotis.co.uk
Indian vegetarian | £13
Cooking score: 1

V £30

A veggie standout among Hall Green's Asian eateries, family-run Jyoti's shines thanks to its rock-bottom prices, friendliness and spot-on food. Out front is a counter loaded with colourful sweetmeats; at the back is a bright eating area where the locals pack in for zingily spiced treats. A host of starters lead the charge (anything from deep-fried lentil kachori to steamed patra leaves), before spiced chickpeas with bhatura bread, assorted masalas and specials including tomato curry with sev. Unlicensed, but you can BYO wine.
Chef/s: Mr and Mrs Joshi. **Open:** all week 12.30 to 10. **Closed:** 25 and 26 Dec, 1 to 5 Jan. **Meals:** alc (main courses £5 to £13). **Service:** not inc. **Details:** Cards accepted. 40 seats. Air-con. Wheelchair access. Music. Children allowed.

NEW ENTRY
Loves Restaurant
An oasis in the city's heart
The Glasshouse, Canal Square, Birmingham, B16 8FL
Tel no: (0121) 4545151
www.loves-restaurant.co.uk
Modern British | £39
Cooking score: 4

£5 OFF 🍾 V

A five-minute walk from bustling Brindleyplace, Loves is located in the quieter Canal Square, and it feels like an oasis in the heart of the city centre with its view of barges and geese. Despite an anonymous modern frontage, it's a comfortable room with chocolate-brown carpet, unclothed dark wood tables and a raised area separated by a waist-high smoked glass wall. Steve Love's contemporary cooking is underpinned by classic techniques, and dishes are intricate and created from high-quality raw ingredients. There is a depth of flavour and contrasting textures in dishes such as slow-cooked breast and braised leg of wood pigeon served with pink almonds, blackberries and chocolate. Elsewhere, a main course of pork belly is served with a crépinette and pig's tail nugget with artichoke purée, spiced apple and black pudding crumble. Finish with an intense rhubarb toffee pudding, gingerbread ice cream and rhubarb yoghurt. The wine list is bursting at the seams with quality, and has plenty below £25.
Chef/s: Steve Love. **Open:** Tue to Sat L 12 to 1.45, D 6 to 9.30. **Closed:** Sun, Mon, 2 weeks Christmas, 2 weeks Aug, 1 week Easter. **Meals:** Set L and D £20

(2 courses) to £25, or £34 (2 courses) to £38.50. Tasting menu £58.50. **Service:** 10% (optional). **Details:** Cards accepted. 40 seats. 14 seats outside. Air-con. No mobile phones. Wheelchair access. Music. Children allowed.

Metro Bar & Grill

Modern classics with a comfort factor
73 Cornwall Street, Birmingham, B3 2DF
Tel no: (0121) 2001911
www.metrobarandgrill.co.uk
Modern British | £23
Cooking score: 2

£30

Despite its imposing Victorian façade, this city-centre bar and restaurant is a bustling and contemporary place. Walk through the friendly, buzzy bar and sit down at the white-clothed tables in the light conservatory-style dining room with its mirrored wall, dark blue banquettes and vibrant modern art. The seasonal and frequently changing menu is stuffed with modern classics, all with a comfort factor – from salmon, prawn and crab cocktail or crispy duck salad to half a spit-roast chicken with piri-piri sauce and hand-cut chips, pan-fried calf's liver or steak and kidney pie with colcannon mash. House wine is £14.95.
Chef/s: Mike Smith. **Open:** Mon to Fri L 12 to 2.30, Mon to Sat D 6 to 10. **Closed:** Sun, 25 Dec to 5 Jan, Easter, bank hols. **Meals:** alc (main courses £13 to £23). Set L and D £14.50 (2 courses) to £17.50. **Service:** 10% (optional). **Details:** Cards accepted. 120 seats. 8 seats outside. Air-con. Separate bar. Wheelchair access. Music. Children allowed.

Opus

Pleasingly simple cooking with deep flavours
54 Cornwall Street, Birmingham, B3 2DE
Tel no: (0121) 2002323
www.opusrestaurant.co.uk
Modern British | £35
Cooking score: 2

The stylish, understated interior has turned what was the lower-ground floor of an office block into a comfortable and welcoming

place. Staff maintain an impressive work rate to ensure things go smoothly, and the cooking draws conscientiously on well-chosen local sources including Birmingham's fine fruit and veg market. The cooking pleases for its simplicity and depth of flavour, seen in earthy duck rillettes, pink-cooked beef rump forestière of impeccable flavour, and turbot with apple purée, roasted salsify and spinach. Desserts usually hit the spot too, along the lines of cranberry crumble served in a cocktail glass. The French-led wine list comes at mostly manageable prices from £14.50.
Chef/s: David Colcombe. **Open:** Mon to Fri L 12 to 2.15, Mon to Sat D 6 to 9.30 (7 to 9.30 Sat). **Closed:** Sun, bank hols, 24 Dec to 4 Jan. **Meals:** alc (main courses £14 to £24). Set L and D £18.50 (3 courses). Market menu (Tue to Fri) £27.50. **Service:** 12.5% (optional). **Details:** Cards accepted. 80 seats. Air-con. Separate bar. No music. Wheelchair access. Children allowed.

Purnell's

Pure brilliance on the plate
55 Cornwall Street, Birmingham, B3 2DH
Tel no: (0121) 2129799
www.purnellsrestaurant.com
Modern British | £42
Cooking score: 6

Cooking on TV seems to have worked a treat for Glynn Purnell, and his fashionable art gallery-style restaurant in Brum's financial district is reaping the benefit of his new-found fame. He has responded by keeping his eye on the ball, maintaining his innovation levels and peppering his menus with witty asides. The tradition of country-house breakfast kedgeree is mercilessly parodied in a starter involving poached egg yolk, smoked haddock milk foam, smoked haddock croquette, curry oil and – yes – cornflakes, while genuine oriental precision defines a dish of cured and slow-cooked mackerel with a mélange of soy, shiitake mushrooms, wasabi and mizuna leaves. Elsewhere, ox cheek might be dusted in liquorice 'charcoal', and mango 'leather' crops up in a dessert of warm dark chocolate mousse and dark chocolate torte. At times it's as

kitschy as a kid's party, but behind the tomfoolery there is serious skill and a feel for the culinary mood of the times that peaks in 'Purnell's Tour' – an eight-course tasting extravaganza with wine pairings. Readers who have taken the trip have returned with tales of the extraordinary as well as the unexpected: the combination of beef carpaccio with cinnamon, brown shrimps, pickled mooli, melon and rocket shoots is pure brilliance on the plate, while a dish of monkfish masala keeps faith with its Asian roots – allowing lentils, coconut, coriander and pickled carrots to have their rightful say. France leads the way on the substantial wine list, which kicks off with a page of house selections from £19.95 (£5.75 a glass).
Chef/s: Glynn Purnell. **Open:** Tue to Fri L 12 to 1.30, Tue to Sat D 7 to 9.30. **Closed:** Sun, Mon, 1 week Easter, first 2 weeks Aug, 1 week Christmas. **Meals:** Set L £21 (2 courses) to £25. Set D £36 (2 courses) to £42. Tasting menu £68 (8 courses). **Service:** 12.5% (optional). **Details:** Cards accepted. 45 seats. Air-con. Separate bar. Wheelchair access. Music.

★ READERS' RESTAURANT OF THE YEAR ★
MIDLANDS

Saffron

Cut-above, stylish Indian
909 Wolverhampton Road, Oldbury, Birmingham, B69 4RR
Tel no: (0121) 5521752
www.saffron-online.co.uk
Indian | £20
Cooking score: 2

£5 OFF V £30

Forget Brummie baltis and garish flock wallpaper, Saffron puts on its stylish Indian show against a backdrop of bold black and red, a 'starlit' ceiling and laminate floors. The food is also a cut above, with tandooris, kormas and biryanis quickly eclipsed by the likes of tawa scallops with cauliflower and red pepper relish or lamb gosht tinged with basil. Sourcing is impressive, and lively ideas abound: free-range chicken is bathed in a garlic and black pepper gravy, Highland venison arrives on

spicy mash, and Barbary duck breast is tossed in a smoky five-spice and hickory sauce. House wine is £10.50.
Chef/s: Gregory Gomes and Sudha Saha. **Open:** Sun to Fri L 12 to 2.30, all week D 5.30 to 11.30. **Meals:** alc (main courses £7 to £19). **Service:** not inc. **Details:** Cards accepted. 95 seats. Air-con. Separate bar. Wheelchair access. Music. Children allowed. Car parking.

Simpsons

Civilised city high-flier
20 Highfield Road, Edgbaston, Birmingham, B15 3DU
Tel no: (0121) 4543434
www.simpsonsrestaurant.co.uk
Modern French | £45
Cooking score: 6

Some serious competitors are staking their gastronomic claims in Birmingham, but Andreas Antona's high-flying restaurant-with-rooms has cemented its reputation as one of the top players in a city that is on the up. The setting is a classically proportioned Georgian mansion in leafy Edgbaston, with a lovely conservatory overlooking a riot of rhododendrons. It's the kind of place where polish and courtesy come with the territory – although the odd niggle about haughty, 'condescending service' has popped up of late. Contemporary French cuisine is the kitchen's business, shored up by generally impeccable technique, oodles of subtlety and a flair for creating unexpected mixed marriages on the plate. Seared Scottish scallops appear with Avruga caviar, orzo pasta and seaweed butter, home-salted cod is exotically paired with coconut basmati rice, coriander and cauliflower salad, while the heady tones of milk-fed Pyrenean lamb, with couscous, semi-dried apricots, aubergine caviar and ras-el-hanout seem to have wafted over on a southerly wind. Stiff Gallic breezes also blow through slow-cooked belly of suckling pig with Agen prunes and a meaty combo of braised beef cheek and fillet with parsley roots and red wine sauce. To finish, exquisite ice

creams point up many of the cleverly crafted desserts – a star anise version with aromatic roasted pear, for example. Five-star French names dominate the majestic wine list, although there is plenty of room for high-strength Super Tuscans and blistering Aussie reds. For best value, visit La Petite Cave – a collection of bottles priced around £30.
Chef/s: Luke Tipping. **Open:** all week L 12 to 2 (2.30 Sat and Sun), Mon to Sat D 7 to 9.30 (10 Fri and Sat). **Closed:** bank hols. **Meals:** alc (main courses £20 to £27). Set L £30. Set D £32.50. Tasting menu £70. **Service:** 12.5% (optional). **Details:** Cards accepted. 70 seats. 10 seats outside. Air-con. No music. No mobile phones. Children allowed. Car parking.

Turners

One of the Midlands' best places to eat
69 High Street, Harborne, Birmingham, B17 9NS
Tel no: (0121) 4264440
www.turnersofharborne.com
Modern British | £45
Cooking score: 6

What Richard Turner's restaurant might lack in dimension, it more than makes up for in culinary ambition. Here, by popular acclaim, is one of the best places to eat out in the Midlands. The long, narrow room may feel a little as though it has the layout of a posh railway carriage, but one with artful mirrors and the proudly trumpeted names of the partners in the business. A reader sums it up: 'dishes are composed of sublime ingredients at their seasonal best, masterfully put together by a kitchen on consistently top form'. Combinations are informed by gastronomic logic and the results are never less than memorable. A sea-fresh first course pairs scallops and tuna, the latter as ceviche, with dabs of oscietre caviar and Japanese seasonings of wasabi, soy and mirin. Main courses are surrounded by supporting casts of ingredients that emphasise their quality, as when new season's lamb comes with dauphinoise, St George's mushrooms, garlic and Madeira, or the roast fillet of locally produced beef is accompanied by caramelised veal sweetbread,

celeriac purée, white asparagus, snails and red wine. To finish, two can share in a dream tarte Tatin served with truffled honey ice cream. Wines are grouped by grape, and include the likes of Zweigelt and Cortese as well as Cabernet and Chardonnay. Prices open at £21.50.
Chef/s: Richard Turner. **Open:** Tue to Fri L 12 to 2, Tue to Sat D 6.45 to 9.30. **Closed:** Sun, Mon. **Meals:** Set L £17.50 (2 courses) to £21.50. Set D £36.50 (2 courses) to £45. **Service:** not inc. **Details:** Cards accepted. 28 seats. Air-con. No mobile phones. Wheelchair access. Music. Children allowed. Car parking.

ALSO RECOMMENDED

▲ Bank

4 Brindleyplace, Birmingham, B1 2JB
Tel no: (0121) 6334466
www.bankrestaurants.com
Modern British

This outpost of a small brasserie group (see entry, London) offers a menu with a contemporary twist on traditional dishes. It's a light, bright space, with a cavernous dining room, an open-to-view kitchen and terrace areas for when the sun shines. Start with beef carpaccio, roast beetroot, watercress and Parmesan (£8.95) and go on to tandoori-baked sea bass (£17.90) or opt for wild mushroom risotto (£10.15). To finish, perhaps Valrhona chocolate soufflé (£6.35) or Malteser ice cream. House wine is £15.50. Open all week.

▲ cielo

6 Oozells Square, Brindleyplace, Birmingham, B1 2JB
Tel no: (0121) 6326882
www.cielobirmingham.com
Italian

In a quiet square among the towering offices and apartments of Brindleyplace, this straightforward and stylish Italian deals in familiar trattoria food without frills. Dishes are comforting and uncomplicated rather than groundbreaking: a starter of king prawns sautéed with white wine, chilli and garlic butter (£11.95) might be followed by veal osso bucco, creamed potatoes, Savoy cabbage and tomato sauce (£16.95). Finish with lemon polenta cake, lemon and lime curd and lemon sorbet (£4.95). Wines from £14.95. Open all week.

READERS RECOMMEND

Lasan

Indian
3-4 Dakota Buildings, James Street, St Paul's Square, Birmingham, B3 1SD
Tel no: (0121) 2123664
www.lasangroup.com
'This is a place you want to keep returning to – the ongoing popularity shows that others think the same'

Pascal's

Modern British
1 Montague Road, Edgbaston, Birmingham, B16 9HN
Tel no: (0121) 4550999
www.pascalsrestaurant.co.uk
'The main course fillet of sea bream was out of this world'

█ Dorridge

The Forest

Food on the right track
25 Station Approach, Dorridge, B93 8JA
Tel no: (01564) 772120
www.forest-hotel.com
Modern European | £23
Cooking score: 2

🛏 V £30

A hot ticket for travel-weary commuters and locals looking for an impromptu supper, this revamped railway hotel does its level best to satisfy all-comers with its easy-going brasserie food. Among the current favourites from the evolving menu are asparagus with a 'crispy egg' and char-grilled piri-piri chicken with Caesar salad; one hardcore fan also drops in regularly for the 'legendary' Forest burger

('rare as requested and without a bun'). Elsewhere, the kitchen raises its game for seared scallops with cauliflower purée and oyster mayo, roast pigeon with confit rabbit, celeriac and lentils, and desserts such as carrot cake with iced banana parfait. Wines start at £12.95.
Chef/s: Dean Grubb. **Open:** all week L 12 to 2.30 (3 Sun), Mon to Sat D 6.30 to 10. **Closed:** 25 Dec. **Meals:** alc (main courses £7 to £18). Set L and D Mon to Fri £13 (2 courses) to £15.50. Sun L £14.50 (2 courses) to £17.50. **Service:** 10% (optional). **Details:** Cards accepted. 70 seats. 70 seats outside. Air-con. Separate bar. Wheelchair access. Music. Children allowed. Car parking.

█ Wolverhampton

ALSO RECOMMENDED
▲ Bilash

2 Cheapside, Wolverhampton, WV1 1TU
Tel no: (01902) 427762
www.thebilash.co.uk
Indian £5 OFF

A venerable family-run institution that has been a Wolverhampton landmark since 1982, Bilash enjoys local renown for classic Bangladeshi and Indian cookery served in smart, contemporary surrounds. 'Excellent and inventive food' includes spicy chicken tikka shahlik, various biryanis (from £12.90), paneer in chilli massala (£9.90) or their own distinctive Goan tiger-prawn masala (£22.90). There are good-value set lunch and dinner menus too, and a short list of international wines from £17. Friendly service. Closed Sun.

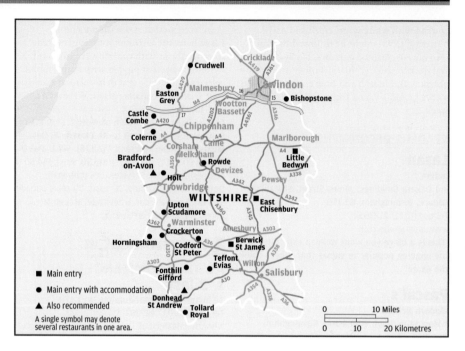

■	Main entry
●	Main entry with accommodation
▲	Also recommended

A single symbol may denote several restaurants in one area.

0   10 Miles

0   10   20 Kilometres

■ Berwick St James

The Boot Inn

Confident, unshowy cooking
High Street, Berwick St James, SP3 4TN
Tel no: (01722) 790243
www.bootatberwick.co.uk
Gastropub | £23
Cooking score: 1

£5 OFF   £30

'Since Giles and Cathy Dickinson came to the Boot Inn, we have become very regular visitors, the food is locally sourced and we never fail to be delighted,' enthuse fans of this traditional brick-and-flint village pub. But don't expect culinary fireworks in this Wiltshire backwater: instead you can look forward to confident, unshowy cooking. Recent successes have included devilled lamb's kidneys and mushrooms on toast, Barnsley chop with bubble and squeak and rosemary gravy, and crispy belly pork with black pudding and mustard mash; good fish, too. Apple and rhubarb crumble has been a successful dessert. Wines from £12.95.

Chef/s: Giles Dickinson. **Open:** Tue to Sun L 12 to 2.15, Tue to Sat D 6.30 to 9 (9.30 Sat). **Closed:** Mon, 25 Dec, 1 to 10 Feb. **Meals:** alc (main courses £10 to £16). Sun L 12.50 (2 courses) to 16.50. **Service:** not inc. **Details:** Cards accepted. 40 seats. 30 seats outside. Wheelchair access. Music. Children allowed. Car parking.

Symbols

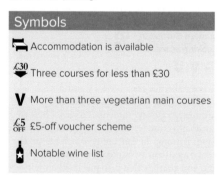

🛏 Accommodation is available

£30 ⬇ Three courses for less than £30

V More than three vegetarian main courses

£5 OFF £5-off voucher scheme

🍷 Notable wine list

▌Bishopstone
Helen Browning at the Royal Oak
Country pub with organic cred
Cues Lane, Bishopstone, SN6 8PP
Tel no: (01793) 790481
www.royaloakbishopstone.co.uk
Gastropub | £28
Cooking score: 3
£5 OFF 🍴 £30 ♨

Scrabble evenings, cheap B&B, slugs of home-produced sloe gin and treks along the Ridgeway are just some of the bonuses at this cheerily revitalised country pub down a narrow lane. Owner Helen Browning is one of England's organic pioneers, and produce from her showpiece Eastbrook Farm is the star turn – aged steaks, glorious pork belly, rare-breed lamb and humanely reared veal all put on a show in tandem with foraged pickings and elite imports including Abruzzese olive oil. The result? Perhaps smoked breast of free-range goose with crab apple jelly or chicken, leek and home-cured bacon pie, portobello mushroom burgers or sticky pork ribs and chilli jam, with top-drawer regional cheeses or sweet treats such as cinnamon-dusted apple fritters to close. A dozen organic wines (from £16.50) do their job admirably.
Chef/s: Liz Franklin. **Open:** all week L 12 to 2.30 (3 Sat and Sun), D 6.30 to 9.30 (8.30 Sun). **Meals:** alc (main courses £10 to £25). **Service:** not inc.
Details: Cards accepted. 45 seats. 25 seats outside. No music. Children allowed. Car parking.

▌Bradford-on-Avon
ALSO RECOMMENDED
▲ Fat Fowl
Silver Street, Bradford-on-Avon, BA15 1JX
Tel no: (01225) 863111
www.fatfowl.com
Modern European £5 OFF

What everybody likes about this cheerful restaurant is its versatility: from morning coffee and pastries via light lunches and tasty tapas to full-blown evening meals. Local and seasonal materials are a strong suit and the cooking shows plenty of flair. Reporters have praised squid with chorizo and tapenade (£8.50), risotto of roasted beetroot, wild garlic and Parmesan, subtly seasoned Moroccan-style lamb, and skate wing with sea beet and a tomato, pepper and paprika broth (£15.50). Plus points, too, for good vegetarian choices, excellent desserts (£5.50) and 'helpful, attentive' staff. Wines from £13.50. Open all week.

▌Castle Combe
The Manor House Hotel, Bybrook Restaurant
Many-layered, luxury dishes
Castle Combe, SN14 7HR
Tel no: (01249) 782206
www.exclusivehotels.co.uk
Modern British | £57
Cooking score: 5
£5 OFF 🍴 V

As one reader observed, this imposing fourteenth-century manor is currently enjoying 'a revival'. The prospect certainly pleases and impresses – a glorious edifice stunningly located amid 365 acres of parkland on the fringes of the Cotswolds, with the river Bybrook running through the grounds and Italianate gardens looking a picture. The Bybrook restaurant proudly displays its stained glass windows, chandeliers and carved stonework, although that's where any backward glances end. Richard Davies is a contemporary chef who cooks in the present, fashioning many-layered, complex ideas from luxurious, top-end ingredients. A brilliant starter of duck 'done three ways' with blobs of peach conserve on the side blew one party away, although the kitchen might also conjure up roast breast of squab pigeon with pumpkin tortellini, red onion tart and jus du vin. Mains sit nearer the mainstream, perhaps 'immaculately timed' halibut with trompettes de mort, spinach and tiny cubes of potato, or slow-cooked loin of Brecon venison partnered in time-honoured fashion by chestnut purée, roast salsify and spiced redcurrant jus, plus a surprise package of truffled potato terrine. To finish, a combo of passion-fruit sorbet and mousse is pure class, or you might prefer cardamom pannacotta with baked plums and plum sorbet. The globetrotting wine list (from £24) deals in serious vintages at serious prices.

Chef/s: Richard Davies. **Open:** Sun to Fri L 12.30 to 2 (2.30 Sun), all week D 7 to 9.30 (10 Fri and Sat). **Meals:** Set L £21 (2 courses) to £25. Set D £49 (2 courses) to £57. Sun L £31. Tasting menu £65. **Service:** 12.5% (optional). **Details:** Cards accepted. 70 seats. 50 seats outside. Separate bar. No music. No mobile phones. Wheelchair access. Children allowed. Car parking.

Codford St Peter

The George Hotel

Classy cooking from a dynamic duo
High Street, Codford St Peter, BA12 0NG
Tel no: (01985) 850270
Modern British | £24
Cooking score: 4

£5 OFF 🍴 £30 🍷

Codford St Peter is more handsomely resourced than many a Wiltshire village. For a start, it boasts this seventeenth-century inn, as well as the Woolstore Theatre just opposite. The George offers log fires in winter, a garden for the summer, and the classy modern British cooking of kitchen partners Boyd McIntosh and Joel Deverill all year round. Expect to find sustaining pub dishes along the lines of deep-fried whitebait with garlic and lemon mayonnaise, or pork cheek terrine with gooseberry chutney to start, followed by a fortifying casserole of local beef and mushrooms in real ale, served with creamy mash, or whole baked plaice with caper butter. Mango pannacotta or well-kept farmhouse cheeses bring up the rear. The short list has four house wines at £13.95 (£3.50 a glass).

Chef/s: Boyd McIntosh and Joel Deverill. **Open:** Wed to Mon L 12 to 2, Mon and Wed to Sat D 6.30 to 9. **Closed:** Tue. **Meals:** alc (main courses £10 to £18).

Service: not inc. **Details:** Cards accepted. 60 seats. 60 seats outside. Music. Children allowed. Car parking.

Colerne

Lucknam Park

Stunning creations and bags of class
Colerne, SN14 8AZ
Tel no: (01225) 742777
www.lucknampark.co.uk
Modern British | £65
Cooking score: 6

🍴 V

Lucknam Park exudes class at every turn, as was noted by the party who enjoyed a Sunday lunch here. They were impressed by the mile-long approach between serried ranks of beech trees, and even more so by the valet parking of their cars in the rain. The central part of the house dates from the Stuart period, with the pillared portico and wings being added later. Inside is as grand as you might expect, but the overall tone is light and easy on the eye, a calming ambience in which to enjoy Hywel Jones's finely crafted modern British food. Sound local and organic supplies, including herbs from Lucknam's own garden, go to make up dishes that deliver a sophisticated sense of adventure. Dinner might begin with a composition of thinly sliced smoked eel, grilled mackerel, potato and horseradish risotto, grilled pancetta and watercress purée, dressed in red wine vinaigrette. Main courses up the ante still further, with some complex but stunning productions: try pot-roast Anjou pigeon with a raviolo of foie gras and baby turnips in a parsnip and Sauternes bouillon. At dessert, a three-way exploration of the classic prune and Armagnac pairing – soufflé, brûlée and ice cream – seems almost straightforward. Prices on the encyclopaedic wine list open at £22.

Chef/s: Hywel Jones. **Open:** Tue to Sat D 7 to 10. **Closed:** Sun, Mon. **Meals:** Set D £65 to £75. **Service:** not inc. **Details:** Cards accepted. 50 seats. No music. Wheelchair access. Children allowed. Car parking.

Crockerton
The Bath Arms
Going from strength to strength
Clay Street, Crockerton, BA12 8AJ
Tel no: (01985) 212262
www.batharmscrockerton.co.uk
Gastropub | £24
Cooking score: 3

It goes from strength to strength, this traditional country pub set in pretty countryside close to Longleat. Dean Carr's cooking is straightforward and unadorned. And it's good; not always perfect, but the heart is in the right places of freshness, value and invention. The menu reads well. Among starters might be crab mayonnaise, baked mushroom Welsh rarebit, and scallops with minted carrots and spiced sultanas, all well reported this year. Sticky beef with braised red cabbage and fillet of red mullet with cauliflower cheese and truffled celeriac are the sort of things to expect for a main course, alongside excellent ribeye steak and a mixed grill. Familiar-sounding desserts might include sticky toffee pudding or bread-and-butter pudding with marmalade ice cream. House wine is £14.50.
Chef/s: Dean Carr. **Open:** all week L 12 to 2 (2.30 Sun), D 6.30 to 9. **Meals:** alc (main courses £7 to £16). **Service:** not inc. **Details:** Cards accepted. 75 seats. 80 seats outside. Wheelchair access. Music. Children allowed. Car parking.

Crudwell
The Rectory Hotel
Quirkiness and quality
Crudwell, SN16 9EP
Tel no: (01666) 577194
www.therectoryhotel.com
Modern British | £30
Cooking score: 3

A keen eye for the cheerful and quirky creates a contemporary feel in this handsome Georgian manor house set in three acres of grounds. Dinner is unhurried, and simple table settings indicate that the focus is on the quality of what you eat rather than any unnecessary frippery (suppliers are listed on the menu, and much comes from a 30-mile radius). Good meat options include roasted pork steak with mustard mash, creamed wild mushrooms and shallot confit, while fish (from the south-west coast) might be sea bass with lemon and chive potato cake with a cream sauce. Scallops with leek and smoked bacon purée, and mulled wine pear with vanilla rice pudding could top and tail the meal. House wine is £13.95.
Chef/s: Peter Fairclough. **Open:** all week D only 7 to 9.30. **Meals:** alc (main courses £14 to £17). **Service:** not inc. **Details:** Cards accepted. 24 seats. 12 seats outside. Separate bar. Wheelchair access. Music. Children allowed. Car parking.

ALSO RECOMMENDED
▲ The Potting Shed
The Street, Crudwell, SN16 9EW
Tel no: (01666) 577833
www.thepottingshedpub.com
Gastropub £5 OFF

A stone-built roadside village pub of the old school, the Potting Shed is all rustic wooden tables and low beams, with a collection of mustard pots and skittles above the fireplace. The food aims for a modern British approach, adding orange-scented cabbage and a pear and grape dressing to honey-glazed wood pigeon for a starter (£6.50), with mains such as an inch-thick, juicy sausage, bacon and sage burger with Montgomery Cheddar, triple-cooked chips and apple compote (£11.95), and finishing with desserts like vanilla and toffee pannacotta with pecan praline and banana and lime sorbet (£5.50). Wines from £13.95. Closed Sun D (though we are told that might change).

Also recommended
Also recommended entries are not scored but we think they are worth a visit.

■ Donhead St Andrew

ALSO RECOMMENDED
▲ The Forester

Lower Street, Donhead St Andrew, SP7 9EE
Tel no: **(01747) 828038**
www.theforesterdonheadstandrew.co.uk
Modern British

Just within the Wiltshire border off the A30, the Forester is a proper village pub, with the two essential features – a garden terrace for outdoor eating in the summer, and roaring fires inside in winter. Locally sourced menus also take in seafood from Devon and Cornwall, and the enterprising cooking is typified by tempura-battered squid in Asian dressing (£6.50), pork belly with apple sauce and potatoes roasted in duck fat (£13.50), and what one reader considers 'the best crème brûlée in the county' (£5.50). Wines from £13.50. Closed Sun D.

■ East Chisenbury
Red Lion

Startlingly accomplished food
East Chisenbury, SN9 6AQ
Tel no: **(01980) 671124**
www.redlionfreehouse.com
Modern British | £28
Cooking score: 5
£5 OFF   £30

Pack an OS map and programme your SatNav if you're heading out to this welcoming thatched freehouse in the wild reaches of Salisbury Plain south of Upavon. Also persevere, because 'startlingly accomplished' modern food is your reward at the sympathetically spruced-up Red Lion (along with ales from Wiltshire's microbreweries). Guy Manning started out as a sous chef at Chez Bruce (see entry), but he and his wife have also done stints with Thomas Keller in New York's Per Se and at Martin Berasategui's self-named restaurant in San Sebastien. Given their pedigree, it's no surprise that the cooking makes you sit up and take notice – roast scallops are partnered by crispy pig's head,

parsnip, apple and meat juices, while desserts such as yoghurt tapioca with roasted pineapple and macadamia granola show the couple's instinct for contrasts. The Mannings' daily menus are driven by impressive local sourcing and what they can produce in-house, although many dishes are given a Mediterranean spin. Roast black bream is served with risotto nero, braised squid and chorizo, while stuffed free-range chicken leg might appear with Ibérico croquettes and braised leeks. Elsewhere, mighty 24oz ribeyes (for two) keep traditional company with béarnaise and hand-cut chips. The nifty, 40-bin wine list comes courtesy of the team at Stone, Vine & Sun. Prices start at £14.50.
Chef/s: Guy and Brittany Manning. **Open:** Tue to Sun L 12.30 to 2.30 (3 Sun), Tue to Sat D 6.30 to 9. **Closed:** Mon, 25 Dec, 2 weeks Jan. **Meals:** alc (main courses £13 to £19). **Service:** 10% (optional). **Details:** Cards accepted. 45 seats. 20 seats outside. Separate bar. Wheelchair access. Music. Children allowed. Car parking.

■ Easton Grey
Whatley Manor

Scintillating food and sensual triumphs
Easton Grey, SN16 0RB
Tel no: **(01666) 822888**
www.whatleymanor.com
Modern French | £69
Cooking score: 8
£5 OFF   🍷 🛏 �

This restored and extended Cotswold manor house is a thing of many parts. Descending from the car park to the interconnecting gravelled inner courtyards, you may feel that it was all built fairly recently and, once inside, the mixed messages continue. The lounges suggest an old-school country house, but the dining room is a wood-floored modern space, softened with Italian silks and concealed uplighting, and decorated with large abstract paintings on rough-textured wood. Martin Burge has set, maintained and now stepped up a cracking pace here, for food that is emphatically contemporary, and yet not given to crackpot combinations or conceptual gimmickry. There are an awful lot of intervening elements, including canapés, amuses, two pre-desserts and two lots of petits fours, but it all seems perfectly judged and executed with scintillating technical acuity. Start with a trio of Scottish langoustine tails, beautifully timed and topped with lemongrass foam, together with accoutrements of cauliflower purée and a large chunk of fat bacon. Main courses evince attention in every bite, from the little cottage pie and puréed parsnip that accompany a pairing of red-rare beef fillet and caramelised kidney to the seared foie gras and cubes of darkly glistening coffee and sherry jelly that form a glorious counterpoint to squab pigeon. At inspection, a starter dish that teamed smoked eel, duck breast and whole foie gras with orange jelly and caramelised walnuts was the only one that appeared to have lost its way a little in terms of overall unity, but the famous dessert-cheese crossover dish of black truffle ice cream with deep-fried goats' cheese, Roquefort cream and cooked pear is a sensual, savoury-sweet triumph. Petits fours arrive with what appears to be a cigar-box that turns out to contain a crown-jewels collection of chocolates (don't miss the prune and Earl Grey). Wines are a broadly based international array, at prices that are varied enough to afford relief, with an excellent selection by the glass. Bottles start at £19.50. Le Mazot is a more informal alternative in the decorative style of a Swiss chalet.

Chef/s: Martin Burge. **Open:** Wed to Sun D only 7 to 10. **Closed:** Mon, Tue. **Meals:** Set D £68.50. Tasting menu £85. **Service:** 10% (optional). **Details:** Cards accepted. 40 seats. Separate bar. Wheelchair access. Music. Car parking.

Please send us your feedback

To register your opinion about any restaurant listed in the Guide, or a new restaurant that you wish to bring to our attention, please visit the web address at the bottom of the page. Your feedback informs the content of the book and will be used to compile next year's reviews.

▮ Fonthill Gifford

NEW ENTRY
The Beckford Arms
Smart inn with a passion for food
Fonthill Gifford, SP3 6PX
Tel no: (01747) 870385
www.beckfordarms.com
British | £22
Cooking score: 2

The team behind Babington House snapped up this eighteenth-century stone-built inn, just a short drive from the A303, in the summer of 2009. Serious investment followed and the result is impressive, with the smart, rustic interior featuring wood floors, blazing log fires and soothing colours. In the kitchen, Mark Blatchford's daily menus show a passion for seasonal foods and local producers. Sound cooking is evident in the likes of wild duck and juniper terrine with fig chutney, Red Poll beef stew or pan-fried black bream with salsify and lemon butter, and rice pudding with homemade jam. Cracking bar snacks and Sunday roasts (booking essential), a super garden and great bedrooms too. House wines from £13.50.

Chef/s: Mark Blatchford. **Open:** all week L 12 to 2.30 (3 Sat, 3.30 Sun), D 6 to 9.30. **Meals:** alc (main courses £9 to £17). **Service:** not inc. **Details:** Cards accepted. 70 seats. 60 seats outside. Separate bar. Music. Children allowed. Car parking.

▮ Holt
The Tollgate Inn
Good value and careful sourcing
Ham Green, Holt, BA14 6PX
Tel no: (01225) 782326
www.tollgateholt.co.uk
Modern British | £25
Cooking score: 2

The sturdy character of this old pub overlooking the green is emphasised within by beams, a wood burner, stone-flagged and oak floors, and by an upstairs dining room housed in the high-raftered former weaver's chapel. The kitchen cares about the provenance of its supplies and there's the option of a snack or a full meal alongside good-value set lunch and dinner menus. One regular visitor has praised scallops on lentil purée and believes they serve 'a great beef Wellington, and the best créme brûlée', but others have complained of 'conveyor belt food' on busy weekends. House wine £14.50.

Chef/s: Alexander Venables. **Open:** Tue to Sun L 12 to 2, Tue to Sat D 7 to 9. **Closed:** Mon, 25 Dec, 1 Jan. **Meals:** alc (main courses £13 to £19). Set L £12.50 (2 courses) to £14.95. Set D £19.75. Sun L £16.95. **Service:** not inc. **Details:** Cards accepted. 60 seats. 40 seats outside. Separate bar. No mobile phones. Wheelchair access. Music. Children allowed. Car parking.

Horningsham

The Bath Arms
Tourist-friendly inn
Longleat Estate, Horningsham, BA12 7LY
Tel no: (01985) 844308
www.batharms.co.uk
Modern British | £30
Cooking score: 2

🛏 V

Standing impressively at the gates of Longleat, the creeper-clad Bath Arms makes a handy refuelling point for visitors to the safari park – although this is no convenience pit stop. The kitchen sources carefully and also takes account of produce from the estate: home-reared pork could turn up in a dish of roast belly with faggot, glazed apples and mash. Dinner might open with scallops with black pudding and cauliflower purée, and there's rhubarb jelly and ice cream for dessert. Lunch is a more informal affair, with bacon baps and ribeye steaks on show. Wines from £14.50.

Chef/s: Chris Gregory. **Open:** all week L 12 to 2.30, D 7 to 9 (9.30 Fri and Sat). **Meals:** alc (main courses £9 to £19). Set L £10 (2 courses) to £15. Set D £24.50 (2 courses) to £29.50. **Service:** not inc. **Details:** Cards accepted. 60 seats. 40 seats outside. Separate bar. Wheelchair access. Music. Children allowed. Car parking.

Little Bedwyn

The Harrow at Little Bedwyn
Fine dining with wines to match
Little Bedwyn, SN8 3JP
Tel no: (01672) 870871
www.theharrowatlittlebedwyn.co.uk
Modern British | £43
Cooking score: 6

🍷 V

The Harrow was a wreck when Roger and Sue Jones bought it in 1998, but they have transformed it into a refined modern restaurant, a restful room with pastel walls and black seating. The couple are avid for as much quality produce as they can get their hands on, from Devon and Scilly Isles seafood to pure-breed Welsh meats and incomparable West Country dairy produce. It all finds its way into Roger Jones's inspired cooking; crisp-fried squid may be teamed with caramelised belly pork and sweet chilli jam, while a wild mushroom risotto may be further deepened with winter notes from chestnuts and Jerusalem artichoke cream. There is resonance to these dishes, and a hit-rate that comes from knowing not to gild the lily; black beef fillet for example, is accompanied by a crépinette sausage and horseradish-spiked potato cake in firm supporting roles. It all lingers long in readers' memories, including finely rendered classic desserts such as lemon tart with vanilla ice cream. The owners' other abiding passion is wine. There are representative runs of vintages from a number of pedigree growers, such as South Africa's Hamilton Russell and New Zealand's Felton Road. Bottles open at £21.

Chef/s: Roger Jones and John Brown. **Open:** Wed to Sun L 12 to 2 (3 Sun), Wed to Sat D 6 to 11. **Closed:** Mon, Tue, 2 weeks Christmas, 2 weeks Aug. **Meals:** alc (main courses £24). Set L £30. Set D £40. Tasting menu £70. **Service:** not inc. **Details:** Cards accepted. 32 seats. 24 seats outside. Wheelchair access. Music. Children allowed.

Rowde
The George & Dragon
Pleasing pub with serious seafood
High Street, Rowde, SN10 2PN
Tel no: (01380) 723053
www.thegeorgeanddragonrowde.co.uk
Modern British | £23
Cooking score: 4

£5 OFF ⊨ V £30 ❦

The frontage looks pretty unpromising, but get through the door of this amenable coaching inn and you'll find log fires ablaze, panelled walls and signs of serious culinary intent. This may be landlocked Wiltshire, but fish is one of the star turns here – and it's worth checking the blackboard for specials. Supplies arrive daily from Cornwall, and the kitchen might work its magic on spicy crab risotto with rocket and crème fraîche, a brochette of char-grilled scallops and black pudding or unflashy grilled skate wing with caper butter. Those with other preferences could veer towards baked fresh figs with goats' cheese and prosciutto, lamb and cider pie or roast chicken breast on bacon and thyme dauphinois potatoes. A few snacks and pubby dishes are offered in the bar, while desserts run the familiar gamut from Eton mess to sticky toffee pudding. Fish-friendly whites outnumber reds on the respectable wine list; prices start at £10.50 (£3.50 a glass).
Chef/s: Christopher Day. **Open:** all week L 12 to 3 (4 Sat and Sun), Mon to Sat D 7 to 10 (6.30 to 10 Sat). **Meals:** alc (main courses £9 to £25). Set L and D £14.50 (2 courses) to £17.50. Sun L £17.50. **Service:** 10% (optional). **Details:** Cards accepted. 32 seats. 25 seats outside. Wheelchair access. Music. Children allowed. Car parking.

Teffont Evias
Howard's House
Country comforts and quietly confident food
Teffont Evias, SP3 5RJ
Tel no: (01722) 716392
www.howardshousehotel.co.uk
Modern British | £45
Cooking score: 3

⊨

An entrancing English idyll complete with its own little stream, gardens and undulating topiary, Howard's House drifts along easily in its own carefree, cocooned world. Inside, this remodelled seventeenth-century dwelling pleases with its country comforts, genuine courtesy and quietly confident, impeccably presented food. 'Utterly tender' rump of lamb and pannacotta with raspberries have satisfied of late, but Nick Wentworth's concise seasonal menus also yield other interesting possibilities. An open lasagne of Devon crab with shellfish foam tips its hat to big-city kitchens, but the chef also keeps faith with his home turf by offering an assiette of Wiltshire pork with thyme-roasted root vegetables. For afters, soak up the exoticism of passion-fruit soufflé, pineapple sorbet and coconut ice cream. A page of house selections from £15.95 (£4.60 a glass) opens the sizeable French-centred wine list.
Chef/s: Nick Wentworth. **Open:** all week L 12.30 to 2, D 7 to 9. **Meals:** Set L £23 (2 courses) to £27.50. Set D £24 (2 courses) to £28.50. Sun L £27.50. **Service:** not inc. **Details:** Cards accepted. 22 seats. 22 seats outside. No mobile phones. Wheelchair access. Music. Children allowed. Car parking.

■ Tollard Royal

NEW ENTRY
The King John Inn
Country virtues aplenty
Tollard Royal, SP5 5PS
Tel no: (01725) 516207
www.kingjohninn.co.uk
Modern British | £25
Cooking score: 3
🛏 £30

Rescued from near dereliction and beautifully refurbished by Alex and Gretchen Boon, this Victorian inn comes with period fireplaces, rug-strewn tiles, country life photos on the walls and copies of the *Shooting Gazette* scattered around the rambling, open-plan interior. Pheasant, partridge and venison from neighbouring Rushmore Estate appear in season, and the robust repertoire also stretches to Dorset lamb with wild mushroom dauphinoise and redcurrant jus or lemon sole with saffron potatoes and mussels. Begin with ox tongue fritters or a bowl of bouillabaisse, and finish with textbook bread-and-butter pudding. House wine is £14.95 – also check out the wine shop across the car park.
Chef/s: Simon Trepass. **Open:** all week L 12 to 2.30 (3 Fri and Sat), all week D 7 to 9.30 (10 Fri and Sat). **Closed:** 26 and 31 Dec. **Meals:** alc (main courss £11 to £18). **Service:** not inc. **Details:** Cards accepted. 70 seats. 70 seats outside. No mobile phones. Wheelchair access. Car parking.

■ Upton Scudamore
The Angel Inn
An updated inn of substance
Upton Scudamore, BA12 0AG
Tel no: (01985) 213225
www.theangelinn.co.uk
Modern British | £29
Cooking score: 3
🛏 V £30

You enter this low-slung, whitewashed inn via a southwest-facing walled garden and terrace, and the spacious interior is easy on the eye, too, with polished floorboards and bare wood tables creating a breezy, modern feel. The kitchen looks to the Mediterranean and beyond for menus that offer fine fresh fish from Brixham – say scallops with cauliflower bhaji or a panache of seafood in saffron consommé. Canny sourcing also brings prime Ashdale Farm beef fillet with foie gras butter, celeriac purée and baby roast onions. Novel touches at dessert stage have included double chocolate bread-and-butter pudding with chocolate sauce and a white chocolate and mixed berry ripple ice cream. House wine is £13.75.
Chef/s: Andy Lee. **Open:** all week L 12 to 2, D 6.30 to 9.30. **Meals:** alc (main courses £12 to £23). Set L £10.95 (2 courses) to £14.95. **Service:** not inc. **Details:** Cards accepted. 68 seats. 40 seats outside. Separate bar. Wheelchair access. Music. Children allowed. Car parking.

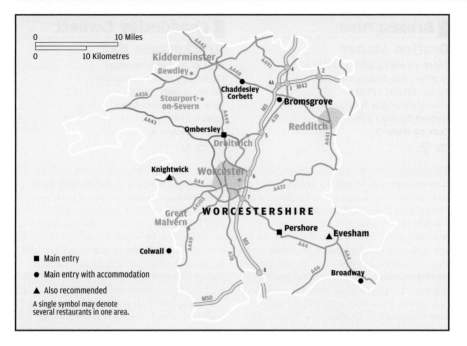

0   10 Miles
0   10 Kilometres

- Main entry
- Main entry with accommodation
- Also recommended

A single symbol may denote
several restaurants in one area.

■ Broadway

Russell's

Boutique brasserie with panache
20 High Street, Broadway, WR12 7DT
Tel no: (01386) 853555
www.russellsofbroadway.co.uk
Modern British | £27
Cooking score: 4

£5 OFF 🛏 £30

Once home to celebrated furniture designer
Gordon Russell, this restored Georgian
building now plies its trade as a boutique
restaurant-with-rooms. The stylish
contemporary dining room occupies the
ground floor, with glass doors opening onto a
secluded courtyard for alfresco meals. Chef
Matthew Laughton cooks with an open mind,
happily reinventing prawn cocktail, dressing
Caesar salads and offering tapas 'slates' to share,
as well as pulling some unexpected brasserie
strokes along the way. Home-cured gravlax is
given a perky lift with pickled vegetable salad,
while dried fruit couscous, butternut squash,
olives and mint yoghurt relish add some warm
Middle Eastern tones to grilled Barnsley chop.
To finish there's coffee pannacotta with
espresso ice cream. Not all reports have been
ecstatic: six spears of asparagus with over-
chilled hollandaise and a hard-boiled duck
egg for £10 wasn't a thrilling start for one
visitor, and others have complained of stale
homemade bread. The 50-bin wine list
includes 11 house recommendations at £18.50
(£4.75 a glass).

Chef/s: Matthew Laughton. **Open:** all week L 12 to
2.30, Mon to Sat D 6 to 9.30 (6.30 Sat). **Meals:** alc
(main courses £12 to £22). Set L and D £12 (2
courses) to £15. Sun L £22.95. **Service:** not inc.
Details: Cards accepted. 60 seats. 30 seats outside.
Air-con. Wheelchair access. Music. Children allowed.
Car parking.

▌Bromsgrove

Grafton Manor
Country cooking with a spicy twist
Grafton Lane, Bromsgrove, B61 7HA
Tel no: (01527) 579007
www.graftonmanorhotel.co.uk
Modern British | £29
Cooking score: 3

The original manor house was built in the sixteenth century by an Earl of Shrewsbury and played centre-stage in the hatching of the Gunpowder Plot. Now a high-end country hotel, it enjoys a tranquil setting, a refined tone and a chef who loves Indian food. So the country cooking often has a spicy twist – and there are sometimes special all-Indian feasts to celebrate festivals. Everyday fixed-price menus feature the likes of seared scallops with spiced pear, pork fillet wrapped in pancetta with champ mash, braised red cabbage and Madeira, and chocolate tart with caramel ice cream to finish. That Indian touch might influence the dessert menu too, so don't be surprised to see Hyderabadi apricots with mango and coriander sorbet. A French-led wine list opens with nine house recommendations, including Ardèche blends at £13.95.
Chef/s: Tim Waldron and Adam Harrison. Open: Sun to Fri L 12 to 2.30, Mon to Sat D 7 to 9. Closed: 30 Dec to 1 Jan. Meals: Set L £22.50. Set D £28.95 to £33.75 (4 courses). Service: not inc. Details: Cards accepted. 50 seats. Separate bar. No music. No mobile phones. Wheelchair access. Children allowed. Car parking.

▌Chaddesley Corbett

Brockencote Hall
Bags of skill and invention
Chaddesley Corbett, DY10 4PY
Tel no: (01562) 777876
www.brockencotehall.com
French | £40
Cooking score: 4

The setting is as attractive as ever: an impressive, classically styled country house overlooking a lake in 70 acres of parkland. Staff are well-informed and personable and chef John Sherry is setting a formidable pace in the kitchen. His cooking makes a virtue of simplicity and economy, and seems to please the great majority on both fronts. There is plenty of skill and invention here too: squab pigeon breast with blood pudding, leg pastilla and black cherry jus makes a strong opener, and there is no bashfulness about serving straightforward main dishes such as cannon of beef with oxtail croquette, horseradish rösti, onion purée, ceps and smoked beef jus. Elsewhere, 'wonderful' crab ravioli opened a spring Sunday lunch for one regular, followed by 'simple but superbly cooked cod'. Accomplished desserts include passion-fruit soufflé with coconut parfait, vanilla yoghurt and banana ice cream. House wines from £18.
Chef/s: John Sherry. Open: all week L 12 to 1.30 (2 Sun), D 7 to 9.30 (8.30 Sun). Meals: alc (main courses £19 to £28). Set L £17 (2 courses) to £22. Set D £39.50. Sun L £27.50 (3 courses) to £44.50. Tasting menu £55 (6 courses). Service: not inc. Details: Cards accepted. 75 seats. Separate bar. No mobile phones. Wheelchair access. Music. Children allowed. Car parking.

■ Colwall

Colwall Park Hotel

Handsome hotel with appealing food
Walwyn Road, Colwall, WR13 6QG
Tel no: (01684) 540000
www.colwall.co.uk
Modern British | £35
Cooking score: 3

£5 OFF 🛒

Smartly turned-out and with views towards the Malvern Hills, this solid mock-Tudor hotel makes a favourable impression on visitors. In the handsome oak-panelled Seasons Restaurant the name of the game is to combine sound ingredients with uncomplicated modern cooking to produce a menu with broad appeal. James Garth carries this off with style, treading a reassuringly safe path through scallops with cauliflower purée and sherry caramel, breast of chicken with wild mushroom and asparagus risotto and tarragon cream sauce, and baked peach cheesecake with raspberry sorbet. Fair prices characterise the international wine list, with bottles from £16.95.
Chef/s: James Garth. **Open:** all week L 12 to 2 (2.30 Sun), D 7 to 9 (8.30 Sun). **Meals:** alc (main courses £19 to £23). Set L £16.95 (2 courses) to £19.95. **Service:** not inc. **Details:** Cards accepted. 40 seats. Air-con. Separate bar. No mobile phones. Wheelchair access. Music. Children allowed. Car parking.

■ Evesham

ALSO RECOMMENDED
▲ The Evesham Hotel

Cooper's Lane, Evesham, WR11 1DA
Tel no: (01386) 765566
www.eveshamhotel.com
Modern British

House and home to the Jenkinson family since 1975, this idiosyncratic Cotswold hotel is run with ebullient hospitality and a real sense of fun. The kitchen goes its own way, offering a lively, allsorts selection of eclectic dishes from around the globe. Tempters might include

Roquefort and fig brûlée with pecans (£5.50) and rump of lamb on crushed sweet potato (£16.50), with perhaps elderflower pannacotta (£5.20) to close. The gargantuan wine list is housed in four photograph albums; prices start at £18. Open all week.

■ Knightwick

ALSO RECOMMENDED
▲ The Talbot

Knightwick, WR6 5PH
Tel no: (01886) 821235
www.the-talbot.co.uk
British

The Clift family has been running this centuries-old, black-and-white inn overlooking the river Teme for 28 years. Honest pub cooking (rather like the bare-bones décor) keeps things simple, making the most of local and homegrown supplies in dishes such as smoked pigeon breast with onion marmalade (£6.50) and rabbit casserole with ginger and cider (£14). Good-value lunches bring leek and potato soup and roast pig's cheek with mash and red cabbage for £12. House wine £12.50. Accommodation. Open all week.

■ Ombersley

The Venture In

Cracking food in a crooked house
High Street, Ombersley, WR9 0EW
Tel no: (01905) 620552
Anglo-French | £37
Cooking score: 3

Toby Fletcher's timbered fifteenth-century inn on the high street is a real crooked house of a building. An inglenook fireplace and low oak beams set the interior scene, and you may not be surprised to hear there's a ghost in the house. Of more obvious substance, however, is Toby's superior country cooking, praised by one reader as the best for many miles around. It's a world away from old pub catering, with scallops and bacon, grilled goats' cheese, or smoked haddock risotto among starters, while main courses might deliver pan-roasted pheasant breast, served with a pheasant and vegetable pasty. Worry about the diet tomorrow with desserts such as sticky toffee pudding, or chocolate mousse with griottine cherries and clotted cream. A fine spread of wines opens at £17.

Chef/s: Toby Fletcher. **Open:** Tue to Sun L 12 to 2, Tue to Sat D 7 to 9.30. **Closed:** Mon, 1 week Christmas, 1 week Feb, 2 weeks Aug. **Meals:** Set L £23 (2 courses) to £27. Set D £37. Sun L £27. **Service:** not inc. **Details:** Cards accepted. 28 seats. Air-con. Separate bar. Music. Car parking.

▌Pershore

Belle House

Lively ideas and good local supplies
Bridge Street, Pershore, WR10 1AJ
Tel no: (01386) 555055
www.belle-house.co.uk
Modern British | £29
Cooking score: 3

£30

This handsome Georgian-fronted restaurant in the centre of town comes with the bonus of an adjoining traiteur. The compact, monthly changing set-price menus incorporate lively ideas and good local supplies. The short roll call of well-sourced ingredients includes tempura of vegetables and seafood (served as a starter with chilli mayonnaise and soy honey dressing), and roasted leg of lamb noisette (with olive oil ricotta, baked beetroot and confit of celeriac). Regulars have praised a spring lunch that included poached pear and blue cheese fritter with mustard and celeriac, lasagne of wild mushrooma, spinach and ricotta with Welsh rarebit, and passion fruit tart with orange granité. They also described the service as 'impeccable'. House wines are £14.95.

Chef/s: Sue Ellis. **Open:** Tue to Sat L 12 to 2, D 7 to 9.30. **Closed:** Sun, Mon, first 2 weeks Jan. **Meals:** Set L £14 (2 courses) to £21. Set D £22.50 (2 courses) to £28.50. **Service:** not inc. **Details:** Cards accepted. 80 seats. Air-con. Separate bar. Wheelchair access. Music. Children allowed.

Happy Birthday!

As *The Good Food Guide* turns 60, our thoughts turn to suitable venues to celebrate a birthday of this magnitude.

Where better to have a boozy do than **Vatika**, Atul Kochhar's restaurant-in-a-vineyard? Plenty of extras and a great wine list make an avant-garde Indian meal feel very special.

If it's a discreetly luxurious celebration you're after, **Kitchen W8**'s stealth glamour and super-rich dishes (try the crème fraîche tart) should do nicely.

Noisy groups won't feel self-conscious at the deliberately utilitarian **Hix Oyster & Chop House**, where pre-arranged 'feast' menus feature roast chicken, suckling pig or asparagus and lobster.

A family affair requires a relaxed atmosphere and a generous hostess, and both are on tap at **Da Piero**, the Wirral Italian where everyone is welcome.

An afternoon in the pub is sometimes all that's required, but why not make it a pub with exceptional local food? **The Nut Tree Inn** at Murcott and **The Highwayman** at Nether Burrow both fit the birthday bill.

For a grown-up sleepover, **The Crown at Woodbridge** offers a communal table that will seat all your closest friends, and the wide-ranging menu, using plenty of local produce, should suit them all. Upstairs, ten smart bedrooms allow for a luxurious rest, much needed after a surfeit of Adnams.

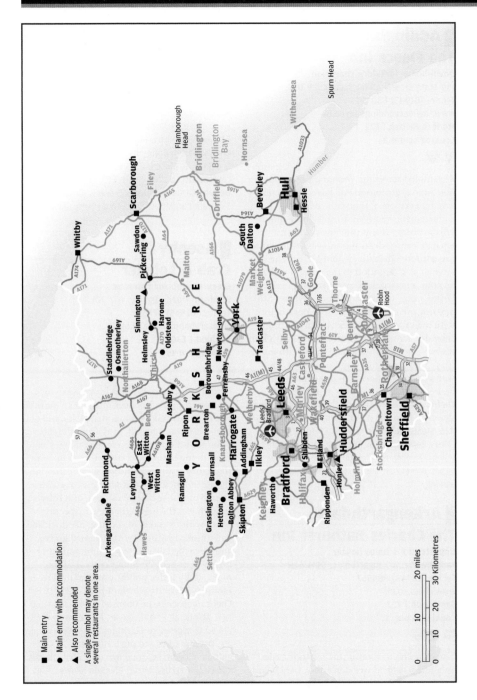

Main entry

Main entry with accommodation

Also recommended

A single symbol may denote
several restaurants in one area.

Addingham

The Fleece Inn

Down-home Yorkshire champion
154 Main Street, Addingham, LS29 0LY
Tel no: (01943) 830491
www.thefleeceaddingham.co.uk
Modern British | £22
Cooking score: 3

V £30

'I stumbled across this restaurant by accident one Sunday afternoon and have completely loved it ever since', is just one of many endorsements received for this down-home village boozer. Requisite low ceilings, a separate bar for drinking and a blazing winter fire reinforce the pub credentials, but the kitchen pays attention to the seasons and has built up a network of specialist suppliers. Dishes range from lamb shank, Whitby fish pie, fish and chips and 'fabulous pork belly with red cabbage' to specials such as seafood chowder, fennel and chorizo risotto with king scallops, and 'a brilliant ham hock with mushy peas'. Staff are friendly and interested, the atmosphere wonderful, and the fairly priced, French-led wine list opens at £13.95.
Chef/s: Andrew Cressey and Chris Monkman. **Open:** all week L 12 to 2.15 (12 to 8 Sun). Mon to Sat D 6 to 9.15. **Meals:** alc (main courses £9 to £23). Sun L £12.95. **Service:** not inc. **Details:** Cards accepted. 90 seats. 50 seats outside. Air-con. Separate bar. No music. Wheelchair access. Children allowed. Car parking.

Arkengarthdale

The Charles Bathurst Inn

Unpretentious Dales boozer
Langthwaite, Arkengarthdale, DL11 6EN
Tel no: (01748) 884567
www.cbinn.co.uk
Gastropub | £23
Cooking score: 1

🛏 **V** £30

There's no pretension at this roadside Dales pub, just scrubbed wooden tables, bare boards and the menu written on a huge mirror over an open fire. But make no mistake, the dishes coming out of the kitchen belie the humble surroundings. Goats' cheese pannacotta with beetroot carpaccio is carefully judged, and wild salmon tart delivers perfect pastry. Chicken with wild rice has pleasing depth of flavour, and the accompanying black bean spring roll provides a shock chilli finish. House wine starts at £12.50.
Chef/s: Gareth Bottomley. **Open:** all week L 12 to 2, D 6.30 to 9. **Closed:** 25 Dec. **Meals:** alc (main courses £10 to £20). Sun L £10. **Service:** not inc. **Details:** Cards accepted. 60 seats. Air-con. Separate bar. Music. Children allowed. Car parking.

Asenby

Crab & Lobster

Eccentric pub for fish fans
Dishforth Road, Asenby, YO7 3QL
Tel no: (01845) 577286
www.crabandlobster.co.uk
Seafood | £30
Cooking score: 2

🛏

With its thatched roof this looks every inch the country pub, but peer in and it's a quirky riot of curios and memorabilia, inside and out. If you can tear yourself away from the sheer volume and variety of ephemera (from fur coats to fog lamps) and study the menu, you'll find fairly traditional dishes, with seafood in the ascendancy. Fillet of wild sea bass with a risotto of smoked haddock, peas and baby spinach was the highlight of an inspection meal, with fishcakes of codling, haddock and oak-smoked salmon (with creamed greens and a poached egg) proving substantial but under-seasoned. Puddings embrace Eton mess, sticky toffee pudding and crème brûlée. House wine starts at a whopping £21.50.
Chef/s: Stephen Dean. **Open:** all week L 12 to 2, D 7 to 9. **Meals:** alc (main courses £16 to £44). Set L £14.50 (2 courses) to £18.50 (exc Sun). **Service:** not inc. **Details:** Cards accepted. 110 seats. 30 seats outside. Air-con. Separate bar. No mobile phones. Wheelchair access. Music. Children allowed. Car parking.

■ Beverley

Whites Restaurant

Wonderfully tasty food goes down well
12a North Bar Without, Beverley, HU17 7AB
Tel no: (01482) 866121
www.whitesrestaurant.co.uk
Modern British | £31
Cooking score: 2

There's much to like about Whites' down-to-earth style: no posh table settings, refreshingly unfussy décor and an absence of pomp or ceremony. It's all about 'a young man happy to be cooking in his simple 30-seat restaurant', observes a fan. A winter meal that began with roasted quail breast served with its own egg, bacon and onion tartlet, and went on to crispy rare-breed pork belly and slow-cooked cheek with candied apple showed 'a wonderful sense of taste', while seasonally tuned desserts might include elderflower jelly with peaches, almond and mint. Readers are quick to applaud the fact that chef/proprietor John Robinson makes his own bread, butter and other staples; his set-up also includes a patisserie. Wines from £16.
Chef/s: John Robinson. **Open:** Tue to Sat L 10 to 3, D 6.30 to 9. **Closed:** Sun, Mon, 25 Dec to early Jan, 1 week Easter, 1 week August. **Meals:** alc (main courses £18 to £20). Set L £13.50 (2 courses) to £15.95. Set D £16 (2 courses) to £20. Tasting menu £45. **Service:** not inc. **Details:** Cards accepted. 28 seats. No mobile phones. Wheelchair access. Music. Children allowed.

■ Bolton Abbey

The Devonshire Arms, Burlington Restaurant

Plush antiquity and über-trendy food
Bolton Abbey, BD23 6AJ
Tel no: (01756) 710441
www.thedevonshirearms.co.uk
Modern British | £60
Cooking score: 5

🍷 ╤ V

There's no doubting the sheer stature of the Devonshire Arms: built of the same stone as nearby Bolton Abbey and with fabulous views towards Lower Wharfedale, it does a grand job as the Duke of Devonshire's flagship destination. Inside all is plush antiquity, heavy drapes and thick carpets, with impeccably drilled service running on castors. By contrast, the food in the prestigious Burlington Restaurant is fiercely modern, and Steve Smith's menus are written in über-trendy, truncated gastrospeak. A dish disarmingly titled 'turbot' is demystified as 'pan-fried turbot – clams – braised veal shin – pumpkin and lemon – cep gnocchi – tonka bean – Madeira', for example. This is accomplished, intricate stuff requiring a great deal of technical nous – cooking salmon mi cuit, curing smoked sirloin or fashioning a cocoa foam to go with poached and roasted teal, salsify, chanterelles and red cabbage purée. It's also the kind of cuisine that involves lots of unlikely collisions and meat/fish pairings (John Dory and langoustines with black pudding), supported by a full panoply of fashionable components (fig fluid gel, crosnes, Amedei chocolate). The 2,000-strong wine list is a sensational tome almost the size of an old volume of *Encyclopaedia Britannica*, bulging with great names and treasured rarities, but it's not all dusty vintages and four-figure price tags. There is a prodigious number of top-drawer house selections from £16.
Chef/s: Steve Smith. **Open:** Tue to Sun D only 7 to 9.30. **Closed:** Mon. **Meals:** Set D £60. Tasting menu £65. Prestige menu £70. **Service:** 12.5% (optional).

Details: Cards accepted. 70 seats. Separate bar. No music. No mobile phones. Wheelchair access. Children allowed. Car parking.

The Devonshire Brasserie

Big-city statement in the Dales
Bolton Abbey, BD23 6AJ
Tel no: (01756) 710441
www.thedevonshirearms.co.uk
Modern British | £25
Cooking score: 2

🛏 V £30

After Wharfedale's rustic vistas, stepping into this casual cousin of the Devonshire Arms can blow your socks off. Forget Barbours and all those other stolid Yorkshire props, this place makes a big-city statement with its hip vibes, dazzling fabrics and brutally frank colour schemes. On the food front, diehards can get their fill of Yorkshire ploughman's and battered cod, but the rest of the menu has a bullish contemporary edge. A warm salad of parsnip and soft-boiled egg might be followed by roasted salmon fillet with crab and pea risotto or loin of venison with celeriac mash and quince jus. Desserts could offer pomegranate pannacotta. Wines from the world-class Devonshire cellar start around £15.
Chef/s: Rob Tegue. **Open:** all week L 12 to 2.30 (3 Sun), D 6 to 10. **Meals:** alc (main courses £10 to £20). Sun L £12.95. **Service:** 12.5% (optional).
Details: Cards accepted. 72 seats. 40 seats outside. Separate bar. Wheelchair access. Music. Children allowed. Car parking.

▌Boroughbridge
The Dining Room

Satisfying dishes from a local favourite
20 St James Square, Boroughbridge, YO51 9AR
Tel no: (01423) 326426
www.thediningroomonline.co.uk
Modern British | £29
Cooking score: 4

£5 £30
OFF

Chris and Lisa Astley have built up an enthusiastic local following since arriving in Boroughbridge more than a decade ago. Their green-painted Queen Anne house is something of a landmark in the town, and they continue to run the place in tandem – she maintains a kindly presence out front while he takes charge of the cooking. Dinner begins with drinks in the comfy first-floor lounge, before guests are ushered downstairs into the restrained dining room. The kitchen doesn't go in for pyrotechnics, but the food provides satisfaction in the form of professional dishes such as crispy confit duck with black pudding mash and cider sauce or Cajun-spiced organic salmon with tomato and red pepper salsa. Start the ball rolling with, say, smoked haddock and herb tart, and conclude with mischievous Snickers crème brûlée or new season's Yorkshire rhubarb and pink Champagne jelly. France and the New World share the honours on the eclectic wine list, with house recommendations from £16.95.
Chef/s: Chris Astley. **Open:** Sun L 12 to 2, Mon to Sat D 7 to 9.15. **Closed:** bank hols, 26 Dec, 1 Jan.
Meals: alc (main courses £14 to £19). Set L £19.70 (2 courses) to £25.65. Set D £23.95 (2 courses) to £28.50. Sun L £25.65. **Service:** not inc.
Details: Cards accepted. 32 seats. 22 seats outside. Separate bar. No mobile phones. Music. Children allowed.

ALSO RECOMMENDED

▲ The Crown Inn

Roecliffe, Boroughbridge, YO51 9LY
Tel no: (01423) 322300
www.crowninnroecliffe.com
Modern British

The sixteenth-century coaching inn with its venerable flagged floors and oak beams is run by a proficient team, and has undergone much upgrading in recent years. An extensive network of local suppliers keeps the kitchen busy, with seafood a strong suit. Start with steamed Shetland mussels and spiced leeks in cream (£7.50), as a prelude to shoulder of Dales lamb slow-cooked in red wine, served with dauphinoise (£14.95), and finish with raspberry mascarpone cheesecake with honeycomb and raspberry coulis (£5.75). Wines from £14.95. Open all week. Accommodation.

▌Bradford

Mumtaz

Kashmiri blockbuster
386-400 Great Horton Road, Bradford, BD7 3HS
Tel no: (01274) 571861
www.mumtaz.co.uk
Indian | £16
Cooking score: 2
V £30

'It's big. Very big!' exclaimed a reader about this sprawling, neon-lit Indian, which feeds hundreds in a glitzy setting of marble floors and Bollywood bling. A takeaway counter dispenses Mumtaz-branded goods and snacks, while the remainder is a series of vast spaces mostly occupied by crowds of Bradford Asians having 'a grand old family time of it'. Kashmiri cooking is the attraction, with biryanis, karahis and 'out of this world' naans as the star turns. Try sharp, spicy channa chaat to start, before murgh makhani topped with pistachios, bhindi gosht or paya (a traditional dish of lamb's trotters). Mumtaz is an alcohol-free zone, although lassis and 'fantastic' tropical mocktails make amends.

Chef/s: Mumtaz Khan. **Open:** all week 11am to midnight (1am Fri and Sat). **Meals:** alc (main courses £6 to £13). **Service:** not inc. **Details:** Cards accepted. 350 seats. Air-con. Wheelchair access. Music. Children allowed. Car parking.

Prashad

Indian veggie treats
86 Horton Grange Road, Bradford, BD7 2DW
Tel no: (01274) 575893
www.prashad.co.uk
Indian Vegetarian | £15
Cooking score: 2
£5 **V** £30
OFF

Kaushy Patel and her family started out by trading in veggie nibbles and sweetmeats before expanding their modest corner site into a sit-down 'chaat house'. Gujarati street snacks and Punjabi specialities are the kitchen's stock-in-trade, with a list that roams from deep-fried pea kachori, stuffed chillies and dhokra (steamed savoury sponge cakes with mustard seed dressing) to 'monster' dosas and bowls of gently spiced lentil and courgette curry. Also check out the meatless 'hara hara' burgers with punchy masala chips, if you fancy a new take on fast-food cliché. All-in thalis are great value and rose-scented faluda adds a sweet note. Unlicensed, but lassi and juices fit the bill if thirst quenching is required.

Chef/s: Minal Patel. **Open:** Tue to Fri L 11 to 3, D 6 to 10.30, Sat and Sun 11 to 10.30. **Closed:** Mon. **Meals:** alc (main courses £6 to £13). **Service:** not inc. **Details:** Cards accepted. 30 seats. Music. Children allowed. Car parking.

Symbols

🛏 Accommodation is available

£30 Three courses for less than £30

V More than three vegetarian main courses

£5 £5-off voucher scheme
OFF

🍾★ Notable wine list

▌Brearton
The Malt Shovel
Tried-and-trusted pub favourites
Main Street, Brearton, HG3 3BX
Tel no: (01423) 862929
www.themaltshovelbrearton.co.uk
Modern British | £25
Cooking score: 3

 £5 OFF **V** £30

The Bleikers' sixteenth-century pub and restaurant does many people very nicely, whether they are locals in for a pint in the candlelit bar, or dressed-up visitors looking for a meal in the elegant red room or conservatory. Ambition is realistic, and the resulting clear focus is much appreciated. The food embraces pub staples, with modifications of tried-and-trusted favourites – say main courses of oxtail and kidney pudding with mashed potato, or beer-battered haddock and chips. But the menu also has wider appeal, running from home-smoked meats and fish via mussels and clams in a fragrant Thai broth, to wiener schnitzel (a reference to Jürg Bleiker's Swiss roots). A dozen interesting house wines open proceedings, from £16.50.
Chef/s: Jürg Bleiker. **Open:** Wed to Sun L 12 to 2 (3 Sun), Wed to Sat D 6 to 9. **Closed:** Mon, Tue. **Meals:** alc (main courses £10 to £23). **Service:** not inc. **Details:** Cards accepted. 70 seats. 15 seats outside. Separate bar. No music. Wheelchair access. Children allowed. Car parking.

▌Burnsall
Devonshire Fell
Panoramic Dales views and skilled food
Burnsall, BD23 6BT
Tel no: (01756) 729000
www.devonshirehotels.co.uk
Modern European | £32
Cooking score: 4

⇆ **V**

Fabulous Wharfedale views are a given at this former pub-turned-busy hotel, which has taken a turn for the better since the arrival of chef Daniel Birk. He runs an industrious kitchen and fills his larder with Yorkshire beef, Dales lamb, Whitby fish, local cheeses and seasonal game as well as home-grown vegetables. Eat in the bar from a menu that focuses on pub staples ranging from fish and chips to pork and apple sausages with creamy mash. Alternatively upgrade to the dining room for 'exquisitely prepared' contemporary dishes along the lines of slow-cooked pig's cheek served with smoked potato, a croquette of black pudding and apple purée or fillet of hake with chorizo cassoulet and sauce vierge. Among desserts, a 'sticky toffee pudding baked Alaska' has appealed to one diner. House wines kick off at £16 and cover the globe without missing a beat.
Chef/s: Daniel Birk. **Open:** all week L 12 to 2.30, D 6.30 to 9.30. **Meals:** alc (main courses £9 to £18). Set L £13.95 (2 courses) to £17.95. Set D £26 (2 courses) to £32. Sun L £26. **Service:** 12.5% (optional). **Details:** Cards accepted. 38 seats. 20 seats outside. Separate bar. No mobile phones. Wheelchair access. Music. Children allowed. Car parking.

▌Chapeltown
Greenhead House
Alluring menus and bags of bonhomie
84 Burncross Road, Chapeltown, S35 1SF
Tel no: (0114) 2469004
www.greenheadhouse.com
Modern European | £42
Cooking score: 2

The Allens maintain the feeling of a country cottage at their seventeenth-century house, with its walled garden and homely interior. Influences from all over Europe, but especially France, inform the alluring menus, which might take in Reblochon- and bacon-topped tartiflette, followed by grilled lemon sole in oyster chowder, or roast partridge with apple, chestnuts and black pudding, sauced with Calvados. Warm cherry and almond pithiviers with vanilla ice cream offers appetising contrasts at dessert stage. It is all served with real Yorkshire bonhomie, and accompanied by a compact wine list starting at £17.90 for Italian and Chilean house selections.

Chef/s: Neil Allen. **Open:** Fri L 12 to 1, Wed to Sat D 7 to 8.30. **Closed:** Sun to Tue, Christmas to New Year, 2 weeks Easter, 2 weeks Aug. **Meals:** Set L £18 (2 courses) to £24. Set D £41 to £44.95 (4 courses). **Service:** not inc. **Details:** Cards accepted. 32 seats. Separate bar. No music. No mobile phones. Wheelchair access. Children allowed. Car parking.

■ East Witton
The Blue Lion
Tastefully converted stone inn
East Witton, DL8 4SN
Tel no: (01969) 624273
www.thebluelion.co.uk
Modern British | £30
Cooking score: 4

🍾 🛏 V

Cattle-drovers tramping through Wensleydale were able to cool their heels at the Blue Lion in the late eighteenth century. It's a stone-built Yorkshire inn not far from Leyburn, tastefully converted and hung with interesting pictures, yet retaining its character as a local hostelry — hand-pumped ales and all. John Dalby offers an extensive repertoire of modern British dishes that keep one foot firmly on the ground, so expect to see a homemade pork pie with pickled onions and piccalilli, or beef and onion suet pudding with wine gravy in among the soft-shell crabs, duck confit terrines and braised masala mutton. One fish option generously combines grey mullet, red snapper and king prawns with gingery noodles and soy butter sauce. Desserts can be just as inventive (liquorice terrine, anyone?), and there are excellent regional cheeses. An entirely commendable wine list, beginning with house French at £16.50, offers a quality-conscious tour of western Europe and the southern hemisphere.
Chef/s: John Dalby. **Open:** all week L 12 to 2.15, D 7 to 9.30. **Closed:** 25 Dec. **Meals:** alc (main courses £11 to £27). **Service:** not inc. **Details:** Cards accepted. 90 seats. 30 seats outside. Separate bar. Wheelchair access. Children allowed. Car parking.

■ Elland
La Cachette
A hidden gem
31 Huddersfield Road, Elland, HX5 9AW
Tel no: (01422) 378833
www.lacachette-elland.com
Modern European | £25
Cooking score: 3

£5 OFF 🍸 V £30

True to its name, which translates as 'the hiding place', this French-style restaurant has plenty of snug booths and candlelit alcoves. But the menu refuses to be constrained by France and roams freely around the globe, offering starters like a warm salad of chorizo sausage or confit duck with plum and hoi sin dressing, and main courses such as tempura king prawns with spiced chilli dip, as well as venison haunch steak with braised parsnip boulangère and Puy lentils. There's also an impressive cheese menu, offering finds from France and the UK, while desserts focus on favourites such as apple tarte Tatin or chocolate fondant. The lengthy wine list, from £13.40, lingers in France before striking out into other parts of Europe and the New World.
Chef/s: Jonathan Nichols. **Open:** Mon to Sat L 12 to 2.30, D 6 to 9.30 (10 Fri and Sat). **Closed:** Sun, 2 weeks Aug, 2 weeks Jan, bank hols (exc 25 and 26 Dec). **Meals:** alc (main courses £10 to £23). Set L £11.95 (2 courses). Set D £20.95. **Service:** not inc. **Details:** Cards accepted. 90 seats. Air-con. Separate bar. Wheelchair access. Music. Car parking.

■ Ferrensby
The General Tarleton
High-profile foodie inn
Boroughbridge Road, Ferrensby, HG5 0PZ
Tel no: (01423) 340284
www.generaltarleton.co.uk
Modern British | £28
Cooking score: 4

🛏 £30

Spawned from the emblematic Angel at Hetton (see entry), this civilised hostelry just off the A1 has established its own identity over the years, thanks largely to the efforts of chef/proprietor John Topham. Known affectionately as 'The GT', it has evolved from country pub to high-profile inn-with-rooms and makes the most of its foodie reputation. Seasonal Yorkshire produce dictates the kitchen's business, and receives a full-blooded airing along the way: depending on the calendar, you might find grilled Lowna goats' cheese tart with truffled leeks, wild mushrooms and winter beetroot, or sticky pork belly with crushed roots, apple and vanilla chutney, or even char-grilled haunch of venison partnered by Yorkshire Blue cheese polenta. 'Little moneybags' packed with seafood continue to get the nod, and desserts promise satisfaction in the shape of lemon tart or bread-and-butter pudding with marinated apricots and Dales clotted cream. The wine list oozes quality without threatening the wallet; 11 house selections start at £14.50 (£2.90 a glass).

Chef/s: John Topham. **Open:** all week L 12 to 2, D 6 to 9 (9.15 Sat, 8.30 Sun). **Meals:** alc (main courses £11 to £24). Set L £10.95 (2 courses) to £15. **Service:** not inc. **Details:** Cards accepted. 150 seats. 80 seats outside. No music. Wheelchair access. Children allowed. Car parking.

▌Grassington

NEW ENTRY

Grassington House Hotel

Keen prices and sharp cooking
5 The Square, Grassington, BD23 5AQ
Tel no: (01756) 752406
www.grassingtonhousehotel.co.uk
Modern British | £25
Cooking score: 3

£5 OFF 🍽 £30

When John and Sue Rudden took over the Grassington House Hotel in 2008 they brought timely refreshment to both its Georgian dining room and the wider Dales restaurant scene with a keenly priced menu and some sharp cooking. A light crab mousse with a contrasting warm crab toast and a compellingly tender pigeon breast with wild mushroom tortellini and crunchy fresh broad

beans opened a meal in July. Generous mains focus on regional steak, rabbit, duck, fish and local lamb (a dish of loin and breast served with dauphinoise potatoes and a piquant anchovy jus was expertly judged). So was their home-reared and deep-flavoured pork fillet and belly with crisp crackling. A marginally under-sweetened summer pudding completed a highly rated dinner that also offered exemplary value. House wine from £13.95.

Chef/s: John Rudden. **Open:** all week L 12 to 2.30 (4 Sat and Sun), D 6 to 9.30 (8.30 Sun). **Closed:** 25 Dec. **Meals:** alc (main courses £12 to £21). Set L and D £12 (2 courses) to £15. Sun L £16. Tasting menu £35.50. **Service:** not inc. **Details:** Cards accepted. 54 seats. 30 seats outside. Separate bar. Wheelchair access. Music. Children allowed. Car parking.

▌Harome

NEW ENTRY

The Pheasant Hotel

Impressive inn with great flavour combinations
Mill Street, Harome, YO62 5JG
Tel no: (01439) 771241
www.thepheasanthotel.com
Modern British | £35
Cooking score: 4

🛏 V

Andrew and Jacquie Pern, of the renowned Star Inn (see entry), breathed new life into the neighbouring inn when they joined forces last year with one-time Star head chef, Peter Neville. It's an impressive transformation, with comfortable public rooms dressed in muted tartans and hunting and shooting paraphernalia. Meals are served in the elegantly formal dining room, the conservatory or the arboured terrace overlooking the village duck pond. Menus reflect region, season and their fulsome vegetable garden, with a discreet nod to France. Witness a cup of vibrant pea and mint soup topped with a ginger ale foam, and a zinging plate of asparagus with tarragon mayonnaise, morels, toasted rye crumbs and sorrel leaves. Neville's sharp sense of combination was confirmed by crisp-skinned, slow-cooked belly pork paired with langoustine, cubed apple, artichoke purée and sorrel. To finish, a beautifully composed dessert of warm apple gratin and brandy sabayon was topped with stem ginger ice cream. All is overseen by a smooth and knowledgeable service team. Wine starts at £17 a bottle.

Chef/s: Peter Neville. **Open:** all week L 12 to 2, D 7 to 9. **Meals:** alc (main courses £13 to £24). Set L and D £30. Sun L £22.50 (2 courses) to £27.50. Tasting menu £55. **Service:** not inc. **Details:** Cards accepted. 40 seats. 20 seats outside. Separate bar. Music. Children allowed. Car parking.

The Star Inn
Still shining brightest
High Street, Harome, YO62 5JE
Tel no: (01439) 770397
www.thestaratharome.co.uk
Modern British | £40
Cooking score: 6

Ever since Andrew and Jacquie Pern turned a forlorn village pub into a destination restaurant, their ambition has rarely gathered dust. Last year they built a new kitchen, dining room, cocktail bar, chef's table and a gorgeous vegetable garden – then co-acquired the Pheasant Hotel across the road. Overstretched? Recently, there have been mutterings about the food: 'Obsessed with shot glasses' and 'miniscule portions', writes one reader. Another regretted uninspiring vegetarian options. But the majority still praise the 'wonderful, imaginative, flavoursome food'. The no-booking, cosy old bar under the thatch is as inviting as ever and if the new dining room's silver trim looks more urban than rural, the menu still flags up exciting treatments of local produce from prime meats, fish and cheese to village duck eggs and Ampleforth apples. Pern's signature of 'black pudding and foie gras' (the title of his book) remains a brilliantly inspired combination. Similarly, more muscular than minimal 'posh fish pie' is chock-full of halibut, shrimp, lemon sole, samphire and peas given added chutzpah by a garnish of crunchy smoked sprats and sweet morsels of lobster. A dessert of ginger parkin with Yorkshire rhubarb, rhubarb ripple ice cream and rhubarb schnapps was further proof that the Star still shines brightest in the firmament of Yorkshire dining pubs. Andrew Pern's well-informed wine list is a treasure trove packed with superb growers and great vintages, wherever you look. You may not get past the glorious house selections, which are worth their weight in gold; there are irresistible choices by the glass (from £4.50) and plenty of peerless drinking from around £20.

Chef/s: Andrew Pern. **Open:** Tue to Sun L 11.30 to 2 (12 to 6 Sun), Mon to Sat D 6.30 to 9.30. **Closed:** 1 Jan. **Meals:** alc (main courses £17 to £24). **Service:** not inc. **Details:** Cards accepted. 66 seats. 38 seats outside. Separate bar. Wheelchair access. Music. Children allowed. Car parking.

▌Harrogate
Orchid Restaurant
Authentic pan-Asian eatery
Studley Hotel, 28 Swan Road, Harrogate, HG1 2SE
Tel no: (01423) 560425
www.orchidrestaurant.co.uk
Pan-Asian | £30
Cooking score: 2
£5 OFF V

Bamboo steamers, claypots, black lacquered chopsticks and upscale oriental design flourishes add authenticity to this pan-Asian eatery in the basement of the Studley Hotel. Diners can spot the chefs at work through an interactive screen, forging dishes from all corners of the Far East: Korea might offer steamed vegetarian dumplings, Thailand could chip in with tom yum soup or lamb massaman curry, Japan is represented by wasabi prawns and pork tonkatsu. There are also sizeable contributions from the Chinese provinces, and it's worth checking out 'sushi Tuesdays'. Wines (from £16.50) have been chosen to match the food – don't miss the fragrant beauties from the Trimbach Estate in Alsace.

Chef/s: Kenneth Poon. Open: Mon to Fri and Sun L 12 to 2, all week D 6 to 10. Closed: 25 and 26 Dec. Meals: alc (main courses £7 to £20). Set L £9.95 (2 courses) to £12.95. Set D £21.95. Sun L £15.70. Service: 10% (optional). Details: Cards accepted. 72 seats. 24 seats outside. Air-con. Separate bar. Wheelchair access. Music. Children allowed. Car parking.

Sasso
Cheerful trattoria with excellent wine
8-10 Princes Square, Harrogate, HG1 1LX
Tel no: (01423) 508838
www.sassorestaurant.co.uk
Italian | £38
Cooking score: 3
£5 OFF V

This cheerful basement trattoria has been deservedly praised in the past for its excellent handmade pasta and good-value lunches. Of late, however, it has shown signs of 'over-excitement' and inconsistency. On the one hand, the kitchen can deliver exemplary tortellini with spring vegetables, pine nuts and pesto, but it also lets itself down with 'heavy-duty, stodgy cannelloni'. Nobody wants Italian food straight off the peg, but Sasso's adventurous impulses risk veering over the top: calf's liver with a bizarre herb and amaretti biscuit crust proved an ill-conceived notion for one recipient. Rabbit wrapped in speck and stuffed with artichokes and Fontina has been more satisfying, although side orders of vegetables (typically, roast potatoes, broccoli and carrots) can seem 'more suited to a Sunday roast'. Desserts redress the balance with the likes of lemon tart and limoncello sorbet. Service is faultless, and wines (from £13.95) are a sound Italian bunch.
Chef/s: Stefano Lancellotti. Open: Mon to Sat L 12 to 2, D 5.45 to 10 (10.30 Fri and Sat). Meals: alc (main courses £14 to £22). Set L £8.95 (2 courses). Service: 10% (optional). Details: Cards accepted. 60 seats. 16 seats outside. Music. Children allowed.

ALSO RECOMMENDED
▲ Hotel du Vin & Bistro
Prospect Place, Harrogate, HG1 1LB
Tel no: (01423) 856800
www.hotelduvin.com
Modern European

Eight Georgian houses make up this contemporary hotel (part of a busily expanding group) overlooking the vast common in the centre of Harrogate. The dining room offers the kind of unfussy modern bistro cooking that guarantees broad appeal – moules marinière (£7.95), cod with butternut gnocchi, hazelnut, sage and girolles (£17.95) and classic roast free-range chicken feature on the French-influenced menu. The group's reputation for fine wines at affordable prices is well-deserved. The extensive, easy-to-navigate list is strong in France, but underpinned by rich pickings from elsewhere; prices from £16.50. Open all week.

■ Haworth
Weavers
Amiable Brontë stop-off
15 West Lane, Haworth, BD22 8DU
Tel no: (01535) 643822
www.weaversmallhotel.co.uk
Modern British | £25
Cooking score: 3
🛏 V £30

Pilgrims to the Brontë museum at Haworth Parsonage are well advised to book ahead at Weavers, which has a fair old welter of custom to deal with. Amalgamated from three Victorian shops and two weavers' cottages, the restaurant-with-rooms is appealingly cosy and amiably run, and the cooking doesn't just rely on British heritage dishes, it also offers a modern spin on regional classics. Carpaccio of Dales beef, caramelised onion tart with melted Yellison goats' cheese, and Pennine lamb stuffed with fennel seeds and coriander on Indian-spiced crushed potatoes are what to expect. 'Afters' include a properly sherry-sodden raspberry trifle. It's also a good place for breakfast, if you're intent on an early start. A serviceable wine list is offered at very fair prices, beginning with wines by the glass from £3.65.

Chef/s: Adam Vendettuoli. **Open:** Wed to Fri L 11 to 2, Tue to Sat D 6 to 9. **Closed:** Sun, Mon, 26 Dec to 10 Jan. **Meals:** alc (main courses £13 to £19). Set L and D £15.95 (2 courses) to £17.95. **Service:** not inc. **Details:** Cards accepted. 65 seats. Air-con. Separate bar. No mobile phones. Music. Children allowed.

▌Helmsley

NEW ENTRY

The Black Swan Hotel

Vamped-up inn with ambitious food
Market Place, Helmsley, YO62 5BJ
Tel no: (01439) 770466
www.blackswan-helmsley.co.uk
Modern British | £33
Cooking score: 2

£5 OFF 🛏

A three-course set menu is the mainstay of dinner at this vamped-up old inn on the town square. Dining can veer between impressive ambition and cheffy fiddling. At inspection, escabèche of mackerel played well enough, but venison carpaccio pushed wise boundaries with an edgy garnish of beetroot, hazelnuts and chocolate, and cod was rendered over-fussy with the addition of aubergine, courgette, tomato, pepper and sauce vierge. At dessert, cherry parfait with cinnamon-poached cherries was satisfying. Prices are high given the inconsistencies, especially if you leave the set menu and opt for the chef's numerous 'specialities' which attract lots of supplements. Wine starts at £19.

Chef/s: Paul Peters. **Open:** Sun L 12 to 2, all week D 7 to 9.30. **Meals:** alc (main courses £7 to £28). Set D £33. Sun L £25. **Service:** not inc. **Details:** Cards accepted. 70 seats. Separate bar. Wheelchair access. Music. Children allowed. Car parking.

Feversham Arms Hotel

Slick country hotel with smart food
High Street, Helmsley, YO62 5AG
Tel no: (01439) 770766
www.fevershamarmshotel.com
Modern European | £40
Cooking score: 4

🛏

Arrive at the Feversham Arms and a small army is mobilised to attend you, from the car park valet to the knowing maître d'. It's a slick operation, whose coaching inn origins have evolved into a top-notch modern country hotel: sumptuous lounges, a floodlit swimming pool and modish spa. Dinner is served in the well-dressed dining room or the snug with its muted heritage colours. The menu is similarly more smart than soulful. A starter of wild rabbit roulade brought a rolled and pressed meaty terrine with miniature leaves. Mains, strong on fish, saw poached fillet of halibut and pea purée lifted by a bold tomato and mussel salsa. Elsewhere, Yorkshire sirloin steak is served fulsomely with braised shin, celeriac and bone marrow. Desserts are a high point, a delicate peanut parfait, dark chocolate mousse and a miniature crème brûlée making up a superior plate. There are well-ripened cheeses on the trolley and a thorough wine list, though no bottles under £23.

Chef/s: Simon Kelly. **Open:** all week L 12 to 2 (12.30 to 2.30 Sun), D 6 to 10. **Meals:** alc (main courses £19 to £26). Sun L £29. **Service:** not inc. **Details:** Cards accepted. 60 seats. 20 seats outside. Air-con. Separate bar. Wheelchair access. Music. Children allowed. Car parking.

Please send us your feedback

To register your opinion about any restaurant listed in the Guide, or a new restaurant that you wish to bring to our attention, please visit the web address at the bottom of the page. Your feedback informs the content of the book and will be used to compile next year's reviews.

Hessle

Artisan

Gimmick-free Humberside treasure
22 The Weir, Hessle, HU13 0RU
Tel no: (01482) 644906
www.artisanrestaurant.com
Modern European | £40
Cooking score: 5

Devotees of this 'fabulous' little restaurant in a Georgian town house are happy to clock up serious miles to experience its memorable charms. Richard Johns works wonders as a one-man show at the stoves, while his wife Lindsey attends to affairs in the pint-sized dining room with real warmth. There's no posturing or gimmickry here, just top-class food cooked with natural acumen and a sharp eye for detail. The supper menu may be pared right back, but it's perfectly balanced and 'right on the money' when it comes to quality and execution. Typically, you might begin with slow-cooked duck egg with truffled wild mushrooms, move on to steak and chips and round off with warm vanilla and cinnamon rice pudding. On Fridays and Saturdays a gourmet tasting menu allows diners to explore the full repertoire. Recent standouts have included stunningly good free-range pork belly with a precise salad of shaved apple, shallot and truffle dressing, and the 'pure bliss' of pheasant three ways (slow-roasted breast alongside confit leg sitting in a pheasant and cider consommé). To conclude, exploding crystals of 'space dust' add a flavour-burst to a Belgian chocolate pot with orange curd ice cream and sticky kumquats. Two dozen wines start at £20.

Chef/s: Richard Johns. **Open:** Wed to Sat D only from 7.15, last Sun of every month L 1 to 2. **Closed:** Mon, Tue, 2 weeks Christmas and New Year, 1 week summer. **Meals:** Set D £40 (3 courses). Sun L £19 (2 courses) to £25. Tasting menu £50 (6 courses). **Service:** not inc. **Details:** Cards accepted. 16 seats. Air-con. No mobile phones. Wheelchair access. Music. Children allowed. Car parking.

Hetton

The Angel Inn

Culinary delight in the Dales
Hetton, BD23 6LT
Tel no: (01756) 730263
www.angelhetton.co.uk
Modern British | £26
Cooking score: 3

£5 OFF 🍷 ⟷ V £30

Fans love the secluded location in a tiny hamlet by Rylstone Fell, and applaud the clever mix of oak-beamed hostelry, brasserie chic and fine dining; they also approve of the 'terrific uniformed staff'. The kitchen blends local ingredients into a multicultural stew of old favourites – say, baked black pudding with deep-fried poached egg and tomato chutney – and more modish ideas such as wild sea bass with braised fennel, crayfish tortellini and citrus foam. Add mutton from Bolton Abbey and Goosnargh duck breast with thyme mash – plus 'the best sticky toffee anywhere' – and it's easy to see why this is still 'one of the hottest places to eat in the area'. Similar food is offered in the no-bookings bar/brasserie. France and Italy are the stupendous wine list's twin peaks, although world-class selections abound, and it's worth investigating the imports from small estates. Prices (from £17) are thoroughly accommodating.

Chef/s: Mark Taft. **Open:** Mon to Sat L 12 to 2, D 6 to 9.15 (9.30 Fri and Sat). Sun 12 to 8.30. **Closed:** 25 Dec, 10 days Jan. **Meals:** alc (main courses £12 to £27). Set L £11.95 (2 courses). Set D £13.95 (2 courses) to £38.50 (4 courses, Sat only). Sun L £26.25. **Service:** not inc. **Details:** Cards accepted. 80 seats. 30 seats outside. Air-con. Separate bar. No music. Wheelchair access. Children allowed. Car parking.

Honley

ALSO RECOMMENDED
▲ Mustard and Punch

6 Westgate, Honley, HD9 6AA
Tel no: (01484) 662066
www.mustardandpunch.co.uk
Modern British £5 OFF

Messrs Richard Dunn and Wayne Roddis have been doing sterling service in Honley for a decade, and their industrious local favourite continues to satisfy most who come here. British produce gets a good outing on a menu that has a certain 1980s ring to it: expect fishcakes with celeriac salad and chive oil, beef Wellington, or sea trout with braised lettuce and mussel chowder, followed by spiced fruit cheesecake with cherry compote. Two courses £18.50, three courses £21.50; house wine is £13.95. Open Mon to Sat D only.

Huddersfield
Bradley's Restaurant

Good-value global food
84 Fitzwilliam Street, Huddersfield, HD1 5BB
Tel no: (01484) 516773
www.bradleysrestaurant.co.uk
Modern British | £30
Cooking score: 2
V

A converted warehouse close to the city centre, Bradley's has a friendly atmosphere and a snappy menu of keenly priced, internationally inspired food. Slow-roast 'Chinese' pork with fondant potatoes, soy, sesame and ginger sits at one end of the spectrum, while fish pie with Fountains Gold cheese glaze sounds a patriotic note at the other. In between there might be breast of chicken with tagliatelle of ceps, tarragon and truffle cream, or a starter of wild mushroom and pea risotto. To finish, maybe cheese and biscuits or bread-and-butter pudding. The international wine list offers plenty by the half-bottle or glass. Bottles start at £13.95. There is a second branch, with identical menus, at 46-50 Highgate, Heaton, Bradford; tel: (01274) 499890.

Chef/s: Eric Paxman. Open: Mon to Fri L 12 to 2, Mon to Sat D 6 to 10 (5.30 Fri and Sat). Closed: Sun, bank hols. Meals: alc (main courses £10 to £19). Set L £5.50 (2 courses) to £7.95. Set D £12.95 (2 courses) to £16.95. Service: not inc. Details: Cards accepted. 120 seats. Air-con. Separate bar. Wheelchair access. Music. Children allowed. Car parking.

Hull
The Boars Nest

Trencherman feasts
22-24 Princes Avenue, Hull, HU5 3QA
Tel no: (01482) 445577
www.theboarsnesthull.com
British | £25
Cooking score: 2
£30

The name is appropriate, since this admirable eatery used to be Hohenriens family butchers back in Edwardian times. Today, some of the ceramic wall tiles and meat rails remain, while the menu promises trencherman helpings of 'interesting and inventive' British food, old and new. Potted Bridlington crab and pigeon with pease pudding tap into the North Country vernacular, but the kitchen also deals in oyster fritters and golden beetroot, slow-roast venison belly with its liver or Label Anglais chicken with Stilton polenta and creamed silverskin onions. To finish, 'proper suet pudding' with custard is a must. The Boars Nest also serves up 'the best-value lunch in the GFG', according to one reader. Wines from £17.50.

Chef/s: Simon Rogers. Open: all week L 12 to 2 (3 Sun), D 6.15 to 10 (9 Sun). Closed: 1 Jan. Meals: alc (main courses £15 to £20). Set L £8 (2 courses) to £10. Set D £23 (3 courses). Service: 10% (optional). Details: Cards accepted. 97 seats. 15 seats outside. Separate bar. Wheelchair access. Music. Children allowed.

> **Also recommended**
> Also recommended entries are not scored but we think they are worth a visit.

Ilkley

The Box Tree

Delivering marvels on the plate
35-37 Church Street, Ilkley, LS29 9DR
Tel no: (01943) 608484
www.theboxtree.co.uk
Anglo-French | £65
Cooking score: 6

The Box Tree has been going about its business famously since 1962, when founding fathers Malcolm Reid and Colin Long converted what was a teashop into one of the country's most idiosyncratic restaurants. Current owners Rena and Simon Gueller set about reviving its flagging fortunes in 2004 and have given the place new vigour. Some of Messrs Reid and Long's decorative eccentricities have been smoothed out along the way, and the kitchen can still deliver marvels on the plate. A 'beautiful' amuse bouche of crab and avocado worked the magic for one reporter, and Gueller's team addresses the Anglo-French repertoire with refinement and technical excellence – witness a risotto of Maine lobster with braised fennel, tarragon and lobster essence or an earthy warm salad of morteau sausage, new potatoes and poached egg. Elsewhere, daube of beef and turbot viennoise show an affection for old-world flavours, while pot-roast squab with Puy lentils and chocolate sauce is seriously modern. To finish it's back to the textbook for caramelised pear tarte Tatin with lime-scented ice cream or hot passion-fruit soufflé with mango sauce. The mood often seems 'very correct', although service can lack experience and prices are rising, according to some reports. Set lunches help to ease any pain, and the pedigree wine list adds some stately lustre to proceedings. Expect some of the greatest terroirs and finest vintages from France, plus thoroughbred Italians and a cracking Aussie contingent. House selections start at £25.
Chef/s: Simon Gueller. **Open:** Fri to Sun L 12 to 2, Tue to Sat D 7 to 9.30. **Closed:** Mon, 1 to 7 Jan. **Meals:** alc (mains £29 to £33). Set L £22 (2 courses) to £30. Set D £34 (3 courses). Sun L £30.

Service: not inc. **Details:** Cards accepted. 56 seats. Air-con. Separate bar. No music. No mobile phones. Wheelchair access. Music. Children allowed.

Farsyde

An impeccably modern urban restaurant
1-3 New Brook Street, Ilkley, LS29 8DQ
Tel no: (01943) 602030
www.thefarsyde.co.uk
Modern British | £25
Cooking score: 3
£30

The bold, broad frontage with its frosted glass panels announces an impeccably modern urban restaurant. Booth seating and a decidedly informal approach enhance the feel, and Gavin Beedham's contemporary British cooking does the rest. Start with braised cod cheeks on pea purée with smoked bacon foam and crispy potato, and then motor on with Gressingham duck in two presentations, the breast with celeriac purée, a leg stuffed with apple and chestnuts, all sauced with Calvados. Look out for the menu of evening specials too (taking in, say, tuna on mango and lychee salsa with stir-fried noodles and a dressing of tomato-chilli jam), before concluding with a slice of pear and almond tart served with Bailey's ice cream. Wines start at £11.95.
Chef/s: Gavin Beedham. **Open:** Tue to Sat L 11.30 to 2, D 6 to 10. **Closed:** Sun, Mon, 25 and 26 Dec, 1 and 2 Jan. **Meals:** alc (main courses £13 to £17). Set L £14.95. Set D £15.50. **Service:** not inc. **Details:** Cards accepted. 82 seats. Air-con. Separate bar. Wheelchair access. Music. Children allowed.

Ilkley Moor Vaults

Brit classics with a modern twist
Stockeld Road, Ilkley, LS29 9HD
Tel no: (01943) 607012
www.ilkleymoorvaults.co.uk
British | £20
Cooking score: 2
£5 OFF £30

A wood-floored pub with chalkboards, a kitchen garden and its own smokehouse, the Vaults sits at the start of the Dales Way, close by the river Wharf. It's a thoroughly modern venue that adds class to the Ilkley scene, reinterpreting classic British fare such as Yorkshire rarebit with bacon, beer-battered haddock with mushy peas, chips and tartare sauce, and roast pork belly with smoked sausage and an inimitably British version of sauerkraut. Revisit your summer holidays at meal's end with Malaga raisin ice cream topped with treacly Pedro Ximénez sherry, or stay home with jam sponge and custard. House French is £11.50.

Chef/s: Sabi Janak. **Open:** all week L 12 to 2.30 (3 Sun), Mon to Sat D 6 to 9 (9.30 Sat). **Meals:** alc (main courses £9 to £18). **Service:** not inc. **Details:** Cards accepted. 60 seats. 50 seats outside. No music. Wheelchair access. Children allowed. Car parking.

▌Leeds

Anthony's Restaurant
Fizzing culinary escapades
19 Boar Lane, Leeds, LS1 6EA
Tel no: (0113) 2455922
www.anthonysrestaurant.co.uk
Modern European | £45
Cooking score: 7

Anthony Flinn's ongoing conquest of the Leeds restaurant scene reached another milestone with the launch of Piazza by Anthony (see entry), although his original venue on Boar Lane is still king of the hill. Anthony's exudes a relaxed, urbane vibe – a low-key backdrop to the fizzing culinary escapades on offer. A meal here fleshes out the bare bones of conventional dining with shot glasses of frothed-up juice, microscopic gustatory distractions and visual jokes. The menu language is fashionably terse, but the results – served on weird and wonderful plates – are dazzlingly complex, audacious and brilliantly evocative: 'I imagined I was somewhere in northern Spain, on my way to Galicia', confessed one reader. There was a time when a meal at Anthony's came with the built-in risk of the odd misfiring dish, but those days are gone and his creations are now triumphantly consistent, exploding on the

taste-buds like firecrackers. Nothing is quite what it seems on the plate, be it the ever-popular risotto of white onion with espresso and Parmesan air or meltingly soft roasted squid paired with squid ink raviolo, gorgeous granola and a couple of curried shallots. Flinn's alchemy is also applied to daring conceptions from the far-out regions of avant-garde gastronomy – pig's tail and ears combined with sushi prawns or sous-vide mackerel with liquorice, tartare and onion won ton. And then come desserts – an extraordinary beetroot pannacotta with orange foam or a bulgur wheat pudding with cardamom milk and apple sorbet. The zany coffee cups may not be to everyone's taste, but no one complains about the truly sublime petits fours. Occasionally a dissenting voice protests that Anthony's is 'pretentious when it doesn't need to be', but most people's reaction is one of genuine amazement and pure delight – even more so when the bill arrives. Prices are remarkable given the stellar quality of the food, and Flinn also deserves a pat on the back for serving designer beers alongside his serious (if hardly head-spinning) wines. Vinous tipples start at £14.70.

Chef/s: Anthony James Flinn. **Open:** Tue to Sat L 12 to 2, D 7 to 9.30 (10 Sat). **Closed:** Sun, Mon, Christmas to New Year. **Meals:** Set L £21 (2 courses) to £24. Set D £36 (2 courses) to £45. Tasting menu £65. **Service:** not inc. **Details:** Cards accepted. 40 seats. Separate bar. No mobile phones. Wheelchair access. Music. Children allowed.

Brasserie Forty 4
On-the-money hot spot
44 The Calls, Leeds, LS2 7EW
Tel no: (0113) 2343232
www.brasserie44.com
Modern European | £30
Cooking score: 3
🍾

A showpiece arched window overlooking the river Aire is a feature of this on-the-money brasserie in the ever-fashionable Calls complex. It's a venue that oozes metropolitan confidence, with mirrors, lacquered floors and a funky curving bar setting the tone. The kitchen's output is pitch-perfect for the location – a mix of stylish, cosmopolitan dishes for diehards and foodies alike. The old guard can fill up with helpings of cottage pie or lamb cutlets with bean casserole; others might prefer pan-fried scallops with minted pea purée and crispy pancetta followed by brill fillet with saffron risotto and coriander beurre blanc. To finish, the famed chocolate fondue with a bonanza of fruit, marshmallows and biscotti is still hard to beat. The 200-bin wine list is a slick performer, touting plenty of glitzy French fizz but favouring brilliant New World performers in other areas. Prices start at £15.75, and 17 are offered by the glass (from £3.95).

Chef/s: Roy Dickinson and Paul Derbyshire. **Open:** Mon to Sat L 12 to 2 (1 to 3 Sat), D 6 to 10 (5 Sun). **Closed:** Sun, bank hols, 25 and 26 Dec. **Meals:** alc (main courses £12 to £18). Early bird Set D £22.50 (3 courses). **Service:** 10% (optional). **Details:** Cards accepted. 120 seats. 18 seats outside. Air-con. Separate bar. Wheelchair access. Music.

Fourth Floor
All this and shopping too...
Harvey Nichols, 107-111 Briggate, Leeds, LS1 6AZ
Tel no: (0113) 2048000
www.harveynichols.com
Modern British | £30
Cooking score: 4

🍾

'Relaxed atmosphere but still feels special', noted a regular to this light, contemporary restaurant on the top floor of Harvey Nichols. That it is still popular, 15 years after opening, is testimony to the consistently good food. Ambitious menus bring contemporary influences to bear on a fundamentally classic style of cooking. This can produce some elaborate constructions – rolled terrine of ham hock with celeriac purée, pickled mushrooms and balsamic onions, say, followed by 'expertly cooked' sea bass poached in coconut and lime, with apple purée, pak choi and lemongrass velouté – although there are simple yet equally appealing ideas,

including 'full of flavour' pot-roast poussin with braised vegetables, white beans and pancetta. Desserts draw praise for sticky toffee pudding 'a notch or two above the usual regular offering'. Service is 'efficient and professional' and the wine list is an engaging, well-chosen mix from all over, with some good drinking under £25. House wine is £18.

Chef/s: Richard Walton-Allen. **Open:** all week L 12 to 3 (4 Sat and Sun), Tue to Sat D 5.30 to 10 (from 7 Sat). **Closed:** 25 Dec, 1 Jan, Easter Sun. **Meals:** alc (main courses £11 to £18). Set L and D £16.50 (2 courses) to £19.50. **Service:** 10% (optional). **Details:** Cards accepted. 80 seats. 20 seats outside. Air-con. Separate bar. Wheelchair access. Music. Children allowed.

The Olive Tree
Fun-loving taverna
Oaklands, 55 Rodley Lane, Leeds, LS13 1NG
Tel no: (0113) 2569283
www.olivetreegreekrestaurant.co.uk
Greek | £25
Cooking score: 1

£5 OFF **V** £30

A Victorian mill owner's mansion is the unlikely setting for George Psarias' fun-loving taverna, which has been feeding families, students and holiday-struck couples with passionate Greek food for more than 20 years. Gargantuan plates of mezze are the star turns, but the menu also touts ample kebabs, grills, pastries and some less familiar regional specialities (lamb stuffed with spinach and feta is a winner). Sticky baklava is the must-order dessert, and retsina tops the international wine list (prices from £13.45). There are branches in Headingley and Chapel Allerton (see website for details).

Chef/s: Andreas Jacouvu and George Psarias. **Open:** Mon to Sat L 12 to 2, D 6 to 10. Sun 12 to 10. **Closed:** 25 and 26 Dec, 1 Jan. **Meals:** alc (main courses £11 to £20). Set L £8.95 (2 courses) to £10.95. Set D £14.95 (3 courses). Sun L £9.95. **Service:** 10% (optional). **Details:** Cards accepted. 140 seats. Separate bar. Wheelchair access. Music. Children allowed. Car parking.

Piazza by Anthony

All-day eatery in a stunning space
The Corn Exchange, Call Lane, Leeds, LS1 7BR
Tel no: (0113) 2470995
www.anthonysrestaurant.co.uk
Modern European | £25
Cooking score: 3

V £30

'Anthony has made excellent use of this
wonderful building, which was in need of a
revamp. It is very Leeds, offering a large bar
with a flexible area in the middle for dining'.
So writes a visitor to the Victorian Corn
Exchange, the site of Anthony Flinn's latest
Leeds-based eatery. A flexible, all-day
operation, there's praise for a 'welcome dish' of
fried whitebait, confit of duck salad, and spit-
roast chicken with spit-roast potatoes and a
'deeply flavoured gravy'. But the cooking can
lack that little bit of sparkle: roast cod with
crayfish and pearl barley, praised at one meal,
has not lived up to expectations at another, and
all reporters dislike being charged for
ungenerous portions of bread. House wine
is £13.95.
Chef/s: Ben Sharp. **Open:** all week 10 to 10
(10.30pm Fri and Sat, 9pm Sun). **Closed:** 25 and 26
Dec, 1 Aug. **Meals:** alc (main courses £8 to £19).
Service: 10% (optional). **Details:** Cards accepted.
118 seats. Separate bar. Wheelchair access. Music.
Children allowed.

Salvo's

Pizzas and pasta worth queueing for
115 Otley Road, Headingley, Leeds, LS6 3PX
Tel no: (0113) 2755017
www.salvos.co.uk
Italian | £24
Cooking score: 2

V £30

Owned and run by the Dammone family
since 1976, this Leeds landmark is big, brash
and noisy; queues are *de rigueur*. Even so, the
crowds still pack in for some of the finest
pizzas in town, as well as gutsy pasta (perhaps
penne with Calabrese salami, fennel sausage
and pecorino) and hearty platefuls such as

twice-cooked pork belly in sweet and sour
pepper and caper confit.'Inexpensive' wines
start at £14.50. Upstairs is Enoteca Nunzia (a
cocktail bar complete with a vintage Vespa),
and the family also run Salumeria – a café/deli
a few doors down at 109 Otley Road.
Chef/s: Gip Dammone and Giuseppe Schirripa.
Open: Mon to Sat L 12 to 2, D 6 to 10.30 (5.30 to 11
Fri and Sat). Sun 12.30 to 9. **Closed:** 25 and 26 Dec,
1 Jan. **Meals:** alc (main courses £8 to £19). Set L
£9.95 (2 courses). Early set D £12.95 (2 courses) to
£15.95. **Service:** not inc. **Details:** Cards accepted. 65
seats. 12 seats outside. Air-con. Separate bar.
Music. Children allowed.

ALSO RECOMMENDED

▲ Hansa's

72-74 North Street, Leeds, LS2 7PN
Tel no: (0113) 2444408
www.hansasrestaurant.com
Indian Vegetarian £5 OFF

Leeds' long-established player on the Indian
scene serves reliable Gujarati vegetarian
cooking from Mrs Hansa Darbhi. Her menus
offer a wide range of snacky starters, including
patudi, a delicate snack comprising savoury
gram flour rolls coated with fried mustard
seeds and served with two types of dips
(£4.95). Among larger dishes are bhaji paneer,
a spinach and Indian cheese curry (£7.50) and
masala dosa with sambar and coconut chutney
(£5.95). Finish with gajjar halva (£4.25).
House wine is £13.35. Open Sun L and Mon
to Sat D.

▲ Sukhothai

8 Regent Street, Chapel Allerton, Leeds, LS7 4PE
Tel no: (0113) 2370141
www.thaifood4u.co.uk
Thai £5 OFF

A full panoply of Thai artefacts, carved
woodwork and waterfalls works its exotic
magic in Sukhothai, and this amicable
restaurant is blessed with sweet staff who are as
charming as you could wish for. The menu is
an accessible trawl through the mainstream
repertoire, with soups, salads, stir-fries and

curries looming large. Expect anything from chicken wrapped in pandan leaves (£4.50) to roast duck with tamarind sauce and a seafood claypot (£9.95). After that, try Thai custard or steamed mango rolls (£3.50). Wines from £11.95. Closed Mon L.

READERS RECOMMEND

Kendells Bistro

French
St Peters Square, Leeds, LS9 8AH
Tel no: (0113) 2436553
www.kendellsbistro.co.uk
'Casual French bistro style, no formal menu, blackboards on one wall with a very extensive choice, and a good range of French wines'

▮ Leyburn

The Sandpiper Inn

Restored hostelry with gutsy dishes
Market Place, Leyburn, DL8 5AT
Tel no: (01969) 622206
www.sandpiperinn.co.uk
Modern British | £27
Cooking score: 3
🛏 £30

Hard by the church on Leyburn's marketplace, the Sandpiper Inn is a beautifully restored seventeenth-century hostelry built of rough brown stone. It has weathered the years well, although the beamed interior has been spruced up with homely touches – especially in the green dining room. The kitchen keeps things seasonal and looks to the region for the likes of venison and rabbit terrine, pressed Dales lamb with roasted root vegetables, and slow-cooked Wensleydale beef with duck-fat potatoes and wild mushrooms. Reporters have also singled out a carefully rendered starter of caramelised pork belly with black pudding and accurately timed roast cod with mussels. For afters, crème brûlée has been warmly endorsed, likewise raspberry and almond tart with homemade ice cream. A few pubby specials are also offered at lunchtime. Georges Duboeuf house French is £13.95.

Chef/s: Jonathan Harrison. **Open:** Tue to Sun L 12 to 2.30, D 6.30 to 9 (9.30 Fri and Sat). **Closed:** Mon, Tue in winter, 25 to 27 Dec and 1 Jan. **Meals:** alc (main courses £11 to £18). **Service:** not inc. **Details:** Cards accepted. 40 seats. 20 seats outside. Separate bar. No mobile phones. Music. Children allowed.

▮ Masham

Samuel's at Swinton Park

Big-city flavours and Gothic grandeur
Swinton Park, Masham, HG4 4JH
Tel no: (01765) 680900
www.swintonpark.com
Modern British | £45
Cooking score: 5
£5 OFF 🛏

The Yorkshire seat of the Cunliffe-Lister family since the 1880s, Swinton Park does Victorian Gothic with a big dollop of lordly grandeur, and flaunts its opulent credentials with a full complement of battlements, towers and gatehouses. The heritage portfolio also embraces a deer park, lake and a fully functioning walled kitchen garden which provides chef Simon Crannage with generous horticultural bounty. The result is a repertoire of artful, intricate modern food, best enjoyed at night in the gleaming glitter of Samuel's restaurant – a blue-blooded extravaganza of heavy portraits, silk brocades and chandeliers dangling from a gilded, gold-leaf ceiling. Big-city flavours collide with country-house luxury on the plate, and the results are seldom dull: fillet of red mullet might appear with potato and rosemary 'soup', verjus jelly, raisins and anchovy, while fillet of locally reared pork is dressed up in eclectic garb with passion-fruit tea, shiitake mushrooms and watermelon. Game from the estate is also a strong suit, be it venison, pheasant or pigeon (perhaps partnered by hedgerow bulgur wheat, soused vegetables and liquorice jus). To finish, the kitchen offers its take on peach Melba as well as the intriguingly named 'smoking pot' – a heady concoction involving dark chocolate and nut caramel, fromage frais and lime ice. The burly wine list starts at £18.50.

Chef/s: Simon Crannage. Open: Wed to Sun L 12.30 to 2, all week D 7 to 9.30. Meals: Set D £45 (3 courses). Sun L £28. Service: not inc. Details: Cards accepted. 60 seats. 20 seats outside. Separate bar. No mobile phones. Wheelchair access. Music. Children allowed. Car parking.

Vennell's

Top cooking, top value
7 Silver Street, Masham, HG4 4DX
Tel no: (01765) 689000
www.vennellsrestaurant.co.uk
Modern British | £23
Cooking score: 5
£5 OFF £30

Six years on, there's a lot to be said for Jon Vennell's restaurant just off Masham's picturesque square. Reporters have emerged full of praise for 'imaginative and well prepared' food and for the 'congenial atmosphere'. It is all neat, uncluttered and unshowy, with neutral colours and white linen providing the backdrop to a short seasonal menu built around excellent raw materials. A refreshing lack of undue fuss characterises dishes such as seared mackerel with celeriac rémoulade and sardine dressing or a main course of roasted roe deer with wilted spinach, cep risotto and port jus. Egg and bacon salad, comprising crisp pancetta, soft poached egg, croûtons and dressed leaves, might be served as a starter, while cod is poached to make an earthy main course with cassoulet. Desserts such as warm ginger pudding with gingerbread ice cream or a dark chocolate trio – warm brownie, mousse, and chocolate and hazelnut ice cream – round things off with style. Tasting notes point the way on a wine list that's arranged by style; eight house selections start at £14.95.

Chef/s: Jon Vennell. Open: Sun L 12 to 4, Tue to Sun D 7.15 to 11. Closed: Mon, 2 weeks Jan. Meals: Set D £19.50 (2 courses) to £26. Sun L £19.95. Service: not inc. Details: Cards accepted. 28 seats. Separate bar. No mobile phones. Music. Children allowed.

■ Newton-on-Ouse
The Dawnay Arms

Brit cooking with verve and gusto
Newton-on-Ouse, YO30 2BR
Tel no: (01347) 848345
www.thedawnayatnewton.co.uk
Gastropub | £25
Cooking score: 4
£5 OFF **V** £30

Built in the 1770s, the Dawnay Arms stands on the main road through a charming little Yorkshire village, with a big garden at the back sloping down to the river Ouse. The décor deploys light wood tones and greys against beams and flagged floors to create an appealing backdrop for Martel Smith's skilfully executed British cooking. Depending on the market and the season, you might kick off with, say, a Whitby crab and salmon fishcake in spicy tomato sauce, before moving on to local pheasant with bacon, rösti and wild mushrooms, or oxtail braised in Hambleton ale with horseradish mash and root vegetables. It's all presented with verve, gusto and the minimum of pretentious guff. The same earthy principles also apply when it comes to desserts – perhaps sticky toffee pudding, apple crumble or banana parfait with chocolate sauce. Yorkshire cheeses are on offer for the less sweet of tooth. House wines start at £12.

Chef/s: Martel Smith. Open: all week L 12 to 2.30 (6 Sun), D 6 to 9.30. Closed: 1 Jan. Meals: alc (main courses £9 to £18). Set L £11.95 (2 courses) to £14.95. Set D £12.95 (2 courses) to £15.95. Sun L £14.95 (2 courses) to £17.95. Service: not inc. Details: Cards accepted. 80 seats. 30 seats outside. Separate bar. Wheelchair access. Music. Children allowed. Car parking.

Oldstead

NEW ENTRY
The Black Swan
Highly capable restaurant with ambitions
Oldstead, YO61 4BL
Tel no: (01347) 868387
www.blackswanoldstead.co.uk
Modern British | £37
Cooking score: 3

🛏 V

The Banks family have farmed this corner of the North York Moors for generations and still do, but three years ago they bought up the failing village pub to create a highly capable restaurant with aspirations well above a gastropub. You can eat in the rustic bar, but more serious stuff goes on in the smarter upstairs dining room. A beautifully presented plate of scallops with miniature shallot rings and a smear of intensely flavoured onion purée shows off chef Adam Jackson to good effect. So does the loin of lamb atop a square of pressed shoulder garnished with asparagus, tomato, olives and potato gnocchi. Desserts have impressed with a textbook chocolate fondant. An interesting wine list starts at £15.50 and includes some 20 by the glass. The whole well-oiled operation is charmingly run by Anne Banks.
Chef/s: Adam Jackson. **Open:** Thur to Sun L 12 to 2 (2.30 Sun), all week D 6 to 9. **Closed:** first 2 weeks Jan. **Meals:** alc (main courses £16 to £22). Sun L £22.95 (2 courses) to £26.95. **Service:** not inc. **Details:** Cards accepted. 50 seats. 20 seats outside. Separate bar. Wheelchair access. Music. Children allowed. Car parking.

Osmotherley

Golden Lion
No fads, just confident, accomplished food
6 West End, Osmotherley, DL6 3AA
Tel no: (01609) 883526
www.goldenlionosmotherley.co.uk
Modern European | £24
Cooking score: 3

🛏 £30

Walkers, tourists and locals rub shoulders in this eighteenth-century sandstone inn overlooking the village square. The menu is a tad retro, but on the bright side this means you get confident, accomplished cooking unswayed by fickle fads and fashions. You could start with prawn cocktail or fresh mussels in white wine cream, ahead of main courses such as a homemade chicken Kiev with chips, grilled sea bass with new potatoes and peas or lasagne with chips. There's also a choice of burgers and several imaginative vegetarian options (warm Roquefort cheesecake with poached pear chutney, for instance). Desserts range from the ubiquitous crème brûlée to Middle Eastern orange cake with marmalade cream. Wines start at £15.95.
Chef/s: Chris and Judy Wright and Sam Hind. **Open:** Wed to Sun L 12 to 2.30, all week D 6 to 9. **Closed:** 25 Dec. **Meals:** alc (main courses £8 to £19). **Service:** not inc. **Details:** Cards accepted. 90 seats. 20 seats outside. Music. Children allowed.

Pickering

NEW ENTRY
The White Swan Inn
Tasteful inn with some gorgeous food
Market Place, Pickering, YO18 7AA
Tel no: (01751) 472288
www.white-swan.co.uk
Modern British | £35
Cooking score: 3

🍷 🛏

Retaining the best of its coaching inn origins with a tasteful modern update, the White Swan envelops you in dark and cosy recesses whether you eat in the bow-windowed front bar among the Turkish rugs and Windsor chairs or in the dining room that glows with glass and polished silver. To start, an impressively delicate platter of pork contained ham hock terrine, potted pork and air-dried ham and celeriac coleslaw, crisp-skinned, salted sea bream was given a zinging salsa verde. A main of monkfish wrapped in York ham on a crab thermidor was bubbling, rich and gorgeous. Only a lumbering pistachio crème brûlée came in for criticism. An excellent wine list stars Quincy Jean-Michel Sorbe Loire and Tasmanian Tamar Ridge Pinot Noir by the glass. Bottles start at 13.95 and hit three figures for the owner's speciality in Saint-Emilion.

Chef/s: Darren Clemmit. **Open:** all week L 12 to 2, D 6.45 to 9. **Meals:** alc (main courses £11 to £21). Sun L £15.95 (2 courses) to £21.95. **Service:** not inc. **Details:** Cards accepted. 55 seats. 20 seats outside. Separate bar. No music. Wheelchair access. Children allowed. Car parking.

▌Ramsgill

The Yorke Arms
Adorable retreat with superb food
Ramsgill, HG3 5RL
Tel no: (01423) 755243
www.yorke-arms.co.uk
Modern British | £55
Cooking score: 6

£5 OFF 🍷 🛏

'Frances and Bill Atkins have created a haven of peace and tranquillity in a delightful part of Nidderdale', was a comment from someone who went on to stress that the total deal is 'a delight'. Simply furnished, soothingly decorated, the creeper-covered former shooting lodge feels restrained but not austere. Freshness, timing and balance combine to give the food vitality, and top quality regional produce is at the heart of the cooking. Most reports praise the set lunch for its 'particularly good value'. There was peerless execution and bold flavours, too, in a winter meal that consisted of rabbit, leek and pancetta press with pineapple relish, then stuffed breast and ballottine of guinea fowl with mozzarella and

herbs, pistou of vegetables and rosemary gnocchi, and finished with ruby red orange charlotte with date and pecan crunch. Technical skills are exemplary: beef fillet, properly rested, and served with small and distinctive accompaniments (wild mushrooms, foie gras and truffle jus) or a thick slab of poached halibut, its centre still slightly translucent, served with langoustine, morels, sweet potato and sesame dauphinoise. The wine list majors in Burgundy, Bordeaux and the Rhône but delivers an exciting mix of highly rated and good-value wines from elsewhere. Prices start from £21. As we went to press, work started on a garden restaurant (the Orangery) to be opened in the autumn of 2010.

Chef/s: Frances Atkins. **Open:** all week L 12 to 2, D 7 to 9 (8 Sun). **Meals:** alc (main courses £20 to £38). Set L £30. Sun L £35. Tasting menu £75. **Service:** not inc. **Details:** Cards accepted. 40 seats. 25 seats outside. Separate bar. Wheelchair access. Music. Children allowed. Car parking.

▌Richmond

The Punch Bowl Inn
Gastropub in a gorgeous spot
Low Row, Richmond, DL11 6PF
Tel no: (01748) 886233
www.pbinn.co.uk
Gastropub | £23
Cooking score: 1

🛏 V £30

The Codys' gorgeously sited seventeenth-century inn in the Swaledale valley is a must-do for anyone walking or touring in the Dales. Inside, it's smartly attired, with antique pine setting the tone, and some locally based cooking offering the likes of fried mackerel with spiced lentils and spinach, and mains of braised local lamb with leek and garlic mash and redcurrant jus. In keeping with the heartiest pub traditions, there's usually something like a beef and red wine casserole hidden under a puff pastry lid, and there are reliable regional cheeses, including properly matured Wensleydale. Wines from £14.50.

Chef/s: Andrew Short. **Open:** all week L 12 to 2, D 6.30 to 9. **Closed:** 25 Dec. **Meals:** alc (main courses £10 to £20). **Service:** not inc. **Details:** Cards accepted. 60 seats. Air-con. No mobile phones. Music. Children allowed. Car parking.

Ripon

Lockwoods
Bright, appealing all-dayer
83 North Street, Ripon, HG4 1DP
Tel no: (01765) 607555
www.lockwoodsrestaurant.co.uk
Modern British | £27
Cooking score: 1

V £30

'Matthew Lockwood has given Ripon just what it wants and needs' reports one who was relieved to find this bright, cheerful café just off the main square. No matter what time of day, you can find a wide range of food from breakfast croissants via lunches of homemade pork sausages, fishcakes or pasta to three-course evening meals, with smoked haddock, bubble and squeak with poached egg and hollandaise as the centrepiece. Puddings are 'fantastic'. House wine is £13.95.
Chef/s: Ronayut Grimshaw. **Open:** Tue to Sat L 12 to 2.30, D 6 to 9.30 (10 Fri and Sat). **Closed:** Sun, Mon, 25 to 26 Dec, 1 Jan. **Meals:** alc (main courses £12 to £20). Set D £17.50 (2 courses) to £19.95. **Service:** not inc. **Details:** Cards accepted. 58 seats. Wheelchair access. Music. Children allowed.

ALSO RECOMMENDED
▲ The Old Deanery
Minster Road, Ripon, HG4 1QS
Tel no: (01765) 600003
www.theolddeanery.co.uk
Modern British

The seventeenth-century, Grade II-listed Deanery stands across the road from the cathedral – it's a big selling point. Guests can enjoy light lunches in the contemporary restaurant (haddock and chips, chicken Caesar salad) or call in for dinner, where the menus are fixed-price for two or three courses

(£26.50/31.50). The line-up of dishes runs from baked queen scallops with garlic butter and Gruyère cheese, via loin of venison with braised red cabbage, to baked chocolate cake. House wine is £14.95. While the Old Deanery does have its supporters, there has been the odd comment about 'inadequate, disorganised' service and lacklustre cooking. Closed Sun D. Reports please.

Ripponden

El Gato Negro Tapas
Spain reigns in the Pennines
1 Oldham Road, Ripponden, HX6 4DN
Tel no: (01422) 823070
www.elgatonegrotapas.com
Spanish | £25
Cooking score: 5

V £30

Simon Shaw's cracking tapas restaurant does the local community proud – and it succeeds without resorting to castanet clichés. The simple dining room has a fairly monochrome look and menus double as placemats on the plain close-packed tables, but the place invariably buzzes with warmth and life. The food has authenticity as well as ambition and modern style. A list of tapas greatest hits is just the start: Padrón peppers, jamón Ibérico, patatas bravas, tortilla and lamb cutlets with romesco sauce and mojo verde are all present and correct, but the kitchen also has a few home-grown tricks hidden behind its matador's cape. Yorkshire beetroot might be paired with young goats' curd, a dish of Cheshire pork 'cheek 'n' belly' is spiced up with pumpkin purée and caramelised shallots, and there's duck with Savoy cabbage too. The output is consistent and quality pin-sharp. An intelligently composed wine list flies the flag for Spain and the Spanish New World, with reasonable mark-ups and plenty available by the glass. Bottles start at £14.95.
Chef/s: Simon Shaw. **Open:** Sat and Sun L 12 to 2 (12.30 to 5 Sun), Wed to Sat D 6 to 9.30 (10 Fri and Sat). **Closed:** Mon, Tue, 24 Dec to 6 Jan, 2 weeks summer. **Meals:** alc (tapas £3 to £13). Set D £35 for

2 (inc wine). **Service:** not inc. **Details:** Cards accepted. 47 seats. No mobile phones. Wheelchair access. Music. Children allowed.

Sawdon

The Anvil Inn

Village pub with big-flavoured food
Main Street, Sawdon, YO13 9DY
Tel no: (01723) 859896
www.theanvilinnsawdon.co.uk
Gastropub | £24
Cooking score: 2

This 250-year-old former blacksmith's works comfortably as a village pub – complete with real fires, real ales and timbers. Its main business is undoubtedly food, and the robustly flavoured cooking combines seasonal supplies of vegetables, leaves and herbs with estate game and meat from local farms. Beetroot-cured salmon and cucumber relish is accompanied by herbed crème fraîche, red chard and rocket salad, and main courses could feature slow-roasted belly pork with apple and sage mash, black pudding and cider and pork jus. Desserts include warm treacle tart and Spanish orange cake with almond ice cream. House wine is £14.95.
Chef/s: Mark Wilson. **Open:** Tue to Sun L 12 to 2 (3 Sun), Tue to Sat D 6.30 to 9. **Closed:** Mon, 25 and 26 Dec, 1 Jan. **Meals:** alc (main courses £10 to £16). **Service:** not inc. **Details:** Cards accepted. 36 seats. 12 seats outside. Separate bar. No mobile phones. Music. Children allowed. Car parking.

Symbols

🛏 Accommodation is available

£30 Three courses for less than £30

V More than three vegetarian main courses

£5 OFF £5-off voucher scheme

★ Notable wine list

Scarborough

Lanterna

Italian all-dayer
33 Queen Street, Scarborough, YO11 1HQ
Tel no: (01723) 363616
www.lanterna-ristorante.co.uk
Italian | £40
Cooking score: 3

V

Bow-fronted Georgian windows mark out Giorgio and Rachel Alessio's small restaurant not far from the Stephen Joseph Theatre. Established in 1973, it's the oldest Italian restaurant in Scarborough – the Alessios have been custodians for the past 14 years. The style is neither old trattoria nor new-wave, but sits happily between the two. Produce imported from Italy (the prized white truffle from Piedmonte holds place of honour in season) is matched with prime Yorkshire ingredients and the carte might take in local fish stew served with homemade crostone, ravioli filled with venison, fillet steak with a sauce of Taleggio cheese, cream and grappa, and baked pears with fruit ice cream and a Barbera wine syrup. The all-Italian wine list opens at £13.50.
Chef/s: Giorgio Alessio. **Open:** Mon to Sat D only 7 to 9.30. **Closed:** Sun, 25 and 26 Dec, 1 Jan, 2 weeks end Oct. **Meals:** alc (main courses £16 to £44). **Service:** not inc. **Details:** Cards accepted. 35 seats. Air-con. Music. Children allowed.

Sheffield

Artisan

A thoroughly modern British bistro
32-34 Sandygate Road, Crosspool, Sheffield, S10 5RY
Tel no: (0114) 2666096
www.relaxeatanddrink.com
Modern British | £27
Cooking score: 3

£5 OFF V £30

Set in a leafy suburb (allegedly Sheffield's oldest village), this restaurant was once the local Co-op, but these days its look is more continental, with polished floors, dark wood

furniture and plenty of wine on show. It bills itself as a 'modern British bistro', which translates into classically based starters such as pressed terrine of confit duck leg or goats' cheese soufflé, followed by steak with hand-cut chips, grilled sea bream with braised leeks, tiger prawns and a creamy white wine sauce, or slow-cooked ox cheek with bourguignon garnish and creamy mash. As for desserts, pecan pie or sticky toffee pudding keep things nicely within the comfort zone. Upstairs is the Canteen, a 'fast-paced diner' offering simple food at affordable prices. Wines from £14.
Chef/s: Daniel Gower. **Open:** all week L 12 to 2 (3 Sun), D 6 to 10 (9 Sun). **Closed:** 26 Dec, 1 Jan. **Meals:** alc (main courses £10 to £25). Set L and D £12 (2 courses) to £15. Sun L £18. **Service:** not inc. **Details:** Cards accepted. 70 seats. Air-con. Separate bar. Wheelchair access. Music. Children allowed.

The Cricket Inn
Reborn boozer with lively food
Penny Lane, Totley, Sheffield, S17 3AZ
Tel no: (0114) 2365256
www.relaxeatanddrink.com
Gastropub | £21
Cooking score: 2

£5 OFF V £30

Part of a small group of eateries that includes Artisan (see entry, Sheffield), this 'outstanding' gastropub is the brainchild of popular restaurateur Richard Smith. Set in a smart suburb on the edge of the Peak District, the building dates from the sixteenth century and in previous incarnations served as a morgue and an asylum. These days, expect a perfectly lucid and lively take on classic pub fare, based on superb local ingredients; maybe belly pork and black pudding croquette with apple sauce and crackling salad, steak and Thornbridge ale pie with dripping-roast potatoes, and treacle tart for pudding. Wines start at £14.
Chef/s: Marco Caires. **Open:** all week L 12 to 3, D 5 to 10 (Sun 9). **Meals:** alc (main courses £9 to £19). Set L and D £12 (2 courses) to £15. Sun L £19. **Service:** not inc. **Details:** Cards accepted. 90 seats. 100 seats outside. Separate bar. Wheelchair access. Music. Children allowed. Car parking.

NEW ENTRY
The Milestone
Characterful corner pub on the up
84 Green Lane, Sheffield, S3 8SE
Tel no: (0114) 2728327
www.the-milestone.co.uk
Modern British | £30
Cooking score: 2

Since Sheffield's historic Kelham Island became a conservation area it has been enjoying its time in the spotlight, with chi-chi apartments and this characterful corner pub dispensing trendy food from a free-thinking kitchen. Much is made of the pig in all its forms: the trotters are stuffed with ham hock, the head is braised and served with scallops, squid and squid ink. Elsewhere, there could be gilthead bream with red quinoa, surf clams, sweet cicely velouté and samphire. Desserts are not a strong suit. House wine £12.50.
Chef/s: James Wallis. **Open:** Downstairs all week 12 to 10 (9 Sun), Upstairs restaurant Tue to Sat D only 6.30 to 9.30. **Closed:** 25 and 26 Dec. **Meals:** alc (main courses £10 to £26). Set L and D £12 (2 courses). Sun L £9.95. **Service:** not inc. **Details:** Cards accepted. 100 seats. Separate bar. Wheelchair access. Music. Children allowed.

Moran's Restaurant
Suburban gem with knockout food
289b Abbeydale Road South, Dore, Sheffield, S17 3LB
Tel no: (0114) 2350101
www.moranssheffield.co.uk
Modern European | £30
Cooking score: 4

£5 OFF

It may remind you of a gussied-up transatlantic diner/wine bar in a Portakabin, but Moran's knows how to put on the gastronomic style. The interior of this unprepossessing suburban gem has been tricked out in shades of aubergine and burnt orange, with bare darkwood tables and a low, tiled ceiling. Service is all smiles and patience, and the food is a knockout. Bryan Moran has fun re-inventing North Country icons –

beer-battered monkfish 'scampi' (in cahoots with chilli tomato jam, mango relish and coriander cress), roast rump of lamb with a dinky steamed lamb and mint suet pud on the side, and jammy Bakewell 'pudding' (a homage to the Derbyshire original). His curiosity also takes him overseas – witness herb-crusted cod on black olive mash with mussel, caper and saffron sauce, or prune and Armagnac crème brûlée. Sunday roasts have been given the nod, and the wine list splits between Europe and the New World, with prices from £12.95.

Chef/s: Bryan Moran. **Open:** Wed to Sun L 12 to 2 (3 Sun), Tue to Sat D 7 to 9 (9.30 Sat). **Closed:** Mon, first 2 weeks Jan. **Meals:** alc (main courses £13 to £21). Sun L £15.95 (2 courses) to £19.95. **Service:** not inc. **Details:** Cards accepted. 60 seats. 10 seats outside. Air-con. Separate bar. Wheelchair access. Music. Children allowed. Car parking.

Rafters Restaurant
Modern British
220 Oakbrook Road, Sheffield, S11 7ED
Tel no: (0114) 2304819
www.raftersrestaurant.co.uk
'The entire experience is of the highest quality and nothing is a problem for Marcus Lane and his team'

▌Shibden
Shibden Mill Inn
Seriously hearty cooking
Shibden Mill Fold, Shibden, HX3 7UL
Tel no: (01422) 365840
www.shibdenmillinn.com
British | £21
Cooking score: 3
£5 OFF 🍴 £30

Deep in a lush Yorkshire valley just a few miles from the urban sprawl of Halifax, this converted seventeenth-century mill has a certain heritage appeal with its lovely outlook and maze of rooms. Judging by recent reports, all is well following another change of chef – although comments on 'extremely slow'

service suggest there's work to do out front. Meanwhile, Darren Parkinson shows his confidence and prowess, sending out bold dishes such as rabbit and black pudding pie with pickled mushrooms, crab and coriander croquettes with samphire or a slab of venison with pan-fried duck's gizzard. This is seriously hearty cooking based on sound local raw materials, and the kitchen follows it up with desserts including lemon curd posset with homemade Eccles cake and warm elderflower jelly. A decent wine list starts at £13.75, with 15 by the glass.

Chef/s: Darren Parkinson. **Open:** all week L 12 to 2 (7.30 Sun), Mon to Sat D 6 to 9.30. **Closed:** 26 Dec. **Meals:** alc (main courses £10 to £18). **Service:** not inc. **Details:** Cards accepted. 120 seats. 40 seats outside. Separate bar. Wheelchair access. Music. Children allowed. Car parking.

▌Sinnington
▲ The Fox & Hounds
Main Street, Sinnington, YO62 6SQ
Tel no: (01751) 431577
www.thefoxandhoundsinn.co.uk
Modern British

A road skirting the edge of the North Yorks Moors leads to this stone-built, eighteenth-century pub. With a comfortable lounge and pleasant dining room, it now focuses on food. Quality local produce is used imaginatively, delivering starters of twice-baked Yorkshire Blue soufflé (£6.25) or scallops with black pudding, baby spinach and sherry dressing, and main dishes such as a casserole of local silverside (£12.50) and slow-braised shoulder of lamb. House wine £13.50. Accommodation. Open all week.

> ### Average price
>
> The average price listed in main-entry reviews denotes the price of a three-course meal, without wine.

Skipton

Le Caveau
Atmospheric subterranean dining
86 High Street, Skipton, BD23 1JJ
Tel no: (01756) 794274
www.lecaveau.co.uk
Anglo-French | £28
Cooking score: 2

£5 OFF £30

Legions of regulars testify to the consistency of this well-regarded local eatery hidden in an ancient, barrel-vaulted 'caveau' beneath Skipton's award-winning high street. 'Eat from the blackboard' is sound advice from those who know: the listings might include anything from smoked haddock and tomato tart to coq au vin or navarin of lamb. Alternatively, pick from the regular menu if you're partial to pork, black pudding and apple terrine followed by crispy roast duck with orange, rhubarb and ginger sauce. Steaks are as tender as can be, and the choice of homely puds runs from fresh fruit vacherin to dark chocolate truffle cake. House French is £13.95.
Chef/s: Richard Barker. **Open:** Tue to Fri L 12 to 2, Tue to Sat D 7 to 9.30 (5 to 9.45 Sat). **Closed:** Sun, Mon, first week Jan, first week Jun, first 2 weeks Sept. **Meals:** alc (main courses £13 to £22). Set L £9.95 (2 courses) to £14.95. Set D £15.95 to £20 (3 courses). **Service:** not inc. **Details:** Cards accepted. 26 seats. Separate bar. Music. Children allowed.

South Dalton

The Pipe & Glass Inn
Fast becoming Yorkshire's favourite chef
West End, South Dalton, HU17 7PN
Tel no: (01430) 810246
www.pipeandglass.co.uk
Modern British | £30
Cooking score: 5

🍽 V

When you find a country pub in a quiet corner of the Yorkshire Wolds packed out on a midweek lunchtime, you know there must be something good going on. And so it is at the Pipe & Glass, where James Mackenzie's stock continues to rise. His menu is packed with confident local and seasonal flavours including everything from wild garlic soup or North Sea lobster Caesar salad to braised crispy Burdass lamb with a mutton and kidney faggot, roast butternut squash purée and autumnal wild mushrooms. Dishes are big, bold and generous, from new season's asparagus with crisp-coated soft-boiled egg, lovage and chorizo butter to a slab of poached halibut with crayfish, wilted sea spinach, caper and sea purslane butter. Elsewhere, one reporter raved over a goats' cheese tart so crisp and light it might have levitated but for its quiveringly soft filling. There's always plenty happening on the plate, but this is food with real character and Mackenzie has an instinct for what works together – note beer-braised oxtail paired with beetroot and a Lindisfarne oyster fritter or a textbook burnt cream with warm orange compote for dessert. The interior comprises a series of drinking and dining areas (including a conservatory), which neatly straddle the gap between a country pub with excellent microbrewery ales and an upwardly mobile restaurant with a sensibly priced wine list, featuring around 20 by the glass. House selections are £13.95.
Chef/s: James Mackenzie. **Open:** Tue to Sun L 12 to 2 (4 Sun), Tue to Sat D 6.30 to 9.30 (6 Sat). **Closed:** Mon, 2 weeks Jan. **Meals:** alc (main courses £10 to £22). **Service:** not inc. **Details:** Cards accepted. 80 seats. 50 seats outside. Air-con. Separate bar. No mobile phones. Wheelchair access. Music. Children allowed. Car parking.

Staddlebridge

McCoys at the Tontine
Idiosyncratic hotel with retro food
Staddlebridge, DL6 3JB
Tel no: (01609) 882671
www.mccoystontine.co.uk
Modern British | £40
Cooking score: 3

🍽

Eugene McCoy has been successfully wooing drivers off the A19 and into this idiosyncratic hotel for 35 years. A total refurb of the bedrooms is underway, but the dark wood dining room remains as beguiling as ever, stuffed with old sideboards, vintage lamps and huge mirrors that reflect the candlelight. The retro menu veers towards France with traditional sauces, sirloin steak and Café de Paris butter, but also harks back to 70s Britain with classic prawn cocktail and seafood pancake in thermidor sauce. Prices are far from retro, but readers continue to praise 'good, unpretentious food' and the likes of foie gras with Madeira and toasted brioche. At inspection, wild mushroom risotto was richly flavoured and fillets of black bream on shellfish linguine with crayfish oil were well-timed and crisp-skinned. A creamy lemon posset spiked with brandy snap came curiously on lemon cake crumbs. House wine £18.50. **Chef/s:** Simon Whalley. **Open:** all week L 12 to 2, D 6.30 to 9 (9.45 Fri and Sat). **Closed:** 25 and 26 Dec, 1 and 2 Jan. **Meals:** alc (main courses £13 to £28). Set L £14.95 (2 courses) to £16.95. Sun L £21.95. **Service:** not inc. **Details:** Cards accepted. 96 seats. Music. Children allowed. Car parking.

▊ Tadcaster

Singers

Musically themed restaurant
16 Westgate, Tadcaster, LS24 9AB
Tel no: (01937) 835121
www.singersrestaurant.co.uk
Modern European | £27
Cooking score: 2

£30

Contrary to what its cottagey frontage would have you expect, Singers has a sleek, understated interior decorated with images of famous vocalists (hence the name). Expect modern brasserie-style cooking with plenty to choose from, be it a starter of balti chicken terrine with onion bhaji, yoghurt and mint dressing followed by baked vegetable lasagne with baba ganoush and peperonata or (for more traditional tastes) hot-smoked salmon with a poached egg and hollandaise ahead of twice-cooked sticky pork belly with black pudding and a cider reduction. To finish,

maybe apple and blackberry crumble or baked chocolate mousse with figs in vanilla syrup. Wines start at £13.95.
Chef/s: Adam Hewitt. **Open:** Tue to Sat D only 6 to 9.30. **Closed:** Sun, Mon, 1 week Christmas. **Meals:** alc (main courses £19 to £23). Early D £16.95. Set D £26.95. **Service:** not inc. **Details:** Cards accepted. 38 seats. Air-con. Separate bar. Music. Children allowed.

▊ West Witton

The Wensleydale Heifer

Big-city seafood in the country
Main Street, West Witton, DL8 4LS
Tel no: (01969) 622322
www.wensleydaleheifer.co.uk
Seafood | £35
Cooking score: 3

🛏 V

This seventeenth-century building combines the log-fired atmosphere of a pub with a chic style that is 'rare in the Dales'. It's still a provider of hospitality with modern bedrooms, but the seafood restaurant and more informal fish bar attract locals and visitors with the quality and worth of the fresh stuff on offer. Straightforward dishes of mussels and lobster have 'gone down extremely well', but more complicated ideas produce plenty of flavours, as in a main course of whole roast chilli sea bass with crab and prawn stuffing. There's choice for meat eaters too, perhaps shoulder of lamb or duck confit, and vegetarians get their own menu. For a resonant finale, try sharing the hot Valrhona fondant. The wine list is a well-spread assortment starting at £16.95.
Chef/s: David Moss. **Open:** all week L 12 to 2.30, D 6 to 9.30. **Meals:** alc (main courses £14 to £20). Set L and D £16.75 (2 courses) to £19.95. Sun L £18.95. **Service:** 10% (optional). **Details:** Cards accepted. 80 seats. 50 seats outside. Separate bar. Wheelchair access. Music. Children allowed. Car parking.

Whitby

Green's
Go-getting
13 Bridge Street, Whitby, YO22 4BG
Tel no: (01947) 600284
www.greensofwhitby.com
Modern British | £30
Cooking score: 3

Rob and Emma Green have added a letting cottage to their go-getting operation close to Whitby harbour, but food remains their primary focus. Visitors can choose to eat casually in the ground-floor bistro from a menu that touts moules marinière, chicken Kiev and other crowd-pleasers, or venture up to the restaurant for something more ambitious. Expect intricately worked dishes along the lines of turbot with rice pilaff, fennel bhaji, crispy langoustines and curried hollandaise or wood pigeon Wellington with turnip fondant, black pudding faggot and game chips. To conclude, perhaps tarte Tatin. Sourcing is admirable – fish from the Whitby trawlers, well-hung meat from Yorkshire farms – but reports of watery sauces and 'black bits' from the frying pan suggest the kitchen doesn't perform well under pressure; service can also veer from bubbly to 'slow and unwelcoming'. Wine drinkers quaff affordably from £13.95.
Chef/s: Rob Green. **Open:** Mon to Fri L 12 to 2, D 6.30 to 9.30 (10 Fri), Sat 12 to 10, Sun 12 to 9.30. **Closed:** 25 and 26 Dec, 1 Jan. **Meals:** alc (main courses £13 to £23). Set D £33.95 (2 courses) to £40.95. Sun L £10.95. **Service:** not inc. **Details:** Cards accepted. 52 seats. Air-con. No mobile phones. Wheelchair access. Music. Children allowed.

Readers recommend

A 'readers recommend' review is a genuine quote from a report sent in by one of our readers. We intend to follow up these suggestions throughout the year to come.

Magpie Café
Doyen of seaside cafés
14 Pier Road, Whitby, YO21 3PU
Tel no: (01947) 602058
www.magpiecafe.co.uk
Seafood | £25
Cooking score: 2

£5 OFF **V** £30

The doughty, irrepressible Magpie has been a Guide stalwart for more than three decades and still sits atop the tree as a purveyor of fish and chips by the sea. It feeds Whitby's throngs handsomely come rain or shine, and families dote on the place despite the queues (bring an umbrella). The cracking quayside location means that ultra-fresh supplies are a given, and the kitchen makes the most of them: supreme battered fish aside, the menu might promise anything from seafood chowder to lobster thermidor or grilled plaice with Puy lentils. Don't leave without sampling one of the Magpie's legendary, lip-smacking desserts. You can drink wine (from £3.25 a glass), but most people prefer a cuppa.
Chef/s: Paul Gildroy. **Open:** all week 11.30 to 9. **Closed:** 25 and 26 Dec, 1 to 28 Jan. **Meals:** alc (main courses £7 to £22). **Service:** not inc. **Details:** Cards accepted. 130 seats. Air-con. Wheelchair access. Music. Children allowed.

York

J. Baker's Bistro Moderne
Affordable fine dining and fun
7 Fossgate, York, YO1 9TA
Tel no: (01904) 622688
www.jbakers.co.uk
Modern British | £29
Cooking score: 5

£5 OFF £30

When it opened in 2006, Jeff Baker's self-styled 'bistro moderne' was hailed as a restaurant for the twenty-first century. It continues to follow a steady upward trajectory, building on a foundation of unshowy but accomplished cooking, a commitment to local produce and affordable prices. At lunchtime, a flexible grazing menu means you can order from an assortment of small plates designed for sharing or a quick snack, say rabbit pie and pease pudding or 24-hour lamb breast with piquillo pepper and anchovy. Evening menus raise the bar and reporters have been generous in praise of Goosnargh duck and white bean hotpot with garlic sausage, and Whitby crab cocktail with avocado, sweet-and-sour apple and seaweed brittle. A main of Old Spot pork cheek slow-cooked with Ampleforth cider and served with homemade black pudding and purple carrots also gets the thumbs-up. Desserts such as an 'outstanding' coconut rice pudding with Yorkshire early rhubarb are in the same comfort zone. Upstairs is a chocolate room, where there's fun to be had with a grown-up knickerbocker glory – chocolate beer, chocolate balsamic, chocolate popping candy – or a wicked white chocolate Martini. Staff are 'friendly and helpful'. Good value extends to the wine list, which opens at £13.95.

Chef/s: Jeff Baker. **Open:** Tue to Sat L 12 to 3, D 6 to 10. **Meals:** Set menu £24 (2 courses) to £28.50. **Service:** not inc. **Details:** Cards accepted. 36 seats. 20 seats outside. Separate bar. Wheelchair access. Music. Children allowed.

Le Langhe
Foodie heaven
The Old Coach House, Peasholme Green, York, YO1 7PW
Tel no: (01904) 622584
www.lelanghe.co.uk
Italian | £35
Cooking score: 3

The spirit of 'cucina' is alive and well in this lovely old building hard by the city walls – thanks to the Bocca family, York's Italian importers *par exellence*: Just look at their mouthwatering display of farm cheeses, cured meats, buckets of olives and shelves stacked with provisions. This is heaven for local foodie shoppers, who pack into the café behind the deli for ciabattas, salads and other lunchtime goodies. Two evenings a week, the place also morphs into a restaurant offering tasting

menus in true 'osteria' style. Dishes come and go depending on the larder, but there's always some pasta – perhaps involving game ragù or even black truffles. You might also find pork and venison terrine or polentina to start, followed by mains fashioned from, say, rabbit loin or skate wing. Wines are also imported direct, with glugging from £14.50.

Chef/s: Ottavio Bocca. **Open:** Mon to Sat L 12 to 3, Fri and Sat D 7 to 9. **Closed:** Sun, 1 to 20 Jan. **Meals:** alc (main courses £16). Set L £19.50 (4 courses). Set D £35 (6 courses). **Service:** not inc. **Details:** Cards accepted. 60 seats. 20 seats outside. No mobile phones. Wheelchair access. Music. Children allowed.

Melton's
Impressively good stuff
7 Scarcroft Road, York, YO23 1ND
Tel no: (01904) 634341
www.meltonsrestaurant.co.uk
Modern British | £30
Cooking score: 5

£5 OFF

Michael Hjort and co have been feeding the York set with 'very fine food' for the last 20 years and show no signs of weakening. The setting for their endeavours – a terraced house not far from the racecourse – is understated, and the dining room can seem cosily intimate or gloomy, depending on your viewpoint. What matters here is the output of the kitchen, and this is impressively good stuff, based emphatically on North Country produce. There is a great deal of sophistication and panache at work here – consider a shepherd's pie served with slices of tender lamb, vacuum-sealed and perfectly cooked in a bain-marie at 58°C ('as good as any lamb I've had from the Rouxs or their protégés', commented one reporter). Seasonality also counts: in January, you might find moorland 'shearling' (young mutton) or confit pork belly with cockle-warming butternut squash, pease pudding and a dressing tinged with smoked rapeseed oil. Fish also finds favour, whether it's a dish of scallops and Jerusalem artichoke rösti or smoked haddock and Whitby crab cake with creamed leeks and fried polenta. Cheeses are British to the core, and desserts play tricks on the classics – perhaps a warm ginger and rhubarb terrine with two custards and iced rhubarb sticks. Melton's reputation for value also extends to the imaginative global wine list. Sub-£20 bottles get special attention, but this is also a happy hunting ground for big spenders in search of quality. Don't miss the Pica Broca, made by a Yorkshireman in the Languedoc.

Chef/s: Michael Hjort and Greg Birch. **Open:** Tue to Sat L 12 to 2, D 5.30 to 10. **Closed:** Sun, Mon, 2 weeks Christmas, 1 week Aug. **Meals:** alc (main courses £14 to £19). Set L and early D £19 (2 courses) to £22.50. **Service:** not inc. **Details:** Cards accepted. 42 seats. Air-con. Music. Children allowed.

Melton's Too
Boisterous bistro for all-comers
25 Walmgate, York, YO1 9TX
Tel no: (01904) 629222
www.meltonstoo.co.uk
Modern European | £18
Cooking score: 2
£30

Expect boisterous babble aplenty at this freewheeling sibling of Melton's (see entry) – especially at peak times, when the bistro is packed. 'Mtoo' is spread over three levels and food is served from breakfast onwards, right through the day: come here for some tapas and a drink at the bar or drop by for the full culinary works. Yorkshire ingredients meet global flavours on the cosmopolitan menu, which travels from Moroccan vegetable tagine to Russian fish pie via herb-crusted lamb on Savoy cabbage and rare-breed beef with black olives and persillade. To finish, perhaps rhubarb sponge pudding. Drinks range from real ales to affordable wines (from £14.50).

Chef/s: Michael Hjort. **Open:** all week 10.30 to 10.30 (9.30pm Sun). **Closed:** 25 and 26 Dec, 1 Jan. **Meals:** alc (main courses £9 to £13). Set L and early D £12.50 (2 courses). **Service:** not inc.

Details: Cards accepted. 120 seats. Air-con. Separate bar. Wheelchair access. Music. Children allowed.

Middlethorpe Hall
The full aristocratic package
Bishopthorpe Road, York, YO23 2GB
Tel no: (01904) 641241
www.middlethorpe.com
Modern British | £43
Cooking score: 3

"'Tis a very pretty [sic] place', quipped Lady Mary Wortley Montagu nonchalantly in 1713 – although most of today's visitors would spout purple prose when describing this majestic Palladian mansion just a canter from York Racecourse. Now owned by the National Trust, Middlethorpe Hall is the full aristocratic package, from its lake and landscaped ha-ha to portraits in oil, antiques and wall-to-wall panelling in the stately dining room. Nicholas Evans cooks with vigour and a modern outlook, serving fillet of sea bream with crab croquettes, shimeji mushrooms and chive butter, or partnering slow-cooked sirloin of beef with rib meat, onions 'five ways' and red wine sauce. Starters might feature diver-caught scallops with maple-glazed pork belly and pumpkin purée, with desserts promising the likes of roast black fig tart with milk jam. The French-led wine list's pedigree is matched by serious prices (from £21.50).

Chef/s: Nicholas Evans. **Open:** all week L 12.30 to 1.45, D 7 to 9.45. **Meals:** alc (main courses £17 to £25). Set L £17 (2 courses) to £23. Sun L £26. **Service:** not inc. **Details:** Cards accepted. 50 seats. 32 seats outside. Separate bar. No music. No mobile phones. Wheelchair access. Children allowed. Car parking.

SCOTLAND

Borders, Dumfries & Galloway,
Lothians (inc. Edinburgh),
Strathclyde (inc. Glasgow), Central, Fife,
Tayside, Grampian, Highlands & Islands

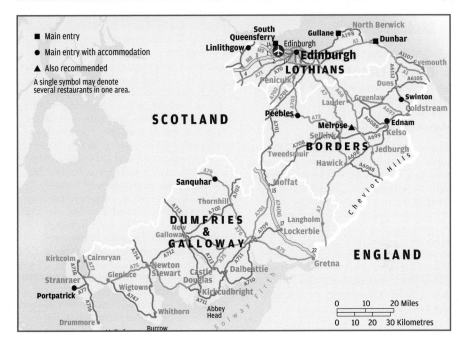

- ■ Main entry
- ● Main entry with accommodation
- ▲ Also recommended

A single symbol may denote several restaurants in one area.

Ednam

Edenwater House

Peaceful rural retreat
Ednam, TD5 7QL
Tel no: (01573) 224070
www.edenwaterhouse.co.uk
Modern European | £36
Cooking score: 4

£5 OFF 🍽 V

The small manse by the church in a village near Kelso was the birthplace of James Thomson, who wrote the lyric to *Rule Britannia* – as starry a claim to fame as any. These days the Kellys run the place as a peaceful rural retreat, with a smart, candlelit dining room, and a set menu offered in the evenings (by prior arrangement). It's a three-course affair, built around an all-stops-out main course, such as suprême of guinea fowl stuffed with cep and foie gras mousse, served on rösti with Savoy cabbage and ham, a roast carrot and butternut squash gâteau and cep-infused jus. Topping and tailing that little lot might be Parmesan-crusted monkfish tails with pickled vegetables, celeriac purée and chicken stock sauce, and bitter chocolate tart with avocado and ginger ice cream. Edenwater now also boasts a wine-tasting room called Le Chai, where you can try before you buy. House wines are £16.

Chef/s: Jacqui Kelly. **Open:** Mon to Sat D only 8 (1 sitting). **Closed:** Sun, 31 Oct to 1 Feb. **Meals:** Set D £36. **Service:** not inc. **Details:** Cards accepted. 16 seats. No music. No mobile phones. Children allowed. Car parking.

Jedburgh

READERS RECOMMEND
The Caddy Mann
Modern British
Mounthooly, Jedburgh, TD8 6TJ
Tel no: (01835) 850787
www.caddymann.com
'Belly pork and scallops cooked to perfection'

Melrose

ALSO RECOMMENDED
▲ Burt's Hotel

Market Square, Melrose, TD6 9PL
Tel no: (01896) 822285
www.burtshotel.co.uk
Modern European £5 OFF

Built in 1722, this town-centre hotel has been a fixture of Melrose life since the Henderson family took over in 1971. Formal restaurant dinners (three courses £35) offer a run through the mainstream repertoire – say smoked pheasant and chicken terrine with tempura vegetables, followed by fillet of halibut and curried mussel nage, with dark chocolate mousse to finish. Service can be 'brutally efficient', but there is the option of taking lunch or supper in the casual bar (mains from £10.50). House wines are £14.95. Open all week.

READERS RECOMMEND
Dryburgh Abbey Hotel, Tweed Restaurant

Modern British
St Boswells, Melrose, TD6 0RQ
Tel no: (01835) 822261
www.dryburgh.co.uk
'A truly beautiful setting only surpassed by the outstanding meal'

Peebles
Cringletie House

Bold style in a baronial pile
Edinburgh Road, Peebles, EH45 8PL
Tel no: (01721) 725750
www.cringletie.com
Modern British | £40
Cooking score: 4

£5 OFF 🍷 🛏 🍽

Cringletie's baronial turrets and gables loom over 25 acres of private grounds complete with a waterfall, dovecote and fully functioning seventeenth-century walled garden which provides the kitchen with abundant seasonal pickings. You can taste the fruits of Craig Gibb's culinary endeavours in the elegantly appointed Sutherland Room on the first floor of the hotel, where fine views, a carved oak fireplace and an exquisite hand-painted trompe l'oeil ceiling provide a lordly backdrop to confident modern food with an emphatic French accent. To start, crispy pork belly and pig's ears might be paired with langoustines, soubise purée and fennel salad, while mains keep up the tempo with, say, roasted halibut, oxtail beignets, pea mousse and tomato fondue. To conclude, you might be taken by hot chocolate fondant with passion fruit and hazelnut ice cream. The wine list reflects the owners' travels to exclusive independent vineyards across the globe; prices start at £20.
Chef/s: Craig Gibb. **Open:** all week L 12 to 2, D 6.30 to 9. **Meals:** alc (main courses £23). Set D £42.50. Sun L £27. Tasting menu £65 (6 courses). **Service:** not inc. **Details:** Cards accepted. 35 seats. Separate bar. No mobile phones. Wheelchair access. Music. Children allowed. Car parking.

NEW ENTRY
The Horseshoe Inn

Local favourite with top comfort food
Eddleston, Peebles, EH45 8QP
Tel no: (01721) 730225
www.horseshoeinn.co.uk
European | £40
Cooking score: 2

£5 OFF 🛏

'There's always a warm welcome', writes a regular visitor to Vivienne and Patrick Bardoulet's converted Victorian smithy. They have a strong, even vociferous, local following. Top billing goes to the comfort food served in the informal bistro, say classic fish soup, then pork belly, sauerkraut and chorizo, with a traditional crumble to finish. The restaurant offers modern dishes evolved out of the French tradition and there's plenty to fire the imagination. Dishes such as carpaccio of smoked scallops with pineapple salsa and coconut sauce ahead of mallard duck breast with a croquette of the leg, served with

chanterelle mushrooms, celeriac fondant and miso caramel show the style. Sunday lunch is well reported. House wine £12.95.
Chef/s: Patrick Bardoulet. **Open:** Tue to Sun L 12 to 2.30, Tue to Sat D 7 to 9 (9.30 Sat and Sun). **Closed:** Mon (except bank hols), 25 Dec, 2 weeks Jan. **Meals:** alc (main courses £16 to £23). Set L £19.50. Sun L £22.50. **Service:** not inc. **Details:** Cards accepted. 43 seats. Separate bar. No mobile phones. Wheelchair access. Music. Children allowed. Car parking.

Geoffrey Smeddle The Peat Inn

▌Swinton

The Wheatsheaf
Village inn with satisfying food
Main Street, Swinton, TD11 3JJ
Tel no: (01890) 860257
www.wheatsheaf-swinton.co.uk
Modern British | £29
Cooking score: 3

£5 OFF 🍷 ⇆ V £30

Stone-built and stoutly traditional, the Wheatsheaf sits opposite the village green in sleepy Swinton. The interior is a rambling series of homely, carpeted rooms, decked out with a mix of modern and antique furniture. Expect all the trappings of a typical country inn, from brass oddments on the walls to a real fire in winter. A lunchtime starter of artichoke and fennel soup came with excellent homemade bread, while a main of monkfish tail wrapped in Parma ham with roast tomato and pesto risotto was well-judged and generously proportioned. A dessert of summer pudding also satisfied. Evening dishes plough a similar furrow, with the likes of guinea fowl and pistachio terrine, and rump of Borders lamb with pea purée, fondant potato and thyme jus. An intelligently compiled wine list (from £11.95) is full of useful tasting notes.
Chef/s: Tim Holmes. **Open:** Wed to Sun L 12 to 2, all week D 5 to 9 (8.30 Sun). **Closed:** 25 and 26 Dec, 1 Jan. **Meals:** alc (main courses £15 to £19). **Service:** not inc. **Details:** Cards accepted. 45 seats. Separate bar. Wheelchair access. Music. Children allowed. Car parking.

What food trends are you spotting at the moment?
Foraging continues to move from being a practice of a few chefs to something more mainstream, hence a lot of wild herbs and seaweeds crop up on an increasing number of menus.

What would be your perfect birthday meal?
Falling in the middle of June, I would love a huge barbecue in the garden with my family and friends – lots of grilled mackerel followed by lamb cutlets.

What do you wish you had known when you started out as a chef?
Doing work experience is not just for students. Work for a few days, even a week if possible, somewhere else once a year. Invigorating!

Could you give us a very simple recipe?
Butter two slices of white bread on both sides, cover one side with smoked salmon, lemon juice and black pepper, sandwich them together then pan fry in foaming butter, cut into fingers and eat at once.

Moffat

READERS RECOMMEND
The Limetree Restaurant
Modern British
Hartfell House, Hartfell Crescent, Moffat,
DG10 9AL
Tel no: (01683) 220153
www.dalbeattie.com/hartfellhouse
'Delightful, robustly flavoured food'

Portpatrick
Knockinaam Lodge
Splendid isolation, splendid food
Portpatrick, DG9 9AD
Tel no: (01776) 810471
www.knockinaamlodge.com
Modern British | £55
Cooking score: 5

£5 OFF 🍷 🛏

In a remote corner of southwest Scotland, in a
private cove overlooking the Irish Sea,
Knockinaam is certainly isolated – sufficiently
isolated to have provided the venue for a secret
meeting between Churchill and Eisenhower
during World War II. It's a greystone mid-
Victorian mansion house of great beauty, a
few miles from the fishing village of
Portpatrick. The dining room has an
atmosphere of quiet intimacy, rather than
dome-flourishing grandeur. There are
soothing sea views, and plenty going on to
arrest the taste-buds; Tony Pierce – head chef
here for 15 years – is an assured culinary
powerhouse. Set menus are the drill,
progressing in the evenings through four
courses, the last a choice of cheese or dessert. A
winter menu opened with wild mushroom
soup with pesto, went on to a grilled fillet of
salt cod with chive hollandaise and reached its
peak with fabulous roast cannon of Galloway
lamb served with rösti, a haggis beignet and a
sauce of juniper and rosemary. The sweet
alternative to British and French cheeses was
pistachio soufflé served with what was
promisingly described as a 'luxury bombe'. It
comes with a wholly commendable wine list

that covers almost all the known vinous
world; selections such as Zind-Humbrecht in
Alsace, Willamette Valley in Oregon and
Lebanon's Château Musar are sound as a bell
throughout. House wines start at £21.
Chef/s: Tony Pierce. Open: all week L 12 to 2, D 7 to
9. Meals: Set L £39.50 (4 courses). Set D £55 (5
courses). Sun L £29.50 (4 courses). Service: not inc.
Details: Cards accepted. 24 seats. Separate bar. No
mobile phones. Wheelchair access. Music. Car
parking.

Sanquhar

NEW ENTRY
Blackaddie House Hotel
Outstanding, first-class food
Blackaddie Road, Sanquhar, DG4 6JJ
Tel no: (01659) 50270
www.blackaddiehotel.co.uk
Modern British | £42
Cooking score: 4

£5 OFF 🛏

Reports have come in thick and fast for this
classy restaurant in an 'out-of-the-way area of
Scotland'. Ian McAndrew is no stranger to the
Guide, though he has been absent from its
pages for some time. Here he is cooking in a
homely country house that dates from the
sixteenth century. Local produce is everything
and the result is 'absolutely first-class food'.
Scallop Waldorf with Chardonnay-soaked
raisins and walnut foam has been praised in
more than one report, crisp belly pork with a
chorizo sauce has been described as 'delectable',
while a test meal produced outstanding herb-
wrapped cannon of lamb with English
asparagus and a herb and caper dressing and a
textbook Bakewell tart. Praise too for 'a
phenomenal rhubarb dish with ginger cream
and candied slivers of rhubarb'. The wine list is
a fluid line-up of quality bottles peppered
with tasting notes; house recommendations
start at £15.75.
Chef/s: Ian McAndrew. Open: all week L 12.30 to 2,
D 6.30 to 9. Meals: alc (main courses £19 to £26).
Service: not inc. Details: Cards accepted. 20 seats.
Separate bar. Wheelchair access. Music. Children
allowed. Car parking.

▌Dunbar

The Creel

Freshness and fish come first
25 Lamer Street, Dunbar, EH42 1HJ
Tel no: (01368) 863279
www.creelrestaurant.co.uk
Modern British | £27
Cooking score: 3

£5 OFF £30

History is all around at this modest wood-panelled bistro, with Dunbar's ancient harbour close by and the castle ruins just a stroll away. Logan Thorburn earned his stripes with the likes of Rick Stein, so it's no surprise that his cooking is based on freshness, locality and – above all – fish (from sources certified by the Marine Stewardship Council). As a supporter of the Slow Food Movement, he keeps it simple with steamed crab claws and bowls of Holy Isle mussels, but flexes his culinary muscles when it comes to dishes such as grilled Eyemouth haddock wrapped in Parma ham with patatas bravas. Spanish tones are also to the fore in a ragoût of Rioja-braised chicken and chorizo, while desserts might promise vanilla pannacotta with sugar-soaked pears. Wines start at £16.95.
Chef/s: Logan Thorburn. **Open:** Thur to Sun L 12 to 2, Thur to Sat D 6.30 to 9. **Closed:** Mon to Wed, 25 Dec. **Meals:** alc D (main courses £14 to £18). Set L £13.50 (2 courses) to £17.50. Sun L £22.50. **Service:** not inc. **Details:** Cards accepted. 36 seats. No mobile phones. Wheelchair access. Music. Children allowed.

▌Edinburgh

Atrium

Menus with real local colour
10 Cambridge Street, Edinburgh, EH1 2ED
Tel no: (0131) 2288882
www.atriumrestaurant.co.uk
Modern British | £38
Cooking score: 4

Hard by the Usher Hall and the Traverse Theatre, this old stager has been feeding Edinburgh's culture vultures and foodies since the 90s. It's still a striking dining room – a bold collage of canvas, dark wood and flickering lamps, with shafts of natural daylight when it's required. The kitchen is shoring up its Scottish allegiances, and the inventory of native ingredients adds real colour to the menu. Here you might find seared Campbeltown scallops with Stornoway black pudding or Hugh Grierson's organic chicken served the old way with wild mushrooms, roast potatoes and bread sauce. Home-baked oatcakes are just dandy with brawn and Cuddybridge apple jelly, and there's home-cured bacon too (try it in a dish of Gressingham duck breast and pearl barley). To finish, sea buckthorn sorbet accompanies dark chocolate fondant, while quince jam goes with artisan British cheeses. The wine list is conspicuously ambitious; prices from £18.50.
Chef/s: Neil Forbes. **Open:** Mon to Fri L 12 to 2, Mon to Sat D 5.30 to 10. **Closed:** Sun, 24 to 26 Dec, 1 Jan. **Meals:** alc (main courses £18 to £24). Set L £15 (2 courses) to £20. Set D £17.50 (2 courses) to £22.50 (3 courses). Tasting menu £55. **Service:** not inc. **Details:** Cards accepted. 70 seats. 90 seats outside. Air-con. No music. Wheelchair access. Children allowed.

The Balmoral, Number One

Star restaurant at a princely address
1 Princes Street, Edinburgh, EH2 2EQ
Tel no: (0131) 5576727
www.restaurantnumberone.com
Modern European | £58
Cooking score: 6

🍷 🍽 V

The Balmoral is a noble leviathan stuffed with grand gestures and marble-hued extravagance. At the heart of things is Number One, an opulent basement dining room designed by Olga Polizzi, with echoes of the Hong Kong Mandarin hotel. It makes a suitably patrician setting for food that never stints on the luxuries of gastronomic life, but keeps its overblown gestures in check. A marvellous truffle risotto with scallops won over one reader immediately, but the kitchen also finds other ingenious uses for the tuberous fungus:

it might appear with flecks of smoked hake in a warm vichyssoise, for example. Those with classically inclined palates do well here, too – especially if top-drawer Scottish meat and game are required. Aberfoyle beef fillet with spätzle and pied bleu mushrooms or Borders venison loin partnered by pommes Anna, spinach and parsley root purée are two seasonal standouts. Chef Craig Sandle also goes boldly into the modern world, matching poached lobster with smoked mango purée, adding a *soupçon* of anise foam to a passion-fruit 'opera', and emblazoning chocolate baba with red pepper reduction and chilli ice cream. Aristocratic Burgundies and Bordeaux are the cornerstones of a heavyweight wine list that also finds room for some marvellous stuff from Italy, Australia and the USA. Prices (from £20) may put a restraining order on the wallet, but numerous by-the-glass offerings and half-bottles offer an easy escape.
Chef/s: Craig Sandle. **Open:** all week D only 6.30 to 10. **Closed:** first 2 weeks Jan. **Meals:** Set D £57.50. Tasting menu £62.50. **Service:** 12.5% (optional). **Details:** Cards accepted. 55 seats. Air-con. Separate bar. No mobile phones. Wheelchair access. Music. Children allowed.

The Bonham
Smart hotel with stimulating menus
35 Drumsheugh Gardens, Edinburgh, EH3 7RN
Tel no: (0131) 2747444
www.thebonham.com
French | £35
Cooking score: 4

The Victorian town house hotel in Edinburgh's West End screams 'boutique', with its sleekly designed public spaces and its collection of well-chosen contemporary art. Some of this is on display in the dining room, where vast mirrors enhance the sense of space, and the cooking is in the hands of French chef Michel Bouyer. Using a cornucopia of Scottish seasonal produce, gently inflected with classical Gallic technique, the menus offer a fresh and stimulating range of dishes. A typical main course might be seared fillet of

wild sea bass with leek and potato Parmentier in a sea-fresh broth of mussels and brown shrimps, or braised pork belly Moroccan-style, served with potato gnocchi, a cucumber salad and carrot purée. Before that, a mosaic of game from the Rutherford Estate may appear in a terrine with dried apricot chutney, and meals end with the likes of white chocolate and almond soufflé and mango sorbet. Wines start at £16.50.
Chef/s: Michel Bouyer. **Open:** all week L 12 to 2.30 (12.30 to 3 Sun), D 6.30 to 10. **Meals:** alc (main courses £15 to £30). Set L £13.50 (2 courses) to £16. Set D £14 (2 courses) to £18. **Service:** not inc. **Details:** Cards accepted. 72 seats. Wheelchair access. Music. Children allowed.

Café St Honoré
Like being in Paris
34 North West Thistle Street Lane, Edinburgh, EH2 1EA
Tel no: (0131) 2262211
www.cafesthonore.com
French | £33
Cooking score: 3
£5 OFF

Café St Honoré is a Parisian bistro that looks like it got off at the wrong Métro stop and somehow ended up in Edinburgh. The tarnished mirror panels and framed cartoons, the tatty net curtains and the smoky tones of Madeleine Peyroux make all the right noises, and the cooking achieves a balance of French modes with accents closer to home. A sausage roll of Perthshire venison and beef isn't exactly Montmartre, but roast free-range pork loin with potato galette, roast courgette and pancetta should reorient you. Fish could run to crisp-skinned Shetland salmon with fennel and tomatoes, and desserts have included a light rhubarb cheesecake with clotted cream ice cream. Wines start at £16 a bottle.
Chef/s: Ben Radford. **Open:** all week L 12 to 2, D 5.15 to 10 (6 Sat and Sun). **Closed:** 25 to 26 Dec, 1 to 2 Jan. **Meals:** alc (main courses £13 to £24). Set L and D £16.50 (2 courses) to £20.50. **Service:** 10% (optional). **Details:** Cards accepted. 48 seats. Music. Children allowed.

Centotre

Buzzing all-day Italian caffè
103 George Street, Edinburgh, EH2 3ES
Tel no: (0131) 2251550
www.centotre.com
Italian | £25
Cooking score: 2

V £30

At fun, easy-going Centotre you'll find 'people of all ages enjoying themselves'. The building was a nineteenth-century grainstore and later a bank; owners Victor and Carina Contini rate its high-ceilinged interior as 'one of the most beautiful rooms in Edinburgh'. Expect simple, down-home Italian food, from pizzas through to pasta dishes such as lasagne alla bolognese or gnocchi all'amatriciana. For more adventurous choices, look to the meat and fish dishes (char-grilled lamb with lemon risotto, for instance) and the five-course tasting menu. 'Top-quality' wines are, naturally, Italian and start at £14.95 a bottle.
Chef/s: Carina Contini. **Open:** Mon to Sat 7.30am to midnight, Sun 10am to 10pm. **Meals:** alc (main courses £9 to £20). Set L £14.95 (2 courses) to £19.95. **Service:** not inc. **Details:** Cards accepted. 156 seats. 50 seats outside. Air-con. Separate bar. No mobile phones. Wheelchair access. Music. Children allowed.

David Bann

On-trend veggie hot spot
56-58 St Mary's Street, Edinburgh, EH1 1SX
Tel no: (0131) 5565888
www.davidbann.co.uk
Vegetarian | £21
Cooking score: 2

V £30

Forget hair-shirted clichés, rough-hewn interiors and stodge, David Bann's veggie crusader off Edinburgh's Royal Mile is a glossy, urbane good-looker and his kitchen scorns leaden quiches in favour of zingy global dishes with on-trend flavours. Vegetarian restaurants love spelling out their ingredients, and DB is no exception: consider 'aromatic spicy Thai fritters of smoked tofu, peas,

ginger, green chilli, lime, sesame and potato, with banana chutney and plum sauce'. Elsewhere, there might be curries loaded with butternut squash, cashews and cauliflower, or tarts involving Jerusalem artichokes, Ardrahan cheese and celeriac – although there's less eulogising when it comes to desserts (perhaps orange jelly with coconut rum sorbet). House wines are £13.50.
Chef/s: David Bann. **Open:** all week 12 to 10 (10.30 Fri to Sun). **Closed:** 25 and 26 Dec, 1 Jan. **Meals:** alc (main courses £10 to £13). **Service:** not inc. **Details:** Cards accepted. 80 seats. Air-con. No music. Children allowed.

The Dogs

Food with plenty of bite
110 Hanover Street, Edinburgh, EH2 1DR
Tel no: (0131) 2201208
www.thedogsonline.co.uk
Modern British | £25
Cooking score: 4

V £30

Restaurateur David Ramsden marked his return to the Edinburgh scene with the opening of this cheap-as-chips eatery housed in a grand-looking Victorian town house. The Dogs is a wonderfully atmospheric, high-ceilinged venue reached via a grand staircase, with canine motifs dotted around. The food also has plenty of bite, and the kitchen plunges straight into the earthy world of pig's cheeks, ox liver and faggots with 'rumbledethumps' (Scots' bubble and squeak). Indigenous ingredients are the building blocks for a full-frontal menu that never minces its words or gestures: creamy cockles and bacon on toast might give way to braised shin of beef with horseradish dumplings, while puds such as toffee tapioca with stewed apple reel in the years. A 'day menu' cherry-picks simpler choices from the full line-up, and there are Scottish beers to quaff – along with wines from £12.95. Sister venue Amore Dogs (a bargain Italian eatery) is at 104 Hanover Street; tel (0131) 2205155, and David Ramsden recently launched fish-friendly Seadogs at 43 Rose Street; tel (0131) 2258028.

Chef/s: James Scott. **Open:** all week L 12 to 4, D 5 to 10. **Closed:** 25 Dec, 1 Jan. **Meals:** alc (main courses £8 to £12). **Service:** not inc. **Details:** Cards accepted. 60 seats. No music. Children allowed.

Forth Floor

Open-plan foodie destination
Harvey Nichols, 30-34 St Andrews Square,
Edinburgh, EH2 2AD
Tel no: (0131) 5248350
www.harveynichols.co.uk
Modern European | £34
Cooking score: 3

Breathtaking views across the capital all the way to the Firth of Forth make this Harvey Nics restaurant an inviting destination, and an outdoor terrace for summer carousing adds to the appeal. What seals the deal is Stuart Muir's capable modern brasserie cooking. This takes in the likes of gnocchi with breaded white Stilton, port syrup and beurre noisette to start, and mains such as roast monkfish with cod brandade and chorizo in red wine butter, or veal fillet with shallots, hazelnuts and celeriac purée. Oysters and langoustine from the seafood bar also prove seasonally popular. Finish with chocolate orange ganache and berry sorbet. The wine list is one of the glories of the place, a treasure trove of goodies to encourage adventurous drinking. Own-label house selections start at £18.
Chef/s: Stuart Muir. **Open:** all week L 12 to 3 (3.30 Sat and Sun), Tue to Sat D 6 to 10. **Closed:** 25 Dec, 1 Jan. **Meals:** alc (main courses £17 to £22). Set L and D £20 (2 courses) to £25. Sat and Sun L £28 (2 courses) to £34. **Service:** 10% (optional). **Details:** Cards accepted. 54 seats. 10 seats outside. Air-con. Separate bar. Wheelchair access. Music. Children allowed. Car parking.

★ READERS' RESTAURANT OF THE YEAR ★
SCOTLAND

La Garrigue

The flavour of Languedoc
31 Jeffrey Street, Edinburgh, EH1 1DH
Tel no: (0131) 5573032
www.lagarrigue.co.uk
French | £24
Cooking score: 3
£30

A waft of the wild, scented landscape of the Midi is evoked by the name of Jean-Michel Gauffre's homely restaurant – which is no surprise as that's where he hails from. It may be a long way from there to the old quarter of the Scottish capital, but the culinary traditions have survived the journey intact, and the subtitled French menu (a user-friendly prix fixe) contains plenty to entice. Rabbit confit with leeks and hazelnuts in mustard dressing and saffron-scented Mediterranean fish soup are among the starting options that may lead on to bourride, cassoulet, or salsify-stuffed duck breast. A rich chocolate tart with cinnamon ice cream will cement your allegiance at dessert stage. Wines from the benchmark Languedoc producer Mas de Daumas Gassac lead off a list that offers a comprehensive beakerful (and more) of the warm south. Prices start at £15.50 (£4.50 a glass).
Chef/s: Jean-Michel Gauffre. **Open:** Mon to Sat L 12 to 3, D 6.30 to 9.30. **Closed:** Sun, 25 and 26 Dec and 1 and 2 Jan. **Meals:** Set L £14 (2 courses) to £16. Set D £24 (2 courses) to £28. **Service:** 10% (optional). **Details:** Cards accepted. 45 seats. Air-con. No music. Wheelchair access. Children allowed. Car parking.

Kalpna

Venerable Indian vegetarian
2-3 St Patrick Square, Edinburgh, EH8 9EZ
Tel no: (0131) 6679890
www.kalpnarestaurant.com
Indian Vegetarian | £19
Cooking score: 2

 £5 OFF **V** £30

This venerable Edinburgh institution marks its twenty-ninth year in the Guide in 2011, and though the culinary landscape has changed greatly since it first opened, Kalpna has not been left behind. As one of the true champions of Indian vegetarian cooking, it is 'very good at what it does', with dishes drawn from Gujarat, South India and Rajasthan. Among starters are dahi poori and pakoras, while main courses include paneer pasanda – cheese infused with sesame seeds, garlic and spices with an onion, cashew nut and saffron sauce. Lunch is a buffet, and thalis are excellent value. Drink lassi, beer or the house wine at £11.75.
Chef/s: Ajay Bhartdwaj and Hukam Dhanai. **Open:** Mon to Sat L 12 to 2, all week D 5.30 to 10.30. **Closed:** 25 and 26 Dec. **Meals:** alc (main courses £5 to £9). Set L £7 (buffet). Set D £15 (3 courses). **Service:** 10%. **Details:** Cards accepted. 50 seats. Air-con. Wheelchair access. Music. Children allowed.

The Kitchin

Waterfront star
78 Commercial Quay, Leith, Edinburgh, EH6 6LX
Tel no: (0131) 5551755
www.thekitchin.com
Modern European | £56
Cooking score: 6

£5 OFF

'In the true traditions of the Festival, Tom Kitchin orchestrated a memorable evening', noted one couple who travelled up from Surrey for Edinburgh's cultural junketings and were blown away by the food at this starry restaurant on the scrubbed-up Leith waterfront. What was an old whisky distillery has been transformed with slate-grey paintwork, sexily intimate lighting and a big dollop of garrulous bonhomie: forget reverential gastronomic gloom, this place buzzes with well-bred, happy chatter – although the odd gripe about lazy service has cropped up of late. Tom Kitchin's food does all the right things – it feeds generously, avoids poncey pretension and celebrates Scotland's home turf. It is also intelligent and ablaze with seasonal counterpoints: 'from nature to plate' is the trademarked mantra. Here you will find Arisaig 'spoots' (razor clams) served respectfully with chorizo and lemon confit alongside stuffed saddle of Dornoch hogget (young mutton) partnered by braised lettuce or roast Humbie roe deer with an endive Tatin, celeriac fondant and pepper sauce. This kitchen is also at home with big, time-honoured flavours – a roasted trio of bone marrow, 'melt-in-the-mouth' grouse and Donald Russell's 28-day aged rib of beef with shallot and parsley compote, although 'tough duck' was a let-down for one reader. To finish, pear Belle Hélène is brought up to date with chocolate ravioli, and Yorkshire rhubarb tart is served with palate-tingling green tea sorbet. Cheeses are stupendous and the seasonally tweaked wine list leans towards France, with gold-standard ballast from elsewhere, a raft of interesting producers and a thrilling choice by the glass. Bottle prices start at £23. Fans of Tom Kitchin will be delighted to hear that he has launched a second restaurant, the Castle Terrace, on the Edinburgh site formerly occupied by Abstract – reports please.
Chef/s: Tom Kitchin. **Open:** Tue to Sat 12.15 to 2, D 6.30 to 10 (10.30 Fri and Sat). **Closed:** Sun, Mon, 24 Dec to 17 Jan. **Meals:** alc (main courses £29 to £34). Set L £24.50 (3 courses). Tasting menu £65. **Service:** not inc. **Details:** Cards accepted. 50 seats. 32 seats outside. Air-con. Separate bar. No mobile phones. Wheelchair access. Music. Children allowed. Car parking.

Average price

The average price listed in main-entry reviews denotes the price of a three-course meal, without wine.

NEW ENTRY

Ondine

Sleek metropolitan seafood restaurant
2 George IV Bridge, Edinburgh, EH1 1AD
Tel no: (0131) 2261888
www.ondinerestaurant.co.uk
Seafood | £32
Cooking score: 4

£5
OFF

Set just off the Royal Mile, this first-floor seafood restaurant is a far cry from your local chippy, but the mosaic tiling around the oyster bar gives a nod in that direction, as does the presence of fish and chips on the menu. The main mood, though, is sleek and metropolitan – and this permeates everything from the efficient, slightly formal service to the snappy, internationally inspired cooking. An inspection meal opened (after excellent breads) with squid tempura with pea shoots, crisp-fried slices of onion and chilli and a Vietnamese dipping sauce. A generous bowlful of mussels in a rich, curried sauce teamed nicely with fine fries cooked in dripping. For dessert, a sophisticated take on pavlova (a plump meringue atop a ring of strawberries in jelly) kept with the classy but fuss-free tone. Wines are divided between the New and Old Worlds, and kick off at £15.50.
Chef/s: Roy Brett. **Open:** all week 12 to 10.
Meals: alc (main courses £14 to £36). Set L £14.95 (2 courses) to £17.95. **Service:** not inc.
Details: Cards accepted. 74 seats. Air-con. Wheelchair access. Music. Children allowed.

Plumed Horse

Real beauty that makes a big impact
50-54 Henderson Street, Edinburgh, EH6 6DE
Tel no: (0131) 5545556
www.plumedhorse.co.uk
Modern European | £48
Cooking score: 5

Tony Borthwick's restaurant on a bend in the road on the way to the Leith development area is a real beauty. Inside is rather smarter than its neighbourhood might lead you to anticipate. The service is good and proper and, despite

the limited dimensions of the irregularly shaped conjoined rooms, tables are well-spaced. A lot of effort goes into dishes that sit squarely in the modern European mainstream, and powerful, clear, sculpted flavours are everywhere. Ideas are good too: a chicken and foie gras 'club sandwich' with celeriac and fennel rémoulade is a witty starter that might be followed by a complex fish course involving sea bream and red mullet alongside saffron and vanilla gnocchi and Solway brown shrimps, in an assertive red mullet soup. Lighter lunch dishes make a big impact too, as when a breast of corn-fed chicken comes with crumbled chorizo, Puy lentils and carefully cooked roots. In-vogue 'ingredient of the year' rhubarb is celebrated in a dessert that combines a lemon crème brûlée with some stewed rhubarb at the bottom with rhubarb candyfloss and ginger-nut ice cream. A good spread of wines starts at £19, or £5.50 a glass.
Chef/s: Tony Borthwick. **Open:** Tue to Sat L 12 to 1.30 (12.30 Tues and Sat), D 7 to 9. **Closed:** Sun, Mon, 25 and 26 Dec, 2 weeks July. **Meals:** Set L £25.50 (4 courses). Set D £48 (3 courses). Tasting menu £59. **Service:** not inc. **Details:** Cards accepted. 36 seats. Air-con. No mobile phones. Wheelchair access. Music. Children allowed.

Restaurant Martin Wishart

The jewel in Edinburgh's crown
54 The Shore, Leith, Edinburgh, EH6 6RA
Tel no: (0131) 5533557
www.martin-wishart.co.uk
Modern French | £60
Cooking score: 8

🍾 V

'Outstanding in every aspect', is a typically glowing response to Martin Wishart's flagship restaurant overlooking Leith's re-energised waterfront. The plaudits continue to stack up, and few would dispute that this is one of the jewels in Scotland's gastronomic crown. There's little to suggest culinary pyrotechnics in the restrained dining room with its light wood panels, flashes of pale blue and mirrored pillars, but once things are under way the

kitchen delivers 'course after course of delights'. Mild-mannered, 'approachable' Martin Wishart is a supremely confident risk-taker, although his highly individual style has its roots in the modern French tradition. He doesn't go in for madcap molecular alchemy or self-conscious showiness, but the results are pure class. It takes a brave chef to dress up native Colchester oysters with sour green apple, pungent sauerkraut and decadent oscietra caviar, or bring together Dover sole, braised pig's trotter, mushroom vinaigrette and a crunchy wheat cracker, but Wishart pulls it off. When it comes to seasonal flavours, his fastidious sourcing yields platinum rewards such as a fabulous pairing of Kilbrannan scallops with Bellota ham, winter truffle and Parmesan velouté, or roast cod with Devon snails and a gratin of salsify. Other masterpieces of intensity have also stunned reporters, including crab Marie Rose and veal tartare with white radish and Basque pepper, as well as more conventional loin of Borders roe deer accompanied by sauce grand veneur with embellishments of braised baby gem and goats' cheese gnocchi. A tasting of three desserts went down a storm with one party, while those wanting something specific might opt for delicate praline soufflé with milk sorbet and jokey praline lollipops, or exotically tinged golden pineapple with star anise cream, poppyseed tuile and warm doughnuts. By and large, service is 'uniformly welcoming', professional and carefully paced – although occasional slip-ups have been noted; one couple had to endure the iciest of receptions and were even told to come back later because they were 15 minutes early for their booking. The patrician wine list roams the world, turning up rare treats including a batch of organics, a mouthwatering array of 'stickies' and plenty of halves. Prices are surprisingly easy on the wallet, with plenty of serious stuff below £30 and by-the-glass offerings from £5.50.
Chef/s: Martin Wishart. **Open:** Tue to Sat L 12 to 2 (1.30 Sat), D 6.30 to 9.30. **Closed:** Sun, Mon, 25 and 26 Dec, 2 weeks Jan. **Meals:** Set L £24.50. Set D

£60. Tasting menu £65 (6 courses). **Service:** not inc. **Details:** Cards accepted. 45 seats. Wheelchair access. Music. Children allowed.

Rhubarb at Prestonfield
Unrestrained opulence and elaborate food
Prestonfield House, Priestfield Road, Edinburgh, EH16 5UT
Tel no: (0131) 2251333
www.prestonfield.com
Modern European | £50
Cooking score: 4

For a Scottish country house experience without leaving the city, Prestonfield Hall is just the ticket. Beyond the kilted doormen is a feast of unrestrained decorative opulence – antique furniture, flock wallpaper, stern oil paintings and a preponderance of red and gold. Rhubarb occupies two sumptuous rooms with views over the grounds, and the food here is as elaborate as the décor. A tray of umpteen excellent homemade breads sets the tone for a cooking style that's occasionally seized by one idea too many. A miniature rabbit pie impressed at inspection, sensibly served with peas and girolles. Noisettes of Borders lamb with spiced shoulder of mutton and crushed butter beans delighted in terms of quality, but the addition of feta was puzzling. In a dessert of rhubarb served many ways, it was the simple elements that really satisfied. Staff are impeccable. The weighty wine list reads like an atlas of the winemaking world, and kicks off at £21.50.
Chef/s: John McMahon. **Open:** all week L 12 to 2 (3 Sun), D 6 to 10 (11 Fri and Sat). **Meals:** alc (main courses £14 to £33). Set L £16.95 (2 courses) to £30. Set D £30. **Service:** not inc. **Details:** Cards accepted. 90 seats. 20 seats outside. Separate bar. Wheelchair access. Children allowed. Car parking.

NEW ENTRY
21212
Culinary premier league's creative midfielder
3 Royal Terrace, Edinburgh, EH7 5AB
Tel no: (0131) 5231030
www.21212restaurant.co.uk
Modern French | £65
Cooking score: 5

Paul Kitching forsook the leafy ambience of Altrincham – where his restaurant Juniper was a major player in the English premier league – for Edinburgh. He has decamped to an old town house hotel in a terrace that sits proud above the road below. It has been designed with a balancing sense of old-fashioned comfort and modern lines. The dining room's main feature is the glass screen painted with Matisse-like blobs of colour behind which Kitching can be seen leading the tuition of a young, eager brigade, at conversational levels that float tantalisingly into the public space. The restaurant name refers to the menu structure, in which a pair of choices is offered for starter, main and dessert, with fixed courses of soup and cheeses intervening. The cooking is undoubtedly still premier league, but if Juniper was the star striker, the position here is more like creative midfielder, with subtle interventions and delicate manoeuvres to pull dishes together. Menu descriptions will take a while. One May main dish offered 'Gloucester Old Spot pork fillet, white pudding, spicy new potatoes, mooli, smoked streaky bacon, dates, jumbo couscous, sage, cauliflower purée, nutmeg, pimento and pumpkin seeds, paprika yoghurt, ginger beurre blanc'. What arrives is a little ovoid dish of ingredients all placed carefully on top of each other, as though waiting to be cross-referenced against the listing. Seasonings are surprisingly delicate, as is the cooking (a couple of slivers of baby halibut baked in a very low oven), but the expected impact may be missing. Desserts pile it all on again, with lemon curd, white beans, macadamias, sweetcorn and more turning up, while the cheese plate intervenes almost

rudely, shouting out its fabulously ripe flavours in the old-fashioned way. In short, we await developments with keen interest. The wine list is a well-chosen array, from £20.
Chef/s: Paul Kitching. **Open:** Tue to Sat L 12 to 1.30, D 6.45 to 9.30. **Closed:** Sun and Mon. **Meals:** Set L £25 (2 courses) to £55. Set D £65 (5 courses). **Service:** not inc. **Details:** Cards accepted. 38 seats. Air-con. Separate bar. No music.

Valvona & Crolla Caffè Bar
Pioneering foodie Godfather
19 Elm Row, Edinburgh, EH7 4AA
Tel no: (0131) 5566066
www.valvonacrolla.co.uk
Italian | £22
Cooking score: 3

The Contini family have been doing Edinburgh proud since setting out their stall as market traders in 1934. Over the years their foodie enterprise has blossomed, and this daytime caffè bar has become a city landmark. All-day shopping and casual chomping is its stock-in-trade, and everything hinges on top-notch Italian ingredients – plus a helping of Scottish produce. Drop in for Venetian cichetti or try some spot-on pasta (perhaps capellini with garlicky cherry tomatoes); otherwise, order a bowl of stufato (salted fish stew with prunes, black olives and potatoes) followed by one of the luscious Milanese ice creams. Breakfasts bring everything from handmade bombolone doughnuts to paesano rolls stuffed with rustic sausage. The Continis have also assembled a fine collection of Italian regional wines offered in the caffè – or you can pick any bottle from the shelves at retail price (plus £6 corkage). The Continis also run the VinCaffè in Multrees Walk shopping complex, tel no: (0131) 5570088.
Chef/s: Mary Contini. **Open:** Mon to Sat 8.30am to 5.30pm (8am to 6.30pm Fri and Sat), Sun 10.30 to 3.30. **Closed:** 25 and 26 Dec, 1 and 2 Jan. **Meals:** alc (main courses £11 to £15). **Service:** not inc. **Details:** Cards accepted. 60 seats. Air-con. Wheelchair access. Music. Children allowed.

Andrew Fairlie Andrew Fairlie at Gleneagles

What is your earliest culinary memory?

Tasting a sauce chasseur as a dishwasher while still at school, it was my eureka moment, I wanted to know how they did that.

How do you relax when out of the kitchen?

I love hillwalking in Scotland. As a form of exercise and relaxation, it is perfect.

What do you think is exciting about the British food scene?

Its diversity, from great pub food to haute gastronomie, Britain is open to all food cultures and styles which makes it really exciting.

Could you give us a very simple recipe?

Jerusalem artichoke purée for fish: 750 ml whole milk, 1 kg artichokes, seeds from a vanilla pod, salt. Peel artichokes, chop, drop into boiled milk, cook 25 minutes, purée, season, add vanilla seeds, reheat and serve with grilled fish.

Sum up your cooking style in three words.

Modern, classic, pure.

The Vintners Rooms
Historic surrounds and confident cooking
The Vaults, 87 Giles Street, Edinburgh, EH6 6BZ
Tel no: (0131) 5546767
www.thevintnersrooms.com
French | £40
Cooking score: 4

People remark on the 'rather fine' setting – an atmospheric old wine merchant's building a short walk for the waterfront in Leith – but save their 'oohs and aahs' for the intricate plasterwork of the candlelit dining room. The kitchen works to a concise Mediterranean / French-influenced repertoire and dishes change with the market and the seasons with confident results. Octopus carpaccio with Scottish lobster and marinated peppers might open proceedings, and centrepieces might be spiced duck pie with celeriac purée and ginger glaze or cod with potato galette and a mussel and vegetable fricassé. For dessert, yoghurt cake has been described as 'perfect', an adjective that describes the service too. Wines are given star treatment here, with big names peppered throughout, but there are plenty of more modest bottles from £19.50.
Chef/s: David Spanner. **Open:** Tue to Sat L 12 to 2, D 7 to 10. **Closed:** Sun, Mon, 25 Dec to 6 Jan. **Meals:** alc (main courses £23 to £30). Set L £19 (2 courses) to £23. **Service:** not inc. **Details:** Cards accepted. 30 seats. Separate bar. No mobile phones. Wheelchair access. Music. Children allowed. Car parking.

The Witchery by the Castle
A dream date with terrific terrace views
Castlehill, Royal Mile, Edinburgh, EH1 2NF
Tel no: (0131) 2255613
www.thewitchery.com
Modern British | £50
Cooking score: 2

One of Edinburgh's most engagingly sited restaurants is to be found on a cobbled rise leading to the Castle. Inside is a dream-date environment of old wood panelling, with a terrace overlooking the city – a beautiful prospect in the evenings. The food essays only cautious forays into the modern world, with the likes of a smoked fish platter (trout, eel and salmon) incoporating crab in crème fraîche, pot-roast duck breast with Puy lentils in curry cream sauce, and passion-fruit and mascarpone trifle served in a Kilner jar. A monster wine list at prices that won't break the bank is on hand, from £17.95.

Chef/s: Douglas Roberts. **Open:** all week L 12 to 4, D 5.30 to 11.30. **Closed:** 25 and 26 Dec. **Meals:** alc (main courses £12 to £35). Set L and D £13.95 (2 courses) to £30. **Service:** not inc. **Details:** Cards accepted. 90 seats. 16 seats outside. Air-con. Music. Children allowed.

ALSO RECOMMENDED

▲ Fishers Bistro

1 Shore, Leith, Edinburgh, EH6 6QW
Tel no: (0131) 5545666
www.fishersbistros.co.uk
Seafood

This former pub is now a well-established and thriving restaurant on the Leith shoreline. It's a fish fan's dream, featuring the likes of oysters, queenie scallops (£6.95), Peterhead plaice (£14.95), Loch Duart salmon, lobster and seafood platters (£17.95). Rack of lamb, slow-roasted pork belly and free-range chicken are on offer if you're not in the mood for fish. To finish there's treacle tart or crème brûlée. The wine list is worth exploring; bottles from £13.50. Open all week.

▌Gullane

La Potinière

Cordial hospitality and top-class food
34 Main Street, Gullane, EH31 2AA
Tel no: (01620) 843214
www.la-potiniere.co.uk
Modern British | £40
Cooking score: 6

The grey-stone austerity of La Potinière's exterior is in sharp contrast to the gentle warmth and low-key cordiality of this ever-popular Guide veteran. Readers continue to voice their support for current owners Mary Runciman and Keith Marley, who have consolidated its reputation for congenial hospitality and top-class food. Dinner is an easy-paced, happy occasion accompanied by conversational chatter rather than hushed tones – the owners' refined, brilliantly executed cooking certainly deserves to be celebrated. High points from recent lauded meals have included a succulent portion of braised halibut on smoked salmon and chive mash with seasonal greens and a distinctive vanilla and saffron sauce, and a textbook apple tart perfectly matched with apple mousse and cinnamon ice cream. On other occasions, the concise menu might promise the pleasures of warm foie gras royale with pineapple, fennel and star anise compote followed by poached and seared fillet of Scotch beef set off by a sauce of shallots and native girolles. The value for money is 'unsurpassed' in the region – especially at lunchtime, when the pared-back choice might take a duo of slow-cooked pork belly and fillet, and lightly salted caramel syllabub with poached pears. The wine list is a strong slate of serious bottles, from £16.50.

Chef/s: Mary Runciman and Keith Marley. **Open:** Wed to Sun L 12.30 to 1.30, D 7 to 8.30. **Closed:** Mon, Tue, 24 to 26 Dec, 3 weeks Jan. **Meals:** Set L £18.50 (2 courses) to £22.50. Set D £40 (3 courses). **Service:** not inc. **Details:** Cards accepted. 24 seats. No music. No mobile phones. Wheelchair access. Children allowed. Car parking.

▌Linlithgow

Champany Inn

Aberdeen Angus reigns
Champany Corner, Linlithgow, EH49 7LU
Tel no: (01506) 834532
www.champany.com
British | £60
Cooking score: 3

Clive and Anne Davidson have developed this cluster of sixteenth-century farm buildings over the last 28 years and turned Champany into a Mecca for fans of Scottish-reared beef.

Prime Aberdeen Angus beef is the main event, hung for three weeks in an ionised chill room and cooked on specially designed stoves – you just choose your preferred cut (perhaps a slab of T-bone, porterhouse or ribeye) and decide if you want a sauce, say wild mushroom and Pommery mustard. The menu also runs to lobsters, salmon and double lamb chops, with prawns, oysters and Brechin black pudding to start. Quality is second to none, but it comes at a price; however, the adjoining Chop and Ale House offers a more wallet-friendly proposition. Good steak demands good wine and Clive Davidson's list is a truly monumental, 600-bin tour of the vinous world, featuring rare French stars, Spanish gold and a glorious array from South Africa. Own-label Cape selections come in at around £20.

Chef/s: David Gibson and Ross Miller. **Open:** Mon to Fri L 12.30 to 2, Mon to Sat D 7 to 10. **Closed:** Sun, 25 and 26 Dec, 1 and 2 Jan. **Meals:** alc (main courses £28 to £48). Set L £19.50 (2 courses) to £27. Set D £39.50. **Service:** 10%. **Details:** Cards accepted. 50 seats. 20 seats outside. Separate bar. No music. No mobile phones. Wheelchair access. Car parking.

South Queensferry
The Boat House
Scottish seafood by the Forth
22 High Street, South Queensferry, EH30 9PP
Tel no: (0131) 3315429
www.theboathouse-sq.co.uk
Seafood | £30
Cooking score: 3

Astonishing views of the Forth Bridge are a perennial talking point at Paul and Suzanne Steward's Boat House – a three-pronged venue pitched right by the river, with a deli-cum-cocktail bar at street level and plenty of culinary action happening below stairs. The bistro/wine bar offers casual sustenance (think hot sandwiches, pasta and sharing platters), while the sparkling white restaurant specialises in Scottish seafood. Expect straightforward ideas along the lines of grilled langoustines with lemon and garlic butter, or

whole wild sea bass with tomato and balsamic dressing. There's also roast Barbary duck breast on sweet braised red cabbage, while puds could range from profiteroles to pannacotta. House wine is £13.95 (£3.75 a glass). The owners did not return their questionnaire so some details may be out of date.

Chef/s: Paul Steward. **Open:** Sat and Sun L 12 to 2.30, all week D 5.30 to 10. Bistro open all week 12 to 9.30 (12.30 to 9 Sun). **Meals:** alc (main courses £16 to £23). **Service:** not inc. **Details:** Cards accepted. 45 seats. Separate bar. Music. Children allowed.

ALSO RECOMMENDED
▲ Dakota Grill
Dakota Hotel Forth Bridge, Ferrymuir Retail Park, South Queensferry, EH30 9QZ
Tel no: (0131) 3193690
www.dakotaforthbridge.co.uk
Modern European

The minimalist Dakota Grill is a striking industrial-style building, providing accommodation and food on the south shore of the river Forth. Crustacea and steaks are the main contenders, with anything from roasted shellfish with garlic butter to char-grilled ribeye steak (£19.95) on offer. Back-up comes from a supporting cast taking in everything from pan-fried squid with chorizo (£6.95) to omelette Arnold Bennett and tagliatelle with rabbit ragù (£11.95). For afters, perhaps glazed orange tart (£5.95). House wine is £15.95. Open all week.

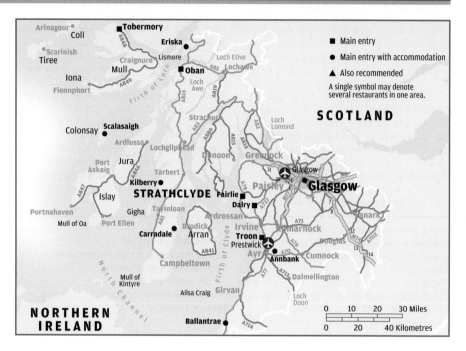

Annbank

Browne's at Enterkine

Enchanting views and oodles of hospitality
Annbank, KA6 5AL
Tel no: (01292) 520580
www.enterkine.com
Modern European | £40
Cooking score: 4

To mark 10 years at Enterkine House, Oscar Browne re-named the hotel's restaurant, but little else has changed at this immaculate 1930s residence – the views over the river Ayr still enchant and visitors are still treated to oodles of personable hospitality. Scottish produce figures prominently on Browne's menu, and the kitchen dreams up some telling ideas: Mr McIntyre's pork is served four ways with a Szechuan sauce, fillet of mature Buccleuch beef is accompanied by white beans, Savoy cabbage and navets (baby turnips), and organic Borders lamb comes with goats' cheese emulsion, baby leeks and olive jus. Elsewhere, seafood waxes strongly in the shape of, say, Kintyre Bay scallops with pig's cheeks, cauliflower and 'angel spice' or loin of monkfish with langoustines, surf clams, mussels and lemongrass foam. The complex approach also feeds through to desserts such as pecan and honey parfait with bee pollen, toffee lemon curd, nougat and gingerbread, for example. House wines start at £21.50 (£5.25 a glass).

Chef/s: Paul Moffat. **Open:** all week, L 12.30 to 2, D 7 to 9. **Closed:** Mon and Tue from Jan to Mar. **Meals:** alc (main courses £10 to £24). Set L £25 (3 courses). Sun L £16.50 (2 courses) to £18.50. **Service:** not inc. **Details:** Cards accepted. 40 seats. No mobile phones. Music. Children allowed. Car parking.

Visit us online

To find out more about
The Good Food Guide, please visit
www.thegoodfoodguide.co.uk

Ballantrae

Glenapp Castle

Dazzling cooking at a top-notch hotel
Ballantrae, KA26 0NZ
Tel no: (01465) 831212
www.glenappcastle.com
Modern British | £60
Cooking score: 6

£5 OFF 🛏

Built for the Deputy Lord Lieutenant of Ayrshire as a grand gesture of Scottish baronial exuberance, this mighty Victorian castle with its castellated walls, turrets, landscaped gardens and fantastic vistas out towards Ailsa Craig and the Mull of Kintyre is a thrilling prospect. As a top-notch country hotel it also looks the part and runs like clockwork, with lavish interiors, original features and dutiful, friendly staff who are praised for their professionalism. Since Adam Stokes' arrival in 2008, the kitchen has upped its game and dazzled visitors with its 'forward-looking', precision-tuned cooking. Dinner is the main event, and the pared-back, six-course menu changes daily. Ingredients have a strong Scottish allegiance, but there's a freewheeling spirit at work – witness roast loin of Ayrshire venison with walnuts, Szechuan flavours and hotpot or loin of hare Wellington with pistachios, Grelot onions, prune and Armagnac sauce. Fish also shows some inspired touches – a salad of West Coast crab with Granny Smith apple, tomato and ginger beer jelly or a vigorous pairing of John Dory with roasted ceps, tartare mash and Parma ham, for instance. To finish, don't miss the masterly soufflés (the 'rice pudding' version comes with raspberry jam, of course); alternatively, chocolate fondant cleverly re-designed as a 'tart' with caramelised banana and bee pollen is a good shout. Lunch is a simpler prospect, but there's no dumbing down when it comes to dishes such as poached sea bass with tomato, fennel, oranges and hazelnuts. France claims pole position on the hefty wine list, although most major producing countries get some coverage. Prices start at £28 (£6.50 a glass).

Chef/s: Adam Stokes. **Open:** all week L 12 to 2, D 7 to 10. **Closed:** Christmas week, 2 Jan to late Mar. **Meals:** Set L £35. Set D £60 (6 courses). **Service:** not inc. **Details:** Cards accepted. 34 seats. No music. No mobile phones. Wheelchair access. Children allowed. Car parking.

Carradale

Dunvalanree

Enchanting home-from-home
Port Righ, Carradale, PA28 6SE
Tel no: (01583) 431226
www.dunvalanree.com
Modern British | £28
Cooking score: 2

£5 OFF 🛏 £30

Dunvalanree's hospitable pedigree dates back more than 70 years, although its current incumbents have only been nurturing the tradition since 1998. Even so, there's a mood of ingrained domesticity about this enchanting home-from-home on the Mull of Kintyre. Alyson Milstead's cooking takes what it can from the region, fashioning the harvest into plain-speaking, unshowy dishes. Fish fans might be drawn to monkfish with fennel and lemon or Kintyre sea bass 'en papillote' with rosemary and lime, while carnivores could veer towards crispy pork belly with apples or rack of Saddell lamb on minted pea purée with Marsala gravy. To finish, nod off with a 'Dunvalanree dream' (essentially chocolate and alcohol). A dozen wines start at £14.50. **Chef/s:** Alyson Milstead. **Open:** all week D only 7.30 (1 sitting). **Closed:** Christmas. **Meals:** Set D £22.50 (2 courses) to £27.50. **Service:** not inc. **Details:** Cards accepted. 20 seats. No mobile phones. Wheelchair access. Music. Children allowed. Car parking.

Average price

The average price listed in main-entry reviews denotes the price of a three-course meal, without wine.

Dalry

Braidwoods
Clear, incisive flavours
Drumastle Mill Cottage, Dalry, KA24 4LN
Tel no: (01294) 833544
www.braidwoods.co.uk
Modern British | £40
Cooking score: 6

Keith and Nicola Braidwood's modest country restaurant still has echoes of bucolic farmhouse ruggedness – not surprising given that it is housed in two remote whitewashed mill cottages. Inside, all is relaxed indulgence and attentive courtesy, with smooth contemporary design features reminding visitors that the place isn't stuck in an archaic groove. Keith's cooking has also moved with the times, although he still has a natural-born sensitivity to the seasons and a feel for native produce. A starter of rabbit stuffed with mushrooms and Parma ham on Puy lentils has impressed with its big, bold flavours, while perfectly seared hand-dived scallops on tomato and coriander dhal strikes a subtler, more exotic note. After that, the kitchen might send out Parmesan tart with red pepper dressing or beautifully balanced spinach, leek and potato soup. Top-drawer Scottish ingredients and clear, incisive flavours re-emerge in main courses based around Ayrshire lamb, pigeon, local roe deer and seafood – perhaps baked fillet of West Coast turbot on smoked salmon risotto with Avruga caviar sauce. To conclude, enjoy the lingering richness of a fine Valrhona chocolate truffle cake with caramel and sea-salt ice cream, or the lighter tones of caramelised pecan parfait. The prestigious wine list offers a pitch-perfect selection from expert growers – including several South African choices sourced by the owners on a recent trip; also check out the page of 'fine and rare' seasonal recommendations. Prices start at £19.95.
Chef/s: Keith Braidwood. **Open:** Wed to Sun L 12 to 1.45, Tue to Sat D 7 to 9. **Closed:** Mon, 24 Dec to 18 Jan, first 2 weeks Sept. **Meals:** Set L £22 (2 courses)

to £25. Set D £40. Sun L £27.50. **Service:** not inc. **Details:** Cards accepted. 24 seats. No music. No mobile phones. Children allowed. Car parking.

Fairlie

Fins
Big-flavoured seafood
Fencefoot Farm, Fairlie, KA29 0EG
Tel no: (01475) 568989
www.fencebay.co.uk
Seafood | £30
Cooking score: 2

Jill and Bernard Thain's seafood restaurant has been an Ayrshire fixture for 17 years and it remains as popular as ever. It's a thoroughly distinctive enterprise, with its own smokehouse, farm shop, and cook/craft shop, and fresh fish delivered from the couple's boat. Classic assemblages are the order of the day, with big-flavoured dishes such as king scallops with black pudding on a grainy mustard sauce or hot-buttered Cumbrae crab, followed by lemon sole with citrus herb crust and lemon butter sauce. For a resonant finale, try the rhubarb cranachan. House Sauvignon Blanc is £14.70
Chef/s: Jane Burns. **Open:** Tue to Sun L 12 to 2.30, Tue to Sat D 6.30 to 9. **Closed:** Mon, 25 and 26 Dec, 1 and 2 Jan. **Meals:** alc (main courses £12 to £33). Set L £13 (2 courses) to £17. Set D £16 (2 courses) to £20. **Service:** not inc. **Details:** Cards accepted. 50 seats. No mobile phones. Wheelchair access. Music. Car parking.

Glasgow

Brian Maule at Chardon d'Or
Attention-grabbing food that speaks for itself
176 West Regent Street, Glasgow, G2 4RL
Tel no: (0141) 2483801
www.brianmaule.com
French | £45
Cooking score: 4

Black seating and wood tones against a pastel backdrop strike a softly contemporary note in the grand Victorian premises that house Brian

Maule's split-level restaurant. The ornate ceilings are worth a 'wow', before the French-inspired food, which uses the cream of Scotland's natural bounty, diverts the attention. Maule is a hands-on chef. He designs the menus and cooks them too, and the results speak for themselves. A roulade of ham hough with peppered foie gras and celeriac rémoulade displays the fruits of his French training, while grilled sea bass with pickled cauliflower and saffron-scented penne pasta evokes a more British Isles approach. Lamb treatments receive praise – perhaps for a serving of the roast fillet with cumin-spiced aubergine – before desserts revert to classic modes for crème brûlée or dark chocolate mousse with griottine cherries. The user-friendly list incorporates an imaginative page of 'wines for the season', before launching off into its varietal sections. Prices start at £19 (£4.10 a glass).
Chef/s: Brian Maule. **Open:** Mon to Fri L 12 to 2 (3 Fri), Mon to Sat D 5 to 10 (11 Sun). **Closed:** Sun, bank hols, 25 and 26 Dec, first 2 weeks Jan. **Meals:** alc (main courses £22 to £27). Set L and D £16.50 (2 courses) to £19.50. Tasting menu £55 (6 courses). **Service:** not inc. **Details:** Cards accepted. 70 seats. Air-con. Separate bar. Wheelchair access. Music. Children allowed.

Gamba

Glasgow seafood stalwart
225a West George Street, Glasgow, G2 2ND
Tel no: (0141) 5720899
www.gamba.co.uk
Seafood | £40
Cooking score: 3

£5
OFF

The name is Spanish for 'prawn', so there's no concealing the foodie allegiances of this long-running Glasgow eatery. Seafood is the name of the game, and Gamba goes about its business in soft-edged, family-friendly surroundings that are in stark contrast to many of the city's post-modern venues. The kitchen's fish soup is a legendary broth loaded with crabmeat and prawn dumplings, but the menu also makes room for organic salmon tartare,

monkfish curry with bananas and sweet potatoes, and classics such as grilled lemon sole. Sirloin of Buccleuch beef satisfies carnivorous cravings and veggies might fancy tomato, olive and haloumi tart. Desserts come good with, say, star anise pannacotta and stewed rhubarb. Fish-friendly whites wax strongly on the substantial wine list, priced from £18.95.
Chef/s: Derek Marshall. **Open:** Mon to Sat L 12 to 2.30 (2.15 Sat), all week D 5 to 10 (10.30 Fri and Sat). **Closed:** 25 and 26 Dec, 1 and 2 Jan. **Meals:** alc (main courses £11 to £24). Set L £15.95 (2 courses) to £19.95. Pre-theatre D £15 (2 courses) to £18. **Service:** not inc. **Details:** Cards accepted. 65 seats. Air-con. Separate bar. No mobile phones. Music. Children allowed.

Michael Caines at ABode Glasgow

Finesse in the heart of the city
129 Bath Street, Glasgow, G2 2SZ
Tel no: (0141) 5726011
www.michaelcaines.com
Modern European | £40
Cooking score: 5

🛏 V

Glasgow's iconic Arthouse was given the luxe treatment in 2006, as Michael Caines and Andrew Brownsword added this dazzling Edwardian edifice to their clutch of boutique ABode hotels. It's the real deal in the heart of the city, with a pulsating late-night bar and a casual grill as well as swish ground-floor restaurant oozing chic refinement. The attention to detail is obvious from the very start, as diners are offered an impressive selection of warm breads and a beautifully presented amuse-bouche such as salmon and avocado mousse. A starter of crab cannelloni with spiced apple purée and crab foam 'dances across the palate', and the excitement continues with mains such as wild stone bass with mushroom agnolotti and baby leeks, or rack and breast of Orkney lamb with swede and potato pavé, artichokes and tapenade jus. Careful execution and intense flavours are the hallmarks of the cooking, with Michael

Caines' fondness for regional produce pointing up just about everything on the menu. To conclude, a pre-dessert of tropical fruit salad and apricot foam could usher in a deliciously light, full-flavoured banana soufflé with rum crème anglaise and exotic fruit sorbet. Wines are housed in a temperature-controlled 'cave', and the list offers a broad choice of fine drinking from £21.50.
Chef/s: Craig Dunn. **Open:** Tue to Sat L 12 to 2.30, D 6 to 10. **Closed:** Sun, Mon, 26 and 27 Dec, 1 to 17 Jan, 11 to 26 Jul. **Meals:** alc (main courses £18 to £28). Set L £12.95 (2 courses) to £15.95. Set D £15.95 (2 courses) to £18.95. Tasting menu £55 (7 courses). **Service:** 12% (optional). **Details:** Cards accepted. 47 seats. Air-con. Separate bar. No mobile phones. Wheelchair access. Music. Children allowed.

Stravaigin

Inventive, good-value food
28 Gibson Street, Glasgow, G12 8NX
Tel no: (0141) 3342665
www.stravaigin.com
Modern British | £25
Cooking score: 2

£5 OFF | V | £30

Well-known and heavily used by regulars, this popular West End café/bar and restaurant was planning an expansion of its ground-floor café/bar as we went to press – knocking through into next door to create extra seating and improved kitchen facilities. The basement restaurant remains one of Glasgow's best options for inventive, good-value food in lively, informal surroundings. Fresh flavours are found in dishes such as wild mushroom and Savoy pierogi with celeriac fondant and beetroot broth, and mains of Balinese slow-cooked belly pork with lemongrass and peanut, coconut congee, choi sum and coriander pesto. Steamed ginger pudding is a great dessert. The wine list is well chosen, well annotated and reasonably priced, with bottles from £15.50. NB: Stravaigin 2, operating on similar lines, can be found at 8 Ruthven Lane; tel: (0141) 3347165.

Chef/s: Douglas Lindsay. **Open:** all week 11 to 10.30. **Closed:** 25 Dec, 1 Jan. **Meals:** alc (main courses £13 to £22). Set pre-theatre D £12.95 (2 courses) to £15.95. **Service:** not inc. **Details:** Cards accepted. 50 seats. 12 seats outside. Air-con. Separate bar. Music. Children allowed.

Ubiquitous Chip

Glasgow icon
12 Ashton Lane, Glasgow, G12 8SJ
Tel no: (0141) 3345007
www.ubiquitouschip.co.uk
Modern British | £40
Cooking score: 4

£5 OFF | 🍷

This fiercely supported Glasgow icon shows no sign of waning, despite the sad death of founder Ronnie Clydesdale in April 2010. The Chip has always been in it for the long haul, expanding its horizons along the way (there is now a maze of four dining zones, including the irresistible cobblestone courtyard). Home-stuffed haggis was on the menu when the place opened its doors back in 1971, and the kitchen still pleases punters with the best from Scotland's larder – Perthshire pork, Scrabster seafood, Argyllshire venison, creel-caught langoustines and more besides. Recent triumphs have included scallops with Rothesay black pudding purée, candied apple, vanilla oil and hazelnut tuile, braised pig's cheek with truffled potato omelette, a superb 'trilogy' of lamb, and 'the most incredible' pear tarte Tatin. 'Friendly professionalism' sums up the enthusiastic service, and the wine list is one of Scotland's vinous treasures. Pedigree clarets and Burgundies vie with mature Italians, Germanic rarities and up-front contenders from the New World. Prices start at £16.95.
Chef/s: Andy Mitchell. **Open:** all week L 12 to 2.30 (12.30 to 3 Sun), D 5.30 to 11 (6.30 Sun). **Closed:** 25 Dec, 1 Jan. **Meals:** Set L £24.85 (2 courses) to £29.95. Set D £34.85 (2 courses) to £39.85. Sun L £19.25. **Service:** not inc. **Details:** Cards accepted. 170 seats. Air-con. Separate bar. No music. Children allowed.

La Vallée Blanche

Cared-for neighbourhood bistro
360 Byres Road, Glasgow, G12 8AY
Tel no: (0141) 3343333
www.lavalleeblanche.com
French | £35
Cooking score: 3

£5
OFF

A French eatery above a shop on frenetic Byres Road hardly sounds inviting, but visitors are instantly converted once they settle into this amenable neighbourhood dining room. The name references an Alpine ski resort and the interior has been fitted out like a chalet – although there's nothing tacky about the result. A lot of care has been lavished on the place and the kitchen is not about to let the side down. Potted rabbit and 'melt in the mouth' pig's cheeks with shallot purée and watercress salad did the business for one reader, but there's also plenty for fish fans (Tarbert halibut with pea purée, wild garlic and blood orange dressing, for example). To finish, spiced pear soufflé is a good call. House wine is £14.95.
Chef/s: Neil Clark. **Open:** Tue to Sun L 12 to 2.30 (3.30 Sat and Sun), D 5.30 to 10. **Closed:** Mon, 25 Dec, 1 Jan. **Meals:** alc (main courses £11 to £20). Set L and pre theatre D £12.95 (2 courses) to £15.50. **Service:** not inc. **Details:** Cards accepted. 80 seats. Air-con. Music. Children allowed.

READERS RECOMMEND

The Dining Room

Modern British
104 Bath Street, Glasgow, G2 2EN
Tel no: (0141) 3326678
www.diningroomglasgow.com
'When I had lunch with my cousin, a notoriously picky eater, she cleared all three plates with great relish – a first in 66 years!'

Isle of Colonsay

The Colonsay

Classy island getaway with star fish
Scalasaigh, Isle of Colonsay, PA61 7YP
Tel no: (01951) 200316
www.colonsayestate.co.uk
Modern British | £25
New Chef

£30

Perched on an island off the Argyll coast, overlooking the harbour and the neighbouring Isle of Jura, this Georgian inn has served the local community for 250 years and it's now a getaway magnet for lovers of the great outdoors. New chef Darren McGuigan arrived in 2010 to head up the classy kitchen, but fish is still a sure-fire bet on the menu. Local crab on toast or squid tempura with lime and garlic mayo could precede halibut with courgettes and chive butter. Meat-eaters can order steak and chips, and there's rhubarb crumble for afters. A serviceable wine list opens at £12.50.
Chef/s: Darren McGuigan. **Open:** all week L 12 to 2, D 6 to 9 (5.30 to 9 Fri and Sun). **Closed:** Jan to Mar, Nov to Christmas. **Meals:** alc (main courses £12 to £18). **Service:** not inc. **Details:** Cards accepted. 40 seats. 20 seats outside. Air-con. Separate bar. No music. Wheelchair access. Children allowed. Car parking.

Isle of Eriska

Isle of Eriska Hotel

Elegant food on a private island
Ledaig, Isle of Eriska, PA37 1SD
Tel no: (01631) 720371
www.eriska-hotel.co.uk
British | £42
Cooking score: 4

The Buchanan-Smiths' towered and turreted Victorian mansion is set on its own 300-acre private island (with access via a vehicular bridge). Reports focus on the merits of the kitchen. Robert MacPherson's four-course dinners display a modern edge and he uses the best seasonal ingredients. As one annual visitor noted: 'the depth of flavours and elegance on the plate really makes an impression that sits comfortably alongside the wonderful ambience of Eriska as a destination in itself'. A typical menu from March shows the style: slow-braised boneless oxtail with shallot and thyme mash, vegetable and port reduction followed by roasted turbot accompanied by local cockles, poached lettuce with celery and cider sauce, then pistachio bavarois with a poached Williams pear and coconut sorbet, before farmhouse cheeses. The wine list is more than adequate in geographical range, and delicate financing is considered too, with house wines from £14. **Chef/s:** Robert MacPherson. **Open:** all week D only 7.30 to 9. **Closed:** 3 to 31 Jan. **Meals:** Set D £42 (4 courses). **Service:** not inc. **Details:** Cards accepted. 49 seats. Separate bar. No music. No mobile phones. Wheelchair access. Children allowed. Car parking.

▌Isle of Mull

Café Fish

Simple, fresh and fabulous seafood
The Pier, Main Street, Tobermory, Isle of Mull, PA75 6NU
Tel no: (01688) 301253
www.thecafefish.com
Seafood | £23
Cooking score: 3

£30

This former shorefront ticket office turned café commands great views over Tobermory Bay. A short climb up external stairs gives you the option of sitting outside on the whitewashed terrace or inside, where pale blue walls, tiled floor and fishing paraphernalia enhance the seaside feel; you can even see the catch arrive at the back door through the open-plan kitchen. The small menu focuses on simplicity and freshness, with favourites like moules marinière or a bowl of sweet, luscious squat lobsters, while Café Fish stew or coley braised with a well-considered combination of baby gem lettuce, peas and pancetta might appear among blackboard

specials. Service is knowledgeable and friendly with a small well-chosen wine list. Bottles start at £14.50. **Chef/s:** Liz McGougan. **Open:** all week L 11 to 3, D 6 to 9. **Closed:** end of Dec to end of March. **Meals:** alc (main courses £10 to £25). **Service:** not inc. **Details:** Cards accepted. 34 seats. 32 seats outside. Music.

▌Kilberry

The Kilberry Inn

No flummery, just good cooking
Kilberry Road, Kilberry, PA29 6YD
Tel no: (01880) 770223
www.kilberryinn.com
Modern British | £28
Cooking score: 3

🛏 £30

The single-track road to Kilberry has stunning views over the Paps of Jura and leads to a fairly ordinary-looking inn that doubles comfortably as a place to eat and a place to stay. It wins for honest food with no pretensions or flummery, just good cooking, and the quality of the raw materials is high. Reporters have praised 'luscious', sweet' scallops with celeriac purée and pancetta, smoked salmon from the Sleepy Hollow smokery (near Ullapool) served with artichoke and toasted sourdough, and gurnard with sage and garlic. Meat cookery runs to duck rillettes, local rabbit with cider and roasted vegetables, or perfectly pink rack of lamb with French-style peas. Puddings are unadorned country creations: vanilla ice cream with slightly spicy Aztec chocolate sauce, for example. A short but wide-ranging wine list opens at £15. **Chef/s:** Tom Holloway and Clare Johnson. **Open:** Tue to Sun L 12.15 to 2.15, D 6.30 onwards. **Closed:** Mon, Christmas, 3 Jan to mid Mar. **Meals:** alc (main courses £12 to 18). **Service:** not inc. **Details:** Cards accepted. 30 seats. No mobile phones. Wheelchair access. Music. Children allowed. Car parking.

▌Oban

Ee-Usk

Fresh seafood without frills
North Pier, Oban, PA34 5QD
Tel no: (01631) 565666
www.eeusk.com
Seafood | £28
Cooking score: 1
£30

The name is phonetic Gaelic for fish, so it's pretty obvious what you can expect at this glassed-in, red-roofed building by the old harbourmaster's office. Big windows look out onto Oban Bay, and the kitchen plunders the local catch for much of its output. Fresh ingredients are given the unadorned treatment they deserve – witness plates of Lissmore oysters, creel-caught langoustines spiked with chilli and ginger, or baked wild halibut with creamed leeks. Seafood platters are a huge draw, while desserts bring on lemon cheesecake or crème brûlée. House wine is £13.50.
Chef/s: Jane Scott. **Open:** all week L 12 to 3 (2.30 winter), D 6 to 9.30 (9 winter). **Closed:** 25 and 26 Dec, 1 Jan. **Meals:** alc (main courses £12 to £20). Set L winter only £10.95 (2 courses) to £13.95. Set D winter only £15.95 (2 courses) to £17.95.
Service: not inc. **Details:** Cards accepted. 102 seats. 24 seats outside. Air-con. Wheelchair access. Music. Children allowed. Car parking.

ALSO RECOMMENDED

▲ Waterfront

1 Railway Pier, Oban, PA34 4LW
Tel no: (01631) 563110
www.waterfrontoban.co.uk
Seafood £5 OFF

Locals and visitors alike appreciate the good value and hospitality in this boisterous bar-cum-eatery. Locally landed fish is the focus, and the kitchen turns its hand to mussels with white wine and cream (£6.95), battered haddock and chips or sole fillets with warm new potato salad (£13.95). Meat lovers might be offered venison or steaks. For dessert, Irn Bru ice cream (£3.95) has won good reports. Wines from £13.95. Open all week.

▌Troon

MacCallums Oyster Bar

Top-drawer Scottish seafood
The Harbour, Troon, KA10 6DH
Tel no: (01292) 319339
Seafood | £25
Cooking score: 2
£30

Owner John MacCallum is a fish merchant by trade, and his connections have stood this converted hydraulic pump house by Troon harbour in good stead. Top-drawer seafood is naturally the star of the show, and the kitchen keeps it simple with an assortment of unfussy dishes dictated by the market and the local catch. Thai-style steamed mussels or a plate of oysters might precede pancetta-wrapped monkfish with barley risotto or Parmesan-crusted cod with lime crème fraîche, while sticky toffee pudding could wrap up proceedings sweetly. Battered haddock fish pie and seafood crêpes please the lunchtime crowd. Fish-friendly wines start at £13.95.
Chef/s: Phillip Burgess. **Open:** Tue to Sun L 12 to 2.30 (3 Sun), Tue to Sat D 6.30 to 9.30. **Closed:** Mon, 3/4 weeks from 22 Dec. **Meals:** alc (main courses £10 to £28). **Service:** not inc. **Details:** Cards accepted. 43 seats. Wheelchair access. Music. Children allowed. Car parking.

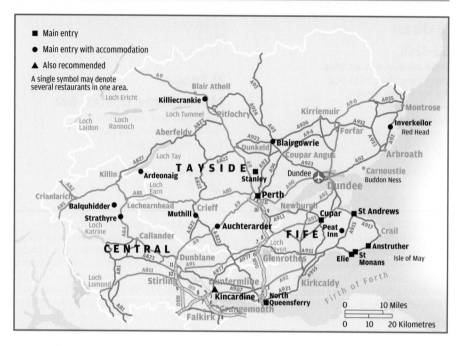

Ardeonaig

Ardeonaig Hotel

South Africa comes to Scotland
South Road, Loch Tay, Ardeonaig, FK21 8SU
Tel no: (01567) 820400
www.ardeonaighotel.co.uk
Modern British | £35
Cooking score: 5

£5 OFF ☗ ☖

'Remote beauty with strong tones of South Africa' is one fan's enigmatic description of this remarkable enterprise, which adds some Cape chic to the bonny banks of Loch Tay. Ardeonaig also comes with an enlightened culinary view of things – thanks to go-getting chef/proprietor Pete Gottgens, a South African with Scottish ancestry, globetrotting instincts and a passion for indigenous produce. The kitchen garners a host of ingredients from regional producers for dishes shot through with creativity and innovative flourishes. Gottgens' way with fish gets plenty of votes – perhaps line-caught Shetland halibut with Loch Fyne crab, almond crust and beetroot raita, or West Coast bream fillet with winter chanterelles, chestnuts and butternut squash. Elsewhere, Ardtalnaig Estate roe deer is served with herb polenta and wild mushrooms, while a trio of home-reared Blackface lamb (loin, bobotie and shoulder) with carrot purée and umngqusho (a Cape 'risotto' made from dried corn kernels and sugar beans) shows off the kitchen's skills. To finish, chocolate 'mielie' pudding with caramelised banana and milk ice cream is a star turn, or you might prefer to complete your culinary adventure with a granadilla soufflé with crème fraîche sorbet and granadilla syrup. By contrast, lunch is a more limited affair, served in the bistro-style 'study'. The wine list provides a palate-challenging tour of the South African winemaking world, with excitement at every turn. Prices start at £19.50. Gottgens has also planted the UK's most northerly vineyard in the grounds of Ardeonaig.

Chef/s: Pete Gottgens. **Open:** all week L 12 to 3.30, D 7 to 9.30. **Meals:** alc (main courses £10 to £18). Set D £35. Tasting menu £50 (6 courses). **Service:** not inc. **Details:** Cards accepted. 56 seats. 42 seats outside. Separate bar. No music. No mobile phones. Wheelchair access. Music. Car parking.

Balquhidder
Monachyle Mhor
Family-run hotel with uncomplicated food
Balquhidder, FK19 8PQ
Tel no: (01877) 384622
www.mhor.net
Modern British | £46
Cooking score: 5

The Lewis family's 2000-acre estate in the heart of the Trossachs National Park has to be one of the more impressively large-scale operations in the Guide. As well as farming their own livestock, they run a fishmonger, a tea room, a bakery and much more besides – including this blush-pink hotel, reached down a single-track lane along the wooded banks of Loch Voil. Tom Lewis goes in for uncomplicated modern cooking. Fixed-price dinner menus may range from cured Shetland salmon with celeriac and apple rémoulade to Mhor's own venison, perhaps a loin cut served with braised chicory, spring greens, carrots and shallots, with a soup such as roast tomato in between. Peanut butter parfait with gingerbread and salted cashews is an unimpeachably modern finale. The whole place is run with warm, enveloping bonhomie, and there is also an admirable wine list to go at, arranged by grape variety and with enough choice below £25 for everyone to feel included. Prices start at £18, and there is a decent handful by the glass from £4.50.
Chef/s: Tom Lewis. **Open:** all week L 12 to 1.45, D 7 to 8.30. **Closed:** Jan. **Meals:** Set L £20 (2 courses) to £25. Set D £46 (5 courses). Sun L £31. **Service:** not inc. **Details:** Cards accepted. 45 seats. 30 seats outside. Separate bar. Music. Children allowed. Car parking.

Port of Menteith
Lake of Menteith Hotel
Modern British
Port of Menteith, FK8 3RA
Tel no: (01877) 385258
www.lake-hotel.com
'Food, location and servce can be summed up in one word – stunning'

Strathyre
Creagan House
Dreamy farmhouse with stand-out food
Strathyre, FK18 8ND
Tel no: (01877) 384638
www.creaganhouse.co.uk
French | £32
Cooking score: 4

'As always it's a lovely relaxing place, and is definitely our favourite both for food (breakfast as well as dinner) and staying.' So runs a satisfied report on the Gunns' seventeenth-century farmhouse that basks in all the majesty the Highlands have to offer. Gordon Gunn's classically expressed menu works out a vein of French cooking with variations, hence slow-braised belly of pork with seared hand-dived scallops and plum sauce topped with fabulously crispy bits of pork crackling, and a 'stand-out' roasted tail of North Sea monkfish with crab and prawn croquette, shellfish and tomato sauce, accompanied by four kinds of 'wonderful veggies'. For dessert, bread-and-butter pudding on a sticky toffee bed or squidgy spiced apple cake, both with homemade vanilla ice cream, are recommended. Cherry Gunn's expertise with the wine selection is appreciated, with bottles from £16.15.
Chef/s: Gordon Gunn. **Open:** Fri to Tue D only 7.30 (1 sitting). **Closed:** Wed, Thur, 24 to 26 Dec, 19 Jan to 10 Mar, 9 to 24 Nov. **Meals:** Set D £31.50. **Service:** not inc. **Details:** Cards accepted. 14 seats. Separate bar. No music. No mobile phones. Wheelchair access. Car parking.

Anstruther

The Cellar

Virtuous seafood and stunning wine
24 East Green, Anstruther, KY10 3AA
Tel no: (01333) 310378
www.cellaranstruther.co.uk
Seafood | £40
Cooking score: 6

£5 OFF 🍷

The location just behind the Scottish Fisheries Museum is appropriate, as here is one of Scotland's premier seafood chefs. Peter Jukes has notched up almost 30 years at the Cellar, an intimate hideaway in a seventeenth-century listed building with a cobbled courtyard. The original beams and candlelit ambience make for an utterly charming experience, and the impeccable seafood dishes (not forgetting some fine Scotch beef too) add to the wholly classy package. One way of starting is with an omelette, creamily filled with Finnan haddock, or you could enjoy the traditional salmon preparations, served as a tripartite plate of oak-smoked, hot-smoked and gravadlax. For main, there might be prime east-coast halibut served with greens, pine nuts, smoked bacon and hollandaise, or pesto-crusted cod with pak choi, basil mash and balsamic, while that beef fillet appears with wild mushrooms, caramelised onions and stovies, sauced in grain mustard. These simple but highly effective dishes are cooked with consummate care and skill, flawlessly timed, and meals conclude with the likes of praline parfait, garnished with fruits in cassis. Wines from £18.50 open a list that knows no boundaries in its line-up of exciting producers and formidable international reach.
Chef/s: Peter Jukes. **Open:** Fri and Sat L from 12.30, Mon to Sat D 6.30 to 9. **Closed:** Sun, 24 to 26 Dec, 1 Jan. **Meals:** Set L £19.50 (2 courses) to £24.50. Set D £34.95 (2 courses) to £39.95. **Service:** not inc. **Details:** Cards accepted. 40 seats. No music. No mobile phones. Children allowed.

Cupar

Ostlers Close

Hidden-away foodie gem
25 Bonnygate, Cupar, KY15 4BU
Tel no: (01334) 655574
www.ostlersclose.co.uk
Modern British | £39
Cooking score: 5

£5 OFF

With nigh on three decades under their belts, James and Amanda Graham should know a thing or two about running a restaurant. This hidden-away, seventeenth-century cottage is their pride and joy — and an understated foodie destination to boot. The mood is homely, but the whole set-up is run with polish and pride — and that includes the careful sourcing of regional ingredients. Over the years, the couple have nurtured links with a network of suppliers and producers who provide the building blocks for James' disarmingly simple, but brilliantly handled seasonal dishes. Woodcock from the shoots might appear with its braised leg meat on Stornoway black pudding mash accompanied by beetroot sauce, while roast breast of free-range Barbary duck comes to the table with red cabbage, roasted butternut squash and orange clove sauce. Fish from Scotland's boats also has its say — perhaps fillet of pollack (with a Puy lentil, potato and coriander broth) or wild halibut (served on hot-smoked salmon risotto with wilted greens). As a finale, the kitchen might serve vanilla pannacotta with damson sorbet and a compote of fruits in homemade damson gin. Off-season, the Grahams also provide a fixed-price supper menu (advance bookings for whole tables only). The handwritten wine list is a well-chosen international selection at realistic prices from £17.
Chef/s: James Graham. **Open:** Sat L 12.15 to 1.30, Tue to Sat D 7 to 9.30 (6.30 Sat). **Closed:** Sun, Mon, 25 and 26 Dec, 1 and 2 Jan, 2 weeks Easter, 2 weeks mid-Oct. **Meals:** alc (main courses £18 to £22). **Service:** not inc. **Details:** Cards accepted. 26 seats. No music. No mobile phones. Wheelchair access. Children allowed.

Elie

Sangster's
Small restaurant with big ideas
51 High Street, Elie, KY9 1BZ
Tel no: (01333) 331001
www.sangsters.co.uk
Modern British | £39
Cooking score: 5

From the moment you set foot in Bruce and
Jacqueline Sangster's agreeable town house,
you can sense this is a small restaurant with big
ideas. Inside, it has been treated to a gentle dose
of cosmopolitan chic, but there's also a
personable homeliness about the squashy
sofas, paintings and open fireplace. The
cooking reflects this mix, overlaying carefully
sourced Scottish produce and garden pickings
with confident, grown-up flavours and an
open-minded philosophy. Bruce's twice-
baked Tobermory cheese soufflé continues to
wow the crowds, and it sets the tone for
concise menus that also find room for honey-
glazed quail breast with lentil salad, sesame
and soy dressing or a tart of confit duck with
red onion marmalade. Simplicity, assured
technique and pretty presentation point up
pitch-perfect main courses of roast turbot
with langoustine, pea and courgette risotto or
saddle of Perthshire venison with a little
helping of shin hotpot, crushed root
vegetables, thyme and Madeira sauce. To
conclude, mango 'gazpacho' surprised one
visitor, but the choice might also extend to hot
pear soufflé with marzipan ice cream or iced
apple crumble parfait with apple and lemon
compote. Superb coffee and moreish
sweetmeats end proceedings on a thoroughly
satisfying note. The admirably annotated,
100-bin wine list garners high-quality
drinking from elite estates and family
growers; choice is spot-on and prices have
been deemed 'excellent'. House
recommendations start at £18.50.
Chef/s: Bruce Sangster. **Open:** Wed to Fri and Sun L
12.30 to 1.30, Tue to Sat D 7 to 8.30. **Closed:** Mon,
25 and 26 Dec, first 2 weeks Jan, first 2 weeks Nov.
Meals: Set L £20 (2 courses) to £25. Set D £30 (2

courses) to £45 (4 courses). Sun L £27.50.
Service: not inc. **Details:** Cards accepted. 28 seats.
No music. No mobile phones. Wheelchair access.
Children allowed.

Kincardine

ALSO RECOMMENDED
▲ The Unicorn
15 Excise Street, Kincardine, FK10 4LN
Tel no: (01259) 739129
www.theunicorn.co.uk
Modern British £5
OFF

The contemporary brasserie in this
seventeenth-century coaching inn tucked off
the main road to Glasgow continues to please
all-comers. The kitchen makes the most of
Scottish produce but looks further afield for
inspiration, spanning everything from tarte
Tatin of goats' cheese (£5.75) and smoked
Caesar salad to coq au vin, and roe deer with
rösti, wild mushroom fricassee and winter
berry jus (£16.95). Homemade ice creams or
toffee ripple cheesecake (£4.95) to finish.
House wine is £14.95. Closed Mon.

North Queensferry

The Wee Restaurant
A diamond under the Forth bridge
17 Main Street, North Queensferry, KY11 1JT
Tel no: (01383) 616263
www.theweerestaurant.co.uk
Modern European | £30
Cooking score: 3

Craig and Vikki Wood have found their niche
in this compact early Victorian building,
which now ticks over as a relaxed, well-
supported neighbourhood restaurant. The
freshness of their ingredients has impressed
and intense flavours come through in dishes
such as slow-cooked collar of pork teamed
with garlic mash, shallot, fennel and pancetta
jus, spiced megrim fillets served with
vermicelli pasta, tomato, white wine and
shellfish velouté. Overall, the food treads a
modern European path, taking in standards
from chicken liver parfait and aged ribeye

steak with mustard butter to baked apple tarte Tatin with homemade Calvados ice cream. House wine is £14.75.

Chef/s: Craig Wood. **Open:** Tue to Sun L 12 to 2, D 6 to 9. **Closed:** Mon, 25 and 26 Dec, 1 and 2 Jan. **Meals:** Set L £16.25 (2 courses) to £19.75. Set D £25 (2 courses) to £30. **Service:** not inc. **Details:** Cards accepted. 36 seats. Music. Children allowed.

Peat Inn

The Peat Inn

Blue-chip food lover's paradise
Peat Inn, KY15 5LH
Tel no: (01334) 840206
www.thepeatinn.co.uk
Modern British | £40
Cooking score: 6

Geoffrey and Katherine Smeddle's tenure at this iconic Scottish inn continues to yield satisfaction – thanks to their good-natured hospitality, the prospect of homely comforts and the surefire brilliance of the food. Muted colours, flowers and domestic touches soften the mood in the three intimate dining rooms, where guests can look forward to carefully honed gastronomic treats aplenty. Geoffrey's artful cooking is defined by invention, panache and sharp seasonal awareness – you don't need a calendar when the menu offers carpaccio of wild venison, pumpkin and Parmesan soup and a dish of roast loin and braised shoulder of hare with roast Jerusalem artichokes, young turnips and sauce salmis. Elsewhere, he might perk up a textbook feuilleté of langoustine and smoked haddock with chorizo compote, offset a warm salad of wood pigeon with prune and Armagnac purée, or dazzle the veggie brigade with a composition involving rosemary polenta, open ravioli of Little Gem and celeriac, wild mushrooms, pomegranate and walnut velouté. When it comes to the sweet end of proceedings, expect the likes of cold Amedei chocolate fondant with dark chocolate and Grand Marnier sorbet, or lemon tart with poached rhubarb and pistachio ice cream.

France is a passion on the global wine list, which shows an acute eye for quality as well as value. Prices start at £19 (£5 a glass).

Chef/s: Geoffrey Smeddle. **Open:** Tue to Sat L 12.30 to 1.30, D 7 to 9.30. **Closed:** Sun, Mon, 25 and 26 Dec, 1 week Nov, 2 weeks Jan. **Meals:** alc (main courses £16 to £26). Set L £16. Set D £32. Tasting menu £55 (6 courses). **Service:** not inc.
Details: Cards accepted. 45 seats. Separate bar. No music. No mobile phones. Wheelchair access. Children allowed. Car parking.

St Andrews

The Seafood Restaurant

Sparkling fresh fruits of the sea
The Scores, Bruce Embankment, St Andrews, KY16 9AB
Tel no: (01334) 479475
www.theseafoodrestaurant.com
Seafood | £45
Cooking score: 4

Perched dramatically like a glass box overlooking West Sands Beach and the North Sea, this fashion-conscious restaurant does exactly what it promises: seafood is the name of the game and the owners are big on provenance, spelling out their sources in meticulous detail: creel-caught Pittenweem crab, halibut farmed on Gigha, cod from sustainable Icelandic fisheries and so on. With all the right ingredients in place, the kitchen goes about its business with discretion and pin-sharp accuracy. Typical offerings on the concise menu might include cured salmon with celeriac rémoulade and apple jelly, halibut with pak choi and shrimp beurre noisette, and stone bass on lemon and parsley risotto with gremolata and razor clams. Meat dishes also feature – perhaps calf's liver with creamed shiitake mushrooms and spinach or rabbit loin and leg with pommes mousseline – and desserts such as poached meringue with green tea and pistachios or tonka bean brûlée with toasted almond milkshake conclude things splendidly. France, Spain and Germany get top billing on the high-ranking wine list, which is sympathetically tilted towards fish-friendly tipples. A page of house selections starts at £22 (£5.50 a glass), and there's a good choice of half-bottles. Sister to the Seafood Restaurant at St Monans (see entry). **Chef/s:** Douglas Sillars. **Open:** all week L 12 to 2.30 (3 Sun), D 6.30 to 10. **Closed:** 25 and 26 Dec, 1 Jan. **Meals:** Set L £22 (2 courses) to £26. Set D £40 (2 courses) to £45. **Service:** not inc. **Details:** Cards accepted. 60 seats. 20 seats outside. No mobile phones. Wheelchair access. Children allowed.

ALSO RECOMMENDED
▲ The Doll's House
3 Church Square, St Andrews, KY16 9NN
Tel no: (01334) 477422
www.houserestaurants.com
Modern European

Versatile, informal all-rounder that adds some fizz to the St Andrews scene with its typically forthright menu of classic and modern dishes. Pressed terrine of ham hough with piccalilli (£5.75), pork loin chop with honey and grain mustard sauce (£13.95) or sea bass fillets on creamy pesto sauce show the style. Good-value set lunches (from £6.95 for 2 courses) and dinners (from £19.95 for 2 courses), plus a good selection of wines by the glass; bottles from £13.95. Open all week.

▲ The Vine Leaf
131 South Street, St Andrews, KY16 9UN
Tel no: (01334) 477497
www.vineleafstandrews.co.uk
Modern British £5 OFF

At the end of a winding lane in the heart of St Andrews, the Hamiltons' eye-catching restaurant is a colourful place, all greens and purples, with a series of effective seascapes on the walls. The cooking is equally diverting, offered as a fixed-price menu (£23.50/25.95 for two/three courses). Dinner might proceed from Cullen skink or garlic-buttered langoustine to Parma-wrapped chicken breast stuffed with goats' cheese on tomato sauce, with hot chocolate cherry fudge cake and whipped cream to finish. Wines from £15.95. Open Mon to Sat D.

St Monans
The Seafood Restaurant
Deliciously simple fish and big flavours
16 West End, St Monans, KY10 2BX
Tel no: (01333) 730327
www.theseafoodrestaurant.com
Seafood | £38
Cooking score: 5
🗒️⭐

Enjoyment pervades this smart, clean-cut restaurant carved out of a 400-year-old whitewashed fisherman's cottage overlooking St Monans harbour. Fish is cooked deliciously simply – for instance precisely timed whole lemon sole served with some Pink Fir potatoes, green beans and a lemon-herb butter. The menu deals in bright, modern flavours, delivering a contemporary classic pairing of scallops on beetroot and pancetta risotto with cauliflower and truffle purée. Careful attention to big flavours shows in dishes such as gilthead bream teamed with peas, beans, bacon, gnocchi and chorizo. Other options might run to fish pie stuffed with cod, salmon, smoked salmon and mussels, and a token meat main course of Gressingham duck breast with prune and citrus polenta, Little Gem, carrot and ginger. More upbeat ideas appear at dessert stage, such as mango parfait with orange and star anise jelly with spiced bread ice cream or ginger and crème fraîche mousse with a compote and sorbet of rhubarb. There are plenty of interesting, fish-friendly bottles on the wide-ranging list. Prices start at £20 and there's a good selection by the glass.
Chef/s: Craig Millar and Roy Brown. **Open:** all week L 12.30 to 2.30 (3 Sun), D 6.30 to 9.30. **Closed:** Mon and Tue from Sept to May, 25 and 26 Dec, 1 Jan. **Meals:** Set L £22 (2 courses) to £26. Set D £33 (2 courses) to £38. **Service:** not inc. **Details:** Cards accepted. 50 seats. 32 seats outside. Separate bar. No music. No mobile phones. Wheelchair access. Children allowed. Car parking.

Auchterarder

Andrew Fairlie at Gleneagles

Meticulously polished cooking
Auchterarder, PH3 1NF
Tel no: (01764) 694267
www.andrewfairlie.com
Modern French | £75
Cooking score: 7

Naturally, you'll have arrived at the Gleneagles Hotel by limo, but if you've given the chauffeur the night off and have to come by train, note that there is no taxi rank at the station (though there is a phone that puts you straight through). Acres of sprawling golf course interspersed with beautiful parkland are the focal point, and the hotel itself has the impress of high-gloss corporate business about it. Its principal gastronomic draw is to be found off one of the ground-floor corridors, where a receptionist waits to admit you to a huge, windowless black space (more cavern than womb), hung with modern art including two oil portraits of 'chef'. It all feels a little too reverential to be fun, but the cooking is what you're here for and for that you can set your faces to 'stunned'. From the first canapés (try the foie gras ice cream cone topped with candied almonds), the intent is posted, and the attention to detail is awe-inspiring. Andrew Fairlie favours deconstructive presentations, with elements of a dish sitting proud of each other, waiting for the diner to combine them – as in a first-course array of pot-roasted scallops, scallop carpaccio, braised pig cheek, coconut purée, radish, apple and a blob of apple and yuzu sorbet. Nit-pickers might say that certain dishes lack the hoped-for wow factor (a couple of collops of venison loin with baby artichokes, truffled leeks and spring veg), but most of the incidentals have it. A serving of gariguette strawberries with pistachio cake and a sorbet of strawberry and rhubarb is fresh and agreeably light. Service is correct to a nicety, but pleasantly chatty too. Wine-drinkers will need to dig deep; prices from £25.

Chef/s: Andrew Fairlie. **Open:** Mon to Sat D only 6 to 10. **Closed:** Sun, 24 and 25 Dec, 3 weeks Jan. **Meals:** Set D £75 to £95 (6 courses). **Service:** not inc. **Details:** Cards accepted. 52 seats. Air-con. Wheelchair access. Music. Car parking.

Blairgowrie

Kinloch House Hotel

Conservative cooking with élan
Dunkeld Road, Blairgowrie, PH10 6SG
Tel no: (01250) 884237
www.kinlochhouse.com
Modern British | £48
Cooking score: 5

Kinloch's family owners have a long tradition of country house hospitality, with the next generation now in charge at this rather grand, early-Victorian stone manor embedded in 25 acres of prime Perthshire real estate. Chef Steve MacCallum (formerly at the Airds Hotel, Port Appin – see entry) is in full flow, delivering food that shows an acute eye for detail and bags of technical know-how. His cooking may be rooted in the conservative world of crab and avocado tian, honey-glazed guinea fowl and duck breast with prune and apple sauce, but it's executed with considerable élan. A June meal in the formal, chandeliered dining room opened with creamy smoked haddock risotto with lightly poached quails' eggs and a textbook chicken liver terrine with classic accompaniments of Cumberland sauce and brioche. First-class Scottish raw materials are the key – witness Loch Duart salmon with pea mash, lobster and watercress sauce or an exemplary main course of roe deer 'cooked to melting perfection' and served with red cabbage, rösti and a red wine sauce. Simplicity rules when it comes to desserts such as baked egg custard with poached rhubarb or strawberry soufflé with white chocolate ice cream. The serious Francophile wine list is particularly strong on Burgundy, but gives full credit to other classic regions; also note the pickings from Ventisquero in Chile. House wines start at £21 (£6.50 a glass) and there's a useful contingent of half-bottles.

Chef/s: Steve MacCallum. **Open:** all week L 12.30 to 1.45, D 7 to 8.30. **Closed:** 12 to 29 Dec. **Meals:** Set L £18.50 (2 courses) to £23.50. Set D £48. Sun L £28. **Service:** not inc. **Details:** Cards accepted. 36 seats. Separate bar. No music. No mobile phones. Wheelchair access. Car parking.

Inverkeilor

Gordon's

Family's thrilling foodie fireworks
Main Street, Inverkeilor, DD11 5RN
Tel no: (01241) 830364
www.gordonsrestaurant.co.uk
Modern British | £45
Cooking score: 5

'Warm and appealing, even in mid-winter', the Watson family's intimate restaurant-with-rooms occupies a sympathetically restored Victorian house in a remote little village close to Lunan Bay. Inside, it sings of domesticity and personal pride, with beamed ceilings and a fire burning in the grate. This is a close-knit enterprise to the core, with Maria Watson tending to the front of house 'in her own well-practised way', while Gordon and son Garry man the stoves. However, any homespun sobriety is blown away by the thrilling fireworks emanating from the kitchen. Twice-baked Isle of Mull Cheddar soufflé is about as mainstream as it gets; otherwise, be prepared to be dazzled by the complexities of quail boudin with Stornoway black pudding, spinach, potato blinis and lentils or home-smoked Gressingham duck breast with confit leg, panko crust, curly kale, vanilla fig and kohlrabi. Desserts add their own exciting contrasts, as in Valrhona chocolate fondant with cherry compote, warm Pedro Ximenez jelly, caramel and balsamic ice cream. Scottish threads are also woven into the favourably reported lunch menu, which has yielded pleasurable platefuls including a tian Loch Duart salmon with parley purée and Cullen skink sauce, and fillet of Forfar beef with veal sweetbreads, ox cheek and butternut squash. Well-annotated wines from £16.

Chef/s: Gordon and Garry Watson. **Open:** Wed to Fri and Sun L 12.30 to 1.30, Tue to Sun D 7 to 8.30 (6.30 Sun). **Closed:** Mon, 2 weeks Jan. **Meals:** Set L £27 (3 courses). Set D £45 (4 courses). **Service:** not inc. **Details:** Cards accepted. 24 seats. No music. No mobile phones. Wheelchair access. Children allowed. Car parking.

Killicrankie

NEW ENTRY

Killiecrankie House

Traditional hotel in a lovely setting
Killicrankie, PH16 5LG
Tel no: (01796) 473220
www.killiecrankiehotel.co.uk
Modern British | £38
Cooking score: 3

All agree that the location of this early Victorian house is superb, set above the river Garry in a wonderful mix of formal gardens and woodland. 'One of its attractions is the delightful friendly and relaxed atmosphere fostered by its owner Henrietta Ferguson, and the other is the quality of the food on offer', reads a report that confirms this is no stiff-necked operation. The 'cosy, beautifully decorated dining room' makes a fine setting for Mark Easton's uniformly straightforward cooking. Reporters have enjoyed memorable starters of twice-baked goats' cheese brûlée, as well as Perthshire lamb, roasted partridge and 'a good fillet of beef'. Fillet of venison with sweet potato fondant, braised carrot, Savoy cabbage, redcurrant and port jus, was 'probably the best venison I have ever tasted'. Desserts are well reported, service good and house wine £18.

Chef/s: Mark Easton. **Open:** all week D only 6 to 8.30. **Closed:** 3 Jan to early Mar. **Meals:** Set D £31 (3 courses) to £38. **Service:** not inc. **Details:** Cards accepted. 34 seats. Separate bar. No music. No mobile phones. Wheelchair access. Children allowed. Car parking.

Muthill

Barley Bree

New life for an old inn
6 Willoughby Street, Muthill, PH5 2AB
Tel no: (01764) 681451
www.barleybree.com
French | £28
Cooking score: 3

Fabrice and Alison Bouteloup have breathed new life into this eighteenth-century coaching inn with their warmth, personality and skilfully crafted food. Inside all is cosy and traditional, with drinks by the open fire setting the tone. The genuine welcome is matched by Fabrice's French-influenced menu, which changes weekly. To start, pea and leek soup with smoked salmon or seared pigeon breast with beetroot and celery could precede wild halibut fillet with squid ink risotto and langoustine sauce or roast Perthshire partridge with Savoy cabbage and baby turnips. Mains come with a novel jar of steamed vegetables on the side, and desserts such as banana tarte Tatin round things off a treat. Sourcing is impressive, and helpings are generous without going overboard. Nine wines by the glass (from £3.95) head the clearly described list.

Chef/s: Fabrice Bouteloup. **Open:** Wed to Sat L 12 to 2, D 6 to 9. Sun 12 to 7.30. **Closed:** Mon, Tue, Christmas, 2 weeks Feb, 2 weeks Oct. **Meals:** alc (main courses £17 to £19). **Service:** not inc. **Details:** Cards accepted. 32 seats. No music. Wheelchair access. Children allowed. Car parking.

Perth

Deans @ Let's Eat

Elaborate food in classic surrounds
77-79 Kinnoull Street, Perth, PH1 5EZ
Tel no: (01738) 643377
www.letseatperth.co.uk
Modern British | £26
Cooking score: 4

Willie Deans cooks with confidence and verve in this smart, slightly formal restaurant on a busy street corner not far from the city centre. His carte and competitive fixed-price deals make the most of enthusiastically garnered global ingredients, and lots of influences are at work: seared scallops might be served on a salad of preserved limes with crab and coriander crème fraîche and oriental caramel, say. Dishes are ingredient-laden, so a breast of French duckling is served alongside orange candied turnip purée, a timbale of black pudding and potato wafers and finished off with sherry vinegar gravy – 'all too much' for one reporter – although beef fillet medallion with caramelised onions, mushrooms and little celeriac croquettes is a simpler option. A hot raspberry soufflé with berry ice cream and vanilla custard is a neat idea for dessert. Service is generally expertly co-ordinated. Wines from £16.50.

Chef/s: Willie Deans. **Open:** Tue to Sat L 12 to 2, D 6.30 to 9.30. **Closed:** Sun, Mon, 2 weeks Jan. **Meals:** alc (main courses £13 to £20). Set L £12.95 (2 courses) to £15.95. Set D £20 (2 courses) to £25. **Service:** not inc. **Details:** Cards accepted. 65 seats. Separate bar. No mobile phones. Wheelchair access. Music. Children allowed.

63 Tay Street

Surprising the locals
63 Tay Street, Perth, PH2 8NN
Tel no: (01738) 441451
www.63taystreet.co.uk
Modern British | £31
Cooking score: 3

£5
OFF

There cannot be many local eateries that offer lamb belly galette with Shetland mussels and whipped goats' cheese in the normal course of events, but Graeme Pallister has the temerity of a good cook at ease with his materials. Visitors to his informal restaurant across the road from the river Tay have also be been bowled over by Jerusalem artichoke velouté served with scallops, a dish of fricassee chicken and ham tortellini, local wood pigeon and ribeye steak. One new regular observes that it takes something special to surprise a seasoned native, but Tay Street has done it. Meals always end on a high note with commendable desserts such as chocolate fondant and sticky toffee pudding, otherwise plump for the Scottish cheeses with homemade oatcakes and quince jelly. The well-spread wine list opens at £14.95.

Chef/s: Graeme Pallister. **Open:** Tue to Sat L 12 to 2, D 6.30 to 9. **Closed:** Sun, Mon, 1 weekend Dec, 1 week Jan, 1 week July. **Meals:** alc (main courses £12 to £21). Set L £22.95 (3 courses). Set D £33.95 (3 courses). **Service:** not inc. **Details:** Cards accepted. 36 seats. No mobile phones. Music. Children allowed. Car parking.

▌Stanley

The Apron Stage

Small is beautiful
5 King Street, Stanley, PH1 4ND
Tel no: (01738) 828888
www.apronstagerestaurant.co.uk
Modern British | £26
Cooking score: 3

£30

The Apron Stage is Shona Drysdale and Jane Nicoll's pride and joy, proof that small is not only beautiful but also highly effective. It couldn't be simpler: one room of a terraced house with a minuscule kitchen, trompe l'oeil mirrors, a few tables and a weekly blackboard menu. Lunches are straightforward – pork and spinach terrine, fishcakes, crème brûlée – but the kitchen rolls up its sleeves for more ambitious culinary adventures in the evening. Glamis asparagus and pea tart with pea shoots might set the scene for a warm salad of seared wild sea bass and dived scallops with sauce vierge, or a fillet of prime Angus beef with caponata and red wine jus. After that, perhaps a trio of apple desserts. The highly seasonal, unpretentious food is backed by a sharp 20-bin wine list, priced from £13.75 (£3.50 a glass).

Chef/s: Shona Drysdale. **Open:** Fri L 12 to 2, Wed to Sat D 6.30 to 9.30. **Closed:** Sun to Tue, 1 week spring, 1 week Sept. **Meals:** alc (main courses £14 to £18). Set L £13.50 (2 courses) to £15.75. **Service:** not inc. **Details:** Cards accepted. 18 seats. No mobile phones. Wheelchair access. Music. Children allowed.

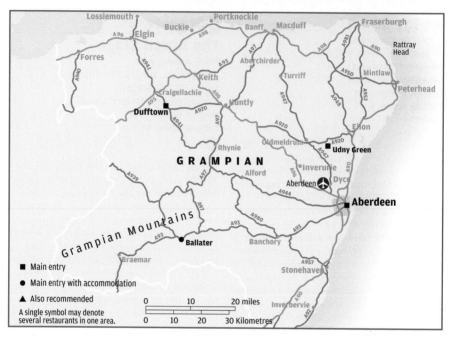

Aberdeen

Silver Darling

Fish-loving harbourside heavyweight
Pocra Quay, North Pier, Aberdeen, AB11 5DQ
Tel no: (01224) 576229
www.thesilverdarling.co.uk
Seafood | £40
Cooking score: 6

It would be hard for any restaurant to get much closer to the source of its supplies than the Silver Darling, which stands at the harbour entrance, its rooftop restaurant affording commanding views of the Aberdeen waterfront. Didier Dejean has been at the helm since 1986 and is justly proud of his commitment to quality Scottish produce, particularly seafood. Lunchtime provides a gentle, set-price limber-up in the shape of tuna and scallop tartare with rocket, Parmesan shavings and a balsamic and hazelnut vinaigrette, and fillet of lemon sole with clams, mussels, seaweed risotto and bisque velouté, but the kitchen pulls out all the stops come dinner. Start with a shellfish gratinée topped with brioche, parsley and garlic crust or confit duck tempura with shiitake mushrooms, coriander and a sweet-and-sour ponzu sauce. Next comes sea bream with a chickpea and fennel croquette, marinated grilled courgettes, herb salad and basil confit garlic dressing, and to finish, steamed carrot and coconut cake with tonka bean ice cream and a carrot and orange sauce. Reports suggest service is hardly sharp enough to warrant the service charge. Wines are predominantly French, with bottles from £21.
Chef/s: Didier Dejean. **Open:** Mon to Fri L 12 to 1.30, Mon to Sat D 6.30 to 8.30 (9 Fri and Sat). **Closed:** Sun, 2 weeks Christmas and New Year. **Meals:** alc (main courses £20 to £22). Set L £15.50 (2 courses) to £19.50. **Service:** 10%. **Details:** Cards accepted. 50 seats. No mobile phones. Wheelchair access. Music. Children allowed. Car parking.

Ballater

Darroch Learg

Bastion of Scottish family hospitality
Braemar Road, Ballater, AB35 5UX
Tel no: (013397) 55443
www.darrochlearg.co.uk
Modern British | £45
Cooking score: 5

Students of Gaelic will know that 'darroch learg' translates as 'the oak wood on the sunny hillside'; it's a romantic prospect that has paid huge dividends for the Franks family over the last 50 years. Since taking over in 1961, they have transformed this Victorian country retreat into a bastion of Scottish family hospitality on fashionable Deeside – although recent reports suggest that standards are starting to slip. Chef David Mutter is a relative new boy, with only 15 years under his belt, but visitors are completely *au fait* with his refined approach to country house cuisine. His daily menus take their cue from the Scottish larder, offering wood pigeon en croûte with shallot and mushroom jam, loin of Glen Muick venison with a pithiviers of boudin, creamed celeriac and red cabbage, and braised local brisket with Vichy carrots, coriander and watercress. He also looks to Scotland's waters for supplies of seafood (grilled fillet of halibut served with butter beans and a smoked haddock chowder, say) and plunders the classics for desserts such as lemon tart, dark chocolate cake or creamed rice pudding with Agen prunes. The Franks' aristocratic, 200-bin wine list was being updated as we went to press, but drinkers can expect a broad global range plus an excellent choice of half-bottles. Prices start at £23.
Chef/s: David Mutter. **Open:** Sun L 12.30 to 2, all week D 7 to 9. **Closed:** 1 week Christmas, last 3 weeks Jan. **Meals:** Set D £35 to £45 (3 courses). Tasting menu £55. Sun L £24 (3 courses). **Service:** not inc. **Details:** Cards accepted. 48 seats. No music. Wheelchair access. Music. Children allowed. Car parking.

The Green Inn

Tantalising restaurant-with-rooms
9 Victoria Road, Ballater, AB35 5QQ
Tel no: (013397) 55701
www.green-inn.com
Modern British | £41
Cooking score: 4

The O'Hallorans' restaurant-with-rooms in the heart of Ballater makes a big impression on those who stop by here. Tartan carpets in both conservatory and main dining room (which also has a throbbing-red colour scheme) tantalise the eye, and Chris O'Halloran's cooking does the same for the palate. The food is built on a bedrock of local ingredients, and is always 'interesting and intelligent', according to one reporter, with portions that are sensibly balanced, 'neither minute and prissy, nor huge and Scottish'. That applies as much to main courses such as wild sea bass with lobster noodles and pak choi, or rack of lamb with roasted garlic purée, dauphinoise and roasting juices as it does to starters like oxtail cannelloni with creamed celeriac and horseradish foam. Desserts worth waiting for may include Calvados soufflé with cider sabayon and apple sorbet. Service is characterised as 'lovely – helpful, but not too much'. An efficiently global wine selection opens at £19.95.
Chef/s: Chris O'Halloran. **Open:** Tue to Sat D only 7 to 9. **Closed:** Sun, Mon, 2 weeks Jan, 2 weeks Nov. **Meals:** Set D £33.50 (2 courses) to £40.50. **Service:** not inc. **Details:** Cards accepted. 26 seats. Separate bar. No mobile phones. Wheelchair access. Music. Children allowed.

Please send us your feedback

To register your opinion about any restaurant listed in the Guide, or a new restaurant that you wish to bring to our attention, please visit the web address at the bottom of the page. Your feedback informs the content of the book and will be used to compile next year's reviews.

Dufftown

La Faisanderie

Crowd-pleasing French cooking
2 Balvenie Street, Dufftown, AB55 4AD
Tel no: (01340) 821273
French | £32
Cooking score: 3

Reliable French cooking and a relaxed atmosphere proves a crowd-pleasing combination at Eric Obry's modest bistro-style restaurant on Dufftown's main square. A seafood platter (smoked salmon and mackerel pâté roulade, salted cod brandade, marinated scallop and langoustine parcel) or grilled pepper and oxtail terrine, for instance, may be followed by a choice of five main courses ranging from pork fillet with creamed Savoy cabbage, Pommery mustard and pancetta crisps to venison with beetroot purée, horn of plenty mushrooms and juniper cream sauce. Simple desserts include apple tarte Tatin with ginger ice cream and toffee sauce and there's always a Scottish and French cheeseboard. The good-value wine list opens at £12.90. Opening times may vary in winter.
Chef/s: Eric Obry. **Open:** all week L 12 to 1.30, D 6 to 8.30 (summer). **Meals:** alc (main courses £18 to £21). Set L £14.95 (2 courses) to £17.50. Set D £32. **Service:** not inc. **Details:** Cards accepted. 30 seats. Wheelchair access. Music. Children allowed.

Udny Green

Eat on the Green

Unhurried vibes and sound cooking
Udny Green, AB41 7RS
Tel no: (01651) 842337
www.eatonthegreen.co.uk
Modern European | £38
Cooking score: 2

£5 OFF

'Unhurried atmosphere in lovely Scottish village', is one reporter's epigrammatic view of this converted neighbourhood inn overlooking the green. The dining room occupies what was the on-site local post office, and chef/proprietor Craig Wilson is generally on hand to oversee matters. The kitchen's approach is to perk up interest using excellent raw materials and menus play to a fairly safe modern European tune – although 'exceptional signature dishes' have also been applauded. Start with marinated sea bass with rocket salad and lemon crème fraîche, go on to loin of lamb served with pomme purée, Puy lentils, confit shallots, braised salsify, crispy pancetta and lamb jus, and finish with honey-roast pear mille-feuille with pear purée. Wines from £14.
Chef/s: Craig Wilson. **Open:** Wed to Fri and Sun L 12 to 1.45 (2 Sun), Wed to Sun D 6 to 9 (5.30 to 10 Sat). **Closed:** Mon and Tue. **Meals:** alc (main courses £19 to £25). Set L £18.95 (2 courses) to £21.95. Sun L £22.95 (2 courses) to £27.95. **Service:** not inc. **Details:** Cards accepted. 70 seats. Air-con. Music. Car parking.

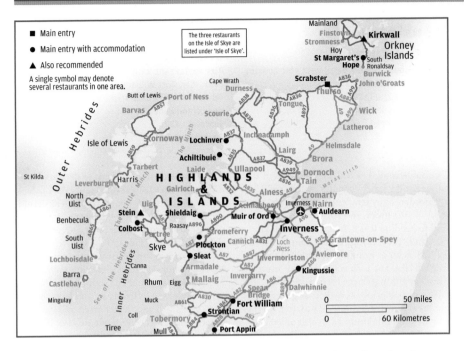

▌ Achiltibuie

Summer Isles Hotel

Magical Highland refuge
Achiltibuie, IV26 2YG
Tel no: (01854) 622282
www.summerisleshotel.com
Modern European | £56
Cooking score: 4

Summer Isles has lost none of its magic since
changing hands in 2008. The views and the
sunsets are as breathtaking as ever, home-
grown produce and freshly caught fish still
define the food, and long-serving chef Chris
Firth-Bernard continues to make a virtue of
simplicity. Light lunches are built around the
seafood harvest, but the kitchen saves its best
shots for fully blown five-course dinners. On
an April evening, you might begin with a
delicate mousse of hand-dived scallops served
with home-baked fennel and raisin bread;
next, grilled breast of quail on wilted spinach
with mushroom purée could precede Ullapool
turbot accompanied by saffron-tinged
steamed mussels. After that, a laden sweet
trolley appears, before exemplary Scottish
cheeses. Each night, guests are offered cherry-
picked wines by the glass from Summer Isles'
fabulous cellar. The full list runs to some 400
bins, with prime pickings from the French
regions and countries as diverse as Switzerland
and Argentina. Prices start at £18.
Chef/s: Chris Firth-Bernard. **Open:** all week L 12.30
to 2, D 8 (1 sitting). **Closed:** 1 Nov to 1 Apr.
Meals: Set L £30 (2 courses). Set D £56 (5 courses).
Service: not inc. **Details:** Cards accepted. 34 seats.
Separate bar. No music. No mobile phones.
Wheelchair access. Children allowed. Car parking.

Please send us your feedback

To register your opinion about any
restaurant listed in the Guide, or a new
restaurant that you wish to bring to our
attention, please visit the web address at
the bottom of the page. Your feedback
informs the content of the book and will be
used to compile next year's reviews.

▌Auldearn

Boath House

Distinguished country hotel with chic cooking
Auldearn, IV12 5TE
Tel no: (01667) 454896
www.boath-house.com
Modern European | £65
Cooking score: 5

☵ **V**

The bow-fronted Georgian house was in rather a sorry state when the Mathesons acquired it. They set about restoring the place to its former glory, and employed a talented chef to head up its kitchen. It's now one of Scotland's most distinguished country hotels, with 20 acres of grounds, including a trout-stocked lake, and a dining room that surveys the scene through large French windows. Charles Lockley cooks daily changing set menus at lunch and dinner. The latter is a six-course deal built around a wealth of local ingredients, in a style that owes more than you may be expecting to urban chic. Begin with celeriac soup with a float of curry oil, before an intermediate serving of rabbit with accompaniments of lentils, bacon and pear. Fish is up next, perhaps mackerel in the piquant company of cauliflower, capers and chickweed, while main-course meat could be a blade of rose veal from Peelham Farm, garnished with morels and salsify. Then, after a plate of British and Irish cheeses, comes the finishing line, in the happily nostalgic form of rhubarb with custard and jelly. The wine list does an efficient job sourcing good producers in western Europe and the southern hemisphere, opening with house selections from £21 (£6.50 a glass).
Chef/s: Charlie Lockley. **Open:** all week L 12.30 to 1.15, D 7.30 (1 sitting). **Meals:** Set L £21 (2 courses) to £28.50. Set D £65 (6 courses). **Service:** not inc. **Details:** Cards accepted. 26 seats. 8 seats outside. Separate bar. No music. No mobile phones. Wheelchair access. Children allowed. Car parking.

▌Fort William

Crannog

Pier restaurant with top-quality seafood
Town Pier, Fort William, PH33 6DB
Tel no: (01397) 705589
www.crannog.net
Seafood | £27
Cooking score: 2
£30

Reporters are often hard put to decide which is the more spectacular, the view over Loch Linnhe or the food, but all agree there should be 'more restaurants like this in the Highlands, please'. Crannog is housed in a converted bait shed on the town pier and the owner runs a fishing boat, so top-quality seafood is the starting point on a daily changing menu that may include sea trout en croûte with samphire salad and lemon hollandaise, and hake served with a shellfish and fennel broth and sweet potato fondant. There's applause, too, for mussels and dhal fritters, salmon en croûte and ribeye steak. House wine is £15.45.
Chef/s: Stewart MacLachlan. **Open:** all week L 12 to 2, D 6.30 to 9.30. **Closed:** 25 Dec, 1 Jan. **Meals:** alc (main courses £13 to £20). Set L £9.95 (2 courses). **Service:** not inc. **Details:** Cards accepted. 60 seats. Separate bar. Wheelchair access. Music. Children allowed. Car parking.

Inverlochy Castle

Turbo-boosted, tour de force cooking
Torlundy, Fort William, PH33 6SN
Tel no: (01397) 702177
www.inverlochycastlehotel.co.uk
Modern British | £65
Cooking score: 6

☵

Inverlochy is a colossal study in Scottish magnificence, built by a big-thinking peer of the realm in the Victorian era. Victoria herself approved: the place inspired her to take up her watercolour brush. The magnificence hasn't in the least been dimmed by time, with chandeliers, oil paintings and layers of fabric gilding the lily within. The views from the dining room over the well-stocked lake to the hills beyond are breathtaking as the sun goes down. Philip Carnegie knows more than a little about taking the breath away himself. Arriving in 2009, he gave the already inventive cooking a turbo-boost, with the result that, on a good day, the performance is nothing short of a *tour de force*. Eclectic thinking might yield a starter of char-grilled tuna with lemon couscous, chorizo, spring onions and pak choi, followed by soup, perhaps Jerusalem artichoke and salsify velouté. Mains tend to be more classically oriented, as in leg of rabbit with white beans in grain mustard sauce, or Gressingham duck breast with spiced lentils and foie gras. Daring flourishes continue with the desserts, as when hazelnut pannacotta turns up with date cake and Cassis-soaked figs. The formal atmosphere (jacket-and-tie order, please) is reflected by a luxurious wine list, from £35.

Chef/s: Philip Carnegie. **Open:** all week L 12.30 to 1.35, D 6 to 10. **Meals:** Set L £28 (2 courses) to £35. Set D £65. **Service:** not inc. **Details:** Cards accepted. 45 seats. Separate bar. No mobile phones. Wheelchair access. Music. Children allowed. Car parking.

ALSO RECOMMENDED

▲ Lochleven Seafood Café
Onich, Fort William, PH33 6SA
Tel no: (01855) 821048
www.lochlevenseafoodcafe.co.uk
Seafood

The draw is outstanding locally caught seafood at this bustling, informal café and shop on the shores of Loch Leven. Straightforward treatments have included razor clams with white wine, lemon and olive oil (£7.25), roasted scallops with ginger, soy and sesame (£15.90) and a superb platter of hot-roasted shellfish with aïoli for two (£78.50). For those who don't feel like fish there's braised lamb with butter beans and summer vegetable broth. Finish with elderflower jelly with berry soup and fruit smoothie. House wine £14.25. Open all week. Opening times may vary in winter.

▌ Grantown-on-Spey

Culdearn House
Modern British
Woodlands Terrace, Grantown-on-Spey, PH26 3JU
Tel no: (01479) 872106
www.culdearn.com
'The cooking was excellent and imaginative... using good wholesome local foods'

▌ Inverness

Abstract at Glenmoriston Town House
Swanky dining with bells and whistles
20 Ness Bank, Inverness, IV2 4SF
Tel no: (01463) 223777
www.abstractrestaurant.com
Modern French | £50
Cooking score: 5

As the posh dining option at one of the town's smartest hotels, Abstract rises to the occasion with a swanky modern-retro interior (all reds and browns and polished wood) and slick French staff. It's a lovely spot, with river views and outdoor seating for sunny days. The cooking here is full of voguish bells and whistles, so expect savoury ice creams, micro-herbs, jellies and foams aplenty. Crucially, though, the kitchen never loses its grip on the basic tenets of taste and texture; nothing jars here, with sensible flavour combinations throughout. A pre-starter of cauliflower velouté with mealie pudding set the tone for a meal that gave more than a passing nod to Scotland's wonderful native ingredients. Not that this rule becomes restrictive: take a starter of pata negra ham, for instance, served with celeriac rémoulade, truffle dressing and sweetcorn sorbet. Slow-cooked loin of Highland venison with creamy spelt, jellied balsamic, quince purée, textured beetroot and peanut butter foam made a patriotic main course, while a dessert of mango rice pudding with passion-fruit sorbet brought things to a refreshing but comforting close. The extensive wine list covers France by region then strikes out to the New World. Prices start at £21 a bottle.

Chef/s: Geoff Malmedy. **Open:** Tue to Sat D only 6 to 10. **Closed:** Sun, Mon. **Meals:** alc (main courses £20 to £28). Tasting menu £55. **Service:** not inc. **Details:** Cards accepted. 40 seats. 20 seats outside. Air-con. Separate bar. Wheelchair access. Music. Children allowed. Car parking.

Rocpool

Fizzy riverside brasserie
1 Ness Walk, Inverness, IV3 5NE
Tel no: (01463) 717274
www.rocpoolrestaurant.com
Modern European | £30
Cooking score: 2

£5
OFF

Not to be confused with the nearby Rocpool Reserve Hotel, this fizzy brasserie by the banks of the river Ness is shot through with metropolitan adrenalin. The kitchen adds some global zing to Scottish ingredients, matching roast monkfish and steamed cockles with spiced coriander couscous, serving poached halibut with crab risotto and brightening up rare beef salad with a chilli-spiked tomato relish. Elsewhere, lamb cutlets are given an Asian edge with Bombay potatoes and curry vinaigrette, venison is paired with black pudding and wild mushrooms, and desserts bring on hot lemon meringue pie or white chocolate and coconut cheesecake. A short, upbeat wine list kicks off at £15.95.
Chef/s: Steven Devlin. **Open:** Mon to Sat L 12 to 2.30, all week D 5.45 to 10. **Closed:** Sun from Oct to Apr, 25 and 26 Dec, 1 and 2 Jan. **Meals:** alc (main courses £9 to £21). Set L £10.95 (2 courses). Early set D £12.95 (2 courses). **Service:** not inc. **Details:** Cards accepted. 60 seats. Air-con. No mobile phones. Wheelchair access. Music. Children allowed.

Average price

The average price listed in main-entry reviews denotes the price of a three-course meal, without wine.

Isle of Harris

READERS RECOMMEND

Anchorage Restaurant

Seafood
The Pier, Leverburgh, Isle of Harris, HS5 3UB
Tel no: (01859) 520225
'Oysters, lobsters, scallops – you name it!'

Scarista House

Modern British
Sgarasta Bheag, Isle of Harris, HS3 3HX
Tel no: (01859) 550238
www.scaristahouse.com
'Organic, local, homegrown – with a set menu changed daily'

Isle of Lewis

READERS RECOMMEND

Digby Chick

Modern British
5 Bank Street, Stornoway, Isle of Lewis, HS1 2XG
Tel no: (01851) 700026
'An unlikely place to find a good restaurant...seafood is the reason for going and the food appears to be locally sourced as much as possible'

Isle of Skye

NEW ENTRY

Kinloch Lodge

Creative cooking and dreamy views
Sleat, Isle of Skye, IV43 8QY
Tel no: (01471) 833214
www.kinloch-lodge.co.uk
Modern European | £55
Cooking score: 5

The family seat of Lord and Lady Macdonald, this centuries-old clan lodge is blessed with dreamy views over Loch na Dal and elemental Highland vistas. Inside, it feels like a family home, with ancestral portraits lining the walls, log fires blazing and service that runs smoothly 'in a low-key, "islands" kind of way'. The kitchen is fronted by Brazilian chef

Marcello Tully, who has given the food a creative shot in the arm. Meals begin with a frothy '*soupçon*' such as celeriac and Achmore Blue cheese or parsnip and Pernod; next, get your vintage cutlery to work on a stunning plate of roast monkfish with melting Moray pork cheeks, crisp belly and passion-fruit jus, before tackling 'Marcello's special' – a tiny taste of steamed organic salmon paired with caramelised banana, say. Centrepiece dishes bring the regional larder into sharp focus with the likes of Mallaig hake partnered by deep-fried red pepper gnocchi and saffron-tinged mussels, or Isle of Muck wild duck with butternut squash, Highland 'burgundy' potatoes and caramelised orange sauce. A pre-dessert heralds the final act, which offers temptation in the form of passion-fruit parfait with bay leaf ice cream or a 'proper' cheese course involving, say, Strathdon Blue with prune and orange mousse, Perthshire honey jellies, cinnamon syrup and poached pears. Each dish comes with the option of something appropriately boozy – choose from malt whisky, beer or a wine flight – and the full list has a broad span with prices from £22 a bottle (£6 a glass).

Chef/s: Marcello Tully. **Open:** all week L 12.30 to 2.30, D 6.30 to 9. **Closed:** 24 to 26 Dec. **Meals:** Set L £24.95 (2 courses) to £27.95. Set D £52 to £55. **Service:** not inc. **Details:** Cards accepted. 40 seats. Separate bar. Wheelchair access. Music. Children allowed. Car parking.

The Three Chimneys
A memorable prospect
Colbost, Isle of Skye, IV55 8ZT
Tel no: (01470) 511258
www.threechimneys.co.uk
Modern British | £55
Cooking score: 5

🍷 🍴

Any visit to the Three Chimneys is bound to be memorable, not least for the remote location, peaceful setting and spectacular views. For 27 years, Shirley and Eddie Spear have held on to the belief that a restaurant should reflect its surroundings, use local and

regional produce and thus respond to the seasons. This gives food its identity, which means seafood is paramount here. John Dory from Mallaig served with crisp rösti, confit fennel, pepper dulce and cockles or Loch Dunvegan langoustines, Colbost Bay crabs and Loch Harport oysters served as a platter of fruits de mer with Glendale mesclun are typical of chef Michael Smith's output. Praise has been registered for west coast monkfish teamed with sea bass and squid with saffron potatoes, carrots, winkle and sorrel butter. Seafood is balanced on the well-constructed menu by roast saddle and Wellington of wild rabbit and hare, with perhaps a starter of winter Russian salad. For dessert, hot marmalade pudding with Drambuie custard is an old favourite. The impressive wine list leans towards France, but when it tilts over to the New World it is perfectly sound. Half-bottles are plentiful, there's good choice by the glass and bottles open at £25.

Chef/s: Michael Smith. **Open:** Mon to Sat L 12.15 to 1.45, all week D 6.15 to 9.45. **Closed:** L Nov to Mar, Jan, first week Feb. **Meals:** Set L £27.50 (2 courses) to £35. Set D £55. Tasting menu £80. **Service:** not inc. **Details:** Cards accepted. 40 seats. 8 seats outside. Separate bar. No music. No mobile phones. Wheelchair access. Car parking.

ALSO RECOMMENDED
▲ Loch Bay
1-2 Macleod Terrace, Stein, Isle of Skye, IV55 8GA
Tel no: (01470) 592235
www.lochbay-seafood-restaurant.co.uk
Seafood

Spanking fresh fish is what to expect at this miniscule terraced restaurant located not 10 yards from the pier in the fishing village of Stein. A regular menu of fish soup (£4.95), organic salmon and various crustacea is bolstered by a daily specials board depending on the catch, say whole sea bass or black bream with olive oil and citrus juices (£13.50). Homely sweets include clootie dumpling. Wines from £14.85. Open Tue to Fri, Easter to mid Oct.

▌Kingussie

The Cross

Old mill with great food and service
Ardbroilach Road, Kingussie, PH21 1LB
Tel no: (01540) 661166
www.thecross.co.uk
Modern British | £50
Cooking score: 5

🍷 🛏

'Good cooking and very friendly service',
noted one visitor to David and Katie Young's
converted tweed mill by a rippling stream.
'Some of the best food we have eaten', admits
another. This is an establishment where
unobtrusive professionalism and hard work
count for a great deal. Dinner is a tried-and-
trusted formula of four courses with a couple
of choices at each stage. One such meal
included a miniature salmon fishcake with
cucumber salsa, a terrine of organic chicken
breast with truffle and prosciutto and spiced
fig chutney, and roast breast of local pheasant
with a bonbon of the leg, quince purée, soured
cabbage and rösti potatoes. On another night,
the plaudits might go to Jerusalem artichoke
soup, then loin slow-roast belly and braised
cheek of Middle White pork with caramelised
walnuts and dates, a 'gratin' of cavolo nero and
sweet potato purée, followed by chocolate
brownie with salted pistachio ice cream. This
cooking shows finesse, depth of flavour and
startling freshness. Fish – for instance, wild
sea bass with honey and mustard dressing,
marsh samphire, orange and beetroot and ratte
potatoes – benefits from this quality. The long
wine list is as wonderful as ever and works its
magic at all price levels. Organisation is by
grape variety or style, whichever suits, and the
choice includes organic and biodynamic wines
with detailed notes. Bottles from £22.
Chef/s: David Young and Becca Henderson. **Open:**
Tue to Sat D only 7 to 9. **Closed:** Sun, Mon,
Christmas, 3 weeks Jan, 1 week Oct. **Meals:** Set D
£50 (4 courses). **Service:** not inc. **Details:** Cards
accepted. 24 seats. No music. No mobile phones.
Wheelchair access. Car parking.

▌Kirkwall, Orkney

ALSO RECOMMENDED
▲ Dil Se

7 Bridge Street, Kirkwall, Orkney, KW15 1HR
Tel no: (01856) 875242
www.dilserestaurant.co.uk
Indian

The sumptuous red interiors of Dil Se, the
most northerly Indian/Bangladeshi restaurant
in the British Isles, are a welcoming haven
amid the bracing climate of Orkney. Local
supplies are celebrated in carefully prepared
classic dishes such as sheek kebab with mint
dip (£5.95), prawn bhuna puri (£4.95), and
the scoop of locally made ice cream that comes
with gulab jamun (£5.95). Otherwise, all
your favourite and familiar main courses are
here, from rogan josh to vindaloo. Wines from
£11.95. Open all week from 4pm.

▌Lochinver

Albannach

Stellar chill-out with impeccable cooking
Baddidarroch, Lochinver, IV27 4LP
Tel no: (01571) 844407
www.thealbannach.co.uk
Modern British | £55
Cooking score: 6

🍷 🛏

Albannach stands in splendid isolation – a tall
white beacon on the wild and windy moors
overlooking Lochinver. Since 1990, it has been
house and home to Colin Craig and Lesley
Crosfield as well as a chill-out *par excellence* for
visitors wanting to get away from it all. The
setting is pure magic, but Albannach's real
trump card is its food: the owners have never
wavered in their dedication to all things local,
wild and free-range, and guests are treated to a
procession of impeccably crafted dishes noted
for their limpid, natural flavours. On a lazy
August night, you might commence with a
ragoût of langoustines scented with ginger,
before a little dish of guinea fowl breast with
'croft' chard, roast red Grelot onion and a sauce
of locally foraged chanterelles. As a leisurely

centrepiece there might be roast wild turbot accompanied by a harvest festival of braised fennel, black potatoes and white asparagus with red wine sauce; then it's on to cheeses (smoked Irish Gubbeen or French Langres, say) and, finally, dessert – perhaps caramelised apple tart with apple crisp, apple and Calvados 'gelato'. At the back end of the year, other flavours emerge – wild mushroom risotto or Morayshire beef fillet with heritage root vegetable parcels and thyme mash, for example. Colin Craig's endlessly fascinating, deeply personal wine list has a French bias, but includes page after page of glorious stuff from elsewhere. Bottle prices start at £16 and there's always plenty of fine drinking by the glass. Note that meals are for residents only on Mondays.

Chef/s: Colin Craig and Lesley Crosfield. **Open:** all week D only 7.30 for 8 (1 sitting only). **Closed:** 3 Jan to 10 Mar, Mon to Wed in Nov and Dec (exc 2 weeks Christmas). **Meals:** Set D £55 (5 courses). **Service:** not inc. **Details:** Cards accepted. 20 seats. No music. No mobile phones. Car parking.

▌Muir of Ord

The Dower House
Homely Highland hideaway
Highfield, Muir of Ord, IV6 7XN
Tel no: (01463) 870090
www.thedowerhouse.co.uk
Modern British | £42
Cooking score: 2

🛏

Robyn and Mena Aitchison have been running this early-Victorian 'cottage orné' as a homely Highland hideaway for more than two decades, and are justly proud of their reputation for personable bonhomie, politesse and simply rendered seasonal food. Dinner revolves around a short menu comprising three courses followed by coffee and Scottish tablet. On a typical evening you might open with warm sea trout salad with tomato and basil vinaigrette, move on to loin of local lamb with crab and dill sauce, and round things off with continental lemon tart and raspberry

sauce. House French is £18, and there are some fine drams waiting to be sampled in the hotel's 'malt cupboard'.

Chef/s: Robyn Aitchison. **Open:** all week D only 7.30 (1 sitting). **Closed:** 2 weeks Nov, 25 Dec. **Meals:** Set D £42. **Service:** not inc. **Details:** Cards accepted. 16 seats. 4 seats outside. No music. No mobile phones. Wheelchair access. Children allowed. Car parking.

▌Plockton

Plockton Inn
Straight-up seafood that speaks for itself
Innes Street, Plockton, IV52 8TW
Tel no: (01599) 544222
www.plocktoninn.co.uk
Seafood | £23
Cooking score: 2

🛏 V £30

Not to be confused with the nearby Plockton Hotel, this amenable pub-with-rooms is situated at the top of the hill by the church. If the sun is shining, grab one of the tables out on the terrace; otherwise stake your claim in the traditional bar or dining room. The barman provides the kitchen with creel-caught Loch Carron prawns from his own boat and the pub's smokehouse produces all manner of goodies for the renowned seafood platters. A few meat and veggie options are also on show, and you can round things off with sticky toffee pudding. There's nothing fancy here, but the food is as fresh as can be. Wash it all down with a pint of Plockton Bay ale or a glass of wine (from £3.50).

Chef/s: Mary Gollan and Susan Trowbridge. **Open:** all week L 12 to 2.15, D 6 to 9. **Closed:** 25 Dec. **Meals:** alc (main courses £9 to £18). **Service:** not inc. **Details:** Cards accepted. 50 seats. 16 seats outside. Separate bar. Wheelchair access. Music. Children allowed. Car parking.

Port Appin

Airds Hotel

Smart, intimate hotel with local food
Port Appin, PA38 4DF
Tel no: (01631) 730236
www.airds-hotel.com
Modern British | £50
Cooking score: 5

Port Appin lies on the Argyll coast between
Oban and Fort William, and this pretty,
white-fronted inn once served the ferries
crossing Loch Linnhe. It's a hauntingly
beautiful setting for a well-run country hotel,
which is all designer fabrics and comfy sofas.
A long, low-ceilinged room with sumptuous
views over the loch is the setting for Paul
Burns' confident modern cooking. Excellent
raw materials are handled with sensitivity and
flair, and locally caught fish (usually
outnumbering meats two-to-one at main
course) is a particular draw. Turbot might
appear with sautéed spinach and mussels in a
sauce spiked with coriander, or there could be
fine wild salmon alongside braised fennel and
a citrus beurre blanc. Crab, lobster and
langoustine also turn up regularly, but if
you're in a meatier mood, dishes like honey-
roast breast of Gressingham duck with rösti
and deep-fried sage might tempt. Desserts
often try out new tricks, as when warm
pineapple is served with a sauce of Kahlùa,
green peppercorns and orange, or you might
opt for an old favourite such as date pudding
with butterscotch sauce. The wine list is one to
treasure. It opens with eight well-chosen
house selections from £18, and goes on to
explore all the premier regions in depth, with
Australia and New Zealand showing as much
care as France.
Chef/s: Paul Burns. **Open:** all week L 12 to 1.45, D
7.30 to 9.30. **Closed:** 2 days each week Nov to Jan.
Meals: Set L £17.95 (2 courses) to £22.95. Set D
£49.50 (4 courses). Sun L £21.95. **Service:** not inc.
Details: Cards accepted. 32 seats. Separate bar. No
music. No mobile phones. Wheelchair access.
Children allowed. Car parking.

St Margaret's Hope, Orkney

The Creel

Stunning local produce, perfectly cooked
Front Road, St Margaret's Hope, Orkney,
KW17 2SL
Tel no: (01856) 831311
www.thecreel.co.uk
Modern British | £38
Cooking score: 7

'A more counter-intuitive restaurant is hard to
imagine in remote St Margaret's Hope',
observed a regular visitor to this spellbinding
oasis overlooking the bay. Alan and Joyce
Craigie have been in residence for 25 years and
there is something irresistibly appealing about
their approach to hospitality and cooking –
no wonder they continue to play to full
houses. Being Orcadians, they know exactly
what to do with seafood from the local boats,
meat reared on their home pastures or plants
pulled from their native soil. The results on the
plate have a shimmering freshness and
simplicity: what could be more harmonious
than a starter of perfectly timed and
beautifully presented queen scallops dressed
with parsley and lemon butter, or a mound of
crabmeat – white over brown – matched with
stunning apple mayonnaise, a dinky fresh-
tasting salad and tiny slices of marinated
cucumber? Alan's miraculously
unembellished seafood cookery also has an
earthier side that shows itself in, say, a dish of
full-flavoured hake fillet partnered by a squid
and brown lentil casserole, and he applies the
same principles to meat – serving slow-
cooked, seaweed-fed North Ronaldsay
mutton with braised carrots and barley, for
instance. Orkney raspberries and strawberries
step into the seasonal spotlight for dessert, and
there are home-baked bannocks to accompany
fine cheeses. Guests have also approved of
Alan's breakfast kippers, smoked over shavings
from an Orkney chair-maker. The short, well-
annotated wine list promises consistency and
value across the range. Prices start at £16.

Chef/s: Alan Craigie. **Open:** Tue to Sun D only 7 to 9. **Closed:** Mon, mid-Oct to April. **Meals:** Set D £32 (2 courses) to £38. **Service:** not inc. **Details:** Cards accepted. 30 seats. No music. No mobile phones. Wheelchair access. Children allowed. Car parking.

▋ Scrabster
The Captain's Galley
Sustainable seafood by the harbour
The Harbour, Scrabster, KW14 7UJ
Tel no: (01847) 894999
www.captainsgalley.co.uk
Seafood | £45
Cooking score: 3

The Cowies can feel justly pleased with themselves at their restoration of the barrel-vaulted, early nineteenth-century building that was once an ice house and salmon bothy. The bounty of the sea – sustainable bounty, that is – is the focus of Jim's fixed-price dinner menus. Steamed mussels with lemongrass, chilli and coconut is a good opener that might be followed by an intermediate dish of grilled oysters or butterflied langoustine tails with herb salad. Mains could offer megrim, fried on the bone and served with spring greens and tarragon butter or, for the meatily inclined, Caithness roe deer with roasted roots and elderberry game jus. Finish with ginger crème brûlée, served with cherry compote and sweet-salty pistachio praline, or Highland cheeses. House wines from Valencia are £14.75.
Chef/s: Jim Cowie. **Open:** Tue to Sat D only 7 to 9. **Closed:** Sun, Mon, 25 and 26 Dec, 1 to 3 Jan. **Meals:** Set D £35 (2 courses) to £44.50. **Service:** not inc. **Details:** Cards accepted. 25 seats. Separate bar. Wheelchair access. Music. Children allowed. Car parking.

▋ Shieldaig
Tigh an Eilean Hotel
Homespun hospitality
Shieldaig, IV54 8XN
Tel no: (01520) 755251
www.tighaneilean.co.uk
Modern British | £45
Cooking score: 3

£5 OFF 🍽

Christopher and Cathryn Field have imbued their 'house by the island' with a mood of domestic intimacy and homespun hospitality, making Tigh an Eilean an enchanting refuge on Scotland's rugged west coast. Chris taps into the regional larder for cooking that highlights locally landed fish, game from the moors and naturally reared meat: the result is a daily changing dinner menu that might take in grilled langoustines with truffled-scented pea risotto, juniper-crusted saddle of venison, and roast fillet of beef with roasted shallots and morels. To conclude, cheeses from Scotland and Spain are alternatives to Euro-inspired desserts such as chocolate marquise or tarte Tatin. House wine is £16.50. Alternatively, soak up the views from the adjoining Shieldaig Bar and Coastal Kitchen, which specialises in seafood and wood-fired pizzas (all week 12 to 9pm).
Chef/s: Christopher Field. **Open:** all week D only 7 to 8.30. **Closed:** Nov to Mar. **Meals:** Set D £45. **Service:** not inc. **Details:** Cards accepted. 26 seats. Separate bar. No music. No mobile phones. Wheelchair access. Children allowed. Car parking.

▋ Stromness, Orkney
READERS RECOMMEND
Hamnavoe Restaurant
Modern British
35 Graham Place, Stromness, Orkney, KW16 3BY
Tel no: (01856) 850606
'The best meal, by far, in a week of eating out in Orkney'

▌Strontian

Kilcamb Lodge

Welcoming full-dress country house
Strontian, PH36 4HY
Tel no: (01967) 402257
www.kilcamblodge.co.uk
Modern European | £48
Cooking score: 5

🛏 V

'It's not just the wonderful building in its wonderful location; it's not just the staff with their cheery disposition and great attention to detail; it's not just the delicious food prepared and presented so beautifully, and complemented so well by the many and varied wines on offer; it's a combination of all of these things .... and more, much, much more.' So wrote one satisfied Christmas visitor, giving an indication of the waves of hospitality that flow from Sally and David Ruthven-Fox's full-dress country house with its welcoming fires, comfy sofas and armchairs, beautiful drapes, and vases full of fresh flowers. Elsewhere, Tammo Siemers brings a more contemporary touch to the food. He is a chef with an eye for detail – just consider roasted loin and braised shoulder of venison with spiced Madeira jus (with smoked and pickled beetroot, purée of roasted shallots and boulangère potatoes) and vanilla-steamed fillet of halibut and brown crab dumplings (with confit tomatoes, sautéed artichokes, garlic and potato mousseline and saffron cappuccino). These might be book-ended by scallops with cauliflower tempura, walnut dressing and sautéed caperberries, and desserts including prune and Armagnac soufflé. Wines continue to hit the spot with a wide-ranging selection that punches its weight from France to the New World with prices from £23.95.
Chef/s: Tammo Siemers. **Open:** all week L 12 to 2, D 7.30 to 10. **Closed:** Jan. **Meals:** Set L £14.75. Set D £48. Sun L £12.50. Tasting menu £55 (6 courses). **Service:** not inc. **Details:** Cards accepted. 28 seats. 4 seats outside. Separate bar. No mobile phones. Music. Car parking.

Fashionable ingredients

Just as certain styles of cooking have gone in and out of fashion over the years, individual ingredients, too, have their moments in the sun. These tend to run in shorter cycles, but can often take on such a ubiquitous character that we can be left wondering how we ever managed without them.

Meats are no longer just elemental categories, but come with specific designations: Angus beef, Old Spot pork, English rose veal, Anjou pigeon. Ingredients from other cultures can become rapidly assimilated too – witness the indispensability of chorizo.

The nation's favourite restaurant shellfish, the scallop, has reigned supreme on menus for some years now, teamed not long ago with black pudding, now more often with a vegetable purée.

Vegetables have their moments too. The Jerusalem artichoke, a boon during winter scarcity, has been brought in from the cold. Beetroot has been rescued from the pickle jar, while rhubarb rules the roost from starters through to dessert.

Dessert ingredients are probably the least susceptible to voguishness (notwithstanding the brief tonka bean craze), perhaps because chocolate, toffee and dairy richness never go out of fashion.

The Good Food Guide 2011

WALES

Glamorgan, Gwent, Mid-Wales, North-East Wales, North-West Wales, West Wales

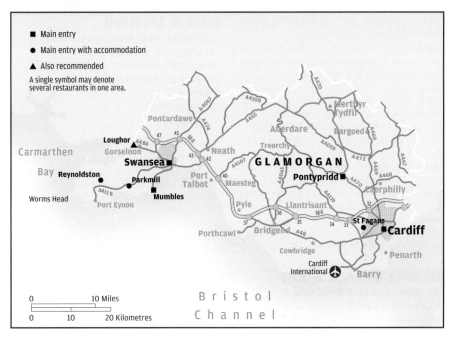

- ■ Main entry
- ● Main entry with accommodation
- ▲ Also recommended

A single symbol may denote several restaurants in one area.

■ Cardiff
Le Gallois
Suave, with seriously stylish food
6-10 Romilly Crescent, Cardiff, CF11 9NR
Tel no: (029) 2034 1264
www.legallois.co.uk
Modern European | £30
Cooking score: 4

A long-standing leader of the Cardiff scene, Le Gallois offers a slick metropolitan take on Gallic cuisine and 'near perfect' service from a French team. Set in a peaceful suburb 10 minutes' walk from the city centre, its chi-chi contemporary style is matched by cooking with serious intent. Here is a kitchen that flirts with the Japanese slow-cooked 'onsen' egg, tweaks Welsh pork with smoked tea sauce, and serves up Rougie foie gras with smoked mackerel, pickled girolles and beetroot glaze. Meanwhile, mainstream offerings can also make the grade, witness a 'stunning' pea and spring vegetable soup ahead of lemon sole, salmon ravioli and razor clams with an

'absolutely beautiful' butter sauce. To finish, perhaps crème caramel with pear cider sorbet and a ginger sablé. The French-accented wine list starts at £16.95.
Chef/s: Grady Atkins. **Open:** Tue to Sat L 12 to 2.30, D 6.30 to 9.30 (10 Fri and Sat). **Closed:** Sun, Mon, 25 Dec to 5 Jan. **Meals:** Set L £20 (2 courses) to £25. Set D £25 (2 courses) to £30. Tasting menu £49. **Service:** 10% (optional). **Details:** Cards accepted. 60 seats. Air-con. Separate bar. Wheelchair access. Music. Children allowed. Car parking.

Garçon Brasserie Française
Bistro flavours and Gallic charm
Mermaid Quay, Cardiff, CF10 5BW
Tel no: (029) 2049 0990
www.garcon-resto.co.uk
French | £20
Cooking score: 1

V £30

Part of the buzzing restaurant scene on Mermaid Quay, Garçon is tucked away up a flight of steps and has views over Cardiff Bay

(there are outdoor tables for sunny days). The Francophile interior convincingly apes a Parisian brasserie and the French staff add to the illusion. The menu follows suit, offering simple classics such as croque-monsieur, salade niçoise or omelettes from the bistro menu (available 12 to 5) and more substantial favourites such as excellent seared foie gras with toasted brioche or tournedos Rossini from the carte. Round it off with tarte Tatin and honey ice cream. Wines from £15.50.
Chef/s: Ross Williams. **Open:** all week 12 to 10 (11 Fri and Sat, 5 Sun). **Closed:** 24 to 26 Dec, 1 Jan. **Meals:** alc (main courses £10 to £50). Set L and D £12.95 (2 courses) to £15.95. Sun L £15.95. **Service:** 10% (optional). **Details:** Cards accepted. 100 seats. 26 seats outside. Air-con. Wheelchair access. Music. Children allowed.

Mimosa Kitchen & Bar

City slicker with good Welsh food
Mermaid Quay, Cardiff, CF10 5BZ
Tel no: (029) 2049 1900
www.mimosakitchen.co.uk
Modern European | £24
Cooking score: 2

V £30

Expect 'straightforward food done well' at Cardiff's self-appointed 'first gastro-bar'. Slate floors and steel surfaces play to the slick city setting, while the menu reminds diners at every course that this is Wales – the land of cockles and laverbread (in this case, cockle fritters with a laverbread sauce), lamb (maybe with dauphinoise potatoes and minted ragoût) and excellent fish – wild turbot, for instance, with asparagus velouté and fresh tagliatelle, or sea bass with rosemary butter sauce and sautéed new potatoes. A nicely balanced wine list starts at £13.95.
Chef/s: Alun Roberts. **Open:** all week 10 to 11 (midnight Fri and Sat, 10.30 Sun). **Closed:** 25 and 26 Dec. **Meals:** alc (main courses £8 to £17). Sun L £13.50 (2 courses) to £15.95. **Service:** not inc. **Details:** Cards accepted. 67 seats. 48 seats outside. Air-con. Separate bar. Wheelchair access. Music. Children allowed. Car parking.

Mint & Mustard

Trailblazing Indian with superb flavours
134 Whitchurch Road, Cardiff, CF14 3LZ
Tel no: (029) 2062 0333
www.mintandmustard.com
Indian | £27
Cooking score: 2

£5 OFF **V** £30

'Superb flavours' and 'unusual dishes' continue to pull the punters at this calm, contemporary Indian restaurant. Chef Anand George trained in Kerala and worked at luxury hotels in Mumbai before heading for the UK. This diverse experience is evident in his cooking, but so is a trailblazing spirit that gives Mint & Mustard a style of its own. Try crispy soft-shell crab dusted with curry leaves and garlic ahead of lamb stew enriched with coconut milk, or (from a superb vegetarian selection) paneer tikka followed by butternut squash and cowpeas in coconut milk gravy. House wine is £14.
Chef/s: Anand George. **Open:** all week D only 6 to 11 (10.30 Sun). **Closed:** 25 and 26 Dec. **Meals:** alc (main courses £6 to £15). Set D £22 (2 courses) to £27. Tasting menu £35. **Service:** not inc. **Details:** Cards accepted. 56 seats. Air-con. Wheelchair access. Music. Children allowed.

Patagonia

South America meets South Wales
11 Kings Road, Cardiff, CF11 9BZ
Tel no: (029) 2019 0265
www.patagonia-restaurant.co.uk
Modern European | £29
Cooking score: 3

£5 OFF £30

Eight years old and still going strong, this smart little restaurant is testament to the power of keeping things small. Owners Joaquin Humaran and Leticia Salina met in a Buenos Aires kitchen then worked all over Europe, eventually landing in Cardiff where they opened Patagonia as a restaurant and coffee shop. The restaurant proved so successful that the coffee shop fell by the wayside, allowing its owners to concentrate on their special brand of eclectic modern cooking. Caramelised scallops with roasted Jerusalem artichokes and hazelnut dressing is typical of their approach, followed perhaps by pork tenderloin and slow-cooked belly pork with honey-roasted parsnip purée and anise jus. Round it off with dulce de leche crème brûlée and caramelised bananas. Wines from a balanced international list start at £13.90. **Chef/s:** Joaquin Humaran. **Open:** Tue to Sat D only 6.30 to 10. **Closed:** Sun, Mon, 24 Dec to 24 Jan. **Meals:** Set D £24.90 (2 courses) to £28.90. **Service:** not inc. **Details:** Cards accepted. 42 seats. Air-con. Wheelchair access. Music. Children allowed.

Woods Brasserie

Local asset with modern menus
The Pilotage Building, Stuart Street, Cardiff, CF10 5BW
Tel no: (029) 2049 2400
www.woods-brasserie.com
Modern European | £30
Cooking score: 2
V

Now into its second decade in the former Pilotage Building, Woods is a long-running asset to the Cardiff Bay scene. Expect a convivial ambience and a short menu that promises colourful modern dishes such as creamed goats' cheese with poached rhubarb, candied walnuts and truffle honey, and slow-cooked lamb rump, shoulder and chorizo pithiviers with Savoy cabbage. Fish-lovers could choose fillet of bream with butterbean and black pudding cassoulet. Desserts include hazelnut tart with ginger biscuit ice cream and bitter chocolate marquise with mint chocolate chip ice cream. House wine is £16. **Chef/s:** Wesley Hammond. **Open:** all week L 12 to 2 (3 Sun), Mon to Sat D 5.30 to 10. **Closed:** 25 and 26 Dec. **Meals:** alc (main courses £11 to £28). Set L £14.50 (2 courses) to £17.50. Sun L £17.95. **Service:** not inc. **Details:** Cards accepted. 100 seats. 30 seats outside. Air-con. Separate bar. Wheelchair access. Music. Children allowed.

Loughor

ALSO RECOMMENDED
▲ **Hurrens Inn on the Estuary**
13 Station Road, Loughor, SA4 6TR
Tel no: (01792) 899092
www.hurrens.co.uk
Modern European

It may look like a little old Welsh pub on a side street, but Hurrens is 'quite a surprise' with its funky contemporary interiors, views of the Loughor estuary and lively, eclectic food. A salad of smoked duck comes with dried cranberries and spiced walnuts (£5.50), seared sea bass is paired with king prawn tempura and celeriac purée (£15.75) and there's local salt marsh lamb too. Desserts might run to lemon posset with grilled figs (£5.95). Wines from £11.95. Closed Sun D and Mon.

Mumbles

NEW ENTRY
The Mermaid
Excellent local food and keen prices
686 Mumbles Road, Mumbles, SA3 4EE
Tel no: (01792) 367744
www.themermaid.co.uk
Modern British | £20
Cooking score: 2
V £30

On the site of the Mermaid Hotel (once a haunt of the poet Dylan Thomas), this stylish modern restaurant looks towards the expansive sweep of Swansea Bay. Keenly priced menus make excellent use of fresh seafood, as well as Gower salt marsh lamb, Welsh black beef and local pork. Chef/proprietor Nick Bevan has a strong following for his inventive cooking style but keeps things safely in the comfort zone, with plenty of classical techniques in evidence. After homemade breads you could try cockle, laverbread and bacon tartlet and then slow-baked Gower pork with homemade pork sausage, roasted loin and a coarse-grain mustard jus. To finish, maybe lemon posset with lemon curd ice cream. Wines start at £12.95.

Chef/s: Nick Bevan. **Open:** all week L 12 to 2.30, D 7 to 9.30. **Closed:** 25 and 26 Dec, 1 Jan. **Meals:** alc (main courses £13 to £22). Set L £12.95 (2 courses) to £14.95. Set D £15.95 (2 courses) to £18.95. Sun L £13.95 (2 courses) to £15.95. **Service:** not inc. **Details:** Cards accepted. 85 seats. 20 seats outside. Air-con. Separate bar. Wheelchair access. Music. Children allowed.

Parkmill

Maes-Yr-Haf
Classic food with modern overtones
Parkmill, SA3 2EH
Tel no: (01792) 371000
www.maes-yr-haf.com
Modern British | £40
New Chef

Deep in the heart of Gower a short stroll away from stunning Three Cliffs Bay, this stylish restaurant-with-rooms has forged a reputation for imaginative cooking backed up by polished, courteous service and an interior that is 'sleek and modern'. We learned a new chef was due to take over too late for us to respond with an inspection, but a last-minute reader's report just before we went to press was full of praise for a 'simply delicious' lunch where 'nothing was too much trouble': gravad lax with lemon and herb oil, chicken breast that was 'full of flavour' and a 'superior' version of Eton Mess. Whole bottles are priced from £13.95.

Open: Tue to Sun L 12 to 2.30, Tue to Sat D 7 to 9.30. **Closed:** Mon, last 2 weeks Jan. **Meals:** alc (main courses £12 to £25). Set L and D £14.95 (2 courses) to £17.95. **Service:** not inc. **Details:** Cards accepted. 44 seats. 40 seats outside. Separate bar. Wheelchair access. Music. Children allowed. Car parking.

Also recommended

Also recommended entries are not scored but we think they are worth a visit.

Pontypridd

Bunch of Grapes
Gastro-slickness in a buzzy pub
Ynysangharad Road, Pontypridd, CF37 4DA
Tel no: (01443) 402934
www.bunchofgrapes.org.uk
Gastropub | £20
Cooking score: 1

£5 OFF   £30

'Great food, great ales and a relaxed atmosphere buzzing with life' make this gastropub a smart choice. Originally a stopping-off point for canal boat tradesmen, it's now an ideal spot for walkers as it stands on the Taff Trail (a rambling and cycling route between Merthyr Tydfil and Cardiff). The interior keeps one foot in the 'traditional pub' camp, but the dining areas have a certain gastro-slickness, with chalkboards displaying the likes of devilled kidneys on toasted focaccia and confit shoulder of new season's lamb with celeriac chips, wilted spinach and beetroot pesto. Wines from £13.25.

Chef/s: Sebastien Vanoni. **Open:** all week L 12 to 2.30 (3 Fri and Sat, 3.30 Sun), Mon to Sat D 6 to 9.30 (10 Fri and Sat). **Meals:** alc (main courses £13 to £23). Sun L £12.50. **Service:** not inc. **Details:** Cards accepted. 66 seats. 24 seats outside. Separate bar. Wheelchair access. Music. Children allowed. Car parking.

Reynoldston

Fairyhill
Special house, special cooking
Reynoldston, SA3 1BS
Tel no: (01792) 390139
www.fairyhill.net
Modern British | £45
Cooking score: 4

A loyal army of followers continues to praise this country house restaurant, whose many constants include 'the welcome, the serenity, the ambience, the service and the food'. An alluring retreat in acres of lovely grounds, it feels special but not stuffy. The cooking follows suit, keeping things simple enough for the ingredients to shine through. 'Visit in May', enthuses one reader, 'and have the seasonal asparagus with the best hollandaise sauce that you will ever taste.' Other choices – such as air-dried Welsh black beef with Parmesan shavings, lemon and capers, or herb-crusted silver hake with buttered spinach, smoked haddock and scallop chowder – highlight the sheer variety of excellent produce available locally. Round it off with hot chocolate fondant and liquorice ice cream. The weighty wine list offers interesting finds from around the world and covers France's major wine-producing areas in detail. Prices start at £19.50 a bottle.

Chef/s: James Hamilton. **Open:** all week L 12 to 2, D 7 to 9. **Closed:** 26 Dec, first 3 weeks Jan. **Meals:** alc (main courses £10 to £18). Set L £15.95 (2 courses) to £19.95. Set D £35 (2 courses) to £45. Sun L £24.50. **Service:** not inc. **Details:** Cards accepted. 60 seats. 35 seats outside. Separate bar. Wheelchair access. Music. Car parking.

▌St Fagans

The Old Post Office

First-class food that's great value
Greenwood Lane, St Fagans, CF5 6EL
Tel no: (029) 2056 5400
www.theoldpostofficerestaurant.co.uk
Modern European | £28
Cooking score: 3

🛏 **V** £30

Looking at the lofty, architect-designed interior it's hard to believe that this smart little restaurant was once a post office and police station. Set in a quiet, leafy village just outside Cardiff, it's a world away from the daily grind but slick enough to compete with the city's best offerings. The 'great value for money' food follows the interior design, tempering tradition with bold modernity in dishes like fresh crab risotto, 'succulent' slow-roast belly of St Fagans pork with cavolo nero and mashed potato, and treats such as almond, lemon and ricotta cake with lemon cream for dessert. Expect to be treated like royalty as

'passionate' chef/patron Simon Kealy and his team go about their duties. Wines from £14.95.

Chef/s: Simon Kealy. **Open:** Wed to Sun L 12 to 3 (7 Sun), Wed to Sat D 6 to 9.30. **Closed:** Mon, Tue, 2 weeks Jan, 2 weeks August. **Meals:** alc (main courses £14 to £18). Set L £12.95 (2 courses) to £16.95. Sun L £16.95 to £21.95. **Service:** not inc. **Details:** Cards accepted. 35 seats. 20 seats outside. Air-con. Separate bar. Wheelchair access. Music. Children allowed. Car parking.

▌Swansea

NEW ENTRY
Charlie's

Sleek new arrival
2 Prospect Place, Swansea, SA1 1QP
Tel no: (01792) 413290
www.charliesdining.co.uk
Modern British | £28
Cooking score: 2

£5 OFF **V** £30

This sleek new arrival has added some fizz to central Swansea since launching. Behind the Georgian frontage is a smart ground-floor bar (think black furniture and modern art) and a basement restaurant where candlelight and cosy corners create an intimate mood. Local ingredients, especially fish, are to the fore: mussels in garlic, cream and white wine impressed at inspection, as did a main course of pork loin with bacon, apple and apple jus. Chocolate fondant also hit the mark. Wines start at £15.

Chef/s: Brian Petrie. **Open:** Wed to Sun L 12 to 3, Wed to Sat D 7 to 9 (9.30 Fri and Sat). **Closed:** Mon, Tue. **Meals:** alc (main courses £7 to £19). Set L £8.95 (2 courses). Set D £18.95 (2 courses). Sun L £11.95 (2 courses) to £14.95. **Service:** not inc. **Details:** Cards accepted. 60 seats. 6 seats outside. Air-con. Separate bar. Music. Children allowed.

Average price

The average price listed in main-entry reviews denotes the price of a three-course meal, without wine.

Welsh produce

Welsh produce

Restaurants in Wales can take their pick from a vast array of local produce. To begin with a cliché, there are sheep – raised not only on the hills but also on the salt marshes, where their meat takes on a distinctive sweet flavour.

The jagged coastline yields porphyra seaweed which, cooked for several hours, becomes laverbread – that traditional breakfast partner for another Welsh speciality, cockles (though in the hands of modern Welsh chefs laverbread finds its way into everything from tarts to sauces).

Lobsters and mussels are another delight, and sea bass caught off the Gower coast is some of the best you'll ever taste.

The Welsh Black is the country's finest source of beef – rich, marbled and full-flavoured thanks to the lush pastures that feed it.

Then there are native crops, from winter sprouts to summer berries and – for the more intrepid chef – wild food including autumn mussels, springtime nettles and wild garlic, and summer elderflowers.

When in Wales, look for menus that champion local produce; there really is no excuse for anything else.

Didier & Stephanie

Delightful French dining
56 St Helen's Road, Swansea, SA1 4BE
Tel no: (01792) 655603
French | £30
Cooking score: 4

This 'consistently good' French restaurant has been delighting Swansea diners for more than a decade. A classy and intimate setting with soft yellow walls and stripped wood floors, it's a perfect choice for a meal for two. 'Very calm, unfussy but precise' service is provided by co-proprietor Stephanie Danvel, while her partner Didier Suvé takes charge of the kitchen. Expect confidently executed and technically accomplished cooking with a strong French accent. The 'quite delicious' croustillant of French black pudding is a perennial star of the starters, while a seasonal offering might be asparagus salad with Parmesan. Some ingredients are specially imported, but local stars also shine – maybe sea bass with a 'well-balanced' seafood sauce or braised shoulder of Welsh lamb with tomato and red wine. Desserts are classic with a twist – witness orange flower blossom crème brûlée. The decent wine list starts at £12.90.
Chef/s: Didier Suvé. **Open:** Tue to Sat L 12 to 2, D from 7 onwards. **Closed:** Sun, Mon, 2 weeks Christmas, 2 weeks summer. **Meals:** alc (main courses £16 to £19). Set L £13.50 (2 courses) to £16.50. **Service:** not inc. **Details:** Cards accepted. 20 seats. Air-con. Music. Children allowed.

Hanson at the Chelsea

Haven with on-the-money food
17 St Mary Street, Swansea, SA1 3LH
Tel no: (01792) 464068
Modern British | £20
Cooking score: 3

V £30

Tucked down a lane just off pub-lined Wind Street, this quiet little restaurant is a haven of peace compared with the bustle and weekend wildness of Swansea's main drinking district. Simple décor (lots of wood) and slick service make for a relaxing, informal atmosphere, and the food is on-the-money, offering a good balance of tradition, trends and international flavours. Fish and seafood are a special strength – a starter of superb fresh mussels with spaghetti in white wine and cream has impressed, likewise a meaty main course comprising a fall-apart tender piece of slow-roasted belly pork set on smooth sage and onion mash with scrumpy apple velouté and Pink Lady compote. The high standard continues to desserts such as baked lemon cheesecake. Wines start at £12.95.

Chef/s: Andrew Hanson. **Open:** Mon to Sat L 12 to 2, D 7 to 9.30. **Closed:** Sun, 25 Dec, bank hols. **Meals:** alc (main courses £12 to £23). Set L £12.50 (2 courses) to £16.95. Set D £19.95. **Service:** not inc. **Details:** Cards accepted. 49 seats. No mobile phones. Music. Children allowed.

NEW ENTRY

Rose Indienne

Raising the Indian bar

73-74 St Helen's Road, Swansea, SA1 4BG
Tel no: (01792) 467000
www.roseindienne.com
Indian | £18
Cooking score: 2

£5 OFF **V** £30

This newcomer has had a big impact in Swansea, raising the Indian bar with its emphasis on home-ground spices, fresh local ingredients and traditional recipes. Chef Liyakat Ali Khan worked in hotels across the Subcontinent before coming to the UK, and his menus draw on this experience. All the favourites are there of course, from chicken tikka masala to lamb rogan josh, but less predictable choices include Ajwani fish tikka, Goan duck curry, and grill pudina macchi (fresh salmon marinated in the chef's 'special green masala', cooked over charcoal and served with mint chutney). Wines start at £11.95.

Chef/s: Liyakat Ali Khan. **Open:** all week L 12 to 2 (5 Sun), D 5.30 to 12 (1am Fri and Sat). **Closed:** 26 Dec. **Meals:** alc (main courses £6 to £13). Sun L buffet £8. **Service:** not inc. **Details:** Cards accepted. 120 seats. Air-con. Wheelchair access. Music. Children allowed.

★ **READERS' RESTAURANT OF THE YEAR** ★
WALES

Slice

Confident, pint-sized contender

72-75 Eversley Road, Swansea, SA2 9DE
Tel no: (01792) 290929
www.sliceswansea.co.uk
Modern British | £32
Cooking score: 3

V

The remit at this diminutive restaurant is to deliver refined but uncomplicated food of consistently high quality. Most reporters would agree they manage it: 'We have been eating at Slice for over 18 months and have enjoyed every meal.' The proprietors set great store by good-quality local produce, with a page of the menu dedicated to all their main suppliers. The short repertoire delivers starters such as twice-baked laverbread soufflé on home-smoked trout fillets and pan-fried duck cake with ginger sauce. Both have impressed visitors, and a main course of marinated chicken breasts on wild garlic risotto is recommended too. Finish with a trio of rhubarb comprising crumble, parfait and ice cream, or a selection of Welsh cheeses. House wine is £12.95.

Chef/s: Philip Leach. **Open:** Thur to Sun L 12 to 2, D 6.30 to 9. **Closed:** Mon to Wed, 4 weeks Dec to Jan, 2 weeks May, 2 weeks Sept. **Meals:** Set L £15 (2 courses) to £20. Set D £32. **Service:** not inc. **Details:** Cards accepted. 18 seats. No mobile phones. Music.

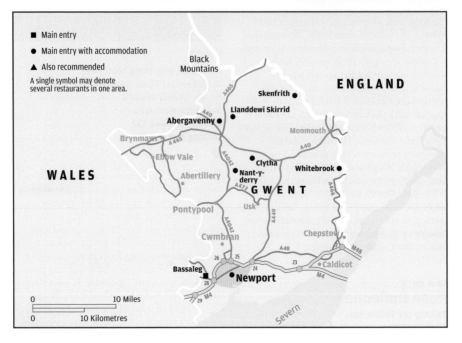

Abergavenny

The Hardwick

Thriving gastropub with imaginative food
Old Raglan Road, Abergavenny, NP7 9AA
Tel no: (01873) 854220
www.thehardwick.co.uk
Modern European | £32
Cooking score: 4

Stephen Terry's thriving gastropub has been extended, but the intimate atmosphere remains; even if it's your first time here you'll feel like one of the locals. Quarry-tiled floors, low beams and a wood-burning stove strike a rustic note that's echoed on the menu with dishes such as Provençal-style fish soup with aïoli, Gruyère and croûtons or homemade local Saddleback pork sausages with Italian farro, bacon and spring greens. Other dishes such as scallops with crispy breadcrumbed Gloucester Old Spot pork belly, black pudding and apple and mustard sauce or local venison four ways are more sophisticated and

nod to Terry's London days, when he worked for Marco Pierre White. Desserts have similar scope, from imaginative homemade ice creams (peanut butter and jelly, for instance) to the 'plate of chocolate loveliness' which includes, among other things, Amedei chocolate mousse and a Valrhona chocolate brownie. An equally classy choice of wines kicks off at £15.60. Plans are afoot to open seven days a week once the ongoing refurbishment and new accommodation are complete – so ring to check opening times.
Chef/s: Stephen Terry. **Open:** Tue to Sun L 12 to 3, Tue to Sat D 6.30 to 10. **Closed:** 25 Dec. **Meals:** alc (main courses £13 to £24). Set L £18.50 (2 courses) to £23.50. Sun L £24.50. **Service:** not inc.
Details: Cards accepted. 65 seats. Separate bar. No mobile phones. Music. Children allowed. Car parking.

Bassaleg
Junction 28
Ex-railway station with eclectic food
Station Approach, Bassaleg, NP10 8LD
Tel no: (01633) 891891
www.junction28.com
Modern European | £25
Cooking score: 2

£30

Once a railway station, this white-painted building stands in a tranquil spot, although it's not far from junction 28 of the M4. These days it plies its trade as a country restaurant, with one area decked out as an old-fashioned railway carriage. Jean Jacques Payel has headed the kitchen for 10 years, and he deals in eclectic dishes with some voguish flourishes. Open, perhaps with sweet-cured mackerel on a potato and crab salad with salsa verde and watercress, move on to rack of Welsh lamb with a Moroccan 'rissole' and finish off with vanilla crème brûlée. House wines are £13.75. **Chef/s:** Jean Jacques Payel. **Open:** all week L 12 to 2 (4 Sun), Mon to Sat D 5.30 to 9.30. **Closed:** 26 Dec, July 26 to Aug 10. **Meals:** alc (main courses £11 to £20). Set L £11.95 (2 courses) to £13.95. Set D (until 7) £16.25 (3 courses). Set D (until 9.30) £19.95 (3 courses). Sun L £12.95 (2 courses) to £14.95. **Service:** not inc. **Details:** Cards accepted. 165 seats. Air-con. Separate bar. Wheelchair access. Music. Children allowed. Car parking.

Clytha
The Clytha Arms
Everything you want from a pub
Clytha, NP7 9BW
Tel no: (01873) 840206
www.clytha-arms.com
Modern British | £32
Cooking score: 1

£5 OFF ☕ V

Everything you could want from an old-style country pub is here: excellent ales, real fires, bare floors and a lively buzz of conversation. Food choices range from a lengthy tapas menu to a full à la carte. The style is eclectic, with

ideas coming thick and fast from around the globe: seafood soup, teriyaki fillet of beef or Caribbean fruit curry are typical choices. At inspection a kebab of pork tenderloin and black pudding made use of decent ingredients but lacked style and precision. Don't expect pinpoint accuracy, but if you're seeking a hearty, oversized pub meal the Clytha won't disappoint. Wines start at £13.95. **Chef/s:** Andrew Canning and Roger Cottrell. **Open:** Tue to Sun L 12 to 3.30, Mon to Sat D 7 to 9.30. **Closed:** Late May and Aug, bank hols. **Meals:** alc (main courses £14 to £20). Set L and D £20 (2 courses) to £23. Sun L £17.50 (2 courses) to £20. **Service:** not inc. **Details:** Cards accepted. 70 seats. 100 seats outside. Separate bar. No music. Wheelchair access. Children allowed. Car parking.

Llanddewi Skirrid
The Walnut Tree
Famous eatery back on form
Llanddewi Skirrid, NP7 8AW
Tel no: (01873) 852797
www.thewalnuttreeinn.com
Modern British | £35
Cooking score: 5

🍷 🛏

Shaun Hill has made a 'spectacular' impact since arriving at Wales' most famous eatery, and the Walnut Tree is now well and truly back on form – 'almost like the old days', mused a visitor who has watched its fortunes ebb and flow. Hill is generally hands-on, dividing his time between overseeing the stoves and playing courteous host at the bar – although he has also brought back one of the redoubtable waitresses from the Franco Taruschio years to run things 'in her own determined way'. The menu is 'wonderfully seasonal' and ingredients are impeccably sourced; expect some Italian influences and a few nods to Hill's back catalogue (scallops with lentil and coriander sauce, say), but no twee flourishes or effete gestures. What you see is what you get – perhaps deep-fried courgette flowers, crab empanadillas with saffron mayo, bowls of bourride, gooseberry fool. Nothing detracts from the emphatically simple approach, even when global influences are at work – witness a limpid starter of organic sea trout tataki with citron salad. Set lunch is astonishing value, and the admirable 70-bin wine list follows the unshowy ethos of the place, with the focus on quality, interest and value from artisan growers, plus plenty by the glass. Prices (from £16) are eminently reasonable.

Chef/s: Shaun Hill and Roger Brook. **Open:** Tue to Sat L 12 to 2.30, D 7 to 10. **Closed:** Sun, Mon, 1 week Christmas. **Meals:** alc (main courses £12 to £23). Set L £17.50 (2 courses) to £23. **Service:** not inc. **Details:** Cards accepted. 50 seats. 20 seats outside. Air-con. Separate bar. No music. Wheelchair access. Children allowed. Car parking.

Nant-y-derry
The Foxhunter
Understated gastropub cool
Nant-y-derry, NP7 9DN
Tel no: (01873) 881101
www.thefoxhunter.com
Modern British | £30
Cooking score: 4

'Proper, honest food' is the order of the day at this former stationmaster's house. Decked out with an air of understated gastropub cool, it's smart inside without feeling formal. Settings don't come much more rural, but there's more than a hint of urban sophistication to the cooking – a throwback to chef-proprietor Matt Tebbutt's time spent under mentors such as Marco Pierre White. As one reader summed up: 'you can expect fantastic locally sourced ingredients presented in both traditional and imaginative ways'. Typically, poached loin of rabbit with black pudding and red wine sauce might precede a main course of slow-cooked pork belly with braised white beans, watercress and crisp onions. A dessert of wild plum soup nods to the restaurant's popular foraging excursions and wild food lunches. The substantial wine list covers the globe and includes a good selection of halves. Prices start at £15.95 a bottle.

Chef/s: Matt Tebbutt. **Open:** Tue to Sun L 12 to 3, Tue to Sat D 7 to 10. **Closed:** Mon, 25 and 26 Dec. **Meals:** alc (main courses £15 to £21). Set L £18.95 (2 courses) to £22.95. Sun L £20.95 (2 courses) to £25.95. **Service:** not inc. **Details:** Cards accepted. 50 seats. 12 seats outside. Separate bar. Wheelchair access. Music. Children allowed. Car parking.

Newport
The Chandlery
Skilled classical cooking
77-78 Lower Dock Street, Newport, NP20 1EH
Tel no: (01633) 256622
www.thechandleryrestaurant.com
Modern British | £36
Cooking score: 4

£5 OFF **V**

A change of hands has noticeably enhanced the appeal of this former ship's chandlery. In the kitchen, long-serving deputy Ryan Mitchell has stepped up to the plate, while the new owner leads front-of-house with genuine charm. The cooking remains classically based, with a high level of technical skill. At inspection homemade breads impressed, as did an amuse-bouche of tomato and basil velouté. A boudin of smoked chicken with truffled potato and chicken consommé made a balanced and comforting starter, followed by a tender fillet of Welsh beef with parsnip purée, braised oxtail gratin and the deep savoury notes of sautéed wild mushrooms. A trio of desserts was on the money, from a classy take on sticky toffee pudding through summer berry trifle to a gloriously boozy prune and Armagnac parfait. The setting remains smartly understated, with pale walls, stripped wood floors and assorted antique furniture. A respectable selection of international wines opens at £16.95

Chef/s: Ryan Mitchell. **Open:** Tue to Sun L 12 to 2.30, Tue to Sat D 7 to 10. **Closed:** Mon. **Meals:** alc (main courses £16 to £25). Set L £16.95 (2 courses) to £19.95. **Service:** not inc. **Details:** Cards accepted. 80 seats. Air-con. Separate bar. Wheelchair access. Music. Children allowed. Car parking.

The Crown

Flagship resort restaurant
The Celtic Manor Resort, Coldra Woods, Newport,
NP18 1HQ
Tel no: (01633) 413000
www.celtic-manor.com
Modern European | £48
Cooking score: 5

£5 OFF 🍷 🛏

Sister to the Crown at Whitebrook (see entry), this Crown is the esteemed flagship of the sprawling Celtic Manor Resort – an extravagant tribute to destination tourism, leisure and corporate hospitality. The interior is a triumph of modish contemporary design with gleaming white walls, walnut floors and sparkling modern chandeliers dangling from coffered ceilings. The kitchen knows its ingredients and is fond of variations on the theme – perhaps seared scallops with pumpkin three ways, a tripartite dish of rabbit with Medjool dates or a porcine alliance of free-range tenderloin and braised pig's head with caramelised chicory, apple and tarragon. Other ideas show a home-grown inclination – roasted pigeon breast with confit duck liver and black treacle or Welsh sirloin steak and braised shoulder glazed with beer. Meals begin with artful canapés and diners can expect the usual array of showy interruptions before the kitchen re-kindles its east-west love affair with desserts such as pineapple tarte Tatin with Szechuan pepper ice cream, pear and toffee soufflé or dark chocolate mousse with basil sorbet and orange. A wine list of biblical proportions covers France's major regions in detail and makes productive forays into countries as diverse as the USA and Portugal. Overseen by an expert sommelier, it kicks off at £23 a bottle.
Chef/s: Tim McDougall. **Open:** Tue to Sat L 12 to 2, D 7 to 10. **Closed:** Sun, Mon, 1 to 12 Jan. **Meals:** Set L £29.95 (2 courses) to £37.50. Set D £47.50.
Service: not inc. **Details:** Cards accepted. 49 seats. Air-con. Separate bar. Wheelchair access. Music. Car parking.

▌Skenfrith

The Bell at Skenfrith

Riverbank inn with luxury cooking
Skenfrith, NP7 8UH
Tel no: (01600) 750235
www.skenfrith.co.uk
Modern British | £30
Cooking score: 4

🍷 🛏 V

Just inside the Welsh border, this whitewashed inn on the banks of the river Monnow is surrounded by wooded hills and boasts a fully accredited organic garden which provides a great deal of produce for the kitchen. Inside it has extensive dining areas as well as relaxing corners. Rupert Taylor's cooking shows vaulting ambition, with luxury items such as foie gras and scallops to the fore, plus canapés and tempters such as a 'tasse' of gazpacho with olive oil before the meal. Presentation aims for maximum impact with a starter of foie gras parfait and mousse, pain d'épices and balsamic reduction, before a main course of pan-fried gurnard with mussel, tomato and baby leek broth. Highly polished desserts take in an acclaimed lemon verbena pannacotta served with beetroot honeycomb and sorrel ice cream. The encyclopaedic wine list reveals a passion for Champagne and essays a comprehensive tour of the great and the good at mostly fair prices (from £13).
Chef/s: Rupert Taylor. **Open:** all week L 12 to 2.30, D 7 to 9 (9.30 Fri and Sat). **Closed:** Tue (Nov to Mar), last week Jan to 12 Feb. **Meals:** alc (main courses £12 to £19). Sun L £20 (2 courses) to £24.
Service: not inc. **Details:** Cards accepted. 60 seats. 30 seats outside. Separate bar. No music. No mobile phones. Wheelchair access. Car parking.

Whitebrook

The Crown at Whitebrook

World-class restaurant-with-rooms
Whitebrook, NP25 4TX
Tel no: (01600) 860254
www.crownatwhitebrook.co.uk
Modern European | £48
Cooking score: 7

The stunning drive along the Wye Valley is enough to blow you away, even before you pitch up at this tranquil oasis surrounded by wooded slopes. It may be squirreled away in deepest Wales, but there's something of a romantic French auberge about the Crown – especially when chef James Sommerin takes time out to personally greet guests. On the food front, this is a Welsh venue 'performing on the international stage', with meals interspersed by all manner of seductive extras – exquisite amuse-bouches, between-course sorbets and heavenly petits fours (served with coffee in the spacious, book-filled lounge). Innovation, flair and consummate accuracy typify everything that emerges from the kitchen, from a sensational starter of butter-poached crab with fried squid, roast red pepper and polenta to textbook mango soufflé with La Beryl Blanc wine and basil ice cream ('a fantastic combination of flavours') or intense baked fig cream with flapjack, caramel and cinnamon. The food is 'heroically seasonal' and there are nods to Welsh provenance in dishes such as roast Longhorn beef with veal sweetbreads, butternut squash and salsify, but James Sommerin is also open to the latest trends from the world's big gastronomic players: salt-baked celeriac (inspired by a visit to Alinea in Chicago) appears in a dish with poached and roast quail, beetroot and watercress. Those who drop in for the superb-value lunch menu might be treated to a less heady line-up that could feature pan-fried sardines with polenta, olive oil and soy, followed by leg of lamb with roast onion, celeriac and rosemary, or roast hake with chorizo, smoked mussels and borlotti beans. High levels of service suit the elevated cooking, although some have found it all rather 'stiff' and impersonal. The top-drawer wine list ('250 of the most interesting bottles we can lay our hands on') is impeccably managed by a clued-up sommelier, who will guide you through the pages of offbeat and classic names. Half-bottles and luscious dessert tipples show up strongly, but there are ample temptations across the board. Prices start at £20 (£5 a glass).

Chef/s: James Sommerin. **Open:** all week L 12 to 2, Mon to Sat D 6 to 9.30. **Closed:** 2 weeks Christmas and New Year. **Meals:** Set L £25 (2 courses) to £28. Set D £48. Sun L £28. Tasting menu £55 to £70. **Service:** 12.5% (optional). **Details:** Cards accepted. 26 seats. No mobile phones. Wheelchair access. Music. Children allowed. Car parking.

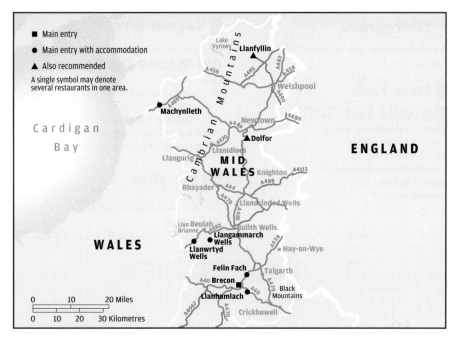

- ■ Main entry
- ● Main entry with accommodation
- ▲ Also recommended

A single symbol may denote
several restaurants in one area.

Lake Vyrnwy **Llanfyllin**
Cambrian Mountains
A458 A495 A483 A458
A490
Welshpool
A489 A470 A489
Machynlleth
A487 A470 **Newtown**
A470 ▲**Dolfor**
C a r d i g a n
B a y
Llanidloes
Llangurig **M I D**
W A L E S Knighton A4113
A44 A488
Rhayader A44
A470 **Llandrindod Wells**
A483
A470 A483
Llyn Beulah A483 **Builth Wells**
Brianne **Llangammarch** A438
WALES **Wells**
Llanwrtyd ● Hay-on-Wye
Wells
Felin Fach **Talgarth**
A40 ■**Brecon**
A40 A479 Black
Llanhamlach Mountains
Crickhowell

ENGLAND

| 0 | 10 | 20 Miles |
| 0 | 10 | 20 | 30 Kilometres |

■ Brecon
Tipple'n'Tiffin
Casual canalside grazing
Canal Wharf, Brecon, LD3 7EW
Tel no: (01874) 611866
Modern British | £22
Cooking score: 1

£5 OFF **V** £30

Custom-built for sharing and grazing,
Richard and Louise Gudsell's laid-back eatery
is tacked on to the Theatr Brycheiniog – but
you don't need to be taking in a show to enjoy
the food (or the lovely canalside views). Global
tapas plates are the mainstays, loaded with
anything from deep-fried Penclawdd cockles
with salsa to crispy duck legs with kumara and
butternut squash rösti. Heartier specials might
take in braised oxtail on mustard mash or
Moroccan spiced chicken, with puds
promising the likes of apple and blackberry
crumble. Wines start at £12.

Chef/s: Louise Gudsell. **Open:** Mon to Sat L 12 to
2.30, D 6 to 9. **Closed:** Sun, 24 to 27 Dec. **Meals:** alc
(main courses £8 to £10). Set L £15 (2 courses) to
£20. Set D £20 (2 courses) to £25. **Service:** not inc.
Details: Cards accepted. 40 seats. 30 seats outside.
No mobile phones. Wheelchair access. Music.
Children allowed. Car parking.

■ Dolfor

ALSO RECOMMENDED
▲ The Old Vicarage Dolfor
Dolfor, SY16 4BN
Tel no: (01686) 629051
www.theoldvicaragedolfor.co.uk
Modern British £5 OFF

Majestic views of the Montgomeryshire hills
are the backdrop to this former vicarage,
where a homely style of modern Welsh
cooking is offered in the form of fixed-price
dinner menus (£30 for three courses, £35 for
four). Expect organic smoked salmon
bavarois, followed by rack of Mochdre lamb
with orange and laverbread on potato rösti.

Sticky toffee pudding is a favourite dessert, and it's as well to leave room for the Welsh farmhouse cheeses too. Wines from £14. Open all week.

Felin Fach
The Felin Fach Griffin
Classic gastropub on the up
Felin Fach, LD3 0UB
Tel no: (01874) 620111
www.thefelinfachgriffin.co.uk
Modern British | £32
Cooking score: 4

£5 OFF ⊨

'I love the atmosphere here – no pretension', writes one reader of this classic gastropub where big leather sofas, real fires and charming staff set the tone for a relaxed trawl through some of the best local produce (a lot of it home-grown). Excellent homemade bread and 'cheese puffs' arrive at the table almost as soon as you're seated and get things off to a swimming start. A change of chef has raised the game and while dishes sound simple, there are some sophisticated and beautifully balanced pairings of texture and flavour at play here. Witness a starter of pressed ham hock terrine with chive flowers, sweet pickled pears, tiny silverskin pickled onions and matchstick strips of gherkin, or ribeye of Welsh beef with onion confit, onion purée, chips and béarnaise sauce. A similar balancing act is seen in desserts such as a rhubarb and buttermilk pannacotta with a brandy-snap tuile. A substantial choice of international wines opens at £15.50.
Chef/s: Simon Potter. **Open:** all week L 12.30 to 2.30, D 6 to 9 (9.30 Fri and Sat). **Closed:** 24 and 25 Dec, 4 days early Jan. **Meals:** alc (main courses £15 to £19). Set L £15.90 (2 courses) to £18.90. Set D £21.50 (2 courses) to £26.50. Sun L £22.
Service: not inc. **Details:** Cards accepted. 60 seats. 16 seats outside. Separate bar. No mobile phones. Wheelchair access. Music. Children allowed. Car parking.

Hay-on-Wye
READERS RECOMMEND
Old Stables Tea Rooms
Café
Bear Street, Hay-on-Wye, HR3 5AN
Tel no: (01497) 821557
www.chefontherunfoods.co.uk
'Food was to a very high standard and I could tell that a lot of heart goes into this place'

Llanfyllin
ALSO RECOMMENDED
▲ Seeds
5 Penybryn Cottages, High Street, Llanfyllin, SY22 5AP
Tel no: (01691) 648604
Modern British

Locals and tourists call in at this long-standing, family-run restaurant for some good-value cooking. The traditional menu takes in potted prawns (£4.95), lamb's kidneys with grain mustard and cream sauce (£12.75) and finishes with a rather good treacle tart. Saturday dinner is fixed price (two courses £22.75, three courses £25.75). Low beams, slate floors and a cheerful woodburner add to the charm, as do puzzles and books. The keenly priced wine list opens at £12.50. Closed Sun, Mon and Tue L.

Llangammarch Wells
Lake Country House
Modern country cooking with some style
Llangammarch Wells, LD4 4BS
Tel no: (01591) 620202
www.lakecountryhouse.co.uk
Modern British | £38
Cooking score: 2

£5 OFF ⊨ V

This is a country house for families, and a no-brainer for weddings, anniversaries and reunions. The gardens are splendid, the lounges comfortable, and visitors can also look forward to eating in a revamped orangery-style dining room. The kitchen might send out rillettes of salmon or a pressing of ham, foie gras and green peppercorns ahead of braised shin of Welsh beef or roast monkfish with braised oxtail, garlic potato purée, red onion jam, capers and rosemary oil. Desserts also put on a show – think green tea and lemon pannacotta with confit lemon, lime sorbet and chocolate croquant. The result is modern country cooking, with some style and enough variation to keep almost everyone happy. House wine is £19.50.

Chef/s: Sean Cullingford. **Open:** all week L 12.30 to 2, D 7 to 9. **Meals:** Set L £15 (2 courses) to £18.50. Set D £32.50 to £38.50. Sun L £18.50. **Service:** not inc. **Details:** Cards accepted. 60 seats. Separate bar. No music. No mobile phones. Wheelchair access. Car parking.

Llanhamlach
Peterstone Court

Great ingredients from the family farm
Brecon Road, Llanhamlach, LD3 7YB
Tel no: (01874) 665387
www.peterstone-court.com
Modern British | £32
Cooking score: 4

🍾 🍽 V

This Georgian house in the Brecon Beacons National Park looks imposing but is very relaxed inside. Outbuildings have been converted to provide more contemporary accommodation than in the main house, the cellars have been made into a spa, while the current dining room looking out onto the terrace and glorious countryside is a more recent addition. Menus incorporate plenty of appealing combinations, often using seasonal raw materials from the nearby family farm. Confit Glaisfer lamb and potato hash could be served as a starter with poached free-range egg and mustard dressing, while slow-cooked breast of chicken, teamed with creamed leek and Savoy cabbage, roast garlic mash and morel mushroom jus makes a satisfying main course. To finish, don't miss the luscious homemade ice creams, and there are fine Welsh

cheeses too. Wines are a reasonably priced, carefully chosen selection from all over the world, with bottles starting at £13.95.

Chef/s: Ian Sampson and Sean Gerrard. **Open:** all week L 12 to 2.30, D 7 to 9.30. **Meals:** alc (main courses £9 to £19). Set L £11.50 (2 courses) to £13.50. Sun L £18.95. **Service:** not inc. **Details:** Cards accepted. 45 seats. 45 seats outside. Separate bar. Wheelchair access. Music. Children allowed. Car parking.

Llanwrtyd Wells
Carlton Riverside

Deeply relaxing riverside retreat
Irfon Crescent, Llanwrtyd Wells, LD5 4ST
Tel no: (01591) 610248
www.carltonriverside.com
Modern British | £39
Cooking score: 6

£5 OFF 🍽

Praise continues to flow for Mary Ann and Alan Gilchrist's riverside restaurant-with-rooms. From the homely lounge with its many books and big squashy sofas to the long dining room with its river views, the atmosphere is traditional, refined and deeply relaxing. The occasional distant ring of laughter signals the existence of a lively bar-bistro below floors (ideal for a post-dinner drink) but in the restaurant all is calm, with Alan providing subtly attentive and 'quietly efficient' service. Expect classic French and British cooking from Mary Ann, with occasional forays further afield (Chinese-spiced braised belly pork with mash and cabbage or fresh egg tagliatelle with wild chanterelles). Local ingredients shine through, whether in a starter of Trealy Farm charcuterie or a main course of roast rack of Irfon Valley lamb and slow-roast breast with sherried lamb jus. Fish is a strength – perhaps paupiette of sole with a 'quite delicious' lobster velouté. Finish with a terrific mango mousse or a 'very rich and satisfying' plum cake with hazelnut ice cream. The wine list is a concise and well-chosen selection with a decent choice by the glass. Prices start at £15 a bottle.

Chef/s: Mary Ann Gilchrist. **Open:** Mon to Sat D only 7 to 8.30. **Closed:** Sun, 19 to 30 Dec. **Meals:** Set D £34 (2 courses) to £39.50. **Service:** not inc. **Details:** Cards accepted. 20 seats. Separate bar. No mobile phones. Wheelchair access. Music. Children allowed.

Lasswade Country House
Confident cooking with great views
Station Road, Llanwrtyd Wells, LD5 4RW
Tel no: (01591) 610515
www.lasswadehotel.co.uk
Modern British | £32
Cooking score: 2

Roger and Emma Stevens' Edwardian country house hotel has great views and an intimate little restaurant where Roger's increasingly confident cooking makes a show of the stunning produce available locally. Expect impressive attention to detail and 'individual, informal service', enhanced by the fact that Roger tends to pop out of the kitchen to chat with his guests. A warm salad of black pudding and smoked bacon with a poached egg and basil oil might be followed by roast cannon of organic mutton with leek soufflé and roasted winter vegetables. To finish, maybe Cognac-scented crème brûlée. A short list of affordably priced wines, grouped by type, starts at £12.
Chef/s: Roger Stevens. **Open:** all week D only 7.30 to 9. **Meals:** Set D £32. **Service:** not inc. **Details:** Cards accepted. 20 seats. No music. No mobile phones. Wheelchair access. Children allowed. Car parking.

■ Machynlleth

The Wynnstay
Bursting with character
Maengwyn Street, Machynlleth, SY20 8AE
Tel no: (01654) 702941
www.wynnstay-hotel.com
Modern British | £26
Cooking score: 2

Every inch the old-fashioned small town hotel, the Wynnstay has bags of character and atmosphere. Gareth Johns sources as much as he can locally and cooks in a relatively straightforward style, although influences are pulled in from far and wide. Pork is teamed with chorizo in a hearty terrine, loin of venison comes with red wine, smoked chocolate and red cabbage. Elsewhere there's a strong Welsh accent to herb-crusted roast cod with laver seaweed velouté, and prime sirloin steaks are considered the best in the area. Sticky toffee pudding shares the billing with Welsh cheeses at dessert stage. House wine is £13.95.
Chef/s: Gareth Johns. **Open:** all week L 12 to 2, D 6.30 to 9. **Closed:** 1 week around New Year. **Meals:** alc (main courses £12 to £16). Sun L £12.95 (2 courses) to £14.95. **Service:** not inc. **Details:** Cards accepted. 80 seats. 30 seats outside. Separate bar. No music. Wheelchair access. Children allowed. Car parking.

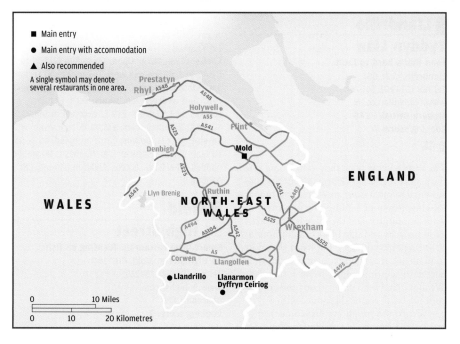

■ Main entry
● Main entry with accommodation
▲ Also recommended

A single symbol may denote several restaurants in one area.

0   10 Miles
0   10   20 Kilometres

▎ Llanarmon Dyffryn Ceiriog

The West Arms Hotel

Remote inn with modern food
Llanarmon Dyffryn Ceiriog, LL20 7LD
Tel no: **(01691) 600665**
www.thewestarms.co.uk
Modern European | £33
Cooking score: 3

🛏 V

This seriously remote hostelry was originally a refuelling point on the old drovers' route that snakes its way around the foothills of the Berwyn Mountains. Today it's a comfortable inn with gardens running down to the river Ceiriog. Inside, flagstone floors, a mighty inglenook and weathered timberwork are reminders of the past, although Grant Williams' kitchen rejects antiquated flavours in favour of mainstream modern dishes. To start, a crostini of duck liver parfait is served with local white pudding and poached Bantam egg, while mains might range from honey-glazed rack of Welsh lamb drizzled with tarragon beurre blanc to breast of guinea fowl with pears, wild mushrooms and an elderberry and port sauce. Desserts keep it simple with the likes of raspberry and chocolate cheesecake. Thirty international wines start at £14.95.
Chef/s: Grant Williams. **Open:** all week L 12 to 2, D 7 to 9. **Meals:** alc (main courses £9 to £19). Set D £27.95 (2 courses) to £32.90. Sun L £15.95.
Service: 10% (optional). **Details:** Cards accepted. 70 seats. 42 seats outside. Separate bar. Wheelchair access. Music. Children allowed. Car parking.

Please send us your feedback

To register your opinion about any restaurant listed in the Guide, or a new restaurant that you wish to bring to our attention, please visit the web address at the bottom of the page. Your feedback informs the content of the book and will be used to compile next year's reviews.

Llandrillo

Tyddyn Llan
Food that's hard to fault
Llandrillo, LL21 0ST
Tel no: (01490) 440264
www.tyddynllan.co.uk
Modern British | £48
Cooking score: 7

The Webbs knew what they were doing when they chose this small Georgian country house at which to pitch camp in Wales. It's a homely-looking greystone building set in prime walking country, and the place is run with great panache and splendid good humour by Susan, a perfect dynamo out front. As to the food, many people find it hard to fault. It isn't necessarily cutting-edge cuisine, but Bryan Webb is a chef who understands and enjoys cooking local, seasonal produce with a confidence and simplicity that come from years of experience. He is a chef for Wales to be proud of, as much as he takes pride in the first-class ingredients that come from local farms or indeed Tyddyn Llan's own garden. An August dinner breathed summer from start to finish, from an outstanding crab and langoustine starter with avocado salsa and a fennel and watercress salad, through wild sea bass with a flawless laverbread beurre blanc, to the closing serving of local raspberries ('the best I have ever tasted') with a just-trembling pannacotta. The extravagant range of choice on the menus suggest this is a formidably hard-working kitchen, and yet the food never seems overworked, the straightforward treatments allowing the quality of ingredients to shine in the best modern manner. Local rose veal might come simply accoutred with shallot and thyme purée, while the fabled Welsh black beef, perhaps served au poivre with chips or dauphinoise, is a firm favourite. Desserts run the gamut from modern classics such as grilled pineapple with chilli syrup and coconut sorbet to classical classics like prune and almond tart. An elegant wine list has been assembled from the best of western Europe and the New

World, with plenty of choice below £30, and many half-bottles on show. Prices start at £19 (£5 a glass).
Chef/s: Bryan Webb. **Open:** Fri to Sun L 12.30 to 2 (12.45 to 2.30 Sun), all week D 7 to 9 (9.30 Fri and Sat). **Closed:** Mon to Thur during Jan, first 2 weeks Feb, third weekend Jan. **Meals:** Set L £24 (2 courses) to £30. Set D £39 (2 courses) to £47.50. Sun L £30. Tasting menu £67.50 (8 courses).
Service: not inc. **Details:** Cards accepted. 40 seats. 10 seats outside. Separate bar. No music. No mobile phones. Wheelchair access. Children allowed. Car parking.

Mold

56 High Street
Smart little restaurant focusing on fish
56 High Street, Mold, CH7 1BD
Tel no: (01352) 759225
www.56highst.com
Seafood | £25
Cooking score: 2
£5 OFF £30

Fish and seafood top the billing at this smart little restaurant in the heart of Mold, opposite the fourteenth-century church. Bare floorboards and simple furniture set a modern tone that's reflected in the cooking. King scallops with shredded pork rillettes and apple might be followed by monkfish fillet wrapped in Parma ham with green herb crumble, pancetta and pea risotto. Roast rump of lamb with brochette of lamb's kidney, black pudding and boulangère potato is a typical meat offering. Wines start at £11.95.
Chef/s: Karl Mitchell, Kirsten Robb and Martin Fawcett. **Open:** Tue to Sat L 12 to 3, D 6 to 9.30 (10.30 Fri and Sat). **Closed:** Sun, Mon, 26 Dec, bank hols. **Meals:** alc (main courses £10 to £18). Set L £9.95 (2 courses) to £14.99. **Service:** not inc. **Details:** Cards accepted. 52 seats. Air-con. No mobile phones. Wheelchair access. Music. Children allowed.

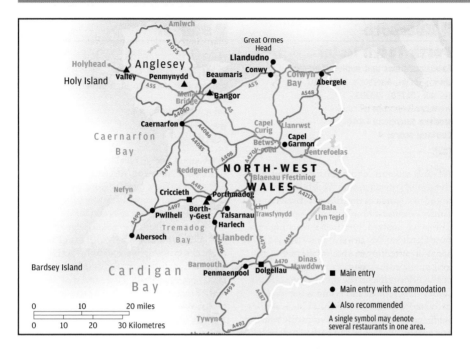

■ Abergele

The Kinmel Arms

Exciting and subtle cooking
St George, Abergele, LL22 9BP
Tel no: (01745) 832207
www.kinmelarms.co.uk
Modern British | £30
Cooking score: 4

⇌ V

Lynn Cunnah-Watson and Tim Watson are
ebullient hosts, and Tim's artistic endeavours
are reflected in the exhibits that enliven the
spacious bar and two dining areas of this
Victorian building. At lunchtime there is a
brasserie-style menu, with more ambitious
offerings in the evening when chef Gwyn
Roberts offers some exciting and subtle
cooking. At inspection a trio of Conwy crab –
a tian, some crispy squid sitting on a crab
rillette, and a spiced crab cake with saffron and
lime aïoli – was meticulously presented, while
roast pork loin was stuffed with an apricot,
sultana and apple mousse and served with a
slow-braised pork shoulder, Hafod cheese
puff-pastry pie, crispy sage dauphinoise
potatoes, creamed celery, red cabbage compote
and rum jus. A chocolate assiette comprising a
spiced fondant, dark mousse, chocolate and
tonka bean ice cream, and Halen Môn
chocolate wafer also revealed high levels of
technical expertise. House wine from £14.40.
Chef/s: Gwyn Roberts. **Open:** Tue to Sat L 12 to 2, D
6.30 to 9.30. **Closed:** Sun, Mon, 25 Dec, 1 Jan, bank
hols. **Meals:** alc (main courses £15 to £24).
Service: not inc. **Details:** Cards accepted. 80 seats.
24 seats outside. Separate bar. Wheelchair access.
Music. Children allowed. Car parking.

Please send us your feedback

To register your opinion about any
restaurant listed in the Guide, or a new
restaurant that you wish to bring to our
attention, please visit the web address at
the bottom of the page. Your feedback
informs the content of the book and will be
used to compile next year's reviews.

▌Abersoch
Porth Tocyn Hotel
Fabulous views and evolving menus
Bwlch Tocyn, Abersoch, LL53 7BU
Tel no: (01758) 713303
www.porthtocynhotel.co.uk
Modern European | £40
Cooking score: 4

A Guide stalwart for 54 years and counting, this grand veteran among Welsh hotels is still in the safe hands of the Fletcher-Brewer family – as it has been since day one. Porth Tocyn has evolved, but the far-reaching views over Cardigan Bay towards Snowdonia's peaks are as breathtaking as ever, whether you are grabbing an alfresco opportunity or relaxing at a window table in the dining room. All is impeccably tended and homely, the food is delivered with grace, and the kitchen applies wide-ranging influences to shrewdly sourced raw materials. A starter of grilled red mullet arrives on a warm escabèche with aubergine won ton, roast venison loin comes with a beetroot potato cake, wild mushrooms and Madeira jus, and locally caught cod is partnered by rhubarb, fennel and tarragon hollandaise. Finish with savoury Welsh rarebit or something sweet – say iced mango parfait with raspberry trifle. Changes are afoot on the wine front, with Tanners now supplying much of the list – although the mark-up ceiling of £12 will remain.
Chef/s: Louise Fletcher-Brewer and John Bell.
Open: all week L 12.15 to 2.30, D 7.15 to 9 (9.30 in high season). **Closed:** early Nov to just before Easter. **Meals:** Set D £33.50 (2 courses) to £40. Sun L £24.50. Light lunch menu. **Service:** not inc.
Details: Cards accepted. 50 seats. 30 seats outside. Separate bar. No music. No mobile phones. Wheelchair access. Children allowed. Car parking.

Also recommended
Also recommended entries are not scored but we think they are worth a visit.

▌Bangor
ALSO RECOMMENDED
▲ Blue Sky Café
Ambassador Hall, 236 High Street, Bangor, LL57 1PA
Tel no: (01248) 355444
www.blueskybangor.co.uk
Eclectic £5 OFF

With wood floors, a real fire and a hotchpotch of wooden furniture, this excellent daytime café strikes a cosy, modern note. At the heart of the menu is a host of 'Blue Sky platters' (£10.95) showcasing splendid local ingredients – from mezze and charcuterie to cheese and smoked fish – with bread and all the accompanying bits and bobs. You'll also find sandwiches, soups (£3.85), burgers and salads (say char-grilled haloumi with sweet chilli drizzle, £6.95) – plus hearty breakfasts too (if you call in before 11.30). Wines start at £10.95. Open Mon to Sat.

▌Beaumaris
Ye Olde Bulls Head Inn, Loft Restaurant
Anglesey aristocrat
Castle Street, Beaumaris, LL58 8AP
Tel no: (01248) 810329
www.bullsheadinn.co.uk
Modern British | £40
Cooking score: 5

Built in 1472 and 'improved' in 1617, this aristocratic old-stager comes with reams of historical baggage. The inn's gastronomic epicentre is the aptly named Loft Restaurant, high up in the eaves of the building. It's a striking, atmospheric space with circular mirrors and arty partitions, overseen by approachable, knowledgeably professional staff. The cooking has suitably lofty aspirations and chef Hefin Roberts impresses visitors with his sharp imagination, respect for ingredients and eye for visual detail. Dinner is interspersed with fashionable extras, and

Welsh ingredients figure strongly across the board: a patriotic starter of Caerphilly cheese soufflé impressed one reader, likewise a crab and scallop lasagne showcasing the best of native seafood. Mains include cannon of lamb with leek porridge, shank ragoût and coriander jus or roast Conwy Valley pork fillet with sweet potato purée, spiced baby apples, Madeira and prune jus. Bringing up the rear are dazzling desserts including Champagne rhubarb mousse with ginger crumbs and Armagnac anglaise. Shrewdly chosen wines from the French regions form the backbone of the impressive list, although fascinating names from elsewhere should also tempt those with a nose for something more adventurous. Prices are very accommodating: house selections weigh in at £13 a carafe.

Chef/s: Hefin Roberts. **Open:** Tue to Sat D only 7 to 9.30 (6.30 Fri and Sat). **Closed:** Sun, Mon, 25 and 26 Dec, 1 Jan. **Meals:** Set D £39.50 (3 courses). **Service:** not inc. **Details:** Cards accepted. 45 seats. Separate bar. No music. No mobile phones. Children allowed. Car parking.

Borth-y-Gest

ALSO RECOMMENDED
▲ Moorings Bistro
4 Ivy Terrace, Borth-y-Gest, LL49 9TS
Tel no: (01766) 513500
www.mooringsbistroborthygest.com
Modern British

This charming bistro with an 'Egyptian sand' colour scheme overlooks the bay. Steve Williams used to be a chef on a ship, and his French-Canadian wife, Nadya Muir-Williams, is a cheerful front-of-house hostess. Start maybe with grilled sea bass and pepper skewer with lime aïoli (£5.50), followed by pot-roasted lamb shank with red wine and rosemary jus (£13.95), and finish with summer pudding (£5.50). Wine starts at £13.95. Open Wed to Sat D, also L on Sun and bank hols.

Caernarfon
Rhiwafallen
Stylish restaurant-with-rooms
Llandwrog, Caernarfon, LL54 5SW
Tel no: (01286) 830172
www.rhiwafallen.co.uk
Modern British | £35
Cooking score: 2

Classy interior design harmonises nicely with the traditional charms of an old farmhouse in this 'superb' restaurant-with-rooms. The 20-seater conservatory dining room has views over magnificent countryside towards the sea, and it's particularly lovely at sunset. A meal might kick off with an amuse-bouche of 'beautiful' homemade soup ahead of 12-hour cooked Anglesey belly pork with lentils, apple and black pudding and mains of rack of Welsh lamb with cauliflower cheese gratin and rosemary-roasted potatoes, followed by 'heavenly' chocolate crème brûlée. Wines from £15.95.

Chef/s: Robert John. **Open:** Sun L 12.30 to 2, Tue to Sat D 7 to 9. **Closed:** Mon. **Meals:** Set D £35 (3 courses). Sun L £19.50. **Service:** not inc. **Details:** Cards accepted. 40 seats. Air-con. Separate bar. No mobile phones. Music. Car parking.

Capel Garmon
Tan-y-Foel Country House
A very personal country house
Capel Garmon, LL26 0RE
Tel no: (01690) 710507
www.tyfhotel.co.uk
Modern British | £46
Cooking score: 5

As you negotiate the winding road up to this secluded restaurant-with-rooms, the stunning views of Snowdonia National Park become widescreen. On arrival, the traditional Welsh stone residence is everything you would expect, so the modern interior ('basic' thought one visitor) is a surprise. The Pitmans have been here for 20 years, and their hard work shows, above all, in the limited choice set dinners, which begin with canapés in the lounge at 7pm. There has always been a sense of season – deep-fried courgette flowers, say, or soft herring roes on spelt croustade with lemon and caper dressing – and Janet Pitman proudly champions local produce, whether it is seafood, meat or vegetables. Typical of the format – and a menu regular – is fillet of Welsh beef 'of excellent quality', perhaps served with sautéed potatoes, beetroot and green beans or with devilled kidneys and puff-pastry pie topping with Anna potatoes, sauté baby greens and rich beef gravy. Desserts can include an intense lemon sponge or a selection of Welsh cheeses. The wine list offers a thorough world survey with some good-value options poured into loose-styled categories. Bottles from £21.

Chef/s: Janet Pitman. **Open:** all week D only 7.30 (1 sitting). **Closed:** Dec, limited availability in Jan. **Meals:** Set D £46 (3 courses). **Service:** not inc. **Details:** Cards accepted. 10 seats. No music. No mobile phones. Car parking.

▌Conwy
Castle Hotel, Dawson's Restaurant
Hearty crowd-pleasers and classics
High Street, Conwy, LL32 8DB
Tel no: (01492) 582800
www.castlewales.co.uk
Modern British | £24
Cooking score: 2
£5 OFF 🍴 £30

A change of format has seen Dawson's take on a brasserie air. Refurbishment has given the setting a modern slant, but the walls are still adorned with the magnificent paintings of Victorian artist and illustrator John Dawson-Watson, who spent his last days in Conwy. The menu spans classic (crispy leg of duckling with a casserole of Puy lentils) and modern (cod terrine and noodle salad), but is weighted towards hearty crowd-pleasers such as sticky braised pork belly on a cassoulet of white

beans, tomato and local sausages with crackling and apple purée, perhaps followed by bread-and-butter pudding. Wines start at £13.95.

Chef/s: Graham Tinsley. **Open:** all week 12 to 9.30 (9 Sun). **Meals:** alc (main courses £11 to £22). Set L and D £17.95 (2 courses) to £23.95. Sun L £14.95 (2 courses) to £17.95. **Service:** 10% (optional). **Details:** Cards accepted. 60 seats. 10 seats outside. Separate bar. Music. Children allowed. Car parking.

▌Criccieth
Tir a Môr
Thriving bistro with comforting food
1-3 Mona Terrace, Criccieth, LL52 0HG
Tel no: (01766) 523084
www.tiramor-criccieth.co.uk
European | £25
Cooking score: 2
£30

'Tir a Môr' translates as 'land and sea' – which neatly sums up this bistro's location and the scope of its menu. Set on a street corner not far from the seafront, it has a simple, uncluttered interior brightened by modern artwork. The Heberts have run the place since 2004, attracting a loyal following with their friendly welcome and honest, comforting European cooking. Influences come from France and the Mediterranean – witness a starter of roasted pepper and goats' cheese tart, followed by seared fillets of sea bass with black olive tapenade and pesto butter sauce. To finish, maybe traditional crème brûlée. Wines from £13.95.

Chef/s: Laurent Hebert. **Open:** Tue to Sat D only 6 to 9. **Closed:** Sun, Mon, 23 Dec to mid Feb. **Meals:** alc (main courses £14 to £23). Set D £19.50 (3 courses). **Service:** not inc. **Details:** Cards accepted. 38 seats. Wheelchair access. Music. Children allowed. Car parking.

Visit us online

To find out more about *The Good Food Guide*, please visit www.thegoodfoodguide.co.uk

Dolgellau
Dylanwad Da
All-rounder with honest food and wine
2 Ffôs-y-Felin, Dolgellau, LL40 1BS
Tel no: (01341) 422870
www.dylanwad.co.uk
Modern British | £27
Cooking score: 1
£5 OFF 🍷 £30

This is a bar, café, bistro and wine shop rolled into one. It operates as a coffee shop during the day, offers a tapas menu for lunch (items such as Serrano ham with tomato salad or marinated anchovies) and good, honest bistro dishes in the evening. Start perhaps with leek and Perl Las blue cheese rarebit, followed by breast of chicken with a cream, saffron and apricot sauce, and finish with blueberry Bakewell tart. Dylan Rowlands runs a wine business, 'Dan y Dylanwad' (Under the Influence), and imports wines directly from Europe. Bottles in-house start at £14.50.
Chef/s: Dylan Rowlands. **Open:** Thur to Sat L 10 to 3, D 7 to 9. **Closed:** Sun to Wed, Feb. **Meals:** alc (main courses £13 to £18). Set L and D £15.50 (2 courses) to £21.50. Tasting menu £45. **Service:** not inc. **Details:** Cards accepted. 28 seats. Separate bar. Music. Children allowed.

Harlech
Castle Cottage
Warmth, congeniality and Welsh food
Y Llech, Harlech, LL46 2YL
Tel no: (01766) 780479
www.castlecottageharlech.co.uk
Modern British | £36
Cooking score: 2
🛏

'A beacon of honest cooking in a wilderness' was one reader's verdict on Glyn and Jacqueline Roberts' unaffected restaurant-with-rooms. The warmth and congeniality of this cottagey place never disappoint, and there's an increasingly light touch in the kitchen by all accounts. Glyn's daily menus are stuffed with as many local ingredients as he

can muster – Menai mussels, roast loin of lamb with herbs and garlic, a duo of Llyn Peninsula pheasant with bubble and squeak, port and chestnut jus, and of course Welsh steaks with chunky chips. Vegetables are now integrated into each main dish, and desserts are crowd-pleasers such as banana and walnut sponge. Wines start at £15.
Chef/s: Glyn Roberts. **Open:** all week D 7 to 9.30. **Closed:** 3 weeks Nov. **Meals:** Set D £34 (3 courses). **Service:** not inc. **Details:** Cards accepted. 35 seats. Separate bar. No mobile phones. Music. Children allowed.

Llandudno
Bodysgallen Hall
Sophisticated, sense-of-occasion food
Llandudno, LL30 1RS
Tel no: (01492) 584466
www.bodysgallen.com
Modern British | £39
Cooking score: 5
🍷 🛏 V

Follies, cascading water features and trimmed box hedges bursting with scented herbs are just part of the full-dress, heritage experience at Bodysgallen Hall – a majestic edifice overlooking Snowdonia. When it comes to matters gastronomic, the focus is the Dining Room – a vision of old-school elegance where guests can sample Gareth Jones' sophisticated, sense-of-occasion food. Meals are replete with mid-course sorbets and other high-end incidentals, but the kitchen keeps its feet on terra firma when it comes to sourcing and execution. Welsh produce has its say in starters such as a tian of Pant ys Gawn goats' cheese with a fig and walnut pastilla and whipped sweet red wine – a theme that is picked up by mains including a roe deer and trompette mushroom boudin served with caramelised cauliflower and truffle jus. Seafood is also treated with refinement and *élan* (seared fillet of sea bass with Aberdaron crab fritter and 'all things fennel', for example). Prettily fashioned desserts aim for surprise with compositions such as dark chocolate fondant, griottine cherry tempura and iced yoghurt. The wine list is a well-travelled, classically schooled aristocrat with an eye for fine Bordeaux and Burgundies as well as tasty vintages from across the globe. House selections start at £19. For something more casual, try the 1620 Bistro in the converted Wynn Rooms coach house. **Chef/s:** Gareth Jones. **Open:** Tue to Sun L 12.30 to 1.45, D 7 to 9.30 (Sun D summer only). **Closed:** Mon. **Meals:** Set L £19.50 (2 courses) to £22.50. Set D £39 (3 courses). **Service:** inc. **Details:** Cards accepted. 60 seats. Air-con. Separate bar. No music. No mobile phones. Wheelchair access. Children allowed. Car parking.

St Tudno Hotel, Terrace Restaurant

Old-school elegance by the sea
Promenade, Llandudno, LL30 2LP
Tel no: (01492) 874411
www.st-tudno.co.uk
Modern British | £30
Cooking score: 3
£5 OFF ♦ 🍴

There's something about this seafront hotel that harks back to a golden age of bandstands and promenades on the pier. Alice Liddell stayed here at the age of eight, the year Lewis Carroll wrote about her in *Alice in Wonderland*. Nowadays, enormous murals of Lake Como dominate the dining room and a modern European influence is evident in the cooking, which makes good use of local produce, notably seafood. Cod quenelles poached in a Hafod cheese sauce with a ham and pease pudding stottie, ahead of loin of roe deer with a game pudding and truffled Welsh honey glaze, and roast pineapple pain perdu with a mango parfait show the style. The wine list covers France's main regions in detail, with some interesting finds from around the world. Bottles start at £15.95.
Chef/s: Ian Watson. **Open:** all week L 12.30 to 2, D 7 to 9.30 (9 Sun). **Meals:** alc (main courses £16 to £20). Set L £18 (2 courses) to £22. Sun L £18.95. **Service:** not inc. **Details:** Cards accepted. 65 seats. Air-con. Separate bar. No mobile phones. Music. Car parking.

▮ Penmaenpool
Penmaenuchaf Hall

Big helpings of country house grandeur
Penmaenpool, LL40 1YB
Tel no: (01341) 422129
www.penhall.co.uk
Modern British | £40
Cooking score: 3
£5 OFF ♦ 🍴

Oak-panelled opulence is the order of the day at this handsome mansion set amid the foothills of Cader Idris. If country house grandeur is your thing, this place offers big helpings without being tired or fusty. The dining room strikes a contemporary note with a Welsh slate floor and tables draped in crisp white linen. Gothic windows look out over immaculate gardens to Snowdonia, and the view provides much of what's on the plate – local pork belly (honey-glazed and served with onion compote and chilli caramel sauce) or seared sirloin of Welsh Black beef (with wild mushrooms, fondant potato and port sauce). Desserts such as cider-poached pears with ginger sauce plough the same trad/ modern furrow. The comprehensive, ever-evolving wine list still puts France at the top of the heap, but Australia and the USA offer increasingly tempting distraction. Eleven house selections – all commendably priced at £19.75 – open the show, and half-bottles are numerous. The hotel also has a thriving wine club and hosts regular tastings.
Chef/s: Justin Pilkington. **Open:** all week L 12 to 2 (2.30 Sun), D 7 to 9.30. **Meals:** alc (main courses £22 to £26). Set L £15.95 (2 courses) to £17.95. Set D £40. Sun L £18.50. **Service:** not inc. **Details:** Cards accepted. 35 seats. 16 seats outside. Separate bar. No mobile phones. Wheelchair access. Music. Car parking.

Penmynydd

ALSO RECOMMENDED
▲ Neuadd Lwyd Country House

Penmynydd, LL61 5BX
Tel no: (01248) 715005
www.neuaddlwyd.co.uk
Modern British

The greystone house on Anglesey was built as a rectory in the early Victorian era, and enjoys magnificent views towards Snowdonia from the handsome dining room. Susannah Woods cooks a set four-course dinner three nights a week. October diners took in smoked haddock chowder, local black beef fillet with creamed courgettes, dauphinoise and red wine sauce, tarte Tatin with Penderyn whisky ice cream, and the standard finishing trio of Welsh farmhouse cheeses (£39). Wines from £13.95. Open Thu to Sat D.

Porthmadog

NEW ENTRY
Peppino's at The Royal Sportsman

Ambitious food in a solid hotel
131 High Street, Porthmadog, LL49 9HB
Tel no: (01766) 512015
www.royalsportsman.co.uk
Modern European | £30
Cooking score: 2

 £5 OFF 🛏 V

The Naudis' town-centre hotel is a solid place with an ambitious restaurant. Although the ambience in Peppino's 'is not the best' – despite its original Victorian wooden floor a visitor found the décor uninspiring – the food is 'rather good'. Red onion and cherry tomato tarte Tatin, with glazed goats' cheese and balsamic vinegar is a good start, followed, perhaps, by a duo of Welsh lamb – pink rack and braised shoulder – with truffle oil mash, Puy lentils, butternut squash purée and rosemary jus. Finish with lemon tart,

raspberry coulis and crème fraîche or Welsh cheeses. A reasonably priced, short wine list starts at £15.25.
Chef/s: Felix Prem. **Open:** all week L 12 to 2.30, D 6 to 9. **Meals:** alc (main courses £9 to £21). Set D £24 (2 courses) to £30. Sun L £13.95 (2 courses) to £16.95. **Service:** not inc. **Details:** Cards accepted. 50 seats. 24 seats outside. Separate bar. Wheelchair access. Music. Children allowed. Car parking.

Pwllheli

Plas Bodegroes

Landmark country hotel with expert food
Nefyn Road, Pwllheli, LL53 5TH
Tel no: (01758) 612363
www.bodegroes.co.uk
Modern British | £43
Cooking score: 5

🍷🛏

Chris and Gunna Chown's tenure of this secluded Georgian manor house spans more than 25 years and, during that time, Plas Bodegroes has become a landmark hotel famed for its lovely location on the Llyn Peninsula, an amazing art collection and expert food. The kitchen chooses its ingredients with consummate care, although a little more seasonal awareness might give the menus added impact. Chris Chown is at his best when he's on familiar territory, producing robustly flavoured guinea fowl, apricot and pistachio terrine with red pepper chutney, or a dish of grilled hake with roast garlic mash and crab sauce – but he's not averse to slipping in the occasional modish idea (roast monkfish with mizuna, pickled carrots and spiced Puy lentil dressing, say). Locally reared meat is also given a good outing, although the results tend to be safe rather than challenging – roast rump of Llyn lamb with devilled kidneys, potato gratin and rosemary jus, or a trio of pork with roast root vegetables and apple sauce, for example. To finish, Grand Marnier parfait with sesame snap sounds more promising than 'out of season' apple and rhubarb crumble with elderflower custard, which smacks of gastropub rather than high-ranking restaurant. Superb home-baked breads and a

prestigious wine list help to redress the balance; the latter favours France, but there is also plenty of impressive drinking from the New World. Twenty house recommendations start at £17.50 (£4.50 a glass).
Chef/s: Chris Chown and Aled Williams. **Open:** Sun L 12.30 to 2, Tue to Sat D 7 to 9. **Closed:** Mon, 28 Nov to 12 Feb. **Meals:** Set D £42.50 (4 courses). Sun L £19.50. **Service:** not inc. **Details:** Cards accepted. 40 seats. Separate bar. No music. No mobile phones. Wheelchair access. Children allowed. Car parking.

ALSO RECOMMENDED
▲ Y Daflod at Tafarn Y Fic
Llithfaen, Pwllheli, LL53 6PA
Tel no: (01758) 750473
www.tafarnyfic.com
Modern British

Set on the first floor of a community-owned pub, this is the domain of self-taught cook Hefina Prichard and her farmer husband Tomos, who handles front-of-house proceedings with genuine charm. Dishes span traditional and international themes, from sweet potato and coconut soup (£3.50) to main courses such as chunks of beef and kidneys slow-cooked in red wine and topped with a pastry crust (£11). Puddings exhibit a similar scope, say crème brûlée with plums, toasted almonds and a hint of star anise (£4.50). Wines start at £10.50. Open Thur to Sat.

▌Talsarnau
Maes-y-Neuadd
Romantic medieval manor
Talsarnau, LL47 6YA
Tel no: (01766) 780200
www.neuadd.com
Modern European | £35
Cooking score: 3
£5 OFF 🍷 🛏

The name means mansion in the meadow and Maes-y-Neuadd's setting delivers on this promise. The granite-built fourteenth-

century manor sits in 85 acres of grounds backed by green hills. Produce from the restored kitchen garden features on the menu; if it isn't home-grown it's caught or raised locally. There's a simple selection of light meals at lunchtime (fisherman's pie, lamb's liver with bacon and mash), but dinner is a more serious affair. Reports this year suggest that standards vary, but at its best the kitchen has turned out well-timed scallops with mash, black pudding and port wine jus followed by loin of venison with a casserole of lentils, roasted shallots and juniper sauce. Desserts appear to excite less interest. The wine list lingers in France and kicks off at £16.95 a bottle.
Chef/s: Peter Jackson. **Open:** all week L 12 to 1.45, D 7 to 8.45. **Meals:** alc (main courses £9 to £15). Set D £30 (2 courses) to £39. Sun L £17.95. **Service:** 10% (optional). **Details:** Cards accepted. 65 seats. 20 seats outside. Separate bar. No music. No mobile phones. Wheelchair access. Music. Children allowed. Car parking.

▌Valley

ALSO RECOMMENDED
▲ Cleifiog Uchaf
Spencer Road, Valley, LL65 3AB
Tel no: (01407) 741888
www.cleifioguchaf.co.uk
Modern British

This sixteenth-century Anglesey longhouse was turned into a smart country hotel by Prydwen and Emyr Parry. Llywelyn's Bistro is at its heart, and on weekdays there is a no-choice, five-course tasting menu (£39.95), supplemented by a carte on Saturdays. The chef creates artistically presented fashionable dishes such as pea, Parmesan and chorizo soup, fillet of beef with lobster and watercress, and a 'deconstructed rhubarb cheesecake'. Open Tue to Sat D only. Wines start at £14.50.

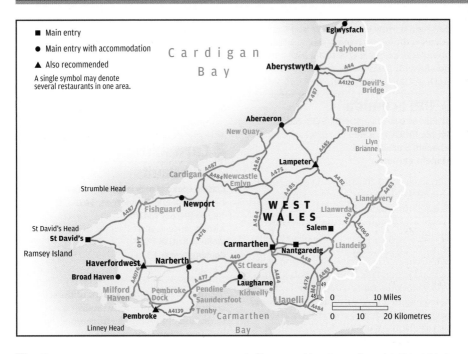

■ Main entry

● Main entry with accommodation

▲ Also recommended

A single symbol may denote
several restaurants in one area.

Aberaeron

Harbourmaster

Sleek harbourside hotel
Pen Cei, Aberaeron, SA46 OBT
Tel no: (01545) 570755
www.harbour-master.com
Modern British | £30
Cooking score: 2

Right at the water's edge in pretty Aberaeron,
this sleek boutique hotel has no shortage of
local fans, who pack its expansive, wood-
floored bar most evenings. Meanwhile, the
restaurant makes the most of native
ingredients for an eclectic repertoire ranging
from steamed mussels with Thai flavours to
rump of Welsh lamb with Puy lentils, spinach
and Pant Mawr goats' cheese. For dessert,
maybe chocolate fondant with vanilla ice
cream. There have been some niggles about
the food (especially the bar menu), but
everyone applauds the 'well-organised,
cheerful service'. The wine list kicks off at £13.

Chef/s: Tom Holden. **Open:** all week L 12 to 2.30, D
6 to 9. **Closed:** 25 Dec. **Meals:** alc (main courses £12
to £23). Set L £13 (2 courses) to £16. Sun L £14 (2
courses) to £18.50. **Service:** not inc. **Details:** Cards
accepted. 55 seats. 15 seats outside. Air-con.
Separate bar. No mobile phones. Wheelchair
access. Music. Car parking.

Aberystwyth

ALSO RECOMMENDED
▲ Treehouse
14 Baker Street, Aberystwyth, SY23 2BJ
Tel no: (01970) 615791
www.treehousewales.co.uk
Café £5 OFF

This daytime bistro-cum-coffee house
occupies the upper floors of what was once the
Victoria Inn in the heart of Aberystwyth.
Downstairs is a superb organic food store, and
the eatery makes excellent use of the produce
sold there. Choices from the unfussy menu
range from butternut squash and celery
Madras soup with coconut (£3.50) to quinoa

and cashew nut rissoles on a mixed vegetable korma with basmati rice (£5.60), with back-up from jacket potatoes filled with hummus to quiche with potato wedges (£6.40). Wines from £9.50. Open Mon to Sat.

▲ Ultracomida

31 Pier Street, Aberystwyth, SY23 2LN
Tel no: (01970) 630686
www.ultracomida.co.uk
Modern European

Ultracomida's well-endowed larder, based around Welsh, Spanish and French produce, drives both restaurant and deli alike. Regularly changing menus show quality from the off. Snack on tapas such as cod and hake fishcake with mojo verde (£4) or a plate of Welsh cheeses, order cod with saffron bomba rice and lemon sauce from the daily set lunch (£8.95 for one course) or look for beef bourguignon on the evening menu (Fri and Sat only; £16 for two courses). Excellent service. House wine £10.95. Open all week.

▍Broad Haven
The Druidstone

Romantic old house with global food
Broad Haven, SA62 3NE
Tel no: (01437) 781221
www.druidstone.co.uk
Global | £30
Cooking score: 2

'The view and the art' are two good reasons to come here. Perched precipitously above St Brides Bay, this romantic old house has a ragged, bohemian air, with an eclectic décor that includes a colourful array of paintings by local artists. The menu is equally diverse, with influences spanning the globe. Vegetable dhal soup, Iranian spinach and potato tortilla, and Moroccan roasted leg of lamb with crushed chickpeas are typical of the scope. Pub-style puds might include banoffi pie or sticky toffee pudding with butterscotch sauce. The wine list includes plenty of organic and biodynamic offerings, with prices from £11.80 a bottle.

Chef/s: Angus Bell, Matt Ash and Richard Janukowicz. **Open:** all week L 12.30 to 2.30, D 7 to 9.30. **Meals:** alc (main courses £14 to £22). **Service:** not inc. **Details:** Cards accepted. 36 seats. 50 seats outside. Separate bar. No music. No mobile phones. Wheelchair access. Music. Children allowed. Car parking.

▍Carmarthen
Angel Vaults

Classic cooking with a modern edge
10 Notts Square, Carmarthen, SA31 1PQ
Tel no: (01267) 238305
www.theangelvaultsrestaurant.co.uk
Modern British | £27
Cooking score: 1

£5 OFF £30

'I cannot speak highly enough of the service', enthused one reader of this stylish restaurant in the heart of town. The fifteenth-century building retains some striking original features, offset by understated modern décor. The cooking is classic with a modern edge: you could kick off with a buckwheat blini with smoked salmon and dill crème fraîche, then move on to confit pork belly with black pudding, apple purée and parsley sauce. To finish, maybe vanilla pannacotta with Champagne-poached rhubarb. Wines start at £12.95.

Chef/s: Andrew Thomas. **Open:** Mon to Sat L 12 to 2.30, Tue to Sat D 6.30 to 9.30. **Closed:** Sun. **Meals:** alc (main courses £15 to £22). Set L £11.95 (2 courses). Set D £24.95 (3 courses). **Service:** not inc. **Details:** Cards accepted. 65 seats. 12 seats outside. Air-con. Separate bar. Music. Children allowed.

Eglwysfach

Ynyshir Hall
Smart dining with thrills and frills
Eglwysfach, SY20 8TA
Tel no: (01654) 781209
www.ynyshir-hall.co.uk
Modern British | £70
Cooking score: 5

£5 OFF

'A big treat', cherished for its personable style, scrupulous attention to detail and blissful tranquillity, Ynyshir Hall was once owned by Queen Victoria – although it now does a right royal job as a country house retreat. The shooting lodge stands amid 14 acres of peachy grounds planted with horticultural rarities, all surrounded by a vast UNESCO Biosphere reserve. Shane Hughes makes the most of 'stunning' produce from the locality and rotates his menus daily – perhaps serving roast red-legged partridge with Brussels sprout tops dressed in foie gras butter or embellishing tender, slow-cooked shoulder of lamb with exemplary potato beignet, onion cream, broad beans and salsify. Fish is also handled with imagination, accuracy and some exotic strokes, witness cod and scallop with curried new potatoes and shallot crisps or roast halibut with crab tortellini and a Thai-style nage. Dinner prices are far from cheap, but meals are peppered with lots of extras (a pre-dessert shot of carrot and gin, say). To finish, 'textbook' pumpkin seed soufflé is perfectly offset by a bitter dark chocolate sauce. Lunch is a more affordable prospect, with a community-conscious 'friends and neighbours' deal on Mondays and Tuesdays. Joan Reen is a perfect hands-on host, and her staff approach their duties without a smidgen of stuffiness or formality. Wine service is also 'superb', and the all-embracing international list is a top-drawer slate that opens with a brilliant choice of house recommendations from £20 (£5 a glass).
Chef/s: Shane Hughes. **Open:** all week L 12 to 2, D 7 to 8.45. **Meals:** Set L £21.50 (3 courses). Set D £70 (5 courses). Tasting menu L £48, D £80. **Service:** not

inc. **Details:** Cards accepted. 27 seats. Separate bar. No mobile phones. Wheelchair access. Music. Children allowed. Car parking.

Haverfordwest

ALSO RECOMMENDED
▲ The George's
24 Market Street, Haverfordwest, SA61 1NH
Tel no: (01437) 766683
www.thegeorges.uk.com
Eclectic £5 OFF

'Always a fantastic welcome', noted one of the many fans of this quirky business. Behind an old-fashioned shop frontage lies a new-age store and a restaurant offering a menu that mixes comfort food with international flavours – maybe goats' cheese salad (£5.50) followed by seafood chowder (£14.50) with bread-and-butter pudding (£5.50) for dessert. Wines from £18 per litre. Open Tue to Sat L, Fri and Sat D.

Lampeter

ALSO RECOMMENDED
▲ Ty Mawr Mansion
Cilcennin, Lampeter, SA48 8DB
Tel no: (01570) 470033
www.tymawrmansion.co.uk
Modern British

An extraordinary find deep in the Ceredigion countryside, Ty Mawr's Georgian splendour chimes well with the dramatic surrounds of the Aeron Valley. The kitchen showcases Welsh produce for a menu that might open with Anglesey Bay seafood chowder before, say, loin of lamb with confit shoulder, shepherd's pie and rosemary jus (£21.95). To finish, the assiette of fruit crumbles and cheesecakes (£7.95) bowled over one party. Wines start at £14.50. Open all week D only. An in-house cinema is the latest attraction for guests.

Laugharne

The Cors

Quirky and very romantic
Newbridge Road, Laugharne, SA33 4SH
Tel no: (01994) 427219
www.the-cors.co.uk
Modern British | £28
Cooking score: 3
£5 OFF 🍴 £30

There's a sense of true dedication about this idiosyncratic and very romantic restaurant-with-rooms set in a fairy glade of a bog garden. For one reader it's a 'real find', run by chef/proprietor Nick Priestland 'in his own inimitable style'. His cooking appeals for its well-executed straightforwardness and dedication to local raw materials. In the dining room there's a relaxed, unpretentious feel. Short, daily-changing dinner menus deliver the likes of seared scallops with tomato and basil sauce, roasted rack of new season's lamb with a rosemary and garlic crust and caramelised red onion gravy, or wild sea trout with asparagus and lemon hollandaise sauce. The compact wine list offers a decent global selection from £14.50.
Chef/s: Nick Priestland. **Open:** Sun L 12 to 3, Thur to Sat D 7 to 9.30. **Closed:** Mon to Wed, last two weeks Nov. **Meals:** alc (main courses £15 to £22). Set L £20. Set D £25. Sun L £20. **Service:** not inc. **Details:** Cards accepted. 28 seats. 12 seats outside. Separate bar. No mobile phones. Music. Car parking.

Nantgaredig

Y Polyn

Remote haven run by foodie couples
Capel Dewi, Nantgaredig, SA32 7LH
Tel no: (01267) 290000
www.ypolynrestaurant.co.uk
Modern British | £29
Cooking score: 3
£5 OFF £30

Out in the sticks, a few miles east of Carmarthen, Y Polyn began life as a remote tollhouse and boozing inn, but two couples

with professional foodie backgrounds have dusted it down and fostered the place as a cottagey restaurant dealing in accomplished (but not 'over-refined') food. The kitchen is in the hands of Susan Manson and Maryann Wright, who fill their larder with good local ingredients and send out confident, well-presented dishes with earthy accents – think pork rillettes, Welsh lamb hotpot and coq au vin. Other ideas such as Tuscan white bean soup or fillet of Brixham pollack with cannellini beans and chorizo strike a sunny Mediterranean note, while soothing desserts might bring warm pear and almond tart. Welsh cheeses are worth a go, and the respectable wine list opens with house selections from £13.50 (£3.50 a glass).
Chef/s: Susan Manson and Maryann Wright. **Open:** Tue to Sun L 12 to 2 (2.30 Sun), Tue to Sat D 7 to 9 (9.30 Fri and Sat). **Closed:** Mon, 25 and 26 Dec. **Meals:** alc (main courses £10 to 17). Set L £12 (2 courses) to £14.50. Set D £29.50. Sun L £22.50. **Service:** not inc. **Details:** Cards accepted. 50 seats. 12 seats outside. Wheelchair access. Music. Children allowed. Car parking.

Narberth

NEW ENTRY

The Grove

Appealing hotel with good local food
Narberth, SA67 8BX
Tel no: (01834) 860915
www.thegrove-narberth.co.uk
Modern European | £34
Cooking score: 2
£5 OFF 🍷 🍴

A visit to this country house begins with drinks in the lounge, with its oversized sofas, modern artwork and rug-strewn wood floors. The wood-panelled dining room has green and leafy views, linen-clad tables and a team of young, charming staff. Expect simple food fuelled by local ingredients – perhaps baked goats' cheese with caramelised pears, honey and salad, followed by an excellent fillet of Welsh beef with fine beans, sautéed potatoes and béarnaise sauce. A dessert of meringue with rich vanilla ice cream, cream and fresh fruit was generous and balanced. The painstakingly annotated wine list is big on quality and value, with a generous sprinkling of southern hemisphere wines supporting the European classics. A quartet of house wines comes at £16 (£4 a glass).

Chef/s: Nigel Marriage. **Open:** all week L 12 to 2, D 6 to 9.30. **Meals:** alc (main courses £18 to £23). Sun L £18 (2 courses) to £21. **Service:** not inc. **Details:** Cards accepted. 50 seats. 12 seats outside. Air-con. Separate bar. Music. Children allowed. Car parking.

ALSO RECOMMENDED

▲ Ultracomida

7 High Street, Narberth, SA67 7AR
Tel no: (01834) 861491
www.ultracomida.com
Modern European

Venture in to bag a seat at this deli-cum-restaurant and you will find yourself passing a veritable takeaway feast of Spanish, Welsh and French produce. Like its counterpart in Aberystwyth (see entry), the kitchen shows its mettle with a repertoire that takes in plates of charcuterie and cheese, tapas such as albondigas (meatballs in tomato sauce, £4), and good-value set lunches, with duck leg cooked with tomato, orange and olives as the centrepiece (£11 for two courses). House wine £10.95. Closed Sun.

■ Newport

Cnapan

Classy, creative home cooking
East Street, Newport, SA42 0SY
Tel no: (01239) 820575
www.cnapan.co.uk
Modern British | £30
Cooking score: 2

£5 OFF 🍴

A family-run restaurant-with-rooms in picture-perfect Newport (think Cornwall with fewer crowds), Cnapan has the small and personal approach of a boutique hotel and a home-from-home appearance. There's

nothing slick about the styling, but it does feel loved and lived-in. Accordingly the food, served in a carpeted dining room decorated with shelves of ornaments, is classy and creative home cooking, inspired by an impressive array of local ingredients. Typical of the style is seafood chowder followed by roast breast of guinea fowl with a fresh pesto stuffing and crispy pancetta. Finish with lemon crème brûlée. Wines start at £14.

Chef/s: Judith Cooper. **Open:** Wed to Mon D only 6.30 to 10. **Closed:** Tue, Christmas, 5 Jan to mid Mar. **Meals:** Set D £24 (2 courses) to £30. **Service:** not inc. **Details:** Cards accepted. 35 seats. Separate bar. No mobile phones. Wheelchair access. Music. Children allowed. Car parking.

Llys Meddyg

Modish, unfussy food
East Street, Newport, SA42 0SY
Tel no: (01239) 820008
www.llysmeddyg.com
Modern European | £35
Cooking score: 4

£5 OFF 🍴

This 'excellent-value' restaurant offers 'outstanding' food in a relaxed, boutique hotel setting. Choose between two dining areas: the downstairs bar has a roaring fire, big leather sofas and relaxed ambience; the dining room above offers a more formal experience. The style throughout is subtly cool, with a harmonious blend of traditional and modern elements. The same could be said of the cooking; expect modish, unfussy food such as smoked haddock soup with a poached egg and parsley or chump of Preseli lamb with cockles and cardamom. To finish, maybe damson soufflé with almond milk ice cream. A separate kitchen garden menu offers light bites ranging from stuffed peppers to a chorizo burger with homemade chutney. The nicely balanced, international wine list kicks off at £14.50. Opening times may vary.

Chef/s: Scott Davis. **Open:** Wed to Sun L 12 to 2 (12.30 Sun), Tue to Sun D 7 to 9. **Meals:** alc (main courses £18 to £22). Set L £15.50 (2 courses) to £18.50. Sun L £12.50. **Service:** not inc.

Details: Cards accepted. 36 seats. 50 seats outside. Separate bar. Wheelchair access. Music. Children allowed. Car parking.

Pembroke

ALSO RECOMMENDED
▲ Old Kings Arms
Main Street, Pembroke, SA71 4JS
Tel no: (01646) 683611
www.oldkingsarmshotel.co.uk
British £5 OFF

The Wheeler family have owned Pembroke's oldest hostelry for 58 years and little seems to change here. A red theme dominates the beamed dining room and the extensive menu majors in tried-and-tested favourites. Hot cockles, laverbread and grilled bacon (£7.95) is a pleasing starter, while approved main courses have included various daily changing fish specials, braised shank of lamb and very good fillet steak au poivre (£21.75). Finish with bread-and-butter pudding. House wine is £12.95. Accommodation. Open all week.

St David's

★ BEST FAMILY RESTAURANT ★

Cwtch
Local cooking with pride
22 High Street, St David's, SA62 6SD
Tel no: (01437) 720491
www.cwtchrestaurant.co.uk
Modern British | £29
Cooking score: 3
£5 OFF   £30

'What a lovely place, simple, informal, welcoming', noted one visitor to this two-tiered restaurant on St David's main street. Pride in carefully sourced local ingredients is much in evidence on the menu, and fish is successful – potted crab with a very good lemon-dill mayonnaise and perfectly cooked local sea trout with sauce vierge have been heartily endorsed. Otherwise, there could be pork belly with black pudding, roasted apples and onion gravy. The foccacia is excellent, and

those with room for dessert have enjoyed clotted cream rice pudding, and lemon curd and white chocolate cheesecake. Families are very welcome (children are really well catered for, with crayons and their own menu). An international selection of wines opens at £14. **Chef/s:** Matt Cox. **Open:** all week D only 6 to 10 (Apr to Oct), Wed to Sat D 6 to 9.30 (Nov to Mar). **Meals:** Set D £24 (2 courses) to £29. **Service:** not inc. **Details:** Cards accepted. 50 seats. Wheelchair access. Music. Children allowed.

Salem

Angel
A splendid village pub
Salem, SA19 7LY
Tel no: (01558) 823394
www.angelsalem.co.uk
Modern British | £25
Cooking score: 4
£30

Rod Peterson and Liz Smith's splendid village pub is the kind of place you dream about having in your home town: casual, honest and uncompromising in pursuit of quality. The mood is cheerful, the décor smart – in a wood-floored, antique furniture kind of way – and the cooking is spot-on for what it offers. Ravioli of smoked haddock and coriander with curried spinach epitomises the teaming of powerful flavours with emphatic spicing. Main courses might turn up roast fillet and confit of pork, with apple charlotte, celeriac and mustard, or braised beef steak with mushroom jus, tarragon dumpling and béarnaise sauce. This being Wales, Welsh rarebit is a must, otherwise there's white chocolate and raspberry trifle with homemade shortbread. The short wine list keeps prices on a short leash from £15.95. Half-a-dozen come by the glass, from £3.90. **Chef/s:** Rod Peterson. **Open:** Wed to Sun L 12 to 2, Wed to Sat D 7 to 9. **Closed:** Mon and Tue. **Meals:** alc (main courses £11 to £17). Set D £21.95 (2 courses) to £24.95. Sun L £18.95 (2 courses) to £22.95. **Service:** not inc. **Details:** Cards accepted. 60 seats. 12 seats outside. Separate bar. Wheelchair access. Music. Children allowed. Car parking.

CHANNEL ISLANDS

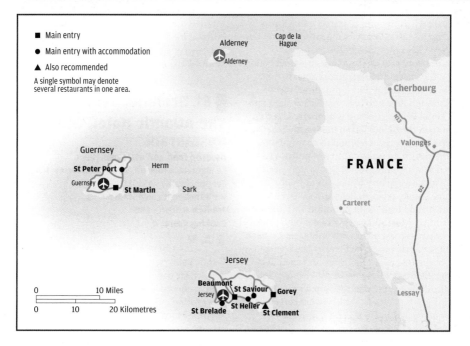

Beaumont, Jersey

Bistro Soleil

Sunny seaside bistro
La Route de la Haule, Beaumont, Jersey, JE3 7BA
Tel no: (01534) 720249
Modern British | £15
New Chef

£30

'Always a pleasure', remarks one regular visitor to this sunny seaside bistro. Overlooking the shimmering expanses of St Aubin's Bay and beyond, it really is a treat – especially if you're basking on the courtyard and eating alfresco when *le soleil* turns up the heat. Locally landed fish features strongly on the menu – perhaps steamed mussels in Jersey cider, cream and leeks followed by a fresh lobster or seafood pie with buttered asparagus and Champagne sauce. Meat fans might consider char-grilled rump steak with chive mash, baked field mushrooms and Café de Paris butter. Wines start at £14.75. A new chef was due to start as the Guide went to press; reports please.

Open: Tue to Sun L 12.15 to 2, D 6.45 to 9.30.
Closed: Mon, bank hols. **Meals:** alc (main courses £9 to £18). Set L £12.50 (2 courses) to £15.00. Set D £15. Sun L £15. **Service:** not inc. **Details:** Cards accepted. 60 seats. 40 seats outside. Separate bar. Wheelchair access. Music. Children allowed. Car parking.

Gorey, Jersey

Suma's

A fairytale setting and polished food
Gorey Hill, St Martin, Gorey, Jersey, JE3 6ET
Tel no: (01534) 853291
www.sumasrestaurant.com
Modern European | £32
Cooking score: 5

V

It may be the easy-going little sister of stately Longueville Manor (see entry) but Suma's has been around long enough to shrug off any inferiority complexes – especially when it's blessed with one of the most fairytale locations on Jersey. Perched high above Gorey's stone-walled harbour and centuries-old Mont Orgeuil castle, it makes the most of gorgeous views over the colourfully decorated waterfront cottages and boats bobbing about on the water. The restaurant's slogan, 'fine food, fun dining' gets it just about right – although this is no brasserie lightweight and Daniel Ward's cooking is up there with the best on the island. Given the waterside setting, you might expect seafood to show up well, and the kitchen adds plenty of polish and panache to native Royal Bay oysters, scallops (with chive beurre blanc), squid (with guacamole, crème fraîche and sweet chilli sauce) and brill (with pumpkin and thyme risotto). Meat and game also get high priority – witness roast quail with bubble and squeak and celeriac purée, best end of lamb with caramelised root vegetables, and even steak pie. Desserts aim to please all-comers, with the likes of apple crumble and lemon tart lining up alongside vanilla pannacotta with orange salad and cranberry compote. The well-spread wine list reflects the kitchen's even-handed approach, with commendable pickings from £9.75.

Chef/s: Daniel Ward. **Open:** all week L 12 to 2.30 (3.30 Sun), Mon to Sat D 6 to 10. **Closed:** Christmas to mid Jan. **Meals:** alc (main courses £12 to £24). Set L £16.50 (2 courses) to £18.50. Sun L £22.50. **Service:** not inc. **Details:** Cards accepted. 40 seats. 16 seats outside. Air-con. No mobile phones. Wheelchair access. Music. Children allowed.

ALSO RECOMMENDED
▲ Castle Green
La Route de la Côte, Gorey, Jersey, JE3 6DR
Tel no: (01534) 840218
www.jerseypottery.com
Gastropub

The pub is part of the Jersey Pottery group, and has a pleasingly informal atmosphere, with bare tables and calming bay views. Seasonal local produce is the watchword, with seafood coming in from the St Helier catch. Expect generous platters in two sizes, perhaps comprising smoked mackerel, roast salmon, king prawns and smoked salmon with spicy

Marie Rose and saffron aïoli (£10.50/13.95). Finish with banana and pecan pudding with honey-crunch ice cream and toffee sauce (£6). Wines from £13.50. Closed Sun D and Mon.

▍St Brelade, Jersey
The Atlantic Hotel, Ocean Restaurant
Assured food and awesome views
Le Mont de la Pulente, St Brelade, Jersey, JE3 8HE
Tel no: (01534) 744101
www.theatlantichotel.com
Modern British | £50
Cooking score: 4

🍷 ⇌ V

Exotic palm trees, an azure pool, colonial-style white shutters and a championship golf course suggest a subtropical, jet-setting playground rather than Jersey, and the swanky Atlantic Hotel also lives up to its name with awe-inspiring sea views. Decked out in maritime blue shades, the cool Ocean Restaurant goes with the flow, offering assured modern food with a fanciful contemporary touch and a feel for island produce. Pan-roasted langoustine tails with caramelised bacon, cauliflower purée and shaved brazil nuts could open the show, ahead of thyme-roasted rump of lamb with lentil cassoulet, garlic and herb gnocchi or fillet of line-caught turbot with a meaty pairing of beef cheeks, butter beans and chicken stock reduction. To finish, Jersey yoghurt semifreddo with crystallised violets and blueberry compote has a summery feel, or you might prefer fig tarte Tatin with mascarpone ice cream. Sommelier Sergio dos Santos is an authoritative guide when it comes to navigating the magisterial wine list – a weighty tome that straddles the globe, flaunts quality and tips its hat to organic producers. House selections from £18.

Chef/s: Mark Jordan. **Open:** all week L 12.30 to 2.30, D 7 to 10. **Closed:** 3 Jan to 5 Feb. **Meals:** Set L £20 (2 courses) to £25. Set D £50. Sun L £30. Tasting menu £70. **Service:** not inc. **Details:** Cards accepted. 65 seats. Separate bar. No mobile phones. Music. Children allowed. Car parking.

ALSO RECOMMENDED
▲ Wayside Café

Le Mont Sohier, St Brelade, Jersey, JE3 8EA
Tel no: (01534) 743915
Café

Renowned for its beachside setting and gorgeous coastal views, this all-day café is a popular destination, especially on fine days when tables on the extensive decked terrace are at a premium. Breakfasts cover everything from porridge to full English, and from noon the café repertoire of sandwiches, salads and burgers is supplemented by the likes of grilled garlic prawns with salad (£8), fillet of sea bass with Spanish-style seafood rice (£13.90) and sweet treats such as orange cake (£4). House wine is £11.95. Open all week.

▮ St Clement, Jersey
ALSO RECOMMENDED
▲ Green Island Restaurant

Green Island, St Clement, Jersey, JE2 6LS
Tel no: (01534) 857787
www.greenisland.je
Seafood

Fresh fish and wide-ranging sea views win the day at this slipway restaurant, billed as the most southerly in the British Isles. You can expect anything from smoked haddock and mascarpone risotto with fresh crevettes (£8.95) to roasted monkfish tail with an oriental vegetable stir-fry, fragrant rice and red Thai curry sauce (£18.95). Otherwise there could be roast rack of lamb or beef fillet for dissenting carnivores, followed by rhubarb and ginger crème brûlée (£6) for dessert. House wine is £14.95. Closed Sun D and Mon.

▮ St Helier, Jersey
Bohemia

Cooking up a storm
The Club Hotel & Spa, Green Street, St Helier,
Jersey, JE2 4UH
Tel no: (01534) 880588
www.bohemiajersey.com
Modern European | £50
Cooking score: 7

🍴 V

An inimitably stylish hotel not far from St Helier beach, the Club boasts all the modern amenities trendsetters like to see, including a state-of-the-art spa and, in Bohemia, one of the Channel Islands' outstanding destination restaurants. The decoration is fashionably muted; wood panelling, banquette seating and a white-tiled floor create a faintly Japanese backdrop for the smartly laid-up tables. The cooking capitalises on Jersey's best products, from unctuous cream to the famous Royal potatoes, and is hardly ever short of brilliant. Shaun Rankin is the kind of cook who makes it all look effortless, with dishes turned out to their best advantage and a talent for making contemporary classic combinations work – and then some. A spin on the scallops and black pudding idea sees the shellfish Indian-spiced and grilled, the pudding puréed, and further elements of apple, coconut and an onion bhaji adding depth. Lightly poached Royal Bay oysters are garnished with Sevruga caviar (at no supplement) and served with saffron noodles and lemon butter. On to main courses, and there may be a reinterpretation of tournedos Rossini in the shape of a slow-cooked Scottish beef fillet adorned with woodland mushrooms and a potato galette, while fashionable pork belly might be teamed with glazed cheek, alongside griddled squid, Savoy cabbage and a purée of quince. Desserts offer nice textural contrasts, adding the crunch of sesame seed brittle to pineapple Tatin, served with coconut and lemongrass ice cream. You will expect a full panoply of appetisers, intermissions and postludes, and you won't be disappointed. Nor will the wine list leave you spoilt for choice on its two closely printed pages. Prices soon shoot out of sight, but there are selections by the glass from £3.25.

Chef/s: Shaun Rankin. **Open:** Mon to Sat L 12 to 2.30, D 6.30 to 10. **Closed:** Sun, 25 to 28 Dec. **Meals:** alc (main courses £28 to £39). Set L £18.50 (2 courses) to £21.50. Set D £42.50 (2 courses) to £49.50. **Service:** 10%. **Details:** Cards accepted. 60 seats. Air-con. Separate bar. No mobile phones. Wheelchair access. Music. Children allowed. Car parking.

ALSO RECOMMENDED

▲ The Green Olive

1 Anley Street, St Helier, Jersey, JE2 3QE
Tel no: (01534) 728198
www.greenoliverestaurant.co.uk
Mediterranean £5 OFF

Paul and Anna Le Brocq run a hospitable restaurant, with Paul constantly developing his modern ideas. His style doesn't test diners, but it seems to satisfy with a repertoire that deals exclusively in vegetarian, seafood and poultry dishes. Expect to find sun-blush tomato and goats' cheese tart (£6.95), Thai vegetable and chickpea curry or scallops with creamy sweetcorn purée, apricot salsa and crisp pancetta (£8.95), plus confit of duck (£14.95) and Cajun chicken. House wine is £13.95. Closed Sat L, Sun and Mon.

▮ St Martin, Guernsey

The Auberge

Taste thrills and big flavours
Jerbourg Road, St Martin, Guernsey, GY4 6BH
Tel no: (01481) 238485
www.theauberge.gg
Modern European | £40
Cooking score: 5

V

Huge picture windows make the most of breathtaking views across Pied du Mur Bay, but this sleekly minimalist, brasserie-style eatery high up on the cliffs has plenty more aces up its sleeve for those seeking taste thrills and bold flavours. Daniel Green's kitchen puts

its faith in top-drawer island produce – especially consignments of seafood fresh from the Guernsey boats – for a repertoire of exciting dishes without frontiers. A starter of crispy lamb breast confit comes with garlicky chickpeas and tzatziki, while grilled red mullet is festooned with an array of cod brandade, black olive toasts, artichokes à la grecque and saffron aïoli. Mains tend to take a more measured view of things – perhaps calf's liver with smoked potato purée, braised endive and caramelised onion jus or Parmesan-crusted brill with basil and shallot salsa and garlic mash. Alternatively, prime steaks with classic sauces and chunky chips satisfy those who like their food with slightly less modish embellishment. To conclude, there are neatly composed desserts such as pear and frangipane tart with Calvados jelly. Forty well-spread wines start at £17.50, and it's worth dipping into the 'special selection' of more prestigious bottles.

Chef/s: Daniel Green. **Open:** all week L 12 to 2, Mon to Sat D 6.30 to 9.45. **Closed:** 25 Dec to 1 Jan. **Meals:** alc (main courses £14 to £23). Set L £14.95 (2 courses). Set D £18.95. Sun L £25. **Service:** 10% (optional). **Details:** Cards accepted. 60 seats. 33 seats outside. Separate bar. Wheelchair access. Music. Children allowed. Car parking.

▮ St Martin, Jersey

READERS RECOMMEND

The Bass & Lobster Foodhouse

Gastropub
Gorey Coast Road, St Martin, Jersey, JE3 6EU
Tel no: (01534) 859590
www.bassandlobster.com
'Gastropub with an emphasis on seafood'

Average price

The average price listed in main-entry reviews denotes the price of a three-course meal, without wine.

▌St Peter Port, Guernsey

La Frégate

Stunning seascapes and detailed dining
Les Cotils, St Peter Port, Guernsey, GY1 1UT
Tel no: (01481) 724624
www.lafregatehotel.com
Modern European | £30
Cooking score: 4

🛏

'From the local hand-dived scallops (so simple, yet perfectly prepared) to the rich yellow Guernsey table butter, it's the detail in dining at La Frégate that is its greatest achievement', comments a loyal supporter of this tastefully upgraded eighteenth-century manor. The setting, perched high above St Peter Port, with the 800-year-old Castle Cornet floodlit at night and the bay looking over to Jersey, Herm, Sark and France, is enviable. Fresh fish is an obvious strength, but it is well matched by the quality of the meat dishes. Rack of lamb and chateaubriand (for two) are as highly praised as the mussel and sweet potato velouté, the sea bass with chilli and ginger or the 'fresh and delicious' lobster with white crabmeat. Desserts usually include a warm apple tarte Tatin and a well reported gin and tonic sorbet. The wine list has a heavy French emphasis, starting at £14.95.
Chef/s: Neil Maginnis. **Open:** all week L 12 to 2, D 7 to 10. **Meals:** alc (main courses £13 to £22). Set L £16.45 (2 courses) to £20. Set D £26.20 (2 courses) to £30. Sun L £20. **Service:** not inc. **Details:** Cards accepted. 80 seats. 35 seats outside. Air-con. Separate bar. No music. No mobile phones. Children allowed. Car parking.

ALSO RECOMMENDED

▲ Da Nello
46 Pollet Street, St Peter Port, Guernsey, GY1 1WF
Tel no: (01481) 721552
www.danello.gg
Italian £5 OFF

A fifteenth-century granite house with glassed-in courtyard extension is the setting for this amiably run Italian restaurant on the Guernsey coast. Look for the chalkboard specials and ask advice from the staff, readers suggest. The result may be sautéed scallops and prawns with ginger gremolata (£6.95), veal cutlet in sage and lemon butter with roasted peppers and mash (£17.95), or sea bass with chorizo and tomato cream sauce, haricot beans and gem lettuce (£18.95). Wines from £14.25. Open all week.

▲ Le Nautique
Quay Steps, St Peter Port, Guernsey, GY1 2LE
Tel no: (01481) 721714
www.lenautiquerestaurant.co.uk
French

Occupying a converted eighteenth-century warehouse overlooking Castle Cornet and St Peter Port quay, Gunter Botzenhardt's suited and booted restaurant flaunts its nautical credentials with themed maritime décor and a menu that gives top billing to local fish. The line-up might include 'plump' scallops with citrus dressing (£8.50), lobster thermidor and grilled brill topped with a seafood ragoût (£18.50), plus meaty options such as pistachio-crusted lamb fillet with port jus. To conclude, try bitter chocolate mousse with lime jelly (£5.50). House wine is £16.50. Closed Sat L and Sun.

READERS RECOMMEND

Brown's Restaurant
European
15 Mansell Street, St Peter Port, Guernsey, GY1 1HP
Tel no: (01481) 727268
www.browns-restaurant.co.uk
'A good-value, local restaurant that is often booked up'

La Piazza Restaurant
Italian
Trinity Square, St Peter Port, Guernsey, GY1 1LX
Tel no: (01481) 725085
'Always great food and very friendly, attentive service'

▮ St Saviour, Jersey

Longueville Manor

Fine country house with impeccable food
St Saviour, Jersey, JE2 7WF
Tel no: (01534) 725501
www.longuevillemanor.com
Modern British | £55
Cooking score: 5

🍷 🛏 V

A Norman manor house set in 15 acres at the foot of its own wooded valley, Longueville is saturated with history, right up to the modern era when German officers quartered themselves here during the Nazi occupation of Jersey. Generations of the Lewis family have since restored and nurtured it into one of the finest country house hotels on the Channel Islands. Andrew Baird has been a constant and commanding presence at the stoves since 1990. The cooking is a gentle take on contemporary British thinking, with impeccable Jersey ingredients (including plenty from the hotel's own kitchen garden) playing the starring roles. Start with a technically agile upside-down crab soufflé, anointed with cheese and crab velouté, before going on to an assiette of various pork preparations, served with a vegetable ragoût and pancetta, or turbot suprême in Champagne beurre blanc with ginger and spring onions. Finish with a parfait made with figs from the garden, accompanied by chocolate crémeux and a port reduction. The wine list is a treasure, not just for its extravagant scope and indisputable quality, but for the commendable effort not to let prices just rip through the roof. Bottles start at £21, glasses at £5.
Chef/s: Andrew Baird. **Open:** all week L 12 to 2, D 7 to 10. **Meals:** Set L £18 (2 courses) to £20.50. Set D £47.50 (2 courses) to £55. Sun L £32.50. Tasting menu £75. **Service:** not inc. **Details:** Cards accepted. 60 seats. 35 seats outside. Separate bar. No music. No mobile phones. Wheelchair access. Children allowed. Car parking.

Sustainable fish

Over the past decade, we have realised that overfishing is one of the biggest threats to marine wildlife and habitats, affecting our future food security, biodiversity and even climate change.

Sustainability has now become part of the definition of good food for people who like to eat fish. But how does one know what to ask for, or what to avoid? By and large, fish that reproduce quickly, like mackerel or herring, are more likely to be sustainable, whereas top predators, such as bluefin tuna or sturgeon, are likely to be vulnerable to overexploitation.

Good advice on which fish to avoid and which to eat can be found on the Marine Conservation Society's website, www.fishonline.org; as the Guide went to press, they were advising:

Some fish to avoid
- haddock from the Faroes and West of Scotland fisheries
- Atlantic cod: avoid wild-caught from all areas except north-east Arctic and Iceland

Some fish to eat
- seabass, line-caught and tagged from Cornwall
- organically farmed Atlantic salmon

You can find out more about restaurants and the sustainability of what they serve at www.fish2fork.com, so you can enjoy fish with a clear conscience.

Charles Clover, author of
The End of the Line, www.fish2fork.com

NORTHERN IRELAND

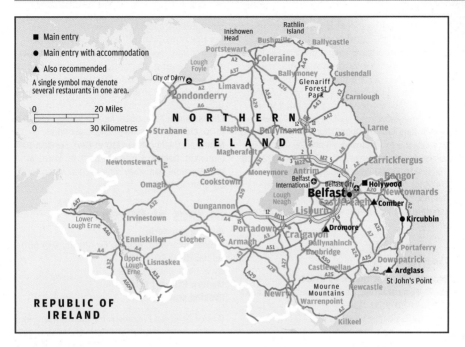

Ardglass, Co Down

ALSO RECOMMENDED
▲ Curran's Bar & Seafood Steakhouse
83 Strangford Road, Chapeltown, Ardglass, Co Down, BT30 7SP
Tel no: (028) 4484 1332
www.curransbar.net
Seafood £5 OFF

Down-to-earth hospitality is to be had at this capacious family-run bar and restaurant, where the menu majors in superb fresh fish and prime Irish beef. Typical dishes might include a hefty bowl of seafood chowder (£7.95), crayfish risotto, seafood linguine and a 10oz sirloin steak with Bushmills whiskey and peppercorn cream sauce (£16.95). To finish, try a chocolate brownie with hot chocolate sauce and vanilla ice cream (£4.50). House wine is £11.95. Open all week.

Belfast, Co Antrim

Cayenne
Spicy, big-flavoured bistro
7 Ascot House, Shaftesbury Square, Belfast, Co Antrim, BT2 7DB
Tel no: (028) 9033 1532
www.cayenne-restaurant.co.uk
Global | £22
Cooking score: 4

⚫ V £30

Paul and Jeanne Rankin's modern bistro is as spicy as it sounds. Its heady mix of Asian, Far Eastern and Mediterranean flavours and the bright, arty interior draws a lively crowd. Some dishes are played fairly straight – goats' cheese soufflé with caramelised fennel and wild mushrooms, or a fillet and daube of beef bourguignon with a colcannon potato cake for example – while others verge on the wacky: Szechuan-peppered Finnebrogue venison with winter fruits, salsify, shiitake and foie gras flan. On the whole combinations work well, and highlights have included a salad of crispy duck with pickled plums, ginger and chilli, and rack of lamb with a masala crust, mint chutney, creamy spiced gratin and Indian salad. A straightforward steamed marmalade pudding with custard provides a welcome break after all the excitement. Care and effort has gone into the sophisticated global wine list, which opens at £19.50 (£4.50 a glass). **Chef/s:** Paul Rankin. **Open:** Thur and Fri L 12 to 2, all week D 5 to 11. **Closed:** 25 and 26 Dec, 1 Jan. **Meals:** alc (main courses £17 to £23). Set L £12.50 (2 courses) to £15.50. Set D £21.50 to £26.50. Sun L £14.50 (2 courses) to £17.50. **Service:** not inc. **Details:** Cards accepted. 80 seats. Air-con. Separate bar. Wheelchair access. Music. Children allowed.

Deanes

Beautiful food at the city's heart
36-40 Howard Street, Belfast, Co Antrim, BT1 6PF
Tel no: (028) 9033 1134
www.michaeldeane.co.uk
Modern British | £30
Cooking score: 5

£5 OFF 🍷 V

Michael Deanes' flagship restaurant, right in the heart of Belfast, is considered one of the most delightful dining spaces in the city. Fronting two streets, the light, high-ceilinged room has recently been freshened up, with deep-red walls and pillars now setting off the grey panelling. An open-to-view kitchen adds to the relaxed mood, and a seafood bar offers some new possibilities – especially if you fancy filling up with moules-frites or crab and celeriac mayo on toast at lunchtime. The main menu is a mix of hardy perennials (Ewing's smoked salmon with potato bread, Lough Erne beef with triple-cooked chips) and more intricate big-city dishes – perhaps Strangford scallops with a purée of Armagh Bramley apples, glazed rare-breed pork belly and black pudding beignets, open ravioli of young pigeon with chanterelles or Gressingham duck breast with confit leg, pak choi, gingerbread and port jus; also ask about the day's fish special. To finish, the dessert menu touts rich raspberry chocolate tart,

pistachio-topped carrot cake and such like. Service is 'wonderful', according to recent reports. The lively modern wine list promises a wide-ranging selection, mainly from France but with more than a nod to the rest of Europe and the New World. House recommendations start at £22 (£5 a glass). **Chef/s:** Simon Toye. **Open:** Mon to Sat L 12 to 3, D 6 to 10. **Closed:** Sun, 1 week July, bank hols. **Meals:** alc (main courses £10 to £24). **Service:** 10% (optional). **Details:** Cards accepted. 80 seats. Air-con. Separate bar. Wheelchair access. Music. Children allowed.

Deanes at Queens

Buzzing brasserie
1 College Gardens, Belfast, Co Antrim, BT9 6BQ
Tel no: (028) 9038 2111
www.michaeldeane.co.uk
Modern British | £30
Cooking score: 3

Part of Michael Deanes' restaurant empire that now flourishes in various prime sites across Belfast (see previous entry), Deanes at Queens makes the most of its College Gardens location. With its cool but functional modern design and muted colours, its modern brasserie look fits the menu to a T. The kitchen starts with sound ingredients and balances their flavours with judgement, thanks in part to some tried and tested combinations, from foie gras and chicken liver parfait to roast pork belly with celeriac and potato gratin. Well-executed dishes range from smoked haddock and leek fishcake with tartare sauce to organic Glenarm salmon with chorizo and pea risotto. Wines are arranged by style and open at £14.95. **Chef/s:** Chris Fearon. **Open:** Mon to Sat L 12 to 3, D 5.30 to 9 (10 Wed to Sat). **Closed:** Sun, 1 Jan. **Meals:** alc (main courses £12 to £20). Early bird D £12.95 (2 courses) to £15. **Service:** 10% (optional). **Details:** Cards accepted. 120 seats. 30 seats outside. Air-con. Wheelchair access. Music.

Touring in Britain?
THE
GOOD FOOD
GUIDE
1951-1952

tells you of 600 places throughout Britain where you can rely on
a good meal at a reasonable price,
recommended by members of the
GOOD FOOD CLUB

Rules for Eating Out

Back in 1951, Raymond Postgate, founder of *The Good Food Guide*, proposed some 'Rules for Eating Out' to help diners get a decent meal and good service. Some of these might even come in handy today!

Fourth Rule: On sitting down at your table, polish the glasses and cutlery with your napkin. Don't do this ostentatiously or with an annoyed expression, do it casually. You wish to give the impression not that you are angry with this particular restaurant, but that you are suspicious, after a lifetime of suffering.

Sixth Rule: Ask the waiter (or waitress) 'What is good today?' or, if you are in Soho: 'What is the *Specialité de la Maison*?'. If he answers the equivalent of 'everything is excellent', then he is a bad waiter and it's probably a bad restaurant. But persist; and he (or she) will probably refer to a seedy-looking man in a boiled shirt (or a cross woman in black silk). That is the person who knows, and from him or her you will find out the one thing that is eatable.

Eighth Rule: This is for wives and girl friends only. There are two expressions from which you must in all circumstances refrain. Do not say, or indicate by your nose or eyelashes: 'Oh Henry, you aren't going to make a *scene!*' Do not, on the other hand, go to the other extreme, and indicate: 'Henry, this is intolerable. Deal with these people as they deserve!' Your escort is engaged in delicate and dangerous warfare.

NEW ENTRY

The Ginger Bistro

Popular bistro with very good fish
7-8 Hope Street, Belfast, Co Antrim, BT12 5EE
Tel no: (028) 9024 4421
www.gingerbistro.com
Modern European | £30
Cooking score: 2

V

Tucked in a side street away from Belfast's main thoroughfare, the Ginger Bistro has rapidly become one of the city's most popular eateries. It's a winning formula: two light and contemporary dining spaces, friendly service and very good fish dishes, plus the likes of ribeye steak ('always consistently good') and reasonably priced lunches. The kitchen deploys excellent, locally sourced ingredients for eclectic Euro-inspired dishes such as mackerel with wilted carrots and citrus dressing or braised and roasted belly of pork with Sauvignon Blanc, fennel and haricot beans. Microbrewery beers complement a wine list that leans towards the New World; bottles start at £14.50 (£4 a glass).
Chef/s: Simon McCance and Tim Moffett. **Open:** Tue to Sat L 12 to 3, Mon to Sat D 5 to 9.30 (9 Mon, 10 Fri and Sat). **Closed:** Sun, 25 and 26 Dec, May Day, Easter Mon. **Meals:** alc (main courses £8 to £20). **Service:** not inc. **Details:** Cards accepted. 70 seats. Air-con. Wheelchair access. Music. Children allowed.

James Street South

Assured big-city food
21 James Street South, Belfast, Co Antrim, BT2 7GA
Tel no: (028) 9043 4310
www.jamesstreetsouth.co.uk
Modern European | £30
Cooking score: 5

Since taking over this one-time Belfast linen mill in 2003, Niall and Joanna McKenna have done a grand job transforming the ground-floor space into one of the most vibrant dining rooms in the city. Displays of contemporary

artwork are emblazoned on the bare white walls, the floors are polished wood, and high arched windows ensure that the interior is bathed in natural light during the day. Niall handed over the reins to his dependable sidekick Stephen Toman in 2010, although he still oversees matters in the kitchen. The changeover has been seamless, and the cooking remains as accomplished and precisely executed as ever. Local produce is taken seriously here, although ingredients are given a European spin – witness lobster salad with radish and confit lemon dressing or a dish of wild Donegal salmon enhanced by fennel, tomato and chickpea nage. The region's farms, estates and moorland also provide rich pickings, from loin of veal with asparagus, sweetbread fritter and bordelaise jus to pigeon with pear, ricotta and pistachio baklava and sherry jus. As for desserts, expect the odd surprise – perhaps strawberry Melba or Tokaji parfait with orange and fig roll. Set menus are great value and the eclectic wine list is a goodly mix of regional varietals and classic vintages. Prices start at £19 (£5 a glass).
Chef/s: Stephen Toman. **Open:** Mon to Sat L 12 to 2.45, all week D 5.45 to 10.45 (5.30 to 9 Sun). **Closed:** 25 and 26 Dec, 1 Jan, 12 Jul. **Meals:** alc (main courses £15 to £23). Set L £14.50 (2 courses) to £16.50. Pre-theatre D £16.50 (2 courses) to £18.50. **Service:** not inc. **Details:** Cards accepted. 60 seats. Air-con. Separate bar. Wheelchair access. Music. Children allowed.

Menu by Kevin Thornton
Classy, user-friendly eatery
Fitzwilliam Hotel Belfast, 1-3 Great Victoria Street, Belfast, Co Antrim, BT2 7BQ
Tel no: (028) 9044 2080
www.fitzwilliamhotelbelfast.com
Modern European | £30
Cooking score: 5
£5
OFF

Kevin Thornton is one of Ireland's top achievers, with a stellar reputation in Dublin and beyond. In 2008 he was lured north of the border to oversee the menu for the Filtzwilliam Belfast's flagship restaurant. Chic

fittings, high-back chairs and moody lighting might suggest chi-chi fine dining, but the food and prices tell a different story. Head chef Patrick Leonard delivers a balanced mix of classy, but user-friendly dishes that chime with the deliberately casual intentions of the place. Bacon and cabbage terrine with shallot vinaigrette and leek purée is a Thornton classic that highlights his wit, wisdom and feel for earthy partnerships. Diners can also feast on plates of Irish stew or confit duck with braised red cabbage and Dijon mustard sauce, but the kitchen gets serious when it comes to fillet of halibut accompanied by ribbons of fennel and soy vinaigrette or mi-cuit of Glenarm organic salmon with spring onion mash, fine beans and capers. Desserts promise the likes of soft-centred chocolate fondant with raspberry sorbet, nougatine with confit orange or moist citrus drizzle cake. The 100-bin wine list offers a global range at inoffensive prices (from £19).
Chef/s: Patrick Leonard. **Open:** Mon to Fri and Sun L 12.30 to 2.30, all week D 5.30 to 9.30 (10 Sat). **Meals:** alc (main courses £12 to £24). Set L £9.99 (2 courses) to £12.99. Set D £15.99 (2 courses) to £18.99. Pre-theatre D £12.99. **Service:** not inc. **Details:** Cards accepted. 130 seats. Air-con. Separate bar. Wheelchair access. Music. Children allowed. Car parking.

NEW ENTRY
Molly's Yard
Charming restaurant with good local food
1 College Green Mews, Botanic Avenue, Belfast, Co Antrim, BT7 1LW
Tel no: (028) 9032 2600
www.mollysyard.co.uk
Modern British | £27
Cooking score: 3
£5
OFF

Pass through a picturesque courtyard (good for summer alfresco) to reach this charming restaurant housed in converted Victorian stables. Of the two dining spaces, downstairs is more casual bistro-style, and the menus are designed to show local produce to advantage. Excellent wheaten bread, for example, is made with Chocolate stout brewed in Lisburn.

Scallops come with homemade fadge – an Ulster-type potato bread – and mains include rump of local lamb with thyme and Chardonnay-braised carrots; daily specials might include a crab and fennel gratin or a traditional Irish stew. Chocolate stout also features in an ice cream served with a Belgian chocolate sauce. A good cheeseboard has cheese from 'the four provinces' with homemade chutney and Ditty's famous oat biscuits. Wine by the glass from £3.50.
Chef/s: Ciarán Steele. **Open:** Mon to Sat 12 to 9 (9.30 Fri and Sat). **Closed:** Sun, 24 to 26 Dec, 12 Jul. **Meals:** alc (main courses £7 to £20). **Service:** not inc. **Details:** Cards accepted. 45 seats. 12 seats outside. Wheelchair access. Music. Children allowed.

Mourne Seafood Bar
A spanking-fresh fishy haul
34-36 Bank Street, Belfast, Co Antrim, BT1 1HL
Tel no: (028) 9024 8544
www.mourneseafood.com
Seafood | £25
Cooking score: 3
V £30

An offshoot of the Dundrum original, this branch of the Mourne Seafood Bar is camped in Belfast city centre next to iconic Kelly's Cellars. Oysters, mussels and cockles are from the owners' beds in Carlingford Lough; the rest of the spanking-fresh fishy haul comes from the boats at Annalong and Kilkeel. Daily specials bolster the regular menu, so expect the likes of squid and chorizo risotto, whole John Dory with mussels and herb butter or roast monkfish with spinach, colcannon and mustard cream alongside staples such as crab claws in chilli butter, seafood 'fish fingers' and chargrilled ribeye steaks – for those who need a red meat fix. Everything comes with an eminently affordable price tag, and wines (from £12) follow suit. There's a third outlet at 107 Central Promenade, Newcastle BT33 0LU, tel: (028) 4372 6401.
Chef/s: Andy Rea. **Open:** all week L 12 to 5 (4 Fri and Sat, 1 to 6 Sun), Tue to Sat D 5 to 9.30 (10 Thur to Sat). **Closed:** 24 to 26 Dec, 1 Jan. **Meals:** alc

(main courses £7 to £17). **Service:** not inc. **Details:** Cards accepted. 66 seats. Air-con. Wheelchair access. Music. Children allowed.

Nick's Warehouse
Local supplies and good ideas
35 Hill Street, Belfast, Co Antrim, BT1 2LB
Tel no: (028) 9043 9690
www.nickswarehouse.co.uk
Modern British | £30
Cooking score: 3
£5 OFF

Originally a bonded whiskey store for Bushmills Distillery and a bolthole for Belfast drinkers looking for a drop of the hard stuff, this converted warehouse is now in the business of peddling modern food and global wines. Set among the city's historic cobbled streets, Nick's has evolved over the years with a new theatre kitchen now providing distraction for the crowds. Chef Sean Craig feeds off local supplies, but gleans ideas from near and far: marinated squid comes with a Thai dressing, grilled salmon is served with an Indian spiced pea and potato cake, and mince with neeps and tatties pleases homesick Scots. You can also get mezze-style 'cold collations', steaks and pasta, plus soup, salads and sandwiches at lunchtime. Affordably priced wines start at £14.25 – also check out the section headed 'Nobody Expects – the Spanish Wine List'.
Chef/s: Sean Craig. **Open:** Tue to Sat L 12 to 3, D 6 to 9.30 (10 Fri and Sat). **Closed:** Sun, Mon, 25 and 26 Dec, 1 Jan, Easter, 12 Jul. **Meals:** alc (main courses £12 to £22). Set D Tue to Thur £16.95 (2 courses) to £19.95. **Service:** not inc. **Details:** Cards accepted. 185 seats. Air-con. Separate bar. Wheelchair access. Music. Children allowed.

Readers recommend

A 'readers recommend' review is a genuine quote from a report sent in by one of our readers. We intend to follow up these suggestions throughout the year to come.

No 27 Talbot Street
Cool, sleek hot ticket
27 Talbot Street, Belfast, Co Antrim, BT1 2LD
Tel no: (028) 9031 2884
www.no27.co.uk
Modern British | £35
Cooking score: 3
£5
OFF

Like its near neighbour Nick's Warehouse (see entry), this address was once a historic bonded liquor store, but it has brushed off the cobwebs since launching as a hot-ticket restaurant in Belfast's energetic Cathedral Quarter. 27 Talbot Street now puts on a trendy face with cool, sleek surrounds, vivid artwork and a daily menu that promotes contemporary food with a brasserie edge. Readers have endorsed the pan-seared lamb salad with new potatoes, green beans and rocket pesto, as well as scallops with artichoke purée and pea shoots, although the open-to-view kitchen also rustles up anything from grilled goats' cheese with apple and vanilla purée to char-grilled ribeye with home-cut chips. To finish, walnut tart with Valrhona chocolate ice cream and crème anglaise has also been given the nod. The well-spread wine list starts at £13.50. A new alfresco space is in the pipeline.
Chef/s: Alan Higginson. **Open:** Mon to Fri L 12 to 3, Tue to Sat D 6 to 10. **Closed:** Sun, 25 and 26 Dec, 1 Jan, 1 May, 12 and 13 Jul. **Meals:** alc (main courses £14 to £23). Set D £19.50 (2 courses) to £25. **Service:** not inc. **Details:** Cards accepted. 70 seats. 14 seats outside. Air-con. Separate bar. Wheelchair access. Music. Children allowed.

ALSO RECOMMENDED
▲ Coco
7-11 Linenhall Street, Belfast, Co Antrim, BT2 8AA
Tel no: (028) 9031 1150
www.cocobelfast.com
Modern British

Very on-show, contemporary restaurant and bar that sets out its stall in the centre of Belfast. Sound modern brasserie dishes range from a lunchtime spicy crayfish Thai-style soup (£4.25) or game sausages with creamy champ

(£7.50) to more ambitious dinner offerings of baby Dover sole with chorizo, shrimp, capers and garlic butter (£6.95), pork belly with apple and celeriac mash or hake with braised fennel, asparagus, char-grilled potatoes, Portavogie prawns and white wine chive velouté (£18.50). House wine is £15.50. Closed Sat L and Sun D.

▌Bushmills
READERS RECOMMEND
Tartine at the Distillers Arms
Modern British
140 Main Street, Bushmills, BT57 8QE
Tel no: (028) 2073 1044
www.distillersarms.com
'**Extremely good value and of a decent standard to encourage further visits**'

▌Comber
ALSO RECOMMENDED
▲ The Old Schoolhouse Inn
100 Ballydrain Road, Comber, BT23 6EA
Tel no: (028) 9754 1182
www.theoldschoolhouseinn.com
French £5
OFF

This cheerful, family-run restaurant-with-rooms in a converted schoolhouse on the shores of Strangford Lough is open only for dinner (and not on Sundays). Set menus are priced at £14.95 for one course to £23.95 for three courses. The kitchen turns its hand to wide-ranging modern brasserie dishes such as lamb's kidneys with a Dijon and red pepper sauce, followed perhaps by whole Dover sole with parsley and lemon butter or chicken breast with tarragon and mushroom sauce. House wine is £13.95. Accommodation.

Also recommended
Also recommended entries are not scored but we think they are worth a visit.

Dromore

ALSO RECOMMENDED
▲ Boyles of Dromore
8-10 Castle Street, Dromore, BT25 1AF
Tel no: (028) 9269 9141
www.boylesofdromore.com
Modern British £5 OFF

It may look like an old boozer from the outside, but Boyles' dramatic pink-and-green frontage gives way to a cottagey restaurant and bar with serious culinary intent. Named after a famous Dromore family, it offers a mix of dishes with local and eclectic overtones. Expect the likes of Fivemiletown Ballyblue cheese brûlée (£6.25), turbot with cockles, oxtail and mash or pheasant cooked in Bushmills whiskey (£19.50). To conclude, perhaps steamed marmalade pudding (£5.95). Wines start at £14.50 (£3.95 a glass). Open Fri to Sun L, Tue to Sun D.

Holywood, Co Down
The Bay Tree
Fizzing all-dayer
118 High Street, Holywood, Co Down, BT18 9HW
Tel no: (028) 9042 1419
www.baytreeholywood.co.uk
Modern British | £22
Cooking score: 2
£5 OFF **V** £30

A fizzing combination of craft shop, art gallery, coffee house and unfettered local restaurant, the Bay Tree has moved with the times since it opened in 1990. Breakfasts give way to a daily line-up of soups with home-baked wheaten bread, organic 'superfood' salads, pasta and casseroles, while evening brings an eclectic choice embracing everything from crab claws with peas, Pernod and chorizo to rosemary-scented crème brûlée via slow-roast belly pork with caramel and ginger sauce. Legendary cinnamon scones and a handful of savoury dishes can also be bought from the adjoining takeaway by the front door. House wine is £13.50.

Chef/s: Dessie Robb. Open: Mon to Sat L 12 to 3, Mon and Wed to Sat D 6 to 9.30. Closed: Sun, 25 and 26 Dec, 12 to 14 Jul. Meals: alc (£9 to £17.50). Service: not inc. Details: Cards accepted. 60 seats. Wheelchair access. Music. Children allowed. Car parking.

Kircubbin
Paul Arthurs
Straight-talking bistro cooking
66 Main Street, Kircubbin, BT22 2SP
Tel no: (028) 4273 8192
www.paularthurs.com
Modern British | £25
Cooking score: 3

🛏 V £30

Paul Arthurs has been going strong in Kircubbin for almost a decade, and his straight-talking, bistro-style food perfectly suits this brick-walled upstairs dining room. The kitchen is happy to glean and garner ideas from all over – so don't be surprised to see French-style bone marrow toast alongside salt and chilli squid, or crispy duck confit with shiitake mushrooms up there with a dish of penne, corn-fed chicken and garlicky chorizo. Bowls of light curried mussels from Strangford Lough are a star turn, the catch of the day is always worth considering, and there's no beating about the bush when it comes to straightforward desserts such as apple crumble or hot chocolate pudding. House wine is £14. A new ground-floor bistro-cum-carvery was due to open as the Guide went to press – reports, please.

Chef/s: Paul Arthurs. Open: Sun L 12 to 2.30, Tue to Sat D 5 to 9 (9.30 Fri and Sat). Closed: Mon, 25 and 26 Dec. Meals: alc (main courses £16 to £19). Service: not inc. Details: Cards accepted. 40 seats. 20 seats outside. Separate bar. Wheelchair access. Music. Children allowed. Car parking.

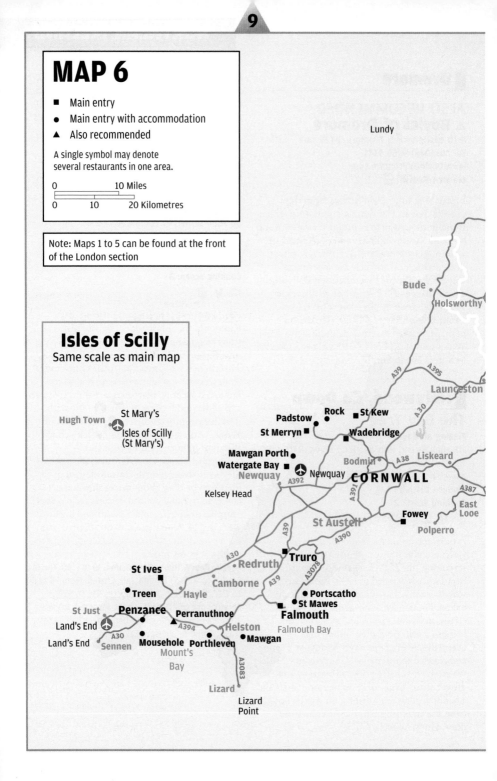

MAP 6

- ■ Main entry
- ● Main entry with accommodation
- ▲ Also recommended

A single symbol may denote
several restaurants in one area.

0   10 Miles

0   10   20 Kilometres

Note: Maps 1 to 5 can be found at the front
of the London section

Isles of Scilly
Same scale as main map

Hugh Town   St Mary's
Isles of Scilly
(St Mary's)

Lundy

Bude
Holsworthy

A39 A395

Launceston

A39 A395

Rock ■ St Kew
Padstow ●
St Merryn ■   Wadebridge ■
A30

Mawgan Porth ●
Watergate Bay ■   Bodmin ● A38 Liskeard
Newquay A392 Newquay C O R N W A L L

Kelsey Head   A387

East
Looe
Fowey ■
St Austell   Polperro
A39   A390

A30 Redruth ■ Truro

St Ives ■   Camborne A39 A3078
● Treen Hayle   ● Portscatho
St Just Penzance Perranuthnoe ▲ ● St Mawes
Land's End   A394 Helston Falmouth
Land's End A30 Sennen Mousehole Porthleven ● Mawgan Falmouth Bay
Mount's
Bay   A3083

Lizard
Lizard
Point

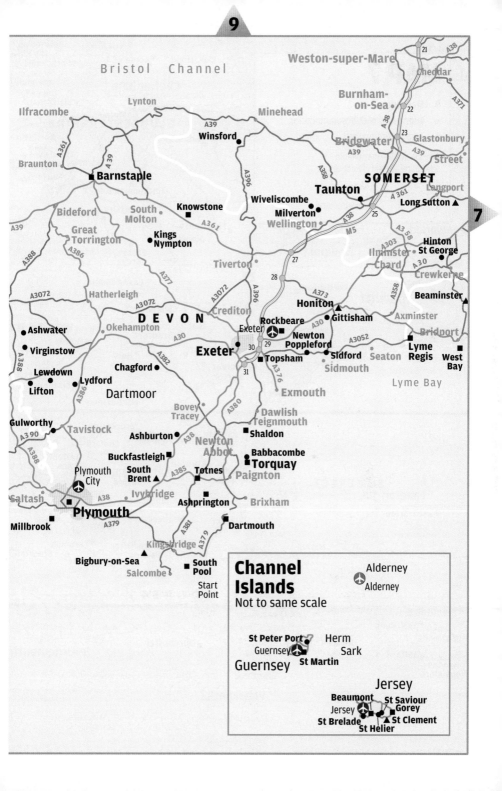

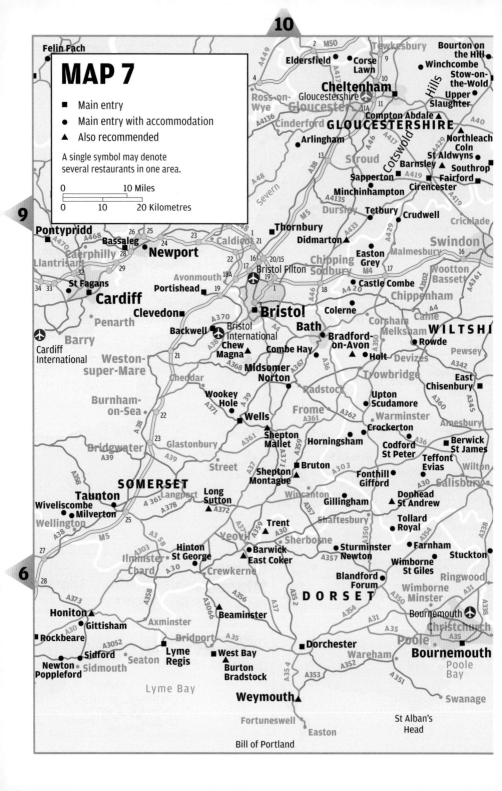

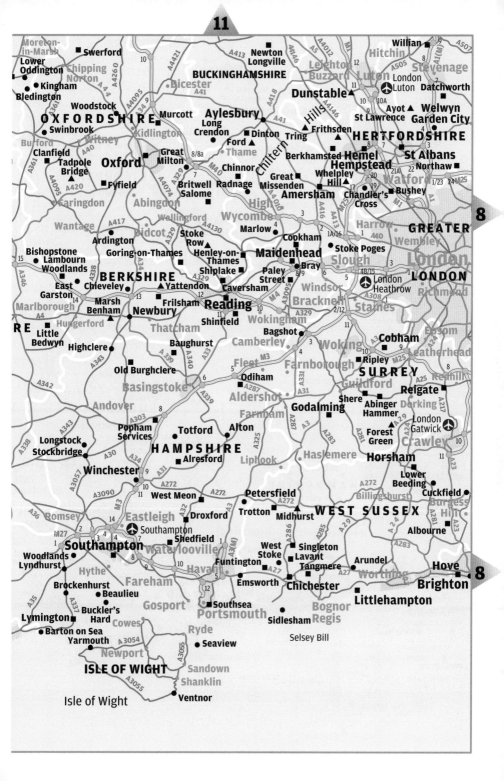

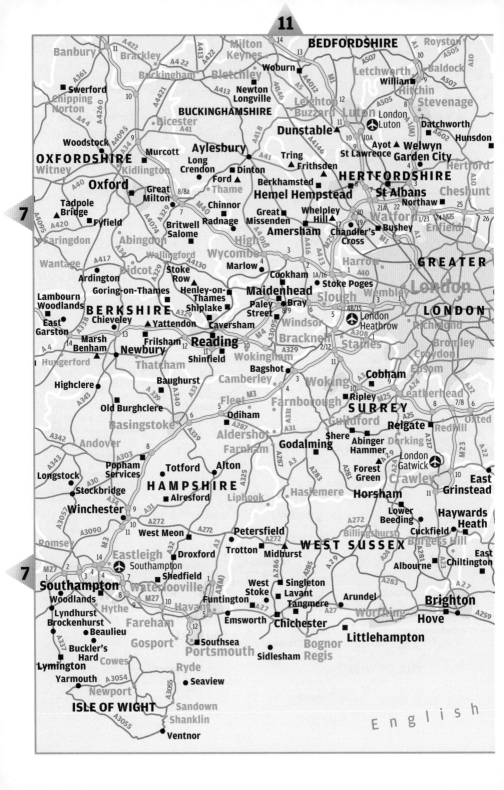

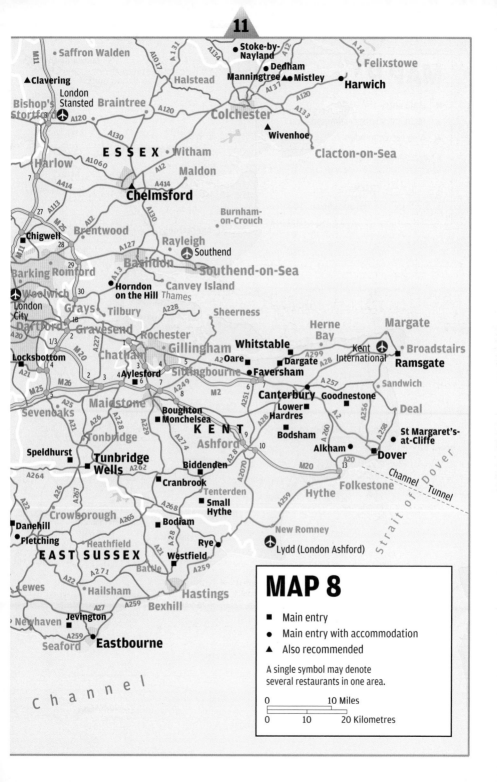

MAP 8

- ■ Main entry
- ● Main entry with accommodation
- ▲ Also recommended

A single symbol may denote
several restaurants in one area.

0   10 Miles

0   10   20 Kilometres

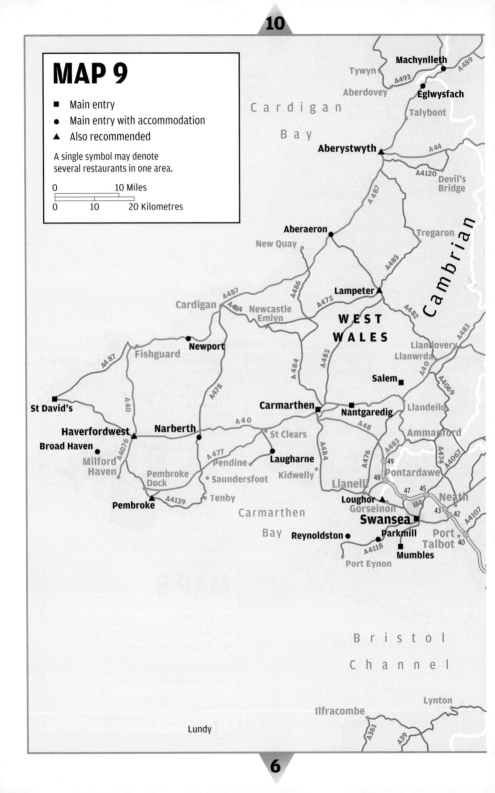

MAP 9

- ■ Main entry
- ● Main entry with accommodation
- ▲ Also recommended

A single symbol may denote
several restaurants in one area.

0   10 Miles

0   10   20 Kilometres

Cardigan Bay

Machynlleth
Tywyn
Aberdovey
Eglwysfach
Talybont
A489
A493
Aberystwyth
A44
A4120
Devil's Bridge
Tregaron
A487
Aberaeron
New Quay
A485
Lampeter
Cardigan
Newcastle Emlyn
A486
A475
A482
A487
A484
WEST WALES
Cambrian
A483
Llandovery
Llanwrda
Newport
Fishguard
A487
A40
A478
A484
A485
Salem
A4069
St David's
Carmarthen
Nantgaredig
Llandeilo
Ammanford
A40
A48
A416
A483
A473
A40067
Haverfordwest
Narberth
St Clears
Broad Haven
A4076
A477
Pendine
Laugharne
A484
Milford Haven
Pembroke Dock
Saundersoot
Kidwelly
Llanelli
49
48
47
45
Pontardawe
Pembroke
A4139
Tenby
Loughor
Gorseinon
Neath
43
42
M4
A4107
Carmarthen Bay
Reynoldston
Swansea
Parkmill
Port Talbot
40
A4118
Mumbles
Port Eynon

Bristol Channel

Ilfracombe
Lynton
A361
A39

Lundy

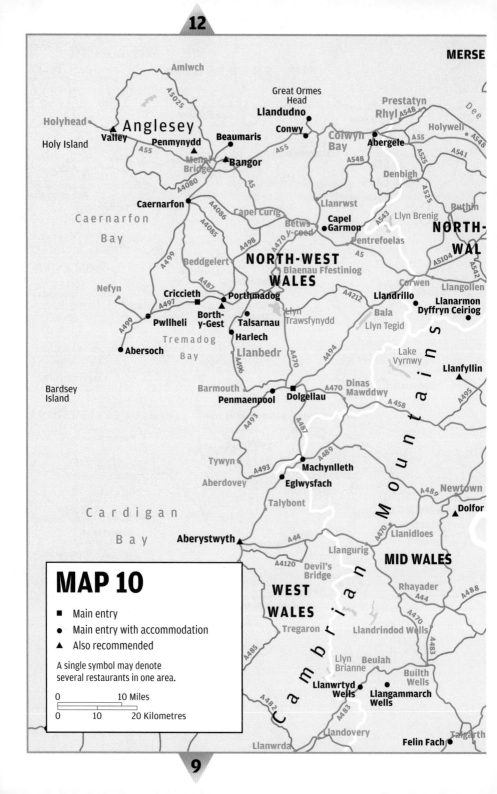

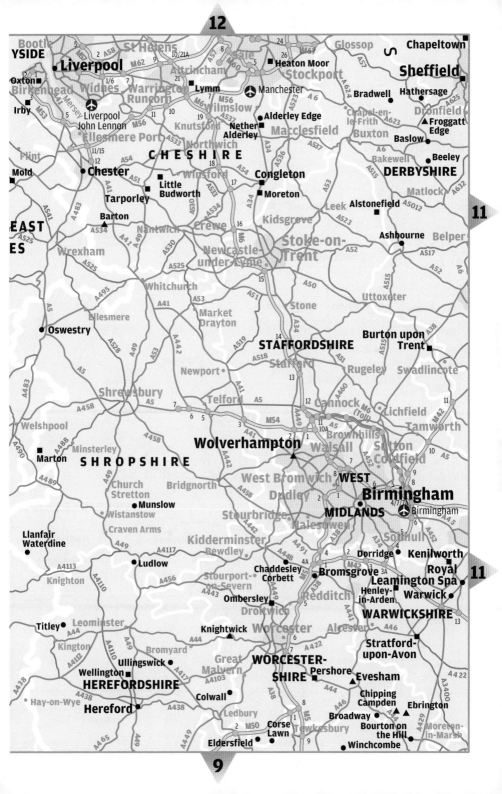

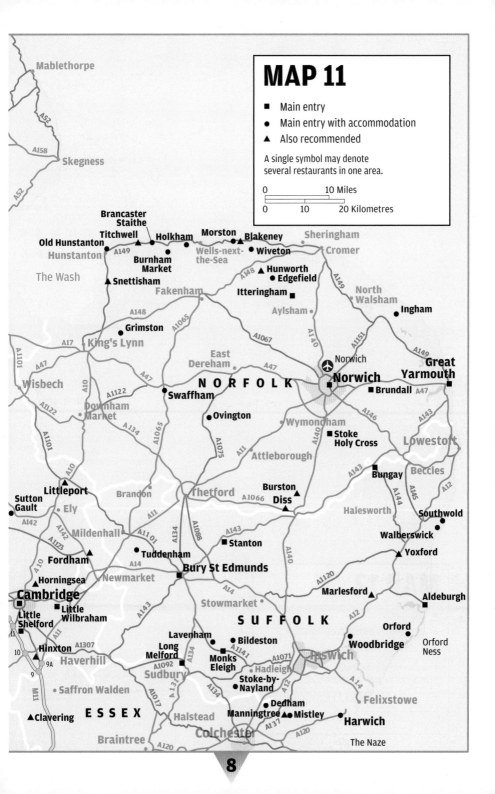

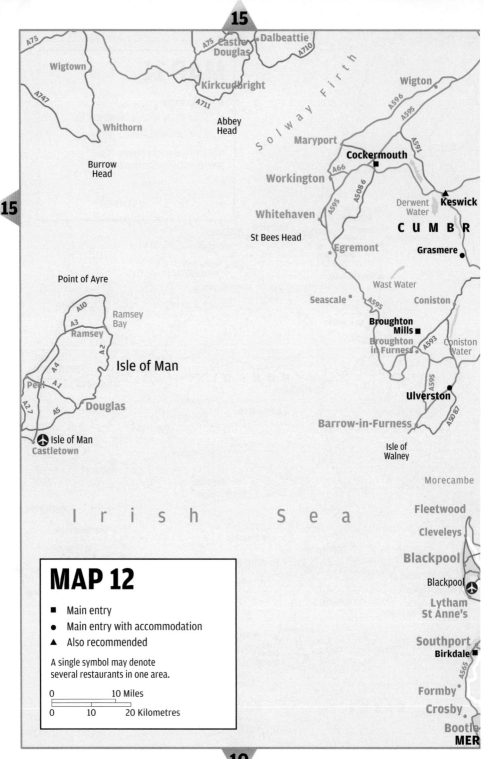

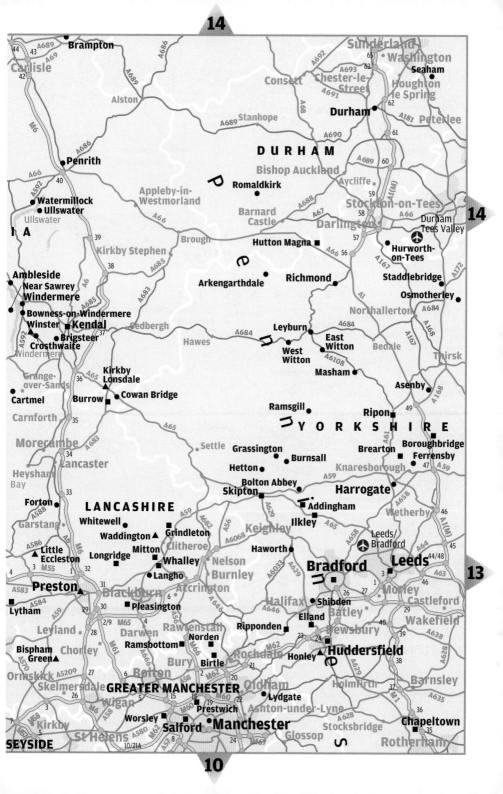

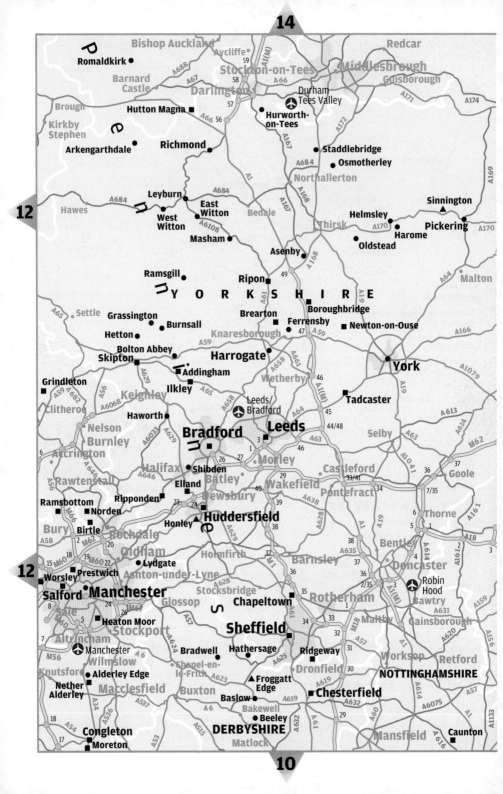

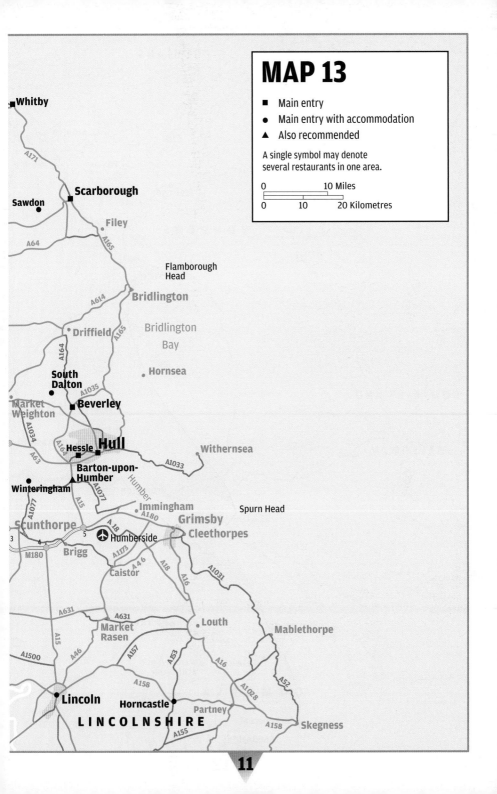

MAP 13

- ■ Main entry
- ● Main entry with accommodation
- ▲ Also recommended

A single symbol may denote
several restaurants in one area.

0   10 Miles

0   10   20 Kilometres

Whitby

A171

Scarborough

Sawdon

Filey

A165

A64

Flamborough
Head

A614

Bridlington

Driffield

A165

Bridlington
Bay

A164

Hornsea

South
Dalton

A1035

Market
Weighton

Beverley

A1034

A63

Hessle   Hull

Withernsea

A1033

Barton-upon-
Humber

Winteringham

A15

A1077

Humber

Immingham

A180

Spurn Head

Scunthorpe

A18

Grimsby

Humberside

Cleethorpes

3   4   5

M180

Brigg

A1173

A446

A18

Caistor

A16

A1031

A631

A631

Louth

Mablethorpe

A15

Market
Rasen

A46

A157

A153

A16

A52

A1500

A158

A1028

Lincoln

Horncastle

Partney

LINCOLNSHIRE

A158

Skegness

A155

11

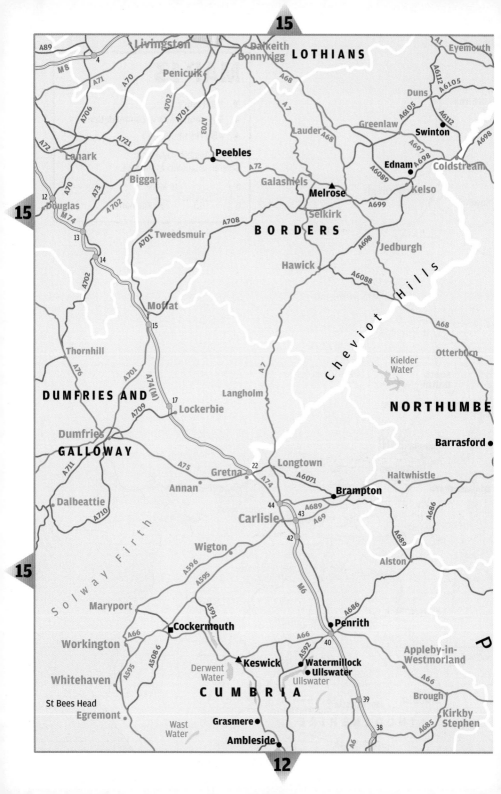

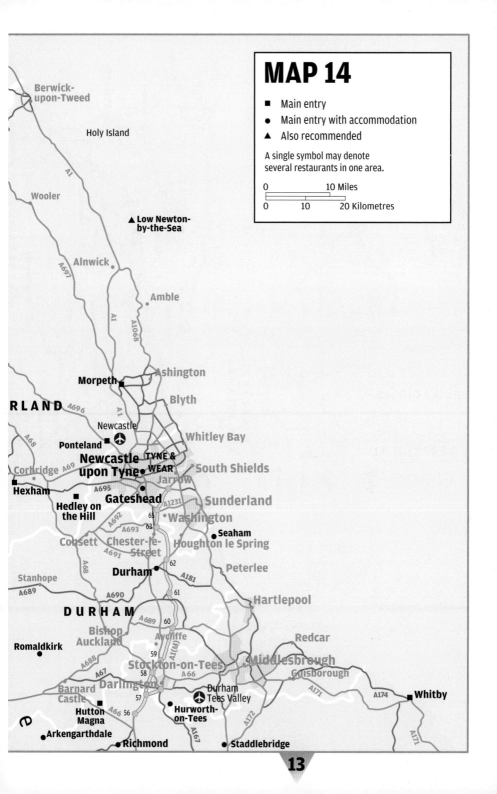

MAP 14

- ■ Main entry
- ● Main entry with accommodation
- ▲ Also recommended

A single symbol may denote
several restaurants in one area.

0   10 Miles

0   10   20 Kilometres

Berwick-
upon-Tweed

Holy Island

A1

Wooler

▲ Low Newton-
by-the-Sea

A697

Alnwick ●

Amble ●

A1

A1068

Ashington

Morpeth ■

RLAND A696

Blyth

A1

Newcastle

Ponteland ■ ✈

Whitley Bay

A68

Corbridge A69

Newcastle
upon Tyne

TYNE &
WEAR ●

South Shields

Jarrow

■
Hexham

A695

Gateshead

A1231

Sunderland

Hedley on
the Hill

A692

64

Washington

A693

63

Consett

Chester-le-
Street

A691

Houghton le Spring

Seaham ●

A68

62

Peterlee

Stanhope
A689

Durham ●

A181

Hartlepool

A690

61

DURHAM

A689

60

Bishop
Auckland

Aycliffe

A11(M)

Redcar

Romaldkirk ●

A688

59

Stockton-on-Tees

Middlesbrough

Guisborough

A67

58

A66

Barnard
Castle

Darlington

A171

A174

Whitby ■

A66

57

Durham
Tees Valley ✈

Hutton
Magna

56

Hurworth-
on-Tees ●

A172

Arkengarthdale ●

A167

A171

Richmond ■

Staddlebridge ●

13

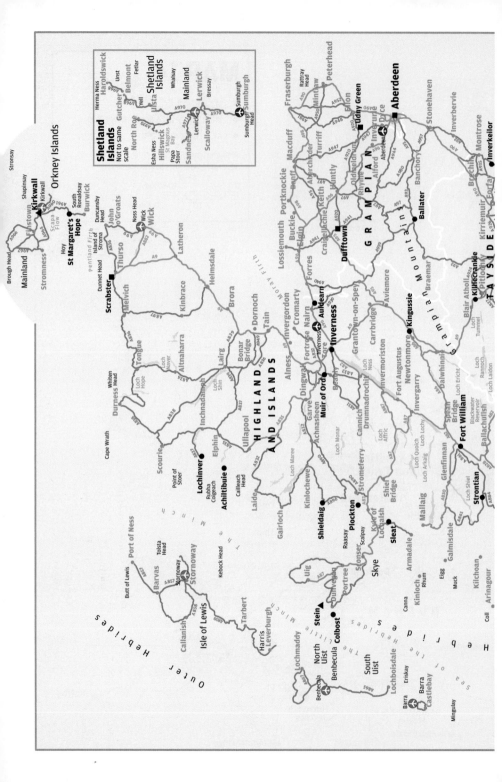

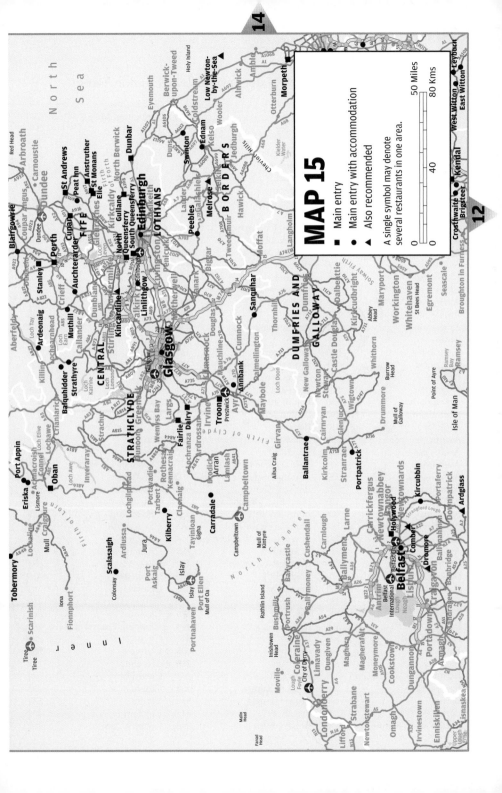

Note: The INDEX BY TOWN does not include London entries.

This book couldn't happen without a cast of thousands. Our thanks are due to the following contributors, amongst many others:

Ms Dolapo Abayomi
Ms Dolly Abbay
Mr David Abbott
Mrs Paula Abbott
Mr Cameron Abernethy
Mr Michael Abolins
Mrs Kathryn Abraham
Mr Anthony Abrahams
Mr Alasdair Adam
Mr Ben Adams
Ms Julie Adams
Mr Richard Adams
Mrs Kristina Adamson
Miss Kirstie Addis
Mrs Vicky Addis
Miss Madeline Adeane
Mrs Beth Aho
Miss Suzanne Aikman
Mrs Valerie Aikman
Mr John R Aird
Miss Vanessa Aitken
Mr Muhammad Akhtar
Mrs Marguerite Akister
Mr Clive Albany
Mr Tony Alden
Mr Justin Alderson
Mrs Helen Aldred-Jones
Mr Brian Alexander
Mr James Alexander
Mr Serge Alexander
Mr John Alflatt
Mr Zak Ali
Mr Douglas Allan
Dr Linda Allan
Ms Hilary Allanson
Mr Ben Allen
Mrs Beverley Allen
Mrs Gaynor Allen
Mr Ian Allen
Mrs Margaret Allen
Mr Oliver Allen
Mr Simon Allen
Mrs Louise Allfrey-Cutcliffe
Mr Peter Allinson
Ms Lynne Allison
Mr Michael Allsop
Mrs Diane Almond
Mr Roger Almond
Mrs Susan Almond
Miss Lubna Altajir
Mr Tom Alves
Mr Stephen Alvis
Mr Carl Ambrose
Mr Edward Ames
Miss Inga Andersen
Mr David Anderson
Mr Gary Anderson
Mr James Anderson
Mr John Anderson
Miss Victoria Anderton
Miss Arianna Andreangeli
Mr Terry Andrew
Mrs Chris Andrews
Miss Libby Andrews
Miss Lynda Andrews
Miss Naomi Andrews
Mr Will Andrews
Mrs Ellen Andronov
Ms Lynda Anfrews
Mrs Gill Anstey
Mr Leighton Anthony
Mrs Gisela Antunes
Mrs Susan Appleton
Mr Richard Applin
Mrs Valerie Arbery
Ms Molly Archer
Mr Patrice Archer
Miss Felicity Aries
Miss Anke Arkenberg
Mr Charlie Arkwright
Mrs Isabel Arlow
Mr David Armstrong
Mr Glen Armstrong
Mrs Louise Armstrong
Mr Daniel Arnell
Ms Hilary Arnold
Mrs Tina Arnold

Mrs Anne-Marie Arpino
Mrs Denise Ashby
Mr Ian Ashcroft
Mrs Margaret Ashcroft
Mr Kenneth Ashken
Mrs Eva Ashmore
Mrs Gill Ashplant
Mr David Ashworth
Ms Sarah Ashworth
Miss Beatrice Asprey
Miss Irina Atanasova
Mr Bryan Atherton
Mr Bryan Atherton
Ms Margaret Atherton
Miss Nichola Atherton
Mr Alan Atkins
Mrs Julie Atkins
Mr Bradley Atkinson
Mrs Lynn Atkinson
Mrs Phyllis Atkinson
Mr Paul Atkinsons
Mr Richard Attwood
Ms Vera Attwooll
Ms Dominique Auge
Miss Rebecca Ault
Mrs Caroline Austin
Mr Colin Austin
Ms Jane Austin
Miss Jen Austin
Miss Lily Austin
Mrs Denise Avent
Mr Maurice Avent
Mr Sam Avery
Mr Anthony Avison
Mrs Brenda Axe
Miss Kim Ayling
Mr Jonathan Bacon
Mrs Victoria Bacon
Mr J Badge
Mrs Susan Bagnall
Mrs Karen Bailey
Mr Keith Bailey
Mr Paul Bailey
Ms Heather Baily
Mr Tim Bain
Mr Thomas Bainbridge
Mr M Bains
Mr James Baird
Mr Jim Baird
Mr Ashley Baker
Mr Barry Baker
Mrs Cara Baker
Miss Caroline Baker
Mrs Catherine Baker
Mrs Connie Baker
Mr George Baker
Mrs Janet Baker
Mrs Linda Baker
Mr Michael J M Baker
Mrs Niki Baker
Mrs Bernadette Balchin
Mrs Janice Balchin
Dr Peter Baldry
Mrs Tania Baldwin-Pask
Mr David Ball
Miss Georgina Ball
Mrs Jennie Ball
Mr Thomas Ball
Miss Catherine Ballard
Mrs Michelle Bamber
Mr Robert Bamberger
Mrs Anne Bangay
Mrs Imogen Banks
Mr Leo Banks
Miss Jade Bann
Mrs Christine Bannatyne
Mr John Banner
Mr Peter Bannister
Mr Michael Banyard
Mr John Barber
Ms Lisa Barber
Mr Benjamin Barclay
Mr Nic Bard
Mr James Barker
Mr John Barker
Mrs Maggie Barker
Mrs Sue Barker

Mrs Claire Barlawau
Mr Alex Barley
Mrs Claire Barlow
Mrs Gaynor Barnden
Mrs Janet Barnes
Mr Kenneth Barnes
Ms Lee-Anne Barnes
Mrs Lindsay Barnes
Mr Margaret Barnes
Mrs Pat Barnes
Mrs Susan Barnes
Mr Stephen Barnett
Mr Robert Barnsley
Mrs Sue Barr
Mr Richard Barraclough
Mr Andrew Barratt
Mrs Annette Barrett
Mrs Clair Barrett
Mr Paul Barrington
Mrs Brigitte Barron
Mr David Barrow
Mrs Jane Barry
Mr William Barry
Mr Jacques Barsi
Mrs Cherry Bartles-Smith
Ms Ann Bartlett
Mr Dominic Barton
Mr Matthew Barton
Miss Nikki Barton
Mr Nick Barton Jayne
Mr Alex Barwise
Miss Francesca Bashall
Mr Bassim Basma
Mr Alex Batchelor
Mr Martin Batchelor
Mr Mike Bateman
Mr Barry Bates
Mr Thomas Bates
Miss Gillian Batey
Ms J Batson
Mr Andrew Batt
Mrs Cynthia Battersby
Mr Tim Battle
Mrs Susi Batty
Mr Iain Baughen
Mrs Helen Baws
Mr Michael Bayston
Ms Lesley Beach
Mrs Linda Beadle
Mr Duncan Beale
Mrs Suzanne Beale
Miss Lucy Beales
Miss Nicola Bean
Mrs Mandy Bear
Mr George Beardow
Mr Glen Beasley
Mr Martin Beaumont
Mrs Marion Beckett
Ms Aura Beckhofer-Fialho
Mr Stephen Beckwith
Mr Steve Bedborough
Ms Amanda Beddows
Mr Bernard Bedford
Mrs Maureen Bednal
Miss S Beeching
Mr Paul Beesley
Mrs Susannah Beeson
Mrs Lisa Behague
Mrs Gina Belcher
Mrs Catherine Bell
Mrs Christine Bell
Mr Alan Bellas
Mr John Bence
Mrs Angela Bending
Mr Frank Benfield
Mrs Lisa Benge
Mrs Davina Benito
Mrs Christine Benner
Mr Duncan Bennett
Mr Jeremy Bennett
Miss Lesley Bennett
Mr Neil Bennett
Mr Stephen Benson
Mr Andrew Benz
Mrs Christina Benz
Mrs Teresa Berkengoff
Mr Marc Berresford

Mrs Jane Berridge
Mr Paul Besaw
Mr Matt Bess
Mr Suzanne Bessant
Mr W J Best
Mrs Christine Bethune
Mr Michael Bettell
Mr Neil Bevan
Mrs Rachael Bewsey
Mr John Bibbings
Mrs Shirley Bibby
Mr Peter Bickley
Miss Alison Bicknell
Miss Joanna Biddolph
Mrs Angela Biggs
Miss Del Bilbar
Mr Percy Billinge
Mr Tracy Bilsland
Mrs Laura Bingham
Mr Paul Bingham
Mr Chris Birch
Sir Robert Birch CBE
QPM
Mr Rob Birchall
Mr Kate Birchenough
Mr Pietro Birindelli
Miss Sharan Birk
Miss Kate Birmingham
Ms Sara Biro
Mr John Birtwistle
Mrs Emma Bishop
Mrs Sandra Bishop
Mrs Janice Bizley
Mrs Beverley Blackburn
Mr Chris Blackburn
Mr Graham Blackburn
Mr Matthew Blackistan
Mr Jon Bladon
Mr Jane Blair
Mrs Diana Blake
Mrs Gillian Blake
Miss Sian Blakmore
Miss Elaine Blanchard
Mr Philip Bland
Mr Jenny Blincoe
Mr Steve Block
Mrs Sandi Bloomfield
Ms Dawn Bloxwich
Mr Christopher Blunden
Mr Tony Blythe
Mrs Kerstin Blythin-
 Cotterill
Mr Andy Boase
Mrs Angela Bobela
Mrs Sara Boddy
Ms Abigail Boisot
Mrs Victoria Boland
Mr Frank Bolger
Mr Michael Bolsover
Mr Bill Bolter
Mrs Eirian Bolton
Mrs Kym Bolton
Mr Steve Bolton
Mrs Gillian Bolton-Allen
Mr David Bolwell
Mrs Julia Bolwell
Mr Dan Bones
Mr Brendan Bonner
Ms Joanna Bonner
Mr Richard Bonwick
Mr Mike Boobier
Mr William Boocock
Mr James Bool
Mr Alan Booth
Mr Antony Booth
Mr Duncan Booth
Mr Peter Booth
Mr Nick Boothman
Miss Nicola Boothman
Mr Andy Borthwick-Clarke
Mr Neville Borton
Mr Gregory Botelho
Mr Mike Bottle
Mr Simon Bottomley
Mrs Caroline Boucher
Mr David Bourdier
Mr Roger Bousfield

Mrs Meggi Bowater
Mrs Helen Bowden
Mrs Valerie Bowden
Mr Bryan Bowen
Mr Brian Bower
Mr Clive Bowman
Mr Simon Bown
Miss Melanie Bowran
Miss Rachael Bowser
Mrs Sophie Boxall
Mrs Emma Boyd
Mrs Leone Boyle
Mr Richard Boyle
Mr Charles Boyles
Mrs Sandra Boynton
Mr Martyn Brabbins
Dr Brian Bracegirdle
Mr Nicolas Bracegirdle
Ms Gill Bracey
Mrs Sheila Bracey
Mr Anthony Bradbury
Mr James Bradbury
Miss Rosanna Bradbury
Mr Sam Bradbury
Mr Julian Bradley
Mr Martyn Bradley
Mr Peter Bradley
Miss Rebecca Bradshaw
Mr John Brady
Mr Christopher Brailsford
Mr Kerry Braithwaite
Mr Roger Braithwaite
Mr Stuart Bramley
Mrs Helen Brandon
Mrs Angie Braney
Mr Frank Branney
Miss Claire Bratcher
Ms Carly Bray
Ms Davina Breaden
Mr Barrie Brears
Mrs Maureen Brears
Mr Gary Brewer
Mr Mark Brian
Mrs Zoe Briant-Evans
Mr Jeff Brice
Mr Stephen Bridge
Miss Emily Bridgewater
Mr John Brierley
Mrs Jennifer Briggs
Mr John Briggs
Mr Miles Brignall
Mrs L C Briscoe
Mr Simon Briscoe
Mr Simon Bristow
Mr Simon Briton
Mr Paul Brittain
Mr Julian Britton
Miss Helen Broadbent
Mr Ray Broadbridge
Mr David Broadfield
Mrs Gillian Brockway
Mr Patrick Bromley
Miss Marion Brondet
Mr Michael Brook
Mrs C Brookes
Mr Tim Brookes
Mrs A Brooks
Miss Elizabeth Brooks
Ms Nicola Brooks
Mr Peter Brooks
Mrs Lynda Broom
Mrs Patricia Broom
Mr Simon Broom
Mr Kenneth Brotherston
Mr Colin Brouwer-Ince
Mrs A J Brown
Mrs Beverley Brown
Mr Bruce Brown
Miss Claire Brown
Mr Dean Brown
Mrs Diane Brown
Mr Elvin Brown
Mrs Helen Brown
Miss Jaclyn Brown
Mr Janice Brown
Mrs Judy Brown
Ms Katie Brown

Mr Michael Brown
Mr Pedro Brown
Mr Peter W Brown
Mr Philip Brown
Mr Sam Brown
Mr Willian Brown
Mr Michael Browne
Mr Robert Brownhill
Miss Sarah Browning
Miss Caroline Bruce
Mrs Pam Brunning
Ms Vera Brunskill
Mr Michael Brunt
Mr Matt Bryant
Mr Ronnie Bryant
Mr Iain Bryce
Mr Ian Buchanan
Mr Anthony Buckland
Mrs Martine Buckler
Ms Maria Buckley
Mr Roger Buckley
Mrs Amadna Bucknall
Mr Abbas Budak
Mr Alan Budd
Miss Eleanor Bull
Mr Peter Bullard
Miss Jessica Bullers
Mrs Daphne Bullock
Mr Peter Bullock
Mr Michael Bunbury
Miss Emily Bunce
Mr Helen Bunter
Mrs Sarah Buntin
Mr David Burford
Miss Carol Burgess
Mr Douglas Burgess
Mrs Helen Burgess
Mr Julian burgess
Miss Lucy Burke
Miss Mischa Burke
Mr Matthew Burlem
Mr Graham Burnett
Miss Katie Burnetts
Mr Tim Burnham
Miss Rachel Burns
Ms Nicola Burns-Thomson
Mrs Ann Burr
Mr David Burr
Mrs Jill Burrington
Mrs Diane Burrows
Mr Harry Burrows
Mr Dave Burton
Mr James Burton
Mrs Lindsay Burton
Mr Mike Burton
Mr Malcolm Busby
Mr Richard Busby
Mr Michael Bushby
Mr David Bushell
Mr Terry Bushell
Mr Tony Bushell
Mr Adam Butcher
Mr Jeremy Butcher
Miss Becka Butler
Mr Jeff Butler
Mr Shaun Butler
Mr Paul Button
Mrs Ann Buxton
Mr John Buxton
Mrs Anne Byard
Miss Amy Byrne
Mr Brendan Byrne
Miss Jodie Byrne
Mr Piers Cadell
Mr James Cadle
Mrs Amanda Cairns
Mr Ian Cairns
Mrs Joanne Caley
Mrs Joanne Caley
Mr Tim Caley
Mr Graeme Callegari
Mr Phil Callender
Mrs Jane Camm
Mrs Nancy Camp
Mrs Alison Campbell
Mr Charles Campbell
Mr Colin Campbell
Mr James Campbell
Mr Norman Canderton
Mrs Carolyn Cannon
Mrs Pat Cannon
Mr Fabien Carbonell

Mrs Helen Carby
Mr Bruce Card
Mr Gordon Cardew
Miss Rachel Care
Mr Chris Carey
Mrs Susan Carlin
Mrs Elaine Carlton
Mrs Nicki Carman-Ellis
Miss Elsa Carneau
Mr Barry Carr
Mr Chris Carr
Mrs Josephine Carr
Miss Michelle Carr
Mr Richard Carr
Mr Rupert Carr
Mr Terry Carr
Mr Brian Carroll
Mr John Carroll
Mr Richard Carroll
Ms Sue Carroll
Mrs Alison Carse
Mrs Laura Carstairs
Mrs Debbie Carter
Miss Gemma Carter
Mrs Judith Carter
Mrs Linda Carter
Mr Robert Carter
Mr Tony Carter
Mrs M J Carthew
Mrs Gila Cartwright
Mrs Judith Cartwright
Mr Neville Cartwright
Mr William Casey
Miss Cally Cass
Mr Des Cass
Ms Anne Cassidy
Miss Helen Cassidy
Mr Alex Castledine
Mr Marcus Catling
Miss Philippa Catt
Miss Kirsty Cattanach
Mr William Catterick
Miss Sarah Cauldwell
Mrs Karen Causton
Mr John Cave
Mrs Susan Cave
Mr Michael Cavendish
Mr Suzanne Cayless
Mrs Thara Cecil
Mr Dave Chaffer
Mr Alaster Chalmers
Mr Richard Chamberlain
Mrs Cheryl Chambers
Mr John Chambers
Mr Cyril Alex Chan
Mrs Lena Chandler
Mrs Alyson Chaney
Mrs Iryna Chapman
Mr Peter Chapman
Mr Philip Chapman
Mr Dave Chappell
Miss Kerry Chapple
Ms Hilary Charlesworth
Mrs Angela Charlton
Mr Colin Chatelier
Mrs Gabrielle Chater
Mrs Sally Chatterjee
Mr Andrew Cheater
Mrs Juliet Cheetham
Mr William Chesneau
Mr James Chespy
Mr Kevin Chester
Mrs Sally Chesters
Miss Sarah Cheung
Mr Adam Chew-Tetlaw
Mrs Sophie Chiappe
Miss Diana Childs
Mr Richard Chinn
Mr Barry Chopping
Mrs Sophie Christelow
Mr Nick Christie
Mr Andy Christmas
Mrs Tracey Christmas
Mr Ernould Christophe
Mrs Amy Church
Mrs Sally Church
Ms Sophia Ciampa
Mr Luke Ciarleglio
Mrs Isabella Cirimpei
Mr Dan Clague
Ms Eleanor M Clamp
Ms Margaret Clancy

Ms Fiona Clapperton
Ms Lesley Clare
Mrs Marjorie Clare
Mr Alan Clark
Mr Gwyn Clark
Miss Helen Clark
Mr Jack Clark
Mr Jim Clark
Mr Jonathan Clark
Mr Roger Clark
Miss Sue Clark
Miss Vivienne Clark
Mrs Anne Clarke
Mrs Else Clarke
Mrs Jackie Clarke
Mr James Clarke
Mrs Libby Clarke
Mr Michael Clarke
Mr Nick Clarke
Mrs Sara Clarke
Miss Sarah Clarke
Mr Tom Clarke
Mrs Jennifer Clayton
Mr John Clayton
Mrs Liz Clayton
Mr Steve Clayton
Mr Brian Clegg
Mrs Barbara Clements
Mrs Judi Clements
Mr Trevor Clements
Mrs Cheryl Clennett
Mr Andrew Cliff
Mrs Kathleen Clifford
Mr Peter Clifford
Mr Simon Clifton
Mrs Helen Clish
Mrs Tina Clough
Mrs Marie Cobb
Mrs Myrtle Cobb
Mr Peter Cobrin
Mr Nicholas Cochran
Mrs Pauline Cochrane
Mr Martyn Cocks
Mr Frances Coe
Mr James Cohen
Mr Ronald Cohen
Mr David Coldicutt
Mrs Claire Cole
Mr Gareth Cole
Mr Jeremy Cole
Mrs Susan Colebrook
Mr John Coleman
Mrs Anne Coles
Miss Heidi Coles
Ms Alexandra Colesby
Ms Yvonne Colgan
Mrs Naomi Colley
Mr Roger Collicott
Mr and Mrs Collier
Mr Gordon Collier
Mr John Collier
Mr Simon Collinge
Mrs Jan Collings
Mrs Ashley Collingwood
Miss Belinda Collins
Mrs C Collins
Mr David Collins
Mr John Collins
Mrs Jane Colston
Mr Matt Colton
Mr Dave Comber
Mr Pat Conneely
Mr Derek Connery
Mrs Rachel Connolly
Mr Mike Connor
Mr Adam Constable
Mr Peter Constable
Mr Alfredo Contarato
Mr Andrew Cook
Mrs Caroline Cook
Mr Colin Cook
Mr Graham Cook
Miss Julia Cook
Mrs Lisa Cook
Miss Lyndsey Cook
Mrs Pauline Cook
Mrs Brenda Cook Harrison
Mrs Caroline Cooke
Mr Michael Cool
Ms Catherine Coombes
Mrs Margaret Coombs
Ms Caron Cooper

Mrs Elizabeth Cooper
Mrs Gai Cooper
Mr John Cooper
Mr Nick Cooper
Mr Norman Cooper
Mr Peter Cooper
Mr Peter Cooper
Mr Rupert Cooper
Miss Sarah Cooper
Miss Shelley Cooper
Mr Simon Cooper
Miss Claire Cope
Mrs April Copeland
Mr David Copley
Mrs Frances Copping
Mr Ron Corbett
Mrs Sheila Corbett
Mr Ken Corcoran
Mrs Sue Corderoy
Mr David Cordon
Mr John Corfield
Mrs Alexia Corkery
Mr Graham Corlett
Mrs Susannah Corley
Mrs Christine Corner
Mrs Ali Cornock
Mr John Corradine
Mrs Gillian Corry
Miss Merlin Costa
Mr Martin Coulson
Mr J R Coulthwaite
Mr Peter Coulton
Mr Wayne Coupland
Miss Michelle Court
Mr Rufus Cove
Mr Roger Cowen
Mrs Evelyn Cowie
Mrs Ana Cox
Ms Georgina Cox
Mrs Jennifer Cox
Miss Louisa Cox
Ms Lucianne Cox
Mr Rob Cox
Mr David Coxon
Mr Brian Coyle
Mr Adrian Crabtree
Mr Stephen Craddock
Mrs Helen Craft
Mr Stephen Cragg
Mr Nathan Crame
Miss Tracey Crampin
Mr John Crane
Mrs Sarah Cranston
Miss Kirsty Crawford
Mr John Crawley
Mrs Valerie Crean
Mr Jonathan Crisp
Mr Roger Critchley
Mr Nigel Crocker
Mr Stephen Cromie
Mr Peter Crook
Mrs Ann Crosbie
Mr Antony Cross
Mrs Nimisha Cross
Mr Tony Cross
Mr James Cruickshank
Mrs Janet Crush
Mrs Naomi Cryer
Mr Joshuah Cudd
Mr Ian Culley
Mr Ian Cullis
Mrs Karen Cunliffe
Mrs Karen Cunningham
Mrs Rothes Currie
Miss Anna Currigan
Mrs Brooke Curtis
Mrs Joanne Curtis
Mr Lee Curtis
Mr Malcolm Curtis
Mr Mark Curtis
Mrs Ruth Curzon
Mr Chris Cusack
Mr Tom Cuthbertson
Miss Patricia Czyzewska
Mrs Anne Da Costa
Mrs Katharine Da Forno
Mr Saf Dad
Mrs Christine Dadd
Mr Sam Daffin
Mrs Jacqueline Daines
Mr Nigel Dakin
Mrs Catherine Dalal

Miss Gemma Dale
Professor J E Dale
Mr James Daley
Mr Peter Daley
Mrs Lauren Dalgleish-Mclaren
Mr Andrew Dalton
Ms Maria D'Amelio
Mrs Meriel Dand
Ms Laura Dandy
Miss Christina Daniel
Miss Claire Daniel
Mr Julian Danskin
Mr Tausif Darbar
Mrs Ann Darby
Ms Elinor Dare
Mr Clifford Darlington
Mr Daniel Darwood
Miss E Dashper
Miss Faye Dasley
Miss Katy Dauden
Mr Nigel Davenport
Mrs Ellie Davidson
Mr Hugh Davidson
Mrs Jan Davidson
Mr John Davidson
Mrs Wendy Davidson
Miss Jackie Davie
Mr Adrian Davies
Mr Alun Davies
Mrs Anne Davies
Mrs Beverley Davies
Ms Catrin Davies
Mr Christopher Davies
Mr Colin Davies
Miss Donna M E Davies
Mr Gareth Davies
Mrs Gay Davies
Mr Graham Davies
Mrs Helen Davies
Ms Linda Davies
Mrs Liz Davies
Mr Martin Davies
Mrs Michelle Davies
Mrs Molly Davies
Mr Roger Davies
Mr Tony Davies
Mrs Eileen Davis
Miss Emma Davis
Mrs Joanne Davis
Mr Julie Davis
Mrs Mandy Davis
Mr Paul Davis
Miss Rose Davis
Mr Brian Davison
Mrs Judith Davison
Miss Sarah Davison
Miss Kelly Davy
Mrs Christine Daw
Mrs Maggie Dawber
Dr Rodney Dawber
Miss Emma Dawes
Mrs Deborah Dawson
Miss Holly Dawson
Mr John Dawson
Ms Lucy Dawson
Miss Alison Day
Mrs Jean Day
Mrs Sallie Day
Mr Nicholas Daykin
Mr Christian de Larringa
Miss Laura Deacon
Mrs Annabel Dearlove
Mr Mark Dearlove
Mr Ian DeBattista
Miss Thomas Debbie
Mr N Dee
Mr Steve DeHavillande
Mr John Delahaye
Mrs Jennifer Delves
Mr James Dempsey
Mr Paul Denham
Mrs Susan Denholm
Mr Roxiy Denim
Mr Philip Dennison
Mrs Lorraine Dent
Mrs Pamela Denwood
Miss Maya Desai
Mrs Gina Desborough
Mrs Anne Devlin
Miss Claire Devlin

Mrs Sandra Devlin
Mr John Dews
Mrs Andrea Dewsbery
Mr Suresh Dhargalkar
Mrs Susan Diamond
Mr Roy Dias
Mr John Dickenson
Mrs Winifred Dickenson
Mrs Helen Dickinson
Mr Graeme Dickson
Mrs Philippa Dickson
Mr Martin Diggins
Mr Richard Dilks
Mrs Kate Dimsey
Miss Stacy Dingain
Mrs Sam Dingley
Mr Frederick Dinmore
Mr Glen Dixon
Mrs Jo Dixon
Mr Michael Dixon
Miss Hannah Dobbs
Miss Chatty Dobson
Mrs Christine Dobson
Mr Geoffrey Dobson
Mrs Jackie Dockreay
Mrs Linda Dodd
Mr Martin Dodd
Mrs Louise Dodds
Mr Gerard Doherty
Mr Byron Dolan
Mr Sean Dolby
Mrs Gaynor Donaldson
Mr Keith Donaldson
Miss Kate Donkersley
Miss Kate Donohoe
Mr Carl Donovan
Mr Frank Doran
Mr Mike Dorka
Mr R W B Douglas
Ms Rebecca Douglas
Mr Anthony Dove
Miss Victoria Dove
Mrs Kelly Dowding
Mr Neil Dowdney
Mrs Debra Down
Mr Mervyn Down
Mr David Downey
Mr Colin Dowse
Mr Robert Dowsett
Ms Sharon Dowson
Miss Trudie Draper
Miss Kat Dray
Mr Dudley Drayson
Mrs Anna Drew
Mr Phil Drew
Miss Rebecca Drew
Mrs Candida Drew-Prior
Mr Doublas Driscoll
Miss Jessica Driscoll
Mrs Sandra Drury
Mrs Arlette DSouza
Mr John Du Cane
Mr Alex du Feu
Miss Vivienne DuBourdieu
Mr John Ducker
Mrs Nina Ducker
Mrs Joanne Duffy
Mr Barrie Dugdale
Mr Andreos Duhart
Mr Michael Duke
Mrs Elizabeth Duller
Mr Ian Duncan
Mrs Linda Dunford
Miss Tracey Dunford
Ms Barbara Dunlop
Mr John Dunn
Mrs Sally Dunn
Ms Judith Dunne
Mr James Dunstan
Mr Paul Dunstan
Mrs Rebecca Dunstan
Mrs Eileen Dunwell
Mrs Elaine Durant
Mr Francis Durham
Mrs Wendy Durrant
Mr Dom Dwight
Mrs Ann Dwyer
Mr Andy Dyble
Mr Bill Dyer
Miss Ella Dyer
Mr Nick Dymoke-Marr
Mrs Gillian Eades

Mr Terry Eagers
Ms June Eakins
Mr Graeme Earl
Mr Andrew Eason-Gibson
Mr John East
Mr Paul Eastham
Mrs Penny Ebdon
Ms Jo Ebdon-Muir
Mr Raul Echavarri
Mrs Anne-Marie Eden
Mrs Gina Eden
Mrs Amanda Edge
Mrs Caroline Edge
Mr Daniel Edge
Mr Stepphen Edge
Mr Neil Edmonds
Miss Sandra Edmonds
Mrs Catherine Edmonds-Hahn
Mr David Edward
Mr Alan Edwards
Mr Andrew Edwards
Miss Anna Edwards
Miss Caitlin Edwards
Mrs Janice Edwards
Mr Jason Edwards
Mrs Jenny Edwards
Ms Liz Edwards
Mrs Michelle Edwards
Mr Robert Edwards
Mr Thomas Egetemeyer
Mr Peter Egli
Mr Eric Eisenhandler
Mr Rob Eisner
Mrs Myra Elderfield
Mr Raymond Elderfield
Mr Gary Elflett
Mrs Cynthia Elkington
Mr Mark Ellam
Mr Michael Elleston
Mr Dan Ellingworth
Mrs Ann Elliot
Mr Don Elliott
Mrs Kathryn Elliott
Ms Alex Ellis
Mrs Christine Ellis
Mr James Ellis
Mr Peter Ellis
Mrs Valerie Ellis
Ms Martine Ellison-Smith
Mr Julian Elloway
Mrs Rebecca Ellwood
Mr Phil Elstob
Ms Jane Elsworth
Miss Tracey Elvidge
Ms Jane Elwood
Mrs Jennifer Emmerson
Miss Lindsay Endean
Mr John Enfield
Mr John England
Mr Stuart Englefield
Mr Nick English
Mrs Karen Ephgrave
Mr Brian Errington
Miss Polly Errington
Mrs Claire Esberger
Miss Claire Evans
Mr David Evans
Ms Elaine Evans
Mr Glynn Evans
Mr Greg Evans
Miss Heulwen Evans
Mrs Julie Evans
Mrs Kath Evans
Mr Michael Evans
Mr Neville Evans
Mr Richard Evans
Mr Rob Evans
Mrs Sally Evans
Mr Tony Evans
Mr William Evans
Mrs Ann Eve
Mrs Susan Everett
Mr Ted Everett
Mr Barry Eves
Mr David Exell
Mr Philip Extance
Mr P Fabb
Mr John Faber
Mr John Fahy
Mrs Anne Fairbairn
Mr John Fairhurst

Mrs Maura Falla
Mr Mick Farmer
Ms Michaela Farquhar
Mrs Beth Farr
Mr Julian Farrall
Mr R A Farrand
Mrs Lydia Farrell
Mrs Erika Farwell
Ms Ana Fass
Mrs Sally Faure Walker
Mr Neil Fazakerley
Mr Geoffrey Fearnehough
Ms Jane Fehler
Mr Mark Feingold
Mr Paul Fella
Mrs Amanda Fellows
Mr Ben Fenner
Mrs Janette Fenner
Mr Kevin Fenner
Mr Hugh Fergie
Mrs Jean Ferguson
Mr Peter Ferguson
Mr Simon Ferguson
Mrs Sam Fermandez
Ms Lynda Fermor
Mr M Fernandes
Mr R. Fernandes
Mr Yohan Fernando
Mrs Rosemary Ferrier Moore
Ms Olivia Field
Mrs Tracey Field
Mrs Lee Michael Fielder
Miss Nicola Fieldsend
Mrs Tracy Figg
Mr Neville Filar
Mr Anthony Fincham
Mr Geoffrey Fink
Ms Catherine Finlay
Mrs Jo Finley
Mrs Anne Finnegan
Mrs Ruth Finney
Mr Roger Firman
Mrs Julia Firth
Mr Arran Fisher
Mr Lee Fisher
Mrs Maddy Fiske
Mrs Julie Fitch
Mrs Ann Fitzgerald
Mr Chris Fitzgibbon
Mrs Rosalind Fitz-Gibbon
Miss Ciara Fitzpatrick
Mrs Rachel Flanagan
Mr Kieran Flatt
Mr Peter Flatter
Mrs Adelaide Flaxman
Miss Rachel Fletcher
Mr Jon Flitney
Mr Ian Floody
Mrs Jean Flowers
Mrs Janet Flucker
Mr James Flynn
Mr Brian Folley
Miss Clara Fontanella
Mr Anthony Forbes
Mr Justin Forbes
Miss Bambina Forciniti
Mr Alan Ford
Mrs Clare Ford
Mrs Kelly Ford
Mr Robert Ford
Mr Gabor Forgacs
Miss Anna Forrest
Mr Rob Forrest
Mr John Forse
Mrs Katie Forster
Mr Kelvin Forster
Mr Ben Foster
Mrs Fiona Foster
Mr Gordon Foster
Mrs Julie Foster
Mrs Lynda Foster
Mr Richard Foster
Mrs Annabel Foulston
Mr John Foulston
Mr Christopher Fowler
Mr David Fowler
Mrs BV Fox
Mr Harry Fox
Mrs Hilary Fox
Miss Nicola Frame
Ms Marilyn Frampton

Mr Roberto Franceschini
Mr Gordon Franklin
Miss Saira Franklin
Mrs Jo Fraser
Mr Nicholas Fraser
Miss Rachel Fraser
Mr Stephen Fraser
Mr Jay Freeborn
Mr Daniel Freedman
Mr David Freedman
Mr Paul Freeman
Mrs Sheila Freeman
Mr John Freer
Mrs Amanda French
Mrs Alice Fretwell
Mr Patrick Frew
Mrs Patricia Friedman
Mr Roger Frier
Mrs Anne Frisby
Mrs Becky Frost
Mrs Margaret Frost
Ms Sarah Frost
Mrs Allison Frown
Mrs Amanda Fryer
Mr Richard Fryer
Mr Des Fulcher
Mrs Chris Fuller
Mr David Furlong
Mrs Isabel Furmston
Ms Lucy Gable
Ms Jane Gaca
Miss Rachel Gadd
Mr Roger Gadsby
Ms Lisa Gagliani
Mr Curtis Galbraith
Ms Caroline Gallagher
Mr Steven Gallagher
Mrs Gillian Galloway
Mr Lee Gamble
Mr Tim Gane
Mr Richard Ganesh moorthy
Mrs Susan Ganley
Mr Tim Garbett
Mr Paul Garcia
Mr Barry Gardiner
Mr Stephen Garner
Miss Katherine Garrity
Mrs Vivien Garside
Mrs Jennifer Garvan
Mrs Margaret Gash
Mrs Rosemary Gaskell
Mrs Jula Gaster
Mr Boyd Gawish
Miss Sarah Gay
Mr Adrian Gazzard
Miss Hayley Gee
Mrs Ann Geen
Mrs Helen Geen
Mrs Priyanca Gela
Mr Sam Geneen
Mr James Geoghegan
Mr Tony Georgakis
Mrs Gillian George
Mrs Christine Gerezdi
Mr Stephen Gerrard
Mr Martyn Gettings
Mrs Jenny Gibbons
Ms Lisa Gibbons
Mr Andrew Gibbs
Mr Michael Gibbs
Mrs Deborah Gibson
Mr Jonathan Gibson
Mrs Shirley Gibson
Mr Kevin Giddings
Mr Alastair Gilman
Mr David Gilbert
Mr Aidan Giles
Ms Marie Giles
Miss Tracy Giles
Ms Jane Gill
Miss Sara Gill
Mr Tony Gill
Mrs Marion Gillette
Mr Theodore Gillick
Mrs Maureen Gilmartin
Mrs Angie Gilmore
Mr Robert Girvan
Mr Joseph Gittos
Mrs Susan Gittos
Dr Helen Gladstone
Ms Sarah Jane Gladwin

Mrs Karen Glasby
Mr Colin Glascoe
Mr Bryan Glastonbury
Mr John Glaze
Mrs Caroline Gleed
Mrs Julie Glenn
Mr Henry Globe
Mr Roger Glover
Mrs Ros Glover
Mr Fred Goat
Mr Nick Godden
Ms M Godfrey
Mr Philip Godfrey
Mr Robert Godfrey
Mrs Liz Godsmark
Miss Jane Golby
Miss Lowri Gold
Mrs Jean Golding
Mr Arnold Goldman
Mr Derek Goldrei
Mr Peter Goldsbrough
Mr Paul Goldschmidt
Mr Mike Goldsmith
Miss Malgorzata Golisz
Miss Keira Goncalves
Mr Robert Good
Mr Vic Good
Mrs Celia Goodchild
Mr Michael Goodchild
Mr Glen Goode
Mr David Goodman
Ms Hilary Goodman
Mrs Sally Goodman
Miss Helen Goodrum
Mrs Gill Goodwillie
Miss Kelly Goosen
Mr Terry Gorman
Mr Chris Gorringe
Miss Sophie Gorton
Mr Noel Gorvett
Mr Keith Gotch
Mr Richard Gottfried
Mrs Stephanie Gottlieb
Mr Bryan Goude
Mrs Diane Goulding
Miss Rebecca Grace
Miss Charmaine Gragasin
Mr Adam Graham
Miss Caroline Graham
Ms Christine Graham
Mr David Grant
Mrs Jeannine Grant
Mrs Joanne Grant
Miss Sam Grant
Mrs Christine Granville-Edge
Mr Michael Graubart
Mrs Jacqui Graves
Miss Devin Gray
Mr Gordon Gray
Mrs Helen Gray
Mr Peter Gray
Mr Richard Gray
Mrs Ruth Gray
Mrs Caroline Greaves
Mrs Dianne Green
Mrs Janet Green
Mrs Kate Green
Mr Lewis Green
Mrs Margaret Green
Mr Peter Green
Mr Steven Green
Mr Garret Greene
Ms Sally Greene
Mr Simon Greene
Mr John Greenhough
Mrs Susan Greenman
Mr David Greenwood
Miss Margaret Greenwood
Mr Tony Greenwood
Miss Emma Gregg
Mrs Charlotte Gregory
Miss Harriet Gregory
Mr John Gregory
Ms Paula Grevett
Mr John Gridley
Mr David Griffiths
Mr Ian Griffiths
Mr John Griffiths
Mr Wayne Griffiths
Mrs Janet Grigg

Mr James Grigor
Mr and Mrs Grimes
Mr Joe Grimshaw
Mrs Maria Grimshaw
Mr N M Grimwood
Mr Nigel Grimwood
Mr Martin Grindell
Mr Peter Grist
Mr David Groome
Mr Nick Grossman
Mrs Sandi Gryce
Mrs Vanessa Grzywacz
Mr James Guest
Mrs Carmen Guevara
Mrs Carol Ann Guilford
Mr Frank Guinn
Mr Derek Gull
Mr Lawrence Gulley
Mrs T Gumbert
Mr Richard Gunn
Mr Joe Gunnett
Mr Ian Gunning
Mrs Claire Gunyon
Mrs Sara Guven
Mr Leconte Guy
Mr David Hackett
Mr Douglas Hacking
Mr Simon Hackney
Mrs Karen Haddock
Miss Kate Haden
Mr Robin Hadley
Mrs Michale Hagard
Mrs Karen Haggarty
Miss Vicky Hague
Mr Ben Haigh
Miss Charlotte Haines
Miss Sophie Haithwaite
Mr Steve Haithwaite
Mrs Sandy Hale
Miss Lauren Hales
Mr Geoffrey Halfhide
Mrs Emma Hall
Mrs Irene Hall
Mr Peter Hall
Ms T Hall
Mr Tim Hall
Mr Simon Halley
Mrs Sally Halsey
Mr Jon Ham
Mr Matthew Hamber
Mr John Hamer
Mr James Hamilton
Mrs Vonney Hamilton
Mrs Callie Hammond
Mr Lee Hammond
Miss Mary Hanahoe
Mr David Hancock
Mrs Judith Hancox
Mr Neal Handforth
Mr Gary Handley
Mr Gordon Hands
Mrs Michelle Hankins
Miss Carol Hanna
Ms Laura Hannan
Miss Zara Hannoun
Mr Ian Hanreck
Mr Ralph Hansby-Patterson
Mrs Maggie Hanson
Mr Brian Harden
Mrs Wendy Hardiman-Evans
Mrs Di Harding
Mrs Laura Harding
Mrs Jane Hardman
Mr Jeremy Hards
Mr Charles Hardy
Miss Jeffie Hardy
Mrs Julie Hardy
Miss Donna Hardyman
Mr John Hargest
Mr Matt Harirngton
Mr Phil Hariss
Mrs Tricia Harker
Mrs Caroline Harnett
Mr Jerald Harpur
Mr Marcus Harpur
Mrs Kathleen Harries
Mr Ken Harries
Mrs Glynis Harris
Mrs Isabelle Harris
Mr James Harris
Mrs Julie Harris

Mrs Karen Harris
Mrs Kirsty Harris
Miss Lisa Harris
Mrs Lynda Harris
Ms Lynn Harris
Mr Paul Harris
Mr Raymond Harris
Mrs Sally Harris
Mrs Shona Harris
Mr Trevor Harris
Mrs Annie Harrison
Mr Chris Harrison
Mrs Elizabeth Harrison
Mr Gordon Harrison
Mrs Lindsay Harrison
Miss Louise Harrison
Mr Patrick Harrison
Ms Tatiana Harrison
Ms Wendy Harrison
Mr Phil Harriss
Ms Jo Hart
Mrs Joan Hart
Mrs Meryl Hart
Mrs Toni Hart
Miss Jenny Harth
Mr John Hartley
Ms Katharine Hartley
Mr Ben Harvey
Mrs Christine Harvey
Mr Colin Harvey
Mrs Janet Harvey
Mrs Jennifer Harvey
Mr Leslie Harvey
Dr Peter Harvey
Mr Phil Harvey
Mr R Harvey
Mrs Rosemary Harvey
Mr John Haslam
Mrs Fleur Haslock
Mr James Hassell
Ms Pam Hastings
Mrs Pamela Hastings
Mr Gus Hatchard
Mr Alun Hatfield
Mr Luke Hawker
Miss Anna Hawkins
Mr Chris Hawkins
Mr Roger Hawkins
Mrs Rachel Hayball
Mrs Julia Hayfield
Mr Andy Hayler
Mr John Haynes
Mrs Clair Hayward
Mr James Hayward
Mrs Hilary Haywood
Mrs Julie Hazell
Mrs Maria Head
Mrs Carole Heath
Ms Marilyn Heath
Ms Tara Heath
Mr David Heaton
Mrs Debra Heaton
Reverend Cannon N C Heavisides
Mr Roland Hebeler
Mrs Tricia Heckingbottom
Mr Don Heeley
Mr Colin Heggie
Ms Jane Hellewell
Mrs Katherine Helliwell
Ms Sara Helm
Mrs C Hemsley
Mrs Carol Hemus
Mr Derek Henderson
Mr Hamish Henderson
Mrs Jacqui Henderson
Mrs Jenny Henderson
Miss Natalie Henderson
Mr Paul Henderson
Mr Steven Henderson
Miss Jemimah Hendrick
Mr Charles Hendry
Ms Christine Hendry
Mrs Jacqui Henness
Mr David Henshaw
Dr M E Henstock
Ms Alicia Herbert
Mr Gerhard Herbst
Mr George Herd
Mr Rod Heron
Mr Malcolm Herring
Mr Piers Herrmann

Mr Michael Hession
Mr Patrick Heuff
Mr Gad Heuman
Mrs Clare Heyes
Miss Layla Heyes
Mrs Betty Heywood
Mrs Sue Hibbard
Mrs Diane Hibbert
Mr Steve Hibbert
Mrs Denise Hickey
Mrs Kathryn Hickey
Ms Ana Higginson
Mrs Jessica Higgs
Mrs Emma Hignett
Mr Allen Hill
Mr Brian Hill
Mrs Camille Hill
Mr David Hill
Mr Ian Hill
Mr Jack Hill
Mr John Hill
Mr Rupert Hill
Miss Wendy Hill
Mr Jonathan Hills
Mr Roy Hillyard
Mr John Hilsum
Ms Lynn Hilton
Mr Nigel Hindley
Mr Eric G Hinds
Mr Wade Hinkley
Mrs Ann Hitchcock
Mrs Rosemarie Hitches
Mr Peter Hoare
Mrs Caroline Hoblyn
Miss Sophie Marie Hochleithner
Ms Dinah Hockridge
Mrs Samantha Hockridge
Mr Alan Hodder
Mr Brendan Hodge
Miss Margaret Hodge
Mrs Annette Hodges
Mr Brian Hodges
Mr Mike Hodges
Mr Michael Hodgson
Mrs Debbie Hodson
Mrs Ursula Hofheinz
Miss Jenny Holbrow
Mrs Pauline Holden
Mrs Suzi Holder
Mrs Kate Holdsworth
Mrs Eileen Holkham
Mrs Carole Holland
Mr Grant Holland
Ms Niki Holland
Mrs Sharon Holland
Mrs Siobhan Holland
Mrs Patsy Hollings
Mr David Hollings
Mrs Sheilagh Hollingsworth
Mrs Jo Holloway
Mrs Diane Holman
Mrs Suzanne Holman
Mrs Fiona Holmes
Mr Geoff Holmes
Mrs Joycelyn Holmes
Mr Andy Holt
Mr Gareth Holt
Miss Olya Homes
Mr Jon Honeyball
Mr Benjamin Hook
Mr Tony Hook
Mr Martin Hooper
Mr Ryan Hooper
Mr Kelvin Hoose
Mrs Rebecca Hope
Mrs Keri Hopkins
Mr Mark Hopkins
Mr Vernon Hopkins
Mrs Dawn Hopkinson
Mrs Anne Hopton
Ms Barbara Horrell
Mr Peter Horrell
Mrs Emma Horrocks
Mr Andrew Horsler
Mr Laszlo Horvath
Ms Zoe Horwich
Mrs Janice Hosegood
Miss Alison Hoskin
Mrs Sue Hoskins Day
Mr D R Houghton
Miss Gemma Houghton

Mrs A Hoult
Mrs Joanne Howard
Mr Ken Howard
Mrs Susan Howard
Mrs Kate Howarth
Mr Michael Howarth
Mr Anthony Howell
Mr Michael Howell
Mr Philip Howell
Mr Vaughan Howells
Mr Alastair Howie
Ms Sophia Howlett
Mrs Elaine Huberry
Mrs Anita Huckle
Mrs Norma Huddy
Mrs Sarah Huddy
Mrs Allison Hudson
Mrs Elaine Hudson
Mr Paul Hudson
Mr Peter Hudson
Mrs Margaret Huelin
Mr Alan Hughes
Mr Ellis Hughes
Mrs Emma Hughes
Miss Lucy Hughes
Mr Marue Hughes
Mr Shane Hughes
Mrs Sharon Hughes
Mr Tristan Hughes
Ms Ann Hulme
Ms Linda Humphrey
Mrs Sarah Humphrey
Mr Ralph Humphries
Miss Alannah Hunt
Mr Martin Hunt
Mr Nick Hunt
Mrs Kate Hunter
Mr Peter Hunter
Mrs Susan Hunter
Miss Kate Hupen
Ms Karen Hurst
Mr Faisal Hussain
Mr Ali Hussan
Mrs Stephanie Hutchings
Mrs Nicola Hutchinson
Mr Paul Hutchinson
Mr Barry Hutt
Mr Charles Hutt
Mrs Dahlia Hutton
Mr Richard Hutton
Mr Reg Huyton
Mrs Joyce Hyam
Mrs Chris Hyett
Mrs Maria Hyrapiet
Miss Lena Ib
Ms Junko Imai-Perkins
Mr Chris Impey
Mr Ian Inch
Mrs Deirdre Ines
Mrs Abby Ingham
Mrs Kristy Ingle
Mr David Ingleby
Miss Jennifer Insley
Mr Ron Ion
Mr Rory Ireland
Mrs Sylvia Ireton
Mrs Ros Irving
Mr Vincent Irwin
Mr David Isaac
Mrs June Ive
Miss Courtney Ives
Ms Jennifer Jack
Mrs Susan Joy Jackett
Mr Andrew Jackson
Mr Darren Jackson
Mr James Jackson
Mrs Lesley Jackson
Mrs Liz Jackson
Miss Nicola Jackson
Mr Peter Jackson
Mrs Su Jacobs
Mrs Swapna Jadhav
Ms Alison Jagger
Mrs Samantha Jaggon
Mrs Bridgit James
Mrs Clare James
Mr David James
Ms Denise James
Mrs Elizabeth James
Ms Julie James
Mr Mark James
Mr Steve James

Mrs Elizabeth Jamieson
Mr Robert Jamieson
Mrs Caecilia Janzen
Mr N Jarvis
Mrs Rita Jarvis
Mr Bharat Jashanmal
Mrs Lesley Jay
Mrs Nick Jeanes
Mrs Annette Jeeves
Mr Martin Jeeves
Mrs Christine Jeffery
Mrs Lucie Jeffery
Mr Terry Jeffries
Mrs Janet Jenkins
Mrs Thelma Jenkin-Jones
Mr Julian Jenkins
Mr Kevin Jenkins
Mr Philip Jenkins
Mrs Pamela Jenkins
Mr Richard Jenkins
Mr Trevor Jenkins
Miss Deborah Jennings
Mrs Diana Jennings
Mr Ronan Jennings
Miss Eleanor Jenvey
Ms Lisa Jerman
Mr David Jervois
Mr Huw Jessop
Mr Nick Jewell
Mrs Hazel Jillings
Miss Raj Johal
Miss Charlotte John
Mr Michael John
Mr Gareth Johns
Mr Benjamin Johnson
Mr Daniel Johnson
Mr David Johnson
Mrs Gillian Johnson
Mrs Jane Johnson
Miss Katie Johnson
Mrs Maria Johnson
Mr Martin Johnson
Miss Samantha Johnson
Mrs Sue Johnson
Mrs Suellen Johnson
Mr Graeme Johnston
Mrs Laura Johnston
Mrs Lesley Johnston
Miss Aimee Jones
Mr Alan Jones
Miss Amanda Jones
Mrs Barbara Jones
Mr Bob Jones
Mrs Carole Jones
Mr Cellan Jones
Miss Ceris Jones
Mr Christopher Jones
Mrs Dalleen Jones
Mrs Dominica Jones
Mr Douglas Jones
Mrs Gaetane Jones
Mr Ian Jones
Mrs Janet Jones
Mr John Jones
Mr Jonathan Jones
Mr Kathryn Jones
Miss Kerry Jones
Miss Laura Jones
Mr Martin Jones
Mr Matthew Jones
Dr Mel Jones
Mr Michael Jones
Mrs Natasha Jones
Mr Peter Jones
Miss Rhiannon Jones
Mr Rod Jones
Mr Ross Jones
Mrs Sarah Jones
Mrs Tahiba Jones
Mrs Vivienne Jones
Mrs Larissa Jonsson
Mr John Jordan
Miss Lisa Jordan
Mrs Margaret Jordan
Mrs Vivien Jouhin
Mrs Verity Jowett
Mrs Barbara Joyner
Mr Nick Joyner
Mrs Lorraine Judge
Mr Michael Judge
Mrs Rachael Jurkiw
Miss Jennifer Kadar

Mr Carl Kaeppner-Smith
Mr Charles Kail
Miss Caoimhe Kane
Miss Hayley Kane
Mr Paul Kane
Mr Rumy Kapadia
Mrs Linda Karlsen
Mrs Penelope Karmel
Mrs Mary Kaspar
Mrs Bernadette Katchi
Ms Tonia Katsantonis
Mr Denis Kavanagh
Mr Andrew Kay
Mrs Gill Kaye
Mrs Helen Kayes
Mr James Kearney
Mrs Natasha Kearney
Mr Christian Keegan
Mr Alan Keighley
Mr Andrew Keil
Ms Ruth Keillar
Mrs Julie Kelley
Mrs Bobbie Kelly
Miss Deborah Kelly
Mrs Maria Kelly
Mrs Martha Kelly
Miss Michelle Kelly
Miss Yasemin Kemal
Ms Eva Kemble
Mrs Jane Kemp
Mr John Kemp
Miss Victoria Kemp
Mr Philip Kempster
Mr Colin Kenealy
Mr Emma Kennedy
Mr James Kennedy
Mrs Karen Kennedy
Mr Christain Kenny
Mr David Kenny
Mrs Edwina Kent
Mrs Fiona Kent
Mr James Kent
Mr Matthew Kent
Mrs Christina Kenward
Mr John Kenward
Mrs Kath Kenyon
Mrs Carol Keohane
Mr Dave Keper
Mr Jack Kerbel
Mrs Moira Kerr-Clemenson
Ms Emily Kerrigan
Miss Katie Kervell
Mr Richard Kettles
Mr Michael Keys
Mr Bijan Khoshabi
Mr Vimal Khosla
Mr Gary Kidd
Mr John Kilby
Mrs Margaret Kilby
Mr Emma Killilea
Miss Leona Kimber
Miss Anna King
Mr Barry King
Mr Graham King
Mrs Helen King
Mrs Helene King
Mrs Judith King
Miss Zena King
Mr Robert Kingman
Mr Iain Kingsley
Mr George Kingston
Mr John Kirk
Mr Ernest Kirkbride
Mr Mark Kirkbride
Miss Marianna Kiss
Ms Esther Kissling
Mr Terry Kitching
Mr Athanasios Kitsios
Mrs Riki Kittel
Mr Martin Kittel
Mr Pieter Kleynhans
Mr Andrew Knight
Mrs Cheryl Knight
Mr Karl Knight
Mr Keith E Knight
Mrs Lyn Knight
Mr Robin Knight
Ms Selena Knight
Mr Stephen Knight
Mr Tom Knight
Mr Chris Knipe
Mrs Helen Knott
Miss Angela Knox

Mrs Heather Kohn
Mr Ebrahim Kolil
Mr Thomas Konopka
Mr Mathew Kopel
Miss Szita Koto
Mr Kristof Kowalski
Mr Piers Krause
Mr Ingo Kresse
Mr Paul Krykant
Mr Paul Krykant
Mrs Roz Krueger Campbell
Mrs Karen Kubran
Mr Peter Kudelka
Mr Pardeep Kumar
Mrs Rachel Kyriazi
Mr Christopher Lacey
Mrs Patricia Lacey
Mrs Amanda Lachlan
Mr Marc Laing
Miss Carol Lamb
Mr Peter Lamb
Ms Layne Lambert
Mrs Tracey Lamberti
Mr Ray Lampkin
Mrs Elisabeth Lancaster
Mr Paul Lancaster
Miss Andrea Lane
Mr Phillip Lane
Ms Susan Lane
Mrs Sylvia Lanfranchi
Mr Jack Lang
Mr Mike Langford
Mr John Langham
Miss Rebecca Langham
Mr David Langston
Miss Hayley Langston
Mr John Lansdowne
Mrs Kay Laskey
Miss Gemma Latham
Mr John Lattimore
Mr Nick Lavelle
Mrs Judith Lavender
Mrs Vivienne Lavis
Mrs Margot Lawlor
Mr Darren Laws
Mr Chris Lawson
Mr G Mark Lawson
Mrs Alison Lay
Ms Janita Lay
Mr Matt Le Fevre
Mr Tony Lea
Mr Alan Leading
Mr Robin Leake
Mr Alan Leaman
Mr Dennis Leaming
Miss Suzanne Leather
Mr Andrew Lee
Mr Darren Lee
Mr David Lee
Mr Roger Lee
Mr Stanley Lee
Mrs Victoria Lee
Mrs Sharon Lee
Mr Chris Leeks
Miss Bonnie Lee-Richards
Ms Helen Lees
Mr Matt Lees
Ms Tanya Lees
Ms Tracey Lees
Mr John Legg
Mr Bob Legit
Mrs Ann Leitch
Ms Julie Leitz
Mrs Gillian Lello
Miss Laura Lemon
Mr Terry Lennox
Mr James Leo
Mr Paul Leonard
Ms Catriona Leslie
Professor K M Letherman
Mrs Michelle Lettall
Miss Anne Lettice
Mr Paul Leverton
Mr Edgar Levy
Mrs Gayle Levy
Mr Jason Levy
Mr Glyn Lewis
Mrs Helen Lewis
Miss Maria Lewis
Mr Noel Lewis
Miss Rhiannon Lewis
Mrs Sandy Lewis
Mr Tom Lewis
Miss Wendy Lewis

Mr Craig Lewis-Bowker
Mr Richard Leworthy
Mr Tony Lewty
Mrs Valerie Leyland
Miss Jiannan Li
Mrs Kathryn Lichtensteiger Keeble
Mr Harry Liddell
Mr Thomas Liedermann
Miss Heather Lightbody
Miss Roxanne Liley
Mrs Denise Limbrick
Miss Ema Linaker
Mrs Ann Lincoln
Mrs Carole Lindey
Mrs Ann Lindsay
Mr Stephen Lindsay
Mr Kim Lingjaerde
Mr David Linnell
Mr Ben Linton
Mr Ian Lipton
Mr Paul Lister
Mr James Littlejohn
Mr Richard Littlejohns
Mrs Vivienne Littley
Ms Marina Livingstone
Mr Alastair Lloyd
Mr Allan Lloyd
Mr Clive Lloyd
Mr David Lloyd
Ms Frances Lloyd
Mr Greg Lloyd
Mr Michael Lloyd
Mrs Pat Lloyd
Miss Sally Lloyd
Mrs Andrea Loasby
Mr Richard Loasby
Mrs Shirley Lobb
Mr Sue Lock
Mr Michael Locke
Mrs Sarah Locke
Miss Amy Lockwood
Mr Adrian Lockyer
Mrs Janet Lomas
Mr David London
Mr Barry Long
Mr Christopher Long
Mrs Linda Long
Miss Nicola Long
Mrs Sally Long
Mr Sue Longfield
Mrs Jackie Longley
Mr Joe Longmuir
Mrs Kate Lopez MBE
Mr Stephen Lorch
Mr Peter Lord
Mr Hubert Losguardi
Miss Mariah Louca
Mr Phil Louch
Mr David Loudoun
Mr Michael Loveday
Mr Richard Lovegrove
Mr Terry Loveless
Mr Keith Lowe
Mr Martin Lowe
Mr Stephen Lowit
Mr Mike Lowndes
Mr Peter Lowry
Mr Adrian Lucas
Miss Louise Lucas
Miss Bettina Lugge
Mr John Luke
Mr Alan Lunn
Mrs Jennifer Lusby
Mr Chris Lutrario
Mrs Sandra Lymburn
Mrs Connie Lynn
Mr James Lynn
Miss Lizzie Mabott
Ms Claire MacArthur
Mr Peter Macaulay
Ms Cathy MacBride
Mrs Anneli MacDonald
Mrs Hilary Macdonald
Mrs Jennifer Macdonald
Ms Liz Macdonald
Mr Michael MacDonald
Mrs Shelley MacDonald
Mr Hugh MacDonald OBE
Mr Fred Macey
Mrs Samantha MacGowan
Miss Katriona MacGregor
Mrs Lesley Maciver

Mr Ian W Mackay
Ms Lisa Mackenzie
Ms Ruth MacKenzie
Mr George MacKerron
Mr Alasdair Mackie
Mr John Mackie
Mr Hugh Mackintosh CBE
Mr Archie Maclean
Mrs Ada MacLeod
Mrs Cathy MacLeod
Mr Robert MacLeod
Mrs Valerie Macniven
Miss Abigail Macolm
Mr Chris Macvie
Mr Christopher Madden
Mr George Madden
Miss Mercedes Maeckelberghe
Ms Nico Maeckelberghe
Miss Vashti Maeckelberghe
Mr Pietro Magliola
Mr James Maguire
Mrs Janet Maguire
Mr Daniel Mahony
Mrs Shelley Mahony
Ms Eleanor Maidment
Miss Marion Main
Mr John Malley
Mr Ian Malone
Mr Matthew Maloney
Ms Donna Manfre
Mrs Maggie Mann
Mr John Manning
Mr Julian Manning
Mrs Linda Manning
Mrs Janet Mansfield
Mrs Susan Mansfield
Mr Michael Mansfield QC
Mrs Joan Manzer
Mr Nick Manzi
Sir Gordon Manzie
Mr Jacques Marchal
Mr Andrew Marcs
Mr Julian Marcus
Miss Chauveu Marion
Mr Raymond Marks
Mr Charles Markus
Mrs Louise Markus
Mr Gavin Markwick
Mr Dennis Marler
Miss Oki Marley
Mrs Anne-Marie Marlow
Miss Vanessa Marriott
Mrs Jill Marsden
Miss Laura Marsden
Miss Kate Marsh
Mr Mike Marsh
Mr Aaron Marshall
Mr Anthony Marshall
Mr John Marshall
Miss Kylie Marshall
Mr Paul Marshall
Miss Philippa Marshall
Mr Sam Marshall
Mr Tim Marshall
Mr Alan Marston
Mr Andrew Martin
Mr David Martin
Mr Graham Martin
Mrs Joan Martin
Mr John Martin
Mr Roger Martin
Mr Stephen Martin
Ms Anne Martinez
Miss Karen Marvin
Mr Roger Marvin
Miss Sarah Mary
Mr David Maslin
Mr David Mason
Mr Edward Mason
Mr Jake Mason
Mr Jon Mason
Mr Robert Mason
Mr Christopher Mason-Watts
Mrs Prue Matchwick
Mrs Colette Mather
Mrs Vicky Mathers
Mrs Sally Matson
Miss Caron Matthews
Mr John Matthews

Miss Susan Matthews
Mr Philip Maude
Mr Jack Maunders
Mr Kevin Maw
Mrs Elaine Maxwell
Mr J D Maxwell
Mr David May
Mrs Hannah May
Mr Ian May
Mr Richard May
Mr Adrian Mays
Miss Bronwyn McAlister
Mr Peter McAllister
Mr Andrew McAlpine
Mr Robert McArdle
Mrs Adeline McBurney
Mrs Lyn McCambley
Mr Mark McCann
Mr Kian McCarthy
Mr Patrick McCarthy
Mrs P V McClen
Miss Victoria McClen
Mrs Elaine McClure
Mr Andrew McDonald
Mr Bruce McDonald
Mrs Elizabeth McDonald
Mr Graeme McDonald
Mr Paul McDonald
Mrs Irene McDougal
Mr David McFadzean
Mr Robert McFadzean
Mrs Penny McGarr
Mr Duncan McGibbon
Mrs Annabel McGinley
Ms Karen McGovern
Mrs Margaret McGuire
Mr Callum McHugh
Mr John R McHugh
Mr Leonie McIntosh
Mr S McIntyre
Mr Sean Mcintyre
Miss Tana McIntyre
Mrs Jackie McKenna
Miss Keira McKenna
Miss Siobhan McKenna
Miss Hayley McKenzie
Miss Simone McKenzie
Mr Robin McKie
Mr Andrew McKnight
Miss Fiona McKnight
Mr Frank McKnight
Mrs Anne McLeean
Mr Peter McMahon
Mrs Angela McManus
Mr Colin McManus
Mr Nicholas McNally
Mrs Pam McNee
Mr Rupert McNeile
Mr Ian McNicoll
Mr Ian McPherson
Mrs Margot McPherson
Miss Liza McQuaid
Mrs Elizabeth McWilliam
Mr Gordon McWilliam
Mr Roger Meacham
Mrs Annie Meager
Mrs Lucille Meah
Mrs Vicki Measom
Miss Chahira Medhkour
Mr John Medlicott
Mr Stephen Medlock
Miss Rita Mehta
Mr Trevor Mehtar
Mr Jonathan Meier
Mr Barry Mellett
Mrs Sian Melvin
Mr David Melzack
Ms Katherine Mendelsohn
Mr Roy Merrell
Mr Andrew Merrett
Mr Craig Merrick
Mr Andrew Merrifield
Mrs Rebecca Messina
Mrs Kay Metcalf
Mrs Helen Metcalfe
Mrs Jenny Metcalfe
Mr Anthony Mew
Mr Jay Miah
Mr Josh Michaels
Mr Andy Middleton
Mrs Anne Middleton
Ms Jane Middleton
Ms Sandie Middleton

Mrs Sara Middleton
Miss Sharon Middleton
Mr Jaz Milano
Miss Jennifer Milbourne
Mrs Lyndsey Millar
Mrs Jo Millard
Mrs Margaret Millbourn
Mrs Sara Millburn
Mrs Barbara Miller
Mrs Carol Miller
Mrs Debbie Miller
Mr John Miller
Mr T A Miller
Mr Ian Millington
Mr Clive Mills
Mr Shaun Mills
Mr Steve Mills
Mrs Eve Milner
Mr Marcus Milton
Mr Alistair Milward
Miss Kate Minshall
Mrs Janice Minton
Mrs Amanda Miscampbell
Mr Jol Miskin
Mr Andrew Mitchell
Miss Louise Mitchell
Miss Rebecca Mitchell
Ms Susanne Mithoefer
Mrs Grace Mizen
Mr Simon Mogg
Mr Rhys Monahan
Mr Alan Montgomery
Mr Stephen Montgomery
Mr David Moor
Mr Alan Moore
Mrs Alison Moore
Ms Caroline Moore
Mr Gerard Moore
Mr Peter Moore
Mrs Susan Moore
Mrs Christelle Moorhouse
Mrs Katherine Moorhouse
Mr Patrick Moorin
Miss Wendy Moran
Mr Anthony Morel
Mrs Claire Morel
Mr David Morgan
Mrs Kate Morgan
Mrs Katie Morgan
Mrs Lindsey Morgan
Mrs Mavis Morgan
Mrs Patricia Morgan
Mr Paul Morgan
Mr R C Morgan
Mr John Moriarty
Mrs Patricia Morley
Mrs Victoria Morley
Mr Fergus Moroney
Ms Christine Morris
Mr David Morris
Mrs Helen Morris
Mrs Kathy Morris
Ms Michelle Morris
Mr Nick Morris
Mr Roderick Morris
Mr Stephen Morris
Mrs Anne Morrison
Ms Katie Morrison
Mr Robert Mortimer
Mr Graham Morton
Mrs Danielle Moss
Mr Gerry Moss
Ms Sandrea Mosses
Mr Marc Mosthav
Mrs Victoria Motlry
Mr Benjamin Mott
Mr Michael Moult
Mr Rodney Mowe
Mrs Lydia Mowll
Mr Martyn Moxley
Mr Terence Muckian
Mrs Kate Mucklow
Ms Vicky Mudford
Mrs Anne Muers
Mr Martin Muers
Mr Kevin Muggleton
Mr Sian Muggridge
Mrs Pamela Muirhead
Miss Vivien Muller
Mr David Mullett
Mrs Julie Munday
Miss Natalie Mundy

Miss Carey Munn
Mr Peter Munro
Mrs Christine Murphy
Ms Gillian Murphy
Miss Kathryn Murphy
Mr David Murray
Mrs Debbie Murray
Mr Gordon Murray
Mr Scott Murray
Miss Samantha Murray-Hinde
Mr Stephen Muse
Mrs Francine Mussell
Mr Aqil Mustafa
Mrs Fiona Myers
Mr Norris Myers
Mrs Patricia Myers
Mr Tim Myers
Miss Melanie Myhill
Ms Natasha Myles
Mr Lukasz Myszkowski
Mr Gary Nathan
Mr Barry Natton
Mrs Caroline Naudi
Mrs Anna Nayler
Mrs Jill Naylor
Miss Lucy Neal
Mr Nathan Neal
Miss Kulsoma Nehar
Mrs Kaye Neill
Mrs Jennifer Nelmes
Mrs Denise Nelson
Miss Helen Nelson
Mr Leigh Nelson
Mr Iain Nesbitt
Mrs Caro Ness
Mrs Kathy Nettleship
Miss Anna Nevill
Mr Jerry Neville
Miss Louise Neville
Mr Michael Newberry
Miss Kirsty Newland
Mr David Newman
Mr Paul Newman
Mr Dave Newth
Mr Keith Newton
Mrs Susan Newton
Miss Catherine Nice
Mr David Nicholas
Mr G C Nicholas
Mr David Nichols
Mr Matthew Nichols
Mr Chnristopher Nicholson
Ms Jennifer Nicholson
Mrs Lucy Nicholson
Mr Andrew Nicklin
Mr Cam Nicolle
Mr Philip Niesluchowski
Miss Tiffany Nieuwland
Mr Mike Nikolaou
Ms Luba Nikulina
Mrs Fiona Nixon
Mrs Pauline Noble MBE
Mr Denis Norgan
Mr Nathaniel Norgren
Mr Hugh Norman
Mrs Michele Norrie
Mr Peter Norrie
Mr Geraint Norris
Ms Janice Norris
Mrs Joan Norris
Mrs Teresa Norsworthy
Mrs Emma North
Mrs Carolyn Northover
Mr Steve Norton
Mr David Nunn
Mrs Marian Nuttall
Mr Eric Nutter
Mrs Joan O'Connor
Mr Anthony Oade
Miss Karen Oake
Miss Jenny Obrien
Mr Luke O'Brien
Mr Thomas O'Brien
Mrs Tineke O'Brien
Mr David Octagon
Ms Aoife O'Donoghue
Mr James Offen
Miss Melissa Offer
Mrs Nicole O'Flaherty
Ms Caroline Ogden
Ms Catherine Ogden
Mr Matt Ogden

Mr Robert Ogles
Mr Bill Oldfield
Mrs Eugenie Olding
Mr Jim O'Leary
Mr Jason Olive
Miss Anne Oliver
Mr Michael. R. Oliver
Mr Peter Oliver
Mrs Sarah Olney
Mr Dirk Michael Olsen
Mrs Lucy O'Neill
Mrs Sarah O'Neill
Mr W B O'Neill MBE
Mr Matthew Oodles
Ms Kath Oram
Mr Gary Orchard
Mr Darren Orian
Mrs Karen O'Riley
Mr Carlos Orzabal
Miss Julie Osborne
Mrs Megan Osborne
Mr Richard Osborne
Mr Columb O'Shea
Ms Blanaid O'Sullivan
Mr Michael O'Sullivan
Mr Alan Owen
Mr Conrad Owen
Miss Jo Owen
Miss Sioned Mai Owen
Mrs Fiona Owen-Jones
Mrs Charlotte Owens
Mr Henry Oxtoby
Mr William Pack
Mr Steve Packer
Mrs Meriel Packman
Mr Stephen Packter
Mrs Yvonne Paddy
Mr Thomas Padfield
Ms Ann Page
Mr Russell Page
Mr Geoff Painting
Mr Desmond Palmer
Mrs Jeannie Palmer
Mrs Nicola Palmer
Mrs Olwen Palmer
Mr Dinesh Panch
Miss Bina Pandit
Mr David pannel
Miss Sharon Papirnyk
Mr Nick Parish
Mrs Christine Parker
Mrs Gayle Parker
Ms Helen Parker
Mr James Parker
Ms Janette Parker
Mr Martin Parker
Mr Nick Parkhouse
Miss Eve Parkin
Miss Rachel Parnham
Mr Neil Parr
Mr Phillip Parr
Mr Derek Parry
Mr Finlay Parry
Miss Rebekah Parry
Mrs Carol Parsons
Mr Steven Parsons
Mr Chris Parton
Mr Henry Partridge
Miss Rebecca Pashley
Mr Mark Passfield
Miss Jessie Passmore
Mr Neal Patell
Mr Shahpur Patell
Mr Pater Pater
Mr Penelope Patrick
Mr Michael Pattison
Mr Reginald Pauffley
Mr Chris Pawlowski
Mr John Pawsey
Mrs Angie Payne
Mrs Christine Payne
Mrs Janet Payne
Mr P Payne
Mrs Tracy Payne
Mr Nigel Peacock
Mr Simon Peacock
Mrs Valerie Peacock
Mrs Tonia Pearce
Mr Andrew Pearson
Mr Joseph Pearson
Mr Mark Pearson
Mr Kenny Peck

Mr Ken Peek
Mrs Patience Pefferberg
Mr John Pelling
Ms Gail Pemberton
Mr John Pembridge
Miss Kristi Penney
Mr Benjamin Penny
Ms Christine Penny
Ms Judith Penny
Mr Thomas Peplinski
Mr Matthew Pepper
Mrs Maureen Percival
Mrs Nicky Percival
Mr Charles Perkins
Miss Margisel Peroza
Mrs Zoe Perrior
Mr Clarke Perry
Mr Brian Perryman
Mr Jeyamurugan Perumal Sengottuvel
Mr Ernesto Pescini
Mr Andrew Peters
Ms Sue Peters
Mr Peter Pett
Mr David Petter
Ms Leishia Pettigrew
Mr Charlie Pettis
Mrs Paula Phelps
Miss Vivienne Pheysey
Mr David Phillips
Ms Eleanor Phillips
Mrs Gillian Phillips
Mr Howard Phillips
Mr Ian Phillips
Ms Kelle Phillips
Ms Liz Phillips
Mr Peter Phillips
Mr Thomas Phillips
Mr Thomas Phillips
Mr John Pickering
Mrs Mary Elizabeth Picot-Guacraud
Mr Wyndham Pidgeon
Mr Willem Pietersen
Mr Christopher Pike
Mr Andy Pilcher
Mrs Shirley Pink
Mrs Julie Piper
Mr Richard Pitts
Mr Gordon Plahn
Mr Graham Plant
Mr Roger Plastow
Mrs Alex Platt
Mrs Ann Platt
Mr Roger Plowden
Mrs Liz Plummer
Ms Victoria Pod
Mr Frederic Poirier
Mr Benjamin Pollard
Mr Brian Pollard
Mr Garth Pollard
Mr Robert Pollock
Mrs Barbara Pond
Mr Alan Ponter
Mrs Kirsty Pook
Mr Robert Poole
Mr Adam Pope
Mrs S Popple
Ms Caroline Portch
Miss Jenny Portch
Mr James Porteous
Mrs Judith Porter
Mr Phillip Porter
Mrs Sarah Porter
Mr Mark Potter
Mr Roy Potter
Mr Andrew Powell
Ms Jackie Powell
Ms Jean Powell
Mrs Rachel Powell
Mr Paul Powell-Jackson
Mr Phillip Power
Mr Simon Powis
Mr Rohit Pratap
Mrs Lynda Preece
Mrs Marie-Louise Preen
Mr William Prentice
Mr Tony Prescott
Mr Robert Prestige
Mr Mike Prew
Miss Gillian Price
Mr Jeremy Price
Mrs Ruth Price

Ms Samantha Price
Mrs Sarah Prideaux
Mrs Karen Priestman
Mr John Prince
Miss Samantha Prince
Mrs Frances Pritchard
Mr Graham Pritchard
Mr Steve Pritchard
Mr Norman Pritchard-Woollett
Mr Simon Prodger
Mrs Mandy Pryke
Mr David Vincent Pullen
Miss Grace Pullen
Mr Mark Pullen
Mr Angi Pyart
Mr Stuart Pybus
Mrs Barbara Pycraft
Mr Charles Pycraft
Mr Jeffrey Pym
Mr Mark Pym
Mrs Jackie Pyrah
Mrs Lisa Quayle
Mr Jeanne Quigley
Mrs Penny Quigley
Mr John Quinn
Miss Sinead Quirke
Mr Mark Quirolo
Mr Jonathan Raby
Mrs Fiona Rackham
Mr Alan Radcliffe
Mr Jak Radice
Mr Serban Radu Florian
Mr Arek Radziszewski
Miss Daisy Rae
Mr Christopher Raeburn
Mr Julia Ragouzeos
Mr Matt Raines
Mrs Isobel Rainey
Mrs Julie Ralph
Mrs Sandra Ramsay
Dr A M Rankin
Mr Thomas Rankin
Mrs Patricia Ranson
Mrs Jane Ranzetta
Mr Stephen Rashid
Mrs Katie Rasmussen
Mr Bernard Ratigan
Mrs Ellen Rau
Ms Avril Raven
Mr Peter Ray
Mr Paul Reach
Miss Jane Read
Mrs Jennie Read
Miss Faye Reade
Mr Arthur Reader
Mr Jackie Reader
Mr Paul Reavley
Mrs Janet Redfern
Mr Jacopo Redi
Mrs Christine Redmayne
Mr Bryan Reed
Mrs Lesley Reed
Mr Lyn Rees
Mrs Angela Reeves
Mrs Gill Reeves
Mr James Reeves
Mr George Reid
Mr Ian Reid
Mr Ken Reid
Mr Mike Reid
Miss Seonaid Reid
Mr Tom Reid
Mr Eugene Reilly
Mr Michael Reilly
Mrs Marika Reinholds
Miss Paola Reita
Mr Jon Rennie
Mr Martin Renshaw
Mr Bunny Retard
Mr Dennis Reygate
Mr Colin Reynolds
Mrs Jane Reynolds
Mrs Jacquelaine Rice
Mr Alex Richadson
Ms Annette Richards
Miss Celine Richards
Mrs Georgia Richards
Mrs Geraldine Richards
Mr Guy Richards
Miss Joanna Richards
Mrs Julie Richards
Mr Kenneth Richards

Mr Ron Richards
Miss Debbie Richards
Mrs Anne Richardson
Mr C John Richardson
Mrs Caroline Richardson
Mr Greg Richardson
Mr Ken Richardson
Mr Alan Richell
Mrs Gail Richmond
Mr Tony Rickaby
Mr J D Rickard
Mrs Joyce Ricketts
Mrs Cathy Riddington
Mr Malcolm Ridge
Mrs Ruth Ridge
Mrs Julie Ridgway
Mr L C Ridgwell
Mr Lloyd Ridgwell
Mr Philip Rigby
Ms Jessica Riggles
Mr Dan Riley
Ms Marie Riley
Mrs Patricia Riley
Mrs Becky Rimmer
Mr Stuart Ritchie
Mrs Cindy Ritson
Mrs Sue Rixon
Mrs Rubia Rizwan
Mr Paul Roach
Mr Ian Robb
Mr Christopher Roberts
Mr Colin Roberts
Mr David Roberts
Mr Geraint Roberts
Miss Heather Roberts
Mr James Trevor Roberts
Mr Jim Roberts
Miss Kirsty Roberts
Mrs Lee Roberts
Mr M Roberts
Mr Martyn Roberts
Mrs Sarah Roberts
Mr Tim Roberts
Mrs Veronica Roberts
Mr David Robertson
Mr Matthew Robertson
Mrs Rebecca Robins
Miss Samantha Robinson
Mrs A Robinson
Mr David Robinson
Miss Heidi Robinson
Mr Michael Robinson
Miss Nicola Robinson
Mr Peter Robinson
Mrs Polly Robinson
Mrs Sue Robinson
Ms Toeni Robinson
Mrs Tracy Robinson
Mrs Louise Robling
Mr Colin Rockall
Mr Rob Rockell
Miss Kat Rodd
Mr Colin Roden
Mr Keith Rodgerson
Mr Chris Roe
Miss Lucy Rogan
Mr Bill Rogers
Mr Colin Rogers
Miss Lindsey Rogers
Ms Lorraine Rogers
Mrs Rachel Rogers
Miss Angela Rolle
Mrs Christine Rollin
Miss Laura Roloson
Miss Birgitta Ronn
Mr Laurence Rooke
Mrs Shirley Rookyard
Mr Jim Rooney
Miss Amanda Rose
Mrs Diana Rose
Mr Ian Rose
Mrs Helen Roskott
Mr Saladin Rospigliosi
Mrs Adrienne Ross
Mr Colin Ross
Miss Kelly Ross
Mrs Lindsay Ross
Miss Sarah Ross
Mr Stephen Ross
Mr Thomas Ross
Mr Christopher Rothery
Mrs Ananda Rousseau
Mr Stefan Rousseau

Mr Andy Rowden
Mrs Mia Rowe
Mr Roger Rowe
Ms Sandra Rowe
Mr Martin Rowland
Ms Vicky Rowland
Mr and Mrs Rowley
Mr David Rowley
Ms Gemma Rowley
Mrs Rachel Rowley
Mr Stephen Rowley
Ms Angela Royle
Miss Vanessa Royle
Ms Krysia Rozanska
Ms Hilary Rubinstein
Mr Grahame Ruddock
Mrs Lynne Ruddock
Ms Sonja Ruehl
Mrs Lizzy Ruffles
Mrs Gabi Rumble
Mr Keith Rusby
Mrs Linda Rush
Mrs Celia Rushforth
Mr Bob Ruskin
Mr Simon Russell
Mrs Alison Rust
Mr Peter Rust
Miss Patricia Rutten
Mrs Ally Ruwell
Ms Anka Ryall
Mr Luke Ryan
Mr Andrew Ryde
Mrs Tracy Ryden
Mrs Amanda Ryder
Mrs Joanne Ryle
Mr Ben Rymer
Mr Graham Sadd
Mrs Sue Sadler
Mrs Nawal Sahouli
Mrs Lyn Sales
Mr Frank Salisbury
Mr Kai Salomaa
Mr Sebino Salvati
Mr Keith Salway
Mr Paul Sampson
Mr Oliver Samuel
Mrs Vivienne Sanders
Miss Kirsty Sanderson
Miss Laura Sanderson
Mr Keith Sandys
Miss Kavita Sangha
Mr Ash Sansom
Mr Alan Sargeant
Mr Ed Sargent
Mrs J Sargent
Mr Trevor Saunders
Mr Vince Saury
Mrs Tessa Sauven
Mr Robert Savage-Hanford
Miss Helen Saville
Mr Martin Saville
Mrs Christine Saxon
Mr Jon Sayers
Mr Michael David Scales
Mrs Ruth Scarr
Mrs Catherine Schade
Miss Tricia Schillaci
Mrs Valerie Schofield
Mr Malcolm Schooling
Mr Wayne Schroeder
Mr Ronald Schwarz
Mr Peter Schwier
Mr Matthew Scobey
Miss Alessandra Scoleri
Mr Ian Scott
Mr John Scott
Mrs Mary Scott
Mr Nigel Scott
Mr R Scott
Mrs Sheila Scott
Mr Stuart Scott
Mrs Thalia Scott
Miss Victoria Scott
Mr David Scrivens
Mr Gordon Scrogg
Mrs Barbara Sculthorpe
Mr Rob Seager
Mr Peter Seagroatt
Mr Steven Searle
Mr Carl Seddon
Mrs Joan Seddon
Mr David Sefton
Mr Barry Selby

Mrs Carol Selby
Mrs Elizabeth Sellers
Mr John Sellwood
Mr Angus Selstrom
Mr Tim Sempers
Mrs Di Semple
Mr Nitesh Senapati
Miss Gillian Seville
Mrs Elaine Sexton
Miss Sherin Shaker
Mrs Nikki Shakespeare
Mr Robert Shannon
Mr Patrick Sharman
Mr Cliff Sharp
Miss Kelly Sharp
Mr Richard Sharp
Mr Robin Sharp
Mr Chris Sharpin
Mr Carl Shavitz
Miss Becky Shaw
Mr Bertram Shaw
Mrs Elaine Shaw
Mr John Shaw
Mrs Kathryn Shaw
Mr Peter Shaw
Mrs Sheilagh Shaw
Mrs Sue Shaw
Mrs Jayne Shawcross
Mr Philip Shawcross
Mr David Shearer
Mr Rory Sheehan
Mrs Jo Sheerin
Mr Peter Sheldrick
Mr Derek Shepherd
Mr Richard Shepherd
Ms Chloe Sheppard
Mrs Lisa Sherwin
Mrs Marcia Sherwin
Mrs Stepanie Sherwood
Mr Anthony Shields
Mrs Sarah Shiers
Miss Joanna Shipley
Mrs Sarah Shipp
Ms Zoe Shipton
Mr Peter Shirtliff
Mrs Manjit Shoker
Mr Michael Shone
Mr Stephen Shore
Mrs Jackie Shorrocks
Mr Gilbert Short
Mrs Victoria Short
Mrs Helen Shorthouse
Mr Robert Shuler
Mr John Sibly
Ms Mandie Sidlin
Ms Theresa Siesun
Ms Carolyn Silberfeld
Miss Tara Silvester
Mr Manfredo Simeoni
Mrs Emma Simes
Mr Peter Simmonds
Mr Richard Simmonds
Mr David Simmons
Mr Jeremy Simms
Mr Kay Simon
Mr Hugh Simons
Mr Steven Simpkins
Mr Brian Simpson
Miss Erica Simpson
Mrs Jackie Simpson
Mr Stephen Simpson
Mr Will Simpson
Mr Drew Sims
Mr Ian M Sinclair
Mrs Joana Sinclair
Mr John Sinclair
Mrs Sue Sinclair
Mr Navtej Sing
Mr M Singh
Ms Emma Sirius
Mr William Sithers
Mr Robert Skeen
Mr Nick Skew
Mrs Carole Skidmore
Ms Wendy Skilton
Miss Kerrie Slater
Mrs Louise Slater
Mr Steve Slater
Mrs Amanda Sleight
Mr David Sleight
Mr Tim Slesinger
Mrs Anita Sloan
Mr Barney Sloane

Mrs Julie Small
Mr Sam Smalley
Ms Judith Smallwood
Mr Ben Smee
Mr Adrian Smith
Mrs Andrea Smith
Mr Andrew Smith
Mrs Anne Smith
Mrs Barbara Smith
Mr Charles Smith
Mr Christopher Smith
Mr D Smith
Mr David Smith
Mr Eliz Smith
Ms Elta Smith
Miss Emily Smith
Mr Fraser Smith
Mrs Gaynor Smith
Mr George Smith
Mr Graeme Smith
Miss H Smith
Mr James Smith
Miss Janet Smith
Mr Jim Smith
Mrs Kay Smith
Miss Louise Smith
Mr Michael Smith
Mrs Michelle Smith
Mr Oliver Smith
Mrs Pamela Smith
Mrs Paula Smith
Mr Peter Smith
Mr Philip Smith
Mr Richard Smith
Mr Ron Smith
Mr Ronald Smith
Mrs Rosalynn Smith
Mr Stephen Smith
Mr Sue Smith
Ms Theresa Smith
Mr Tim Smith
Miss Victoria Smith
Mrs Yvonne Smith
Mr Jamie Smith
Mr Jason Smithers
Mrs Christina Smyth
Ms Michelle Smyth
Mr Ken Smythe
Miss Linda Sneddon
Mr Gordon Snell
Miss Rebecca Snow
Mr Abdul Sobur
Mr Nick Solomides
Ms Eppie Somers
Mr Miguel Somoza
Mr Lester Sonden
Mr Abi Sonkour-Bohey
Miss Elaine Sosna
Miss Nawal Souli
Miss Georgina Southern
Mrs Helen Southgate
Mr Sam Southwick
Mr Jamie Southworth
Mr Ann Sowerby
Ms Leanne Spackman
Mrs Eileen Spalding
Miss Karen Speight
Mrs Angela Spence
Mrs Linda Spencer
Mrs Meryl Spencer
Miss Kate Spicer
Mrs Helen Spiers
Mr Nick Spoliar
Mr Paul Springer
Mr David Spurling
Mr Steve Squibb
Mr Robin St Clair Jones
Mr Ray St John
Mr Guy Stainton
Mrs Valerie Stamp
Mr Anthony Stanbridge
Mr Anthony Stanbury
Ms Pam Stanier
Mr Michael Stanley
Mr Paul Stanley
Mrs Valerie Stanley
Mrs Jenny Staples
Mrs Nancy Stark
Mr Sarah Starkey
Miss Kelly Starrs
Miss Aferdita Statovic
Mr Kirk Steel
Miss Bronwen Steele

Mr Lawson Steele
Mrs Kim Steenson
Mr Daniel Steer
Mrs Dawn Steer
Ms Venetia Stent
Mr John Stephany
Mrs Billie Stephens
Mrs Elizabeth Stephenson
Mrs Judith Stephenson
Mr Michael Stephenson
Mr Christopher Stevens
Miss Fi Stevens
Miss Gemma Stevens
Ms Helen Stevens
Mr Richard Stevens
Mr Roy Stevens
Mrs Jane Stevensen
Mr Andrew Stevenson
Mr John Stevenson
Mrs Mary Stevenson
Mr Robin Stevenson
Miss Lauren Steventon
Mrs Rosemary Stewart
Ms Samantha Stewart
Mr Clive Stickells
Mr Allen Stidwill
Mrs Fiona Stillington
Mrs Donella Stirling
Mr Iain Stirling
Miss Marianne Stirrat
Mr Peter Stoakley
Mr Douglas Stoddart
Mr John Stoker
Mr Martin Stoker
Mr Alex Stone
Mrs Caroline Stone
Mr Trevor Stone
Mrs Salakchome Stones
Mrs Sheilagh Stones
Miss Ella Stonley
Mrs Rachael Storey
Mr Micheal Stott
Miss Nicola Stott
Mrs Debbie Strachan
Mrs Linda Strachan
Mr Richard Stradling
Mr Nick Stranks
Mrs Sheila Stranks
Mrs Jane Straw
Mr Ben Street
Mr Charles Stride
Mrs Elizabeth Strilkowski
Mr Robert Stroud
Mr Charles Struthers
Mr David Stuart
Mrs Sally Stuart
Mrs Eileen Stuart-Clarke
Mrs Helen Sturdy
Mrs Helen Style
Miss Sarah Styles
Mr Bernard Sulzmann
Ms Judy Summers
Mr Rob Summers
Mrs Maria Summerscales
Mrs Catriona Sutherland-Hawes
Mrs Jean Sutton
Mr Richard Swainson
Mr Wayne Swiffin
Mrs June Swindell
Mr Gavin Swonnell
Mr Christopher Syer
Mrs Sabrina Sykes
Mrs Lorraine Syme
Mr Carl Symonds
Ms J Syne
Mr Adam Szafranek
Miss Tehmzin Taha
Mr Sarthak Takalkar
Mrs P Talati
Mr Gavin Talbot-Smith
Mr Douglas Talintyre
Mrs Jacqueline Tame
Miss Geraldine Tan
Mr Kelvin Tan
Mrs Karen Tanner
Mr Geoff Tapper
Mr Mike Tarbard
Mrs Olwynne Tarlow
Mrs Amanda Tate
Mr Anne Tate
Mr Denis W Tate
Mr John Taverner

THANK YOUS

Mrs Judy Tayler-Smith
Mrs Angela Taylor
Mr Bill Taylor
Mrs Catherine Taylor
Mr Howard Taylor
Mr Jake Taylor
Mrs Jean Taylor
Ms Julie Taylor
Miss Lucy Taylor
Mrs Lynn Taylor
Mrs Maureen Taylor
Mrs Nimi Taylor
Mrs Shiralee Taylor
Mr Simon Taylor
Mrs Sue Taylor
Mr Tim Taylor
Mr Tom Taylor
Mr George Tee
Ms Flora Teh-Morris
Mr Bryan Telfer
Mr Alan Templeton
Ms Patricia Terry
Ms Alison Terry-Evans
Mrs Mathilde Texier
Ms Anne Thirlwelll
Mrs Angela Thomas
Mr Hefin Thomas
Miss Hilary Thomas
Mr Ieuan Thomas
Mr Joy Thomas
Ms Judith Thomas
Mrs June Thomas
Mr Michael Thomas
Mr Neville Thomas
Mr Paul Thomas
Miss Sarah Thomas
Mrs Tracy Thomas
Ms Viv Thomas
Ms Wendy Thomas
Mrs Carole Thompson
Mrs Diane Thompson
Mr Dickon Thompson
Mr James Thompson
Mrs Judi Thompson
Mrs Judy Thompson
Mr Paul Thompson
Mr Roger Thompson
Mrs Tina Thompson
Miss Heather Thomson
Mrs Marlyn Thomson
Mr Robert Thomson
Mr John Thornburn
Miss Samantha Thorndike
Mr Christopher
    Thorneycroft-Smith
Mrs Marcelline
    Thorneycroft-Smith
Mr Phil Thornley
Mr Rich Thornton
Mr Graham Thorpe
Mr Gwion Thorpe
Miss Hannah Thorpe
Miss Alexandra Thrower
Mr Bob Thurlow
Mrs Linda Thurlow
Mr Andy Ticer
Miss Louise Tillett
Miss Kathleen Timbs
Mrs Gail Timewell
Mrs Sarah Titcomb
Mr Philip Titheridge
Mrs Roongtip To
Miss Jenna Todd Jones
Ms Helena Tolkien
Mrs Barbara Tolley
Mr Barry Tomkins
Mr Peter Tomkins
Mr Mark Tomkinson
Mr Martin Tomlinson
Mr Michael Tomlinson
Mr Stephen Tomlinson
Mr David Tonge
Miss Janet Tonge
Mr Paul Toomer
Miss Lorna Torrance
Mr Nevill Towler
Mr Peter Townend
Mrs Joanna Townson
Miss Anne Tozer
Mrs Verity Travers
Mr Paul Treby
Ms Kate Trelawny
Mrs Linda Trenouth

Mrs Sarah Tricks
Mr Phil Tristram
Mrs Susan Tristram
Mr Charles Trotereau
Mr Allan Trotter
Mr Christopher Trotter
Mr Chris Trow
Mr Michael Trudgill
Mrs Selina Truman
Mr Andrew Trythall
Mrs Julie Tuck
Mr Robert Tuck
Mr Jonathan Tudor
Mr Robert Tunnard
Mrs Deborah Tunnicliffe
Mr David Turgoose
Mr Geoff Turner
Mr Gordon Turner
Mr John Turner
Mr John G Turner
Mrs June M Turner
Mr K Turner
Miss Kirsty Turner
Mrs Moira Turner
Mr Roger Turner
Mr Shaun Turner
Ms Jill Turton
Mrs Helen Tweedy
Mr Brian Tye
Miss Gemma Tyler
Ms Mary Tyler
Ms Jenny Tyndall
Mrs Lesley Tyre
Mrs Elizabeth Tyrrell
Mr Moin Uddin
Mr Martin Underdown
Mr Peter Underdown
Mr Brian Underwood
Mr Victor Underwood
Mrs Philippa Unwin
Ms Lorraine Ure
Mr Peter Urquhart
Mr David Uwins
Mr Mark Uytenhaak
Mr Nick Vadis
Mrs Cristina Valenzuela
    Luna
Mr Michel Van Damme
Mr Mark van Gelderen
Mr Bob van Gulik
Mr Dick Vardy
Ms Wendy Varley
Miss Yana Vatska
Mrs Deborah Vaudin
Mr John Vaughan
Mr Mark Vaughan
Mr Robert Vaughan
Mrs Alison Vella
Mrs Claire Venables
Mr Graham Venables
Mrs Dee Venner
Mr Paul Venner
Dr G I Verney
Mr D F Verney
Mrs Rosalind Vernon
Ms Barbara Vesey
Mr Andrew Vick
Miss Dace Viesture
Mr John Vinall
Mr Julian Vince
Mr Mark Vincent
Mrs Alyson Viner
Mrs Maureen Vizer
Miss Jessica Vogelsberg
Mr Ludwig Von Sembach
Mr Deepak Vyas
Mrs Anne Wade
Mrs Jennifer Wade
Mrs Ruth Wadley
Mrs Suzanne Waggett
Mr Tom Waldron-Lynch
Mrs Susie Wales
Mrs Alison Walker
Mr Anthony Walker
Mrs Christine Walker
Ms Christine Walker
Mr David Walker
Mrs Diane Walker
Mrs Karen Walker
Mr Peter Walker
Mr Ray Walker
Mr Samuel Walker
Mr Simon Walker

Miss Susie Walker
Mr Richard Wall
Mr Frank Wallace
Mrs Joanne Wallace
Mr Russell Wallace
Mr Nigel Wallace-Mason
Ms Heather Waller
Mrs Emily Wallis
Mr Graham Wallis
Mrs K Wallis
Mr Darren Walsh
Mr James Walsh
Mr John Walsh
Mrs Lorraine Walsh
Mrs Samantha Walsh
Mr Tony Walsh
Ms Joy Walton
Mrs Susan Waple
Mr Paul Warburton
Mrs Amanda Ward
Mrs Beverley Ward
Mr Chris Ward
Mr David Ward
Mr Hilary Ward
Mrs Ira Ward
Miss Kim Ward
Miss Natasha Ward
Mr Steve Ward
Mrs Tracy Ward
Mr Neil Warden
Mr Fraser Wardlaw
Mr Steve Wardle
Ms Julia Warin
Miss Rebecca Warne
Mrs Beccy Warner
Mrs Christine Warner
Mrs Victoria Warner-Smith
Mrs Carol Warrant
Mr Bernard Warren
Mr Bruce Wass
Mr Kenneth Waters
Mr Brian Wates
Mr Andrew Watson
Mr David Watson
Mrs Jane Watson
Miss Karen Watson
Mr Michael Watson
Mrs Noreen Watson
Mr Peter Watson
Mr Robert Watson
Mrs Sue Watson
Mr Colin Watson
Mr David Watters
Miss Helen Watts
Mr Ian Watts
Miss Melissa Watts
Mrs Christine Way
Mr T Weaver
Mrs Nicola Webb
Mr Don Webber
Mr Edward Webster
Miss Jackie Weeks
Mr Nigel Weeks
Mrs Devindar Weerasooriya
Mrs Audrey Weir
Ms Hannah Welch
Mr John Welch
Mr Geoff Wellens
Mr Bill Wellings
Mr Carol Wells
Mr Keith Wells
Miss Daniela Wesenberg
Mrs Louise Wesley
Mr J F M West
Mr John West
Dr Margaret West
Miss Nichola West
Mrs Sally West
Miss Erica Westerman
Mr Simon Westerman
Mrs Emma Westmoreland
Mrs Valerie Weston
Mrs Claire Westrop
Mrs Helen Wheatcroft
Mrs Carol Wheeler
Miss Georgina Wheeler
Mr Joe Wheeler
Mr Oliver Wheeler
Mrs Vicky Wheeler
Mrs Lynne Whiston
Miss Claire Whitaker
Mrs Tara Whitaker
Mr Christopher White

Mr George White
Mr Harrison White
Mrs Hester White
Mrs Melanie White
Miss Nicky White
Mr Peter White
Mrs Ruth White
Mrs Virginia White
Mr Paul Whitehead
Mrs Christina Whiteway
Ms Belinda Whitfield
Ms Teresa Whitfield
Miss Alison Whitley
Mr James Whitmore
Mr Stephen Whittaker
Mrs Shirley Whittem
Mr Matthew Whittington
Mr Stephen Whittle
Mr Roy Whitworth
Mr John Whyman
Mr John Whyman
Mr David Wibberly
Ms Kirsty Wichary
Mr Paul Wickham
Mr Mobray Wiffin
Mrs Elizabeth Wiffin
Miss Lucy Wiggins
Miss Eleanor Wigmore
Mr Nigel Wilcox
Mrs Trish Wilczak
Mr Andrew Wildey
Mr Jeff Wilding
Mrs Dianne Wilkins
Mr Geoffrey Wilkins
Miss Helen Wilkins
Mr John Wilkinson
Mr Nick Wilkinson
Mr Paul Willan
Mr Alan Williams
Miss Alison Williams
Mrs Andrea Williams
Mr Asodah Williams
Mrs Barbara Williams
Mrs Christine Williams
Ms Cynthia Williams
Mr Daniel Williams
Mr David Williams
Mr Edwyn Williams
Mrs Heather Williams
Mrs Isobel Williams
Mrs Jaki Williams
Mr Janice Williams
Miss Karen Williams
Miss Katie Williams
Mr Lindsay Williams
Mr Mathew Williams
Mr Philip Williams
Mrs Rhian Williams
Mr Robin Williams
Mr Teresa Williams
Mr Tim Williams
Mrs Serena Williams-Ellis
Mr Andrew Williamson
Mr Brian Williamson
Miss Charlie Williamson
Mrs Gill Williamson
Mrs Helen Williamson
Mr Ian Williamson
Mr John Williamson
Mrs Sarah Williamson
Mr David Willingham
Mr John Willingham
Mr Mick Willis
Mr Darren Willmott
Mrs Adele Wills
Mrs Shelagh Wills
Mr Adrian Willson
Mr Robert Willson-
    Pemberton
Mr Alan Wilson
Mr Andrew Wilson
Mrs Annette Wilson
Mr Ben Wilson
Mrs Caroline Wilson
Ms Catriona Wilson
Mr Derek Wilson
Miss Janette Wilson
Mrs Janis Wilson
Mr John Wilson
Miss Naomi Wilson
Mr Neil Wilson
Miss Nicola Wilson
Mrs Pauline Wilson

Mrs Petra Wilson
Mr Richard Wilson
Mrs Wendy Wilson
Mrs Roberta Wilson
Miss Susannah Wilson
Mr Tony Wilson
Mrs Esme Wilson Staniforth
Mr Barry Wiltshire
Mr Robert Wiltshire
Mr John Window
Mr John Windsor
Mr Mike Winser
Ms Lesley Winship
Mr Roger Winstanley
Mr Steve Wise
Miss Amanda Wiseman
Mr Andrew Wiseman
Mr Paul Withers
Mrs Ann Withinshaw
Mrs Bronwen Wolton
Mr Alen Wong
Ms Angelina Wong
Mrs Sibella Wonnacott
Mr David Wood
Mrs Eleanor Wood
Ms Gail Wood
Mrs Helen Wood
Mrs Jane Wood
Mrs June Wood
Mrs Karen Wood
Mr Keith Wood
Mrs Mary Wood
Mr Rose Wood
Mrs Sue Wood
Mr Thomas Wood
Mr David Woodbridge
Ms Ruth Woodhead
Mrs Anita Woodhouse
Mr Roger Woodhouse
Mrs Pauline Woods
Mr Richard Woods
Ms Rosie Woods
Mrs Rosemary Woodward
Miss Rebecca Woof
Mrs Letitia Woolacott
Mrs Wendy Woolgar
Mr Martin Wooller
Mrs Carol Woolley
Mrs Alex Woollings
Mr Gordon Worcester
Mr Roderick Wordie
Mr Stephen Worgan
Ms Amanda Wragg
Mrs Anni Wray
Mr Andrew Wright
Ms Berni Wright
Mr David Wright
Mr Glynn Wright
Mrs Laura Wright
Mr Nick Wright
Ms Paula Wright
Mrs Sally Wright
Mr Timothy Wright
Mr Tish Wright
Mrs Kate Wrightson
Miss Kaja Wunder
Mrs Fiona Wyatt
Mr Jeremy Wyatt
Mr Norman Wyatt
Mrs Tina Wyatt
Mr Richard Wyndham
Mr Roderick Wyness
Mrs Laura Wysling
Mr Imura Yakamoto
Ms Marina Yaseen
Mr John Yearley
Miss Danielle Youds
Mrs Andrea Young
Ms Colleen Young
Mr Justin Young
Mr Philip Young
Mr Roger Young
Mr Stephen Young
Mr David Zerdin
Mr Jia Zhang
Miss Fifi Ziane
Mr A Zimmerman
Mrs Kiki Zobl
Mr John Zoo

Special thank yous

We would like to extend special thanks to the following people:

Kirstie Addis, Hilary Armstrong, Francesca Bashall, Iain Barker, Elizabeth Bowden, Chris Bulman, Andy Burge, David Carter, Martin Chapman, Ruth Coombs, Katy Denny, Grace Duffy, Alex Ellis, Nicola Gardner, Alix Godfree, Natalie Goodrick, Matthew Grey, Alan Grimwade, Nicole Gross, Verity Hartley, Ben Kay, Janice Leech, Michelle Lyttle, David Mabey, Angela Newton, Jeffrey Ng, Deborah Prince, John Rowlands, John Rudkin, Kate Stuart-Cox, Emma Sturgess, Mark Taylor, Judi Turner, Rochelle Venables, Stuart Walton, Martin Webster, Erin Wheeler, Jenny White, Blânche Williams, Emma Wilmot and Jane Wilson.

Picture credits
Nikki English (David Everitt-Matthias, Nathan Outlaw, Will Holland)
Jason Lowe (Mark Hix)
Shutterstock (Features: Fine dining, Great trolleys, Grow-your-own, Happy birthday, London's Italian bargains, Saké, Sustainable fish, Welsh produce, Wine lists then and now, Kitchen tables, Fashionable ingredients)

Map credits
Maps designed and produced by Cosmographics Ltd, www.cosmographics.co.uk
UK digital database © Cosmographics Ltd, 2010
Greater London map © Cosmographics Ltd, 2010
North and South London maps © Collins Bartholomew 2010
West, Central and East London maps © BTA (trading as VisitBritain) 2010
produced by Cosmographics Ltd and used with the kind permission of
VisitBritain.

Please send updates, queries, menus and wine lists to:
editors@thegoodfoodguide.co.uk or write to:
The Good Food Guide, 2 Marylebone Road, London, NW1 4DF

WIN!
A GREAT GOURMET PRIZE

To celebrate the 60th anniversary of *The Good Food Guide*, we're offering two readers the chance to win a day at the exclusive Raymond Blanc Cookery School, located at his world-renowned restaurant Le Manoir aux Quat'Saisons in Oxfordshire.

This once-in-a-lifetime experience will include a full day's cookery course with hands-on tuition from Raymond's experienced cookery school chefs, an exclusive goodie bag and a chance to meet Raymond himself.

This is a rare opportunity to develop your culinary skills and tap into the secrets of one of the country's finest chefs.

For more details about the prize and how to enter, log on to our website: **www.thegoodfoodguide.co.uk/competition**